Garage Sale & Flea Market Annual

Second Edition

Cashing in on Today's Lucrative Collectibles Market

NOSTALGIA PUBLISHING COMPANY

The current values in this book should be used only as a guide. They are not intended to set prices, which vary from one section of the country to another. Auction prices as well as dealer prices vary greatly and are affected by condition as well as demand. Nostalgia Publishing Co., Inc. does not assume responsibility for any losses that might be incurred as a result of consulting this guide.

On the cover top to bottom, left to right:

Bracelet, 7", marked sterling, orchid design. $60.00. Courtesy of Kay Smith.

Brooch, marked sterling, poppy design. $40.00. Courtesy of Kay Smith.

Head vase, 6", marked #C 7472 Napcoware. $37.50. Courtesy of Beth Ray.

Chalkware cat with fishbowl, 7" tall, 8" wide. $35.00. Courtesy of BJ and Beth Summers.

Thermometer, camel cigarettes, 13½" tall, 6" wide. $35.00. Courtesy of BJ and Beth Summers.

Christmas oil lamp, 10", 1950's, unmarked. $15.00. Courtesy of Kay Smith.

Hopalong Cassidy Rocking Horse, $175.00. Courtesy of Roszella Jones.

Ruby vase, 9", $17.50. Courtesy of BJ and Beth Summers.

• • • ● • • • ● • • ● • • • ● • • • ● • • ● • • • ● • • • ● • • •

Nostalgia Publishing Co. Inc.
P.O. Box 277
La Center, Kentucky 42056

• • • ● • • • ● • • ● • • • ● • • • ● • • ● • • • ● • • • ● • • •

A Word from the Editor

The collectibles market is alive and healthy! Let me assure you that there is no shortage of activity at any level. New collector clubs are constantly being formed, attendance is up at antique shows all around the country, there are more and more huge flea markets – some with thousands of dealers – and small towns that once had one antique store may now have several co-ops. In fact, downtown areas that for years have been practically vacant due to the country's economic slowdown have found new life for no other reason – oftentimes to the degree that the entire town profits through the additional revenue generated by the tourists who are drawn there to shop for antiques. It naturally follows that as the traffic increases, filling station owners benefit, the restaurant business expands, and many times new shops are opened featuring merchandise such as crafts, gifts, specialty foods, home decorating items, reproduction oak furniture, and so forth – ventures that no one would dare to undertake without first being assured that those antique shops and malls were doing a successful, thriving business.

If you decide to seize the opportunity to be a part of this economic subsystem for whatever reason – investment potential, to increase your income, or for the pure enjoyment of collecting – we're going to see that this publication is just what you'll need to learn how. First of all, we'll tell you how to finance that first step – how to raise a little cash by having a garage sale to get you started. Then we'll give you some tips on how to take that little nest egg and turn it into a one a little bigger – what to buy, where and how to sell. We're going to introduce you to hundreds of types of collectibles. Not expensive antiques but those things that are still readily available, often at bargain prices. Items that you can turn a profit on. This book contains nearly 25,000 descriptions and values for just that type of merchandise. At the beginning of each category, you'll find some background information – a little history, collecting tips, and most of the time references to definitive collector books. They're written by many of today's experts and leading authorities and are a must for every seller, buyer, dealer, collector, or an individual who is just trying to develop a feel for the market. Remember, study is the key to being a successful collector or antiques merchant. You must be willing to learn; the time you spend in studying the field will be the investment that will make the difference between success and mediocrity. We'll list hundreds of clubs and newsletters that cater to people who are avid, active collectors. You'll find an organization for virtually every area of interest, be it Barbie Dolls, Depression Glass, Railroadiana, or the more esoteric fields such as barbed wire. In the back of the book, we'll list our *Interested Buyers*. They're organized by topic, and they invite you to contact them if you find yourself in possession of the type of merchandise they seek.

We've tried to keep our format as simple as possible and our abbreviations to a minimum. If you have trouble locating a subject, please refer to the index. We've organized our topics alphabetically, following the most simple logic, usually by manufacturer or type of product. Exceptions to this may occur when a subject is better served by having its own narrative. For instance, rather than let 'Barbie' get lost in the 'Dolls' category, she has her own space – jadite glass, instead of being with the rest of the kitchen glassware, has its own. We've used cross-references when this happens, and I think on the whole you'll be able to find things very easily. So read, observe, get motivated! There can be no doubt about it, the antiques and collectibles industry is continually expanding, and there has never been a better time for you to get involved.

Even if you've never collected anything, never held your own garage sale, never sold one collectible, the majority of the people you know probably have. They belong to an entire socioeconomic subculture conservatively estimated at more than 20,000,000 people, turning millions of dollars back into the economy each year. Any one of them will tell you that the antiques market has made drastic changes over the past ten years. That's because the majority of today's buyers are baby boomers with the wherewithal to buy whatever they want. And what they want is nostalgia. Few are interested in in genuine antiques; they hold little or no meaning for them. What they do want are things they associate with their childhood days. In nearly every field, it's items from the forties through the seventies that are selling.

How To Hold Your Own Garage Sale

Having a garage sale can be fun as well as profitable. Everyone has items they no longer use, and you can turn them into extra cash that can finance your induction into the collectibles buying and selling market. Here's how.

Get Organized. Gather up and price your merchandise. Though there's not a lot of money in selling clothing, this is the perfect time to unload things you're not using. Kids' clothing sells well, since it's usually outgrown before it's worn out. Realistically, about all you can ask is 25% (tops) of the original retail price on items that are still in good condition. Were your parents savers? Check their attics and basements for your old Brady Bunch game, or maybe you'll find a your old Batman costume or some Hot Wheels – surely some Little Golden Books. Even if you're still a newlywed, you yourself may have some fast food collectibles, Avon bottles, or a poster from a rock concert. Apply a little creative thinking and see what all you can come up with. Use pressure-sensitive labels or masking tape for price tags. Unless a friend or a neighbor is going in on the sale with you, you won't have to remove them, the profit will all be yours. Of course, you'll have to keep tabs if others are involved. You can use a sheet of paper divided into columns, one for each of you, and write the amount of each sale down under the appropriate person's name, or remove the tags and restick them on a large piece of poster board, one for each seller. I've even seen people use straight pins to attach small squares of paper which they remove and separate into plastic butter tubs. When several go together to have a sale, the extra help is nice, but don't let things get out of hand. Your sale can get *too* big. Things become too conjested, and it's hard to display so much to good advantage.

Clothing should of course be clean and pressed to sell at all, and try to get the better items on hangers. If you have good brand-name clothing that has been worn very little, you would probably do better by taking it to a resale or consignment shop. They normally price things at about one-third of retail, with their cut being 30% of that. Still considerably better that you could reasonably expect at a garage sale.

Supposing that you're following our plan to use this garage sale as a 'leg-up' to a more aggressive career as an 'antique' dealer, price any low-end collectibles you have at about one-third of 'book' price. This will give the dealers who buy from you a margin for profit without their having to try to get 'top book' when they sell, and you won't be giving them away either. Remember, if what you're selling is relatively common, there will be lots of competition from other garage sales. If your neighbor is pricing her Hot Wheels at $1.00 each, unless yours are noticeably better, you probably won't sell many at $2.00. If you do your research and you find you have some things that you think have good resale potential, you might want to hold out for at least half of 'book.' If they don't sell for you at your garage sale, take them to a flea market or consign them to a shop. The same people who balk at paying $5.00 for a board game at a garage sale will pay $10.00 for it at a flea market. It's a totally different mind-set. Refer to our listings to help you price your things; you'll be surprised at what you are able to retain by researching tangible items. The connection between the mind and the eye reinforces memory, and the values you learn will stay with you for a long time.

Advertise. Place your ad in your local paper or on your town's cable TV information channel. It's important to make your ad interesting and upbeat. Though most sales usually start early on Friday or Saturday mornings, some people are now holding their sales in the early evening, and they seem to be having good crowds. This gives people with day jobs an opportunity to attend. You *might* want to hold your sale for two days, but you'll do 90% of your selling during the first two or three hours, and a two-day sale can really drag on. Make signs – smaller ones for street corners near your home to help direct passersby and a large one for your yard. Be sure that you use a wide-tipped felt marker and print in letters big enough that the sign can be read from the street. Put the smaller signs up a few days in advance unless you're expecting rain. (If you are, you might want to include a rain date in your advertising unless your sale will be held under roof.) Make sure you have lots of boxes and bags and plenty of change. If you will price your items in increments of 25¢, you won't need anything but a few rolls of quarters, maybe ten or fifteen ones, and a few five-dollar bills. Then on the day of the sale, put the large sign up in a prominent place out front with some balloons to be sure to attract the crowd. Take a deep breath, brace yourself, and raise the garage door!

What To Do With What's Left. After the sale, pack any good collectibles that didn't sell until you've decided on your next strategy. Sort out the better items of clothing for Goodwill or a similar charity, unless your city has someone who will take your leftovers and sell them on consignment. This is a fairly new concept, but some of the larger cities have such 'bargain centers.' Now for the next step.

What's Hot on the Market Today, Where To Make a Profit

If you aspire to become a dealer or if you just want to invest your money wisely, you'll need to know what areas have the most activity. The successful dealer is diversified. They know they can't rely on only two or three types of merchandise to run a lucrative business. Obviously no one can be an expert in every field, so what you'll need to do is choose the areas that you find most interesting and learn just what particular examples or types of items are most in demand within that field. Concentrate on the top 25%. There is where you'll do 75% of your business. Quality will always be a sure seller.

From my own observations, we'll recommend some areas that you should concentrate on. All of them are the focus of a substantial amount of interest right now; chances are they will be the ones you personally find appealing. We will list them alphabetically, since to rank them in any other way would probably only reflect my own preferences.

Advertising – There's no question about it, advertising collectibles are hot. There are scores of cataloged auctions listing thousands of items relating to this field, and record prices are constantly being realized. Vintage items from the turn of the century sometimes bring in 4- and 5-digit prices. For instance, a rare Hires Rootbeer dispenser made by Mettlach and decorated with the 'Hires boy' sold at auction last year for a very substantial sum of almost $25,000.00. A Sun Cured pipe tobacco pocket tin sold for $1,375.00, and a 1907 Coca-Cola tray with a lady in an off-the-shoulder gown went for $3,900.00 in near mint condition. Granted, items like these are generally sold today only when someone is dispersing of a collection that was built years ago, but it is not out of the realm of possibilty to find a good tin at a garage sale or flea market now and then. The same qualities that make collectors willing to pay such sums today prompted the housewife to save some tins over the years for storing her buttons, stashing her pennies, or what have you.

There are literally hundreds of subdivisions within the advertising field, all of which have their own band of interested followers searching out and willing to pay for items they want. The first rule you should remember: Always use the term 'want,' 'need' being a four-letter word that has absolutely no application in the collector's world. Example: (spouse speaking – 'You don't 'need' that.) For instance, there are Coca-Cola collectors by the score, Planters Peanuts fans who have nationwide clubs and publish newsletters, and those that specialize in such areas as breweriana (including cans, bottles, trays, labels, posters, mugs, glasses, coasters, and dozens of other items) and automobilia (for instance, pamphlets introducing new models, license plates, gear shift knobs, and the like). The field is so vast that no one could possibly feel confident of the entire spectrum, but here are some general guidelines.

Colorful graphics are important. The quality of the artwork is the first thing that will catch the eye of the potential buyer. Vintage advertising collectors become excited over strong colors and images, and they prefer some types of subject matter over others. If the focus is on beautiful ladies or babies, modes of transportation (a train or an automobile, for instance), types of sports, or Black Americana, the item will most certainly generate lots of interest. Some products are more attractive to collectors than others. Among them (and in addition to those we've already mentioned) are peanut butter, talcum powder, tobacco, and soft drinks.

The slogans themselves interest some collectors even more than the graphics. Remember the Burma Shave signs? So simple, yet how persuasive. But not all messages are so obvious. Sometimes all it took to get the point across was to show the product being used in a happy or up-beat situation. Subtlety can be an art form in itself.

There's another type of advertising collectible currently in the foreground, relatively easy to find and extremely popular with many people right now, and that's those items that bear the likeness of or are modeled in the form of a well-known character logo. Reddy Killowat, Poppin' Fresh, Charlie Tuna, the Campbell Kids, Elsie the Cow – there are hundreds of them, all as familiar as the kid next door. Many are not at all old, and the majority of these items can be purchased for less than $50.00. Watch for these items at garage sales. I've picked up a plastic Planters Peanut mug for a dime, a vinyl Poppin' Fresh toy for 25¢, and an ice cream sundae dish with Elsie the Cow that was mixed in with a boxful of some other goodies for just $1.00 for the lot.

I can't stress enough to be critical of condition. It's a very important consideration when buying and selling advertising items. Whether paper, glass, tin, plastic or only those pieces in really great condition can be counted on to attract buyers. There's just too much of it around to expect rusty tin, stained paper, or cracked and chipped glassware and plastic items to have worth. We'll talk more about the importance of condition later.

American Pottery – Good Roseville, Rookwood, and Weller have been solid ground for investment for years, and there is a nationwide network of collectors for art pottery of all types. But because of this long-sustained interest, much of it has been bought up, and though it's not entirely inconceivable that you may yet stumble across a steal during your next garage sale outing, chances are not in your favor. However we heard from one very lucky man a few weeks ago who for the price of one thin dime made off with a 15" Second Line Dickensware (Weller) vase (decorated with a shepherdess and her flock and valued at about $1,800.00) that he found among odds and ends at a neighborhood sale, and this summer I myself found a large, early, mint condition Roseville Matt Green wall pocket, still stuffed with the plastic flowers it had obviously held for years. I got it for $1.00. The last listed price I could find for it was $275.00, and that was by no means current. I found a 5" Bushberry (Roseville) vase down the block for 25¢, worth probably about $35.00 – certainly not as thrilling as the wall pocket, but still lots of fun. So those things still happen, and if you take the time to educate yourself, the next time, it may happen to you!

But what you're more likely to find are small vases and flowerpots made perhaps by Haeger, McCoy, or Shawnee, for instance. Or dinnerware by Hull, Pfaltsgraff, Homer Laughlin, Harker, or any number of companies who produced literally hundreds of different dinnerware lines. There's a steady market for just about any of these items, espcially if they're marked. People seem to want to know just what it is they're buying.

Black Americana – always hot! And it's such a broad field. Magazine covers featuring prominent Black entertainers and sports stars, sheet music, linens, advertising and kitchenware items, toys, books, banks – and the list goes on. Because some of the prices in this field have gone so high, reproductions are everywhere. Cookie jars, salt and pepper shakers, prints, banks and doorstops have all been reproduced, so be alert as you examine your finds, especially at flea markets. There are good books on the subject that will help you become familiar with these items, and the time you invest studying them will be well spent. A friend of mine found a chalkware Mammy-face string holder at a garage sale for 50¢, located one of our 'Interested Buyers,' and sold it for $90.00, making both buyer and seller very happy.

Celebrity Memorabilia – Movie stars, rock 'n roll singers and musicians, sports greats. There are several that have sustained the interest of their fans though most of them are now gone. Items of memorabilia featuring Elvis (my personal favorite) and the Beatles have skyrocketed this year, prompting the release of a new price guide for each. The Elvis postage stamp sales were phenomenal. Almost 600 million were printed. Also offered were first-day covers, art prints, full-sheets, and special holders. Because of the huge amount of stamps printed, don't expect them to hold much promise of ever becoming valuable. But there are good Elvis collectibles to be had, and more than enough fans to buy them. One of my saddest 'should'a bought it, didn't' experiences of this past summer was passing up an Elvis record player for $150.00 in good working order. Rosalind Cranor, author of the new Elvis book, assured me it was worth $1,000.00. Ouch!

From every decade since the fifties, celebrity memorabilia is selling – James Dean, Marilyn Monroe, and Buddy Holly right on through Janis Joplin and John Lennon and up to modern day icons like Michael Jackson and Madonna. Prices realized at the larger auction galleries like Butterfield's for items such as original song lyrics, guitars, and costumes often reach $20,000.00 and up (in fact, handwritten lyrics for a Beatles tune made $96,000.00!) But what you will be finding are concert posters, 45 rpm picture sleeves, celebrity dolls, book, magazines, jewelry, toys and games, all priced on a level everyone can afford.

Character-Related Items – especially toys, board games, and puzzles featuring TV and movie characters from the fifties through the seventies, Disney characters in particular, are really moving. Also look for CHIPS, Laverne and Shirley, Happy Days, Mork and Mindy, The Fugitive, Underdog, Mister Ed, Scooby-Doo, et al.The better-known the character, the more in demand they will be. Age doesn't figure in nearly as much as the character factor. Even Roger Rabbit and Teenage Ninja Turtles are hot. When you buy games and puzzles, be sure what you're buying is complete, even if you have to count the pieces. You'll usually be able to find an inventory of game pieces, either on the instruction sheet or printed inside the lid.

The cowboy craze has been sweeping the country, and virtually everything representing the American West is now bringing top dollar. Radio and TV cowboys that sparked the airwaves in the '40s and '50s have again become the favorites of those same kids, now grown, who raced in from school just in time to glue themselves to the radio for the adventures of Tom Mix, Straight Arrow, Roy Rogers, Hopalong Cassidy, and scores of others. Guns and holsters, secret code rings, pin-back buttons, costumes, dinnerware and what have you, are selling like hot cakes!

Cookie Jars – we told you about these last year; they're still hot, hot, hot! The rare ones keep going higher and higher, and even this late in the game there are new collectors coming on all the time. Character-related jars are high on the price scale, with the American Bisque Flintstones and Popeyes, for instance, selling in the $900.00 and up range. Sweet Pea (American Bisque) went for $4,000.00 at auction this year. Black Americana jars are always in demand, and four-figure asking prices are not uncommon. Even with such extreme and sustained hunting pressure, you're still going to find good cookie jars that are well underpriced. Get to those garage sales early, though, they won't set there long. It was an early bird who bought Eeyore (copyright Walt Disney) for $2.00. Eeyore, by the way, goes for about $175.00 minimum.

You will have to be aware of reproductions to be a wise cookie jar buyer. There are already many, many of the better jars being reproduced, and more are coming out every day. Roger Jensen of Rockwood, Tennessee, is making several which he marks 'McCoy.' Because the real McCoy company never registered their trademark, he was able to get federal approval to begin using the mark in 1992. Though he added '#93' to some of the pieces he made last year, the majority are undated. He is using molds of now-defunct potteries to produce several popular cookie jars. Here are some of his reproductions, there may be others: McCoy Mammy, Clown, Dalmations, Indian Head; Hull Little Red Riding Hood; Pearl China Mammy; and the Mosaic Tile Mammy. To anyone who is thinking of collecting or dealing in cookie jars we recommend *The Cookie Jar Newsletter*, edited and published by Joyce Roerig, author of *The Collector's Encyclopedia of Cookie Jars*. It's really a remarkable newsletter, and you'll learn enough by reading it to keep you aware of rarities, reproductions, and values.

Fast Food Collectibles – McDonald's, Arby's, Wendy's, Burger King, and so forth. We're talking about the kiddie meal toys, the posters used in the restaurant to promote each series, and sometimes even the box the meals came in. These were just coming on when we did the first edition, but this past summer saw even more collector activity. Dealers were snatching them up at garage sales at ten for $1.00, sorting them out into plastic laundry baskets and taking them to the flea markets where they were selling for $2.00 up to as much as $10.00. There was always several buyers buzzing around those baskets; I myself was guilty. I'd found an Archie 'bendee' and looked all summer for Veronica, Jughead, and Betty, and I still haven't found them. Some of the ones you'll want to concentrate on are Barbies, old familiar Disney characters and certainly the new ones (Aladdin and Beauty and the Beast toys are bound to be good), Star Trek, and popular characters such as My Little Pony. If you can find them still in unopened packages, so much the better.

Figural Pottery – banks, wall pockets, planters, clothes sprinkler bottles, figurines, and so forth. Parents who had lived through the Depression years understood the importance of teaching their children to save and gave them banks modeled after their favorite characters. These are the ones to look for today. Some were made by American companies, and many were imported from Japan. There's a Popeye by American Bisque that sells for about $250.00, but most of the good character-related banks are in the $20.00 to $50.00 range. Wall pockets sell well, especially the larger, more detailed ones with exotic birds, and those with out-of-the-ordinary themes. Stay away from the small, run-of-the mill variety. Flea market dealers tell us that figural planters are coming on, and clothes sprinkler bottles, especially the good ones, usually go out about as quickly as they hit the tables. Before the advent of the steam iron in the 1950s, housewives used these to dampen their laundry before ironing. Some, such as the Chinamen (who were nearly all inscribed 'Sprinkle Plenty') are relatively common but still sell in $35.00 to $45.00 range. The harder-to-find exampes are more pricey. For instance, there's a Black Mammy in a pink-trimmed white dress that often goes for around $150.00 and a Victorian lady with her purse that sells for $100.00 up to $125.00. Don't pass up any, if you find them at a bargain. These are selling!

Head vases – vases and planters shaped like the heads of beautiful ladies, children, clowns, and even animals – seem to be very attractive to an ever-growing number of fans who have organized clubs, newsletters, and annual conventions. Values have been climbing; price guides that were originally issued only four or five years ago have been updated, and examples that were at first in the $25.00 to $35.00 range are now up by 50%. Most of these were imported from Japan and bear the mark of any one of a number of import companies, but a few were made in the States as well. The most desirable are extra large examples, 7" and up, those with special features such as a fur collar, pearl jewelry, or an umbrella alongside, and especially those that represent a popular cartoon character or look like one of several well-known personalities. There are head vases of Howdy Doody, Alice in Wonderland, Snow White, and Mary Poppins, for instance, and others that bear a striking resemblance to Doris Day, Jackie Kennedy, Marilyn Monroe, and Lucy.

Figurines by Rosemeade, Ceramic Arts Studios, Mortens Studios, and scores of California potteries such as Hedi Shoop, Sascha Brastof, Kay Finch, Max Weil (Weilware), Howard Pierce, Florence Ceramics, and Brayton Laguna are high on the want list of many collectors today. You can be sure that a piece by any of these companies will have good resale potential. Learn to recognize examples of each – this is an area that many dealers are still unsure of! I bought a beautiful Ceramic Arts Studio lady (actually a bell) for a quarter this year at a garage sale, a gold igloo-style Sascha Brastoff ashtray for little more than that, and a Rosemeade creamer and sugar bowl in the corn pattern for an equally ridiculous sum. I've seen the bell priced from $75.00 to $100.00, the ashtray for about $35.00, and the creamer and sugar bowl should easily be worth $30.00 to $35.00. I picked up a Florence girl from an antique co-op at 80% under book and passed up a Kay Finch cat at about half price (one of those things I should have bought but didn't.) There's money to be made here, especially on the California pottery. It's just now coming on, and since there's been relatively little published on the subject, there are bargains to be had.

Salt and Pepper Shakers – always a popular collectible, always in demand. You'll see tables and tables of them at flea markets, but knowing which to buy might take some thought. If you're a collector buying for the sheer pleasure of collecting, by all means buy the ones that appeal to you. But if you're looking for bargains for resale, some are better than others. There are shakers that will draw the attention of cross-over buyers, people who specialize in lines made by a particular manufacturer – Rosemeade,

Ceramic Arts Studios, and Shawnee, for instance. Black Americana and Disney collectors are another cross-over group, so are advertising buffs. There are several good books on the market, national clubs and conventions, and interest continues to be high in this area.

Toys – without doubt the hottest items of the '90s. Not the toys from the turn of the century (though they continue to hold their value), but toys from the forties on. Toys that many of us grew up with – Barbie dolls, slot cars, Japanese wind-ups, model kits, GI Joes and other action figures, Matchbox, Tootsietoys, Tonka Toys, Fisher-Price, trains, cars, boats, and so on.

Vintage Barbies have been expensive for several years. Now a mint-in-box 1959 Barbie (the blond) books at $2,000.00. But even a much more recent version, the Happy Holiday Barbie issued in 1988, will bring $400.00 to $500.00 (MIB). There are auctions offering nothing but Barbie dolls (and her friends Ken, Kelly, Allan, PJ, Skipper, and Scooter, of course) and their accessories. There's a lot you'll need to learn if you're going to collect or deal extensively in this field. There are several good books available to you, and you'd do well to study them all. You can't go a day doing garage sales without seeing some decent Barbie doll items, and you'll need to know where to invest your money and what to pass up.

Slot cars are really taking off. Cars that sold for $5.00 only a year ago are now carrying price tags of $25.00 to $30.00 at toy shows. Look for names like AMT, Aurora, Eldon, and Strombecker.

Model kits is another segment of toy collecting that's recording strong sales. Figure-type kits have increased in price and popularity in just the past five years or so. Prices vary according to who is buying and selling, subject matter, and above all condition. It's best to look for mint-in-the-box examples; built-ups are worth only about half as much.

Japanese wind-ups attract a great number of toy collectors, the more actions they perform, the better. Watch for those that still work and are rust-free. If you can find them mint-in-box, so much the better.

Die-casts such as Matchbox and Hot Wheels can easily be found at garage sales and flea markets, and there's a ready market for any of them. Early Hot Wheels were known as 'redlines' because the sidewalls of the tires had a red line around them similar to whitewall tires. Dinky toys were made from 1933 until 1979, so they're becoming scarce today; Corgi is the newcomer – they've been made since 1956. Tootsietoys are not as detailed as most of the others, but they're affordable and very popuar among collectors. Most of them issued from the 1940s through the 1960s were either 3", 4", or 6" long. Look for examples in at least very good condition.

Transformers were introduced to the toy shelves of America in 1984. They were products of Japan, produced by Hasbro. They were discontinued by 1990, but their fans continue to buy them on the secondary market, and there are Transformer clubs with members allover the world. The basic Transformer was either a car or a robot that with the twist of the wrist could become a jet airplane or a hand gun. Make sure the one you buy has all its parts. One still in its original box is usually worth about twice as much as a 'loose' one.

If you're especially interested in toys, read books, attend toy shows, study tradepapers and magazines, and talk with dealers and collectors. They're a great bunch of people, and I've found them very willing to share their knowledge.

The fields we've mentioned above are only a few of the newer collecting areas with major amounts of activity. There are many more, and all of them are covered in the following pages. Some of the old standbys are still strong: carnival, elegant, and Depression glassware; kitchen items; comic books; coin-operated machines; militaria; sports collectibles; costume jewelry; anything from the '50s; fishing lures; banks; lunch boxes; radios; and pocketknives. The thousands of current values found in this book will increase your awareness of today's wonderful world of buying, selling, and collecting antiques and collectibles. Use it to educate yourself to the point that you'll be the one with the foresight to know what and how to buy as well as where and how to turn those 'sleepers' into cold cash if that is your goal.

Where To Find the Bargains

This is the fun part. Get you a partner (if you don't already have one), and just go for it! You can easily spend a whole day going from garage sale to garage sale, consignment shop to flea market, maybe attend a mall show, or even catch an estate sale. It's good excercise, gets you out to enjoy the sun, meet new people, and it's a learning process.

Garage sales are absolutely wonderful for finding bargains. But you'll have to get up early! Don't expect those treasures to wait until you get there. Even non-collectors can spot quality merchandise, and at those low, low garage sale prices, collectible items will be the first to move.

In order for you to be a successful garage sale shopper, you have to learn how to get yourself organized. It is important to conserve your time. The sales you hit during the first early morning hour will prove to be the best nine times out of ten, so you must have a plan before you ever leave home. Plot your course. Your local paper will have a section on garage sale ads, and local cable TV channels may also carry garage sale advertising. Most people hold their sales on the weekend, but some may start earlier in the week, so be sure to turn to the 'Garage Sales' ads daily. Write them down and try to organize them by areas – northwest, northeast, etc. At first you'll probably need your city map, but you'll be surprised at how quickly the streets will become familiar to you. Upper middle-class neighborhoods generally have the best sales and the best merchandise, so concentrate on those areas. When you've decided where you want to start, go early! If the ad says 8:00, be there at 7:00. This may seem rude and pushy, but if you can bring yourself to do it, it will pay off. And chances are when you get there an hour early, you won't be their first customer. If they're obviously not ready for business, just politely inquire if you may look. If you're charming and their nerves aren't completely frayed from trying to get things ready, chances are they won't mind.

Competition can be fierce during those important early-morning hours; learn to scan the tables quickly, then move to the area that looks the most promising. Don't be afraid to ask for a better price if you feel it's too high, but most people have already priced garage sale merchandise so that it will sell. Keep a notebook to jot down items you didn't buy the first time around but think you might be interested in if the price were reduced later on. After going through dozens of sales (I've done as many as thirty or so in one morning), you won't remember where you saw what! Often by noon, at least by mid-afternoon, veteran garage sale buyers are finished with their rounds and attendance becomes very thin. Owners are usually much more receptive to the idea of lowering their prices, so it may pay you to make a second pass. In fact, some people find it advantageous to go to the better sales on the last day as well as the first. They'll make an offer for everything that's left, and since most of the time the owner is about ready to *pay* someone to take it at that point, they can usually name their price. Although most of the collectibles will normally be gone at this point, there are nearly always some useable household items and several pieces of good, serviceable clothing left. The household items will sell at flea markets or consignment shops, and re-sale clothing shops usually charge about 30% on items that they sell for you. A new approach used by some 'pre-used clothing' shops is to buy the items outright for about half of what they feel they can price them at. Because they want only clothing that is in style, in season, and like new, their prices are a little higher than other shops, so half of that asking price is a good deal.

Tag sales are common in the larger cities. They are normally held in lieu of an auction, when estates are being dispersed, or when families are moving. Sometimes only a few buyers are admitted at one time, and as one leaves another is allowed to take his place. Just as is true of garage sales, the early bird gets the goodies. But since it's customary to have tag sale items appraised before values are set, be prepared to pay higher prices. That's not to say, though, that you won't find bargains here.

Auctions can go either way. Depending on the crowd and what items are for sale, you can sometimes spend all day and never be able to buy anything anywhere near 'book' price.On the other hand, there are often 'sleepers' that can be bought cheaply enough to resell at a good profit. Toys, dolls, Hummels, Royal Doultons, banks, cut glass, and other 'high-profile' collectibles usually go high; but white ironstone, dinnerware sets from the '20s through the '50s, silverplated hollowware, books, records, and linens, for instance, often pass relatively unnoticed by the majority of the buyers.

If there is a consignment auction house in your area, check it out. These are usually operated by local auctioneers, and the sales they hold in-house often involve low-income estates. You won't find something every time, so try to investigate the merchandise ahead of schedule to see if it's going to be worth your time to attend. Competition is probably less at one of these than in any of the other types of sales we've mentioned, and wonderful buys have been made from time to time.

Flea markets, I would have to say, are my favorite places to find bargains. I don't like the small ones – not that I don't find anything there, but I've learned to move through them so fast (to beat the crowd), I don't get my 'fix'; I just leave wanting more. If you've never been to a large flea market, you don't know what you're missing. Even if you're not a born-again collector, I guarantee you will love it.

Flea markets are excellent places to study the market. You'll be able to see where the buying activity is, you can check and compare prices, talk with dealers and collectors, and do hands-on inspections. I've found that if I first study a particular subject by reading a book or a magazine article, this type of exposure to that collectible really 'locks in' what I have learned.

Because there are many types of flea market dealers, there are plenty of bargains. The casual, once-in-a-while dealer may not always keep up with changing market values. Some of them simply price their items by what they themselves had to pay for it. Just as being early at garage sales is important, here it's a must. If you've ever been in line waiting for a flea market to open, you know that cars are often backed up for several blocks. At Brimfield last spring, there were so many people standing in line when they opened the gate, for safety's sake they had to let them pour through for several minutes without stopping them to collect admission. Browsers? Window shoppers? Not likely. Competition. So if you're going to have a chance at all, you'd better be in line yourself. It's a good idea for you and your partner to split up for the first pass. It's a common sight to see the serious buyers conversing with their partners via walkie-talkies, and if you like to discuss possible purchases with each other before you actually buy, this is a good way to do it.

Learn to bargain with dealers. Their prices are usually negotiable, and most will come down by 10% to 20%. Be polite and fair, and you can expect the same in return. Unpriced items are harder to deal for. I have no problem offering to give $8.00 if an item is marked $10.00, but it's difficult for me to have to ask the price and then make a counter offer. So I'll just say 'This isn't marked. Will you take..?' I'm not an aggressive barterer, so this works for me.

Learn to be suspicious of anything that looks too new! There are fakes and reproductions everywhere nowadays. Just about any field of collecting has a few. Black Americana, banks, wind-up toys, teddy bears, lamps, glassware, doorstops, cookie jars, prints, advertising items – and there are many, many, more. Check for telltale signs – paint that is too bright, joints that don't fit, variations in colors or size, creases in paper that you can see but not feel. Remember that zip codes have been used only since 1963, and this can sometime help you date an item in question. Check glassware for areas of wavy irregularities often seen in new glass. A publication we would highly recommend to you is called *Antique and Collector Reproduction News*, a monthly report of 'Fakes, Frauds, and Facts.' To subscribe, call 1-800-227-5531. Rates are very reasonable compared to the money you may save by learning to recognize reproductions.

Antique malls and co-ops should be visited on a regular basis. Many mall dealers restock day after day, and traffic and buying competition is usually fierce. As a rule, you won't often find great bargains here; what you do save on is time. And if time is what you're short of, you'll be able to see lots of good merchandise under one roof, on display by people who've already invested *their* time, hence the higher prices. But there are always items that are underpriced, and if you've taken the time to study the market, you'll be able to spot them right away. I bought a Roseville jardiniere and pedestal for $300.00 (sold it for $575.00) and a Pennsburv pretzel bowl for $8.00 (it books at $85.00) from antique malls just recently.

Prices at malls and co-ops are usually firm, though many dealers often run sales – '20% off everything in booth #101.' If you have a dealer's license, and you really should get one, most will give you a courtesy 10% discount, unless you want to pay with a credit card.

Antique shows are exciting to visit, but obviously if a dealer is paying several hundred dollars to set up for three days, he's going to be asking top price to offset expenses. So even though the bargains will be few, the merchandise is usually superior, and you may be able to find that special item you've been looking for.

Mail order buying is not only very easy, but most of the time economical as well. Many people will place an ad in 'For Sale' sections of tradepapers. Some will describe and price their merchandise in their ad, while others offer lists of the items they have in exchange for a SASE (stamped, self-addressed envelope). You're out no gas or food expenses, their overhead is minimal so their prices are usually very reasonable, so it works out great for both buyer and seller. I've made lots of good buys this way, and I've always been fairly and honestly dealt with. You may want to send a money order or a cashier's check to save time, otherwise (especially on transactions involving larger sums of money) the seller might want to wait until your personal check clears.

Goodwill stores and re-sale shops are usually listed in the telephone book. When you travel, it will pay you to check them out. I found a Purington cookie jar for $7.00, lots of Avon's Cape Cod (very cheap), Moon and Star, signed costume jewelry, Mirror Brown and Gourmet dinnerware by Hull and Pfaltzgraff, Annalee dolls (Santa and Mrs. Claus at $50.00 for the pair), good records, and a wonderful Florence figurine at about one-third its value on the shelves of Goodwill stores.

Turning Those Bargains Into Profit

Pricing Your Merchandise. In addition to this one, there are several other very fine price guides on the market. One of the best is *Schroeder's Antiques Price Guide*, another is *The Flea Market Trader*. Both are published by Collector Books. *The Antique Trader Antiques and Collectibles Price Guide*, *Warman's Antiques and Their prices*, and *Kovel's Antiques and Collectibles Price List* are others. You may want to invest in a copy of each. Where you decide to sell will have a direct bearing on how you price your merchandise, and nothing will affect an item's worth more than condition.

First of all, locate a listing for the item in question. If you don't find the exact piece, look until you find a few similar items. For instance, if it's a McCoy rabbit planter you're researching, go through the McCoy section and see what price range other animal planters are in. Or if you have a frame-tray puzzle with Snow White and the Seven Dwarfs, see what other Disney frame-trays are priced at. Just be careful not to compare apples and oranges! Once you have found 'book' price, decide how much less you can take for it. A collectible will often change hands many times, and obviously it will not always be sold at book price. It may have been first discovered at a garage sale. That person may have taken it to a small flea market where the overhead was low and priced it to sell fast. Perhaps the next buyer was a dealer who specialized in just that type of merchandise and whose customer was willing to pay book or near book, just for the convenience of buying from someone with a large inventory. After these four transactions, the book price may have finally been realized. Another thing to remember is that within a particular line of glassware or type of pottery, prices are relative. That magical 'top 25%' we referred to will probably always bring top dollar. And even though relative worth between a 10" dinner plate and a saucer seems equitable at $30.00 to $8.00, you may have to price your saucer at $4.00 just to get rid of it, simply because the saucer is more common and less desirable.

Nothing affects value more than condition. Most people, especially unexperienced buyers and sellers, have a tendency to overlook some flaws and to overrate merchandise. Mint condition means that an item is complete and undamaged, in effect, just as it looked the day it was made. Glassware, china, and pottery may often be found in mint condition, though signs of wear will downgrade anything. Unless a toy is still in its original box and has never been played with, you seldom see a toy in mint condition. Paper collectibles are almost never found without deterioration or damage. Most price guides will list values that apply to glass and ceramics that are mint (unless another condition is specifically indicated within some descriptions). Other items are usually evaluated on the assumption that they are in the best as-found condition common to that particular area of collecting. Grade your merchandise as though you were the buyer, not the seller. You'll be building a reputation that will go a long way toward contributing (or hindering) your success. If it's glassware or pottery you're assessing, an item in less than excellent condition will be mighty hard to sell at any price. Just as a guideline (a basis to begin your evaluation, though other things will factor in), use a scale of one to five with Good being a one, Excellent being a three, and Mint being a 5. As an example, a beer tray worth $250.00 in mint conditon would then be worth $150.00 if excellent and $50.00 if only good. Remember, the first rule of buying is 'Don't put your money in damaged goods.'

Decide where you're going to sell. There are many options (the same ones we recommended to you as a buyer). Overhead and expenses will vary with each and must be factored into your final pricing. If you have some especially nice items and can contact a collector willing to pay top dollar, that's obviously the best of the lot. Or you may decide to sell to a dealer who is willing to pay you only half of book. Either way, your expenses won't amount to much more than a little gas or a phone call.

Another way to get a good price for your more valuable merchandise without investing much money or time is to place a 'For Sale' ad or run a mail bid in one of the collector magazines or newsletters, several of which are listed in the back of this book. Many people have excellent results this way. One of the best to reach collectors in general is *The Antique Trader Weekly* (P.O. Box 1050, Dubuque, Iowa 52004). It covers virtually any and all types of antiques and collectibles and has a very large circulation. If you have glassware, china, or pottery from the Depression era, you should have good results through *The Depression Glass Daze* (Box 57, Otisville, Michigan 48463). If you have several items and the cost of listing them all is prohibitive, simply place an ad saying (for instance) 'Several pieces of Royal Copley (or whatever) for sale, send SASE for list. Be sure to give your correct address and phone number.

When you're making out your list or talking with a prospective buyer by phone, try to draw a picture with words. Describe any damage in full; it's much better than having a disgruntled customer to deal with later, and you'll be on your way to establishing yourself as a reputable dealer. Sometimes it's wise to send out photographs. Seeing the item exactly as it is will often help the prospective buyer make up his or her mind. Send a SASE along and ask that your photos be returned to you, so that you can send them out again, if need be. A less expensive alternative is to have your item photocopied. This works great for many smaller items, not just flat shapes but things with some dimension as well. It's wonderful for hard-to-describe dinnerware patterns or for showing their trademarks.

If you've made that 'buy of a lifetime' or an item you've hung onto for a few years has turned out to be a scarce, highly sought collectible, a mail bid is often the best way to get top dollar for your prize. This is how you'll want your ad to read. 'Mail Bid. Popeye cookie jar by American Bisque, slight wear (or 'mint' – briefly indicate condition), closing 6/31/94, right to refuse' (standard self-protection clause meaning you will refuse ridiculously low bids), and give your phone number. Don't commit the sale to any bidder until after the closing date, since some may wait until the last minute to try to place the winning bid.

Be sure to let your buyer know what form of payment you prefer. Some dealers will not ship merchandise until personal checks have cleared. This delay may make the buyer a bit unhappy. So you may want to request a money order or a cashier's check.

Be very careful about how you pack your merchandise for shipment. Breakables need to be well protected. There are several things you can use. Plastic bubble wrap is excellent, or scraps of foam rubber such as carpet padding (check with a carpet-laying service or confiscate some from family and friends who are getting new carpet installed). I've received items wrapped in pieces of egg-crate mattress pads. (Watch for these at garage sales!) If there is a computer business near you, check their dumpsters for discarded foam wrapping and other protective packaging. It's best not to let newspaper come in direct contact with your merchandise, since the newsprint may stain certain types of items. After you've wrapped them well, you'll need boxes. Find smaller boxes (one or several, whatever best fits your needs) that you can fit into a larger one with several inches of space between them. First pack your well-wrapped items snuggly into the smaller box, using crushed newspaper to keep them from shifting. Place it into the larger box, using more crushed paper underneath and along the sides, so that it will not move during transit. Remember, if it arrives broken, it's still your merchandise, even though you have received payment. You may want to insure the shipment; check with your carrier. Some have automatic insurance up to a specified amount.

After you've mailed it out, it's good to follow it up with a phone call after a few days. Make sure the box arrived in good condition and that your customer is pleased with the merchandise. Most people who sell by mail allow a 10-day return privilege, providing their original price tag is still intact. You can simply initial a gummed label or use one of those pre-printed return address labels that most of us have around the house.

For very large or heavy items such as furniture or slot machines, ask your buyer for his preferred method of shipment. If the distance involved is not too great, he may even want to pick it up himself.

Flea Market Selling can either be lots of fun, or it can turn out to be one of the worst experiences of your life. Obviously you will have to deal with whatever weather conditions prevail, so be sure to listen to weather reports so that you can dress accordingly. You'll see some inventive shelters you might want to copy. Even a simple patio umbrella will offer respite from the blazing sun or a sudden downpour. I've recently been seeing stands catering just to the needs of the flea market dealer – how's that for being enterprising! Not only do they carry specific items the dealers might want, but they've even had framework and tarpaulins for shelters to erect right on the spot!

Be sure to have plastic table covering in case of rain and some large clips to hold it down if there's much wind. The type of clip you'll need depends on how your table is made, so be sure to try them out before you actually have need for them. Otherwise your career as a flea market dealer may be cut short for lack of merchandise!

Price your things, allowing yourself a little bargaining room. Unless you want to collect tax separately on each sale (for this you'd need lots of small change), mentally calculate the amount and add this on as well. Sell the item 'tax included.' Everybody does.

Take snacks, drinks, paper bags, plenty of change, and somebody who can relieve you occasionally. Collectors are some of the nicest people around. I guarantee that you'll enjoy this chance to meet and talk with them, and often you can make valuable contacts that may help you locate items you're especially looking for yourself.

Auction Houses are listed in the back of this book. If you have an item you feel might be worth selling at auction, be sure to contact one of them. Many have appraisal services; some are free while others charge a fee, dependant on number of items and time spent. We suggest you first make a telephone inquiry before you send in a formal request.

In Summation

If you've been considering buying and selling antiques and collectibles as a sideline or a hobby, let me assure you without a doubt that there is money to be made by doing just that. Aside from monetary gain, you'll find that there's lots of enjoyment and satisfaction to be had as well. I recommend it highly. It's a hobby the whole family can enjoy together. Join the ranks of the millions who are already searching for 'today's collectibles, tomorrow's antiques.'

Abbreviations

MIB - Mint in (original) box
M - Mint Condition
NM - Near Mint Condition
EX - Excellent Condition
VG - Very Good
G - Good
lg - large
sm - small
med - medium
oz - ounce
pt - pint
qt - quart
gal - gallon
pr - pair
dia - diameter
w/ - with

Abingdon Pottery

You may find smaller pieces of Abingdon around, but it's not common to find many larger items. This company operated in Abingdon, Illinois, from 1934 until 1950, making not only nice vases and figural pieces but some kitchen items as well. Their cookie jars are very well done and popular with collectors. They sometimes used floral decals and gold to decorate their wares; a highly decorated item is worth about 25% more than the same shape with no decoration. Some of their glazes also add extra value. If you find a piece in black, bronze, or red, you can add 25% to those as well.

If you talk by phone about Abingdon to a collector, be sure to give him the mold number on the base. To learn more about Abingdon cookie jars, we recommend *The Collector's Encyclopedia of Cookie Jars* by Joyce and Fred Roerig.

Ashtray, chick, #615 ....$15.00
Ashtray, leaf, black & yellow, #660 ....$35.00
Bookends, horse head, #441, pr $50.00
Bookends, sea gull, #305, pr $60.00
Bowl, bulb; oval, #542 ....$35.00
Bowl, Panel, #460 ....$40.00
Bowl, Ribbon, #462 ....$12.00
Bowl, Scroll, #480, minimum value $20.00
Bowl, Streamliner, #546, lg..$20.00
Bowl, 6½", leaf, beige, #408, 1937 ....$65.00
Candle holders, Panel, #461, pr $17.50
Candle holders, sunflower, #384, pr $35.00
Candlestick, bamboo, #716, introduced in 1939, pr $28.00
Cookie Jar, Choo Choo, locomotive $150.00

Cookie jar, Clock, marked Abingdon USA $95.00
Cookie jar, Hobby Horse, #502....................................$235.00
Cookie jar, Jack-in-the Box, #611 (Illustrated) ...$265.00
Cookie jar, Little Old Lady $235.00
Cookie jar, Money Bag, #588, 1947 ....$85.00
Cookie jar, Three Bears, #696.......................................$100.00
Cornucopia, low, #569...$25.00
Cornucopia, 7", black, #565, 1942-47 ....$25.00
Figurine, 7", peacock, celadon green, #416 ....$45.00
Jar, turquoise, Ming, #301..$80.00

Mint compote, 6", pink, footed, #568, 1942-47 ....$28.00
String holder, mouse, #712..$72.50
Vase, Acadia, #516...$20.00
Vase, Alpha Classic, #101 ....$20.00
Vase, fluted, #550...$26.00
Vase, ship, #494, plain, sm..$22.50
Vase, Star, #463..$16.00
Vase, Wheel, handled, #466..$25.00
Vase, 10½", highly decorated w/decals & much gold .$90.00
Vase, 5½", Classic, blue, mini, #142.............................$25.00
Vase/bookend, dolphin, #444, each..............................$29.50
Wall bracket, Acanthus, #649..$65.00
Wall pocket, #493, double, turquoise...........................$65.00
Wall pocket, shell, #508 ....$40.00
Wall pocket, 7¾", double morning-glory, white, #375.$45.00
Wall vase, book, #676...$35.00
Wall vase, Calla, decorated, #586 ....$65.00

Advertising Collectibles

If you're a beginning advertising collector, you have probably been drawn into this field because of a special attraction you have for a particular advertising character, or maybe you have a certain product in mind. But were you to attempt to be more generalized in your collecting, you'd want to keep some of these things in mind:

Graphics are very important. Watch for bright colors, well-placed subjects, and good detail. There are some products that are generally considered more collectible than others – tobacco, talcum powder, beer, peanut butter, and many soft drinks, for instance. Items with character logos are always good. There's the Red Goose Shoe's goose, RCA's Nipper, the Campbell Kids, and Buster Brown, just to name a few. Anything that depicts sports, patriotic or Western themes, famous people, modes of transportation, or has a Black Americana connection will be very desirable to collectors. Watch for condition; it's very important. A mint condition item may bring twice what the same item in only very good condition will, and often (unless they're rare or especially sought after) things that are damaged are very slow to sell.

You'll find ashtrays, dolls, pin-back buttons, and tons of other small items from the past few decades that have a market value of $50.00 or less, and these are the types of things that make up a good percentage of today's sales.

There are several books we recommend: *Huxford's Collectible Advertising* by Sharon and Bob Huxford, *The Book of Moxie* by Frank Potter, *American Sporting Advertising, Vol I, Posters and Calendars,* by Bob and Beverly Strauss, *Antique Advertising Encyclopedia, Vols 1* and *2,* and *Antique Advertising Handbook,* both by L-W Promotions, *Advertising Dolls Identification and Value Guide* by Joleen Ashman Robison and Kay Sellers, *Pepsi-Cola Collectibles* by Bill Vehling and Michael Hunt, and *The Collector's Guide to Key-Wind Coffee Tins* by James H. Stahl.

See also Airline Memorabilia; Automobilia; Avon; Beer Cans; Breweriana; Bubble Bath Containers; Cereal Boxes;

Character and Promotional Drinking Glasses; Coca-Cola Collectibles; Cookbooks; Cracker Jack Collectibles; Dairy Bottles; Decanters; Fast Food Toys and Figurines; Gas Globes and Collectibles; Keen Kutter; Labels; Pez Candy Containers; Pin-Back Buttons; Planters Peanuts; Playing Cards; Pepsi–Cola; Posters; Soda Bottles; Soda Fountain Collectibles; Typewriter Ribbon Tins; Vending Machines; Watch Fobs.

Almanac, GG Green, 9x6¾", Health Is Happiness, multicolor cover, 1900, NM $15.00

Ashtray, Player's Navy Cut Tobacco, 1x5½" dia, Player's Please in red script, logo in bottom, ceramic, EX. **$22.50**

Ashtray, 4¼" dia, Meyer Furnace Co, Snuffarette **$12.50**

Bank, Amoco, 3", product name in center oval, 586 Special Piston & Valve Stem Oil below, tin, NM **$12.50**

Bank, Captain Crunch Cereal, 7x4", 3-D full figure w/orange stopper, plastic, late 1960s-early '70s, M **$30.00**

Bank, Curad, 7½", molded vinyl Taped Crusader figure, 1977 .... **$35.00**

Bank, Donald Duck Orange Juice, 3¾", resembles a juice container, cardboard w/metal ends, NM **$7.50**

Bank, Emerson, 2½x4", television shape, plastic, NM. **$30.00**

Bank, Esso, 9x3", saluting 3-D Esso man w/logo on his chest, bright red plastic, 1960s, EX+ **$45.00**

Bank, Eveready, black cat figural, plastic, EX **$5.00**

Bank, Howard Johnson's, 5x4", 3-D image of restaurant, orange & blue on white, plastic, 1960s, NM **$25.00**

Bank, Hush Puppy Shoes, Bassett Hound figural, EX. **$24.00**

Bank, Kentucky Fried Chicken, 9½x4½", Colonel Sanders figural, 3-D, plastic, late 1960s-early '70s, NM **$40.00**

Bank, Kool-Aid, 7", pitcher man w/mug on square yellow base, mechanical, 1970s **$25.00**

Bank, Peter's Weatherbird Shoes premium, 2", tin & paper, EX **$12.50**

Bank, Pillsbury, Poppin' Fresh, ceramic, 1985, M **$20.00**

Bank, Pizza Hut, Pizza Pete figural, plastic, 1969, VG. **$10.00**

Bank, Red Goose Shoes, 3¾", goose, cast iron, EX **$50.00**

Bank, Sun Maid Raisins, 7", California Raisin man in red glasses & shoes stands by box, vinyl, 1980s, M **$25.00**

Bank, Thermo Anti-Freeze, 2¾", pictures a smowman w/product & company name below, tin, NM **$16.50**

Bank, Weatherbird Shoes, filled w/candy, plastic, 1940s, EX **$15.00**

Bendee, Quick Bunny, bendable plastic figure, M **$8.00**

Birthday candles, Tony the Tiger, MIB **$8.00**

Blotter, Boston Rubbers, 6½x3¾", lady w/umbrella, ca 1906 .... $8.00

Blotter, Carter's Ink, 6x3", The Old Bookeeper's Verdict, unused, M **$6.50**

Book, Pillsbury Doughboy, Sticker & Activity w/Iron-On Transfer, M **$15.00**

Booklet, Seagram's, Fun At Cocktail Time, 1934, EX... **$12.00**

Bottle topper, Canada Dry, 9x7", little girl & boy drink through straws, Good Sippin'..., cardboard, 1950s, NM **$10.00**

Bottle topper, Dad's Root Beer, 12x8", smiling man w/mustache, ...Old Fashioned Draft..., cardboard, 1950s, M **$30.00**

Bottle topper, Goody Root Beer, 7x5½", little boy's face in center, Golly It's Good below, cardboard, 1940s, NM **$6.00**

Bottle topper, Hires Root Beer, 11x8½", man & woman w/tray, Toast to Good Taste, die-cut cardboard, 1940s, M **$40.00**

Bottle topper, 7-Up, bunny rabbit w/umbrella, Easter Fresh-Up lettered below, cardboard, 1954, EX **$5.00**

Calendar, Dr Pepper, 100th Anniversary, full pad, 1985, EX **$5.00**

Calendar, Esso Gasoline, 15x10", pictures Esso truck & old cars, 1969, full pad, EX **$9.50**

Calendar, Kik Cola, 26x13", little boy w/baseball bat & glass of Kik, full pad, 1955, NM **$40.00**

Calendar, Royster Fertilizers, 8x4¾", pictures baby girl w/wooden doll, full pad, 1949, NM **$16.00**

Calendar, Squirt, Be Healthy, Be Happy, Drink Squirt, 1949, full pad, EX..............$35.00

Camera, instamatic; Kraft Velveeta Shells & Cheese Dinner premium, made like the box, 1980s, MIB $25.00

Catalog, Borden's Premiums, 6x5", Elsie the Cow, 1955, 39-page, EX $25.00

Chalkboard, Campbell's Soups, 24x18", Campbell's boy & bowl of soup, Good N' Hearty..., metal, 1950s, EX........$225.00

Chalkboard, Sun-Drop Soda, 28x20", logo atop, metal, 1972, EX..............$20.00

Clock, Friskies, pictures winking dog, light-up, '50s, M..............$175.00

Clock, Kist Soda, metal & glass light-up, 1940s, working, EX $165.00

Clock, Prestone Anti-Freeze, 10" dia, product name & numbers in silver on blue, metal, wind-up, EX+..........$65.00

Clock, Purina, reverse-painted glass light-up, working, M..............$155.00

Coaster, Vernor's Ginger Ale, from Branson's Welcome Inn, West Union OH, heavy cardboard, 1948, EX..........$5.00

Container, Bosco, 7½", plastic rabbit figure, white w/red letters, 1960s..............$20.00

Container, Nestle's Quick, 8½", brown plastic bunny figure w/yellow cap, 1980s $5.00

Cookie cutter, Elsie the Cow, 2½" dia, hard yellow plastic, NM $17.50

Cookie jar, Tony the Tiger, painted orange plastic head, M..............$40.00

Crate, Hires Root Beer, 11½x17", Hires embossed on sides, holds 24 bottles, metal, 1950s, EX+ $40.00

Creamer, Ken-L-Ration, 3", yellow plastic dog's head, 1950s..............$15.00

Decal, Kist Soda, 7x15", Kist in lg white letters on red die-cut lips, 1940s, EX..............$15.00

Decal, Orange-Crush, 10x10", Enjoy a Fresh New Taste lettered above logo, 1967, EX $6.00

Decal, Sprite, 14", hand holding bottle, 1963, EX..........$7.50

Decal, Whistle Soda, 4½x4½", bottle cap w/lettering below, 1950s, EX $2.50

Display, Kodak Film, 18", side view of girl in swimsuit, Don't Forget..., die-cut cardboard, 1940s, EX........$45.00

Display, Packard Automatic Windshield Washer, lady driving w/windshield wipers on, cardboard trifold, EX.....$45.00

Display, Uncle John's Syrup, 12x16½", elderly gentleman behind counter, die-cut cardboard, NM $16.50

Display, Westinghouse Electric Blankets, 3-D cardboard stand-up w/autumn pumpkin patch setting, light-up, 1950s, EX..............$125.00

Display, Whistle Soda, 13x12", 3 elves carrying lettered banners, die-cut cardboard, holds 1 bottle, 1948, NM..$65.00

Display stand, Clark's Teaberry Gum, 3¼x7x4¾", product name embossed on 4 sides of pedestal, vaseline glass, EX..............$60.00

Doll, Aim Toothpaste, Smokey Bear, 8", vinyl w/denim pants, 1976, M..............$25.00

Doll, Archie Comics, Archie, 18", cloth, M $15.00

Doll, Atlas Van Lines, Atlas Annie, 15½", cloth w/2-toned blue pantsuit, 1977, M $12.00

Doll, Aunt Jemima, Wade, 9", vinyl w/red & white striped shirt holding a lollipop, 1950, M..............$50.00

Doll, Beech-Nut's Fruit Stripe Gum, Zebra, 12", plush w/trademark stripes, 1972, M..............$15.00

Doll, Blue Bonnet Margarine, Sue, 8", dark blue taffeta dress & bonnet w/braid trim, 1970s, M..............$8.00

Doll, Borden's, Beauregard (Elsie's calf), 8½", Guernsey-colored plush w/vinyl head, 1950s, M..............$25.00

Doll, Bumble Bee Tuna, Yum Yum Bumble Bee, 24", inflatable vinyl, M..............$12.00

Doll, Frito-Lay's, Chee-tos Mouse, 12", cloth w/lg felt ears, blue suit & orange tie, 1974, M..............$10.00

Doll, General Mills, Boo Berry, 7½", molded vinyl ghost, 1975, M..............$20.00

Doll, General Mills, Sippin' Sue, 6", vinyl w/molded hair, western outfit, manufactured by Kenner, 1972, M..$7.50

Doll, Hamburger Helper, Helpin' Hand, 14", white plush w/3 fingers & a thumb, 1976, M..............$10.00

Doll, Kellogg's Frosted Flakes, Tony the Tiger, 8", molded & painted vinyl w/red neckerchief, 1974, M............$20.00

Doll, Kellogg's Rice Krispies, Snap, Crackle, & Pop, 8", vinyl squeaker w/molded features, 1975, M, set of 3 ....$36.00

Doll, Mountain Dew, Hillbilly, 18", vinyl head w/sm white beard, round cloth sticker on back, M $65.00

Doll, Nestlé Quik, Little Hans, cloth, 1970, M..............$20.00

Doll, Pillsbury, Poppin' Fresh, knit velour over a foam core, molded nose & mouth, plastic eyes, 1972, M.......$15.00

Doll, Play Doh Boy, 15", cloth, smiling w/arms up, red outfit & hat, Rainbow Craft Inc, 1969, M..............$15.00

Doll, Quake, 12", rag type, 1960s, EX $30.00

Doll, Ralston Purina Dog Chow, Shaggy DA, 21", white plush w/felt eyes, nose & tongue, 1977, M............$8.00

Doll, Razzle Dazzle Bubble Gum, Razzle, 13½", white cloth w/maroon trim on shirt, blue shoes, 1970s, M $10.00

Doll, Revlon, Little Miss Revlon, 10½", vinyl w/cotton print dress, rooted hair, Ideal Toy Co, 1950, M $75.00

Doll, Sergeant's Sentry IV Flea Collar, Sergeant Dog, 20", gold plush w/plastic eyes & nose, 1976, M..........$10.00

Doll, Shakey's Pizza, Shakey Chef, 18", white fabric w/lines outlining apron, hands & facial features, M..........$10.00

Doll, Sunbeam Bread, Little Miss Sunbeam, 17", stuffed cloth w/short blue dress & Mary-Jane shoes, M.............$20.00

Doll, Trix Rabbit, 8½", jointed vinyl, General Mills premium, 1977, EX..............$28.00

Doll kit, Mennen's Baby Magic, Snuggly Sammy, 24", cloth, 1975, M..............$30.00

Door plate, Bubble-Up, 30x4", Drink Bubble-Up, Kiss of Lemon-Kiss of Lime, metal, 1950s, EX..............$50.00

Door plate, Hires Root Beer, 11½x3½", Hires on lg circle, Made w/Roots... below, metal, flanged, 1940s, M..$90.00

Door plate, Robin Hood Flour, product name in red on white ground, EX+..............$40.00

Door plate, Schweppes Ginger Ale, Ask for Schweppes Dry Ginger Ale, gold, black, green & white, NM.........$55.00

Door plate, Squirt, 8½x3½", embossed bottle w/Drink Squirt lettered above, tin, 1941, M..............$75.00

Door plate, Wonder Bread, 2x20", red lettering on white ground, 1940s, EX..............$25.00

Duffle bag, Squirt, inflatable plastic, M $15.00

Fan, Perl Sweeny Steel & Wood, 10¾x8", girl looking over shoulder, cardboard $9.00
Figurine, Marky Maypo, 9", painted vinyl, NM $35.00
Figurine, 7-Up Spot, Bendee, M.......................................$8.00
Figurine, 7-Up Spot, 4", PVC man's face is red disk w/black sunglasses, white hands & feet, 1980s.....................$3.00
Hot pad holder, 5¾", composition Campbell's Kid $12.50
Letterhead, Orange-Crush, 11x8½", amber crinkle bottle in top left corner, ...Carbonated Beverage, 1950s $5.00
Mask, Whisky Mussolini, Seagrams, 1940s, EX $15.00
Match holder, De Laval Cream Separator, 6 x 4 x 1", embossed die-cut tin cream separator, NM........$220.00
Match holder, Dr Shoop's Coffee, 5", encircled portrait of Dr Shoop, ...Health Coffee above & below, tin litho, EX+ $175.00
Match holder, Kool Cigarettes, 8x7", penguin lighting a cigarette, ...For That Clean Kool Taste, tin, EX $16.00
Memo board, Pillsbury, 12x9", Poppin' Fresh, w/magnets & wipe-off pen, M $20.00
Memo board, Pillsbury Doughboy, 8x10", M...............$12.00
Menu, Dybala's Ginger Ale, ...Pale, Dry & Golden Ginger Ale lettered above list of flavors, waxboard, NM..$12.50
Menu board, Crown Beverages, 22x9½", Enjoy... above list of various sodas, cardboard, 1940s, M $110.00
Menu board, Squirt, 28x20", logo & bottle atop, ...Never an After-Thirst, metal, 1973, EX.................................$20.00
Mirror, Skeezix, Skeezix Shoes & figure on celluloid..$22.50
Mug, Borden's, pictures Elsie the Cow, ceramic, M.....$25.00
Mug, Nestlé Quick, 4½", brown plastic bunny face, ears are handles, 1980s...$10.00
Mug, Pillsbury, ceramic, 1980s, MIB $8.00
Mug, Pillsbury Doughboy, painted plastic figural, 1979, EX $10.00
Mug, Quaker Oats, 3¾", plastic head of Quaker man, marked F&F..$12.50
Mug, Quick Rabbit, painted plastic, M $4.50

Paperweight, Emerson Piano Co, rectangular, pictures red building, horse-drawn wagon & trolley, glass, NM..$35.00
Paperweight, Fruit of the Loom, assorted fruits in center, product name arched above, mirror on reverse, EX......$15.00

Paperweight, Johnston Glass Co, 2½x4" $50.00
Paperweight, Merchants Awning Co, 3x4½", ...Montreal, glass, oval, VG..$20.00
Paperweight, Morton's Salt, container w/product name arched above, mirror on reverse, EX....................$25.00
Paperweight, Penn Central Railroad, pictures railroad engine, 1963, EX..$10.00
Plaque, Cap'n Crunch, 8x10", Oath of Allegiance on high-grade document paper, Quaker, 1964, M............$25.00
Playing cards, Elsie the Cow, original box, EX...........$75.00
Pocket mirror, Angelus Marshmallows, 2⅜" long, 2 cherubs leaning on box of marshmallows, oval, VG.........$50.00
Pocket mirror, Boston Varnish Company, 3½" dia, man's faces turn from happy to sad w/movement, EX...$25.00
Pocket mirror, Buster Brown Shoes, 1¾" dia, pictures Buster & Tige, ...For Boys & Girls, NM $150.00
Pocket mirror, Carmen Complexion Powder, 1¾" dia, bust portrait of girl in oval, product name above, EX..$20.00
Pocket mirror, Copper Clad Ranges, 3" long, ...World's Greatest Ranges in horizontal oval flanked by figures, EX..$15.00
Pocket mirror, Cunningham Pianos, 2¾", piano w/lettering above & below, oval, EX......................................$20.00
Pocket mirror, Hires Root Beer, 3" long, lady holding pink roses, Put Roses in Your Cheeks, gold border, EX $200.00
Pocket mirror, Huntley & Osborne Crackers, 2⅛" dia, shaped to look like cracker, EX..........................$25.00
Pocket mirror, Litholin Water Proofed Linen, 2¾", collar & bow tie w/lettering, 25¢ in center, oval, VG.........$15.00
Pocket mirror, Old Reliable Coffee, 2¼" dia, dock worker resting on coffee crate, EX $60.00
Pocket mirror, Rosary Chocolates, 2¼" dia, product name above box of candy, company name below, EX..$15.00
Pocket mirror, Skeezix Shoes, 2⅛", I Wear Skeezix Shoes w/character in center, colorful, 1930s, EX............$62.50
Pocket tin, Bankers Smoking Mixture, product name w/coins above & below, red, gold & white, VG+ $32.00
Pocket tin, Briggs Pipe Mixture, hand holding pipe, 1932 patent date on hinged lid, EX $16.50

Pocket tin, Bugler Tobacco, 3x3", Bugler Cigarette Case lettered in center of gold diagonal bands, EX............**$8.50**

Pocket tin, Edgeworth Tobacco, 4½x1⅛", ...Extra High Grade Plug Slice, blue & silver, VG......................**$14.50**

Pocket tin, Half & Half Tobacco, product name on diagonal center band, Bright & Burley in circle above, EX+..**$9.00**

Pocket tin, Tuxedo Tobacco, man in tuxedo encircled in center, yellow lettering on green ground, EX+.....**$24.00**

Pocket tin, Union Leader Tobacco, 4¼x3", eagle logo, EX **$7.50**

Pot holder, Reddy Kilowatt, M.......................................**$17.50**

Puppet, Elsie the Cow, 14", vinyl head w/plush body, premium offered for $2.50 w/ice cream carton flap, 1958, EX..**$30.00**

Puzzle, Quaker Muffets Cereal premium, clown on swing & clown w/balloons, steel w/clear plastic lid, EX....**$14.00**

Radio, Polaroid 600 Plus Film premium, film pack figural, AM/FM w/built-in antenna, 1980s, NM................**$40.00**

Ruler, Garfield Tea, 12", Cures Constipation & Sick Headache, wood, EX **$6.00**

Ruler, Tums, 12", wood, EX **$5.00**

Salt & pepper shakers, Elsie the Cow, 4", ceramic bust, painted features on white, 1950s, pr **$90.00**

Salt & pepper shakers, Elsie the Cow & Elmer, 4½", painted ceramic figurals, pr **$70.00**

Salt & pepper shakers, Poppin' Fresh, 3½", Doughboy figurals, 1980s, pr **$20.00**

Shoe stretcher, Buster Brown, plastic w/figural face on handle, 1950s, NM..**$38.00**

Sign, Borden, 15" dia, Elsie's face in center of a daisy, cardboard, EX...**$45.00**

Sign, Brooke Bond Tea, 30x20", product name in black on red ground, black & white checked border, porcelain, EX+ **$130.00**

Sign, Butter Nut Bread, 13½x27½", loaf of bread w/Enriched Bread above & below, embossed metal, 1930s, VG **$50.00**

Sign, Calumet Baking Powder, removable price wheels, cardboard, EX..**$15.00**

Sign, Chew Pay Car Scrap, 14x11", The Best Flavor, red & green on white, pictures trolley car............$85.00

Sign, Clabber Girl Baking Powder, 12x34", 2-sided, tin, 1940s, NM..**$55.00**

Sign, Coleman's Ginger Ale, 12x24", embossed tin, yellow, green, blue & red, EX...**$40.00**

Sign, Dad's Root Beer, pictures Elizabeth Montgomery, cardboard, 1960, M **$35.00**

Sign, Dr Pepper, 10½x26", Drink...Good For Life! in white letters on checked ground, porcelain, 1940s, EX.....**$150.00**

Sign, Five Roses Flour, 8½x27½", Five Roses in bold red letters above The All Purpose... in black, tin, M.......**$25.00**

Sign, Frostie Root Beer, 15x29½", little girl reaching for bottle of root beer, self-framed cardboard, VG..........**$25.00**

Sign, Good Year Rubber Heels, 10x18", 2-sided, ...Applied Here, yellow, blue & white, porcelain, G **$40.00**

Sign, Grapette Soda, 8x12", embossed lettering in oval center, purple, red & white, tin, 1940s, NM................**$30.00**

Sign, Green River Whiskey, 17x23", Black man & horse, metal, 1989, EX...**$8.00**

Sign, Green Spot Orange-Aid, 12x20", Green Spot lettered in black circle atop bottle neck, tin, 1940s, NM........**$95.00**

Sign, Happy Foot Socks, 14x29", Santa admiring his sock, ...Health Socks by McGregor, cardboard, EX+......**$26.00**

Sign, Hazel Club Cream Soda, 9" dia, frothy mug of soda w/lettering arched above & below, celluloid, 1940s, NM...**$40.00**

Sign, Hi-Plane Tobacco, 12x35", product name in lg letters, tobacco tin at left, embossed tin, 1930s, EX..........**$60.00**

Sign, Hires Root Beer, 28½x20", lady w/hot dog & 6-pack of Hires, Top It Off w/Hires, cardboard, 1950s, EX+..**$35.00**

Sign, Jic Jac, 9" dia, Drink Jic Jac, green, red & white, celluloid, 1940s, NM **$40.00**

Sign, Kist Beverages, 10x2½", Drink Kist Beverages, bottle shape, orange, white & red, cardboard, 1940s, M..**$15.00**

Sign, Lemmy Lemonade, ...5¢, tin, 1930s, EX.............**$45.00**

Sign, Lift Soda, 12x7", labeled bottle in center w/Drink above & It's Good for You below, embossed tin, 1940s, NM...**$40.00**

Sign, Lord Maxwell Ginger Ale, 13x23", red, green & white, embossed tin, EX **$50.00**

Sign, Moore's Ice Cream, 9x20", waitress w/ice cream scoop, ...Hand Packed To Take Out, paper, 1950s, EX....**$12.50**

Sign, Moxie, 13x8", boy in baseball cap w/vintage Moxie bottle, die-cut cardboard, 1930s, EX...................**$125.00**

Sign, Nehi Beverages, 21½x13½", lady's leg beside bottle of Nehi, ...Quality Beverages, cardboard, 1940s, EX.**$100.00**

Sign, Nesbitt's, 10x28", tilted bottle & Nesbitt's in lg script, black, orange & white, embossed metal, 1956, EX.**$90.00**

Sign, Nichol Kola, 12x36", America's Taste Sensation, tin, 1930s, EX..**$100.00**

Sign, Orange-Crush, 19" dia, Enjoy Orange Crush, bottle cap shape, embossed metal, 1940s, NM....................**$120.00**

Sign, Orange-Crush, 21x21", Real Fresh! Drink Orange-Crush, diamond shape, metal, dated 1939, NM..**$120.00**

Sign, Pop-Kola, 16½x10½", girl holding bottle, white, black, red & blue, cardboard, 1940s, NM.....................**$35.00**

Sign, Quaker Boy Cigars, 9x7¼", Quaker Boy in center square, Smoke...Best 5¢ Cigar above & below, cardboard, EX..**$30.00**

Sign, Ramsay's Floor Finish, 9x12", text in center w/color chart each side, celluloid over metal, EX+ $16.00

Sign, Red Goose Shoes, 10½x6", red goose above Half the Fun of Having Feet!, cardboard, 1950s, M............$20.00

Sign, Red Rose Coffee, 19x27", product name in bold letters, Really Fresh lettered below, tin, NM...................$80.00

Sign, Red Spot Coffee, 3x20", embossed metal, '40s, EX.$15.00

Sign, Royal Crown Cola, 11x28", girl w/RC bottle talking on telephone, Yes...Bring RC, cardboard, 1940s, EX .$35.00

Sign, Royal Crown Cola, 12x30", Drink...Best By Taste Test, labeled bottle in oval at right, tin, 1947, EX+........$65.00

Sign, Royal Crown Cola, 28x11", couple w/RC & chips watching TV, Enjoy RC w/TV!, cardboard, '40s, EX.........$35.00

Sign, Texaco, keyhole shape, 1939, EX......................$160.00

Sign, Texo Feeds, 12x6", It's in the Bag, tin, EX..........$18.00

Sign, Timberline Smokeless Tobacco, 22" dia, When You're Up to Great Taste Every Time, metal, 1982, EX....$15.00

Sign, Ward's, Orange-Lemon-Lime Crush, embossed tin, self-framed, EX...$275.00

Sign, 7-Up, 12x8½", girl watching grandmother knit, We're a Fresh Up Family!, cardboard easel-back, 1946, NM .$10.00

Sign, 7-Up, 8" dia, 7-Up Likes You, red, green & white, reverse-painted glass w/metal frame & hanging chain, NM $75.00

Spoon, Campbell Kid, International Silverplate, EX $15.00

Spoon, Gerber Baby, silverplate, M...........................$12.50

Stafford's Universal Ink, hold-to-light, sleeping child's eyes open, EX...$15.00

Statue, Reddy Kilowatt, 12", wooden 'lightning bolt' man, 1950s...$375.00

Store display, Elsie the Cow, 10", composition bust, head turned, daisy necklace, white dress, 1950s.........$400.00

Sundae dish, Elsie the Cow, portrait on clear glass, footed, EX $28.00

Sunglasses, Pillsbury Doughboy, M...........................$12.50

Tape measure, Frigidaire, man carrying refrigerator encircled by This Modern..., text on back, celluloid, EX......$30.00

Tape measure, John Deere, celluloid, EX $14.00

Tape measure, Nancy Lynn Hosiery, celluloid, ca 1951, EX $12.00

Telephone, Poppin' Fresh, 14", Doughboy figural, 1980s, M...$90.00

Thermometer, B1 Lemon-Lime, 16x4½", More Zip in Every Sip above, logo below, red, white & blue, tin, 1950s, M...$35.00

Thermometer, Canada Dry, 12" dia, bottle in center, metal & glass, dated 1961, M..$70.00

Thermometer, Carter White Lead Paint, 27x7", can of paint at bottom, product name atop, porcelain, EX.....$140.00

Thermometer, Double-Cola, 12" dia, Enjoy Double-Cola in center, metal & glass, 1950s, M..............................$95.00

Thermometer, Dr Pepper, Frosty Cold, 1960s, EX.......$60.00

Thermometer, Dr Pepper, 12" dia, Dr Pepper Hot or Cold in white letters, metal & glass, 1950s, NM $95.00

Thermometer, Haines Dairy Farm, 5¾x2½", milk bottle shape, product name & letters below, NM in box $35.00

Thermometer, Maxwell House Coffee, 12" dia, product name in center, glass front, 1950s, NM $65.00

Thermometer, Orange-Crush, 16x6", pictures bottle cap at top, metal, 1950s, NM...................................$55.00

Thermometer, Quicky Soda, 16x6", labeled bottle in center, Quicky lettered in oval atop, metal, 1950s, EX.....$35.00

Thermometer, Royal Crown Cola, 12" dia, RC logo in center, metal & plastic, 1960s, M...$40.00

Thermometer, Squirt, 13½x5½", Squirt boy beside lg bottle, logo above, embossed metal, 1961, NM................$95.00

Thermometer, Tums, ...For the Tummy, EX................$22.00

Thermometer, Wolfschmidt Vodka, round, glass face, 1950s, NM $25.00

Thermometer, 7-Up, 13" dia, logo in center w/Fresh Clean Taste below, glass, 1950s, M $95.00

Tin, A&P Paprika, 3x2" dia, 1½-oz, red w/gold lettering & lg logo, shaker top, VG...$12.50

Tin, American Breakfast Coffee, 9x7", 5-lb, product & company name on front, coffeepot on back, slip lid & bail, EX+.$28.00

Tin, Benson's Candies, 5x8", full color litho of the Queen Mary, canted corners, EX+ $18.00

Tin, Best Talking Machine Needles, old victrola beside product name in gold on red background, NM............$10.00

Tin, Betsy Ross Tea, Betsy Ross flanked by lettering on red background, VG..$10.00

Tin, Blue Ribbon Pure Marjoram, blue ribbon in center, product name in white above & below, red ground, slip lid, EX+...$4.00

Tin, Brach's, 10", 5-lb, candies & factory scenes, Candies of Quality..., gold on gold, screw lid, 1930s-40s, EX .$55.00

Tin, Calumet Baking Powder, 3½x2" dia, Indian in on orange paper label, embossed lid, EX...................$16.50

Tin, Christie's Butter Wafers, 6", wafers w/product name above, company name below, blue & beige, slip lid, VG...$6.00

Tin, Cleopatra Chocolates, 1x6½x9", 1½-lb, lady's face in gold & red on dark blue, 1930s-40s, EX...............$25.00

Tin, Defender Motor Oil, 2-gal, WWI sentry guarding tents, EX...$50.00

Tin, Gardenia & Sweet Pea Blended Talc, 6", 5-oz, colorful gardenias & sweet peas, shaker top, 1930s, EX....$20.00

Tin, Granger Tobacco, 6x4¾" dia, 14-oz, tobacco leaf on front, pointing dog on finial & back, EX...............$22.50

Tin, Lipton Tea, 5x5x5", 100th anniversary, limited edition, 1990, M in original box..$5.00

Tin, Manor House Coffee, 1-lb, paper label w/product name over landscape w/horse & rider, slip lid, EX $30.00

Tin, Peak Coffee, 6x4", 1-lb, mountain scene above product name, red, white & blue, pry lid, EX+..................$28.00

Tin, Rawleigh's Fan-Jang Talc, oriental lady w/open fan surrounded by flowers, EX...$35.00

Tin, Red Rose Coffee, pictures a rose; red, white, blue & yellow, key-wind lid missing, VG $9.00

Tin, Sailor Boy Oysters, 5-gal, M $40.00

Tin, Simoniz Car Kleener, 4", early touring car & product name in black on green ground, EX....................$15.00

Tin, Squirrel Peanut Butter, 3-lb, squirrel logo w/lettering above & below, press lid, VG $50.00

Tip tray, Maxwell House Instant Coffee, 7x9", red on white, Kaldi & Goats story on back, EX $7.50

Tip tray, Prudential Insurance, 3½x2½", oval, EX........**$25.00**

Tip tray, Wrigley's Soap, pictures a cat, EX **$175.00**

Toy, Ernie, The Keebler Elf, 7", vinyl figural, 1974......**$15.00**

Toy, Good Humor Bar, 8", vinyl figural ice cream bar w/smiley face, 1975..**$250.00**

Toy, Poppin' Fresh, 6½", Doughboy, molded rubber, 1970s..**$8.00**

Tray, 7-Up, featuring Sugar Ray Leonard, tin, 1981, EX .**$2.50**

Trolley sign, Walter Neilly & Co, 11x20¾", girl w/book & dish of ice cream, ...Fig Walnut Sundae, EX.........**$60.00**

Tumbler, Elsie the Cow, 6x3" dia, tapered clear glass w/head portrait, 1950s, EX................................**$17.50**

Watch, Goodyear, revolving Goodyear Blimp, 1960s, EX **$40.00**

Wristwatch, Ritz, Olympic Quartz, Ritz in yellow letters on black ground in center, working, EX+ **$34.00**

Advertising Trade Cards

During the last decade of the 19th century, these trade cards became a popular way to advertise merchandise of all types. They were collectible even then. They were often packaged in with the products they advertised, and many were available directly from the corner grocery store and other places of business. Children as well as adults delighted in pasting the colorful cards in albums, so when you buy today, be sure they've not been damaged by having been once pasted down. Many people collect cards related to a particular theme (cats, transportation, children, or a favorite product).

Ad cards range in size from 2" x 3" up to 4" x 6", though some may be larger. Many common examples may be bought for under $5.00. Metamorphics (mechanicals), die-cuts, and hold-to-lights will be more pricey. Those listed here are among the more expensive.

Ansonia Clock Co, metamorphic, unhappy sleepless man opens to happy man, ...Peep O' Day...above, EX **$22.00**

Brooks Spool Cotton, 3 cats w/instruments, EX............**$10.00**

Bush Hill Creamery Butter, ranch scene, red & green on white, advertising on reverse, EX **$10.00**

Buttermilk Toilet Soap, opens down to 4 panels w/story of Jack & Jill, wallet shape, EX................................**$20.00**

Carl Dunder Cigars, elderly man & children, EX **$6.50**

Cooley's Globe Corset, metamorphic, unhappy woman opens to happy woman, Dressing for the Ball..., EX.........**$15.00**

Foster Pianos, die-cut girl w/jump rope, pull head & hands move, EX...**$12.00**

Globe Clothing Co, St Bernard in center square, This Dog Don't Bite!... above & below, EX.............................**$20.00**

Hoods Sarsaparilla, 3x5", First Lesson, dog family ponders capture of mouse **$8.00**

Merchant's Gargling Oil, 3 horses drinking from trough, $1000 Reward... upper left, advertising on revererse, EX ..**$20.00**

New Brunswick Tires, 3 women on a bicycle in shades of sepia brown, advertising on reverse, G.................**$35.00**

Palmer's Perfumes, die-cut vase of flowers, advertising on reverse, EX **$15.00**

Quaker Oats, folder, Quaker Oats man front & back, Quaker White Oats..., advertising inside, EX........**$40.00**

Royal Lawn Mower, girl in bonnet pushing mower, The Boss of All... above, advertising on reverse, EX ...**$10.00**

Sandwich Manufacturing Co, Clean Sweep Hay Loader upper left, advertising on back, VG **$15.00**

Schimmel's Fruit Preserves, product name above & below various fruits, VG **$15.00**

Scott's Emulsion, little girl twins holding flag & standing on boxes of product, advertising on reverse, EX.......**$25.00**

Soapine, shows a dog kissing a horse, advertising on reverse, EX **$15.00**

Sohmer Pianos, head portraits of leading artists surrounding piano, Preferred by the... below, VG.....................**$10.00**

Stafford's Universal Ink, hold-to-light, sleeping child's eyes open, EX...**$15.00**

Sunflower Baking Powder, die-cut sunflower w/girl's face in center, advertising on reverse, rare, EX.................**$35.00**

Tarrant's Seltzer Aperient, metamorphic, sick family opens to healthy one, Home Made Happy... below, EX.**$15.00**

Van Houton's Cocoa, little girl in her bed playing w/puppies, Early Visitors, EX..**$30.00**

Van Houton's Cocoa, metamorphic, man w/cup labeled Imitation opens to man w/Van Houton's, VG...........**$25.00**

Airline Memorabilia

Items from commercial airlines such as dinnerware, flatware, playing cards, and pins and buttons worn by the flight crew represent a relatively new field of collector interest. Anything from before the war is rare and commands a high price. Advertising material such as signs, models of airplanes from travel agencies, and timetables are included in this area of collecting as well.

See also Playing Cards.

Bag, Pan American, 1st-class complimentary w/toiletries **$5.00**

Ballpoint pen, Western Airlines, New Non-stop to San Diego, M...**$10.00**

Booklet, TWA, 1935, EX..**$15.00**

Booklet of maps & schedules, American Airlines, 1946, EX.**$22.00**

Card, Eastern, Occupied, plastic w/compass-like logo, 1961, NM...**$2.00**

Corkscrew/knife, Eastern..**$10.00**

Cup, Air Canada, Royal Stafford bone china, gold details, M **$12.00**

Cup, American, Syracuse China, Airlite, 1940s, blue & white **$35.00**

Drink stirrer, TWA, Gold Plate Service ....**$.50**

Emergency card, Delta, folder, B-757, 1988 ....**$3.50**

Emergency card, United, plastic, DC-8, 1973 ....**$4.00**

Flight schedule, Transtar, 1987...**$2.00**

Folder, TWA, shows air routes, back shows 10 different airplanes & configurations, DC-4 ....**$14.00**

Fork, United, winged badge at top, United Air Lines at bottom, 1930s, EX **$10.00**

Globe, 8", tin, w/22 different airline logos on base, M .**$12.00**

Hat badge, Eastern, Ground Hostess...........................**$25.00**

Hat badge, 2", Trans Canada Airlines, maple leaf w/white metal overlay initials TCA, EX..............................**$75.00**

Hatpin, Eastern, Flight Attendant................................**$25.00**

Highball glass, TCA, oval logo w/line name inside.......**$5.00**

Knife, American, DC-3 handle **$30.00**

Luggage sticker, Airways Cuba, pictures airplane & world globe **$7.50**

Medal, Mohawk, bronze, observation pilot, ground workers, flight attendant, back: motto, 45mm.....................**$25.00**

Menu, Air France, Indies cover, 1962, EX **$2.50**

Menu, Pan-Am, first class, cities in script on cover, 1971, M **$3.00**

Mug, Air France, glass, inscribed Air France, Houston-Paris 747 Non-Stop, 1970s **$5.00**

Pin-back button, 2¼" dia, Alaska Airlines, white on blue, 1960s...**$15.00**

Plaque, Scandinavian Airlines System, shaped as rear tail, silver **$35.00**

Plate, American, Syracuse China, Airlite, ca 1940s, blue & white **$125.00**

Plate, Pan-Am Clipper..**$45.00**

Plate, salad; Eastern, Rosenthal, Made in Germany.......**$5.00**

Plate, service; 7", British Airways, trimmed w/blue & gold pattern of stylized Concords, EX........................**$25.00**

Playing cards, American, Ford Tri-Motor picture, NM ...**$4.50**

Postcard, American, DC-4..**$10.00**

Ring, American, Junior Pilot..**$15.00**

Roly-poly, Aeroflot, gold logo, EX..............................**$25.00**

Shot glass, Eastern..**$2.00**

Tumbler, Eastern, 1950, Rickenbacker, M **$15.00**

Tumbler, Frontier, frosted logo, footed, EX **$7.00**

Tumbler, juice; Eastern, etched logo, early..................**$25.00**

Tumbler, Northwest, lg NWA on side, tall **$4.00**

Wine glass, Air Canada, maple leaf logo, EX................**$4.00**

Wings, Eastern, child's, plastic **$2.00**

Akro Agate

Everybody remembers the 'Aggie' marbles from their childhood; this is the company that made them. They operated in West Virginia from 1914 until 1951, and in addition to their famous marbles they made children's dishes as well as many types of novelties – flowerpots, powder jars with scotty dogs on top, candlesticks, and ashtrays, for instance – in many colors and patterns. Though some of their glassware was made in solid colors, their most popular products were made of the same swirled colors as their marbles. Nearly everything they made is marked with their logo: a crow flying through the letter 'A' holding an Aggie in its beak and one in each claw. Some children's dishes may be marked 'JP,' and the novelty items may instead carry one of

these trademarks: 'JV Co, Inc,' 'Braun & Corwin,' 'NYC Vogue Merc Co USA,' 'Hamilton Match Co,' and 'Mexicali Pickwick Cosmetic Corp.'

In the children's dinnerware listings below, you'll notice that color is an important worth-assessing factor. As a general rule, an item in green or white opaque is worth only about a third when compared to the same item in any other opaque color. Blue marbleized pieces are about three times higher than solid opaques, and of the marbleized colors, blue is the most valuable. It's followed closely by red, and green is about 25% under red. Lemonade and oxblood is a good color combination, and it's generally three times higher item for item than the transparent colors of green or topaz.

For further study we recommend *The Collector's Encyclopedia of Akro Agate Glassware* by Gene Florence and *The Collector's Encyclopedia of Children's Dishes* by Margaret and Kenn Whitmyer.

Children's Dishes

Chiquita, creamer, 1½", opaque colors other than green.**$15.00**

Chiquita, cup, 1½", opaque green................................**$3.50**

Chiquita, plate, 3¾", transparent cobalt.......................**$6.00**

Chiquita, sugar bowl, 1½", opaque colors other than green, no lid **$15.00**

Chiquita, teapot, 3", baked-on colors, w/lid **$19.00**

Chiquita, 22-piece boxed set, opaque green................**$70.00**

Concentric Rib, creamer, 1¼", opaque green or white..**$9.00**

Concentric Rib, cup, 1¼", opaque other than green or white..**$7.00**

Concentric Rib, saucer, 2¾", opaque other than green or white..**$2.00**

Concentric Rib, teapot, 3⅜", opaque other than green or white, w/lid...**$13.00**

Concentric Rib, 8-piece set in original box, opaque green or white..**$30.00**

Concentric Ring, creamer, 1⅜", transparent cobalt, lg...**$27.50**

Concentric Ring, cup, 1¼", marbleized blue, sm **$33.00**

Concentric Ring, cup, 1¼", transparent cobalt, sm **$28.50**

Concentric Ring, plate, 4¼", marbleized blue, lg.........**$22.00**

Concentric Ring, saucer, 2¾", transparent cobalt, sm....**$9.00**

Concentric Ring, sugar bowl, 1⅞", solid opaque colors, w/lid, lg...**$23.00**

Concentric Ring, teapot, 3⅜", solid opaque colors, w/lid, sm **$30.00**

Interior Panel, cereal bowl, 3⅜", marbleized green & white, lg...**$20.00**

Interior Panel, creamer, 1¼", transparent green or topaz, sm **$17.50**

Interior Panel, creamer, 1⅜", marbleized blue & white, lg...**$32.00**

Interior Panel, cup, 1¼", marbleized red & white, sm.**$26.00**

Interior Panel, cup, 1⅜", lemonade & oxblood, lg **$22.50**

Interior Panel, cup, 1⅜", pink or green lustre, lg.........**$14.50**

Interior Panel, pitcher, 2⅞", transparent green or topaz, sm **$13.00**

Interior Panel, plate, 3¾", marbleized green & white, sm **$9.00**
Interior Panel, plate, 3¾", pink lustre, sm **$5.00**
Interior Panel, plate, 4¼", marbleized red & white, lg . **$15.00**
Interior Panel, plate, 4¼", pink or green lustre, lg **$7.50**
Interior Panel, saucer, 3⅛", pink or green lustre, lg **$3.50**
Interior Panel, teapot, 3¾", lemonade & oxblood, w/lid, lg **$60.00**
Interior Panel, teapot, 3⅜", marbleized blue & white, w/lid, sm **$37.00**
Interior Panel, 8-piece boxed set, green lustre, sm **$50.00**
JP, creamer, 1½", baked-on colors **$7.00**
JP, creamer, 1½", transparent red or brown **$42.00**
JP, cup, light blue or clear, 1½" **$16.50**
JP, plate, 4¼", transparent green **$9.00**
JP, teapot, 2¾", baked-on colors, w/lid **$16.00**
JP, 17-piece boxed set, baked-on colors **$84.00**
Miss America, creamer, 1¼", forest green **$53.00**
Miss America, cup, 1⅝", white **$37.00**
Miss America, plate, 4½", white w/decal **$42.00**
Miss America, saucer, 3⅝", marbleized orange & white . **$13.50**
Miss America, sugar bowl, 2", forest green, w/lid **$60.00**
Miss America, teapot, 3¼", white, w/lid **$67.00**
Octagonal, cereal bowl, 3⅜", green, white or dark blue, lg **$8.50**
Octagonal, creamer, 1½", pink or yellow, closed handle, lg **$9.00**
Octagonal, cup, 1½", beige or light blue, closed handle, lg **$13.50**
Octagonal, cup, 1½", lemonade & oxblood, closed handle, lg **$23.50**
Octagonal, cup, 1½", pumpkin, closed handle, lg **$22.50**
Octagonal, cup, 1¼", dark green, blue or white, sm **$9.00**

Octagonal, cup, 1¼", pumpkin, sm $11.00
Octagonal, cup, 1¼", yellow or lime green, sm **$22.00**
Octagonal, pitcher, 2¾", dark green, blue or white, sm. **$16.50**
Octagonal, plate, 3⅜", pumpkin, yellow or lime green, sm **$5.50**
Octagonal, plate, 4¼", beige, pumpkin or light blue, lg (illustrated) $8.50
Octagonal, plate, 4¼", lemonade & oxblood, lg **$13.00**
Octagonal, saucer, 2¾", dark green, blue or white, sm. **$3.50**
Octagonal, saucer, 2¾", pumpkin, yellow or lime green, sm (illustrated) $3.50
Octagonal, saucer, 3⅜", lemonade & oxblood, lg **$5.50**
Octagonal, sugar bowl, 1½", pink or yellow, w/lid, closed handle, lg **$12.00**
Octagonal, teapot, 3⅝", green, white or dark blue, w/lid, closed hdl, lg **$17.00**
Octagonal, tumbler, 2", dark green, blue or white, sm . **$9.00**
Octagonal, tumbler, 2", pumpkin, yellow or lime green, sm **$16.00**
Octagonal, 16-piece boxed set, dark green, blue or white, sm **$115.00**
Raised Daisy, creamer, 1¾", yellow **$42.00**
Raised Daisy, cup, 1¾", blue **$42.00**
Raised Daisy, cup, 1¾", green **$16.50**
Raised Daisy, plate, 3", blue **$12.00**
Raised Daisy, saucer, 2½", beige **$8.50**
Raised Daisy, saucer, 2½", yellow **$9.00**
Raised Daisy, sugar bowl, 1¾", yellow **$42.00**
Raised Daisy, tumbler, 2", beige **$28.00**
Stacked Disc, creamer, 1¼", opaque green or white, sm **$9.00**
Stacked Disc, creamer, 1¼", pumpkin, sm **$19.00**
Stacked Disc, cup, 1¼", opaque green or white, sm **$5.00**
Stacked Disc, sugar bowl, 1¼", pumpkin, no lid, sm .. **$20.00**
Stacked Disc, teapot, 3⅜", pumpkin, w/lid, sm **$19.00**
Stacked Disc, tumbler, 2", pumpkin, sm **$19.00**
Stacked Disc & Interior Panel, cereal bowl, 3⅜", transparent green, lg **$21.00**
Stacked Disc & Interior Panel, creamer, 1⅜", marbleized blue, lg **$40.00**
Stacked Disc & Interior Panel, cup, 1⅜", transparent green, lg **$19.00**
Stacked Disc & Interior Panel, plate, 3¼", transparent cobalt, sm **$26.00**
Stacked Disc & Interior Panel, plate, 3¼", transparent green, sm **$16.00**
Stacked Disc & Interior Panel, plate, 4¾", marbleized blue, lg **$19.00**
Stacked Disc & Interior Panel, plate, 4¾", transparent cobalt, lg **$15.00**
Stacked Disc & Interior Panel, saucer, 3¼", transparent green, lg **$6.50**
Stacked Disc & Interior Panel, sugar bowl, 1¼", solid opaque colors, sm **$17.00**
Stacked Disc & Interior Panel, teapot, 3¾", transparent cobalt, w/lid, lg **$65.00**
Stacked Disc & Interior Panel, tumbler, 2", transparent green, sm **$11.00**
Stacked Disc & Interior Panel, 7-piece boxed water set, transparent cobalt, sm **$110.00**
Stippled Band, creamer, 1½", transparent green, lg **$19.00**
Stippled Band, cup, 1½", transparent amber, lg **$11.00**
Stippled Band, pitcher, 2⅞", transparent amber, sm **$17.00**

Stippled Band, pitcher, 2⅞", transparent green, sm.....**$13.50**

Stippled Band, plate, 3¼", transparent amber, sm.........**$5.00**

Stippled Band, plate, 4¼", transparent azure, lg..........**$15.00**

Stippled Band, plate, 4¼", transparent green, lg............**$5.50**

Stippled Band, saucer, 3¼", transparent amber, lg **$5.50**

Stippled Band, sugar bowl, 1⅞", transparent azure, w/lid, lg...**$43.00**

Stippled Band, teapot, 3⅜", transparent amber, w/lid, sm .**$19.00**

Stippled Band, tumbler, 1¾", transparent green, sm **$7.00**

Stippled Band, 8-piece set in original box, transparent green, sm...**$40.00**

Other Lines of Production

Apothecary jar, pink, w/lid **$65.00**

Ashtray, 3", green, Edison Hotel................................**$40.00**

Basket, white, 2-handled..**$15.00**

Bell, 5¼", white **$50.00**

Bowl, 5¼", Ribs & Flutes, cobalt or pumpkin, footed .**$20.00**

Candlesticks, 3¼", cobalt or pumpkin, pr **$125.00**

Cup & saucer, demitasse; yellow **$8.00**

Flowerpot, 2½", black amethyst, Banded Dart............**$35.00**

Flowerpot, 2½", cobalt or pumpkin, Banded Dart.......**$20.00**

Flowerpot, 2¼", marbleized, ribbed top **$3.00**

Flowerpot, 3", cobalt or pumpkin, Graduated Darts, scalloped top..**$10.00**

Flowerpot, 3", marbleized, Graduated Darts.................**$5.00**

Flowerpot, 4", green, ribbed top..................................**$7.50**

Flowerpot, 5½", pumpkin, Ribs & Flutes, scalloped top .**$20.00**

Flowerpot, 5½", marbleized, Stacked Disc **$15.00**

Jardiniere, 4½", light blue, rectangular, tab handles **$20.00**

Jardiniere, 5", marbleized, Graduated Dart, scalloped.**$15.00**

Mug, black...**$30.00**

Planter, marbleized, rectangular, rounded bottom, embossed floral decor **$4.00**

Planter, 6", light blue w/factory floral decoration, scalloped, oval **$32.50**

Planter, 6", pumpkin color, scalloped, rectangular......**$10.00**

Powder jar, black, allover ribbing, w/lid....................**$30.00**

Powder jar, blue, allover ribbing, w/lid......................**$20.00**

Powder jar, white, allover ribbing, w/lid **$10.00**

Puff box, Colonial Lady, 1939-1942, any transparent color **$325.00**

Puff box, Colonial Lady, 1939-1942, blue (several shades, any other than cobalt or ice blue) **$60.00**

Puff box, Colonial Lady, 1939-1942, cobalt blue or ice blue...**$225.00**

Puff box, Scotty Dog, 1939-1942, dark green **$150.00**

Puff box, Scotty Dog, 1939-1942, white or pink.........**$60.00**

Vase, 6¼", cobalt or pumpkin, tab handles.................**$50.00**

Vase, 8", yellow, Ribs & Flutes **$100.00**

Vase, 8¾", cobalt or pumpkin, 7 darts.......................**$60.00**

Vase, 8¾", marbleized, 7 darts **$35.00**

Aluminum

This is an exciting, relatively new field of collecting, and your yard sale outings will often yield some nice examples at very little expense. You'll find all types of serving pieces and kitchenware, most of which will be embossed with fruit or flowers. Some will have a hand-hammered texture; these pieces are generally thought to be from the fifties, though aluminum ware was popular from the late 1930s on. The best buys are those with a backstamp; a good one to watch for is Wendell August Forge. Russel Wright and Royal Hickman were two highly renowned designers of dinnerware and ceramics that used this medium for some of their work; items signed by either are very collectible. For more information we recommend the newsletter *The Aluminist* published by Dannie Woodard, author of *Hammered Aluminum, Hand Wrought Collectibles.* Although Book I is now out of print, Book II will soon be available. Another new book on the subject is *Collectible Aluminum, An Identification and Value Guide,* by Everett Grist (Collector Books).

Ashtray, 5½" dia, tulip design, feet curve over top to make 3 cigarette rests, Rodney Kent..................................**$14.00**

Basket, 8½" dia, wild rose design on inside bottom, square knot handle, Early American Style #6...................**$15.00**

Bowl, fruit; 11", embossed flowers & fruit, handles...**$17.50**

Bowl, 11" dia, shallow w/deeply carved curvilinear design, Canterbury Arts **$18.00**

Bowl, 6½" dia, embossed pine trees & mountain, Arthur Armour..**$14.00**

Bowl, 7½" dia, round base flared to hexagonal rim, Everlast...**$6.00**

Bread tray, 13" long, embossed blackberries on leaf shape, Everlast...**$14.00**

Butter dish, ¼-lb, Rodney Kent.................................**$12.00**

Butter tub, embossed leaves, hammered **$18.00**

Candle holder, tulip blossom pattern on base, low style holds lg candle, Rodney Kent..............................**$8.00**

Candy dish, 7½" dia, box shape w/3-part glass insert, Everlast...**$18.00**

Casserole, hammered design, w/lid, Buenilum **$12.50**

Cigarette box, cast gun as decoration, Palmer-Smith **$55.00**

Coaster, 4" dia, embossed flying goose design, Arthur Armour..**$4.00**

Coaster, 4" dia, embossed pine cone, Wendell August Forge...**$4.00**

Coasters w/tray, embossed flowers, marked Everlast Forged Aluminum, set of 8 ....**$18.00**

Compote, 6", 3 sections, each w/flowers & fruits design, beaded rim, Cromwell **$12.00**

Dresser tray, hammered design, w/2 glass powder-jar inserts, Kent...**$25.00**

Electric urn, chrysanthemum, #22, Continental..........**$65.00**

Ice bowl, 8", slotted bottom, embossed flower garlands, w/insert & slotted spoon, Everlast.......................**$18.00**

Ice bucket, 8x7", pyrex-lined w/mahogany knob, Buenilum...**$20.00**

Nut dish, 11", round, unmarked.................................**$8.50**

Nut dish, 9" long, 'figure - 8' shape, chrysanthemum design, molded leaf & floral handle, Continental, #754 ....**$20.00**

Percolator, 1-cup size, w/basket, wood handle...........**$17.50**

Pitcher, water size, hand hammered, Buenilum **$15.00**

Pitcher, 7½", plain (no embossing), Everlast..............**$15.00**

Plate/wall plaque, embossed wild turkeys, Wendell August Forge...............**$40.00**

Punch bowl & ladle, Wendell August Forge.............**$225.00**

Punch ladle, 11", twisted stem finial, Buenilum..........**$18.00**

Server, 16", tile inset, Cellini Craft **$100.00**

Smoking stand, Wendell August Forge **$125.00**

Tidbit, 8" & 11" tiers, embossed roses & forget-me-nots, Everlast **$15.00**

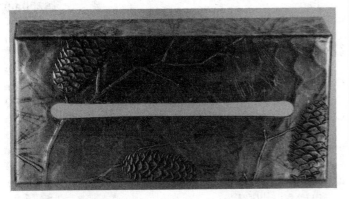

Tissue box, 5x10", pine cones, Wendell August Forge, paper sticker **$75.00**

Tray, fluted rim w/embossed horse, Arthur Armour ...**$50.00**

Tray, hammered design, embossed tulips, w/lid, Rodney Kent, #440.................**$25.00**

Tray, 10x14", embossed butterfly & dogwood, Arthur Armour...................**$55.00**

Tray, 11¾" dia, embossed dogwood, design Wendell August Forge.................**$20.00**

Tray, 14½x21½", embossed fox hunters & hounds, Arthur Armour...................**$95.00**

Tray, 8x11", embossed grapes, unmarked Everlast.....**$15.00**

Tray, 9x14", embossed thistles, Wendell August Forge.**$35.00**

Tray/plate, 10" dia, dogwood blossom design, rim curved up, Stede...................**$14.00**

Trivet, 7¼x5½", embossed ivy, Everlast......................**$10.00**

Warming dish, hammered design w/acorns, w/lid, Bakelite handles **$40.00**

Water goblet, stemmed, hammered design, unmarked.**$8.00**

Anodized

Ashtray, 8" dia, 4 rests, coaster in center......................**$5.00**

Butter dish, ¼-lb, 6½" long, marked Bascal **$6.50**

Coasters, marked Colorcraft, set of 8" **$10.00**

Funnel, 4", gold...............................**$2.50**

Measuring cups, Colorcraft, set of 4 ....**$4.00**

Mug, 3", gold, marked Hong Kong.................................**$3.00**

Pitcher, juice; 7½", no mark **$9.00**

Pitcher, water; 12½", marked Bascal...........................**$12.00**

Salt & pepper shakers, 4", gold w/black tops, marked Westbend, pr **$4.50**

Shaker, graduated measurements to 2 cups, w/lid........**$6.00**

Sherbet, glass liner, no mark.......................................**$10.00**

Spoon rest, heart shape, marked Colorcraft...................**$3.00**

Teakettle, maroon-red, marked Regal, M.....................**$30.00**

Tumbler, 3¼", flares at rim...**$3.00**

Tumbler, 5½", straight sides, marked Perma Hues **$2.50**

Animal Dishes

Glass dishes with animal and bird figures on the lids are a common sight at flea markets today, but you'll need to study the subject thoroughly to be able to tell the old ones from the new. Many were made in the latter 1800s and the early years of this century. Some of the smaller ones were sold to food processors who filled them with products such as mustard or baking powder. Several companies have recently made reproductions. In the 1960s, Kemple made a cat, duck, dove, fox, hen, lamb, lion, rabbit, rooster, and turkey; Westmoreland was making some in the 1980s, and some you'll see were made yesterday! Beware. *Covered Animal Dishes* by Everett Grist will help you in your study. If no color is given in the descriptions, assume that the following examples are clear.

Bird on round basketweave base, 6½", milk glass, Vallerysthal **$95.00**

Cat, 5¼", milk glass head w/blue body & base, Westmoreland....................**$120.00**

Chick emerging from horizontal egg, milk glass, unmarked **$95.00**

Chick in vertical egg, 3¾", milk glass **$125.00**

Donkey powder jar, clear, attributed to Jeannette Glass, from Depression era **$20.00**

Elephant, 9" long, walking, trunk up, fancy headgear, clear, from Depression era **$45.00**

Flat fish on ribbed base, 8½", milk glass, attributed to Fostoria....................**$100.00**

Hand & dove, milk glass, marked WG on base..........**$95.00**

Hen, beaded-edge base, dark blue carnival, Indiana Glass Company **$20.00**

Hen, 2", milk glass, Vallerysthal..................................**$35.00**

Hen, 8", milk glass, Fenton **$150.00**

Hen on cattail base, 5½", milk glass, unmarked **$65.00**

Hen w/chicks, 5½", milk glass, oval base, unmarked Mckee **$165.00**

Horse, 5½", milk glass, reproduction, attributed to St Clair Glass **$75.00**

Lion on picket base, milk glass, Westmoreland..........**$85.00**

Lovebirds on sm compote-like base, clear, recent, Westmoreland **$15.00**

Mother Eagle, milk glass, Westmoreland, marked WG ..**$75.00**

Poodle powder jar, amber carnival glass, Jeannette Glass, 1950s **$22.00**

Quail on scroll base, 5½", milk glass, unmarked.........**$65.00**

Rabbit, clear, marked Vallerysthal...............................**$95.00**

Rabbit, mule-eared, on picket base, pink ears & eyes, Westmoreland reproduction marked WG.....................**$85.00**

Rabbit, 8", on nest w/eggs, attributed to Atterbury **$65.00**

Robin on pedestal base, blue opaque, Vallerysthal...**$125.00**

Rooster, goofus glass w/milk glass base, unmarked ...**$65.00**

Rooster, standing, clear w/red comb & waddle, attributed to LE Smith..**$55.00**

Rooster on basketweave base, milk glass, Challinor, Taylor & Co...**$125.00**

Rooster on wide-ribbed base, 5¼", milk glass, unmarked.**$85.00**

Sheep, on split-rib base, head to right, recent............**$20.00**

Squirrel finial on fancy dish, milk glass, unmarked.....**$95.00**

Swan, milk glass, head on breast, closed-in neck, Westmoreland Specialty Co **$75.00**

Swan, 5½", clear frosted, Vallerysthal......................**$95.00**

Swan, 7" long, head on breast, open neck, knobby basketweave base, Patent Appl'd For inside, attributed to Belmont **$165.00**

Swan powder jar, ribbed lid & base, blue to green, Jeannette Glass, late 1960s **$20.00**

Turkey, very sm, squatting, milk glass, marked IG **$45.00**

Turtle, lg, amber, unmarked **$100.00**

Art Deco Collectibles

During the period from about 1925 until 1950, popular taste and fashions favored architecture, home furnishings and decorations, jewelry, appliances, and even automobiles with sleek aerodynamic lines, cubist forms, or sweeping curves. Lightning bolts, slender nudes, sleek greyhounds, and geometrics were preferred decorative motifs. Chrome, vinyl, and plastic was high style, though at the other end of the spectrum, lush fabrics and exotic woods were used as well. When Art Deco furnishings began showing up in some of our leading home decorating magazines a few years back, collector demand for authentic pieces ran high. Many moderately priced items are around today, but signed pieces often carry high-dollar price tags.

For further study we recommend *The Collector's Guide to Art Deco* by Mary Frank Gaston.

See also Chase.

Ashtray, cast metal seated nude w/painted gold finish holding round amber glass tray, marked Nu Art, Imperial Glass **$125.00**

Ashtray, 4" dia, clear glass Manhattan pattern w/red heart in center, Anchor Hocking....................................**$10.00**

Ashtray, 5" dia, blue glass base w/chrome sailboat, marked FD Co..**$50.00**

Belt buckle, oval shape w/repetitive enameled crescent designs in shades of green, gold trim, Germany ..**$20.00**

Bookends, 7", sailboat figurals, Bronze Art, pr.........**$200.00**

Bowl, 10½" long, oval-shaped serving dish w/multicolor leaves on orange, gold handles, Japanese lustre ..**$35.00**

Bowl, 3x11" long, ceramic oval-shaped centerpiece w/cameo outlined in black, black & green swag & tassel details...**$70.00**

Brush & comb set, man's set in black fitted case, brushes have monogrammed nickel silver tops................**$75.00**

Candle holder, 6", porcelain w/hand-painted stylized birds & geometric patterns, attached dish, black handle....**$85.00**

Candle holders, 5½", frosted blue glass sailboats, pr...**$60.00**

Candy jar, green glass, Manhattan pattern, urn shape w/lid & pedestal foot, late 1930s, Anchor Hocking.......**$25.00**

Cheese board, 6½" dia, chrome dome-shaped cover w/celluloid handle on wooden base, Chase **$75.00**

Cigarette box, 5½" long, black & red plastic half-circle shape w/molded Deco details **$55.00**

Cigarette holder, 2½" long, individual style, black plastic w/narrow gold bands **$20.00**

Clock, brass candle lights flank round clock face on oval onyx base, bird motif, electric, 1930s, marked Silvox, Paris **$200.00**

Compact, blue, green & cream enamel decorated w/roses, brass-plated trim on stair-step perimeter............**$150.00**

Compact, brass-plated octagon w/silver & black designs on green enamel, marked Richard Hudnut **$60.00**

Cracker jar, 7", porcelain w/orange & yellow flowers on white band, blue background, Japanese lustre.....**$45.00**

Creamer & sugar bowl on double octagon tray w/center handle, green glass, Cambridge **$100.00**

Evening bag, square top w/long orange mesh body, chain handle, 1920s, Whiting & Davis, New York.........**$56.00**

Fan, 12" dia, oscillating electric w/brass blades, round base, marked Gilbert...**$175.00**

Figurine, ceramic figure modeled after Dorothy Lamour wearing sarong, light green glaze, 1940s, Clark Pottery, Ohio..**$150.00**

Figurine, pr of birds in green high-gloss glaze on rectangular base, signed Ch Lemanceau...........................**$275.00**

Frame, 17x14½", easel back, beveled glass w/etched florals, picture in lower right corner, 1940s.....................**$95.00**

Head, 5½", of ceramic vanity doll, w/dark tan skin & white hair, marked G&K Keramik, made in Austria **$175.00**

Ice bucket, 6", glass window-pane style w/decorative chrome handle, unmarked **$50.00**

Inkwell, 3½x6", brass, w/attached tray.......................**$80.00**

Jewel box, 2½x6½", plain rectangular shape w/column-like corners, nickel silver w/black velvet interior **$40.00**

Perfume bottle, 6½", gold Deco woman & child on round black glass bottle w/round gold ribbed stopper, 1927, Lanvin **$150.00**

Pick holder for onions & olives, chrome swan on pedestal base, red plastic ball for head, unmarked............**$25.00**

Pin, 3", figural woman tennis player in sterling silver **$55.00**

Pocket lighter, tortise shell w/chrome trim, made by Ronson **$75.00**

Powder box, ceramic, round w/abstract design on yellow ground, black handle & trim, artist signed, Czechoslovakia **$75.00**

Salt & pepper shakers, 3½", ceramic, white glaze w/gold S&P, sit side by side w/rounded outer corners.....**$25.00**

Silent butler, 11½" long, chrome tear-drop shape w/yellow Bakelite handle, marked Chase................................**$60.00**

Table lighter, chrome elephant figural w/trunk up, black oval base **$125.00**

Toaster, chrome w/black base & handles, electric, Sunbeam...$80.00

Tumbler, 2½", chrome holder w/cobalt blue glass insert $20.00

Tumbler, 3", cobalt blue glass on ribbed chrome cone-shaped base, unmarked...$25.00

Vase, 6", black amethyst glass w/hand-painted silver band on cylinder shape w/flared-out top & bottom......$30.00

Vase, 6½", clear glass cornucopia shape by New Martinsville $35.00

Vase, 7", white-glazed pottery, 5-tiered cone shape on round base, 2 'zigzag' handles, Made in Japan.....$35.00

Vase, 8½", ballerina figure by disk receptacle, ceramic $20.00

Wall sconce, 10", 2-tiered brass half-circles ranging from lg to sm on round mount, theater type, American .$175.00

Autographs

Philography is an extremely popular hobby, one that is very diversified. Autographs of sports figures, movie stars, entertainers, and politicians from our lifetime may bring several hundred dollars, depending on rarity and content, while John Adams' simple signature on a document from 1800, for instance, might bring thousands. A signature on a card or photograph is the least valuable type of autograph; a handwritten letter is the most valuable, since in addition the signature, you also get the handwritten message as well. Content is also important. Depending upon what it reveals about the personality involved, it can make a major difference in value.

Many times a polite request accompanied by an SASE to a famous person will result in receipt of a signed photo or a short handwritten note that might in several years be worth a tidy sum!

Obviously as new collectors enter the field, the law of supply and demand will drive the prices for autographs upward, especially when the personality is deceased. There are forgeries around, so before you decide to invest in expensive autographs, get to know your dealers.

Aaron, Henry; signed 3x5" card $8.00
Agnew, Spiro; signed 3x5" card $10.00
Allen, Woody; signed lobby card, Play It Again Sam, 1972, 11x14"...$20.00
Backus, Jim; signed 3x5" card $8.00
Bankhead, Tallulah; signed black & white photo, 8x10" .$95.00
Banks, Ernie; signed color photo, 8x10" $20.00
Bardot, Brigitte; signed black & white photo, 9x11" ...$40.00
Bench, Johnny; signed 3x5" card................................$14.00
Berra, Yogi; signed 3x5" card.....................................$8.00
Blue, Vida; signed 8x10" color photo...........................$10.00
Borman, Frank; color photo, signed in black on corner of image, 3x5"..$6.00
Bush, George; signed typed copy of Presidential Oath on quality paper, 8½x11"..$185.00
Byrd, Admiral RE; inscribed & signed 3x5" card, 1927..$25.00
Caan, James; signed lobby card, from Alien Nation, 1988, 11x14" $20.00
Carter, Rosalyn; signed color photo, portrait as First Lady, 8x10" $25.00
Clapton, Eric; signed black & white bust portrait photo, 8x10" $40.00
Cosby, Bill; signed 3x5" card......................................$5.00
Cruise, Tom; signed color close-up portrait photo, late 1980s, 8x10"...$45.00
Dali, Salvador; photograph taken from book, boldly signed, 6x8" $125.00
Dean, Dizzy; signed 3x5" card.....................................$65.00
Diddley, Bo; record album, Go Bo Diddley, boldly signed on cover, VG...$65.00
Dietrich, Marlene; signed black & white full-length photo, 1940s..$30.00
DiMaggio, Joe; signed 3x5" card..................................$25.00
Donahue, Phil; signed color photo, 8x8" $8.00
Douglas, Kirk; signed lobby card, Last Train From Gun Hill, 1959, 11x14"...$15.00
Drysdale, Don; signed 3x5" card...................................$6.00
Duke, Patty; signed 8x10" color photo.........................$24.00
Eastwood, Clint; signed 3x5" card................................$5.00
Ford, Harrison; signed color photo, dressed as Indiana Jones, 8x10"...$75.00
Ford, Tennessee Ernie; inscribed signed black & white photo, 8x10"..$10.00
Funicello, Annette; black & white signed photo, close-up portrait as Mouseketeer, 11x13" $40.00
Gardner, Eva; cover of vintage Song Hits magazine, boldly signed next to her photo, M.......................................$25.00
Garner, James; signed lobby card, from Up Periscope, 1959, 11x14" $12.00
Garson, Greer; signed black & white photo, 1950s, 8x10"..$35.00
Gibson, Mel; signed color photo, 8x10" $55.00

Gillespie, Dizzy; record album, Endlessly, boldy signed on cover **$175.00**

Grove, Lefty; signature cut from document................**$35.00**

Harris, Bucky; signature cut from document **$20.00**

Harrison, Rex; boldly signed black & white portrait, 8x10" **$25.00**

Hefner, Hugh; inscribed signed color photo, 8x10" **$25.00**

Hepburn, Audrey; signed 3x5" card **$18.00**

Hershiser, Orel; signed 8x10" color photo **$15.00**

Hoffman, Dustin; color photograph, scene from All the President's Men, boldly signed, 8x10" **$35.00**

Holmes, Oliver Wendell; inscription & signature, dated 1879 by Holmes **$50.00**

Hopkins, Anthony; signed black & white photo, original still from When Eight Bells Toll, 8x10" **$20.00**

Howdy Doody & Buffalo Bob, signatures on framed black & white photograph................................**$95.00**

Huston, John; signed black & white photo, profile portrait w/cigar in mouth, 8x10" **$45.00**

Kelly, Gene; signed black & white photo, 1950s film scene, dancing w/Cyd Charisse, 8x10" **$15.00**

Koufax, Sandy; signed 3x5" card.............................**$8.00**

Lamarr, Hedy; signed contract for personal appearance, 1965 ....**$80.00**

Lancaster, Burt; signed 3x5" card............................**$12.00**

Lemmon, Jack; signed lobby card, from Bell, Book & Candle, 1958, 11x14" **$15.00**

Maclaine, Shirley; black & white 1950s portrait w/signature attached, 8x10" **$10.00**

Mantle, Mickey; signed 3x5" card **$25.00**

Martin, Mary; signed 3x5" card.............................**$8.00**

Martin, Steve; signed lobby card, from Roxanne, 1987, 11x14" **$15.00**

Mays, Willie; signed 3x5" card **$10.00**

McCrae, Joel; signed black & white photo, vintage matt-finish portrait, 8x10" **$25.00**

McEnroe, John; signed black & white photo, action pose swinging racquet, 8x10" **$20.00**

Mitchum, Robert; signed lobby card, from The Angry Hills, 1959, 11x14" **$15.00**

Newman, Paul; signed lobby card, from Sometimes a Great Notion, 1971, 11x14".......................................**$50.00**

Nicklaus, Jack; sports trading card, boldly signed, M **$25.00**

Nixon, Richard M; book, Leaders, boldy signed on title page, M...**$175.00**

North, Oliver; inscribed signed photo, seated at desk during Iran-Contra hearings, color, 8x10" **$25.00**

O'Connor, Carroll; signed 3x5" card.......................**$10.00**

Olivier, Sir Laurence; signed 3x5" card....................**$20.00**

Pacino, Al; signed color portraits, scenes from The Godfather, 8x10" **$15.00**

Paige, Satchel; signature cut from document **$50.00**

Palmer, Arnold; sports trading card, boldy signed, M **$20.00**

Pavarotti, Luciano; black & white photo, full-length pose on stage, boldly signed, 8x10" **$35.00**

Peck, Gregory; signed 3x5" card.............................**$9.00**

Pickford, Mary; photo reproduction of a fine portrait drawing, bold vintage signature, 4x5", M **$35.00**

Radner, Gilda; cover of Rolling Stone Magazine, November 1978, very boldly inscribed & signed, NM **$95.00**

Reese, Pee Wee; signed 3x5" card **$8.00**

Robinson, Brooks; signed color photo, 8x10".............**$10.00**

Rogers, Roy; signed color portrait, early 1950s, 8x10" **$25.00**

Roosevelt, Eleanor; signed 3x5" card........................**$35.00**

Sandberg, Ryne; signed 8x10" color photo **$15.00**

Savage, Fred; color portrait, young pose, bold signature, 8x10" **$20.00**

Schoendienst, Al 'Red'; signed 3x5" card.................**$7.00**

Scorsese, Martin; boldly signed black & white photo, close-up portrait from Round Midnight, 8x10" **$40.00**

Seuss, Dr; signed 3x5" card **$20.00**

Stanwyck, Barbara; inscribed signed black & white half-length portrait, 1940s, 8x10" **$25.00**

Stewart, Patrick; color portrait from Star Trek the Next Generation, boldly signed, 8x10"...............................**$45.00**

Streep, Meryl; original still from Sophie's Choice, 1982, signed in ink **$50.00**

Streisand, Barbra; signed black & white photo, portrait from Funny Lady, 8x10" **$50.00**

Thomas, Danny; signed 3x5" card **$6.00**

Turner, Kathleen; signed 3x5" card **$12.00**

Turner, Tina; record album, Private Dancer, boldy signed on cover **$25.00**

Van Doren, Mamie; inscribed signed black & white photo, sexy 1950s portrait, 8x10".......................................**$20.00**

Van Dyke, Dick; signed lobby card, from Cold Turkey, 1971, inscribed, 11x14"...**$12.00**

West, Mae; newspaper photo, 1936, signed in ink......**$50.00**

Wilder, Billy; signed 3x5" card...............................**$10.00**

Williams, Ted; signed card from diner, 1988 ....**$30.00**

Williams, Ted; yellow Hall of Fame plaque postcard, boldly signed along top **$75.00**

Yastrzemski, Carl; signed 3x5" card..........................**$10.00**

Automobilia

A specialized field that attracts both advertising buyers and vintage car buffs alike, 'automobilia' is a term collectors use when referring to auto-related items and accessories such as hood ornaments, gear shift and steering wheel knobs, owner's manuals, license plates, brochures, and catalogs. Many figural hood ornaments bring from $75.00 to $200.00 – some even higher. Things from the thirties through the fifties are especially popular right now.

Ashtray, Ford, shield logo in red & white on clear glass, square **$15.00**
Bank, Whiz Motor Rhythm, 3x2" dia, tin....................**$45.00**
Belt buckle, Cab Co safe driving award, 3x2", enameled 1950s era cab on chrome, initialed GED, 3x2" **$22.00**
Blotter, Ford Motor Co, 6x3", ...Last Longer lettered on logs protruding from back of truck, unused, NM **$4.00**
Booklet, Datsun 1600 Sports Road Test, 4 pages...........**$6.00**
Booklet, Ford V-8 Comfort Economy Performance, 1933, 8 pages...**$20.00**
Booklet, Atwater Kent ignition system types K-2 & H, 18 pages...**$15.00**
Booklet, Knowing Your Saab, Model 93, 28 pages **$10.00**
Booklet, Lincoln V-8 Engine, 1950, 12 pages.................**$8.00**
Booklet, Pennsylvania Turnpike, 1953, 16 pages **$10.00**
Booklet, Things You Don't Want To Forget About Chrysler at the Century of Progress Exposition, illustrated, 24 pages...**$15.00**
Brochure, 1964 Corvette Stingray, 8¾x12", color photos & specifics, 8 pages **$16.50**
Brochure, 1969 Corvette Stingray, 18x11", color photos & specifics **$28.00**
Calendar, 17x7" Gilmore Gasoline, 1947, red lion logo, 17x7" **$16.50**
Cigar box, Illinois Automobile Club, wood..................**$20.00**
Compass, Airglide Nomad Deluxe, self-illuminating w/mounting bracket, M in original box **$35.00**
Compass, Taylor Navigator, self-illuminated w/swivel mount, M in original box **$25.00**
Compass, Union 76 Auto, orange, blue & white w/suction cup mount...**$12.00**

Foldout, Plymouth for 1953 ....**$12.00**
Gearshift knob, black plastic w/facets........................**$25.00**

Gearshift knob, simulated onyx w/brass St Christopher medallion in center **$25.00**

Hood ornament, Packard, Goddess of Speed, metal.$300.00
Horn, Sparton SOS Deluxe, 16" long, 6-volt **$55.00**
Ink blotter, Ford, pictures touring car & family on picnic, Have a Good Time on a Picnic w/Ford **$25.00**
Instruction book, Triumph TR-3, 5th edition, 2nd printing, late 1940s, VG **$8.00**
Key chain/flashlight, Buick in block letters w/eagle above, tan & black **$12.00**
Key holder, Dodge, enameled logo on leather...........**$12.00**
Key holder, Ford, oval script logo on blue & white tube shape **$20.00**
Key holder, Nash, green & white plastic w/script logo.**$10.00**
Lapel button, 3" dia, Chrysler-Plymouth Dealers Joy to You, From Us, black, orange & white **$10.00**
Lapel pin, Renault Regie Nationale, diamond logo, red on brass..**$30.00**
Lapel pin, Studebaker, bird & crown logo, red, black & gold, enameled..**$35.00**
License plate, motocycle; Iowa, 1960 ....**$15.00**
License plate topper, Chrysler-Plymouth Sales & Service, blue & white..**$25.00**
Lighter, Pontiac, 1950s-style chief's head logo, yellow & black, M in original box **$35.00**
Lighter, Zippo, Ford 300-500 Club, M in original box.**$35.00**
Magazine, Buick, features First Look at the Golden Anniversary Buicks, January 1953.............................**$10.00**
Magazine, Harley Davidson Enthusiast, May 1950.......**$12.00**
Matchbook, Plymouth, 1940...**$5.00**
Mechanical pencil, Jeep Willy's Motors, pictures red jeep..**$20.00**
Medallion, Chrysler, You Get Good Things First From Chrysler, full color **$20.00**
Medallion, Futuramic 88 Oldsmobile, Driving & Seeing Is Believing, brass **$5.00**
Medallion, Your Rambler Dollar Is a Bigger Dollar, aluminum..**$5.00**
Money clip, Ford, oval script logo, green & black, heavy metal...**$15.00**
Owner's manual, 1979 Eldorado **$6.00**
Pencil clip, REO Speed-Wagon, red, white & blue......**$35.00**
Postcard, F-85 Cutlass Ragtop & Coupe **$2.00**
Postcard, Ford Rotunda by Night at the Chicago World's Fair, EX **$6.00**
Promotional car, 1965 Chevy Impala SS, M **$110.00**

Radiator emblem, Hudson Super Six, triangular, black & white w/ornate border, enameled $65.00

Ruler, Chevrolet advertising, celluloid, 1930s, 6", M....$25.00

Screwdriver, Chevrolet Sales & Service w/bow tie logo, metal handle...$25.00

Screwdriver, Nash in script, Here Is That Handy Tool for Your Glove Compartment, red, green & white plastic handle..$20.00

Shoe horn, Chevrolet, 1979 Theme Line, bow tie logo, plastic...$6.00

Stick pin, Volkswagon logo, aluminum w/blue background $15.00

Tape measure, Cadillac CSI Action Program, 5 ft, in original box...$10.00

Trunk emblem, Dodge Brothers, 6" wide, 6-point star logo, black, gold & silver enameled..........................$40.00

Windshield scraper, Chevrolet, bow tie logo, plastic w/rubber squeegee & clip for attaching to sun visor $6.00

Windshield scraper, Pontiac, 1957 ....$5.00

Wrench, Ford 5-Z-152, script logo $8.00

Autumn Leaf Dinnerware

A familiar dinnerware pattern to just about all of us, Autumn Leaf was designed by Hall China for the Jewel Tea Company who offered it to their customers as premiums. In fact, some people refer to the pattern as 'Jewel Tea.' First made in 1933, it continued in production until 1978. Pieces with this date in the backstamp are from the overstock that was in the company's warehouse when production was suspended. There are matching pitchers, tumblers, and stemware all made by the Libbey Glass Company, and a set of enameled cookware that came out in 1979. You'll find blankets, tablecloths, metal canisters, clocks, playing cards, and many other items designed around the Autumn Leaf pattern. All are collectible.

Since 1984 the Hall Company has been making items for the National Autumn Leaf Collectors Club. So far, these pieces have been issued: a teapot (their New York style); a restyled vase; candlesticks; a (Philadelphia) teapot, sugar bowl and creamer set; a sugar packet holder; a tea-for-two set; a Solo tea set; a donut jug; a punch bowl with 12 cups; a Donut teapot; and a large oval casserole. All are plainly marked and dated.

Limited edition items (by Hall) are being sold by China Specialties, a company in Ohio; but once you become familiar with the old pieces, these are easy to identify, since the molds have been redesigned or were not previously used for Autumn Leaf production. These are the pieces I'm aware of: the Airflow teapot, the Norris refrigerator pitcher, a square-handled beverage mug, a restyled Irish mug, 'teardrop' salt and pepper shakers, a mustard jar, a set of covered onion soup bowls, sherbets, an ashtray, the automobile teapot, a tankard-shaped beer pitcher, and a 1-handle (2½-pint) bean pot. In glassware they have had made water and wine goblets, juice tumblers, and beer pilsners. These are crystal (not frosted) and are dated '92 at the base

of one of the leaves. Their accessory items include playing cards that are dated in the lower right-hand corner.

For further study, we recommend *The Collector's Encyclopedia of Hall China* by Margaret and Kenn Whitmyer.

Baker, 3-pint, French fluted $14.00
Baker, 4½", French fluted $7.00
Ball jug, #3 ....$25.00
Bowl, cereal; 6½" $11.00
Bowl, fruit; 5½" $5.00
Bowl, oval $16.00
Bowl, oval, divided..$85.00
Bowl, salad $14.00
Bowl, soup; 8½", flat...$13.00
Bowl, 7½", Radiance $12.00
Bowl, 9", round..$85.00
Bowl covers, plastic, 8-piece set..........................$85.00
Bowls, Glasbake, 4-piece set $35.00
Bread box, metal $225.00
Butter dish, 1-lb, regular......................................$325.00

Butter dish, 8½", ¼-lb $145.00
Cake plate..$13.00
Cake safe, 1935-41 ....$40.00
Cake safe, 1950-53, no pattern on top of lid..............$30.00
Cake stand, metal base..$125.00
Canister, short, round, copper-color lid $55.00
Canister, tall, round, copper-color lid....................$75.00
Canister, tea or coffee; 4", square, each $20.00
Casserole, 2-qt, round...$25.00
Coaster, 3⅛" dia $4.50
Coffeepot, all china...$295.00
Coffeepot, 9-cup, Rayed......................................$35.00
Condiment, marmalade; w/underplate....................$47.00
Condiment, mustard; w/underplate.......................$45.00
Cookie jar, Rayed..$130.00
Creamer, Rayed...$16.00
Creamer, ruffled-D..$10.00
Cup, ruffled-D...$6.50
Cup, St Denis $16.00
Cup & saucer, Melmac...$8.00
Custard, Radiance..$5.50
Drip jar $17.00
Dutch oven, 5-qt, porcelain-clad steel.......................$175.00
Fondue set, wooden lid knob & handle, complete $55.00
Gravy boat...$20.00
Gravy boat underplate..$17.00
Hot pad, 7¼" felt back..$12.00
Mixer cover, standard $25.00

Mixing bowl set, 2-qt, porcelain-clad steel..................$65.00
Mug, conic...$57.00
Napkin, 16" square...$40.00
Pie baker $20.00
Place mat, plastic $27.00
Plate, dinner; 10", Melmac...$8.00
Plate, salad; 7", Melmac...$6.00
Plate, 10"...$14.00
Plate, 6"..$4.50
Plate, 7¼"..$7.00
Plate, 9"...$8.50
Platter, 11½", oval..$18.00
Platter, 13½", oval..$20.00
Platter, 14", Melmac...$10.00
Saucepan, 1½-qt, wooden handle, no lid..................$95.00
Saucer, ruffled-D $1.50
Saucer, St Denis..$5.00
Shaker, range; each..$10.00
Shaker, regular, ruffled, each $9.00
Sifter...$290.00
Silverware, stainless, 24-piece set $225.00
Sugar bowl, Rayed...$20.00
Sugar bowl, ruffled-D..$13.00
Tablecloth, 54x54" or 72x54", plastic.......................$145.00
Tablecloth, 72x54", sailcloth.....................................$110.00
Tea towel, 33x16" $25.00
Teakettle, wooden lid knob & handle $210.00
Teapot, Aladdin...$45.00

Teapot, Newport, 1930s.....................................$145.00
Teapot, Newport, 1970s...$100.00
Thermos, bail handle, spigot.....................................$225.00
Tidbit, 2-tier...$37.00
Tin, holiday fruit cake; round $9.00
Tray, 18¼", oval..$50.00
Tumbler, 10-oz, Libbey...$30.00
Tumbler, 5½", frosted $14.00
Tumbler, 9-oz, Brockway...$22.00
Vase, regular decal $165.00
Warmer, round...$100.00

Avon

You'll find Avon bottles everywhere you go! But it's not just the bottles that are collectible – so are jewelry, awards, magazine ads, catalogs, and product samples. Of course the better items are the older ones (they've been called Avon since 1939 – California Perfume Company before that), and if you can find them mint in box (MIB), all the better.

For more information refer to *Hastings Avon Collector's Price Guide* by Bud Hastings. See also Cape Cod.

Aladdin's Lamp Foaming Bath Oil, 6-oz green glass bottle w/gold cap, 1971, MIB $8.50
Avonshire Blue Cologne, 6-oz blue opaque glass vase shape w/white trim, 1971, MIB...........................$10.00
Bird of Paradise Cologne Fluff, 5½" aqua plastic coating over glass bottle, gold cap, 1969, MIB.....................$3.50
Blue Lotus After Bath Freshener, 8" clear glass bottle w/blue cap, 1967, MIB.............................$7.50
Bright Night Beauty Dust, white plastic container w/gold stars on lid, 1959-61...........................$9.50
Brocade Beauty Dust, round, brown plastic ribbed container w/paisley pattern on lid, 1967-71...........................$7.50
Brocade Cologne, 2⅝" clear glass bottle w/gold screw-on lid, 1970, MIB...........................$3.00

California Perfume Co, Anniversary Keepsake (1975 Anniversary), original box $10.00
Charisma Soap, 3 pink soaps in Christmas-decorated box, 1975, MIB.............................$9.50
Close Harmony, 8-oz white glass barber bottle, gold lettering & neck band, Spicy & Original after shave, 1963, MIB.............................$25.00
Cotillion Perfume Talc, 3½-oz, cardboard, pink w/gold lettering, 1974-77 ....$2.50
Cotillion Sachet, 2¾" clear glass bottle w/aqua label & plastic screw-on lid, 1940..............................$14.00
Daisies Won't Tell Cream Sachet, pink glass container w/raised daisy on white plastic lid, 1963-64, MIB.$12.50
Double Dare Nail Polish, 1-oz, clear glass w/red paper label & black cap, 1946-47 ....$8.50
Double Dip Bubble Bath, 5-oz, plastic ice cream cone shape, orange & white w/red cap, 1968-70, MIB ...$5.50

Elegante Toilet Water, 2-oz, glass bottle w/silver cap, neck tag & ribbon, red & silver box, 1957-59, MIB **$40.00**

Flamingo, 5-oz glass figural decanter w/gold cap, various cologne, 1971-72, MIB **$5.50**

Floral Perfumed Talc, lavender & white container w/floral design, 1959-60, MIB..........................**$7.50**

Forever Spring Cologne, 4-oz, clear w/yellow tulip-shaped cap, green painted label, 1951-56, MIB.................**$25.00**

Fragrant Mist set, 2-oz toilet water w/green & gold atomizer, various colognes, turquoise & gold box, 1950, M.......................................**$50.00**

Her Prettiness Talc, 3½-oz, white plastic rabbit w/pink fluffy tail, 1969-72, MIB **$7.50**

Here's My Heart Soap, 2 heart-shaped soaps in blue & white box, 1962-65, MIB.........................**$30.00**

Jasmine Bath Salts, 9-oz, clear glass w/pink flower on black paper label, black lid, 1945-52 ....**$35.00**

Kitchen Crock Candle, milk glass w/flowered border, 1974.......................................**$5.00**

Lip Pop Cola, plastic bottle shape, various lip pomades, 1973-74, MIB.........................**$3.50**

Liquid Rouge, ⅛-oz, clear glass w/painted label & embossed gold cap, 1954-59, MIB........................**$6.50**

Merry Fingertips set, 2 bottles of nail polish in pink velvet box w/floral design, 1967, M **$10.50**

Miss Lollipop Hand Cream, 2-oz, Miss Lollipop w/umbrella on white plastic tube, 1968 ....**$4.00**

Nearness Body Powder, frosted glass bottle w/blue paper label & cap, 1956-58 ....**$10.50**

Occur! Perfumed Bath Oil, 6-oz, black plastic container w/painted label & gold cap, 1964-65, MIB.............**$5.00**

Original Soap on a Rope, white w/embossed carriage, 1966-68, MIB **$30.00**

Persian Wood Perfumed Talc, red & gold container w/brass cap & trim, 1958-62, MIB.........................**$4.50**

Precious Slipper, ¼-oz frosted glass figural decanter w/gold cap, Sonnet or Moonwind cologne, 1973-74...........**$7.50**

Pretty Peach Cologne, 2-oz, glass bottle w/painted label & figural peach lid, 1964-67, MIB **$7.50**

Rollin' Great Roller Skate, 2-oz glass figural decanter w/red cap, Zany or Lover Boy cologne, 1980-81, MIB **$4.00**

Skin-So-Soft Bath Oil, 6-oz, urn shape, Nile blue, 1972 .**$8.00**

Skin-So-Soft Compliments set, 3-oz box of Satin Talc & 2 bars of soap, 1967, MIB...........................**$9.50**

Somewhere Powder Sachet, frosted bottle w/paper label & gold cap, 1965-55 ....**$6.50**

Sports Rally Hair Dress, 4-oz, red & white tube picturing football players, red cap, 1966-68, MIB..................**$4.50**

Talc for Men, 3-oz, carriages on white background, red shaker top, 1962-65........................**$8.50**

To a Wild Rose Perfumed Bath Oil, 8-oz, white plastic bottle w/pink cap, 1959-61, MIB **$6.00**

Topaze Perfume Oil, ½-oz, glass w/painted label & canted corners, gold cap, 1963-69, MIB...................**$7.50**

Twice Spice set, 4-oz bottle of Spicy after shave & talc in brown striped box, 1967, MIB **$16.50**

Wild Country Soap on a Rope, ivory w/bull's head in center, round, 1967-76, MIB **$6.00**

Wishing Bath Oil, 6-oz, white plastic bottle w/gold lettering, 1964-66, MIB **$11.50**

Wishing Scented Hair Spray, 7-oz, white w/gold lettering & highlights, 1966-67 ....**$11.50**

1926 Checker Cab, 5-oz, painted glass decanter w/stick-on decals, held Everest or Wild Country after shave, 1977-78, MIB **$8.50**

Azalea Dinnerware

Although this line of dinnerware was made earlier than most of the collectibles we're dealing with, it was made in huge quantities, and you're likely to find a piece or two now and then. It was manufactured by the Noritake Company from 1916 until about 1935 and was offered through the catalogs of the Larkin Company who gave it away as premiums to club members and home agents.

Collectors use the catalog order numbers Larkin assigned to each piece. There were more than seventy items in the dinnerware line as well as six pieces of matching, hand-painted crystal.

Bonbon dish, 6¼", #184..............................**$50.00**
Bowl, #310, deep **$70.00**
Bowl, salad; 10", #12 ....**$45.00**
Bowl, vegetable; 10½", #172, oval **$62.00**
Butter tub, #54, w/insert.........................**$50.00**
Cake plate, 9¾", #10 ....**$42.00**
Comport, #170.....................................**$100.00**
Condiment set, #14 ....**$68.00**
Creamer & sugar bowl, berry; #122.................**$160.00**
Gravy boat, #40...................................**$50.00**
Pickle or lemon set w/fork, #121..................**$26.00**
Pitcher, syrup; #97, w/underplate.................**$135.00**
Plate, bread & butter; 6½", #8 ....**$12.00**
Plate, breakfast; 8½", #98........................**$25.00**
Plate, tea; 7½", #4...............................**$12.00**
Platter, 12", #56.................................**$60.00**
Refreshment set, #39..............................**$50.00**
Saucer, fruit; 5¼", #9............................**$12.00**
Shakers, #89, bulbous, pr.........................**$32.00**

Sugar bowl, #401, gold finial, scarce **$85.00**
Teapot, #15, regular.................................**$112.00**

Teapot tile, #169 ....$50.00
Toothpick/match holder, #192, rare $132.00
Tray, celery or roll; 12", #99 ....$58.00
Vase, #187, fan shape, footed, rare $190.00

Banks

There are several types of collectible banks: mechanical, these are the ones with parts that move when the coin is inserted – still, advertising, and registering, those that tabulate the amount of money as you deposit it. This is a very diverse field, with literally thousands of shapes and variations available. If you find yourself drawn toward collecting banks, careful study and observation of the market is a must. Reproductions, though not very good ones, abound at flea markets all over the country. Since many of these banks were produced from the 1870s until about 1940, pass right on by any bank with paint that is too bright. Examine their construction; parts fit together well in the old banks. If the parts fit loosely and the designing is crude, they're new.

Prices for old banks continue to accelerate rapidly. Several of the auction houses we list in the back, especially those that specialize in toys, will often hold large cataloged bank auctions. Condition is of the utmost importance; good paint can mean the difference of hundreds of dollars. And they must be complete and original to bring top price. Repaired banks or those with replaced parts are worth much less.

Although the mechanicals are at the top of the price structure, still banks are widely collected as well. Cast iron examples are preferred, but lead banks are coming on, and tin and pottery banks are attracting more and more collector interest.

There are a number of good books on the market for further study; among them are: *The Dictionary of Still Banks* by Long and Pitman, *The Penny Bank Book* by Moore, *The Still Bank Book* by Norman, *Penny Lane* by Davidson, *The History of Antique Mechanical Toy Banks* by Al Davidson, and *The Collector's Encyclopedia of Toys and Banks* by Don Cranmer. In our listings, 'M' numbers refer to the Moore book, 'L' to the book by Long and Pitman, 'N' to the Norman book, and 'D' to Davidson's.

See also Advertising Collectibles.

Mechanical Banks

Cabin, 3½", D-93, painted cast iron, Black man stands at door of cabin, yellow & green variations, J&E Stevens, VG $300.00
Dinah, 7", D-153, painted cast iron, bust & head form of a Black lady whose mouth receives coin, variations, Harper, VG $370.00
Hall's Excelsior, 5¼", D-228, painted cast iron & wood, figure pops out of building to receive coin, G..........$65.00
Humpty Dumpty, 7½", D-248, painted cast iron, coin goes from hand to mouth, Shephard Hardware, VG+ .$800.00
Milking Cow, 9⅝" long, painted cast iron, seated figure milking cow by fence, Book of Knowledge reproduction...$65.00

Monkey w/Tray, N-4000A, painted cast iron, Germany, ca 1910, NM $350.00
Owl Turns Head, 7½", D-375, cast iron, yellow eyes, on tree-branch base, color & metal variations, VG ..$300.00

Rooster, 6¼", D-419, cast iron w/paint traces, VG.$250.00
Tammany, 5¾", D-455, painted cast iron, chubby man in black coat sits in red chair, J&E Stevens, VG $125.00
Trick Pony, 7⅛" long, G-272, painted cast iron, pony stands before trough, retangular base, J&E Stevens, VG...$425.00
William Tell, 10½" long, D-565, painted cast iron, stands ready to shoot apple from boy's head, J&E Stevens, VG...$325.00

Registering Banks

Bed Post, M-1305, 5¢ register.....................................$70.00

Dopey Dime Register, 2½" square, holds $5.00 in dimes, copyright 1938, Walt Disney Productions $75.00
Gem, embossed eagle, 10¢ register, EX $20.00
NY World's Fair, M-1566, tin, 1¢ register, M on card ..$55.00
Phoenix Dime Register Trunk, 5" long, nickel-plated cast iron, working, Piaget, VG......................................$50.00
Snow White & the Seven Dwarfs, holds up to $5.00 in dimes, marked copyright 1938, Walt Disney Ent (illustrated) $85.00

Uncle Sam's Register Bank, 6¼", painted rolled steel cash register form w/red & gold details, VG $20.00

Still Banks

Angry Bear, 3", M-704, painted lead, w/padlock, G $165.00

Bank building, 4½", red-painted cast iron, VG....$50.00
Bank building, 3¼", cast iron w/traces of gold paint (illustrated)..$65.00
Bear, 3¼", M-697, painted lead, arms folded, VG......$185.00
Billy Bounce, 4¾", M-14, painted cast iron, Wing, EX ..$650.00
Bird on Stump, 4¾", M-644, cast iron, gold paint, VG .$175.00
Boston Bull Terrier, 5¼", M-421, painted cast iron, VG .$100.00
Brink's Truck, 8¼" long, M-1500, painted metal, VG ..$85.00
Buick Fireball Eight, 4⅜", lithographed tin, key lock, VG .$65.00
Captain Kidd, 5⅝", M-38, painted cast iron, G...........$250.00
Cat, W-248, cast iron w/paint traces, seated $195.00
Circus Elephant, 5⅛", tin litho, sits on round drum base, semimechanical, trunk receives coin, no trap, Chein, G $55.00
Clown, 5", tin litho, semimechanical, tongue receives coin, Chein, VG $45.00
College Hat, 4⅛", M-1391, painted tin, G $55.00
Dime Bullet, 7¼", M-1407, brass, conversion, G..........$80.00
Drum, 2¼", tin litho, Remember Pearl Harbor, VG $45.00
Dutch Boy, 5½", M-180, painted cast iron, EX.............$75.00
Elephant on Tub Without Blanket, 5¼", M-483, painted cast iron, VG $175.00
English Throne, 3⅜", M-1327, gold-painted aluminum, VG $15.00
Fido, 5", painted cast iron, Hubley, 1914, VG............$145.00
Football Player, 5⅞", M-11, cast iron, Williams, G.....$325.00
Horse (Beauty), 4¼", M-532, painted cast iron, Beauty in raised letters on sides, Arcade, ca 1932, G..........$100.00
Horse on Tub Without Blanket, 5⅜", M-509, cast iron, black, AC Williams, ca 1932, EX $225.00
Ideola Juke Box, 6¼", M-1580, plastic, music box, G..$25.00
Indian Bust, 3½", M-221, lead, full headdress, VG $55.00
Jiminy Cricket, 5⅞", M-284, painted composition material, EX $110.00
Kewpie, 3¼", M-301, glass w/paint traces, tin lid, VG..$50.00
Labrador Retriever, 4½", M-412, cast iron, black w/gold collar, red trim, EX $375.00
Lion, 4⅛", M-747, painted cast iron, on tub, worn $140.00

Mary & Little Lamb, 4½", M-164, painted cast iron, G .$95.00
Metropolitan, 5⅞", M-904, painted cast iron, broken lock, G $185.00
Monkey Tips Hat, 5", tin litho, red, yellow & brown, semimechanical, hat receives coin, Thank You on base, Chein, VG+...$35.00
Mulligan, 5¾", M-177, painted cast iron policeman, G...$55.00
Professor Pug Frog, 3¼", M-311, painted cast iron, minor wear, EX..$245.00
Punch & Judy, 2⅞", M-1298, tin, EX...........................$150.00
Quilted Lion, 5", M-758, gold-painted cast iron, EX..$245.00
Recording Bank, 6⅝", M-1062, nickel-plated cast iron, worn finish $195.00
Scottie, 4½", M-432, nickel-plated lead, Deco style, EX..$165.00
Scotties (6 in a basket), 4½", M-427, white metal, VG...$55.00
Seal on Rock, 3½", M-732, cast iron, gold or black paint, EX..$450.00
Snowman, 4⅝", M-92, aluminum, w/broom, Reynolds, NM .$70.00
Spaniel, 4⅝", white metal, World's Fair label, G..........$25.00
Spitz, 4", M-409, cast iron w/paint traces, light rust, VG..$175.00
State Bank, 3⅛", M-1085, cast iron w/bronze finish, VG.$175.00
Terrier, 5½", white metal, trap missing, VG $100.00
Three Little Pigs, 3", lithographed tin, G $100.00
Treasure Chest, 2", M-928, cast iron, red, VG $195.00
Underwood Typewriter, 1⅜", M-1272, white metal in gold, black or white, VG..$95.00
US Mail, 4⅛", M-849, painted cast iron, w/eagle, worn paint, VG+..$200.00
White City Safe #10, 4⅝", M-913, painted cast iron, EX $200.00
Woolworth Building, 8", M-1041, gold-painted cast iron, some wear, EX...$95.00

Barbie and Her Friends

Barbie dolls are some of the 'hottest' collectible toys on the market today. There are auctions devoted entirely to selling vintage Barbies and accessory items. The first Barbie, issued in 1959, books at $2000.00 mint in the box. If she happens to be a brunette instead of a blond, tack on another $500.00. Even dolls made more recently can be pricey! For instance, the Happy Holiday Barbie from 1988 commands at least $400.00 to $500.00.

Barbie was first introduced in 1959, and soon Mattel found themselves producing not only dolls but tiny garments, fashion accessories, houses, cars, horses, books, and games as well. Today's Barbie collectors want them all. Though the early Barbies are very hard to find, there are many of her successors still around; don't overlook Ken, Skipper, or any of her other friends.

You'll need to do lots of studying and comparisons to learn to distinguish one Barbie from another, but this is the key to making sound buys and good investments. If you compare our Barbie doll values to those in many other price guides, you'll notice they are much lower. This is because we have priced them as you'll probably be finding them: not mint in box as most other guides do, but nude and in good condition. A doll that is mint in box may be worth at least twice as much as our listed values, and in some cases even more. But even when the box has simply been opened, the value drops about 20%. If you need to price a mint in box Barbie (or one of her companions) or want good sources for study, refer to one of these fine books: *The Wonder of Barbie* and *The World of Barbie Dolls* by Paris and Susan Manos; or *The Collector's Encyclopedia of Barbie Dolls and Collectibles* by Sibyl DeWein and Joan Ashabraner.

Our values are given just for the doll (unless noted otherwise), but we've included information within parentheses describing originial clothing and accessories that each doll came out with, in case you're lucky enough to find some of those. In the section on accessories, values are for mint condition items; worn examples are generally worth at least 50% less.

Allan (multicolored striped jacket & blue trunks), red molded hair, straight legs, 1964 ....**$40.00**

Allan (red jacket & blue trunks), red molded hair, bendable knees, 1965 ....**$175.00**

Barbie, (black & white striped jersey swimsuit, wire stand was included), bubble-cut hair, painted lips & nails, 1961..**$50.00**

Barbie, Angel Face (white lace blouse & pink skirt, black belt & pink handbag), twist waist, straight legs, 1983, MIB **$25.00**

Barbie, Beautiful Bride, blond hair, bendable knees, twist waist, 1976...**$25.00**

Barbie, Crystal (white evening gown & stole), black skin, twist waist, 1983, MIB...**$30.00**

Barbie, Deluxe Quick Curl (Jergen's beauty kit included), blond hair, bendable knees, twist waist, 1976 ......**$10.00**

Barbie, Fashion Queen (1-piece gold & white striped swimsuit & beach bandana, 3 wigs & stand included), 1963 ....**$35.00**

Barbie, Free Moving (playsuit & print skirt, tennis racket & golf club), red hair, pull tab in back for movement, 1975 ....**$15.00**

Barbie, Gold Medal Skier (US Olympic-styled outfit & gear, doll-size medal included), Sears Exclusive, 1975..**$10.00**

Barbie, Great Shape (blue exercise suit & headband, striped leg warmers), 1983, MIB...**$25.00**

Barbie, Hair Happenin's (white & rose-colored dress, 3 hair pieces & stand included), bendable knees, 1971 ..**$200.00**

Barbie, Happy Holidays (white satin evening gown w/fur trim & stole), 1989, MIB **$45.00**

Barbie, Hawaiian (floral bikini w/matching skirt & lei, grass skirt, ukulele & sailboat), limited edition, 1975 ....**$25.00**

Barbie, Live Action on Stage (fringed outfit & headband, 45 rpm record & microphone), blond hair, swivel joints, 1971 ....**$25.00**

Barbie, Malibu (1-piece swimsuit), suntanned skin & long blond hair, bendable knees, twist waist, 1971-72.**$10.00**

Barbie, Miss (pink swimsuit & cap, 3 wigs & stand, lawn swing & planter), open & close eyes, bendable knees, 1964 ....**$150.00**

Barbie, Music Lovin' (yellow & white outfit w/radio & head phones), 1985, MIB...**$30.00**

Barbie, My First (yellow outfit w/blue trim, comb & brush), twist waist, straight legs, 1980-present, MIB.........**$25.00**

Barbie, Pony Tail, 1963 (M, unopened, $300.00) nude, in good condition **$75.00**

Barbie, Quick Curl Miss America (evening gown & crown), brunette hair, blue eyes, twist waist, bendable knees, 1973 ....**$35.00**

Barbie, Spanish Talking (2-piece red vinyl swimsuit & net jacket), 1970 ....**$25.00**

Barbie, Sweet 16 (pink & white party dress, make-up compact & barrettes included), bendable knees, twist waist, 1974 ....**$20.00**

Barbie, Talking (2-piece swimsuit w/gold midi-coat), straight facing eyes, rooted eyelashes, bendable knees, 1971 ....**$25.00**

Barbie, Twist 'N Turn (salmon vinyl bikini & white net cover-up), rooted eyelashes, bendable knees, 1967...**$35.00**

Barbie, Walk Lively Miss America (evening gown & red cape w/imitation ermine, walk 'n turn stand included), 1972...**$35.00**

Barbie (red jersey swimsuit & high-heeled shoes, pearl earrings, wire stand), blond w/ponytail & curly bangs, 1963 ....**$75.00**

Barbie (1-piece yellow swimsuit), from Canada, long straight blond hair, 1975 ....**$12.00**

Brad (reddish-orange tricot shirt & multicolored shorts), black skin, molded black hair, bendable knees, 1970 ....**$35.00**

Cara, Ballerina (pink tutu & stand), black skin, legs constructed for pirouettes, swivel-jointed head & arms, 1976 ....**$20.00**

Carla (orange dress w/white trim), black skin & hair w/bangs & 2 ponytails, bendable, 1976 ....**$35.00**

Christie, Talking, dull brown hair, (M, unopened, $125.00) nude, in good condition...**$20.00**

Christie, Twist 'N Turn (1-piece pink & yellow swimsuit), black skin, bendable knees, 1970 ....**$35.00**

Curtis (1-piece white & orange sport suit, golf club & tennis racket), black skin, pull tab in back for movement, 1975 ....**$25.00**

Francie, Growin' Pretty Hair (pink satin & net party dress), pull hair to lengthen or shorten, bendable knees, 1970 ....**$25.00**

Francie (1-piece swimsuit w/teal background), rooted eyelashes, bendable knees, 1st edition, 1966 ....**$35.00**

Julia, Talking (gold & silver jumpsuit), rooted eyelashes, bendable knees, 1969 ....**$25.00**

Kelly, Yellowstone (dotted blouse & striped shorts, camp gear included), suntanned, long red hair, 1974 ....**$75.00**

Ken, Funtime (blue trunks), pink skin, dark brown hair, 1976 ....**$15.00**

Ken, Gold Medal Skier (US Olympic-styled outfit & gear, doll-size medal included), 1975 ....**$4.00**

Ken, Live Action (fringed outfit, motorized stage included), loosely jointed waist, bendable knees, 1971 ....**$20.00**

Ken, Mod Hair (checked jacket & brown pants, 4 hair pieces & posing stand), rooted hair, bendable knees, 1973 ....**$12.00**

Ken, Spanish Talking (blue jacket w/orange trim & orange shorts), molded brown hair, 1970 ....**$25.00**

Ken, Sun Valley (blue & red ski outfit, ski gear included), molded hair, 1974 ....**$10.00**

Ken, Walk Lively (blue shirt & plaid pants, walk 'n turn stand included), bendable knees, 1972 ....**$15.00**

Midge (1-piece multicolored striped swimsuit), bubble-cut hair, freckled face, bendable knees, 1965 ....**$150.00**

Midge (2-piece multicolored swimsuit), freckled face w/blue eyes, rooted Saran hair, straight legs, 1963 ....**$20.00**

PJ, Gold Medal Gymnast (US Olympic-styled outfit & gear, doll-size medal included), 1975 ....**$10.00**

PJ, Groovy Talking (floral mini-dress), blond hair, real eyelashes, bendable knees, 1969 ....**$20.00**

PJ, Live Action (fringed outfit, pink motorized stage & guitar included), bendable knees & elbows, swivel waist, 1971 ....**$20.00**

PJ, Malibu (1-piece lavender swimsuit, glasses & towel included), blond hair, suntanned skin, 1972 ....**$10.00**

Ricky (blue shorts w/multicolored striped jacket & sandals), molded red hair, straight legs, 1965.....................**$35.00**

Skipper, Funtime (2-piece yellow swimsuit), pink skin, long blond hair, bendable knees, twist waist, 1967 ......**$15.00**

Skipper, Growing Up (red & white skirt w/red blouse), by turning left arm she grows ¾" & develops bustline, 1975 ....**$12.00**

Skipper, Living (1-piece blue & rose tricot swimsuit), blond hair, swivel joints, bendable knees, elbows & ankles, 1970 ....**$12.00**

Skipper, Malibu (2-piece swimsuit, sunglasses & towel), blond hair, suntanned, bendable knees, 1971-72...**$10.00**

Skipper, Sensational Malibu (1-piece purple swimsuit & sunglasses), 1981, MIB **$65.00**

Skipper, Western (red shirt, blue jeans & boots, cowboy hat & lasso included), 1981, MIB **$65.00**

Skooter, Funtime (2-piece blue swimsuit), dark red hair, blue eyes, bendable knees, twist waist, 1976 ......**$50.00**

Skooter (2-piece red & white swimsuit, comb, brush & stand included), brown eyes, freckles, straight legs, 1965 ....**$20.00**

Stacey, Talking (1-piece multicolored swimsuit), short flip, real eyelashes, bendable knees, 1969.................**$30.00**

Stacey, Twist 'N Turn (1-piece red swimsuit w/button trim), rooted eyelashes, molded teeth, bendable knees, 1968 ....**$35.00**

Truly Scrumptious, Talking (old-fashioned pink & rose dress w/fancy hat), bendable knees, 1969...................**$250.00**

Accessories

Airplane, Barbie, 1964 ....**$300.00**
Ballerina Stage, Barbie, 1976.............................**$35.00**
Bathe 'N Beauty Place, Barbie, Sears special, 1975 .....**$30.00**
Beauty Kit, Barbie, 1961 ....**$20.00**
Book, Barbie & Ghost Town Mystery, Random House.**$8.00**
Book, Barbie Solves a Mystery, Random House **$8.00**
Book, The World of Barbie, Random House **$15.00**
Bunk Bed, Skipper & Skooter, 1965-67.................**$150.00**
Carrying case, Miss Barbie, red...........................**$50.00**
Clock, wristwatch shape w/Barbie in center, electric..**$40.00**
Color Magic Fashion Designer Set, Barbie & Francie.**$250.00**
Country Camper, Barbie, 1971 to present **$50.00**
Dancer, Barbie's horse, 1971-72...........................**$75.00**
Display set, Barbie & Stacey Fashion Boutique, 1969.**$500.00**

Fashion Embroidery Set, made by Standard Toycraft under license from Mattel, M....................$25.00
Fashion Magazine, Barbie, miniature, 1964-65............**$10.00**
Fashion Plaza, Barbie, 1976................................**$50.00**
Fishing Boat, Barbie, Sears exclusive, 1973-76 ....**$75.00**
Friend Ship, Barbie, 1973 to present **$45.00**

Gift set, Skipper on Wheels, 1964 ....**$300.00**

Gift set, Walking Jamie Strollin' in Style, 1972...........**$475.00**

Good Grooming Manicure Set, Barbie **$35.00**

Hair Originals, Barbie, 1973 to present **$15.00**

Heirloom Service Play Set, Barbie, 1961....................**$50.00**

Jumbo Trading Cards, Barbie & Ken, 1962 ....**$45.00**

Lunch box & thermos, Barbie & Midge, black, 1963...**$45.00**

Mattel-a-Phone, Barbie **$50.00**

Miss America Beauty Center, Barbie, Sears special, 1974 to present..**$15.00**

Mountain Ski Cabin, Barbie, Sears Exclusive **$35.00**

Nurse Kit, Barbie, Pressman.....................................**$75.00**

Patio Picnic Case, Tutti & Chris.................................**$25.00**

Photo album, Barbie, black, 1963.............................**$30.00**

Playhouse, Tutti, 1967...**$75.00**

Room-fulls, Barbie's Country Kitchen, 1975-76...........**$50.00**

Schoolroom, Barbie & Skipper, Sears Christmas catalog, rare, 1965..**$275.00**

Sew-Free Fashion-Fun, Barbie, each **$25.00**

Teen Dream Bedroom, Barbie **$35.00**

Ten Speeder, Barbie, 1974 to present.........................**$15.00**

2-in-1 Bedroom, Growing Up Skipper, 1976 ....**$40.00**

Barware

This field covers cocktail shakers, decanters, ice buckets, and the like that were designed to use in mixing and serving drinks. These items are diverse enough that they appeal to a variety of tastes and collecting interests. Some examples are from the Depression era, some carry advertising messages, and others are very Deco or ultramodern, made of chrome, Bakelite, and aluminum.

Cocktail shakers were made in many forms. The lady's leg was a popular design, and you may find some modeled as penguins, roosters, golf bags, zeppelins, and airplanes. You'll find that *Kitchen Glassware of the Depression Years* and *The Collector's Encyclopedia of Depression Glass,* both by Gene Florence, show several examples of glass decanters as well as ice buckets.

Cocktail shaker, transparent green glass w/chrome top, pinched-in sides...**$40.00**

Cocktail shaker, transparent pink glass **$70.00**

Cocktail shaker, transparent red glass w/chrome stopper, Duncan Miller..**$50.00**

Cocktail shaker, 12", hammered aluminum w/chrysanthemum design, pour spout, screw cap, Continental Hand Wrought #530 ....**$50.00**

Cocktail shaker, 4½" dia reamer top, transparent green glass, Speakeasy..**$40.00**

Cocktail shaker, 4½" dia reamer top, transparent pink glass w/chrome lid, Party Line **$85.00**

Decanter w/shot glass stopper, transparent red glass ..**$100.00**

Decanter w/stopper, transparent green, bulbous shape horizontally ribbed from top to bottom **$40.00**

Hors d'oeuvres server, 11½", chrome holder w/yellow Bakelite handle holds 4 trays, 2 middle trays swivel, unmarked..**$125.00**

Ice bucket, black glass, ring design on knobed lid & bucket, rattan handle **$75.00**

Ice bucket, hammered aluminum w/glass liner, knobed lid, knotched edge on base, banded design at rim, Keystone Ware...**$40.00**

Ice bucket, transparent pink glass, vertically ribbed, chrome handle, no lid...**$22.50**

Liqueur set, 14" overall, encased in replica of bowling ball, marbleized plastic, chrome dispenser, color-trimmed shots...$100.00

Mixer, Southern Comfort promotional sales item, electric, 1950s, $100.00 up to $125.00

Stem, cocktail; 5", pink glass bowl on dancing nude figural stem, unmarked, American......................................**$65.00**

Tray & tumbler set, dark green glass tumblers & tray w/chrome handles & holders, American............**$100.00**

Baseball Cards

How do we see the baseball card market? Perhaps softening, but certainly not dead. Since 1987 the new-card market has been literally flooded, and obviously with such an influx, the investment potential of these more current cards may be slim. But many of the older examples continue to climb in value. For instance, Hank Aaron (#128) 1954 Topps card sells at a minimum of $2,000.00, up by about 75% in only one year. But after 1980, you'll find some that have fallen off by about the same percentage. Hundreds of cards have been printed and many are worth less than 20¢, so as you can see, if you're going to collect, you must stay on top of the market by study and observation.

A good card can often represent a significant investment. It wouldn't be unusual to have to pay as much as $50.00 for a early Topps or Bowman superstar, and a 1952 Topps Jackie Robinson books today at $12,000.00, though this is probably a minimum value. Some of the more valuable cards have been reproduced, so beware. Except for only a few, the entire 1952 Topps set was reissued in the early 1980s, but these are clearly marked. You'll need a good price guide before you start to collect; one of the best is *Gene Florence's Standard Baseball Card Price Guide*.

If you are totally unfamiliar with cards, you'll need to know how to determine the various manufacturers. 1) Bowman; All are copyrighted Bowman or B.G.H.L.I., except a few from the fities that are marked '. . . in the series of Baseball Picture Cards.' 2) Donruss: All are marked with the Donruss logo on the front. 3) Fleer: From 1981 to 1984 the Fleer name is on the backs of the cards; after 1985 it was also on the front. 4) Score & Sportflics; Score written on front, Sportflics on back of each year. 5) Topps: 1951 cards are baseball game pieces with red or blue backs (no other identification). After that either Topps or T.G.C. appears somewhere on the card. 6) Upper Deck: Marked front and back with Upper Deck logo and hologram.

Learn to judge the condition of your card, since its condition is a very important factor when it comes to making an accurate evaluation. Our values are for mint condition cards. One that is judged to be in only good condition may be worth only one-tenth as much. Superstars' and Hall of Famers' cards are most likely to appreciate, and the colored photocards from the thirties are a good investment as well. Buy modern cards by the set while they're inexpensive; who knows what they may be worth in years to come. Any of today's rookies may be the next Babe Ruth.

Aaron, Hank; #212, Topps, 1959, M **$40.00**
Abbott, Jim; #88, Score, 1989, M **$1.00**
Abernathy, Ted; #187, Topps, 1971, M ....**$.80**
Abner, Shawn; #223, Sportflics, 1988, M..................**$.25**
Abrams, Cal; #55, Bowman, 1955, M **$7.00**
Adcock, Joe; #563, Topps, 1967, VG **$6.00**
Aguilera, Rick; #441, Donruss, 1986, M ....**$.75**
Aguirre, Hank; #6, Topps, 1963, M **$1.80**
Ainge, Dan; #418, Fleer, 1981, M **$1.00**
Alcala, Santo; #589, Topps, 1976, M **$2.00**
Allen, Dick; #210, Topps, 1975, M **$1.60**
Allison, Bob; #290, Topps, 1964, VG ....**$.45**
Alomar, Roberto; #299, Fleer, 1989, M......................**$.75**
Alomar, Roberto; #346, Upper Deck, 1990, M..........**$.75**

Alou, Felipe; #240, Topps, 1967, M **$3.00**
Alou, Matty; #720, Topps, 1971, M **$4.50**
Alyea, Brant; #383, Topps, 1972, M ....**$.40**
Amoros, Sandy; #93, Topps, 1958, VG **$1.75**
Anderson, Brady; #563, Score, 1989, M ....**$.25**
Andrews, Mike; #42, Topps, 1973, M ....**$.40**
Aparicio, Louis; #61, Topps, 1974, M **$2.00**
Arlin, Steve; #159, Topps, 1975, M ....**$.40**
Ashburn, Richie; #15, Bowman, 1954, VG..................**$7.50**
Ashburn, Richie; #300, Topps, 1959, M **$14.00**
Aspromonte, Ken; #464, Topps, 1963, M **$10.00**
August, Don; #392, Topps, 1985, M............................**$.40**
Avery, Steve; #109, Score, 1990, VG ....**$.50**
Bacsik, Mike; #103, Topps, 1977, M ....**$.25**
Baerga, Carlos; #443, Donruss, 1990, M **$3.50**
Bagwell, Jeff; #702, Upper Deck, 1991, M................**$1.00**
Bailey, Bob; #580, Topps, 1968, VG ....**$.65**
Baines, Harold; #347, Topps, 1981, M **$3.50**
Baker, Dusty; #5, Fleer, 1984, M ....**$.35**
Baker, Floyd; #146, Bowman, 1950, VG......................**$4.50**
Baldschun, Jack; #284, Topps, 1970, M **$1.40**
Banks, George; #348, Topps, 1965, M........................**$1.60**
Barr, Jim; #308, Topps, 1976, M ....**$.25**
Bateman, John; #417, Topps, 1970, M **$1.40**
Becker, Joe; #463, Topps, 1960, M **$4.00**
Bedrosian, Steve; #222, Sportflics, 1988, M ....**$.75**
Bell, Derek; #81, Score, 1981, M................................**$2.00**
Bell, Gary; #273, Topps, 1962, M **$2.00**
Bell, George; #148, Fleer, 1984, M **$1.50**
Bell, Juan; #1, Donruss, 1991, M................................**$2.00**
Bench, Johnny; #584, Fleer, 1983, M **$1.00**
Beniquez, Juan; #496, Topps, 1976, M ....**$.25**
Bernhardt, Cesar; #179, Topps, 1992, M ....**$.25**
Berra, Yogi; #351, Donruss, 1981, M..........................**$.30**
Biggio, Craig; #103, Score, 1988, VG ....**$.40**
Biggio, Craig; #49, Topps, 1989, M ....**$.35**
Bilko, Steve; #206, Bowman, 1954, M **$12.00**
Black, Joe; #178, Topps, 1956, VG..............................**$3.50**
Black, Joe; #49, Topps, 1989, M ....**$.35**
Blue, Vida; #200, Topps, 1976, M **$1.40**
Blyleven, Bert; #554, Topps, 1981, M ....**$.50**
Boggs, Wade; #29, Fleer, 1987, M..............................**$1.50**
Boggs, Wade; #371, Donruss, 1986, M **$2.00**
Bolin, Bobby; #574, Topps, 1970, M **$1.40**
Bonds, Barry; #440, Upper Deck, 1989, M **$1.00**
Bonilla, Bobby; #116, Score, 1988, M ....**$.35**
Bonilla, Bobby; #357, Donruss, 1991, M....................**$.25**
Boone, Bob; #131, Topps, 1974, M **$3.00**
Boudreau, Lou; #11, Bowman, 1949, EX....................**$16.00**
Bouton, Jim; #562, Topps, 1968, M **$3.00**
Branca, Ralph; #56, Bowman, 1951, EX **$6.00**
Breazeale, Jim; #33, Topps, 1973, M ....**$.40**
Brett, George; #1, Topps, 1977, M **$4.00**
Brett, George; #108, Fleer, 1983, M **$1.25**
Brett, George; #215, Upper Deck, 1989, M................**$.75**
Brett, George; #34, Donruss, 1982, M **$1.50**
Brewer, Jim; #571, Topps, 1970, M **$1.40**
Brooks, Hubie; #476, Donruss, 1982, M ....**$.60**

Brown, Kevin; #47, Donruss, 1990, M ....**$.25**	Donneis, Chris; #104, Score, 1991, M.....................**$.25**
Browning, Tom; #634, Donruss, 1985, M **$1.50**	Downing, Al; #584, Topps, 1970, M **$1.40**
Buckner, Bill; #18, Fleer, 1984, M ....**$.35**	Dozier, DJ; #97, Score, 1990, M..........................**$.35**
Buechele, Steve; #544, Donruss, 1986, M ....**$.35**	Dressen, Charlie; #124, Bowman, 1953, VG.............**$15.00**
Buford, Don; #81, Topps, 1965, M.......................**$1.20**	Dunston, Shawon; #280, Topps, 1985, M.................**$2.00**
Burgess, Forrest (Smoky); #209, Bowman, 1955, M **$8.00**	Dunston, Shawon; #311, Donruss, 1986, M.............**$.75**
Burks, Ellis; #121, Donruss, 1988, M ....**$.50**	Durham, Leon; #5, Donruss, 1984, M ....**$.25**
Butler, Bill; #377, Topps, 1970, M......................**$1.40**	Eckersley, Dennis; #639, Donruss, 1984, M.............**$.75**
Cain, Bob; #197, Bowman, 1951, VG.....................**$3.50**	Edwards, Bruce; #165, Bowman, 1950, VG.............**$4.50**
Calderon, Ivan; #182, Donruss, 1988, M ....**$.25**	Ellsworth, Dick; #59, Topps, 1970, M....................**$.80**
Calderon, Ivan; #382, Topps, 1986, M ....**$.75**	Ennis, Del; #127, Bowman, 1954, EX....................**$8.00**
Callison, Johnny; #133, Topps, 1969, M................**$1.20**	Erickson, Scott; #201, Fleer, 1992, M....................**$.25**
Campanella, Roy; #22, Bowman, 1955, M.............**$100.00**	Espinoza, Alvaro; #240, Donruss, 1990, M.............**$.25**
Candiotti, Tom; #197, Fleer, 1984, M ....**$.50**	Espy, Cecil; #73, Score, 1988, M..........................**$.25**
Canseco, Jose; #178, Sportflics, 1986, VG..............**$2.25**	Estrada, Chuck; #560, Topps, 1962, M.................**$20.00**
Canseco, Jose; #97, Donruss, 1987, M...................**$8.00**	Evans, Al; #38, Bowman, 1951, VG **$6.00**
Carlton, Steve; #183, Donruss, 1986, M ....**$.50**	Evans, Dwight; #293, Fleer, 1982, M....................**$.25**
Carlton, Steve; #641, Fleer, 1982, M ....**$.75**	Evans, Dwight; #614, Topps, 1973, M.................**$80.00**
Carlton, Steve; #67, Topps, 1973, M.....................**$6.00**	Everett, Carl; #386, Score, 1991, M......................**$.25**
Carter, Gary; #70, Topps, 1980, M **$2.00**	Farrell, John; #620, Score, 1988, M......................**$.25**
Carty, Rico; #655, Topps, 1975, M ....**$.60**	Feller, Bob; #27, Bowman, 1949, VG **$45.00**
Cedeno, Andujar; #753, Score, 1991, M ....**$.35**	Fernandez, Alex; #645, Upper Deck, 1991, M..............**$.50**
Chamberlain, Wes; #258, Fleer, 1991, M...............**$1.25**	Fielder, Cecil; #442, Donruss, 1989, M...................**$.35**
Clancy, Jim; #19, Donruss, 1984, M......................**$.25**	Fingers, Rollie; #21, Topps, 1975, M....................**$4.00**
Clark, Jack; #460, Topps, 1982, M ....**$.35**	Fingers, Rollie; #485, Fleer, 1981, M...................**$1.00**
Clark, Will; #78, Score, 1988, M ....**$.50**	Finley, Chuck; #407, Donruss, 1987, M...............**$1.50**
Clayton, Royce; #4, Upper Deck, 1991, M ....**$.35**	Finley, Steve; #37, Topps, 1989, M.......................**$.35**
Clemens, Roger; #207, Sportflics, 1988, M.............**$1.00**	Fisk, Carlton; #193, Topps, 1973, M...................**$40.00**
Clemens, Roger; #276, Donruss, 1987, M **$3.00**	Fisk, Carlton; #204, Fleer, 1986, M......................**$.75**
Coan, Gil; #40, Bowman, 1954, VG......................**$2.00**	Fisk, Carlton; #495, Donruss, 1982, M................**$1.50**
Cochrane, Dave; #158, Sportflics, 1987, M.............**$1.50**	Fisk, Carlton; #609, Upper Deck, 1989, M.............**$.75**
Coleman, Joe; #127, Topps, 1970, M......................**$.80**	Fitzgerald, Ed; #168, Bowman, 1954, M...............**$12.00**
Coleman, Ray; #250, Bowman, 1950, VG................**$4.50**	Ford, Curt; #648, Fleer, 1986, M.........................**$.30**
Coleman, Vince; #651, Donruss, 1986, M ....**$.50**	Foster, Alan; #266, Topps, 1969, M.....................**$1.60**
Cosman, Jim; #384, Topps, 1967, M **$2.00**	Fox, Charlie; #129, Topps, 1972, M......................**$.40**
Cox, Billy; #56, Bowman, 1955, VG......................**$1.75**	Fox, Howie; #180, Bowman, 1951, VG..................**$3.50**
Cox, Danny; #449, Donruss, 1984, M.....................**$.35**	Franco, John; #156, Sportflics, 1986, M..................**$.30**
Cruz, Henry; #590, Topps, 1976, M ....**$.60**	Franco, Julio; #216, Donruss, 1986, M...................**$.50**
Cuyler, Milt; #583, Score, 1990, M.......................**$.25**	Friend, Bob; #520, Topps, 1962, M......................**$4.00**
Daniels, Kal; #646, Fleer, 1986, M **$5.00**	Friend, Owen; #189, Bowman, 1950, VG...............**$4.50**
Dark, Al; #34, Bowman, 1952, M **$24.00**	Fryman, Travis; #96, Fleer, 1990, M....................**$1.25**
Darling, Ron; #27, Topps, 1984, M **$3.00**	Furillo, Carl; #24, Bowman, 1952, VG..................**$7.50**
Darling, Ron; #434, Donruss, 1985, M ....**$.25**	Galarraga, Andres; #33, Donruss, 1986, M.............**$.75**
Davis, Alvin; #488, Fleer, 1985, M.......................**$1.00**	Gant, Ron; #590, Fleer, 1989, M.........................**$.50**
Davis, Eric; #325, Donruss, 1985, VG **$3.75**	Gant, Ron; #647, Score, 1988, M.........................**$2.50**
Davis, Glenn; #30, Donruss, 1990, M.....................**$.30**	Garagiola, Joe; #27, Bowman, 1952, VG...............**$17.50**
Davis, Mike; #586, Fleer, 1981, M.........................**$.25**	Garber, Gene; #444, Topps, 1975, M.....................**$.40**
Davis, Storm; #268, Topps, 1983, M......................**$.25**	Garcia, Mike; #128, Bowman, 1955, M **$7.00**
Dawson, Andre; #139, Sportflics, 1987, M ....**$.50**	Gardenshire, Ron; #623, Topps, 1982, M...............**$.25**
Dawson, Andre; #97, Donruss, 1984, M **$4.00**	Gardner, Mark; #371, Donruss, 1990, M...............**$.25**
Decker, Steve; #441, Donruss, 1991, M...................**$.50**	Garver, Ned; #29, Bowman, 1952, VG...................**$4.50**
Delock, Ike; #336, Topps, 1960, M **$3.00**	Garvey, Steve; #110, Fleer, 1981, M......................**$.75**
Delsing, Jim; #55, Bowman, 1954, VG...................**$2.00**	Gehrig, Lou; #881, Score, 1992, M.......................**$.25**
DeShields, Delino; #27, Fleer, 1990, M ....**$.35**	Gibson, Bob; #72, Topps, 1971, VG.....................**$1.00**
Dibble, Rob; #334, Donruss, 1989, M ....**$.25**	Gibson, Kirk; #407, Donruss, 1982, M..................**$1.00**
Dibble, Rob; #83, Fleer, 1988, M.........................**$1.25**	Gladden, Dan; #607, Fleer, 1985, M......................**$.35**
Ditmar, Art; #374, Topps, 1959, VG.....................**$1.00**	Glavine, Tom; #267, Bowman, 1989, M..................**$.35**
Dobson, Joe; #44, Bowman, 1950, VG **$12.50**	Gomez, Preston; #74, Topps, 1969, M..................**$1.20**

Gonzalez, Jose; #525, Donruss, 1987, M	$.25
Gonzalez, Juan; #637, Score, 1990, M	$1.50
Gonzalez, Luis; #567, Upper Deck, 1991, M	$.75
Gooden, Dwight; #26, Donruss, 1986, M	$.50
Gordon, Sid; #60, Bowman, 1952, VG	$3.75
Gordon, Tom; #736, Upper Deck, 1989, M	$.50
Grace, Mark; #426, Fleer, 1989, M	$.25
Greene, Tommy; #640, Score, 1990, M	$.25
Greenwell, Mike; #221, Sportflics, 1989, M	$.75
Greenwell, Mike; #233, Topps, 1988, M	$.35
Griffey, Ken Jr; #192, Donruss, 1989, M	$3.50
Griffey, Ken Jr; #481, Bowman, 1990, M	$1.25
Gruber, Kelly; #444, Donruss, 1987, M	$1.50
Gruber, Kelly; #458, Topps, 1987, M	$.25
Guerrero, Pedro; #174, Donruss, 1984, M	$.50
Guidry, Mike; #185, Sportflics, 1986, M	$.60
Gumpert, Randy; #59, Bowman, 1951, M	$20.00
Gwynn, Tony; #13, Sportflics, 1986, M	$1.00
Hairston, Jerry; #391, Topps, 1976, M	$.25
Hall, Mel; #126, Donruss, 1983, M	$1.25
Hamilton, Darryl; #301, Upper Deck, 1989, M	$.25
Hammond, Chris; #421, Fleer, 1990, M	$.25
Hanson, Erik; #430, Donruss, 1990, M	$1.00
Hardy, Carroll; #341, Topps, 1960, M	$3.00
Harvey, Bryan; #53, Donruss, 1988, M	$.35
Harvey, Bryan; #87, Score, 1988, M	$1.50
Hassler, Andy; #207, Topps, 1976, M	$.25
Hatcher, Billy; #649, Fleer, 1985, M	$5.00
Hawblitzel, Ryan; #59, Upper Deck, 1992, M	$.25
Haynes, Joe; #223, Topps, 1954, M	$15.00
Hearn, Jim; #49, Bowman, 1952, M	$15.00
Henderson, Dave; #489, Fleer, 1985, M	$.35
Henderson, Rickey; #35, Donruss, 1983, M	$4.50
Hendrick, George; #406, Topps, 1972, M	$1.60
Hernandez, Keith; #62, Sportflics, 1986, M	$.75
Hernandez, Keith; #68, Donruss, 1985, M	$.25
Herschiser, Orel; #226, Donruss, 1986, M	$.75
Higgins, Dennis; #529, Topps, 1966, M	$20.00
Hiller, John; #209, Topps, 1966, VG	$.50
Hodges, Gil; #158, Bowman, 1955, VG	$10.00
Hodges, Gil; #183, Topps, 1971, M	$4.00
Holman, Brian; #100, Fleer, 1988, M	$.25
Horton, Willie; #494, Topps, 1972, M	$.40
Hosey, Steve; #62, Upper Deck, 1992, M	$.25
Hundley, Todd; #76, Score, 1990, M	$.25
Hunter, Brian; #359, Fleer, 1992, M	$.50
Hunter, Brian; #366, Upper Deck, 1992, M	$.35
Hunter, Jim; #330, Topps, 1972, VG	$1.25
Hurst, Bruce; #23, Donruss, 1990, M	$.25
Incaviglia, Pete; #231, Donruss, 1990, M	$.25
Incaviglia, Pete; #48, Topps, 1986, M	$.25
Jackson, Bo; #119, Donruss, 1988, M	$.75
Jackson, Bo; #540, Topps, 1989, M	$.35
Jackson, Reggie; #535, Donruss, 1982, M	$1.75
Jackson, Reggie; #93, Fleer, 1983, M	$1.25
Jackson, Sonny; #244, Topps, 1966, M	$1.20
James, Chris; #42, Donruss, 1987, M	$.35
Jansen, Larry; #162, Bowman, 1951, VG	$3.50
Jefferies, Gregg; #38, Fleer, 1989, M	$.25
Jefferson, Jesse; #47, Topps, 1976, M	$.25
John, Tommy; #423, Donruss, 1985, M	$.25
Johnson, Earl; #188, Bowman, 1950, VG	$4.50
Johnson, Howard; #582, Upper Deck, 1989, M	$.25
Johnson, Lance; #37, Fleer, 1988, M	$.25
Johnson, Walter; #417, Topps, 1979, M	$.60
Jones, Tracy; #651, Fleer, 1987, M	$.40
Jorgensen, Mike; #117, Topps, 1976, M	$.25
Joyner, Wally; #24, Donruss, 1990, M	$.75
Joyner, Wally; #75, Sportflics, 1987, M	$1.00
Justice, Dave; #650, Score, 1990, M	$2.00
Kasko, Eddie; #193, Topps, 1962, M	$3.00
Keane, Johnny; #131, Topps, 1965, M	$1.20
Kelly, Roberto; #212, Fleer, 1988, M	$1.50
Kelly, Roberto; #590, Upper Deck, 1989, M	$.35
Key, Jimmy; #193, Topps, 1985, M	$1.00
Key, Jimmy; #559, Donruss, 1985, M	$1.25
Kingman, Dave; #360, Donruss, 1984, M	$.25
Kirkland, Willie; #17, Topps, 1964, M	$1.80
Kluszewski, Ted; #178, Topps, 1958, M	$14.00
Knoblauch, Chuck; #37, Fleer, 1991, M	$.50
Knoblauch, Chuck; #39, Donruss, 1991, M	$.50
Koosman, Jerry; #64, Topps, 1976, M	$.40
Laboy, Jose; #238, Topps, 1970, M	$.80
Landis, Jim; #375, Topps, 1957, VG	$1.50
Langston, Mark; #589, Fleer, 1987, M	$.35
Lankford, Ray; #731, Score, 1991, M	$.25
LaPoint, Dave; #544, Donruss, 1983, M	$.30
Larkin, Barry; #239, Fleer, 1988, M	$1.00
Law, Vance; #291, Topps, 1982, M	$.25
Lee, Manny; #370, Donruss, 1990, M	$.25
Lefebvre, Jim; #553, Topps, 1970, M	$1.40
Leibrandt, Charlie; #208, Fleer, 1981, M	$.35
Leonard, Dennis; #205, Topps, 1978, M	$.80
Lind, Jose; #334, Fleer, 1988, M	$.25
Lindros, Eric; #100, Score, 1990, VG	$1.75
Livingstone, Scott; #53, Upper Deck, 1991, M	$.25
Logan, Johnny; #205, Topps, 1960, M	$3.00
Lonborg, Jim; #94, Topps, 1975, M	$.40
Maddux, Greg; #36, Donruss, 1987, M	$1.50
Maddux, Greg; #361, Topps, 1987, M	$.75
Magadan, Dave; #648, Fleer, 1987, M	$1.00
Martinez, Buck; #314, Topps, 1975, M	$.40
Martinez, Carmelo; #623, Donruss, 1984, M	$.40
Martinez, Edgar; #378, Fleer, 1988, M	$1.00
Martinez, Edgar; #768, Upper Deck, 1989, M	$.75
Martinez, Ramon; #224, Sportflics, 1989, M	$.75
Martinez, Ramon; #635, Score, 1989, M	$1.00
Mattingly, Don; #176, Bowman, 1989, M	$.25
Mattingly, Don; #2, Sportflics, 1986, M	$2.50
Mattingly, Don; #52, Donruss, 1987, M	$1.00
Mays, Willie; #50, Topps, 1968, M	$60.00
McCaskill, Kirk; #163, Fleer, 1986, M	$.25
McDowell, Jack; #85, Score, 1988, VG	$2.50
McGee, Willie; #625, Donruss, 1984, M	$.75
McGwire, Mark; #385, Score, 1990, M	$.25
McIntosh, Joe; #497, Topps, 1976, M	$.25

McRae, Brian; #152, Fleer, 1991, M............**$1.00**
Mikkelsen, Pete; #177, Topps, 1965, M.........**$1.20**
Milacki, Bob; #402, Donruss, 1990, M............**$.25**
Mitchell, Kevin; #120, Donruss, 1990, M..........**$.75**
Mohorcic, Dale; #131, Fleer, 1987, M.............**$.25**
Moon, Wally; #210, Topps, 1954, M **$4.00**
Moore, Mike; #482, Fleer, 1983, M............**$.75**
Morris, Jack; #415, Donruss, 1984, M..........**$.75**
Morris, Jack; #475, Fleer, 1981, M.............**$1.00**
Munson, Thurman; #442, Topps, 1972, VG...........**$2.50**
Murphy, Dale; #443, Fleer, 1982, M............**$1.00**
Murphy, Dale; #47, Donruss, 1983, M..........**$.75**

Musial, Stan; #290, Topps, 1961, M....................$100.00
Naehring, Tim; #87, Score, 1990, M ....**$.25**
Neagle, Denny; #34, Upper Deck, 1991, M.........**$.50**
Nelson, Dave; #435, Topps, 1975, M ....**$.40**
Nelson, Gene; #477, Donruss, 1990, M..........**$.25**
Nettles, Graig; #324, Topps, 1971, M..........**$3.00**
Nettles, Graig; #82, Fleer, 1984, M............**$1.00**
Newfield, Marc; #391, Score, 1991, M............**$.50**
Newfield, Marc; #64, Upper Deck, 1992, M..........**$.50**
Niekro, Phil; #83, Fleer, 1984, M............**$4.00**
Nuxhall, Joe; #312, Topps, 1965, M...........**$1.60**
O'Brian, Pete; #281, Donruss, 1984, M...........**$.75**
Oldis, Bob; #269, Topps, 1962, M............**$2.00**
Olerud, John; #2, Donruss, 1990, M...........**$.75**
Olerud, John; #589, Score, 1990, M............**$.50**
Olson, Greg; #161, Topps, 1989, M ....**$.35**
Orsulak, Joe; #85, Fleer, 1985, M ....**$.35**
Pagliarulo, Mike; #638, Topps, 1985, M..........**$.25**
Palmeiro, Rafael; #47, Donruss, 1987, M **$2.50**
Palmer, Jim; #69, Fleer, 1983, M............**$1.00**
Parker, Wes; #344, Topps, 1965, M............**$1.60**
Parrish, Lance; #15, Donruss, 1984, M ....**$.35**
Pasqua, Dan; #86, Fleer, 1985, M............**$.35**
Pendleton, Terry; #260, Donruss, 1990, M...........**$.35**
Pendleton, Terry; #44, Fleer, 1986, M ....**$.50**
Perry, Jim; #385, Topps, 1973, M............**$.80**
Pettis, Gary; #157, Sportflics, 1987, M............**$.50**
Plantier, Phil; #406, Score, 1992, M............**$.35**
Porter, Darrell; #52, Topps, 1975, M ....**$.40**
Presley, Jim; #500, Fleer, 1985, M ....**$.50**
Puckett, Kirby; #149, Donruss, 1987, M...........**$1.75**

Puckett, Kirby; #236, Upper Deck, 1990, M ....**$.25**
Puckett, Kirby; #633, Fleer, 1987, M ....**$.75**
Queen, Mel; #33, Topps, 1964, M............**$1.80**
Quinones, Ray; #595, Fleer, 1987, M............**$.25**
Quintana, Carlos; #26, Upper Deck, 1989, M............**$.50**
Quisenberry, Dan; #222, Donruss, 1981, M............**$.30**
Quisenberry, Dan; #667, Topps, 1980, M............**$1.75**
Raines, Tom; #164, Topps, 1982, M............**$1.00**
Reardon, Jeff; #547, Donruss, 1982, M............**$1.25**
Redus, Gary; #481, Fleer, 1984, M............**$.25**
Reed, Howie; #398, Topps, 1971, M............**$.80**
Reed, Jody; #360, Fleer, 1988, M............**$.50**
Reuschel, Rick; #153, Topps, 1975, M............**$.60**
Reynolds, Harold; #484, Donruss, 1986, M............**$.65**
Reynolds, RJ; #97, Fleer, 1984, M............**$1.00**
Rhodes, Arthur; #17, Upper Deck, 1992, M............**$.25**
Ricketts, Dick; #236, Topps, 1960, M............**$3.00**
Rijo, Jose; #143, Fleer, 1985, M............**$2.00**
Ripken, Cal Jr; #15, Score, 1989, M............**$.35**
Ripken, Cal Jr; #89, Donruss, 1987, VG............**$1.25**
Roberts, Bip; #427, Fleer, 1987, M............**$.35**
Robinson, Brooks; #202, Topps, 1975, M............**$1.00**
Rodriguez, Henry; #21, Upper Deck, 1991, M............**$.25**
Rollins, Rich; #90, Topps, 1965, M............**$1.20**
Rose, Pete; #1, Fleer, 1981, M............**$2.50**
Rose, Pete; #600, Topps, 1985, M............**$.75**
Ruffin, Bruce; #151, Donruss, 1990, M............**$.25**
Ryan, Nolan; #250, Score, 1990, M............**$.50**
Ryan, Nolan; #419, Donruss, 1982, VG............**$1.50**
Ryan, Nolan; #486, Bowman, 1990, M............**$.40**
Sabo, Chris; #100, Score, 1988, VG............**$1.25**
Sabo, Chris; #317, Donruss, 1989, M............**$.50**
Sadecki, Ray; #26, Topps, 1966, M............**$1.00**
Samuel, Juan; #183, Donruss, 1985, M............**$.75**
Samuel, Juan; #634, Fleer, 1985, M............**$1.00**
Sandberg, Ryne; #1, Donruss, 1985, M............**$3.00**
Sanders, Deion; #13, Upper Deck, 1990, M............**$.50**
Sanders, Ken; #366, Topps, 1975, M............**$.40**
Sanders, Reggie; #421, Fleer, 1992, M............**$.25**
Santiago, Benito; #644, Fleer, 1986, VG............**$.35**
Sax, Steve; #104, Donruss, 1984, M............**$1.00**
Sax, Steve; #21, Fleer, 1982, M............**$4.00**
Schmidt, Dave; #381, Topps, 1982, M............**$.50**
Schmidt, Mike; #11, Donruss, 1981, M............**$2.50**
Schmidt, Mike; #21, Sportflics, 1989, M............**$.75**
Schmidt, Mike; #641, Fleer, 1982, M............**$.75**
Schofield, Dick; #105, Fleer, 1984, M............**$.75**
Schooler, Mike; #91, Score, 1988, M............**$.50**
Scioscia, Mike; #598, Donruss, 1982, M............**$.50**
Scott, Mike; #109, Topps, 1981, M............**$.50**
Seaver, Tom; #422, Donruss, 1981, M............**$2.00**
Seitzer, Kevin; #652, Fleer, 1987, M............**$.50**
Sheffield, Gary; #31, Donruss, 1989, M............**$.25**
Sierra, Ruben; #113, Score, 1988, M............**$.35**
Sierra, Ruben; #771, Topps, 1988, M............**$.35**
Simmons, Ted; #154, Topps, 1972, VG............**$.50**
Simmons, Todd; #650, Fleer, 1988, M............**$.25**
Smith, Lee; #403, Donruss, 1983, M............**$1.00**

Smith, Lee; #603, Fleer, 1982, VG ....**$.35**
Smith, Lonnie; #317, Topps, 1981, M.........................**$.50**
Smith, Ozzie; #44, Donruss, 1989, M ....**$.25**
Smoltz, John; #74, Fleer, 1988, M..............................**$2.50**
Sosa, Sammy; #558, Score, 1990, M ....**$.25**
Staton, Dave; #66, Upper Deck, 1991, M...................**$.25**
Stefero, John; #652, Fleer, 1987, M............................**$.50**
Stenhouse, Dave; #304, Topps, 1965, M.....................**$1.60**
Stieb, Dave; #71, Donruss, 1984, M ....**$.50**
Strawberry, Darryl; #118, Donruss, 1987, M..............**$1.00**
Strawberry, Darryl; #93, Fleer, 1985, VG **$2.75**
Sutton, Don; #47, Fleer, 1983, M.................................**$.35**
Sutton, Don; #605, Topps, 1981, M.............................**$.75**
Swift, Bill; #219, Score, 1989, M **$1.00**
Swindell, Greg; #319, Topps, 1987, M ....**$.50**
Swindell, Greg; #644, Fleer, 1987, M ....**$.75**
Tanana, Frank; #204, Topps, 1976, M..........................**$.60**
Tapani, Kevin; #87, Upper Deck, 1990, M..................**$.75**
Tartabull, Danny; #117, Fleer, 1987, M ....**$.35**
Tartabull, Danny; #147, Donruss, 1987, M.................**$.35**
Tartabull, Danny; #23, Sportflics, 1987, M ....**$.75**
Thomas, Darrel; #457, Topps, 1972, M........................**$.40**
Thomas, Frank; #712, Fleer, 1991, M..........................**$1.25**
Tidrow, Dick; #241, Topps, 1975, M............................**$.40**
Toliver, Fred; #647, Fleer, 1986, M.............................**$.75**
Trammell, Alan; #76, Donruss, 1982, M......................**$1.00**
Tresh, Tom; #69, Topps, 1968, M **$2.00**
Tudor, John; #311, Fleer, 1982, M...............................**$.35**
Turner, Jerry; #619, Topps, 1975, M...........................**$.40**
Unser, Del; #336, Topps, 1970, M...............................**$1.40**
Vail, Mike; #655, Topps, 1976, M................................**$.25**
Valenzuela, Fernando; #510, Topps, 1982, M..............**$.25**
Valenzuela, Fernando; #53, Donruss, 1988, M ....**$.25**
Van Poppel, Todd; #12, Upper Deck, 1991, M ....**$.50**
Van Slyke, Andy; #242, Fleer, 1985, M ....**$.75**
Vaughn, Maurice; #275, Bowman, 1990, M..................**$.75**
Vaughn, Maurice; #430, Donruss, 1991, M..................**$.50**
Ventura, Robin; #595, Score, 1990, M.........................**$.75**
Versalles, Zoilo; #38, Topps, 1969, M.........................**$1.20**
Viola, Frank; #291, Fleer, 1985, M..............................**$.50**
Viola, Frank; #99, Sportflics, 1986, M.........................**$.50**
Vitiello, Joe; #73, Upper Deck, 1992, M.....................**$.50**
Wagner, Leon; #495, Topps, 1968, M **$1.20**
Walker, Greg; #73, Fleer, 1984, M..............................**$.50**
Walker, Jerry; #357, Topps, 1962, VG.........................**$.50**
Wallach, Tim; #140, Donruss, 1982, M **$1.00**
Ward, Gary; #113, Donruss, 1990, M...........................**$.25**
Wathan, John; #218, Topps, 1977, M...........................**$.80**
Welch, Bob; #178, Donruss, 1981, M...........................**$.40**
Whisenant, Pete; #201, Topps, 1961, VG.....................**$.60**
Whitaker, Lou; #293, Donruss, 1985, M......................**$.35**
White, Devon; #123, Fleer, 1987, M............................**$.35**
Whiten, Mark; #607, Donruss, 1991, M.......................**$.25**
Wickersham, Dave; #647, Topps, 1969, M **$1.20**
Williams, Bernie; #44, Fleer, 1991, M.........................**$1.00**
Williams, Matt; #118, Score, 1988, M **$1.50**
Williams, Matt; #628, Donruss, 1988, M.....................**$1.50**
Wilson, Willie; #128, Sportflics, 1986, M....................**$.50**

Wine, Bobby; #332, Topps, 1970, M...........................**$1.40**
Winfield, Dave; #409, Donruss, 1983, M.....................**$.75**
Witt, Bobby; #129, Fleer, 1986, M...............................**$.35**
Wood, Wilbur; #342, Topps, 1972, M..........................**$.40**
Wynn, Jim; #260, Topps, 1968, M...............................**$1.20**

Yastrzemski, Carl; #287, Topps, 1961, M.............$150.00
Yastrzemski, Carl; #94, Donruss, 1981, M....................**$1.50**
Yeager, Steve; #593, Topps, 1974, M ....**$.40**
Young, Matt; #16, Donruss, 1984, M ....**$.25**
Yount, Robin; #601, Fleer, 1985, M.............................**$1.50**
Zahn, Geoff; #294, Topps, 1975, M.............................**$.40**
Zauchin, Norm; #422, Topps, 1958, M.........................**$4.00**
Zeile, Todd; #31, Donruss, 1990, M.............................**$.30**
Zimmer, Don; #493, Topps, 1961, M **$4.00**
Zuvella, Paul; #651, Fleer, 1985, M ....**$.75**

Bauer Pottery

Undoubtedly the most easily recognized product of the Bauer Pottery Company who operated from 1909 until 1962 in Los Angeles, California, was their colorful 'Ring' dinnerware (made from 1932 until sometime in the early sixties). You'll recognize it by its bright solid colors: Jade Green, Chinese Yellow, Royal Blue, Light Blue, Orange-Red, Black and White; and by its pattern of closely aligned ribs. They made other lines of dinnerware as well; they're collectible, too, although by no means as easily found.

They also made a line of Gardenware vases and flowerpots for the florist trade. To give you an idea of their values, a 12" vase from this line would bring about $75.00.

To further your understanding of Bauer, we recommend *The Collector's Encyclopedia of California Pottery* by Jack Chipman.

Al Fresco, bowl, vegetable; 9¼" dia, coffee brown or Dubonnet..**$18.00**
Al Fresco, casserole, 1½-qt, w/lid, green or gray.........**$22.00**
Al Fresco, cup & saucer, coffee brown, or Dubonnet **$12.00**
Al Fresco, hostess tray & cup, speckled, green or gray..**$12.00**
Al Fresco, plate, 8", speckled, green or gray.................**$5.00**
Contempo, gravy boat, all colors **$8.00**

Contempo, individual casserole, French; w/lid, all colors, sm **$15.00**
El Chico, plate, 7½", all colors **$15.00**
Hi-Fire, rose bowl, 5½x6½", white........................**$40.00**
La Linda, creamer, new shape, burgundy or brown....**$20.00**
La Linda, teapot, 6-cup, light brown, ivory or olive **$35.00**
Mat Carlton, vase, 7½", ruffled rim, yellow...............**$125.00**
Monterey, ashtray, 3", black **$50.00**
Monterey, tumbler, 8-oz, all colors but white.............**$15.00**

Oil jar, 22", #100, orange-red **$850.00**
Ring, butter dish, ¼-lb, dark blue, burgundy or white.**$125.00**
Ring, candlestick, 2½", orange-red, dark blue or burgundy **$45.00**
Ring, pickle dish, all colors but black **$35.00**

Ring, plate, 6", all colors but black.....................**$10.00**
Ring, platter, 12", oval, dark blue, burgundy or white .**$30.00**
Ring, salt & pepper shakers, barrel form, orange-red, ivory or white, pr..**$30.00**

Ring, sherbet, orange-red, dark blue or burgundy **$40.00**
Ring, soup plate, 7½", jade green or turquoise...........**$45.00**
Ring, teapot, 6-cup, yellow, jade green or turqoise (illustrated) **$60.00**

Beatles Collectibles

Possibly triggered by John Lennon's death in 1980, Beatle's fans, recognizing that their dreams of the band ever reuniting were gone along with him, began to collect memorabilia of all types. Recently some of the original Beatles material has sold at auction with high-dollar results. Handwritten song lyrics, Lennon's autographed high school textbook, and even the legal agreement that was drafted at the time the group disbanded are among the one-of-a-kind multi-thousand dollar sales recorded.

Unless you plan on attending sales of this caliber, you'll be more apt to find the commercially produced memorabilia that literally flooded the market during the sixties when the Fab Four from Liverpool made their unprecedented impact on the entertainment world. A word about their records: they sold in such mass quantities that unless the record is a 'promotional,' made to send to radio stations or for jukebox distribution, they have very little value. Once a record has been played very often and has lost much of its original gloss, becomes scratched, or has writing on the label, its value is minimal. Even in near-mint condition, $4.00 to $6.00 is plenty to pay for a 45 (much less if its worn) unless the original picture sleeve is present. The exception to this is the white-labeled Swan recording of 'She Loves You/I'll Get You,' which in great condition may go as high as $50.00. The picture sleeves are usually valued at $30.00 to $40.00, except for the rare 'Can't Buy Me Love,' which is worth ten times that amount. Beware of reproductions!

For more information we recommend the *Beatles: A Reference and Value Guide,* by Michael Stern, Barbara Crawford, and Hollis Lamon.

Apron, paper-like fiber w/faces in stars, musical scores, NEMS Ent, G..**$350.00**
Ball, 14" inflated, rubber, made by Seltaeb, VG **$850.00**
Belt, vinyl, repetitive faces of all, any color, EX..........**$90.00**
Binder, 3-ring; group portrait, facsimile signatures on white, EX (purple $175; turquoise $250) **$125.00**
Bracelet, 5 charms, 4 Beatles & 1 musical note, EX ..**$135.00**
Bubble bath container, 9", Paul, Soaky, NM **$200.00**
Button, 1", I'm 4 Beatles, blue variety, Green Duck Co (or similar)...**$12.50**
Button, 3", group portrait w/names below each, EX...**$20.00**
Candy cigarette box, 2½x1", 1 figure on various background colors, made by World Candies Inc, EX..............**$120.00**
Cigar band, w/Beatles face, made in Jamaica, VG **$80.00**
Clutch purse, allover pattern of musicians w/instruments, black & white, EX..**$325.00**
Coloring book, official, Saalfield, EX........................**$75.00**
Comb, 14½" long, plastic, made by Lido Toys, EX......**$80.00**

Computer, cardboard, move inner card to line up trivia, Capital Records, 1970, EX...............................**$45.00**

Disk Go Case, plastic, round w/all 4 & facsimile signatures, Charter Industries, any color, EX.......................**$125.00**

Dolls, 13", inflatable plastic, caricature faces, set of 4, EX..**$125.00**

Dolls, 6½", plastic, w/instruments, made by Remco, EX, set of 4...**$375.00**

Dolls, 9", bobbin' heads, composition, made by Carmascot Co, EX, set of 4..**$350.00**

Flasher ring, EX..**$15.00**

Game, Flip Your Wig, Milton Bradley, game board, 48 cards & 4 player pieces, EX..**$165.00**

Handkerchief, cloth, 4 faces, song titles, printed diagonally in black on various colors, EX............................**$200.00**

Lunch box, metal, pictures all 4, w/thermos, Aladdin Industries, VG...**$300.00**

Model kit, Ringo, made by Revell Co, EX..................**$250.00**

Pen, ballpoint; red plastic w/faces of all 4, made in Denmark, EX...**$130.00**

Pencil pouch, vinyl w/portraits & facsimile signatures, by Standard Plastics, in yellow or gray, EX (red or blue, $175)...**$145.00**

Pennant, 22" long, group & facsimilie signatures, red & black on white, EX **$125.00**

Pin, w/portrait of the Beatles, M.........................$135.00

Plate, 11", 4 girls styling boys' hair, red, green & black on natural, Bamboo Tray Specialist Co, VG **$120.00**

Postcard, any, EX...**$25.00**

Pressbook, Help, complete, NM **$50.00**

Record player, 4-speed, group picture in lid, NM ..**$1,800.00**

Scarf, 26" square, face in each corner, red & black on white, by Blackpool Publishers, EX...............................**$165.00**

Scrapbook, pictures all 4, by Whitman, 29¢ original price, EX..**$95.00**

Tray, each Beatle in colored square on white, made by Worcester Ware (watch for reproductions), EX **$60.00**

Bedroom and Bathroom Glassware

This type of glassware was produced in large quantities during the Depression era by many glasshouses who were simply trying to stay in business. They made puff jars, trays, lamps, and vanity sets for the bedroom; towel bars, soap dishes, and bottles of all types for the bath. These items came in much the same color assortment as the Depression glass dinnerware that has been so popular with collectors for more than twenty years. For the most part, it's not terribly expensive, though prices for items that can be traced to some of the more prestigious companies such as Heisey, Cambridge, Fostoria, or Akro Agate are already climbing.

For more information we recommend *Bedroom and Bathroom Glassware of the Depression Years* by Margaret and Kenn Whitmyer.

Ashtray, green & black opaque, square w/canted corners..**$20.00**

Atomizer, 6½", ebony w/metal collar, Cambridge.....**$115.00**

Barber bottle, vaseline, Vertical Stripe, made by Fenton for LG Wright, 1960 ....**$120.00**

Cabinet knob, lg, amber glass, hexagonal.................**$6.50**

Clock, frosted crystal w/gold-decorated square body.**$60.00**

Clock, 5½x6½", frosted green, elongated 8-sided base w/pinwheel-shaped body, foreign **$120.00**

Cold cream jar, blue opalescent, Coin Dot pattern, Fenton #91 ....**$85.00**

Cologne, opaque blue, bell shape w/basketweave design, Akro Agate...**$50.00**

Cologne, satin blue, Swirled Feather pattern, frosted crystal stopper, Fenton..**$70.00**

Cologne, 3½", crystal w/horizontal concentric ribs, jadite beehive stopper, New Martinsville........................**$22.00**

Cologne, 6½", sapphire blue, American Hobnail pattern, Duncan & Miller..**$30.00**

Cotton ball dispenser, frosted blue, bunny rabbit figural w/ears back..**$90.00**

Doorknob, topaz w/cut center, hexagonal **$95.00**

Guest set, pitcher: 6", tumbler: 3⅜", crystal w/etched flowers, handled, Heisey #517 ....**$140.00**

Guest set, water bottle: 5¾", tumbler: 3", topaz, stretch glass, Fenton #401..**$55.00**

Lamp, nodder, Oriental Lady, fired-on pink or blue, weighted figural head rocks............................**$130.00**

Lamp, Southern Belle, fired-on pink or blue, figural w/clip-on shade...**$55.00**

Lamp, Sunbonnet Girl, frosted crystal, figural.............**$25.00**

Lamp, 8", pseudo Rombic, pink transparent **$60.00**

Lamp, 8½", Hexagonal, green transparent **$30.00**

Lamp, 9¼", pink, English Hobnail pattern, Westmoreland #555 ....**$85.00**

Mirror, 4¼" dia, crystal, Candlewick pattern w/beaded edge, Imperial **$80.00**

Night light, frosted amber, football shape.................**$110.00**

Perfume, emerald green satin w/gold encrusted foot & stopper, Cambridge..**$50.00**

Perfume, 4½", crystal w/orange enamel & gold trim, Fostoria #2323...**$35.00**

Perfume, 5", green, hexagon stem base w/beehive stopper, Lancaster Glass Co...**$50.00**

Perfume lamp, 7", multicolored glass insert w/nude figures in graceful motion...**$225.00**

Powder jar, frosted green, court jester head finial on lid, round base w/12 square tab-like feet...................$60.00

Powder jar, frosted green, horizontal ridges around base, embossed leaves on dome lid, 3-footed...............$30.00

Powder jar, frosted pink, embossed fish on base, mermaid & cockleshell finial on lid.......................................$45.00

Powder jar, frosted pink, triangular w/3-tiered triangular-shaped finial, 3-footed, Ramses-Paris-NY.............$50.00

Powder jar, Royal Coach, black glass figural w/crown finial on lid...$175.00

Powder jar, transparent pink, embossed waves & sailboat finial on lid...$75.00

Powder jar, 3¾" square, frosted pink w/embossed birds on base, dove finial on round lid, Dermay Inc..........$40.00

Powder jar, 4¼" dia, black glass, applied crystal seated nude (Simone) finial on lid.......................................$165.00

Powder jar, 5½", frosted green, flapper girl (Wendy) finial on lid, oval 3-footed base.......................................$90.00

Powder jar, 5½" dia, frosted crystal, lady (Lillian I) torso finial on paneled lid, smooth base, Hazel Atlas....$65.00

Powder jar, 6" dia, frosted green ribbed design, elephant finial on lid...$55.00

Powder jar, 6¾" dia, transparent pink rippled design, lg owl finial on lid...$130.00

Puff box, crystal, Colonial pattern, disk shape finial on lid, LE Smith...$10.00

Puff box, 6½x3½" dia, opaque blue, embossed Scotties on base, seated Scottie finial on lid, Akro Agate........$75.00

Soap dish, frosted amber w/black glass base $25.00

Soap holder, 4x6", frosted green, seated nude figural.$45.00

Torchiere, flashed orange w/black screw base............$45.00

Torchiere, 12½", frosted blue w/cone-shaped top.......$30.00

Towel bar, Jadite w/metal clips $25.00

Towel bar holder, green clambroth.............................$45.00

Tray, 11½" long, milk glass w/Jenny Lind figure in beaded oval, Fostoria #824 ....$40.00

Tray, 13" long, emerald w/Winged Scroll pattern & gold highlights, Heisey...$175.00

Tumbler, milk glass w/Jenny Lind figure in beaded oval, Fostoria #835 ....$20.00

Vanity box, cranberry w/enameled dots, hinged lid, 3-footed metal base, Wave Crest...........................$140.00

Vanity set, 7½", vaseline w/gold encrusted decor, hexagonal pointed stopper, Fostoria #2276............................$75.00

Beer Cans

In the mid-1930s, beer came in flat-top cans that often carried instructions on how to use the triangular punch-type opener. The 'cone-top' can was patented about 1935, and in the 1960s both types were replaced by the aluminum beer can with the pull-tab opener. There are hundreds of brands and variations available to the collector today. Most are worth very little, but we've tried to list a few of the better ones to help you get a feel for the market.

Condition is very, very important! Collectors grade them as follows: 1) rust-free, in 'new' condition; 2) still no rust, but a few scratches or tiny dents are acceptable; 3) a little faded, minor scratching, maybe a little rusting; 4) all of the above only more pronounced. Our prices are for cans in Grade 1 condition. Billy Beer? Unopened it's still worth only little more than $1.00 a can.

A-1, 16-oz $1.95
ABC Beer, 16-oz, Garden State brewery.......................$3.00
Ballantine Ale, 16-oz..$1.50
Beer Drinker's Beer, 12-oz $2.25
Big Iron, 16-oz, Pittsburgh brewery...........................$3.00
Black Horse Ale, 12-oz, Dunkirk............................$175.00
Blackhawk Topping, cone top, 12-oz, M $95.00
Brown Derby, 16-oz..$16.50
Budweiser Malt Liquor, 12-oz $3.50
Burger By Burger, 12-oz...$2.00
Burkhardt's Beer, cone top, EX...............................$100.00
Clyde Cream Ale, cone top, original cap, 1920s, EX.$150.00
Coor's, 8-oz...$1.00
Coor's Cutter, 12-oz $1.00
Gambrinus Gold, 12-oz...$1.25
Huber Buck, 12-oz, 1971..$3.00
Iron City, 12-oz..$1.35
King Snedley, 12-oz..$3.50
Knickerbocker, 12-oz, 1970s $2.00
Knickerbocker, 16-oz..$1.25
Long Life, 15½-oz...$1.65
Miller Malt Liquor, 16-oz, red $4.00
Molson's Special Dry, 12-oz $1.25
Narragansett, 16-oz $1.25
New Castle Brown Ale, 16-oz $1.95
Old Froth, 12-oz, bear rug...$1.50
Old Frothingslush, 12-oz, gray...................................$1.75
Old Frothingslush, 12-oz, red.....................................$4.00
Old Tap Ale, cone top, original cap, 1920, EX..........$300.00
Owen Brew, 12-oz, yellow...$1.50
Point Bicentennial, 12-oz...$2.50
Polish Count, 12-oz, red $1.00
Rhinelander, 12-oz, 1974...$1.95

Robin Hood Cream Ale, 16-oz, pull tab $3.50
Rolling Rock, 8-oz...$1.00

Sawdust City, 12-oz, 1979............................**$1.25**
Schell's Golden, 16-oz **$2.50**
Schell's Light, 12-oz..................................**$1.50**
Schlitz Malt Liquor, 16-oz, 1973 ....**$1.75**
Stag Premium Dry, cone top, 12-oz, M **$22.50**
Topper, 12-oz **$2.00**
Valley Forge, 16-oz **$1.00**
West Virginia Bicentennial, 12-oz **$1.95**
World's Fair, 12-oz, purple & white................**$1.85**
900 Malt Liquor, 16-oz ....**$.95**

Big Little Books

The Whitman Publishing Company started it all in 1933 when they published a book whose format was entirely different than any other's. It was very small, easily held in a child's hand, but over an inch in thickness. There was a cartoon-like drawing on the right hand page, and the text was printed on the left. The idea was so well accepted that very soon other publishers – Saalfield, Van Wiseman, Lynn, World Syndicate, and Goldsmith – cashed in on the idea as well. The first Big Little Book hero was Dick Tracy, but soon every radio cowboy, cartoon character, lawman, and space explorer was immortalized in his own adventure series.

When it became apparent that the pre-teen of the fifties preferred the comic book format, Big Little Books were finally phased out; but many were saved in boxes and stored in attics, so there's still a wonderful supply of them around. You need to watch condition carefully when you're buying or selling.

Andy Panda, Whitman, 1942, G....................**$22.00**
Blaze Brandon w/the Foreign Legion, Whitman, 1938, G .**$12.00**
Blondie, Baby Dumpling & Daisy, Whitman, 1939, VG...**$42.50**
Brick Bradford w/Brocco Modern Buccaneer, Whitman,
  1938, G **$12.50**
Bronc Peeler the Lone Cowboy, 1937, VG..................**$35.00**
Buccaneer (w/Frederick March), Paramount, movie tie-in,
  color cover, G **$40.00**
Buccaneers, Whitman, 1958, NM **$10.00**
Chester Gump at Silver Creek Ranch, 1933, spine wear &
  scuffing on covers..................................**$19.00**
Cinderella & the Magic Wand, Whitman, 1950, VG.....**$25.00**
Dan Dunn Secret Operative 48, On the Trail of Wu Fang,
  1938, G **$17.50**
Desert Eagle Rides Again, Whitman, 1939, VG...........**$27.50**
Flint Roper & 6 Gun Showdown, Whitman, 1941, VG..**$22.50**
Gene Autry, Red Bandits Ghost, Whitman, 1949, EX..**$22.00**
Harold Teen Swing at Sugar Bowl, Whitman, 1939, EX...**$30.00**
Junior Nebb & the Diamond Bar Ranch, Whitman, 1938,
  NM..**$22.00**
Li'l Abner in New York, Whitman, 1936, VG...............**$42.50**
Little Orphan Annie & Chizzler, published by Big Little
  Books, VG **$35.00**
Little Orphan Annie & the Big Train Robbery, Whitman,
  1934, EX..**$42.50**

Little Orphan Annie & the Ghost Gang, 1935, VG **$45.00**
Lone Ranger & the Red Renegades, VG....................**$32.50**
Lone Ranger & the Secret Killer, bright colors on front &
  back covers, VG......................................**$38.00**
Mac of the Marines in Africa, 1936, VG....................**$35.00**
Mandrake the Magician & the Flame Pearls, Whitman, 1946,
  EX...**$30.00**
Men w/Wings, movie version, Whitman, 1938, VG.....**$17.50**

**Mickey Mouse & Pluto, The Racer; Walt Disney Enter-
  prises, 1936, EX**.....................................**$35.00**
Mickey Mouse, Walt Disney Enterprises, ca 1938, EX.$25.00
Peggy Brown, Mystery Basket, Whitman, 1941, EX.....**$28.00**
Pioneers of the Wild West, World Syndicate, 1933, G ..**$30.00**
Red Barry Undercover Man, Whitman, 1939, NM........**$32.00**
Secret Agent X-9, Whitman, 1936, VG.....................**$37.50**
Skyroads by Lt Dick Calkins, Russell Keaton art, 1936..**$35.00**
Skyroads w/Hurricane Hawk, Whitman, 1936, EX **$28.00**
Smitty Golden Gloves Tournament, 1934, printed for Coco-
  malt, G **$20.00**
Snow White & Seven Dwarfs, Whitman, 1938, VG......**$45.00**
Son of Mystery, Muheim illustrations, Saalfield, 1939,
  VG...**$38.00**
SOS Coast Guard, Henry E Valley illustrator, 1936, G.**$35.00**
Sybil Jason in Little Big Shot, Warner Bros, movie tie-in,
  1935, VG..**$35.00**
Tailspin Tommy, Dirigible Flight to North Pole; Whitman,
  1934, EX..**$35.00**
Tailspin Tommy & the Hooded Flyer, G....................**$40.00**
Tailspin Tommy in the Famous Pay-Roll Mystery, original
  copyright 1923, G.....................................**$35.00**
Tarzan of the Screen, Johnny Weissmuller Story; Whitman,
  1934, EX..**$80.00**
Tarzan Twins, Edgar Rice Burroughs, 1935, Racine, 1st edi-
  tion, G..**$57.50**
Texas Bad Man, movie version, Five Star Library, 1934,
  VG...**$42.50**
Tom Mix & His Circus on the Barbary Coast, Whitman,
  1940, EX..**$36.00**
Treasure Island, #1141, Jackie Cooper & Wallace Beery on
  full-color cover, movie tie-in, 1934.....................**$87.50**
Treasure Island, #720, 1933, M............................**$62.50**
Two-Gun Montana, Whitman, 1936, VG...................**$27.50**
Walt Disney's Dumbo the Flying Elephant, soft cover, Dell,
  1941, G..**$25.00**

Wash Tubbs & Captain Easy Hunting the Whales, Whitman, 1938, EX..............$38.00

Wells Fargo (w/Joel McCrea), Paramount, movie tie-in, 1938, VG..............$30.00

Zane Grey's King of the Royal Mounted, G.............$35.00

Zip Saunders King of the Speedway, Whitman, 1939, NM..............$28.00

Black Americana

There are many avenues one might pursue in the broad field of Black Americana and many reasons that might entice one to become a collector. For the more serious, there are documents such as bills of sales for slaves, broadsides, and other historical artifacts. But by and far, most collectors enjoy attractive advertising pieces, kitchenware items, toys and dolls, and Black celebrity memorabilia.

It's estimated that there are at least 50,000 collectors around the country today. There are large auctions devoted entirely to the sale of Black Americana. The items they feature may be as common as a homemade potholder or a magazine or as rare as a Lux Dixie Boy clock or a Mammy cookie jar that might go for several thousand dollars. In fact, many of the cookie jars have become so valuable that they're being reproduced; so are salt and pepper shakers, so beware.

For further study, we recommend *Black Collectibles Sold in America* by P.J. Gibbs.

See also Sheet Music; Postcards.

Advertising sign, 19½x13½", Amos & Andy for Campbell's Soups, ...Sho, Sho Amos, Ain't Dey Somp'n, ca 1930s, NM..............$135.00

Apron, adult size, rubberized canvas, Aunt Jemima Pancake Jamboree lettered in red on yellow, 1950s, EX.....$85.00

Ashtray, 4½", man playing bongo drums, iridescent trim, Japan, EX..............$65.00

Bank, 4½", embossed glass Joe Lewis image, lid w/coin slot advertising Nash's Mustard, 1930-50, EX.............$50.00

Beer bottle, 9½", glass, label w/brown-skinned waiter serving Sparkling Atlantic Ale, EX.............$55.00

Bell, 5¾", metal, covered w/red polka dot cloth dress, white apron, black cloth face, red scarf, 1910s-40s, EX..$65.00

Bells, 3½", ceramic, brown-skinned Mammy & Chef, in white, she w/red bow on head, blue shoes, ca 1920-45, EX, pr..............$75.00

Block set, Acrobatic Balance Toys, w/Black porter, Anchor Toy Company, MIB..............$225.00

Book, 6¼x8¾", hardcover, Gigi & Gogo, about a Black boy & a giraffe, 15 pages, illustrated, 1943, EX.........$70.00

Brooch, 2", sterling silver, full-length caricature of Johnny Griffin eating watermelon, marked Sterling, M.....$90.00

Button, tin, features Aunt Jemima's face, Aunt Jemima's Breakfast Club, Eat a Better Breakfast, M.............$15.00

Can label, 4x5½", Black man w/white hair & beard serving Old Black Joe Butter Beans, 1920-45, EX.............$12.00

Charm, 1¼", rubber, black-skinned Mammy in red bandana, ca 1920s, EX..............$45.00

Cigarette caddy, 2½x3¼", ceramic, boy at side of clothes line featuring Ashes, Cigarettes, Matches, 1920s-40s, G..............$45.00

Circus figure (Negro Dude), 9", molded composition head w/hat, clothed wooden body, Schoenhut, VG...$350.00

Clothes brush, 7", plastic Mammy figural, EX.............$45.00

Condiment set, china, salt, pepper, & mustard, 3-piece chef in blue suit, white hat & collar, brown face, EX.$140.00

Cookbook, de Knight, A Date w/a Dish, American Negro Recipes, 1948, 426 pages..............$15.00

Cookie jar, 11½", painted plastic, Aunt Jemima figural holding serving tray, F&F Mold & Die Works, EX- ...$325.00

Creamer, 2", black-skinned Mammy in white dress w/red details, cream pours from mouth, EX.............$50.00

Creamer & sugar bowl, plastic, Aunt Jemima & Uncle Mose figurals attached to yellow cups, F&F Mold & Die Works, G+..............$70.00

Decanter, 8½", for Green River Whiskey, Black man in bowler hat, 6 shot glasses & swizzle stick, ca 1930s, EX..............$125.00

Doll, 15", molded plastic head & body w/cloth suit, Louis Armstrong w/trumpet, Effanbee, in original box, EX......$60.00

Doll, 18", hard plastic, dark brown skin w/rooted black hair, jointed, Beatrice Wright, ca 1967, EX.............$145.00

Door knocker, metal, black-skinned boy caught w/his pants down, gold trim, ca 1940s, MIB..............$110.00

Egg timer, wood die-cut chef's head glancing at egg timer, white hat & scarf w/black details, red lips, EX.....$80.00

Fan, die-cut cardboard, Black man's smiling face, Coon Chicken Inn, M..............$85.00

Figure, 8½", Mammy w/cotton ball, wood, lithographed face, red dress, w/New Orleans on apron, EX.....$40.00

Figurine, Angel of Africa figure, tan skin & black hair, skirt of leaves, gold halo & trim, Artgift Co, 1958, EX..$55.00

Figurine, 1½x2", bisque, 3 boys sitting side by side, attached, Hear, See, Speak No Evil, EX..............$60.00

Figurine, 2", ceramic, Black boy in red pants sits on white potty, Mat de Mer, Japan, 1920s-40s, EX **$35.00**

Figurine, 5", celluloid, brown-skinned girl in dark rose dress, jointed arms, appears to be dancing, ca 1920s-30s, G.................**$40.00**

Figurine, 6⅛", plastic, little Black boy w/nodding head sitting on round orange base marked Florida, 1940s-50s, G **$45.00**

Figurines, papier-mache, mother clapping, father playing banjo, boy & girl dancing, EX, 4-piece set..........**$155.00**

Figurines, wax folk figures on wooden bases, female cotton picker, male chimney sweep, colorful attire, pr .**$250.00**

Figurines, 2", wood, carved musical caricatures on round wood-grain bases, 1 plays violin, 1 plays horn, EX, each **$85.00**

Figurines, 5¼", ceramic, 2 boys in white angel's robes, gold trim, one w/book, one w/star, Japan, 1940-55, EX ..**$75.00**

Game, From the Cultural Heritage of Ancient Africa, Milton Bradley, complete, MIB **$60.00**

Hand puppet, 10", Sammy Davis Jr, rubber head, VG ..**$25.00**

Head vase, pottery, lady w/tan skin & lg red lips, upswept black hair, eyes closed, Kindell, ca 1940s, M........**$90.00**

Head vase, 6¼", lady's head w/sepia-toned skin, black hair, & pink lips, pearl earrings, ca 1960s, M **$70.00**

Incense burner, 3", bisque, boy on elephant, VG **$50.00**

Kitchen towel, cotton, black-skinned Mammy holding watermelon slice above little boy's head, ca 1930s, M..**$45.00**

Magazine, Life, Lewis Armstrong playing trumpet on cover, April 15, 1966, EX **$35.00**

Magazine, Time, Martin Luther King feature, Man of the Year issue, January 3, 1964, EX....................**$35.00**

Marionette puppet, 12", plastic & cloth, black face, white hands & legs, shirt & striped pants, black shoes, 1945-55, EX **$115.00**

Menu, die-cut paper, Black man's smiling face, Coon-Chicken Inn lettered on teeth, EX **$150.00**

Noisemaker, 4" dia, painted Sambo-type face in yellow w/red, twirl to make noise, 1920-40, EX **$65.00**

Note holder, Mammy, painted plastic, wall mount, marked F&F Plastics, M....................**$95.00**

Note holder, wood, man stands behind half-door scratching head, ...Jus' Leave a Note w/Me, ca 1940s, EX **$75.00**

Note holder, 10½", die-cut wood, Mammy in green scarf holding roll of paper, Japan, EX **$85.00**

Pancake maker, 8½" dia, makes 4 different animals, Aunt Jemima, EX....................**$145.00**

Pendant, 1½", sterling silver, embossed face of Black boy in hat, marked Sterling, early 20th century, M **$80.00**

Pennant, 28" long, felt, 2 children, red ground, Lub Me Just A Lil' Bit, An I Will Lub Yu Mo, 1900, EX...........**$110.00**

Pin, 1½", gold-toned enameled metal, features golliwog, black-skinned fellow in red pants & blue jacket, red lips, EX....................**$50.00**

Pincushion, 3", bisque, kneeling man in red pants holding oversized dice, pincushion on man's back, ca 1920s-40s, EX....................**$35.00**

Playbill, 9x6", Shubert Theater, Pearl Bailey & Cab Calloway illustrating Hello, Dolly!, January 1, 1970, EX **$25.00**

Playbill, 9x6", stylized horn player & dancer w/bubbles illustrating the play Bubbling Brown Sugar, 1925-50, EX.....**$25.00**

Playing cards, features Carribean dancers & band, in holder, EX....................**$40.00**

Postcard, I Am Completely in the Dark, 1¢ stamp .$15.00

Postcard, 5½x3½", backside view of young boy & girl in embrace looking at ocean, Two Loving Hearts, 1930s-50s, EX .**$15.00**

Poster, 20x14", Black Panther Party, native w/gun & sword illustrates Afro-American Solidarity..., 1969, EX ..**$125.00**

Poster, 22x17", political, close-up backview of woman in scarf holding young child w/gun, Emory 67, EX.........**$100.00**

Print, face of Black boy in tattered hat sitting sideways facing front, circle mat, framed, ca 1900, EX **$60.00**

Puppet theater, heavy cardboard, features push-out puppet of Little Black Sambo & book w/dialogue, dated 1942, MIB **$195.00**

Record, 13¼x12½", LP, bust photo of Fats Domino in green plaid jacket, When I'm Walking, ca 1969, EX **$30.00**

Record, 13¼x12½", LP, many faces of Ray Charles, Have a Smile w/Me, ABC Paramount, ca 1960, EX **$35.00**

Restaurant table card, die-cut cardboard, features Aunt Jemima's face, ...Time for Aunt Jemima Pancakes, dated 1953, M....................**$25.00**

Salt & pepper shakers, Brayton Laguna pottery, stylized Latin look in brown, white & yellow, EX, pr **$70.00**

Salt & pepper shakers, ceramic, busts of boy & girl w/brown skin, she in yellow straw hat, he w/blue straps, pr....................**$90.00**

Salt & pepper shakers, ceramic, chef standing on base w/2 trays holding watermelon slices (shakers), 3-piece set, EX....................**$90.00**

Salt & pepper shakers, ceramic, girl shaker sitting on chair holding watermelon slice (shaker), glossy, 2-piece set, EX....................**$60.00**

Salt & pepper shakers, ceramic, Mammys w/black skin, 1 in yellow w/red, 1 in blue w/red, marked S&P, pr ..**$45.00**

Salt & pepper shakers, Mammy & chef in gray, gold trim, black faces, marked S&P, EX, pr....................**$70.00**

Salt & pepper shakers, 3½", ceramic, clowns w/green pants & hats, EX, pr....................**$45.00**

Salt & pepper shakers, 4", red clay, Mammy & Chef w/brown skin & rose lips, white bandana & chef's hat, EX, pr...**$95.00**

Salt & pepper shakers, 4¼", boy & girl, matt black skin, red & yellow attire, winking action eyes, earrings, EX, pr **$60.00**

Salt & pepper shakers, 5", Aunt Jemima & Uncle Mose, premiums, F&F Mold & Die Co, pr **$65.00**

Salt & pepper shakers, 5", Mammy & Chef, red & green on cream attire, EX, pr......................................$55.00

Salt & pepper shakers, 5¼", Mammys serving Luzianne tea, gold-tone blouses & green skirts, F&F, EX, pr....**$185.00**

Salt dip spoon, 2¼" features detailed bust of Black boy in hat on spoon handle, ca 1900, EX+.....................**$110.00**

Sheet music, 12x9", features the Mills Brothers in a vertical row, Don't Be a Baby, Baby, 1946, EX.................**$25.00**

Sheet music, 9¾x7", Summertime, from play Porgy & Bess, Gershwin Publishing Corp, ca 1935-45, EX...........**$35.00**

Shoe polish, for Mason's White Dressing Shoe Polish, Black man & dog graphics on box & bottle, ca 1920s, unused, EX+ **$35.00**

String holder, 6½", ceramic, full-figure Mammy in off-white dress w/green & red details, USA NS CO, G+ **$100.00**

Toaster cover, 8", cloth doll, w/hands on hips, G+.....**$30.00**

Toothpick holder, 2¾", pot metal, boy sitting w/watermelon, & boy standing by cotton bale receptacle, EX.....**$125.00**

Toothpick holder, 5¾x6", boy & girl attached to corn-shaped holder, he holds watermelon, she holds corn, 1930-40, EX **$75.00**

Toy, Dapper Dan, 10¼", tin litho, colorful jointed figure on trunk marked Coon Jigger, Marx, working, G+ ..**$325.00**

Toy, Jazzbo Jim, 10¼", tin litho, colorful jointed banjo-playing figure on top of cabin, Unique Art, VG **$400.00**

Toy, Trumpet Player, 10½", tin litho feet & hands, painted rubber head & hands, wind-up, Japan, original box, VG+..**$275.00**

Wall pocket, ceramic, boy's head in green hat w/white polka dots, Japan, EX **$155.00**

Watch, features the Little Rascals, 1986, MIB **$85.00**

Black Cats

Kitchenware, bookends, vases, and many other items designed as black cats were made in Japan during the 1950s and exported to the United States where they were sold by various distributors who often specified certain characteristics they wanted in their own line of cats. Common to all these lines were the red clay used in their production and the medium used in their decoration – their features were applied over the glaze with 'cold (unfired) paint.' The most collectible is a line marked (or labeled) Shafford. Shafford cats are plump and pleasant looking. They have green eyes with black pupils; white eyeliner, eyelashes, and whiskers; and red bow ties. The same design with yellow eyes was marketed by Royal, and another fairly easy-to-find 'breed' is a line by Wales with yellow eyes and gold whiskers. You'll find various other labels as well. Some collectors buy only Shafford, while others like them all.

When you evaluate your black cats, be critical of their paint. Even though no chips or cracks are present, if half of the paint is missing, you have a half-price item. Remember this when using the following values which are given for cats with near-mint to mint paint.

Ashtray, 3-dimensional head, open mouth w/cigarette rest, Shafford **$15.00**

Creamer, 5½", yellow eyes, gold whiskers & eyebrows, red bow tie, lifted paw is the spout, Wales **$22.50**

Cruets, 8", sitting upright, 1 has O eyes for oil, other has V eyes for vinegar & red hairbow, Shafford, pr **$50.00**

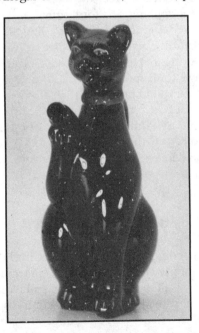

Decanter, 8", sitting upright, right paw lifted holding small bottle which is the spout, w/label, Shafford.......$50.00

Decanter, 8", upright w/lift-off head, white-lined green eyes, red bow & allover red polka dots, +6 shot glasses, set ...**$25.00**

Salad set, 2 cruets, salt & pepper shakers in wireware rack w/handle..**$45.00**

Salt & pepper shakers, sitting upright w/legs together, tail handle, yellow eyes, red bow tie, pr.....................**$10.00**

Salt & pepper shakers, 5", facing each other w/heads turned forward, white slit eyes, white dot nose, white S&P, pr...**$12.00**

Salt & pepper shakers, 5½", slim & upright w/wide gold bow tie, red polka dots on neck, tail handle, gold S&P, pr...**$8.00**

Salt & pepper shakers, 6" long, very slim w/rhinestone eyes, pr...**$8.00**

Spoon, for rack, cat's face attached to wooden handle, pierced for draining, Shafford, scarce....................**$50.00**

Sugar bowl, 4¾", crouching full-body figural, no lid, green eyes (Shafford), marked RD, 1951 ....**$22.50**

Teapot, 5", upright, panther-like sleek face w/gold slanty eyes, paws form spout..**$20.00**

Teapot, 5¾", fat round body, 1951, Shafford **$40.00**

Teapot, 6½", fat body, w/label, Shafford.....................**$45.00**

Teapot, 8¼", upright full body, left paw forms spout, yellow eyes, red bow tie, made for Wales **$45.00**

Toothpick holder, small cat on book by vase, marked Occupied Japan **$12.00**

Blair Dinnerware

The Blair company operated in Ozark, Missouri, only briefly, opening in 1946 and closing sometime during the fifties. Blair himself was a modernistic painter-turned-potter, and his dinnerware designs reflect his approach to art. He favored square shapes over round, straight-sided hollowware pieces, and simple color combinations and patterns. His work was sold through some of the country's leading department stores, Neiman-Marcus and Marshall Field's among them.

His most popular pattern and the one most easily found today was Gay Plaid. The concept was very simple: intersecting vertical and horizontal brush strokes in brown, dark green, and chartreuse on white. He used twisted rope-like handles and applied leaves as knobs on lids. Yellow Plaid was simlilar; the same colors were used with yellow added. Rick-Rack featured hand-painted zigzags and diagonals. Bamboo was a bit more artistic with a stalk of bamboo and a few large leaves, and Autumn featured leaves as well. A departure from his earlier lines and the hardest to find today, Bird (except for still using the colors he obviously preferred – browns, white, and green) is different in that he used red clay for the body of the ware and the primitive bird designs were carved in the clay (a process called sgraffito) rather than hand painted. You'll have no problem identifying this dinnerware, since it is clearly marked 'Blair, Decorated by Hand.'

For further study, we recommend *The Collector's Encyclopedia of American Dinnerware* by Jo Cunningham.

Autumn Leaf, cup..**$10.00**
Autumn Leaf, nut dish..**$8.00**
Bamboo, creamer...**$15.00**
Bird, celery dish...**$20.00**
Bird, cruet, no stopper **$25.00**
Bird, salt & pepper shakers, pr...................................**$15.00**
Gay Plaid, bowl, onion soup; w/lid **$18.00**

Gay Plaid, creamer, watering can form................**$12.00**
Gay Plaid, cup & saucer...**$12.00**
Gay Plaid, milk (or utility) pitcher (illustrated) ...**$14.00**
Gay Plaid, plate, dinner...**$12.00**
Gay Plaid, salt & pepper shakers, pr.........................**$12.00**
Gay Plaid, tumbler (illustrated) **$12.00**
Rick-Rack, bowl, onion soup; w/lid **$20.00**
Rick-Rack, cup & saucer...**$20.00**

Blue and White Stoneware

Though it hasn't been made since the 1930s, blue and white stoneware is a popular collectible today and carries price tags hefty enough that reproductions are everywhere, so we wanted to forewarn you. Beware of too bright colors, sloppy workmanship, and anything that looks unused. This was strictly utilitarian pottery, and it would be a rare piece indeed that showed no signs of wear. It was made as early as the turn of the century by many of the well-known potters of the era, among them Roseville, Brush McCoy, and Uhl.

For further study, we recommend *Blue and White Stoneware* by Kathryn McNerney.

Bedpan, 12x12", Diffused Blue................................$120.00
Bowl, berry; 2½x4½", Diffused Blue $75.00
Bowl, dough; lg, dark blue scalloped rim..................$85.00
Bowl, 10¾", Daisy & Waffle..................................$95.00
Bowl, 11", plain..$65.00
Bowl, 3x4½", advertising sample, minimum price.......$85.00
Butter crock, Apricot, original lid & bail $200.00
Butter crock, Cow, stenciled, original lid & bail........$150.00
Butter crock, 3x6½", Grapes & Leaves, double ring around
    trim $175.00
Canister, Basketweave, Raisins, original lid $225.00
Canister, Snowflake, Rice, original lid......................$150.00
Cookie jar, 9x8", Turkey Eye color drip, Diffused Blue
    bands $250.00
Cup, 3½x3", Paneled Fir Tree, spurs on applied handle,
    minimum value $75.00
Cup, 3¾x3½", Bow Tie, bird transfer $95.00
Cup & saucer, Flowerpot, deep, ca 1820 ....$125.00
Custard cup, 5x2½", Fishscale...................................$75.00
Egg storage rack, 5½x6", Barrel Staves, bail handle..$185.00
Match holder, 5x5½", duck form...............................$95.00
Measuring cup, 6x6¾", Spearpoint & Flower Panels.$120.00
Measuring pitcher, 8½x7", ½-gal, Acid Proof Measure, wide
    lip $95.00
Milk bowl, 4x8", Daisy & Lattice, NM......................$125.00
Mug, plain $65.00

Pitcher, 8", Apricots, EX $165.00
Pitcher, 9", Cattails $185.00
Pitcher, 9", Iris $175.00
Pitcher, 9½", Pine Cone..$200.00
Planter jug, 4½x3", Diffused Blue $75.00
Potty, Beaded Rose..$110.00
Roaster, 8½x12", Wildflower, domed lid....................$195.00
Roaster, 9x16", Grooved Band.................................$175.00
Rolling pin, Wildflower & Blue Band........................$250.00
Salt crock, Blackberry, original lid...........................$145.00
Salt crock, Oak Leaf, original lid..............................$125.00
Salt crock, 6½x6", Daisy & Snowflakes, original lid ..$220.00
Salt crock, 6x5", Blue Band, printed letters................$135.00
Slop jar, Bow Tie $125.00
Soap dish, cat's head $165.00
Soap dish, Fishscale w/Flower Cluster $150.00
Spittoon, Peacock & Fountain.................................$275.00
Toothbrush holder, Bow Tie, stenciled flower $50.00
Toothpick holder, 3¼x4", swan form $65.00
Tumbler, 6x3", Diffused Blue...................................$75.00
Vinegar/cider crock, 19x16", Brushed Leaves, stippled
    ground $175.00
Wash set, Rose on Trellis, 2-piece $300.00
Water cooler, Blue Band, original lid.........................$175.00
Water cooler, 17x15", Polar Bear, brass nickel-plated spigot,
    EX $700.00

**Mug, 5½", Windy City (Fannie Flagg), Robinson Clay
    Products, M** $175.00
Pickle crock, 8x8", Heart Band, w/advertising message,
    rolled rim...$225.00
Pie plate, 10½", Blue Walled Brick-Edge star embossed base,
    EX $100.00
Pitcher, Dutch Landscape, stenciled, tall..................$175.00
Pitcher, Wildflower, stenciled $200.00
Pitcher, 10", Cherry Cluster & Basketweave..............$175.00
Pitcher, 4¾x4¾", Lincoln, allover deep blue..............$175.00

Blue Ridge Dinnerware

Blue Ridge has long been popular with collectors, and prices are already well established; but that's not to say there aren't a few good buys left around. It was made by a company called Southern Potteries, who operated in Erwin, Tennessee, from sometime in the latter thirties until the mid-fifties. They made literally hundreds of patterns, all hand decorated. Some collectors prefer to match up patterns, while some like to mix them together for a more eclectic table setting.

One of the patterns most popular with collectors (and the most costly) is called French Peasant. It's very much like Quimper with simple depictions of the little peasant fellow with his staff. They made many lovely floral patterns, and it's around these where most of the buying and selling activity is centered. You'll also find roosters, plaids, and simple textured designs, and in addition to the dinnerware, some vases and novelty items as well.

Nearly every piece is marked 'Blue Ridge,' though occasionally you'll find one that isn't. Watch for a similar type of ware often confused with Blue Ridge that is sometimes (though not always) marked Italy.

The values suggested below are for the better patterns. To evaluate the French Peasant line, double these figures; for the simple plaids and textures, deduct 25% to 50%, depending on their appeal. If you'd like to learn more, we recommend *Southern Potteries Inc., Blue Ridge Dinnerware,* by Betty and Bill Newbound.

Ashtray, china, individual, artist signed	**$12.00**
Ashtray, w/rest	**$18.50**
Bonbon, china, flat shell, artist signed	**$60.00**
Bowl, fruit; 5¼"	**$4.00**
Bowl, mixing; 8½"	**$30.00**
Bowl, salad; 11½"	**$45.00**
Bowl, soup; 8", flat	**$12.50**
Bowl, vegetable; w/lid	**$60.00**
Bowl, vegetable; 9", oval	**$18.50**
Box, Seaside	**$90.00**
Butter dish	**$40.00**
Butter pat/coaster	**$18.50**
Cake lifter	**$20.00**

Candy dish, 6", French Peasant	**$180.00**
Celery, china, leaf shape, artist signed	**$30.00**
Celery, Skyline	**$24.00**
Cigarette box	**$65.00**
Creamer, demitasse; china, artist signed	**$55.00**
Custard	**$12.00**
Gravy boat	**$18.50**
Mug, child's	**$24.00**
Pitcher, Abby, china, artist signed	**$80.00**
Pitcher, Grace	**$40.00**

Pitcher, Milady, china, artist signed	**$110.00**
Pitcher, Virginia, china, artist signed	**$70.00**

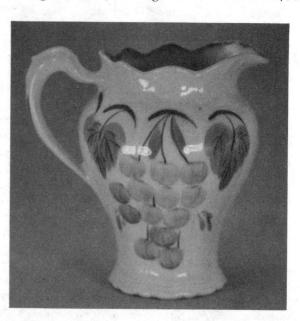

Pitcher, 6", Wisteria (exceptional pattern)	**$145.00**
Plate, cake; 10½"	**$28.00**
Plate, child's	**$28.00**
Plate, Christmas or Turkey	**$65.00**
Plate, dinner; 9½"	**$10.00**
Plate, Language of Flowers	**$65.00**
Plate, 6" square, novelty pattern	**$38.00**
Platter, Turkey w/Acorns	**$190.00**
Platter, 12½"	**$14.50**
Powder box, round, w/lid	**$120.00**
Ramekin, 7½", w/lid	**$28.00**
Relish, china, heart shape, artist signed	**$42.00**
Relish, Mod Leaf, china, artist signed	**$60.00**
Salad fork	**$30.00**
Salad spoon	**$30.00**
Salt & pepper shakers, Bud Top, pr	**$32.50**
Salt & pepper shakers, Mallards, pr	**$145.00**
Sherbet	**$12.50**
Sugar bowl, demitasse; china, artist signed	**$35.00**
Syrup jug, w/lid	**$80.00**
Tea tile, 6", round or square	**$22.50**
Teapot, ball shape	**$48.00**
Teapot, Colonial shape	**$80.00**
Teapot, Woodcrest	**$100.00**
Tidbit, 3-tier	**$25.00**
Tumbler, glass	**$12.00**
Vase, china, tapered, artist signed	**$85.00**
Vase, 5½", china, artist signed, round	**$70.00**
Wall sconce	**$65.00**

Blue Willow Dinnerware

Blue Willow dinnerware has been made since the 1700s, first by English potters, then Japanese, and finally American companies as well. Tinware, glassware, even paper 'go-withs' have been produced over the years – some fairly recently, due to ever-popular demand. It was originally copied from the early blue and white wares made in Nanking and Canton in China. Once in awhile you'll see some pieces in black, pink, red, or even multicolor.

Obviously the most expensive will be the early English wares, easily identified by their backstamps. You'll be most likely to find pieces made by Royal or Homer Laughlin, and even though comparatively recent, they're still collectible, and their prices are very affordable.

For further study, we recommend *Blue Willow Identification and Value Guide* by Mary Frank Gaston.

Bowl, cream soup; 5¾", w/7" underplate, no mark **$25.00**
Bowl, fruit; 5½", Royal **$4.00**
Bowl, salad; 3⅝x9¾", Japan, w/china-handle serving fork & spoon **$65.00**
Bowl, salad; 3x10", unmarked.......................................**$42.50**

Bowl, vegetable; 10", Allerton, w/lid $235.00
Bowl, 10¼", Royal...**$16.00**
Bowl, 5", thick, unmarked..**$3.50**
Bowl, 8½", Royal...**$14.00**
Creamer, Royal, tapered base...**$5.00**
Creamer & sugar bowl, Japan, w/lid **$40.00**
Cruet, vinegar; 5½", Japan, w/stopper.........................**$24.00**
Cup & saucer, demitasse; Japan.....................................**$10.00**
Cup & saucer, Japan...**$15.00**
Cup & saucer, Royal, angular handle **$7.50**
Cup & saucer, stacking, USA..**$3.25**
Gravy boat, Royal, double spout **$8.00**
Mug, 3¼", unmarked Japan...**$12.00**
Plate, grill; 11¼", Japan..**$12.00**
Plate, 10", rolled edge, unmarked...................................**$4.75**
Plate, 10", Royal..**$10.00**
Plate, 10½", Royal, handles **$10.00**
Plate, 6", Allerton **$16.00**
Plate, 6", Japan **$3.00**
Plate, 6", Royal..**$3.50**
Plate, 7", Homer Laughlin...**$4.00**
Plate, 7¼", Occupied Japan..**$6.00**
Plate, 8", Homer Laughlin..**$5.75**
Plate, 9", Occupied Japan...**$8.00**
Plate, 9", Royal **$7.50**

Plate, 9¼", unmarked...**$5.00**
Platter, 12½", England..**$30.00**
Platter, 13", USA **$19.00**
Platter, 15", Maastricht, oval **$120.00**
Sugar bowl, England, w/lid..**$22.00**

Bookends

You'll find bookends in various types of material and designs. The more inventive their modeling, the higher the price. Also consider the material. Normally bronze and brass examples are higher than cast iron, though elements of design may override the factor of materials. If they are signed by the designer or marked by the manufacturer, you can about triple the price. Those with a decidedly Art Deco appearance are often good sellers, so are cast iron figurals in good paint.

Boy in armchair, Nu Art **$75.00**
Buddha, 7¾", cast metal w/bronze finish....................**$65.00**
Deer (standing), 6", Deco style, bronze, Frankart **$140.00**
Dutch boy & girl, 5", brass, marked Frankart **$125.00**
Eagle (sitting on sphere), bronze, marble base **$120.00**
Flower basket, painted cast iron....................................**$40.00**
German shepherd, brass...**$58.00**
Horse & foal, metal on wooden base.............................**$65.00**
Indian head, painted cast iron, MN **$125.00**
Leda & the Swan, 4½x8x2¼", cast iron, gold paint **$85.00**
Log cabin amid pines, 6½", painted cast iron, 1920s...**$45.00**
Masonic symbols, cast metal **$60.00**
Mayflower, #381...**$65.00**
Owl, 5¼", cast iron...**$40.00**
Pirate w/parrot, copper clad, marked Verona **$45.00**
Sailor boy, Frankart, EX paint **$95.00**
Spaniel, 4", white metal w/ebony & bronze finish.....**$75.00**
Spanish man serenading lady at window, 5½", cast iron, 1920s...**$55.00**
Sunbonnet Girl, painted cast iron.............................**$125.00**

Books

Books have always occupied the mind's imagination. Before television lured us out of the library into the TV room, everyone enjoyed reading the latest novels. Western, horror, and science fiction themes are still popular to this day — especially those by such authors as Louis L'Amour, Stephen King, and Ray Bradbury, to name but a few. Edgar Rice Burrough's Tarzan series and Frank L. Baum's Wizard of Oz books are regarded as classics among today's collectors. A first edition of a popular author's first book (especially if it's signed) is especially sought after, so is a book that 'ties in' with a movie or television program.

On the whole, ex-library copies and book club issues (unless they are limited editions) have very low resale values.

For further information, we recommend *Huxford's Old Book Value Guide* by Sharon and Bob Huxford. This book is designed to help the owners of old books evaluate their holdings, and it also lists the names of prospective buyers.

See also Children's Books; Paperback Books; Cookbooks.

Adams, Richard; Nature Day & Night, 1978, Viking, 1st US edition, w/dust jacket, M............................$12.50

Aiken, Conrad; Kid, 1947, Duell Sloan Pearce, 1st edition, w/dust jacket, VG $20.00

Allen, Woody; Four Films of Woody Allen, 1982, Random House, illustrated, EX $50.00

Asimov, Isaac; ABCs of Space, 1969, NY, Walker, illustrations & photos, w/dust jacket, G $5.00

Austin, Richard L; Yearbook of Landscape Architecture, 1984, NY, VG $35.00

Baker, Houston A Jr; Journey Back, 1980, Chicago, 1st edition, inscribed, w/dust jacket, M $50.00

Baldwin, James; Little Man, Little Man; 1976, Dial, 1st edition, 95 pages, w/dust jacket, M $40.00

Banks, Russell; Continental Drift, 1985, NY, Harper, 1st edition, w/dust jacket, NM $10.00

Barth, John; End of the Road, 1969, NY, 1st revised edition, in wrapper, NM..............................$30.00

Blake, Pamela; Peep Show, 1973, Macmillan, 1st edition, w/dust jacket, VG $15.00

Block, Lawrence; Burglar's Can't Be Choosers, 1977, Random House, 1st edition, w/dust jacket, NM.........$25.00

Booth, Philip; Letter From a Distant Land, 1957, Viking, 1st edition, author's 1st book, w/dust jacket, VG.......$25.00

Bourne, Peter; Twilight of the Dragon, 1954, Putnam, 1st edition, w/dust jacket, NM $7.50

Bradbury, Ray; Martian Chronicles, 1974, Cordova Press, Mugnaiani illustrator, signed, w/slipcase, M.......$185.00

Bradbury, Ray; Something Wicked This Way Comes, 1963, Rupert Hart Davis, 1st English edition, w/dust jacket, M...............................$125.00

Brautigan, Richard; Sombrero Fallout, 1976, Simon & Schuster, 1st edition, w/dust jacket, VG $25.00

Broner, EM; Her Mothers, 1974, Hold Rinehart Winston, 1st edition, w/dust jacket, NM $45.00

Buchwald, Art; Gift From the Boys, 1958, Harper, 1st edition, w/dust jacket, VG $8.50

Buck, Frank; All in a Lifetime, 1941, NM, 1st edition, signed, w/dust jacket, VG $45.00

Buck, Pearl S; Kennedy Women, 1970, NY, pictured dust jacket, M $20.00

Burroughs, William S; Ticket That Exploded, 1967, NY, Grove, 1st US edition, w/dust jacket, M.............$40.00

Caldwell, Taylor; Grandmother & the Priests, 1963, Doubleday, 469 pages, EX..............................$8.50

Carmichael, Hoagy; Sometimes I Wonder, 1965, NY, 1st edition w/dust jacket, VG..............................$17.50

Carter, Rosalynn; First Lady From Plains, 1984, NY, limited edition signed, w/dust jacket, VG.................$35.00

Cather, Willa; Death Comes for the Archbishop, 1947, Knopf, 299 pages, EX $8.50

Chandler, David; Captain Hollister, 1973, Macmillan, 1st edition, w/dust jacket, M..............................$45.00

Christie, Agatha; At Bertram's Hotel, 1965, NY, Dodd Mead, 1st edition, w/dust jacket, M $35.00

Clancy, Tom; Patriot Games, 1987, NY, Putnam, w/picture wrapper, M..............................$75.00

Clarke, Arthur C; Promise of Space, 1968, Harper Row, photos, 325 pages, w/dust jacket, G $5.00

Clower, Jerry; Ain't God Good, 1975, Waco TX, Word Book Publishing, hard cover, 179 pages, M.........$4.00

Conklin, Groff; Giants Unleashed, 1965, Grosset, 1st edition, w/dust jacket, M..............................$27.00

Conroy, Pat; Prince of Tides, 1986, Houghton Mifflin, 1st edition, w/dust jacket, M $40.00

Cook, Thomas H; Orchids, 1982, Houghton Mifflin, 1st edition, w/dust jacket, M $30.00

Costain, Thomas B; Son of a Hundred Kings, 1951, Chicago, Peoples, w/dust jacket, M.................$5.00

Cousteau, Jacques-Yves; Whales, 1972, NY, 1st US edition, illustrated, 304 pages, w/dust jacket, M.........$15.00

Cristie, Agatha; Endless Night, 1967, Dodd Mead, 1st edition, w/dust jacket, M $40.00

Darwin, Charles; On the Origin of Species: Facsimile of First Edition, 1963, Heritage, 470 pages, w/slipcase, M...$38.00

Davis, Lindsey; Silver Pigs, 1989, NY, Crown, 1st US edition, w/dust jacket, M..............................$25.00

Derleth, August; Over the Edge, 1964, Arkham House, 1st edition, 297 pages, w/dust jacket, M $65.00

Dickens, Emily; Poems, 1952, Heritage, illustrated, w/slipcase, VG..............................$22.00

Dixon, Franklin W; Masked Monkey, 1972, Grosset Dunlap, 1st printing, picture binding, VG.................$5.00

Donleavy, JP; Onion Eaters, 1971, Delacorte, 1st printing, 306 pages, w/dust jacket, M $20.00

Douglas, Lloyd C; Robe, 1944, Chicago, Peoples, w/torn dust jacket, M $5.00

Du Bois, William Pene; Lion, 1956, Viking, 1st edition, w/dust jacket, M $75.00

Du Maurier, Daphne; Parasites, 1950, Doubleday, 1st US edition, w/dust jacket, VG..............................$10.00

Eastman, Max; Great Companions, 1959, Farrar, Straus & Cudahy, illustrated, 312 pages, w/dust jacket.......$23.00

Edwards, Frank; Strange People, 1961, Stuart, 1st edition, w/dust jacket, NM $12.00

Eisenhower, Dwight D; Crusade in Europe, 1948, Doubleday, 1st edition, 559 pages, w/dust jacket, M.......$20.00

Eliot, TS; Cocktail Party, 1950, London, 1st edition, error on page 29, w/dust jacket..............................$90.00

Elliot, Lawrence; George Washington Carver, 1966, Prentice Hall, 1st edition w/dust jacket, VG $8.50

Ellroy, James; LA Confidential, 1990, Mysterious, 1st edition, w/dust jacket, M..............................$18.00

Engle, Paul; Midland, 1961, Random House, 1st edition, w/dust jacket, VG $20.00

Estleman, Loren D; Kill Zone, 1984, Mysterious, 1st edition, signed, w/dust jacket, M..............................$30.00

Falkner, David; Short Season, 1986, Times, 1st edition, w/dust jacket, M $12.50

Farber, James; Texans w/Guns, 1940, Naylor, index, drawings, 196 pages, VG $16.50

Farrell, James T; Yet Other Water, 1952, Vanguard, 1st edition, w/dust jacket, M................................$25.00

Faulkner, William; Reivers, 1962, Random House, 1st edition, clipped dust jacket, M................................$75.00

Faulkner, William; Wishing Tree, 1967, Random House, 2nd printing, w/dust jacket, M $20.00

Ferber, Edna; Giant, 1952, Doubleday, 1st edition, w/dust jacket, VG................................$30.00

Field, Edward; Other Walker, 1971, Georgetown CA, 1st edition, author's 1st book, inscribed, w/dust jacket, M.**$10.00**

Fleming, Ian; Golden Gun, 1965, London, Cape, 1st United Kingdom edition, w/dust jacket, M................$60.00

Fleming, Ian; Spy Who Loved Me, 1962, Jonathan Cape, 1st English edition, w/dust jacket, M................$125.00

Foster, Stephen; Treasury of Stephen Foster, 1946, Random House, William Sharp illustrator, 222 pages, w/dust jacket, NM................................$17.50

Fowles, John; French Lieutenant's Woman, 1969, Little Brown, 1st US edition, w/dust jacket, VG............$20.00

Francis, Dick; Hot Money, 1987, London, Michael Joseph, 1st edition, w/dust jacket, M $40.00

Francis, Dick; In the Frame, 1977, Harper Row, 1st US edition, w/dust jacket, M................................$45.00

Frank, Pat; Hold Back the Night, 1952, Lippincott, w/dust jacket, M $6.00

Frost, Robert; Birches, 1988, Holt, Ed Young illustrator, 1st edition, 32 pages, w/dust jacket, M................$17.50

Frost, Robert; Stories for Leslie, 1984, VA University, Warren Chappell illustrator, 1st edition, w/dust jacket, M...**$30.00**

Gaines, Ernest; Autobiography of Miss Jane Pitmann, 1971, Dial, 1st edition, w/dust jacket, M $75.00

Gann, Ernest K; Aviator, 1981, Arbor House, 1st edition, w/dust jacket, VG................................$12.50

Gardner, Erle Stanley; Human Zero, 1981, Morrow, 1st edition, w/dust jacket, M................................$30.00

Gardner, Erle Stanley; Neighborhood Frontiers, 1954, Morrow, 1st edition, w/dust jacket, NM................$20.00

Gardner, John; License Renewed, 1981, London, Cape/Hodder Stoughton, 1st edition, w/dust jacket, M.........$40.00

Gardner, Piece of the Action, 1958, Simon Schuster, 1st edition, w/dust jacket, M................................$12.50

Garnett, David; Aspects of Love, 1956, Harcourt Brace, 1st US edition, w/dust jacket, M................................$45.00

Gisnberg, Louis; Morning in Spring & Other Poems, 1970, Morrow, review 1st edition, w/dust jacket, VG $20.00

Gordon, Caroline; Glory of Hera, 1972, Doubleday, 1st edition, w/dust jacket, VG................................$20.00

Graham, Billy; How To Be Born Again, 1977, Carmel NY, Guideposts, 184 pages, w/dust jacket, M $5.50

Greene, Graham; End of the Affair, 1951, Viking, 2nd printing, w/dust jacket, M $10.00

Grey, Zane; Blue Feather, '61, Harper, 1st edition, VG.**$60.00**

Grey, Zane; Horse Heaven Hill, 1959, Harper, 1st edition, w/dust jacket, VG................................$85.00

Grubb, Davis; Tree Full of Stars, 1965, Scribner, 1st edition, w/dust jacket, M................................$50.00

Hammond, Arthur; Secret Tunnel Treasure, 1962, Little Brown, Secret Circle Mystery, w/dust jacket, VG....**$7.00**

Hannah, Barry; Captain Maximus, 1985, Knopf, 1st edition, w/dust jacket, VG $15.00

Hansen, Joseph; Gravedigger, 1982, NY, Holt Rinehart, 1st edition, w/dust jacket, M................................$35.00

Harris, Harry; Plague From Space, 1965, Doubleday, 1st edition, w/dust jacket, VG................................$75.00

Harris, Thomas; Black Sunday, 1975, Putnam, 1st edition, w/dust jacket, M................................$75.00

Harrison, Jim; Sundog, 1984, Dutton/Lawrence, 1st edition, w/dust jacket, M................................$12.50

Hawdon, Robin; Rustle in the Grass, 1984, Dodd Mead, 1st US edition, w/dust jacket, VG................................$12.50

Hayden, Robert; Angle of Ascent, 1975, Liveright, 1st edition, w/dust jacket, M................................$50.00

Healy, Jeremiah; So Like Sleep, 1987, Harper Row, 1st edition w/dust jacket, M................................$16.00

Heinlein, Robert A; Cat Who Walks Through Walls, no date, Putnam, 7th printing, w/dust jacket, M $15.00

Heinlein, Robert A; To Sail Beyond the Sunset, 1987, NY, 1st edition, 416 pages, w/dust jacket, M $12.50

Hemingway, Ernest; For Whom the Bell Tolls, 1940, Scribner, 1st edition, G................................$100.00

Hemingway, Ernest; Moveable Feast, 1964, Scribner, 1st edition, w/dust jacket, M................................$50.00

Henderson, David; Felix of Silent Forest, 1967, NY, 1st edition, author's 1st book, signed, w/wrappers, VG .**$25.00**

Henie, Sonja; Wings on My Feet, 1940, Prentice Hall, 1st edition, 177 pages, w/dust jacket, M $75.00

Herriot, James; All Creatures Great & Small, 1972, NY, 1st edition, w/dust jacket, VG................................$20.00

Hersey, John; Marmot Drive, 1953, Knopf, 1st edition, w/dust jacket, VG $15.00

Higgins, Jack; Season in Hell, 1989, Simon Schuster, 1st edition, w/dust jacket, NM $19.00

Hillerman, Tony; Dark Wind, 1982, Harper Row, 1st edition, w/dust jacket, M................................$100.00

Hillyer, Robert; Suburb by the Sea, 1952, Knop, 1st edition, w/dust jacket, VG................................$15.00

Himes, Chester; Heat's On, 1966, Putnam, 1st edition, w/dust jacket, M................................$150.00

Himes, Chester; Rage in Harlem, 1985, London, Allison Busby, 1st hardcover edition, w/dust jacket, M....**$30.00**

Hitchcock, Alfred; Stories That Go Bump in the Night, 1977, Random House, 1st edition, w/dust jacket, VG $17.50

Hoffman, Abbie; Woodstock Nation, 1969, NY, Vintage, 4th printing, w/wraps, VG................................$15.00

Holton, Leonard; Corner of Paradise, 1977, St Martin, 1st edition, w/dust jacket, M................................$15.00

Howard, Robert E; Sowers of the Thunder, 1976, Donald Grant, 2nd edition, w/dust jacket, NM $25.00

Hubbard, L Ron; Enemy Within, 1986, Bridge, 1st edition, w/dust jacket, M................................$25.00

Hughes, Dorothy B; Candy Kid, 1940, Duell Sloan, book club edition, w/worn dust jacket, M................$4.50

Hughes, Monica; Iris Pedlar, 1983, Atheneum, 1st US edition, as issued, M................................$17.00

Hugo, Victor; Hunchback of Notre Dame, no date, Al Burt photoplay edition, VG................................$30.00

Hunter, Evan; Horse's Head, 1967, Delacorte, 1st edition, w/dust jacket, VG **$35.00**

Huxley, Aldous; Genius & the Goddess, 1955, Harper, 1st US edition, w/dust jacket, VG **$15.00**

Huxley & Capa, Farewell to Eden, 1964, Harper, 1st edition, 244 pages, w/dust jacket, G **$20.00**

Infield, Glenn B; Unarmed & Unafraid, 1970, NY, Macmillan, 1st edition, 308 pages, w/dust jacket, NM............**$15.00**

Innes, Michael; Appleby & Honeybath, 1983, Gollancz, 1st edition, w/dust jacket, M....................................**$17.50**

Innes, Michael; Sheiks & Adders, 1982, Dodd Mead, 1st edition, w/dust jacket, M **$15.00**

Isherwood, Christopher; World in the Evening, 1954, Random House, 1st edition, w/dust jacket, VG **$30.00**

Jaffe, Rona; Away From Home, 1960, Simon Schuster, 1st edition, w/dust jacket, VG **$7.50**

James, PD; Skull Beneath the Skin, 1982, Scribner, 2nd edition, w/dust jacket, VG **$12.50**

Jensen, Joan; Price of Vigilance, 1968, Chicago, Rand McNally, 1st edition, 367 pages, w/dust jacket, VG...............**$12.50**

Josephson, Matthew; Union House, Union Bar; 1956, Random House, 1st edition, VG **$12.50**

Kallen, Lucille; Tanglewood Murder, 1980, Wyndham, 1st edition, w/dust jacket, M...............................**$15.00**

Kaminsky, Stuart; Fala Factor, 1984, St Martin, 1st edition, w/dust jacket, VG **$12.50**

Kane, Henry; Laughter in the Alehouse, 1968, Macmillan, 1st edition, w/dust jacket, M...............................**$20.00**

Kanin, Garson; Thousand Summers, 1973, Doubleday, book club edition, w/dust jacket, M..........................**$5.00**

Keating, HRF; Bedside Companion to Crime, 1989, Mysterious Press, 1st US edition, w/dust jacket, M...........**$25.00**

Keeling, Jill A; Old English Sheep Dog, 1961, London, Foyles, 1st edition, 94 pages, VG.........................**$15.00**

Keene, Carolyn; Haunted Lagoon, 1959, Grosset Dunlap, G **$15.00**

Kennedy, John F; Strategy of Peace, 1960, NY, Harper, 1st edition, w/dust jacket, M....................................**$40.00**

Kennedy, Robert F; Just Friends & Brave Enemies, 1962, Harper Row, 1st edition, w/dust jacket, VG.........**$15.00**

Kenrick, Tony; Faraday's Flowers, 1985, Doubleday, 1st edition, w/dust jacket, M **$15.00**

Kherdian, David; Settling America, 1974, Macmillan, 1st edition, 126 pages, w/dust jacket, M **$20.00**

Kidder, Tracy; Road to Yuba City, 1974, Doubleday, 1st edition, 317 pages, w/dust jacket, VG **$20.00**

King, Frank; Operation Honeymoon, 1950, Robert Hale, 1st edition, w/dust jacket, VG.....................................**$17.50**

King, Stephen; Eyes of the Dragon, 1987, Viking, 1st edition, w/dust jacket, M.......................................**$20.00**

King, Stephen; It, 1986, Viking, 1st edition, 1138 pages, w/plastic-covered dust jacket, VG **$22.50**

King, Stephen; Stand, 1978, Doubleday, 1st edition, 823 pages, w/dust jacket, VG.....................................**$35.00**

Kline, Otis Adelbert; Outlaws of Mars, 1961, Avalon, 1st edition, w/dust jacket, VG **$30.00**

Knight, Damon; Beyond Tomorrow, 1965, Harper Row, 1st edition, w/dust jacket, VG....................................**$20.00**

Koontz, Dean R; Midnight, 1989, Putnam, 1st edition, w/dust jacket, VG **$20.00**

Kosinski, Jerzy; Hermit of 69th Street, 1988, Seaver Books, 1st edition, 529 pages, VG....................**$15.00**

Kyle, Duncan; Black Camelot, 1978, Collins, 1st edition, w/dust jacket, M...**$15.00**

L'Amour, Louis; Flint, no date, Bantam, imitation leather cover, NM **$15.00**

L'Amour, Louis; Haunted Mesa, 1987, Bantam, w/dust jacket, VG **$19.00**

Lamb, Harold; Mighty Manslayer, 1969, Doubleday, 1st edition, w/dust jacket, VG.....................................**$22.00**

Langart, Darrel; Anything You Can Do, 1963, Doubleday, 1st edition, w/dust jacket, VG...........................**$18.00**

Langton, Jane; Paper Chains, 1977, Harper Row, 1st edition, w/dust jacket, VG **$20.00**

Lathen, Emma; Ashes to Ashes, 1971, Simon Schuster, book club edition, w/dust jacket, M............................**$5.00**

Lawrence, DH; Lady Chatterly's Lover, 1959, Grove, no printing, w/dust jacket, M **$10.00**

Le Carre, John; Little Drummer Girl, 1983, Knopf, 4th edition, w/dust jacket, VG **$15.00**

Le Carre, John; Smiley's People, 1980, Hodder Stoughton, 1st edition, w/dust jacket, VG...........................**$25.00**

Leary, Timothy; Psychedelic Prayers, 1966, University Books, VG **$35.00**

Lee, Tanith; Silver Metal Lover, 1981, Nelson Doubleday, 1st edition, w/dust jacket, M................................**$12.00**

Lehmann, John; Open Night, 1952, Harcourt Brace, 1st US edition(?), w/VG dust jacket, M............................**$7.50**

Leiber, Fritz; Night's Black Agents, 1975, Neville Spearman, w/dust jacket, M...**$25.00**

Lewin, Michael; Late Payments, 1986, Morrow, 1st edition, w/dust jacket, M...**$20.00**

Lewis, Peter; John Le Carre, 1985, NY, Unger, 1st edition, w/dust jacket, M...**$22.50**

Lindbergh, Ann Morrow; Earth Shine, 1969, Harcourt Brace World, 1st edition, 73 pages, w/dust jacket, VG.....**$8.00**

Llewellyn, Richard; Few Flowers for Shiner, 1950, Macmillan, 1st edition, w/dust jacket, VG...................**$15.00**

Lopez, Barry Holstun; Of Wolves & Men, 1978, Scribner, 2nd printing, signed, w/dust jacket, NM **$40.00**

Lovesy, Peter; Keystone, 1983, Pantheon, 1st edition, w/dust jacket, M **$15.00**

Ludlum, Robert; Icarus Agenda, 1988, NY, Random House, 1st edition, M..**$25.00**

Lupoff, Richard A; Sword of the Demon, 1977, Harper Row, 1st edition, w/dust jacket, M **$17.50**

Lyall, Gavin; Conduct of Major Maxim, 1983, Viking, 1st edition, w/dust jacket, VG....................................**$15.00**

MacDonald, John D; Cinnamon Skin, 1982, Harper Row, 1st edition, w/dust jacket, M...............................**$20.00**

MacDonald, John D; One More Sunday, 1984, Knopf, 1st edition, w/dust jacket, VG....................................**$20.00**

MacKenzie, Donald; Raven Feathers His Nest, 1979, Macmillan, 1st edition, w/dust jacket, M........................**$15.00**

MacLean, Alistair; Athabisca, 1980, Collins, 1st edition, w/dust jacket, M **$25.00**

MacLean, Alistair; Partisans, 1983, Doubleday, 1st edition, w/dust jacket, G $15.00

Mailer, Norman; American Dream, 1965, Dial, 1st edition, w/dust jacket, VG $20.00

Mailer, Norman; Prisoner of Sex, 1971, Little Brown, 1st edition, w/dust jacket, M...$10.00

Mankowitz, Wolf; Laugh Till You Cry, 1955, Dutton, 1st US edition, w/dust jacket, VG $10.00

Marshall, Catharine; Man Called Peter, 1951, McGraw Hill, 354 pages, G...$4.00

Maugham, W Somerset; Trio, 1950, Doubleday, 1st edition, w/dust jacket, VG $20.00

McMurtry, Larry; Anything for Billy, 1988, Simon Schuster, 1st edition, w/dust jacket, M $30.00

McMurtry, Larry; Last Picture Show, 1989, Simon Schuster, 2nd edition, w/dust jacket, M $45.00

McMurtry, Larry; Terms of Endearment, 1989, Simon Schuster, new preface, picture wrapper, VG.................$15.00

Michener, James A; James Michener's USA, 1981, Crown, 1st edition, 342 pages, w/dust jacket, NM $35.00

Miller, Henry; Sexus, 1962, Grove, 1st US edition, w/dust jacket, M $25.00

Milsap, Ronnie; Almost Like a Song, 1990, NY, 1st edition, signed, w/dust jacket, M..$25.00

Moore, Pamela; Chocolates for Breakfast, 1956, Rinehart, NM $5.00

Muller, Marcia; Cavalier in White, 1986, St Martin, 1st edition, w/dust jacket, M...$32.50

Musial & Broeg, Stan Musial: The Man's Own Story, 1964, Doubleday, 1st edition, M $25.00

NASA, Exploring Space w/Camera, 1968, NASA, NM $15.00

Nichols, John; Ghost in the Music, 1979, Harcourt Rinehart Winston, 1st edition, w/dust jacket, M $12.50

Nixon, Richard; Six Crises, 1962, Doubleday, 1st edition, w/dust jacket, M..$20.00

Nugent, Tom; Death at Buffalo Creek, 1973, Norton, 1st edition, 191 pages, w/dust jacket, NM.....................$12.50

Nutting, Wallace; Pennsylvania Beautiful, Garden City Publishing, NY, copyright 1924-1935, EX.......$67.50

O'Hara, John; From the Terrace, 1958, Random House, 1st edition, w/dust jacket, M.......................................$15.00

O'Neill, Eugene; Iceman Cometh, 1981, Limited Edition Club, Baskin illustrations, w/slipcase, M.............$150.00

O'Rourke, Frank; Catcher & the Manager, 1953, Barnes, 1st edition, w/dust jacket, VG.................................$20.00

Oates, Joyce Carol; Miracle Play, 1974, Black Sparrow, 1st edition, w/dust jacket, M.......................................$45.00

Oates, Joyce Carol; Them, 1969, Vanguard, 1st edition, w/dust jacket, NM..$65.00

Page, Martin; Day Kruschchev Fell, 1965, NY, Hawthorn, 224 pages, w/dust jacket, EX................................$15.00

Pasquarelli, John; Temporary Wife, 1954, New Voices, 1st edition, w/dust jacket, M.......................................$20.00

Peters, Ellis; Leper of St Giles, 1982, NY, Morrow, 1st US edition, w/dust jacket, M.......................................$35.00

Poe, Edgar A; Great Tales of Horror & Suspense, 1974, Galahad, w/dust jacket, M...$12.00

Price, Anthony; Prospect of Vengeance, 1988, London, Gollancz, 1st edition, w/dust jacket, M.......................$30.00

Queen, Ellery; King Is Dead, 1952, Little Brown, 1st edition, w/dust jacket, M..$65.00

Quentin, Patrick; Black Widow, 1952, Simon Schuster, book club edition, w/worn dust jacket, M.................$4.50

Rathbone, Basil; In & Out of Character, 1962, NY, w/dust jacket, VG $45.00

Rendell, Rugh; Sleeping Life, 1978, Doubleday, 1st US edition, w/dust jacket, M...$35.00

Reynolds, William J; Moving Targets, 1986, St Martin, 1st edition, w/dust jacket, M.......................................$25.00

Rice, Anne; Feast of All Saints, 1979, Simon Schuster, 1st edition, author's 2nd book, w/dust jacket, M $55.00

Richter, Conrad; Light in the Forest, 1953, Knopf, 1st edition, w/dust jacket, VG...$25.00

Roberts, Janice; Irish Setter, 1978, NY, Arco, 1st edition, 192 pages, w/dust jacket, VG...................................$25.00

Roberts, Kenneth; Boon Island, 1956, Doubleday, clipped dust jacket, G $15.00

Rose, Pete; Pete Rose: My Life in Baseball, 1979, Doubleday, 1st edition, w/dust jacket, M...............................$20.00

Roth, Phillip; Great American Novel, 1973, Harcourt Rinehart Winston, 1st edition, w/dust jacket, M...........$17.50

Ruark, Robert; Poor No More, 1949, NY, Holt, 1st edition, w/dust jacket, M...$40.00

Rushdie, Salman; Satanic Verses, 1988, London, Viking, true 1st edition, w/dust jacket, M.............................$250.00

Ryder, Stephanie; Blind Jack, 1961, Houghton Mifflin, 1st edition, w/dust jacket, M.......................................$12.50

Sanchez, Sonia; I've Been a Woman, 1978, Sausalito, Black Scholar Press, 1st edition, w/dust jacket, M $30.00

Saroyan, William; Laughing Matter, 1953, Doubleday, 1st edition, w/dust jacket, VG......................................$30.00

Sarton, Mary; Land of Silence, 1953, Rinehart, 1st edition, signed, w/dust jacket, NM.....................................$75.00

Schute, Nevil; On the Beach, 1957, Morrow, 1st US edition, w/dust jacket, M...$35.00

Scott, Evelyn; Escapade, 1987, Penguin, Lisa St Aubin de Terand introduction, 1st edition, w/wrapper, M...$10.00

Segal, Erich; Love Story, 1970, Harper Row, book club edition, w/dust jacket, M **$6.00**

Settle, Mary Lee; Blood Tie, 1977, Houghton Mifflin, 1st edition, w/dust jacket, VG **$15.00**

Settle, Mary Lee; Know Nothing, 1961, London, Heinemann, 1st United Kingdom edition, w/dust jacket, M......**$35.00**

Shannon, Dell; Unexpected Death, 1970, Morrow, book club edition, M..**$7.00**

Silverberg, Robert; Threads of Time, 1974, Nelson, 1st edition, w/dust jacket, M **$17.00**

Sinclair, Upton; Dragon's Teeth, 1942, Viking, 1st edition, w/dust jacket, VG **$40.00**

Sinclair, Upton; World To Win, 1946, Viking, M............**$5.00**

Skinner, Ainslie; Harrowing, 1980, Rawson-Wade, 1st US edition, w/dust jacket, M **$12.00**

Smith, H Allen; Waikiki Beachnick, 1960, Little Brown, 1st edition, w/dust jacket, VG **$5.50**

Solomita, Stephen; Force of Nature, 1979, Putnam, 1st edition, w/dust jacket, M **$25.00**

Southern, Terry; Blue Movie, 1970, NY, 1st edition, w/dust jacket, M **$17.50**

Spillane, Mickey; Deep, 1961, Dutton, 1st edition, w/dust jacket, M **$50.00**

Stark, Richard; Deadly Edge, 1971, Random House, 1st edition, w/dust jacket, NM **$45.00**

Stark, Richard; Somebody Owes Me Money, 1969, Random House, 1st edition, w/dust jacket, M **$40.00**

Steel, Danielle; Message From Nam, 1990, Delacort, 1st edition, w/dust jacket, M **$25.00**

Steinbeck, John; Pearl, 1947, Viking, 1st edition, w/dust jacket, VG **$75.00**

Steinbeck, John; Winter of Our Discontent, 1961, Heinemann, 1st English edition, w/dust jacket, VG **$55.00**

Stengel & Paxton, Casey at the Bat, 1962, Random House, book club edition, VG **$10.00**

Stieglitz, Alfred; Georgia O'Keefe: A Portrait, 1978, NY, 1st edition, w/slipcase, M..............................**$60.00**

Stone, Irving; Immortal Wife, 1944, Doubleday Doran, 1st edition, 450 pages, w/worn dust jacket, M..........**$35.00**

Stone, Robert; Children of Light, 1986, Knopf, 1st US edition, author's 4th novel, w/dust jacket, M.............**$65.00**

Stone, Robert; Dog Soldiers, 1974, Houghton Mifflin, 1st edition, author's 2nd book, w/dust jacket, M **$150.00**

Stout, Rex; Death of a Doxy, 1966, Viking, 1st edition, w/dust jacket, M..**$30.00**

Straub, Peter; Ghost Story, 1979, Coward McCann, 1st edition, w/dust jacket, VG **$17.00**

Strauss, Victoria; Lady of Rhuddesmere, 1982, Warne, 1st edition, w/dust jacket, M **$16.00**

Sutton, Margaret; Haunted Road, 1954, Grosset Dunlap, brick tweed binding, w/dust jacket, VG **$35.00**

Swift, Jonathan; Gulliver's Travels, 1947, NY, Crown, 1st edition, w/dust jacket, VG **$15.00**

Tate, Elizabeth; Angel, 1957, Viking, 1st US edition, w/dust jacket, VG **$15.00**

Taylor, Frank; From Land & Sea, 1975, San Francisco, Chronicle Books, 1st edition, 288 pages, w/dust jacket, M **$15.00**

Taylor, Robert Lewis; Journey to Matecumbe, 1961, NY, 1st edition, w/dust jacket, VG..............................**$15.00**

Thomas, Ross; Out on the Rim, 1982, Mysterious, 1st edition, w/dust jacket, M **$25.00**

Thomas, Ross; Twilight at Mac's Place, 1990, Mysterious, 1st edition, w/dust jacket, M **$22.50**

Thompson, Jim; More Hard Core, 1986, NY, Donald Fine, Omnibus edition, w/dust jacket, M.....................**$25.00**

Thorn, Ronald S; Twin Serpents, 1965, Macmillan, book club edition, w/dust jacket, M **$5.00**

Traven, B; White Rose: A Novel, 1979, Westport, 1st edition, 209 pages, VG **$35.00**

Trublood, Ted; Fishing Handbook, 1951, Greenwich, illustrated, 144 pages, G **$4.00**

Tyler, Anne; Celestial Navigation, 1974, Knopf, 1st edition, w/repaired dust jacket, NM **$125.00**

Ullman, James Ramsey; White Tower, 1945, Lippincott, M **$3.50**

Updike, John; Bech: A Book, 1970, Knopf, 1st edition, w/dust jacket, VG **$20.00**

Updike, John; Pigeon Feathers, 1979, Logan IA, 1st separate book edition, w/wrapper, M **$35.00**

Updike, John; Rabbit Is Rich, 1981, Knopf, 1st edition, w/dust jacket, M **$35.00**

Updike, John; 16 Sonnets, 1979, Cambridge, Halty Ferguson, w/wrapper, M **$85.00**

Vachss, Andrew; Blossom, 1990, Knopf, 1st edition, w/dust jacket, M **$15.00**

Van Gulik, Robert; Haunted Monastery, 1968, Scribner, 1st US edition, w/dust jacket, M **$50.00**

Van Vogt, AE; Slan, 1951, Simon Schuster, 1st trade edition, w/dust jacket, VG **$50.00**

Vidal, Gore; Creation, 1981, Random House, 1st edition, w/slipcase, M **$50.00**

Vidal, Gore; Empire, 1987, Franklin Library, leather cover, M **$65.00**

Vonnegut, Kurt; Cat's Cradle, 1963, Harcourt Rinehart Winston, 1st edition, w/dust jacket, G **$60.00**

Vonnegut, Kurt; Palm Sunday, 1981, Delacorte, 1st edition, w/dust jacket, M **$15.00**

Wagoner, David; Baby Come on Inside, 1968, Farrar, Straus & Giroux, 1st edition, w/dust jacket, M...............**$7.50**

Walker, Keith; Piece of My Heart, 1985, Novato, Presidio, 1st edition, w/dust jacket, M **$35.00**

Wallace, Irving; Fabulous Originals, 1955, Knopf, 1st edition, w/dust jacket, M **$20.00**

Warren, Robert Penn; Band of Angels, 1955, Random House, 1st edition, w/dust jacket, M **$45.00**

Warren, Robert Penn; Night Rider, 1939, Random House, early reprint, w/dust jacket, M **$35.00**

Welch, James; Indian Lawyer, 1990, NY, Norton, 1st edition, w/dust jacket, M **$35.00**

West, Elizabeth; Garden in the Hills, 1980, London, Faber, 1st edition, 204 pages, w/dust jacket, M **$12.50**

West, Morris; Summer of the Red Wolf, 1968, Morrow, 1st edition, w/dust jacket, M **$7.50**

West, Rebecca; Birds Fall Down, 1966, Viking, 1st US edition, w/dust jacket, VG **$15.00**

Wilder, Thornton; Ides of March, 1948, Harper, 1st edition, w/dust jacket, VG **$17.00**

Willeford, Charles; I Was Looking for a Street, 1988, Woodstock VT, Countryman Press, 1st edition, w/dust jacket, M **$30.00**

Williams, Tennessee; Roman Spring of Mrs Stone, 1950, New Directions, 1st edition, w/dust jacket, M **$35.00**

Williams, Tennessee; Twenty-Seven Wagons Full of Cotton, 1953, New Directions, revised edition, w/dust jacket, VG **$50.00**

Wilson, Jeremy; Minorities, 1971, Jonathan Cape, 1st edition, w/dust jacket, M..**$55.00**

Wolfe, Thomas; Of Time & the River, 1935, Scribner, 1st edition, VG **$20.00**

Woods, Stuart; Deep Lie, 1986, NY, Norton, 1st edition, w/dust jacket, M...**$30.00**

Woolf, Virginia; Writer's Diary, 1953, Hogarth, Leonard Woolf edition, NM **$75.00**

Wouk, Herman; Don't Stop the Carnival, 1965, Doubleday, 1st edition, w/dust jacket, M **$40.00**

Yerby, Frank; Griffin's Way, 1962, Dial, book club edition, w/dust jacket, M...**$3.00**

Yerby, Frank; Treasure of Pleasant Valley, 1955, NY, Dial, 1st edition, w/dust jacket, M **$65.00**

Young, Al; Who Is Angelina?, 1975, Harcourt Rinehart Winston, 1st edition, w/dust jacket, M.........................**$45.00**

Young, Kenneth; Greek Passion, 1969, London, 1st edition, 542 pages, cloth cover......................................**$22.50**

Zanger, Jack; Ken Boyer, 1965, Nelson, 1st edition, w/dust jacket, VG **$20.00**

Bottle Openers

A figural bottle opener is one where the cap lifter is an actual feature of the model being portrayed – for instance, the bill of a pelican or the mouth of a 4-eyed man. Most are made of painted cast iron or aluminum, though some were chrome or brass plated. Some of the major bottle opener producers were Wilton, John Wright, L&L, and Gadzik. They have been reproduced, so beware of any examples with 'new' paint. Condition of the paint is an important consideration when it comes to evaluating an opener. There are some rare ones – faces of a winking boy, a skull, an Amish man, a coyote, and an eagle (these are wall mounts); 3-dimensional stand-up figures of college students and cheerleaders, a girl in a bathing suit, a dodo bird, and a beer drinker with an apron-string opener. These are worth from $100.00 to $400.00 or so (if the paint is good) to the right collector.

For more information, read *Figural Bottle Openers, Identification Guide,* by the Figural Bottle Opener Collectors. They're listed in the Directory under Clubs, Newsletters, and Catalogs.

Alligator & boy, F-133, 2¾x3⅞", painted cast iron, Black boy being bitten by alligator, scarce, 1947 ....**$200.00**

Amish boy, F-31, 4x2", painted cast iron, standing, wearing black hat & pants & bright red shirt, 1953, rare..**$225.00**

Bear head, F-426, 4x3", wall mount, painted cast iron, fierce looking w/open mouth & bulging white eyes, 1950, common..**$65.00**

Billy goat, F-47, painted cast iron, J Wright **$150.00**

Black man's head, painted cast iron, wall mount, Wilton, EX...**$125.00**

Bulldog, 4x3¾", mouth open, painted cast iron, white w/brown accents, green collar............................**$115.00**

Clown head, F-417, 4½x4", painted cast iron, laughing face, white bow tie w/red polka dots, 1950, common **$95.00**

Cowboy w/guitar, F-27, 4¾", painted cast iron, 1950, common, VG **$80.00**

Donkey, F-60, 3½x3½", painted cast iron, laughing, oversize head on sm body, brown, 1947, common **$35.00**

Donkey, 3¾", sm body, sitting, lg head & open mouth, painted cast iron **$25.00**

Drunk at lamppost, 4⅛", leg down, painted cast iron, Wilton products..**$17.50**

False teeth, F-420, 2⅜x3⅜", wall mount, painted cast iron, red & white, 1954, common..................................**$65.00**

Foundry Man, F-29, 3⅛x2⅝", painted cast iron, pouring molten metal in mold, 1950, scarce....................**$120.00**

Lady standing by lamppost, 4½", painted cast iron, J Wright Co, From $60.00 to **$80.00**

Lamppost Drunk, F-1, 4⅛x2½", painted cast iron, 1 leg up, 1950s, common..**$25.00**

Mademoiselle at lamppost w/sign, F-10, 4½x2¾", painted cast iron, skirt above knee, 1960s, common.........**$35.00**

Mallard duck on base, painted cast iron, Wilton **$50.00**

Palm tree, F-21, 4½x2⅝", painted cast iron, 1947 ......**$140.00**

Parrot, 3", full figure, sitting on perch, notched crest & long plumage, painted cast iron, J Wright, EX **$25.00**

Pelican, F-129, 3⅜x3¾", painted cast iron, red & black w/closed yellow beak, 1947, common.................**$50.00**

Pelican, 2½", cast metal w/VG paint...........................**$45.00**

Pheasant head, 4", cast metal w/M paint $40.00

Sailor, F-17, 3¾", painted cast iron, appears to be hitchhiking by sign reading Sailor's Ball '56, 1950s **$75.00**

Sea horse, F-140, 3¼", painted cast iron, green, 1950, EX $85.00

Squirrel, F-91, painted cast iron, J Wright $82.50

Tennis racquet form, brass................................$22.00

Bottles

You could spend thousands of dollars and come home with very few bottles to show for your money. As you can see in our listings, certain types of old bottles (many bitters, historical flasks, and the better antique figurals, for instance) are very expensive, and unless you're attending one of the big bottle auctions in the East, you're not too likely to see these around. But flea markets are full of bottles, and it's very difficult to know how to start buying.

Mold seams are a good indicator of age. Bottles from ca 1800 normally will have seams that stop at the shoulder. From about 1875 until approximately 1890 the seam ended between the shoulder and the top of the neck. The line crept gradually on up until about 1910, when it finally reached the top of the neck. Bottles have been reproduced, but 'dug' bottles with these characteristics are most certainly collectible.

Color is an important consideration when collecting old bottles. Aqua, amethyst, yellow, and pink tints are desirable, and deep tones are better yet. When old clear glass is exposed to the sun, it will often turn amethyst (because of its manganese content), so this can also be an indicator of age.

Unlike many antiques and collectibles, bottles with imperfections are appreciated for flaws such as crooked necks, bubbles in the glass, or whittle marks (caused from blowing glass into molds that were too cold for the molten glass to properly expand in.) But glass that is stained, cloudy, or sick (having signs of deterioration) is another matter entirely.

Check for mold marks. Three-mold bottles were made in one piece below the shoulder, while the top was made in two. This type of bottle is very old (from the first half of the 19th century) and expensive. Colored examples command premium prices!

There are several types of old bottles – an applied lip (a laid-on-ring), while others are simply 'sheared' (snapped off the blow pipe, reheated, and hand tooled). Pushed-up bottoms (called 'kick-ups' by collectors) were made that way so that they could be easier packed in layers. The necks of the bottom layer of bottles would easily fit into the pushed-up bottoms of the layer on top. A 'blob seal' is a blob of applied glass that has a die-stamped product or company name.

If you find yourself interested in collecting bottles, you'll need to study. Go to bottle shows, talk to dealers, and read all you can. There are several books available on this subject: *Collecting Barber Bottles* by Richard Holiner, *The Standard Old Bottle Price Guide* by Carlo and Dorothy Sellari, and *Bottle Pricing Guide* by Hugh Cleveland.

See also Avon; Coca-Cola; Dairy Bottles; Decanters; Pepsi-Cola; Perfume Bottles; and Soda Bottles.

Barber, 6⅝", Coin Spot on sapphire blue, melon ribs, American, ca 1900.....................................$90.00

Barber, 7", Coin Spot on emerald green, tooled top, smooth base, American, ca 1900.....................$100.00

Barber, 7", gold & white enamel flowers on deep amethyst, tooled top, open pontil, American, ca 1900........$100.00

Barber, 8½", multicolored scene on milk glass, tooled top, open pontil, American, ca 1900 ....$130.00

Barber, 8⅛", cobalt w/melon ribs, tooled top, smooth base, American, ca 1910..............................$100.00

Barber, 8⅛", emerald green w/melon ribs, tooled top, smooth base, American, ca 1910 ....$110.00

Bitters, Atwood's Jaundice Bitters, 6", clear...................$5.00

Bitters, Aunt Charity's Bitters, 8", clear, oval $65.00

Bitters, Baker's Premium Bitters, 6½", aqua, oval $55.00

Bitters, Beecham's Bitters, 8", amber, rectangular.......$12.50

Bitters, Berring Bitters, 9½", brown.............................$7.50

Bitters, Bonekamp Bitters, 12¼", amber, cylindrical....$15.00

Bitters, Caroni Bitters, 8", black, cylindrical $18.00

Bitters, Columbo Peptic Bitters, 9½", amber $27.50

Bitters, Damiana Bitters, 11½", aqua..........................$30.00

Bitters, Hanlan's Tuna Bitters, 9⅛", clear, cylindrical ..$22.50

Bitters, Higby Tonic Bitters, 9⅜", amber, square $22.00

Bitters, Lash's Bitters, 11", amber $15.00

Bitters, Malt Bitters, 8¼", green, cylindrical.................$15.00

Bitters, Peruvian Bitters, 9", amber, square $65.00

Bitters, plain, 8¾", amber $5.00

Bitters, Poland Bitters, ¾-qt, green w/label, cylindrical..$30.00

Bitters, Prickly Ash Bitters, 9½", amber $30.00

Bitters, Stag Bitters (labeled only), 9½", amber, square.$6.00

Bitters, Tuft's Tonic Bitters, ½-pt, aqua, cylindrical $15.00

Bitters, West Indian Stomach Bitters, 10", amber, square.$50.00

Food, Airline Trademark, 2⅝", clear $3.00

Food, California Olive Oil, 9½", amethyst.....................$3.00

Food, Curtis Bros Perserves, 8", sun-colored amethyst, ribbed, Rochester NY embossed in seal $2.50

Food, Evangeline Pepper Sauce, 12-sided....................$5.00

Food, Hire's Household Extract, 4¾", aqua...................$2.50

Food, Hot Dog Sauce, 4½", clear................................$7.50

Food, Knight's Extracts, 4½", clear.............................$2.00

Food, Old Mission Olive Oil, 8¾", amethyst.................$5.00

Food, Re Umberto Olive Oil, 6¾", clear.......................$2.00

Food, Spark's Horseradish, 7", aqua $3.00

Food, Tillman's Extract, 7", aqua................................$2.00

Food, Whitehouse Vinegar, 8", clear $8.00

Food, Yacht Club Salad Dressing, 7½", sun-colored amethyst $5.00

Gin, Cosmopoliet, 9¾", man holding cup embossing, JJ Melchers WZ Schiedam, olive green, bubbly $290.00

Household, Ayer's Hair Vigor, 6½", deep green..........$25.00

Household, Beach & Clarridge Co, 9¼", amethyst.........$2.50

Household, Bixby, 3½", aqua......................................$5.00

Household, Calder's Dentine, 3", clear.........................$2.00

Household, Clair's Hair Lotion, 7¼", cobalt.................$8.00

Household, Creme Simon, 2¼", milk glass...................$3.00

Household, Crown Perfumery Co, 2½", green............$17.50

Household, Epsey's Fragrant Cream, 4½", clear...........$3.00

Household, Frostilla Cosmetic, 4⅜", clear $3.00

Household, Graduated Nursing Bottles, 7" **$10.00**
Household, Palmer's Parfume (sic), peacock green **$12.50**
Household, Pompeian Cream, 2⅞", amethyst **$2.50**
Household, Purola Toilet Preparation, 7½", amethyst ...**$2.50**
Household, Reven Gloss Shoe Dressing, 5", green........**$5.00**
Household, Wakelee's Carmalline, 4¾", amber..............**$3.00**
Ink, Arnold's, 2½", amethyst, cylindrical........................**$4.00**

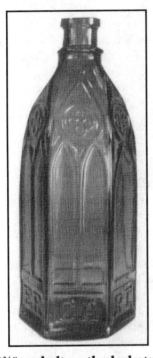

Ink, Carter's, 9¾", cobalt, cathedral style, applied lip, smooth base, NM **$60.00**
Ink, Carter's No 8, 3-oz, 2¾", sun-colored amethyst......**$4.00**
Ink, Caw's Ink Co, 2¼", aqua **$4.00**
Ink, Diamond & Onyx, 3", aqua **$4.00**
Ink, Higgins Inks, Brooklyn NY, 2", amethyst, cylindrical.**$3.00**
Ink, J&IE Moore, 1½", aqua..**$9.00**
Ink, Johnson Ink Co, 5⅞", dark green, sheared top **$24.00**
Ink, Keller Ink, Detroit, 2", amethyst, square w/screw-on lid **$8.50**
Ink, Pomeroy Ink, 2½", aqua...**$8.00**
Ink, Sanford's Fountain Pen Ink, 2" (1½" chimney), clear, machine-made **$6.00**
Ink, Superior Ink, 2", tan & brown pottery **$7.50**
Ink, Waterman's Ideal, NY, 3", sun-colored amethyst ...**$5.00**
Medicine, Abernathy's Ginger Brandy, 10½", amber, cylindrical...**$5.00**
Medicine, Ayer's Cherry Pectoral Lowell, 7", aqua, rectangular **$2.50**
Medicine, Ayer's Sarsaparilla, 8½", blue **$10.00**
Medicine, Bliss Liver & Kidney Cure, 9½", clear, rectangular **$15.00**
Medicine, Bosanko's Cough & Lung Syrup, 6", aqua, rectangular **$2.50**
Medicine, Bromo Seltzer, 4", blue..................................**$3.00**
Medicine, Cadler's Dentine, 3", clear, cylindrical..........**$1.50**
Medicine, Chamberlain's Colic Cholera & Diarrhea Remedy, 4½", aqua..**$4.00**
Medicine, Cod Liver Oil, 7⅜", brown.............................**$8.00**

Medicine, Daniels' Cough Cold & Fever Drops, 4½", clear, rectangular...**$3.00**
Medicine, Drake's Cough Remedy, 6¼", aqua, rectangular .**$3.00**
Medicine, Ferrol, The Iron Oil Food, 9½", aqua, rectangular **$2.50**
Medicine, Graham's Dyspepsia Cure, 8¼", clear, rectangular **$16.00**
Medicine, Hagan's Magnolia Balm, 5", milk glass, rectangular **$12.50**
Medicine, Harter's Iron Tonic, 9", amber, rectangular ...**$8.00**
Medicine, Kendall's Spavin Cure, 5½", amber, 12-sided..**$9.00**
Medicine, Kilmer's Swamp Root, 8⅜", blue.................**$10.00**
Medicine, Lindsey's Blood Searcher, aqua, rectangular..**$10.00**
Medicine, Melvin & Badger Apothecaries, 6¾", cobalt, 6-sided **$10.00**
Medicine, Myer's Angelo, 6", purple **$9.00**
Medicine, Old Reliable Eye Water, 3¼", blue.................**$4.50**
Medicine, Perry's Dead Shot Vermifuge, 4", aqua, oval .**$10.00**
Medicine, Pierce's Favorite Prescription, 8¼", aqua, rectangular **$5.00**
Medicine, Pond's Extract, 7⅞", blue...............................**$2.00**
Medicine, Prairie Weed Balsam, aqua **$7.50**
Medicine, Royaline Oil, 5", aqua, rectangular **$3.00**
Medicine, Scovill Blood & Liver Syrup, 9½", aqua, rectangular **$4.50**
Medicine, Skoda's Concentrated Extract Sarsaparilla, 9", amber, rectangular **$20.00**
Medicine, St Luke's Hospital, 4⅛", clear, rectangular.....**$2.50**
Medicine, Warner's Safe Kidney & Liver Cure, 9¼", amber, oval **$12.50**
Medicine, Wistar's Balsam of Wild Cherry, 5", blue.......**$8.00**
Mineral water, Adam's Springs Mineral Water, 11½", aqua, glob top, cylindrical **$8.00**
Mineral water, Allen Mineral Water, 12", amber, applied top, vertical lettering...**$8.00**
Mineral water, Apollinaris Mineral Water, 12", green, crown top, paper label **$3.00**
Mineral water, Bethesda Water, 12", light green, cylindrical w/pear-shaped label **$3.00**
Mineral water, Congress & Empire Spring Co, Saratoga NY, 8", green, applied top, embossed C in center......**$25.00**
Mineral water, Distilled Water Co, Cuyamaca San Diego, 1-gal, 12½", aqua...**$6.00**
Mineral water, Gettysburg Katalysing Water, 9½", olive green, cylindrical..**$8.00**
Mineral water, Humboldt Artesian Mineral Water, 7½", aqua, applied top **$5.00**
Mineral water, John Clark NY Spring Water, 7", green, cylindrical...**$55.00**
Mineral water, Quinan Mineral Water, 7¾", cobalt, cylindrical...**$30.00**
Mineral water, Saratoga Red Springs Water, 1-pt, emerald green, cylindrical...**$45.00**
Mineral water, 7½", Lynde & Putnam, San Francisco Cal, teal blue, Union Glass Works, Philada, worn, ca 1850, VG **$95.00**
Poison, Carbolic Acid embossed on side, Use w/Caution on other, 3-oz, 5", cobalt, 6-sided **$50.00**

Poison, Cobolt Owl Poison, sm size, triangular...........**$65.00**

Poison, Poison embossed, 3¼", blue, triangular.........**$65.00**

Poison, Poison Tinct Iodine, 2½", amber, embossed skull & crossbones...**$12.50**

Poison, 4", bright blue, rectangular w/raised ridges....**$57.50**

Snuff, Garrett Snuff Co, blown mouth.........................**$2.50**

Snuff, Levi Garrett & Sons, 4", dark amber.................**$1.00**

Snuff, 4", yellow..**$20.00**

Snuff, 4⅛", green..**$20.00**

Snuff, 5¾", amber...**$10.00**

Soda, Bacon's Soda Works, Sonora CA, 7", light green, blob top...**$8.00**

Spirits, Binswager, Simon & Bros, 6¾", clear.............**$7.50**

Spirits, Catto's Whiskey, 9", olive green......................**$8.00**

Spirits, Crown Distilleries Company, 4½", amber, cylindrical...**$6.00**

Spirits, De Kuyper Gin, 10½", dark amber, labeled.....**$12.00**

Spirits, Duffy Malt Whiskey Co, 3⅝", amber, w/cork..**$15.00**

Spirits, Garrett's AM Wines, 11¾", clear, screw-on lid...**$6.00**

Spirits, Harvest King Distilling Co, 12", aqua, heavy embossed letters, cork stopper...........................**$30.00**

Spirits, Hawley Glass Co, 8¼", amber.........................**$12.00**

Spirits, Juniper Leaf Gin, 10½", amber, case type........**$22.50**

Spirits, Little Brown Jug, 2¾", Brown pottery..............**$22.50**

Spirits, North Pole, The Anderson Bros, 7", clear, cork stopper..**$10.00**

Spirits, Red Top Whiskey, 6½", aqua, flask shape.........**$8.00**

Spirits, Rucker Dry Gin, 9", aqua..................................**$7.50**

Spirits, Rutherford & Kay, 10½", olive green, 3-piece mold, cork stopper...**$7.50**

Spirits, UDL, Old Rye Whiskey, 11", amber, paper label.$16.00

Spirits, Wakelee's Magnolia Spirit, cobalt......................**$7.50**

Utility, 10", olive green, VR (upsidedown anchor) embossed in seal, applied square collar lip, cylindrical.......**$100.00**

Whiskey, Queen Mary, 10⅜", olive green, bust of queen on front, EX...**$75.00**

Boy Scout Collectibles

The Boy Scouts of America was organized in 1910. It was originated in England by General Baden-Powell and inspired by his observations during the Boer War. He believed boys wanted and needed to learn about outdoor activities. The first Boy Scout Jamboree was held in Washington DC in 1937. Today people who are or have been active in Scouting are interested in all types of items that relate to its history, for example: patches, uniforms, pins, medals, books and magazines, Jamboree items, Explorer items, pictures, and paper items.

For more information, refer to *Guide to Scouting Collectibles* by R.J. Sayers. See the Interested Buyers section in the back of the book for his address.

Badge, Sea Scout Apprentice, black felt.........................**$5.50**

Belt, Official Scout, olive green, webb type, FC on buckle, early...**$20.00**

Belt buckle, Official Boy Scout, double knot type, no patent date..**$7.50**

Book, Boy Scout Adventure Stories, by Irving Crump, 1950, EX..**$4.00**

Book, The Ransom of Red Chief, Every Boy's Library edition, hard-bound, O'Henry...................................**$20.00**

Bookends, Official Boy Scout, #1703, painted brass, 1937-45, pr..**$20.00**

Calendar, A Good Sign All Over the World, Rockwell cover, 1963, complete...**$15.00**

Calendar, Come & Get It, Rockwell cover, 1970, NM.**$20.00**

Card, Baden-Powell & Dutch Queen reviewing Scouts, 1937, NM...**$10.00**

Christmas cards, #3081, 1933-37, boxed set..................**$5.00**

Compass, Leedawl #1202, white metal, 1918-24.........**$20.00**

Handbook, Lion or Bear Cub Scouts, 2nd edition, 1948, either...**$5.00**

Handbook for Boys, Rockwell cover, green, 4th edition, 1940...**$7.50**

Hat badge, Scoutmasters, #263, dark green enamel, screw-back type, 1924-29 ....**$20.00**

Key chain, National Jamboree souvenir, w/logo, 1950 .**$5.00**

Manual, Air Explorer, edited by Holstein, Dec 1953 .....**$7.00**

Match holder, Official Boy Scout, #1437, seamless brass, 1925-32 ....**$10.00**

Medal, Official Boy Scout archery contest, bronze, 1925-32 ....**$25.00**

Neckerchief, National Jamboree, cotton, 4 variations, 1969, each **$8.00**

Pamphlet, The Scouts First Book, 1921 ....**$12.00**

Patch, Emergency Service Explorer, red felt **$5.00**

Patch, National Jamboree, woven, 1964.....................**$10.00**

Patch, National Jamboree Sea Scout, square, 1973......**$20.00**

Patch, National Jamboree Security Staff, 1981..............**$15.00**

Patch, Official Boy Scout Eagle, type 2, BSA on tan square, 1925-32 ....**$90.00**

Pillowcase, National Jamboree, silk, w/logo, 1964........**$7.00**

Pocketknife, #1996, red bone-like handle, round Tenderfoot shield w/belt loop, 4-blade, 1970-79 ....**$5.00**

Pocketknife, Official Boy Scout, Hammer brand, stag handle, 4-blade, 1925-32..**$22.00**

Postcard, Baden-Powell & Son in uniform, full color, 1950s, NM..**$7.00**

Watch fob, Second Class Scout, for Patrol leaders **$100.00**

Whistle, Official Scout, #1006, brass, cylinder type **$15.00**

Wristwatch, #1544, Waltham model, 7-jewel type, 1925-32 ....**$22.00**

Boyd Crystal Art Glass

After the Degenhart glass studio closed (see the Degenhart section for information), it was bought out by the Boyd family, who added many of their own designs to the molds they acquired from the Degenharts and other defunct glasshouses. They are located in Cambridge, Ohio, and the glass they've been pressing in the more than 225 colors they've developed since they opened in 1978 is marked with their 'B in diamond' logo. Since 1988, a line has been added under the diamond. All the work is done by hand, and each piece is made in a selected color in limited amounts – the production run lasts only about six weeks or less. Items in satin glass or an exceptional slag are especially collectible; so are those with hand-painted details.

Basket Toothpick Holder, Classic Black.........................**$8.50**

Boyd Airplane, Heather Grey..**$17.50**

Bull Dog's Head, Persimmon **$9.00**

Buzz Saw, Wine, Katydid **$8.50**

Cat Slipper, Buckeye...**$9.00**

Chick Salt, Grape Parfait Carnival **$12.00**

Chick Salt, Pebble Beige **$9.00**

Chick Salt, Thistlebloom **$9.00**

Chicken Covered Dish, Buckeye......................................**$7.50**

Colonial Man, Edward, Milk White **$17.50**

Duck Covered Dish, Blue Carnival **$7.50**

Duck Salt, Cobalt..**$9.00**

Forget-Me-Not Toothpick, Cardinal Red......................**$9.00**

Hambone Ashtray, Heliotope.....................................**$17.50**

JB Scotty, Cornsilk **$10.00**

JB Scotty, Crystal **$9.00**

Miss Cotton the Kitten, Shasta White **$8.00**

Rose Puff Box, Kumquat **$13.50**

Statue of Liberty Plate, Ruby **$9.50**

Tear Drop Wine, Golden Delight...................................**$7.50**

Tub Salt Dip, Patriot White...**$4.00**

Brass

Because it has become so costly to produce things from brass (due to the inflated price of copper, one of its components), manufacturers have largely turned to plastics and other less-expensive materials. As a result, nearly anything made of brass is becoming collectible.

If you'd like a source for further study, we recommend *Antique Brass and Copper Identification and Value Guide* by Mary Frank Gaston.

Ashtray, squatty urn shape w/push-down center, 2 rests, decorative rim, ca mid-20th century **$25.00**

Ashtray, 1x1⅔" dia, individual hand-held type, cast construction, American, ca 1920s, EX **$15.00**

Bell, for table, store or hotel desks, EX.......................**$40.00**

Bell, school; 12", brass w/wooden handle, worn......**$100.00**

Bowl, 10" dia, shallow round shape w/engraved floral & leaf design, marked China....................................**$75.00**

Cabinet pull, plain, lg, EX..**$12.00**

Cabinet pull, rope design...**$22.00**

Door handle, 14½", commercial type, marked Push ...**$70.00**

Door knocker, 6", lion's head w/ring through nose....**$35.00**

Grain measure, 8½x4½" dia, smooth straight sides, smooth swing handle w/hook, marked Howe, EX.........**$135.00**

Horse brasses, any design, each $25.00

Inkwell w/tray, 3½", tray 6" long, 1950s, EX..............**$75.00**

Kettle, apple butter; 10x17", iron handle, American, worn/mended on bottom....................................**$150.00**

Letter holder, 3½x5", horizontal oval shape, plain, marked Bradley & Hubbard, American, ca 1920s, EX........**$60.00**

Match holder, 4", round cup w/attached tray **$65.00**

Nozzle for hose, 3", EX..**$25.00**

Pail, milk or water; 9x10" dia, lip rim forms loops to hold bail handle, slightly worn......................................**$100.00**

Scoop used on spring or weight-type scales, 20" long, pedestal base, some pitting, VG **$90.00**

Spittoon, 5x7" dia, hammered rim, flat bottom **$60.00**
Tobacco jar, 8", round, tapers at bottom, slip lid w/smooth flat top, mid-20th century, EX **$25.00**
Umbrella stand, smooth cylinder shape w/flared rim & base, ring handles attached to lion heads, mid-20th century, EX **$125.00**
Washboard, wooden frame w/brass rub board, worn ..**$50.00**

Sascha Brastoff

California has always been a big producer of dinnerware and decorative pottery items, and those from the thirties, forties, and fifties are attracting lots of collector interest right now. Designer wares such as those by Sascha Brastoff, Marc Belaire, and their contemporaries are especially in demand. Brastoff's career was diversified, to say the least. Although he is best-known in our circles for his high-style ceramic, enamelware, and resin pieces which even then (1940s-50s) were expensive, he was also a dancer, costume designer, sculptor, painter, and jeweler.

Brastoff's wares are signed in two ways. If the item was signed with his full signature, it was personally crafted by Brastoff himself. These are much more valuable than items simply stamped 'Sasha B,' a mark used on production pieces that were made by his staff under his supervision. Unless our listings contain the phrase 'full signature,' values that follow are for pieces with the 'Sasha B' stamp.

Jack Chipman has written a book on California potteries in which he devotes a chapter to Brastoff. It is entitled *The Collector's Encyclopedia of California Pottery*, we highly recommend it for further study.

Ashtray, ceramic, horse decoration on gray **$40.00**
Ashtray, lg, ceramic, Eskimo in parka **$40.00**
Ashtray, 8½" long, ceramic, free-form, light blue speckled matt w/abstract gold leaf design, signed **$30.00**
Bowl, ceramic, Star Steed (horse), footed **$43.00**
Cigarette box, ceramic, bird decoration on white w/gold trim, signed Sascha Brastoff (full signature)........**$100.00**
Cigarette box, ceramic, horse decoration.....................**$48.00**
Cigarette holder & lighter, ceramic, turquoise, set.......**$45.00**
Compote, 9½", ceramic, gold & silver dove on ivory ..**$65.00**
Figurine, 6", bear, red resin, rare **$150.00**

Plate, 11x11" square, ceramic, horse decoration, signed Sascha B on front, presentation inscription & 1950 on back **$150.00**

Tray, 17" dia, ceramic, matt multicolored abstracts ...**$125.00**
Tray, 17¾", enamelled copper w/embossed grapes....**$75.00**
Tray, 8" square, ceramic, circus elephant design w/multi-color on gray mottle **$45.00**
Vase, 10", resin, amber w/grapes & vines...................**$80.00**
Vase, 20", ceramic, slender form w/husky dog............**$95.00**
Vase, 5¾", emerald green resin w/grape decoration...**$50.00**

Brayton Laguna

Brayton was the potter, Laguna Beach, California, his residence. Durlin Brayton began making dinnerware in the 1920s and is credited for being the one to introduce the concept of the mixed, solid-color dinnerware lines made later by Bauer and Homer Laughlin (the manufacturer of Fiesta). His pieces were rather crudely designed, and it is said that he simply erected stands and sold the ware in his front yard or carried it in the trunk of his car to wherever people were apt to congregate.

When he married in 1936, his wife helped him develop his business into a larger, more lucrative enterprise. They started producing quality figurines, some of them licensed by Walt Disney Studios. They also made vases, cookie jars, various household items, and larger figurines that they referred to as sculptures. Some of their decorating was done by hand, some by the airbrush-painting method. Finishes varied and included a white crackle as well as a woodtone (stained) bisque among their more standard glazes.

All of their marks include either the word 'Brayton,' 'Laguna,' or both, except for the stamp used on their Pinocchio series. These pieces were marked 'Geppetto Pottery' in an oval. Not everything they made was marked, though, simply because very often there wasn't enough room. But there will be an incised or painted decorator's initial to clue you, and as you see and handle more of the ware, you'll be able to recognize Brayton's unique appearance.

The company did quite well until after WWII, when vast amounts of Japanese imports spelled doom for many small American potteries. They closed in 1968.

For further study, read *The Collector's Encyclopedia of California Pottery* by Jack Chipman.

Cookie jar, Goose Woman, marked **$145.00**

Cookie jar, Mammy...$395.00
Creamer, cat figural...$45.00

Creamer & sugar bowl, Provincial **$70.00**

Figurine, abstract man w/cat, 21", satin-matt black, in-mold mark, ca 1957 ....**$200.00**

Figurine, mule, 7¼x10", honey-colored body w/black & purple details, A Anderson **$70.00**

Figurine, Pedro, 6½", from Francis Robinson's childhood series, stamp marked **$60.00**

Figurine, sniffing Pluto, 3¼x6", Walt Disney line **$150.00**

Figurine, St Bernard, late 1930s, Andy Anderson **$90.00**

Figurine, Toucan, 9½", wood-tone & high-gloss colors, 1950s-60s **$80.00**

Flower holder, Sally **$30.00**

Flowerpot, 5½", flares out to larger ruffled rim, deep purple, Durlin Brayton **$35.00**

Pitcher, 5", bulbous shape w/burgundy semigloss glaze, Durlin Brayton **$45.00**

Pitcher, 7¼", squatty round shape w/lg loop handle, 2-tone blue high-gloss glaze, Durlin Brayton **$80.00**

Tile, 4½x4½", colorful cats on a rooftop carved on yellow w/black edging, ca 1928, Durlin Brayton **$70.00**

Tile, 6½x6½", fanciful palm tree on purple w/dark purple edging, ca 1928, Durlin Brayton **$95.00**

Toothpick holder, Gingham Dog **$75.00**

Vase, 5½", bulbous, yellow glaze, Durlin Brayton **$50.00**

Breweriana

'Breweriana' is simply a term used by collectors to refer to items (usually freebies) given away by breweries to advertise their products. Some people prefer pre-prohibition era bottles, pocket mirrors, foam scrapers, etched and enameled glasses, mugs, steins, playing cards, postcards, pin-back buttons, and the like; but many collectors like the more available items from the past few decades as well. Some specialize either in breweries from a particular state, specific items such as foam scrapers (used to clean the foam off the top of glasses or pitchers of beer), or they might limit their buying to just one brewery.

The book we recommend for this area of collecting is *Back Bar Breweriana* by George J. Baley.

Bank, 11", Hamm's Beer, ceramic black & white bear figure, 1980s **$25.00**

Bank, 7", Foremost Sales Promotions, plaster bottle man, red, white & black, 1970s **$75.00**

Bottle, Oconto Brewing Co, amber, blob top **$6.00**

Bottle, 11", Reno Brewing Co, Reno NV, dark amber, blob top **$5.00**

Bottle, 11½", amber opalescent, applied top **$8.00**

Bottle, 11½", Henninger, amber, machine made **$3.00**

Bottle, 12", Pabst Brewing Co of Milwaukee, amber.....**$6.00**

Bottle, 7½", Jos Schlitz Brewing Co **$3.00**

Bottle, 8", El Paso Brewery, amber **$6.00**

Bottle, 9", Maryland Brewing Co, amber **$6.00**

Bottle, 9", Nebraska Brewing Co, Omaha NE, reddish amber, blob top **$9.00**

Bottle, 9", Texas Brewing Co, Property of TBC Fort Worth TX, frosted, crown top **$4.00**

Bottle, 9½", Anheuser-Busch Inc, amber **$1.50**

Bottle, 9½", York Brewing Co, aqua w/embossed eagle on barrel logo, crown top, ca 1893-1920, VG **$12.00**

Bottle, 9¼", Burkhardt, Boston MA, amber, blob top....**$9.50**

Bottle, 9¼", Wisconsin Select Beer, aqua **$4.00**

Bottle opener, 3⅜" long, Duquesne Pilsner/Silver Top Beer, Bull #E-12-4, NM **$5.00**

Calendar, 12x5½", Black Label Beer, 1969, NM **$40.00**

Clock, Dawson's Ale & Beer, round w/glass front & metal frame, king's portrait in circle below lettering, VG **$65.00**

Coaster, 4½" dia, Ruppert Beer & Ale, 2 lg hands holding beer mugs, cardboard, NM **$7.50**

Corkscrew, 2¾", Anheuser-Busch, bottle-shaped, nickel-plated brass & brass label w/eagle over A **$70.00**

Decanter, 10¾", Hamm's bear figural dressed in suit & tie as bartender, marked 1973, EX..............**$60.00**

Display, Pabst Blue Ribbon, street scene w/embossed bottle, light-up, plastic & metal, 1960, NM **$125.00**

Foam scrapper, 8½x1", printed Drink Stegmaier's Beers Wilkes-Barre PA, celluloid, EX............**$18.00**

Mug, Busch Bavarian Beer, can shape, metal, 1970....**$10.00**

Mug, 6", features the Hamm's bear celebrating the 1973 Octoberfest, brown & white, EX............**$22.00**

Playing cards, Schaefer, America's Oldest Lager Beer, complete, M.............$10.00

Pocket mirror, 2¾", oval, Mathie Red Ribbon Beer, Mathie lettered diagonally over neck of bottle, VG..........**$45.00**

Postcard, shows colorful aerial view of Pabst Brewery in Milwaukee, 1935, EX............**$2.50**

Puzzle, 5", Miller High Life, can form, unopened........**$10.00**

Saloon token, ¾", frothy mug & JW on sides, EX........**$12.50**

Shelf sign, 11", Ask for American All Grain Beer on barrel end, bottle to left, 1958............**$65.00**

Shelf sign, 3x9", Champagne Velvet in cursive above ..Beer w/the Million Dollar..., 1952............**$35.00**

Shelf sign, 5", Weber Beer, Indian & pine trees, bottle & glass to right, 1959 ....**$65.00**

Shelf sign, 7", E&B Premium Beer on cap shape above On Tap for Tops in Taste on base, 1955 ....**$35.00**

Sign, 11x7", Budweiser, bottle & glass on tray, cardboard, 1950s, EX............**$10.00**

Sign, 14x19", Highlander Beer, pictures bottle & glass, tin, EX+ **$145.00**

Sign, 9x12", McGovern Beer, kicking mule & labeled bottle, paper, framed, VG **$30.00**

Sign, 9x19", Silver Spring Ale, bottle & glass flanked by product name, tin, NM............**$40.00**

Statue, 12½", Metz Beer, barrel shape, premium, Omaha NE, 1956............**$35.00**

Statue, 14½", Black Horse Beer, figure of a horse on oval base, Montreal Canada, 1960............**$85.00**

Statue, 15", Bud Light, Spuds MacKenzie sitting on haunches, St Louis, 1987 ....**$50.00**

Statue, 16½", Falstaff Beer, Falstaff holds shield-shaped sign, 1954............**$100.00**

Statue, 17", Blatz Beer, 'bottle' man & 'can' man hold mugs, do 'chorus line' kick, 1968 ....**$75.00**

Statue, 6", Goebel Beer, crowing rooster on rectangular base, 1953............**$75.00**

Statue, 6", Hensler Beer, whale atop, ...Is a Whale of a Beer, Newark, 1951 ....**$235.00**

Statue, 6¾", Drewry's Beer, mountie astride beer bottle, South Bend IN, 1955............**$75.00**

Statue, 7", Acme Beer, cowgirl kneeling on top of rectangular base, 1940 ....**$135.00**

Statue, 8½", American All Grain Beer, bar scene, 1 customer & bartender, ca 1958 ....**$100.00**

Stein, 8½", Anheuser-Busch, ceramic Bud Man figural, 1989 ....**$30.00**

Store display, Drewry's Beer, plastic figure of a man in a grey hat & suit, looking & pointing to the right, on base, 1957 ....**$150.00**

Store display light, 15", Bud Light, Spuds MacKenzie polyethylene figure, 1980s **$100.00**

Tap knob, 9", Anheuser-Busch, molded vinyl Bud Man figure, 1991............**$75.00**

Thermometer, 15x6", Old Export Beer, colorful bottle, Cumberland Brewing Co, EX............**$45.00**

Tray, Budweiser, pictures long-neck bottle, 1940s-50s .**$55.00**

Tray, 11¾" dia, Duquesne Pilsner, pictures uniformed prince w/raised glass, EX............**$25.00**

Tray, 12" dia, Beverwyck Beer, lettered graphics in red & gold on green & black ground, deep-dish, EX.....**$60.00**

Tray, 12" dia, Duquesne Beer, white lettering in orange ribbon, Finest Beer in Town on rim, 1960s, VG........**$25.00**

Tray, 13" dia, Narragansett Ale, lettering in gold w/black on red background, gold & black hops on rim, EX...**$80.00**

Tray, 13x11", Pabst Beer, old man pouring glass of beer, EX **$85.00**

Tray, 13x13", Encore Beer, Monarch Brewing Co, EX ..**$45.00**

Tray, 13x13", Iroquois Beer, Indian in headdress, VG .**$45.00**

Tray, 13x13", Olympia Beer, lady on bottle, Capitol Brewing Co, VG **$20.00**

Tumbler, 4x2¼" dia, Bartholomy Rochester Beer & Ale & winged wheel logo in white on crystal, EX..........**$25.00**

Breyer Horses

Breyer horses have been popular children's playthings since they were introduced in 1952, and you'll see several at any large flea market. The earlier horses had a glossy finish, but after 1968 a matt finish came into use. You'll find domestic animals as well. They are evaluated by condition, rarity, and desirability; some of the better examples may be worth a minimum of $150.00.

Abdullah Famous Trakehner #817, limited edition, 1989, MIB **$35.00**

Andalusian Family, MIB............**$45.00**

Appaloosa stock horse foal #238, gray w/black points, EX **$17.00**
Basset hound #326, EX.................................**$20.00**
Brahma bull #70, glossy, EX.........................**$30.00**
Buckskin mustang stallion #87, black mane, tail & hooves, pink nose, EX...**$35.00**
Classic Arabian family, Animal Creations series, MIB..**$50.00**
Clydesdale #80, red & white bobs on mane, VG.........**$17.00**
Clydesdale mare & foal stable, MIB...........................**$60.00**
Family Arab foal #6, glossy palomino, EX..................**$10.00**
Family stallion glossy palomino #4, caramel color, w/saddle, EX..**$14.00**
Fighting stallion, MIB...**$45.00**
Fighting stallion #30, white w/gray hooves, EX..........**$20.00**
Foundation stallion #64, black, EX **$22.50**
Grazing palomino mare, pink muzzle & ears, EX **$22.00**
Jumping bay stallion #300, jumping over wall, EX......**$29.00**
Lady Phase #40, EX..**$25.00**
Long Horn Texas steer #75, EX..................................**$20.00**
Lying buckskin foal #166, EX.....................................**$23.00**
Man O' War stallion #47, EX **$18.00**
Morgan black stallion #48, EX...................................**$22.50**
Nursing foal, light matt chestnut, EX.........................**$50.00**
Old-Timer gray mare #205, harness & blinders, glossy, EX.**$28.00**
Prancing palomino Arabian stallion #812, 1988, MIB..**$35.00**
Proud Arab mare #215, dark dapple gray w/bold speckles, tail attached to left leg at knee, EX.................**$28.00**
Proud Arabian stallion #211, white, EX **$22.00**
Rider horse, miniature, semirearing, black accessories, EX.**$12.50**
Running Appaloosa stallion #210, black w/white rump w/black speckles, pink nose, color #127, EX **$22.50**
Running Black Beauty stallion #89, right front sock, EX.**$18.00**
Running mare #124, brown w/black mane, EX...........**$18.50**
San Domingo stallion #67, EX....................................**$25.00**
Scratching Appaloosa foal #168, black w/white, EX ...**$18.00**

Sorrel foal..**$12.00**
Sorrel mare, 5½x9½" (illustrated)........................**$15.00**
Western pony, sm, black w/chain & snap-on brown saddle, EX...**$20.00**
Western prancing horse #110, gray, chain reins & slip-on saddle, EX..**$27.50**

British Royal Commemoratives

While seasoned collectors may prefer the older pieces using circa 1840 (Queen Victoria's reign) as their starting point, even present-day souvenirs make a good inexpensive beginning collection. Ceramic items, glassware, metalware, and paper goods have been issued on the occasion of weddings, royal tours, birthdays, christenings, and many other celebrations. Food tins are fairly easy to find and range in price from about $30.00 to around $75.00 for those made since the 1950s.

For more information, we recommend *British Royal Commemoratives* by Audrey Zeder.

Beaker, Edward VII's coronation, King's Dinner, marked Royal Doulton **$125.00**
Beaker, 3¾", Victoria's 1897 Jubilee, enameled........**$170.00**
Booklet, Victoria's Diamond Jubilee, ILN..................**$150.00**
Bookmark, Victoria's 81st birthday, celebrated in Canada, silk **$100.00**
Bowl, 4x6½", Victoria, pressed & cut glass, 1887......**$125.00**
Bowl, 9½", Elizabeth's coronation, pressed glass w/some cutting **$35.00**
Bust, 3¾x3", Victoria, amber glass, 1887....................**$165.00**
Calendar, George V, in Scottish clothing, 1911...........**$35.00**
Covered dish, Elizabeth's coronation, embossed portrait on cobalt, marked Wedgwood............................**$75.00**
Cup & saucer, Elizabeth's coronation, official, 1953....**$45.00**
Cup plate, 3½", Albert & Victoria's 1840 wedding, clear glass **$190.00**
Cup plate, 3½", Charles & Diana, pressed glass **$25.00**
Cup plate, 3½", Prince William's 10th birthday, amber glass, pressed...**$20.00**
First Day cover, Charles' 1969 Investiture **$60.00**
Magazine, Elizabeth's coronation, Illustrated **$25.00**
Magazine, Elizabeth's years on the throne, Official.....**$15.00**
Magazine, Margaret's 1960 wedding, ILN...................**$45.00**
Medal, 1", George III's 1809 Jubilee **$50.00**
Medal, 1½", Victoria's portrait w/War generals, 1900..**$90.00**
Medal, 1¾", Victoria reviewing Scottish troops, 1860.**$190.00**
Mug, Charles & Diana's 1981 wedding, multicolor portraits on china..**$30.00**
Mug, cider; Diana's 30th birthday, sepia portrait, marked LE 250 ....**$40.00**
Mug, Elizabeth's 1991 visit to United States, multicolor portraits of Elizabeth & George Bush........................**$60.00**
Mug, Queen Mother Elizabeth's 90th birthday, multicolor portrait on china **$30.00**
Novelty, Elizabeth's coronation, hand mirror, w/color portrait..**$25.00**
Novelty, Victoria, match safe, relief portrait on gutta percha, 1901 ....**$175.00**
Novelty, Victoria, velvet frame, 4 generations **$250.00**
Novelty, 12", Victoria, brewery bottle, portrait embossed in glass **$100.00**
Novelty, 2½", Charles & Diana's wedding, music box, plays Camelot..**$50.00**
Paperweight, 3½", Diana's 30th birthday, dome-shaped clear glass **$45.00**
Pin dish, 4¾", Princess Anne as a child, glass.............**$50.00**
Plate, Victoria, hand-painted portrait, signed MBW ..**$175.00**
Plate, 10", Edward VII's 1902 coronation, color portrait, marked Royal Doulton, pr...................................**$250.00**

Plate, 10", Elizabeth's 1991 visit to United States, color portrait w/George Bush **$110.00**

Plate, 10", Victoria, pressed glass, 1887.....................**$175.00**

Plate, 10½", Charles & Diana's 1981 wedding, engagement portrait..**$150.00**

Plate, 10½", Queen Elizabeth's 1939 Canada visit, Royal Winton...$50.00

Plate, 8", Diana's 30th birthday, sepia portrait, marked LE 250 ....**$40.00**

Plate, 8", Prince William's christening, marked Royal Crown Derby & LE...**$125.00**

Plate, 8", 3 royal ladies' August 1990 birthdays, w/color portrait...**$50.00**

Playing cards, Charles & Diana's 1981 wedding, color engagement photo..**$25.00**

Postcard, Edward II in uniform, embossed portrait.....**$30.00**

Postcard, Elizabeth & Philip's 40th wedding anniversary, colorful, marked LE 1000.......................................**$10.00**

Postcard, Elizabeth's 1988 Australia visit, LE 500 ....**$10.00**

Postcard, George V in uniform w/Queen Mary, colorful, marked Tuck **$20.00**

Postcard, George VI w/teenage Elizabeth in garden...**$10.00**

Postcard, Princess Diana, Tears That Tell the Truth, marked LE **$5.00**

Postcard, Victoria's 1901 memorial **$25.00**

Puzzle, 11x14", Charles & Diana's wedding, collage of tins .**$25.00**

Puzzle, 6", Diana's 30th birthday **$10.00**

Scarf, Charles & Diana's 1981 wedding, silhouettes printed on silk..**$40.00**

Spoon, Charles & Diana's 1981 wedding, color portrait on silverplate **$25.00**

Spoon, Prince Henry's 1984 birth celebration, relief design on silverplate...**$15.00**

Spoon, Princess Beatrice's birth celebration, relief design on silverplate...**$15.00**

Spoon, Victoria, 1883 Canadian coin in bowl, twist design in handle...**$75.00**

Statue, Elizabeth II on horse, lead on wood plinth.....**$40.00**

Tankard, Charles & Diana's 1981 wedding, multicolor graphics on clear glass...**$25.00**

Teapot, 2-cup, Queen Mother's 90th birthday, w/color portrait...**$50.00**

Teapot, 4-cup, Edward VII's 1901 coronation, color portrait & design **$295.00**

Thimble, Charles & Diana w/William & baby Henry, color portraits on china...**$10.00**

Thimble, Queen Mother's 90th birthday, enameled stanhope...**$30.00**

Tin, Charles & Diana's 1981 wedding, color portraits on royal blue octagon form.....................................**$35.00**

Tin, George VI's coronation, George, Elizabeth & 2 princesses in sepia portraits on lid **$45.00**

Tin, Princess Elizabeth...Trooping the Colours, Huntley & Palmer...**$75.00**

Tin, Queen Mother's 90th birthday, color portrait, Walkers **$35.00**

Tin, 6" long, St Lawrence Seaway Opening, map on bottom, Harner & Co $45.00

Toby mug, Diana, hand-painted portrait, Kevin Francis, marked LE **$250.00**

Toby mug, 2¾", George VI, creamware, miniature **$50.00**

Tray, 12" dia, Victoria, embossed portrait & design on brass, 1887 ....**$175.00**

Tray, 16x12", Elizabeth's coronation, color portrait & royal residences...**$50.00**

Bubble Bath Containers

By now you're probably past the state of being incredulous at the sight of these plastic figurals on flea market tables with price tags twenty time higher than they carried when new and full. There's no hotter area of collecting today than items from the fifties through the seventies that are reminiscent of early kids TV shows and hit movies. Most of these were made in the 1960s. The Colgate-Palmolive Company produced the majority of them – they're the ones marked 'Soaky' – and these seem to be the most collectible.

Other companies followed suit; Purex also made a line, so did Avon.

The prices below are for bottles in excellent to near-mint condition. Be sure to check for paint loss, and look carefully for cracks in the brittle plastic heads of the Soakies.

Alvin, Colgate-Palmolive, marked Soaky, 1963, M **$28.00**
Augie Doggie, 10", marked Purex, EX..........................**$38.00**
Bozo the Clown, 9½", blue & white w/Bozo on each arm, Colgate-Palmolive, early 1960s, VG **$20.00**
Broom Hilda, marked Colgate-Palmolive, EX.............**$17.50**
Brutus, marked Colgate-Palmolive, NM......................**$25.00**
Bugs Bunny, marked Colgate-Palmolive, EX..............**$18.00**
Cinderella, w/moveable arms, Soaky, M.....................**$28.00**
Creature from the Black Lagoon, 10", metallic green plastic w/painted details, marked Soaky, ca 1960s, NM ..**$92.50**

Deputy Dawg, 8½", marked Colgate-Palmolive, EX.$18.00
Dick Tracy, 10", painted hard plastic, marked Colgate-Palmolive w/1965 copyright, M **$37.50**
Dopey, painted hard plastic, marked Colgate-Palmolive, 1960s, EX..**$15.00**
Felix the Cat, 9½", hard plastic, marked Colgate-Palmolive, EX..**$27.50**
Frankenstein, 10", marked Colgate-Palmolive, ca 1950s, NM, NM **$100.00**
Goofy, marked Soaky, EX...**$18.00**
Hulk Hogan...**$10.00**
Jiminy Cricket, marked Soaky, M..............................**$28.00**
Lippy the Lion, marked Purex, NM............................**$25.00**
Little Orphan Annie, marked Soaky, M **$32.00**
Mickey Mouse, marked Avon.....................................**$25.00**
Mickey the Bandleader, 9½", silver on red w/flesh-colored face, marked Soaky, 1960s, EX **$20.00**
Mouseketter, girl w/Mickey Mouse-ears hat, marked Colgate-Palmolive, VG **$15.00**
Mr Jinks w/Pixie & Dixie, 10", Purex, 1962, NM.........**$22.00**
Mr Magoo, 11", Colgate-Palmolive, marked Soaky, M.**$30.00**

Pinocchio, painted hard plastic, marked Colgate-Palmolive, EX..**$18.00**
Pluto, marked Soaky, M **$20.00**
Porky Pig, 9", marked Soaky, 1960s, M.....................**$25.00**
Rocky the Flying Squirrel, Colgate-Palmolive, marked Soaky, M **$30.00**
Smokey Bear, marked Lander Co, 1970s, EX.............**$20.00**

Smokey Bear, 8½", 'Smokey' on Ranger hat, marked Colgate-Palmolive, ca 1960s, EX $20.00
Snow White, marked Soaky, M..................................**$22.00**
Superman, marked Avon, 1978, MIB..........................**$30.00**
Top Cat, Colgate-Palmolive, marked Soaky, 1960s, NM **$22.50**
Top Cat, Colgate-Palmolive, marked Soaky, 1960s, VG.**$10.00**
Touche Turtle, 5x6x10", soft vinyl, marked Purex, ca 1960s, EX..**$40.00**
Wendy, 10", marked Soaky, VG................................**$20.00**
Wolfman, marked Colgate-Palmolive, 1963, EX..........**$60.00**
Woodsy Owl, marked Lander Co, NM **$30.00**
Woody Woodpecker, marked Colgate-Palmolive, M...**$22.00**

Butter Pats

Tiny plates made to hold individual pats of butter were popular in Victorian times; as late as the 1970s, some were still being used by hotels, railroads, and steamship lines. They're becoming a popular item of collector interest because they are so diversified (you'll find them in china, silverplate, pewter, and glass), their small size makes them easy to display, and right now, at least, their prices are relatively low.

The new collector might choose to concentrate on pats made of a particular material or those from only one manufacturer or country. Don't confuse them with children's toy dishes, coasters, or small plates intended for other uses; and don't buy them if they're at all damaged.

Blue Willow, Booths...$25.00
Blue Willow, Buffalo Pottery.................................$18.00
Bluebird, Buffalo Pottery.....................................$12.50
Commercial type, Astor Hotel, 3½", top mark, logo, vitrified china $7.50
Commercial type, B&O, Centenary, Shenango $32.00
Commercial type, B&O Railroad, Capitol, no back stamp..$95.00
Commercial type, Pennsylvania Railroad, Purple Laurel, bottom stamped..$48.00
Commercial type, San Diego Hotel, 3¼", logo, top mark, vitrified china...$7.50
Commercial type, Union Pacific, Streamliner..............$25.00
Commercial type, Waldorf, 3¼", ironstone, Meakin $2.50
Cut glass, Cypress pattern $32.50
Early American pattern glass, Daisy & Button, crystal...$7.50
Flow Blue, Aldine, Grindley....................................$12.50
Flow Blue, Scinde, Alcock......................................$25.00
Haviland, Ranson...$15.00
Haviland, wild flowers, 2½", scalloped rim................$12.00
Heisey, Ipswich, Sahara, square..............................$19.00
Heisy, Narrow Flute, 3", pink.................................$15.00
Ironstone, square, plain..$3.50
Ironstone, 2½" square, brown scenic transfer.............$10.00
Majolica, pansy shape..$45.00
Nippon, leaf & stem border, M-in-wreath mark............$7.50
Pewter, 3", plain, beaded edge $6.00
Rosenthal, 3⅝", Carmen, hand-painted forget-me-nots .$7.50
Shelley, Archway of Roses $45.00
Shelley, Rosebud, 6 flutes......................................$55.00
Shelley, 2¾", Dainty Blue......................................$40.00
Shelley, 2¾", Maytime...$39.00
Silverplate, beaded edge..$8.00
Sterling, plain w/rolled edge...................................$14.50
Sterling, 3½", embossed rose border, monogram center, Gorham...$22.50
Tea Leaf Ironstone, Wilkinson $12.00
Tea Leaf Ironstone, 2¾" square, Meakin $14.00

Camark Pottery

You may occasionally find a piece of pottery marked 'Camark,' though it's fairly scarce. This was an Arkansas company based in the city of Camden, from whence came its name – 'Cam' from the city, 'ark' from the state. They operated from the mid-twenties until they closed in the early 1960s, mainly producing commercial wares such as figurines, vases, and novelty items, though artware was attempted for the first few years they were in existence. This early artware, marked 'Lessell' (for John Lessell, the decorator) or 'Le-Camark' is very similar to lines by Weller and Owens, and when a piece comes up for sale, it is usually tagged at somewhere between $300.00 to $500.00, depending on its size and decoration.

Basket, 5x3", embossed florals on cream....................$13.50

Bowl, centerpiece; w/figural bird flower flog $22.50
Candle holder, triple; molded as a leaf, white glaze ...$12.50
Ewer, 16", irises, hand painted in pink, white, red & green $37.50
Figurine, 8", cat beside fish bowl, white gloss............$30.00
Pitcher, 6½", w/parrot handle, blue gloss $65.00
Salt & pepper shakers, steamships, red, white & blue ..$30.00
Salt & pepper shakers, the salt shaped as the letter S, the pepper as P $12.50
Sign, 6½", shaped as the state of Arkansas $55.00
Teapot, 8", bulbous w/deep swirls, matching warmer..$22.50
Vase, 8", fish form w/orange & brown mottle $45.00
Vase, 8", 3 joined cylinders, Deco styling $25.00
Wall pocket, 8", flour scoop, pink...........................$12.00

Cambridge Glassware

If you're looking for a 'safe' place to put your investment dollars, Cambridge glass is one of your better options. But as with any commodity, in order to make a good investment, knowledge of the product and its market is required. There are two books we would recommend for your study, *Colors in Cambridge Glass,* put out by the National Cambridge Collectors Club, and *The Collector's Encyclopedia of Elegant Glass* by Gene Florence.

The Cambridge Glass Company (located in Cambridge, Ohio) made fine quality glassware from just after the turn of the century until 1958. They made thousands of different items in hundreds of various patterns and colors. Values hinge on rarity of shape and color. Of the various marks they used, the 'C in triangle' is the most common. In addition to their tableware, they also produced flower frogs representing ladies and children and models of animals and birds that are very valuable today. To learn more about them, you'll want to read *Glass Animals and Figural Flower Frogs from the Depression Era* by Lee Garmon and Dick Spencer.

See also Glass Animals.

Apple Blossom, amber, compote, 7" $45.00
Apple Blossom, amber, plate, dinner; square..............$65.00
Apple Blossom, amber, tumbler, 10-oz, #3130, footed .$25.00
Apple Blossom, blue, bowl, cream soup; w/liner plate $45.00
Apple Blossom, blue, cup $35.00
Apple Blossom, blue, stem, water; 8-oz, #3135 ....$42.00

Apple Blossom, clear, bowl, finger; #3025, footed, w/plate liner..$20.00

Apple Blossom, clear, cheese compote & 11½" plate for crackers...$40.00

Apple Blossom, clear, pitcher, 64-oz, #3025.............$110.00

Apple Blossom, clear, plate, sandwich; 11½", w/tab handles...$22.00

Apple Blossom, clear, platter, 13½" rectangular, w/tab handles...$40.00

Apple Blossom, clear, salt & pepper shakers, pr.........$37.50

Apple Blossom, clear, sugar, tall, footed...................$11.00

Apple Blossom, green, creamer, tall, footed...............$25.00

Apple Blossom, green, plate, grill; 10".......................$50.00

Apple Blossom, green, tumbler, 9-oz, #3400, footed ..$27.50

Apple Blossom, pink, bowl, 10", 2-handled................$75.00

Apple Blossom, pink, plate, 6" square, 2-handled.......$10.00

Apple Blossom, pink, tumbler, 4-oz, #3025 ....$19.00

Apple Blossom, pink, vase, 5" $45.00

Apple Blossom, yellow, bowl, bonbon; 5½", w/2 handles...$25.00

Apple Blossom, yellow, pitcher, 80-oz, ball shape....$135.00

Apple Blossom, yellow, stem, low sherbet; 6-oz, #3130.$15.00

Apple Blossom, yellow, tumbler, 10-oz, #3135, footed..$25.00

Candlelight, clear, bowl, 11½", #3900/28, footed, w/2 handles...$65.00

Candlelight, clear, candle holder, 6", #3900/72, 2-light.$37.50

Candlelight, clear, compote, 5½", #3900/136 ....$50.00

Candlelight, clear, creamer, #3900/41........................$20.00

Candlelight, clear, cup, #3900/17................................$27.50

Candlelight, clear, hurricane lamp, #1603, keyhole, w/bobeche $150.00

Candlelight, clear, mayonnaise, #3900/19, 2-piece $47.50

Candlelight, clear, plate, dinner; 10½", #3900/24.........$65.00

Candlelight, clear, plate, 14", #3900/166, rolled edge .$60.00

Candlelight, clear, plate, 8", #3900/131, 2-handled......$25.00

Candlelight, clear, relish, 7", #3900/123, 2-handled.....$32.50

Candlelight, clear, salt & pepper shakers, #3900/1177, pr...$45.00

Candlelight, clear, saucer, #3900/17 ....$5.00

Candlelight, clear, stem, claret; 4½-oz, #3776 ....$32.50

Candlelight, clear, stem, low sherbet; 7-oz, #3111.......$17.50

Candlelight, clear, stem, tall sherbet; 7-oz, #3776........$20.00

Candlelight, clear, stem, water; 9-oz, #3776................$30.00

Candlelight, clear, stem, wine; 2½-oz, #3776..............$30.00

Candlelight, clear, sugar bowl, #3900/41 ....$17.50

Candlelight, clear, tumbler, iced tea; 12-oz, #3776......$22.50

Candlelight, clear, tumbler, juice; 5-oz, #3111, footed ..$20.00

Candlelight, clear, vase, bud; 10", #274.....................$42.50

Candlelight, clear, vase, 6", #6004, footed..................$35.00

Caprice, blue, bowl, 8", #49, 4-footed $60.00

Caprice, blue, candlestick, 2½", #67 ....$35.00

Caprice, blue, compote, 7", #136.................................$85.00

Caprice, blue, mayonnaise, 6½", #129, 3-piece set....$100.00

Caprice, blue, plate, cabaret; 14", #33, 4-footed $80.00

Caprice, blue, stem, low sherbet; 5-oz, #4 ....$85.00

Caprice, blue, stem, wine; 2½-oz, #300, blown $60.00

Caprice, blue, tumbler, 5-oz, #180..............................$45.00

Caprice, blue, vase, 3½", #249 ....$130.00

Caprice, clear, ashtray, 2¾", #213, shell shape, footed..$6.00

Caprice, clear, bonbon, 6" square, #154, 2-handled $12.00

Caprice, clear, bowl, jelly; 5", #151, 2-handled............$15.00

Caprice, clear, bowl, 10" square, #58, 4-footed $30.00

Caprice, clear, cake plate, 13", #36, footed...............$150.00

Caprice, clear, candy dish, 6", #165, 3-footed, w/lid...$42.50

Caprice, clear, creamer, lg, #41.................................$10.00

Caprice, clear, cruet, oil; 5-oz, #100, w/stopper..........$65.00

Caprice, clear, cup, #17 ....$13.00

Caprice, clear, mayonnaise, 8", #106, 3-piece set........$40.00

Caprice, clear, pitcher, 80-oz, #183, ball shape...........$90.00

Caprice, clear, plate, bread & butter; 6½", #21 ....$10.00

Caprice, clear, plate, dinner; 9½", #24.......................$40.00

Caprice, clear, salt & pepper shakers, individual; #90, ball shape, pr...$30.00

Caprice, clear, saucer, #17...$2.50

Caprice, clear, stem, cocktail; 3½-oz, #3 ....$24.00

Caprice, clear, stem, parfait; 5-oz, #300, blown...........$75.00

Caprice, clear, sugar bowl, lg, #41..............................$10.00

Caprice, clear, tumbler, tea; 12-oz, #301, blown..........$17.00

Caprice, clear, tumbler, 3-oz, #12, footed $20.00

Caprice, clear, vase, 3½", #249..................................$45.00

Caprice, clear, vase, 6½", #338, crimped....................$90.00

Caprice, pink, bowl, 13", #66, crimped, 4-footed $75.00

Caprice, pink, coaster, 3½", #13.................................$25.00

Caprice, pink, cup, #17...$32.00

Caprice, pink, plate, salad; 7½", #23...........................$22.00

Caprice, pink, saucer, #17 ....$5.50

Caprice, pink, stem, water; 9-oz, #300, blown............$37.50

Caprice, pink, sugar bowl, med, #38...........................$15.00

Caprice, pink, tumbler, 12-oz, #9, footed....................$45.00

Caprice, pink, vase, 4½", #344, crimped $165.00

Chantilly, clear, bowl, bonbon; 7", 2-handled, footed.$16.00

Chantilly, clear, bowl, 12", 4-footed, flared...............$32.50

Chantilly, clear, candlestick, 5" $17.50

Chantilly, clear, candy box, round, w/lid....................$55.00

Chantilly, clear, creamer, individual; #3900, scalloped..$12.50

Chantilly, clear, cup...$17.50

Chantilly, clear, marmalade, w/lid..............................$55.00

Chantilly, clear, mustard, w/lid...................................$45.00

Chantilly, clear, pitcher, ball shape $120.00

Chantilly, clear, plate, dinner; 10½".............................$55.00

Chantilly, clear, plate, salad; 8".................................$12.50

Chantilly, clear, plate, service; 12", 4-footed $30.00

Chantilly, clear, salt & pepper shakers, footed, pr.......$30.00

Chantilly, clear, saucer..$2.50

Chantilly, clear, stem, claret; 4½-oz, #3625...............$35.00

Chantilly, clear, stem, cocktail; 2½-oz, #3600.............$24.00

Chantilly, clear, stem, cordial; 1-oz, #3625.................$50.00

Chantilly, clear, stem, low oyster cocktail; 4½-oz, #3600..$15.00

Chantilly, clear, stem, tall sherbet; 6-oz, #3779...........$17.50

Chantilly, clear, stem, water; 10-oz, #3625.................$25.00

Chantilly, clear, stem, wine; 2½-oz, #3775 ....$30.00

Chantilly, clear, sugar bowl.......................................$13.50

Chantilly, clear, sugar bowl, individual; #3900, scalloped edge $11.00

Chantilly, clear, tumbler, juice; 5-oz, #3600, footed.....$15.00

Chantilly, clear, tumbler, tea; 12-oz, #3625, footed $22.00

Chantilly, clear, tumbler, water; 10-oz, #3775, footed .**$15.00**
Chantilly, clear, tumbler, 13-oz **$22.00**
Chantilly, clear, vase, bud; 10" **$30.00**
Cleo, amber, candlestick, 2-light **$35.00**
Cleo, amber, pitcher, 62-oz, #955, w/lid **$225.00**
Cleo, amber, sugar bowl, footed **$20.00**
Cleo, amber, tray, serving; 12", handled **$150.00**
Cleo, amber, vase, 9½" **$100.00**
Cleo, blue, basket, 11", Decagon shape, upturned sides, 2-handled **$50.00**
Cleo, blue, bowl, cranberry; 6½" **$37.50**
Cleo, blue, bowl, 11", oval **$75.00**
Cleo, blue, ice pail **$95.00**
Cleo, blue, plate, 11", Decagon shape, 2-handled **$110.00**
Cleo, blue, stem, cordial; 1-oz, #3077 ....**$150.00**
Cleo, blue, tumbler, 12-oz, #3022, footed **$65.00**
Cleo, green, bowl, miniature console; 8" **$125.00**
Cleo, green, decanter, w/stopper **$225.00**
Cleo, green, stem, wine; 3½-oz, #3077 ....**$60.00**
Cleo, green, tumbler, 5-oz, #3115, footed **$25.00**
Cleo, pink, bowl, fruit; 5½" **$15.00**
Cleo, pink, creamer, 6", ewer style **$75.00**
Cleo, pink, plate, 11", Decagon shape, 2-handled **$30.00**
Cleo, pink, tray, for sugar & creamer, oval **$50.00**
Cleo, yellow, bowl, vegetable; 9", w/lid **$125.00**
Cleo, yellow, mayonnaise, Decagon shape, w/liner & ladle **$45.00**
Cleo, yellow, stem, fruit; 6-oz, #3115 ....**$15.00**
Cleo, yellow, tumbler, 12-oz **$35.00**
Crown Tuscan, bowl, 12", #3400/4, 4-footed, Charleton decoration **$125.00**
Crown Tuscan, candelabrum, #1307, 3-light, gold trim, Crown Tuscan signature **$100.00**
Crown Tuscan, decanter, 40-oz, Nautilus, #3450 ....**$300.00**
Crown Tuscan, Doulton jug, 76-oz, #2400/152 ....**$750.00**
Crown Tuscan, epergne vase, #2355 ....**$75.00**
Crown Tuscan, ice bucket, Cascade, #4000/671 ....**$350.00**
Crown Tuscan, novelty basket, 4", #1506/1 ....**$65.00**
Crown Tuscan, vase, 12", embossed tulips, paper label, #1253 ....**$250.00**
Crown Tuscan, vase, 7½", Everglade, #21 ....**$165.00**
Decagon, cobalt blue, bowl, bonbon; 5½", 2-handled ..**$17.00**
Decagon, cobalt blue, creamer, footed **$20.00**
Decagon, cobalt blue, cup **$10.00**
Decagon, cobalt blue, plate, dinner; 9½" **$30.00**
Decagon, cobalt blue, stem, cordial; 1-oz **$60.00**
Decagon, cobalt blue, tray, service; 11", oval **$15.00**
Decagon, green, bowl, cereal; 6", flat rim **$10.00**
Decagon, green, creamer, footed **$9.00**
Decagon, green, cup **$6.00**
Decagon, green, plate, 7", 2-handled **$9.00**
Decagon, green, saucer **$1.00**
Decagon, green, stem, low sherbet; 6-oz **$9.00**
Decagon, green, tray, flat pickle; 8", 2-handled **$10.00**
Decagon, green, tumbler, 8-oz, footed **$12.00**
Decagon, pink, bowl, berry; 10" **$12.00**
Decagon, pink, bowl, individual almond; 2½" **$17.50**
Decagon, pink, creamer, tall, lg foot **$10.00**

Decagon, pink, mayonnaise, 2-handled, w/2-handled liner & ladle **$25.00**
Decagon, pink, plate, grill; 10" **$8.00**
Decagon, pink, stem, cocktail; 3½-oz **$12.00**
Decagon, pink, sugar bowl, lightning bolt handles **$7.00**
Decagon, pink, tumbler, 10-oz, footed **$15.00**
Decagon, pink, tumbler, 2½-oz, footed **$12.00**
Decagon, red, bowl, berry; 10" **$20.00**
Decagon, red, bowl, cream soup; w/liner **$22.00**
Decagon, red, creamer, lightning bolt handles **$12.00**
Decagon, red, plate, 7", 2-handled **$15.00**
Decagon, red, saucer **$2.50**
Decagon, red, stem, water; 9-oz **$30.00**
Decagon, red, tumbler, 12-oz, footed **$35.00**
Diane, clear, bowl, berry; 5" **$20.00**
Diane, clear, bowl, bonbon; 6", 2-handled, footed **$17.00**
Diane, clear, bowl, 12", flared, 4-footed **$40.00**
Diane, clear, butter dish, round **$115.00**
Diane, clear, candlestick, 6", 3-light **$35.00**
Diane, clear, cup **$20.00**
Diane, clear, pitcher, ball shape **$125.00**
Diane, clear, plate, salad; 8" **$10.00**
Diane, clear, plate, 13½", 2-handled **$30.00**
Diane, clear, saucer **$5.00**
Diane, clear, stem, cocktail; 3-oz, #3122 ....**$14.00**
Diane, clear, stem, cordial; 1-oz, #1066 ....**$55.00**
Diane, clear, stem, low sherbet; 7-oz, #3122 ....**$11.00**
Diane, clear, stem, water; 11-oz, #1066 ....**$20.00**
Diane, clear, stem, wine; 3-oz, #1066 ....**$25.00**
Diane, clear, tumbler, iced tea; 12-oz, #3135, footed ..**$25.00**
Diane, clear, tumbler, juice; 5-oz, #3106, footed **$13.00**
Diane, clear, tumbler, 8-oz, footed **$22.00**
Diane, clear, vase, 9", keyhole base **$45.00**
Elaine, clear, bowl, relish; 6½", 3-part **$15.00**
Elaine, clear, bowl, 11½", tab handled, footed **$30.00**

Elaine, clear, bowl, 15", gold encrusted $125.00
Elaine, clear, candy box, round, w/lid **$70.00**
Elaine, clear, compote, 5⅜", blown **$40.00**
Elaine, clear, creamer **$11.00**
Elaine, clear, oil cruet, 6-oz, handled, w/stopper **$60.00**
Elaine, clear, plate, 8", 2-handled, footed **$15.00**
Elaine, clear, salt & pepper shakers, footed, pr **$30.00**
Elaine, clear, stem, claret; 4½-oz, #3104 ....**$65.00**
Elaine, clear, stem, cordial; 1-oz, #3121 ....**$55.00**
Elaine, clear, stem, low sherbet; 6-oz, #3121 ....**$15.00**
Elaine, clear, stem, oyster cocktail; 4½-oz, #3500 ......**$14.00**
Elaine, clear, stem, water; 10-oz, #3121 ....**$21.00**

Elaine, clear, stem, wine; 3-oz, #1402............................**$25.00**
Elaine, clear, tumbler, water; 9-oz, #1402, footed........**$17.00**
Elaine, clear, vase, 6", footed **$30.00**
Flower frog, amber, 8½", lady w/roses on round base.**$165.00**
Flower frog, amber, 8½", draped lady on round base .**$160.00**
Flower frog, Crown Tuscan, 3" dia, #2899 ....**$50.00**
Flower frog, Gold Krystol, 3" dia, #2899 ....**$20.00**
Flower frog, light emerald, 4" dia, #2899 ....**$19.00**
Flower frog, peachblow, 2¼" dia, #2899 ....**$13.00**
Flower frog, peachblow, 5½", eagle on round base..**$185.00**
Gloria, clear, bowl, fruit; 11", 2-handled **$30.00**
Gloria, clear, bowl, relish; 8", 2-part, 2-handled **$15.00**
Gloria, clear, compote, 6", 4-footed............................**$19.00**
Gloria, clear, cup, round or square **$15.00**
Gloria, clear, cup, square, 4-footed **$25.00**
Gloria, clear, finger bowl..**$15.00**
Gloria, clear, mayonnaise, 4-footed, w/liner & ladle.**$35.00**
Gloria, clear, pitcher, 80-oz, ball shape......................**$135.00**
Gloria, clear, plate, chop or salad; 14" **$40.00**
Gloria, clear, plate, dinner; 9½" **$50.00**
Gloria, clear, salt & pepper shakers, tall, w/glass tops, pr.**$27.50**
Gloria, clear, stem, claret; 4½-oz, #3035 ....**$25.00**
Gloria, clear, stem, low sherbet; 6-oz, #3120 ....**$10.00**
Gloria, clear, syrup, tall, footed **$50.00**
Gloria, clear, tray, pickle; 9", tab handled..................**$15.00**
Gloria, clear, tumbler, juice; 5-oz, #3115, footed........**$12.00**
Gloria, clear, vase, 12", keyhole base, flared rim........**$50.00**
Gloria, green, bowl, salad; 9", tab handled..................**$55.00**
Gloria, green, creamer, tall, footed **$20.00**
Gloria, green, plate, 6", 2-handled **$13.50**
Gloria, green, stem, tall sherbet; 6-oz, #3130 ....**$11.00**
Gloria, green, stem, wine; 2½-oz, #3035 ....**$40.00**
Gloria, green, vase, 12", keyhole base, flared rim **$110.00**
Gloria, pink, bowl, 13", flared rim **$55.00**
Gloria, pink, cup, round or square **$25.00**
Gloria, pink, plate, 8½"...**$14.00**
Gloria, pink, stem, water; 9-oz, #3035......................**$30.00**
Gloria, pink, tumbler, 12-oz, #3115, footed **$30.00**
Gloria, yellow, compote, fruit cocktail; 4"..................**$20.00**
Gloria, yellow, cup, square, 4-footed **$60.00**
Gloria, yellow, plate, dinner; 9½" **$70.00**
Gloria, yellow, stem, goblet; 9-oz, #3115 ....**$26.00**
Gloria, yellow, tumbler, juice; 5-oz, #3135..................**$20.00**
Imperial Hunt Scene, amber, creamer, footed **$30.00**
Imperial Hunt Scene, amber, sugar bowl, footed........**$30.00**
Imperial Hunt Scene, clear, bowl, cereal; 6".............**$15.00**
Imperial Hunt Scene, clear, candlestick, 2-light, keyhole,
    each **$17.50**
Imperial Hunt Scene, clear, cup................................**$45.00**
Imperial Hunt Scene, clear, mayonnaise, w/liner........**$30.00**
Imperial Hunt Scene, clear, plate, 8" **$12.00**
Imperial Hunt Scene, clear, saucer **$10.00**
Imperial Hunt Scene, clear, stem, cocktail; 3-oz..........**$40.00**
Imperial Hunt Scene, clear, stem, 14-oz, #1402.........**$50.00**
Imperial Hunt Scene, clear, sugar bowl, footed..........**$15.00**
Imperial Hunt Scene, clear, tumbler, 10-oz, #1402.....**$23.00**
Imperial Hunt Scene, green, bowl, cereal; 6"..............**$25.00**
Imperial Hunt Scene, green, plate, 8"..........................**$22.00**

Imperial Hunt Scene, green, tumbler, 8-oz, footed **$25.00**
Imperial Hunt Scene, pink, candlestick, 3-light, keyhole.**$55.00**
Imperial Hunt Scene, pink, stem, sherbet; 6-oz, #3085.**$27.50**
Mr Vernon, amber, candlestick, 5", #110, 2-light **$20.00**
Mt Vernon, amber, bowl, 11", #136, oval, 4-footed.....**$27.50**
Mt Vernon, amber, box, 3" dia, #16, w/lid **$25.00**
Mt Vernon, amber, cigarette holder, #66.....................**$15.00**
Mt Vernon, amber, compote, 8", #81..........................**$25.00**
Mt Vernon, amber, creamer, #86 ....**$10.00**
Mt Vernon, amber, finger bowl, #23...........................**$10.00**
Mt Vernon, amber, pitcher, 50-oz, #90.......................**$75.00**
Mt Vernon, amber, relish, 8", #101, 2-part, handled....**$17.50**
Mt Vernon, amber, stem, low sherbet; 4½-oz, #42 ....**$7.50**
Mt Vernon, amber, stem, wine; 3-oz, #27 ....**$13.50**
Mt Vernon, amber, tumbler, cordial; 1-oz, footed **$22.00**
Mt Vernon, amber, tumbler, old-fashioned; 7-oz, #57.**$15.00**
Mt Vernon, amber, vase, 10", #46, footed **$50.00**
Mt Vernon, amber, vase, 5", #42................................**$15.00**
Mt Vernon, clear, bowl, 12", #118, oblong, crimped...**$32.50**
Mt Vernon, clear, butter tub, #73, w/lid **$60.00**
Mt Vernon, clear, candy dish, 1-lb, footed, w/lid........**$50.00**
Mt Vernon, clear, cocktail icer, #85, 2-piece **$22.50**
Mt Vernon, clear, creamer, #8, footed **$10.00**
Mt Vernon, clear, cup, #7 ....**$6.50**
Mt Vernon, clear, plate, dinner; 10½", #40 ....**$27.50**
Mt Vernon, clear, rose bowl, 6½", #106......................**$18.00**
Mt Vernon, clear, saucer, #7......................................**$7.50**
Mt Vernon, clear, stem, oyster cocktail; 4-oz, #41 ....**$9.00**
Mt Vernon, clear, stem, water; 10-oz, #1....................**$15.00**
Mt Vernon, clear, tumbler, juice; 3-oz, #22, footed........**$9.00**
Mt Vernon, clear, tumbler, water; 10-oz, #3, footed....**$15.00**
Mt Vernon, clear, vase, 6", #50, footed......................**$25.00**
Nude stem, ashtray, Royal Blue w/clear stem **$190.00**
Nude stem, brandy, 1-oz, amber w/frosted clear stem.**$125.00**
Nude stem, candlestick, 9", Windsor Blue **$300.00**
Nude stem, claret, 4½-oz, #7, Royal Blue w/clear stem.**$125.00**
Nude stem, cocktail, 3-oz, Mandarin Gold w/clear
    stem..**$75.00**
Nude stem, cocktail, 3-oz, Tahoe Blue w/clear stem..**$145.00**
Nude stem, cocktail, 3-oz, #9, ebony bowl & foot, w/clear
    stem..**$350.00**
Nude stem, ivy ball, #25, Carmen bowl w/clear stem.**$175.00**
Nude stem, mint dish, 4", amber shell, clear stem **$300.00**
Nude stem, saucer champagne, #3, pink w/clear stem.**$200.00**
Portia, clear, bowl, bonbon; 6", 2-handled, footed......**$16.00**
Portia, clear, bowl, cranberry; 3½" square...................**$20.00**
Portia, clear, bowl, relish; 7", 2-part **$16.00**
Portia, clear, bowl, 10", flared, 4-footed......................**$35.00**
Portia, clear, cake plate, 13½", 2-handled **$35.00**
Portia, clear, cup, square, footed **$18.00**
Portia, clear, pitcher, ball shape **$125.00**
Portia, clear, plate, salad; 8" **$12.50**
Portia, clear, salt & pepper shakers, pr **$25.00**
Portia, clear, saucer, square or round..........................**$3.00**
Portia, clear, stem, brandy; 1-oz, #3121, low footed ...**$40.00**
Portia, clear, stem, claret; 4½-oz, #3126 ....**$35.00**
Portia, clear, stem, cocktail; 3-oz, #3124 ....**$15.00**
Portia, clear, stem, cordial; 1-oz, #3130......................**$55.00**

Portia, clear, stem, goblet; 9-oz, #3126.........................$20.00
Portia, clear, stem, parfait; 5-oz, #3121.......................$35.00
Portia, clear, stem, tall sherbet; 7-oz, #3124...............$15.00
Portia, clear, tray, celery; 11".....................................$27.50
Portia, clear, tumbler, juice; 5-oz, #3130....................$16.00
Portia, clear, tumbler, tea; 12-oz, #3130 ....$22.00
Portia, clear, tumbler, water; 10-oz, #3126 ....$15.00
Portia, clear, vase, 11", pedestal foot..........................$55.00
Rosalie, amber, bowl, bonbon; 6½", 2-handled...........$15.00
Rosalie, amber, bowl, console; 15", oval.....................$60.00
Rosalie, amber, compote, 5½", 2-handled....................$15.00
Rosalie, amber, creamer, tall, ewer shape, footed.......$20.00
Rosalie, amber, cup..$25.00
Rosalie, amber, finger bowl, footed, w/liner $30.00
Rosalie, amber, ice tube $50.00
Rosalie, amber, plate, bread & butter; 6¾"...................$5.00
Rosalie, amber, plate, dinner; 9½" $30.00
Rosalie, amber, platter, 15"...$65.00
Rosalie, amber, saucer...$4.00
Rosalie, amber, stem, high sherbet; 6-oz, #3077.........$14.00
Rosalie, amber, tumbler, 8-oz, #3077, footed.............$16.00
Rosalie, amber, vase, 6½", footed $45.00
Rosalie, blue, creamer, tall, ewer shape, footed..........$30.00
Rosalie, blue, relish, 11", 2-part.................................$35.00
Rosalie, blue, tray, 11", center handled $30.00
Rosalie, green, bowl, 12", Decagon shape $95.00
Rosalie, green, cup $35.00
Rosalie, green, plate, salad; 7½".................................$10.00
Rosalie, green, saucer $5.00
Rosalie, green, stem, goblet; 10-oz, #801 ....$30.00
Rosalie, green, tumbler, 10-oz, #3077, footed............$27.00
Rosalie, pink, bowl, cream soup...................................$22.50
Rosalie, pink, candlestick, 5", keyhole $35.00
Rosalie, pink, ice bucket $65.00
Rosalie, pink, plate, dinner; 9½" $55.00
Rosalie, pink, stem, low sherbet; 6-oz, #3077............$15.00
Rosalie, pink, tumbler, 5-oz, #3077, footed................$25.00
Rosalie, pink, vase, 5½", footed $45.00
Rose Point, clear, ashtray, 4", #3500/130, oval...........$80.00
Rose Point, clear, bowl, bonbon; 7", #3900/130, tab han-
   dled, footed $35.00
Rose Point, clear, bowl, cereal; 6", #3500/11 ....$55.00
Rose Point, clear, bowl, nappy; 5½", #3400/56...........$42.50
Rose Point, clear, bowl, 12½", #3400/2, flared, rolled
   edge..$135.00
Rose Point, clear, cake plate, 13½", #3900/35, handles.$70.00
Rose Point, clear, candlestick, 6", 3-light, keyhole $45.00
Rose Point, clear, celery, 12", #3500/652....................$47.50
Rose Point, clear, cigarette box, #615, w/lid.............$120.00
Rose Point, clear, coaster, 3½", #1628 ....$50.00
Rose Point, clear, compote, 6", #3400/13, 4-footed.....$37.50
Rose Point, clear, finger bowl, #3121, w/liner............$75.00
Rose Point, clear, mayonnaise, #3900/111, divided, w/liner
   & 2 ladles...$75.00
Rose Point, clear, pitcher, 76-oz, #3900/115 ....$185.00
Rose Point, clear, plate, salad; 8½", #3500/5................$20.00
Rose Point, clear, relish, 6½", #3500/61, 3-part, w/han-
   dles $37.50

Rose Point, clear, relish, 7", 3-part w/center handle.$125.00
Rose Point, clear, salt & pepper shakers, #1468, egg shape,
   pr...$80.00
Rose Point, clear, stem, parfait; 5-oz, #3500, low foot..$75.00
Rose Point, clear, stem, sherry; 2-oz, #3106................$40.00
Rose Point, clear, stem, water goblet; 10-oz, #3106 ....$35.00
Rose Point, clear, sugar bowl, individual; #3500/15, pie crust
   edge...$22.50
Rose Point, clear, tumbler, iced tea; 12-oz, footed $50.00
Rose Point, clear, tumbler, 8-oz, #498, straight sides...$45.00
Rose Point, clear, tumbler, 9-oz, #3106, footed $25.00
Rose Point, clear, vase, 10", #274, slender $55.00
Rose Point, clear, vase, 9", #1237, keyhole, footed $85.00

Tally Ho, ruby, mug $40.00
Valencia, clear, basket, 6", 2-handled, footed.............$22.00
Valencia, clear, cigarette holder, #1066, footed $38.00
Valencia, clear, cup, #3500/1 ....$17.50
Valencia, clear, plate, sandwich; 11½", #1402, handled.$22.50
Valencia, clear, salt & pepper shakers, #3400/18, pr...$50.00
Valencia, clear, stem, oyster cocktail; 4½-oz, #3500....$15.00
Valencia, clear, sugar bowl, #3500/14 ....$15.00
Valencia, clear, tumbler, 10-oz, #3500, footed $14.00
Wildflower, clear, bowl, 11", #3900/34, 2-handled......$40.00
Wildflower, clear, candlestick, #3400/638, 3-light $35.00
Wildflower, clear, candy box, #3900/165, round, w/lid..$50.00

Wildflower, clear, compote, 5⅜", #3121, blown **$40.00**
Wildflower, clear, cup, #3900/17 or #3400/54 ....**$16.50**
Wildflower, clear, pitcher, 80-oz, #3400/38, ball type.**$125.00**
Wildflower, clear, plate, bread & butter; 6½"................**$7.50**
Wildflower, clear, plate, dinner; 10½", #3900/24.........**$65.00**
Wildflower, clear, stem, wine; 3½-oz, #3121 ....**$30.00**
Wildflower, clear, sugar bowl, #3900/41.....................**$12.50**
Wildflower, clear, tray, for sugar & creamer, #3900/37.**$15.00**
Wildflower, clear, tumbler, iced tea; 12-oz, #3121 ......**$22.00**
Wildflower, clear, vase, bud; 10", #1528 ....**$30.00**

Cameras

To make good investments when buying cameras, several criteria are involved. Those that hold their values best and have a better resale potential are usually the more unusual, more obscure models in fine condition. Most camera buffs build their collections around either a particular type of camera (those with the same sort of shutter, for instance), or they might limit their buying to cameras made by only one company. But even if you can afford to buy only inexpensive, mass-produced cameras, you'll find it to be a very interesting hobby. You can (many do) add viewers, photography supplies and advertising, projectors, and accessories of all types to round out your collection.

Agfa Ambi Silette, 35mm range finder, interchangeable Coulor Solina lens, Synchro Compur shutter, 1950s, EX **$17.50**
Agfa Isolette V, EX in original leather case **$15.00**
Agfa Silette Rapid I, 35mm view finder, Colour Agnar 45mm lens, Parator shutter, metal case, 1965, NM..........**$15.00**
Agfa Synchro, box style, EX....................................**$5.00**
Agfa-Ansco B-2 Cadet, box style, leather strap worn otherwise EX **$4.00**
Ansco Clipper, VG **$6.00**
Ansco Shur-Flash, EX..**$6.00**
Argus A, 35mm, gold-colored case, ca 1940s, EX........**$22.00**

Bolsey B 35mm w/rangefinder, common..........$125.00
Canonex, leaf shutter fixed lens, 1960s, EX..............**$120.00**
Canonflex R2000, Canomatic lenses, 1960s, M **$145.00**
Foca Standard, 35mm lens, later model w/rewind lever, EX **$95.00**

Graphic 35, 35mm, range finder, Graflex 50mm lens, ca mid-1950s, EX..**$200.00**

Keystone Movie Camera 16mm, oval $30.00
Kodak #3-A, folding pocket type, autographic, Anastigmat lens, ballbearing shutter, original case, EX............**$10.00**
Kodak Autographic Jr #2-C, folding, Anastigmat lens, ballbearing shutter, original case, EX **$18.00**
Kodak Baby Brownie Special, EX.................................**$5.00**
Kodak Brownie 2A Model C, VG **$5.00**
Kodak Bullet, meniscus lens, takes 127 roll film, NM.**$12.50**
Kodak Junior Six-20 Series II, 8.8 lens, #1 Kodex shutter, NM in G box **$24.00**
Kodak Monitor Six-16, Anastigmat Special lens, Supermatic shutter, takes 616 roll film, 1940s, EX...................**$12.00**
Kodak Pocket #1A Series II, folding, fixed focus, Meniscus acromatic lens, original leather & brass case, EX..**$18.00**
Kodak Retina I, Stuttgart type #141, 35mm, view finder, Ektar lens, late 1930s, M.................................**$50.00**
Kodak Signet 50, Ektanar 50mm lens, Synchro 250 shutter, ca mid-50s to 1960, NM...**$35.00**
Kodak Six-20, Anastigmat 100mm lens, takes 620 roll film, EX **$12.00**
Kodak Vest Pocket Series III, takes 127 film, 1930, EX **$35.00**
Kodascope Eight Model 50, 8mm movie projector, 1930s, NM **$15.00**
Konan 16 Automat, 25mm, 1950s, EX **$100.00**
Olympus Ace, 35mm, range finder, interchangeable lenses, NM **$85.00**
Sears Kewpie Kamera, takes 120 roll film, leatherette covered box type, 1920s, EX................................**$10.00**
Tower 35, 35mm, range finder, Nikkor 50mm lens, w/wind lever, 1956, M..**$250.00**
Twinflex, meniscus lens, sector shutter, reflex veiw, uses 00 roll film, M...**$30.00**
Universal Mercury II, 35mm, view finder, metal body, Universal Tricor lens, uses 35mm film, EX................**$55.00**

Voigtlander Bessamatic, 35mm, single lens reflex, built-in light meter, 1959, EX...................................**$75.00**
Yashica 44LM, 60mm lens, knob advance, built-in light meter, takes 127 roll film, ca 1962, EX **$65.00**

Candlewick Glassware

This is a beautifully simple, very diverse line of glassware made by the Imperial Glass Company (a division of Lenox Inc., Bellaire, Ohio) from 1936 until the company closed in 1982. It was named for the tufted needlework done by the Colonial ladies in early America. Rows of small crystal balls surround rims of bowls and plates, foot rings of tumblers, and decorate the handles of pitchers. Some pieces have stems of stacked balls. Though most was made in crystal, a few pieces were made in color as well, while others had a gold wash. Imperial made two etched lines, Floral and Valley Lily, that utilized the Candlewick shapes; both are very scarce.

Among the hardest-to-find items are the desk calendar (made as gifts for company employees and customers), the chip and dip set, and the dresser set containing a cologne bottle, powder jar, clock, and mirror.

There were more than 740 items in all, and collectors often use the company's mold numbers to help identify all those variations and sizes. Gene Florence's *Collector's Encyclopedia of Elegant Glassware* has a chapter that gives this line of glassware very good coverage.

From the 1940s through the sixties, Hazel Atlas produced sherbets, cocktail glasses, wines, and water goblets that are being mistaken for Candlewick, so beware. You'll find these in malls and antique shops, priced and labeled as Candlewick. They were made with a crystal, green, amber, or ruby top on a crystal foot ringed with small glass balls. But the flared part of the foot is ribbed, unlike any Candlewick foot, so you can tell the difference. These are becoming very collectible in their own right, but they're certainly not worth Candlewick prices, and you won't want them in your collection. Gene Florence calls them 'Boopie' and indicates values in the $3.00 to $7.00 range for crystal and in the $7.00 to $17.00 range for colors.

Ashtray, 4", #400/33, round...**$10.00**
Ashtray, 6½", #400/174, heart shape............................**$15.00**
Ashtray set, #400/550, 3-piece nester, clear or colors .**$20.00**
Basket, 6½", #400/40/0, handled **$27.50**
Bell, 4", #400/179...**$75.00**
Bottle, bitters; 4-oz, #400/117.......................................**$55.00**
Bowl, finger; #3400, footed **$25.00**
Bowl, fruit; 6", #400/3F...**$11.00**
Bowl, pickle/celery; 7½", #400/57 ....**$25.00**
Bowl, relish; 6½", #400/84, 2-part................................**$22.00**
Bowl, salad; 10½", 400/75B...**$40.00**
Bowl, sauce; 5½", #400/243, deep...............................**$35.00**
Bowl, 10", #400/13F...**$40.00**
Bowl, 10", #400/75F, cupped edge...............................**$40.00**
Bowl, 12", #400/92B, round **$40.00**

Bowl, 4¾", #400/42B, round, 2-handled **$10.00**
Bowl, 5", 400/49H, heart shape w/handle **$17.50**
Bowl, 7", #400/62B, round, 2-handled **$15.00**
Bowl, 8½", #400/69, round..**$32.50**
Butter dish, 5½", #400/144, w/lid, round **$30.00**

Cake stand, 11", #400/103D....................................$70.00
Candle holder, #400/100, 2-light..................................**$20.00**
Candle holder, 4½", #400/207, 3-toed **$37.50**
Candle holder, 5", #400/40HC, heart shape **$40.00**
Candy box, 5½", #400/59, round **$42.50**
Cigarette box, #400/134, w/lid......................................**$30.00**
Coaster, 4", #400/78 ....**$6.00**
Compote, 4½", #400/63B...**$25.00**
Compote, 5½", #400/66B, low, plain stem **$18.00**
Creamer, #400/18, domed foot **$110.00**
Creamer, #400/31, plain foot..**$9.00**
Cup, after dinner; #400/77...**$17.50**
Cup, punch: #400/211..**$7.50**
Cup, tea; #400/35 ....**$8.00**
Egg cup, #400/19, beaded foot......................................**$45.00**
Hurricane lamp, #400/76, w/candle base & ring handle, 2-piece **$135.00**
Ladle, marmalade; #400/130, 3-bead stem **$10.00**
Mayonnaise set, #400/23, bowl & spoon, 2-piece **$35.00**
Mustard jar, #400/156, w/spoon **$30.00**
Oil, 6-oz, #400/166, beaded base **$65.00**
Party set, #400/98, oval plate w/cup indent, 2-piece ..**$30.00**

Pitcher, water size..$165.00
Pitcher, 20-oz, #400/416, plain.....................................**$40.00**
Plate, bread & butter; 6", #400/1D...............................**$8.00**

Plate, dinner; 10", #400/10D...........................**$35.00**
Plate, luncheon; 9", #400/7D..........................**$12.50**
Plate, torte; 14", #400/17D............................**$40.00**
Plate, 4½", 400/34..**$6.00**
Plate, 6¾", #400/52C, 2-handled, crimped.........**$25.00**
Plate, 7½", #400/52D, 2-handled......................**$10.00**
Plate, 8½", #400/62D, 2-handled......................**$12.00**
Relish & dressing set, 10½" relish w/marmalade, #400/1112,
    4-piece...**$90.00**
Salt & pepper shakers, footed, beaded base, pr.........**$45.00**
Salt dip, 2", #400/61......................................**$9.00**
Salt spoon, 3", #400/616.................................**$9.00**
Saucer, tea or coffee; #400/35 or #400/37.........**$2.50**
Stem, claret; 5-oz, #3400................................**$40.00**
Stem, cocktail; 4-oz, #400/190........................**$18.00**
Stem, cordial; 1-oz, #400/190..........................**$65.00**
Stem, tea; 12-oz, #4000..................................**$20.00**
Stem, water; 9-oz, #3800................................**$25.00**
Stem, wine; 5-oz, #400/190.............................**$22.50**
Sugar bowl, #400/126, flat, beaded handle.........**$27.50**
Sugar bowl, #400/31, plain foot.......................**$6.50**
Tidbit, #400/2701, 2-tier, cupped.....................**$45.00**
Tray, celery; 13½", #400/105, 2-handled, oval.........**$30.00**
Tray, 5½", #400/42E, upturned handles..............**$18.00**
Tray, 6½", #400/29..**$15.00**
Tumbler, cocktail; 3-oz, #400/19, footed.............**$15.00**
Tumbler, juice; 5-oz, #400/18..........................**$35.00**
Tumbler, sherbet; 6-oz, #400/18.......................**$37.00**
Tumbler, tea; 12-oz, #400/18...........................**$40.00**
Tumbler, 5", beaded foot (illustrated on page 76).$18.00
Vase, 6", #400/287C, flat, crimped edge..............**$20.00**
Vase, 6", #400/287F, fan shape.........................**$27.50**
Vase, 7", #400/87R, rolled rim, beaded handle.........**$35.00**

Candy Containers

Most of us can recall buying these glass toys as a child, since they were made well into the 1960s. We were fascinated by the variety of their shapes then, just as collectors are today. Looking back, it couldn't have been we were buying them for the candy, though perhaps as a child those tiny sugary balls flavored more with the coloring agent than anything else were enough to satisfy our 'sweet tooth.'

Glass candy containers have been around since our country's centennial celebration in 1876 when the first two, the Liberty Bell and the Independence Hall, were introduced. Since then they have been made in hundreds of styles, and some of them have become very expensive. The leading manufacturers were in the East – Westmoreland, Victory Glass, J.H. Millstein, Crosetti, L.E. Smith, Jack Stough, T.H. Stough, and West Bros. made perhaps 90% of them – and collectors report finding many of them in the Pennsylvania area. Most of them are clear, but you'll find them in various other colors as well.

If you're going to deal in candy containers, you need a book that will show you all the variations available. The books called *An Album of Glass Candy Containers* (there

are two volumes) by Jennie Long, are excellent references. They use a numbering system that has become universal among collectors. Numbers in our listings refer to Jennie's book. Another good book is *The Compleat American Glass Candy Containers Handbook* by Eikelberner and Agadjainian, recently revised by Adele Bowden.

Because of their popularity and considerable worth, many of the original containers have been reproduced. Beware of any questionable glassware that has a slick or oily touch. Among those that have been produced are: Amber Pistol (#144), Auto (#355 and #377), Carpet Sweeper (#242 and #243), Chicken on Nest (#12), Display Case (#246), Dog (#24), Drum Mug (#255), Fire Engine (#386), Happifats on Drum (#89), Independence Hall (#76), Jackie Coogan (#90), Kewpie (#91), Mail Box (#254), Mantel Clock (#114), Mule and Waterwagon (#38), Peter Rabbit (#55), Piano (#289), Rabbit Pushing Wheelbarrow (#47), Rocking Horse (#58), Safe (#268), Santa (#103), Santa's Boot (#233), Station Wagon (#378), Uncle Sam's Hat (#168). Others are possible.

Our values are given for candy containers that are undamaged, in good original paint, and complete (with all original parts and closure). Repaired or repainted containers are worth much less.

See also Christmas; Easter; Halloween.

Airplane, Passenger, #323.............................**$275.00**
Automobile, rear trunk, G paint, #367.............**$140.00**
Barney Google on Pedestal, #78......................**$220.00**
Basket, flower design, #224............................**$40.00**

Battleship, #377..**$28.00**
Bear on Circus Tub, original blades, #1.............**$350.00**
Bell, Hand; wooden handle, #494......................**$165.00**
Black Cat Sitting, #5.......................................**$770.00**
Bottle, Baby Dear, #64....................................**$10.00**
Bugler or Megaphone, #278..............................**$25.00**
Candelabrum, #202...**$30.00**
Candy Cane, mercury glass, #613......................**$80.00**
Car, Ribbed-Top Sedan, closure, #376................**$25.00**
Chicken on Oblong Basket, closure, green, #10.........**$50.00**
Clock, Alarm; #11, #549..................................**$110.00**
Dog by Barrel, closure, original paint, #13.............**$220.00**
Dog w/Glass Hat, lg, #22.................................**$25.00**
Don't Park Here, #314.....................................**$185.00**
Fire Engine, blue glass, #381...........................**$100.00**
Flatiron, closure, original paint, #249.................**$385.00**
Flossie Fisher Chair, #128................................**$300.00**

Gun, metal, #157 ....$80.00
Horn, Millsteins, #282 ....$20.00
Horn, 3-Valve; w/mouthpiece, #281 ....$175.00
Ice Truck, #458 ....$650.00

Jeep, 4¼" long, Millsteins $20.00
Lantern, barn type #2, #178 ....$75.00
Lantern, brass cap, #184 ....$17.50
Locomotive, screw cap, #411 ....$110.00
Model Cruiser, original closure, #339 ....$22.00
Naked Child w/Derby, #95 ....$45.00
Owl, closure, glass eyes, #37 ....$110.00
Piano, w/paint, #289 ....$225.00
Pumpkin Head Witch, #265 ....$565.00
Rabbit Nibbling Carrot, #53 ....$35.00
Rabbit Running on Log, gold paint, #42 .....$200.00
Racer or Convertible, #433 ....$50.00
Rubber Boot, #234 ....$90.00
Scottie Dog, #17 ....$12.00
Spark Plug, no paint, #109 ....$90.00
Telephone, Stough's #3, #308 ....$40.00

Telephone, 5", Victory Glass #5, red paint, wooden receiver, #302 ....$55.00
Volkswagen, #373 ....$40.00
Wheelbarrow, closure, #273 ....$85.00
Windmill, pewter top, #443 ....$400.00

Canes

If you want to collect canes, your collection could certainly be diversified. There are canes that are simple and primitive, while others have hidden compartments that house a collapsible umbrella, a portable bar, or even a weapon. Some had complicated patented mechanisms of one sort or another. Materials used in cane-making are just as varied. Glassblowers made canes of glass that were carried in parades and proudly displayed as evidence of their artistic abilities. Natural formations of tree branches and roots, precious metals, and man-made compositions were also used.

Bamboo, 36", curved handle, end finished w/incised circles, heavy $30.00
Bamboo, 36", root end, 9 Chinese characters & calligraphy on side $40.00
Blackthorn, 36½", thorns removed, bulbous handle ...$45.00
Bone & horn, 34½", steel core, variegated brown & cream stripes, braided leather top, silver tip $100.00
Cactus wood, 36", root end, incised vertically $30.00
Gadget type, 1939 World's Fair, map inside $250.00
Glass, 35", black, blue & white spiral threads in clear .$100.00

Glass, 36", blue & brownish amber central core, ca 1850-70, EX..$200.00
Glass, 58", burgundy swirl stripes, baton top $175.00
Glass, 59", white, yellow & mahogany loops in clear.$150.00
Malacca, 34", porcelain handle, marked French $265.00
Malacca, 35", carved lady's leg handle $135.00
Maple, 36", wide gold ferrule, horn handle & tip......$125.00
Pussy willow, 39", natural w/gall growths $20.00
Rattlesnake skin cover, 33½", EX $130.00
Rosewood w/cat's eye handle, sterling ferrule w/crown bezel $275.00
Tiger maple, 35", chrome repousse flashlight handle, metal tip, Austria $175.00
Tortoise veneer, 32¾", braided silver knob $550.00
Walnut, 36", twisted w/2 grooved sides, lady's $15.00

Cape Cod

You can't walk through any flea market or mall now without seeing volumes of this ruby red glassware. It has been issued by Avon since the seventies, the small cruet and tall candlesticks, for instance, filled originally with one or the other of their fragrances, the wine and water goblets filled with scented candlewax, and the dessert bowl with guest soap. Many 'campaigns' since then have featured accessory tableware items such as plates, cake stands, and a water pitcher, and obviously it has been a very good seller for them, judging from the sheer volume of it around and the fact that they still feature some pieces in their catalogs.

I've found some nice pieces at garage sales, so I've bought it with an eye to the future, since it was so cheap. The dealers I've talked with about it tell me that it moves sporadically. I expect it to come into its own. The glassware is of good quality, there's a nice assortment of items in the line, and it's readily available. Even at mall prices, it's not expensive. That's about all it takes to make a collectible.

Bell, 6½", marked 'Christmas 1979' on bottom **$20.00**
Bowl, dessert; 5" **$7.50**
Bowl, serving; 8¾" dia...**$18.00**
Bowl, soup/cereal; 1½x7½" dia.....................................**$12.50**
Butter dish, 7" long, holds ¼-lb stick, w/lid.................**$17.50**
Cake plate, 3½x10¾" dia **$40.00**
Candle holder, hurricane type w/clear straight-sided chimney **$20.00**
Candle holder, 3¾" dia, squat form, each **$6.00**

Creamer, 4", footed...**$7.50**
Cruet, 5-oz..**$10.00**
Cup, 3¼"...**$7.50**
Decanter, 10½-oz, w/stopper..**$15.00**
Dessert server, 8", wedge-shaped stainless steel w/red plastic handle..**$12.00**
Goblet, champagne; 5¼" **$12.50**
Goblet, water; 6"..**$10.00**
Goblet, wine; 4½" **$6.00**
Mug, 5", w/pedestal foot..**$10.00**
Napkin rings, set of 4 ....**$20.00**
Pie plate server, 1½x11" **$30.00**
Pitcher, water; 8¼", footed..**$30.00**
Plate, bread & butter; 5¾" **$5.00**
Plate, dessert; 7½"...**$6.00**
Plate, dinner; 11"...**$15.00**
Platter, 10¾x13½"..**$20.00**
Salt & pepper shakers, footed, pr (illustrated).....$12.00
Saucer, 3¼"...**$3.00**
Shaker, may or may not be dated 'May 1978' on bottom, each.**$6.00**
Sugar bowl, 3½", footed (illustrated) $7.50
Tumbler, 3¾", footed **$7.00**

Tumbler, 5½", straight sided..**$8.50**
Vase, 8", footed **$16.50**
Wine glass, 5¼", footed **$7.50**

Cardinal China Company

This was the name of a distributing company who had their merchandise made to order and sold it through a chain of showrooms and outlet stores in several states from the late 1940s through the 1950s. (Although they made some of their own pottery very early on, we have yet to find out just what they themselves produced.) They used their company name to mark cookie jars (some were made by the American Bisque Company), novelty wares, and kitchen items, many of which you'll see as you make your flea market rounds. Their primary colors were yellow and green, and their spoon holders came complete with colorful plastic measuring spoons.

The Collector's Encyclopedia of Cookie Jars by Joyce and Fred Roerig shows a page of their jars.

Cookie jar, Clown, pointed hat w/I Want Some Cookies, sad expression, marked Cardinal USA #302.................**$85.00**
Cookie jar, Garage, brown, Free Parking for Cookies over door, marked Cardinal, USA #306......................**$75.00**
Cookie jar, Little Girl, pink hat is lid, freckles, licking lips, marked Cardinal USA #301...................................**$85.00**
Cookie jar, Pig, Go Ahead Make a Pig of Yourself on lid w/ears, marked Cardinal USA #304 ....**$85.00**

Cookie jar, Round House, marked USA Cardinal .$75.00
Cookie jar, Soldier, marked #312 USA Cardinal (illustrated) $95.00
Measuring spoon holder, flowerpot form, plain (not basketweave) base **$10.00**
Measuring spoon holder, shaped to look like a window sill planter (illustrated) $15.00
Salt & pepper shakers, Chinese man & lady, green & yellow, pr..**$22.00**

Scissors holder, nest w/chicken figural $25.00
Spoon holder, shaped as a flowerpot w/a basketweave
  base...$12.00
String holder, chicken figural......................................$25.00

Carnival Chalkware

From about 1910 until in the fifties, winners of carnival games everywhere in the United States were awarded chalkware figures of Kewpie dolls, the Lone Ranger, or any one of a vast assortment of animals and birds. The earliest were made of plaster with a pink cast. They ranged in size from about 5" up to 16".

They were easily chipped, so when it came time for the carnival to pick up and move on, they had to be carefully wrapped and packed away, a time consuming, tedious chore. When stuffed animals became available, concessionists found that they could simply throw them into a box without fear of damage, and so ended an era.

Today the most valuable of these statues are those modeled after Disney characters, movie stars, and comic book heroes.

Chalkware figures are featured in the book *The Carnival Chalk Prize* written by Thomas G. Morris, who has also included a fascinating history of carnival life in America.

Abraham Lincoln bust, 12", dated 1940......................$57.50
Charley McCarthy, 7½", sitting $20.00
Cowboy, 12", full chaps, gun & 10-gallon hat, 1940s..$37.50
Dog w/flower bank, 10¾", unmarked, 1935-45...........$25.00
Donald Duck's Nephew, copyrighted as Junior,
  unmarked, 6½"..$15.00
Dutch girl, 11½", hands in pockets, hat tilted, marked 1934
  on bottom...$52.50
Easter Bunny bank, 11¾", marked Deluxe No 1024 Chattanooga, Tenn...$25.00
End of the Trail lamp, 6½" figure of cowboy on horse, ca
  1930-45 ....$52.50
Frenchie, voluptuous lady w/hands on hips, glass lamp
  back, ca 1934, 15"..$150.00
Horse head, 6¾", w/bridle, ears up, ca 1940s.............$12.00
Hula Hula girl, 17", lady in grass skirt & lei, left hand in
  hair, 1940s $32.50

Lone Ranger, 16", unmarked.............................$100.00
Papa, 14", marked Call Me Papa, ca 1935-45 ....$15.00
Pluto, 7½", comic dog, unmarked, ca 1930-45.............$25.00
Popeye, 9½", hands folded over chest $32.00
Shirley Temple, 14½", dressed as Little Colonel $200.00
Snuffy Smith, 9¼", in bib overalls & sloppy hat...........$70.00
Wimpy, 13½", comic figure w/hands behind back......$60.00

Carnival Glass

From 1905 until late in the twenties, many companies (Northwood, Fenton, Imperial, Millersburg, Dugan, and others) produced huge quantities of this type of press-molded iridescent glassware. Because it was so inexpensive, lots of it was given away at carnivals, and that's where it got its name. Even today you're apt to find a piece stuck away in Grandma's cabinet or at a tag sale, so we want you to be at least a little familiar with it. It's been widely reproduced over the past twenty-five years, and even the new glass is collectible. A few of the companies that have reproduced it are Indiana Glass, Westmoreland, and Imperial. Just be sure you know what you're buying. It's one thing to buy 'new' glass if you like it, but if you have your heart set on the genuine article, you certainly don't want to make mistakes.

To educate yourself so that this doesn't happen, attend antique shows, go to the better shops in your area, and get to know reputable dealers. Read and study *The Standard Encyclopedia of Carnival Glass* by Bill Edwards. You'll soon find yourself confident and able to recognize both old carnival glass as well as the newer reproductions.

See also Indiana Glass Carnival Ware.

Acorn (Fenton), bowl, 8½", green, ruffled edge $90.00
Acorn Burrs (Northwood), bowl, 10", marigold, flat.$100.00
Apple Blossoms (Dugan), bowl, 7½", marigold, ruffled $35.00
April Showers (Fenton), vase, blue, ruffled $55.00
Arcs (Imperial), compote, marigold, geometric design on
  exterior $45.00

Autumn Acorns (Fenton), bowl, 8¾", amethyst, deeply fluted edge **$50.00**

Balloons (Imperial), perfume atomizer, marigold........**$55.00**

Banded Diamond & Fan (English), toothpick holder, marigold...**$70.00**

Banded Grape & Leaf (English), tumbler, marigold, slightly flared rim, rare **$100.00**

Banded Panels (Crystal), sugar bowl, marigold...........**$40.00**

Beaded Bull's Eye (Imperial), vase, 14", amethyst, flared top w/fluted edge **$45.00**

Beaded Panels (Imperial), powder jar, marigold, w/lid.**$55.00**

Beaded Shell (Dugan), bowl, 9", amethyst, footed....**$100.00**

Beaded Spears (Crystal), tumbler, marigold, flared rim.**$80.00**

Beaded Swirl (English), compote, blue, fluted edge ...**$60.00**

Bells & Beads (Dugan), nappy, peach opalescent **$80.00**

Big Basketweave (Dugan), vase, 14", amethyst...........**$45.00**

Birds & Cherries (Fenton), bowl, 5", marigold, rare....**$65.00**

Blackberry Spray (Fenton), compote, green **$55.00**

Border Plants (Dugan), bowl, 8½", amethyst, footed..**$75.00**

Bouquet (Fenton), tumbler, blue **$55.00**

Boutonniere (Millersburg), compote, amethyst, ruffled .**$225.00**

Broken Arches (Imperial), bowl, 8½", green................**$65.00**

Butterflies (Fenton), bonbon, marigold.......................**$45.00**

Butterfly & Berry (Fenton), sugar bowl, marigold, w/lid .**$110.00**

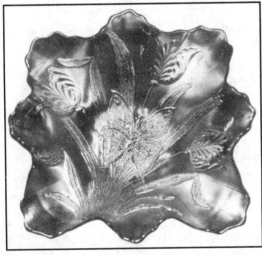

Butterfly & Tulip (Dugan), bowl, 10½", marigold .$475.00

Buttermilk, Plain (Fenton), goblet, marigold...............**$55.00**

Cane (Imperial), pickle dish, marigold........................**$30.00**

Capitol (Westmoreland), bowl, blue, footed, sm.........**$70.00**

Carnival Honeycomb (Imperial), bowl, marigold, 6", handled **$35.00**

Cathedral (Sweden), creamer, marigold, footed **$50.00**

Checkerboard Bouquet, plate, 8", amethyst.................**$55.00**

Cherry (Millersburg), bowl, 7", green, rare **$130.00**

Cherry & Cable Intaglio (Northwood), bowl, 5", marigold...**$55.00**

Circle Scroll (Dugan), hat shape, amethyst, rare **$130.00**

Cobblestones (Dugan), bowl, 5", marigold **$42.00**

Coin Spot (Dugan), compote, blue, ruffled edge **$75.00**

Corinth (Dugan), bowl, 9", amethyst...........................**$55.00**

Crackle (Imperial), spittoon, marigold, lg **$42.00**

Daisy & Plume (Northwood), candy dish, green.........**$65.00**

Diamond Lace (Imperial), bowl, 10", amethyst...........**$70.00**

Diamond Ovals (English), compote, marigold, fluted .**$40.00**

Diamond Points (Northwood), vase, 14", blue, deeply fluted edge **$45.00**

Diamonds (Millersburg), tumbler, marigold.................**$65.00**

Double Dutch (Imperial), bowl, 9", marigold, footed **$50.00**

Double Stem Rose (Dugan), bowl, 8½", green, dome shaped base **$55.00**

Dutch Twins, ashtray, marigold **$50.00**

Enamelled Grape (Northwood), tumbler, blue **$45.00**

Engraved Grapes (Fenton), vase, 8", marigold **$45.00**

Fanciful (Dugan), bowl, 8½", amethyst **$65.00**

Fanciful (Dugan), plate, marigold, 9", fluted edge **$245.00**

Feathers (Northwood), vase, 12", amethyst, ruffled.....**$45.00**

Fentonia Fruit (Fenton), bowl, 6", blue, footed **$60.00**

File (Imperial & English), sugar bowl, marigold.........**$130.00**

Floral & Optic (Imperial), bowl, 8", marigold, footed .**$32.00**

Flute #3 (Imperial), tumbler, blue................................**$90.00**

Four Flowers, plate, 6½", green, fluted edge **$80.00**

Garland (Fenton), rose bowl, amethyst, footed **$75.00**

Golden Flowers, vase, 7½", marigold............................**$55.00**

Grape (Imperial), plate, 8½", amethyst, ruffled edge ..**$85.00**

Grape (Northwood's Grape & Cable), shot glass, amethyst..**$200.00**

Grapevine Lattice (Fenton), tumbler, marigold, rare ...**$58.00**

Heavy Prisms (English), celery vase, 6", blue **$90.00**

Hexagon & Cane (Imperial), sugar bowl, marigold, w/lid...**$70.00**

Hobstar (Imperial), sugar bowl, amethyst, w/lid.......**$100.00**

Hobstar Panels (English), creamer, marigold...............**$50.00**

Honeycomb & Clover (Fenton), bonbon, blue............**$52.00**

Horses Head (Fenton), bowl, 7", marigold, footed......**$90.00**

Intaglio Daisy (English), bowl, 7½", marigold.............**$52.00**

Interior Rays (Westmoreland), butter dish, marigold, w/lid...**$70.00**

Inverted Strawberry, bowl, 5", green............................**$50.00**

Iris (Fenton), compote, amethyst..................................**$65.00**

Jeweled Heart (Dugan), bowl, 10", amethyst..............**$105.00**

Kokomo (English), rose bowl, green, footed................**$65.00**

Lacy Dewdrop (Westmoreland), creamer, pastel.......**$100.00**

Lattice & Prisms, cologne, marigold, w/stopper **$60.00**

Leaf & Beads (Northwood-Dugan), candy dish, amethyst, fluted edge, footed..**$60.00**

Little Beads, bowl, 8", marigold **$20.00**

Little Stars (Millersburg), bowl, 7", amethyst, rare **$75.00**

Long Prisms, hatpin, amethyst **$40.00**

Lotus & Grape (Fenton), bonbon, green.......................**$50.00**

Louisa (Westmoreland), candy dish, green, footed **$70.00**

Lustre & Clear (Imperial), vase, 8", marigold, footed ..**$92.00**

Lustre Rose (Imperial), bowl, 12", amethyst, footed....**$60.00**

Magnolia Drape, tumbler, marigold..............................**$55.00**

Many Prisms, perfume, marigold, w/stopper **$70.00**

Maple Leaf (Dugan), bowl, 4½", green, stemmed **$45.00**

Mayflower, compote, pastel **$65.00**

Maypole, vase, 6¼", green...**$62.00**

Milady (Fenton), tumbler, marigold............................**$105.00**

Mirrored Lotus (Fenton), bowl, 8½", marigold............**$50.00**

Mitered Diamond & Pleats (English), bowl, 8½", marigold, shallow **$40.00**

Moonprint (English), sugar bowl, marigold, stemmed **$55.00**

Near Cut Souvenir (Cambridge), mug, marigold **$200.00**

Nell (Higbee), mug, marigold **$70.00**

Nippon (Northwood), bowl, 8½", blue **$65.00**

Northwood Jester's Cap, vase, blue **$65.00**

Number 4 (Imperial), bowl, marigold, footed **$30.00**

Octagon (Imperial), toothpick holder, amethyst, rare .**$95.00**

Open Rose (Imperial), bowl, 9", amethyst, footed **$46.00**

Orange Tree (Fenton), compote, marigold, sm **$35.00**

Oriental Poppy (Northwood), tumbler, amethyst **$50.00**

Palm Beach (US Glass), bowl, 5", marigold **$35.00**

Panelled Hobnail (Dugan), vase, 10", green **$75.00**

Pansy (Imperial), pickle dish, green, oval **$50.00**

Panther (Fenton), bowl, 5", marigold, footed **$60.00**

Peach (Northwood), tumbler, blue **$90.00**

Peacock & Urn (Fenton), bowl, 8½", marigold **$55.00**

Peacock & Urn (Northwood), bowl, amethyst, 9" **$105.00**

Peacock at the Fountain (Northwood), orange bowl, marigold, footed **$175.00**

Persian Medallion (Fenton), rose bowl, green **$70.00**

Pine Cone (Fenton), plate, 6½", amethyst **$75.00**

Plain Jane, paperweight, marigold **$85.00**

Pretty Panels (Fenton), tumbler, marigold, handled **$55.00**

Propeller (Imperial), compote, marigold **$35.00**

Quartered Block, creamer, marigold **$55.00**

Rays & Ribbons (Millersburg), bowl, 8½", amethyst, round or ruffled **$90.00**

Ripple (Imperial), vase, amethyst, ruffled, any 1 of several various sizes **$50.00**

Rising Sun (US Glass), sugar bowl, marigold, ear-type handles, w/lid **$95.00**

Rose Spray (Fenton), compote, marigold **$175.00**

Royalty (Imperial), punch bowl, marigold, w/base **$140.00**

Ruffled Rib (Northwood), bowl, 10", amethyst **$65.00**

S-Repeat (Dugan), creamer, sm, amethyst **$65.00**

Scotch Thistle (Fenton), compote, blue, ruffled **$50.00**

Scroll Embossed (Imperial), bowl, 8½", marigold **$40.00**

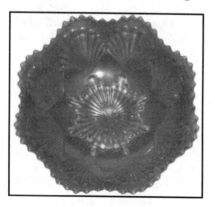

Shell, bowl, marigold..**$40.00**

Shell & Jewel (Westmoreland), sugar bowl, green, w/lid **$65.00**

Singing Birds (Northwood), bowl, 5", marigold **$35.00**

Small Rib (Dugan), rose bowl, green, stemmed **$45.00**

Smooth Rays (Westmoreland), bowl, 5", green, dome-shaped base **$55.00**

Springtime (Northwood), bowl, 5", amethyst, fluted ...**$55.00**

Stag & Holly (Fenton), bowl, 9", marigold, footed **$105.00**

Star Medallion (Imperial), bonbon, marigold **$50.00**

Starfish (Dugan), compote, green **$65.00**

Stippled Rambler Rose (Dugan), nut bowl, blue, fluted edge, footed **$80.00**

Stork & Rushes (Dugan), basket, marigold, handled ...**$55.00**

Strawberry (Northwood), bowl, 5", blue **$45.00**

Swirl (Northwood), tumbler, marigold **$55.00**

Thistle (English), vase, 6", marigold, flared rim...**$35.00**

Three Fruits (Northwood), bowl, 8⅝", amethyst, dome base **$85.00**

Three-In-One (Imperial), plate, 6½", marigold **$60.00**

Tree Bark (Imperial), pickle jar, 7½", marigold **$40.00**

Tree of Life (Imperial), basket, marigold, handled **$35.00**

Tree Trunk (Northwood), vase, 12", blue **$55.00**

Tulip & Cane (Imperial), goblet, 8-oz, marigold, rare .**$85.00**

Two Flowers (Fenton), bowl, 8", green, footed **$55.00**

US Diamond Block (US Glass), salt & pepper shakers, marigold, pr **$65.00**

Valentine, ring tray, marigold **$90.00**

Vineyard (Dugan), pitcher, marigold **$100.00**

Vintage (Fenton), plate, 11", marigold, ruffled **$195.00**

Waffle Block (Imperial), parfait glass, marigold **$35.00**

Water Lily (Fenton), bonbon, amethyst **$50.00**

Weeping Cherry (Dugan), bowl, marigold, flat base ...**$45.00**

Whirling Star (Imperial), compote, green **$70.00**

Wide Panel (Northwood-Fenton-Imperial), cake plate, marigold, 12" **$75.00**

Wide Panel Bouquet, basket, 3½", marigold **$72.00**

Wild Rose (Northwood), bowl, 6", amethyst, open edge, footed **$55.00**

Wild Strawberry (Dugan), bowl, lg, marigold **$85.00**

Wild Strawberry (Dugan), bowl, 6", marigold, rare **$46.00**

Windmill (Imperial), tray, green, flat **$72.00**

Wise Owl, bank, marigold **$50.00**

Wishbone (Northwood), bowl, 9", marigold, footed ...**$85.00**

Wreath of Roses (Fenton), bonbon, marigold, stemmed .**$48.00**

Wreathed Cherry (Dugan), bowl, 5", amethyst, oval ...**$42.00**

Zig Zag (Millersburg), bowl, 9½", marigold, round or ruffled, each **$255.00**

Cat Collectibles

I have no doubt that every cat-lover in America is in some small way a 'cat' collector. More than any other species, cats have enjoyed tremendous popularity over the years. They were revered in Ancient Egypt and the Orient, and from Biblical times up to the present day they have been modeled in marble, bronze, pottery, and porcelain. They have been immortalized in paintings and prints and used extensively in advertising.

There are several 'cat' books available on today's market; if you want to see great photos of some of the various aspects of 'cat' collecting, you'll enjoy reading *Collectible Cats, An Identification and Value Guide,* by Marbena Fyke.

Bank, 5x8", figural black cat, Save w/The Cat lettered in white, plastic, 1981 Union Carbide giveaway **$15.00**
Bank, 6½" long, black & white striped cat w/red sneakers, Kliban, 1979..**$22.00**
Bath salts bottle, 6½", figural white cat w/black facial features & bow tie, w/original contents, 1940s..........**$18.00**
Book, Four Little Kittens, Rand McNally, 1935.............**$12.00**

Butter dish, cat lying on fish-shaped base, airbrushed colors, 1950s **$15.00**
Figurine, 4", figural cat, sitting plastic w/mixed quarry stones, movable eyes...**$15.00**
Figurine, 5½" long, Roly Poly, cat w/ball of yarn, Dakin Mint Cats of Character Series, bone china, 1987 ....**$15.00**
Figurine, 5¼", Mirror Mirror, cat looking in mirror, Dakin Mint Cute Cat Series, bisque, 1989.......................**$29.00**
Figurine, 6½", Sandy, Danbury Mint Kittens Series, stone bisque w/glass eyes, 1988.....................................**$75.00**
Jim Beam whiskey bottle, 11½", figural Siamese cat, bone china, 1975 ....**$18.00**
Night light, 5", figural cat in sitting position w/paw up, light fits in belly, cast metal, 1940s...............................**$25.00**
Nodders, flocked Siamese twins in wicker basket, blue glass eyes, 1940s **$35.00**
Painting, 12x9", brown & white kitten on red background, oil on canvas, signed Balneba, 1920......................**$65.00**
Paperweight, clear glass w/brown kitten on green marbleized pattern in center, round, Joe St Clair, 1985.............**$25.00**
Paste brush, 3½", hand-carved head w/glass eyes, black w/red & gold hightlights, 1930 ....**$22.00**
Pencil sharpener, 2x1½", chalkware kitten, 1940s.......**$12.00**
Perfume bottle, 6", satin glass w/cat finial, 1988 ....**$18.00**

Pin, figural cat in sitting position, gold-tone w/rhinestone eyes...**$6.00**
Pin, figural cat lying on a chair, pewter, marked JJ.....**$10.00**
Pin, 1½", figural cat, sterling w/marcasite & onyx highlights, ruby eyes..**$20.00**
Plate, 9½" dia, titled Dominic, pictures black cat laying in front of flowerpot, 1980....................................**$25.00**
Puzzle, 7x5½", die-cut of 2 yellow & white kittens, wood, 1940 ....**$10.00**
Salt & pepper shakers, Art Deco cats, pr **$10.00**
Salt & pepper shakers, brown kittens w/white faces & pink flowers in their hair, bisque, pr............................**$6.00**
Salt & pepper shakers, seated Siamese w/rhinestone eyes, hand-painted ceramic, pr....................................**$9.00**
Spoon rest/ashtray, cat face, yellow w/red ears & black facial features, ceramic, 1940s...........................**$14.50**
Tic-Tac-Toe set, board: 6" square, cats & mice: 1½-2", brass, 1987 ....**$25.00**
Toothpick holder, 2" long, figural cat, pink & beige lusterware, 1940s..**$15.00**
Toothpick holder, 3¾", figural black cat w/yellow eyes & red highlights on yellow base, painted wood, 1940s...**$18.00**
Toy, 5" long, black & white cat w/ball, tin wind-up, celluloid head & tail, 1940s..**$35.00**
Wall pocket, 6½", cat playing banjo, hand-painted lusterware, porcelain, Japan, 1940s **$28.00**
Wine decanter, 13", figural cat, green glass, 1950s......**$25.00**

Cat-Tail Dinnerware

Cat-Tail was a dinnerware pattern popular during the late twenties until sometime in the forties. So popular, in fact, that ovenware, glassware, tinware, even a breakfast table set was made to coordinate with it. The dinnerware was made primarily by Universal Potteries of Cambridge, Ohio, though even a catalog from Hall China circa 1927 shows a 3-piece coffee service, and there may have been others. It was sold for years by Sears Roebuck and Company, and some items bear a mark with their name.

The pattern is unmistakable: a cluster of red cattails (usually six, sometimes one or two) with black stems on creamy white. Shapes certainly vary; Universal used a minimum of three of their standard mold designs, possibly more. If you're trying to decorate a forties vintage kitchen, no other design could afford you more to work with. To see many of the pieces that are available and to learn more about the line, read *The Collector's Encyclopedia of American Dinnerware* by Jo Cunningham.

Bowl, berry; 5" **$4.00**
Bowl, 7"...**$10.00**
Bowl, 9"...**$12.00**
Butter dish, 1-lb, w/lid..**$40.00**
Cake server..**$25.00**
Casserole, 8¼", w/lid **$22.00**
Cup & saucer..**$12.00**
Custard, individual **$5.50**

Gravy boat, w/liner..**$28.00**
Jug, refrigerator; w/stopper.................................**$28.00**
Pie plate, deep..**$18.00**
Pitcher, red & black on clear glass, w/ice lip **$95.00**
Pitcher, 6", utility or milk....................................**$20.00**
Plate, 6"..**$3.00**
Plate, 9"..**$5.00**
Plate serving; on Laurella shape, Universal Potteries ..**$30.00**
Platter, 11½"...**$12.00**
Platter, 14½"...**$15.00**
Refrigerator jar, 4"..**$10.00**
Salt & pepper shakers, pr......................................**$20.00**

Scales, kitchen; decal on white-painted metal......$35.00

Shaker set, salt, pepper, sugar, & flour; black lids, all same
    size..**$32.00**
Shaker set, short salt & pepper, tall flour & sugar, red lids,
    w/red metal rack..**$40.00**
Sugar bowl, handled..**$6.00**
Tablecloth, NM..**$75.00**
Teapot, Oxford shape..**$25.00**
Tray, utility; 11½"...**$15.00**
Tumbler, iced tea; red & black design on clear glass..**$30.00**
Tumbler, marked Universal Potteries, scarce..............**$37.00**

Catalin Napkin Rings

Plastic (Catalin) napkin rings topped with heads of cartoon characters, animals, and birds are very collectible, especially examples in red and orange; blue is also good, and other colors can be found as well.

Band, 1¾", lathe turned, amber, red or green, each......**$8.00**
Chicken, no inlaid eye..**$25.00**
Donald Duck, w/decal..**$58.00**
Elephant, no ball on head.......................................**$25.00**
Elephant, w/ball on head...**$35.00**
Mickey Mouse, w/decal..**$58.00**
Rabbit, inlaid eye rod..**$35.00**
Rocking horse, inlaid eye rod..................................**$66.00**
Schnauzer dog..**$25.00**
Scotty dog, inlaid eye rod..**$38.00**

Catalina Island

Located on the island of the same name some twenty-five miles off the Los Angeles coastline, this pottery operated for only ten years after it was founded in 1927. The island was owned by William Wrigley, Jr. (the chewing gum tycoon), who with his partner David Renton established the pottery with the purpose in mind of providing year-round employment for residents while at the same time manufacturing brick and tile to use in the island's development. Using the native red clay, they went on to produce garden ware, vases, decorative accessories, and eventually dinnerware. They made a line of hand-painted plates featuring island motifs such as birds, flying fish, and Spanish galleons that are today highly collectible. They developed some remarkable glazes using only oxides available on the island. Even though the red clay proved to be brittle and easily chipped, at Mr. Wriggley's insistence, they continued to use it until after he died in 1932. To make a better product, they began importing a tougher white-burning clay from the mainland; ironically the added expense was a major contributing factor to their downfall. In 1937 the company was sold to Gladding McBean.

Various types of marks were used over the years, but without enough consistency to indicate a production date. Marks are 'Catalina' or 'Catalina Island.' Paper labels were also used. Pieces marked 'Catalina Pottery' were produced by Gladding McBean.

If you'd like to learn more about this pottery, refer to *The Collector's Encyclopedia of California Pottery* by Jack Chipman.

Ashtray, cowboy hat, matt green...............................**$100.00**
Bowl, berry; Catalina Island line................................**$25.00**
Casserole, w/lid, Rope Edge line...............................**$50.00**
Creamer, Catalina Island line **$35.00**
Cup, Rope Edge line...**$20.00**
Cup & saucer, Rope Edge line....................................**$35.00**
Custard cup, Catalina Island line **$25.00**
Flowerpot, 6", Ring style...**$55.00**
Pitcher, squat base, Catalina Island line.....................**$75.00**
Plate, bread & butter; 6", coupe shape, Catalina Island
    line...**$15.00**
Plate, dinner; 10½", Rope Edge line **$25.00**

Plate, 10½", underwater scene, bright yellow rim .$300.00

Sugar bowl, Catalina Island Line..............................$45.00
Teapot, 4-cup, Rope Edge line................................$75.00
Tumbler, 4", Catalina Island line............................$20.00
Vase, 5½", flowerpot shape, Monterey brown............$60.00
Vase, 6", Toyon red, bulbous base.........................$175.00
Wall pocket, 9", basketweave................................$200.00
Wine cup, w/handle, Catalina Island line..................$23.00

Catalogs

Right now, some of the most collectible catalogs are those from the the fifties, sixties, and seventies, especially those Christmas 'wish books.' They're full of the toys that are so sought after by today's collector's – battery ops, Tonkas, and of course, GI Joes and Barbies. No matter what year the catalog was printed, its value will hinge on several factors: subject, illustrations and the amount of color used, collector demand, size, rarity, and condition. Generally, manufacturer's catalogs are more valuable than those put out by a jobber.

Aldens, 1939, general, Spring & Summer, EX..............$60.00
American Flyer, 1952, toy trains, EX.........................$35.00
Atwater Kent Radio Catalog, ca 1927, 28 pages, VG...$18.00
Beals, McCarthy & Rogers, 1934, hardware, hardcover, EX.$36.00
Belknap Hardware, 1961, Louisville, KY, M................$60.00
Black & Decker Mfg, 1954, power tools, 24 pages, EX..$10.00
Brooks Mfg Co, 1916, boats & boat building kits & motors,
      64 pages, no back cover...$30.00
Burgess Seeds & Plants, 1949, EX..............................$18.00
Chicago Mail Order, 1932, fashions, Spring & Summer, 312
      pages, VG..$65.00
Craftsman & Companion Power Tools & Accessories, 1933,
      41 pages, EX..$18.00
Emeralite, early 1900s, desk lamps, color illustrations, 28
      pages, lightly soiled $18.00
FAO Schwartz, 1961, toys, Christmas, EX...................$65.00
Firestone Home & Auto, 1942, EX.............................$35.00
General Electric Refrigerators, ca 1928, color illustrations, 22
      pages, EX...$18.00
Griffith Tool Works, 1926, solid forged hammers & hachets,
      line illustrations, 36 pages, EX $35.00
JC Penney, 1964, Summer, EX $20.00
JC Penney, 1969, Christmas, NM................................$85.00
Jung's Seed, 1940, color illustrations, 72 pages, EX.......$8.00
Kodak Supplies, 1930, EX..$25.00
Lionel Trains, 1949, EX..$45.00
LL Bean, 1958, 108 pages, VG...................................$35.00
Manny Pruskauer, 1958, wholesale fur fashions, wholesale &
      retail prices, original mailing envelope, 24 pages.$22.00
Marshall Fields & Co, 1978, fashions, Christmas, 72 pages,
      VG..$25.00
Milton Bradley, 1931, school supplies, 128 pages, EX ..$24.00
Montgomery Ward, 1942, Fall & Winter, EX................$45.00
Montgomery Ward, 1965, Spring & Summer, EX.........$32.00
Montgomery Ward Plumbing, 11x8½", 1920s $38.00
National Bellas Hess, 1970, Spring & Summer, EX......$30.00

RCA Radiolas & Loudspeakers, 1929-30, full-page illustra-
      tions in sepia, 34 pages, EX $28.00
S&H Green Stamps, 1950, EX....................................$15.00
Sears, 1950, Christmas, EX..$65.00
Sears, 1964, Christmas, EX..$85.00
Sears, 1965, Spring & Summer, EX $35.00
Sears, 1972, EX..$30.00
South Bend, 1935, fishing equipment, EX...................$40.00
Spiegel, 1960, Fall & Winter, EX................................$28.00
Tru Value Hardware, 1974, toys, EX...........................$45.00
Victor Records, 1930, 5x7", EX..................................$10.00
Winchester, 1968, guns, EX.......................................$10.00
Wolverine Shoe & Tanning Corp, 1954, dress shoes, inserted
      dealer price list, original mailer, 48 pages.............$15.00
Woolworth's, 1954, Christmas, 16 pages, EX $15.00

Ceramic Arts Studio

American-made figurines are very popular now, and these are certainly among the best. They have a distinctive look you'll soon learn to identify with confidence, even if you happen to pick up an unmarked piece. They were first designed in the forties and sold well until the company closed in 1955. (After that, the new owner took the molds to Japan, where he made them for only a short time.) The company's principal designer was Betty Harrington, who modeled the figures and knicknacks that so many have grown to love. In addition to the company's mark, 'Ceramic Arts Studios, Madison Wisconsin,' many of the character pieces she designed also carry their assigned name on the bottom.

The company also produced a line of metal items to accessorize the figurines; these were designed by Liberace's mother, Zona.

Though prices continue to climb, once in awhile there's an unmarked bargain to be found, but first you must familiarize yourself with your subject! BA Wellman has compiled *The Ceramic Arts Studio Price Guide* as well as an accompanying video tape that we're sure you'll enjoy if you'd like to learn more.

Arched window, metal accessory piece for Madonna
      w/child $40.00
Ashtray, hippo, 3½" $40.00
Bank, Paisley Pig, 3" $75.00
Bank, Tony, 4¼", razor disposal $42.50
Bell, Lillibelle, 6½" $75.00
Bell, Winter Belle, 5¼"...$60.00
Bowl, 2¼", shallow, rectangular...............................$25.00
Bowl, 5", any Pixie series, shield shape $45.00
Candle holder, Bedtime boy & girl, 4¾", pr..............$55.00
Figurine, Bali Gong, 5½" $55.00
Figurine, bass viol boy, 4¾" $45.00
Figurine, Bo-Peep, 5½"...$28.00
Figurine, bride & groom, 4¾", 5", pr $65.00
Figurine, Comedy & Tragedy, 10", pr.......................$160.00
Figurine, Cupid, 5"..$45.00
Figurine, Daisy donkey, 4¾".....................................$38.00

Figurine, drummer girl, 4¼" $35.00
Figurine, duck mother & baby, 3¼", 2¼", pr $75.00
Figurine, flute girl, 4¾" $55.00
Figurine, fox, modern, 3" $50.00
Figurine, French boy & girl, 3", pr $40.00
Figurine, frog, 2" $20.00
Figurine, Indian girl, 3¼" $26.00
Figurine, Inkey skunk, 2" $22.00
Figurine, Little Miss Muffet, 4½" $30.00
Figurine, Modern Dance man & woman, 9½", pr $125.00
Figurine, Mr Skunky, 3" $32.00
Figurine, pekingese, 3", pr $36.50
Figurine, Peter Rabbit, 3¾" $30.00
Figurine, Polish boy & girl, 6¾", 6", pr $38.00
Figurine, Promenade woman, 7¾" $45.00
Figurine, scotties, 2¾", 1-pc $32.00
Figurine, St George on Charger, 8½" $150.00
Figurine, toadstool, 3" $16.00
Figurine, turtle w/cane, 3¼" $28.00
Figurine, Winter Willy, 4" $35.00
Figurine, zebra, 5" $42.00
Jug, Aladdin, 2" $27.50
Jug, Miss Forward, 4" $65.00
Jug, rose, 2¾" $17.50
Jug, 2", swan body, handle & spout $17.50
Lamp, Zorina, on base $95.00
Planter, Bonnie, 7" $50.00
Planter, Manchu, 7½" $60.00

Planter head, 6", Svea $45.00
Plaque, Attitude & Arabesque, 9½", pr $68.00
Plaque, fish, 4½" $40.00
Plaque, mermaid, 6" $55.00
Plaque, Neptune, 6" $125.00
Plaque, Shadow Dancers, 7", pr $75.00
Salt & pepper shakers, bunnies, 4", 2½", kissing, pr ... $38.00
Salt & pepper shakers, chick & nest, 2¾" overall, pr .. $27.50
Salt & pepper shakers, chihuahua & doghouse, 1¾" overall,
    pr $38.00
Salt & pepper shakers, Chinese boy & girl, 4", pr $27.50

Salt & pepper shakers, dog & doghouse, pr $40.00
Salt & pepper shakers, elephant & young native boy, 5",
    2¾", pr $165.00
Salt & pepper shakers, elephant boy & girl, 3½", pr . $35.00
Salt & pepper shakers, Eskimo boy & girl, 3", pr $30.00
Salt & pepper shakers, fish, 4", up on tail, pr $45.00
Salt & pepper shakers, frog & toadstool, 2", 3", pr $35.00
Salt & pepper shakers, horse head, 3½", pr $32.00
Salt & pepper shakers, Mr & Mrs Penguin, 3¾", pr $36.00
Salt & pepper shakers, Scottish boy & girl, 3¼", pr $30.00
Salt & pepper shakers, snuggle kitten & cream pitcher, 2½",
    pr $40.00
Salt & pepper shakers, snuggle mother & baby bear, 4¼",
    white, pr $45.00
Salt & pepper shakers, snuggle mouse & cheese, 3" long,
    pr $35.00
Salt & pepper shakers, snuggle sea horse in coral, 3½", 3",
    pr $40.00
Shadow box, 13" square, metal w/wood $30.00
Shelf sitter, boy w/dog, girl w/cat, 4¼", pr $78.00
Shelf sitter, Chinese boy & girl, 4", pr $35.00
Shelf sitter, Greg & Grace, pr $75.00
Shelf sitter, Mexican boy & girl, pr $58.00
Shelf sitter, spaniel, 1¾", recumbent, pr $50.00
Shelf sitter, Tuffy & Fluffy, pr $85.00
Star, 9", metal accessory to hold any 1 of angel trio ... $20.00
Vase, 2", duck motif, round $22.00
Vase, 2", modern style, square $22.00
Vase, 2¼", rose motif, round $20.00

Cereal Boxes

Yes, cereal boxes – your eyes aren't deceiving you. But think about it. Cereal boxes from even the sixties have to be extremely scarce. The ones that are bringing the big bucks today are those with a well-known character emblazoned across the front. Am I starting to make more sense to you? Good. Now, say the experts, is the time to look ahead into the future of your cereal box collection. They recommend going to your neighborhood supermarket to inspect the shelves in the cereal aisle today! Choose the ones with Batman, Quisp, Ninja Turtles, or some other nineties phenomenon. Take them home and (unless you have mice) display them unopened, or empty them out and fold them up along the seam lines. If you want only the old boxes, you'll probably have to find an old long-abandoned grocery store, or pay prices somewhere around those in our listings when one comes up for sale.

Store displays and advertising posters, in-box prizes or 'send-a-ways,' coupons with pictures of boxes, and shelf signs and cards are also part of this field of interest.

If you want to learn more about this field of collecting, we recommend *Toys of the Sixties* by Bill Bruegman.

Addams Family, cereal box w/shrink-wrapped toy on front,
    ca 1990, M $5.00

Cheerios, Star Trek Next Generation on front, 1987, M .**$10.00**
Corn Flakes, 18-oz, Kellogg's, w/Wally & the Beaver on front, 1984 ....**$24.00**
Dunkin' Donuts, 13-oz, Ralston, 1988 ....**$24.00**
GI Joe Action Stars, 11-oz, 1985.....................................**$35.00**
Grant's Hygienic Breakfast Food, 4x8x2", product & strawberries on the front, health claims, ca 1915, EX ...**$17.50**
Mother's Oats, round, w/Roy Rogers ad, ca 1951, NM..**$50.00**
Nabisco Shreaded Wheat, w/airplane on panel, 1942, EX.**$25.00**

Pac-Man, Series #3, full..$10.00
Quisp, 10x7x2½", Space Trivia #2 game on back of box, marked Quaker Oats Co, copyright 1985, M.........**$37.50**
Rainbow Brite, 11-oz, Ralston, 1984 ....**$35.00**
Smurf Magic Berries, 11-oz, Post **$25.00**
Wheaties, features NFL Champions-New York Giants, 1991, EX **$10.00**

Wheaties, features World Champions, Minnesota Twins, 1987 ....$30.00
Wheaties, Larry Bird on front, 1992, M.........................**$25.00**

Character and Promotional Drinking Glasses

In any household, especially those with children, I would venture to say, you should find a few of these glasses. Put out by fast-food restaurant chains or by a company promoting a product, they have for years been commonplace. But now instead of glass, the giveaways are nearly always plastic. If a glass is offered at all, you usually pay 99¢ for it.

You can find these for small change at garage sales, and at those prices, pick up any that are still bright and unfaded. They will move well on your flea market table. Some are worth more than others. Among the common ones are Camp Snoopy, B.C. Ice Age, Garfield, McDonald's, Smurfs, and Coca-Cola. The better glasses are those with superheroes, characters from Star Trek and thirties movies such as 'Wizard of Oz,' sports personalities, and cartoon characters by Walter Lantz and Walt Disney. Some of these carry a copyright date, and that's all it is. It's not the date of manufacture.

Many collectors are having a good time looking for these glasses; if you want to learn more about them, we recommend _The Collector's Guide to Cartoon and Promotional Drinking Glasses_ by John Hervey.

There are some terms used in the descriptions that may be confusing. 'Brockway' style refers to a thick, heavy glass that tapers in from top to bottom. 'Federal' style, on the other hand, is thinner, and the top and bottom diameters are the same.

A&W Root Beer, The Great Root Bear, tumbler, 16-oz, Brockway style **$8.00**
American Greetings, Strawberry Shortcake, mug, 4", Apple Dumplin' on milk glass, Anchor Hocking **$4.00**
Arby's, BC Ice Age, tumbler, 3½", Zot, pinch-creased base, ca 1970s **$5.00**
Arby's, Bicentennial, tumbler, 16-oz, Bullwinkle to the Defense, Brockway style, 1976 ....**$15.00**
Arby's, Christmas (Holly & Berries), stemware, 6¾", leaves & berries above red strip w/gold trim at flared top....**$5.00**
Arby's, Currier & Ives, tumbler, 4⅝", Christmas Snow, marked Arby's Museum of the City of NY, thick heavy base...**$5.00**
Arby's, Loony Tunes, tumbler, 6", Daffy Duck saying You're Disspicable, name in banner at top, rounded bottom, 1980 ....**$10.00**
Arby's, Norman Rockwell Saturday Evening Post Summer Scenes, tumbler, 6¼", Gone Fishing, straight sides, 1987 ....**$5.00**
Arby's, Zodiac, Aries, 6¼", stylized graphics w/name at bottom, Brockway style **$5.00**
Baltimore Orioles, tumbler, 6", Cal Ripken Jr portrait w/facsimile signature & Our Great Comeback, 1984.......**$8.00**
Big Top Peanut Butter, Children's Songs, tumbler.........**$5.00**
Big Top Peanut Butter, Song Series, tumbler, 5⅛", After the Ball, heavy round base, 1940s-50s **$5.00**
Big Top Peanut Butter, State Glasses, tumbler, Montana, state w/mascot, flower, flag & state capitol.............**$5.00**
Blakely Gas, Arizona Cactus, Organ Pipe, 6½", graphics on frosted glass, 1959...**$8.00**
Borden Dairy, tumbler, 3½", Aunt Elsie in red & blue graphics w/blue verse **$25.00**

Burger Chef, Cincinnati Bengals NFL, tumbler, 5⅝", Cleveland Browns helmet on smoke glass, 1979 .... **$5.00**

Burger Chef, Endangered Species, tumbler, 5⅝", Giant Panda, indented base, marked w/Libbey Glass logo in base, 1978 .... **$5.00**

Burger Chef, Men of Mount Rushmore, tumbler, 4¼", Paul Revere, indented base, 1975 .... **$10.00**

Burger King, Bicentennial, tumbler, 5½", Eagle & Shield w/1776-1976, heavy pedestal base **$5.00**

Burger King, Denver Broncos, tumbler, 5⅝", Randy Gradeshar portrait, indented base, straight sides, 1977 .... **$8.00**

Burger King & Coca-Cola, Return of the Jedi, tumbler, 5⅝", Han Solo, indented base, straight sides, 1983 .... **$5.00**

Burger King & Dr Pepper, Dallas Cowboys, tumbler, 6", portrait & name w/ring at top, indented base, any of set of 12 .... **$5.00**

Coca-Cola, Centennial Calendar Girls, tumbler, 4⅛", 1916, lead crystal w/square base, ca 1975-76 .... **$15.00**

Coca-Cola, Disneyland, tumbler, 5⅛", full-length character w/name & Disneyland at base, Federal Glass **$25.00**

Coca-Cola, Heritage Collector Series, tumbler, 5½", Betsy Ross & Old Glory, indented base, 1976 .... **$5.00**

Coca-Cola, Heritage Collector Series, tumbler, 6", John Paul Jones, I Have Not Yet Begun To Fight, indented base, 1976 .... **$5.00**

Coca-Cola, Holly Hobbie Holidays, tumbler, A Gift of Love Especially for You, dated 1981 .... **$5.00**

Coca-Cola, Holly Hobbie Merry Christmas, tumbler, 5¾", Christmas Is Fun for Everyone, flared, heavy base **$5.00**

Coca-Cola, Holly Hobbie Simple Pleasures, tumbler, 5⅝", Make Every Day a Picnic, indented base **$5.00**

Coca-Cola, National Flag Foundation & Herfy's Food, Heritage, tumbler, 6", Alamo, colorful graphics, rounded bottom, '76 .... **$5.00**

Coca-Cola, Norman Rockwell Santa, tumbler, 6", Santa w/finger to mouth, marked 1 of 3 Series I **$2.00**

Coca-Cola, Olympics' Sam the Eagle, tumbler, 6¾", Sam in kayak, straight sided, 1980 .... **$5.00**

Coca-Cola & Walt Disney, Mickey's Christmas Carol, tumbler, 6⅛", Scrooge McDuck, flared rim, 1982 .... **$8.00**

Country Time Lemonade, Saturday Evening Post (Rockwell), tumbler, Low & Outside, indented base **$5.00**

DC Comics, Super Heroes Action Series, tumbler, 6¼", Aquaman, thick, dated 1978 .... **$10.00**

Domino's Pizza & Will Vinton Productions, Noids, tumbler, 5", indented base, straight sides, Libbey Glass logo, 1988 .... **$8.00**

Dr Pepper & Paramount Pictures, Happy Days, tumbler, Potsie, no record on back, deep indented base, 1977 .... **$5.00**

Godfather's Pizza, Seattle Supersonics, tumbler, 5⅝", Kesler, Shelton & Talbert portraits, rounded bottom **$5.00**

Godfather's Pizza & Warner Brothers, The Goonies, tumbler, 5⅝", Sloth Comes to the Rescue, indented base, 1985 .... **$5.00**

Hallmark, Charmers, tumbler, 5", It's Good To Take Time, slightly flared top, 1975 .... **$8.00**

Hardee's, The Chipmunks, tumbler, 6", Alvin, name at bottom, rounded base, marked Bagdesarian Productions, Libbey, 1985 .... **$5.00**

Harvey Cartoon, Action Series, tumbler, 5", Big Baby Hubey & barbells, thick, flared sides, Brockway Glass Company **$15.00**

Holiday Freeze, Davy Crockett, 4¼" **$10.00**

Kellogg's, tumbler, 4¼", Dig 'Em, deep indented base, mail-in premium, 1977 .... **$8.00**

Knox Gas, Oklahoma Indians, tumbler, 6½", Hen-Toh Wyandot on frosted glass, late 1950s **$10.00**

Libbey Glass Company, M*A*S*H Series, tumbler, 6", Hot Lips, straight sided w/slightly flared, Libbey logo **$60.00**

Little Ceasar's, Detroit Tigers, tumbler, 3 players w/names, indented base, flared, 1984, any of set of 4 .... **$15.00**

Marriott's, Shot Glass w/Moon, tumbler, 4¾", Buggs Bunny w/orange moon & black letters, 1975 .... **$8.88**

Mattel & Libbey Glass Company, Masters of the Universe, tumbler, 5⅝", indented base, straight sides, 1986 .... **$8.00**

McDonald's, Garfield Mug Series, mug, 4", Use Your Friends Wisely & colorful graphics on clear, 1987 .... **$5.00**

McDonald's, McDonaldland Action, tumbler, 6⅛", Grimace on pogo stick, indented base, 1977 .... **$10.00**

McDonald's, Milwaukee Brewers, tumbler, 5⅝", Gorman Thomas & Cecil Cooper, indented base, straight sides, 1982 .... **$8.00**

McDonald's, Olympic Mugs, mug, 4", 4 graphically stylized events & logos on back on clear glass, 1984 .... **$5.00**

McDonald's, Pittsburgh Steelers, tumbler, on-the-rocks; 4¾", portraits & names, 1 of 4, Libbey logo, 1982 .... **$15.00**

Michael Jackson, tumbler, 5¼", Pepsi-Cola promotion for Thriller video, straight sides, minimum value **$150.00**

Mickey Mouse Club, Walt Disney Film Strip, tumbler, 5", Mickey on skates, indented base, Libbey logo **$8.00**

Mobile Oil & National Football League, NFL Helmets, tumbler, 5½", Atlanta Falcons, indented base, Libbey Glass, 1988...**$4.00**

Mountain Dew, Wisconsin Badger Series, tumbler, Hockey, rounded bottom, flared sides, ca 1979-80 ....**$40.00**

Nintendo, Super Mario 2, tumbler, 6¼", 1989 ....**$2.00**

Pancho's Mexican Restaurant, tumbler, 5½", Pancho in yellow hat, rounded bottom, no Pepsi logo **$8.00**

PAT Ward Productions, Action Series, tumbler, 5⅛", Bullwinkle w/balloons, thick.......................................**$15.00**

Pepsi-Cola, Flintstones, tumbler, 1977, Hanna-Barbera, any..$15.00

Pepsi-Cola, goblet, blue script on clear, footed **$4.00**

Pepsi-Cola, The 12 Days of Christmas, tumbler, 6⅛", 1st Day, straight sides **$4.00**

Pepsi-Cola, tumbler, Taco Time w/cactus, simple graphics, rounded base, straight sides **$4.00**

Pepsi-Cola, Warner Brothers Looney Tunes Action Series, tumbler, 5⅞", Tweety & Sylvester, rounded bottom, 1979...**$5.00**

Pepsi-Cola & DC Comics, Super Heroes, Moon Series, tumbler, 6¼", Batman, thick, flared sides, 1976 ....**$15.00**

Pepsi-Cola & Herfy's Foods, tumbler, Herfy's 20th Anniversary, 1982 Seattle World's Fair premium **$25.00**

Pepsi-Cola & Shakey's Pizza, tumbler, 5⅞", logos in stained glass design, rounded bottom, straight sides...........**$4.00**

Pepsi-Cola & Visual Creations, Friends Are Us, tumbler, 6¼", You Give Me a Life at bottom, thick, no logo **$10.00**

Pizza Hut, Care Bears, tumbler, 6", Grumpy Bear w/Hugs Welcome at bottom, Libbey logo in bottom, 1983..**$5.00**

Pizza Hut & Hanna-Barbera, Flintstones Kids, tumbler, 6", Betty, round bottom, 1986.......................................**$2.00**

Pizza Hut & National Football League, Green Bay Packers, tumbler, 6¼", Bart Star portrait, straight sides.......**$15.00**

Pizza Hut & Universal Studios, ET, tumbler, 6", I'll Be Right Here, flared top, 1982 ....**$2.00**

Sears & Walt Disney, Winnie-the-Pooh, tumbler, 5", Tigger & Pooh planting tree, round bottom **$2.00**

Sneaky Petes in Alabama, Li'l Abner, tumbler, 6¼", full-length Daisy Mae w/lamb, Brockway style, 1975.**$40.00**

Sonoco Gas, Batman, tumbler, 4¼", Batman's car & logo, marked Canada, 1989 ....**$5.00**

Sunoco Canadian Gas Co, Ghostbusters II, tumbler, 5", Nunzio Scoleri portrait, indented base **$8.00**

Sunoco Gas & Walt Disney, Mickey Thru the Ages, tumbler, 5⅛", 1928 Steamboat Willie, indented base, 1988...**$8.00**

United Oil, Baseball Past Greats, tumbler, 5", Babe Ruth (1936), rounded bottom, 1988......................**$15.00**

Universal City Studios, Monster Series, tumbler, 6⅝", Creature from the Black Lagoon, straight sides, 1960s.........**$25.00**

Universal Studios, Battlestar Galactica, tumbler, 6", Apollo, rounded bottom, 1979 ....**$5.00**

Walt Disney, All Star Parade, tumbler, 4¼", Big Bad Wolf & the 3 Little Pigs, banner at top, 1939 ....**$60.00**

Walt Disney, Davy Crocket, tumbler, 4¼", green graphics & Steady Nerves verse..**$15.00**

Walt Disney, Davy Crockett, tumbler, 5⅝", green & white graphics, fighting Indian, ribbed interior................**$8.00**

Walt Disney, Davy Crockett, tumbler, 7", chasing Indians w/words Holiday Freeze, slightly tapered.............**$10.00**

Walt Disney, Donald Duck, tumbler, 4¾", Donald Cooking, Nephews on back, banner at top, 1930s...............**$80.00**

Walt Disney, Sleeping Beauty, tumbler, 5", Briar Rose & Friends, slightly curved heavy base, 1958 ....**$15.00**

Walt Disney, The Rescuers, tumbler, 6¼", Brutus & Nero, thick, slightly flared, 1977......................................**$25.00**

Walt Disney, Wonderful World, tumbler, 6", 101 Dalmations, rounded bottom **$10.00**

Walter Lantz, tumbler, 5¾", Andy Panda & Miranda, thick, indented base, straight sides, no logo **$8.00**

Welches Jelly, Archies, tumbler, 4¼", Archie Takes the Gang for a Ride, embossed face in bottom, 1971 ....**$5.00**

Welches Jelly, Flintstones, tumbler, 4¼", Fred & Barney Play... around top w/graphics below, tapered sides **$4.00**

Welches Jelly, Howdy Doody, tumbler, Ding Dong Dell Ring the Bell..., face in bottom, dated 1953 ....**$10.00**

Wendy's, Cleveland Browns, tumbler, 6¼", Brian Sipe portrait in star, Wendy's logo around top, straight sides, 1981...**$8.00**

Wendy's & 7-Up, Indiana Jones & Temple of Doom, tumbler, 5¾", High Priest Mola, straight sides, 1984 .....**$8.00**

7-11 & Marvel Comics, tumbler, 5⅝", Fantastic Four, indented base, straight sides, 1977.......................**$8.00**

9 Lives, Morris the Cat, tumbler, portrait & Morris on Glass Is Like Sterling on Silver, indented base, flared......**$8.00**

Character Collectibles

Any popular personality, whether factual or fictional, has been promoted through the retail market to some degree. Depending upon the degree of their popularity, we may be deluged with this merchandise for weeks, months, even years. It's no wonder, then, that the secondary market abounds with these items or that there is such wide-spread collector demand for them today. There are rarities in any field, but for the beginning collector, many nice items are readily available at prices most can afford. Western heroes, TV and movie personalities, superheroes, comic book characters, and sports greats are the most sought after.

For more information, we recommend *Character Toys and Collectibles* by David Longest and *Toys of the Sixties* by Bill Bruegman.

See also Beatles Collectibles; Betty Boop Collectibles; Bubble Bath Containers; Character and Promotional Drinking Glasses; Character Watches; Dionne Quintuplets; Disney Collectibles; Elvis Presley Memorabilia; Gone with the Wind; Holly Hobbie; Movie Stars; Paper Dolls; Peanuts Collectibles; Pez Candy Containers; Popeye Collectibles; Puzzles; Radio Personalities; Rock 'n Roll Memorabilia; Shirley Temple; Star Trek Memorabilia; Star Wars Trilogy Collectibles; Three Stooges Memorabilia; Toys; Western Heroes; Wizard of Oz Collectibles.

Alphonse & Gaston, bandana, 12x12", printed cloth, VG .**$65.00**
Andy Gump, nodder, 4", bisque, marked Germany, EX..**$65.00**
Andy Gump & Min, figurines, 7", painted bisque, 1930s, pr **$120.00**
Atom Ant, push puppet, marked Kohner, NM.............**$28.00**
Baba Louie, bank, marked Knickerbocker & Hanna Barbera, 1970s, EX **$10.00**
Baba Louie, doll, marked Knickerbocker, 1959, EX....**$30.00**
Babar & Pom, figural hand-painted soap, 1930s, MIB .**$20.00**
Baby Barry (Li'l Abner), puppet, EX...........................**$52.00**
Bam Bam, doll, 12½", Ideal, EX...................................**$75.00**
Barney Google, figurine, 4", china, marked Germany, EX **$65.00**
Batman, bank, bust figural, Mego, EX.......................**$32.50**

Batman, belt, made by Morris Belt Company, Long Island City, 1966, MIB.......................................$40.00
Batman, charm bracelet, 6", gold metal w/small painted charms, marked National Periodical Publications, 1966, M on card **$50.00**
Batman, Colorforms, 1976, VG...................................**$15.00**
Batman, doll, 24", marked Presents, NM **$20.00**
Batman, fork, silverplate, figural handle, 1966, NM.....**$15.00**
Batman, Magic Slate, 1966, VG **$22.50**
Batman, marked Spectra Star, 1989, M on card **$7.50**
Batman, pen, 6", baseball bat form w/Batman logo & Bat Pen in black, unmarked, late 1960s, EX **$15.00**
Batman, postcard, color photo w/facsimile autographs, 1966, EX..**$15.00**

Batman, puppet, vinyl, Ideal, ca 1960s, M **$45.00**
Batman, ring, 1¼x2¼", dark red rubber bat figural, marked Samsons Products & dated 1966, VG.....................**$15.00**
Batman, slippers, 10" long, acrylic sock top w/vinyl sole, marked DC Comics Inc, M **$32.00**
Batman, stickers, 4x4", Bat Stickers, marked Allen-Whitney Co, 1966 copyright, set of 4 in original cellophane bag, M..**$30.00**
Batman, switchplate, dated 1975, M **$8.00**
Batman & Robin, mask, reversible printed cardboard, dated 1966, NM **$15.00**
Beany & Cecil, chalkboard, 20x30", marked Pressman, 1966, EX..**$37.50**

Betty Boop, cloth doll, sewn-on earrings, removable panties & dress, c King Features, made by Colorforms, 1977, M...$60.00
Betty Boop, doll, 9", plastic w/vinyl head, marked Hong Kong on back, 1976-77, M in package **$15.00**
Betty Boop, film, Cinderella, Duracolor, made for home projector, 1930s..**$45.00**
Betty Boop, pin, 2⅜x1¾", figural celluloid w/flat metal back, unmarked, G **$25.00**
Betty Boop, playing cards, 3½x2¼", Betty portrait on orange or blue & white design, 1930s, 52-card set, EX **$75.00**
Betty Boop, sheet music, Aint'cha, Helen Cane portrait on cover, from Pointed Heels, 1929 movie, EX.........**$17.50**
Betty Boop, transfer, colorful, 1930s, M **$10.00**
Betty Boop & Koko, saucer, 3", glazed china, 1930s, EX..**$35.00**
Bimbo, figurine, 3", painted bisque, playing violin, 1930s, EX...**$35.00**
Blondie, figurine, 2½", cast lead, ca 1940s, EX...........**$22.00**
Bonzo, tablet, A Dog's Life, 1930s **$42.50**

Bozo the Clown, coloring book, #1185, M...................$15.00

Bozo the Clown, mask, 10½x12½", full-color die-cut paper, ad for Capitol Records on back, 1950s, EX...........$20.00

Bringing Up Father, coloring book, Whitman, 1936, EX.$27.50

Buck Rogers, battle cruiser, Tootsietoy #1032, EX $125.00

Buck Rogers, binoculars, Super Sonic Glasses, 1953, M .$80.00

Buck Rogers, Colorforms, 1979, MIB...........................$17.50

Buck Rogers, Halloween pail, 1970s, EX.......................$6.00

Buck Rogers, model, 9x11½x3" box, Marauder, marked Monogram & Universal Studios, copyright 1979, MIB...$20.00

Buck Rogers, pencil box, red & blue, 1935, EX...........$60.00

Buck Rogers, sunglasses, unmarked, 1940s, M on card..$55.00

Bugs Bunny, magic slate, marked Eldco, 1975, M.........$6.00

Bugs Bunny, paper plates, 7", 1965, M in package $12.50

Bugs Bunny, pencil sharpener, marked Janex, battery operated, 1975, VG...$12.50

Bugs Bunny, planter, 5", ceramic, Shaw, Los Angeles..$85.00

Bullwinkle, bulletin board, marked Magee Company, 1960s, NM $38.00

Bullwinkle, coloring book, Make Way for Bullwinkle, 1972, EX $10.00

Bullwinkle, doll, 14", stuffed cloth, Gund, 1970, EX ...$52.50

Bullwinkle, playset, Make Your Badge, marked Laramie, 1979, M on card $10.00

Bullwinkle, spelling & counting board, marked Laramie, 1969, M on card $10.00

Captain America, coloring book, Whitman, 1966, NM .$12.50

Captain Marvel, model, Buzz Bomb airplane, original envelope, M $20.00

Captain Marvel, party horn, paper, marked Fawcett Publications, EX $30.00

Captain Meteor, gun & holster set, Cosmic Ray Gun, boxed, EX...$60.00

Captain Midnight, cup, marked Beetleware, EX.........$55.00

Captain Midnight, stamps, Skelly Air Heroes, set of 16, NM $30.00

Casper the Friendly Ghost, record, 78 rpm, 1962, EX ...$8.00

Casper the Ghost, figurine, rubber, marked Sutton, M in package $40.00

Cecil, puppet, talking, Mattel, 1961, M $60.00

Charlie McCarthy, bubble gum wrapper, EX.................$4.00

Charlie McCarthy, doll, rubber, marked Effanbee, M ..$90.00

Charlie McCarthy, game, Radio Party, complete w/original envelope, EX...$26.00

Charlie McCarthy, get well card, 1930s, EX................$17.50

Charlie McCarthy, mask, molded gauze, complete w/separate monocle, EX...$75.00

Charlie McCarthy, paint book, 11x13", Whitman, 1938, EX...$45.00

Chester Gump, nodder, 2½", painted ceramic, 1930s, EX..$65.00

Chipmunks, magic slate, Alvin at top, 1960s, EX.........$22.50

Churchy (Pogo), figurine, 4½", plastic, 1969, M...........$15.00

Clarabell, wash mitt, 7x8", terry cloth puppet, marked Bernhard Ullmann Co, 1950s, NM $40.00

Cookie (Blondie's daughter), figure, 3", wood, dated 1944, EX...$35.00

Dagwood Bumstead, planter, 5", head figural, marked KFS, EX...$30.00

Daisy Mae, bank, 7", full-color ceramic figural, NM $37.50

Dennis the Menace, doll, 7", Hall, 1957, M.................$45.00

Dennis the Menace, spoon, silverplate, EX.................$15.00

Dick Tracy, activity book, Sparkle Plenty Cutouts, ca 1948, NM $37.50

Dick Tracy, book, Manual & Code, dated 1939, EX....$62.50

Dick Tracy, book Snowflake & Shaky, Fawcett Publishing, paperback, EX..$15.00

Dick Tracy, camera, marked Seymour, early 1950s, VG ..$40.00

Dick Tracy, candy bar wrapper, ca 1950, NM.............$30.00

Dick Tracy, coloring book, 11x14", Whitman, 1935, EX ..$45.00

Dick Tracy, comic book, Wheaties premium, 1938, NM $15.00

Dick Tracy, crime lab, marked Ja-Ru, ca 1980s, M on card...$12.50

Dick Tracy, film viewer, w/2 films, 1940s, EX.............$90.00

Dick Tracy, police station, 6x9x3", wind-up toy, made by Marx, EX in original box $150.00

Dick Tracy, puppet, Ideal, 1961, M $50.00

Dick Tracy, televiewer, marked Laramie, dated 1978, M on card...$25.00

Dr Seuss, alarm clock, Cat in the Hat, metal, ca 1978, EX.$110.00

Dr Seuss, book bag, 1960s, NM $17.50

Dr Seuss, record, 33 1/3 rpm, How the Grinch Stole Christmas, dated 1975, M...$15.00

Dudley Do-Right, bop bag, MIP **$17.50**

Dudley Do-Right, coloring book, Artcraft, 1962, NM ..**$20.00**

Dudley Do-Right, figurine, marked Wham-O, 1972, EX ..**$15.00**

Elmer Fudd, figurine, painted ceramic, marked Shaw, 1940s, EX..**$70.00**

Farmer Alfalfa (Terrytoons), doll, 17½", stuffed body w/vinyl head & hands, ca 1950, M..................................**$60.00**

Felix the Cat, book, Comic Adventures of Felix, dated 1923, VG..**$70.00**

Felix the Cat, flashlight, marked Bantamlite, M on card...**$60.00**

Felix the Cat, tablecloth, illustrations on paper, 1960s, NM..**$27.50**

Flash Gordon, belt, rocket ship on lg plastic buckle, 1950s, M..**$45.00**

Flash Gordon, coloring book, Saalfield, 1958, NM **$25.00**

Flash Gordon, gun, 1½", red-painted aluminum w/decal, marked Budson Company, EX................................**$55.00**

Flash Gordon, water pistol, plastic, 1950s, M **$40.00**

Flub-A-Dub, figurine, 3", plastic, MIB........................**$40.00**

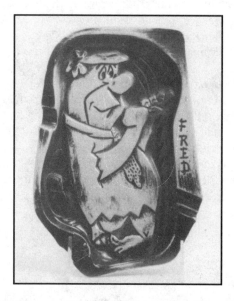

Fred Flintstone, ashtray, 8", ceramic, black & white, Hanna-Barbera, 1961......................................$18.00

Fred Flintstone, night light, figural, marked Hanna-Barbera, M in package..**$10.00**

Green Hornet, bracelet, dated 1966, M on card..........**$60.00**

Green Hornet, coloring book, Kato's Revenge, marked Watkins, 1966, VG **$17.50**

Green Hornet, playing cards, 1966, EX **$20.00**

Green Hornet, spoon, silverplated, dated 1966, EX **$15.00**

Gumby, hand puppet, marked Lakeside, dated 1965, NM..**$25.00**

Happy Hooligan, pencil holder, 8½", painted bisque figural, NM..**$150.00**

Happy Hooligan, puppet, 9¼", cast iron & cloth, M ...**$70.00**

Happy Hooligan, stick pin, 1¼", detailed metal, ca 1920s, EX..**$50.00**

Harold Teen, puppet, 17", painted folding cardboard, moving eyes & mouth, NM..**$40.00**

Heathcliff, bank, figural plastic, M **$10.00**

Heckle, squeeze toy, 1950s, M **$55.00**

Henry Hawk, coloring book, marked Warner Brothers #670, M..**$20.00**

Herby, doll, 10", oilcloth, M......................................**$40.00**

Howdy Doody, activity book, Follow the Dots, Whitman, 1950s, EX...**$10.00**

Howdy Doody, activity book, Fun Book, Whitman, 1951 .**$15.00**

Howdy Doody, cake decoration set, marked Kagran, 1950s, M on card..**$38.00**

Howdy Doody, child's place setting, ceramic, marked Taylor, 3 pieces...**$50.00**

Howdy Doody, pennant, 15", marked Kagran, NM.....**$35.00**

Howdy Doody, shoe polish, marked Kunkel, boxed, 1950s, EX...**$15.00**

Howdy Doody, ukulele, plastic, marked Emenee, 1950s, EX..**$75.00**

Huckleberry Hound, ring, portrait on brass, adjustable, marked Hanna-Barbera 1961 copyright, NM........**$32.00**

Huckleberry Hound, spoon, 6", marked Old Company Plate, 1960s, EX...**$15.00**

Jeff, stick puppet, 12", EX..**$60.00**

Jiggs, figurine, 1¾", gold-tone metal, EX...................**$35.00**

Jiggs, figurine, 3", hard plastic, 1960s, M...................**$12.00**

Joe Palooka, doll, 4", jointed wood, M.......................**$70.00**

Jolly Blinker, figurine, 10", vinyl clothespin w/painted features & chef hat, EX..**$12.50**

Katzenjammer Kids, coloring book, 1930s, EX **$37.50**

King Leonardo, coloring book, Whitman, 1965, EX **$30.00**

Lamb Chop, puppet, 11", 1960s, EX **$22.00**

Li'l Abner, greeting cards, 1940s, set of 15, all different, original illustrated envelopes, M...............................**$48.00**

Li'l Abner, mask, painted rubber, marked Al Capp, 1950s, EX..**$22.50**

Li'l Abner, paint set, contains paints, crayons, brush, coloring sheets, 1957, M...**$145.00**

Li'l Abner, tray, 12" dia, Dogpatch USA w/characters & scenes on black, plastic, Capp Ent, ca '68.............**$30.00**

Linus the Lionhearted, doll, 10", stuffed plush, Post premium, 1965, M...**$32.50**

Linus the Lionhearted, record, 33 1/3 rpm, colorful sleeve, 1964, EX...**$35.00**

Little Audrey, puppet, cloth w/vinyl head, VG...........**$12.50**

Little Lulu, book, Shape Book, Whitman, #1970, 1971, M..**$20.00**

Little Lulu, standee, 10", cardboard, Kleenex promotion, 1950s, M...**$37.50**

Little Lulu, valentines, 8½x11" sheet, punchouts, set of 4, M..**$20.00**

Little Orphan Annie, decoder, 1¾x1¼", badge type w/secret compartment, Ovaltine premium, 1936, EX..........**$55.00**

Little Orphan Annie, mug, 3", marked Beetleware, NM..**$25.00**

Little Red Riding Hood, pencil box, die-cut figural, marked Dixon, 1934, EX...**$100.00**

Loopy De Loop, coloring book, Whitman, 1965, NM..**$28.00**

Maggie, figurine, 3", hard plastic, 1960s, M..................**$12.00**

Magilla Gorilla, coloring book, Whitman, 1965, NM ...**$25.00**

Magilla Gorilla, doll, 19", Ideal, 1960s, EX................**$300.00**

Magilla Gorilla, push puppet, marked Kohner, EX......**$28.00**

Major Matt Mason, coloring book, Whitman, 1968, EX.**$28.00**

Mammy Yokum, bank, M..**$17.50**

Mammy Yokum, tumbler, 5", colorful graphics & name on clear glass, EX $15.00

Mary Poppins, doll, marked Horsman, 1968, original box, NM $65.00

Max Headroom, mask, plastic, 1970s, NM $5.00

Mighty Mouse, coloring book, marked Terrytoons Treasure Coloring Book #301, copyright 1957, EX $10.00

Miss Piggy, hand puppet, 16", Fisher-Price, MIB $20.00

Moon Mullins, baking set, Pillsbury, 1937, boxed, EX ..$50.00

Moon Mullins, book, Drawing & Tracing, McLoughlin Brothers, 1932, EX............................$32.50

Moon Mullins, mask, 1933, M $40.00

Mortimer Snerd, figurine, 13", composition & wire, Ideal, EX $112.00

Mr Magoo, coloring book, Whitman, 1965, EX............$12.50

Mr Magoo, hand puppet, M $50.00

Mr Magoo, sign, advertising Stag Beer, dated 1958, NM ...$58.00

Mr Potato Head, pencil case, plastic figural, Hasbro, EX....$45.00

Noid, figure, Bendee, bendable plastic, M $8.00

Olive Oyl, hand puppet, marked Gund, EX $25.00

Olive Oyl, marionette, 11", Gund, M $70.00

Olive Oyl, mask, cardboard, 1940s, M....................$40.00

Olive Oyl, mask, cardboard cut from cereal box, 1950s, VG............................$15.00

Olive Oyl, push puppet, marked Kohner, M $25.00

Oliver Hardy, hand puppet, Knickerbocker, M $40.00

Oscar Goldman, doll, 13", EX $22.50

Oswald Rabbit, doll, 7½", Sun Rubber, 1950s, M in package $27.50

Ozark Ike, Christmas card, ca 1950s, M....................$7.00

Pee Wee Herman, beach towel, 60", M....................$25.00

Pee Wee Herman, growth chart, MIP $8.00

Pepe Le Pew, doll, 24", Columbia Pictures promotion item, 1950, NM $45.00

Pink Panther, hand puppet, cloth body, Gund, early, M............................$30.00

Pogo Possum, figurine, 4", vinyl, marked Walt Kelley Made in Japan, w/1969 copyright, NM $12.00

Pogo Possum, mug, painted plastic, 1970s, NM...........$6.00

Pokey, figurine, marked Bendee, ca 1960s, M...........$20.00

Pokey, hand puppet, marked Lakeside, 1965, NM $22.50

Popeye, bank, 9½", vinyl figural, dated 1979, EX........$45.00

Popeye, bubble pipe, early plastic, EX....................$5.00

Popeye, charm, figural celluloid, 1930s, M $15.00

Popeye, Colorforms, #2110, 1957, M $60.00

Popeye, doll, cloth w/vinyl head, Uneeda, 1979, M....$40.00

Popeye, doll, 10", plush w/vinyl face, musical, marked Gund, 1950s, EX............................$45.00

Popeye, kazoo, color lithograph on tin, EX.................$65.00

Popeye, mask, cardboard, 1940s, EX....................$45.00

Popeye, paint book, McLoughlin Brothers, 1932, EX ..$45.00

Popeye, paint set, American Crayon, 1949, EX...........$17.50

Rootie Kazootie, hand puppet, 1950s, EX.................$60.00

Samson & Goliath, coloring book, Whitman, 1967, NM ..$22.50

Scrappy, 3½", painted bisque figure, marked Japan, 1930s, EX............................$40.00

Shadow, bookmark, 3", 1940s, EX....................$10.00

Shmoo, doll, 15", inflatable vinyl, 1940s, EX.............$90.00

Shmoo, key chain, 1½", green plastic figural w/painted features $45.00

Skippy, sheet music, 1930s, EX............................$20.00

Skippy, toothbrush holder, 6", figural bisque, 1930s, EX...$85.00

Smilin' Jack, coloring book, Saalfield, copyright 1946, EX..$30.00

Smokey Bear, ashtray, 6" dia, figure standing on forest scene, marked Norcrest Japan on foil sticker, M ..$35.00

Smokey Bear, booklet, Fire Safety Manual, dated 1955, EX $5.00

Smokey Bear, bookmark, dated 1965, M....................$5.00

Smokey Bear, figurine, 6", painted vinyl, marked Bendee, EX............................$8.00

Sniffles the Mouse, planter, marked Moss Metals, 1950s, EX $100.00

Snuffy Smith, charm, silver metal figure, EX..............$17.50

Snuffy Smith, puppet, cloth body w/rubber head, marked Gund & King Features, M............................$60.00

Spiderman, puppet, Ideal, 1967, EX $45.00

Tarzan, mask, paper, Northern Paper Mills, 1933, EX...$100.00

Tennessee Jed, blotter, Tip Top Bread, framed........$25.00

Terry & the Pirates, pop-up book, Blue Ribbon Press, 1935, EX............................$15.00

Tillie the Toiler, book, drawing type, 1930s, EX..........$30.00

Tom & Jerry, bookends, marked Gorham, 1981, NM..$25.00

Tom & Jerry, paint book, 1952, M $20.00

Tom Corbett Space Cadet, coloring book, 12x15", Saalfield, 1950, M $70.00

Tony the Tiger, doll, 25", straw-stuffed cloth, 1960s, EX..$30.00

Topo Gigio, doll, 11", vinyl, 1960s, EX....................$15.00

Topo Gigo, nodder, EX............................$45.00

Underdog, doll, 15", Gund, 1970, EX $60.00

Walter Lantz, stamp set, 12 different rubber stamps, M ..$24.00

Wendy (Casper the Ghost), coloring book, Artcraft, 1960, NM $20.00

Wendy (Peter Pan), hand puppet, 1950s, EX.............$15.00

Wile E Coyote, eraser, 2¼", green rubber figure, 1971, EX $2.00

Willie the Weatherman, Colorforms, #2109, 1957, M ..$50.00

Wimpy, figurine, 3", hard plastic, 1960s, M.............$24.00

Wimpy, mask, cardboard, 1940s, M....................$20.00

Wimpy, puppet, Gund, EX............................$38.00

Wonder Woman, coloring book, Whitman, 1979, M...$12.50

Wonder Woman, valentine, 1940s, EX $15.00

Woody Woodpecker, bowl & mug set, graphics on wood-grained plastic, F&F Mold & Die Works, EX........$32.50

Woody Woodpecker, doll, 16", Knickerbocker, 1960s, NM $45.00

Woody Woodpecker, lamp, 20", figural plastic, M $40.00

Woody Woodpecker, magic slate, w/wooden stylus, 1960s, VG............................$10.00

Woody Woodpecker, spoon, silverplate, NM $18.00

Yellow Kid, ad card, 3½x5", early, EX....................$45.00

Yogi Bear, doll, 7½", Knickerbocker, 1973, M...........$25.00

Yogi Bear, hand puppet, marked Knickerbocker, 1961, EX $17.50

Yogi Bear, paint set, Presto, 1964, MIB $30.00

Yogi Bear, spoon, 6", marked Old Company Plate, 1960s, EX............................$15.00

Yogi Bear, yo-yo, marked Justen Products, dated 1976, M on card **$15.00**

Yosemite Sam, mug, glazed ceramic, marked Japan, 1960s, EX...**$40.00**

Zero (Beetle Bailey), puppet, vinyl & cloth, Gund, 1960s, EX...**$45.00**

Character Watches

There is a growing interest in the comic character watches and clocks produced from about 1930 into the fifties and beyond. They're in rather short supply simply because they were made for children to wear (and play with). They were cheaply made with pin-lever movements, not worth an expensive repair job, so many were simply thrown away. The original packaging that today may be worth more than the watch itself was usually ripped apart by an excited child and promptly relegated to the wastebasket.

Condition is very important in assessing value. Unless a watch is in like-new condition, it is not mint. Rust, fading, scratching, or wear of any kind will sharply lessen its value, and the same is true of the box itself. Good, excellent, and mint watches can be evaluated on a scale of one to five, with excellent being a three. In other words, a watch worth $25.00 in good condition would be worth five times that if it were mint ($125.00). Beware of dealers who substitute a generic watch box for the original. Remember that these too were designed to appeal to children and (99% of the time) were printed with colorful graphics.

Some of these watches have been reproduced, so beware. When the description includes the term 'die-debossed' (die-stamped) back, make sure the watch you're trying to evaluate has this design. Otherwise, it's probably not authentic. For more information, we recommend *Comic Character Clocks and Watches* by Howard S. Brenner.

Pocket Watches

Cinderella, US Time, w/original inside box display .$80.00

Hopalong Cassidy, US Time, 1950, M **$175.00**

Mickey Mouse, Bradley, 1976, Bicentennial, MIB........**$50.00**

Mickey Mouse, Ingersoll, 1938, decal on back, EX ...**$285.00**

Popeye, New Haven, 1934, characters around dial, EX.**$210.00**

Superman, Bradley, 1959, M **$200.00**

Three Little Pigs, Ingersoll, 1934, wolf's eye blinks, die-debossed back, red dial, EX...........................**$270.00**

Tom Mix, Ingersoll, 1934, Always Find Time for a Good Deed on die-debossed back, w/original fob, very rare, G **$120.00**

Wristwatches

Babe Ruth, Exacta Time, 1949, MIB **$300.00**

Batman, Timex, 1978, MIB.......................................**$50.00**

Captain Liberty, Liberty Watch Company, 1951, EX **$60.00**

Dale Evans, Ingraham, 1951, expansion band, EX **$30.00**

Davy Crockett, US Time, 1954, w/figural powder horn holder, MIB **$150.00**

Donald Duck, Ingersoll, 1948, 1 of 10 in birthday series, MIB **$275.00**

Dopey, Ingersoll, 1948, 1 of 10 in birthday series, EX **$75.00**

Goofy, Helbros, 1972, numbers & hands run backwards, 17 jewels, MIB...**$225.00**

Howdy Doody, Patent Watch Co, 1954, moving eyes, $7.95 original price, MIB...**$250.00**

Joe Carioca, Ingersoll, 1953, 1 of 10 in birthday series, EX **$75.00**

Joe Palooka, New Haven, 1947, EX...........................**$90.00**

Little Pig, US Time, 1947, EX....................................**$75.00**

Mary Marvel, Fawcett, 1948, MIB..............................**$200.00**

Mickey Mouse, US Time, 1958, w/porcelain figural, MIB...**$150.00**

Mickey Mouse Club, Bradley, 1982, Mickey Mouse on face, MIB **$40.00**

Orphan Annie, New Haven, 1948, EX.........................**$60.00**

Robin, Timex, 1978, M..**$35.00**

Robin Hood, Viking, 1938, M.....................................**$100.00**

Rocky Jones, Ingraham, 1954, EX..............................**$75.00**

Smitty, New Haven, 1935, EX **$100.00**

Superman, Timex, 1976, MIB.....................................**$50.00**

Tom Corbett, Ingraham, 1951, M **$50.00**

Chase Brass and Copper Company

In the thirties, this company began to produce quality products styled in the new 'modernist' style that had become so dominate in the European market. They turned to some of the country's leading designers, Russel Wright and Rockwell Kent among them, and developed a wonderful assortment of serving pieces, smoking accessories, and various other items for the home which they marketed at prices the public could afford. They favored chromium over more expensive materials such as silver, copper, brass, and nickel plate (though these continued to be used in limited amounts). Handles were made of Bakelite or some other type of plastic, and many pieces had glass inserts.

Many newlyweds received Chase products as wedding gifts, and now sadly they've reached the time in their lives where they're beginning to unload some of the nice things they've held on to for years. So it's not uncommon to find some very good examples on the market today. Many show little or no sign of use. Most are marked; if you don't find it right away, look on the screws and rivets. Sets may contain only one marked piece. Unmarked items should be carefully evaluated to see if they meet the high Chase standards of quality. It's best to compare them with pictures of verified pieces or similar items that are marked to be sure. Many items are shown in *The Chase Era* and *Art Deco Chrome, Book 2, A Collector's Guide, Industrial Design in the Chase Era,* both by Richard J. Kilbride.

Aristocrat ashtray, 4" dia bowl, 5½" across handles, polished chromium w/black plastic handles, #835 .... **$60.00**

Automatic table lighter, 3¼x1½" dia, polished chromium w/black, red or tortoise enamel, #825 .... **$70.00**

Barnegat lamp, 11¼", polished brass w/red or green base light, 9½" parchment shade w/map motif, #6314 .... **$90.00**

Blue Moon cocktail cup, 3½x2¼" dia, polished chromium & deep blue glass, holds 3 ozs, #90067 .... **$40.00**

Bubble candlestick, 2½x2½" square base, polished chromium w/dark blue glass, #17063 .... **$100.00**

Bubble cigarette server, 2¼x2⅜" dia, polished chromium & blue glass, holds 20 cigarettes, #860 .... **$43.00**

Butter dish, 2⅝x6" dia, polished chromium w/white plastic knob, #17067 .... **$95.00**

Calyx vase, 7⅞x5½" dia, polished chromium or copper, flared rim, #3011 .... **$65.00**

Candy dish, 3⅛x7" dia, satin brass or copper w/white plastic knob, glass liner, Gerth design, #90011 .... **$55.00**

Cannonball humidor, 6¾x6¼", polished chromium or copper, sponge moistener in plastic lid, #17094 .... **$65.00**

Canterbury bell, 3¾x2¼" dia, polished copper or polished chromium w/white plastic handle, #13008 .... **$37.00**

Chester lamp, 11¾", polished brass, 9" parchment shade, w/socket reducer, #6194 .... **$75.00**

Cocktail cup, 2x2¾", polished chromium, #26002 .... **$15.00**

Cocktail set, 11½" shaker, 16" tray, 4 2" cups, polished chromium decorated w/black, #90064 .... $250.00

Cocktail tray, 15⅞x5⅜", polished chromium, #9013 .... **$55.00**

D'Orsay lamp, 18¼", polished brass or tole red, 13½" metalized parchment shade, polished brass finish, #6317 .... **$65.00**

Diana flower bowl, 10" dia, polished chromium or copper w/white plastic base, #15005 .... **$60.00**

Fairfax relish dish, 1x8½", polished chromium w/white plastic handles, glass liner, #90128 .... **$50.00**

Ice crusher, polished chromium, 6" long, can be used as ice tongs as well, #90135 .... **$30.00**

Jubilee syrup jug, 4¼x3½" dia, on 5⅝" dia plate, polished chromium & clear ribbed glass, #26004 .... **$45.00**

Masthead lantern, 8⅝x4¾", polished brass w/clear crystal, red or green globe, electric, #25008 .... **$32.00**

Midas cigarette box, 1⅛x9⅛x2¾", black plastic w/satin brass cover, holds 3 packs, #878 .... **$50.00**

Mt Vernon hurricane lamp, 8½", polished brass or satin silver w/hand-cut crystal chimney, #6316 .... **$65.00**

Old-fashioned cocktail cup, 2⅞, polished chromium w/red, green, black or white muddler knob, #90063 .... **$30.00**

Pendant plant bowl, 5½x6¼" dia, polished copper or English bronze, complete w/chain, #4004 .... **$65.00**

Pilot bookends, 6⅜x4⅜x3½", polished brass w/natural walnut & brown plastic, modeled as a ship's wheel form, #90138, pr **$150.00**

Puritan candle snuffer, 15½" long, polished brass or satin silver w/white plastic, #90151 .... **$26.00**

Rippled flowerpot, 4¾x6⅛" dia, polished brass or copper, ripple design on lower half, #4007 .... **$28.00**

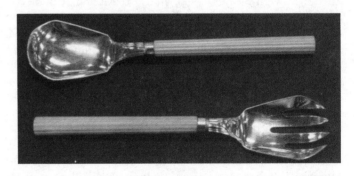

Salad fork & spoon, chrome w/celluloid handle .$50.00

Sconce light (battery), 7⅜", polished brass or combination of polished brass & copper, white candle, #16004 .... **$70.00**

Sentinel lamp, 15⅞", polished brass w/red or blue plastic, 8⅞" parchment shade, #17112 .... **$200.00**

Serving fork & spoon, 10⅛", polished chromium, white or walnut-colored plastic handles, #90076, pr **$65.00**

Silent butler, 1½x11⅜x5⅝", polished copper w/white plastic handle, #17111 .... **$95.00**

Sunbird desk lamp, 9¼", polished chromium or brass w/black plastic, 5½" metal shade, #6320 .... **$100.00**

Tarpon fishbowl, 7⅞x7⅞" dia, amber bronze base w/clear glass bowl, Dennis design, #90125 .... **$45.00**

Tea ball, 5" long, polished chromium w/white plastic handle, #90118 .... **$60.00**

Three Anchors ashtray, 3½ dia, polished brass, red or green glass liner, #889, pr **$50.00**

Triple tray, 7⅛x13x11" (open), satin chromium or copper, white plastic handle, #9001 .... $125.00

Tulip serving dish, 4¼x7⅝x5½", polished chromium or copper, almond shaped, scroll handle, #90095 .... $45.00

Whisk broom, 8⅛", English bronze or polished brass, brown whisks, #90133 .... $15.00

Children's Books

There's lots of interest in children's books; some collectors limit themselves to specific authors or subject matter while others prefer to concentrate on the illustrators. Series books from the twenties and the thirties such as The Rover Boys, The Bobbsey Twins, and Nancy Drew have their own aficionados. They were produced by the Stratemeyer Syndicate and penned under the name Carolyn Keene. As with any book, first editions are the most valuable, and condition is extremely important.

A Is for Anna Belle, 1954, Tasha Tudor, Henry Z Walck Inc, w/dust jacket, VG $15.00

Adventure for Beginners, 1944, Margaret Friskey, Wilcox & Follett, Katherine Evans illustrator, 26 pages, VG. $20.00

Airplane Boys at Platinum River, 1931, EJ Craine, World Syndicate Publishing Co, G $4.00

Ali Baba & the 40 Thieves, 1940s?, Raphael Tuck, pop-up, NM $75.00

All the Mowgli Stories, 1936, Rudyard Kipling, Doubleday Doran, Wiese illustrator, 1st edition, VG $40.00

Along the Laughing Brook/On the Green Meadows, 1954, Thornton Burgess, Little Brown, Cady illustrator, dust jacket, M $200.00

Alphabet Dreams, 1976, Judith Brown, Prentice-Hall, illustrated by author, 1st edition, w/dust jacket, M $15.00

Alphabet from A to Z, 1944, Leah Gale, Artists/Writers Guild, 7th printing, 41 pages, VG $7.50

Alphabet of Garden Flowers, 1987, Marie Angel, London, Pelham Books, author illustrated, w/dust jacket, M $25.00

Animal Alphabet, 1984, Bert Kitchen, Dial, illustrated by author, 1st edition, 32 pages, w/dust jacket, M $30.00

Animals' Merry Christmas, 1950, Kathryn Jackson, Simon Schuster, Giant Golden Book, 1st edition $50.00

Ann at Highwood Hall, 1964, Robert Graves, Doubleday, Ardizzone illustrator, 1st US edition, dust jacket, M . $65.00

Anno's Alphabet, 1975, Mitsumasa Anno, NY, Crowell, illustrated by author, w/dust jacket, NM $35.00

Ant & Bee & the ABC, 1966, Angela Banner, NY, Watts, 1st American edition, 94 pages, w/dust jacket, NM.... $20.00

Ape in a Cape, 1952, Fritz Eichenberg, illustrated by author, reprint, w/dust jacket, M $25.00

Babar & Father Christmas, 1950s, Wonder Book #592, early edition, VG $6.00

Baby Elephant, 1950, Wonder Book #541, 1st edition, NM $6.00

Bambi's Big Day, 1960s, Disney, mini pop-up, NM $15.00

Barry Dare & the Mysterious Box, 1929, Gardner Hunting, Saalfield, VG $7.00

Beasts From a Brush, 1955, Juliet Kepes, Pantheon, illustrated by author, 1st edition, 32 pages, w/dust jacket, NM $55.00

Betty Gordon at Boarding School, 1932, Alice B Emerson, Cupples & Leon, 4th in series, G $6.00

Bible Story of the Creation, 1940, Mary Jones, Rand McNally, 1st edition, 39 pages, w/dust jacket, VG $20.00

Bird's Last Song, 1976, Judith Liberman, Addison-Wesley, illustrated by author, 1st printing, dust jacket, M.. $20.00

Black Beauty, 1986, Anne Sewell, Random House, Susan Jeffers illustrator, 1st edition, folio, 69 pages, w/dust jacket, M $28.00

Black Stallion's Filly, 1952, Walter Farley, Random House, 1st printing, VG $20.00

Blue Willow, 1940 Doris Cates, Viking, many illustrations, 4th printing, w/dust jacket, EX $8.00

Bomba the Jungle Boy, 1934, Roy Rockwood, Cupples & Leon, ragged, VG $12.00

Brave Tin Soldier, 1973, V Kubasta, Artia, pop-up, as issued, NM $30.00

Breakfast, Books & Dreams; 1981, MP Hearn editor, Warne, Barbara Garrison illustrator, 1st edition, w/dust jacket, M $25.00

Brer Rabbit & the Tar Baby, 1980, Pavlin & Seda, Octopus, M $10.00

Buddy & the Secret Cave, 1934, Howard R Garis, Cupples & Leon, worn cover binding $4.00

Bunny Hopwell's First Spring, 1953, Wonder Book #614, 1st edition, NM $7.00

Campfire Girls in the Alleghany Mountains, no date, Stella M Francis, Donohue, picture board, VG $4.00

Caves of Fear, 1951, John Blane, Grosset & Dunlap, worn cover, G $4.00

Cherry Ames Boarding School Nurse, 1944, Helen Wells, Grosset & Dunlap, tweed binding, G $12.50

Cherry Ames Night Supervisor, 1950, Julie Tatham, Grosset & Dunlap, 1st printing, picture binding, VG $6.00

Chester the Little Pig, 1951, Rand McNally Elf Book, 1st edition, VG $3.00

Child's Garden of Verses, 1924, Stevenson, Saalfield, VG.................. $12.00

Children's Picture ABCs, 1940s, anonymous, London, Higham illustrator, 93 pages, VG $15.00

Christmas ABC, 1962, Florence Johnson, Golden Press, 1st edition, picture board, M..$15.00

Christmas Carol, ca 1952, Charles Dickens, Grosset & Dunlap, Maraja illustrator, 106 pages, dust jacket, M ..$35.00

Cinderella, 1974, Izawa & Hijikata, Grosset & Dunlap, puppet pop-up, VG..$15.00

Cinderella, 1985, Perrault, Susan Jeffers illustrator, 1st edition, folio, w/dust jacket, M $30.00

Clue in the Patchwork Quilt, 1941, Margaret Sutton, Grosset Dunlap, red tweed binding, torn dust jacket, VG.$10.00

Clue of the Broken Blossom, 1950, Julie Tatham, Grosset & Dunlap, Vicki Barr #5, w/dust jacket, VG $10.00

Clue of the Coiled Cobra, 1951, Bruce Campbell, Grosset & Dunlap, 5th in series, G...............................$5.00

Complete Story of Three Blind Mice, 1987, John Ivemy, Clarion, P Galdone illustrator (his last book), w/dust jacket, M $20.00

Connie Benton, Reporter; 1941, Betty Baxter Anderson, Cupples Leon, w/dust jacket, G $6.50

Cops & Robbers, 1978, Janet & Allan Ahlberg, Greenwillow, 1st American edition, cloth, 32 pages, M.............$20.00

Counting Book, 1957, Wonder Book #692, NM..........$10.00

Country Colic, 1944, Robert Lawson, Little Brown, 2nd printing, 70 pages, cloth, NM....................................$15.00

Cowboy Andy, 1959, Edna Walker Chandler, Beginner Books (Random House), G $5.00

Digger the Badger Decides To Stay, 1972, Thornton Burgess, Whitman, Harrison Cady illustrator, 30 pages, VG $60.00

Donald Duck & the Chipmunks, 1980, Walt Disney, mini pop-up, VG $15.00

Donald Duck Full Speed Ahead, 1953, Walt Disney Productions, Whitman Tell-a-Tale Book, VG.....................$5.00

Down-Adown-Derry, 1922, Walter dela Mare, Henry Holt, Dorothy Lathrop illustrator, gilt-lettered cloth, VG ..$65.00

Dumbo of the Circus, 1941, Walt Disney, Garden City, red cloth, VG $45.00

Early in the Morning, 1986, Charles Causley, Viking, M Foreman illustrator, 1st edition, 64 pages, w/dust jacket, M..$20.00

Easy Way To Draw, 1958, Walter Lantz, Whitman, VG.$25.00

Elephant & the Kangaroo, 1947, TH White, Putnam, 1st edition, w/dust jacket, VG.......................................$30.00

Emerald City of Oz, ca 1940s, Frank L Baum, Reilly Lee, John R Neill illustrator, red cloth cover, VG..........$38.00

Empire Strikes Back, 1980, Patricia Wynne, Random House, pop-up, NM...$25.00

Fairy Tale Alphabet Book, 1983, Nancy Hall, Macmillan, John O'Brien illustrator, 57 pages, dust jacket, M.$20.00

Fairy Went A-Marketing, 1986, Rose Fyleman, EP Dutton, Jamichael Henterly illustrator, 24 pages, w/dust jacket, M...$17.50

Five Little Peppers at School, 1937 (1950 printing), Margaret Sidney, Grosset & Dunlap, G $4.00

Flash Gordon & the Tournament of Death, 1935, Blue Ribbon, Pleasure Book Series, rare, VG $625.00

Flower Book, 1935, June Head, Mueller, Morpugo illustrator, unpaged, M $25.00

Forgetful Wishing Well, 1985, XJ Kennedy, Atheneum, Monica Incisa illustrator, 1st edition, 88 pages, w/dust jacket, NM $15.00

Frankenscience Monster, 1969, Forrest J Ackerman, Ace, paperback, w/wrapper, M.....................................$20.00

Gandy Goose, 1957, Wonder Book #695, CBS Television, VG $4.50

Gene Autry & Arapaho War Drums, 1957, Lewis B Patton, Whitman, EX $35.00

Gene Autry & the Big Valley Bears, 1957, Whitman, EX .$35.00

Girl I Loved, James Whitcomb Riley, Christy illustrator, Bobbs Merrill, EX..$45.00

Golden Bible for Children, New Testament; 1953, Elsa J Werner, Simon & Schuster, Provenson illustrator, 1st edition, M $45.00

Golden Touch, 1937, Walt Disney, Whitman, 212 pages, G $25.00

Gray Menace, 1953, Betsy Allen, Grosset & Dunlop, 8th in Connie Blair series, w/dust jacket, VG $5.00

Greek Gods & Heroes, 1960, Robert Graves, Doubleday, Davis illustrator, 1st edition, w/dust jacket, NM ...$30.00

Guinea Pig ABC, 1983, Kate Duke, NY, EP Dutton, 1st edition, 32 pages, w/wrapper, M...............................$25.00

Hand in Hand We'll Go, 1965, Robert Burns, Crowell, Lonny Hogrigian illustrator, cloth, 31 pages, NM............$15.00

Hansel & Gretel, 1981, Anthony Browne, Knopf, 1st US edition, NM..$16.00

Hansel & Gretel: Story of the Forest, 1944, Grimm & Grimm, Knopf, Warren Chappell illustrator, 1st edition $45.00

Happy Story Book, 1918, Platt & Monk, #666, VG+.......$10.00

Haunted Road, 1954, Margaret Sutton, Grosset & Dunlap, Judy Bolton #25, G $18.00

Hiawatha, 1950 (1956 edition), Rand McNally, Elf Book #565, VG..$6.00

Holly Saunders, Designer; 1947, Betty Baxter Anderson, Cupples & Leon, VG..$12.50

Honey Bunch & Norman on Lighthouse Island, 1949, Helen Thorndyke, Grosset & Dunlap, w/dust jacket, VG.**$5.00**

Horse for Johnny, 1952, Charlotte Bookman, Wonder Book #754, VG...**$3.00**

Hunting of the Snark, 1970, Lewis Carrol, Watts, Oxenbury illustrator, 1st American edition, dust jacket, M....**$45.00**

I Like Weather, 1963, Aileen Fisher, Crowell, Janina Domanska illustrator, 1st edition, w/dust jacket, M.........**$25.00**

I Love Spring, 1965, Clara Lewis, Little Brown, Dick Lewis illustrator, 1st edition, w/dust jacket, M **$17.50**

I Saw a Ship A-Sailing, 1972, Janina Domanska, Macmillan, author illustrated, 1st edition, reinforced cloth, M..**$45.00**

Is There a Mouse in the House?, 1965, Josephine Gibson, Macmillan, Bocecker illustrator, 1st edition, w/dust jacket, M **$20.00**

Island Stallion's Fury, 1951, Walter Farley, Random House, 1st printing, 243 pages, w/dust jacket, VG...........**$20.00**

Jack the Runaway, 1937, Saalfield, Frank V Webster, frayed edges, VG **$7.00**

Jim Flying High, 1979, Mari Evans, Doubleday, Ashley Bryan illustrator, 1st edition, 32 pages, dust jacket, M....**$25.00**

John Burningham's ABC, 1985, John Burningham, NY, Crown, 1st American edition, 29 pages, M...........**$15.00**

Jolly Jump-Up's Number Book, 1940, McLoughlin Brothers, Clyne illustrator, pop-up, repaired, G...................**$30.00**

Jungle Book, 1963, Rudgard Kipling, Grosset & Dunlap, EX...**$12.00**

Kate Greenaway's Mother Goose, 1974, Kate Greenaway, London/NY, Routledge, James Thorp introduction, facsimile, M **$15.00**

Katie's Magic Glasses, 1965, Jane Goodsell, Houghton Mifflin, Cooney illustrator, 6th printing, dust jacket, M........**$30.00**

King Who Saved Himself From Being Saved, 1965, John Ciardi, JB Lippincott, Edward Gorey illustrator, 1st edition, M **$35.00**

Latch Against the Wind, 1985, Victoria Forrester, Atheneum, illustrated by author, 1st edition, dust jacket, M ...**$17.50**

Let's Play Indian, 1950(1952), Wonder Book #538, VG.**$3.50**

Little Bears Playtime, 1922, Frances Margaret Fox, Rand McNally, G **$7.50**

Little Black Sambo, 1950, Helen Bannerman, Whitman, Suzanne illustrator, unpaged, soft cover, VG.......**$15.00**

Little Book of Bedtime Songs, 1947, Jeanette Brown, Abingdon-Cokesbury, Merwin illustrator, 1st edition, 26 pages, VG **$12.50**

Little Book of Necessary Ballads, 1930, Wilhelmina Harper (compiler), Harper & Bros, Evers illustrator, 1st edition, NM **$35.00**

Little Brown Koko Has Fun, 1945, Seale Hunt, Chicago, 1st edition, VG **$32.50**

Little Chameleon, 1966, Silvia Cassedy, World, Rainey Bennett illustrator, w/soiled dust jacket, NM...............**$20.00**

Little Children's Bible, December 1924, Macmillan, 2nd printing, 121 pages, VG.......................................**$12.50**

Little Christmas Book, 1931, Rose Fyleman, Doubleday Doran, Hummel illustrations, 41 pages, G **$12.00**

Little House in the Big Woods, 1953, Laura Ingalls Wilder, Harper & Brothers, VG **$6.00**

Little Man & the Big Thief, 1969, Erick Kastner, Knopf, Stanley Mack illustrator, 1st edition, 162 pages, M......**$28.00**

Little Orphan Annie & Jumbo the Circus Elephant, 1935, Blue Ribbon, Pleasure Book Series, as issued, M.........**$300.00**

Little Pete's Adventure, 1941, Thornton Burgess, McLoughlin, Cady illustrator, VG **$25.00**

Little Prince, 1943, De Saint-Exupery, Harcourt Brace, VG.**$35.00**

Little Red Riding Hood, 1937, Whitman, linen-like, unpaged, VG..**$8.00**

Littlest Angel, 1946, Charles Tazewell, Children's Press, Katherine Evans illustrator, G..................................**$6.00**

Littlest Christmas Tree, 1953, Flora Strousse, Morehouse Gorham, Cooke illustrator, 1st edition, NM..........**$25.00**

Littlest Christmas Tree, 1954, Thornton Burgess, Wonder Book #625, 1st edition, M.......................................**$5.00**

Lolly's Pony Ride, 1959, Charlotte Steiner, Doubleday, 1st edition, VG **$18.00**

Lullaby for Eggs, 1955, Betty Bridgman, Macmillan, Elizabeth Orton Jones illustrator, 1st printing, w/dust jacket, M **$30.00**

Mammy Cottontail & Her Bunnies, 1934, Allen Chaffee, McLoughlin Bros, G **$4.00**

Meadow Brook Girls, 1913, Janet Aldridge, Saalfield, VG.**$6.50**

Merry Mouse Book of Nursery Rhymes, 1981, P Hillman, Doubleday, illustrated by author, 1st edition, w/dust jacket, M **$15.00**

Mickey Mouse, 1978, Walt Disney Studios, Abbeville, Gottfredson introduction, Disney illustrations, w/dust jacket, M **$85.00**

Miranda's Music, 1968, Jean Boudin & Lillian Morrison, Crowell, Helen Webber illustrator, cloth, 69 pages, M **$15.00**

Mother Goose, 1984, Michael Hague, Holt Rinehart Winston, illustrated by author, 1st edition, 61 pages, w/dust jacket, M **$30.00**

Mother Goose As Told by Kellogg's Singing Lady, 1933, Vernon Grant, Kellogg Co, unpaged, w/wrapper, VG .**$45.00**

Mother Goose Treasury, 1966, Raymond Briggs, Coward-McCann, 1st American edition, reinforced cloth, 220 pages, VG **$75.00**

Mrs Roo & the Bunnies, 1953, Rachel Leanard, Houghton Mifflin, Tom Funk illustrator, 1st edition review copy, M......**$35.00**

My Caravan, 1934, Eulalie Grover, Albert & Whitman, Florence Sampson illustrator, 4th printing, VG..........**$15.00**

My Skyscraper City, 1963, Penny Hamond, Doubleday, Katrina Thomas photographs, 1st edition, w/dust jacket, M...**$25.00**

My Song Is a Piece of Jade, 1981, Toni de Gerez, Little Brown, Wm Stark illustrator, 1st American edition, 48 pages, M **$25.00**

New Book of Days, 1961, Eleanor Farjeon, Walck, Philip Gough & MW Hawes illustrators, 1st American edition, VG...**$35.00**

New Fun w/Dick & Jane, 1951, W Gray, Scott Foresman, school book, G...**$36.00**

Night & the Cat, 1950, Elizabeth Coatsworth, Macmillan, Fougita illustrator, 1st printing, 115 pages, w/dust jacket, M **$35.00**

Night Before Christmas, 1932, Clement Clark Moore, Whitman, McNaughton illustrator, color picture wrapper, G **$10.00**

Night Before Christmas, 1950, Clement Clark Moore, Golden Press, Big Golden Book, NM **$18.00**

Night Before Christmas, 1965, Clement Clark Moore, Whitman, Tell-a-Tale Book, 30 pages, VG **$8.00**

Nursery Rhymes, 1975, Nichola Bayley, Knopf, 1st edition, w/dust jacket, M...**$25.00**

Once Upon a Rhyme, 1982, Sara & Stephen Corrin, Faber & Faber, Jill Bennett illustrator, 1st edition, w/dust jacket, M **$20.00**

Once Upon A to Z, 1991, Jody Linscott, Doubleday, 1st edition, C Holland illustrator, w/dust jacket, M **$16.00**

One, Two, Three, & Four, No More?; 1988, Catherine Gray, Houghton Mifflin, Marissa Moss illustrator, 1st edition, M **$15.00**

Over in the Meadow, 1986, Paul Galdone, Prentice-Hall, illustrated by author, 1st edition, 41 pages, w/dust jacket, M **$20.00**

Oz Scrapbook, 1977, Green & Martin, Random House, 1st edition, VG **$95.00**

Patchwork Girl of Oz, 1940, Frank L Baum, Reilly Lee, JR Neill ilustrator, w/dust jacket, VG............................**$75.00**

Peacock Pie, 1961, Walter dela Mare, Knopf, Barbara Cooney illustrator, cloth, 117 pages, frayed dust jacket, VG **$45.00**

Penny Fiddle, 1960, Robert Graves, Doubleday, Edward Ardizzone illustrator, 1st American edition, w/dust jacket, M **$55.00**

Peter Goes to School, 1953, Wonder Book #600, early edition, M...**$4.00**

Peter Pan in Kensington Gardens, 1951, JM Barrie, London, Hodder Stoughton, Racham illustrator, VG **$55.00**

Pied Piper of Hamelin, 1910 (1927 edition), Robert Browning, Rand McNally, Hope Dunlap illustrator, 56 pages, NM **$45.00**

Pinnacled Tower, 1974, Thomas Hardy, Macmillan, C Leighton illustrator, H Plotz editor, 1st edition, w/dust jacket, M **$25.00**

Playtime for Nancy, 1951, Wonder Book #560, 1st edition, short split in spine, EX...**$3.00**

Pleasant Field Mouse, 1964, Jan Wahl, Harper Row, Sendak illustrator, probable 1st edition, dust jacket, NM ..**$50.00**

Poems of Thomas Hood, 1968, William Cole, Crowell, S Fischer illustrator, 1st edition, reinforced cloth, w/dust jacket, M **$20.00**

Pollyanna's Western Adventure, 1929 (1940 4th printing), Harriet Lummis Smith, Grosset & Dunlap, 6th in series, VG **$4.00**

Popular Folk Tales, 1978, Grimm, Doubleday, 1st American edition, EX..**$27.50**

Prairie Colt, no date, Stephen Holt, Grosset & Dunlap, Wesley Dennis illustrator, blue binding, G **$10.00**

Prayer for a Child, 1944, Rachel Field, Macmillan, Elizabeth Orton Jones illustrator, Caldecott 1945 Medal Winner, M **$85.00**

Red House Mystery, 1965, AA Milne, Dutton, VG **$8.00**

Reluctant Dragon, 1941, Walt Disney, Garden City, Benchley introduction, unpaged, VG......................................**$55.00**

Rime of the Ancient Mariner, 1971, Samuel Coleridge, Coward, McCann & Geoghegan, Hodges illustrator, w/dust jacket, M **$35.00**

Robin Family, 1954, Miss Frances, Rand McNally & Co, Ding Dong School, 1st edition, M.....................................**$6.00**

Roy Rogers & The Sure 'Nough Cowpoke, 1952, Roy Rogers Enterprises, Whitman Tell-a-Tale Book, G **$4.50**

Sally Riddle School, no date, Hallmark, Marianne Smith illustrator, pop-up, VG **$30.00**

Santa Claus Book, 1976, Willis E Jones, Walker, 1st edition, 127 pages, red boards, VG **$30.00**

Sesame Street ABC Book of Words, 1988, Random House, Harry McNaught illustrator, 1st edition, 40 pages, M.**$12.50**

Sesame Street ABC Book of Words, 1988, Random House, Jim Henson's muppets, McNaught illustrator, 1st edition, M **$12.50**

Short Walk From the Station, 1951, Viking, McDonald illustrator, EX..**$15.00**

Simon's Song, 1969, Barbara Emberley, Prentice-Hall, Ed Emberley illustrator, 1st edition, cloth, NM...........**$35.00**

Singing Rails, 1934, Francis J Concidine, Black Cat Press, unpaged, cloth, VG...**$45.00**

Six Little Possums, A Birthday ABC; 1982, Golden Press, Cyndy Szerkeres, 1st edition, 24 pages, NM **$17.50**

Sleeping Beauty, 1983, Anne G Johnstone, Dean, pop-up, VG..**$10.00**

Small Wonders, 1979, Norma Farber, Coward, McCann & Geoghegan, Mizumura illustrator, 1st edition, w/dust jacket, VG **$30.00**

Snow White, no date, Hallmark, Arlene Noel illustrator, pop-up, VG **$20.00**

Snow White & the 7 Dwarfs, 1949, Julian Wehr, Saalfield, pop-up, VG **$30.00**

Songs & Games of the Americas, 1943, Frank Henius, Scribners, Oscar Fabres illustrator, torn dust jacket, VG..**$17.50**

Songs of Innocence, 1961, William Blake, AS Barnes, Harold Jones illustrator, 32 pages, w/dust jacket, M.........**$25.00**

Stand By for Mars, 1952, Carey Rockwell, Grosset & Dunlap, Tom Corbett Space Cadet series, dust jacket, VG ...**$5.00**

Story of Applby Capple, 1940, Anne Parrish, Harper & Brothers, illustrated by author, 1st edition, 184 pages, NM **$65.00**

Strange Monsters of the Sea, 1979, Richard Armour, McGraw-Hill, Galdone illustrator, 1st edition, 42 pages, M **$15.00**

Strange Room, 1964, Claudia Lewis, Whitman, Altschuler illustrator, 38 pages, w/dust jacket, M **$15.00**

Summer's Coming In, 1970, Natalia Belting, Harcourt Rinehart Winston, Adams illustrator, 1st edition, 48 pages, M.**$30.00**

Surprise for Howdy Doody, 1951, Kagran Corp, Whitman Tell-a-Tale Book, G...**$6.00**

Sword in the Stone, 1939, Putnam, Lawson illustrator, 1st American edition...**$35.00**

T'was the Night Before Christmas, 1953, Clement Clark Moore, Samuel Lowe, Bonnie Book, plaid binding, VG..**$14.00**

Tale of Master Meadow Mouse, 1921, Arthur Scott Bailey, Grosset & Dunlap, Fagan illustrator, picture cloth, VG **$20.00**

Tarzan & the City of Gold, 1947, Edgar Rice Burroughs, Harcourt Brace, EX **$35.00**

Tarzan & the Forbidden City, 1952, Edgar Rice Burroughs, Whitman, light wear...**$7.50**

The Way Things Are & Other Poems, 1974, Myra Livingston, Atheneum, J Oliver illustrator, 1st edition, w/dust jacket, NM **$17.50**

Thing in B-3, 1969, Talemage Powell, Whitman, EX...**$15.00**

Three Little Pigs, 1904, Altemus, illustrator JK Neill, EX..$45.00

Three Little Pigs, 1983, V Kubasta, Brown Watson, reprint of Artia edition, pop-up, VG **$18.00**

Through the Looking Glass, 1953, Lewis Carroll, London, Macmillan, Tenniel illustrator, 235 pages, VG **$8.00**

Thumper, 1942, Walt Disney, Grosset & Dunlap, VG .**$42.00**

Tinker Tim the Toy Maker, 1934, Vernon Grant, Whitman, illustrations, picture board, VG **$60.00**

Tom Swift & His Diving Seacopter, 1956, Victor Appleton II, Grosset & Dunlap, 7th in series, VG........................**$3.00**

Topsy Turvy, 1987, Monika Beisner, Farrar, Straus & Giroux, 1st American edition, cloth, 32 pages, M..............**$17.50**

Trixie Beldon & the Black Jacket Mystery, 1961, Katheryn Kenny, Whitman, EX **$15.00**

Tucky the Hunter, 1978, James Dickey, Crown, Marie Angel illustrator, cloth, 44 pages, M **$35.00**

Tuggy the Tugboat, 1958, Wonder Book #696, 1st edition, NM...**$7.00**

Ugly Duckling, no date, Arlene Noel illustrator, pop-up, VG **$20.00**

Victoria's ABC Adventure, 1984, Cathy Warren, NY, Patience Brewster illustrator, 1st edition, w/dust jacket, M.**$17.50**

Visit From St Nicholas, 1981, Clement Clark Moore, Kitemaug Press, 1st edition, 20 pages, w/green wrapper, M.**$15.00**

Walt Disney's Stormy, 1954, Walt Disney, Cozy Corner Book, VG **$7.50**

West of Boston, Yankee Rhymes & Doggerel, 1956, James Daugherty, Viking, 1st edition, cloth, VG.................**$20.00**

What Katy Did, 1976, Susan Coolidge, Purnell Books, English edition, picture binding, VG......................**$4.00**

What the Good Man Does Is Always Right, 1968, Hans Christian Anderson, Dial, Schreiter illustrator, NM........**$30.00**

When the Pie Was Opened, 1968, Jean Little, Little Brown, 2st edition, w/dust jacket, NM **$25.00**

Wind Has Wings, 1968, Mary Downie & Barbara Robertson, Walck, Elizabeth Cleaver illustrator, rebound, 95 pages, M...**$12.50**

Wind in My Hand, 1970, Fududa, Golden Gate Jr Books, EX..**$15.00**

Wings of Rhyme, 1967, Lloyd Frankenberg editor, Funk & Wagnalls, 1st edition, 96 pages, w/dust jacket, M.**$17.50**

Wizard in the Well, 1956, Harry Behn, Harcourt Brace, 1st edition, 62 pages, NM...**$35.00**

Wizard of Oz, 1983, Frank L Baum, Weekly Reader Classics, illustrated, 206 pages, G **$10.00**

Wonder Book of Christmas, 1951, Wonder Book #651, WT Mars illustrator, NM...**$6.00**

Wonder Why, 1971, Ruth Harnden, Houghton Mifflin, E Livermore illustrator, 1st printing, w/dust jacket, M..**$25.00**

Year Santa Went Modern, 1964, Richard Armour, McGraw Hill, 32 pages, picture boards, VG **$10.00**

Young Reader's Bible, 1965, Nashville, Abingdon, hard cover, 871 pages, VG **$6.50**

10 Rabbits, 1957, Wonder Book #648, early edition, M.**$4.50**

Children's Dinnerware

Little girls have always enjoyed playing house, and glassware and chinaware manufacturers alike have seen to it that they're not lacking in the dinnerware department. Glassware 'just like Mother's' was pressed from late in the 19th century until well into the 20th, and much of it has somehow managed to survive to the present. China was made in England, Japan, and the United States in patterns that ranged from nursery-rhyme themes to traditional designs such as Blue Willow and Tea Leaf. Both types are very collectible today.

For further study, we recommend *The Collector's Encyclopedia of Children's Dishes* by Margaret and Kenn Whitmyer and *Children's Glass Dishes, China, and Furniture, Vols 1 and 2*, by Doris Anderson Lechler.

China

Blue Banded, bowl, 4", octagonal, blue band on ironstone, backstamped Iron Stone......................................**$18.00**

Blue Banded, canister, 2½", blue on white.................**$25.00**

Blue Marble, plate, 4", blue 'marbleizing' on white, England **$15.00**

Blue Onion, cup, blue on white **$20.00**

Bowl, Barnyard Scene, 5⅜", Royal Windsor, England.**$13.50**

Children on Carousel Horse, plate, 8", 2 handles, ribbed rim, Salem China Co **$9.00**

Circus, cup & saucer, performing bear, blue, yellow & red on white, Edwin M Knowles China Co.......$9.50

Circus, plate, 6½", clown w/balloons, lg parrot beside him, Edwin M Knowles China Co (illustrated) .$5.00

Circus, teapot, 4½", clown w/balloons, Edwin M Knowles China Co (illustrated) $27.50

Dimity, soup bowl, 4¼", green 'woven look' pattern on creamy yellow **$10.00**

Elsie the Cow, hot plate, 9⅛" **$19.00**

Flow Blue, platter, Dogwood, 6¾", Minton.................**$47.00**

Flow Blue Dogwood, casserole, 4½", blue on white, Minton......................**$90.00**

Gaudy Ironstone, plate, 6", England......................**$40.00**

Jack Be Nimble, plate, 9", Shenango China **$16.00**

Kite Flyers, plate, 3½", blue transfer on white **$47.50**

Mary Had a Little Lamb, teapot, 3½", Brentleigh Ware, Staffordshire England......................**$33.00**

Merry Christmas, plate, 5", pink lustre on white w/gold trim **$10.00**

Mill Scene, teapot, brown transfer, David Methvin & Sons, Scotland **$45.00**

Myrtle Wreath, bowl, 5", blue wreaths on white, oval......................**$25.00**

Myrtle Wreath, platter, 6½", blue wreaths on white **$27.50**

Pembroke, platter, 4¼", reddish brown floral on cream, Bistro, England......................**$25.00**

Peter Cottontail, mug, 2⅞", Knowles China Co............**$11.00**

Pink Luster, chamber pot, gold trim, England **$22.00**

Pink Rose, creamer, 2¼", pink rose transfer on creamy eggshell, Homer Laughlin......................**$15.00**

Pink Rose, teapot, 6¼", pink roses transfer on white......................**$45.00**

Playful Dog, mug, 2⅝", comic transfer on white, Warwick China......................**$17.50**

Silhouette, cup & saucer, girl pushing stroller, black trim, Noritake **$17.00**

Silhouette Children, cup & saucer, Victoria Czechoslovakia **$8.00**

Snow White, plate, 4⅜", character transfer on white...**$10.00**

Tan Lustre, cup & saucer, red, blue & yellow dots **$3.50**

Teddy Bear, sugar bowl, 4", transfer Teddy bear scene w/yellow at rim, w/lid......................**$40.00**

Waterfront Scenes, sugar bowl, 4⅛", blue transfer on white, w/lid **$10.00**

Whirligig, plate, 5", red & white flower w/dark green leaves, green rim, Southern Potteries......................**$10.00**

Glassware

Banana dish, marigold, Kittens, kitten border, Fenton Glass Co **$145.00**

Bowl, 5", Gulliver's Travels, red decal on white, Anchor Hocking **$21.00**

Butter dish, 2¼", crystal, Bucket, Wooden Pail, Bryce Brothers **$275.00**

Butter dish, 2¼", crystal, Hawaiian Lei, intricate, JB Higbee Glass Co......................**$37.00**

Butter dish, 2⅜", crystal, Buzz Saw #2697, swirled, Cambridge Glass......................**$35.00**

Butter dish, 2⅞", green, Clear & Diamond Panel.........**$60.00**

Creamer, 1⅜", clear green, Little Tots Tea Set, horizontal rings, 1950s, CODEG Series, Made in England **$10.00**

Creamer, 2½", crystal, Button Panel #44, George Duncan's Sons **$50.00**

Creamer, 2½", French Ivory, colored ring, Laurel, McKee Glass Co......................**$22.00**

Creamer, 2¼", crystal, Fine Cut Star & Fan, pressed stars & fans, Higbee **$25.00**

Creamer, 2¼", crystal, Horizontal Threads **$40.00**

Creamer, 2¾", blue, Clear & Diamond Panel.............**$37.00**

Creamer, 2⅞", crystal, Lamb, embossed lambs **$70.00**

Creamer, 3⅛", crystal, Lion, embossed lion, Gillinder & Sons **$68.00**

Creamer, 3⅜", crystal, Hobnail w/Thumbprint Base #150, Doyle & Co......................**$40.00**

Cup, 1½", clear green, Little Tots Tea Set, horizontal rings, 1950s, CODEG, Made in England **$6.00**

Cup, 1½", jade green, Laurel, 1930s, McKee Glass **$25.00**

Cup, 1½", pink, Homespun, vertical ribs, Jeannette Glass Co......................**$30.00**

Mug, 2x2", Butterfly, Bryce Higbee $40.00

Mug, 3", Child's Prayer, God Is Great..., Anchor Hocking, 3" **$5.50**

Mug, 3", Scottie Dog, blue decal on milk glass, Hazel Atlas Co **$9.00**

Plate, 2¾", crystal, ice cream Set, Ice Cream bowl in middle w/alphabet border, Federal Glass Co **$45.00**

Plate, 4½", crystal, Homespun, vertical ribs, Jeannette Glass Co **$5.00**

Plate, 5½", Scottie Decal, Laurel, 1930s, McKee Glass.**$35.00**

Punch Bowl, crystal, Flattened Diamond & Sunburst Thumbelina, Westmoreland Glass Co **$35.00**

Punch bowl, 3⅜", crystal, Inverted Strawberry, Cambridge Glass Co...**$52.00**

Saucer, 3¼", crystal w/frosted head, Lion, embossed lion, Gillinder & Sons **$20.00**

Saucer, 3¼", pink, Homespun, vertical ribs, Jeannette Glass Co **$5.00**

Saucer, 3⅜", clear green, Little Tots Tea Set, horizontal rings, 1950s, CODEG Made in England **$3.00**

Saucer, 4½", blue, Kittens, kitten border, Fenton Glass..**$65.00**

Saucer, 4⅜", jade green, Laurel, 1930s, McKee Glass **$5.50**

Spooner, 2⅛", crystal, Chimco **$60.00**

Spooner, 2⅛", crystal, Flattened Diamond & Sunburst Thumbelina, Westmoreland Glass Co **$25.00**

Spooner, 2⅜", crystal, Liberty Bell, embossed bells ..**$150.00**

Spooner, 2⅜", decorated white milk glass, Cloud Band, floral design, Gillinder & Sons, Inc **$70.00**

Spooner, 3", frosted crystal, Lion, embossed lion, Gillinder & Sons **$95.00**

Sugar bowl, 1⅛", clear green, Little Tots Tea Set, horizontal rings, 1950s, CODEG Made in England.................**$10.00**

Sugar bowl, 2⅜", French Ivory, Laurel, 1930s, McKee Glass Co **$20.00**

Sugar bowl w/lid, 3½", Clear & Diamond Panel..........**$40.00**

Teapot w/lid, pink, Homespun, vertical ribs, Jeannette Glass Co **$110.00**

Teapot w/lid, 3¾", clear green, Little Tots Tea Set, horizontal rings, 1950s, CODEG Made in England.................**$14.00**

Tray, 7⅜", crystal, Hobnail w/Thumbprint Base #150, rows of thumbprints, Doyle & Co....................................**$40.00**

Tumbler, alphabet, D Is for Duckling, Hazel Atlas......**$11.00**

Children's Kitchenware

Just as plentiful as their dinnerware, children's kitchenware items such as those we've listed here always seem to bring good prices. Because of their small scale, they're easy to display in very little space, and miniature collectors as well as collectors of children's things snap these goodies right up!

All the books mentioned in the Children's Dinnerware narrative above show wonderful examples.

Bean pot, 2¾", stoneware, Albany glaze (dark brown), w/lid..**$48.00**

Bowl, 1½", stoneware, blue band on cream w/cream interior **$65.00**

Bowl, 1¾", stoneware, embossed ribs on cream w/blue interior **$22.00**

Bread baker, Glasbake, clear w/red trim, rectangular.**$20.00**

Canister, 2½", blue bands on white china, Germany...**$25.00**

Canister, 3", Jadite, Jeannette **$95.00**

Casserole, 6" oval, cast iron, Griswold.................**$55.00**

Creamer, blue speckled graniteware **$30.00**

Cup & saucer, 1⅝", 3½", Frolicking Children on creamy graniteware, Germany **$40.00**

Custard cup, 5-oz, Fire-King, light blue......................**$2.50**

Kettle, 4¾", aluminum, w/lid, Griswold (illustrated).**$45.00**

Muffin pan, aluminum, 6-cup..**$10.00**

Pan, 1¼", 'hammered' aluminum, w/lid **$12.00**

Percolator set, Kiddy Kook, Aluminum Specialty Co, serves 6, complete...**$50.00**

Pie plate, tin **$8.00**

Pitcher, 1½", stoneware, dark blue **$22.00**

Plate, tin..**$7.50**

Plate, 5⅛", blue banded graniteware w/gold trim.......**$12.00**

Salt box, 1⅞", painted floral on white china, Germany.**$35.00**

Scoop, blue graniteware **$5.00**

Silverware, metal, unmarked USA, each piece............**$1.00**

Skillet, 1⅛" dia, 'hammered' aluminum **$12.00**

Skillet, 4¾", heavy aluminum, Griswold (illustrated).**$18.00**

Strainer, blue graniteware...**$35.00**

Sugar bowl, white graniteware w/blue band..............**$17.50**

Teapot, blue graniteware, w/lid....................................**$80.00**

Teapot, 2¾", copper **$75.00**

Teapot, 3¾", cast iron, Wagner.....................................**$80.00**

Tray, 2x4⅝", light blue speckled graniteware.............**$40.00**

Chocolate Molds

Molds used to shape chocolate are usually tin, though copper and occasionally even pewter molds were made as well. They are quite often very detailed (on the inside, of course), and variations are endless. Some are as simple as an Easter egg, others as complex as a rabbit hunter equipped with his gun and pouch or a completely decorated Christmas tree.

These seem to be regional; if you live in the East, you're bound to see them.

Bear in overalls, 7½", #166, standing.........................**$135.00**

Bride & groom, 10", #23344 & #23342, pr..................**$285.00**

Bulldog, 5"..**$75.00**

Burro, 7", #15919, Holland..**$50.00**

Cat, 8", marked #8230, Made in USA, 'top' mark for Eppelsheimer, clamped, rare..............................**$85.00**

Chick, 3½", #8060..**$30.00**

Chick w/hat, 5½"...**$37.50**

Chick w/hat & clothes, 5½"...**$60.00**

Cross w/flowers, 5"	$25.00
Dog, 11½", #287	$255.00
Dog, 4½", Scottie	$45.00
Dog, 4x6", #4804, Irish Setter	$60.00
Dog, 6", #24347, Basset Hound	$70.00
Dog w/hat, 6½", #25896	$90.00
Duck, 4½x5½", floating	$42.50
Duck w/basket, 6½x9½"	$75.00
Duck w/hat, 5"	$32.00
Duck w/hat, 6x6"	$60.00
Elephant, 3½"	$50.00
Elephant, 5", #602	$80.00
Girl w/veil & robe, 7", #28106	$85.00
Hen & chick pulling egg cart, 7", #16110, Holland	$45.00
Hen on nest, 14x8"	$275.00
Hen on nest, 5x5"	$45.00
Horse w/cart, 4x7"	$80.00
Indian, 5¼", American Chocolate Mould Co	$80.00
Kewpie, 10"	$125.00
Kewpie, 11½"	$180.00
Lamb, 6½x9", recumbent	$60.00
Men in speed boat, 10", #26476	$80.00
Rabbit, 10", standing	$80.00
Rabbit, 11½", #230, standing	$98.00
Rabbit, 16", standing	$335.00
Rabbit, 4x5", #3091, eating grass	$42.50
Rabbit, 5½", #8016, running	$37.50
Rabbit, 6", dancing	$42.50
Rabbit, 6", playing drum	$75.00
Rabbit, 6", playing mandolin	$65.00
Rabbit, 7", #31608, standing	$38.00
Rabbit, 7", #8189, smoking pipe	$65.00
Rabbit, 7", pulling cart	$75.00
Rabbit on egg, 8½", #4011	$65.00
Rabbit on toadstool w/basket, 13x10"	$230.00
Rabbit w/basket, 12½x9", standing	$255.00
Rabbit wearing clothes, 6¼", #8213	$50.00
Rabbit w/egg basket, 6½"	$45.00
Rooster, 10½", #6184	$160.00
Rooster, 6"	$45.00

Santa, 3½" $50.00

Santa, 4", #8049, detailed	$90.00
Sheep, 4½x3½", #806, EX detail	$67.50
Spaceman, 4½", ca 1950s	$47.50
Squirrel, 4½"	$45.00
Teddy bear, 11½"	$395.00
Train, 3x6"	$87.50

Christmas Collectibles

Christmas is nearly everybody's favorite holiday, and it's a season when we all seem to want to get back to time-honored traditions. The stuffing and fruit cakes are made like Grandma always made them, we go caroling and sing the old songs that were written two hundred years ago, and the same Santa that brought gifts to the children in a time long forgotten still comes to our house and yours every Christmas Eve.

So for reasons of nostalgia, there are thousands of collectors interested in Christmas memorabilia. Some early Santa figures are rare and may be very expensive, especially when dressed in a color other than red. Blown glass ornaments and Christmas tree bulbs were made in shapes of fruits and vegetables, houses, Disney characters, animals, and birds. There are Dresden ornaments and candy containers from Germany, some of which were made prior to the 1870s, that have been lovingly preserved and handed down to our generation. They were made of cardboard that sparkled with gold and silver trim.

Artificial trees made of feathers were produced as early as 1850 and as late as 1950. Some were white, others blue, though most were green, and some had red berries or clips to hold candles. There were little bottle brush trees, trees with cellophane needles, and trees from the sixties made of aluminum.

Collectible Christmas items are not necessarily old, expensive, or hard to find. Things produced in your lifetime have value as well. To learn more about this field, we recommend *Christmas Collectibles* by Margaret and Kenn Whitmyer, and *Christmas Ornaments, Lights, and Decorations* by George Johnson.

Advertising trade card, 2 die-cut girl Christmas figures w/ tree & bag of toys, WI Potter lettered on bag, EX	$35.00
Book, children's, Santa Claus & the Lost Kitten, Whitman Publishing Co, 1952, EX	$8.00
Book, children's pop-up, Santa's Circus, Santa emerges when book is opened, spiral-bound, 1952, EX	$10.00
Bowl, milk glass banded w/red Christmas decorations, Corning Glass, EX	$8.00
Box, 11", Santa figure on lid, either as shown	$15.00
Cake mold, 11½", Santa w/gifts emerging from chimney, aluminum, Nordic-Ware, EX	$20.00
Cake mold, 3" dia, embossed reindeer & lettering, aluminum, EX	$9.00
Cake mold, 9", tree shape, marked Mirro-Finest Aluminum, EX	$8.00

Candy container, foil cone w/white fur-trimmed opening, celluloid face of Santa on front, EX......................$25.00

Candy container, 3¾", mica-covered ball w/bell on lid sits on flat base w/Santa figure, West Germany, EX...$25.00

Candy container, 3x4x2", cardboard box resembles brick-red fireplace w/silhouette of children, 1930s-50s, EX...$4.00

Candy container, 4", chenille boot w/mesh top, drawstring opening, EX...$40.00

Candy container, 4", Santa w/celluloid face in wicker basket w/mesh drawstring top, EX...................................$75.00

Candy container, 9", snowman, mica-covered cardboard w/wooden carrot nose, black snow-covered top hat & scarf, EX...$48.00

Decoration, red chenille wreath, green candle w/red light bulb in center, holly trim, electrical, original box, EX...$20.00

Decoration, 14", angel holding branch, die-cut cardboard, very realistic figure w/white wings & pink flowing gown, EX...$35.00

Decoration, 6", Santa, celluloid face w/cotton cloth body & suit, composition boots, EX $110.00

Fence, 2½x18x24", folding type, wood w/red & green paint, EX $125.00

Figure, 3¼", Santa w/lantern, bisque, red suit w/white trim, dark brown boots, white bag, German, EX...........$95.00

Garland, 60" long, glass beads in various shapes & colors, EX...$30.00

Lamp, 6", Santa on round base holding sm green tree & pointing finger upward, plastic, EX $12.00

Lamp, 8", Santa figure holding a bubble light, plastic, 1950s, EX...$27.00

Light bulb, acorn, clear glass w/multicolored paint, EX.$32.00

Light bulb, apricot, clear glass w/yellow & orange paint.$18.00

Light bulb, Betty Boop, painted milk glass, EX...........$85.00

Light bulb, bubble type, fluid in blown glass candle on ribbed glass base, late 1940s-50s, EX.......................$5.00

Light bulb, choir girl, painted milk glass, EX...............$45.00

Light bulb, Dismal Desmond, milk glass w/painted polka dots, M..$55.00

Light bulb, Donald Duck, painted clear glass, EX.......$55.00

Light bulb, Dutch Girl, painted milk glass............$55.00

Light bulb, Santa w/pack, painted milk glass, EX........$45.00

Light bulb, Jester in red suit pointing to a playing card (illustrated) $90.00

Light bulb, Oriental lantern, ribbed cylinder shape, colors graduate from green to pink, black base, VG.........$8.00

Light bulb, pear, brass base, ivory insulator, EX..........$25.00

Light bulb, sm lantern, painted milk glass, Japan, NM..$22.00

Light bulb, sm rose bud, painted milk glass $28.00

Light bulb, 2", Santa's head, painted milk glass, Japan, EX $35.00

Light bulb, 2½", cottage, painted milk glass, EX.........$12.50

Light bulb, 3", bell w/3 Santa faces, painted milk glass, EX $35.00

Light bulb, 3¼", grapes w/leaves, painted milk glass..$25.00

Light bulbs, 8 Disney characters, painted glass, licensed to Parmount, 1960s, original box, EX, set.................$95.00

Lights, Noma Mazda Christmas Candles, string of 5 parallel lights (burn independently), 1940s, EX................$45.00

Lights for window or mantel, 9 bubble lights on red 5-tiered base, 1950s, EX $50.00

Nativity scene, 14x22", heavy cardboard, folds flat, depth expands when opened, EX.................................$110.00

Ornament, glass-beaded star in gold w/lg blue beads in points, Occupied Japan, EX $20.00

Ornament, star, wire wrapped w/gold tinsel, 1950s, EX...$7.00

Ornament, 2½", kugel ball, cobalt, baroque cap.......$110.00

Ornament, 2½", pearly white blown glass ball, raised windmill w/red blades & base on flat side, 1920s, VG.$55.00

Ornament, 2½", rocking horse, coated cardboard, blue w/red star on silver saddle, EX............................$12.00

Ornament, 2¼", blown glass ball, knobby silver surface w/raised painted cat heads front & back, 1929, G.$65.00

Ornament, 2¼", drum, mold-blown glass w/silver, green, gold & red, VG..$45.00

Ornament, 2¼", rectangular metal basket w/handle, intricate cut-out design, silver-tone, EX $25.00

Ornament, 2¾", apple w/leaf, pressed cotton, sparkling white, w/pink shading, VG $20.00

Ornament, 3", angel, mold-blown glass w/pink & yellow frost..$65.00

Ornament, 3", blown glass ribbed stocking, pearly white w/pink at top, blue-green toe, 1910-20, G............$95.00

Ornament, 3", flower, painted mold-blown glass, unsilvered, NM $65.00

Ornament, 3", pine cone, mold-blown glass, green $45.00

Ornament, 3½", butterfly, blue mold-blown glass body w/spun glass wings, painted blue & orange decoration on wings, EX...$125.00

Ornament, 3½", candle, free-blown glass, red, w/clip, 1940s, EX $12.00

Ornament, 3½", Santa w/tree, mold-blown glass, blue suit w/white & gold trim, 1930s, EX............................$35.00

Ornament, 4", red chenille wreath w/silver paper foil candle, red chenille flame, EX $8.00

Ornament, 4", street lamp, mold-blown glass, gold knobby top w/snow, silver base, ca 1930-40, VG $30.00

Ornament, 4½", die-cut cardboard angel on tinsel cross, VG..$45.00

Ornament, 4¼", reddish pink mold-blown Malaga bottle w/decorative paper label, matt silver top, EX.......$60.00

Ornament, 4¼x6½", swan w/indents on sides, painted free-blown glass, black annealed hanger, ca 1910, VG .**$18.00**

Ornament, 5", black celluloid dirigible w/Santa & doll on drum in passenger compartment, EX **$30.00**

Ornament, 5", deer, free-blown glass, gold-tone w/black antlers, ca 1930s, EX **$50.00**

Ornament, 5", icicle, clear glass, EX **$12.00**

Ornament, 5", kugel ball, embossed brass hanger **$85.00**

Ornament, 6", icicles, pressed cotton, early 1900s, EX ..**$18.00**

Ornament, 6", kugel, grape cluster, blue, EX............**$100.00**

Ornament, 6½", Lady Liberty head atop cone-shaped ornament, mold-blown glass, gold-tone & red, real hair, 1920s, EX...**$125.00**

Ornament, 6¼", glass candy cane w/blue & gold spiral bands, EX...**$8.00**

Ornament, 8", Santa, clay face w/blue & red chenille body, EX...**$25.00**

Ornament, 8½" long, bird w/crest, spun glass tail, VG .**$45.00**

Reflectors, foil, various colors, made in Germany, 1900s, in original box, EX **$45.00**

Signal lantern, full-length Santa on round base, battery operated, late 1940s-early 50s, EX.................................**$27.00**

Store display, 18", Santa head, papier-mache, gold glitter on beard, brows & hat, EX **$65.00**

Store display, 21", Santa w/bag of toys reading want list, die-cut cardboard covered w/velvet, Whitman Co, EX...**$25.00**

Tin, rectangular, Blue Bird Toffee, winter scene w/children in oval, black w/decorative gold trim, EX.............**$40.00**

Tin, round, Huntley & Palmer lettered on side, close-up of Santa w/bag of toys on lid, VG.............................**$30.00**

Tin, 8" dia, Mackintosh's Christmas Festival Chocolate Assortment, black w/close-up of Santa, G **$45.00**

Toy, 12", Happy Santa, plastic face, tin body, red cotton flannel suit, Cragston, 1950s $95.00

Toy, 5½", Santa holding gift, tin litho, red & white w/yellow belt, green boots, Chein wind-up, 1920-30, EX...**$100.00**

Tree, 18", aluminum, branch tips fan out, 1960s, EX ..**$18.00**

Tree, 19", plastic base, cellophane needles, decorated w/bubble lights, 1950s, EX..................................**$60.00**

Tree, 23", paper-wrapped wood center post, heavy wire branches w/cloth needles, revolves on music box base, 1950s, EX..**$65.00**

Tree, 8½", bottle-brush type w/2-tiered square wooden base, decorated w/pressed cotton ornaments, EX..........**$35.00**

Tree stand, 14", tin, Santa lithos, VG.........................**$150.00**

Tree stand, 15" dia, tin, manger litho, 1920s, EX.......**$150.00**

Tree topper, 6" dia, angel w/gold wings & angel-hair skirt on burst of spun glass, Germany, late 1940s, EX..**$15.00**

Tree topper, 8¾", sun face, mold-blown glass, Germany, MIB **$145.00**

Village piece, 4", house, cardboard, red w/snow-covered roof, no base, Japan, EX..**$15.00**

Cigarette Collectibles

Cigarette companies have been among the most vigorous in promoting their products, and the many items they issued with their advertising slogans and logos represent a specialized area that can yield up interesting and eclectic collections.

Ashtray, Chesterfield Cigarettes, 6" long, tin, football stadium encircles tray, They Satisfy, 1930-50, EX **$20.00**

Ashtray, Winston Cigarettes, embossed tin....................**$8.00**

Booklet, Lucky Strike Cigarettes, 8x5", The Story of, by Roy C Flannagan, 1939 New York World's Fair logo, 94 pages, EX..**$12.50**

Cigarette cards, Uniforms of Territorial Army, '50s, set of 50 .**$75.00**

Door plate, 9x4", tin litho, lg pack, More Than Ever They Satisfy, 1945-55, VG **$60.00**

Lighter, gold-tone metal, lady's, Evans **$8.00**

Lighter, marble, silver decoration, Ronson, table size .**$45.00**

Lighter, sea horses & shells in clear Lucite, Evans.......**$25.00**

Lighter, 4", commode figural, chrome **$20.00**

Pack, Half & Half Cigarettes, 1960s, unopened, NM ...**$12.50**

Pack, Milla Egyptian Cigarettes, exotic lady pictured, unopened, EX **$15.00**

Package, Country Gentleman Pipe & Cigarette Tobacco, cloth sack w/paper label, sealed, EX.......................**$6.00**

Playing cards, Kent Cigarettes, depicts soft pack of Kents in front of chess set, complete, M.............................**$10.00**

Playing cards, Marlboro Cigarettes, 2 logos, 1 upside down, black, red & white, complete, M.............................**$9.00**

Playing cards, Winston Cigarettes, rodeo cowboy on horse, Rodeo Awards, black on red & white Winston background, M..**$20.00**

Pocket mirror, Lucky Strike, 2" dia, cowboy standing by Lucky Strike window sign, ca 1920s, VG+ **$22.00**

Poster, Cavalier King Size, 20x28", cavalier & lg pack of cigarettes, EX..**$22.00**

Sign, Camel Cigarettes, 11x21", full color image of James Daly, Have a Real Cigarette, paper, 1960s, EX......**$25.00**

Sign, Camel Lights, 21½x17½", pack of cigarettes w/lettering above & below, metal, 1978, EX..............................**$7.50**

Sign, Egyptian Deities Cigarettes, 21x15", tin, still life w/pack of cigarettes, Plain End or Cut Tip, self framed, G $120.00

Sign, London Life Cigarettes, 37x19", Most Extraordinary, EX $600.00
Sign, Lucky Strike Flat Fifties, 39x26", tin, EX............$275.00
Sign, Marvel Cigarettes, 15x10", open pack of cigarettes, multicolored, tin, 1950s, EX $35.00
Thermometer, Camel Cigarettes, 13½x5¾", embossed pack of cigarettes, ...Have a Real Cigarette..., tin, EX....$40.00
Thermometer, 13x6", tin, embossed pack of Chesterfields, They Satisfy, EX $110.00
Tin, Black Cat Cigarettes, 4x3x2", black cat on lid $45.00
Tin, Camel Cigarettes, Turkish & Domestic Blend, round, VG...$30.00
Tin, Caravan Plain Cigarettes, held 50, green, VG.......$12.00
Tin, Caravan Cigarettes, held 50, red, Canada, VG......$15.00

Cleminsons Pottery

One of the several small potteries that operated in California during the middle of the century, Cleminsons was a family-operated enterprise that made kitchenware, decorative items, and novelties that are beginning to attract a considerable amount of interest. At the height of their productivity, they employed 150 workers, so as you make your 'rounds,' you'll be very likely to see a piece or two offered for sale just about anywhere you go. Prices are not high; this may be a 'sleeper.'

They marked their ware fairly consistently with a circular ink stamp that contains the name 'Cleminsons.' But even if you find an unmarked piece, with just a little experience you'll be able to easily recognize their very distinctive glaze colors. They're all strong, yet grayed-down, dusty tones. They made a line of bird-shaped tableware items that they marketed as 'Distlefink,' and several plaques and wall pock-

ets that are decorated with mottos and Pennsylvania Dutch-type hearts and flowers.

In Jack Chipman's *The Collector's Encyclopedia of California Pottery*, you'll find a chapter devoted to Cleminsons Pottery; and Roerig's *The Collector's Encyclopedia of Cookie Jars* has some more information.

Bank, sm, modeled as a doghouse...............................$12.50
Butter dish, Distlefink..$25.00
Canister, tea size, cherries on tree branch....................$25.00
Child's set, 8¼", waffle dish w/lid lettered Big Circus, sugar bowl modeled as clown, +4½" bowl $35.00
Cookie jar, potbellied stove $75.00
Cookie jar, Winter House, EX $80.00
Creamer & sugar bowl, King & Queen of Hearts........$35.00

Cup & saucer, girl w/hair in rollers, Shine!..........$15.00
Darner, 5", motto $15.00
Egg cup, cylinder w/hand-painted face of man, his feet protrude..$25.00
Egg cup, lady figural, early $25.00
Jar, 7", girl figural, opens at waist................................$25.00
Pitcher, 7", Gala Gray, red figures & leaves on gray ...$20.00
Pitcher, 9½", Distlefink, bird shape..............................$30.00
Plaque, 8", hand-painted fruit, holes for hanging..........$8.50
Plate, 9½", crowing rooster in center............................$8.00
Spoon rest, leaf form $12.50
String holder, heart form, You'll Always Have Pull.....$25.00

Clothes Sprinkler Bottles

In the days before perma-press, the process of getting wrinkles out of laundered clothing involved first sprinkling each piece with water, rolling it tightly to distribute the moisture, and packing it all down in a laundry basket until ironing day. Thank goodness those days are over!

To sprinkle the water, you could simply dip your fingers in a basin and 'fling' the water around, or you could take a plain old bottle with a screw-on cap, pierce the cap a few times and be in business. Maybe these figural bottles were made to add a little cheer to this dreary job. Anyway, since no one does all this any more, they represent a little bit of history, and collectors now take an interest in them. Prices are already fairly high, but there still may be a bargain or two out there!

Black Mammy, white dress, pink trim, minimum value.**$125.00**

Cat, 8", marble eyes, tail curled around to side **$75.00**

Cat, 9", jeweled eyes, seated w/front legs between hind feet...**$70.00**

Chinaman, holding iron, green or white pants, made in Japan...**$85.00**

Chinaman, red flowers w/black trim, Sprinkle Plenty.**$35.00**

Chinaman, 8", Sprinkle Plenty in vertical printing on vest, hands at sides...**$55.00**

Chinaman, 8", yellow & green, hands folded across chest, Cardina China...**$30.00**

Chinaman, 8½", white clothing, blue frog, blue cuffs, hands folded..**$35.00**

Clothespin, 8", painted-on facial features.....................**$65.00**

Dutch boy, 8", hands in pocket, airbrushed multicolors, Cleminsons **$75.00**

Dutch girl, 8", hands folded at waist, long dress & apron.**$75.00**

Elephant, grey w/pink airbrushing, seated, w/feet together...**$55.00**

Elephant, 7½", seated, Sprinkles written across tummy, hand-painted details **$65.00**

Flatiron, girl & ironing board on sole....................**$45.00**

Iron, w/ivy trim..**$25.00**

Mandarin, flowing pink robe **$55.00**

Matilda, Pfaltzgraff **$80.00**

Merry Maid, 7½", plastic, lady w/hands on hips, hoop skirt, marked USA...**$15.00**

Rooster, 10", long neck, airbrushed multicolors **$65.00**

Siamese cat, 9", airbrushed natural colors...................**$75.00**

Victorian lady w/purse **$95.00**

Clothing and Accessories

Vintage clothing shops are everywhere; have you noticed? And what's especially exciting are the forties, fifties, and sixties items that look so familiar. Hawaiian shirts have been hot for some time, and when padded shoulders became fashionable for women, thirties and forties clothing became very 'trendy.'

While some collectors buy with the intent of preserving their clothing and simply enjoy having and looking at it, many buy it to wear. If you do wear it, be very careful how you clean it; they're not made of polyester!

Apron, tea style, pink silk w/embroidered violets & lace trim, EX...**$20.00**

Blouse, sheer batiste, much lace, Peter Pan collar, long sleeves, 1920s, EX...**$30.00**

Blouse, white nylon w/satin trim, long sleeves, 1930s..**$20.00**

Cape, black crocheted wool w/sequins, short, 1950s .**$25.00**

Coat, black brocade, full length, 1950s, EX..................**$8.00**

Coat, cashmere, full length, wide collar, 1950s, EX.....**$10.00**

Collar, linen, V-neck shawl style, tatted lace edging, 1930s, M **$5.00**

Collar & cuff set, cotton w/cutwork, Peter Pan style.....**$8.00**

Dress, baby's, white w/cross-over smocking, EX **$20.00**

Dress, black crepe, short sleeves, 'V' neck w/rosette front, 1930s, EX...**$60.00**

Dress, cream crepe w/rhinestones, 1930s, EX **$70.00**

Dress, lace w/silk lining, beads & sequins, long sleeves, jewel neck, 1950s, EX..**$75.00**

Dress, silk, cream top w/peach skirt, shell buttons, V neck, sleeveless, 1930s, EX..**$35.00**

Dress, silk chiffon, flapper style, scoop neckline w/bow, fabric flower at hip, layered & pleated skirt, 1920s, M **$50.00**

Dress, silk faille, self-bow at neck, sleeveless, 1950s ..**$50.00**

Fur coat, brown Persian lamb w/mink trim, long, EX .**$225.00**

Hat, flapper-style cloche, blue fine-textured straw, EX ..**$45.00**

Hat, pillbox, simulated Persian lamb, EX **$7.50**

Levi jacket, w/single pocket & pleats, pre-1971 (look for lg E on red tab: LE, not Le), VG, minimum value.....**$75.00**

Levi jeans, non-vintage, 501, VG **$10.00**

Levi jeans, w/visible rivets inside, single pocket, pre-1971, lg E on tab, VG, minimum value.............................**$50.00**

Nightgown, peach rayon, 1940s, EX............................**$10.00**

Robe, rayon print, 1940s-50s **$5.00**

Shawl, black lace, 1920s, 12x66"................................**$55.00**

Shawl, embroidered pastel flowers on silk, China **$100.00**

Shell, black w/sequins, EX..**$12.00**

Shirt, man's, cotton w/Hawaiian print, 1960s.................**$3.00**

Shirt, man's, rayon, w/Hawaiian print, 1940s, minimum value **$15.00**

Shoes, fake black alligator, high platform & heel, 1960s..**$7.00**

Shoes, red snakeskin, open toes, sling back, 1950s **$10.00**

Sweater, black w/long fur trim **$15.00**

Sweater, heavily beaded, pink-lined, EX......................**$50.00**

Sweater, lightly beaded cardigan, 1950s, EX...............**$10.00**

Teddy, rose print on white rayon, French lace yoke ..**$50.00**

Coca-Cola Collectibles

Coca-Cola was introduced to the public in 1886. Immediately an advertising campaign began that over the years and to the present day has literally saturated our lives with a never-ending variety of items. Some of the earlier calendars and trays have been known to bring prices well into the four figures. Because of these heady prices and the extremely wide-spread collector demand for good Coke items, reproductions are everywhere, so beware! Some of the items that have been reproduced are pocket mirrors (from 1905, 1906, 1908-11, 1916, and 1920), trays (from 1899, 1910, 1913-14, 1917, 1920, 1923, 1926, 1934, and 1937), tip trays (from 1907, 1909, 1910, 1913-14, 1917, and 1920), knives, cartons, bottles, clocks, and trade cards. Currently being produced and marketed are an 18" brass 'button,' a 24" brass bottle-shaped thermometer, cast iron toys and bottle-shaped door pulls, Yes Girl posters, a 12" 'button' sign (with one round hole), a rectangular paperweight, a 1949-style cooler radio, and there are others.

In addition to reproductions, 'fantasy' items have also been made, the difference being that a 'fantasy' never existed as an original. Don't be deceived. Belt buckles are 'fantasies.' So are glass doorknobs with an etched trademark, bottle-shaped knives, pocketknives (supposedly from the 1933 World's Fair), a metal letter opener stamped 'Coca-Cola 5¢,' a cardboard sign with the 1911 lady with fur (9x11"), and celluloid vanity pieces (a mirror, brush, etc.)

When the company celebrated its 100th anniversary in 1986, many 'centennial' items were issued; they all carry the '100th Anniversary' logo. Many of them are collectible in their own right, and some are already high-priced.

If you'd really like to study this subject, we recommend these books: *Goldstein's Coca-Cola Collectibles* by Sheldon Goldstein, *Huxford's Collectible Advertising* by Sharon and Bob Huxford, and *Collector's Guide to Coca-Cola Items, Vols I and II*, by Al Wilson.

Apron, 1960s, Enjoy Coca-Cola w/contour logo, 2 pockets, M **$10.00**

Ashtray, 1960s, gray metal round dish w/a Coke bottle & Drink Coca-Cola embossed in center, EX...............**$8.00**

Ashtray, 1960s, silver lettering on red metal square shape w/rounded corners, Things Go Better..., EX.........**$10.00**

Ashtrays, 1950s, ruby glass, Drink Coca-Cola embossed on diamond, spade, club & heart shapes, set of 4 in box, EX **$350.00**

Bank, 1950s, bottle cap form, EX.................................**$10.00**

Bank, 1980, plastic, soda-dispenser type, in original box, NM **$110.00**

Baseball bat, 1968, Compliments of Coca-Cola... on lg end of bat, EX...**$35.00**

Blotter, 1935, train engineer drinking bottle of Coke, The Drink That Keeps You Feeling Fit, For Duty Ahead, dated, EX+ **$20.00**

Blotter, 1940, features clown drinking bottle of Coke, The Greatest Pause on Earth, button logo at right, EX..**$45.00**

Blotter, 1953, features the Sprite boy, Good!, EX **$6.00**

Blotter, 1960, Over 60 Million Sold, VG **$2.00**

Book, copyright 1928, Alphabet book of Coca-Cola, features children wearing cards lettered A-B-C, nice images & poems **$60.00**

Book cover, 1960, 60 Million a Day, VG **$4.00**

Book cover, 1986, features Max Headroom, VG...........**$2.00**

Bottle, 1976, 75th Anniversary, Louisville KY, VG.........**$2.00**

Bottle, 1980, commemorating the Georgia Bulldogs...**$60.00**

Bottle, 1982, commemorating Penn State.......................**$4.00**

Bottle, 1983, commemorating Washington Redskins Super Bowl 17 ....**$20.00**

Bottle, 1984, commemorating the Dallas Cowboys' 25 yrs in NFL..**$10.00**

Bottle, 1989, commemorating Bill Elliot's Winston Cup Championship **$20.00**

Bottle cap set, 6 from various countries representing the Coca-Cola Export Corp set in Lucite, w/original box, NM **$25.00**

Bottle carrier, ca 1939, cardboard, red, white & green w/Season's Greetings on handle, holds 6, G **$30.00**

Bottle carrier, 1930s, wood painted yellow, features 1923 Christmas bottle in red on ends, lettered logo on sides, G **$65.00**

Bottle carrier, 1950s, aluminum, silver w/red & white logo on front & back, includes 6 green bottles, EX......**$35.00**

Box of jumbo straws, 1960s, Be Really Refreshed & fishtail logo on 4 sides, EX..**$60.00**

Calendar, 1936, old fisherman sitting on edge of red boat enjoys Coke w/girl, 50th anniversary, full pad, VG...........**$575.00**

Calendar, 1944, pictures girl in hat w/rim flattened on 1 side lifting bottle of Coke, full double pad, EX..........**$200.00**

Calendar, 1973, tin, perpetual 1950s style w/button atop reading Drink Coca-Cola In Bottles, full pad, G.**$140.00**

Calendar, 1975, square Coca-Cola logo, It's the Real Thing, pad w/single number & day, 15x7½", NM **$40.00**

Calendar, 1986, 100th Anniversary, VG **$8.00**

Calendar top, 1930, bathing beauty w/bottle of Coke seated on rock, her feet in water, EX.............................**$110.00**

Can, commemorating the new Oriole Park stadium/Camden Yards **$5.00**

Can, 1984, University of Washington, Husky Fever.......**$3.00**

Can carton, commemorating the 1984 Olympics, holds 12 cans..**$4.00**

Car plate, 1950s, white on red or red on white, Drink Coca-Cola, EX...**$20.00**

Change apron, 1940s, EX..**$60.00**

Charm bracelet, 1950s, features Cleveland Browns.....**$75.00**

Cigar box, inside label & end panel feature Lillian Russell her name above, 2 for 5¢ in corner, G.................**$25.00**

Clock, 1950s, metal, numbers on white background surround red disk w/Drink Coca-Cola in white, 17" **$145.00**

Clock, 1960s, brass w/light-up glass face on fishtail logo base, 12x11", NM **$135.00**

Clock, 1970s, electric pendulum style light-up base, wood-look plastic case, logo below pendulum, EX+......**$45.00**

Cookie jar, can shape, MIB **$50.00**

Cuff links, bottle shape in sterling silver **$65.00**

Decal, 1960s, foil peel-back, Drink Coca-Cola, Please Pay When Served, 6x13", EX...**$8.00**

Dish, 1976, smoked glass, a bicentennial piece featuring 100 Years of Free Enterprise, EX **$15.00**

Doll, 1960, Santa, EX...**$60.00**

Drinking glasses, 1986, Coca-Cola Classic Whataburger glasses in the yellow rose design, set of 4 ....**$6.00**

Fan, 1930s, cardboard w/wooden handle featuring Coke bottle over sun logo, Drink Coca-Cola above, EX......**$40.00**

Fan, 1950s, cardboard, M **$30.00**

Fan pull, 2-sided bell shape, Regular Size, Serve Coca-Cola, Sign of Good Taste, EX **$13.00**

Festoon, 1934, features wood flowers, Drink Coca-Cola, Be Alert, original envelope, NM, 3-piece.................**$475.00**

First aid kit, 1950s, First Aid Kit in raised letters on red lid w/Coca-Cola in white letters, rounded corners, EX.**$35.00**

Flashlight, bottle shape, EX...........................**$15.00**

Fly swatter, 1950s, EX....................................**$14.00**

Game, 1957, Shanghi, MIB..............................**$10.00**

Golf tee set, 1950s, 4 white golf tees in white case, Enjoy Coke lettered in red, EX...............................**$10.00**

Ice bucket, 1960, Drink Coca-Cola in Bottles lettered on white circle on side of bucket, EX...................**$12.00**

Kite, 1930s, High Flyer featuring 6-oz bottle of Coke w/Coca-Cola lettered above, some major tears, G.............**$45.00**

Lighter, Scripto butane, features applied gold Coke bottle, EX **$15.00**

Lighter, 1960s, Coke can style, M.......................$20.00

Lunch box, vinyl, w/thermos, Coca-Cola in various languages, EX...**$15.00**

Magic lantern picture, 1920s, hand-colored image of couple toasting w/bottles of Coke, Good Company!, EX .**$100.00**

Magnifying glass, 1950s, round glass in red tongue-shaped case w/white Coca-Cola in script, snap closure, EX **$20.00**

Marbles, 1950s, mesh bag, M **$20.00**

Matchbook, 1965, reproduction of 1908 matches, EX ...**$3.00**

Mechanical pencil, 1950s, bottle floating in liquid, EX..**$20.00**

Menu board, 1930s, logo above Specials To Day w/double yellow lines down left side, red double lines across bottom, G..**$150.00**

Menu board, 1960s, tin, fishtail logo w/Sign of Good Taste & bottle in upper right, EX+ **$180.00**

Menu holder, 1940s, plastic, 1940s Silhouette Girl insert, EX **$70.00**

Mileage table, 1960s, shows the distance between major cities in the southeastern United States, Better w/Coke, NM **$60.00**

Miniature 6-pack, 1950s, cardboard carrier w/wire handle holds 6 bottles painted to look full of Coke, NM .**$85.00**

Needle case, 1925, shows profile of lady lifting a glass of Coke, VG **$35.00**

Opener, 1930s, skate-key type w/Coca-Cola embossed on handle...**$45.00**

Opener, 1950s, bottle-shaped handle, octagonal opener.**$25.00**

Opener & ice pick, 1940s, metal loop at end of wooden handle w/red lettering, EX **$15.00**

Opener spoon, 1930s, lettering on handle that serves as opener **$60.00**

Pillow, 1950s, cloth, bottle shape, EX.........................**$40.00**

Pin-back button, 1976, Happy Birthday America, 3" **$3.00**

Placemats, 1950s, Around the World, set of 4, EX......**$12.00**

Playing cards, 100th Anniversary, double deck, unopened, M...**$20.00**

Playing cards, 1951, Party Girl w/head tilted holding bottle of Coke, in unopened box, stamp intact, box NM, cards M **$80.00**

Playing cards, 1963, shows couple at fireplace, complete, w/box, EX...**$55.00**

Playing cards, 1971, features girl in the grass, It's the Real Thing, EX...**$25.00**

Playing cards, 1979, features the Sprite boy, EX..........**$40.00**

Pocket comb, 1950s, red w/Drink Coca-Cola 5¢ lettered in gold, NM...**$5.00**

Pocket mirror, 1906, Juanita w/high collar & lg necklace lifts glass of Coke, 2¼x1¾", G.....................**$160.00**

Pocket mirror, 1916, Elaine seated holding Coke bottle while peering over shoulder, 2¾x1¾", VG+ **$175.00**

Pocketknife, 1940s, Drink Coca-Cola in Bottles in red lettering on white handle, EX...............................**$75.00**

Postcard, 1940s, pictures a Coca-Cola truck, EX..........**$20.00**

Poster, features Willie Màys, 24x18", EX **$12.00**

Poster, 1960s, cardboard, 2-sided, Things Go Better w/Coke, couple sunning on deck, 2 bottles in snow, EX...**$55.00**

Push plate, yellow Thanks Call Again...& white Coca-Cola diagonally on red, rounded ends, 11½x4", VG **$50.00**

Push plate, 1941, red porcelainized metal w/yellow lettering & border, Merci Revenez Pour Un..., EX.............**$135.00**

Puzzle, 1970s-80s, An Old Fashioned Girl (1901 calendar girl), in original box w/plastic wrapper, NM.........**$12.00**

Radio, 1970s-80s, bottle form, in original box, NM **$30.00**

Radio, 1982, vending machine style, AM-FM transistor, in original box, NM **$40.00**

Record, 1967, 45 rpm, Trini Lopez, record sleeve advertises Fresca...**$14.00**

Record, 1971, 45 rpm, Buy the World a Coke, It's the Real Thing...**$8.00**

Salesman's training guide, 1960s, red spiral notebook w/fishtail cover, 8x4", EX **$18.00**

Seltzer bottle, 1950s, glass, metal top, Coca-Cola Bottling Works, Alliance Ohio, Content 26 Fl Oz on shield logo, EX **$135.00**

Shot glass, 1979, Coke Adds Life to Christmas...............**$3.00**

Sign, neon, red & white, Enjoy Coca-Cola, M............**$350.00**

Sign, 1926, self-framed tin, front view of girl offering a bottle of Coke over lettered logo, G **$170.00**

Sign, 1941, cardboard, singer at mike holding bottle of Coke, button logo upper right, Entertain Your Thirst, EX+ **$525.00**

Sign, 1941, cardboard, 1920s couple walking past touring car, enclosed Coca-Cola logo at left of lady, 30x50", VG+..**$320.00**

Sign, 1941, embossed tin sidewalk type w/6-pack in circle, Take Home a Carton lettered below, vertical rectangle, NM **$425.00**

Sign, 1950, cardboard, Home Refreshment, pictures girl beside refrigerator, some nicks & holes, G **$140.00**

Sign, 1950s, cardboard, Cheese Treats on band above button logo over display of cheeses, 24x18", EX **$30.00**

Sign, 1950s, cardboard, button type lettered Drink Coca-Cola, Sign Of Good Taste, 6" dia, EX **$30.00**

Sign, 1950s, die-cut tin fishtail shape w/Coca-Cola in white script on red background, 7½x15½", EX+...........**$150.00**

Sign, 1950s, metal, free-standing whirlygig style w/4 double-sided buttons attached to common base, NM.....**$750.00**

Sign, 1950s, metal button shape w/Drink lettered above Coca-Cola in script on red background, 16", NM...........**$250.00**

Sign, 1950s, 2-sided paper pennant w/fishtail point showing hamburger & glass of Coke, Drink Coca-Cola, 14x12", EX+ **$45.00**

Sign, 1955, cardboard, girls having a beach party around cooler of Coke, Coke Time, Join the Friendly Circle, 20x36", EX **$300.00**

Sign, 1955, cardboard, Sprite boy looking around Coke bottle above button logo & bottle, Now! Family Size Too!, NM **$100.00**

Sign, 1956, 2-sided hanger type, pictures elves w/6-pack of Coke on toboggan, NM **$70.00**

Sign, 1958, cardboard, 2-sided w/Enjoy the Party More on 1 side & Cookouts on the other, 27x56", EX............**$55.00**

Sign, 1960, metal flange w/Drink Coca-Cola in script on fishtail logo on white background, 15x18", NM.**$170.00**

Sign, 1960s, metal, Coke bottle at right of fishtail logo, Coca-Cola in white script, Ice Cold above, 20x28", NM.**$130.00**

Sign, 1960s, metal, outdoor type w/fishtail logo, Sign of Good Taste, 36x50", NM...................................**$110.00**

Sign, 1960s, 2-sided hanger type, Enjoy Coke Ice Cold, shows a Coke bottle in the snow, EX...................**$90.00**

Sign, 1962, die-cut metal fishtail w/Coca-Cola logo, 16" long, NM **$275.00**

Sign, 2-sided stenciled steel flange w/Coke bottle against yellow circle, Drink Coca-Cola, 24" long, G+ **$190.00**

Stadium vendor, 1950s, handled metal box w/opener on side holds 20 bottles, VG **$130.00**

Sunglasses, Coca-Coca logo on lenses, EX...................**$12.00**

Tap knob, 1960s-70s, 2-sided, round w/Coke lettered in red on white, EX..**$10.00**

Tape measure, heart shape, EX **$18.00**

Telephone, 1984, cube shape featuring the USA Olympics logo, 12 sectioned-off numbers & Coca-Cola ribbon logo, MIB...**$35.00**

Thermometer, 1930s, porcelain, silhouette of girl drinking Coke, Thirst Knows No Season, 18x6", EX **$300.00**

Thermometer, 1948, tin, red button logo at top on white, In Bottles, Serve Coke at Home, 9", NM...................**$185.00**

Thermometer, 1950s, die-cut metal, bottle shape, 16", EX+ **$75.00**

Thermometer, 1950s, flat metal bottle shape w/thermometer on bottom half of bottle, 16x5", NM.....................**$80.00**

Thermometer, 1959, metal w/glass face, degree numbers surround fishtail logo, 12" dia, NM.....................**$220.00**

Tip tray, 1914, Betty in a bonnet, oval, NM..............**$275.00**

Toy car, 1960s, Ford friction sedan, Refresh w/Zest, in original box, NM...**$195.00**

Toy train car, 1970s, Tyco, MIB **$5.00**

Toy truck, 1961, cast steel, Matchbox, fishtail logo, 2", NM **$75.00**

Toy truck, 1976, Buddy-L set, MIB **$50.00**

Train set, 1974, Lionel, red Coke engine & caboose w/Fanta, Tab & Sprite boxcars **$135.00**

Tray, 1930, close-up of girl w/legs crossed talking on phone, rectangular w/rounded corners, G............**$80.00**

Tray, 1938, girl in yellow dress & picture hat, American Art Works, NM..$200.00

Tray, 1939, bathing beauty sitting on diving board lifting a bottle of Coke, rectangular, rounded corners, EX.......**$165.00**

Tray, 1941, pretty ice skater sitting on snowy log holding a bottle of Coke, rectangular, rounded corners, NM......**$285.00**

Tray, 1942, girl in plaid jacket leaning against car talking to friend, rectangular w/rounded corners, NM........**$340.00**

Tray, 1950-52, close-up portrait of smiling girl on solid background lifting bottle of Coke to mouth, rectangular, VG..**$170.00**

Tray, 1959, Drive In for Coke on rim w/fishtail logo in center, Goes Good w/Food, rectangular, NM..........**$425.00**

Tray, 1961, features hand pouring bottle into glass among pansies, Here's a Coke for You, NM....................**$15.00**

Tray, 1961, Thanksgiving, EX..**$30.00**

Tray, 1966, deep-dish, woman holding bottle close to face, NM **$45.00**

Tray, 1968, deep-dish, Coca-Cola bottles on ice, EX+.**$50.00**

Tray, 1970, deep-dish, shows a Coke bottle displayed w/party food, NM..**$8.00**

Tray, 1972, reproduction of Betty, 1914, oval, EX.......**$12.00**

Tray, 1976, features Bobby Knight & Indiana's NCAA championship, EX...**$8.00**

Tray, 1981, features early Coca-Cola items, Springtime in Atlanta, EX **$6.00**

Tray, 1984, pictures Santa & young girl, EX...................**$6.00**

Tray, 1985, features calendar girls, round, EX...............**$6.00**

Tray, 1990, pictures Santa & a bunny, rectangular, EX..**$8.00**

Wallet, 1940s, pigskin, original box, EX.......................**$45.00**

Wallet, 1960s, black leather fold-over type w/Drink Coca-Cola Delicious Refreshing in gold lettering..........**$20.00**

Watch fob, 1920s, embossed brass w/Coke bottle flanked by 5¢, logo above, rare, 1¾", EX....................................**$95.00**

Writing tablet, 1936, 50th Anniversary logo, EX **$6.00**

Comic Books

Though just about everyone can remember having stacks and stacks of comic books as a child, few of us ever saved them for more than a few months. At 10¢ a copy, new ones quickly replaced the old, well-read stacks; we'd trade them to our friends, but very soon, out they went. If we didn't throw them away, Mother did. So even though they were printed in huge amounts, few survive. Today they're a very desirable collectible. The 1938 Action No.1 comic that introduced Superman has a recorded sale of over $82,000.00!

Factors that make a comic book valuable are condition (as with all paper collectibles, extremely important), content, and rarity, but not necessarily age. In fact, comics printed between 1950 and the late 1970s are most in demand by collectors who prefer those they had as children to the earlier comics. They look for issues where the hero is first introduced, and they insist on quality. Condition is first and foremost when it comes to assessing worth. Compared to a book in excellent condition, a mint issue might be worth six to eight times as much, while one in only good condition should be priced at less than half. We've listed some of the more collectible (and expensive) comics, but many are worth very little. You'll really need to check your bookstore for a good reference book before you actively get involved in the comic book market.

Annie Oakley & Tagg, #18, Dell, VG.............................**$6.50**
Army War Heroes, #38, Charlton Comics, M.................**$8.00**

Atom, #1, DC Comics, EX.......................................$150.00
Battle Beasts, Four Color, #4, Blackthorne, M...............**$2.00**
Battle Ground, #12, Atlas Comics, EX............................**$6.50**
Beagle Boys Versus Uncle Scrooge, #1, Gold Key, M ...**$2.50**
Beverly Hillbillies, #20, photo cover, Dell, M **$18.00**
Bewitched, #12, photo cover, Dell, EX **$10.00**
Big Valley, #1, photo cover, VG **$4.00**
Buck Jones & the Iron Horse Trail, Four Color, #299, Dell, M **$80.00**
Buck Rogers, #7, Toby Press, VG **$18.50**
Burning Romances, Fox Giants, EX..............................**$85.00**
Captain America, #101, Marvel Comics, M **$60.00**
Captain Marvel & the Horn of Plenty, Fawcett Minatures, G..**$4.50**
Captain Marvel Jr, #4, Fawcett Publications, VG..........**$50.00**
Captain Nice, #1, Gold Key, EX....................................**$12.00**
Casper the Ghost, #2, Harvey Publications, EX **$25.00**
Cave Kids, #16, Gold Key, EX...**$3.50**
Chief Victorio's Apache Massacre, #1, Avon, VG.........**$25.00**
Classic Comics, Black Arrow, #87, EX **$6.50**
Classics Illustrated, #47, David Copperfield, VG..........**$12.50**
Classics Illustrated, Treasure Island, #62, VG..............**$10.00**
Classics Illustrated, White Fang, #79, EX.....................**$16.50**
Classics Illustrated Jr, Aladdin & His Lamp, #516, EX..**$10.00**
Commando Adventures, #2, Atlas Comics, M **$18.00**
Courtship of Eddie's Father, #2, photo cover, Dell, M ..**$16.50**
Crime Patrol, #7, EC Comics, VG **$38.50**
Daniel Boone, #15, Gold Key, EX....................................**$3.50**
Dark Shadows, #15, Gold Key, EX **$8.50**
Darkhawk, #1, Marvel Comics, M **$6.00**
Date w/Danger, #5, Standard Comics, VG **$4.00**

David Cassidy, #14, photo cover, Charlton Comics, M..**$6.50**

Dennis the Menace, #45, Fawcett Publications, EX **$5.00**

Devil Dog Dugan, #3, Atlas Comics, EX......................**$7.50**

Dinky Duck Comics, #2, St John Publishing Co, M.....**$16.50**

Dixie Dugan, V3#1, Prize Publications, EX **$15.00**

Dolly Dill, #1, Marvel Comics, G...............................**$8.00**

Doomsday, #6, Charlton Comics, EX **$2.50**

Dudley Do-Right, #7, Charlton Comics, EX..................**$9.50**

E-Man, #3, Comica, M...**$3.00**

Eddie Stanky, Baseball Hero, photo cover, Fawcett Publications, EX **$42.00**

El Bombo Comics, #1, Standard Comics, EX...............**$18.50**

Elfquest, #5, Epic Comics, M **$3.50**

Ella Cinders, #5, United Features Syndicate, EX **$12.00**

Emerald Dawn, #5, DC Comics, M..............................**$6.50**

Enchanting Love, #2, photo cover, Kirby Publishing, EX.**$10.00**

Everything's Archie, #2, Archie Publications, M...........**$18.00**

Fairy Tale Parade, #2, Dell, VG.................................**$50.00**

Fashion in Action, Winter Special, Eclipse Comics, M...**$3.00**

Fightin' Army, #16, Charlton Comics, EX....................**$6.50**

Film Stars Romances, #1, Rudy Valentino story, Star Publications, VG..**$18.00**

Flaming Western Romances, #2, Star Publications, EX.**$35.00**

Flash Gordon, #2, Harvey Publications, EX **$40.00**

Flintstones Kids, #5, Marvel Comics, M **$2.00**

Flipper, #2, Gold Key, M...**$18.00**

Flying Nun, #4, photo cover, Dell, EX........................**$4.50**

Forever People, #4, DC Comics, M **$1.75**

Fraggle Rock, #8, Star Comics, M..............................**$1.50**

Freddy, #3, Dell, M **$6.50**

Gang Busters, Four Color, Dell, EX **$65.00**

Gene Autry in Outlaw Trail, Four Color, #83, Dell, M .**$200.00**

Get Smart, #1, photo cover, Dell, EX.........................**$20.00**

Godzilla, #10, Marvel Comics, M...............................**$4.50**

Green Hornet, #3, photo cover, Gold Key, EX...........**$30.00**

Gulliver's Travels, #2, Dell, M **$12.50**

Happy Days, #6, Dell, EX..**$1.50**

Heckle & Jeckle, #1, Gold Key, EX............................**$12.50**

Hercules, #8, Charlton Comics, M..............................**$18.50**

Hollywood Secrets, #2, Quality Comics, M **$80.00**

Hot Rod Racers, #5, Charlton Comics, EX **$4.00**

Howdy Doody, #5, photo cover, Dell, VG....................**$9.50**

Huckleberry Hound Summer Fun, #31, Dell Giant, EX..**$32.00**

Huey, Dewey, & Louie Back to School, #22, Dell Giant, VG..**$18.00**

Ideal Romance, #8, Key Publications, EX.....................**$6.50**

Incredible Hulk & Wolverine, #1, Marvel Comics, M ..**$12.50**

Ironjaw, #1, Atlas Publications, M...............................**$2.00**

Jiggs & Maggie, #22, Harvey Publications, EX **$9.50**

Johnny Jason, Four Color, #1302, Dell, M...................**$10.00**

Jughead's Diner, #5, Archie Comics, M **$1.50**

Jungle Jim, Four Color, #490, Dell, EX **$15.00**

Kid Eternity, #2, Quality Comics, EX **$60.00**

King Louie & Mowgli, #1, Gold Key, EX.....................**$6.50**

Labyrinth, #3, Marvel Comics, M...............................**$1.50**

Land of the Lost Comics, #2, EC Comics, EX **$35.00**

Laugh Comics Digest, #1, Archie Publications, M..........**$6.50**

Little Archie, #6, Archie Publications, VG....................**$7.50**

Little Lizzie, #4, Marvel Comics, M............................**$20.00**

Love Mystery, #1, George Evans photo cover, Fawcett Publications, EX...**$35.00**

March of Comics, Bullwinkle, #233, M.......................**$65.00**

March of Comics, Oswald the Rabbit, #38, EX **$20.00**

March of Comics, Three Stooges, #280, photo cover, M.**$45.00**

Marvin Mouse, #1, Atlas Comics, EX **$14.00**

Mighty Bear, #13, Star Publications, VG **$5.50**

Mighty Mouse in Outer Space, #43, Dell Giant, EX.....**$50.00**

Molly Manton's Romances, #1, photo cover, Marvel Comics, EX...**$18.50**

My Little Margie, #2, photo cover, Charlton Comics, M .**$40.00**

New Teen Titans, #3, DC Comics, M..........................**$3.00**

Night Rider, #5, Marvel Comics, M............................**$1.50**

Nukla, #1, Dell, M **$15.00**

Outlaws of the West, #11, Charlton Comics, EX..........**$14.00**

Oz-Wonderland Wars, #3, DC Comics, M **$2.50**

Partridge Family, #4, Charlton Comics, EX..................**$4.00**

Patty Powers, #7, Atlas Comics, EX...........................**$7.50**

Phantom Stranger, #4, DC Comics, M.........................**$1.50**

Prize Comics, #3, VG **$40.00**

Prize Comics, #33, VG **$15.00**

Quick-Draw McGraw, #8, Charlton Comics, EX **$6.00**

Richie Rich & Casper, #2, Harvey Publications, M.........**$3.50**

Richie Rich Gems, #10, Harvey Publications, M............**$5.00**

Robot Battalion 2050, #1, Eclipse Comics, M **$2.50**

Roger Rabbit's Toontown, #6, Disney Comics, M.........**$2.00**

Rootie Kazootie, Four Color, #459, Dell, M.................**$38.00**

Roots of the Swamp Thing, #5, DC Comics, M.............**$3.00**

Saga of the Swamp Thing, #53, DC Comics, M.............**$4.50**

Scooby Doo, #2, Marvel Comics, M............................**$2.00**

Secret Agent, #2, photo cover, Gold Key, EX.............**$10.00**

Silver Kid Western, #3, Key Publications, EX...............**$7.50**

Six-Gun Heroes, #5, Fawcett Publications, VG **$14.50**

Smilin' Jack, Four Color, #14, EX **$90.00**

Soldier Comics, #5, Fawcett Publications, NM **$14.50**

Star Trek, #2, DC Comics, NM...................................**$2.50**

Stumbo the Giant, #63, Harvey Hits, M **$26.00**

Stumbo Tinytown, #5, Harvey Publications, VG............**$6.00**

Supercar, #2, Gold Key, VG......................................**$9.50**

Suspense Detective, #5, Fawcett Publications, EX.......**$22.00**

Tales From the Crypt, #2, Gladstone Publishing, EX.....**$2.00**

Tarzan, Vol 1, #52, EX..**$15.00**

Texas Slim, #9, A-1 Comics, M.......................$18.50
Tillie the Tioler, Four Color, #8, EX..........................$50.00
Tiny Tots Comics, #1, Dell, EX $95.00
Tom & Jerry Back to School, #1, Dell Giant, NM $60.00
Tomb of Dracula, #2, Marvel Comics, EX.....................$9.50
Tweety & Sylvester, #10, Gold Key, EX.......................$3.00
Untold Legend of Batman, #3, DC Comics, NM.............$3.00
Voodoo, #3, Ajax, EX..$38.00
Wagon Train, Four Color, #895, photo cover, Dell, M..$50.00
War & Attack, #1, Charlton Comics, VG......................$2.50
Wendy the Witch, #16, Harvey Hits, EX......................$14.00
Werewolf, #1, Dell, EX $3.00
Wild Boy of the Congo, #11, Approved Comics, EX...$12.50
Wild Wild West, #3, Gold Key, EX $16.50
101 Dalmations, Four Color, #1183, Dell, M $30.00

Compacts

Very new to the collectibles scene, compacts are already making an impact. When 'liberated' women entered the workforce after WWI, cosmetics, previously frowned upon, became more acceptable, and as as result the market was engulfed with compacts of all types and designs. Some went so far as to incorporate timepieces, cigarette compartments, coin holders, and money clips. All types of materials were used, mother-of-pearl, petitpoint, cloisonne, celluloid, and leather among them. There were figural compacts, those with wonderful Art Deco designs, souvenir compacts, and compacts with advertising messages.

For further study, we recommend *Ladies' Compacts of the 19th and 20th Centuries* by Roselyn Gerson.

Best & Co, 2¾x2¾", horse design in smooth gold & white on brushed gold-plated finish $30.00
Bliss, oval, black enamel w/carved jade & pearl centerpiece, holds powder & rouge, some wear $38.00
Bourjois France, 1½" dia, partially nude woman etched in red on chrome...$20.00
Coty, 1¾" dia, textured chrome finish $22.00
Daniel, oblong w/gold-tone satin finish, 3-D plastic courting scene under raised plastic dome...........................$75.00
Elgin, 4x3", brushed silver w/gold grapes....................$50.00
Flato, gold-tone w/open umbrella design, fitted black faille case, includes lipstick...$120.00
Girey, 3¼x1½x¾", beige leather figural camera w/chrome trim, push button opens to powder & rouge........$60.00
Harriet Hubbard Ayer, square shape w/black & white crosshatching on gold...$18.00
Houbigant, enameled, sliding comb on lid, minimum value $80.00
Lin-Bren, 3¼x3¼", gold-plated circle within square, metal filigree, lg cabochon turquoise & rhinestones..........$40.00
Majestic, sm square shape w/copper-colored basketweave design $40.00
Max Factor, rectangular, gold-tone metal w/woven texture, bar-shaped centerpiece encrusted w/rhinestones $28.00

Mondaine, red enamel, lipstick on lid, 1920s-30s, minimum value $60.00
Pilcher, square shape w/black & white mother-of-pearl checkerboard design...$40.00
Souvenir, 2¾x2¾", Golden Gate International Expo, San Francisco, 1939, view of Expo w/blue enamel border, MIB $75.00

Sterling, 3", w/engraved swirled feathers.............$85.00
Terri, blue plastic square shape w/silver silhouette of dancers on blue metal lid......................................$35.00
Yardley, gold-tone & enamel finish w/swivel mirror, 1930s, minimum value $40.00
Yardley, rectangular metal case, colonial design in center, holds powder & rouge $48.00

Consolidated Glass

The Consolidated Lamp and Glass Company operated in Coraopolis, Pennsylvania, from 1894 until 1964. At first much of what they made was oil lamps and shades, although they also made Cosmos, a limited line of milk glass tableware decorated with pastel flowers.

By the mid-twenties they were making glassware with 'sculptured' designs, very similar to a line made by a nearby competitor, the Phoenix Glass Company located in Monaca, Pennsylvania. Unless you're a student of these two types of glassware, it's very difficult to distinguish one from the other. The best clue (which is not foolproof) is the fact that most of the time Consolidated applied color to the relief (raised) design and left the background plain, while the reverse was true of Phoenix.

One of their lines was called Ruba Rombic. It has a very distinctive 'cubist' appearance; shapes are free-form with jutting dimensional planes. It was made in strong colors to compliment its Deco forms, and collectors value anything from this line very highly.

For more information we recommend *Phoenix and Consolidated Art Glass, 1926-1980,* by Jack D. Wilson.

Bowl, salad; 9", Catalonian, emerald, straight sides.....**$55.00**
Bowl, 9", Mermaid, amethyst stain on crystal...........**$155.00**
Goblet, Five Fruits, green wash **$32.00**
Jug, Iris, sepia stain...**$200.00**

Katydid, vase, 7", gold iridescent wash...............$100.00
Plate, 6", Iris, green stain...**$37.50**
Plate, 8", Dancing Nymphs, teal blue **$60.00**
Plate, 8", Olive, green stain on crystal.........................**$38.00**
Plate, 8¼", Bird of Paradise, yellow wash....................**$47.50**
Sundae, Vine/Line 700, light green stain on crystal.....**$22.50**
Tumbler, Iris, transparent green over white.................**$95.00**
Vase, 6", Dragonfly, green cased..................................**$175.00**
Vase, 6½", Ruba Rombic, jungle green.........................**$175.00**
Vase, 6¼", Jonquil, pink flowers & green leaves on white
satin **$80.00**

Cookbooks and Recipe Leaflets

If you've ever read a 19th-century cookbook, no doubt you've been amused by the quaint way the measurements were given. Butter the size of an egg, a handful of flour, a pinch of this or that – sounds like a much more time-efficient method, doesn't it? They'd sometimes give household tips or some folk remedies, and it's these antiquated methods and ideas that endear those old cookbooks to collectors, although examples from this circa are not easily found.

Cookbooks from the early 20th century are scarce, too, but even those that were printed thirty and forty years ago are also well worth collecting. Food and appliance companies often published their own, and these appeal to advertising buffs and cookbook collectors alike. Some were die-cut to represent the product, perhaps a pickle or a slice of bread. The leaflets we list below were nearly all advertising giveaways and premiums. Condition is important in any area of paper collectibles, so judge yours accordingly.

For further study, we recommend *A Guide to Collecting Cookbooks* by Colonel Bob Allen, and *Price Guide to Cookbooks and Recipe Leaflets* by Linda Dickenson.

All About Baking, 1937, hardcover, 144 pages **$16.00**

American Cookery, J Beard, 1972, hardcover, 877 pages,
EX **$30.00**
American Family Cookbook, L Wallace, 1949, hardcover,
831 pages..**$18.00**
American Way of Progress, Kraft, NY World's Fair, 1939, 20
pages, VG **$6.00**
Amy Vanderbilt's Complete Cookbook, 1961, hardcover, 811
pages..**$15.00**
Art of Making Bread at Home, NW Yeast, ca 1930, black &
white cover, 28 pages, VG **$5.00**
Aunt Jenny's Full Flavor Recipes, Spry, 1940s, trifold pamphlet, VG **$2.00**
Baking Easy & Delicate, Parker, HP Books, 1982, 240 pages,
EX..**$8.00**
Better Homes & Garden Cookbook, 1968, hardcover, 160
pages..**$10.00**
Betty Crocker Frankly Foods, 1959, 26 pages, VG.........**$3.00**
Betty Crocker Guide to Easy Entertaining, 1959, 1st edition,
hardcover, 178 pages..**$12.00**
Biscuits & Biscuits Glorified, Rumford, 1941, 16 pages.**$6.00**
Bond Bread Cookbook, 1933, 22 pages, G **$5.00**

Book for a Cook, Pillsbury Flour, 1905, 128 pages .$25.00
Boston Cooking School, Fanny Farmer, 1923, hardcover, 806
pages..**$22.00**
Calumet Baking Book, 1931, paperback, 31 pages, VG..**$5.00**
Carefree Cooking w/Frigidare Electric Range, 1940, paperback, 48 pages..**$6.00**
Cheese & Ways To Serve It, M Dahnke, 1931, 46 pages,
EX..**$5.00**
Chinese Cooking Secrets, E Chen, ca 1960, hardcover, 177
pages..**$8.00**
Coconut Dishes That Everybody Loves, Baker's, 1931, 39
pages, VG **$6.00**
Cooking by the Calendar, Hensen, Family Weekly, 1978,
hardcover, 308 pages..**$8.00**
Cooking Without Mother's Help, Clara Ingram Judson, 1920,
hardcover, 103 pages..**$25.00**
Corn Products Cookbook, 1916.................................**$14.00**

Delineator Cookbook, Delineator Home Institute, 1928, hardcover, 788 pages..............................**$28.00**

Dinah Shore Cookbook, 1973, 386 pages **$8.00**

Esquire Handbook for Hosts, 1953, hardcover, 288 pages, EX...**$14.00**

Fireside Cookbook, 1949.............................**$25.00**

Ford Times Cookbook, Nancy Kennedy, 1968, hardcover, 253 pages...**$18.00**

Given's Modern Encyclopedia of Cooking, 1947, hardcover, 1724 pages...**$15.00**

Glenna Snow's Cookbook, 1938, 1st edition, 396 pages..**$20.00**

Good Enough To Eat w/a Spoon, Slade's Peanut Butter, 1931, 8 pages, VG **$5.00**

Good Housekeeping Book of Cake Decorating, Dorothy B Marsh, 1961, hardcover, 199 pages........................**$12.00**

Good Housekeeping Cookbook, Marsh, 1935, 4th edition, 254 pages...**$18.00**

Good Meals & How To Prepare Them, K Fisher, 1927, hardcover, 256 pages **$18.00**

Good Things To Eat, Arm & Hammer Baking Soda, 1935, 32 pages, G...**$6.00**

Jello-O, It's So Simple, 1922 ....**$15.00**

Joy of Cooking, Rombauer, 1963, hardcover, 1013 pages.**$16.00**

Knox Gelatin Recipes, 1936, 55 pages, EX.....................**$8.00**

Kraft Cookery – Salads, Desserts, Main Dishes, Sandwiches, 1960s, 12 pages, VG.............................**$3.00**

Magic Chef Cooking, America Stove, 1937, hardcover, 200 pages...**$12.00**

Margaret Rudkin Pepperidge Farm Cookbook, 1963, 450 pages...**$20.00**

Most for Your Money Cookbook, B Brown, 1938, 1st edition, 228 pages...**$28.00**

Mrs Beeton's Cookery & Household Management, 1967, 1344 pages...**$15.00**

Mrs Schlorer's Salad Secrets, 1924, nice pictures, 24 pages, VG...**$10.00**

New York Times Cookbook, C Clairborne, 1961, 1st edition, 716 pages...**$15.00**

Pillsbury Bake-off, 1950, 1st edition, paperback.........**$65.00**

Pressure Cooking, Ida Bailey Allen, 1947, hardcover, 403 pages...**$18.00**

Ransom's Family Receipt Book, 1914, 32 pages, EX ...**$14.00**

Rector's Naughty '90s Cookbook, A Kirkland, 1949, hardcover, 247 pages **$18.00**

Rumford Complete Cookbook, L Wallace, 1923, 241 pages. EX...**$12.00**

Savannah Cookbook, H Colquitt, introduction by Ogden Nash, 1933...**$10.00**

Stocking Up, Organic Garden, 1977, hardcover, 532 pages, EX...**$15.00**

Thoughts for Festive Foods, 1964, hardcover, 687 pages.**$10.00**

Treasury of Great Recipes, Vincent & Mary Price, Doubleday, 1965, hardcover, 455 pages........................**$20.00**

Watkins Cookbook, Allen, 1936, hardcover, 192 pages.**$18.00**

Welch's Howdy Doody Cookbook, dated 1952, EX....**$30.00**

What Mrs Dewy Did With the New Jell-O, 1933, 24 pages, VG...**$6.00**

White House Cookbook, Kennedy, hardcover, 287 pages, EX...**$20.00**

World's Modern Cookbook for the Busy Woman, M Claire, 1942, hardcover, 312 pages **$8.00**

10,000 Snacks, Brown, 1948, hardcover, 593 pages **$10.00**

13 Colonies Cookbook, A Donovan, 1975, hardcover, 270 pages...**$10.00**

20th Century Cookbook, M Cooke, 1897, hardcover, 608 pages...**$35.00**

200 Dishes for Men to Cook, A Deute, 1944, paperback, 254 pages...**$5.00**

201 Tasty Dishes for Reducers, V Lindlahr, 1950, paperback, 128 pages...**$6.00**

250 Delectable Desserts, Culinary Arts Institute, 1940, 48 pages, VG...**$4.00**

365 Ways To Cook Hamburger, D Nickerson, 1960, hardcover, 189 pages **$6.00**

44 Wonderful Ways To Use Philadelphia Brand Cream Cheese, 1950s, 20 pages, VG.............................**$6.00**

49 Delightful Ways To Enjoy Karo, 1937, 30 pages.......**$7.00**

60 Ways To Serve Ham, Armour, 1920s, nice pictures, 26 pages, VG **$8.00**

66 Delicious Money Saving Recipes for Use w/Club Aluminum, 1930s, 16 pages, VG.............................**$4.00**

Cookie Cutters

Although the early tin cookie cutters from the 1700s are nearly all in museums by now, collectors still occasionally find a nice examples of the thinner, handmade cutters from the turn of the century. Unless they're especially large or well detailed, most are worth about $15.00. What you're more apt to find today, of course, are the plastic and aluminum cookie cutters, many of which we've listed below. Though certainly not in the same class as the handmade tin ones, they are becoming collectible. Since the first were issued in the early seventies, Hallmark has sold more than 300 different styles, many available for only a short time.

Molds, instead of cutting the cookie out, impressed a design into the dough. To learn more about both (and many other old kitchenware gadgets as well), we recommend *300 Years of Kitchen Collectibles* by Linda Campbell Franklin and *Kitchen Antiques, 1790 to 1940,* by Kathryn McNerney.

Ball shape w/6 cutters, Ekco Holland **$6.50**
Bell, 2½", aluminum w/green wood handle, ca 1930s ..**$4.00**
Bird, 4", tin, flat back w/strap handle, ca late 1930s ...**$17.50**

Cartoon characters (Sylvester, Elmer Fudd & Bugs Bunny shown), orange plastic, 1978, each.......$6.00
Cat, 3½x3½", tin, open type w/no back or handle, handmade **$15.00**
Chick, tin, back & strap handle, simple **$15.00**
Christmas tree, red plastic, no mark, 1970s-80s **$1.00**
Circular shape, 4" dia, tin, crimped edge, flat back w/knob handle..**$10.00**
Dog, aluminum, 1930s-40s, metal handle......................**$3.50**
Dog, lg, tin, back & strap handle, simple....................**$15.00**
Eagle, lg, tin, wings spread, strap handle....................**$45.00**
Gingerbread boy, 7½", tin, 1980s................................**$2.00**
Goose, lg, tin, strap handle...**$18.00**
Hatchet, aluminum, wood handle, 1935.......................**$4.00**
Heart, tin, sm, open back, strap handle, marked Fries **$20.00**
Heart, 2½", aluminum w/green wooden knob handle, ca 1930s-40s **$3.00**
Leaf, sm, tin, crimped, w/veins................................**$15.00**
Lion, tin, shaped back, strap handle, simple...............**$22.00**

Maple leaf, red plastic, no mark, 1970s-80s.....................**$.75**
Rabbit, sm, tin, running, strap handle **$20.00**
Set of 4, 8½", plastic, Hasboro **$12.00**
Star, sm, tin, 8-pointed...**$15.00**

Cookie Jars

This is an area where we've seen nearly unprecedented growth of both interest and pricing. Rare cookie jars sell for literally thousands of dollars. Even a common jar from a good manufacturer will fall into the $40.00 to $100.00 price range. At the top of the list are the Black-theme jars, then come the cartoon characters such as Popeye, Howdy Doody, or the Flintstones. Any kind of a figural jar from an American pottery is extremely collectible right now. There have been several large collections dispersed at auction this year, and though the results sometimes sent mixed signals, there is no question that they continue to hold their own. Some of the highest prices were realized for Sweet Pea by American Bisque ($4,000.00), Wilma Flintstone, also by American Bisque ($1,700.00) and the Leprechaun by McCoy ($3,000.00). Among the Black cookie jars that sold, Mammy with Caulifowers by McCoy sold twice, once at $1,100.00 and once with a chip at $800.00.

The American Bisque company was one of the largest producers of these jars from 1930 until the 1970s. Many of their jars have no marks at all; those that do are simply marked 'USA,' sometimes with a mold number. But their airbrushed colors are easy to spot, and collectors look for the molded-in wedge-shaped pads on their bases – these say 'American Bisque' to cookie jar buffs about as clearly as if they were marked.

The Brush Pottery (Ohio, 1946-71) made cookie jars that were decorated with the airbrush in many of the same colors used by American Bisque. These jars are strongly holding their values, and the rare ones continue to climb in price. McCoy, Abingdon, Cardinal, Shawnee, and Red Wing cookie jars are listed in categories of their own, and there are lots of wonderful jars by many other companies. Joyce and Fred Roerig's book, *The Collector's Encyclopedia of Cookie Jars,* covers them all beautifully, and Ermagene Westfall's *An Illustrated Value Guide to Cookie Jars II* is a recent release you won't want to miss out on.

Warning! The marketplace abounds with reproductions these days. Roger Jensen of Rockwood, Tennessee, is making a line of cookie jars as well as planters, salt and pepper shakers, and many other items which he marks McCoy. Because the 'real' McCoys never registered their trademark, he was able to receive federal approval to begin using this mark in 1992. Though he added '#93' to some of the pieces he made last year, the majority of his wares are undated. He is using old molds, and novice collectors are being fooled into buying the new for 'old' prices. Here are some of his reproductions that you should be aware of: McCoy Mammy, Clown, Dalmations, Indian Head; Hull Little Red Riding Hood; Pearl China Mammy; and the Mosaic Tile Mammy. There are sure to be others.

See also Abingdon; Cardinal; McCoy; Shawnee; Red Wing.

Alice in Wonderland, marked Japan, red hair bow, Alice's Adventures in Wonderland lettered on front **$75.00**

Avon Bear, unmarked, figural brown teddy bear in red sweater, made by California Originals in 1979 .....**$45.00**

Basket Handle Mammy, marked Mauhon Ware (K) Hand Painted, Japan..**$1,000.00**

Bear, marked Pearl China Co Hand Decorated 22k Gold USA, blue w/heavy gold decor..........................**$190.00**

Betsy Ross, Imports, Enesco Japan paper label........**$165.00**

Blackboard Clown, marked USA, American Bisque, Don't Forget lettered in black **$145.00**

Bubble Gum Machine, 890 USA, California Originals..**$45.00**

Cadillac, unmarked, pink convertible w/black features, made by North American Ceramics....................**$125.00**

Cat, marked USA, American Bisque, Hands-in-the-Pockets series, pink **$55.00**

Cat on Safe, marked 2630, Cookie Safe lettered on door, California Originals **$30.00**

Cat w/Hands in Pocket, marked USA, light green w/black facial features, eyes closed **$55.00**

Chef, National Silver, marked NSCO **$235.00**

Child in Shoe, marked Twin Wintons copyright Calif USA, 1965 ....**$35.00**

Chipmunk, marked Japan 2863, brown w/red cap **$25.00**

Cinderella Pumpkin, marked W 32 Brush, 1967.......**$165.00**

Clown, marked Deforest of Calif, copyright USA, brown w/pastel features, Kookie Klown in yellow **$30.00**

Clown, Sierra Vista...**$50.00**

Cookie Barn, Twin Wintons, California USA, various animals at windows, brown w/yellow trim **$45.00**

Cookie Bear, unmarked, Cookie Bear lettered in white on blue cap..**$25.00**

Cookie House, marked W 31 Brush, green roof, 1962..**$65.00**

Cookie Monster, marked copyright Muppets Inc, 1970, California Originals **$50.00**

Cookie Sack, The Twin Wintons, Grandmas Cookies lettered in yellow...**$35.00**

Cookie Time Clock, unmarked Twin Wintons, mouse as finial..**$35.00**

Cop, marked USA, round body, American Bisque **$100.00**

Cow on Moon, marked J 2 USA, yellow w/black features, Doranne of California, 1950s...............................**$135.00**

Cow w/Cat Finial, marked W 10 Brush USA, brown, early 1950s...**$110.00**

Cream of Wheat Chef, stamped Japan **$850.00**

Daisy Cow, marked copyright OCI, black & white w/lg round body, Omnibus **$60.00**

Dancing Elephant, unmarked American Bisque, pink dress & facial highlights **$100.00**

Davy Crockett, marked Sierra Vista of Calif, copyright, minimum value **$350.00**

Davy Crockett, marked USA, Brush, gold trim, 1956, minimum value **$385.00**

Designosaur, unmarked, red dinosaur w/white feet & knob finial **$40.00**

Dog on Drum, marked Twin Wintons Calif USA.........**$45.00**

Donald Duck & Pumpkin, marked Walt Disney Productions 805, California Originals **$225.00**

Donkey & Cart, marked W33 Brush USA, 1965.........**$300.00**

Donkey w/Sack of Oats, marked CJ 108, Doranne of California, Farmyard Follies series, 1984 ....**$55.00**

Duck w/Mixing Bowl, marked Twin Wintons copyright Calif USA **$65.00**

Dumbo's Greatest Cookies on Earth, marked copyright Walt Disney Prod USA 969, California Originals **$265.00**

Dutch Girl, marked USA, American Bisque, wearing blue dress, 1958..**$40.00**

Elephant, w/Ice Cream Cone, marked W 8 USA, Brush, blue baby bonnet, early 1950s **$375.00**

Elephant, unmarked American Bisque, gold trim......**$220.00**

Engine, marked USA, American Bisque, white, black & yellow..**$85.00**

Ernie, California Originals, c Muppets Inc #973 ..$65.00

Fancy Cat, straightening bow tie, wearing suspenders, marked J5 USA, Doranne of California.................**$40.00**

Friar Tuck, Twin Winton, high-gloss version, paper label missing..**$35.00**

Frog w/Bow Tie, marked 2645, California Originals...**$40.00**

Frosty the Snowman, marked RRP Co.....................**$450.00**

Fruit Basket, marked Shawnee 84, yellow basket w/assorted fruit, designed by Bob Heckman........................**$125.00**

Funshine Bear, marked Funshine Bear, One of the Care Bears, copyright MCMLXXXIV American Greetings Corp, Cleveland Ohio **$65.00**

Gift Box, marked USA, American Bisque, white w/blue bow & ribbon, 1958 ....**$65.00**

Gingerbread House, marked Treasure Craft Compton California Made in USA on paper label **$40.00**

Goldilocks, marked 405 Goldilocks, Pat Pending, Regal China **$220.00**

Grandfather Clock, marked Treasure Craft, copyright Made in USA, key-shaped finial **$40.00**

Grapes, marked Red Wing USA, light green...............**$70.00**

Great Northern Dutch Girl, marked Great Northern USA 1026, Shawnee **$165.00**

Hen on Basket, unmarked Brush, 1969 ....**$110.00**

Hi Diddle Diddle, marked RRP Co #386 ....$250.00

House w/Avon lady at door, blue roof **$65.00**

Howdy Doody, winking, marked Vandor, Made in Japan on paper label **$270.00**

Humpty Dumpty, marked W 18 Brush USA, yellow beanie & bow tie, 1956-61..**$235.00**

Jug, marked USA, light blue, Shawnee........................**$75.00**

Ketchup Bottle, marked CJ 68 USA, Kids Catchup Cookies embossed on front, Doranne of California, 1984..**$35.00**

Lamb w/Flower, marked USA, American Bisque.......**$130.00**

Lunch Box, unmarked Doranne of California, royal blue top w/light blue bottom **$35.00**

Mary Poppins, marked copyright, MCMLXIV, Walt Disney Productions, minimum value **$375.00**

Miss Muffet, marked Little Miss Muffet #705, Regal...**$300.00**

Monk, unmarked, Thou Shalt Not Steal! in white.......**$35.00**

Muggsy, marked Muggsy, Terrace Ceramics, USA, white w/black nose & eyes **$55.00**

Nite Owl, marked W 40 Brush, 1967.....................**$95.00**

Old Clock, marked W 20 Brush USA, 1956 ....$185.00

Owl, marked Treasure Craft, Made in USA, Cookies lettered in yellow..**$30.00**

Pancake Mammy, marked 1987 CG Carol Gifford.....**$130.00**

Panda Bear, unmarked Metlox..................................**$70.00**

Peek-a-Boo, Regal China, c Van Telligen $1,100.00

Persian Kitten, marked Twin Wintons Calif USA copyright '63, sitting w/paw up......................................**$50.00**

Pinocchio, Made in Calif, Poppytrail Pottery by Metlox on paper label **$250.00**

Pinocchio, marked, Walt Disney Productions...........**$350.00**

Polka Dot Topsy, marked Metlox, Calif USA, blue, yellow or red trim...**$335.00**

Popeye, marked USA, American Bisque **$950.00**

Professor Ludwig Von Drake, marked Walt Disney USA 1961, American Bisque, minimum value.............**$500.00**

Pumpkin, marked Holiday Designs **$30.00**

Puppy, marked Treasure Craft, copyright USA, sitting position w/blue & yellow cap & yellow neckerchief..**$35.00**

Puzzled Monkey, marked Maurice of Calif USA, red lips & bow tie...**$35.00**

Rabbit, marked USA, American Bisque, Hands-in-the Pocket series **$90.00**

Raccoon, marked Twin Wintons Calif USA, 1965 ....**$55.00**

Raggedy Ann, marked W 16 USA, Brush, 1956 ....**$465.00**

Red Riding Hood, marked K 24 Brush USA, gold trim, lg size, 1956 ....**$700.00**

Sailor, marked GOB USA, Shawnee, minimum value ..**$450.00**

Sailor Elephant, marked TW 86, Twin Winton 60, c Made in USA **$40.00**

Sailor Elephant, marked USA, American Bisque ..**$65.00**

Santa Head, marked Mallory copyright Inc **$45.00**

Schoolhouse, marked USA, American Bisque, After School Cookies lettered in black, bell in lid **$40.00**

Sheriff Bear, marked Twin Wintons Collectors Series, copyright, California USA **$85.00**

Sheriff on Safe, marked CJ USA, Cookie Safe lettered on door **$28.00**

Smiley Pig, marked USA, white w/blue neckerchief, Shawnee **$150.00**

Smiling Pear, marked 6 C 30, Japan **$18.00**

Snow White, marked Walt Disney Production, Enesco label, minimum value **$400.00**

Squirrel on Pine Cone, marked Made in USA, Metlox.**$50.00**

Standing Santa, marked Metlox Calif USA **$135.00**

Strawberry Shortcake, marked MCMLXXXIII, American Greetings Corp, Cleveland Ohio **$120.00**

Toby Cookies, unmarked Regal, Toby Cookies lettered in gold on cap **$550.00**

Treasure Chest, marked USA, American Bisque, 1959 ..**$90.00**

Trolley, marked Treasure Craft copyright, made in USA, smiley-face finial **$45.00**

Watermelon Mammy, marked copyright 1986 CG Carol Gifford **$130.00**

Whale, marked RRP Co, wearing blue cap **$350.00**

Winking Cat, unmarked Japan, embossed daisies & daisy finial on lid **$20.00**

Winnie the Pooh, marked 900 Walt Disney Productions USA, California Originals **$125.00**

Wonder Woman, marked USA 847, copyright DC Comics Inc 1978, California Originals **$335.00**

Woody Woodpecker, marked A3391/ww Napco, barrel shape w/Woody Woodpecker finial **$260.00**

Yellow Cab, unmarked California Originals **$95.00**

Coors Rosebud Dinnerware

Golden, Colorado, was the site for both the Coors Brewing Company and the Coors Porcelain Company, each founded by the same man, Adolph Coors. The pottery's beginning was in 1910, and in the early years they manufactured various ceramic products such as industrial needs, dinnerware, vases, and figurines, but their most famous line and the one we want to tell you about was 'Rosebud.'

The Rosebud 'Cook 'n Serve' line was introduced in 1934. It's very easy to spot; after you've once seen a piece, you'll be able to recognize it instantly. It was made in solid colors – rose, blue, green, yellow, ivory, and orange. The 'rose bud' and leaves are embossed and hand-painted in contrasting colors. There are nearly fifty different pieces to collect, and prices are still fairly reasonable.

Apple baker, 4¾" dia **$25.00**

Baker, 4¾" dia **$20.00**

Bowl, cereal; 6" **$12.50**

Bowl, fruit; 5" **$8.00**

Bowl, pudding; 5" **$12.50**

Cake knife, 10" **$22.50**

Cup & saucer, 4" **$22.00**

Egg cup, 6-oz **$25.00**

Jar, utility; 2½-pt **$25.00**

Plate, 7¼" **$7.50**

Plate, 9" **$15.00**

Platter, 12x9" **$15.00**

Salt & pepper shakers, 4½", straight sides, pr **$18.00**

Saucer, 5½" **$6.00**

Soup plate, 8" **$15.00**

Spoon, 6" **$32.00**

Teapot, 6-cup **$48.00**

Tumbler, 12-oz, footed...$24.00
Tumbler, 8½-oz, handle...$22.50

Cottage Ware

Made by several companies, cottage ware is a line of ceramic table and kitchen accessories, each piece styled as a cozy cottage with a thatched roof. At least three English potteries made the ware, and you'll find pieces marked 'Japan' as well as 'Occupied Japan.' From Japan you'll also find pieces styled as windmills and water wheels, though the quality is inferior. The better pieces are marked 'Price Brothers' and 'Occupied Japan.' They're compatible in coloring as well as in styling, and values run about the same. Items marked simply 'Japan' are worth slightly less.

Bank, square w/coin slot in side of roof, English........$45.00
Bowl, salad; English..$50.00
Butter dish, square, English.....................................$45.00

Chocolate pot, Price Brothers, England.............$135.00
Cookie jar, 8", round, English $85.00
Cookie jar, 8½x5½", pink, brown & green, Japan $65.00
Cookie or biscuit jar, square, Occupied Japan............$85.00
Creamer & sugar bowl, 2½", 4½", English...................$45.00
Egg cups (2) & salt & pepper shakers on shaped plate
   w/handles, English...$60.00
Marmalade, lid notched for spoon, English $35.00
Marmalade & jelly, co-joined, 2 lids, English, rare $100.00
Pin tray, 4", embossed & painted cottage, English $20.00
Pitcher, water; English...$150.00
Platter, 11¾x7½", oval, English $45.00
Sugar box, for cubes, 5¾" long, English.....................$45.00
Teapot, 6½", English or Occupied Japan....................$50.00
Toast rack, English..$45.00

Cracker Jack Collectibles

Cracker Jack has been around for over one hundred years. For ninety of those years, there's been a prize inside each box. If you could see the toys from over the years,

you'd see the decades of the 20th century unfold. Tanks in wartime, sport's cards and whistles in peacetime, and space toys in the sixties. In addition to the prizes, collectors also look for dealer incentives, point of sale items, boxes, cartons, and advertising.

'Cracker Jack' in the following descriptions indicates that the item in question actually carries the Cracker Jack mark.

Ad, comic book, Cracker Jack, each..............................$9.00
Bookmark, tin, 4 designs, Cracker Jack, each.............$25.00
Box, popcorn; red scroll border, ca 1920....................$85.00
Canister, Cracker Jack Commemorative, white w/red scroll,
   1980s, each..$9.00
Canister, 10-oz, tin, Cracker Jack Coconut Corn Crisp ..$65.00
Dealer incentive, cart w/2 movable wheels, wooden dowel
   tongue, marked Cracker Jack...............................$49.00
Dealer incentive, jigsaw puzzle, 7x10", Cracker Jack or
   Checkers, any 1 of 4, M in envelope.....................$35.00
Dealer incentive, mask, 10" or 12", Halloween face, Cracker
   Jack, each $18.00
Dealer incentive, pencil top clip, metal & celluloid, tube
   shape w/package..$190.00
Decal, cartoon or nursery rhyme figure, paper, marked
   Cracker Jack, 1947-49..$7.00
Lunch box, 4½x5x6", tin, 2 handles, Cracker Jack, 1980s,
   M...$25.00
Pie plate, tin, Cracker Jack $15.00
Popcorn popper, Pop-It $165.00
Premium, pocketbook, jester on cover, Cracker Jack..$62.00
Premium, recipe book, Angelus, 1930s.......................$22.00
Prize, American flag, tin oval standup, 1 of 4, unmarked,
   1936-46 ....$37.00
Prize, badge, 1¼", silvery cast metal 6-pointed star, marked
   Cracker Jack Police, 1931 ....$35.00
Prize, baseball player, 1½", molded blue or gray plastic, #d,
   1958..$7.00
Prize, booklet, stickers, wise cracks, riddles, Borden,
   Cracker Jack, 1965 on..$1.00
Prize, chair, mini, painted cast metal, T (Tootsie) any 1 of 3
   different sectional pieces.....................................$12.00
Prize, circus figure, plastic, stands on base, series of 12,
   Nosco, 1951-54, each...$1.75
Prize, clicker, aluminum, Noisy Cracker Jack Snapper, pear
   shape, 1949...$32.00
Prize, fob, 1½", plastic alphabet letter w/loop on top, 1 of
   26, 1954..$2.25
Prize, glasses disguise, paper, w/eyeballs, 1933 ....$6.00
Prize, helicopter, 2⅝", tin, yellow propeller, wooden stick,
   unmarked, 1937 ....$18.00
Prize, magic game book, paper, erasable slate, made in
   series of 13, 1946, each $27.00
Prize, Midget Auto Race game, 3⅜", paper, wheel, Cracker
   Jack, 1949 ....$45.00
Prize, picture card, 1¼x2¾", full-color mechanical chef
   w/die-cut eyes & mouth, ca 1920s, VG $37.50
Prize, pinball game, paper, lever shoots ball, score in holes,
   1964 to recent...$2.00

Prize, pistol, 2⅛", soft lead, inked, Cracker Jack on barrel, early **$180.00**

Prize, riddle card, paper, 2 series of 20, in package, from factory, Cracker Jack, each **$7.00**

Prize, rocking horse w/boy, 1½", cast metal, 3-D, inked, early **$29.00**

Prize, soldier, tin litho, die-cut standup, any rank, unmarked, each **$17.00**

Prize, spinner, paper, varied colors, 10 designs, from 1948, each..**$1.50**

Prize, spinner, 1¾", die-cut cardboard, product & colorful geometric designs, ca 1920s-30s, EX....................**$62.50**

Prize, train, tin litho coach, red, unmarked, 1941........**$22.00**

Prize, various animals, plastic, stand-up type, letter on back, series of 26, Nosco, 1953, each..............................**$3.50**

Prize, wagon shape, Tank Corps No 47, tin w/green & black paint, 1941 ....**$30.00**

Prize, whistle, paper, Razz Zooka, C Carey Cloud design, Cracker Jack, 1949....................$32.00

Prize, whistle, 1⅜", paper, tube w/animals on top, Cracker Jack, 1 of 6, 1950-53, each......................................**$6.50**

Radio, Tune In, tin, Cracker Jack..................................**$130.00**

Sign, Santa & prizes, lg, multicolor cardboard, Cracker Jack, early **$250.00**

Stamp box, girl, tin, Cracker Jack **$150.00**

Crooksville China

American dinnerware is becoming a very popular field of collectibles, and because many of the more well-established lines such as Fiesta, LuRay, and those designed by Russel Wright have become so expensive, people are now looking for less costly patterns. If you've been at all aware of the market over the past twenty years or so, you know the same thing occured in the Depression glass field. Lines that we were completely disinterested in during the late sixties have come into their own today.

Crooksville China comes from a small town in Ohio by the same name. They made many lines of dinnerware and kitchen items, much of which carried their trademark, until they closed late in the fifties. One of their more extensive lines is called 'Silhouette,' made in the mid-thirties. It is very similar to a line by Hall China, but you can easily tell the difference. Crooksville's decal is centered by the silhouette of a begging dog. Another nice line is 'House,' so named because of the English cottage featured in the petitpoint-style decal. There are many different floral lines, and don't be surprised if you find the same decal on more than one of their standard shapes.

If you'd like to learn more about the various dinnerware companies we've included in this book, we recommend you read *The Collector's Encyclopedia of American Dinnerware* by Jo Cunningham.

Apple Blossom, bean pot, w/lid, handled **$35.00**

Apple Blossom, coffee server, Pantry Bak-In line **$40.00**

Apple Blossom, plate, 6", Iva-Lure shape....................**$4.00**

Avenue, saucer..**$3.00**

Black Tulip, plate, serving..**$40.00**

Blossoms, plate, 6¾", Fruits shape..............................**$6.00**

Border Rose, bowl, vegetable; w/lid, handled............**$25.00**

Border Rose, platter, 11½", oval..................................**$15.00**

Brilliance, plate, dinner; 10" **$6.00**

Calico Chick, plate, dinner; 10¾", coupe shape............**$8.00**

California James Poppy, casserole, 8", w/lid..............**$20.00**

California James Poppy, plate, dinner **$8.00**

Carnival, plate, 9½" **$8.00**

Country Home, sugar bowl..**$15.00**

Flamingo, creamer, Gray Lure shape..........................**$8.00**

Gold Drape, creamer **$6.00**

Homestead in Winter, plate, chop; 10"........................**$15.00**

Kaleidoscope, bowl, soup; 8", Birds shape..................**$8.00**

Little Bouquet, plate, 9¾", La Grande shape................**$6.00**

Medallion, saucer..**$3.00**

Oriental, creamer **$6.00**

Petit Point House, bowl, berry; 5¼"..............................**$7.50**

Petit Point House, bowl, vegetable; 9" **$25.00**

Petit Point House, cookie jar..**$55.00**

Petit Point House, pie or cake server............................**$20.00**

Petit Point House, platter, 11½" **$22.50**

Petit Point House, sugar bowl, w/lid............................**$10.00**

Posies, bowl, utility..**$6.00**

Posies, cup & saucer, La Grande shape........................**$8.00**

Rose Garland, bowl, utility; 3" tall **$5.00**

Rose Garland, bowl, vegetable; 8" **$25.00**

Silhouette, dinner plate, 10"....................................$10.00

Silhouette, pie baker, 10", Pantry Bak-In Line **$12.00**

Silhouette, plate, dinner; 10" $12.00
Silhouette, tumbler, 8-oz $20.00
Southern Belle, plate, 6¾", coupe shape $4.00
Southern Belle, sugar bowl, Iva-Lure shape.................$8.00
Spray, plate, dinner; 10¾", pink coupe shape.............$8.00
Spring Blossom, plate, salad...................................$8.00
Spring Blossom, platter....................................$20.00
Spring Blossom, serving bowl............................$18.00
Trellis, pitcher, batter; 8", 'duck-bill' shape, w/lid.......$50.00
Trellis, tray, utility; 11¼", handled $25.00
Trotter, plate, dinner; 10¼", coupe shape $4.00
Willow, saucer, coupe shape $2.00

Currier and Ives Dinnerware

This dinnerware has for the past two or three years been the focus of a great amount of collector interest. It was made by the Royal China company of Sebring, Ohio, and was given away as premiums for shopping at A&P stores. It is decorated with blue and white renditions of early American scenes by Currier and Ives, and so fits not only into the 'country' look now so popular in home decorating but its color schemes as well. Besides the dinnerware, Fire-King baking pans and accessories, glass tumblers, and vinyl placemats were also offered by A&P. Most pieces are relatively easy to find, but the casserole and the teapot are considered 'prizes' by collectors.

Ashtray..$12.00
Bowl, cereal; 6⅜", tab handle $25.00
Bowl, soup; 8½", flat..$8.00
Bowl, 10"..$20.00
Bowl, 6⅜", lug soup $20.00
Bowl, 9"...$18.00
Butter dish, ¼-lb...$25.00
Casserole, w/lid...$60.00
Chop plate, 11" $20.00
Cup & saucer...$4.00
Gravy boat, w/ladle & liner.................................$35.00
Mug...$18.00
Pie plate, 10"..$15.00
Plate, 10½"..$5.00
Plate, 6"..$3.00
Plate, 7⅜"...$7.00
Plate, 9"...$10.00
Platter, 13" $22.00
Salt & pepper shakers, pr...................................$15.00
Sugar bowl, w/lid $12.00
Teapot..$75.00
Tumbler, juice $10.00
Tumbler, old fashioned; 3¼".................................$10.00
Tumbler, 4¾", 9-oz..$12.00

Czechoslovakian Glass and Ceramics

Established as a country in 1918, Czechoslovakia is rich in the natural resources needed for production of glassware as well as pottery. Over the years it has produced vast amounts of both. Anywhere you go, from flea markets to fine antique shops, you'll find several examples of their lovely pressed and cut glass scent bottles, Deco vases, lamps, kitchenware, tableware and figurines.

More than thirty five marks have been recorded; some are ink stamped, some etched, and some molded in. Paper labels have also been used. *Czechoslovakian Glass and Collectibles* by Diane and Dale Barta and *Made in Czechoslovakia* by Ruth Forsythe are two books we highly recommend for further study.

Ceramics

Basket, 4¼", white pearlescent w/raised braid design, black trim on rim & handle $40.00
Basket, 5¾", blue to beige in mottled variegated design, black base, V-shape handle.....................$60.00
Coaster, 3" dia, red w/white floral design in center, set of 4 ....$100.00
Creamer, 3¼", yellow w/colorful flowers in oval inset, black rim & handle $65.00
Creamer, 3⅝", brown barrel shape w/black bands......$40.00
Creamer, 4¾", cow figural in sitting position, white w/rust spots, open mouth spout, black handle $40.00
Dish, 4¾", light brown raised basketweave design, high relief fruit design on lid, ring handles $60.00

Pitcher, 10½", aqua & oatmeal textured glaze.....$175.00
Pitcher, 10½", turquoise mottling w/rust & cream mottling in alternating bands, double handle $170.00
Pitcher, 5¼", bright yellow w/high gloss, ball form $45.00
Pitcher, 5¾", bright floral design on cream, black trim on top & bottom, gourd form w/flared top, curved black handle $60.00
Sugar bowl, 2¼", white pearl luster, shell design, ear-type handle, 4-footed, open $55.00
Sugar bowl, 3⅜", white pearl lusterware finish, black ear-type handles, w/lid................................$35.00
Tumbler, 4¼", black w/orange, blue & yellow floral design around top $55.00
Vase, 4¼", raised pink & green floral design on cream, gold trim, fan form on tier base $30.00
Vase, 4⅞", red w/high gloss finish, 6-sided $35.00

Vase, 6½", orchid & cream swirled floral design, luster finish, bulbous w/ear-type handles..............................$55.00

Vase, 7¼", orange, cream & purple sawtooth design, bulbous w/flared rim & base.....................................$125.00

Vase, 7¾", cone shape w/triangular panels, red, yellow, black & blue (illustrated on page 118)............$95.00

Vase, 8", beige, black & orange mottling on lustre, black design down side panels, handles..........................$90.00

Glassware

Atomizer, 3", cased, bright orange w/gold trim...........$70.00

Basket, 6½", blue w/applied black rim, clear handle..$90.00

Bowl, 3¼", cobalt w/silver design & rim......................$65.00

Bowl, 4½", cased, cream w/multicolored design.........$75.00

Bowl, 6", cased, white w/applied maroon on ruffled rim, stemmed foot $130.00

Candlestick, 8½", cased, varicolored shades of red, slim form w/round foot...$75.00

Candy dish, 7", cased, red, black medallion designs on sides, black knob finial...$90.00

Candy dish, 8", mottled colors, applied black 4-footed pedestal base...$120.00

Perfume, 2", crystal covered w/metal filigree & enamel, blue jeweled stopper...$85.00

Perfume, 3½", iridescent w/painted light green stripes, graduated bell shape, faceted drop stopper..............$170.00

Perfume, 4", cut crystal base, prism-cut stopper..$60.00

Perfume, 4¼", clear cut base, red cut drop stopper ..$175.00

Perfume, 4¾", clear cut base, amethyst drop stopper w/intaglio cut design..$145.00

Perfume, 4⅞", clear cut base, prism cut drop stopper .$110.00

Perfume, 5½", black opaque cut base & stopper.......$140.00

Perfume, 5½", green cut base, clear cut leaf design on stopper.$100.00

Perfume, 5¾", cut amber base, amber drop stopper w/intaglio-cut design..$130.00

Pitcher, 10⅛", cased, red w/applied black handle, flared cylinder w/collar-type rim...................................$165.00

Pitcher, 5", cased, orange w/applied cobalt rim & handle, tricorner top $75.00

Powder box, 2½", black w/red rose design on lid......$55.00

Toothpick holder, 2¼", cased, orange w/black & green decoration $35.00

Vase, bud; 10", cased, yellow w/silver floral design, clear base, gourd form..$85.00

Vase, bud; 8", cased, orange w/black base, slim cylinder form w/slightly flared rim.....................................$65.00

Vase, bud; 8", orange w/enamel decoration, slim cylinder form w/flared base..$65.00

Vase, 10½", cased, red w/applied crystal & cobalt decoration, flared bottom...$85.00

Vase, 4¼", cased, red w/multicolored mottling on top, applied black serpentine, ruffled rim $95.00

Vase, 4¼", cased, varicolored shades of red & yellow, applied cobalt rim, ear-type handles $70.00

Vase, 5", crystal w/intaglio-cut design, ball form.........$80.00

Vase, 6", cased, green w/brown design, ball form w/sm flared rim...$115.00

Vase, 6", cased, red & yellow variegated design, applied black rim on petal-shaped top.............................$75.00

Vase, 6½", cased, red w/blue & yellow mottling.........$60.00

Vase, 6½", cased, shades of orange, applied cobalt 3-footed pedestal base, gourd form w/flared rim..............$110.00

Vase, 6¼", cased, green w/applied black design, bulbous w/flared rim...$95.00

Vase, 6¾", cased, light blue w/pink interior, ruffled ...$95.00

Vase, 7½", cased, orange w/applied flower decoration, gourd form w/ruffled top $95.00

Vase, 7½", cased, red & varicolored, slim flared cylinder w/ruffled rim...$65.00

Vase, 7¼", cased, varicolored, applied 3-footed clear glass pedestal base...$75.00

Vase, 8", cased, orange, flared cylinder with applied black serpentine decoration $85.00

Vase, 8", pale blue crystal, ridged design, flared rim ..$90.00

Vase, 8½", clear w/variegated blue design, ball form w/sm flared rim...$175.00

Vase, 8½", cobalt w/red overlay, cobalt base $100.00

Vase, 8⅜", cased, yellow & brown variegated design, applied 3-footed black pedestal base, flared rim..$95.00

Vase, 9", cased, yellow w/applied green decoration...$75.00

Dairy Bottles

Between the turn of the century and the 1950s, milk was bought and sold in glass bottles. Until the twenties, the name and location of the dairy was embossed in the glass. After that it became commonplace to pyro-glaze (paint and fire) the lettering onto the surface. Farmers sometimes added a cow or some other graphic that represented the product or related to the name of the dairy.

Because so many of these glass bottles were destroyed when paper and plastic cartons became popular, they've become a scarce commodity, and today's collectors have begun to take notice of them.

begun to take notice of them. It's fun to see just how many you can find from your home state – or try getting one from every state in the union!

What makes for a good milk bottle? Collectors normally find the pyro-glaze decorations more desirable, since they're more visual. Bottles from dairies in their home state hold more interest for them, so naturally New Jersey bottles sell better there than they would in California, for instance. Green glass examples are unusual and often go for a premium, so do those with the embossed baby faces. (Watch for reproductions here!) And those with a 'Buy War Bonds' slogan or a patriot message are always popular.

Some collectors enjoy adding 'go-alongs' to enhance their collections, so the paper pull tops, advertising items that feature dairy bottles, and those old cream-top spoons will interest them as well. The spoons usually sell for about $6.00 each. For more information, we recommend *Udderly Delightful* by John Tutton.

Alta Crest Farms, Brookfield MS, ½-pt, cow's head label front & back, Dacro top, round, maroon pyro **$15.00**

Blue Ribbon Dairies, Freehold NJ, qt, square, red pyro.**$4.00**

Borden's, Phoenix store jug, ½-gal, 3-arm cactus in square on front, round, yellow-brown pyro.....................**$18.00**

Braley's (on front) Creamery (on back), pt, embossed, round **$6.00**

Brookdale Dairy, Seymour CT, qt, Farmer Producer WF Molsick to City Consumer & farm scene on back, round, orange pyro..**$15.00**

Cloverdale Farms, qt, cream top, plain back, square, red pyro...**$20.00**

Cloverleaf, Stockton CA, qt, ribbed cream top, safety slogan on back, round, orange pyro **$20.00**

Crystal Dairy, ¾-oz creamer, square, stars in yellow...**$18.00**

Dairylea, qt, Hoppy's Favorite, Hopalong Cassidy & horse, short, square, black pyro..**$75.00**

Dubin Coop Dairies, Dublin GA (state not printed on label), pt, war slogan on back, squat & round, red pyro.**$27.50**

East Side Creamery, Saratoga Springs NY, qt, round w/vertical ribs, embossed..**$7.00**

EF Mayer, 289 Hollenbeck & phone #, qt, amber, round, embossed..**$75.00**

Evans Dairy, Syracuse NY, qt, dairy building on front, product list on back, square, orange pyro **$7.00**

Faircroft Dairy, Ridgway PA, qt, Best for Baby, Best for You, w/lg baby, round, orange pyro...........................**$16.00**

Fenns Gurnsey Milk, Fenns Bros Inc, Sioux City Falls SD, qt, amber w/white pyro..**$12.00**

Ferndale, Grand Ledge MI, qt, amber w/white pyro, lettering, square..**$10.00**

Frye's Dairy Inc, Leominster MS, qt, double baby top, square, orange pyro.......................................**$85.00**

Gillette & Sons Dairy, pt, phone # on back, America First Last & Always w/eagle, round, orange pyro.........**$45.00**

Goshen Dairy Co, New Phila OH, qt, Registered, round, embossed..**$20.00**

Hillcrest West Bridgewater (embossed around shoulder), qt, square **$3.00**

Knudsen Bros (at shoulder on 2 sides), qt, square, red pyro, lettering..**$3.00**

Lake View Dairies, Ithaca NY, pt, lake (front), baby on globe (back), Moderntop embossed on shoulder, round, orange pyro..**$25.00**

Lang's Creamery Inc, Buffalo NY, qt, green (rare) **$300.00**

Lonce's, Hanover PA, qt, Health Is Our First Line of Defense..., cream top, round, orange pyro..........**$74.00**

Maple City Dairy, Monmouth IL, qt, cream top, A Nourishing Treat..., red pyro $18.00

Martin Farms, Rochester VT, qt, cow's face on front & back, square, orange pyro...**$8.50**

Milford Creamery, Milford NH, ½-pt, elongated teardrops on shoulder, round, embossed....................................**$6.00**

Model Dairy, Bowling Green OH, qt, Cream Separator Bottle & Pat 7-8-30, round, embossed..........................**$90.00**

Needham Dairy, qt, Milk That Is Milk, RH Chambers, Store on back, embossed..**$7.00**

Nickels Dairy, Lowell MA, qt, Produced by Local Farmers & cow's head in circle, cream top, square, red pyro.**$22.00**

Oatman's Good Homogenized Milk, ½-gal, good front design, rectangular, amber w/white pyro..............**$8.00**

Pellissier, Riverside, qt, circle w/3-leaf symbol, round, orange pyro..**$14.00**

Purity Maid Products Co, ¾-oz creamer, round, blue pyro, lettering..**$15.00**

Reehl's Dairy, East Greenbrush NY, qt, square, amber w/white pyro..**$10.00**

Ruff's Dairy, St Clair MI, qt, little girl & safety slogan spelled out in blocks on back, round, orange pyro **$8.00**

Seneca Dairy Corp, Syracuse NY, qt, Indian chief on front, square, orange pyro...**$8.50**

Shadow Lawn Dairy, East Providence RI, pt, standing cow on back, round, red pyro **$14.00**

Sunnymede Farm, Bismark MO, ½-pt, Missouri Pacific Lines & seal on back, squat, round, red pyro...............**$28.00**

Thatcher Farms, Milton MA (state not on label), qt, cream top, square, maroon pyro......................**$18.00**
United Farms, Albany NY, ½-pt, allover diamond designs, round **$6.00**
White's Farm Dairy, qt, Quality Products, baby top, square, red & yellow pyro front, yellow back **$70.00**
Wroblinski Farm, Acushnet MS, pt, cow & barn on front, bottle w/boy & girl on back, Health in Every Bottle, orange pyro **$8.00**

De Vilbiss

The lovely perfume bottles, lamps, and vanity accessories you'll find marked De Vilbiss were not actually made by that company (De Vilbiss made only the metal hardware), but rather by a variety of glasshouses. Fenton provided some, so did Cambridge and Imperial. Others were imported from Italy, Czechoslovakia, and West Germany. They were sold by De Vilbiss both here and abroad. You'll find several variations of the company's paper labels, and rarely an item that will be marked 'DeV' in gold enamel.

Values hinge on two factors: the type of glass that was used and the design. The most valuable are those made in Aurene glass by Steuben. (Aurene is primarily found in gold or blue and is characterized by its strong iridescence.) Perfumes with figural stems or those with strong Art Deco influence are usually near the top of the price scale. Gold-colored glass with a crackled appearance was often used, and the smaller, less-strikingly designed examples made of this type of glass are more common.

A good source for further study is *Bedroom and Bathroom Glassware of the Depression Years* by Margaret and Kenn Whitmyer.

Atomizer, 3", transparent blue pillow shape w/cut-glass design, gold bulb attached to gold sprayer...........**$55.00**
Atomizer, 4¼", black w/crystal stem & foot.................**$55.00**
Atomizer, 5", blue w/3 gold flamingos.........................**$50.00**
Atomizer, 5½", deep blue enamel w/black decoration, shaped like a genie's bottle, w/cord & bulb.........**$60.00**
Atomizer, 5½", enameled dark green w/black enamel floral decoration, octagon shape, brass fitting, w/bulb..**$85.00**

Atomizer, 5¼", clear w/geometric cuttings, blue pyramid stopper...$95.00

Atomizer, 6", gray w/gold duck, paper label...............**$58.00**
Atomizer, 6¼", decorated green bulbous body on long green footed stem **$80.00**
Atomizer, 6¾", orange & black enamel elongated body over frosted crystal stem & foot, black cord & bulb...**$145.00**
Atomizer, 6⅜", transparent tangerine, elongated teardrop form on round flared base **$125.00**
Ginger jar, Chinese red w/gold floral decoration........**$95.00**
Perfume bottle, black w/chrome neck **$45.00**
Perfume dropper, crystal w/blue floral decoration......**$25.00**
Perfume dropper, green enamel bulbous body w/gold design on long gold encrusted stem on round flared base .**$85.00**
Perfume dropper, yellow opaque w/black triangle design around bottom of octagonal bell form **$40.00**
Perfume dropper, 5⅝", orange enamel on elongated teardrop shape w/round flat base..........................**$55.00**
Pin tray, 3¼x5⅝", orange enamel w/black & gold decoration on oval shape..**$25.00**
Puff box, 4¾" dia, gold-encrusted bowl-shaped body on rounded footed base, green enamel domed lid w/gold design **$65.00**
Puff box, 4¾" dia, orange enamel bowl-shaped body on round footed base, orange dome lid w/black & gold decoration..**$55.00**

Decanters

The first company to make figural ceramic decanters was the James Beam Distilling Company, who now own their own china factory here in the United States. They first issued their bottles in the mid-fifties, and over the course of the next twenty-five years, more than twenty other companies followed their example. Among the more prominent of these were Brooks, Hoffman, Lionstone, McCormick, Old Commonwealth, Ski Country, and Wild Turkey. In 1975 Beam introduced the 'Wheel Series,' cars, trains, and fire engines with wheels that actually revolved. The popularity of this series resulted in a heightened interest in decanter collecting.

There are various sizes, the smallest (called miniatures) hold two ounces, and there are some that hold a gallon! A full decanter is worth no more than an empty one, and the absence of the tax stamp will not lower its value either. Just be sure that all the labels are intact and that there are no cracks or chips. You might want to empty your decanters as a safety precaution (many collectors do) rather than risk the possibility of the inner glaze breaking down and allowing the contents to wick into the porous ceramic body.

All of the decanters we've listed are fifths unless we've specified 'miniature' within the description.

Aesthetic Specialties (ASI), Cadillac, white, 1903.........**$50.00**
Aesthetic Specialties (ASI), Oldsmobile, black, 1910 model.**$75.00**
Aesthetic Specialties (ASI), Stanley Steamer, black, 1909 model..**$30.00**
Beam, Casino Series, Golden Gate Casino, 12½", almond shape, gambling scenes, gold lettering, 1969........**$80.00**

Beam, Casino Series, Harvey Hotel, 11½" **$10.00**

Beam, Casino Series, Horseshoe Club, 9¼", 1969..........**$7.00**

Beam, Centennial Series, Cheyenne, 11", grazing buffalo embossed on circular form, 1967.............................**$6.00**

Beam, Centennial Series, Civil War North, 10¾", fort scene, Genuine Regal China, 1961 ....**$20.00**

Beam, Centennial Series, Dodge City, 10", Regal China, 1972 ....**$9.00**

Beam, Centennial Series, Laramie, 10½", cowboy & bucking bronco embossed on front, 1968 ....**$5.00**

Beam, Centennial Series, Lombard, 12½", flowers embossed on front, Illinois shape embossed on back, 1969 ...**$6.00**

Beam, Centennial Series, Statue of Liberty, 1985.........**$24.00**

Beam, Clubs Series, Beaver Valley, beaver sitting on stump, 1977 ....**$10.00**

Beam, Clubs Series, Monterrey Bay Club, 7½", 1977...**$10.00**

Beam, Convention Series, Detroit, #3, 1973 ....**$10.00**

Beam, Convention Series, Gibson Girl, #13, yellow **$50.00**

Beam, Convention Series, Kentucky Colonel, #17, gray .**$75.00**

Beam, Convention Series, Reno Cowboy Fox, #21......**$65.00**

Beam, Convention Series, Waterman, #10, pewter......**$30.00**

Beam, Customer Series, Bohemian Girl, 14½", white skirt, blue vest, Regal China **$10.00**

Beam, Customer Series, Harry Hoffman **$5.00**

Beam, Customer Series, Osco Drugs **$15.00**

Beam, Customer Series, Travelodge Bear......................**$9.00**

Beam, Customer Series, Zimmerman Oatmeal Jug **$45.00**

Beam, Executive Series, Antique Pitcher, 1982 ....**$20.00**

Beam, Executive Series, Barry Berish, 1985 ....**$75.00**

Beam, Executive Series, California Mission, 14", mission w/Indian & priest at door, Regal China, 1970.......**$12.00**

Beam, Executive Series, Golden Chalice, 12½", Genuine Regal China, 1961 ....**$50.00**

Beam, Executive Series, Golden Jubilee, 1977.............**$10.00**

Beam, Executive Series, Gray Cherub, 12", Genuine Regal China, 1958..**$225.00**

Beam, Executive Series, Presidential 1968, 12¾", Genuine Regal China, 1968 ....**$10.00**

Beam, Executive Series, Regency, 1972.........................**$9.00**

Beam, Executive Series, Royal Rose, 17", Genuine Regal China, 1963..**$40.00**

Beam, Executive Series, White Fox, 12¼", fox is wearing a white Nehru jacket & medallion, 1969 ....**$30.00**

Beam, Foreign Series, Australia, Galah Bird, 1979......**$24.00**

Beam, Foreign Series, Australia, Sydney Opera...........**$20.00**

Beam, Foreign Series, Germany, Pied Piper **$10.00**

Beam, Foreign Series, Samoa **$5.00**

Beam, Organization Series, Bartender's Guild **$8.00**

Beam, Organization Series, Kentucky Colonel..............**$5.00**

Beam, Organization Series, Shriner, Indiana **$5.00**

Beam, Organization Series, Telephone #4, Dial, 1919 ....**$45.00**

Beam, Organization Series, Yuma Rifle Club.............**$20.00**

Beam, People Series, Captain & Mate, captain w/arm around sm boy, 1980...**$10.00**

Beam, People Series, Hanna Dustin, 14½", Regal China, 1973 ....**$20.00**

Beam, People Series, Paul Bunyan.................................**$10.00**

Beam, Political Series, Donkey & Elephant, 10", Genuine Regal China, screw-on lids, 1956, pr **$15.00**

Beam, Political Series, Donkey Clown, 1968...........$9.00

Beam, Political Series, Spiro Agnew Elephant, elephant on pedestal, trunk & 1 leg raised, Regal China, 1970.**$1,200.00**

Beam, Sports Series, Bowling Pin **$10.00**

Beam, Sports Series, Hula Bowl.....................................**$9.00**

Beam, Sports Series, Sahara Golf **$10.00**

Beam, State Series, Arizona, 12", Grand Canyon scene on circular form, Genuine Regal China, 1968..............**$6.00**

Beam, State Series, Colorado, 10¾", covered wagon & mountain scene, Regal China, 1959......................**$30.00**

Beam, State Series, Idaho, 12¼", state's shape w/mountain scene, gold lettering, 1963................................**$50.00**

Beam, State Series, Nebraska, 12¼", oxen-drawn covered wagon, Genuine Regal China, 1967......................**$8.00**

Beam, Trophy Series, Bluegill.......................................**$15.00**

Beam, Trophy Series, Cardinal, 13½", 1968.................**$35.00**

Beam, Trophy Series, Eagle...**$10.00**

Beam, Trophy Series, Green Fox, 12¼", green & white hunter's outfit, Genuine Regal China, 1965 (reissued in 1967)..**$25.00**

Beam, Trophy Series, Horse, white mustang w/flowing tail, 1967 (reissue of 1962 bottle) **$10.00**

Beam, Trophy Series, Kentucky Cardinal, 13½", red w/black wing on brown stump, Regal China, 1968 ....**$35.00**

Beam, Trophy Series, Sailfish..**$15.00**

Beam, Trophy Series, Tabby **$10.00**

Beam, Trophy Series, Woodpecker, 13½", Genuine Regal China, 1969...**$10.00**

Beam, Wheel Series, Chevrolet '57 Convertible, black **$90.00**

Beam, Wheel Series, Dodge Challenger, blue **$95.00**

Beam, Wheel Series, Ford Model-A 1930 Fire Truck.**$150.00**

Beam, Wheel Series, Grant Locomotive **$75.00**

Beam, Wheel Series, Train, Baggage Car **$40.00**

Beam, Wheel Series, Train, Lumber Car.......................$24.00

Brooks, Automobiles & Transportation Series, Sprint Racer, #21 ....$55.00

Brooks, Automobiles & Transportation Series, Duesenberg, 1979 ....$24.00

Brooks, Automobiles & Transportation Series, Thunderbird, blue $80.00

Brooks, Firearms Series #1, 1859 Pepperbox, 10", red background, 1969 ....$4.00

Brooks, Firearms Series #1, 1873 Colt .45 Peacemaker, 10", blue background, 1969 ....$4.00

Brooks, Golden Grizzly Bear, 13½", figural, 1968..........$6.00

Brooks, Indian Ceremonial, 12½", Indian dancer figural, 1970 ....$15.00

Brooks, New Hampshire State House, 11¾", state house form w/gold eagle & dome on stopper, 1970.........$8.00

Brooks, Oil Gusher, 16½", oil derrick form, 1969..........$7.00

Brooks, Potbellied Stove, 10", ceramic figural, 1968......$7.00

Brooks, Trout & Fly, 12", Heritage China figural trout leaping to catch a fly, 1970..$8.00

Garnier, Apollo, 13½", china quarter-moon form w/silver Apollo near top, cloud forms base, 1969 ....$16.00

Garnier, Jockey, 12¼", majolica jockey & horse leaping over a hurdle, 1961 ....$24.00

Garnier, Valley Quail, 11", china quail perched on tree figural, 1969 ....$8.00

Grenadier, Automobiles & Transportation, Van, blue .$22.50

Grenadier, Mr Spock Bust......................................$36.00

Grenadier, Teddy Roosevelt....................................$27.50

Grenadier, Valley Forge..$25.00

Hoffman, Automobiles & Transportation Series, Distillery Truck...$72.50

Hoffman, Mr Lucky Series, Bartender..........................$32.50

Hoffman, Mr Lucky Series, Cobbler.............................$20.00

Hoffman, Mr Lucky Series, Doctor..............................$27.50

Hoffman, Mr Lucky Series, Mechanic..........................$32.00

Kontinental, Dentist..$27.50

Kontinental, Lumberjack..$25.00

Lionstone, Bird Series, Cap Swallow $22.50

Lionstone, Bird Series, Quail....................................$12.00

Lionstone, Clown Series, Lampy, #6...........................$35.00

Lionstone, Clown Series, Salty Tails, #4......................$37.50

Lionstone, Dog Series, Golden Retriever.....................$17.50

Lionstone, Old West Series, Bartender $22.50

Lionstone, Old West Series, Casual Indian..................$10.00

Lionstone, Old West Series, Frontiersman...................$17.50

Lionstone, Old West Series, Jessie James $15.00

Lionstone, Oriental Worker, Chinese Laundryman......$22.50

McCormick, Elvis Series, #1, '77................................$75.00

McCormick, Elvis Series, #2, pink, '55 ....$65.00

McCormick, Elvis Series, #3, black, '68.......................$70.00

McCormick, Elvis Series, Christmas Tree....................$165.00

McCormick, Elvis Series, Designer #1.........................$100.00

McCormick, Elvis Series, Encore #1, gold $365.00

McCormick, Elvis Series, Hound Dog.........................$465.00

McCormick, Elvis Series, Teddy Bear $465.00

Old Commonwealth, Coal Miner #3, w/shovel............$80.00

Old Commonwealth, Coal Miner #5, Coal Shooter......$27.50

Old Commonwealth, Firefighter #3 ....$80.00

Pacesetter, Automobile & Transportation Series, Distillery Truck $122.50

Pacesetter, Automobile & Transportation Series, John Deere Tractor $125.00

Pacesetter, Automobiles & Transportation Series, Camaro Z-28, gold..$55.00

Regal China Specialties, Antique Trader, 10½", newspaper shape w/red & black lettering, 1968.....................$6.00

Regal China Specialties, Blue Daisy, 12¼", 3 daisies embossed on straw-like background, 1967............$6.00

Regal China Specialties, Germany Land of Hansel & Gretel, children embossed on front, 1971..........................$8.00

Regal China Specialties, Green China Jug, 12½", pussy willows embossed on green, 1965................................$8.00

Regal China Specialties, Ponderosa, 7½", log cabin house from TV series Bonanza, 1969.................................$8.00

Regal China Specialties, Pony Express, 11", pony express rider embossed on front, map on back, 1968.......$10.00

Regal China Specialties, Pussy Willow, Genuine Regal China, 1970..$10.00

Regal China Specialties, Seattle World's Fair, 13½", Space Needle shape, 1962..$15.00

Regal China Specialties, Texas Rabbit, Genuine Regal China, 1971 ....$10.00

Ski Country, Animal Series, Kangaroo $42.50

Ski Country, Animal Series, Polar Bear......................$78.00

Ski Country, Animal Series, Raccoon.........................$65.00

Ski Country, Bird Series, Dove..................................$72.50

Ski Country, Bird Series, Golden Pheasant $67.50

Ski Country, Bird Series, Great Gray Owl $75.00

Ski Country, Bird Series, Peace Dove.........................$88.00

Ski Country, Bird Series, Peacock.............................$130.00

Ski Country, Bird Series, Pintail Duck, Ducks Unlimited..$112.50

Ski Country, Bird Series, Wood Duck, 1974 ....$245.00

Ski Country, Christmas Series, Cardinals $70.00

Ski Country, Christmas Series, Chickadees..................$82.50

Ski Country, Christmas Series, Mrs Cratchit................$80.00

Ski Country, Christmas Series, Scrooge $80.00

Ski Country, Circus Series, Circus Wagon $55.00

Ski Country, Circus Series, Palomino Horse................$68.00

Ski Country, Circus Series, Tiger on Ball.....................$45.00

Ski Country, Circus Series, Tom Thumb, mini $16.00

Ski Country, Indian Series, Basket Dancer..................$98.00

Ski Country, Indian Series, Eagle Dancer....................$235.00

Ski Country, Indian Series, Great Spirit $148.00

Ski Country, Indian Series, Lookout Indian................$95.00

Ski Country, Wildlife Series, Fox Family $72.50

Ski Country, Wildlife Series, Mountain Goat..............$98.00

Wild Turkey, #10, w/Coyote $72.50

Wild Turkey, #12, w/Skunk`......................................$80.00

Wild Turkey, #2, w/Bobcat $140.00

Wild Turkey, #3, Fighting $80.00

Wild Turkey, #3, Fighting, mini $30.00

Wild Turkey, #7, w/Fox...$30.00

Wild Turkey, Flying Turkey, 1973 ....$42.50

Wild Turkey, Lore Series #2 ....$27.50

Wild Turkey, Standing Turkey, 1971, mini..................$10.00

Degenhart

John and Elizabeth Degenhart owned and operated the Crystal Art Glass Factory in Cambridge, Ohio. From 1947 until John died in 1964, they produced some fine glassware; John himself was well known for his superior paperweights. But the glassware that collectors love today was made after '64, when Elizabeth restructured the company, creating many lovely molds and scores of colors. She hired Zack Boyd, who had previously worked for Cambridge Glass, and between the two of them, they developed almost 150 unique and original color formulas.

Complying with provisions she had made before her death, close personal friends at Island Mould and Machine Company in Wheeling, West Virginia, took Elizabeth's molds and removed the familiar 'D in heart' trademark from them. She had requested that ten of her molds be donated to the Degenhart Museum, where they remain today. Zack Boyd eventually bought the Degenhart factory and acquired the remaining molds. He has added his own logo to them and is continuing to press glass very similar to Mrs. Degenhart's.

For more information, we recommend *Degenhart Glass and Paperweights* by Gene Florence, published by the Degenhart Paperweight and Glass Museum, Inc., Cambridge, Ohio.

Beaded Oval Toothpick, Fawn $22.50
Bicentennial Bell, Amberina.........................$15.00
Bicentennial Bell, Blue Fire.........................$10.00
Bicentennial Bell, Cobalt $17.50

Bicentennial Bell, Crown Tuscan......................$16.00
Bicentennial Bell, Misty Brown.....................$15.00
Bicentennial Bell, Vaseline............................$10.00
Bird Salt w/Cherry, Daffodil.........................$20.00
Bird Salt w/Cherry, Orchid...........................$20.00
Bow Slipper, Blue Marble Slag $25.00
Bow Slipper, Mint Green...............................$17.50
Candy Dish, Cobalt, unmarked.....................$22.00
Candy Dish, Holly Green $24.00
Chick Salt, Lemon Custard, 2".......................$60.00
Colonial Drape Toothpick, Milk Blue............$25.00
Daisy & Button Salt, Emerald Green.............$14.00
Daisy & Button Salt, Tomato.........................$18.00
Daisy & Button Toothpick, Amberina $25.00

Daisy & Button Toothpick, Dark Chocolate Creme.....$25.00
Daisy & Button Toothpick, Emerald (illustrated).$16.00
Daisy & Button Wine, Crown Tuscan, unmarked........$25.00
Face Plate, Sapphire......................................$30.00
Forget-Me-Not Toothpick, Amberina $25.00
Forget-Me-Not Toothpick, Dark Chocolate Creme $25.00
Forget-Me-Not Toothpick, Jade.....................$25.00
Forget-Me-Not Toothpick, Milk Blue.............$20.00
Forget-Me-Not Toothpick, Tomato $32.00
Gypsy Pot Toothpick, Crown Tuscan, hand stamped.$15.00
Gypsy Pot Toothpick, Opalescent, unmarked $8.00
Hand, Crown Tuscan......................................$18.00
Hand, Crystal..$6.00
Heart Box, Baby Pink....................................$30.00
Heart Box, Blue Jay $35.00
Heart Box, Caramel Custard Slag..................$40.00
Heart Box, Frosty Jade..................................$35.00
Heart Box, Milk Blue....................................$25.00
Heart Box, Old Custard, unmarked $25.00
Heart Box, Persimmon...................................$17.50
Heart Toothpick, Amberina............................$18.00
Hen Covered Dish, Brown Sparrow Slag, 3".......$30.00
Kat Slipper, Amberina, unmarked..................$25.00
Kat Slipper, Caramel $27.50
Kat Slipper, Ivorene......................................$28.00
Kat Slipper, Jade Green $28.00
Kat Slipper, Tiger $28.00
Kat Slipper, Tomato $32.00
Kat Slipper, Vaseline.....................................$18.00
Mug, Amberina...$15.00
Owl, Amberina..$50.00
Owl, Baby Green $48.00
Owl, Bluebell $30.00
Owl, Cobalt $35.00
Owl, Crown Tuscan.......................................$35.00
Owl, Heatherbloom $75.00
Owl, Milk Blue (illustrated) $32.50
Owl, Mint Green $28.00
Owl, Mulberry...$45.00
Owl, Pigeon Blood $45.00
Owl, Vaseline..$30.00
Pooch, April Green $20.00
Pooch, Fantastic..$35.00
Pooch, Gray Marble $20.00
Pooch, Gun-metal Blue $25.00
Pooch, Old Lavender.....................................$18.00
Pooch, Tomato...$37.50
Pottie Salt, Henry's Blue $20.00
Pottie Salt, Nile Green $17.50
Priscilla, Daffodil..$90.00
Priscilla, Jade..$110.00
Priscilla, Periwinkle......................................$85.00
Seal of Ohio Plate, Apple Green....................$10.00
Seal of Ohio Plate, Vaseline..........................$10.00
Star & Dewdrop Salt, Heatherbloom $15.00
Texas Boot, Sapphire.....................................$16.00
Wine, Amber $14.00
Wine, Bittersweet..$38.00

Wine, Cobalt	$22.00
Wine, Custard	$24.00
Wine, Dichromatic	$30.00
Wine, Forest Green	$20.00
Wine, Mosser Green	$16.00
Wine, Opalescent, unmarked	$14.00
Wine, Peach Glo	$16.00
Wine, Pistachio	$20.00
Wine, Red	$25.00
Wine, Rose Marie Pink	$20.00
Wine, Taffeta	$34.00

Depression Glass

Since the early sixties, this has been a very active area of collecting. Interest is still very strong, and although values have long been established, except for some of the rarer items, Depression Glass is still relatively inexpensive. Some of the patterns and colors that were entirely avoided by the early wave of collectors are now becoming popular, and it's very easy to reassemble a nice table setting of one of these lines today.

Most of this glass was produced during the Depression years. It was inexpensive, mass-produced, and was available in a wide assortment of colors. The same type of glassware was still being made to some extent during the fifties and sixties, and today the term 'Depression Glass' has been extended to include the later patterns as well.

Some things have been reproduced, and the slight variation in patterns and colors can be very difficult to detect. For instance, the Sharon butter dish has been reissued in original colors of pink and green (as well as others that were not original); and several pieces of Cherry Blossom, Madrid, Avocado, Mayfair, and Miss America have also been reproduced. Some pieces you'll see in 'antique' malls and flea markets today have been recently made in dark uncharacteristic 'carnival' colors, which of course are easy to spot.

For further study, Gene Florence has written several informative books on the subject, and we recommend them all: *The Pocket Guide to Depression Glass, The Collector's Encyclopedia of Depression Glass,* and *Very Rare Glassware of the Depression Years.*

Adam, green, bowl, 7¾"	$20.00
Adam, green, candlesticks, 4", pr	$85.00
Adam, green, pitcher, 8", 32-oz	$40.00
Adam, green, plate, sherbet; 6"	$7.50
Adam, green, platter, 11¾"	$18.00
Adam, green, sugar bowl	$17.00
Adam, green, sugar or candy lid	$35.00
Adam, green, vase, 7½"	$45.00
Adam, pink, ashtray, 4½"	$25.00
Adam, pink, bowl, 10", oval	$22.50
Adam, pink, bowl, 7¾"	$18.00
Adam, pink, cake plate, 10", footed	$20.00

Adam, pink, coaster, 3¾"	$18.00
Adam, pink, cup	$21.00
Adam, pink, pitcher, 8", 32-oz	$35.00
Adam, pink, plate, dinner; 9", square	$22.50
Adam, pink, plate, sherbet; 6"	$7.00
Adam, pink, sugar bowl	$15.00
Adam, pink, sugar or candy lid	$20.00
Adam, pink, vase, 7½"	$225.00
American Pioneer, green, bowl, 9", handled	$22.50
American Pioneer, green, candlesticks, 6½", pr	$80.00
American Pioneer, green, coaster, 3½"	$27.50
American Pioneer, green, creamer, 3½"	$20.00
American Pioneer, green, cup	$11.00
American Pioneer, green, goblet, wine; 4", 3-oz	$45.00
American Pioneer, green, plate, 6", handled	$15.00
American Pioneer, green, sherbet, 3½"	$17.00
American Pioneer, green, sherbet, 4¾"	$32.00
American Pioneer, green, sugar bowl, 3½"	$20.00
American Pioneer, green, tumbler, 5", 12-oz	$45.00
American Pioneer, pink, bowl, 9", handled	$17.50
American Pioneer, pink, candy jar, 1-lb, w/lid	$75.00
American Pioneer, pink, coaster, 3½"	$25.00
American Pioneer, pink, creamer, 2¾"	$17.50
American Pioneer, pink, cup	$9.00
American Pioneer, pink, goblet, wine; 4", 3-oz	$33.00
American Pioneer, pink, plate, 6"	$12.00
American Pioneer, pink, sherbet, 3½"	$15.00
American Pioneer, pink, sherbet, 4¾"	$24.00
American Pioneer, pink, sugar bowl, 3½"	$17.50
American Sweetheart, monax, bowl, cereal; 6"	$10.00
American Sweetheart, monax, bowl, cream soup; 4½"	$95.00
American Sweetheart, monax, creamer, footed	$9.00
American Sweetheart, monax, cup	$9.00
American Sweetheart, monax, plate, salver; 12"	$15.00
American Sweetheart, monax, plate, 15½"	$175.00
American Sweetheart, monax, platter, 13", oval	$55.00
American Sweetheart, monax, saucer	$3.00
American Sweetheart, pink, bowl, cereal; 6"	$12.50
American Sweetheart, pink, bowl, cream soup; 4½"	$65.00
American Sweetheart, pink, creamer, footed	$10.00
American Sweetheart, pink, cup	$14.00
American Sweetheart, pink, plate, bread & butter; 6"	$4.50
American Sweetheart, pink, plate, salad; 8"	$9.50
American Sweetheart, pink, platter, 13", oval	$40.00
American Sweetheart, pink, saucer	$4.00
American Sweetheart, pink, sugar bowl, open, footed	$9.50
American Sweetheart, pink, tumbler, 3½", 5-oz	$65.00
Anniversary, clear, bowl, berry; 4⅞"	$3.00
Anniversary, clear, butter dish, w/lid	$25.00
Anniversary, clear, cake plate, 12½"	$6.50
Anniversary, clear, cup	$3.50
Anniversary, clear, plate, dinner; 9"	$5.00
Anniversary, clear, sugar bowl	$2.50
Anniversary, clear, sugar lid	$5.00
Anniversary, clear, vase, 6½"	$12.00
Anniversary, pink, bowl, soup; 7⅜"	$14.00
Anniversary, pink, butter dish, w/lid	$50.00
Anniversary, pink, creamer, footed	$8.50

Anniversary, pink, pickle dish, 9" **$10.00**

Anniversary, pink, sherbet, footed **$7.00**

Anniversary, pink, sugar bowl **$7.00**

Anniversary, pink, sugar lid **$9.00**

Anniversary, pink, wine glass, 2½-oz **$15.00**

Aunt Polly, blue, bowl, 2x4¾" **$18.00**

Aunt Polly, blue, bowl, 8⅜", oval **$80.00**

Aunt Polly, blue, creamer **$40.00**

Aunt Polly, blue, pitcher, 8", 48-oz **$155.00**

Aunt Polly, blue, plate, luncheon; 8" **$17.50**

Aunt Polly, blue, salt & pepper shakers, pr **$195.00**

Aunt Polly, blue, tumbler, 3⅝", 8-oz **$25.00**

Aunt Polly, green, bowl, handled pickle; 7¼", oval **$10.00**

Aunt Polly, green, bowl, 8⅜", oval **$35.00**

Aunt Polly, green, creamer **$25.00**

Aunt Polly, green, plate, sherbet; 6" **$5.00**

Aurora, cobalt, bowl, 5⅜" **$14.00**

Aurora, cobalt, creamer, 4½" **$17.50**

Aurora, cobalt, cup **$10.00**

Aurora, cobalt, saucer **$5.00**

Aurora, cobalt, tumbler, 4¾" **$17.50**

Avocado, green, bowl, relish; 6", footed **$24.00**

Avocado, green, bowl, 8", 2-handled, oval **$25.00**

Avocado, green, creamer, footed **$32.00**

Avocado, green, cup, footed **$30.00**

Avocado, green, plate, sherbet; 6¾" **$15.00**

Avocado, green, saucer **$26.00**

Avocado, green, sherbet **$52.00**

Avocado, pink, bowl, 5¼", 2-handled **$24.00**

Avocado, pink, bowl, 8", 2-handled, oval **$18.50**

Avocado, pink, creamer, footed **$30.00**

Avocado, pink, cup, footed **$28.00**

Avocado, pink, plate, luncheon; 8¾" **$16.00**

Avocado, pink, saucer **$24.00**

Avocado, pink, sugar bowl, footed **$30.00**

Beaded Block, green, bowl, 4½" **$9.00**

Beaded Block, green, bowl, 5½", w/handled **$7.00**

Beaded Block, green, bowl, 7½", fluted edges **$18.00**

Beaded Block, green, creamer **$15.00**

Beaded Block, green, pitcher, 5¼", 1-pt jug **$95.00**

Beaded Block, green, plate, 7¾", square **$6.50**

Beaded Block, green, stemmed jelly, 4½", flared top ..**$10.00**

Beaded Block, green, sugar bowl **$14.00**

Beaded Block, opalescent, bowl, jelly; 4½", 2-
    handled **$16.00**

Beaded Block, opalescent, bowl, 6¼" **$16.00**

Beaded Block, opalescent, bowl, 7½", fluted edges **$25.00**

Beaded Block, opalescent, creamer **$27.50**

Beaded Block, opalescent, plate, 8¾" **$19.00**

Beaded Block, opalescent, stemmed jelly, 4½", flared ..**$18.00**

Beaded Block, opalescent, vase, bouquet; 6" **$22.50**

Block Optic, green, bowl, cereal; 5¼" **$11.00**

Block Optic, green, candlesticks, 1¾", pr **$95.00**

Block Optic, green, compote, mayonnaise; 4" wide ...**$26.00**

Block Optic, green, creamer, 3 styles **$12.50**

Block Optic, green, cup, 4 styles **$6.50**

Block Optic, green, goblet, 5¾", 9-oz **$19.00**

Block Optic, green, ice bucket **$35.00**

Block Optic, green, pitcher, 8", 80-oz **$55.00**

Block Optic, green, plate, dinner; 9" **$17.50**

Block Optic, green, salt & pepper shakers, footed, pr.**$35.00**

Block Optic, green, saucer, 2 sizes, cup ring **$9.00**

Block Optic, green, sherbet, 3¼", 5½-oz **$5.00**

Block Optic, green, tumbler, 6", 10-oz, footed **$24.00**

Block Optic, green, tumbler, 9-oz, footed **$16.00**

Block Optic, pink, bowl, berry; 4¼" **$6.50**

Block Optic, pink, bowl, berry; 8½" **$20.00**

Block Optic, pink, candlesticks, 1¾", pr **$70.00**

Block Optic, pink, candy jar, w/lid, 2¼" **$45.00**

Block Optic, pink, creamer, 3 styles **$12.50**

Block Optic, pink, goblet, 5¾", 9-oz **$25.00**

Block Optic, pink, pitcher, 8½", 54-oz **$35.00**

Block Optic, pink, plate, luncheon; 8" **$4.00**

Block Optic, pink, salt & pepper shakers, footed, pr..**$70.00**

Block Optic, pink, sherbet, 3¼", 5-oz **$7.00**

Block Optic, pink, tumbler, 9-oz **$12.00**

Block Optic, pink, whiskey, 2¼", 2-oz **$24.00**

Bowknot, green, bowl, berry; 4½" **$13.00**

Bowknot, green, cup **$7.00**

Bowknot, green, tumbler, 5", 10-oz, footed **$16.00**

Bubble, blue, bowl, cereal; 5¼" **$12.00**

Bubble, blue, creamer **$30.00**

Bubble, blue, pitcher, 64-oz, w/ice lip **$50.00**

Bubble, blue, plate, dinner; 9⅜" **$6.50**

Bubble, blue, platter, 12", oval **$15.00**

Bubble, blue, sugar bowl **$17.50**

Bubble, blue, tumbler, juice; 6-oz **$8.00**

Bubble, blue, tumbler, lemonade; 16-oz **$17.50**

Bubble, clear, bowl, berry; 4" **$3.50**

Bubble, clear, bowl, berry; 8⅜" **$6.00**

Bubble, clear, creamer **$5.00**

Bubble, clear, plate, bread & butter; 6¾" **$2.00**

Bubble, clear, sugar bowl **$5.00**

Bubble, clear, tumbler, iced tea; 12-oz **$10.00**

Bubble, red, pitcher, 64-oz, w/ice lip **$50.00**

Bubble, red, tumbler, juice; 6-oz **$8.00**

Cameo, green, bowl, cream soup; 4¾" **$85.00**

Cameo, green, bowl, vegetable; 10", oval **$20.00**

Cameo, green, cake plate, 10", footed **$18.00**

Cameo, green, candlesticks, 4", pr **$90.00**

Cameo, green, cookie jar, w/lid **$45.00**

Cameo, green, creamer, 3¼" **$19.00**

Cameo, green, creamer, 4¼" **$22.50**

Cameo, green, cup, 2 styles **$13.00**

Cameo, green, goblet, water; 6" **$45.00**

Cameo, green, jam jar, 2", w/lid **$140.00**

Cameo, green, pitcher, syrup or milk; 5¾", 20-oz **$170.00**

Cameo, green, pitcher, water; 8½", 56-oz **$45.00**

Cameo, green, plate, grill; 10½", w/closed handles.....**$60.00**

Cameo, green, plate, sandwich; 10" **$12.00**

Cameo, green, plate, sherbet; 6" **$4.00**

Cameo, green, plate, 8½", square **$35.00**

Cameo, green, relish, 7½", 3-part, footed **$25.00**

Cameo, green, salt & pepper shakers, footed, pr **$60.00**

Cameo, green, saucer, w/cup ring **$150.00**

Cameo, green, sherbet, 4⅞" **$30.00**

Cameo, green, sugar bowl, 3¼" **$16.00**
Cameo, green, tumbler, juice; 3¾", 5-oz....................**$25.00**
Cameo, green, tumbler, 5", 9-oz, footed **$22.00**
Cameo, green, tumbler, 5¼", 15-oz....................**$57.50**
Cameo, green, vase, 8" **$25.00**
Cameo, yellow, bowl, cereal; 5½"....................**$26.00**
Cameo, yellow, bowl, console; 11", footed....................**$75.00**
Cameo, yellow, bowl, vegetable; 10", oval **$35.00**
Cameo, yellow, creamer, 3¼"....................**$16.00**
Cameo, yellow, cup, 2 styles, each....................**$7.00**
Cameo, yellow, plate, grill; 10½", w/closed handles **$6.00**
Cameo, yellow, plate, luncheon; 8" **$9.50**
Cameo, yellow, plate, sherbet; 6" **$3.00**
Cameo, yellow, plate, 8½", square **$125.00**
Cameo, yellow, sherbet, 3⅛"....................**$35.00**
Cameo, yellow, sugar bowl, 3¼" **$13.00**
Cameo, yellow, tumbler, 5", 11-oz....................**$42.00**
Cameo, yellow, tumbler, 5", 9-oz, footed....................**$14.00**
Cherry Blossom, green, bowl, flat soup; 7¾"....................**$47.50**
Cherry Blossom, green, bowl, vegetable; 9", oval **$30.00**
Cherry Blossom, green, butter dish **$75.00**
Cherry Blossom, green, cup....................**$17.00**
Cherry Blossom, green, pitcher, 8", pattern around top.**$50.00**
Cherry Blossom, green, plate, grill; 9" **$22.00**
Cherry Blossom, green, platter, 11", oval **$35.00**

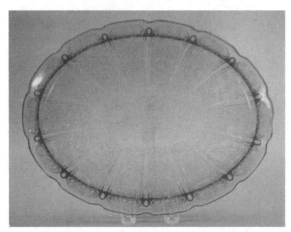

Cherry Blossom, green, platter, 13", oval $60.00
Cherry Blossom, green, sherbet....................**$16.00**
Cherry Blossom, green, tray, sandwich; 2-handled **$19.00**
Cherry Blossom, green, tumbler, 3¾", 4-oz, allover pattern, footed **$16.00**
Cherry Blossom, green, tumbler, 4½", 8-oz, allover pattern, scalloped foot....................**$30.00**
Cherry Blossom, pink, bowl, cereal; 5¾" **$26.00**
Cherry Blossom, pink, bowl, 9", 2-handled **$25.00**
Cherry Blossom, pink, butter dish **$60.00**
Cherry Blossom, pink, cake plate, 10¼", footed..........**$24.00**
Cherry Blossom, pink, cup....................**$15.00**
Cherry Blossom, pink, pitcher, 6¾", 36-oz, allover pattern, round or scalloped bottom....................**$45.00**
Cherry Blossom, pink, plate, salad; 7" **$16.00**
Cherry Blossom, pink, platter, 13"....................**$55.00**
Cherry Blossom, pink, sugar bowl....................**$12.00**
Cherry Blossom, pink, sugar lid....................**$14.00**

Cherry Blossom, pink, tumbler, 4½", 8-oz, allover pattern, scalloped foot....................**$26.00**
Cherry Blossom, pink, tumbler, 4¼", 9-oz, pattern around top....................**$16.00**
Cherryberry, pink or green, bowl, berry; 4"....................**$8.00**
Cherryberry, pink or green, compote, 5¾"....................**$22.50**
Cherryberry, pink or green, creamer, lg, 4⅝"....................**$32.50**
Cherryberry, pink or green, creamer, sm **$16.00**
Cherryberry, pink or green, pitcher, 7¾" **$140.00**
Cherryberry, pink or green, sugar bowl, lg....................**$22.00**
Cherryberry, pink or green, sugar bowl, sm, open **$16.00**
Cherryberry, pink or green, sugar lid....................**$50.00**
Cherryberry, pink or green, tumbler, 3⅝", 9-oz..........**$30.00**
Chinex Classic, ivory, bowl, salad; 7"....................**$14.00**
Chinex Classic, ivory, bowl, vegetable; 9"....................**$10.00**
Chinex Classic, ivory, creamer **$5.00**
Chinex Classic, ivory, plate, sandwich; 11½" **$7.50**
Chinex Classic, ivory, sherbet, low footed **$7.00**
Chinex Classic, ivory decorated, bowl, cereal; 5¾" **$7.50**
Chinex Classic, ivory decorated, bowl, vegetable; 9" ..**$20.00**
Chinex Classic, ivory decorated, cup....................**$6.50**
Chinex Classic, ivory decorated, plate, dinner; 9¾".......**$8.00**
Chinex Classic, ivory decorated, sugar bowl, open.......**$9.00**
Christmas Candy, clear, creamer....................**$8.50**
Christmas Candy, clear, plate, dinner; 9⅝"....................**$9.50**
Christmas Candy, clear, sugar bowl....................**$8.00**
Christmas Candy, teal, bowl, soup; 7⅜"....................**$27.50**
Christmas Candy, teal, plate, bread & butter; 6"..........**$10.00**

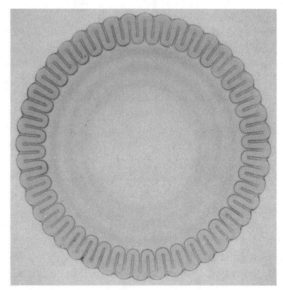

Christmas Candy, teal, plate, 9½" $25.00
Christmas Candy, teal, sugar bowl................................**$18.00**
Circle, pink or green, bowl, 5½", flared **$10.00**
Circle, pink or green, cup....................**$4.50**
Circle, pink or green, pitcher, 80-oz....................**$30.00**
Circle, pink or green, saucer **$1.50**
Circle, pink or green, sugar bowl **$8.00**
Circle, pink or green, tumbler, water; 8-oz **$9.00**
Cloverleaf, green, bowl, salad; 7" **$35.00**
Cloverleaf, green, creamer, 3⅝", footed **$9.00**
Cloverleaf, green, cup....................**$7.00**

Cloverleaf, green, plate, luncheon; 8".............................$7.00
Cloverleaf, green, salt & pepper shakers, pr..............$27.50
Cloverleaf, green, saucer $3.50
Cloverleaf, green, sugar bowl, 3⅝", footed $9.00
Cloverleaf, yellow, bowl, dessert; 4"..........................$23.00
Cloverleaf, yellow, bowl, salad; 7"..............................$45.00
Cloverleaf, yellow, creamer, 3⅝", footed....................$15.00
Cloverleaf, yellow, salt & pepper shakers, pr $95.00
Cloverleaf, yellow, sugar bowl, 3⅝", footed $15.00
Cloverleaf, yellow, tumbler, 5¾", 10-oz, footed..........$27.50
Colonial, green, bowl, berry; 9"..................................$25.00
Colonial, green, bowl, cream soup; 4½" $55.00
Colonial, green, cup $10.00
Colonial, green, goblet, wine; 4½", 2½-oz $24.00
Colonial, green, pitcher, 7", 54-oz $47.50
Colonial, green, plate, grill; 10"..................................$24.00
Colonial, green, plate, luncheon; 8½"...........................$9.00
Colonial, green, sugar bowl, 5"...................................$12.00
Colonial, green, sugar lid $18.00
Colonial, green, tumbler, iced tea; 12-oz $45.00
Colonial, green, tumbler, 3¼", 3-oz, footed $20.00
Colonial, pink, bowl, berry; 4½" $12.00
Colonial, pink, bowl, berry; 9"....................................$22.00
Colonial, pink, cup $10.00
Colonial, pink, pitcher, 7¾", 68-oz, ...$55.00
Colonial, pink, plate, luncheon; 8½".............................$8.50
Colonial, pink, platter, 12", oval $27.50
Colonial, pink, sugar bowl, 5".....................................$22.50
Colonial, pink, sugar lid $45.00
Colonial, pink, tumbler, water; 4", 9-oz......................$19.00
Colonial, pink, tumbler, 5¼", 10-oz, footed $40.00
Colonial Block, pink or green, bowl, 4".........................$6.00
Colonial Block, pink or green, pitcher $35.00
Colonial Block, pink or green, sugar bowl $10.00
Colonial Block, pink or green, sugar lid $10.00
Colonial Fluted, green, bowl, berry; 7½"......................$15.00
Colonial Fluted, green, cup $4.50
Colonial Fluted, green, plate, luncheon; 8" $5.00
Colonial Fluted, green, sherbet $6.00
Columbia, clear, bowl, 10½", ruffled edge $18.00
Columbia, clear, cup..$8.00
Columbia, clear, plate, chop; 11¾" $9.00
Columbia, clear, tumbler, 4-oz....................................$16.00
Columbia, pink, cup $18.00
Columbia, pink, plate, luncheon; 9½" $25.00
Columbia, pink, saucer..$8.00
Coronation, pink, bowl, berry; 8"..................................$7.00
Coronation, pink, plate, luncheon; 8½"..........................$4.00
Coronation, pink, sherbet...$4.00
Coronation, pink, tumbler, 5", 10-oz, footed $18.00
Coronation, red, bowl, nappy; 6½"..............................$10.00
Coronation, red, plate, luncheon; 8½"...........................$8.00
Cremax, ivory, bowl, vegetable; 9"................................$6.00
Cremax, ivory, cup...$4.00
Cremax, ivory, plate, dinner; 9¾".................................$4.00
Cremax, ivory decorated, creamer $7.50
Cremax, ivory decorated, plate, dinner; 9¾"................$9.00

Cremax, ivory decorated, sugar bowl, open $7.50
Cube, green, bowl, salad; 6½" $13.00
Cube, green, butter dish...$55.00
Cube, green, creamer, 3"..$8.00
Cube, green, powder jar, footed, w/lid........................$22.00
Cube, green, sherbet, footed $7.00
Cube, green, sugar bowl, 3"...$7.00
Cube, green, sugar/candy lid.......................................$12.00
Cube, pink, bowl, dessert; 4½" $5.50
Cube, pink, coaster, 3¼"...$6.00
Cube, pink, salt & pepper shakers, pr.........................$32.50
Cube, pink, sherbet, footed..$6.50
Cube, pink, sugar bowl, 3"...$6.00
Cube, pink, sugar/candy lid...$12.00

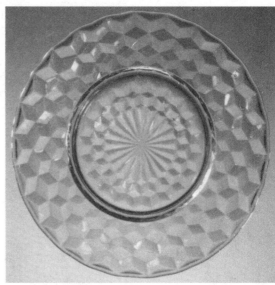

Cube, plate, 8", green...$6.00
Daisy, amber, bowl, cream soup; 4½" $12.00
Daisy, amber, bowl, vegetable; 10", oval $15.00
Daisy, amber, cup...$6.00
Daisy, amber, plate, luncheon; 8⅜" $6.00
Daisy, amber, platter, 10¾"...$14.00
Daisy, amber, sherbet, footed $8.50
Daisy, amber, sugar bowl, footed..................................$8.00
Daisy, clear, bowl, cereal; 6".......................................$10.00
Daisy, clear, bowl, vegetable; 10", oval.........................$9.00
Daisy, clear, cup...$4.00
Daisy, clear, plate, dinner; 9⅜" $5.00
Daisy, clear, platter, 10¾"..$7.00
Daisy, clear, relish dish, 8⅜", 3-part...........................$12.00
Daisy, clear, tumbler, 12-oz, footed............................$19.00
Diamond Quilted, blue, bowl, 5½", 1-handled $15.00
Diamond Quilted, blue, candlesticks, 2 styles, pr........$45.00
Diamond Quilted, blue, creamer $16.00
Diamond Quilted, blue, cup $15.00
Diamond Quilted, blue, plate, luncheon; 8" $11.00
Diamond Quilted, blue, sugar bowl $14.00
Diamond Quilted, green, bowl, cereal; 5".....................$6.50
Diamond Quilted, green, bowl, console; rolled edge .$18.00
Diamond Quilted, green, candlesticks, 2 styles, pr $22.00
Diamond Quilted, green, creamer $7.50

Diamond Quilted, green, cup $9.00

Diamond Quilted, green, goblet, wine; 3-oz.............$10.00

Diamond Quilted, green, mayonnaise set: ladle, plate, 3-footed dish $35.00

Diamond Quilted, green, pitcher, 64-oz...................$45.00

Diamond Quilted, green, plate, luncheon; 8" $5.00

Diamond Quilted, green, sugar bowl $7.50

Diamond Quilted, green, tumbler, 9-oz, footed..........$12.00

Diamond Quilted, green, whiskey, 1½-oz....................$8.00

Diana, amber, bowl, cream soup; 5½" $12.00

Diana, amber, bowl, 12", scalloped edge...................$15.00

Diana, amber, creamer, oval $8.00

Diana, amber, plate, dinner; 9½" $8.00

Diana, amber, platter, 12", oval................................$12.00

Diana, amber, tumbler, 4⅛", 9-oz $28.00

Diana, pink, ashtray, 3½"..$3.50

Diana, pink, bowl, console fruit; 11"........................$32.50

Diana, pink, coaster, 3½"..$7.00

Diana, pink, cup $11.00

Diana, pink, plate, dinner; 9½" $12.00

Diana, pink, plate, sandwich; 11¾" $20.00

Diana, pink, sugar bowl, open, oval $10.00

Dogwood, green, bowl, cereal; 5½" $22.00

Dogwood, green, creamer, 2½" $40.00

Dogwood, green, cup...$32.00

Dogwood, green, plate, grill; 10½", allover pattern or border design $17.00

Dogwood, green, saucer $6.50

Dogwood, green, sugar bowl, 2½" $40.00

Dogwood, pink, bowl, berry; 8½" $47.50

Dogwood, pink, creamer, 3¼" $18.00

Dogwood, pink, cup...$12.00

Dogwood, pink, plate, bread & butter; 6" $7.00

Dogwood, pink, plate, dinner; 9¼" $25.00

Dogwood, pink, saucer $6.00

Dogwood, pink, sugar bowl, 2½" $15.00

Dogwood, pink, sugar bowl, 3¼" $14.00

Dogwood, pink, tumbler, 3½", 10-oz, decorated........$32.50

Doric, green, bowl, vegetable; 9", oval $25.00

Doric, green, candy dish, 8", w/lid..............................$32.50

Doric, green, creamer, 4"...$13.00

Doric, green, plate, dinner; 9" $14.00

Doric, green, salt & pepper shakers, pr $32.50

Doric, green, sugar bowl..$11.00

Doric, green, sugar lid...$20.00

Doric, green, tray, relish; 4x4".......................................$8.00

Doric, green, tray, serving; 8x8"..................................$20.00

Doric, pink, bowl, cereal; 5½" $40.00

Doric, pink, bowl, vegetable; 9", oval $20.00

Doric, pink, bowl, 9", 2-handled.................................$12.00

Doric, pink, coaster, 3"..$15.00

Doric, pink, pitcher, 6", 36-oz.....................................$25.00

Doric, pink, plate, salad; 7" $15.00

Doric, pink, platter, 12", oval......................................$18.00

Doric, pink, sherbet, footed $10.00

Doric, pink, sugar bowl..$10.00

Doric, pink, sugar lid...$12.00

Doric, pink, tray, 10", handled $12.00

Doric & Pansy, pink, bowl, 9", handled.....................$14.00

Doric & Pansy, pink, plate, sherbet; 6"........................$7.00

Doric & Pansy, ultramarine, bowl, berry; 4½".............$15.00

Doric & Pansy, ultramarine, cup................................$16.00

Doric & Pansy, ultramarine, plate, dinner; 9"............$25.00

Doric & Pansy, ultramarine, saucer..............................$5.00

Doric & Pansy, ultramarine, tray, 10", handled...........$20.00

English Hobnail, pink or green, ashtray......................$20.00

English Hobnail, pink or green, bowl, cream soup.....$14.00

English Hobnail, pink or green, candlesticks, 3½", pr.$35.00

English Hobnail, pink or green, celery dish, 9" $21.00

English Hobnail, pink or green, creamer $22.00

English Hobnail, pink or green, cup $16.00

English Hobnail, pink or green, goblet, cocktail; 3-oz.$17.00

English Hobnail, pink or green, pitcher, 23-oz.........$145.00

English Hobnail, pink or green, plate, 8" $8.00

English Hobnail, pink or green, salt & pepper shakers, round or square base, pr.....................................$77.50

English Hobnail, pink or green, saucer $4.00

English Hobnail, pink or green, sherbet $14.00

English Hobnail, pink or green, sugar bowl $24.00

English Hobnail, pink or green, tumbler, iced tea; 4".$16.00

English Hobnail, pink or green, tumbler, 7-oz, footed.$15.00

English Hobnail, pink or green, whiskey, 3-oz...........$25.00

Floragold, iridescent, bowl, fruit; 5½", ruffled.............$8.00

Floragold, iridescent, bowl, 8½", square $12.50

Floragold, iridescent, butter dish, ¼ -lb, oblong, w/lid .$22.50

Floragold, iridescent, creamer $8.50

Floragold, iridescent, cup..$5.50

Floragold, iridescent, pitcher, 64-oz $32.50

Floragold, iridescent, plate, dinner; 8½" $30.00

Floragold, iridescent, platter, 11¼" $17.50

Floragold, iridescent, salt & pepper shakers, pr $45.00

Floragold, iridescent, sugar bowl................................$6.00

Floragold, iridescent, sugar lid....................................$9.50

Floragold, iridescent, tumbler, 10-oz, footed $17.50

Floral, green, bowl, berry; 4" $15.00

Floral, green, bowl, vegetable; 9", oval $15.00

Floral, green, candy jar, w/lid......................................$35.00

Floral, green, cup $11.00

Floral, green, pitcher, 8", 32-oz, footed.....................$32.00

Floral, green, plate, salad; 8".......................................$10.00

Floral, green, platter, 10¾", oval................................$15.00

Floral, green, salt & pepper shakers, 4", footed, pr.....$47.50

Floral, green, saucer $10.00

Floral, green, tray, 6", closed handles, square $15.00

Floral, green, tumbler, water; 4¾", 7-oz, footed $19.00

Floral, pink, bowl, salad; 7½"......................................$15.00

Floral, pink, bowl, vegetable; 8", w/lid.......................$30.00

Floral, pink, coaster, 3¼"...$12.00

Floral, pink, creamer...$12.00

Floral, pink, pitcher, 8", 32-oz, footed.......................$30.00

Floral, pink, plate, dinner; 9" $14.00

Floral, pink, plate, salad; 8"..$10.00

Floral, pink, platter, 10¾", oval..................................$15.00

Floral, pink, sugar bowl..$8.00

Floral, pink, sugar or candy lid...................................$15.00

Floral, pink, tumbler, juice; 4", 5-oz, footed...............$15.00

Floral & Diamond Band, green, bowl, berry; 8" **$13.00**

Floral & Diamond Band, green, creamer, sm **$10.00**

Floral & Diamond Band, green, creamer, 4¾" **$18.00**

Floral & Diamond Band, green, plate, luncheon; 8" ... **$30.00**

Floral & Diamond Band, green, tumbler, water; 4" **$22.00**

Floral & Diamond Band, pink, bowl, nappy; 5¾", w/handle **$10.00**

Floral & Diamond Band, pink, compote, 5½" tall **$14.00**

Floral & Diamond Band, pink, sherbet **$6.00**

Floral & Diamond Band, pink, sugar bowl, sm **$9.00**

Floral & Diamond Band, pink, sugar bowl, 5¼" **$13.00**

Floral & Diamond Band, pink, sugar lid **$45.00**

Florentine No 1, green, ashtray, 5½" **$20.00**

Florentine No 1, green, bowl, berry; 8½" **$20.00**

Florentine No 1, green, creamer, ruffled **$35.00**

Florentine No 1, green, cup **$8.50**

Florentine No 1, green, plate, salad; 8½" **$7.00**

Florentine No 1, green, salt & pepper shakers, pr **$35.00**

Florentine No 1, green, sugar bowl, ruffled **$30.00**

Florentine No 1, green, tumbler, juice; 3¾", footed **$13.00**

Florentine No 1, pink, salt & pepper shakers, pr **$50.00**

Florentine No 1, yellow, bowl, berry; 5" **$13.00**

Florentine No 1, yellow, bowl, 9½", oval, w/lid **$55.00**

Florentine No 1, yellow, creamer **$11.00**

Florentine No 1, yellow, pitcher, 6½", 36-oz, footed ... **$45.00**

Florentine No 1, yellow, plate, dinner; 10" **$20.00**

Florentine No 1, yellow, sugar bowl **$12.00**

Florentine No 1, yellow, sugar lid **$20.00**

Florentine No 1, yellow, tumbler, iced tea; 5¼", 12-oz, footed **$28.00**

Florentine No 2, green, bowl, berry; 4½" **$10.00**

Florentine No 2, green, candlesticks, 2¾", pr **$40.00**

Florentine No 2, green, coaster, 3¼" **$12.00**

Florentine No 2, green, compote, 3½", ruffled **$20.00**

Florentine No 2, green, cream soup; 4¾" **$12.00**

Florentine No 2, green, pitcher, 7½", 28-oz, footed **$28.00**

Florentine No 2, green, plate, grill; 10¼" **$10.00**

Florentine No 2, green, sherbet, footed **$9.00**

Florentine No 2, green, tumbler, water; 4", 9-oz **$11.00**

Florentine No 2, yellow, bowl, berry; 4½" **$17.00**

Florentine No 2, yellow, bowl, berry; 8" **$25.00**

Florentine No 2, yellow, candlesticks, 2¾", pr **$55.00**

Florentine No 2, yellow, coaster, 3¼" **$20.00**

Florentine No 2, yellow, gravy boat **$47.50**

Florentine No 2, yellow, pitcher, 7½", 28-oz, footed ... **$29.00**

Florentine No 2, yellow, plate, dinner; 10" **$13.00**

Florentine No 2, yellow, salt & pepper shakers, pr **$46.00**

Florentine No 2, yellow, sugar bowl **$9.00**

Florentine No 2, yellow, sugar lid **$20.00**

Florentine No 2, yellow, tumbler, 3¼", 5-oz, footed ... **$15.00**

Flower Garden & Butterflies, blue, candy dish, heart shape w/lid **$1,250.00**

Flower Garden w/Butterflies, pink or green, bowl, console; 10", footed **$85.00**

Flower Garden w/Butterflies, pink or green, candlesticks, 4", pr **$50.00**

Flower Garden w/Butterflies, pink or green, candy dish, 6", open **$25.00**

Flower Garden w/Butterflies, pink or green, cup **$60.00**

Flower Garden w/Butterflies, pink or green, plate, 8", 2 styles, each **$16.00**

Flower Garden w/Butterflies, pink or green, saucer ... **$25.00**

Flower Garden w/Butterflies, pink or green, sugar bowl **$65.00**

Forest Green, bowl, dessert; 4¾" **$5.00**

Forest Green, cup **$4.00**

Forest Green, pitcher, 3-qt **$25.00**

Forest Green, plate, dinner; 10" **$25.00**

Forest Green, plate, luncheon; 8⅜" **$5.00**

Forest Green, sugar bowl **$6.00**

Forest Green, tumbler, 10-oz **$6.50**

Forest Green, vase, 9" **$6.00**

Fortune, pink, bowl, 4½", handled **$4.00**

Fortune, pink, candy dish, w/lid **$22.50**

Fortune, pink, cup **$4.00**

Fortune, pink, plate, luncheon; 8" **$8.50**

Fruits, green, cup **$7.00**

Fruits, green, pitcher, 7" **$65.00**

Fruits, green, sherbet **$7.50**

Fruits, green, tumbler, 4", combination of fruits **$25.00**

Fruits, green, tumbler, 4", 1 fruit **$15.00**

Fruits, pink, bowl, cereal; 5" **$20.00**

Fruits, pink, plate, luncheon; 8" **$6.00**

Fruits, pink, tumbler, 4", combination of fruits **$20.00**

Fruits, pink, tumbler, 4", 1 fruit **$12.00**

Georgian, green, bowl, 6½", deep **$60.00**

Georgian, green, butter dish, w/lid **$72.50**

Georgian, green, creamer, 3", footed **$10.00**

Georgian, green, creamer, 4", footed **$13.00**

Georgian, green, plate, dinner; 9¼" **$24.00**

Georgian, green, plate, dinner; 9¼", center design **$19.00**

Georgian, green, sugar bowl, 3", footed **$8.50**

Georgian, green, sugar lid, 3" **$30.00**

Georgian, plate, dinner; green **$25.00**

Harp, clear, cake stand, 9" **$22.50**

Harp, clear, coaster **$3.50**

Harp, clear, vase, 6"...$17.50

Heritage, clear, bowl, fruit; 10½".........................$12.50

Heritage, clear, plate, luncheon; 8".......................$8.50

Heritage, clear, sugar bowl, open, footed...............$17.50

Hex Optic, pink or green, bowl, berry; 4¼", ruffled $5.00

Hex Optic, pink or green, cup, 2 handle styles, each...$4.50

Hex Optic, pink or green, pitcher, 5", 32-oz, sunflower motif
    in bottom...$20.00

Hex Optic, pink or green, platter, 11"....................$12.00

Hex Optic, pink or green, salt & pepper shakers, pr..$25.00

Hex Optic, pink or green, sugar bowl......................$5.00

Hex Optic, pink or green, tumbler, 5¾", footed...........$8.50

Hobnail, clear, cup..$4.00

Hobnail, clear, goblet, iced tea; 13-oz....................$7.50

Hobnail, clear, pitcher, milk; 18-oz.......................$17.50

Hobnail, clear, saucer...$2.00

Hobnail, clear, sugar bowl, footed.........................$4.00

Hobnail, clear, tumbler, cordial; 5-oz, footed $6.00

Holiday, pink, bowl, soup; 7¾".............................$40.00

Holiday, pink, butter dish $35.00

Holiday, pink, cup, 2 sizes $6.50

Holiday, pink, plate, dinner; 9".............................$15.00

Holiday, pink, sugar bowl......................................$9.00

Holiday, pink, sugar lid..$13.50

Holiday, pink, tray, sandwich; 10½".......................$15.00

Homespun, pink, bowl, 4½", closed handles...............$9.50

Homespun, pink, creamer, footed...........................$10.00

Homespun, pink, platter, 13", closed handles $14.00

Homespun, pink, sugar bowl, footed.......................$8.50

Homespun, pink, tumbler, water; 4", 9-oz...............$16.00

Homespun, pink, tumbler, 6½", 15-oz, footed...........$23.00

Indiana Custard, ivory, bowl, flat soup; 7½".............$28.00

Indiana Custard, ivory, cup...................................$35.00

Indiana Custard, ivory, saucer................................$8.00

Indiana Custard, ivory, sugar bowl.........................$10.00

Indiana Custard, ivory, sugar lid...........................$18.00

Iris, clear, bowl, fruit; 11", ruffled.......................$14.00

Iris, clear, creamer, footed....................................$10.00

Iris, clear, demitasse cup......................................$30.00

Iris, clear, goblet, wine; 4¼"...............................$16.00

Iris, clear, pitcher, 9½", footed...........................$35.00

Iris, clear, plate, sandwich; 11¾"..........................$25.00

Iris, clear, vase, 9"..$25.00

Iris, iridescent, bowl, berry; 4½", beaded.................$8.00

Iris, iridescent, creamer, footed............................$11.00

Iris, iridescent, cup...$12.00

Iris, iridescent, pitcher, 9½", footed.....................$35.00

Iris, iridescent, sugar bowl...................................$10.00

Iris, iridescent, sugar lid......................................$11.00

Iris, iridescent, tumbler, 6", footed.......................$15.00

Jubilee, topaz, creamer...$20.00

Jubilee, topaz, cup...$14.00

Jubilee, topaz, goblet, 6", 10-oz............................$37.50

Jubilee, topaz, plate, salad; 7".............................$13.00

Jubilee, topaz, saucer...$6.00

Jubilee, topaz, tray, cake; 11", 2-handled................$40.00

Lace Edge, pink, bowl, 9½", plain or ribbed.............$17.50

Lace Edge, pink, candy jar, ribbed $42.50

Lace Edge, pink, compote, 7".................................$20.00

Lace Edge, pink, cookie jar...................................$55.00

Lace Edge, pink, cup...$20.00

Lace Edge, pink, plate, grill; 10½".........................$16.00

Lace Edge, pink, platter, 12¾", 5-part....................$25.00

Lace Edge, pink, saucer...$10.00

Lace Edge, pink, sugar bowl..................................$20.00

Lake Como, blue scene on white, bowl, cereal; 6" $20.00

Lake Como, blue scene on white, creamer, footed.....$25.00

Lake Como, blue scene on white, cup......................$25.00

Lake Como, blue scene on white, salt & pepper shakers,
    pr...$37.50

Laurel, green, bowl, 6", footed..............................$13.00

Laurel, green, candlesticks, 4", pr.........................$27.50

Laurel, green, creamer, tall...................................$11.00

Laurel, green, plate, sherbet; 6"............................$4.00

Laurel, green, platter, 10¾", oval.........................$18.00

Laurel, green, sherbet...$9.00

Laurel, green, tumbler, 4½", 9-oz..........................$40.00

Laurel, ivory, bowl, cereal.....................................$9.00

Laurel, ivory, bowl, vegetable; 9¾", oval................$16.00

Laurel, ivory, creamer, short.................................$10.00

Laurel, ivory, cup..$7.00

Laurel, ivory, plate, dinner; 9⅛"...........................$11.00

Laurel, ivory, salt & pepper shakers, pr..................$45.00

Laurel, ivory, saucer..$3.00

Lincoln Inn, blue or red, bonbon, handled, square.....$14.00

Lincoln Inn, blue or red, bowl, 6", crimped.............$12.00

Lincoln Inn, blue or red, creamer...........................$20.00

Lincoln Inn, blue or red, cup.................................$16.00

Lincoln Inn, blue or red, goblet, wine.....................$26.00

Lincoln Inn, blue or red, nut dish, footed................$16.00

Lincoln Inn, blue or red, plate, 8"..........................$12.00

Lincoln Inn, blue or red, saucer.............................$4.00

Lincoln Inn, blue or red, sugar bowl.......................$19.00

Lincoln Inn, blue or red, tumbler, 7-oz, footed..........$18.00

Lincoln Inn, other than blue or red, ashtray.............$11.00

Lincoln Inn, other than blue or red, bowl, 6", crimped.$8.00

Lincoln Inn, other than blue or red, candy dish, pedestal
    foot, oval..$12.00

Lincoln Inn, other than blue or red, creamer.............$14.00

Lincoln Inn, other than blue or red, cup...................$9.00

Lincoln Inn, other than blue or red, plate, 12" $15.00

Lincoln Inn, other than blue or red, saucer...............$3.00

Lincoln Inn, other than blue or red, sugar bowl.........$13.00

Lincoln Inn, other than blue or red, tumbler, water; 12-oz,
    footed...$19.00

Lorain, green, bowl, vegetable; 9¾", oval................$35.00

Lorain, green, creamer, footed...............................$15.00

Lorain, green, cup..$10.00

Lorain, green, plate, dinner; 10¼"..........................$35.00

Lorain, green, sherbet, footed...............................$18.00

Lorain, yellow, bowl, salad; 7¼"...........................$54.00

Lorain, yellow, cup..$14.00

Lorain, yellow, plate, dinner; 10¼".........................$48.00

Lorain, yellow, tumbler, 4¾", 9-oz, footed..............$26.00

Madrid, amber, bowl, sauce; 5"..............................$6.00

Madrid, amber, candlesticks, 2¼", pr......................$20.00

Madrid, amber, jello mold, 2⅛" high $12.00
Madrid, amber, tumbler, 5½", 10-oz, footed $23.00
Madrid, green, bowl, vegetable; 10", oval $16.00
Madrid, green, cup $8.00
Madrid, green, plate, relish; 10¼" $16.00
Madrid, green, sugar bowl $8.00
Madrid, green, sugar lid $35.00
Manhattan, clear, ashtray, 4" $10.00
Manhattan, clear, ashtray, 4½", square $18.00
Manhattan, clear, bowl, fruit; 9½", open handle $32.00
Manhattan, clear, coaster, 3½" $14.00
Manhattan, clear, pitcher, 24-oz $25.00
Manhattan, clear, salt & pepper shakers, 2", pr $25.00
Manhattan, clear, vase, 8" $16.00
Manhattan, pink, bowl, berry; 5⅜", handled $15.00
Manhattan, pink, candy dish, footed $10.00
Manhattan, pink, salt & pepper shakers, 2", pr $40.00
Manhattan, pink, tray, relish; 14", 5-part $15.00

Manhattan, tumbler, 5¼", pink $16.00
Mayfair (Federal), amber, bowl, sauce; 5" $8.00
Mayfair (Federal), amber, cup $8.00
Mayfair (Federal), amber, plate, grill; 9½" $13.00
Mayfair (Federal), amber, sugar bowl, footed $12.50
Mayfair (Federal), green, bowl, cream soup; 5" $18.00
Mayfair (Federal), green, creamer, footed $15.00
Mayfair (Federal), green, cup $8.00
Mayfair (Federal), green, plate, dinner; 9½" $12.00

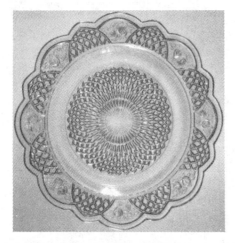

Mayfair (Federal), plate, dinner; amber $12.50
Mayfair (Open Rose), blue, bowl, cereal; 5½" $42.00
Mayfair (Open Rose), blue, bowl, vegetable; 10" $60.00

Mayfair (Open Rose), blue, cake plate; 12", handled .. $55.00
Mayfair (Open Rose), blue, celery dish, 10", divided .. $50.00
Mayfair (Open Rose), blue, cup $45.00
Mayfair (Open Rose), blue, plate, luncheon; 8½" $40.00
Mayfair (Open Rose), blue, relish, 8⅜", 4-part or non-partitioned $55.00
Mayfair (Open Rose), blue, sherbet, 4¾", footed $65.00
Mayfair (Open Rose), blue, vase $95.00
Mayfair (Open Rose), pink, bowl, cream soup; 5" $38.00
Mayfair (Open Rose), pink, bowl, 9½", oval $25.00
Mayfair (Open Rose), pink, cake plate, footed $25.00
Mayfair (Open Rose), pink, cookie jar $45.00
Mayfair (Open Rose), pink, cup $16.00
Mayfair, (Open Rose), pink, pitcher, 8", pink $45.00
Mayfair, (Open Rose), pink, pitcher, 8½", pink $95.00
Mayfair (Open Rose), pink, plate, grill; 9½" $35.00
Mayfair (Open Rose), pink, salt & pepper shakers, pr $55.00
Mayfair (Open Rose), pink, saucer, w/cup ring $27.50
Mayfair (Open Rose), pink, sugar bowl, footed $25.00
Mayfair (Open Rose), pink, tumbler, iced tea; 5¼", ... $40.00
Miss America, clear, bowl, vegetable; 10", oval $14.00
Miss America, clear, coaster, 5¾" $15.00
Miss America, clear, creamer, footed $9.50
Miss America, clear, cup $9.50
Miss America, clear, salt & pepper shakers, pr $28.00
Miss America, clear, saucer $4.00
Miss America, clear, tumbler, iced tea; 5¾", 14-oz $24.00
Miss America, pink, bowl, berry; 6¼" $19.00
Miss America, pink, compote, 5" $22.00
Miss America, pink, plate, dinner; 10½" $22.00
Miss America, pink, plate, sherbet; 5¾" $8.00
Miss America, pink, relish, 8¾", 4-part $20.00
Miss America, pink, sherbet $13.00
Miss America, pink, sugar bowl $15.00

Miss American, candy jar, 11½", pink, w/lid $130.00
Moderntone, amethyst, bowl, berry; 8¾" $35.00
Moderntone, amethyst, creamer $9.00

Moderntone, amethyst, cup.................................$9.00

Moderntone, amethyst, plate, salad; 7¾".................$9.00

Moderntone, amethyst, salt & pepper shakers, pr.......$32.00

Moderntone, amethyst, tumbler, 9-oz....................$22.00

Moderntone, cobalt, bowl, cream soup; 5", ruffled.....$40.00

Moderntone, cobalt, cup.................................$10.00

Moderntone, cobalt, plate, luncheon; 7¾"...............$12.00

Moderntone, cobalt, platter, 11", oval.................$35.00

Moderntone, cobalt, sherbet............................$12.00

Moderntone, cobalt, tumbler, 5-oz......................$35.00

Moondrops, blue or red, ashtray........................$30.00

Moondrops, blue or red, bowl, berry; 5¼"...............$12.00

Moondrops, blue or red, bowl, 9¾", 2-handled, oval..$50.00

Moondrops, blue or red, compote, 4"....................$20.00

Moondrops, blue or red, creamer, 2¾", miniature.......$17.50

Moondrops, blue or red, creamer, 3¾", regular.........$15.00

Moondrops, blue or red, cup............................$15.00

Moondrops, blue or red, goblet, wine; 4", 4-oz.........$20.00

Moondrops, blue or red, mug, 5⅛", 12-oz...............$35.00

Moondrops, blue or red, pitcher, 6⅞", 22-oz...........$150.00

Moondrops, blue or red, plate, luncheon; 8½"...........$14.00

Moondrops, blue or red, sugar bowl, 2¾", miniature..$14.00

Moondrops, blue or red, sugar bowl, 4", regular........$15.00

Moondrops, blue or red, tumbler, juice; 3¾", footed..$15.00

Moondrops, other than blue or red, cup.................$9.00

Moondrops, other than blue or red, goblet, wine; 5⅛", metal stem $10.00

Moondrops, other than blue or red, mug, 5⅛", 12-oz.$22.00

Moondrops, other than blue or red, plate, dinner; 9½".$15.00

Moondrops, other than blue or red, sugar bowl, 2¾", miniature..$9.00

Moondrops, other than blue or red, sugar bowl, 4"......$9.00

Moondrops, other than blue or red, tumbler, 4⅞", 9-oz, handled..$15.00

Moonstone, opalescent hobnail, bowl, cloverleaf.......$12.00

Moonstone, opalescent hobnail, candle holders, pr....$16.00

Moonstone, opalescent hobnail, cup.....................$7.00

Moonstone, opalescent hobnail, sugar bowl, footed.....$8.00

Moonstone, opalescent hobnail, vase, bud; 5½".........$12.00

Moroccan Amethyst, ashtray, 6⅝", triangular............$9.00

Moroccan Amethyst, bowl, 7¾", rectangular.............$13.00

Moroccan Amethyst, cup.................................$5.00

Moroccan Amethyst, plate, dinner; 9⅜"..................$7.50

Moroccan Amethyst, tumbler, water; 9-oz................$10.00

Moroccan Amethyst, vase, 8½", ruffled.................$35.00

Mt Pleasant, black amethyst or cobalt, bowl, 8", 2-handled, square...$27.50

Mt Pleasant, black amethyst or cobalt, candlesticks, double; pr...$40.00

Mt Pleasant, black amethyst or cobalt, cup.............$10.00

Mt Pleasant, black amethyst or cobalt, plate, grill; 9"..$10.00

Mt Pleasant, black amethyst or cobalt, plate, 8", scalloped or square...$14.00

Mt Pleasant, black amethyst or cobalt, salt & pepper shakers, either of 2 styles, pr........................$40.00

Mt Pleasant, black amethyst or cobalt, sugar bowl......$17.50

New Century, green, ashtray or coaster, 5⅜".............$27.50

New Century, green, bowl, cream soup; 4¾".............$16.00

New Century, green, butter dish........................$55.00

New Century, green, pitcher, 8", 80-oz.................$37.50

New Century, green, platter, 11", oval.................$14.00

New Century, green, salt & pepper shakers, pr..........$35.00

New Century, green, tumbler, 4", 5-oz, footed.........$15.00

Newport, amethyst, bowl, cereal; 5¼"...................$25.00

Newport, amethyst, creamer.............................$13.00

Newport, amethyst, cup.................................$9.00

Newport, amethyst, platter, 11¾", oval.................$28.00

Newport, amethyst, saucer..............................$5.00

Newport, cobalt, bowl, berry; 4¼".....................$15.00

Newport, cobalt, creamer...............................$15.00

Newport, cobalt, cup...................................$10.00

Newport, cobalt, plate, sandwich; 11½"................$35.00

Newport, cobalt, saucer................................$5.00

No 610 Pyramid, pink, bowl, berry; 8½"................$27.00

No 610 Pyramid, pink, sugar bowl.......................$22.00

No 610 Pyramid, pink, tumbler, 8-oz, footed............$27.50

No 610 Pyramid, yellow, bowl, berry; 4¾"..............$30.00

No 610 Pyramid, yellow, creamer........................$30.00

No 610 Pyramid, yellow, tumbler, 11-oz, footed.........$65.00

No 612 Horseshoe, green, bowl, salad; 7½"..............$17.50

No 612 Horseshoe, green, creamer, footed...............$13.50

No 612 Horseshoe, green, cup...........................$9.00

No 612 Horseshoe, green, plate, sandwich; 11¼"........$14.00

No 612 Horseshoe, green, relish, 3-part, footed........$18.00

No 612 Horseshoe, green, sugar bowl, open..............$13.50

No 612 Horseshoe, yellow, bowl, berry; 9½"............$30.00

No 612 Horseshoe, yellow, plate, luncheon; 9⅜"........$12.00

No 612 Horseshoe, yellow, sherbet......................$14.00

No 612 Horseshoe, yellow, tumbler, 9-oz, footed........$17.00

No 616 Vernon, green, creamer, footed..................$23.00

No 616 Vernon, green, plate, luncheon; 8"..............$8.50

No 616 Vernon, green, tumbler, 5", footed..............$30.00

No 616 Vernon, yellow, cup.............................$14.00

No 616 Vernon, yellow, saucer..........................$5.00

No 618 Pineapple & Floral, amber, bowl, vegetable; 10", oval...$18.00

No 618 Pineapple & Floral, amber, plate, dinner; 9⅜".$14.00

No 618 Pineapple & Floral, amber, platter, 11", closed handles...$17.00

No 618 Pineapple & Floral, amber, sugar bowl, diamond shaped $9.00

No 618 Pineapple & Floral, clear, ashtray, 4½"..........$16.00

No 618 Pineapple & Floral, clear, bowl, cereal; 6"......$23.00

No 618 Pineapple & Floral, clear, cup..................$10.00

No 618 Pineapple & Floral, clear, plate, dinner; 9⅜"..$15.00

No 618 Pineapple & Floral, clear, tumbler, 5", 12-oz..$37.50

No 622 Pretzel, clear, cup.............................$5.00

No 622 Pretzel, clear, plate, dinner; 9⅜"..............$8.00

No 622 Pretzel, clear, tumbler, juice; 5-oz............$20.00

Normandie, amber, bowl, vegetable; 10", oval...........$14.00

Normandie, amber, plate, sherbet; 6"...................$4.00

Normandie, amber, sherbet..............................$6.00

Normandie, amber, sugar bowl...........................$7.00

Normandie, amber, sugar lid............................$80.00

Normandie, amber, tumbler, juice; 4", 5-oz.............$18.00

Normandie, pink, bowl, berry; 5".......................$6.00

Normandie, pink, cup...**$8.00**
Normandie, pink, plate, grill; 11".......................**$16.00**
Normandie, pink, salt & pepper shakers, pr.............**$65.00**
Normandie, pink, tumbler, water; 4¼", 9-oz.........**$35.00**
Old Cafe, pink, candy dish, 8", low.....................**$8.00**
Old Cafe, pink, cup...**$5.00**
Old Cafe, pink, tumbler, water; 4"........................**$10.00**
Old Cafe, pink, vase, 7¼"......................................**$12.00**
Old Cafe, red, cup...**$7.00**
Old Cafe, red, lamp **$22.00**
Old Cafe, red, tumbler, juice; 3"...........................**$7.50**
Old English, green, pink, or amber, bowl, 9", footed .**$25.00**
Old English, green, pink, or amber, candlesticks, 4", pr.**$30.00**
Old English, green, pink, or amber, pitcher, w/lid ...**$110.00**
Old English, green, pink, or amber, sherbet...............**$18.00**
Old English, green, pink, or amber, sugar bowl.........**$17.00**
Old English, green, pink, or amber, sugar lid.............**$32.00**
Ovide, black, bowl, cereal; 5½" **$7.00**
Ovide, black, salt & pepper shakers, pr **$26.00**
Ovide, black, sugar bowl, open...............................**$6.00**
Ovide, green, cup...**$3.00**
Ovide, green, plate, luncheon; 8"...........................**$2.00**
Ovide, green, sherbet **$2.00**
Oyster & Pearl, pink, bowl, 5", w/handled, heart shape.**$7.00**
Oyster & Pearl, pink, candle holders, 3½", pr.............**$20.00**

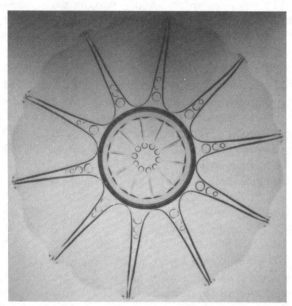

Oyster & Pearl, pink, plate, sandwich; 13½".........$16.00
Oyster & Pearl, pink, relish dish, 10¼", oblong.............**$8.00**
Oyster & Pearl, red, candle holders, 3½", pr.............**$40.00**
Oyster & Pearl, red, plate, sandwich; 13½"...................**$37.50**
Parrot, amber, bowl, soup; 7" **$28.00**
Parrot, amber, creamer, footed **$32.50**
Parrot, amber, cup...**$30.00**
Parrot, amber, jam dish, 7".....................................**$30.00**
Parrot, amber, plate, grill; 10½", square **$22.00**
Parrot, amber, saucer **$12.00**
Parrot, green, bowl, berry; 5"..................................**$20.00**
Parrot, green, plate, dinner; 9"................................**$40.00**
Parrot, green, sherbet, footed, cone shaped **$20.00**

Parrot, green, sugar bowl **$30.00**
Parrot, green, sugar lid...**$120.00**
Patrician, amber, bowl, vegetable; 10", oval **$30.00**
Patrician, amber, cookie jar.....................................**$80.00**
Patrician, amber, salt & pepper shakers, pr **$50.00**
Patrician, amber, sugar bowl....................................**$9.00**
Patrician, amber, sugar lid......................................**$48.00**
Patrician, green, bowl, berry; 8½".............................**$30.00**
Patrician, green, pitcher, 8", 75-oz...........................**$100.00**
Patrician, green, plate, sherbet; 6" **$7.00**
Patrician, green, sherbet **$12.00**
Patrician, green, tumbler, 4½", 9-oz.........................**$24.00**
Patrick, pink, creamer..**$120.00**
Patrick, pink, plate, luncheon; 8"..............................**$115.00**
Patrick, pink, plate, sherbet; 7"................................**$16.00**
Patrick, pink, sherbet, 4¾".......................................**$125.00**
Patrick, yellow, bowl, fruit; 9", handled **$40.00**
Patrick, yellow, creamer **$35.00**
Patrick, yellow, goblet, cocktail; 4".............................**$45.00**
Patrick, yellow, tray, 11", 2-handled **$50.00**
Petalware, monax, bowl, cereal; 5¾"..........................**$6.00**
Petalware, monax, plate, dinner; 9"...........................**$6.00**
Petalware, monax, plate, salver; 11" **$7.00**
Petalware, monax, sherbet, low, footed **$6.50**
Petalware, monax, sugar bowl, footed **$6.00**
Petalware, pink, bowl, berry; 8¾"...............................**$14.00**
Petalware, pink, bowl, cream soup; 4½" **$10.00**
Petalware, pink, creamer, footed **$7.00**
Petalware, pink, plate, salad; 8" **$5.00**
Petalware, pink, platter, 13", oval..............................**$14.00**
Primo, yellow or green, bowl, 4½" **$9.00**
Primo, yellow or green, coaster or ashtray...................**$7.50**
Primo, yellow or green, cup......................................**$8.00**
Primo, yellow or green, plate, dinner; 10" **$15.00**
Primo, yellow or green, saucer **$3.00**
Primo, yellow or green, tumbler, 5¾", 9-oz **$15.00**
Princess, green, cake stand, 10"................................**$20.00**
Princess, green, coaster **$30.00**
Princess, green, cookie jar..**$50.00**
Princess, green, relish, 7½", divided **$22.00**
Princess, green, salt & pepper shakers, 4½", pr..........**$45.00**
Princess, green, tumbler, iced tea; 5¼", 13-oz **$32.00**
Princess, green, vase, 8" **$28.00**
Princess, pink, bowl, 9½", hat shaped........................**$30.00**
Princess, pink, pitcher, 8", 60-oz...............................**$48.00**
Princess, pink, plate, grill; 9"....................................**$12.00**
Princess, pink, platter, 12", closed handles **$20.00**
Princess, pink, sugar bowl **$10.00**
Princess, pink, sugar lid...**$18.00**
Princess, pink, tumbler, 4¾", 9-oz, square footed **$45.00**
Queen Mary, clear, butter dish **$22.00**
Queen Mary, clear, candlesticks, 4½", 2-branch, pr.....**$14.00**
Queen Mary, clear, coaster, 3½"................................**$2.50**
Queen Mary, clear, plate, dinner; 9¾".........................**$13.00**
Queen Mary, clear, salt & pepper shakers, pr **$17.50**
Queen Mary, clear, sherbet, footed **$4.00**
Queen Mary, clear, tumbler, 5", 10-oz, footed............**$25.00**
Queen Mary, pink, ashtray, 2x3¾", oval.....................**$4.50**

Queen Mary, pink, compote, 5¾"............................$12.00
Queen Mary, pink, cup...$7.00
Queen Mary, pink, saucer......................................$2.00
Queen Mary, pink, sugar bowl, oval $7.00
Queen Mary, pink, tray, serving; 14"...................$18.00
Queen Mary, pink, tumbler, water; 4", 9-oz...........$10.00
Radiance, blue or red, bowl, nut; 5", 2-handled.........$15.00
Radiance, blue or red, candlesticks, 2-light, pr...........$55.00
Radiance, blue or red, cup....................................$16.00
Radiance, blue or red, sugar bowl.............................$20.00
Radiance, blue or red, tray, oval..............................$30.00
Radiance, blue or red, tumbler, 9-oz..........................$25.00
Radiance, other than blue or red, compote, 5"...........$15.00
Radiance, other than blue or red, cruet, individual.....$30.00
Radiance, other than blue or red, mayonnaise, w/liner &
    ladle, 3-piece set $25.00
Radiance, other than blue or red, plate, luncheon; 8"...$9.00
Radiance, other than blue or red, salt & pepper shakers,
    pr $45.00
Radiance, other than blue or red, vase, 10", flared.....$28.00
Raindrops, green, bowl, berry; 7½" $35.00
Raindrops, green, cup...$5.00
Raindrops, green, sugar bowl $6.00
Raindrops, green, sugar lid $35.00
Raindrops, green, whiskey, 1⅞"..............................$7.00
Ribbon, black, bowl, berry; 8".................................$30.00
Ribbon, black, plate, luncheon; 8"...........................$12.00
Ribbon, black, salt & pepper shakers, pr $37.50
Ribbon, green, creamer, footed $12.00
Ribbon, green, salt & pepper shakers, pr....................$25.00
Ribbon, green, tumbler, 5½", 10-oz $12.00
Ring, clear, cup $4.00
Ring, clear, ice tub..$13.00
Ring, clear, salt & pepper shakers, 3", pr....................$16.00
Ring, clear, sherbet, 4¾", footed $4.50
Ring, clear, tumbler, water; 5½", footed $5.00
Ring, clear, vase, 8"...$15.00
Ring, clear w/decoration, salt & pepper shakers, 3",
    pr $35.00
Ring, clear w/decoration, sandwich server, upright center
    handle...$24.00
Ring, clear w/decoration, sugar bowl, footed.............$5.00
Ring, clear w/decoration, tumbler, iced tea; 6½", footed .$13.00
Ring, green, pitcher, 8", 60-oz................................$19.00
Ring, green, salt & pepper shakers, 3", pr..................$55.00
Ring, green, tumbler, 5⅛", 12-oz.............................$8.00
Rock Crystal, clear, bonbon, 7½", scalloped $17.50
Rock Crystal, clear, candelabra, 2-light, pr................$38.00
Rock Crystal, clear, creamer...................................$18.00
Rock Crystal, clear, cup, 7-oz..................................$16.00
Rock Crystal, clear, goblet, iced tea; 11-oz, low foot ..$18.00
Rock Crystal, clear, saucer.....................................$7.00
Rock Crystal, clear, tumbler, whiskey; 2½-oz $15.00
Rock Crystal, red, bowl, celery; 12", oblong.............$55.00
Rock Crystal, red, cake stand, 2¾x11", footed.............$95.00
Rock Crystal, red, compote, 7"...............................$60.00
Rock Crystal, red, cup, 7-oz...................................$65.00
Rock Crystal, red, jelly, 5", footed, scalloped.............$45.00

Rock Crystal, red, saucer......................................$20.00
Rock Crystal, red, sundae, 6-oz, low footed $32.00
Rose Cameo, green, bowl, berry; 4½" $8.00
Rose Cameo, green, sherbet....................................$10.00
Rose Cameo, green, tumbler, 5", footed $16.00
Rosemary, amber, bowl, cream soup; 5"....................$14.00
Rosemary, amber, bowl, vegetable; 10", oval $13.00
Rosemary, amber, cup...$5.00
Rosemary, amber, plate, dinner $8.50
Rosemary, amber, sugar bowl, footed $8.00
Rosemary, green, bowl, vegetable; 10", oval $25.00
Rosemary, green, cup...$9.00
Rosemary, green, platter, 12", oval..........................$18.00
Rosemary, green, tumbler, 4¼", 9-oz.........................$28.00
Roulette, green, cup...$6.00
Roulette, green, plate, sandwich; 12" $12.00
Roulette, pink, pitcher, 8", 64-oz..............................$30.00
Roulette, pink, tumbler, iced tea; 5⅛", 12-oz.............$22.00
Roulette, pink, tumbler, juice; 3¼", 5-oz $18.00
Round Robin, green, plate, sandwich; 12" $7.00
Round Robin, green, sugar bowl $5.50
Round Robin, iridescent, bowl, berry; 4"....................$4.50
Round Robin, iridescent, cup, footed $5.00
Roxana, yellow, plate, 6".......................................$6.00
Roxana, yellow, sherbet, footed...............................$8.00
Roxana, yellow, tumbler, 4", 9-oz............................$15.00
Royal Lace, blue, bowl, berry; 10" $55.00
Royal Lace, blue, cup...$32.50
Royal Lace, blue, plate, dinner; 10" $38.00
Royal Lace, blue, sherbet, footed.............................$42.00
Royal Lace, blue, sugar bowl $35.00
Royal Lace, blue, sugar lid $140.00
Royal Lace, blue, tumbler, 3½", 5-oz $45.00
Royal Lace, pink, bowl, 10", rolled edge, footed.........$40.00
Royal Lace, pink, candlesticks, straight edge, pr $38.00
Royal Lace, pink, cookie jar $45.00
Royal Lace, pink, creamer, footed $16.00
Royal Lace, pink, cup...$12.00
Royal Lace, pink, pitcher, 48-oz, straight sides............$60.00
Royal Lace, pink, plate, dinner; 10" $18.00
Royal Lace, pink, salt & pepper shakers, pr................$55.00
Royal Lace, pink, sugar bowl $12.00
Royal Lace, pink, sugar lid $35.00
Royal Lace, pink, tumbler, 4⅛", 9-oz........................$15.00
Royal Ruby, bowl, soup; 7½"..................................$12.00
Royal Ruby, cup, round or square $4.50
Royal Ruby, goblet, ball stem..................................$9.00
Royal Ruby, pitcher, 3-quart, tilted $35.00
Royal Ruby, pitcher, 3-quart, upright $45.00
Royal Ruby, plate, dinner; 9" or 9¼".........................$10.00
Royal Ruby, sugar bowl..$7.00
Royal Ruby, sugar bowl, footed...............................$8.00
Royal Ruby, sugar lid..$9.00
Royal Ruby, tumbler, iced tea; 13-oz.........................$14.00
Royal Ruby, tumbler, juice; 5-oz, 2 styles..................$5.00
Royal Ruby, vase, 4", ball shaped $4.50
S Pattern, amber, cake plate, 11" $38.00
S Pattern, amber, sugar bowl $6.00

S Pattern, amber, tumbler, 5", 12-oz $12.00
S Pattern, clear, bowl, berry; 8½" $8.50
S Pattern, clear, pitcher, 80-oz $45.00
S Pattern, clear, plate, dinner; 9¼" $5.00
Sandwich (Hocking), clear, bowl, cereal; 6" $26.00
Sandwich (Hocking), clear, butter dish, low...............$40.00
Sandwich (Hocking), clear, cookie jar.......................$35.00
Sandwich (Hocking), clear, pitcher, ½-gal, w/ice lip .$65.00
Sandwich (Hocking), clear, plate, dinner; 9" $16.00
Sandwich (Hocking), clear, sugar bowl $20.00
Sandwich (Hocking), clear, tumbler, water; 9-oz..........$7.50
Sandwich (Hocking), green, creamer $22.00
Sandwich (Hocking), green, cup, coffee or tea $18.00
Sandwich (Hocking), green, plate, dinner; 9" $65.00
Sandwich (Hocking), green, saucer............................$11.00
Sandwich (Hocking), green, tumbler, juice; 5-oz..........$3.50
Sandwich (Indiana), clear, butter dish, w/domed lid ..$20.00
Sandwich (Indiana), clear, cup $3.00
Sandwich (Indiana), clear, goblet, 9-oz......................$12.50
Sandwich (Indiana), clear, plate, sandwich; 13" $10.00
Sandwich (Indiana), clear, sugar bowl $8.50
Sandwich (Indiana), clear, tumbler, 8-oz, footed...........$8.00
Sandwich (Indiana), pink, bowl, console; 9" $15.00
Sandwich (Indiana), pink, candlesticks, 3½", pr.........$13.00
Sandwich (Indiana), pink, plate, dinner; 10½"............$12.00
Sandwich (Indiana), pink, sandwich server, upright center
    handle...$25.00
Sharon, amber, bowl, berry; 5" $7.50
Sharon, amber, bowl, cream soup; 5" $25.00
Sharon, amber, butter dish..$43.00
Sharon, amber, cup..$9.00
Sharon, amber, plate, salad; 7½" $15.00
Sharon, amber, salt & pepper shakers, pr...................$38.00
Sharon, amber, saucer $6.00
Sharon, amber, sugar bowl...$8.00
Sharon, amber, sugar lid...$20.00
Sharon, pink, bowl, fruit; 10½" $32.00
Sharon, pink, creamer, footed...................................$16.00
Sharon, pink, cup...$12.00
Sharon, pink, plate, dinner; 9½" $16.00
Sharon, pink, salt & pepper shakers, pr.....................$45.00
Sharon, pink, saucer $9.00
Sierra, green, bowl, vegetable; 9½", oval $85.00
Sierra, green, cup...$13.00
Sierra, green, pitcher, 6½", 32-oz $95.00
Sierra, green, salt & pepper shakers, pr $35.00
Sierra, green, sugar bowl...$20.00
Sierra, green, sugar lid..$14.00
Sierra, pink, bowl, cereal; 5½" $10.00
Sierra, pink, bowl, vegetable; 9½", oval $35.00
Sierra, pink, cup...$10.00
Sierra, pink, pitcher, 6½", 32-oz $65.00
Sierra, pink, platter, 11", oval $35.00
Sierra, pink, salt & pepper shakers, pr $35.00
Sierra, pink, tray, serving; 2-handled.........................$13.00
Sierra, pink, tumbler, 4½", 9-oz, footed $40.00
Spiral, green, bowl, mixing; 7" $8.00
Spiral, green, cup...$5.00

Spiral, green, ice or butter tub.............................$25.00
Spiral, green, pitcher, 7⅝", 58-oz $28.00
Spiral, green, plate, luncheon; 8" $3.00
Spiral, green, salt & pepper shakers, pr $30.00
Spiral, green, sugar bowl, flat or footed $7.00
Spiral, green, tumbler, 5⅞", footed $13.00
Starlight, clear, bowl, salad; 11½" $16.00
Starlight, clear, cup $4.00
Starlight, clear, plate, dinner; 9" $6.00
Starlight, clear, salt & pepper shakers, pr...................$20.00
Starlight, clear, saucer $1.50
Starlight, clear, sugar bowl, oval $5.00
Starlight, pink, bowl, cereal; 5½" $8.00
Starlight, pink, plate, sandwich; 13" $13.00
Strawberry, pink or green, compote, 5¾" $18.00
Strawberry, pink or green, creamer, lg, 4⅝" $30.00
Strawberry, pink or green, creamer, sm $16.00
Strawberry, pink or green, pitcher, 7¾" $135.00
Strawberry, pink or green, sugar bowl, lg....................$30.00
Strawberry, pink or green, sugar bowl, sm, open $15.00
Strawberry, pink or green, sugar lid $45.00
Strawberry, pink or green, tumbler, 3⅝", 9-oz............$27.50
Sunflower, green, ashtray, 5", design in center only ...$12.00
Sunflower, green, cake plate, 10", footed $14.00
Sunflower, green, sugar bowl $17.00
Sunflower, pink, cup...$10.00
Sunflower, pink, saucer $6.00
Sunflower, pink, tumbler, 4¾", 8-oz, footed $22.50
Swirl, pink, bowl, cereal; 5¼"......................................$9.00
Swirl, pink, cup..$6.00
Swirl, pink, plate, sandwich; 12½"..............................$11.00
Swirl, pink, saucer..$3.00
Swirl, pink, sugar bowl, footed $7.00
Swirl, pink, tumbler, 9-oz, footed $16.00
Swirl, ultramarine, bowl, cereal; 5¼" $14.00
Swirl, ultramarine, cup...$14.00
Swirl, ultramarine, plate, dinner; 9¼" $15.00
Swirl, ultramarine, saucer $4.50
Swirl, ultramarine, sugar bowl, footed $14.00
Swirl, ultramarine, tumbler, 4", 9-oz $25.00
Swirl, ultramarine, vase, 8½", footed $25.00
Tea Room, green, candlesticks, low, pr $45.00
Tea Room, green, cup $45.00

Tea Room, green, ice bucket $55.00
Tea Room, green, plate, sherbet; 6½"..........$30.00
Tea Room, green, plate, 10½", 2-handled $45.00
Tea Room, green, salt & pepper shakers, pr....$50.00
Tea Room, green, saucer..........................$25.00
Tea Room, green, sherbet, 3 styles..............$25.00
Tea Room, green, tumbler, 8½ -oz $80.00
Tea Room, green, vase, 9".........................$55.00
Tea Room, pink, bowl, vegetable; 9½", oval $55.00
Tea Room, pink, cup................................$45.00
Tea Room, pink, goblet, 9-oz......................$60.00
Tea Room, pink, pitcher, 64-oz...................$120.00
Tea Room, pink, plate, luncheon; 8¼" $28.00
Tea Room, pink, relish, divided...................$18.00
Tea Room, pink, salt & pepper shakers, pr $45.00
Tea Room, pink, saucer.............................$25.00
Tea Room, pink, tumbler, 11-oz, footed $35.00
Tea Room, pink, vase, 9"............................$45.00
Thistle, green, plate, grill; 10¼"..................$20.00
Thistle, green, plate, luncheon; 8" $16.00
Thistle, pink, bowl, cereal; 5½"...................$18.00
Thistle, pink, cup...................................$18.00
Thistle, pink, saucer................................$9.00
Twisted Optic, pink or green, bowl, salad or soup; 7" .$9.00
Twisted Optic, pink or green, candlestick, 3", pr........$17.50
Twisted Optic, pink or green, candy jar, w/lid...........$25.00
Twisted Optic, pink or green, cup.....................$3.50
Twisted Optic, pink or green, plate, luncheon; 8".........$3.00
Twisted Optic, pink or green, saucer $1.50
Twisted Optic, pink or green, sugar bowl $6.00
Twisted Optic, pink or green, tumbler, 5¼", 12-oz........$8.00
US Swirl, green, butter dish.........................$52.50
US Swirl, green, creamer $12.00
US Swirl, green, sugar bowl $30.00
US Swirl, green, vase, 6½"..........................$15.00
US Swirl, pink, bowl, 5½", 1-handled.................$10.00
US Swirl, pink, pitcher, 8", 48-oz $40.00
US Swirl, pink, salt & pepper shakers, pr $40.00
US Swirl, pink, tumbler, 4⅝", 12-oz $14.00
US Swirl, pink, vase, 6½"...........................$18.00
Victory, blue, cup...................................$30.00
Victory, blue, plate, salad; 7".......................$16.00
Victory, blue, saucer $9.00
Victory, blue, sugar bowl $40.00
Victory, pink, bonbon, 7"............................$10.00
Victory, pink, cup $8.00
Victory, pink, goblet, 5", 7-oz......................$18.00
Victory, pink, mayonnaise set, 3½" tall, 5½" across, 8½"
    indented plate, w/ladle..........................$40.00
Victory, pink, sherbet, footed.......................$12.00
Victory, pink, sugar bowl $12.00
Vitrock, white, bowl, vegetable $10.00
Vitrock, white, cup.................................$3.00
Vitrock, white, plate, luncheon; 8¾"................$4.00
Vitrock, white, sugar bowl, oval $4.00
Waterford, clear, ashtray............................$6.50
Waterford, clear, butter dish........................$24.00
Waterford, clear, cup $6.00

Waterford, clear, cup $6.00
Waterford, clear, goblet, 5¼" or 5⅝"..............$15.00
Waterford, clear, pitcher, 80-oz, tilted, w/ice lip $30.00
Waterford, clear, salt & pepper shakers, either of 2 styles,
    pr...$8.50
Waterford, pink, bowl, berry; 4¾" $12.00
Waterford, pink, creamer, oval......................$10.00
Waterford, pink, plate, dinner; 9⅝".................$16.00
Waterford, pink, tumbler, 4⅞", 10-oz, footed..............$18.00
Windsor, clear, bowl, 7⅛", footed....................$7.00
Windsor, clear, candlesticks, 3", pr..................$16.00
Windsor, clear, coaster, 3¼".........................$3.00
Windsor, clear, pitcher, 4½", 16-oz..................$19.00
Windsor, clear, salt & pepper shakers, pr.............$15.00
Windsor, clear, sugar bowl...........................$8.00
Windsor, clear, tumbler, 3¼", 5-oz...................$7.50
Windsor, pink, bowl, berry; 4¾".......................$8.00
Windsor, pink, butter dish............................$46.00
Windsor, pink, cup..................................$9.00
Windsor, pink, pitcher, 6¾", 52-oz...................$25.00
Windsor, pink, plate, sandwich; 10¼", handled..........$15.00
Windsor, pink, platter, 11½", oval....................$6.00
Windsor, pink, sugar bowl............................$24.00
Windsor, pink, tray, 8½x9¾"..........................$22.50
Windsor, pink, tumbler, 5", 12-oz....................$25.00

Dionne Quintuplets

These famous babies were born on May 28, 1934, in Ontario, Canada, and immediately became the center of worldwide focus. They were the first quintuplets ever delivered who survived longer than a few days. In order to protect them from being expoited as infants, they became wards of King George V. A private nursery was built nearby, equipped with glassed-in viewing areas which were visited by thousands of people every week.

Their parents were very poor people who took advantage of their fame to better themselves financially, allowing the children to endorse a variety of products. By the time they were ten years old, the children returned to live with their parents in a mansion built with money they had earned.

Though many companies made similar dolls, Madame Alexander was the only company ever authorized to market Dionne Quintuplet dolls. They made more than thirty sets of 'Quints,' from babies up through the toddler stage. Scores of books, toys, and souvenirs of all types were issued over the years, and today all are very collectible.

Of the five, only Yvonne, Cecile, and Annette are alive today. Emily died in 1954 and Marie in 1970.

Blotter, Illinois Bankers Life, black & white photo, dated
    1934, EX................................$6.50
Book, Here We Are Three Years Old, Whitman, 1937,
    paperback, VG $22.50
Book, We're Two Years Old, Willis Thornton, Whitman,
    1936, unpaginated, G.....................$12.00

Book, 9½x10", Story of the Dionne Quintuplets, Whitman, softcover, photos copyright NEA Service Inc, 1935, 40-page $37.50

Calendar, color group portrait, marked King Features, dated 1953, EX................$22.50

Calendar, dated 1942, full-color print at top, advertising The City Coal Co, VG........................$15.00

Dish, 5½" dia, ceramic, New Home of Dionne Quintuplets, Callender, Ontario, Canada, multicolor graphics w/gold trim................$25.00

Doll, Mrs Andrews, 18", w/3¼" quint babies, cheap plastic w/inset blue eyes, marked Hong Kong/218, EX...$15.00

Doll, 12", Madame Alexander, name pin on chest, each (M $225.00) EX..................................$150.00

Hair ribbon, 1936, M on card........................$75.00

Magazine, Life, May 17, 1937, NM..............................$35.00

Magazine, Modern Screen, Christy cover, 1936..........$28.00

Magazine, Movie Mirror, 1936, NM........................$17.50

Magazine, Sunset Magazine, 1935, September, Dionnne Quints ads, EX........................$9.50

Paper dolls, All Aboard for Shut-Eye Town, Palmolive Soap premium, NM........................$24.00

Sign, advertising Puretest Cod Liver Oil, marked NEA Service Inc, dated 1936, VG........................$75.00

Spoon, silverplate, plain bowl w/figural handle & name, Palmolive Soap premium, EX................$22.50

Tray, 2x3½x2", quints seated on rim, painted china, Souvenir of Callander, Japan, 1930s $150.00

Disney

The largest and most popular area in character collectibles is without doubt Disneyana. There are clubs, newsletters, and special shows that are centered around this hobby. Every aspect of the retail market has been thoroughly saturated with Disney-related merchandise over the years, and today collectors are able to find many good examples at garage sales and flea markets.

Disney memorabilia from the late twenties until about 1940 was marked either 'Walt E. Disney,' or 'Walt Disney Enterprises.' After that time, the name was changed to 'Walt Disney Productions.' Some of the earlier items have become

very expensive, though many are still within the reach of the average collector.

During the thirties, Mickey Mouse, Donald Duck, Snow White and the Seven Dwarfs, and the Three Little Pigs (along with all their friends and cohorts) dominated the Disney scene. The last of the thirties' characters was Pinocchio, and some 'purists' prefer to stop their collections with him.

The forties and fifties brought many new characters with them – Alice in Wonderland, Bambi, Dumbo, Lady and the Tramp, and Peter Pan were some of the major personalities featured in Disney's films of this era.

Even today, thanks to the re-releases of many of the old movies and the popularity of Disney's vacation 'kingdoms,' toy stores and department stores alike are full of quality items with the potential of soon becoming collectibles.

If you'd like to learn more about this fascinating field, we recommend *Stern's Guide to Disney Collectibles, First and Second Series,* by Michael Stern, *The Collector's Encyclopedia of Disneyana* by Michael Stern and David Longest, *Character Toys and Collectibles* and *Toys, Antique and Collectible,* both by David Longest.

See also Character and Promotional Drinking Glasses; Character Watches; Pin-Back Buttons.

Andy Burnett, coloring book, marked, 1958, EX.........$10.00

Bambi, ashtray, figure at rim, marked Goebel w/stylized bee, ca 1957-60 ....$250.00

Bambi, planter, figure w/tree stump planter, painted & glazed ceramic, marked WDP, NM........................$50.00

Bambi, print, 18x21", Bambi Meets His Forest Friends, printed by New York Graphic Society, NM..........$45.00

Brer Rabbit, paint book, 1940s, M $40.00

Captain Hook, marionette, 1950s, EX........................$112.50

Cinderella, paint book, Whitman & Walt Disney, dated 1950, EX........................$25.00

Cinderella, sheet music, 9x12", Bibbidi-Bobbidi-Boo, marked Walt Disney Music Co w/1949 copyright, EX.......$20.00

Cleo the Goldfish, tumbler, juice; marked WDP, ca 1940, EX........................$20.00

Disneyland, booklet, guide; INA Insurance Co of North America, 1971, NM..$10.00

Doc (of Snow White & the 7 Dwarfs), doll, 13", Knickerbocker, NM $200.00

Doc (of Snow White & the 7 Dwarfs), mask, paper, marked Walt Disney Enterprises, 1938, EX.........................$18.00

Donald & His Nephew, 5½", toy, Linemar, pull-string action, 1950s, EX..$560.00

Donald Duck, Bubble Duck, squeeze him & he blows bubbles, Morris Plastic Corporation, NM $45.00

Donald Duck, figure in relief w/name, painted glazed ceramic, EX...$15.00

Donald Duck, pencil sharpener, figural Bakelite, marked WDE, NM...$85.00

Donald Duck, pencil sharpener, 1" dia, decal on plastic w/metal cutter, Plastic Novelties, 1940s, VG........$42.50

Donald Duck, sand pail, 3", colorful lithographed tin, marked Ohio Art, G $50.00

Donald Duck, straws, Sunshine Straws, 1950s, in original box, EX..$12.00

Donald Duck, tea set, lithographed tin, marked Ohio Art Company, 1940s, 4-piece, EX..............................$65.00

Donald Duck, tea tray, colorful lithographed tin, marked Ohio Art & Walt Disney Productions, G................$25.00

Donald Duck, thermometer, 6x6", Donald bowling & verse on tile plaque, Kemper-Thomas, 1940s, M............$45.00

Donald Duck, valentine, mechanical w/Donald wearing sombrero, dated 1938, EX $20.00

Donald Duck & Daisy, valentine, 4½x5", die-cut heart w/mechanical tab moves Daisy riding donkey, marked, 1939, EX..$37.50

Donald Duck & Flower, tablet, 8x10", color cover, 1940s, NM $87.50

Donald Duck & Mickey Mouse, book, Annual for 1975, full-color comic strip-style stories & puzzle pages, M.$12.50

Dopey (of Snow White & 7 Dwarfs), figurine, 4½", painted ceramic, Enesco label, 1960s, NM........................$45.00

Dopey (of Snow White & 7 Dwarfs), playing cards, green trim, marked Disney, ca 1938, standard deck, EX..$65.00

Dopey (of Snow White & 7 Dwarfs), playset, Disneykin TV scene, complete, 1960s, NM..............................$30.00

Dumbo, hand puppet, 10", Gund, ca 1955, M............$18.00

Fantasia, paint book, marked Walt Disney, 1940s, EX..$75.00

Fiddler Pig, cup & saucer, 2" cup & 5" dia saucer, marked Patriot China & Walt Disney, 1930s, EX...............$65.00

Figaro, mask, paper, Gillette premium, 1939, EX........$12.50

Fox & the Hound, studio stationery, 1981, M $8.00

Gepetto, figurine, 5x3x3", seated pose, marked Multi Products Chicago, ca 1940, EX $125.00

Goofy, ball, graphics & Goofy Ball, Swish, Goofy Scores Again on box, EX...$30.00

Goofy, Mickey Mouse & Donald Duck, plate, Christmas 1980, marked Schmid, EX................................$25.00

Goofy, wind-up, painted plastic figural, Marx, EX $85.00

Happy (of Snow White & 7 Dwarfs), figurine, painted ceramic, Walt Disney Enterprises, ca 1937, M.......$65.00

Jiminy Cricket, mug, figural plastic w/moving eyes, Walt Disney Productions, 1960s, EX..............................$12.00

Jiminy Cricket, record, 45rpm, Addition Made Easy, marked WDP w/1964 copyright, in original sleeve, EX.......$8.00

Lady & the Tramp, record, 45 rpm, Siamese Cat Song, marked Disneyland Record, 1962, original picture sleeve, EX $7.50

Ludwig Von Drake, Ring Toss Game, 18" die-cut figural target, marked Transogram & WDP, 1961 copyright, VG ..$25.00

Mary Poppins, bath powder set, MIB.........................$17.50

Mary Poppins, coloring book, 8x11", Whitman, 1964, 64-page, NM...$12.50

Mary Poppins, spoon, 6", silver metal w/portrait handle, marked WDP w/1964 copyright, EX.....................$20.00

Mickey Mouse, ad card, Mickey Mouse Soap, marked Walt Disney, ca 1930s, EX...............................$60.00

Mickey Mouse, alarm clock, animated feet, wind-up type, marked Bradley, dated 1983, MIB........................$35.00

Mickey Mouse, alarm clock, oversized pocket watch form, marked Bradley, 1979, M................................$25.00

Mickey Mouse, ball, sm, face in relief, marked Sun Rubber, EX...$20.00

Mickey Mouse, bank, figural plastic w/Mickey Mouse decal on shirt, EX.................................**$20.00**

Mickey Mouse, bank, 9", plastic head on square base, marked Hasbro, 1968, EX.....................**$37.50**

Mickey Mouse, barometer, Mickey Mouse Weather House, Pluto in top window, Mickey & Donald revolve through doors, EX.................................**$65.00**

Mickey Mouse, book, 8½x10½", Walt Disney's Paint Book, Mickey w/artist brush on cover, Whitman, 1946, 96-page.................................**$37.50**

Mickey Mouse, bottle warmer, marked Hankscraft, electric, original box, VG.................................**$15.00**

Mickey Mouse, fabric transfer, Simplicity Pattern, 1945, unused.................................$15.00

Mickey Mouse, figural soap, marked Kerk Guild, 1950s, set of 2, EX.................................**$75.00**

Mickey Mouse, flashlight, figural rocket ship, red, white & blue plastic, marked Arco, M on card.................**$5.00**

Mickey Mouse, gumball machine, figural head on cylinder base, EX.................................**$15.00**

Mickey Mouse, plate, child's size, full-color figure on white ground w/black trim on rim, plastic, EX.............**$6.00**

Mickey Mouse, postcard, Birthday Wishes, 1930s, EX .**$25.00**

Mickey Mouse, sheet music, Wedding Party, 1930s, EX .**$58.00**

Mickey Mouse, tablet, Powers Paper, 1930s, EX.........**$40.00**

Mickey Mouse, top, lithographed tin, marked Chein & Walt Disney Productions, 1950s, EX.........................**$65.00**

Mickey Mouse, tumbler, 4¾", black pyro on clear......**$35.00**

Mickey Mouse, valentine, What's Better Than a Kiss?, marked Hall Brothers, 1935, EX.........................**$35.00**

Mickey Mouse Club, pencil case, 4x8½x1½", full-color paper label at top, interior tray, ca late 1950s, EX.........**$37.50**

Minnie Mouse, birthday card, 4x5", die-cut figure at mailbox, marked Hall Brothers, w/envelope, 1930s, M.......**$37.50**

Minnie Mouse, bisque figurine, 5½", Japan, VG.........**$60.00**

Minnie Mouse, spoon, child's, steel plated w/figural handle, EX.................................**$10.00**

Mouseketeers, hat, wood & rayon blend, marked Denay-aluee, 1950s, M.................................**$60.00**

Pete's Dragon, studio stationery, 1970s, M.....................**$6.00**

Pinocchio, alarm clock, marked Bayard, 1967, EX......**$50.00**

Pinocchio, color box, Transogram, w/watercolor paints, ca 1940s, EX.................................**$40.00**

Pinocchio, doll, jointed wood, Disney Design, Ideal Novelty & Toy Co, EX.................................**$125.00**

Pinocchio, doll, 13", Knickerbocker, plush & cloth, M .**$135.00**

Pinocchio, mask, paper, marked Walt Disney & Gillette, 1939, VG.................................**$20.00**

Pinocchio, pipsqueak, colorful plastic, Marx, MIB.......**$8.00**

Pinocchio, sheet music, When You Wish Upon a Star, 1940, EX.................................**$20.00**

Pinocchio, valentine, 3x4¾", die-cut Geppetto at work-bench, mechanical, marked Paper Novelty Mfg, 1939, EX.................................**$27.50**

Pluto, coloring book, Whitman, 1960s, EX.....................**$7.50**

Pluto, cookie cutter, 3½", plastic, marked Loma Plastics & WDP, 1950s, on colorful 4½x5½" card, NM.........**$20.00**

Pluto, mug, ceramic, made by Patriot China Co, M.$50.00

Pluto, scissors, figural plastic handles, M in package.................................**$10.00**

Prince Charming, puppet, 9", vinyl w/cloth & felt body, marked Gund & WDP, ca 1959, EX.....................**$37.50**

Roger Rabbit, mug, painted ceramic, marked Applause, 1987, boxed, M.................................**$20.00**

Scamp, figure, 7½x6", soft vinyl, marked WDP & Japan, early 1960s, EX.................................**$22.50**

Silly Symphony, record, 78 rpm, The Grasshopper & the Ants on Side A, w/Bluebird label, 1930s, VG.......**$37.50**

Snow White, planter, 5½", Walt Disney Productions .$225.00

Snow White, press book, lg, 1958 re-release, VG........**$25.00**

Snow White, purse, 7x5", colorful graphics on red vinyl, metal clasp & chain, marked Walt Disney Enterprises, 1938, EX...**$62.50**

Snow White, record, Decca #A-368, w/illustrated 16-page booklet, 1944 copyright, EX.....................................**$37.50**

Snow White, storybook, 9x11½", Turn & Learn, vinyl covered w/carrying handle, marked WDP, ca 1970s, EX....**$37.50**

Snow White, watch stand, painted plastic figure, marked Walt Disney Productions, 1960s, EX......................**$15.00**

Snow White & the Prince, postcard, The Day That My Dreams Come True, 1938, G................................**$25.00**

Snow White & the 7 Dwarfs, book, Jingle Book, Deitzen's Vitamin D Bread premium, ca 1938, EX................**$45.00**

Snow White & the 7 Dwarfs, charm set, figural celluloid, Japan, set of 8, 1930s, EX..................................**$40.00**

Snow White & the 7 Dwarfs, hand mirror, paper decal on early plastic, marked c Walt Disney, G **$35.00**

Snow White & the 7 Dwarfs, paint book, lg format, copyright 1983, G...**$50.00**

Snow White & the 7 Dwarfs, tablet, marked Walt Disney Enterprises, 1937, G **$60.00**

Thumper, planter, marked Leeds, 1940s, NM **$27.00**

Walt Disney World, map, lg, Magic Kingdom, dated 1987, NM **$15.00**

Zorro, coloring book, 8½x11", Whitman, 1958, EX **$37.50**

Zorro, flashlight, 3¼x1" dia, colorful stickers on plastic w/metal chain, marked WDP, 1950s, EX...............**$52.50**

Dollhouse Furniture

Some of the mass-produced dollhouse furniture you're apt to see on the market today was made by Renwal and Acme during the forties and Ideal in the 1960s. All three of these companies used hard plastic for their furniture lines and imprinted most pieces with their names. Strombecker furniture was made of wood, and although it was not marked, it has a certain recognizable style to it. Remember that if you're lucky enough to find it complete in the original box, you'll want to preserve the carton as well.

Armchair, tin, pink paint **$22.50**
Bath scales, ivory, Renwal..**$7.50**
Bed, 3x6", tin, blue paint, w/mattress, Germany **$45.00**
Chair, bentwood w/upholstered seat **$17.50**
Chair, dining; Strombecker, set of 4, EX **$40.00**
Chair, slat back, green, Tootsietoy...............................**$10.00**
Couch, 11", wooden fold-out type w/green upholstery, Strombecker **$35.00**
Crib, 2x3½", blue w/colorful tin mattress & pillow **$45.00**
Fireplace, Petite Princess, EX.....................................**$20.00**
Grand piano & bench, Tootsietoy, red w/leopard print upholstery..**$65.00**
Grandfather clock, Petite Princess, missing folding screen, M in NM box **$30.00**
Highchair, painted cast iron, Kilgore.........................**$45.00**
Kitchen table, green, Strombecker, EX........................**$10.00**
Kitchen table & chair, Arcade, worn cream paint........**$85.00**

Medicine chest, wooden, door w/mirror, shelves inside, EX white paint **$30.00**
Piano, grand; tin, green paint, w/bench, sm...............**$45.00**

Piano & bench, Petite Princess **$20.00**
Potty chair, painted cast iron, Kilgore **$45.00**
Refrigerator, green, coil top, Tootsietoy, 1930s............**$40.00**
Rocker, brown w/tall back, Little Hostess, EX............**$12.50**
Rocker, Tootsietoy...**$18.00**
Sofa, Tootsietoy, green..**$17.50**
Step ladder, painted cast iron, Kilgore **$45.00**
Stove, My Pet, tin, 4 curved feet **$95.00**
Table, tin w/wire legs, 4 matching chairs, sm **$30.00**
Tricycle, red & yellow, Renwal.......................................**$7.50**

Dolls

Doll collecting is one of the most popular hobbies in the United States. Since many of the antique dolls are so expensive, even modern dolls have come into their own and can be had at prices within the range of most budgets. Today's thrift shop owners know the extent of 'doll mania,' though, so you'll seldom find a bargain there. But if you're willing to spend the time, garage sales can be a good source for your doll buying. Granted most will be in a 'well loved' condition, but as long as they're priced right, many can be redressed, rewigged, and cleaned up. Swap meets and flea markets may sometimes yield a good example or two, depending upon whether the dealer is a professional or someone just trying to peddle his 'junk.'

Modern dolls, those made from 1935 to the present, are made of rubber, composition, magic skin, synthetic rubber, and many types of plastic. Most of these materials do not stand up well to age, so be objective when you buy, especially if you're buying with an eye to the future. Doll repair is an art best left to professionals. But if yours is only dirty, you can probably do it yourself. If you need to clean a composition doll, do it very carefully. Use only baby oil and follow up with a soft dry cloth to remove any residue. Most types of wigs can be shampooed with wig shampoo and lukewarm water. Be careful not to matt the hair as you shampoo, and follow up with hair conditioner or fabric softener. Comb gently and set while wet, using small soft rubber or metal curlers. Never use a curling iron or heated rollers.

In our listings, unless a condition is noted in the descriptions, values are for dolls in excellent condition except for the Cabbage Patch dolls. Those are priced mint in box. (Even if a Cabbage Patch is in super condition but is without its original box, its value would be only about 25% of what we've listed here).

For further study, we recommend these books, all by Patricia Smith: *Patricia Smith's Doll Values, Antique to Modern; Modern Collector's Dolls* (five in the series), *Vogue Ginny Dolls, Through the Years with Ginny;* and *Madame Alexander Collector's Dolls.* Patikii Gibbs has written the book *Horsman Dolls, 1950 - 1970,* and Estelle Patino is the author of *American Rag Dolls, Straight from the Heart;* both contain a wealth of information on those particular subjects.

See also Liddle Kiddles; Barbie and Friends; Male Action Figures; Shirley Temple; and Toys.

Alexander, Argentine Girl, 8", hard plastic, jointed knees, Wendy Ann face, all original, 1965-72.................$450.00

Alexander, Betsy Ross, 8", hard plastic, jointed knees, Wendy Ann face, all original, 1967-72.................$125.00

Alexander, Betty Blue, 8", Storybook Series, straight legs, Maggie face, all original, 1987-88..........................$60.00

Alexander, Caroline, 14", vinyl, rooted blond hair, blue sleep eyes, open/closed mouth, all original, 1961........$400.00

Alexander, Cheerleader, 8", Americana Series, Wendy Ann face, all original, 1990.................................$55.00

Alexander, Christening Baby, 13", vinyl, molded hair, 1-piece stuffed body, sleep eyes, redressed, 1954.$125.00

Alexander, Cissette, 10", white dress w/red flowers, gold shoes, 1958.................................$250.00

Alexander, Flapper, 10", Portrette Series, Cissette face, 1988 to present................................$60.00

Alexander, German, 8", white face, all original, 1986 .$65.00

Alexander, Heidi, 14", Classic Series, plastic & vinyl, Mary Ann face, all original, 1969-88.................$65.00

Alexander, Iris, 10", hard plastic, Cissette face, all original, 1987-88 ....$60.00

Alexander, Jenny Lind, 14", plastic & vinyl, rooted blond hair, blue sleep eyes, all original, 1970 ....$450.00

Alexander, Kathy, 18", hard plastic, blond wig, blue sleep eyes, original bodysuit & skates, 1951.................$650.00

Alexander, Kathy Tears, 12", vinyl, new face, all original, 1960-61 ....$100.00

Alexander, Little Genius, 8", hard plastic & vinyl, nude, good face color, clean condition, 1956-62 ....$85.00

Alexander, Lucinda, 12", plastic & vinyl, Janie face, 1969-70 ....$450.00

Alexander, Maggie, 17", plastic & vinyl, rooted brown hair, blue sleep eyes, all original, 1966.................$450.00

Alexander, Mary Ann Ballerina, 14", plastic & vinyl, all original, 1973-82.................................$175.00

Alexander, Miss Muffett, 8", straight legs, marked Alex, all original, 1973-75.................................$60.00

Alexander, Paulette, 10", Portrette Series, Cissette face, all original, 1989 to present..............................$60.00

Alexander, Rebecca, 14", Classic Series, plastic & vinyl, Mary Ann face, pink tiered skirt, all original, 1968-69 .$225.00

Alexander, Snow Queen, 10", Portrette Series, Cissette face, all original, 1991.................................$60.00

Alexander, Sweet Tears, 14", vinyl, in trunk/trousseau, all original, 1967-74, minimum value $200.00

Alexander, Tommy Snooks, 8", Storybook Series, Wendy Ann face, all original, 1988-91...............................$55.00

Alexander, Welcome Home Desert Storm, 8", boy or girl soldier, all original, 1991, each $75.00

Alexander-Kins, Billy, 8", all original, 1957...............$400.00

Alexander-Kins, Wendy, 8", brown hair, blue sleep eyes, red polka-dot dress, all original, ca 1964...................$225.00

American Character, American Beauty, 22", hard plastic, blond saran hair, sleep eyes, all original, 1955...$385.00

American Character, Baby Lou, 8", plastic 1-piece head & body, molded hair, redressed, 1950...................$20.00

American Character, Baby Tiny Tears, 13½", hard plastic & rubber, molded hair, all original, 1950..............$125.00

American Character, Betsy McCall, 14", vinyl, rooted black hair, sleep eyes, high-heel feet, all original, 1961.$265.00

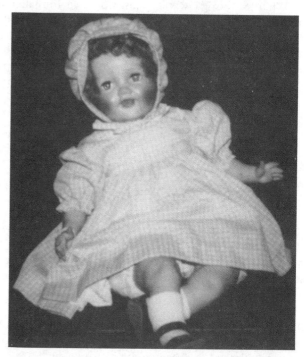

American Character, Chuckles, 24", cloth body, vinyl head & limbs, rooted hair, open mouth w/teeth...$85.00

American Character, Cricket, 9½", plastic & vinyl, rooted blond hair w/grow feature, painted blue eyes, all original.$30.00

American Character, Freckles, 13", plastic & vinyl, rooted blond hair, blue painted eyes, all original, 1966...$45.00

American Character, Groom, 20", hard plastic & vinyl, wool wig, Sweet Sue as a groom, partially redressed..$450.00

American Character, Hoss Cartright, 8", hard vinyl, molded-on clothes, painted hair & features, 1966..............$85.00

American Character, Margaret-Rose, 17", plastic & vinyl, rooted blond hair, sleep eyes, all original, 1966...$30.00

American Character, New Tiny Tears, 17", vinyl, rooted blond hair, sleep eyes, open mouth/nurser, redressed, 1961-64.....$60.00

American Character, Ricky Jr, 13", vinyl, 1-piece body, molded & painted hair, blue sleep eyes, redressed, 1955 ....$85.00

American Character, Sally Says, 19", plastic & vinyl, blond hair, sleep eyes, battery-operated talker, all original, 1964 ....**$95.00**

American Character, Sweet Sue, 17", vinyl, curly brown hair, dressed in original ski outfit, 1955 ....**$325.00**

American Character, Sweet Sue, 20", vinyl, curly brown hair, sleep eyes, all original, 1956, minimum value **$325.00**

American Character, Sweet Susanne, 17", hard plastic, blond wig, blue sleep eyes, all original, 1953 ....**$325.00**

American Character, Teeny Betsy McCall, 8", hard plastic, rooted hair, blue sleep eyes, all original, 1958, minimum value **$250.00**

American Character, Teeny Weeny Tiny Tears, 8½", vinyl, blond hair, sleep eyes, open mouth/nurser, all original, 1964 ....**$25.00**

American Character, Tony, 10½", vinyl, rooted brown hair, sleep eyes, all original, 1955 ....**$110.00**

American Character, Toodles, 22", vinyl, dark brown curly hair, brown flirty sleep eyes, nurser mouth, redressed, 1956 ....**$200.00**

American Character, Whimette, 7½", plastic & vinyl, rooted red hair, painted green eyes, nude, 1963 ....**$30.00**

Annalee, Candy Boy & Girl, 18", holding felt lollipops, 1984, each, M **$150.00**

Annalee, Little Baby, felt w/oil-painted features, flannel blanket, 1980s, minimum value **$90.00**

Annalee, monk w/ski, 9", synthetic fur beard, red clothes, green ski, ca 1970, minimum value **$90.00**

Annalee, mouse wearing diaper & holding baby bottle, late 1970s, minimum value **$95.00**

Annalee, 10", Go Go Girl, felt w/painted features, NM, minimum value **$115.00**

Annalee, 7", felt w/painted features, glued-on hair, felt clothes, original tag, ca 1984, minimum value **$115.00**

Applause, Raggedy Ann or Andy, 12", tag sewn in seam, 1981, M, each **$30.00**

Arranbee, Angeline, 18", hard plastic, mohair wig, sleep eyes, closed mouth, walker, all original, 1952 ....**$285.00**

Arranbee, Littlest Angel, 11", vinyl head, plastic jointed body, rooted hair, sleep eyes, all original, 1959 ....**$125.00**

Arranbee, Miss Cody, 10", hard plastic & vinyl, rooted brown hair, blue sleep eyes, high-heel feet, walker, all original **$125.00**

Arranbee, Nanette, 14", hard plastic, blond wig, sleep eyes, original sailor outfit, 1955, minimum value **$285.00**

Arranbee, Nanette, 17", vinyl, blond wig, in original ball gown & fur cape, 1953 ....**$285.00**

Arranbee, New Happytot, 16", vinyl, molded & painted brown hair, blue sleep eyes, redressed, 1955 ....**$45.00**

Arranbee, Peachy, 10", hard plastic, molded hair w/hole on left side for ribbon, 1-piece head & body, redressed, 1950 ....**$25.00**

Arranbee, Susan, 15", stuffed vinyl, brown wig, blue sleep eyes, toddler legs, all original, 1952 ....**$75.00**

Arranbee, Susan, 15", vinyl, glued-on brown wig, blue sleep eyes, toddler legs, all original, 1952 ....**$85.00**

Arrow Plastics, Baby Doo, 9", vinyl, molded hair, sleep eyes, open mouth/nurser, redressed, 1957 ....**$35.00**

Arrow Plastics, Bye-Bye Baby, 17", vinyl & latex, rooted blond hair, sleep eyes, redressed, 1957 ....**$45.00**

Arrow Plastics, Candy, 8", all vinyl w/molded hair & clothes, painted eyes, closed mouth, 1958 ....**$6.00**

Arrow Plastics, Pouty, 13", vinyl, molded & painted brown hair, blue sleep eyes, open/closed mouth, all original, 1958 ....**$30.00**

Baby Berry, Li'l Abner, 12", vinyl, molded & painted hair, painted features, all original, 1957 ....**$250.00**

Cabbage Patch, baldie w/freckles, 1983, MIB, from $100.00 up to **$125.00**

Cabbage Patch, Black baldie, 1983, MIB, from $100.00 up to **$125.00**

Cabbage Patch, Black boy or girl w/shaggy hair, 1983, MIB, from $125 up to **$125.00**

Cabbage Patch, Black boy w/shaggy hair & freckles, 1983, MIB **$600.00**

Cabbage Patch, Black w/pacifier, 1984, MIB, from $175.00 up to **$225.00**

Cabbage Patch, boy or girl w/no dimples, 1983, MIB, each, from $50.00 up to **$75.00**

Cabbage Patch, boy or girl w/popcorn hairdo, 1985, MIB, each, from $100.00 up to **$125.00**

Cabbage Patch, boy or girl w/1 dimple, lg eyes, 1983, MIB, each, from $50.00 up to **$75.00**

Cabbage Patch, boy or girl w/2 dimples & pacifier, 1983, MIB, each, from $50.00 up to..............................**$75.00**

Cabbage Patch, boy w/red shaggy hair & pacifier, 1983, MIB, from $400.00 up to **$500.00**

Cabbage Patch, boy w/tan shaggy hair & freckles, 1983, MIB **$150.00**

Cabbage Patch, girl w/blond loop ponytail & freckles, 1983, MIB **$150.00**

Cabbage Patch, girl w/brunette ponytail, single tooth, 1985, MIB, from $150.00 up to **$200.00**

Cabbage Patch, girl w/gold hair & freckles, 1985, MIB..**$75.00**

Cabbage Patch, girl w/gray eyes, 1985, MIB, $50.00 to ..**$75.00**

Cabbage Patch, girl w/single auburn ponytail & pacifier, 1983, MIB **$150.00**

Cabbage Patch, girl w/2 blond ponytails & freckles, 1983, MIB, from $175.00 up to **$300.00**

Cameo, Kewpie, 3½", vinyl, molded in sitting position w/elbows on knees, chin resting on hands, marked, 1971 ....**$15.00**

Cameo, Kewpie Doll, 7½", rubber, glass set eyes, squeaker in back, marks on feet....................................**$55.00**

Cameo, Kewpie Doll Beanbag, 10", vinyl w/filled cloth body, M **$45.00**

Cameo, Kewpie Gal, vinyl w/molded hair & glued-on ribbon, jointed neck, shoulders, & hips, marked S71 on neck, 1971 ....**$80.00**

Cameo, Miss Peep, 19", brown vinyl, inset brown eyes, all original, 1973..**$35.00**

Cameo, Ragsy Kewpie Re-Issue, 8", vinyl w/jointed neck, painted features, marked 065 JLK on head, Cameo 65 on body, 1971 ....**$60.00**

Cosmopolitan, Ginger, 7½", hard plastic, glued-on blond wig, blue sleep eyes, walker, all original, 1950s...**$35.00**

Cosmopolitan, Miss Ginger, 8½", vinyl, rooted blond hair, blue sleep eyes, closed mouth, all original, 1956 .**$45.00**

Cragstan, Trike Tike, 4½", plastic, pin-jointed hips & knees, rooted brown hair, painted eyes, all original........**$20.00**

Deluxe, Paula Marie, 24", vinyl, rooted blond hair, blue sleep eyes, marked VH-25, all original, 1959......**$100.00**

Deluxe, Sweet Rosemary, 29", vinyl, rooted blond hair, blue sleep eyes, high-heel feet, all original, 1957-59 ....**$95.00**

Deluxe Reading, Baby Boo, 21", plastic & vinyl, blond hair, blue sleep eyes, battery-operated cryer, redressed, 1965 ....**$40.00**

Deluxe Reading, Baby Magic, 18", plastic & vinyl, blond hair, sleep eyes, smiles & frowns, redressed, 1966........**$45.00**

Deluxe Reading, Penny Brite, 8", vinyl, rooted blond hair, painted eyes, all original, 1963............................**$30.00**

Deluxe Reading, Susie Homemaker, 21", plastic & vinyl, jointed hips & knees, sleep eyes, 5 teeth, all original, 1966 ....**$40.00**

Deluxe Topper, Baby Bunny, 20", plastic & vinyl, white hair, stationary eyes, waves arms & legs, redressed, 1969 ....**$40.00**

Deluxe Topper, Hot Canary, 7", vinyl, blond wig, painted features, all original, 1966....................................**$25.00**

Deluxe Topper, Tickles, 20", plastic & vinyl, blond hair, blue sleep eyes, battery-operated talker, redressed, 1963 ....**$40.00**

Deluxe Toys, Sweet Rosemary, 29", vinyl, rooted blond hair, blue sleep eyes, not jointed, all original, 1957-59.**$70.00**

Eegee, Andy, 12", plastic & vinyl, painted side-glancing eyes, all original (dressed as pilot), 1961 ....**$35.00**

Eegee, Babette, 23", vinyl & cloth, rooted white hair, painted features, 2 painted lower teeth, all original, 1969 ....**$20.00**

Eegee, Baby Susan, 10½", vinyl, molded hair, lg blue sleep eyes, open mouth/nurser, redressed, 1958 ....**$15.00**

Eegee, Chubby Schoolgirl, 10½", hard plastic & vinyl, rooted hair, blue sleep eyes, walker, redressed, 1957......**$15.00**

Eegee, Cuddlekins, 10", plastic & vinyl, molded hair, inset stationary blue eyes, open mouth/nurser, all original, 1970..**$8.00**

Eegee, Gemette, 15", plastic & vinyl, rooted brown hair, blue molded eyes, adult hands, all original, 1963..........**$45.00**

Eegee, Georgette, 22", vinyl & cloth, rooted orange hair, green sleep eyes, freckles, all original, 1971........**$55.00**

Eegee, Gigi Perreaux, 17", hard plastic & vinyl, brown hair, sleep eyes, open mouth w/teeth, original, 1951 ..**$600.00**

Eegee, Grace, 17", latex & vinyl, rooted blond hair, sleep eyes, unjointed, high-heel feet, all original, 1957 .**$50.00**

Eegee, Janie (also sold as Sherry), 8½", vinyl, rooted blond hair, blue sleep eyes, all original, 1956 ....**$20.00**

Eegee, Kid Sister, 9¼", plastic & vinyl, rooted ash blond hair, painted features, freckles, all original **$15.00**

Eegee, Mary Kay, 10½", plastic & vinyl, rooted blond hair, blue sleep eyes, open mouth/nurser, redressed **$5.00**

Eegee, Miss Debby, 14", vinyl, rooted long blond hair, blue sleep eyes, all original (as bride), 1958 ....**$30.00**

Eegee, Miss Flexie, 20", vinyl, rooted reddish hair, blue sleep eyes, open/closed mouth, all original, 1956 ....**$30.00**

Eegee, Miss Sunbeam, 17", plastic & vinyl, rooted hair, blue sleep eyes, painted teeth, dimples, all original.....**$50.00**

Eegee, Pix-I-Posie, 18", Dublon & vinyl, rooted blond hair, sleep eyes, open/closed mouth, redressed, 1966 .**$10.00**

Eegee, Play Pen Pal, 10½", vinyl, molded hair, painted features, open mouth/nurser, jointed hips, redressed, 1956 ....**$5.00**

Eegee, Playpen Baby, 14", plastic & vinyl, rooted blond hair, sleep eyes, nurser hole in mouth, all original, 1968..**$5.00**

Eegee, Posi-Playmate, 18", vinyl head & hands, all foam body, rooted white hair, molded eyes, all original, 1969..**$20.00**

Eegee, Robert, 21", latex & vinyl, molded & painted hair, blue sleep eyes, jointed arms, all original, 1956 ...**$60.00**

Eegee, Shelly, 12", plastic & vinyl, rooted blond hair w/grow feature, blue painted eyes, all original, 1964 ....**$15.00**

Eegee, Tandy Talks, 21", plastic & vinyl, rooted blond hair, blue eyes, pull-string talker, all original, 1961 ......**$75.00**

Eegee, Terri Talks, 19½", plastic & vinyl, blond hair, sleep eyes, battery-operated walker, all original, 1965 ..**$20.00**

Effanbee, Allyssia, 20", hard plastic & vinyl, walker, all original, 1958 ....**$285.00**

Effanbee, Baby Cuddleup, 20", vinyl & vinyl-coated cloth, all original, 1953...**$95.00**

Effanbee, Candy Twins, 11", vinyl, molded & painted hair, blue stationary eyes, all original, 1954, pr.............**$85.00**

Effanbee, character type, 8", composition, jointed, painted features & hair, chubby face, all original **$235.00**

Effanbee, Formal Honey, 27", composition, glued-on blond wig, blue sleep eyes, all original, 1949 ....**$500.00**

Effanbee, Gumdrop, 15", plastic & vinyl, all original, ca 1962 ....**$45.00**

Effanbee, Happy Boy, 10", vinyl, molded hair, closed painted eyes, freckles, redressed, 1960 ....**$60.00**

Effanbee, Honey, 21", composition & hard rubber, human hair wig, blue flirty sleep eyes, all original (missing her hat)...**$485.00**

Effanbee, Honey Bun, 17", vinyl & cloth, rooted blond hair, sleep eyes, extended fingers, redressed, 1967 ......**$20.00**

Effanbee, Honey Walker, 14", hard plastic, brown hair, blue sleep eyes, all original, 1953 ....**$300.00**

Effanbee, Little Lady, 18", composition, original wig, sleep eyes, original bridal clothes **$400.00**

Effanbee, Little Lady, 18", composition, red human hair wig, sleep eyes, closed mouth, redressed, 1941 ....**$295.00**

Effanbee, Mommy's Baby, 27", plastic & cloth, blue sleep eyes, swivel neck, 2 upper teeth, felt tongue, redressed, 1952 ....**$65.00**

Effanbee, My Fair Baby, 12", vinyl, molded hair, sleep eyes, open mouth/nurser, toddler legs, redressed, 1968.**$25.00**

Effanbee, My Precious Baby, 20", vinyl & cloth, blond hair, blue sleep eyes, cryer, all original, 1960 ....**$30.00**

Effanbee, Peaches, 15", vinyl & cloth, rooted blond hair, blue sleep eyes, dimples, redressed, 1965 ....**$50.00**

Effanbee, Portrait Doll, 12", composition, auburn mohair wig, blue sleep eyes, fully jointed, all original ...**$245.00**

Effanbee, Precious New Born, 14", vinyl & cloth, rooted white hair, blue painted eyes, all original, 1962 ...**$35.00**

Effanbee, Skippy, wood composition (EX $85), NM.$125.00

Effanbee, Sugar Plum, 16", vinyl & cloth, rooted brown hair, blue sleep eyes, all original, 1969.........................**$35.00**

Effanbee, Sugar Plum, 18", vinyl & cloth, rooted brown hair, blue sleep eyes, original dress, 1964 ....**$35.00**

Effanbee, Susie Sunshine, 18", rooted brown hair, blue sleep eyes, original clothes, 1966 ....**$75.00**

Effanbee, Suzanne, 13½", composition, blond human hair wig, sleep eyes, closed mouth, all original **$265.00**

Effanbee, Tiny Tubber, 10", vinyl, rooted blond hair, blue sleep eyes, open mouth/nurser, redressed, 1968 ....**$25.00**

Effanbee, Twinkie, 15", vinyl, molded hair, blue sleep eyes, open mouth/nurser, redressed, 1959 ....**$25.00**

Effanbee, Twinkie, 18", vinyl & cloth, rooted white hair, blue sleep eyes, cryer, all original **$50.00**

Fisher-Price, Audrey, 14", vinyl & cloth, rooted red hair, blue painted eyes, freckles, all original, 1973 ....**$20.00**

Fisher-Price, Baby Ann, 14", vinyl & cloth, rooted blond hair, painted brown eyes, all original, 1973 ....**$20.00**

Fisher-Price, Elizabeth, 14", brown vinyl & cloth, rooted black hair, brown painted eyes, all original, 1973 ....**$25.00**

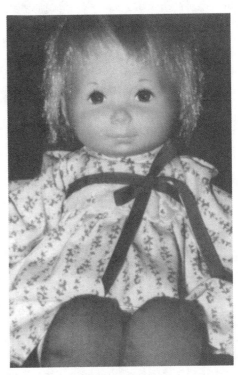

Fisher-Price, 14", Baby Ann, cloth & vinyl w/rooted blond hair, painted brown eyes, marked 60/188460/1973 on head $20.00

Half doll, Germany, 12", arms & hands completely away from body, minimum value.................................**$900.00**

Half doll, Germany, 3", arms & hands completely away from body, minimum value...**$125.00**

Half doll, Germany, 3", arms & hands attached to body, common type, minimum value **$30.00**

Half doll, Germany, 3", arms extended, hands attached to body, minimum value...**$65.00**

Half doll, Germany, 5", arms & hands attached to body, common type, minimum value **$40.00**

Half doll, Germany, 5", arms & hands completely away from body, minimum value......................................**$250.00**

Half doll, Germany, 5", arms extended, hands attached to body, minimum value...**$75.00**

Half doll, Germany, 8", arms & hands attached to body, common type, minimum value **$55.00**

Half doll, Germany, 8", arms & hands completely away from body, minimum value...$425.00

Half doll, Germany, 8", arms extended, hands attached, minimum value...$95.00

Half doll, Japan mark, 3", minimum value..................$20.00

Half doll, Japan mark, 5", minimum value..................$30.00

Half doll, Japan mark, 8", minimum value..................$50.00

Hasbro, Aimee, 18", plastic & vinyl, jointed waist, brown sleep eyes, all original w/jewelry, 1972.............$75.00

Hasbro, Baby Ruth, 10½", vinyl w/beanbag body, painted features, all original, 1971....................................$10.00

Hasbro, Leggy Nan, 10", vinyl, brown hair up in lg curls, original halter & bell-bottom pants, 1972.............$20.00

Hasbro, Love, 9", vinyl, long blond hair, original nickers outfit, 1971..$15.00

Hasbro, Sunday, 4¼", hard & soft vinyl, painted eyes, socks, shoes & gloves, all original, 1965 ....$12.00

Hong Kong, Heidi, 8", plastic & vinyl, rooted hair, painted eyes, all original, 1973 ....$8.00

Hong Kong, Pixie, 7", vinyl, rooted brown hair, painted features, jointed arms & legs, striped sleeper, 1965.....$8.00

Horsman, Anthony Pipsqueak, 12", plastic & vinyl, rooted brown hair, painted features, redressed $25.00

Horsman, Baby Precious, 17", vinyl & cloth, rooted blond hair, blue sleep eyes, cryer, redressed, 1967.........$20.00

Horsman, Baby Tweaks, 20", vinyl & cloth, blond hair, stationary eyes, squeakers in legs, all original, 1967.$45.00

Horsman, Betty Ann, hard plastic & cloth, stapled-on mohair wig, blue sleep eyes, black eyeshadow, all original, 1951 ....$35.00

Horsman, Chubby Baby, 20", vinyl, rooted blond hair, blue sleep eyes, jointed arms, redressed, 1954 ....$15.00

Horsman, Cinderella, 11½", plastic & vinyl, blue eyes painted to side, all original, 1965............................$45.00

Horsman, Cindy, 15", hard plastic, blond hair, head turns, sleep eyes, walker, original, 1953, minimum value........$185.00

Horsman, Floppy, 18", foam body & legs, rooted blond hair, blue sleep eyes, dimples, all original, 1965...........$30.00

Horsman, Grow Up Miss (called Sub-Teen Beauty), 18", vinyl, rooted black hair, blue sleep eyes, all original, 1962 ....$30.00

Horsman, Life Size Baby, 26", latex & vinyl, blue sleep eyes, open/closed mouth w/tongue, all original, 1953..$75.00

Horsman, Marc Pipsqueak, 12", plastic & vinyl, red hair, blue painted eyes, freckles, redressed, 1967.........$25.00

Horsman, Molly, 16", plastic & vinyl, brown rooted hair, blue sleep eyes, posable head, original clothes (shoes missing) $25.00

Horsman, New Baby Tweaks, 19", vinyl & cloth, rooted white hair, blue painted eyes, open/closed mouth, all original...$25.00

Horsman, Peggy, 25", vinyl, rooted light brown hair, sleep eyes, jointed arms, straight legs, all original, 1957..$95.00

Horsman, Penny Penpal, 18", plastic & vinyl, blond hair, painted eyes, fully jointed, holds pencil, all original, 1970 ....$35.00

Horsman, Perfume Pixie, 3", vinyl, rooted white hair, blue painted eyes, all original $10.00

Horsman, Pippi Longstocking, 18", vinyl & cloth, orange hair, painted features, freckles & dimples, all original, 1972 ....$45.00

Horsman, Renee Ballerina, 18", stuffed vinyl, rooted hair, blue sleep eyes, high-heel feet, all original...........$45.00

Horsman, Sleepy Baby, 24", vinyl & cloth, rooted dark blond hair, closed sleeping eyes, tag on body, all original, 1965 ....$50.00

Horsman, Softy Skin, 16", Dublon & vinyl, rooted white hair, blue sleep eyes, all original, 1971.........................$10.00

Horsman, Teensie Baby, 12", plastic & vinyl, blue painted eyes, dimples, nurser, all original, 1964 ....$9.00

Horsman, Thirstee Baby, 18", plastic, rooted light brown hair, blue sleep eyes, open mouth/nurser, all original, 1963 ....$15.00

Horsman, Tiny Baby, 6", vinyl, rooted dark blond hair, blue stationary eyes, open/closed mouth, all original ..$12.00

Horsman, Twin Tot, 11", plastic & vinyl, rooted blond hair, blue sleep eyes, nurser, original dress, 1963........$10.00

Horsman, Twin Tot, 11", plastic & vinyl, rooted blond hair, blue sleep eyes, nurser, baby legs, original dress $10.00

Horsman, Tynie Toddler, 15", plastic & vinyl, rooted blond hair, blue sleep eyes, redressed, 1964...................$10.00

Horsman, Wee Bonnie Baby, 11", plastic & vinyl, rooted hair, black eyes (no pupils), redressed, 1963........$10.00

Horsman, Yvonne Lullabye Baby, 12", plastic & vinyl, molded hair, blue stationary eyes, nurser, music box, redressed $10.00

Ideal, April Showers, 14", plastic & vinyl, battery operated, all original, 1968..$32.00

Ideal, Baby Belly Button, 9", plastic & vinyl, rooted blond hair, painted eyes, redressed, 1970.....................$25.00

Ideal, Baby Gurglee/Tousle Head, 19", plastic & latex, wig over molded hair, sleep eyes, coo voice, all original, 1951 ....$40.00

Ideal, Baby Herman, 9", plastic & vinyl, molded hair, painted features, all original, 1965.........................$35.00

Ideal, Baby Snookie, 9½", latex body, vinyl head w/molded hair, blue painted eyes, original diaper, 1950.......$15.00

Ideal, Betsy Wetsy, 13", plastic & vinyl, molded hair, blue sleep eyes, tear ducts, coo/nurser mouth, all original, 1955 ....$75.00

Ideal, Betsy Wetsy, 23", vinyl, rooted light brown hair, blue sleep eyes, open mouth/nurser, redressed, 1959..$35.00

Ideal, Bonnie Braids, 13", hard plastic & vinyl, saran braids pulled through holes in head, all original, 1951 ...$60.00

Ideal, Bonnie Walker, 23", hard plastic, pin-jointed hips, open mouth, flirty eyes, redressed........................$50.00

Ideal, Brandi, 18", plastic & vinyl, rooted blond hair w/grow feature, painted eyes, swivel waist, all original.....$80.00

Ideal, Busy Lizzy, 17", plastic & vinyl, rooted hair, blue sleep eyes, plug in (in back), all original, 1970....$40.00

Ideal, Bye Bye Baby, 12", vinyl, redressed...................$55.00

Ideal, Cinnamon, 12", plastic & vinyl, red hair w/grow feature, blue painted eyes, original clothes, 1971......$70.00

Ideal, Cream Puff, 18", vinyl, rooted reddish hair, blue sleep eyes, crossed baby legs, all original, 1961............$50.00

Ideal, Cricket, 15½", plastic & vinyl, red hair 'grows,' sleep eyes, jointed waist, original clothes, 1970 ....**$60.00**

Ideal, Cuddly Kissy, 17", vinyl & cloth, puckers up when stomach is pressed, all original, 1964 ....**$60.00**

Ideal, Dew Drop, 20", plastic & vinyl, brown hair, blue sleep eyes, open mouth/nurser, cries tears, all original, 1961 ....**$30.00**

Ideal, Dina, 15", plastic & vinyl, rooted blond hair w/grow feature, painted eyes, all original, 1971 ....**$90.00**

Ideal, Dodi, 9", plastic & vinyl, rooted blond hair, blue painted eyes, all original, 1964................................**$40.00**

Ideal, Giggles, 17", brown plastic & vinyl, rooted black hair, flirty eyes, painted teeth, all original, 1967 ....**$150.00**

Ideal, In a Minute Thumbelina, 10", vinyl & cloth, molded-on shoes & socks, blond hair, painted eyes, pull string, 1970 ....**$18.00**

Ideal, Jiminy Cricket, 9", composition & wood, all original, 1939-40, M..**$300.00**

Ideal, Joan Palooka, 14", vinyl & latex, molded blond hair w/saran tuft on top, sleep eyes, all original, 1952..**$75.00**

Ideal, Lazy Dazy, 12", vinyl & cloth, rooted blond hair, blue sleep eyes, closed mouth, all original, 1971..........**$20.00**

Ideal, Little Miss Revlon, 10½", plastic & vinyl, blond hair, blue sleep eyes, jointed waist, all original, 1957...**$95.00**

Ideal, Look Around Crissy, plastic & vinyl, rooted red hair w/grow feature, brown painted eyes, all original.**$60.00**

Ideal, Look Around Velvet, 15½", plastic & vinyl, hair w/grow feature, violet sleep eyes, pull string, all original **$70.00**

Ideal, Lovely Liz (also called Jackie), 16", plastic & vinyl, blond rooted hair, sleep eyes, all original, 1961...**$60.00**

Ideal, Magic Lips, 24", vinyl w/vinyl-coated cloth body, blond hair, sleep eyes, 3 teeth, all original, 1955 ....**$95.00**

Ideal, Mia, 15½", plastic & vinyl, rooted brown hair w/grow feature, blue sleep eyes, all original, 1970 ....**$80.00**

Ideal, Miss Clairol Glamour Misty, 12", plastic & vinyl, rooted hair, painted eyes, high-heel feet, all original, 1965 ....**$65.00**

Ideal, Miss Curity, 14", hard plastic, blue sleep eyes, original dress, 1950s..**$350.00**

Ideal, Miss Revlon, 18", plastic & vinyl, dressed in Cherries ala Mode outfit, 1955 ....**$95.00**

Ideal, Mitzi, plastic & vinyl, rooted reddish-brown hair, blue painted eyes, redressed, 1970 ....**$85.00**

Ideal, New Tiny Tears, 13", vinyl, rooted hair, inset eyes, nurser mouth, cries tears, w/diaper & bottle **$20.00**

Ideal, Newborn Thumbelina, 10½", vinyl & cloth, blond hair/painted eyes, pull string & she squirms, all original, 1967 ....**$15.00**

Ideal, Patty, 9", plastic & vinyl, rooted brown hair, blue painted eyes, all original **$15.00**

Ideal, Patty Petite, 19", vinyl, rooted dark brown hair, blue sleep eyes, posable head, all original....................**$75.00**

Ideal, Patty Playpal, 36", plastic & vinyl, rooted blond hair, blue sleep eyes, redressed **$285.00**

Ideal, Pebbles, 12", vinyl & plastic, rooted blond hair, painted eyes, all original, 1963.................................**$30.00**

Ideal, Pebbles, 8", plastic & vinyl, rooted hair, painted eyes, all original, 1963...**$20.00**

Ideal, Pixie, 16", vinyl w/1-piece foam body, gauntlet hands, red hair, blue painted eyes, all original, 1967.......**$20.00**

Ideal, Pos'n Pete, 7½", plastic & vinyl, molded brown hair, brown painted eyes, freckles, nude, 1964.............**$35.00**

Ideal, Posie, 23", hard plastic & vinyl, rooted brown hair, blue sleep eyes, nearly all original **$145.00**

Ideal, Posie, 23", plastic & vinyl, rooted brown hair, blue sleep eyes, original dress **$145.00**

Ideal, Princess Mary, 17", hard plastic & vinyl, rooted blond hair, sleep eyes, cryer in tummy, all original, 1954.**$150.00**

Ideal, Real Live Lucy, 20", vinyl, rooted white hair, blue sleep eyes, bobbing head, original dress, 1965 ....**$40.00**

Ideal, Rock Baby Coos, 21", vinyl & cloth, rooted blond hair, blue sleep eyes, yawning, all original, 1962..**$15.00**

Ideal, Samantha the Witch, 12", plastic & vinyl, rooted white hair, green painted eyes, original dress, 1965.......**$85.00**

Ideal, Sara Ann, 12", hard plastic, glued-on blond saran wig, blue sleep eyes, not a walker, all original, minimum value **$400.00**

Ideal, Saucy Walker, 22", hard plastic, mohair wig, blue sleep eyes, 2 teeth, felt tongue, Mama cryer, all original, 1953 ....**$185.00**

Ideal, Spinderella Flatsy, 5", vinyl, rooted blond hair, painted features, posable, pull-string, 1969..........**$15.00**

Ideal, Suzy Playpal, 24", vinyl, rooted blond hair, all orignal, 1960 ....**$175.00**

Ideal, Tabatha, 15", vinyl & cloth, rooted blond hair, painted eyes, open/closed mouth, all original, 1966 ....**$65.00**

Ideal, Talking Goody Two Shoes, 27", plastic & vinyl, sleep eyes, lg feet, battery operated, all original..........**$200.00**

Ideal, Tammy, 12", vinyl, rooted blond hair, painted eyes, closed mouth, high-heel feet, all original, 1962....**$50.00**

Ideal, Tara, 16, brown plastic & vinyl, black hair w/grow feature, brown painted eyes, all original, 1970.....**$50.00**

Ideal, Tearful Thumbelina, 15", vinyl w/stuffed vinyl body, sleep eyes, cries tears, redressed, 1966 ....**$30.00**

Ideal, Tubbsy, 18", plastic & vinyl, blond hair, painted eyes, battery operated, hands splash, head bobs, redressed, 1966 ....**$40.00**

Ideal, Upsy-Dazy, 15", vinyl head, foam body, rooted hair, painted features, non-removable clothes, 1972.....**$20.00**

Ideal, Velvet, plastic & vinyl, rooted blond hair w/grow feature, lavender sleep eyes, all original, 1969 ....**$60.00**

Imperial Crown, Baby Perry, 14", hard plastic & latex, caracul wig, sleep eyes, felt tongue, 1951, all original.........**$15.00**

Imperial Toy Corp, Pan Am Air Hostess, 5", plastic & vinyl, rooted hair, painted features, all original, 1971.......**$6.00**

Jolly Toys, Cutie, 14", vinyl, rooted hair in ponytails, sleep eyes, open hands, stubby legs, redressed, 1965 ...**$20.00**

Jolly Toys, Cutie Pie, 11", plastic & vinyl, rooted blond hair, black sleep eyes, toddler legs, all original, 1967...**$12.00**

Jolly Toys, Jolly Doll, 11", plastic & vinyl, blond hair, painted eyes, molded teeth, all original, 1967, MIB............**$10.00**

Jolly Toys, Kimberly, 14", plastic & vinyl, rooted blond hair, blue painted eyes, all original, 1972 ....**$8.00**

Jolly Toys, Little Love, 14", plastic & vinyl, rooted blond hair, blue sleep eyes, all original, 1962 ....**$10.00**

Jolly Toys, Lovely Lisa, 15", vinyl & cloth, rooted white hair, blue sleep eyes, all original, 1962 ....**$5.00**

Jolly Toys, Miss Grow-Up, 12", plastic & vinyl, rooted blond hair, inset stationary eyes, all original, 1963............**$5.00**

Jolly Toys, Mommy's Baby, 19", vinyl & cloth, rooted blond hair, blue sleep eyes, all original, 1969 ....**$10.00**

Jolly Toys, Trudy, 13", plastic & vinyl, rooted blond hair, blue sleep eyes, closed mouth, all original, 1962 .**$15.00**

Jolly Toys, Twistee, 16", vinyl w/molded foam body, rooted dark hair, black sleep eyes, closed mouth, all original, 1964 ....**$25.00**

Kay Sam, Barbara, 17", plastic & vinyl, rooted white hair, blue sleep eyes, dimples, all original, 1963...........**$10.00**

Kay Sam, Carol Channing, 24", plastic & vinyl, blue sleep eyes w/blue eyeshadow, all original, 1961 ....**$120.00**

Kay Sam, Catherine, 20", plastic & vinyl, rooted brown hair, blue sleep eyes, high-heel feet, all original, 1961.**$75.00**

Kay Sam, Gigi (Juliet Prowse), 15", plastic & vinyl, rooted blond hair, blue sleep eyes, all original, 1961 ....**$120.00**

Kay Sam, Miss Sweet, 14", plastic & vinyl, rooted white hair, sleep eyes, open mouth/nurser, all original, 1963 ....**$10.00**

Kay Sam, Patty Girl, 13", vinyl, molded hair, panties, shoes, & socks, nude, 1955...**$6.00**

Kenner, Blythe, 11½", plastic & vinyl, rooted blond hair, jointed waist, pull string causes eye changes, all original..**$45.00**

Kenner, Charlie Chaplin, 14", all cloth, w/walking mechanism, all original, 1973...**$75.00**

Kenner, Crumpet, 18", plastic & vinyl, blond hair, sleep eyes, jointed wrists & waist, battery & pull string, all original..**$40.00**

Kenner, Gabbigale, 18", plastic & vinyl, blond hair, painted eyes, battery & pull string, all original, 1972........**$45.00**

Kenner, Meadow, 7", vinyl, rooted brown hair, brown painted eyes, right arm holds watering can, all original, 1972 ....**$15.00**

Kenner, Sippin' Bam Bam, 6", vinyl, jointed neck & shoulders, hole in mouth for straw, Hong Kong, 1972 .**$12.00**

Kenner, Strawberry Shortcake, sleep eyes, all original..**$25.00**

Knickerbocker, Hansel, 17", cloth, painted features, sewn-on mohair wig & clothes, wool dust filler, 1969 ....**$5.00**

Knickerbocker, I Dream of Jeannie (Barbara Eden), 20", plastic & vinyl, blond hair, blue sleep eyes, all original, 1966 ....**$95.00**

Knickerbocker, Levi Rag Doll, 15", all cloth, M **$20.00**

Knickerbocker, Multi-Face, 12", cloth w/vinyl heads, topsy-turvy type, yarn hair, painted features, 1962........**$10.00**

Knickerbocker, Raggedy Ann or Andy, 12", red yarn hair, printed features, tag in seam, all original, each ..**$165.00**

Knickerbocker, Raggedy Ann or Andy, 16", all original, 1950s, each...**$225.00**

Knickerbocker, Soupy Sales, 13", vinyl & cloth, non-removable clothes, M...**$145.00**

Knickerbocker, Talking Raggedy Ann or Andy, 12", all original, 1974, each **$45.00**

Lorrie, Baby, 10", plastic & vinyl, molded hair, blue sleep eyes, nurser, Eugene Doll & Novelty Co, redressed, 1963..**$8.00**

Lorrie, Bonnie Jean, 14", plastic & vinyl, rooted blond hair, sleep eyes, nurser, toddler legs, all original, 1961 ..**$7.00**

Lorrie, Cuddly Infant, 14", vinyl & cloth, molded hair, blue sleep eyes, Made by Eugene, redressed, 1963......**$10.00**

Lorrie, Debbie Trix, 15", brown plastic & vinyl, original wig (came w/3), sleep eyes, dimpled chin, redressed...**$8.00**

Lorrie, Louise, 12", brown vinyl & plastic, black hair, brown sleep eyes, nurser, Eugene Doll & Novelty, redressed, 1964..**$9.00**

Lorrie, Mary Jane, 11½", plastic & vinyl, rooted blond hair, blue sleep eyes, palms down, redressed **$5.00**

Lorrie, My Baby, 19", plastic & cloth, rooted blond hair, sleep eyes, fingers curled on left hand, redressed, 1960 ....**$10.00**

Lorrie, Pretty, 19", plastic & vinyl, rooted red hair, blue sleep eyes, all original, 1966 ....**$12.00**

Lorrie, Sweet Candy, 19", plastic & vinyl, rooted blond hair, blue sleep eyes, baby legs, all original, 1964..........**$7.00**

Majestic, Jack & Jill, 12", stuffed oilcloth w/painted features, marked 1950, each...**$9.00**

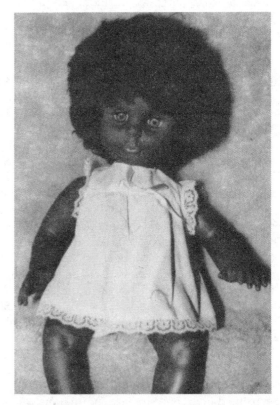

Marx, First Love, 17", Black version w/brown sleep eyes & black rooted hair, 1978-79 ....$30.00

Marx, Miss Toddler, 21", plastic, molded hair & clothes, paper eyes, battery-operated walker, rollers on feet, 1965 ....**$70.00**

Mattel, Baby Beans, 11", beanbag body, arms & legs, vinyl head w/1 row of rooted hair, sewn-on clothes....**$20.00**

Mattel, Baby Beans, 11", vinyl w/beanbag body, blond bangs, blue painted eyes, sewn-on clothes, 1971.**$18.00**

Mattel, Baby Colleen, vinyl & cloth, rooted orange hair, blue painted eyes, pull-string talker, all original, minimum value **$30.00**

Mattel, Baby First Step, 18", plastic & vinyl, blond hair, sleep eyes, battery-operated walker, redressed, 1964 ....**$35.00**

Mattel, Baby Fun, 8", vinyl, rooted blond hair, painted eyes, blows air from mouth, all original, 1968 ....**$20.00**

Mattel, Baby Go Bye Bye, 10", plastic & vinyl, rooted white hair, blue painted eyes, redressed, 1968 ....**$25.00**

Mattel, Baby Love Light, 16", vinyl & cloth, blond hair, blue painted eyes, battery-operated, all original, 1971 .**$40.00**

Mattel, Baby Pattaburp, 13", vinyl & cloth, rooted red hair, sleep eyes, pat on back to burp, redressed, 1963 .**$40.00**

Mattel, Baby Secret, 18", vinyl w/foam body, red hair, blue painted eyes, pull-string talker, all original, 1965 .**$45.00**

Mattel, Baby Tenderlove, 15", 1-piece Dublon foam, painted eyes, open mouth nurser, all original, 1969 ....**$15.00**

Mattel, Baby Walk 'N Play, 11", plastic & vinyl, rooted blond hair, painted eyes, battery operated, all original...**$30.00**

Mattel, Baby's Hungry, 17", plastic & vinyl, blond hair, blue eyes, battery operated, all original, 1966..............**$30.00**

Mattel, Big Jack, 9½", plastic & vinyl, molded & painted hair, painted eyes, fully jointed, all original, 1971........**$75.00**

Mattel, Black Dancerina, 24", brown plastic & vinyl, rooted black hair, painted eyes, all original, 1968...........**$85.00**

Mattel, Bouncy Baby, 11", plastic & vinyl, rooted hair, painted eyes & teeth, spring action, all original, 1968........**$15.00**

Mattel, Chatty Cathy, 20", plastic & vinyl, rooted brown hair, brown sleep eyes, open hands, all original, 1960.**$85.00**

Mattel, Cynthia, 20", plastic & vinyl, rooted hair, painted eyes, battery operated, w/records, all original......**$45.00**

Mattel, Dr Doolittle, 6", vinyl, molded hair, painted features, all original, 1967..**$25.00**

Mattel, Drowsy, 15", vinyl & cloth, rooted blond hair, blue painted eyes, pull-string talker, redressed, 1966...**$25.00**

Mattel, Lilac Rockflower, 6½", vinyl, rooted red hair, brown painted eyes, all original, 1970, minimum value ..**$30.00**

Mattel, Living Baby Tenderlove, 20", 1-piece Dublon body & head, jointed at shoulders & hips, painted eyes, all original **$20.00**

Mattel, Randy Reader, 19", plastic & vinyl, white hair, blue eyes, hands are curled, battery operated, redressed, 1967 ....**$40.00**

Mattel, Saucy, 16", plastic & vinyl, blond hair, rotating arm causes eyes & mouth to move, all original, 1972 .**$65.00**

Mattel, Shoppin' Sheryl, 14½", plastic & vinyl, rooted hair, painted eyes, magnet in right palm, all original ...**$35.00**

Mattel, Sister Belle, 17", plastic & cloth, yellow yarn hair, painted eyes, pull string talker, all original, 1961 .**$35.00**

Mattel, Sister Small Talk, 10", plastic & vinyl, rooted blond-hair, painted eyes & teeth, all original, 1967........**$25.00**

Mattel, Sister Small Walk, 11½", plastic & vinyl, rooted hair, painted eyes, battery-operated walker, all original **$25.00**

Mattel, Small Talk Cinderella, 11", plastic & vinyl, rooted brown hair, painted eyes, all original, 1967.........**$35.00**

Mattel, Sweet 16, 11½", vinyl & plastic, blond hair, painted eyes, non-bendable legs, all original, 1975 ....**$85.00**

Mattel, Talking Baby First Step, 18", plastic & vinyl, painted eyes, battery operated, all original, 1964..............**$45.00**

Mattel, Talking Baby Tenderlove, 16", vinyl, 1-piece Dublon body, rooted hair, pull-string talker, all original ...**$30.00**

Mattel, Tiny Baby Tenderlove, 11½", 1-piece molded Dublon, glued-on blond wig, blue painted eyes, all original..**$35.00**

Mattel, Tiny Cheerful-Tearful, 6½", vinyl, white hair, painted eyes, press stomach, face changes, redressed, 1966.**$25.00**

Mattel, Tutti, 6", vinyl, rooted brown hair, blue painted eyes, original clothes (apron missing), 1965..................**$65.00**

Mattel, Wet Noodles, 3½", vinyl, rooted orange hair, painted eyes, all original, 1969 ....**$15.00**

Mattel, 6", Chris, vinyl, 1-piece body, rooted brown hair, blue painted eyes, original dress, 1966 ....**$60.00**

Mego, Camelot figure, 8", 5 in series, all original, 1974, each **$20.00**

Mego, Dina Mite, 7½", plastic & vinyl, rooted hair, all original, 1973 ....**$20.00**

Mego, Laine, 19", jointed waist, battery operated, all original, 1973 ....**$50.00**

Mego, Ms Fashion, 24", plastic & vinyl, rooted white hair, stationary eyes, jointed waist, all original, 1973....**$40.00**

Mego, Planet of Apes character, 8", 5 in series, all original, 1974-75, each **$15.00**

Mego, Tanya, 11", plastic & vinyl, rooted hair, painted eyes, dimples, jointed waist, original swimsuit, 1972.....**$20.00**

Mollye, Airline Doll, 14", hard plastic, redressed.......**$100.00**

Mollye, baby, 14", hard plastic, redressed...................**$65.00**

Mollye, baby, 15", composition, redressed...................**$65.00**

Mollye, baby, 15", vinyl, all original **$35.00**

Mollye, baby, 8½", vinyl, all original **$15.00**

Mollye, Baby Joan, 21", plastic, cloth & latex, blond hair, sleep eyes, 2 teeth, all original, minimum value ..**$165.00**

Mollye, bride, 23", hard plastic, red saran wig, sleep eyes, teeth, felt tongue, all original, minimum value ...**$350.00**

Mollye, Business Girl, 17", hard plastic, blond wig, blue sleep eyes, all original, 1952, minimum value **$250.00**

Mollye, child, 15", cloth, redressed.............................**$65.00**

Mollye, child, 8", vinyl, redressed **$10.00**

Mollye, Dancing Deb, 19", plastic & vinyl, glued-on wig, music box base, all original, minimum value **$300.00**

Mollye, Lone Ranger, 22", all original........................**$200.00**

Mollye, Martha Washington, 9", hard plastic, white mohair wig, hand-painted features, all original................**$15.00**

Mollye, Olivie DeHaviland as Melanie, 19", plastic & vinyl, sleep eyes, all original, minimum value..............**$400.00**

Mollye, Polly Ann, 36", plastic & vinyl, rooted white hair, sleep eyes, all original, 1961, minimum value **$100.00**

Mollye, Raggedy Ann or Andy, 15", red yarn hair, printed features, multicolored socks, blue shoes, all original, minimum value **$700.00**

Mollye, Spanish Lady, 15", plastic & vinyl, sleep eyes, slight smile, all original..**$35.00**

Mollye, toddler, 15", composition, all original **$175.00**

Remco, Baby Crawlalong, 20", plastic & vinyl, blond hair, blue sleep eyes, head mounted on ball socket, redressed, 1967 ....**$20.00**

Remco, Baby Grow-A-Tooth, 14", all original, 1969....**$30.00**

Remco, Baby Know-It-All, 17", redressed, 1969...........**$15.00**

Remco, Baby Stroll-A-Long, 15", plastic & vinyl, white hair, sleep eyes, battery operated, all original, 1966....**$20.00**

Remco, Black Jumpsy, 14", all original..........................**$22.00**

Remco, Dr John of Littlechap Family, 14½", redressed, 1963 ....**$20.00**

Remco, Gingersnap, 18", brown plastic & vinyl, curly hair, brown painted eyes, all original **$50.00**

Remco, Heidi, 5½", vinyl, rooted white hair, black painted eyes, button makes arm raise, all original, 1965 ...**$15.00**

Remco, Hildy, 4¾", vinyl, blond hair, painted eyes, all original, 1966 ....**$20.00**

Remco, Hug-a-Bug, 3½", green vinyl, painted clothes & features, plastic clip on back, 1971.............................**$6.00**

Remco, Laurie Partridge, 19", plastic & vinyl, long light brown hair, blue painted eyes, all original, 1973..**$75.00**

Remco, LBJ, 5½", vinyl, molded-on clothes, painted features, removable hat, 1964..**$40.00**

Remco, Linda Lee, 10", vinyl & cloth, rooted blond hair, blue painted eyes, dimples, all original, 1970.......**$30.00**

Remco, Mimi, 19", plastic & vinyl, blond hair, blue painted eyes, all original **$65.00**

Remco, Orphan Annie, 15", plastic & vinyl, rooted red hair, plastic disk movable eyes, no ears, all original.....**$70.00**

Remco, Snugglebun, 16", plastic & vinyl, rooted blond hair, blue eyes, open/closed mouth, redressed, 1965...**$15.00**

Remco, Spunky, 5½", vinyl, brown hair, painted eyes, all original including glasses, 1966.............................**$20.00**

Remco, Sweet April, 5½", vinyl, rooted blond hair, stationary eyes, button makes arms move, redressed, 1971....**$6.00**

Remco, Winking Heidi, 6", plastic & vinyl, blue sleep eyes, button in chest for winking, all original, 1968......**$20.00**

Roberta, Debutant Bride, 25", plastic & vinyl, rooted brown hair, sleep eyes, high-heel feet, all original, 1959 ....**$35.00**

Roberta, Dr Ben Casey's Nurse, 17", plastic & vinyl, rooted brown hair, blue sleep eyes, all original, 1963 .....**$35.00**

Roberta, Dr Kildare's Nurse, 13", plastic & vinyl, rooted blond hair, blue sleep eyes, all original, 1964 ......**$30.00**

Roberta, Roberta Ann, 15", hard plastic, brown wig, blue sleep eyes, open mouth w/teeth, all original, 1952, minimum value **$250.00**

Royal, Debbie, 15", vinyl, blond hair, blue sleep eyes, open mouth, dimples, strung, all original, 1961 ....**$60.00**

Royal, Granny, 19", rooted black/gray hair, blue sleep eyes, pierced ears, all original **$65.00**

Royal, Lilo, 19½", vinyl, jointed waist, rooted brown hair, sleep eyes, high-heel feet, all original, 1958 ....**$65.00**

Royal, Lisa Toddler, 23", plastic & vinyl, rooted white hair, blue sleep eyes, posable head, all original, 1962 .**$25.00**

Royal, Merry Lee, 12", vinyl, molded & painted hair, blue sleep eyes, open mouth, wetting hole, all original, 1964..**$15.00**

Royal, Polly, 21½", plastic & vinyl, blond rooted hair, blue sleep eyes, jointed waist, all original....................**$40.00**

Royal, Raggy Muffin Baby, 9½", vinyl, rooted brown hair, blue painted eyes, all original, 1960 ....**$7.00**

Sayco, baby, 22", stuffed vinyl, molded hair, blue sleep eyes, pouty mouth, disk jointed narrow shoulders, all original...**$60.00**

Sayco, Carrie Cries, 19", plastic & vinyl, rooted hair, blue sleep eyes, battery operated, all original, 1963.......**$8.00**

Sayco, Mother, 19", vinyl, glued-on wig, blue sleep eyes, all original, 1957..**$90.00**

Sayco, Peter Pan, 27", vinyl & latex, molded red hair, blue sleep eyes, turned-up nose, all original, 1953-56..**$95.00**

Sayco, Play Girl, 26", hard plastic w/latex limbs & cloth body, blue sleep eyes, teeth, all original, 1950.....**$85.00**

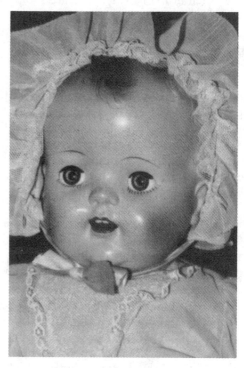

Sayco, Playgirl, 26", cloth body, latex arms & legs, hard plastic head, blue sleep eyes, 2 teeth, marked 750 USA on head...$85.00

Shindana, Kim, 16", brown plastic & vinyl, rooted black hair, brown painted eyes, original ball gown & hat, 1973 ....**$50.00**

Shindana, Lea, 11", cloth w/brown vinyl face mask, molded hair, painted features, all original, 1973 ....**$50.00**

Shindana, Malaika, 15", brown plastic & vinyl, rooted black hair, brown painted eyes, all original, 1969..........**$25.00**

Shindana, Wanda Career Girl Nurse, 9", brown vinyl, rooted black hair, brown painted eyes, snapping knees, all original..**$45.00**

Starr, Cowgirl Annie, 7½", hard plastic, black wig, blue sleep eyes, all original, 1953 ....**$12.00**

Starr, Dorothy Collins, 14", hard plastic, blond wig, sleep eyes, walker, head turns, all original, 1954........**$250.00**

Starr, Miss Christmas, 7½", hard plastic, brown wig, blue sleep eyes, all original, 1954 ....**$5.00**

Sun Rubber, Baby, 8", vinyl, molded in 1 piece, molded-on diaper, shocks, & shoes, painted features, 1956...**$12.00**

Sun Rubber, Chunky, 8", vinyl, molded hair, blue painted eyes, molded & painted clothes & shoes, 1954 ......**$4.00**

Sun Rubber, Colored Sun-Dee, 17", brown vinyl, molded-on hair, brown sleep eyes, nurser, all original **$65.00**

Sun Rubber, Peter Pan, 10", rubber, molded-on clothes, marked Disney, 1953 ....**$15.00**

Sun Rubber, So Wee, 10", vinyl, molded hair, blue stationary eyes, redressed, 1957..**$12.00**

Sun Rubber, Sunbabe, 11", rubber, molded hair, painted eyes, open mouth/nurser, original diaper, 1950...**$45.00**

Sunland, Baby Skin Doll, 20", vinyl, rooted blond hair, blue sleep eyes, all original **$45.00**

Super Doll, Baby Debbi, 16", brown vinyl & cloth, rooted black hair, brown sleep eyes, redressed, 1965........**$8.00**

Super Doll, Carrie, 9½", plastic & vinyl, rooted blond hair, blue painted eyes, all original **$8.00**

Super Doll, Little Debbi Eve, 16", plastic & vinyl, rooted blond hair, blue sleep eyes, all original, 1963.........**$6.00**

Super Doll, Melody Baby Debbi, 17", vinyl & cloth, blond sleep eyes, music box in back, redressed, 1965 .....**$8.00**

Terri Lee, Baby Linda, 9", vinyl, molded & painted hair, black painted eyes, open/closed mouth, redressed, 1951 ....**$185.00**

Terri Lee, Benji, 10", brown hard plastic, lamb's wool wig, sleep eyes, walker, all original, minimum value.**$300.00**

Terri Lee, Connie Lynn, 19", hard plastic, glued-on fur hair, sleep eyes, open/closed mouth, all original, 1955 .**$365.00**

Terri Lee, Gene Autry, 16", rigid plastic, painted hair & eyebrows, blue decal eyes, all original, 1950........**$1,200.00**

Terri Lee, Jerri Lee, 18", hard plastic, inset scalp w/black caracul hair, painted features, all original, 1950, minimum value **$300.00**

Terri Lee, Talking Terri Lee, 16", hard plastic, brown wig, attaches to record player, 1950, MIB **$500.00**

Terri Lee, Terri Lee, 18", hard plastic, white hair, painted features, all original, 1950 ....**$250.00**

Terri Lee, Walking Terri Lee, 10", hard plastic, glued-on wig, sleep eyes, original dress, 1950............................**$200.00**

Terri Lee, Walking Tiny Jerry Lee, 10", hard plastic, blond caracul hair, sleep eyes, original sunsuit, 1950...**$295.00**

Tomy, Cindy, 14½", plastic & vinyl, rooted brown hair, brown sleep eyes, pull-string talker, all original **$6.00**

Tomy, Cycling Cheri, 10", plastic & vinyl, rooted red hair, blue painted eyes, battery operated, all original...**$30.00**

Topper, Black Dale, 6", rooted black hair, brown painted eyes, jointed waist, snapping knees, all original...**$15.00**

Topper, Dinah, 6", vinyl, rooted blond hair, painted eyes, jointed waist, snapping knees, all original, 1970 ..**$25.00**

Topper, Glori, 6", vinyl, rooted long red hair, painted eyes, jointed waist, snapping knees, all original, 1970 ..**$10.00**

Topper, Longlocks Head to Toe, 6", vinyl, rooted hair, painted eyes, jointed waist, all original **$25.00**

Uneeda, Betsy McCall, 11½", plastic & vinyl, rooted red hair, brown sleep eyes, posable head, all original......**$100.00**

Uneeda, Betsy McCall, 29", plastic & vinyl, rooted blond hair, blue sleep eyes, jointed, all original, 1961..**$450.00**

Uneeda, Bridal Time, 5", plastic & vinyl, rooted blond hair, blue painted eyes, all original, 1967 ....**$10.00**

Uneeda, Bride Sue, 10½", vinyl, rooted blond hair, blue sleep eyes, high-heel feet, all original **$35.00**

Uneeda, Bride Time Pee Wee, 3½", rooted blond hair, blue painted eyes, all original, 1965................................**$6.00**

Uneeda, Connie, 15", plastic & vinyl, rooted red hair, blue sleep eyes, nurser, all original, 1968-69................**$15.00**

Uneeda, Dance Time Pee Wee, 3½", rooted blond hair, painted eyes, all original, 1965...............................**$6.00**

Uneeda, Donna Fashion Doll, 5½", plastic & vinyl, rooted blond hair, painted eyes, all original, 1970 ....**$10.00**

Uneeda, Fun Time, 5", rooted brown hair, brown painted eyes, all original, 1967...**$10.00**

Uneeda, Hee Wee, 3½", vinyl, molded hair, painted eyes, mark on right foot, nude, 1965 ....**$6.00**

Uneeda, Impish Elfy, 7", rigid vinyl, molded purple hair, slanted eyes, all original, 1964 ....**$5.00**

Uneeda, Lin, 4", vinyl, rooted black hair, black almond-shaped painted eyes, all original, 1971....................**$5.00**

Uneeda, Little Miss Dollikin, 6½", plastic & vinyl, rooted blond hair, blue painted eyes, all original, 1971...**$30.00**

Uneeda, Little Sophisticate Kristina, 8", plastic & vinyl, rooted brown hair, closed painted eyes, all original, 1967 .**$6.00**

Uneeda, Littlest So-Soft, 6", vinyl & cloth, rooted brown hair, blue painted eyes, all original, 1970 ....**$4.00**

Uneeda, Lovable Lynn, 11", plastic & vinyl, rooted reddish hair, blue sleep eyes, all original, 1970 ....**$5.00**

Uneeda, Magic Meg, 16", plastic & vinyl, rooted frosted blond hair w/grow feature, blue sleep eyes, all original, 1971......**$35.00**

Uneeda, Moonmaid, 11½", plastic & vinyl, rooted blond hair, brown painted eyes, all original, 1966.........**$45.00**

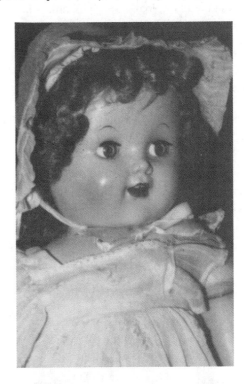

Uneeda, Needa Toddles, 22", composition upper arms & legs, wired-on arms & legs of vinyl, marked 20 on hard plastic head..$55.00

Uneeda, Patti-Cake, 20", plastic & vinyl, rooted white hair, blue sleep eyes, key-wind music box, wiggles, all original **$8.00**

Uneeda, Pretty Portrait, 11", plastic & vinyl, rooted blond hair, painted eyes, all original, 1966......................**$35.00**

Uneeda, Prom Time, 5", plastic & vinyl, rooted dark blond hair, blue painted eyes, all original, 1967..............**$10.00**

Uneeda, Sunny Face, 15", vinyl, rooted blond hair, blue stationary eyes, teeth, dimples, all original, 1963......**$40.00**

Uneeda, Suzette, 11½", plastic & vinyl, rooted red hair, painted eyes, high-heel feet, nearly all original....**$75.00**

Uneeda, Teenie Toddles, 12", brown plastic & vinyl, rooted dark brown hair, brown sleep eyes, pouty mouth, redressed..**$5.00**

Uneeda, Toddles, vinyl & plastic, rooted blond hair, blue sleep eyes, hinged legs, redressed, 1952...............**$20.00**

Uneeda, Weepsy, 4", plastic & vinyl, molded hair, painted features, nurser, cries when tummy is pressed, all original.**$3.00**

Uneeda, Wish-Nik, 7", vinyl, rooted brown hair, brown painted eyes, jointed at neck, nude, 1964..............**$5.00**

Unique, Calico Lass, 12", plastic & vinyl, rooted blond hair, painted eyes, breasts, all original (minus shoes) ..**$20.00**

Unique, Ellie Mae Clampet, 11½", plastic & vinyl, rooted hair, painted eyes, breasts, all original, 1964 ....**$20.00**

Unique, Vickie, 12", plastic & vinyl, rooted brown hair, blue painted eyes, all original **$15.00**

Valentine, Happi-Time Walker, 17½", hard plastic, glued-on blond wig, sleep eyes, 4 teeth, all original, 1953 .**$175.00**

Valentine, Luann Simms, 14", hard plastic, long dark hair, sleep eyes, walker, all original, minimum value.**$200.00**

Valentine, Roxanne, 14", hard plastic, saran hair, sleep eyes, teeth, walker, all original, 1953, minimum value..**$185.00**

Vogue, Angel Baby, 14", vinyl, rooted reddish-blond hair, blue sleep eyes, all original, 1965...........................**$25.00**

Vogue, Baby Dear, 18", vinyl & cloth, light brown hair, brown sleep eyes, original aqua outfit **$35.00**

Vogue, Black Ginny, 8", brown vinyl, all original **$95.00**

Vogue, Black Ginny Baby, 12", brown vinyl & cloth, black hair, sleep eyes, closed mouth, all original, 1964.**$25.00**

Vogue, Brickette, 18", reissue, rooted hair, sleep eyes, original clothes, 1979-1980............................$85.00

Vogue, character baby, 16", vinyl, molded & painted hair, sleep eyes, all original, 1966 ....**$65.00**

Vogue, Ginny, 8", hard plastic, blond wig, original skating outfit, all original, ca 1950s, minimum value **$300.00**

Vogue, Ginny, 8", vinyl, blond wig, blue sleep eyes, all original as Tyrolean girl, 1965 ....**$80.00**

Vogue, Hug a Bye Baby, 16", all original, 1975...........**$40.00**

Vogue, Jan, 10", vinyl, rooted hair, sleep eyes, jointed waist, high-heel feet, all original, minimum value **$125.00**

Vogue, Jeff, 9", plastic & vinyl, molded hair, blue sleep eyes, all original...**$65.00**

Vogue, Littlest Angel, 13", brown plastic & vinyl, rooted black hair, brown sleep eyes, all original, 1963....**$30.00**

Vogue, Miss Ginny, 10", plastic & vinyl, light brown hair, sleep eyes, red & white gown, all original............**$50.00**

Vogue, Miss Ginny, 15", vinyl, rooted blond hair, blue sleep eyes, all original, 1970 ....**$30.00**

Vogue, New Baby Dear, 17", vinyl & cloth, rooted blond hair, blue sleep eyes, dimples, all original, 1960 ..**$45.00**

Vogue, Precious Baby, 12", vinyl, rooted hair, sleep eyes, all original, 1975...**$45.00**

Vogue, Wee Imp, 8", hard plastic, original wig, green sleep eyes, freckles, all original, minimum value........**$400.00**

Wright, Patricia, 18", brown plastic & vinyl, black hair, brown painted eyes, all original, 1967...................**$55.00**

Doorstops

There are three important factors to consider when buying doorstops – rarity, desirability, and condition. Desirability is often a more important issue than rarity, especially if the doorstop is well designed and detailed. Subject matter often overlaps into other areas and can appeal to collectors of Black Americana and advertising, for instance, tending to drive prices upward. Most doorstops are made of painted cast iron, and value is directly related to the condition of the paint. If there is little paint left or if the figure has been repainted or is rusty, unless the price has been significantly reduced, pass it by.

Be aware that Hubley, one of the largest doorstop manufactuers, sold many of their molds to the John Wright Company who makes them today. Watch for seams that do not fit properly, grainy texture, and too-bright paint.

The doorstops we've listed here are all of the painted cast iron variety unless another type of material is mentioned in the description. For further information, we recommend *Doorstops, Identification and Values,* by Jeanne Bertoia.

Blowfish, 8x7¼", full figure, glass eyes, orange & white, Hubley, minor paint chips...................................**$300.00**

Boston Terrier, 8¼x8", full figure, black & white, glass eyes, EX..**$90.00**

Bulldog, 5¾x8½", porcelainized, full figure, white w/black features, EX **$95.00**

Cinderella Carriage, 9¾x19", NM **$250.00**

Cinderella Slipper, 4x9", gold metallic paint shows minor wear..**$125.00**

Clown, 10x4½", hands on his knees, red, white & blue, NM **$500.00**

Colonial Dame, 8x4½", pink & blue dress holding multicolored flowers, Hubley, EX **$200.00**

Cottage w/Fence, 6x8", multicolored, National Foundry, marked 32, EX...**$125.00**

Doberman Pinscher, 8x8½", full figure, Hubley, EX .**$300.00**

Drum Major, 13½x6½", full figure, solid, red & white uniform w/yellow baton, minor paint wear.............**$375.00**

Duck, 4x13", full-figured mallard, minor paint wear.**$300.00**

Fruit Basket, 10x7½", multicolored, Albany Foundry, minor rust..**$150.00**

Giraffe, 15½x4¾", brass, wedge back, EX.................**$160.00**

Little Girl by Wall, 5¼x3¼", full figure, solid, green dress, Albany Foundry, NM **$160.00**

Owl, 10x4½", Hubley...**$245.00**

Poppies & Cornflowers, 7¼x6½", multicolored, Hubley, marked 265, minor paint chips...........................**$110.00**

Rabbit by Fence, 7x8", side view, Albany Foundry, EX original paint **$325.00**

Reclining Kitten, 4x8⅛", full figure, black w/red & black ribbon around neck, National Foundry, EX **$200.00**

Rhumba Dancer, 11x6½", NM...................................**$500.00**

Rose Basket, 11x8", multicolored, Hubley, marked 121, minor rust...**$140.00**

Scottie, 8x8¼", seated in side view, black, NM.........**$150.00**

Squirrel, 8x5½", eating a nut in side view, marked Emig 1382, NM **$160.00**

Swan, 16x6¾", NM...**$275.00**

Tropical Woman, 12x6", NM.....................................**$260.00**

Windmill, 7x7", green, orange, & cream, National Foundry, marked 10 Cape Cod, minor paint wear.............**$120.00**

Woman w/Muff, 9¼x5", solid, brown paint, NM.......**$200.00**

Duncan and Miller Glassware

Although the roots of the company can be traced back to as early as 1865 when George Duncan went into business in Pittsburg, Pennsylvania, the majority of the glassware that collectors are interested in was produced during the twentieth century. The firm became known as Duncan and Miller in 1900. They were bought out by the United States Glass Company, who continued to produce many of the same designs through a separate operation which they called the Duncan and Miller Division.

In addition to crystal, they made some of their wares in a wide assortment of colors including ruby, milk glass, some opalescent glass, and a black opaque glass they called Ebony. Some of their pieces were decorated by cutting or etching. They also made a line of animals and bird figures; for information on these, see Glass Animals.

Canterbury, bowl, 9", oval, clear..............................**$18.00**

Canterbury, cruet, crystal, w/stopper **$25.00**

Canterbury, mayonnaise, blue, w/ladle.....................**$20.00**

Canterbury, mayonnaise set, crystal, 3-piece $45.00
Canterbury, relish, 3-part, clear.................................$15.00
Canterbury, relish, 9", 3-part, blue opalescent $32.00
Caribbean, ashtray, clear $9.00
Caribbean, bowl, 5", blue $32.00
Caribbean, champagne, blue.....................................$45.00
Caribbean, creamer, blue $35.00
Caribbean, nappy, 5", handled, blue $35.00
Caribbean, plate, 6", blue $18.00
Caribbean, relish, blue, 2-part, round.......................$30.00
Caribbean, salt & pepper shakers, 3", blue, pr $85.00
First Love, candlesticks, #304, 2-light, clear, pr...........$75.00
First Love, candy dish, 3-part, clear $45.00
First Love, cordial, clear...$65.00
First Love, relish, 8", #115, 2-part, clear...................$30.00
Georgian, mug, 5", clear w/amber handle $20.00
Georgian, sugar bowl, amber.....................................$10.00
Grecian, urn, 5⅜", square footed, ring handles $38.00
Hobnail, cocktail, clear...$8.00
Hobnail, nappy, 6", shallow, clear.............................$8.00
Hobnail, wine, pink opalescent $27.50
Language of Flowers, comport, clear, footed..............$28.00
Language of Flowers, compote, cheese; clear $18.50
Language of Flowers, creamer & sugar bowl, clear.....$35.00
Language of Flowers, mayonnaise set, 3-piece, clear..$27.00
Language of Flowers, relish, 2-part, clear...................$35.00
Mardi Gras, champagne, 4½" $20.00
Mardi Gras, sherbet, clear, cupped............................$20.00
Plaza, bowl, 8", pink, deep $145.00
Plaza, cocktail, clear $12.50
Plaza, finger bowl, amber..$12.00
Plaza, sugar bowl, clear..$15.00
Plaza, tumbler, 12-oz, amber, flat..............................$15.00
Radiance, cup & saucer, light blue.............................$25.00
Radiance, plate, 8⅝", light blue................................$20.00
Radiance, sugar bowl, light blue................................$20.00
Sandwich, basket, 6x5½", clear.................................$70.00
Sandwich, bowl, nut; 3¼", clear................................$14.00
Sandwich, box, trinket; 3¾x5", clear $75.00
Sandwich, candlesticks, 4", 1-light, clear, pr $27.00
Sandwich, coaster, clear...$10.00

Sandwich, cruet, clear..$35.00
Sandwich, cup & saucer, clear...................................$12.00
Sandwich, goblet, 9-oz, clear $8.00
Sandwich, ice cream dish, 4¼", clear.........................$10.00
Sandwich, mustard, etched, w/lid...............................$30.00
Sandwich, relish, 5½", 2-part.....................................$15.00
Sandwich, salt & pepper shakers, 2½", clear, pr..........$25.00
Sandwich, wine, 4¼", clear $20.00
Seahorse, cocktail, 3-oz, clear, footed $35.00
Seahorse, whiskey, 2-oz, clear, footed $45.00
Spiral Flutes, bowl, almond; footed, green $18.00
Spiral Flutes, bowl, bouillon; 3¾", pink $15.00
Spiral Flutes, bowl, 7", flat rim, amber $8.00
Spiral Flutes, compote, tall, green..............................$22.00
Spiral Flutes, compote, 4⅜", amber $15.00
Spiral Flutes, goblet, 6¼", green................................$16.00
Spiral Flutes, pickle dish, green.................................$15.00
Spiral Flutes, tumbler, ginger ale; 11-oz, 5½", pink $50.00
Spiral Flutes, vase, 8½", pink $17.50
Spring Beauty, goblet, 6¼", clear...............................$22.50
Sylvan, mint dish, 7½", clear w/cobalt handle.............$15.00
Sylvan, relish, 3-part, clear w/cobalt handle $40.00
Sylvan, swan, 7", clear...$30.00
Tear Drop, ashtray, individual; clear............................$3.00
Tear Drop, candlesticks, #301, 4", clear, pr.................$30.00
Tear Drop, champagne, clear $9.00
Tear Drop, compote, cheese; clear.............................$14.00
Tear Drop, creamer & sugar bowl, w/tray, clear........$18.00
Tear Drop, cup & saucer, clear....................................$8.00
Tear Drop, plate, 10½", clear.....................................$28.00
Tear Drop, plate, 8", handles, clear............................$15.00
Tear Drop, relish, 3-part, clear...................................$14.00
Tear Drop, sweetmeat dish, clear...............................$18.50
Tear Drop, tumbler, iced tea; flat, clear $15.00
Terrace, ashtray, red, square $35.00
Terrace, cordial, clear $45.00
Terrace, creamer, red..$42.50
Terrace, plate, 5", clear, handles................................$30.00
Terrace, plate, 5", handles, cobalt..............................$35.00
Terrace, plate, 7½", clear $9.00

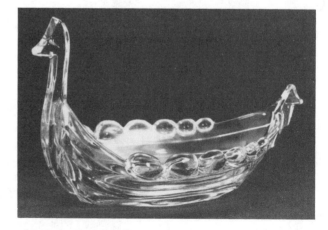

Viking Boat, 12" long $145.00
Waterford, bowl, 5", green $8.00
Waterford, goblet, 6", green, footed $10.00

Easter Collectibles

The egg (a symbol of new life) and the bunny rabbit have long been part of Easter festivities; and since early in the twentieth century, Easter has been a full-blown commercial event. Postcards, candy containers, toys, and decorations have been made in infinite varieties. In the early 1900s, many holiday items were made of papier-mache and composition and imported to this country from Germany. Rabbits were made of mohair, felt, and velveteen, often filled with straw, cotton, and cellulose.

For more information, we recommend *A Guide to Easter Collectibles* by Juanita Burnett.

Bank, figural plastic rabbit, flocked, made in Hong Kong, 1960s-70s **$7.50**
Bank, figural plastic rabbit w/plush ears, red bow tie, marked Roys Des of Fla, 1976 .... **$20.00**
Bank, figural plastic rabbit w/felt skirt, marked Roy Des of Fla, 1968 .... **$20.00**
Basket, rectangular, metal w/floral design, 2 handles, made in USA, 1940s **$25.00**
Booklet, Easter Ideals, bouquet of roses on front, Ideal Publishing Co, $5 up to **$15.00**
Candy container, chick, 3½", cotton batten, glass eyes, wooden beak, blue & yellow feathers, removable head is lid . **$80.00**
Candy container, chick nodder on rooster, 4", composition, multicolor paint, Germany **$160.00**
Candy container, clown chick, 4", composition, yellow in multicolored clothes, head removes, Germany .. **$160.00**
Candy container, figural clear glass rabbit, seated, JH Millstein Co, 1940s **$65.00**
Candy container, papier-mache, rabbit on a log, Germany, 1930s-40s **$130.00**
Candy container, papier-mache, rabbit w/basket of eggs on his back, 1930s-40s **$60.00**
Cookie cutter, figural metal rabbit w/handle, 1930s **$5.00**
Egg, glass w/embossed chick, Goebel, 1978 .... **$20.00**
Egg, metal, rabbits, chicks & ducklings on green background, 1940s.. **$20.00**

Egg, milk glass w/fired-on rabbit & Easter greetings .$25.00
Egg, musical, metal, Mattel Inc, 1950s **$30.00**
Egg, papier-mache, Disney characters, 1930s, each **$30.00**
Greeting card, rabbit painting eggs surrounded by chicks,

die-cut floral frame, Sincere Greetings **$20.00**
Hen on nest, papier-mache, Burt Co, 1920s **$75.00**
Horn, 5", metal, witch, boy w/pumpkin, owls, EX...... **$10.00**
Pipsqueak, rooster, 7", celluloid, on pink squeaker **$85.00**
Postcard, little girl feeding lamb, Easter Greetings, early 1900s **$5.00**
Pot holder, handmade w/embroidered rabbit, 1940s..**$18.00**
Pull toy, figural hand-crafted wood rabbit, 1930s........**$75.00**
Puzzle, Bonnie & Bunnie, Perfect Picture, 1940s..........**$15.00**
Rabbit, light brown mohair w/pink felt clothing, 1950s.**$40.00**
Rabbit, Plush Pals, purple & yellow plush w/rubber head, My-Toy Co, w/original tag, 1950s **$35.00**
Rabbit, short-haired pink plush w/green outfit, button eyes, attached Happy Easter card, 1960s **$25.00**
Rabbit, straw-stuffed plush, button eyes, felt tuxedo & bow tie, 1940s.. **$125.00**
Rabbit, plush, musical wind-up, American, 1950s **$50.00**
Rabbit, stuffed plush, Scottish attire, 1940s **$85.00**
Rabbit, 3", celluloid, in blue egg, early, EX.............. **$120.00**
Rabbit, 4", tan celluloid, multicolor paint, made up as doctor w/bag & cigar.. **$65.00**

Rabbit, 6½", boy or girl, plastic, 1940s, each $20.00
Rabbit, 9", papier-mache, white w/yellow trim, EX.....**$45.00**
Rabbit in car, 4", chalkware, EX.................................. **$45.00**
Rabbit in shoe, 4", celluloid, pink & white **$55.00**
Rabbit on egg, 4", celluloid, yellow w/flowers.......... **$150.00**
Rabbit roly poly, 4", celluloid, yellow w/red & green flowers, EX **$145.00**
Rabbit smoking pipe, papier-mache composition, bright red & yellow outfit, 1940s.. **$90.00**
Rattle, tissue over wood rattle w/wood hdl, Germany..**$40.00**
Tin, advertising, White Rabbit Rolls, 2 rabbits pulling & pushing basket, made in China, 1980s **$15.00**
Wind-up, plastic rabbit on metal tricycle, 1970s..........**$35.00**

Egg Cups

Egg cups were at one time a standard piece in many lines of dinnerware, but most of them you'll see today are the novelty type that were produced in Japan, Germany, or

Czechoslovakia. They take up very little room, so they appeal to apartment dwellers or those of us who simply have no room left for bigger things! They're very inexpensive, and many darling examples can be bought for under $10.00.

Obviously the single-size cup was just right to hold a soft-boiled egg. But if you preferred two for breakfast, you needed a double. You could either have them boiled or poached, and it wasn't considered at all rude to dip your toast points into the soft yolks.

Bone china, Phoenix Bird, Noritake............................$17.00
Ceramic, yellow chick pulling cup modeled as a cart...$6.00
Chinaware, blue band & gold trim on white, Noritake .$14.00

Chinaware, Lowestoft Bouquet, 3½", Royal Doulton .$12.00
Chinaware, Maria pattern, attached saucer, Rosenthal ..**$18.50**

Chinaware, seated boy, 2⅜", Occupied Japan.......$12.00
Cut glass, clear $12.50
Pottery, simple form, green glaze, Universal $12.00
Pottery, simple shape, floral decoration on cream, Southern
    Pottery..$27.50

Pottery, simple shape w/embossed decoration, green glaze,
    Vistosa..**$17.50**

Elvis Presley Memorabilia

Since he burst upon the fifties scene wailing 'Heartbreak Hotel,' Elvis has been the undisputed 'King of Rock 'n Roll.' The fans that stood outside his dressing room for hours on end, screamed themselves hoarse as he sang, or simply danced till they dropped to his music are grown-up collectors today. Many of their children remember his comeback performances, and I'd venture to say that even their grandchildren know Elvis on a first-name basis.

There has never been a promotion to equal the manufacture and sale of Elvis merchandise. By the latter part of 1956, there were already hundreds of items that appeared in every department store, drugstore, specialty shop, and music store in the country. There were bubble gum cards, pin-back buttons, handkerchiefs, dolls, guitars, billfolds, photograph albums, and hundreds of other items. You could even buy sideburns from a coin-operated machine. Look for the mark 'Elvis Presley Enterprises' (along with a 1956 or 1957 copright date); you'll know you've found a gold mine.

Due to the very nature of his career, paper items are usually a large part of any 'Elvis' collection. He appeared on the cover of countless magazines. These along with ticket stubs, movie posters, lobby cards, and photographs of all types are sought after today, especially those from before the mid-sixties.

Though you sometime see Elvis 45s with $10.00 to $15.00 price tags, unless the record is in very good to excellent condition this is just not realistic. In fact, the picture sleeve itself (if it's in good condition) will be worth more than the record. The exceptions are, of course, the early Sun label records that collectors often pay $400.00 to $500.00 for, some of the colored vinyls, promotional records, and EPs and LPs with covers and jackets in excellent condition.

For more information refer to *Elvis Collectibles* and *Best of Elvis Collectibles* by Rosalind Cranor, P.O. Box 859, Blacksburg, VA 24063. ($19.95+$1.75 postage each volume.)

Book, 4x6", Hillman Books, paperback, 32 pages black &
    white photos, includes listing of records, 1960, 160-
    page, M...**$37.50**
Bracelet, 7", linking-type metal w/4 figural charms, marked
    Made in Canada, Elvis Presley Enterprises 1956 on card,
    M **$135.00**
Calendar, 1963, pocket size, full-color cover, marked RCA
    Victor, NM **$50.00**
Commemorative coin, w/literature, M.........................**$28.00**
Concert ticket, 1¼x4", black & red letters on purple ground,
    for San Antonio Convention Center, 1974, M.......**$62.50**
Doll, Elvis World Doll Supergold, from edition of twenty-
    five thousand, 1984, MIB....................................**$225.00**

Hat, western type, w/original tag, dated 1956, EX....**$225.00**
Menu, International Hotel, Las Vegas, 1971, M............**$40.00**
Menu, 8x11", Sahara Tahoe, color photo, 1973, M......**$55.00**
Necklace, gold heart, EX...**$150.00**
Newspaper supplement, 1977, 16-pages of articles & photos, 1977, NM...**$8.50**
Ornament, brass plated, marked Hallmark, MIB.........**$45.00**
Pen, ballpoint, marked Elvis Now & RCA, 1972, EX...**$15.00**

Pennant, I Love Elvis, felt, early **$45.00**
Photo, black & white still from Girl Happy....................**$7.00**
Photo, wallet size, color...**$15.00**
Photo charm, black & white photo of Elvis under clear plastic in brass-plated frame, has facsimile signature, 1950s, EX **$24.00**

Picture, 5x7", in gold & white plastic frame, marked Copyright 1956 Elvis Presley Enterprises.....$330.00
Pillowcase, dated 1976, M in package.............................**$7.50**
Pin-back button, black I Hate Elvis on white band centered between 2 dark blue bands, NM............................**$50.00**
Postcard, black & white, from Germany, M.................**$10.00**

Postcard, Christmas, color, late 1960s, M **$25.00**

Record album, RCA Cal-2428, Elvis' Christmas Album, 1970, EX...$20.00
Record catalog, 1966, EX..**$20.00**

Scrapbook, 14½x12", marked Copyright 1956 by Elvis Presley Enterprises...$500.00
Sheet music, Jailhouse Rock, M **$28.00**
Sheet music, Love Me Tender, M..................................**$25.00**
Sheet music, 9x12", Heartbreak Hotel, photo cover, marked Tree Publishing Co w/1956 copyright, 2-page, EX.**$25.00**
Stamps, Tanzania postage, set of 9 in block, M...........**$25.00**
Tape measure, heart form, from 1977 concert, NM.....**$15.00**
Wallet card, 2½x3½", black & white uniformed Elvis, marked Staring in King Creole w/facsimile signature, ca 1958 ....**$37.50**

Eyewinker

Designed along the lines of an early pressed glass pattern by Dalzell, Gilmore and Leighton, Eyewinker was one of several attractive glassware assortments featured in the catalogs of L. G. Wright during the sixties and seventies. The line was extensive and made in several colors: amber, blue, green, crystal, and red. It was probably pressed by Fostoria, Fenton, and Westmoreland, since we know these are the companies who made Moon and Star for Wright, who was not a glass manufacturer but a distributing company. Red and green are the most desirable colors and are priced higher than the others we mentioned. The values given here are for red and green; deduct about 20% for examples in clear, amber, or light blue.

Bowl, 2½x5", 4 toes **$12.00**
Butter dish, 5x7½"..**$35.00**
Compote, 5x6", pedestal foot.....................................**$18.00**
Compote, 6¾x4", footed, w/lid..................................**$25.00**
Compote, 6¾x7½", fancy pedestal foot.......................**$30.00**
Compote, 8x5", pedestal foot, w/lid............................**$30.00**
Creamer & sugar bowl, 3¾", 4¼", w/lid......................**$40.00**
Honey dish, 6x5½", ribbed lid w/patterned edge........**$35.00**
Marmalade, 5¼x4", w/lid...**$25.00**
Pickle tray, 9½" dia, scalloped edge **$32.00**

Pitcher, water; 1-qt..**$35.00**
Salt & pepper shakers, 4", pr **$22.00**
Sherbet, 4½x3½"..**$8.00**
Tumbler, 8-oz..**$10.00**
Vase, 6", scalloped edge, 3-footed..............................**$32.00**

Fast Food Collectibles

Since the late 1970s, fast food chains have been catering to their very young customers through their kiddie meals. The toys tucked in each box or bag have made a much longer lasting impression on the kids than any meal could. Today it's not just kids but adults (sometimes entire families) who're clamoring for them. They're after not only the kiddie meal toys but also boxes, promotional signs used by the restaurant, the promotional items themselves (such as Christmas ornaments you can buy for 99¢, a collector plate, a glass tumbler, or a stuffed animal), or the 'under 3' (safe for children under 3) toys their toddler customers are given on request.

There have been three kinds of promotions: 1) national – every restaurant in the country offering the same item, 2)

regional, and 3) test market. While, for instance, a test market box might be worth $20.00, a regional box might be $10.00, and a national, $1.00. Supply dictates price.

To be most valuable, a toy must be in the original package, just as it was issued by the restaurant. Beware of dealers trying to 'repackage' toys in plain plastic bags. Most original bags were printed or contained an insert card. Vacuform containers were quickly discarded, dictating a premium price of $10.00 minimum. Toys without the original packaging are worth only about half or less than those mint in package.

Toys representing popular Disney characters draw cross-collectors, so do Star Trek, My Little Pony, and Barbie toys. It's not always the early items that are the most collectible, because some of them may have been issued in such vast amounts that there is an oversupply of them today. At the same time, a toy only a year or so old that might have been quickly withdrawn due to a problem with its design will already be one the collector will pay a good price to get.

As I'm sure you've noticed, many flea market dealers are setting out huge plastic bins of these toys, and no one can deny they draw a crowd. It's going to be interesting to see what develops here! If you'd like to learn more about fast-food collectibles, we recommend *The Illustrated Collector's Guide to McDonald's® Happy Meal® Boxes, Premiums, and Promotions©* by Joyce and Terry Lonsonsky.

McDonald's

Boat, Sailors Happy Meal, Grimace submarine, purple, 1987...**$3.00**
Book, Disney Favorites Happy Meal, Disney's The Sword in the Stone Activity, 1987 ....**$3.00**
Box, Beach Ball Happy Meal, Having a Wonderful Time by the Sea, 1986 ....**$4.00**
Box, Good Sports Happy Meal, 1984 ....**$5.00**
Box, Santa Claus the Movie Happy Meal, 1985 ....**$4.00**
Box, School Days Happy Meal, 1984...........................**$4.50**
Box, Young Astronauts Happy Meal, 1986....................**$8.00**
Car, Stomper Mini 4x4 Push-Along Happy Meal, Dodge Rampage, blue & white w/rubber tires, 1986.........**$5.00**
Car, Stomper Mini 4x4s Happy Meal, Toyota Tercel SR-5, blue w/yellow stripes, 1986.....................................**$4.00**

Christmas ornament, 3", Jacque (stuffed mouse), Cinderella ornament promotion, 1987, MIB..........$6.00

Cup, 16-ounce, Dukes of Hazzard Happy Meal, Uncle Jesse, graphics on white plastic, 1982...............................$5.00

Doll, Ronald McDonald, 13", cloth, 1977 ....$9.00

Figurine, Astrosnicks '83 Happy Meal, Robo-Robot, gold, 1983...$8.00

Figurine, Flintstones Kids Happy Meal, Wilma in purple dragon car, 1987.......................................$6.50

Figurine, Muppet Babies '87 Happy Meal, Kermit on red skateboard, 1987 ....$3.00

Figurine, Old West Happy Meal, Frontier Man, any color, 1981..$7.00

Figurine, Safari Adventure Happy Meal, Safari Lion, any color, 1980 ....$.75

Figurine, 2", Adventures of Ronald McDonald Happy Meal, Birdie, hard rubber, 1981...$4.00

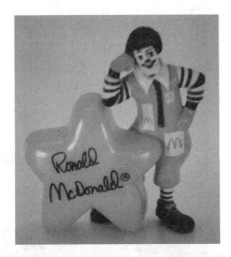

Glow Star, 3", Ronald by lg star, Bedtime Happy Meal, 1988, M in package $4.00

ID bracelet, Circus Wagon Happy Meal, Hamburglar, plastic w/alphabet sticker sheet, 1979.............................$5.00

Legos, Lego Building Set Happy Meal, Airplane, set D, green, 1986, 19-piece $4.00

Pail, Happy Pail Happy Meal, Treasure Hunt, McDonald characters in a forest, plastic, 1986 ....$3.00

Poster, Ronald McDonald House & Snow White 50th Anniversary, 1987, NM...$6.00

Sand mold, 8", Sand Castle Happy Meal, blue domed plastic, 1987 ....$12.50

Spaceship, Young Astronauts Happy Meal, Space Shuttle, white, 1986 ....$5.00

Stencil, Crayola Happy Meal, triangle w/10 cutouts, w/marker, 1986 ....$5.00

Sticker, Sticker Club Happy Meal, Scratch & Sniff, sheet w/set of 5, 1985...$4.00

Toothbrush, Bedtime Happy Meal, Ronald figural handle, w/.85-oz tube of Crest Sparkle toothpaste, 1988 ......$3.00

Yo-yo, Animal Riddles Happy Meal, Grimace 1979.......$3.00

Other Fast Food Chains

Arby's, box, Looney Tunes Collectible World Series $2.00

Arby's, car, 3½", Road Runner Racer, 1989, M $3.50

Arby's, Christmas ornament, 2½", Tweety figural, 1989...$3.00

Arby's, figurine, Firecat Sylvester, M $3.50

Arby's, figurine, Little Miss Series, Miss Sunshine, yellow w/red bows, 1981 ....$2.00

Arby's, figurine, Looney Tunes, Porky Pig, 1987 ....$2.00

Arby's, figurine, Looney Tunes, Wile E Coyote, 1988....$2.00

Arby's, pencil eraser, Pilot Tax figural, 1988, M.............$2.50

Burger King, ball, 1½", Alvin & the Chipmunk Adventure Series, 1987, M in package $5.00

Burger King, crown hat, graphics on paper...................$1.00

Burger King, display, Beauty & Beast w/4 toys, M......$25.00

Burger King, doll, Rodney Reindeer & Friends Series, Ramona, stuffed cloth, 1987 ....$3.00

Burger King, doll, 15", stuffed cloth, 1973, EX............$10.00

Burger King, dolls, Simpson Series, set of 5, M...........$20.00

Burger King, figure, Nerfuls Series, Officer Bob, 1985 ..$3.00

Burger King, mug, 3½", Super Hero Series, Superman, figural handle, 1988..$7.00

Burger King, pencil case, 1982, M in package...............$8.00

Burger King, pencil topper, Alvin & the Chipmunks' Adventure Series, 1987 ....$3.00

Burger King, record, 45 rpm, Pledge of Allegiance by Red Skelton, 1969, M $15.00

Burger King, wind-ups, Celebration Parade Series, Mickey, Minnie, Donald & Roger Rabbit, set of 4, each M in package $20.00

Denney's, car, Flintstone Vehicle Series, Dino, 1990.....$3.00

Denney's, dolls, 4", Flintstones Series, Barney & Betty, stuffed cloth, set of 2, M in package.......................$5.00

Dominos, figurine, Series, noid holding bomb, 1987 ....$4.00

Hardee's, book, Little Red Caboose, Little Golden Book, M $4.00

Hardee's, book & record set, Gremlin Adventure Series, Gift of the Mogwai, Story 1, M $3.00

Hardee's, doll, 6", Raisin Men Series, Conga Dancer, stuffed plush, 1988 ....$3.00

Hardee's, doll, 7", Shirt Tales Series, Bogey, plush........$3.00

Hardee's, figurine, Halloween Hideaway, cat in pumpkin, 1989..**$3.00**

Hardee's, figurine, Raisin Men Series, Dancer w/blue & white shoes, 1st set, 1987 ....**$2.00**

Hardee's, figurine, Raisin Men Series, Surfer w/red sneakers, 1988, 2nd set **$2.00**

Hardee's, figurine, Tang Mouth Series, Flap, 1989.........**$2.00**

Hardee's, toy, Pound Puppies Series, any color **$2.00**

Kentucky Fried Chicken, football, w/Colonel Sanders portrait, M...**$10.00**

Long John Silvers, box, Water Blasters, 1990 ....**$1.00**

Long John Silvers, car, yellow plastic fish figural, 1989.**$2.00**

Pizza Hut, cup, tall, Rocketeer graphics on plastic, NM ..**$2.00**

Pizza Hut, puppet, Land Before Time Series, Cara, yellow rubber, 1988 ....**$4.00**

Pizza Time, coin holder, Chuck E Cheese, orange **$2.00**

Shoney's, comic book, Shoney Bear & Friends, 1991....**$1.00**

Show Biz, figurine, Billy Bob w/banjo, plastic **$4.00**

Taco Bell, doll, Hugga Bunch Series, Fluffer, plush **$3.00**

Wendy's, Alien Mix-up Characters, loose, any $2.00

Wendy's, book, World Wide Life Series, All About Koalas, 1988...**$2.00**

Wendy's, box, Wendy & the Good Stuff Gang, 1989 ....**$2.00**

Wendy's, figurine, All Dogs Go to Heaven Series, Anne Marie, 1989 ....**$3.00**

Wendy's, figurine, Definitely Dinosaurs Series, Apatosaurus, pink plastic, 1989 ....**$3.00**

Wendy's, figurine, Glo Friends Series, Book Bug, 1988 .**$2.00**

Wendy's, figurine, Happy Moodie Series, yellow, 1984 ..**$2.00**

Wendy's, figurine, Potato Head Series, Daisy, 1987 ......**$3.00**

Wendy's, figurine, World of Teddy Ruxpin Series, Grubby Worm, orange, 1987....................................**$3.00**

White Castle, Cosby Kids, 1990 (EX loose $2.50), in original package, M, each $5.00

Fenton Glass

Located in Williamstown, West Virginia, the Fenton company is still producing glassware just as they have since the early part of the century. Nearly all fine department stores and gift shops carry an extensive line of their beautiful products, many of which rival examples of finest antique glassware. The fact that even their new glassware has collectible value attests to its fine quality.

Over the years they have made many lovely colors in scores of lines, several of which are very extensive. Paper labels were used exclusively until 1970; since then some pieces have been made with a stamped-in logo.

Numbers in the descriptions correspond with catalog numbers used by the company. Collectors use them as a means of identifying subtle variations, such as a goblet with a particular style of stem. If you'd like to learn more about the subject, we recommend *Fenton Glass, The Second Twenty-Five Years*, by William Heacock.

Amber Crest, console set, 3-piece..............................**$125.00**

Apple Tree, vase, 12", topaz opalescent, ruffled **$195.00**

Aqua Crest, plate, 8¼" **$22.00**

Aqua Crest, vase, 4", #36 ....**$27.50**

Blotter, donkey, yellow **$75.00**

Blotter, elephant, ebony **$35.00**

Blotter, sailboat, cobalt **$60.00**

Blotter, scotty, jadite **$35.00**

Blue Overlay, top hat, 3¼" **$24.00**

Blue Overlay, top hat, 4" **$35.00**

Blue Overlay, vanity set, #192A, 3-piece....................**$95.00**

Burmese, jack-in-the pulpit vase, 10", decorated, signed Louise Piper..**$190.00**

Butterfly & Berry, basket, #9234, blue opalescent.......**$22.00**

Button & Braids, pitcher, water; green opalescent....**$175.00**

Chinese Yellow, bowl, 12", #1663, oval, flared edge ..**$75.00**

Coin Dot, basket, 7", #1437, cranberry opalescent **$95.00**

Coin Dot, top hat, #1492, Persian Blue opalescent **$38.00**

Coin Dot, vase, 6", #1456, cranberry opalescent, flared at top...**$95.00**

Coin Spot, vase, 11", clear opalescent **$95.00**

Crystal Crest, vase, 6½", fan form **$95.00**

Daisy & Button, boot, #1990, Colonial Blue $14.00

Daisy & Button, cat slipper, emerald green $12.00

Daisy & Button, creamer, Colonial Blue.......................$18.00

Daisy & Button, high-top shoe, Electric Blue $250.00

Daisy & Button, slipper, Provincial Blue opalescent ...$16.00

Diamond Lace, candlesticks, French opalescent, 2-piece single light, pr...$30.00

Diamond Lace, compote, French opalescent, footed ..$75.00

Diamond Lace, epergne, French opalescent, footed, 2-piece $25.00

Diamond Optic, bowl, 14", #1502, blue opalescent, rolled edge $40.00

Diamond Optic, vase, 7½", #192, ruby overlay, double-crimped edge $45.00

Dolphin, bowl, 9", pink w/cut decoration, handles.$500.00

Dolphin, candlestick, 3½", #1623, rose.......................$22.50

Dot Optic, pitcher, water; #1424, blue opalescent $145.00

Emerald Crest, compote, 7"...$30.00

Emerald Crest, creamer & sugar bowl..........................$85.00

Emerald Crest, server, 8" & 12" tiers $45.00

Emerald Crest, sugar bowl $40.00

Emerald Crest & Beaded Melon, jug.............................$45.00

Gold Crest, bowl, 11", decoration.................................$50.00

Gold Crest, bowl vase, 5¼x6", ribs, double-crimped rim $24.00

Gold Crest, sugar bowl...$35.00

Hobnail, basket, 4", blue opalescent $50.00

Hobnail, bonbon, #3630, milk glass $10.00

Hobnail, cake salver, 13", yellow opalescent............$115.00

Hobnail, candle bowl, 6½", milk glass $12.00

Hobnail, candlesticks, #389, blue opalescent, pr.........$45.00

Hobnail, candy dish, milk glass, footed, w/lid $20.00

Hobnail, compote, #3768, plum opalescent..................$78.00

Hobnail, cruet, 4½", French opalescent.......................$20.00

Hobnail, cruet, 6", cranberry opalescent $100.00

Hobnail, jug, #3965, 5½", cranberry opalescent.........$125.00

Hobnail, mustard jar, blue opalescent, w/lid...............$25.00

Hobnail, nappy, 6½", ribbed, double-crimped edge ...$35.00

Hobnail, pitcher, 6½", green opalescent......................$42.00

Hobnail, pitcher, 8", #389, cranberry opalescent.......$175.00

Hobnail, rose bowl, 4", green opalescent $65.00

Hobnail, salt & pepper shakers, #3806, milk glass, pr...$14.00

Hobnail, salt & pepper shakers, blue opalescent, pr...$35.00

Hobnail, salt & pepper shakers, #3806 cranberry opalescent, pr...$90.00

Hobnail, shoe, vaseline, low, signed............................$15.00

Hobnail, vase, swung; 14", plum opalescent $100.00

Hobnail, vase, 10¾", cranberry opalescent $125.00

Hobnail, vase, 3", cranberry opalescent, double-crimped edge $35.00

Hobnail, vase, 3", milk glass..$4.00

Hobnail, vase, 5", blue opalescent, footed, fan shape.$30.00

Hobnail, vase, 5", French opalescent, triangular..........$20.00

Hobnail, vase, 8", #3858, cranberry opalescent, double-crimped edge $145.00

Ivory Crest, bowl, 7" $60.00

Ivory Crest, plate, 11½"..$75.00

Ivory Crest, plate, 8½"...$40.00

Ivy, vase, 11", #194 ....$50.00

Jamestown Blue, vase, 12"...$90.00

Leaf Tiers, bowl, 10", #1790, milk glass, ca 1934-36....$50.00

Lily of the Valley, rose bowl, #8453, blue opalescent.$28.00

Lily of the Valley, vase, #8450, cameo opalescent, handkerchief form $18.00

Lincoln Inn, tumbler, 9-oz, red, footed $24.00

Lincoln Inn, vase, 10", jade green...............................$185.00

Mandarin Red, bowl, 12", #950, flared edge, handles .$85.00

Melon Rib, pitcher, 9", blue overlay $60.00

Milk glass, bowl, berry; #3928......................................$7.00

Milk glass, chip & dip set, #3748 ....$12.00

Peach Crest, basket, 7x5", milk glass handle, 1924......$70.00

Peach Crest, rose bowl, 5"..$45.00

Peach Crest, shell bowl, 10¼", #9020 ....$70.00

Peach Crest & Beaded Melon, basket, 7" $120.00

Polka Dot, vase, 7¾", #2251, cranberry opalescent, double-crimped edge $135.00

Rib Optic, top hat, 10", French opalescent $225.00

Rose Crest, basket, 5" $45.00

Rose Overlay, basket, 5", #1924 ....$75.00

Rose Overlay, ivy ball, #1021, footed..........................$85.00

Sheffield, bowl, 12", #1800, French opalescent, crimped edge $38.00

Silver Crest, basket, 7" $30.00

Silver Crest, bowl, salad; 10".......................................$46.00

Silver Crest, cake salver, 13".......................................$32.00

Silver Crest, candle holders, low, ruffled, pr.............$20.00

Silver Crest, candlesticks, cornucopia shape, pr.........$55.00

Silver Crest, finger bowl, #202 ....$18.00

Silver Crest, plate, 12", #680.......................................$47.50

Silver Crest, plate, 15"..$45.00

Silver Crest, sherbet, ftd..$16.00

Snow Flake, rose bowl, lg, cobalt opalescent, made for LG Wright $48.00

Sophisticated Ladies, vase, 10¼", black.....................$175.00

Spiral, hurricane lamp, 11", French opalescent w/milk glass base...$75.00

Star & Stripe, tumbler, 4", flat.....................................$90.00

Stretch, candlestick, 10½", white..................................$27.00

Thumbprint, goblet, 10-oz, cobalt blue $8.00

Thumbprint, wine, 5", Colonial Blue $15.00

Fiesta

You still can find Fiesta, but it's hard to get a bargain. Since it was discontinued in 1973, it has literally exploded onto the collectibles scene; and even at today's prices, new collectors continue to join the ranks of the veterans.

Fiesta is a line of solid-color dinnerware made by the Homer Laughlin China Company of Newell, West Virginia. It was introduced in 1936 and was immediately accepted by the American public. The line was varied; there were more than fifty items offered, and the color assortment included red (orange-red), cobalt, light green, and yellow. Within a short time, ivory and turquoise were added. (All these are referred to as 'original colors.')

As tastes changed during the production years, old colors were retired and new ones added. The colors collectors refer to as 'fifties' colors are dark green, rose, chartreuse, and gray, and today these are very desirable. Medium green was introduced in 1959 at a time when some of the old standard shapes were being discontinued. Today medium green pieces are the most expensive. Most pieces are marked. Plates were ink stamped, and molded pieces usually had an indented mark.

In 1986 Homer Laughlin reintroduced Fiesta, but in colors different than the old line: white, black, cobalt, rose (bright pink), and apricot. Many of the pieces had been restyled, and the only problem collectors have had with the new colors is with the cobalt. But if you'll compare it with the old, you'll see that it is darker. Turquoise, periwinkle blue, yellow, and seamist green have since been added, and though the turquoise is close, it is a little greener than the original.

New items that have not been restyled are being made from the original molds. This means that you may find pieces with the old mark in the new colors. When an item has been restyled, new molds had to be created, and these will have the new mark. So will any piece marked with the ink stamp. The new mark is a script 'FIESTA' (all letters upper case), while the old is 'Fiesta.' Compare a few, the difference is obvious. Just don't be fooled into thinking you've found a rare cobalt juice pitcher or individual sugar and creamer set, they just weren't made in the old line.

For further information, we recommend *The Collector's Encyclopedia of Fiesta* by Sharon and Bob Huxford.

Ashtray, '50s colors	**$65.00**
Ashtray, original colors	**$37.50**
Ashtray, red, cobalt, or ivory	**$45.00**
Bowl, covered onion soup; cobalt or ivory	**$425.00**
Bowl, covered onion soup; yellow or light green	**$300.00**
Bowl, cream soup; '50s colors	**$55.00**
Bowl, cream soup; original colors	**$32.50**
Bowl, cream soup; red, cobalt, or ivory	**$45.00**
Bowl, dessert; 6", '50s colors	**$40.00**
Bowl, dessert; 6", medium green	**$250.00**
Bowl, dessert; 6", original colors	**$32.00**
Bowl, dessert; 6", red, cobalt, or ivory	**$40.00**
Bowl, footed salad; original colors	**$190.00**
Bowl, footed salad; red, cobalt, or ivory	**$230.00**
Bowl, fruit; 11¾", original colors	**$130.00**
Bowl, fruit; 11¾", red, cobalt, or ivory	**$170.00**
Bowl, fruit; 4¾", '50s colors	**$22.00**
Bowl, fruit; 4¾", medium green	**$275.00**
Bowl, fruit; 4¾", original colors	**$22.00**
Bowl, fruit; 4¾", red, cobalt, or ivory	**$25.00**
Bowl, fruit; 5½", '50s colors	**$28.50**
Bowl, fruit; 5½", medium green	**$60.00**
Bowl, fruit; 5½", original colors	**$22.50**
Bowl, fruit; 5½", red, cobalt, or ivory	**$25.00**
Bowl, individual salad; 7½", medium green	**$75.00**
Bowl, individual salad; 7½", red, turquoise, & yellow	**$57.50**
Bowl, nappy; 8½", '50s colors	**$42.00**

Bowl, nappy; 8½", medium green	**$85.00**
Bowl, nappy; 8½", original colors	**$28.00**
Bowl, nappy; 8½", red, cobalt, or ivory	**$38.00**
Bowl, nappy; 9½", original colors	**$35.00**
Bowl, nappy; 9½", red, cobalt, or ivory	**$45.00**
Bowl, Tom & Jerry; ivory w/gold letters	**$215.00**
Bowl, unlisted; red, cobalt, or ivory	**$250.00**
Bowl, unlisted; yellow	**$70.00**
Candle holder, bulbous; original colors, pr	**$65.00**
Candle holder, bulbous; red, cobalt, or ivory, pr	**$85.00**

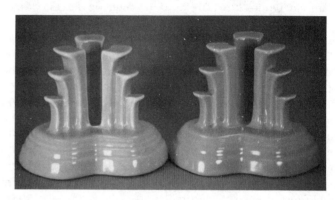

Candle holder, tripod; original colors, pr	**$300.00**
Candle holder, tripod; red, cobalt, or ivory, pr	**$365.00**
Carafe, original colors	**$140.00**
Carafe, red, cobalt, or ivory	**$175.00**
Casserole, '50s colors	**$225.00**
Casserole, French; standard colors other than yellow, minimum value	**$450.00**
Casserole, French; yellow	**$200.00**
Casserole, medium green	**$375.00**
Casserole, original colors	**$100.00**
Casserole, red, cobalt, or ivory	**$150.00**
Coffeepot, '50s colors	**$210.00**
Coffeepot, demitasse; original colors	**$175.00**
Coffeepot, demitasse; red, cobalt, or ivory	**$225.00**
Coffeepot, original colors	**$125.00**
Coffeepot, red, cobalt, or ivory	**$165.00**
Compote, sweets; original colors	**$45.00**
Compote, sweets; red, cobalt, or ivory	**$60.00**
Compote, 12", original colors	**$105.00**
Compote, 12", red, cobalt, or ivory	**$125.00**
Creamer, '50s colors	**$25.00**
Creamer, individual; red	**$135.00**
Creamer, individual; turquoise	**$215.00**
Creamer, individual; yellow	**$48.00**
Creamer, medium green	**$47.50**
Creamer, original colors	**$16.00**
Creamer, original colors, stick handled	**$28.00**
Creamer, red, cobalt, or ivory	**$20.00**
Creamer, red or cobalt, stick handled	**$35.00**
Cup, demitasse; '50s colors	**$210.00**
Cup, demitasse; original colors	**$45.00**
Cup, demitasse; red, cobalt, or ivory	**$50.00**
Egg cup, '50s colors	**$115.00**
Egg cup, original colors	**$40.00**
Egg cup, red, cobalt, or ivory	**$50.00**

Lid, for mixing bowl #1–#3, minimum value..............$500.00
Lid, for mixing bowl #4, minimum value.................$550.00
Marmalade, original colors.......................................$135.00
Marmalade, red, cobalt, or ivory..............................$180.00
Mixing bowl, #1, original colors $82.50
Mixing bowl, #1, red, cobalt, or ivory $110.00
Mixing bowl, #2, original colors $65.00
Mixing bowl, #2, red, cobalt, or ivory $75.00
Mixing bowl, #3, original colors $72.50
Mixing bowl, #3, red, cobalt, or ivory $80.00
Mixing bowl, #4, original colors $82.50
Mixing bowl, #4, red, cobalt, or ivory $90.00
Mixing bowl, #5, original colors $95.00
Mixing bowl, #5, red, cobalt, or ivory $100.00
Mixing bowl, #6, original colors $115.00
Mixing bowl, #6, red, cobalt, or ivory $130.00
Mixing bowl, #7, original colors $152.50
Mixing bowl, #7, red, cobalt, or ivory $175.00
Mug, Tom & Jerry, '50s colors...................................$78.00
Mug, Tom & Jerry; original colors $45.00
Mug, Tom & Jerry; red, cobalt, or ivory $60.00
Mustard, original colors...$115.00
Mustard, red, cobalt, or ivory...................................$160.00
Pitcher, disk juice; gray..$1,100.00
Pitcher, disk juice; red..$240.00
Pitcher, disk juice; yellow...$35.00
Pitcher, disk water; '50s colors.................................$185.00
Pitcher, disk water; medium green...........................$550.00
Pitcher, disk water; original colors $75.00
Pitcher, disk water; red, cobalt, or ivory $110.00
Pitcher, ice; original colors..$75.00

Pitcher, ice; red, cobalt, or ivory $100.00
Pitcher, jug, 2-pt, '50s colors.....................................$90.00
Pitcher, jug, 2-pt, original colors................................$48.00
Pitcher, jug, 2-pt; red, cobalt, or ivory.......................$65.00
Plate, cake; light green or yellow $550.00
Plate, cake; red, cobalt, or ivory $575.00
Plate, calendar; 10", 1954 or 1955............................$32.50
Plate, calendar; 9", 1955 ....$37.50
Plate, chop; 13", '50s colors.......................................$55.00
Plate, chop; 13", medium green.................................$105.00
Plate, chop; 13", original colors $25.00

Plate, chop; 13", red, cobalt, or ivory $35.00
Plate, chop; 15", '50s colors.......................................$70.00
Plate, chop; 15", original colors $30.00
Plate, chop; 15", red, cobalt, or ivory $45.00
Plate, compartment; 10½", '50s colors.....................$42.50
Plate, compartment; 10½", original colors.................$25.00
Plate, compartment; 12", original colors...................$45.00
Plate, compartment; 12", red, cobalt, or ivory...........$40.00
Plate, deep; '50s colors...$42.00
Plate, deep; medium green $80.00
Plate, deep; original colors..$27.50
Plate, deep; red, cobalt, or ivory...............................$40.00
Plate, 10", '50s colors..$38.50
Plate, 10", medium green $75.00
Plate, 10", original colors...$25.00
Plate, 10", red, cobalt, or ivory..................................$32.00
Plate, 6", '50s colors...$7.00
Plate, 6", medium green $12.00
Plate, 6", original colors...$4.00
Plate, 6", red, cobalt, or ivory......................................$6.00
Plate, 7", '50s colors...$10.00
Plate, 7", medium green $22.00
Plate, 7", original colors...$7.00
Plate, 7", red, cobalt, or ivory......................................$8.50
Plate, 9", '50s colors...$16.00
Plate, 9", medium green $35.00
Plate, 9", original colors...$8.00
Plate, 9", red, cobalt, or ivory....................................$15.00
Platter, '50s colors...$37.50
Platter, medium green $80.00
Platter, original colors...$22.50
Platter, red, cobalt, or ivory..$32.00
Salt & pepper shakers, '50s colors, pr $32.00
Salt & pepper shakers, medium green, pr..................$65.00
Salt & pepper shakers, original colors, pr $16.50
Salt & pepper shakers, red, cobalt, or ivory, pr..........$23.00
Sauce boat, '50s colors $50.00
Sauce boat, medium green...$85.00

Sauce boat, original colors $32.50
Sauce boat, red, cobalt, or ivory................................$45.00
Saucer, '50s colors..$5.00
Saucer, demitasse; '50s colors $60.00
Saucer, demitasse; original colors.............................$12.00
Saucer, demitasse; red, cobalt, or ivory....................$12.50
Saucer, regular, medium green $8.00

Saucer, regular, original colors................................$3.00
Saucer, regular, red, cobalt, or ivory.........................$4.00
Sugar bowl, individual; turquoise...........................$235.00
Sugar bowl, individual; yellow................................$72.50
Sugar bowl, 3¼x3½", w/lid, '50s colors.....................$42.00
Sugar bowl, 3¼x3½", w/lid, medium green.................$90.00
Sugar bowl, 3¼x3½", w/lid, original colors.................$30.00
Sugar bowl, 3¼x3½", w/lid, red, cobalt, or ivory........$40.00
Syrup, original colors...$190.00
Syrup, red, cobalt, or ivory..................................$220.00
Teacup, '50s colors..$30.00
Teacup, medium green..$45.00
Teacup, original colors...$22.50
Teacup, red, cobalt, or ivory..................................$26.00
Teapot, lg, original colors....................................$110.00
Teapot, lg, red, cobalt, or ivory.............................$140.00
Teapot, med, '50s colors......................................$195.00
Teapot, med, medium green..................................$400.00
Teapot, med, red, cobalt, or ivory..........................$130.00
Teapot, med; original colors.................................$110.00
Tray, figure-8; cobalt...$55.00
Tray, figure-8; turquoise......................................$175.00
Tray, figure-8; yellow..$190.00
Tray, relish; mixed colors, no red...........................$160.00
Tray, utility; original colors..................................$27.50
Tray, utility; red, cobalt, or ivory...........................$32.00
Tumbler, juice; chartreuse, Harlequin yellow, or dk green .$32.00
Tumbler, juice; original colors...............................$27.50
Tumbler, juice; red, cobalt, or ivory........................$32.00
Tumbler, juice; rose..$37.50
Tumbler, water; original colors..............................$40.00
Tumbler, water; red, cobalt, or ivory.......................$50.00
Vase, bud; original colors.....................................$44.00
Vase, bud; red, cobalt, or ivory..............................$60.00
Vase, 10", original colors....................................$425.00
Vase, 10", red, cobalt, or ivory.............................$475.00
Vase, 12", original colors....................................$500.00
Vase, 12", red, cobalt, or ivory.............................$600.00
Vase, 8", original colors......................................$350.00
Vase, 8", red, cobalt, or ivory...............................$400.00

Kitchen Kraft

Bowl, mixing; 10", light green or yellow....................$80.00
Bowl, mixing; 10", red or cobalt.............................$90.00
Bowl, mixing; 6", light green or yellow......................$55.00
Bowl, mixing; 6", red or cobalt...............................$60.00
Bowl, mixing; 8", light green or yellow......................$70.00
Bowl, mixing; 8", red or cobalt...............................$80.00
Cake plate, light green or yellow.............................$42.00
Cake plate, red or cobalt......................................$48.00
Cake server, light green or yellow............................$80.00
Cake server, red or cobalt.....................................$90.00
Casserole, individual; light green or yellow...............$115.00
Casserole, individual; red or cobalt.........................$130.00
Casserole, 7½", light green or yellow........................$70.00
Casserole, 7½", red or cobalt..................................$80.00
Casserole, 8½", light green or yellow........................$85.00

Casserole, 8½", red or cobalt..................................$90.00
Covered jar, lg, light green or yellow.......................$210.00
Covered jar, lg, red or cobalt................................$230.00
Covered jar, med, light green or yellow.....................$190.00
Covered jar, med, red or cobalt..............................$210.00
Covered jar, sm, light green or yellow......................$200.00
Covered jar, sm, red or cobalt...............................$225.00
Covered jug, light green or yellow...........................$170.00
Covered jug, red or cobalt....................................$180.00
Fork, light green or yellow.....................................$70.00
Fork, red or cobalt..$78.00
Metal frame for platter...$22.00
Pie plate, 10", light green or yellow.........................$38.00
Pie plate, 10", red or cobalt...................................$42.00
Pie plate, 9", light green or yellow..........................$35.00
Pie plate, 9", red or cobalt....................................$40.00
Salt & pepper shakers, light green or yellow, pr.........$75.00
Salt & pepper shakers, red or cobalt, pr...................$85.00
Spoon, light green or yellow..................................$75.00
Spoon, red or cobalt...$85.00
Stacking refrigerator lid, light green or yellow...........$45.00
Stacking refrigerator lid, red or cobalt.....................$50.00
Stacking refrigerator unit, light green or yellow.........$32.00
Stacking refrigerator unit, red or cobalt...................$36.00

Kay Finch

Wonderful ceramic figurines signed by artist-decorator Kay Finch are among the many that were produced in California during the middle of the century. She modeled her line of animals with much expression and favored soft color combinations. Some of her models were quite large; they range in sizes from 12" down to a tiny 2". She made several animal 'family groups' and, though limited, some human subjects as well. Sadly, Ms. Finch passed away last year, and values for her work seem to be climbing.

She used a variety of marks and labels, and though most pieces are marked, some of the smaller animals are not; but you should be able to recognize her work with ease, once you've seen a few marked pieces.

For more information, we recommend *The Collector's Encyclopedia of California Pottery* by Jack Chipman.

Cat, 11", pink & white, long hair w/much detail.......$150.00
Cookie jar, Cookie Pup, 12¾"................................$200.00
Godey man, 7½", holding flowers..............................$72.00
Lamb, 2½", white w/pink & black details....................$35.00
Rabbit, 2½", white w/black eyes, pink ears & nose....$40.00
Rabbit family, 8½" mother, 3-piece..........................$195.00
Rooster, 11", purple, blue & green on white.............$150.00
Yorky pup, 6¾", white w/black & pink details, 1 paw uplifted..$95.00

Fire-King Dinnerware

This is a new area of collecting interest that you can enjoy without having to mortgage the home place. In fact, you'll be able to pick it up for a song, if you keep you're eyes peeled at garage sales and swap meets.

Fire King was a tradename of the Anchor Hocking Glass Company, located in Lancaster, Ohio. As its name indicates, this type of glassware is strong enough to stand up to high oven temperatures without breakage. From the early forties until the mid-seventies, they produced kitchenware, dinnerware, and restaurant ware in a variety of colors. (We'll deal with two of the most popular of these colors, peach lustre and jadite, later on in the book.) Blues are always popular with collectors, and Anchor Hocking made two, turquoise blue and azurite (light sky blue). They also made pink, forest green, ruby, gold-trimmed lines, and some with fired-on colors. During the late sixties they made Soreno in avocado green to tie in with home decorating trends.

Bubble (made from the thirties through the sixties) was produced in just about every color Anchor Hocking made. You may also hear this pattern referred to as Provincial or Bullseye.

Alice was an early forties line; it was made in jadite and a white that was sometimes trimmed with blue or red. Cups and saucers were given away in boxes of Mother's Oats, but plates had to be purchased (so they're scarce today).

In the early fifties, they produced a 'laurel leaf' design in peach and 'Laurel Gray' lustres (the gray is scarce), followed later in the decade and into the sixties with several lines made of white glass and decorated with decals – Honeysuckle, Fleurette, Primrose, and Game Bird to name only a few. The same white glass was used for lots of kitchen items such as bowl sets, range shakers, grease jars, etc. decorated in bold designs and colors. (See Kitchen Glassware and Reamers.)

So pick a pattern and get going. These are the antiques of the future! If you'd like to study more about Anchor Hocking's dinnerware, we recommend *Collectible Glassware of the 40s, 50s, and 60s* by Gene Florence.

Alice, cup, embossed flowers on white w/blue trim, early 1940s **$8.00**

Alice, plate, 9½", embossed flowers on white w/blue trim, early 1940s..**$15.50**

Alice, saucer, embossed flowers on white w/blue trim, early 1940s **$3.00**

Anchorwhite, bowl, vegetable; 8¼", swirled design, ca 1955-early 1960s **$4.50**

Anchorwhite, creamer, swirled design, footed, ca 1955-early 1960s **$2.50**

Anchorwhite, plate, salad; 7⅜", swirled design, ca 1955-early 1960s **$2.00**

Anniversary Rose, bowl, vegetable; 8¼", 2-tone roses on white, 22k gold trim, 1964-65...................................**$7.00**

Anniversary Rose, plate, dinner; 10", 2-tone pink roses on white, 22k gold trim, 1964-65...............................**$6.00**

Anniversary Rose, platter, 9x12", 2-tone pink roses on white, 22k gold trim, oval, 1964-65 ....**$7.50**

Blue Mosaic, bowl, dessert; 4⅝", circular mosaic tile design on white, 1967..**$3.50**

Blue Mosaic, bowl, vegetable; 8¼", circular mosaic tile design on white, 1967..**$10.00**

Blue Mosaic, creamer, circular mosaic tile design on white, 1967..**$5.00**

Blue Mosaic, plate, dinner; 10", circular mosaic tile design on white, 1967..**$4.50**

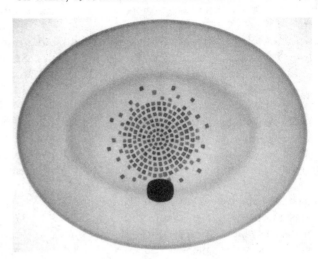

Blue Mosaic, platter, 12", blue motif on white, late 1960s..$12.50

Blue Mosaic, platter, 9x12", circular mosaic tile design on white, 1967 ....**$12.50**

Blue Mosaic, sugar bowl, circular mosiac tile on white, w/lid, 1967...**$2.50**

Charm, bowl, dessert; 4¾" square, Azurite (light blue), 1950-54 ....**$6.50**

Charm, creamer, Azurite (light blue), ear-type handle, 1950-54 ....**$9.50**

Charm, plate, salad; 6⅝" square, Azurite (light blue), 1950-54 ....**$4.00**

Charm, platter, 11x8", Azurite (light blue), 1950-54.....**$12.50**

Fleurette, plate, bread & butter; 6¼", floral decal on white, 1958-60 ....**$1.00**

Fleurette, plate, soup; 6⅝", floral decal on white, 1958-60 .**$3.00**

Fleurette, platter; 12", floral decal on white, 1958-60 ....**$7.50**

Fleurette, sugar bowl, floral decal on white, 1958-60....**$4.50**

Game Bird, bowl, dessert; 4⅝", bird decal on white, 1959-62 ....**$3.75**

Game Bird, bowl, vegetable; 8¼", bird decal on white, 1959-62 ....**$10.00**

Game Bird, mug, 8-oz, bird decal on white, 1959-62....**$7.50**

Game Bird, sugar bowl, bird decal on white, w/lid, 1959-62 ....**$7.00**

Golden Anniversary, bowl, dessert; 22k gold trim on swirled rim, 1955-ca 1963 ....**$2.50**

Golden Anniversary, plate, dinner; 9⅛", 22k gold trim on swirled rim, 1955-ca 1963 ....**$3.25**

Golden Anniversary, sugar bowl, 22k gold trim on swirled rim, open handles, footed, 1955-ca 1963.................**$3.00**

Golden Shell, bowl, soup; 6⅜", scalloped 22k gold trim on white, 1963-late 1970s **$2.50**

Golden Shell, bowl, vegetable; 8½", scalloped 22k gold trim on white, 1963-late 1970s **$5.00**

Golden Shell, plate, salad; 7¼", scalloped 22k gold trim on white, 1963-late 1970s...**$2.00**

Golden Shell, sugar bowl, scalloped 22k gold trim on white, footed, 1963-late 1970s **$2.50**

Gray Laurel, cup, 8-oz, embossed leaf band around rim, 1952-63...**$3.50**

Gray Laurel, plate, salad; 7⅜", embossed leaf band around rim, 1952-63 ....**$3.00**

Gray Laurel, plate, serving; 11", embossed leaf band around rim, 1952-63 ....**$9.50**

Gray Laurel, plate, soup; 7⅝", embossed leaf band around rim, 1952-63 ....**$3.50**

Harvest, bowl, vegetable; 8¼", dark & light gray grain sheaves on white, 1968-71.......................**$7.50**

Harvest, creamer, dark & light gray grain sheaves on white, 1968-71..**$5.00**

Harvest, plate, dinner; 10", dark & light gray grain sheaves on white, 1968-71............................**$5.00**

Homestead, bowl, vegetable; 8¼", red, black & gray scroll design on white, 1968-70......................**$7.50**

Homestead, plate, dinner; 10", red, black & gray scroll design on white, 1968-70.......................**$6.00**

Honeysuckle, bowl, vegetable; 8¼", decal on white, 1958-60 ....**$5.50**

Honeysuckle, creamer, decal on white, 1958-60 ....**$3.00**

Honeysuckle, plate, dinner; 9⅛", decal on white, 1958-60.**$3.50**

Honeysuckle, tumbler, water; 9-oz, decal on clear glass, 1958-60...**$4.00**

Ivory, coffee mug, 7-oz, 2 styles, 1942-50s **$25.00**

Ivory, custard cup, 6-oz, 1942-50s **$3.00**

Ivory, plate, salad; 7¾", plain, 1945-57 ....**$4.00**

Ivory, platter, 9x12", plain, oval, 1945-57 ....**$10.00**

Ivory, sugar bowl, plain, open, 1945-57 ....**$6.50**

Meadow Green, plate, dinner; 10", floral design on white, 1968-76...**$4.50**

Meadow Green, platter, 9x12", floral design on white, oval, 1968-76...**$5.50**

Meadow Green, saucer, 5¾", floral design on white, 1968-76...**$2.00**

Milk White, bowl, cereal; 5⅞", smooth surface, 1950s ..**$4.50**

Milk White, creamer, smooth surface, 1950s.................**$4.00**

Milk White, platter, 9x12", smooth surface, oval, 1950s ..**$7.50**

Pink Swirl, bowl, dessert; 4⅞", swirled lustre design, 1956-early 1960s **$3.75**

Pink Swirl, creamer, swirled lustre design, 1956-1960s .**$6.50**

Pink Swirl, plate, serving; 11", swirled lustre design, 1956-early 1960s **$10.00**

Pink Swirl, saucer, 5¾", swirled lustre design, 1956-early 1960s **$1.00**

Pink Swirl, tumbler, iced tea; 12-oz, swirled lustre design, 1956-early 1960s **$6.00**

Primrose, creamer, floral decal on white, 1960-62.........**$3.00**

Primrose, cup, 8-oz, floral decal on white, 1960-62 ......**$3.00**

Primrose, plate, salad; floral decal on white, 1960-62 ...**$2.50**

Primrose, tumbler, iced tea; 13-oz, floral decal on clear glass, 1960-62 ....**$5.00**

Royal Ruby, cup, 8-oz, plain, 1940s.............................**$5.50**

Royal Ruby, plate, dinner; 9⅛", plain, 1940s.............**$10.00**

Sapphire, bowl, cereal; 5⅜", 1942-50s.........................**$12.00**

Sapphire Blue, bowl, soup or salad; 6⅝", 1957-58 .....**$12.00**

Sapphire Blue, creamer, 1957-58 ....**$5.00**

Sapphire Blue, egg plate, 9¾", gold trim, 1957-58.......**$12.50**

Sapphire Blue, mug, 8-oz, 1957-58 ....**$8.00**

Swirl, bowl, 7⅝", white w/gold trim **$2.00**

Swirl, cup, 4", white w/gold trim **$1.75**

Swirl, plate, 7¾", white w/gold trim **$1.50**

Swirl, plate, 9⅛", white w/gold trim **$2.50**

Swirl, platter, 12x8⅞", white w/gold trim **$5.00**

Swirl, sugar bowl, 3½", white w/gold trim **$2.00**

Turquoise Blue, ashtray, 5¾" square, 1957-58 ....**$12.50**

Turquoise Blue, bowl, cereal; 5", 1957-58....................**$8.00**

Turquoise Blue, divided relish, 7½x11", gold trim .$12.00

Wheat, bowl, dessert; 4⅝", wheat spray on white, 1962-late 1960s **$2.00**

Wheat, bowl, vegetable; 8¼", wheat spray on white, 1962-late 1960s **$5.50**

Wheat, creamer, wheat spray on white, open handle, 1962-late 1960s **$3.00**

Wheat, cup, wheat spray on white, 1962-late 1960s......**$3.00**

Wheat, custard, low or dessert; 6-oz, wheat spray on white, 1962-late 1960s **$2.00**

Fire-King Ovenware

Anchor Hocking made ovenware in many the same colors and designs as their dinnerware. Their most extensive line (and one that is very popular today) was made in Sapphire Blue, clear glass with a blue tint, in a pattern called Philbe. Most pieces are still very reasonable, but some are already worth in excess of $50.00, so now is the time to start your collection. Gene Florence's book, *Collectible Glassware of the 40s, 50s, and 60s,* is a good source for more information.

Ivory, baker, 1½-qt, round, 1942-50s **$5.50**

Ivory, casserole, 1-qt, knob handle on lid, 1942-50s **$9.50**

Ivory, casserole, 2-qt, knob handle on lid, 1942-50s ...**$13.00**

Ivory, pie plate, 1½x9" dia, 1942-50s **$6.50**

Ivory, table server/hot plate, tab handles, 1942-50s **$8.50**

Meadow Green, baking dish, 2-qt, floral design on white, 1968-76...**$6.50**

Meadow Green, casserole, 1½", floral design on white, knob handle on clear glass lid, 1968-76..........................**$6.00**

Primrose, baking dish, 8x12½", floral decal on white, 1960-62..**$10.00**

Primrose, cake pan, 8", floral decal on white, 1960-62..**$7.50**

Primrose, casserole, 1-pt, floral decal on white, knob on cover, 1960-62...**$4.50**

Sapphire Blue, baker, 1-qt, round, 1942-50s.................**$6.00**

Sapphire Blue, bowl, utility; 10⅛" dia, 1942-50s..........**$15.00**

Sapphire Blue, casserole, individual; 10-oz, 1942-50s.**$12.50**

Sapphire Blue, casserole, 1-pt, w/lid $11.00

Sapphire Blue, casserole, 1-qt, w/pie plate lid (illustrated)..$16.00

Sapphire Blue, casserole, 2-qt, w/pie plate lid (illustrated)..$20.00

Sapphire Blue, pie plate, 1½x9⅝" dia, 1942-50s **$9.50**

Sapphire Blue, refrigerator jar, 5⅛x9⅛", 1942-50s **$30.00**

Wheat, baking dish, 5x9", wheat sprays on white, w/lid, 1962-late 1960s...**$10.00**

Wheat, baking dish, 6½x10½x1½", wheat sprays on white, 1962-late 1960s...**$8.00**

Wheat, cake pan, 8x8", wheat spray on white, 1962-late 60s...**$7.50**

Wheat, casserole, 2-qt, wheat sprays on white, knob handle on lid, 1962-late 1960s...**$10.00**

Fishing Lures

This is a hobby that has really caught on over the past five years. There is a national collectors club, newsletters, and several informative books for the serious buyer of old fishing lures.

There have been literally thousands of lures made since the turn of the century. Some have bordered on the ridiculous, and some have turned out to be just as good as the manufacturers claimed. Other than buying outright from a dealer, try some of the older stores in your area – you just might turn up a good old lure. Go through any old tackle box that might be around; and when the water level is low, check out the river banks.

If you have to limit your collection, you might want to concentrate strictly on wooden lures, or you might decide to try to locate one of every lure made by a particular company. Whatever you decide, try to get examples with good original paint and hardware.

For further information, we recommend *Old Fishing Lures and Tackle* by Carl F. Luckey.

Abbey & Imbrie Minnehaha, #1100, wood, red back w/white belly, nose-mounted propeller, 3 treble hooks..**$15.00**

Abbey & Imbrie Whippet, #2400, white w/red head, nose & tail-mounted propeller, 2 treble hooks...................**$5.00**

Brook's Jointed Topwater, scale finish, 2 treble hooks .**$4.00**

Carter's Mouse, single belly-mounted treble hook, flexible tail **$8.50**

Clark's Popper Scout, #700, wood, trailing treble & belly hook..**$4.00**

Creek Chub Big Bug Wiggler, #1400, wood, belly-mounted double hook, 3 tail-mounted strings......................**$25.00**

Creek Chub Midget Pikie Minnow, #2200, floater, scale finish, reversible metal lip blade, 2 treble hooks........**$8.50**

Creek Chub Open Mouth Shiner, #500, scale finish, cut-out notch mouth, belly & tail-mounted double hook **$35.00**

Creek Chub Plunker, #3200, natural perch w/scale finish, belly-mounted & trailing treble hook **$8.00**

Creek Chub Pop 'N Dunk, #6300, natural frog finish, lg glass eye, metal lip, 2 treble hooks................................**$8.00**

Creek Chub Striper Pikie, #6900, white w/red head, jointed, 3 treble hooks **$4.00**

Eger's Stump Knocker, #1400-½, yellow w/polka dots, concave belly, notched mouth, 3 treble hooks.............**$4.00**

Eger's Wiggle Tail, #1100, white w/red head, line tie on top of head, 2 treble hooks....................................**$4.50**

Heddon's Baby Vamp, #7400, rainbow finish, metal lip, 2 treble hooks **$10.00**

Heddon's Black Sucker Minnow, #1300, rainbow finish, glass eyes, 3 treble hooks **$100.00**

Heddon's Crab Wiggler, #1800, rainbow finish, O-shaped collar, glass eyes, 2 treble hooks **$15.00**

Heddon's Flaptail, #7000, white red, 2 treble hooks .**$12.50**

Heddon's Go-Deeper Crab, #D1900, orange w/red & black spots, deep diving lip, 2 treble hooks...................**$10.00**

Heddon's Meadow Mouse, #4000, gray w/white belly, black bead eyes, metal collar, 2 treble hooks.................**$20.00**

Heddon's Midget Digit, #B-110, wood w/weighted body, black w/white head, painted eyes, 2 treble hooks.**$3.50**

Heddon's Sea Runt, #610, yellow w/red head, line tie at top of nose, 2 treble hooks....................................**$18.00**

Heddon's SOS Wounded Minnow, #160, banana shape, white w/red head, glass eyes, 3 treble hooks......**$20.00**

Heddon's Surface Minny, #260, rainbow finish, glass eyes, 2 treble hooks **$65.00**

Heddon's Weedless Widow, #1300, wood, bull frog color, bead eyes, detachable double hook on belly.......**$15.00**

Jamison Quiverlure, #1920, transparent plastic w/red head, 3 treble hooks..**$8.50**

Jos Doodle Bug, white w/red head, painted eyes, cup & screw eye hook hardware, 1 treble hook..............**$18.00**

Millsite Minnow, floater, transparent, deep diving lip, 2 treble hooks..**$6.00**

Pflueger, Wizard Wiggler (EX $25.00), MIB **$40.00**

Shakespeare's Bass-Kazoo, metal, no eyes, sloped head, 3 treble hooks **$12.50**

Shakespeare's Darting Shrimp, #135, natural frog finish, jointed, 2 treble hooks...**$20.00**

Shakespeare's Egyptian Wobbler, #6635, natural pickerel finish, metal lip & ventral fin, 3 treble hooks...........**$10.00**

Shakespeare's Fisher Bait, #6509, floater, yellow perch scale finish, metal lip & ventral fin, 2 treble hooks **$20.00**

Shakespeare's Kazoo Chub Minnow, glass eyes, metal lip, 2 treble hooks **$25.00**

Shakespeare's Swimming Mouse (EX $15.00), MIB .$25.00

South Bend Ketch Oreno, #909, red blend w/scale finish, belly-mounted double hook **$4.00**

South Bend Muskie Surf-Oreno, #964, rainbow finish, nose & tail-mounted propellers, 3 treble hooks **$8.50**

South Bend Surface Minnow, #920, luminous finish, nose-mounted propeller, 2 treble hooks **$8.50**

Wilson's Fluted Wobbler, white w/red flutes, 3 treble hooks **$10.00**

Wilson's Sizzler, metal w/winged metal piece hinged at nose & under body, 2 single hooks, stamped Pat Aug 24-1904 .... **$18.00**

Florence Ceramics

During the forties, Florence Ward began modeling tiny ceramic children as a hobby at her home in Pasadena, California. She was so happy with the results that she expanded, hired decorators, and moved into a larger building where for two decades she produced the lovely line of figurines, wall plaques, busts, etc. that have become so popular today. The 'Florence Collection' featured authentically detailed models of such couples as Louis XV and Madame Pompadour, Queen Elizabeth and King Arthur, Pinkie and Blue Boy, and Rhett and Scarlett. Nearly all of the Florence figures have names which are written on their bases.

Many figures are decorated with 22k gold and lace. Real lace was cut to fit, dipped in a liquid material called slip, and fired. During the firing it burned away, leaving only hardened ceramic lace trim. The amount of lacework that was used is one of the factors that needs to be considered when evaluating a 'Florence.' Size is another. Though most of the figures you'll find today are singles, a few were made as groups, and once in awhile you'll find a lady seated on a divan. The more complex, the more expensive.

If you'd like to learn more about the subject, we recommend *The Collector's Encyclopedia of California Pottery* by Jack Chipman.

Amber, 10", mint green, w/parasol **$200.00**

Clarissa, 7½", gray dress, plum & gold trim **$90.00**

David, 7½", white suit, holds white top hat, extensive gold trim **$78.00**

Delia, 8" **$85.00**

Elaine, 6" **$45.00**

Gentleman (Rhett?) by fence, 9" **$100.00**

Girl, 7½", applied lace & flowers **$45.00**

Irene, 5½", gray & dark green clothes w/gold trim **$65.00**

Irene, 7", wall pocket **$115.00**

Jim, 6¼", gray & maroon clothes w/gold trim **$58.00**

Jim, 6¼", rose & pale rose clothes w/gold trim **$65.00**

June, planter..$40.00
Marilyn, 8¼", lavender, w/hat box $160.00
Melanie, planter $65.00
Patsy, 6", planter $65.00
Rebecca, 7½", seated $95.00
Suzette, 6¾", white, green & pink, holds basketweave vase/planter..$58.00
Vivian, 9½", purple shaded, w/parasol $150.00

Flower Frogs

The purpose of a flower frog is to support long stems of flowers in an arrangement. They are often figural – a nude, a leaf or a mushroom; some are actually modeled as a frog, and birds were popular subjects as well. All have deep holes where the stems were to be inserted, and they were sold with a matching flower bowl or vase. The figurals are becoming very collectible. The most valuable are the nudes, many of which are very Deco and stylized.

Bashful nude, 4¼ on 3" scalloped oval base, September Morn style, ivory, stands in foliage........................$17.50
Basket, 3x4½", mother-of-pearl glass, black handle, Made in Czechoslovakia..$15.00
Bird, 2½", red w/black trim & beak, perched on black base, Japan..$7.00
Bird, 2⅝", blue & yellow lustre w/black trim, Japan $8.00
Bird, 3¾x3", red w/black mask, perched on blue lustre stump, Made in Japan.............................$10.00
Bird, 3x2½', yellow w/black trim, on round black base, unmarked...$8.00
Bird, 4¼x3¼", yellow w/red & gray trim, sits on craggy brown rock, Japan $15.00
Cockatoo, 2⅝x1¾", magenta w/yellow lustre breast & turquoise beak, perched on orange lustre stump, Made in Japan $24.00
Deco-style dancing nude, 8¾x6½" on oval base, white, flowing scarf..$45.00

Deco-style nude, 13½", holding full-length veil, marked Coronet..$125.00

Flowers & leaves, 4x4", ivory, corset-shaped base surmounted by trailing flowers & leaves...................$10.00
Lotus blossom & butterfly, 2x2¾" dia, yellow & blue petals, orange center, green leafy base $14.00
Pelican, 4", purple, green & gold on brown stump, majolica-type glaze, Japan.......................................$12.00
Stump, 2½x3½", orange lustre, Japan $6.00
Turtle, 5x1½", dark green, pottery, Japan.....................$7.00
Water lily, 1⅞x2½", cobalt petals, red & yellow center, green leafy base..$14.00
Water lily bud, 2¼x3¾" dia, pink & yellow on blue & orange lustre pool, Japan $16.00

Fostoria

This was one of the major glassware producers of the twentieth century. They were located first in Fostoria, Ohio, but by the 1890s had moved to Moundsville, West Virginia. By the late thirties, they were recognized as the largest producers of handmade glassware in the world. Their glassware is plentiful today and, considering its quality, not terribly expensive.

Though the company went out of business in the mid-eighties, the Lancaster Colony Company continues to use some of the old molds – herein is the problem. The ever-popular American and Coin Glass patterns are currently in production and even experts have trouble distinguishing the old from the new. Before you invest in either line, talk to dealers. Ask them to show you some of their old pieces. Most will be happy to help out a novice collector. Read *Elegant Glassware of the Depression Era* by Gene Florence. If there is a Fostoria outlet within driving distance, it will be worth your time just to see what is being offered there.

You'll be seeing lots of inferior 'American' at flea markets and (sadly) antique malls. It's often priced as though it is American, but in fact it is not. It's been produced since the 1950s by Indiana Glass who calls it 'Whitehall.' Watch for pitchers with only two mold lines, they're everywhere. (Fostoria's had three.) Remember that Fostoria was hand-made, so their pieces were fire polished. This means that if the piece you're examining has sharp, noticeable mold lines, be leery. There are other differences to watch for as well. Fostoria's footed pieces were designed with a 'toe,' while Whitehall feet have a squared peg-like appearance. The rays are sharper and narrower on the genuine Fostoria pieces, and the glass itself has more sparkle and life. And if it weren't complicated enough, the Home Interior Company has recently offered 'American'-like vases, covered bowls, and a footed candy dish that were produced in a foreign country, but at least they've marked theirs.

Coin Glass was originally produced in crystal, red, blue, emerald green, olive green, and amber. It's being reproduced today in crystal, green, blue, and red. The green and blue are 'off' enough to be pretty obvious, but the red is close. Beware. Here are some (probably not all) of the items currently in production: bowl, 8" diameter; bowl, 9" oval; candlesticks, 4½"; candy jar w/lid, 6¼"; creamer and sugar bowl; footed comport; wedding bowl, 8¼". Know your dealer!

Numbers included in our descriptions were company-assigned stock numbers that collectors use as a means to distinguish variations in stems and shapes.

American, clear, ashtray, 5", square $35.00
American, clear, bottle, cordial; 7¼", 9-oz, w/stopper...$85.00
American, clear, bowl, bonbon; 7", 3-footed $10.00
American, clear, bowl, cream soup; 5", 2-handled $45.00
American, clear, bowl, fruit; 10½", 3-footed $25.00
American, clear, bowl, fruit; 4¾", flared $15.00
American, clear, bowl, vegetable; 9", oval $25.00
American, clear, bowl, 11½", rolled edge $40.00
American, clear, box, 4½x4½", w/lid...........................$200.00
American, clear, butter dish, 7¼" dia plate, w/lid $100.00
American, clear, cake plate, 12", 3-footed...................$22.50
American, clear, candle lamp, 8½" $110.00
American, clear, candlestick, 6½", 2-light, bell base....$85.00
American, clear, candy dish, pedestal foot, w/lid........$30.00
American, clear, cheese & cracker set, 5¾" compote w/11½" plate $50.00
American, clear, compote, jelly; 5", flared...................$12.00
American, clear, creamer, 9½-oz..................................$11.00
American, clear, cup, 7-oz, footed $9.00
American, clear, goblet, iced tea; #2056, 12-oz, 5¾", low foot..$14.00
American, clear, goblet, sherbet; #2056, 5-oz, 3¼", low foot, flared..$9.00
American, clear, goblet, water; #2056, 10-oz, 6⅞", hexagonal foot...$12.00
American, clear, goblet, wine; #2056, 2½-oz, 4⅜", hexagonal foot...$12.00
American, clear, mug, beer; 12-oz, 4½".......................$65.00
American, clear, napkin ring..$12.50
American, clear, oil cruet, 5-oz $32.50
American, clear, pitcher, 1-qt, flat................................$25.00
American, clear, pitcher, ½-gal, 8", footed $65.00
American, clear, plate, cream soup liner......................$12.00
American, clear, plate, dinner; 9½"..............................$20.00
American, clear, platter, 12", oval...............................$55.00
American, clear, sauce boat, w/liner $45.00
American, clear, sugar bowl, 3¼", handled..................$8.50
American, clear, sugar shaker $45.00
American, clear, tray, sandwich; 12", center handle....$35.00
American, clear, tray, 10", square $110.00
American, clear, tray, 6", oval, handled.......................$35.00
American, clear, tumbler, iced tea; #2056½, 12-oz, 5", straight sides...$16.00
American, clear, tumbler, water; #2056, 4⅞", footed...$13.00
American, clear, tumbler, whiskey; #2056, 2-oz, 2½" ..$10.00
American, clear, vase, sweet pea; 4½"..........................$80.00
American, clear, vase, 8", flared...................................$80.00
American, clear, vase, 9", square pedestal foot............$40.00
American, vase, 10", flared..$95.00
Baroque, blue, ashtray..$15.00
Baroque, blue, bowl, vegetable; 9½", oval...................$60.00
Baroque, blue, candy dish, 3-part, w/lid......................$95.00

Baroque, blue, compote, 4¾"..$30.00
Baroque, blue, creamer, 3¾", footed $14.00
Baroque, blue, cup..$30.00
Baroque, blue, plate, 9½"..$50.00
Baroque, blue, salt & pepper shakers, pr $120.00
Baroque, clear, bowl, jelly; 7½", w/lid..........................$30.00
Baroque, clear, candlestick, 6", 3-light $17.50
Baroque, clear, cup..$9.00
Baroque, clear, oil cruet, 5½", w/stopper.....................$85.00
Baroque, clear, plate, 9½"..$15.00
Baroque, clear, tray, 11", oval.......................................$15.00
Baroque, yellow, bowl, cream soup..............................$70.00
Baroque, yellow, bowl, rose; 3¾".................................$45.00
Baroque, yellow, candlestick, 4½", 2-light $50.00
Baroque, yellow, cup $20.00
Baroque, yellow, ice bucket..$60.00
Baroque, yellow, plate, 9½"..$40.00
Baroque, yellow, sugar bowl, 3½", footed....................$11.00
Century, clear, bowl, bonbon, 7¼", 3-footed $15.00
Century, clear, bowl, salad; 10½"................................$30.00
Century, clear, butter dish, ¼-lb, w/lid........................$30.00
Century, clear, cake plate, 10", handled......................$20.00
Century, clear, candlestick, 7", double $27.50

Century, clear compote, 10½", crystal...................$45.00
Century, clear, cup, 6-oz, footed..................................$15.00
Century, clear, pitcher, 16-oz, 6⅛".................................$50.00
Century, clear, plate, dinner; 10½"...............................$27.50
Century, clear, plate, luncheon; 8½".............................$12.50
Century, clear, plate, small dinner; 9½".........................$20.00
Century, clear, stem, sherbet; 5½-oz, 4½" $11.00
Century, clear, stem, wine; 3½-oz, 4½".........................$27.50
Century, clear, tray, 11½", center handle.....................$27.50
Century, clear, tumbler, iced tea; 12-oz, 5⅞", footed...$25.00
Chintz, clear, bowl, cream soup, #2496.......................$37.50
Chintz, clear, bowl, fruit; #2496, 5"...............................$25.00
Chintz, clear, candlestick, #2496, 6", triple.................$39.50
Chintz, clear, compote, #2496, 5½"..............................$35.00
Chintz, clear, cup, #2496, footed $20.00
Chintz, clear, plate, dinner; #2496, 9½".......................$45.00
Chintz, clear, plate, salad; #2496, 7½" $14.00
Chintz, clear, relish, #2419, 5-part..............................$37.50
Chintz, clear, stem, cocktail; #6026, 4-oz, 5" $25.00
Chintz, clear, stem, water goblet; #6026, 9-oz, 7⅝".....$30.00
Chintz, clear, sugar bowl, #2496, 3½", footed.............$15.00
Chintz, clear, tumbler, iced tea; #6026, 13-oz, footed .$30.00

Chintz, clear, vase, #4128, 5"...............................$75.00
Coin Glass, amber or olive, ashtray, 7½" dia $35.00
Coin Glass, amber or olive, bowl, 8"......................$75.00
Coin Glass, amber or olive, creamer, 3½"...................$15.00
Coin Glass, amber or olive, pitcher, quart, 6½" $65.00
Coin Glass, amber or olive, salt & pepper shakers, pr..$35.00
Coin Glass, amber or olive, sugar bowl, 5⅜", w/lid....$35.00
Coin Glass, clear, ashtray, 5".............................$18.00
Coin Glass, clear, bowl, nappy; 4½"........................$25.00
Coin Glass, clear, bowl, 8" $25.00
Coin Glass, clear, cigarette box, w/lid....................$25.00
Coin Glass, clear, tumbler, 12-oz, 5⅛".....................$35.00
Coin Glass, emerald green, ashtray, 10" $55.00
Coin Glass, emerald green, bowl, 5⅜", handled.........$40.00
Coin Glass, emerald green, bowl, 9", oval $70.00
Coin Glass, emerald green, candy box, 6⅜", w/lid $75.00
Coin Glass, ruby or blue, ashtray, 5" $22.50
Coin Glass, ruby or blue, bowl, 8½", footed...............$70.00
Coin Glass, ruby or blue, bowl, 9", oval $55.00
Coin Glass, ruby or blue, candlesticks, 4½", pr $65.00
Coin Glass, ruby or blue, candy jar, 6¼", w/lid..........$70.00
Coin Glass, ruby or blue, jelly, 3¾" $25.00
Coin Glass, ruby or blue, sugar bowl, 5⅜", w/lid........$45.00

Coin Glass, ruby or blue, urn, 13", w/lid $100.00
Colony, clear, bowl, cream soup; 5"........................$40.00
Colony, clear, bowl, fruit; 10" $32.50
Colony, clear, bowl, olive; 7", oblong.....................$10.00
Colony, clear, butter dish, ¼-lb...........................$32.50
Colony, clear, candlestick, 9" $30.00
Colony, clear, compote, 4".................................$15.00
Colony, clear, cup, 6-oz, footed...........................$7.50
Colony, clear, ice bucket..................................$60.00
Colony, clear, pitcher, 1-qt, ice lip $95.00
Colony, clear, plate, luncheon; 8".........................$10.00
Colony, clear, plate, torte; 13"...........................$27.50
Colony, clear, relish, 10½", handled, 3-part $20.00
Colony, clear, stem, cocktail; 3½-oz, 4"...................$11.00
Colony, clear, sugar bowl, 3½" $5.00
Colony, clear, tumbler, iced tea; 12-oz, 4⅞" $22.50
Colony, clear, vase, cornucopia; 9"........................$55.00
Fairfax, amber, ashtray, 4"................................$10.00
Fairfax, amber, bowl, centerpiece; 15" $20.00
Fairfax, amber, cup, footed $6.00
Fairfax, amber, plate, grill; 10¼" $12.00
Fairfax, amber, salt & pepper shakers, pr $30.00

Fairfax, amber, sugar bowl, footed.........................$6.00
Fairfax, blue, bowl, cereal; 6" $20.00
Fairfax, blue, plate, chop; 13" $17.50
Fairfax, blue, stem, high sherbet; 6-oz, 6"................$20.00
Fairfax, green, butter dish, w/lid.........................$90.00
Fairfax, green, cup, flat..................................$6.00
Fairfax, green, stem, wine; 3-oz, 5½"......................$22.50
Fairfax, orchid, ice bucket................................$50.00
Fairfax, orchid, platter, 12", oval........................$35.00
Fairfax, orchid, stem, cocktail; 3-oz, 5¼"................$24.00
Fairfax, rose, baker, 9", oval.............................$25.00
Fairfax, rose, plate, dinner; 10¼" $40.00
Fairfax, rose, plate, salad; 8¾"...........................$10.00
Fairfax, topaz, compote, 5" $17.00
Fairfax, topaz, plate, dinner; 10¼" $25.00
Fairfax, topaz, tumbler, 9-oz, 5¼", footed $13.00
Hermitage, amber, bowl, fruit; #2449½, 5" $8.00
Hermitage, amber, ice tub, #2449, 6".......................$30.00
Hermitage, amber, stem, high sherbet; #2449, 3¼" $11.00
Hermitage, blue, bowl, soup; #2449½, 7"....................$20.00
Hermitage, blue, tumbler, iced tea; #2449, 12-oz, 5¼",
    footed...$25.00
Hermitage, clear, compote, #2449, 6".......................$12.00
Hermitage, clear, pitcher, #2449, 1-pt.....................$22.50
Hermitage, clear, stem, high sherbet; #2449, 3¼" $8.00
Hermitage, green, creamer, #2449, footed $6.00
Hermitage, green, plate, #2449½, 9"........................$20.00
Hermitage, green, tumbler, old-fashioned; 3¼" $9.00
Hermitage, topaz, bowl, cereal; #2449½, 6" $9.00
Hermitage, topaz, pitcher, #2449, 3-pt $50.00
Hermitage, topaz, stem, water goblet; #2449, 5¼".......$15.00
Hermitage, Wisteria, plate, sandwich; #2449, 12" $20.00
Hermitage, Wisteria, sugar bowl, #2449, footed $10.00
June, clear, bowl, baker; 10", oval........................$40.00
June, clear, compote, #2400, 5"............................$18.00
June, clear, cup, footed $15.00
June, clear, goblet, wine; 3-oz, 5½" $25.00
June, clear, plate, grill; 10" $30.00
June, clear, platter, 15" $45.00
June, rose or blue, bowl, bouillon; footed.................$35.00
June, rose or blue, cup, footed............................$30.00
June, rose or blue, goblet, cocktail; 3-oz, 5¼" $45.00

June, rose or blue, oyster cocktail.....................$35.00
June, rose or blue, plate, dinner; 10¼"....................$85.00
June, rose or blue, plate, luncheon; 8¾"...................$15.00

June, rose or blue, sherbet, high foot (illustrated on page 175) **$35.00**
June, rose or blue, tumbler, 12-oz, 6", footed.............**$50.00**
June, topaz, bowl, bonbon...**$20.00**
June, topaz, cup, footed **$22.00**
June, topaz, goblet, wine; 3-oz, 5½".............................**$50.00**
June, topaz, plate, sm dinner; 9½"..................................**$18.00**
June, topaz, sugar bowl, footed......................................**$20.00**
June, topaz, tumbler, 2½-oz, footed **$35.00**
Kashmir, blue, compote, 6"..**$45.00**
Kashmir, blue, cup...**$20.00**
Kashmir, blue, stem, water; 9-oz **$35.00**
Kashmir, green, ashtray..**$25.00**
Kashmir, green, ice bucket..**$65.00**
Kashmir, green, plate, grill; 10"..**$35.00**
Kashmir, yellow, bowl, baker; 9".....................................**$37.50**
Kashmir, yellow, candlestick, 3" **$20.00**
Kashmir, yellow, stem, juice; 5-oz, footed **$15.00**
Navarre, clear, bowl, bonbon; #2496, 7⅜", footed **$25.00**
Navarre, clear, cake plate, #2440, 10½", oval..............**$45.00**
Navarre, clear, candlestick, #2496, 5½" **$27.50**
Navarre, clear, cup, #2440..**$17.50**
Navarre, clear, plate, luncheon; #2440, 8½" **$17.50**
Navarre, clear, relish, #2496, 6", 2-part, square...........**$30.00**
Navarre, clear, stem, cocktail; #6106, 3½-oz, 6"..........**$25.00**
Navarre, clear, sugar bowl, #2440, 3⅝", footed...........**$17.50**
Navarre, clear, tumbler, iced tea; 5⅞", footed.............**$30.00**
Romance, clear, bowl, salad; #2364, 10½"....................**$40.00**
Romance, clear, candlestick, #2594, 8", 3-light **$37.50**
Romance, clear, compote, cheese; #2364, 3¼" **$22.50**
Romance, clear, cup, #2350½, footed.............................**$20.00**
Romance, clear, plate, #2337, 9" **$45.00**
Romance, clear, salt & pepper shakers, 2⅝", pr **$45.00**
Romance, clear, stem, wine; #6017, 3-oz, 5½" **$27.50**
Romance, clear, tumbler, #6017, 5-oz, 4¾", footed **$17.50**
Royal, amber, bowl, baker; #2350, 9", oval..................**$37.50**
Royal, amber, candlestick, #2324, 9" **$45.00**
Royal, amber, pitcher, #5000, 48-oz **$250.00**
Royal, amber, plate, chop; #2350, 15" **$40.00**
Royal, amber, sugar bowl, flat, w/lid **$150.00**
Royal, black, cup, #2350½, footed..................................**$19.00**
Royal, blue, ashtray, #2350, 3½" **$33.00**
Royal, blue, plate, luncheon; #2350, 8½" **$12.00**
Royal, blue, tumbler, #5000, 9-oz, footed **$24.00**
Royal, green, bowl, console; #2329, 11"........................**$22.00**
Royal, green, compote, jelly; 1861½, 6".........................**$25.00**
Royal, green, pickle dish, #2350, 8"...............................**$20.00**
Royal, green, salt & pepper shakers, #5100, pr **$60.00**
Royal, green, tumbler, #869, 5-oz, flat..........................**$22.50**
Seville, amber, ashtray, #2350, 4"....................................**$17.50**
Seville, amber, bowl, salad; #2350, 10" **$30.00**
Seville, amber, celery, #2350, 11"...................................**$15.00**
Seville, amber, cup, #2350½, footed................................**$10.00**
Seville, amber, platter, #2350, 12" **$35.00**
Seville, green, bowl, vegetable; #2350............................**$25.00**
Seville, green, candlestick, #2324, 2" **$17.50**
Seville, green, compote, #2327, 7½", twisted stem **$22.50**
Seville, green, cup, #2350½, footed.................................**$12.50**

Seville, green, egg cup, #2350...**$35.00**
Seville, green, stem, water; #870.....................................**$22.50**
Trojan, pink, bowl, #2354, 6", 3-footed.........................**$30.00**
Trojan, pink, compote, #2375, 7".....................................**$45.00**
Trojan, pink, goblet, wine; #5099, 3-oz, 5½"................**$55.00**
Trojan, pink, sugar bowl, #2375½, footed.......................**$22.50**
Trojan, yellow, bowl, soup;, #2375, 7" **$50.00**
Trojan, yellow, cup, #2375½, footed **$18.00**
Trojan, yellow, plate, luncheon; #2375, 8¾" **$15.00**
Trojan, yellow, relish, #2375, 8½" **$15.00**
Trojan, yellow, tumbler, #5099, 12-oz, 6", footed........**$27.50**
Versailles, blue, ashtray, #2350.......................................**$30.00**
Versailles, blue, cup, #2375½, footed..............................**$21.00**
Versailles, blue, relish, #2375, 8½" **$40.00**
Versailles, pink or green, bowl, cream soup; footed...**$22.00**
Versailles, pink or green, cake plate, 10", 2-handled ..**$26.00**
Versailles, pink or green, tumbler, #5098 or #5099, 12-oz, 6", footed...**$30.00**
Versailles, yellow, bowl, mint; 4½", 3-footed..............**$25.00**
Versailles, yellow, celery, #2375, 11½"...........................**$40.00**
Versailles, yellow, sugar bowl, #2375½, footed **$15.00**
Vesper, amber, candlestick, #2324, 2" **$22.50**
Vesper, amber, cheese, #2368, footed...........................**$20.00**
Vesper, amber, cup, #2350½, footed **$15.00**
Vesper, amber, platter, #2350, 10½" **$35.00**
Vesper, amber, tumbler, #5100, 5-oz, footed **$18.00**
Vesper, blue, bowl, baker; #2350, 9", oval....................**$50.00**
Vesper, blue, plate, sm dinner; #2350, 9½"..................**$20.00**
Vesper, blue, tumbler, #5100, 12-oz, footed **$40.00**
Vesper, green, bowl, cereal; #2350, 6½" **$18.00**
Vesper, green, celery, #2350 ....**$17.00**
Vesper, green, compote, #2327, 7½", twisted stem **$27.50**
Vesper, green, plate, chop; 13¾".....................................**$32.00**
Vesper, green, stem, water; #5093 ....**$25.00**

Fountain Pens

Fountain pens have been made commercially since the 1880s. Today's collector usually prefer those from before 1950, but some of the later ones are collectible as well. Pens by major manufacturers are most desirable, especially Conklin, Mont Blanc, Parker, Sheaffer, Swan, Wahl-Eversharp, and Waterman. Extra large and extra fancy pens, such as those with silver or gold overlays, filigrees, or mother-of-pearl, are at the top of most collectors' lists and can easily run into several hundred dollars, some even thousands. Unless the pen is especially nice and the price is right, avoid buying examples with cracks, missing parts, or other damage all of which drastically affects value.

For more information, we recomend *The 1992 Official P.F.C. Pen Guide* by Cliff and Judy Lawrence.

Aiken Lambert, hard black-chased rubber, gold-filled trim, eye-drop filler, 1910...**$70.00**
Burnham, emerald marbled pattern, gold-filled trim, lever filler, English, 1947..**$70.00**

Camel, No 5, black, gold-filled trim, button & ink pellet filler, 1936...**$375.00**

Carter INX, No 2223, black, gold-filled trim, lever filler, 1928 ....**$95.00**

Chilton, No 16, black, gold-filled trim, touchdown filler, 1930 ....**$250.00**

Chilton Chiltonian, green pearl marbled pattern w/gold-filled trim, touchdown filler, 1941 ....**$265.00**

Conklin, emerald pearl marbled pattern, gold-filled trim, lever filler, 1931 ....**$95.00**

Diamond Medal, No 4, pearl & black, gold-filled trim, lever filler, 1932..**$150.00**

Dunn Camel Society, hard black-chased rubber, pump filler, 1924 ....**$120.00**

Eagle EP31, green pearl marbled pattern, gold-filled trim, plunger filler, 1937 ....**$60.00**

Eclipse, gold-filled w/gold-filled trim, lever filler, 1927.**$150.00**

Eversharp, Dubonnet red mounted w/gold-filled trim, lever filler, 1949 ....**$50.00**

Eversharp, red marbled pattern w/gold-filled trim, lever filler, 1937 ....**$95.00**

Eversharp Gold Seal Doric, black mounted w/gold-filled trim, 1935 ....**$150.00**

Eversharp Ladies, maroon w/gold-filled trim, lever filler, 1941 ....**$130.00**

Eversharp Skyline, gold stripes w/gold-filled trim, lever filler, 1943 ....**$60.00**

Gold Medal, black-lined pearl marbled pattern, gold-filled trim, lever filler, 1931.....................................**$165.00**

Gold Medal, No 636, black w/gold-filled trim, lever filler, 1936 ....**$65.00**

Inkograph Stylographic, No 15M, hard red-mottled rubber, gold-filled trim, lever filler, 1926.....................**$175.00**

John Holland, No 2, vertical green stripes, gold-filled trim, lever filler, 1940 ....**$90.00**

Lady Sheaffer Skripsert AC10E, ivory corduroy w/cartridge, 1958 ....**$40.00**

Laughlin #1, black chased hard rubber, eye-drop filler, 1899 ....**$85.00**

Mont Blanc Masterpiece, No 142, black, gold-filled trim, piston filler, 1955 ....**$275.00**

Moore, lined emerald pearl, gold-filled trim, lever filler, 1944 ....**$100.00**

Moore, onyx marbled pattern, gold-filled trim, lever filler, 1930 ....**$95.00**

Moore Acme, No 721R, hard black-lined rubber, gold-filled trim, lever filler, 1925.....................................**$75.00**

Moore Colonial, No 784C, hard black rubber, gold-filled trim, lever filler, 1925.....................................**$150.00**

Moore 282G, maroon, mounted w/gold-filled trim, lever filler, 1925 ....**$125.00**

Parker, No 25, Jack-Knife in hard black rubber, gold-filled trim, button filler, 1920..................................**$185.00**

Parker, Writefine, black w/gold-filled trim, button filler (matching pencil: $20.00), 1941 ....$50.00

Parker Duofold Debutante, green, gold-filled trim, vacumatic filler, 1941..**$110.00**

Parker Duofold Jr, mandarin yellow, gold-filled trim, button filler, 1927..**$270.00**

Parker Duofold Sr, burgundy & black, gold-filled trim, button filler, 1934..**$450.00**

Parker Lady Duofold, jade, gold-filled trim, button filler, 1930 ....**$125.00**

Parker Major Blue Diamond, golden pearl, gold-filled trim, vacumatic filler, 1940...................................**$260.00**

Parker Parkette, gray w/stainless cap, chromium-plated trim, lever filler, 1950..**$20.00**

Parker Senior Vacumatic, golden pearl, gold-filled trim, vacumatic filler, 1936....................................**$325.00**

Parker Vacumatic Jr, blue pearl stripes, gold-filled trim, vacumatic filler **$75.00**

Parker 61, red w/Lustraloy cap, capillary filler, 1960 ....**$55.00**

Pick Exceptional, No 2002, red, gold-filled trim, lever filler, 1928 ....**$285.00**

Sheaffer, No 21, hard black-chased rubber, gold-filled trim, lever filler, 1918 ....**$185.00**

Sheaffer, No 3-25, silver pearl marbled pattern, nickel-plated trim, lever filler, 1936....................................**$70.00**

Sheaffer Lifetime, emerald marbled pattern, gold-filled trim, lever filler, 1932 ....**$350.00**

Sheaffer Lifetime, No J84C, jade, gold-filled trim, lever filler, 1928 ....**$250.00**

Sheaffer Lifetime, No 1000, marine green, gold-filled trim, lever filler, 1938 ....**$195.00**

Sheaffer Lifetime Skyboy, black, lever filler, 1941 ....**$95.00**

Sheaffer R 46SC, mounted w/coral, gold-filled trim, lever filler, 1924 ....**$200.00**

Sheaffer Self Filling, No 2, hard black rubber, solid gold trim, lever filler, 1923......................................**$200.00**

Sheaffer Signature TM-121S-6, black, 14K band & gold-filled trim, touchdown filler, 1950.....................**$150.00**

Sheaffer White Dot Triumph, black, gold-filled trim & mounted cap, touchdown filler, 1949...................**$95.00**

Sheaffer 28LC, solid gold mounted w/solid gold trim, lever filler, 1924 ....**$240.00**

Swan, No 2, gold-filled mounted w/gold-filled trim, lever filler, 1922 ....**$140.00**

Swan 44 ETN, burgundy, black, & white marbled pattern, gold-filled trim, lever filler, 1933......................**$120.00**

Wahl, No 2, gold-filled mounted w/gold-filled trim, lever filler, 1925 ....**$130.00**

Wahl, No 74, hard black-chased rubber, gold-filled trim, lever filler, 1928 ....**$325.00**

Waterman, No 21, hard black-chased rubber, gold-filled trim, twist filler, 1915.......................................**$120.00**

Waterman, No 24, hard black-chased rubber, nickel-plated trim, twist filler, 1915..............................**$90.00**

Waterman, No 5, jet black mounted w/gold-filled trim, lever filler, 1933...**$150.00**

Waterman, No 54, red mottled hard rubber w/gold-filled trim, lever filler, 1925...............................**$225.00**

Waterman Ideal, black w/gold-filled mounted cap, capillary filler, 1954...**$85.00**

Waterman Ideal, No 52V, black chased hard rubber w/nickel-plated trim, lever filler, 1925.................**$75.00**

Waterman Safety, No 12½VS, black hard rubber, eye-drop filler, 1915...**$165.00**

Waterman Thorobred Deluxe, blue w/chromium-plated trim, lever filler, 1940....................................**$65.00**

Webster Four Star, silver pearl stripes w/gold-filled trim, touchdown filler, 1940................................**$95.00**

Frames

There always seems to be a market for antique picture frames. Some that seem to sell especially well are the tiny ones that decorators like to group together (these may be made of silver, chrome, glass-bead mosaics, etc.), the large oak frames that are often decorated with gilded gesso reliefs, and the crossed-corner Victorians with the applied leaves.

Brass, 14x20", oval, convex glass, EX...........................**$50.00**

Brass, 5½x8", filigree, Victorian stand-up type............**$45.00**

Brass, 5x4¾", ornate border, metal back.....................**$30.00**

Brass & copper, 6¼" dia, rope design edge, stand-up type-easel back...**$60.00**

Cast iron w/gilt, 11½x8¼", reticulated leaves, metal back, desk type...**$55.00**

Cherry wood, 19x16", 2" wide **$80.00**

Curly maple wood, 15x19"...**$150.00**

Laminated mahogany & pine, 9x13", shaped perimeter w/applied bosses **$35.00**

Mahogany veneer, 16x18", 2" wide.............................**$40.00**

Pine wood, 12x14", original finish, gilt liner, pr........**$140.00**

Pine wood w/original gray smoke grain paint, 9x11", 1½" wide, square nails...**$150.00**

Polychrome artificial grain paint, 19x13", 1930s.$90.00

Walnut wood, 13x11", 3" wide, worn........................**$20.00**

Franciscan Dinnerware

Franciscan is a tradename of Gladding McBean, used on their dinnerware lines from the mid-thirties until it closed its Los Angeles-based plant in 1984. They were the first to market 'starter sets' (four place settings), a practice that today is commonplace.

Two of their earliest lines were El Patio (simply styled, made in bright solid colors) and Coronado (with swirled borders and pastel glazes). In the late thirties, they made the first of many hand-painted dinnerware lines. Some of the best known are Apple, Desert Rose, and Ivy. From 1941 to 1977, 'Masterpiece' (true porcelain) china was produced in more than 170 patterns.

Many marks were used, most included the Franciscan name. An 'F' in a square with 'Made in U.S.A.' below it dates from 1938, and a double-line script F was used in more recent years.

For further information, we recommend *The Collector's Encyclopedia of California Pottery* by Jack Chipman.

Almond Cream, cup & saucer.....................................**$10.00**

Almond Cream, plate, 10" **$10.00**

Almond Cream, plate, 8"...**$8.00**

Apple, batter bowl..**$50.00**

Apple, bowl, vegetable; 9" **$20.00**

Apple, bowl, 7½"...**$30.00**

Apple, coaster, 3¾"...**$15.00**

Apple, compote, lg...**$40.00**

Apple, cup & saucer, demitasse.................................**$50.00**

Apple, egg cup..**$18.00**

Apple, plate, 10½"...**$18.00**

Apple, plate, 8"..**$14.00**

Apple, relish, 3-part, 11"...**$45.00**

Apple, sugar bowl, open, sm.....................................**$30.00**

Autumn, salt & pepper shakers, pr............................**$16.00**

Blueberry, cup & saucer...**$8.00**

Bountiful, cup & saucer...**$18.00**

Cafe Royal, canister, tea **$95.00**

Cafe Royal, coffeepot...**$85.00**

Cafe Royal, mug, 7-oz..**$20.00**

Cafe Royal, napkin rings, boxed set of 4 ....**$85.00**

Cafe Royal, plate, 10½"..**$20.00**

California Poppy, bowl, salad; lg...............................**$145.00**

California Poppy, cup & saucer **$25.00**

California Poppy, plate, bread & butter.......................**$12.00**

California Poppy, plate, 10"...**$25.00**

Coronado, ashtray, turquoise gloss............................**$5.00**

Coronado, butter dish, round, w/lid...........................**$35.00**

Coronado, casserole, w/lid..**$28.00**

Coronado, coffeepot, demitasse.................................**$50.00**

Coronado, creamer & sugar bowl..............................**$30.00**

Coronado, cup & saucer, demitasse **$22.00**

Coronado, demitasse pot..**$50.00**

Coronado, nut cup, footed **$16.00**

Coronado, plate, chop; 14".........................$35.00
Coronado, plate, 7½".................................$10.00
Coronado, platter, 11½".............................$25.00
Coronado, sherbet $10.00
Coronado, sugar bowl, w/lid $12.00
Coronado, teapot $40.00
Desert Rose, ashtray, individual...................$12.00
Desert Rose, bowl, vegetable; w/lid..............$50.00
Desert Rose, casserole, stick handles, 12-oz.......$35.00
Desert Rose, coffeepot..............................$85.00
Desert Rose, mug, lg................................$22.00
Desert Rose, pickle dish, 10¼".....................$35.00
Desert Rose, plate, 6½"..............................$10.00
Desert Rose, platter, 12½" $35.00

Desert Rose, water pitcher.......................$70.00
Duet, bowl, 8" oval..................................$20.00
Duet, plate, bread & butter $2.50
Echo, bowl, 9"..$20.00
El Patio, bowl, cereal................................$12.00
El Patio, bowl, vegetable; oval.....................$30.00
El Patio, butter dish $35.00
El Patio, creamer $10.00
El Patio, plate, 10½"..................................$15.00
El Patio, sugar bowl, w/lid $18.00
Forget-Me-Not, bowl, soup; flat $18.00
Forget-Me-Not, bowl, 8¼"...........................$40.00
Forget-Me-Not, coaster, 3¾".........................$15.00
Forget-Me-Not, mug, lg..............................$22.00
Forget-Me-Not, plate, 10½"..........................$25.00
Forget-Me-Not, sugar bowl, w/lid, lg $35.00
Forget-Me-Not, tray, 3-tier $40.00
Fresh Fruits, bowl, cereal; 6"........................$15.00
Fresh Fruits, casserole, stick handles, 12-oz..........$35.00
Fresh Fruits, pickle dish, 10¼".......................$35.00
Fresh Fruits, plate, chop; 14".........................$60.00
Fresh Fruits, plate, 10½"..............................$25.00
Fresh Fruits, plate, 6½"...............................$10.00

Fresh Fruits, salt shaker.............................$18.00
Fresh Fruits, sugar bowl, open, sm.................$30.00
Fresh Fruits, tumbler, 5⅛"...........................$22.00
Hacienda Gold, butter dish, w/lid $25.00
Hacienda Gold, mug, lg..............................$9.00
Honey Dew, cup & saucer...........................$8.00
Honey Dew, plate, 10½"..............................$10.00
Ivy, ashtray, individual $12.00
Ivy, bowl, 7½"..$30.00
Ivy, coaster, 3¾"......................................$15.00
Ivy, creamer, lg $15.00
Ivy, cup & saucer, jumbo............................$35.00
Ivy, pitcher, water....................................$65.00
Ivy, plate, 10½".......................................$25.00
Ivy, salt & pepper shakers, tall, pr.................$35.00
Ivy, tumbler, 5⅛".....................................$22.00
Madeira, creamer......................................$7.00
Madeira, cup & saucer...............................$5.00
Madeira, plate, 10¼"..................................$6.50
Madeira, plate, 8½"...................................$5.00
Madeira, platter, 14".................................$18.00
Madeira, sugar bowl, open..........................$4.00
Meadow Rose, bowl, lug handle, sm...............$18.00
Meadow Rose, casserole, stick handles, 12-oz..........$35.00
Meadow Rose, creamer, lg $15.00
Meadow Rose, goblet.................................$26.00
Meadow Rose, gravy boat............................$45.00
Meadow Rose, pitcher, 1-pt $30.00
Meadow Rose, plate, 9½".............................$20.00
Meadow Rose, salt & pepper shakers, Rosebud, pr....$25.00
Metropolitan, cream soup............................$15.00
Metropolitan, cup, demitasse $12.00
Oasis, plate, 8"...$8.00
October, bowl, cereal; 6".............................$18.00
October, cup & saucer................................$25.00
October, plate, 8".....................................$18.00
October, platter, 14"..................................$65.00
Rosette, bowl, dessert................................$12.50
Rosette, plate, 10½"...................................$20.00
Shady Lane, gravy boat...............................$18.00
Shady Lane, salt & pepper shakers, pr.............$18.00
Shady Lane, sugar bowl...............................$15.00
Starburst, cup & saucer...............................$10.00
Starburst, plate, dinner...............................$10.00
Strawberry, batter bowl..............................$50.00
Strawberry, bowl, vegetable; sm....................$15.00
Strawberry, compote, lg $40.00
Strawberry, egg cup..................................$18.00
Strawberry, plate, 6½".................................$10.00
Strawberry, plate, 9½".................................$20.00
Strawberry, salt & pepper shakers, Rosebud, pr.........$25.00
Strawberry, tumbler, 5⅛".............................$22.00
Twilight Rose, cup & saucer $18.00
Twilight Rose, plate, 10½"............................$20.00
Wheat Gold, plate, chop.............................$35.00
Wheat Gold, plate, salad.............................$7.50
Wheat Gold, plate, 10½"..............................$12.00

Frankoma Pottery

This pottery has operated in Oklahoma since 1933, turning out dinnerware, figurines, novelties, vases, bicentennial plates and plaques, and political mugs in various lovely colors.

Their earliest mark was 'Frankoma' in small block letters; but when fire destroyed the pottery in 1938, all of the early seals were destroyed, so new ones had to be made. The new mark was similar, but slightly larger, and the 'O' (rather than being perfectly round) was elongated. Some of their early wares (1936-38) were marked with a 'pacing leopard'; these are treasured by collectors today. By the mid-1950s the mark was no longer impressed by hand but became instead part of the mold. Paper labels have been used since the late forties, and since 1942 nearly every item has had an impressed mold number.

In 1954 Frankoma began digging their clay from another area of the neighboring countryside. The early clay had been a light golden brown color; it was mined near the town of Ada, and collectors refer to this type of clay as 'Ada' to distinguish it from the red-firing Sapula clay that has been used since 1954.

Their glazes have varied over the years due in part to the change in the color of the clay, so with a knowledge of the marks and color variances, you can usually date a piece with a fair amount of accuracy. If you'd like to learn more, we recommend *Frankoma Treasures* by Phyllis and Tom Bess.

Ashtray, 3½x4½", White Sand, Ada clay	**$15.00**
Bookends, Mountain Girl, 5¾", #425, pr	**$200.00**
Bowl, Plainsman, 12"	**$7.00**
Candle holder, Oral Roberts	**$12.00**
Carafe, all colors, w/lid	**$20.00**
Christmas card, 1958	**$60.00**
Creamer, Guernsey, 3½", #93-A	**$25.00**
Donkey mug, Woodland Moss, 1978	**$25.00**
Elephant mug, 1970, blue	**$65.00**

Figurine, Rodeo Cowboy, 7½"	**$400.00**
Flower arranger, 8½", green abstract	**$15.00**
Flower candlestick, Old Gold	**$6.00**

Flower holder, Boot, 3½", stars on sides, Ada clay	**$12.00**
Honey jar, Beehive, 12-oz, #803, Ada clay	**$25.00**
Lamp base, from Wagon Wheel sugar bowl	**$45.00**
Mug, Proctor & Gamble advertising	**$8.00**
Mug, Red Bud	**$12.00**
Pitcher, batter; 4½", #87	**$35.00**
Pitcher, Snail, mini, Old gold	**$15.00**
Plaque, Indian, 3¾"	**$10.00**
Plate, Peter the Fisherman, 1977	**$25.00**
Plate, Symbols of Freedom	**$20.00**

Plate, Teenagers of the Bible Series, Dorcas the Seamstress, 1976	**$25.00**
Plate, Wagon Wheel, 9"	**$8.00**
Sculpture, Circus Horse, Desert Gold, red clay	**$75.00**
Sculpture, Flower Girl, 5½", #700, 1942-52	**$75.00**
Sculpture, Greyhound, 14", 6 petals on back base, 1983 reproduction	**$50.00**
Sculpture, seated puma, 7½", Prairie Green	**$85.00**
Sculpture, Swan, mini, Peacock Blue	**$40.00**
Teapot, Aztec, green	**$20.00**
Tumbler, Lazybone, 2⅞"	**$3.00**
Vase, #72, 10½", brown horizontal ridges	**$12.00**
Vase, bud; 5", snail decoration, early	**$15.00**
Vase, Ring, 2¾", #500	**$25.00**
Wall pocket, Leaf, 8½", #197	**$45.00**

Fruit Jars

Did you know that we have Napoleon to thank for the invention of the fruit jar? History has it that it was because of a reward he offered to anyone who could come up with a palatable way of preserving food for him and his army during wartime. The money was claimed by a fellow by the name of Appert in 1812, whose winning ideas have been altered or copied more than 4,000 times since.

One of the more successful adaptations ever conceived was patented by John Mason on November 30, 1858. His jar wasn't perfect, but many years and several improvements later (after he'd sold the rights to a company who subsequently let them expire), the Ball Brothers picked it up and began to market them nationwide. They were made by the thousands and are very common today. Just remember that most of them date to the twentieth century (not to 1858, which is simply the patent date), and unless they're made in an uncommon color, they're worth very little. Most fruit jars are clear or aqua blue; other colors, for instance emerald green, amber, cobalt, milk glass, or black, are unusual. Values are based on condition, age, rarity, color, and special features.

ABGA Perfect Mason, Made in USA, aqua, minor lip flake, 1-qt..**$25.00**

Acme (on shield w/stars & stripes), clear, ½-gal **$12.00**

Amazon Swift Seal, blue, 1-qt.......................................**$12.00**

Anchor (in block letters) below anchor, clear, 1-qt.....**$48.00**

Atlas E-Z Seal, aqua, 48-oz..**$15.00**

Atlas E-Z Seal (in circle), aqua, 1-qt **$28.00**

Atlas Good Luck, clear, full wire bail, midget.............**$18.00**

Atlas Mason, clear, midget..**$3.00**

Atlas Mason Improved Pat'd, green, 1-pt **$38.00**

Atlas Whole Fruit, clear, 1-pt.......................................**$2.00**

Ball (in script), Patent Apld For, aqua, original tin lid (slightly rusted) & wire closure, minor lip chipping, qt $300.00

Ball (leaning L's) Perfect Mason, aqua, 1-qt.................**$12.00**

Ball (underlined) Mason, light olive green, 1-qt..........**$22.00**

Ball (underlined) Perfect Mason, blue, w/ribs, 1-qt.......**$6.00**

Ball (3 L loop) Mason, aqua, ½-gal...............................**$4.00**

Ball Ideal (Bicentennial Medallion Edmund F BSLL on reverse), blue, 1-qt...**$75.00**

Ball Ideal (Bicentennial Medallion on back), blue, 1-qt..**$2.00**

Ball Mason (letters double outlined), aqua, ½-gal.......**$28.00**

Ball Perfect Mason (in dual line letters), clear, 1-qt.....**$72.00**

Ball Special, blue, 1-qt..**$8.00**

Boyd Perfect Mason, light green, 1-qt **$25.00**

Brockway Clear VU Mason, clear, 1-qt.........................**$2.00**

Calcutt's Pat's Apr 11th Nov 7th 1893 (on lid), clear, qt..**$38.00**

Clark's Peerless, aqua, 1-qt...**$6.00**

Clarke Fruit Jar Co Cleveland O, aqua, lid damage, qt .**$48.00**

Cohansey (arched), aqua, lip fracture, midget.............**$98.00**

Cohansey (arched), aqua, ½-gal **$30.00**

Crown (emblem) over Crown, aqua, plain aqua insert, midget...**$20.00**

Crown Mason, clear, midget **$18.00**

Crystal Jar, clear, screw on glass lid, ½-gal **$34.00**

Dexter (surrounded by fruits & vegetables), aqua, zinc lid, 1-qt...**$58.00**

Doolittle Patented Dec 3 1901 (on lid), clear, ½-gal....**$25.00**

Drey Improved Everseal, clear, glass ears, 1-qt **$2.00**

Drey Pat'd 1920 Improved Everseal, ½-gal..................**$15.00**

DSG Co 1 (on base), aqua, ½-gal **$34.00**

Durham (in circle), aqua, 1-pt......................................**$28.00**

Electric (World) Globe Fruit Jar, aqua, original lever clamp, 1-qt...**$148.00**

Empire (in stippled cross), clear, 1-qt...........................**$8.00**

Eureka Pat'd Dec 27th 1864, aqua, 1-qt **$68.00**

Excelsior Improved, aqua, 1-qt.....................................**$48.00**

Flaccus Bros Steers Head Fruit Jar, clear, 1-pt **$40.00**

Franklin Dexter Fruit Jar, aqua, 1-qt............................**$32.00**

Fruit Commonwealth Jar, light green, no closure, qt ..**$68.00**

Gem (block G), aqua, midget..**$35.00**

Gem (Mason's Improved Trademark), ground lip, glass insert & zinc lid, aqua, midget, M....................$55.00

Gem CFG Co, aqua, 1-qt..**$18.00**

Glassboro Trade 1 Mark Improved, aqua, ½-gal, EX...**$18.00**

Grandma Wheaton's Old Fashioned Recipes Canning Jar, clear, 1-pt..**$3.50**

Haines Combination, aqua, no lid, 1-qt **$138.00**

Hero (over cross), clear, 1-pt **$58.00**

Jeannette J (in square) Mason Home Packer, clear, 1-qt, EX...**$2.50**

Kerr Economy (Sand Springs Okla on back), clear, pt..**$3.00**

Keystone (Improved), aqua, 1-qt.................................**$18.00**

King (on banner below crown), clear, side clamps, 1-pt.**$14.00**

Kline's Pat'd Oct 27 63 (blown stopper), aqua, 1-qt.**$124.00**

Lafayette (script), aqua, ½-gal....................................**$148.00**

Large Star & A (on base), aqua, 1-qt............................**$25.00**

LG Co (on base), aqua, lip chips, ½-gal......................**$18.00**

Mason (in straight line), amber, 1-pt **$75.00**

Mason Fruit Jar (3 lines), aqua, 1-qt **$10.00**

Mason's (keystone) Pat Nov 30th 1858, aqua, midget.**$30.00**

Mason's (lg keystone), aqua, midget **$38.00**

Mason's BGCO Improved, aqua, 1-qt.....................**$58.00**

Mason's CFJ Co Patent Nov 30th, light olive, 1-qt **$45.00**

Mason's CJGCo (monogram) Patent Nov 30th 1858, aqua, ground lip, zinc lid, midget $55.00

Mason's Cross Improved (over erased Glassboro), aqua, 1-qt...**$18.00**

Mason's GL Patent Nov 30th 1858, aqua, 1-qt **$24.00**

Mason's H Patent Nov 30th 1858, aqua, 1-qt **$24.00**

Mason's KGBCo Patent Nov 30th 1858, aqua, ½-gal ...**$28.00**

Mason's LGW Improved, clear, 1-qt **$20.00**

Mason's Patent Nov 30th 1858, aqua, midget **$25.00**

Mason's Patent Nov 30th 1858 (HGW on reverse), aqua, 1-qt...**$18.00**

Mason's Patent Nov 30th 1858 (hourglass on reverse), aqua, midget...**$85.00**

Mason's 21 (underlined) Pat Nov 30th 1858, aqua, 1-qt.**$22.00**

Mason's 25 (underlined) Pat Nov 30th 1858, aqua, 1-qt..**$30.00**

Mason's 6 Patent Nov 30th 1858, clear, 1-qt **$12.00**

Michigan Mason (MG on base), aqua, 1-pt.................**$28.00**

Millville Atmospheric Fruit Jar, aqua, 1-qt...................**$32.00**

Millville WTCo Improved, aqua, 1-qt **$68.00**

Mission (bell) Mason Jar Made in Calif, aqua, 1-qt......**$10.00**

Monarch (on shield w/stars & stripes in framework), clear, 1-qt..**$10.00**

New Paragon, aqua, 1-qt.......................................**$125.00**

Ohio Quality Mason, clear, 1-qt...................................**$9.50**

Pacific Mason, clear, 1-qt...**$20.00**

Pat July 11 1893 VJC Co (on base), light aqua, no closure, 1-qt **$7.50**

Pat'd Feb 9th 1864 WW Lyman 12, aqua, w/ lid, 1-pt.**$75.00**

Pat'd Mar 26th 1867 BB Wilcox, aqua, 1-qt.................**$70.00**

Potter & Bodine Philadelphia (script), aqua, reproduction lid, 1-qt **$123.00**

Princess (on shield in frame), clear, 1-qt.....................**$25.00**

Putnam (on base), amber, 1-qt, VG............................**$28.00**

Putnam Glass Works Zanesville O (on base), aqua, qt.**$32.00**

Root Mason, green, 1-qt **$48.00**

Safe Seal Pat'd (in circle) July 14 1908, blue, 1-qt.........**$5.00**

Samco (in circle) Genuine Mason, clear, 1-qt.............**$2.00**

Schram Automatic Sealer (script), aqua, 1-pt..............**$15.00**

Simplex (in diamond), clear, 1-pt **$14.00**

SKO Queen Trademark, clear, midget........................**$12.00**

Smalley's (Royal in crown) Royal Trademark Nu-Seal, clear, 1-pt..**$9.00**

Star Glass Co New Albany Ind, aqua, ½-gal **$48.00**

Sun (in circle w/radiating rays), aqua, 1-qt.................**$68.00**

Swayzee's Improved Mason, green, ½-gal **$50.00**

The American (NAG Co), aqua, porcelain-lined interior, midget...**$148.00**

The Haserot Company Cleveland Mason Pat, aqua, qt.**$12.00**

The Hazel (on milk glass lid), clear, ½-gal.................**$15.00**

The Ideal Imperial, aqua, 1-qt....................................**$24.00**

The Queen, aqua, 1-qt...**$22.00**

The Vacuum Seal Pat Nov 1st 1904 Detroit, clear, 1-qt **$125.00**

The Victor Pat Feb, 20 1900 (M in diamond), aqua, clear lid, ½-gal..**$58.00**

Trade Mark The Dandy, amber, 1-qt......................**$142.00**

Trademark Mason's CFJ Improved, aqua, midget........**$24.00**

Woodbury WGW, aqua, ½-gal..................................**$50.00**

Worchester, aqua, outside stopper chips, 1-qt..........**$180.00**

Fry Oven Glassware

First developed in 1920, Ovenglass was a breakthrough in cooking methods, allowing the housewife to cook and serve in the same dish. The glassware was advertised as 'iridescent pearl' in color; today we would call it opalescent. Some pieces were decorated with engraved designs, and these are more valuable. It carried one of several marks; most contained the 'Fry' name, and some included a patent number as well as a mold number. (Though these might be mistaken for the date of manufacture, they're not!)

A matching line of kitchenware was also made – platters, sundae dishes, reamers, etc. – but these were usually marked 'Not Heat Resistant Glass' in block letters.

The company was sold in 1934, but the glassware they made is being discovered by collectors who will cherish it and preserve it for years to come.

To learn more about this subject, we recommend *The Collector's Encyclopedia of Fry Glassware* by the H.C. Fry Glass Society and *Kitchen Glassware of the Depression Years* by Gene Florence.

Apple baker, #1937, orange enamel trim **$30.00**

Au gratin, #1952, 9", oval w/tab handles.....................**$30.00**

Baker, #1917, 6", oval, opalescent **$15.00**

Baker, #1932, 12", oval, w/lid, opalescent **$35.00**

Cake pan, #1939, round, opalescent............................**$15.00**

Cake pan, #1947, square, crystal.................................**$15.00**

Casserole, #1932, 8", w/lid, opalescent w/blue trim....**$35.00**

Casserole, #1935, square w/embossed grapes on lid ..**$40.00**

Casserole, #1938, round, w/lid, transparent green **$75.00**

Casserole, #1938, 8" dia, w/lid, footed metal holder w/pointed ear-shaped handles, opalescent...........**$25.00**
Casserole, #1941, 6" dia, w/lid, opalescent.................**$35.00**
Casserole, sm, w/lid, etched floral & leaf design........**$35.00**
Cocotte, #1926, 4½" dia, straight-sided, opalescent.....**$22.50**
Grill plate, #1957, 8", 3-part, opalescent w/blue trim..**$25.00**
Hot roll dish, #1953, 6", boat shape...........................**$30.00**

Measuring cup, 1-cup..............................$50.00
Meat platter, lg oval w/well & tree design, etched floral & leaf design on rim...................................**$65.00**

Meatloaf pan, 8", embossed w/grapes...................**$30.00**
Pudding baker, #1948, 7" dia, opalescent **$25.00**
Relish dish, 4-pt divided oval, opalescent...................**$40.00**
Shirred egg, #125, round w/tab handles, opalescent ..**$30.00**

Fulper

Founded around the turn of the century, the Fulper Pottery entered into the art pottery market about 1909 and produced a considerable quantity of fine art ware vases, bowls, lamps, etc., many of which were styled in the Arts and Crafts tradition and glazed in outstanding color combinations and textures. Today these pieces are evaluated on the basis of form, size, and glaze. Most pieces are marked in ink under the glaze or with a paper label.

Bookends, 7½", Ramses, matt green, pr....................**$350.00**
Bowl, centerpiece; Chinese blue-green, 3-footed, incised mark....................................**$210.00**
Bowl, 2x13", green & gun-metal crystalline, twisted edge, black vertical mark **$110.00**
Bowl, 3x11", green w/gun-metal crystalline, brown swirls inside, vertical mark.................................**$200.00**

Bowl, 3x13½", green, gray & lavender w/embossed geometrics......................................$325.00
Bowl, 3x14", blue to cream flambe interior, blue over matt gray exterior (illustrated)......................**$500.00**
Fan vase, 8", glossy mocha over matt brown **$150.00**
Fan vase, 8", mirror black over butterscotch, handles, ink stamp **$130.00**
Flower bowl, 5x9", aqua to green matt, ink stamp ...**$250.00**
Flower frog, Indian maiden in canoe, matt green to blue, block stamp................................**$250.00**
Flower frog & bowl, pelican on rock, blue & green crystalline, both pieces marked...............................**$160.00**
Vase, bud; 5", brown & blue crystalline over speckled blue gloss, vertical black mark....................................**$100.00**
Vase, bud; 8", twig shape, matt green over wisteria blue, vertical ink stamp...............................**$125.00**
Vase, 10", plum, gray & pink matt, handles..............**$190.00**
Vase, 12", matt teal blue to semigloss crystalline, repaired handles, incised mark................................**$300.00**
Vase, 5x9", green crystalline over pink famille rose, vertical mark, paper label w/#657 ....**$350.00**
Vase, 6", green semigloss over watermelon, 3 handles, horizontal mark **$110.00**
Vase, 6", mirror green over blue, 3 loop handles, horizontal mark................................**$160.00**
Vase, 6½", blue wisteria mirror glaze **$120.00**
Vase, 6x8", purple crystalline, 3 loop handles at top, raised vertical mark................................**$190.00**
Vase, 7", light brown crystalline, 3 handles, black vertical mark................................**$125.00**
Vase, 7", mirror black over butterscotch, 3 handles, ink stamp **$150.00**
Vase, 7", thick feathered blue crystalline, beaded design at neck, vertical mark **$185.00**

Vase, 7¼x8", green & gun-metal gray mottle w/some iridescence (illustrated on page 183)............$350.00

Vase, 7¾", cat's-eye brown over wheat w/green drip, handles, incised mark.................$190.00

Vase, 8", brown & caramel flambe w/blue...............$115.00

Vase, 8", copper dust, 2 open handles, impressed mark, #864.........$155.00

Vase, 8", famille rose w/aqua drip, handles...............$190.00

Vase, 9", dark blue & brown glossy, handles.............$95.00

Vase, 9", dark brown glossy drip on yellow, 7-sided, cylindrical, impressed mark......................$150.00

Vase, 9", semigloss rose & gray flambe....................$140.00

Whiskey jug, 10", silver overlay golfer, music box missing, unmarked.......................$150.00

Furniture

A piece of furniture can often be difficult to date, since many 17th- and 18th-century styles have been reproduced. Even a piece made early in the 20th century now has enough age on it that it may be impossible for a novice to distinguish it from the antique. Even cabinetmakers have trouble identifying specific types of wood, since so much variation can occur within the same species; so although it is usually helpful to try to determine what kind of wood a piece has been made of, results are sometimes inconclusive. Construction methods are usually the best clues, so watch for evidence of 20th-century tools – automatic routers, lathes, carvers, and spray guns.

To learn about furniture and accessories from the twenties, thirties, and forties, we recommend *Furniture of the Depression Era* by Robert and Harriett Swedberg.

Armchair, Country, ladderback w/4 arched slats, turned feet & stretcher, paper seat....................$275.00

Armchair, Hitchcock type, brown paint w/crest decoration, rush seat, EX.......................$175.00

Armchair, lacy restored caning on back & seat, arms w/notched hand rests, baluster stiles.................$250.00

Armchair, ladderback, cleaned down to old red, sausage turnings, repairs....................:.........$550.00

Armchair, Sheraton, red & black grainpaint w/striping, EX details, repairs & replacements.........................$375.00

Armchair, Windsor, bamboo turnings, medallion back, refinished.......................$225.00

Armchair, Windsor, bow back w/spindles, splayed base, turned legs, shaped seat, old black repaint........$500.00

Armchair, Windsor, bow back w/9 spindles, bamboo turnings, saddle seat, refinished.................$375.00

Armchair, Windsor, bow back w/9 spindles, continuous arms, black paint, breaks & repairs....................$700.00

Armchair, Windsor, comb back w/9 spindles, red stain, repairs & replacements, worn finish....................$500.00

Armchair, 25¼", ladderback w/3 slats, worn cane seat, old black repaint, child's....................$80.00

Armchair, 35", mahogany, Rococo Revival, reupholstered, dark finish, laminated back (minor damage)........$75.00

Armchair rocker, 25", 3 arched slats, replaced woven splint seat, child's.......................$140.00

Armchair rocker, 34", Country, 3 shaped slats, turned posts, splint seat (some damage), old refinishing, late...$85.00

Armchair rocker, 45", oak, 5 graduated arched slats, turned arm posts, shaped arms, replaced woven splint seat, repairs.......................$250.00

Bed, day; 77x24", curly maple w/walnut headboard, Country, upholstered cushion, old refinish.................$500.00

Bed, day; 83x33", beechwood, Louis XV style..........$600.00

Bed, oak, full size, lattice-type cutouts, applied factory carvings on flat head & footboard, square posts.......$575.00

Bed, oak, Mission, 3 wide slats in head & footboards, original finish.......................$175.00

Bed, oak, Mission style, 56" wide, 52" high headboard, 40" high footboard, 1920s.......................$195.00

Bed, quarter-sawn oak, blanket roll along curved top of head and footboards, carved, shaped feet, full size......$350.00

Bed, rope; 76x46" mattress, old red & black grainpaint, red & gold stenciled flowers, turned posts.................$400.00

Bed, 54" wide, 48" high headboard, artificially grained, floral designs on head & footboard, 1930s.....................$75.00

Bed, 76x53", maple & poplar, tall turned posts, replaced headboard, replaced tester frame.........................$380.00

Bench, piano; 20x36x15", oak, lift lid, cabriole legs & paw feet, 1920s.......................$225.00

Bench, water; 48x48x15", poplar, cut-out feet, paneled doors, open shelf, 2 dovetailed drawers, cast iron pulls.......................$1,000.00

Bench, 53x72", settle, pine w/re-grainpaint (as oak), Country English, minor damage.................$400.00

Bench, 61", pine, primitive, weathered brown finish, cut-out legs.......................$150.00

Bench, 64", yellow pine w/worn red paint, Country, cut-out feet, scalloped apron.......................$150.00

Bin, 27x25", poplar w/worn red & green paint, 2 compartments.......................$395.00

Bookcase, mahogany w/inlay, Federal style, tambour, flip-up top in base.......................$1,200.00

Bookcase, oak, 4 sections, 1920s, restored...............$500.00

Bookcase, oak, 4 stacked sections, 4 hinged glass doors lift & roll into recessed tracks.......................$600.00

Bookcase, 4 sections, 3 hold books, 2nd section w/drop door serves as secretary desk w/compartments.$750.00

Bookcase, 62x19x12", oak, 1 glass door, early 1900s.$295.00

Buffet, 38x42x19", solid & quarter-sawn oak, 2 drawers over 1 over 2 arched panel doors, wooden knobs, scrolled feet.......................$350.00

Cabinet, china; lg, oak w/curved glass front, mirror, many press carvings.......................$1,250.00

Cabinet, medicine; 24x24x7", oak, double doors w/mirrors, 1920s.......................$225.00

Candlestand, walnut, Federal, birdcage, 3 cabriole legs, 19" tilt top.......................$325.00

Candlestand, 28x20x17", hardwood base w/yellow pine top, Country, tripod base w/cut-out feet...................$200.00

Candlestand, 38¾x20½" dia, birch base w/mismatched mahogany top, spider legs, repairs, refinished...$125.00

Cedar chest, 21x48x19", Macassar ebony veneer on front, applied decorations, 1930s $225.00

Chair, captain's, 22" arm to arm, 28" high, pine & maple, EX finish **$95.00**

Chair, curly maple, Country Sheraton, rush seat, VG.**$100.00**

Chair, desk; oak, Mission style, swivel base, restored, refinished **$325.00**

Chair, desk; swivel type, upholstered in green leather, modern...**$65.00**

Chair, desk; 37", walnut veneer & walnut-stained hardwoods, vase-shaped splat, pressed cane seat, French legs, 1920s **$65.00**

Chair, hourglass splat, shaped crest rail, plank seat, Pennsylvania, 4 for **$200.00**

Chair, invalid's, 42x21x18½", chestnut, pressed back, drop door for chamberpot **$165.00**

Chair, kitchen; 32x17x15", pine, shaped headpiece, 2 slats, rush seat **$60.00**

Chair, kitchen; 33x15x15", pine, straight headpiece, 4 plain turned spindles, round side posts, shaped seat ..**$110.00**

Chair, side; bird's wings pressed pattern on straight headpiece, 7 spindles, restored cane seat, simple **$125.00**

Chair, side; oak, ornate pressed pattern on back w/6 spindles, pressed cane seat, M, set of 4 ....**$575.00**

Chair, side; oak, single splat back, leather seat w/brass tacks, Dayton OH, 1920s **$85.00**

Chair, side; pine, 3 slats, original upright button finials, replaced woven seat, worn **$95.00**

Chair, side; quarter-sawn oak, Arts & Crafts style, leather seat & back w/brass tacks, set of 4 ....**$300.00**

Chair, side; quarter-sawn oak, vase-shaped splat, caned seat, set of 4...**$300.00**

Chair, side; reproduction, oak, pressed back, 5 spindles, turned rails & legs, faithful details to appear old **$95.00**

Chair, side; stenciled fruit & foliage on brown, half-spindle back, EX **$150.00**

Chair, side; vase-shaped splat, slim legs & frame, pressed cane bottom, simple style, set of 4 ....**$300.00**

Chair, side; Windsor, bow back w/7 spindles, saddle seat, repainted w/striping **$350.00**

Chair, side; 33", mahogany stain w/mahogany veneered lyre back, Duncan Phyfe style, 1940s, set of 4...........**$595.00**

Chair, side; 36¼", oak, English Country Chippendale, repairs to seat, old finish..**$95.00**

Chair, side; 36x16x16", oak, scalloped & pressed stay rail & headpiece hold 6 turned spindles **$200.00**

Chair, side; 38", arched slats, woven splint seat (w/damage), varnish over red paint traces **$75.00**

Chair, side; 38", hardwood, 3 arched slats, turned finials, replaced woven splint seat, refinished, 38"...........**$45.00**

Chair, side; 38", mahogany, English Chippendale, fluted legs, upholstered seat, carved back, old finish ...**$385.00**

Chair, side; 38½", Country Queen Anne, turned legs & posts vase splat & yoke crest, repaint w/gold striping **$385.00**

Chair, side; 39", Country Queen Anne, vase splat & yoke crest, replaced rush seat, old black repaint.........**$105.00**

Chair, side; 43½", banister back, replaced paper rush seat, old black repaint w/yellow striping....................**$100.00**

Chest, blanket; 20x40x18", mahogany veneer & bird's-eye maple veneer front & top on hardwood case.....**$225.00**

Chest, blanket; 25x37x18", poplar & pine, paneled construction, red grainpaint **$500.00**

Chest, blanket; 25x42x18", pine, 6-board construction, staple hinges (loose), putty-filled surface, till **$250.00**

Chest, blanket; 33", poplar w/old red paint, turned feet, dovetailed, applied edge molding, till................**$450.00**

Chest, blanket; 33x46", pine, red repaint, 6-board dovetailed drawer, replaced brasses **$250.00**

Chest, blanket; 38", pine & poplar w/red paint, turned feet, detailed, till, EX...**$275.00**

Chest, blanket; 43", poplar w/brown grainpaint over white, dovetailed, till, EX...**$325.00**

Chest, blanket; 48", poplar, dovetailed, bracket feet, scrolled apron, yellow w/brown combed graining, lg till ..**$650.00**

Chest, cherry w/inlay, Country Hepplewhite, 2 false drawers, 2 drawers, restored, replacements **$650.00**

Chest, curly maple, Empire, scroll feet & pilasters, 4 drawers, wooden pulls, EX **$650.00**

Chest, immigrant's, 26" long, pine, worn brown finish, blue striping...**$295.00**

Chest, maple w/some curl, Empire, 1 deep drawer over 3, half pilasters, EX **$500.00**

Chest, mule; 33x42x18", pine, Country, 6-board construction, cut-out feet, dovetailed drawer, brass pulls, restored...**$450.00**

Chest, mule; 42", red washed-pine, turned feet, paneled, 1 drawer, replaced molding **$385.00**

Chest, mule; 43x39x17", pine, Country, 6-board construction, 2 dovetailed drawers, 2 false drawers.........**$500.00**

Chest, utility; 22x38x15", pine, 6 drawers (3 over 3), restored finish, replaced porcelain knobs, ca 1800s **$450.00**

Chest, 19x36x20", cedar, mohair upholstery covering, 1930s, EX original condition....................................**$225.00**

Chest, 36x27x22", Country Empire, rounded corners, 4 ogee dovetailed drawers, refinished, replacements **$350.00**

Chest, 36x28x14", oak, 2 short drawers over 3, ornate brass pulls, factory dovetailing, golden finish **$295.00**

Chest, 36x43x19", bleached oak, 2 drawers over 4, Lammerts of St Louis, 1950s...**$695.00**

Chest, 40x30x19", oak veneer, 4 bow-front drawers, modified cabriole feet **$350.00**

Chest, 41x40x16", oak, 2 short drawers over 3, square nails, original wooden button knobs, refinished, 1880s .**$800.00**

Chest, 42", butternut, 2 sm step-back drawers over 3, bracket feet, repainted & refinished **$500.00**

Chest, 44x39", cherry & walnut, Country Sheraton, turned feet, paneled ends **$500.00**

Chifforette, 50x34x19", burl mahogany veneer on doors & drawer, pull-out drawers behind doors, 1920s **$245.00**

Coat rack, oak, square upright w/iron hooks, X base .**$150.00**

Commode, 18½x17", mahogany, Country Hepplewhite, lift lid has interior seat, turned feet......................**$135.00**

Cradle, 33", pine, primitive, old worn brown paint, age cracks & edge damage **$250.00**

Cupboard, corner; 85x41", poplar, 2-piece, scalloped base, paneled doors, porcelain knobs, 12 panes of glass in top door **$2,700.00**

Cupboard, corner; 85x45", pine, Country, 4 paneled doors, molded cornice, restoration, stripped **$1,250.00**

Cupboard, hanging; 29x34x17", pine, dovetailed case, raised panel doors, 2 dovetailed drawers, old red paint **$950.00**

Cupboard, jelly; 40", poplar w/red repaint, simple cut-out feet, paneled door **$485.00**

Cupboard, jelly; 50x42x21", pine, Country, narrow paneled board end & board, brass latch, porcelain knob.**$325.00**

Cupboard, jelly; 54x38", pine, Country, blue-green repainted over red, board & batten door............................**$600.00**

Cupboard, kitchen safe; 38x24x11", pine, handmade, 2-board door, iron hinges, bootjack legs, paint traces, 1910s......................**$375.00**

Cupboard, 41", pine, curved shelves w/spoon cutouts, restored......................**$600.00**

Cupboard, 44" wide, pine, Country, 1-piece, 2 paneled doors over 2 drawers over 2 paneled doors, step-back shelf **$750.00**

Cupboard, 70x19x37", pine, tongue & grooved 3-panel door w/brass turn latch, open-shelf top, iron hinges, paint traces **$1,200.00**

Cupboard, 81x38x19", pine, 1-piece, open top, 2 raised panel doors, scalloped top, repairs **$500.00**

Desk, lady's, oak, drop front, curved legs, simple **$450.00**

Desk, oak, partner's, 3 drawers each pedestal, simple .**$485.00**

Desk, 21x31x25½", cherry & poplar, Country Sheraton, dovetailed drawer, slant-top lid, scrolled gallery, refinished **$495.00**

Desk, 29x44x18", maple, kneehole type, 1950s........**$350.00**

Desk, 30x60x30", mahogany, Traditional style, high-quality reproduction, leather inserts, plate glass top **$935.00**

Desk, 38x38x10", Country Hepplewhite, dovetailed drawer, slant-top drop lid (replaced), refinished..............**$400.00**

Desk, 40x30x115", oak, drop lid, 3 drawers, original wooden knobs, simple styling **$545.00**

Desk, 44x24x15", oak, drop front, bow-front drawer, beveled gallery mirror, brass fixtures **$400.00**

Desk, 66", teak, Traditional style, double pedestal, 8 drawers, glass top **$500.00**

Dresser, oak, lg oval mirror in lyre frame, base w/2 drawers over lg drawer..........................**$400.00**

Dresser, 67x45x20", hardwoods, 2-tone walnut finish, router lines & panel decorations on drawers, attached mirror, 1920s..........................**$245.00**

Dresser, 75x42x21", oak, lg round mirror in lyre frame, 2 short drawers over 2, paneled sides..................**$375.00**

Dressing table, Deco style, kidney shape, 3 drawers, 3-way mirror..........................**$500.00**

Dry sink, 30x38", pine, Country, 1-board door w/battens, cast iron thumbpiece, refinished, EX..................**$350.00**

Dry sink, 33x52x19", pine, narrow paneled doors, old worn blue repaint over gray **$350.00**

Dry sink, 46", pine & poplar, cut-out feet, 2 panel doors, galleried well..........................**$450.00**

Footstool, 13", curly maple, exceptional detail, scalloped apron **$525.00**

Footstool, 24" long, pine, primitive, late, age cracks **$85.00**

Footstool, 8¼x17x9½", pine, wire-nail construction, mellow finish **$75.00**

Highchair, 32", Country, 2 slats, rabbit ear posts, simple turnings, rush seat (repaired), refinished..............**$99.00**

Highchair, 42x18", hard rock maple, 1950s..............**$125.00**

Ice box, oak, 4 doors, lg **$500.00**

Ice box, 39x21x18", oak, shiny brass fixtures, White Mountain on brass, reproduction **$350.00**

Desk, S-roll top; 48x50x30", oak, 1920s **$1,500.00**

Linen press, 78x46x22", pine, England, ca 1900, refinished, replaced feet, repairs **$1,500.00**

Piano stool, 15" dia seat, oak, 3 claw feet w/glass balls, 1930s..**$135.00**

Pie safe, 50", butternut & poplar, 6 star-punched tin panels, EX **$700.00**

Pie safe, 57x42x14", pine, 2 doors each w/3 punched tin panels, 2 drawers, gallery top, repairs, refinished......**$500.00**

Rocker, oak, 3-slat back, armless, pressed cane seat **$175.00**

Rocker, platform; 43", oak, pressed headpiece, 9 spindles, turned posts, 1900s..**$500.00**

Rocker, worn red & black grainpaint w/gold & yellow striping, turned legs **$150.00**

Rocker, 28", Boston type, old reproduction w/black paint & decal-decorated crest, child's **$50.00**

Rocker, 33x26", Mission type, original leather & brass tacks, dark stain...**$250.00**

Rocker, 37x26", Mission type, shaped center splat, reupholstered seat **$195.00**

Rocker, 38x19", plain & quarter-sawn oak, pressed back w/oak leaves & beading, splayed arms, restored cane seat...**$250.00**

Rocker, 39", Mission Oak, branded Limbert mark, restored & refinished.......................................$700.00

Rocker, 40", oak, woven splint back, side stretchers wood-pinned to outer side of splayed legs, saddle seat, dark stain **$225.00**

Rocker, 43x21x17", plain & quarter-sawn oak, Shaker-type, oval finials, 3 slats, woven rush seat **$150.00**

Rocker, 44", Man of the Wind pressed into top rail, maple, 1900s $475.00

Secretary, poplar, Country, refinished to yellow grainpaint, 2 glaze doors over pigeonhole over 2 doors, EX ..**$550.00**

Settle, 84", plank seat, simple turnings, refinished **$400.00**

Shelf, 23x25", hardwood w/red stain, very simple style, 3 tiers, wall mount...**$200.00**

Shelf, 28x30", soft wood w/old red stain, molded & curved sides, wall mount..**$800.00**

Sideboard, oak, free-standing column each side of mirror, press-carved trim...**$700.00**

Sideboard, quarter-sawn oak, 2 sm drawers over 2 doors over 1 lg drawer, rectangular mirror in top **$500.00**

Sideboard, quarter-sawn oak, 3 center drawers w/leaded glass door on sides, lg drawer below, beveled glass mirror, EX **$1,200.00**

Stand, cherry & mahogany veneer, Sheraton, 2 drawers, turned legs, 1-board top, refinished **$350.00**

Stand, corner, 63", Adirondak, black, red & gold paint, 4 tiers **$210.00**

Stand, plant; 40x52", Adirondak, original green paint w/orange & gold...**$550.00**

Stand, sewing; 26x12x12", hardwood, Priscilla style, dark mahogany finish, late 1920s **$95.00**

Stand, walnut, Country, tilt 1-board top (w/crack), turned column, 4 carved feet..**$200.00**

Stand, 14" top, birch, Country, tripod base w/flaring legs, chip carving..**$175.00**

Stand, 18" 1-board top, pine w/red repaint, Country Hepplewhite, square tapered legs **$250.00**

Stand, 18x20" top, cherry, Country Hepplewhite, replaced drawer w/walnut front, replacements **$200.00**

Stand, 19", curly maple, Sheraton, cock-beaded drawer, reeded molding...**$700.00**

Stand, 19x17", walnut, Country, 2 dovetailed drawers, 1-board top, turned legs, refinished **$285.00**

Stand, 20" dia 2-board top, walnut, Country, spool-turned column, tripod feet..**$185.00**

Stand, 22" 1-board top, curly maple, Country Sheraton, turned legs, dovetailed drawer **$700.00**

Stand, 29x16x16", oak, button & bulb turnings, scalloped-edge shelf..**$125.00**

Stand, 29x22x16", pine & poplar, Country, 2 dovetailed drawers, 2 turned legs, old repaint w/green stripes, minor damage...**$200.00**

Stand, 31x16x16", oak, narrow pressed apron on all 4 sides, reeded turned legs, tiny brass claw & glass ball feet...**$195.00**

Stand, 37x19x19", pine & poplar, Country, boldly turned legs, drawer, 2-board top, worn red finish **$495.00**

Stand, 38x17x19", cherry & poplar, Country, 4 curved legs joined midway flair out to support turtle-shaped top, stains...**$200.00**

Stool, 28", 9" dia top, oak, primitive, worn finish........**$75.00**

Table, breakfast drop leaf; 36x21x10", oak, turned legs, scalloped apron, 1920s...**$175.00**

Table, breakfast; 31x40x15", porcelain top w/white painted wooden base, 1940s, 2 10" leaf extensions, +4 white chairs **$165.00**

Table, card; cherry w/inlay, Hepplewhite, demilune, repaired veneer.................................**$350.00**

Table, coffee; 17x26x14", bleached mahogany & 2-toned figured walnut veneer, canted corners, square legs, 1940s...**$355.00**

Table, console; striped mahogany veneer & black paint, 4 scrolled legs w/joined cross pieces, 1920s..........**$145.00**

Table, dining; oak, pedestal w/4 cut-out scroll legs, round top...**$650.00**

Table, drop leaf; birch, Country, drawer, turned legs, round top, 10" leaves, refinished **$450.00**

Table, drop leaf; 27¼x41x14½" w/17" leaves, mahogany, English Queen Anne, swing legs, refinished.......**$325.00**

Table, drop leaf; 27x15x22", plain-cut mahogany, Pembroke, figured mahogany drawer front, 1940s................**$285.00**

Table, drop leaf; 47" top (replaced), cherry w/inlay, Hepplewhite, 6 legs...**$600.00**

Table, end; 25x14x12", mahogany, w/book trough **$125.00**

Table, end; 9x8x6", hardwoods, 3 turned legs, late 1920s, refinished..**$110.00**

Table, gate-leg; 29x34x12", original enamel finish, 1920s, 15" drop leaves..**$265.00**

Table, hutch; 28x48x35", pine, box compartment w/lift-off lid, 2-board top, shoe feet, wrought iron nails, old paint..**$700.00**

Table, hutch; 39x42" 4-board top, pine, Country, 1-board ends, bootjack feet **$1,250.00**

Table, kitchen drop leaf; 31x40x24", decorated enamel porcelain top, drawer each end, painted wooden base, 1930s..**$175.00**

Table, library; 29x48", Mission Oak, in the manner of Charles Rohlfs, 1910....................................$1,300.00

Table, occasional; 20x14" dia, tooled leather top, selected hardwood base, 1920s...**$175.00**

Table, tavern; 22x26" 1-board top, maple w/red traces, losses **$400.00**

Table, tavern; 28x23x30", curly maple top, red base, handmade reproduction **$295.00**

Table, tavern; 30" long 2-board pine top (replaced), birch, Country Hepplewhite, 1 drawer, EX...................**$350.00**

Table, tavern; 36", maple & pine w/red traces, Country Queen Anne, turned legs **$750.00**

Table, tea; 28x33" dia, mahogany, Chippendale, tilt top, tripod base w/snake feet, repairs, refinished.........**$800.00**

Table, tea; 29x26" dia, walnut, Country, tripod base w/spider legs, 2-board top, refinished....................**$200.00**

Table, work; 27x47x35", poplar, Country, tapered pencil post legs, H stretcher, replaced breadboard top, refinished **$275.00**

Table, work; 31x53x32", southern pine, Country Hepplewhite, 1 nailed & 1 beveled edge drawer, 3-board top, beaded apron...**$450.00**

Table, work; 58" (replaced) top, walnut, Country Queen Anne, turned legs, duck feet, 2 drawers **$400.00**

Table, 17x19" tilt top, curly maple, Empire, tripod base, sabre legs..**$450.00**

Table, 18x47x38", dark teak finish w/burl veneer top, Oriental style, plate glass cover, contemporary **$110.00**

Table, 20x30" 1-board top w/beaded edge, pine sawbuck, refinished..**$450.00**

Table, 29x44x19", pine, Country Hepplewhite Pembroke, square tapered legs, replaced top, refinished w/old red traces..**$250.00**

Table, 30x29x21", poplar, Pennsylvania Country, turned legs, stretcher base, button face, mortised & pinned, refinished..**$350.00**

Table, 38x41" dia, oak plain-sliced veneer top, quarter-sawn oak veneer apron & base, extension, 1920s **$375.00**

Table, 40", maple w/bird's-eye veneer inlay at edge, Country, demilune..**$750.00**

Table, 42x19" 2-board top, cherry, Pembroke Country Hepplewhite, 13" leaves....................................**$500.00**

Wardrobe, 65x24x21", V-matched oriental walnut veneer on door, veneer cabinet, 1930s **$255.00**

Wardrobe, 77x53x20", southern pine, raised panel doors, molded cornice, bracket feet, old refinishing **$400.00**

Washstand, cherry, Country Sheraton, base drawer, cutout w/ironstone bowl **$175.00**

Washstand, cherry, Country Sheraton, gallery, base shelf, 4-board replaced top **$325.00**

Washstand, pine, Sheraton, original paint decoration, gallery, base drawer, bowl cutout **$200.00**

Washstand, tiger maple, back splash, drawer, replaced lower shelf, EX..**$500.00**

Washstand, 25x32x17", oak, 1 drawer over 2 flat panel doors, original brasses.....................................**$245.00**

Washstand, 28x25x17", poplar, Country, turned feet & posts, dovetailed drawer & gallery, old cherry finish....**$340.00**

Washstand, 36x29x14", cherry & other woods, folk art, 1 drawer, towel bars, scrolled crest, wire nails......**$395.00**

Games

Games from the 1870s to the 1970s and beyond are fun to collect. The early games are beautifully lithographed. Some of their boxes were designed by well-known artists and illustrators of the time. Many times these old games are appreciated more for their artwork than for their entertainment value. Some represent a historical event or a specific era in the social development of our country. Characters from the early days of radio, television, and movies have been featured in hundreds of games designed for children and adults alike.

If you're going to collect games, be sure that they're reasonably clean, free of water damage, and complete. Most have playing instructions printed inside the lid or on a separate piece of paper that include an inventory list. Check the contents, and remember that the condition of the box is very important, too.

If you'd like to learn more about games, we recommend *Toys, Antique and Collectible,* by David Longest and *Toys of the Sixties* by Bill Bruegman.

The sizes listed with board game descriptions indicate the dimensions of the boxes.

See also TV.

$10,000 Pyramid, Milton Bradley, 2nd edition, '74, M.**$15.00**
Abbott & Costello's Who's on First, Parker Brothers, 1970s, MIB **$45.00**
Alfred Hitchcock Presents, Milton Bradley, 1958, EX..**$25.00**
All Star Basketball, Whitman, 1935, NM **$57.50**
Around the World in 80 Days, Transogram, 1957, NM .**$40.00**
Barney Miller, Milton Bradley, 1977, EX.....................**$12.50**
Baseball, Parker Brothers, 1950, VG...........................**$22.50**
Bash, Ideal, 1967, MIB...**$22.50**
Basketball, Cadeco, 1955, NM.....................................**$22.50**
Battleship, Milton Bradley, 1971, MIB **$25.00**
Beat the Clock, Milton Bradley, 1960s, MIB.................**$16.00**
Bionic Woman, Parker Brothers, 1976, EX....................**$5.00**
Black Beauty, Transogram, 1957, M **$45.00**
Blondie Goes to Leisureland, Westinghouse Corporation premium, EX **$40.00**
Bonkers, Parker Brothers, 1964, MIB............................**$25.00**
Bozo the World's Most Famous Clown, Parker Brothers, 1967, EX...**$35.00**
Bruce Jenner Decathlon, Parker Brothers, NM **$12.00**
Calling All Cars, Parker Brothers, ca 1930s, EX...........**$45.00**
Camelot, Parker Brothers, 1930, EX.............................**$45.00**
Captain America, Milton Bradley, 1977, EX..................**$25.00**

Captain Video, 10x19", Milton Bradley, VG...........$60.00
Car 54 Where Are You?, 10x22x1½", marked Eupolis Productions Inc w/1961 copyright, 18x18" board, complete, EX..**$100.00**
Casper the Friendly Ghost, Milton Bradley, 1959, EX .**$12.50**

Charlie's Angels, 8½x19x1½", marked Milton Bradley & Spelling-Goldberg Production, 1977, NM.............**$17.50**
Charlie's Angels Board Game, Milton Bradley, 1977, complete, EX..**$12.50**
Chinese Checkers, Milton Bradley, 1958, NM **$10.00**
CHIPS, 9½x18½x1½", marked Metro-Goldwyn-Mayer Film Co & Ideal w/1981 copyright, 18x18" board, complete, NM **$20.00**
Close Encounters of the Third Kind, Parker Brothers, 1978, EX...**$7.50**
Columbo Detective Game, 9½x19x1½", marked Milton Bradley & Universal Television, 1973, M..............**$20.00**
D-Day, marked Avalon Hill, 1961, EX......................**$25.00**
Daredevil Trik-Track, Transogram, 1965, NM **$80.00**
Dick Tracy Pinball, Marx, 1967, VG.............................**$50.00**
Dig Gold Mining, Parker Brothers, 1949, NM **$30.00**
Doctor Trump Card Game, in original box, 1970s, EX..**$15.00**
Don't Tip the Waiter, Colorforms, 1979, M **$15.00**
Donald Duck Party, Parker Brothers, 1938, VG...........**$42.50**
Donkey Party, Whitman, 1941, EX..............................**$15.00**
Dr Kildare Medical Game, Ideal, 1962, VG **$30.00**
Duck Shooting, Parker Brothers, 1930s, NM..............**$100.00**
Dukes of Hazzard Board Game, Ideal, 1981, NM........**$12.50**
Electric Baseball, Tudor, 1960, EX..............................**$27.50**
Emergency Board Game, Milton Bradley, 1974, EX **$12.50**
Fantasyland, Parker Brothers, 1956, EX......................**$25.00**
Fascination, Remco, 1965, M.......................................**$25.00**
Ferdinand the Bull Chinese Checkers, Walt Disney, copyright, 1938...**$65.00**
Fibber McGee & Molly Wistful Vista Mystery Game, Milton Bradley, 1940, NM..**$45.00**
Finance, Parker Brothers, 1948, NM **$15.00**
Flintstones Animal Rummy, marked Ed-U-Cards, 1961, complete, NM...**$25.00**
Flip-It 21, Aurora, 1973, M...**$20.00**
Flying Nun, Sally Fields full-color photo on lid, Milton Bradley, NM..**$55.00**
Foot Ball Game of Pigskin, Parker Brothers, 1960, EX..**$25.00**
Frontierland, Parker Brothers & Walt Disney's Official Game, 1950s, EX...**$32.50**
Game of the States, Milton Bradley, 1979, MIB **$25.00**
Game of Three Blind Mice, Milton Bradley, 1925, EX.**$48.00**
Game of Tom Sawyer, Milton Bradley, 1930s, EX.......**$45.00**
Going to Jerusalem, Parker Brothers, 1955, NM **$30.00**
Gomer Pyle, Transogram, 1960s, EX **$40.00**
Homestretch Horse Racing, Hasbro, MIB....................**$25.00**
I Dream of Jeannie, Milton Bradley, 1965, EX.............**$45.00**
I'm George Goebel, 10x20x1", marked Edwards & Deutsch Lithographing Co w/1955 copyright, complete, EX.**$55.00**
Interstate Highway, Selchow & Righter, 1979, NM......**$17.50**
Jeopardy, 9½x12x2", marked Milton Bradley & January Enterprises Inc, 3rd edition, 1964, complete, EX..**$20.00**
Jerry Lewis Las Vegas Game of Skill & Chance, 26x26", 1975, VG...**$25.00**
Jumping DJ, Mattel, 1961, NM....................................**$40.00**
Kojak, Telly Savalas color photo on lid, Milton Bradley, 1975, NM **$18.00**
Land of Sea War Games, Samuel Lowe, 1940s, EX......**$48.00**

Leverage, Milton Bradley, 1982, MIB..........................$10.00
Looney Tunes Balloon Game, Whitman, 1977, MIB....$25.00
Mad Magazine Card Game, Milton Bradley, 1980, MIB.$10.00
Masterpiece Art Auction, Parker Brothers, 1971, MIB .$15.00
Merv Griffin's Word for Word Game, 13x15x1½", black & white photo on lid, marked National Broadcasting Co, 1963, EX..............................$17.50
Mighty Mouse, Milton Bradley, 1978, NM $20.00
Milton the Monster, Milton Bradley, 1966, NM $55.00
Mind Over Matter ESP, Ideal, 1967, VG......................$15.00
Moon Rocket Express, Citation Products, 1962, EX.....$20.00
Mork & Mindy, full-color photo on lid, Parker Brothers, 1979, MIB $15.00
Mr Ed the Talking Horse, Parker Brothers, 1962, complete, NM $45.00
Mr Novak, Transogram, 1963, EX $22.00
Mr Potato Head, Hasbro, 1976, complete, NM............$17.50
Mr Ree, Shelchow & Righter, 1957, MIB $85.00

Munsters Card Game, Milton Bradley, #4531, copyright 1964, NM..$50.00
My First Game, Gabriel, 1977, EX...............................$8.00
National Velvet, 9x18x2", marked Transogram & Metro-Goldwyn-Mayer, copyright 1961, 17x17" board, complete, EX...$37.50
Operation, Milton Bradley, 1965, EX...........................$10.00
Park & Shop, Milton Bradley, 1960, EX.......................$20.00
Password, Milton Bradley, 1962, EX............................$18.00
Peter Gunn, 9x17½x2", marked Spartan Productions, Lowell 1960 copyright, 17x17" board, EX......................$45.00
Philmore Electronic Project Game, 1960s, EX.............$25.00
Pop Yer Top, Milton Bradley, 1968, EX $20.00
Poppin' Hoppies, Ideal, 1968, NM...............................$20.00
Price Is Right, dated 1958, EX.....................................$20.00
Prince Valiant Game of Valor, 8x15x1½", Transogram, 1956, EX...$25.00
Rifleman Game, 1959, VG $45.00
Roy Rogers Horseshoes, Ohio Art, EX..........................$35.00
Royal Rummy, Whitman, 1976, MIB $8.00
Shindig, Remco, M...$28.00
Slap-Trap, Ideal, 1967, M...$17.50
Sleeping Beauty, Walt Disney, ca 1959, EX $30.00
Smurf Game, Milton Bradley, 1981, M.........................$10.00
Snakes in the Grass, Kohner, 1969, EX $18.00
Space Race Card Game, marked Edu Cards, 1957, EX..$27.50

Stratego, Milton Bradley, 1961, NM $25.00
Sunken Treasure, Parker Brothers, 1949, EX................$22.50
Terry & the Pirates Sunday Funnies Board Game, Ideal, 1972, MIB $17.50
Toonerville Trolley, 9x17", Milton Bradley, 1927, EX..$162.50
Twister, Milton Bradley, 1st year box, 1st issue, 1966, complete, EX..$15.00
Undersea World of Jacques Cousteau, Parker Brothers, 1968, NM $12.50
Voodoo Doll, 12x13x5", plastic board w/doll, marked Schaper, 1960s, VG $25.00
Welcome Back Kotter, Up Your Nose w/a Rubber Hose Game, Ideal, 1976, EX....................................$12.50
Wipe Out Hot Wheels Race, Mattel, 1968, NM $20.00
Wizard of Oz, Cadaco, 1974, complete, EX $12.50
Wonderful Game of Oz, Parker Brothers, 1920s, EX.$150.00
Yogi Bear Board Game, Milton Bradley, 1971, EX $22.00
Zorro, dated 1958, VG $20.00
101 Dalmations, 8½x15½x1½", marked Whitman & WDP w/1960 copyright, 15x23" board, complete, EX....$35.00

Gas Station Collectibles

Items used and/or sold by gas stations are included in this specialized area of advertising memorabilia. Collector interest is strong here, due to the crossover attraction of these items to both advertising fans and automobilia buffs as well. Over the past few years, there have been several large auctions in the east that featured gasoline-related material, much of which brought very respectable selling prices.

If you're interested in learning more about these types of collectibles, we recommend *Huxford's Collectible Advertising* by Sharon and Bob Huxford.

See also Tire Ashtrays.

Ashtray, Victor Gaskets, 4" dia, metal, green w/red gaskets embossed in center..............................$20.00
Belt buckle, Gulf, brushed brass w/enameled orange, blue, & white logo, in original box................................$45.00
Booklet, Sinclair & the Exciting World of Dinosaurs, copyright 1967, 16 pages..................................$6.00
Box, Dreadnaught Tire Chains, 7x7x5", heavy cardboard, pictures battleship sailing through tire & factory $35.00
Can, Ace High Motor Oil, 4" dia, 1-qt, tin, sunburst logo w/ Ace High arched above car & plane in clouds, ca 1935-45, G $60.00
Can, Air Race Motor Oil, 4" dia, 1-qt, tin, Air Race above yellow plane, Deep Rock below, 1935-45, VG...$100.00
Can, Archer Lubricants, 4" dia, 1-qt, tin, red Indian w/bow & arrow on tan background, lettering below, ca 1935-45, EX+ $65.00
Can, Cert-O-Lene Motor Oil, 4" dia, 1-qt, rocket logo on banded silver, red & green, ca 1970s, NM $20.00
Can, En-Ar-Co Motor Oil, 14", 5-gal, yellow & black lettering, VG $40.00

Can, Heart O'Pennsylvania, 4" dia, 1-qt, product name over red heart on silver, lettered bands below, ca 1935-45, EX+ **$50.00**

Can, Keystone Condensed Oil, tin w/tall spout, red logo on blue & white...**$15.00**

Can, Mobil Handy Oil, 4-oz, tin w/plastic spout, red Pegasus logo **$10.00**

Can, National En-Ar-Co Motor Oil, 4" dia, 1-qt, tin, lettering & logo on cream, turquoise & red bands, ca 1935-45, EX..**$30.00**

Can, Penn-Wynn Motor Oil, 6⅝" dia, 5-qt, Penn-Wynn on diagonal over shield logo, ca 1920s, VG+...........**$250.00**

Can, Pennant Oils, 6¼", ½-gal, rectangular, Pennant logo encircled by Pierce Oil Corp, ca 1915-25, EX **$75.00**

Can, Pennsylvania 100% Pure Motor Oil, 11½x8½", 2-gal, tin, product name above river scene, handled, 1925-45, VG..**$85.00**

Can, Royal Triton Union 76 Oil, 1-qt, tin, top removed, purple, silver & orange...**$15.00**

Globe, D-X Ethyl Lubricating Motor Fuel, 13½" dia, 3-pc glass body, black, red & white lettering over red diamond, NM **$425.00**

Globe, Esso, 15" dia, blue metal body, Esso in blue script, red border on milk glass lens, NM **$500.00**

Globe, Hudson Oil Co Transport Gasoline, 13½", 3-pc, Hudson Oil over Hi-Octane Gas truck, EX+ **$1,100.00**

Globe, Indian Gas, 13½", 3-pc glass, Indian Gas in blue lettering encircles red dot on white, NM.................**$400.00**

Globe, Marathon, 15" dia, red metal body, green Marathon lettered over orange running figure, EX+............**$950.00**

Globe, Mobilgas Ethyl, 16½" dia, red metal body, black & red letters below red Pegasus on white lens, EX........**$425.00**

Globe, Phillips 66 Ethyl, 13½" dia, cream plastic body, Ethyl in black on band below 66 logo on milk glass lens, NM **$400.00**

Globe, Purol Pep, 15" dia, metal body, Purol Pep encircled by Pure Oil Co USA & zig-zag border, EX..........**$330.00**

Globe, Sinclair Gasoline, 13½" dia, 1-pc milk glass w/white & green bars encircled by Sinclair Gasoline, G ..**$700.00**

Globe, Sky Chief, 13" dia, white plastic body, Sky Chief lettered on white band, Texaco logo below, EX+ ..**$155.00**

Globe, Tydol, 14" dia, black metal body, Tydol on white lens w/orange & black border, 1935-45, EX+ **$175.00**

Hat, Mobiloil, brown policeman style w/patch featuring Mobil above red Pegasus, bill cracked, minor soil on patch..**$175.00**

Ink blotter, Atlantic Lubrication White Flash Motor Oil, pictures 3 men in top hats jumping hurdles.................**$6.00**

Key chain, Peter Penn, the Aristocrat of Lubrication, red & white, plastic **$15.00**

Lapel pin, Mellinger Tires, tire encircling globe **$20.00**

Lighter, Zippo, Gulf logo, M in original box...............**$45.00**

Map holder, Caslo Gasoline Road Maps, 20x12½", 3-tiered metal wall shelf, red w/white logo & letters, VG...**$95.00**

Map holder, Texaco Touring Service, 9x4x2½", green painted metal, vertical mailbox style w/lettered red shield, EX...**$80.00**

Mechanical pencil, Pennzoil, w/perpetual calendar, green, yellow, red & black...**$20.00**

Medallion, Dual-8 Tires, The World's Quickest Stopping Tire, aluminum...**$15.00**

Money clip, Delco Battery Silver Anniversary, embossed battery..**$25.00**

Mug, GM Delco Electronics logo, Building on 75 Years of Excellence, glass, blue & white............................**$10.00**

Penknife w/key chain loop, Phillips 66 logo & station name, orange, black & cream.....................................**$25.00**

Pocketknife, Socony-Vacuum Oil Co, Gargoyle Oil, 2 blades, simulated mother-of-pearl handle............**$25.00**

Pump sign, Bay Regular, 13x11", die-cut porcelain, Bay lettered diagonally on shield, Regular on horizontal bar below, G...**$75.00**

Pump sign, Blue Sunoco, 8x12", porcelain, Blue Sunoco lettered on horizontal diamond w/arrow over vertical diamond, EX+...**$130.00**

Pump sign, Dynafuel, 8x12", die-cut porcelain, blue Dynafuel lettered over oval w/red border, EX **$120.00**

Pump sign, Pennsylvania 100% Pure Oil, 9¾x12", 2-sided die-cut porcelain, Pennsylvania on band across oval logo, G+..**$130.00**

Pump sign, Sea Chief, 10x15", 6-sided embossed painted tin, Sea Chief on white w/gold band, Texaco logo below, EX+..**$200.00**

Pump sign, Sterling Quality Gasoline, 8½x11", porcelain, oval, Sterling Gasoline around Sterling symbol, EX **$270.00**

Pump sign, Texaco, 15" dia, porcelain, Texaco logo on white w/black border, G.................................**$350.00**

Ruler, Cities Service Quality Petroleum Products, 12", metal, M..**$6.00**

Sign, Deep Rock Motor Oil, 32x24", porcelain, 2-sided, red, white & blue, rare, G..**$125.00**

Sign, Fire-Chief Gasoline, 18x12", porcelain, red & black lettering above round Texaco logo & fireman's hat, 1940, G...**$35.00**

Sign, Sun Oil Company, 4x24", porcelain, blue lettering on yellow background, EX...**$50.00**

Sign, Texaco, 12x11", ca 1946, EX.......................$175.00

Sign, Texaco Motor Oil, 18x23", porcelain, die-cut 2-sided flange type, red, white & black, few chips, some fading, EX..**$125.00**

Sign, Union Gasoline, 26x32", porcelain, die-cut, 2-sided, red & blue on white, some chips & holes **$175.00**

Spark plugs, Motometer, in original box.....................**$12.00**

Thermometer, Amalie Motor Oil, 9" dia, product name below, metal rim, glass front, VG **$65.00**

Thermometer, Prestone Anti-Freeze, 36x8¾", 6-sided Prestone logo above, You're Set Safe Sure in oval below, 1940s, EX...**$100.00**

Tire gauge, Peerless logo & gold eagle w/raised wings, dial type, 0-50 lbs **$85.00**

Geisha Girl China

During the decade before the turn of the century, Western interest in Oriental and Japanese artwork, home furnishings, and accessories had increased to the point that imports were unable to keep pace with demand. In the country of Japan, years of internal strife and the power struggle that resulted had diverted the interests of the feudal lords away from the fine porcelains that had been made there for centuries, and many of the great kilns had closed down. As a result, tiny household kilns sprang up around the country, worked by both skilled artisans and common laborers, all trying to survive in a depressed economy.

The porcelain they designed to fill the needs of this market was decorated with scenes portraying the day-to-day life of the Japanese people. There were hundreds of different patterns, some simple and others very detailed, but common to each were the geishas. So popular was the ware with the American market that its import continued uninterrupted until WWII. Even after the war, some of the kilns were rebuilt, and a few pieces were manufactured during the Occupied Japan period.

Each piece of this porcelain has a border of a particular color. Some colors are connected with certain time periods, and collectors often use this as a method of dating their pieces. For instance, reds, maroon, cobalt blue, and light and nile green borders were early. Pine green, blue-green, and turquoise were used after about 1917 or so, and in the late 1920s and '30s, a light cobalt was popular. Some pieces from the Occupied era have a black border. (Border colors are given directly after pattern descriptions.)

Even if you're not sure of the name of your pattern, you can use the following listings as a general guide. If you'd like to learn more about this porcelain and its many variations, we recommend *The Collector's Encyclopedia of Geisha Girl Porcelain* by Elyce Litts.

Biscuit jar, Basket of Mums B, lady & child w/flower basket approach 2 ladies on balcony, red w/gold trim....**$50.00**

Bonbon dish, Battledore, ladies & children playing game, olive green, mum shape...**$22.00**

Bowl, berry; Chinese Coin, scenic reserves w/stylized Chinese coins, green w/gold on red-orange ground .**$15.00**

Bowl, 10½" dia, Geisha in Sampan D, lady reading in sampan w/lg sail w/plum blossom reserve of geisha on bench..**$45.00**

Box, 6", Garden Bench B, 2 ladies on bench among others in chrysanthemum garden, 6-sided, red sides.......**$22.50**

Butter pat, Geisha Face, head or bust of lady is sole decoration, flower & butterfly backdrop **$9.00**

Creamer, Boy w/Scythe, boy cuts shrubs to allow 2 ladies to pass, cobalt w/gold trim.....................................**$15.00**

Creamer & sugar bowl, Kite A, 2 ladies fly kites w/child, brown w/gold trim..**$30.00**

Cup & saucer, cocoa; Fan D, 4 ladies w/fans talking in garden, fluted cup, flower-shaped saucer, cobalt & gold border **$25.00**

Jug, 4½", Garden Bench Q, lady on bench, child at side, geometric, multicolor border w/gold trim............**$10.00**

Marmalade, 5", Cloud A, clouds form backdrop for ladies & children, melon ribs, red-orange w/yellow...........**$28.00**

Pin tray, 5x3", Boat Dance, lanterned boat, 2 lady musicians & 1 dancer, green w/gold lacing, molded edges..**$14.00**

Plate, 11", Gardening, 3 ladies tending chrysanthemum garden, foliate edging, wavy cobalt border...............**$48.00**

Plate, 6", Bicycle Race, 2 ladies riding bicycles, red orange w/gold trim...**$8.00**

Plate, 7", Duck Watching B, lady & child by stream, lady on bench, blue-green w/white, thin **$12.00**

Relish dish, 8x5", Courtesan Processional, courtesans & servants on bridge, cobalt border w/gold lacing.......**$28.00**

Salt shaker, Basket A, 4 ladies w/baskets beside river, sea green..**$8.00**

Sauce dish, Bamboo Trellis, 3 ladies at water's edge w/lg trellis behind, red w/gold trim, 8-lobed **$10.00**

Saucer, demitasse; Bamboo Trellis, ladies at water's edge w/lg trellis behind $3.00

Tea set, Fan Dance B, 2 ladies & boy w/fans dancing to musicians on stage, royal cobalt & blue background, 5-piece **$50.00**

Teacup & saucer, Bamboo Trellis, 3 ladies at water's edge, floral interior, red w/gold trim **$22.00**

Teacup & saucer, Child Reaching for Butterfly, 2 ladies & child in garden, orange-red band, modern **$5.00**

Glass Animals and Figurines

Nearly every glasshouse in America has produced beautiful models of animals and birds – many are still being made today. Heisey was one of the largest manufacturers, and some of their more expensive figures are valued at $2,000.00 and higher. As these companies closed, the molds were often bought by others who used them to press their own lines. Although some are marked so that you can identify the maker, many are not, and even advanced collectors are sometimes unable to make a positive identification.

Unless you're sure of what you're buying, we recommend you read *Glass Animals of the Depression Era* by Lee Garmon and Dick Spencer.

American Glass Co, Angelfish, bookend, 8¼", crystal.**$65.00**

American Glass Co, Boxer Dog, 4¾", sitting, crystal ...**$60.00**

Cambridge, Blue Jay, flower holder, 5½", crystal **$135.00**

Cambridge, Bridge Hound, 1¾", amber **$25.00**

Cambridge, Buddha, 5½", amber...............................**$225.00**

Cambridge, Draped Lady, 8½", crystal........................**$60.00**

Cambridge, Draped Lady, 8½", light emerald satin ...**$110.00**

Cambridge, Eagle, bookend, 5½x4", wings uplifted & head turned, crystal..**$70.00**

Cambridge, Heron, 9", crystal **$60.00**

Cambridge, Mandolin Lady, 9½", peachblo satin.......**$395.00**

Cambridge, Rose Lady, 8½", light emerald.................**$185.00**

Cambridge, Scottie, bookend, 6½x5", head turned, hollow, crystal..**$85.00**

Cambridge, Swan, 6½", crystal **$30.00**

Cambridge, Turtle, flower holder, 5¼" long, ebony..**$210.00**

Co-Operative Flint Glass Co, Elephant, 2-piece dish, 4½x7", Ritz blue, ca 1930, rare color **$135.00**

Co-Operative Flint Glass Co, Elephant, 2-piece dish, 4½x7", amber, 1927..**$40.00**

Duncan & Miller, Dove, head down, crystal.............**$165.00**

Duncan & Miller, Duck, ashtray, 4", ruby **$50.00**

Duncan & Miller, Swan, candle holder, 7", ruby **$70.00**

Duncan & Miller, Swan, 7", open back, chartreuse **$40.00**

Duncan & Miller, Swordfish, ashtray, crystal **$300.00**

Duncan & Miller, Sylvan Swan, 5½", blue opalescent.**$70.00**

Duncan & Miller, Tropical Fish, ashtray, 3½" long, pink opalescent..**$45.00**

Fenton, Alley Cat, 11", velva rose **$85.00**

Fenton, Cardinal Head, 6½", ruby, 1984......................**$95.00**

Fenton, Fish, vase, 7", milk glass w/black tail & eyes, ca 1953, rare..**$425.00**

Fenton, Novelty Fish, 2½", ruby w/amberina-type tail & fins, 1935-36 ....**$50.00**

Fenton, Peacock, bookends, 5¾", crystal satin, pr **$160.00**

Fenton, September Morn Nymph, flower frog, 6¼", jade, 1928 ....**$100.00**

Fenton, Turtle, flower frog, 4" long, green, 1929.........**$45.00**

Fostoria, Commemorative Pelican, amber, 1987..........**$40.00**

Fostoria, Dolphin, 4¾", blue, #2821/410, 1971-73 ....**$20.00**

Fostoria, Eagle, bookend, 7½", crystal, 1940-43...........**$90.00**

Fostoria, Flying Fish, vase, 7", teal green, #2497, 1965..**$30.00**

Fostoria, Madonna, 10", crystal, #2635/471, 1950s.......**$50.00**

Fostoria, Penguin, 4⅝", topaz, #2531, 1935-36..........**$110.00**

Fostoria, Polar Bear, 4⅝", crystal, #2531, 1935-44........**$60.00**

Fostoria, Rearing Horse, bookends, 7¾", crystal, #2564, 1939-58, pr..**$40.00**

Fostoria, Reclining Deer, 2⅜", silver mist, 1940-43......**$40.00**

Heisey, Bunny, 2½x2½", head up, crystal, 1948-49...**$175.00**

Heisey, Clydesdale, 7½x7", crystal, 1942-48..............**$350.00**

Heisey, Colt, 4x3½", kicking, crystal, 1941-45...........**$175.00**

Heisey, Fighting Rooster, 7½x5½", crystal, 1940-46...**$175.00**

Heisey, Fish, bookends, 6½x5", crystal, 1942-52, pr..**$200.00**

Heisey, fish bowl, 9" **$450.00**

Heisey, Giraffe, 10¾x3", crystal, 1942-52 ....**$195.00**

Heisey, Horse Head, bookend, 6⅞x6¼", frosted crystal, 1937-55 ....**$85.00**

Heisey, Madonna, 9", frosted crystal, 3" square base, 1942-56 ....**$80.00**

Heisey, Pouter Pigeon, 6½x7½", crystal, 1947-49 ......**$600.00**

Heisey, Sparrow, 2¼x4", crystal, 1942-45 ....**$85.00**

Imperial, Angelfish, bookend, 6⅝", ruby, 1984..........**$300.00**

Imperial, Dragon, candle holders, crystal & frosted crystal combination, signed Virginia B Evans, 1949, pr.**$375.00**

Imperial, Elephant, 4½", pink satin, marked LIG, 1980.**$65.00**

Imperial, Gazelle, 11", clear ultra blue, made for Mirror Images, marked ALIG, 1982................................**$110.00**

Imperial, Mother Pig, 3⅛", ultra blue, made for Mirror Images, 1983..**$95.00**

Imperial, Owl, 2-piece, 6½", caramel slag w/glass eyes.**$60.00**

Imperial, Rabbit, paperweight, 2¾", milk glass, made for HCA, IG, 1977..**$20.00**

Imperial, Scottie Pup, 2½", amber, commemorative issue dated 1983, initialed NIGCS **$40.00**

KR Haley Glassware Co, Kemple Rooster, 9", head down, amber, hollow base **$30.00**

KR Haley Glassware Co, Llama, 6", sitting, crystal.......**$15.00**

KR Haley Glassware Co, Ringneck Pheasant, 11½", crystal, hollow base, 1947..**$20.00**

LE Smith, Rearing Horse, bookend, 8", emerald.........**$50.00**

LE Smith, Turkey, 2-piece candy dish, 7¼", crystal **$35.00**

New Martinsville, Baby Seal w/Ball, 4½", ruby, 1980s .**$50.00**
New Martinsville, Eagle, 8", crystal, #509, ca 1938 ......**$70.00**
New Martinsville, Mama Bear, 4x6", crystal, 1938-51 .**$200.00**
New Martinsville, Police Dog (German Shepherd), 5", crystal, #733, 1937-50 ....**$65.00**

New Martinsville, Seal, w/ball, 7" $65.00
New Martinsville, Starfish, 7¾", crystal **$75.00**
New Martinsville, Swan, ashtray, ebony body w/crystal neck & head, indents in tail for cigarette rest **$25.00**
New Martinsville, Tiger, 6½", head up, crystal **$180.00**

Paden City, Chanticleer, 9"....................................$175.00
Paden City, Chinese Pheasant, 13¾" long, blue, 1940..**$145.00**
Paden City, Goose, 5", light blue, ca 1940, scarce.....**$110.00**
Paden City, Polar Bear on Ice, 4½", crystal, #611 ....**$55.00**
Tiffin, Cat, 6¼", black satin w/raised bumps, #9445, 1924, rare...**$95.00**
Tiffin, Frog, candlestick, 5½", black satin, 1924-34......**$75.00**
Viking, Angelfish, 6½", crystal, #1301, 1957.................**$65.00**
Viking, Bird, 12", ruby, #1310, 1960s..........................**$30.00**
Viking, Duck, 9", ruby, #1317, 1960s..........................**$45.00**

Viking, Rabbit, 6½", emerald green, 1960s..................**$30.00**
Westmoreland, Bulldog, 2½", crystal mist w/gold-painted collar, rhinestone eyes, #75, ca 1910 ....**$30.00**
Westmoreland, Butterfly, 4½" wide, crystal, #3...........**$25.00**
Westmoreland, Pouter Pigeon, 2½", crystal, #9, 1970s ..**$20.00**
Westmoreland, Starfish, candle holders, 5" wide, almond, #1063, pr...**$30.00**
Westmoreland, Turtle, 4" long, green mist, #10, 1970.**$25.00**

Glass Knives

Popular during the Depression years, knives made of glass were produced in many of the same colors as the glass dinnerware of the era – pink, green, light blue, crystal, and once in awhile even amber or forest green. Some were decorated by hand with flowers or fruit. Collectors will accept reground, resharpened blades as long as the original shape has been maintained. By their very nature, they were naturally prone to chipping, and mint condition examples are very scarce.

Aer-flo, 7½", crystal, decorative diamond design imprinted on handle **$18.00**
Aer-flo, 7½", pink, decorative diamond design imprinted on handle...**$32.00**
Block pattern on handle, 8¼", green...........................**$28.00**
Butter, crystal handle w/pinwheel, green blade..........**$10.00**
Butter, green handle w/crystal blade...........................**$25.00**
Candlewick, 8½", crystal, ornate handle **$175.00**
Dagger, 9¼", crystal, hand-painted flowers.................**$70.00**

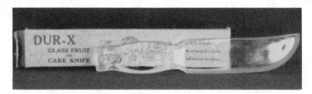

Dur-X, 8½", crystal, imprinted flower & leaf design on handle, in original box $10.00
Dur-X, 9¼", pink, imprinted flower & leaf design.......**$22.00**
Plain handle, 8½", crystal **$14.00**
Plain handle, 9¼", pink **$30.00**
Rose Spray, 8½", amber...**$135.00**
Rose Spray, 8½", crystal...**$45.00**
Steel-ite, pink, sm checks & L imprinted on handle....**$80.00**
Stonex, 8¼", green, horizontal ribs on handle **$55.00**
Stonex, 8¼", white, horizontal ribs on handle..........**$135.00**
Vitex, 8½", crystal, imprinted stars & diamond pattern on handle...**$10.00**
Vitex, 9¼", blue, imprinted stars & diamond pattern on handle...**$22.00**
Westmoreland, 9¼", crystal, hand-painted flowers & leaves on handle, w/thumbguard **$28.00**
Westmoreland, 9¼", crystal, horizontal ribs on handle, w/thumbguard **$90.00**

Glass Shoes

Little shoes of glass were made as early as 1800. In 1886 a patent was issued to John E. Miller for his method of pressing a glass slipper; George Duncan pressed a shoe in the Daisy and Button pattern, and soon every glasshouse in the country was following in their 'footsteps.' Even today, contemporary glass artists like Boyd and Mosser are making shoes very much like the older ones. You'll find shoes of every color and design imaginable. Some have been used to convey an advertising message. There are ladies' slippers and men's house shoes, high-top shoes and roller skates, babies' booties, 'wooden' shoes, shoes with lids, and shoes that are bottles.

To learn more about them all, we recommend *Shoes of Glass* by Libby Yalom.

Boyd's, Cat Slipper, #26, Dark Pippin Green, 1982 .....**$12.50**

Bryce, Chinese Shoe, 5" long, Daisy & Button, amber .$40.00
Bryce Brothers, low cut crystal shoe, 1⅞x7¼", Daisy & Button pattern w/ribbed toe **$65.00**
Central Glass Co, roller skate, 4¼x3⅜", crystal, diamond mesh pattern w/plain top edge & toe **$42.00**
Degenhart, Kat Slipper, dark amethyst.........................**$25.00**
Fenton, Baby Bootee, #1994BO, blue opalescent, ca late 1930s **$30.00**
Fenton, covered dish, 5¼x6½", #3700MB, blue marble Hobnail pattern, 1971-73 ....**$30.00**
Fenton, Kitten Slipper, 3x5⅞", #3995PS, old milk glass, Hobnail pattern, 1949-58 ....**$18.00**
Fenton, Kitten Slipper, 3x5⅞", #3995PS, purple slag, Hobnail pattern, 1970-72 ....**$30.00**

Fenton, Kitten Slipper, 3⅞x5⅜", Daisy & Button, blue opalescent **$25.00**

Kanawha Glass Co, Bow Slipper, 2¼x5¾", amberina, Daisy & Button pattern **$8.00**
Kanawha Glass Co, 2½x5⅝", heavy opaque, cream & salmon w/raised leaves & flowers on vamp, scalloped top, ca 1970 ....**$15.00**
King Glass Co, crystal bow slipper, 2½x5⅞", diamond pattern, diamond mesh sole, ca 1880 ....**$34.00**
Sowerby, 3½x7½", crystal w/3 sunbursts on each side, hobnails around top, embossed peacock head inside.........**$130.00**
Westmoreland, cat in man's shoe, 3½x4", frosted green, ca 1972 ....**$25.00**

Goebel

The Hummelwork Porcelain Manufactory (the same company that produces Hummel figures) has been located in Rodental since 1871, in the area formerly referred to as West Germany. In addition to the Hummels, they're also famous for their Disney characters, Art Deco pieces, bird and animal figures, and two types of novelty kitchenware lines designed as Friar Tuck (brown-robed) monks and Cardinal (red-robed) monks.

The Goebel marks are indicative of particular time periods; see the section on Hummels for information concerning marks.

Ashtray/bowl, Friar Tuck, ZF-43, stylized bee **$35.00**
Cigarette jar, Friar Tuck, RX-99, stylized bee **$195.00**
Cookie jar, Friar Tuck, 9", K-29, full bee....................**$150.00**
Creamer, yellow chick, child's, 1950 mark..................**$30.00**
Cruet tray, Friar Tuck, w/handle, stylized bee............**$55.00**
Decanter, Friar Tuck, KL-95, stylized bee....................**$57.50**
Egg cup, Friar Tuck, E-95/A, stylized bee...................**$25.00**
Egg timer, Friar Tuck, single, 3-line mark **$48.00**
Figurine, cat, 3½", white w/brown spots.....................**$35.00**
Figurine, Colonial couple, 10", crown mark **$275.00**

Figurine, poodle, 7x8" **$65.00**

Figurine, rabbit family, tallest: 3", stylized bee in V mark, 3 pieces $75.00

Jug, Friar Tuck, 2½", S-141-2/0, full bee $25.00

Jug, Friar Tuck, 4", S-141/0, full bee $32.00

Jug, Friar Tuck, 5½", S-141/1, stylized bee $40.00

Matchbox holder, Friar Tuck, RX-111, stylized bee $68.00

Mug, Friar Tuck, 8", T-74/III, stylized bee $75.00

Mustard pot, Cardinal Tuck, S-183, stylized bee $65.00

Mustard pot, Friar Tuck, 3¾", full bee $50.00

Oil & vinegar cruets, Cardinal Tuck, 5", pr $160.00

Pitcher, Cardinal Tuck, 4", stylized bee $75.00

Pitcher, Friar Tuck, 5", stylized bee $35.00

Salt & pepper shakers, Santa Claus, full bee, pr $50.00

Graniteware

Though it really wasn't as durable as its name suggests, there's still lots of graniteware around today, though much of it is now in collections. You may even be able to find a bargain. The popularity of the 'country' look in home decorating and the exposure it's had in some of the leading decorating magazines has caused graniteware prices, especially on rare items, to soar in recent years.

It's made from a variety of metals coated with enameling of various colors, some solid, others swirled. It's the color, the form, and of course the condition that dictates value. Swirls of cobalt and white, purple and white, green and white, and brown and white are unusual, but even solid gray items such as a hanging salt box or a chamberstick can be expensive because pieces like those are rare. Decorated examples are uncommon – so are children's pieces and salesman's samples.

For further information, we recommend *The Collector's Encyclopedia of Graniteware, Colors, Shapes, and Values,* by Helen Greguire.

Baking pan, 10⅞x17", cobalt blue & white swirl, black trim, molded handles, rare, NM $265.00

Baking pan, 11⅞x18¼", gray mottle, applied handles, seamless body, VG $75.00

Baking pan, 11x15¾", blue & white mottle, black trim & handles, imprinted heart-shaped bottom, rare shape, NM $275.00

Bowl, 4⅞", yellow & white swirl, black trim, 1950s $45.00

Bowl, 5⅞", blue & white swirl, black trim, VG $130.00

Bowl, 6½", yellow & green mottle, black trim, 1980s, VG $15.00

Bread pan, 6x11", cobalt blue & white mottle, cobalt trim, End of Day, extremely rare, VG $295.00

Bread plate, 6¼" dia, blue & white mottle w/gray interior, black trim, rare, VG $95.00

Butter dish, 4¾x8⅞" dia, white w/cobalt blue trim, seamless body & spun knob, L&G Mfg Co, rare, M $185.00

Chamber pot, 8", blue mottle, EX $150.00

Chamberstick, 7", gray mottle, w/push-up, VG $285.00

Coffee boiler, 9½x9" dia, blue & white swirl, black trim & handles, wooden bail handle, ca 1940, NM $195.00

Coffeepot, 10¼x6⅛" dia, reddish-brown w/white specks, riveted spout & handle, seamless body, VG $155.00

Coffeepot, 6¾", cream w/black trim & handle, Kook King Vollrath Ware label, ca 1920, M $115.00

Coffeepot, 7⅞x4½" dia, dark green & white swirl, dark blue trim, seamless body, Chrysolite, rare, VG $425.00

Colander, 4x11⅜" dia, blue & white mottle, blue riveted handles & feet, VG $165.00

Cream can, medium blue & white lg swirl, EX $265.00

Creamer, 3½x3¾" dia, yellow w/black trim, 1970s, VG . $30.00

Creamer, 3¼x4" dia, squatty shape, red & white mottle, black trim, ca 1980, rare, M.....................$65.00
Creamer, 5x3⅜" dia, squatty shape, white w/blue chicken wire pattern, riveted handle, marked B, VG.......$165.00
Cup, 2⅛x4¼" dia, deep violet shading to light, NM $45.00
Cup, 4¼" dia, blue & white mottle, black trim, M.....$110.00
Cuspidor, 4x9⅜" dia, dark blue shading to light blue, black trim, seamless body, VG.....................$125.00
Custard cup, 2⅛x4¼" dia, blue & white swirl, cobalt blue trim, Blue Diamond Ware, rare, VG $115.00
Dipper, 5" dia, blue & white mottle, black trim & flat handle, VG.....................$75.00
Egg cup, 2¾x2" dia, light blue w/white interior, VG...$40.00
Egg pan, 12" dia, gray mottle, 5 eyes, riveted handle, rare, NM $275.00
Funnel, 5¾x5¼" dia, squatty shape, blue & white swirl, black trim & handle, seamed spout, VG $165.00
Grater, 10" long, red, flat handle, VG.....................$95.00
Measure, 2¼" dia, black & white mottle, applied strap handle & lip, IGIL embossed on side, rare, M..........$135.00
Measure, 4½x3½" dia, deep sea green shading to moss green, riveted handle, seamless body, rare.........$235.00
Measure, 6¾x5¾" dia, white w/black trim, marked 4 ozs to 64 ozs inside, M $65.00
Mug, 2¾x2¾" dia, green & white swirl, dark blue trim, riveted handle, seamless, Emerald Ware, VG..........$150.00
Mug, 3½x3¾" dia, red w/black trim, ca 1960, VG $10.00
Mug, 3½x3⅞" dia, green & white mottle, black trim, ca 1950, VG.....................$30.00
Mug, 3⅛x3⅞" dia, cobalt blue & white swirl, black trim, NM $95.00
Mug, 3¾" dia, red & white swirl, black trim, 1950s, VG.$55.00
Mug, 4" dia, marbleized gray & white, seamless body, rare color, VG $75.00
Pie plate, 8½" dia, blue & white wavy mottle, black trim, rare, NM.....................$110.00
Pie plate, 8¾" dia, gray mottle, Ideal Wonder Plate embossed in center, rare, VG.....................$195.00
Pie plate, 9" dia, brown & white mottle, black trim, VG.$20.00
Pie plate, 9¾" dia, red & white swirl, cobalt blue trim, extremely rare, NM $400.00
Pitcher, water; 7½x5⅜", brown & white mottle, cobalt blue trim, seamless body, rare, VG $160.00
Plate, 9" dia, blue & white swirl, black trim, VG.......$155.00
Platter, 8⅜x12", gray mottle, Iron City label, M $165.00
Roaster, 5x7" dia, gray mottle, seamless, rare, NM....$110.00
Sauce pan, 3¾x7½" dia, cream w/green trim & handle, ribbed sides, Leader, Easy To Clean on label, M $60.00
Sauce pan, 5" dia, cobalt blue w/white interior, seamless body, VG $30.00
Sauce pan, 5⅜" dia, red & white swirl, black trim & handle, seamless body, ca 1930, M.....................$95.00
Spoon, 13" long, green & white swirl, Emerald Ware, rare, VG.....................$115.00
Spoon, 13¼" long, blue & white mottle, VG................$65.00
Spoon, 13¼" long, red w/black handle, NM................$35.00
Spoon, 13⅜" long, brown & white swirl, rare, NM....$135.00

Stew pan, 7¾" dia, light blue & white dapple-type mottle, black riveted handle & trim, rare color, VG........$180.00
Sugar bowl, 6x3¾" dia, deep sea green shading to light moss, riveted handles, seamless, rare, VG $265.00
Tea strainer, 3¾" dia, blue & white mottle, screen bottom, rare color & shape, VG.....................$185.00
Tea strainer, 5⅛" long x 4" dia, white, scalloped shape w/fancy perforated bottom, rare, VG $75.00
Teakettle, 5x5¾" dia, cream w/light green trim & handle, NM.....................$65.00
Teapot, 11x5½" dia, white w/multicolored castle scene, metal mountings & bands, M $325.00
Teapot, 6½x3¾" dia, aqua & white swirl, cobalt blue trim, riveted rolled handle, rare, VG $265.00
Teapot, 9x6" dia, blue & white mottle, black trim & riveted handle, ribbed tin lid w/wood acorn knob, VG.$295.00
Tumbler, 4x3" dia, yellow & white swirl, black trim, ca 1950, rare, M.....................$60.00
Wash basin, salesman's sample, 4⅜" dia, blue & white mottle, blue trim, eyelet for hanging, M...................$110.00
Wash bowl, 13⅜" dia, mauve & white swirl, dark brown trim, extremely rare color, M $395.00

Griswold Cast Iron Cooking Ware

Late in the 1800s, the Griswold company introduced a line of cast iron cooking ware that was eventually distributed on a large scale nationwide. Today's collectors appreciate the variety of skillets, cornstick pans, Dutch ovens, and griddles available to them, and many still enjoy using them to cook with.

Several marks have been used; most contain the Griswold name, though some were marked simply 'Erie.'

If you intend to use your cast iron, you can clean it safely by using any commercial oven cleaner. (Be sure to re-season it before you cook in it.) A badly pitted, rusy piece may leave you with no other recourse than to remove what rust you can with a wire brush, paint the surface black, and find an alternate use for it around the house. For instance, you might use a kettle to hold a large floor plant or some magazines. A small griddle or skillet would be attractive as part of a wall display in a country kitchen.

For more information, we recommend *Griswold Cast Collectibles* by Bill and Denise Harned.

Ashtray, #00, sm emblem, unused.....................$700.00
Bundt pan, #965, for Frank Hay $400.00
Casserole, 2⅜x9⅜x7⅜", #69, lg emblem, w/lid............$40.00
Cornstick pan, 1x14x7⅝", #283.....................$150.00
Cornstick pan, 13", #273.....................$115.00
Cornstick pan, ¾x8½x4⅛", #262, 1950s.....................$95.00
Danish cake pan, #21, rimless, early $125.00
Deep fat fryer, 2½-qt, #1003.....................$60.00
Dutch oven, 15-qt, #12, Tite Top.....................$55.00
Dutch oven, 4¼x9¾", #9, Erie.....................$165.00
Food grinder, #0, EX.....................$75.00
French roll pan, #11.....................$55.00

French roll pan, 7½x5", #17, Erie $68.00
Fruit press, 4-qt $85.00
Griddle, #9, round $100.00
Griddle, 10½" dia, #609A, lg emblem $65.00
Griddle, 16¾x10", #18, Erie, sm emblem $50.00
Griddle, 19x8½", #8, aluminum, rectangular $140.00
Griddle, 19x9⅛", #8, diamond mark, bail handle $88.00
Grill, barbeque; 12¼", #10, lg emblem $100.00
Grill, hibachi; 30x18x12", #903, mark $95.00
Juicer, #9 .... $135.00
Kettle, 3", #0 .... $50.00
Kettle, 6-qt, #8, Erie, Maslin shape, 6-quart $65.00
Kettle, 7-qt, #8, Erie, lg emblem, flat bottom $60.00
Lemon squeezer, 7½", #1, nickeled $45.00
Meat loaf pan, 1⅝x9½x5½", #18, Erie $85.00
Mold, lamb form, 7½x11", #866 .... $175.00
Patty mold, MIB $55.00
Platter, 14½x8½", well & tree style, oval $45.00
Popover pan, 1⅝x9½x6½", #18, Erie $100.00
Popover pan, 7⅝" long, #10, makes 11 popovers $75.00
Roaster, 6½-qt, #5, oval $55.00
Roll pan, 12⅞", #950, makes 12 rolls $85.00
Skillet, #13, lg emblem, no smoke ring $150.00
Skillet, #2, sm emblem, no smoke ring $65.00
Skillet, #34, 7-egg $60.00
Skillet, #5, lg emblem, no smoke ring $45.00
Skillet, egg; #52, square $38.00
Skillet, Odorless; 14" dia, #8 .... $110.00
Skillet, 12½" dia, #11, lg emblem, smoke ring $150.00
Skillet, 13¼", #12, Erie, w/smoke ring $150.00
Skillet, 13¼" dia, #12, Erie, w/smoke ring $45.00
Skillet, 8¾" dia, #6, Erie $45.00
Skillet, 9½" dia, #9, w/smoke ring $60.00
Skillet griddle, 12¾", #110, Erie, lg emblem $115.00
Skillet lid, Griswold #4 .... $35.00
Teakettle, 4-qt, #6, Erie $65.00
Teakettle, 5-qt, #7, Safety Fill, Erie $55.00

Waffle iron, #6 .... $185.00
Waffle iron, #8, wire handle, w/base $85.00
Waffle iron, 8½" pans, #19, Heart & Star $165.00
Wax ladle, 8", Erie $30.00
Wheat stick, 13½", #280, Erie $115.00

Haeger Pottery

Many generations of the Haeger family have been associated with the ceramic industry. Starting out as a brickyard in 1871, the Haeger Company (Dundee, Illinois) progressed to include artware in their production line as early as 1914. That was only the beginning. In the thirties they began to make a line of commercial artware so successful that as a result a plant was built in Macomb, Illinois, devoted exclusively to its production.

Royal Haeger was their premium line, whose chief designer was Royal Arden Hickman. He was a talented artist who worked in mediums other than just pottery. For Haeger he designed a line of wonderfully stylized animals and birds, high-style vases, and human figures and masks with extremely fine details.

Paper labels were used extensively before the mid-thirties. Royal Haeger ware has an in-mold script mark, and their Flower Ware line (1954-1963) is marked 'RG' (Royal Garden).

For those wanting to learn more about this pottery, we recommend *Collecting Royal Haeger* by Lee Garmon and Doris Frizell.

Ashtray, 4" wide, fish form, R-688 .... $6.00
Ashtray, 7", pear shape, R-1359 .... $12.00
Candle holder, 10¾", dolphin, R-511 .... $15.00
Figurine, dappled horse, 5", R-402 .... $12.00
Figurine, duck, 10", inebriated, fallen, R-158 .... $26.50
Figurine, Polar Bear, 16" long, R-702 .... $36.00
Figurine, rooster, 12", head down, R-101 .... $24.00

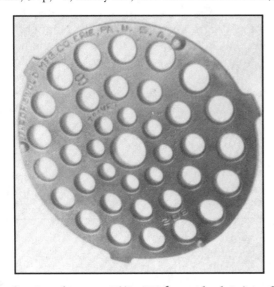

Trivet for Dutch oven, 7¾", #206, marked Griswold Mfg Co Erie, PA USA $25.00
Vienna roll bread pan, #26, marked Griswold Mfg Co. $85.00

Figurine, Russian Wolfhound, 8½", R-319, white matt. $30.00
Figurine, St Francis, 10½", R-1231 .... $30.00

Figurine, stag, 7", R-991 ....$12.00
Figurine, stallion, 8", head up, R-171......................$21.50
Flower frog, 13", nude w/seal, R-364 ....$36.00
Planter, 6", fish form, R-205...............................$8.00
Planter, 8½", fish form, R-752.............................$15.00

Vase, fan form; 16½" wide, R-523, aqua blue w/drip glaze at rim..............................**$25.00**
Vase, 13", gazelle form, R-115.............................$22.00
Vase, 14", double-leaf design on fan shape, R-34........$18.00
Vase, 14", lily form, R-466 ....$27.50
Vase, 7", embossed leaves, R-1123 ....$12.00

Hall China Company

Hall China is still in production in East Liverpool, Ohio, where they have been located since around the turn of the century. They have produced literally hundreds of lines of kitchen and dinnerware items, for both home and commercial use. Several of these in particular have become very collectible.

They're especially famous for their teapots, some of which were shaped like automobiles, basketballs, donuts, and footballs. Each teapot was made in an assortment of colors, often trimmed in gold. Many were decaled to match their dinnerware lines. Some are quite rare, and collecting them all would be a real challenge.

During the 1950s Eva Zeisel designed dinnerware shapes with a streamlined, ultra-modern look. Her lines, Classic and Century, were used with various decals as the basis for several of Hall's dinnerware patterns. She also designed kitchenware lines with the same modern styling; they were called Casual Living and Tri-Tone. All of her designs are popular with today's collectors.

Although some of the old kitchenware shapes and teapots are being produced today, you'll be able to tell them from the old pieces by the backstamp. To identify these new issues, Hall marks them with the shaped rectangular 'Hall' trademark they've used since the early 1970s.

For more information, we recommend *The Collector's Encyclopedia of Hall China* by Margaret and Kenn Whitmyer.

Acacia, bean pot, New England, #4...........................$80.00
Acacia, casserole, Radiance........................$32.00
Acacia, teapot, Radiance...........................$100.00
Arizona, ashtray, Tomorrow's Classic $4.00
Arizona, bowl, open baker; 11-oz, Tomorrow's Classic..$9.00
Arizona, casserole, 2-qt, Tomorrow's Classic $18.00
Arizona, onion soup, w/lid, Tomorrow's Classic.........$18.00
Beauty, bowl, salad; 12".................................$35.00
Beauty, casserole, Thick Rim $35.00
Beauty, teapot, Rutherford $85.00
Blue Blossom, ball jug, #1, #2, or #3.....................$50.00
Blue Blossom, bowl, 8½", Thick Rim $35.00
Blue Blossom, creamer, New York......................$25.00
Blue Blossom, sugar bowl, New York...................$45.00
Blue Bouquet, ball jug, #3.............................$30.00
Blue Bouquet, bean pot, New England #4.................$85.00
Blue Bouquet, bowl, 7¾", flared.......................$30.00
Blue Bouquet, cake plate $18.00
Blue Bouquet, coffeepot, Five Band.....................$50.00
Blue Bouquet, leftover, rectangular....................$35.00
Blue Bouquet, pretzel jar..............................$95.00
Blue Garden, bean pot, New England, #4 ....$120.00
Blue Garden, casserole, Sundial, #4 ....$25.00
Blue Garden, leftover, loop handle $65.00
Blue Garden, sugar bowl, New York $30.00
Blue Willow, ashtray...................................$7.00
Blue Willow, teacup, Chinese, 2 styles..................$20.00
Bouquet, butter dish, Hallcraft $45.00
Bouquet, coffeepot, 6-cup, Hallcraft....................$55.00
Bouquet, cup, Hallcraft................................$8.00
Bouquet, plate, 11", Hallcraft $12.00
Bouquet, salt & pepper shakers, Hallcraft, pr.............$18.00
Buckingham, bowl, soup; 9", Tomorrow's Classic........$8.00
Buckingham, candlestick, 8", Tomorrow's Classic.......$20.00
Buckingham, cup, Tomorrow's Classic.....................$8.00
Buckingham, vinegar bottle, Tomorrow's Classic........$25.00
Cactus, bowl, batter; Five Band $30.00
Cactus, bowl, 9", Radiance $18.00
Cactus, onion soup, individual.........................$45.00
Cameo Rose, bowl, cream soup; 5".......................$20.00
Cameo Rose, creamer $8.00
Cameo Rose, plate, 10"................................$10.00
Cameo Rose, sugar bowl $14.00
Caprice, bowl, fruit; 5¾", Tomorrow's Classic...............$4.00
Caprice, bowl, 8¾", square, Tomorrow's Classic........$14.00
Caprice, candlestick, 8", Tomorrow's Classic $20.00
Caprice, egg cup, Tomorrow's Classic....................$18.00
Caprice, salt & pepper shakers, Tomorrow's Classic, pr.$16.00
Carrot/Golden Carrot, ball jug, #3 ....$40.00
Carrot/Golden Carrot, casserole, Radiance.................$30.00
Clover/Golden Clover, bowl, 9", Radiance.................$16.00
Crocus, baker, French fluted..........................$20.00
Crocus, bowl, fruit; 5½"...............................$6.00
Crocus, bowl, 6", Radiance............................$9.00
Crocus, cake plate....................................$18.00
Crocus, creamer, modern $10.00
Crocus, cup...$9.00
Crocus, platter, 11¼", oval............................$16.00

Crocus, sugar bowl, modern $12.00
Fantasy, ball jug, #1, #2, or #3 ....$50.00
Fantasy, bowl, fruit; lg, footed, Tomorrow's Classic....$20.00
Fantasy, coffeepot, 6-cup, Tomorrow's Classic...........$45.00
Fantasy, creamer, New York $18.00
Fantasy, drip jar, w/lid, Thick Rim...................$27.00
Fantasy, sugar bowl, Morning $22.00
Fantasy, vase, Tomorrow's Classic $16.00
Fern, ashtray, Hallcraft..............................$5.00
Fern, bowl, vegetable; divided, Hallcraft.............$12.00
Fern, butter dish, Hallcraft..........................$25.00
Fern, plate, 10", Hallcraft...........................$6.00
Fern, relish, 4-part, Hallcraft.......................$14.00
Five Band, bowl, 7¼", red or cobalt $10.00
Five Band, cookie jar, canary $25.00
Five band, salt & pepper shakers, ivory, pr $16.00
Five Band, syrup, red or cobalt $40.00
Flamingo, bowl, 7½", Five Band $12.00
Flamingo, creamer, Viking $16.00
Flamingo, sugar bowl, Viking $22.00
Floral Lattice, bowl, batter; Five Band...............$20.00
Floral Lattice, casserole, #76, round.................$30.00
Floral Lattice, syrup, Five Band $22.00
Frost Flowers, bowl, salad; 14½", Tomorrow's Salad ..$20.00
Frost Flowers, casserole, 2-qt, Tomorrow's Classic.....$22.00
Frost Flowers, egg cup, Tomorrow's Classic $22.00
Frost Flowers, platter, 17", Tomorrow's Classic $20.00
Gold Label, baker, French-fluted $12.00
Gold Label, cookie jar, Zeisel-style..................$22.00
Golden Glo, bean pot, New England, #4 ....$25.00
Golden Glo, bowl, salad; 9¾" $10.00
Golden Glo, jug, Five Band $11.00
Golden Glo, teapot, Boston $27.00
Harlequin, bowl, salad; 14½" $16.00
Harlequin, cup $7.00
Harlequin, saucer $1.50
Harlequin, vase $20.00
Heather Rose, bowl, cereal; 6¼" $4.00
Heather Rose, bowl, 8¾", Flare-shape $11.00
Heather Rose, coffeepot, 12-oz, Washington $20.00
Heather Rose, mug, Irish coffee.......................$14.00
Heather Rose, pickle dish, 9" $8.00
Heather Rose, pie baker $14.00
Heather Rose, platter, 15½", oval $15.00
Holiday, ball jug #3..................................$30.00
Holiday, candlestick, 4½" $12.00
Holiday, cookie jar...................................$60.00
Holiday, plate, 11"...................................$8.00
Meadow Flower, bowl, 8½", Thick Rim $22.00
Meadow Flower, custard, Thick Rim $10.00
Meadow Flower, teapot, Streamline.....................$200.00
Medallion, bowl, #2, lettuce $4.00
Medallion, bowl, #4, ivory............................$5.00
Medallion, bowl, #6, Chinese red $15.00
Medallion, custard, lettuce $7.00
Medallion, drip jar, ivory $9.00
Medallion, leftover, square, Chinese red..............$45.00
Medallion, stack set, ivory...........................$27.00

Medallion, teapot, lettuce $55.00
Morning Glory, bowl, 6", straight sides $9.00
Morning Glory, custard, straight sides $10.00
Morning Glory, teapot, Aladdin $55.00
Mulberry, bowl, fruit; 5¾", Hallcraft.................$4.00
Mulberry, butter dish, Hallcraft $35.00
Mulberry, shakers, Hallcraft, each....................$7.00
Mulberry, vase, Hallcraft $18.00
Mums, bowl, cereal; 6" $8.00
Mums, casserole, Radiance $35.00
Mums, cup $8.00
Mums, custard $7.00
Mums, drip jar, w/lid, Medallion $18.00
Mums, plate, 9".......................................$8.00
Mums, platter, 13¼", oval $18.00
No 488, bowl, fruit; 5½"..............................$6.00
No 488, casserole, Five Band $32.00
No 488, cookie jar, Five Band $70.00
No 488, creamer, modern $9.00
No 488, cup $9.00
No 488, plate, 9" $10.00
No 488, platter, 13¼", oval $20.00
No 488, sugar bowl, modern $18.00
Orange Poppy, bowl, fruit; 5½", C-style...............$5.50
Orange Poppy, bowl, vegetable; 9¼", round, C-style..$25.00
Orange Poppy, bowl, 10", Radiance $25.00
Orange Poppy, bread box, metal $35.00
Orange Poppy, cake plate $18.00
Orange Poppy, canisters, metal, 4-piece set $40.00
Orange Poppy, cup, C-style $9.00
Orange Poppy, custard $5.50
Orange Poppy, match safe, metal.......................$20.00
Orange Poppy, saucer, C-style $2.00
Pastel Morning Glory, ball jug, #3 ....$35.00
Pastel Morning Glory, bowl, salad, 9" $12.00
Pastel Morning Glory, bowl, soup; 8½", flat, D-style..$12.00
Pastel Morning Glory, gravy boat, D-style.............$20.00
Pastel Morning Glory, leftover, rectangular...........$35.00
Pastel Morning Glory, pie baker $20.00
Pastel Morning Glory, plate, 9", D-style..............$8.00
Peach Blossom, bowl, 8¾", square, Hallcraft...........$14.00
Peach Blossom, gravy boat, Hallcraft $14.00
Peach Blossom, platter, 17", Hallcraft................$20.00
Peach Blossom, vinegar bottle, Hallcraft..............$20.00
Pine Cone, bowl, celery; oval, Tomorrow's Classic.....$12.00
Pine Cone, bowl, 9", round, E-style...................$16.00
Pine Cone, gravy boat, Tomorrow's Classic.............$14.00
Pine Cone, plate, 9¼", E-style $7.00
Pine Cone, platter, 15", Tomorrow's Classic...........$16.00
Pine Cone, teapot, 6-cup, Tomorrow's Classic..........$45.00
Primrose, bowl, fruit; 5¼"............................$4.00
Primrose, cake plate $12.00
Primrose, plate, 6½" $2.50
Primrose, platter, 13¼", oval $12.00
Radiance, refrigerator jug, red, w/lid, 6" $40.00
Red Poppy, baker, French-fluted.......................$16.00
Red Poppy, bowl, fruit; 5½", D-style $5.00
Red Poppy, bowl, 9¼", round, D-style..................$25.00

Red Poppy, bowl covers, plastic, 8-piece set...............$40.00
Red Poppy, cake plate...$15.00
Red Poppy, cake safe, metal, several styles $35.00
Red Poppy, canister, 1-gal, glass..................................$22.00
Red Poppy, cup, D-style $9.00
Red Poppy, plate, 6", D-style $3.50
Red Poppy, platter, 11¼", oval.......................................$17.00

Red Poppy, salt & pepper shakers, w/handle, pr .$18.50
Red Poppy, saucer, D-style $1.50
Red Poppy, tumbler, frosted glass, 2 styles.................$16.00
Rose Parade, baker, French-fluted................................$28.00
Rose Parade, bean pot, tab handles $45.00
Rose Parade, creamer, Pert..$12.00
Rose Parade, jug, 7½", Pert $32.00
Rose Parade, sugar bowl, Pert $12.00
Rose White, bowl, 6", straight sides................................$8.00
Rose White, salt & pepper shakers, Pert, pr $18.00
Rose White, teapot, 3-cup, Pert $27.00
Royal Rose, ball jug, #3 ....$35.00
Royal Rose, bowl, 9", straight sides $18.00
Royal Rose, teapot, French..$45.00
Sears' Arlington, bowl, cream soup; 5"..........................$12.00
Sears' Arlington, bowl, vegetable; w/lid.......................$25.00
Sears' Monticello, bowl, fruit; 5¼".................................$4.00
Sears' Monticello, bowl, 9¼", oval $14.00
Sears' Monticello, cup...$5.00
Sears' Monticello, plate, 10"...$6.00
Sears' Monticello, saucer...$1.50
Sears' Mount Vernon, bowl, cereal; 6¼".........................$5.50
Sears' Mount Vernon, bowl, 9¼", oval...........................$14.00
Sears' Mount Vernon, gravy boat, w/underplate $16.00
Sears' Mount Vernon, pickle dish, 9"..............................$7.00
Sears' Mount Vernon, platter, 15½", oval $16.00
Sears' Richmond/Brown-Eyed Susan, baker, fluted.....$12.00
Sears' Richmond/Brown-Eyed Susan, bowl, salad; 9" .$12.00
Sears' Richmond/Brown-Eyed Susan, creamer..............$5.00
Sears' Richmond/Brown-Eyed Susan, plate, 10" $5.00
Serenade, bean pot, New England #4 ....$55.00
Serenade, bowl, cereal, 6", D-style $7.00
Serenade, bowl, fruit; 5½", D-style................................$4.50
Serenade, coffeepot, Terrace...$35.00
Serenade, creamer, Art Deco..$10.00

Serenade, plate, 9", D-style...$6.00
Serenade, sugar bowl, Art Deco $16.00
Shaggy Tulip, coffepot, drip; all china, Kadota...........$60.00
Shaggy Tulip, shirred egg dish......................................$20.00
Shaggy Tulip, teapot, Radiance...................................$115.00
Silhouette, bowl, vegetable; 9¼", round, D-style.........$27.00
Silhouette, gravy boat, D-style $22.00
Silhouette, mug, beverage...$37.00
Silhouette, plate, 9", D-style $10.00
Silhouette, sifter...$45.00
Silhouette, tumbler, 10-oz, crystal................................$18.00
Spring, bowl, cereal; 6", Tomorrow's Classic $5.00
Spring, butter dish, Tomorrow's Classic $35.00
Spring, casserole, 2-qt, Tomorrow's Classic $20.00
Springtime, bowl, cereal; 6", D-style...............................$6.00
Springtime, bowl, salad; 9"..$12.00
Springtime, casserole, Thick Rim $22.00
Springtime, custard $4.00
Springtime, gravy boat, D-style.....................................$18.00
Springtime, plate, 7¼", D-style $4.00
Springtime, platter, 15", oval, D-style $18.00
Stonewall, drip jar, #1188, open $22.00
Stonewall, leftover, square $40.00
Stonewall, teapot, Radiance $125.00
Sunglow, bowl, soup; 8", Hallcraft..................................$6.00
Sunglow, bowl, vegetable; divided, Hallcraft..............$12.00
Sunglow, gravy boat, Hallcraft......................................$12.00
Sunglow, relish, 4-part, Hallcraft..................................$12.00
Syrup, Five Band..$40.00

Teapot, 8-cup, Airflow, cobalt w/gold flowers......$55.00
Teapot, 10-12 cup, New York, common colors...........$30.00
Teapot, 2-cup, Manhattan, stock brown, side handle .$45.00
Teapot, 4-cup, Bellvue, cobalt w/gold trim $35.00
Teapot, 6-cup, Airflow, red or cobalt $55.00
Teapot, 6-cup, Albany, pink w/Gold Label.................$55.00
Teapot, 6-cup, Boston, rose w/gold Trailing Astor......$40.00
Teapot, 6-cup, Globe, no-drip, marine w/gold trim....$55.00
Teapot, 6-cup, Modern, ivory w/gold trim...................$16.00
Teapot, 6-cup, Nautilus, Chinese red w/gold trim $135.00
Teapot, 6-cup, Surfside, emerald green w/Special gold deco-
   ration..$85.00
Teapot, 6-cup, Windshield, ivory w/Gold Label polka
   dot $30.00

Teapot, 6-cup, Windshield, ivory w/pheasant decal ...**$80.00**

Tri-Tone, jug, 9", pink, blue & white, Zeisel design .$35.00
Tulip, baker, French-fluted....................................$17.00
Tulip, bowl, fruit; 5½", D-style $5.00
Tulip, bowl, soup; 8½", flat, D-style $11.00
Tulip, creamer, modern...$8.00
Tulip, plate, 10", D-style.......................................$18.00
Tulip, platter, 13¼", D-style..................................$20.00
Tulip, stack set, Radiance $55.00
Tulip, sugar bowl, modern......................................$15.00
Wild Poppy, baker, oval..$45.00
Wild Poppy, bowl, 7½", Radiance $15.00
Wild Poppy, casserole, 10½", round.......................$50.00
Wild Poppy, creamer, Hollywood $30.00
Wild Poppy, sugar bowl, w/lid, Hollywood $45.00
Wild Poppy, teapot, 2-or 4-cup, New York $155.00
Wildfire, bowl, cereal; 6" $9.00
Wildfire, bowl, 7½", straight-sided........................$10.00
Wildfire, cake plate..$12.00
Wildfire, cup...$7.00
Wildfire, drip jar, tab handles...............................$15.00
Wildfire, salt & pepper shakers, Pert, pr $24.00
Wildfire, saucer, D-style...$1.50
Wildfire, tidbit, 3-tier, D-style..............................$50.00
Yellow Rose, bowl, vegetable; 9¼", round, D-style.....$16.00
Yellow Rose, bowl, 6", Radiance $8.00
Yellow Rose, coffeepot, Dome $30.00
Yellow Rose, custard $5.00
Yellow Rose, gravy boat..$20.00
Yellow Rose, plate, 9", D-style...............................$6.00
Yellow Rose, stack set, Radiance............................$55.00

Hallmark Ornaments

Some of the Hallmark Christmas ornaments that have been made since they were first introduced in 1973 are worth many times their original price. This is especially true of the first one issued in a particular series. For instance, Cardinals, first in the Holiday Wildlife series issued in 1982 has a value today of $400.00 (MIB).

If you'd like to learn more about them, we recommend *The Secondary Price Guide to Hallmark Ornaments* by Rosie Wells.

Our values are for ornaments that are mint and in their original boxes (otherwise deduct about 10% to 20%).

1973, Elves, #XHD-103-5, ice skating elves on white glass ball **$55.00**
1973, Santa w/Elves, #XHD 101-5, white glass sphere, 3¼" dia **$60.00**
1973, Yarn Ornament (Blue Girl), #XHD 85-2............**$20.00**
1973, Yarn Ornament (Mr Snowman), #XHD 76-5, wearing blue scarf & black top hat, 4½"............................**$23.00**
1974, Charmers, #QX 109-1, white glass ball decorated w/carolers, dated **$40.00**
1974, Currier & Ives, #QX 112-1, white glass balls w/winter farmstead & horse-drawn sleigh, set of 2.............**$45.00**
1974, Snowgoose, #QX 107-1, white glass ball...........**$77.00**
1974, Yarn Ornament (Mrs Santa), #QX 100-1.............**$22.00**
1975, Adorable Adornments (Raggedy Ann), #QX159-1, hard to find **$300.00**
1975, Betsy Clark Series, #QX 168-1, Christmas 1975, scenes of children w/animals & birds, set of 4 ....**$45.00**
1975, Marty Links, #QX 136-1, Merry Christmas 1975 on back of white glass ball **$33.00**
1975, Nostalgia Ornaments (Rocking Horse), #QX128-1, reissued in 1976..**$145.00**
1976, Betsy Clark Series, #QX 210-1, Christmas 1976 on white glass ball...**$40.00**
1976, Cardinals, #QX 205-1, cardinals perched on pine branches on white glass ball **$40.00**
1976, Norman Rockwell, #QX 196-1, Santa rests from his travels & feeds reindeer on white glass ball **$60.00**
1976, Nostalgia Ornaments (Locomotive), #QX 222-1, same design as 1975..**$160.00**
1977, Beauty of America Collection (Mountains), #QX 158-2, mountain scenes w/captions on white glass ball..**$35.00**
1977, Christmas Expressions (Bell), #QX 154-2, I Heard the Bells on Christmas Day... on white glass ball **$45.00**
1977, Colors of Christmas (Candle), #QX 203-5, acrylic, 3 candles w/stained glass look.................................**$57.50**
1977, Grandson, #QX 209-5, Santa decorated on white satin ball, A Grandson Is...a Joy Bringer **$30.00**
1978, Angel, #QX 139-6, hand-crafted bread-dough look barefoot angel in blue & white holding star.........**$80.00**
1978, Betsy Clark Series, 3¼" ball, The Christmas Season Seems To Bring a Cheerful Glow to Everything **$50.00**
1978, Calico Mouse, #QX 137-6, hand-crafted smiling red calico mouse w/green ears & nose holding sprig of holly...**$185.00**
1978, Little Trimmers (Drummer Boy), #QX 136-3, hand-crafted drummer boy in red, green & blue **$2.50**
1978, Peanuts, #QX 204-3, Snoopy & Woodstock decorate Christmas tree on dated white satin ball **$47.00**

1979, Angel Music, #CX 343-9, sewn fabric, angel w/pink & white wings in blue gown carrying harp **$18.00**

1979, Baby's First Christmas, #QX 208-7, satin ball pictures toys & gifts on sleigh & bird decorated tree **$18.50**

1979, Downhill Run, #QX 145-9, hand-crafted squirrel & rabbit on red toboggan...**$140.00**

1979, Friendship, #QX 203-9, ice skating & sleigh ride scene on white glass ball, w/caption **$20.00**

1980, A Heavenly Nap, #QX 139-4, hand-crafted frosted acrylic sleeping moon holding sleeping angel, reissued 1981 ....**$45.00**

1980, Beauty of Friendship, #QX 303-4, caption encircled by pine branches, acrylic...**$58.00**

1980, Frosted Images (Drummer Boy), #QX 308-1, frosted acrylic figure of Santa w/bag on his back.............**$16.00**

1980, Granddaughter, #QX 202-1, scene, caption & date on ecru soft-sheen satin ball......................................**$18.00**

1981, Betsy Clark Blue Cameo, #QX 512-2, little girl pets fawn, w/caption & date...**$22.00**

1981, Calico Kitty, #QX 403-5, kitty sewn in yellow print fabric w/red bow **$15.00**

1981, Cardinal Cutie, #QX 400-2, bird sewn in red fabric w/white dots **$20.00**

1981, Christmas Fantasy, #QX 155-4, hand-crafted elf rides white goose w/brass ribbon in bill, reissued 1982 .**$55.00**

1981, Fiftieth Christmas Together, #QX 708-2, dated caption surrounded by flowers on gold glass ball **$12.50**

1982, Arctic Penguin, #QX300-3, clear acrylic penguin molded to resemble an ice sculpture **$15.00**

1982, Brass Bell, #QX460-6, polished brass bell w/stamped holly leaves & berries, red bow hanger **$18.00**

1982, Embroidered Tree, #QX 494-6, green fabric tree w/flowers trimmed in red braided cord **$28.00**

1982, Holiday Highlights (Angel), #QX 309-6, acrylic angel playing harp, gold foil caption...............................**$22.50**

1982, Teacher, #QX 214-3, Elves cast shadows to spell Christmas 1982 on white glass ball, w/caption.....**$10.00**

1983, Angels, #QX 219-7, gold tinsel starburst inside clear glass ball, outside has pastel angels **$18.00**

1983, Bell Wreath, #QX 420-9, solid brass holly wreath w/7 sm bells..**$25.00**

1983, Christmas Joy, #QX 216-9, little girl presents carrot to bunny on ecru soft-sheen ball, w/caption **$18.00**

1983, Mailbox Kitten, #QX 415-7, kitten w/letters pops out of red mailbox, 1983 Peppermint Lane **$60.00**

1984, A Christmas Prayer, #QX 246-1, Mary Hamilton's angels chase stars on blue satin ball, w/caption...**$15.00**

1984, Cuckoo Clock, #QX 455-1, hand-crafted clock w/pine cone pendulums & brass face................................**$45.00**

1984, Holiday Jester, #QX 437-4, hand-crafted in black & white costume, movable arms & legs....................**$30.00**

1984, Katybeth, #QX 463-1, hand-painted porcelain angel w/freckles holds star..**$25.00**

1984, Napping Mouse, #QX 400-5, white mouse holding his 'teddy mouse' as he sleeps in walnut shell..........**$47.50**

1985, Doggy in Stocking, #QX 474-2, hand-crafted terrier poking head out of red & green striped stocking..**$32.50**

1985, First Christmas Together, #QX400-5, polished brass locket w/embossed hearts surrounding caption...**$25.00**

1985, Holiday Heart, #QX 498-2, white porcelain puffed heart w/Christmas greenery around Love caption **$22.50**

1985, Nostalgic Houses (Toy Shop), #QX 497-5, upstairs apartment, store displays & furniture **$55.00**

1985, Tin Locomotive, #QX 497-2, black w/colorful decorations & jingle bell, dated, fourth in series **$60.00**

1986, Cookies for Santa, #QX 414-6, plate w/For Santa sign, dated star cookie & gingerbread man **$19.00**

1986, Joy of Friends, #QX 382-3, ice skaters on padded satin oval resembling folk art, chrome frame **$12.50**

1986, Merry Koala, #QX 415-3, hand-crafted flocked koala in oversized Santa's hat..**$15.00**

1987, Clothespin Soldier (Sailor), #QX 480-7, hand-crafted sailor waving red flags w/green trees...................**$16.00**

1987, Country Wreath, #QX 470-9, wood straw wreath is tied w/red yarn & decorated w/wooden shapes ..**$20.00**

1987, From Our House to Yours, #QX 279-9, decorated doorways around white frosted glass ball, dated **$12.00**

1987, Goldfinch, #QX 464-9, hand-painted porcelain bird poised in flight **$40.00**

1988, Chrismas Cardinal, #QX 494-1, cardinal suspended from golden beads inside reserve of evergreen....**$12.50**

1988, Christmas Memories Photoholder, #QX 372-4, silver foil snowflakes & bow, w/date & caption.............**$15.00**

1988, Kiss the Claus, #QX 486-1, Santa in chef's garb serving up cheeseburgers, caption on apron....................**$12.50**

1988, Squeaky Clean, #QX 475-4, mouse bathing in footed walnut shell tub w/shower..................................**$13.50**

1989, Baby Partridge, #QX 452-5, designed by artist John Francis, attached to tree w/special clip **$13.50**

1989, Christmas Carousel Horse Collection (Ginger), #XPR 972-2, palomino w/white mane, #4 of 4 ....**$12.50**

1989, Christmas Kitty, #QX 544-5, porcelain kitty in light green dress w/white apron trimmed in red **$20.00**

1989, Gentle Fawn, #QX 548-5, flocked fawn w/shiny eyes wearing ribbon & holly **$17.00**

1989, Norman Rockwell, #QX 275-2, ...Famous Holiday Covers From Saturday Evening Post, gold glass ball...**$12.50**

1989, Nostalgic Houses (US Post Office), #QX 458-2, w/furnished upstairs office, dated, 6th in series **$32.50**

1990, Across the Miles, #QX 317-3, happy raccoon carries poinsettia on acrylic oval, caption **$10.00**

1990, Bearback Rider, #QX 548-3, penguin w/red hat riding polar bear on red & white rockers **$17.50**

1990, Brother, #QX 449-3, puppy sitting in ball glove marked MVB (Most Valuable Brother), dated.......**$11.50**

1990, Christmas Partridge, #QX 524-6, partridge dangles inside dimensional brass pear w/lg etched leaves **$12.00**

1990, Cozy Goose, #QX 496-6, white goose in goose-down vest..**$12.00**

1990, Donder's Diner, #QX 482-3, Donder serving Santa a hamburger in diner, dated................................**$20.00**

1990, Fabulous Decade, #QX 446-6, squirrel displaying brass 1990, 1st in series..**$17.50**

1990, Garfield, #QX 230-3, blue chrome glass ball w/Garfield ice skating, Merry Christmas...Happy New Year..**$8.00**

Halloween

Next to Christmas, you probably have more happy childhood recollections of Halloween than any other holiday of the year. If somehow you've managed to hang onto some old party decorations or one of the jack-o'-lanterns that we used to collect candy in, you already have a good start on a collection that you'll really enjoy.

Candy bag, cat face, 7x8x3", thin cardboard w/wire handle, EX...$55.00
Candy container, cat, 5½", composition, black w/yellow hat, red nose, holds orange pumpkin, Germany.......**$210.00**
Candy container, cat on skull, 6", composition, black cat w/green eyes, Germany, EX...............................**$350.00**
Candy container, pumpkin, 5", papier-mache, cone shape, 1950s..**$27.50**
Clacker, 2 wooden balls strike tin witch, cats handle .**$45.00**
Cookie cutters, boxed set of 6 metal cutters in various Halloween shapes, EX...**$40.00**
Decoration, bat w/honeycomb, Beistle........................**$20.00**
Decoration, skeleton, life size, embossed cardboard diecut, Luhrs, 1940s..**$40.00**
Decoration, witch diecut, 8", jointed, w/orange tissue wings, M...**$20.00**
Jack-o'-lantern, med size, tin lithograph, EX...............**$65.00**
Jack-o'-lantern, 4", papier-mache lantern w/insert **$55.00**
Lantern, glass owl form..**$45.00**
Lantern, skull, 10", cardboard & tissue, M...................**$55.00**
Nodder, cat, 6", mohair w/glass eyes, wooden neck, early, Germany...**$195.00**
Noisemaker, cat, 7", wood w/orange & black paint, Japan, ... NM...**$20.00**

Noisemaker, clown playing drums, lithograph on tin, USA, NM...**$25.00**
Noisemaker, girls in costumes, tin & wood, Barone Toy Mfg, NM...**$18.00**
Salt & pepper shakers, devil, chalkware, 1930s, pr.....**$55.00**
Tambourine, 5½", dancers around pumpkin face lithograph on tin..**$65.00**
Tambourine, 7", tissue over wooden frame, marked Germany...**$120.00**

Halloween Costumes

If you can find one of these still in the original box and the price is right, buy it! During the fifties and sixties, Collegeville and Ben Cooper made these costumes to represent popular TV and movie characters of the day, and these are the more collectible. If your costume shows even a minimum amount of wear or damage, it's worth only 65% to 75% of one mint in box.

Andromeda Lady Space Fighter, Bland Charnas Company, MIB...**$20.00**
Bamm Bamm, 1971, boxed, EX...................................**$18.00**

Batman, Ben Cooper, 1973, EX in VG box $15.00
Batman, Ben Cooper, 1973, MIB.................................**$35.00**
Beany, Ben Cooper, M...**$55.00**
Blondie, Collegeville, EX..**$55.00**
Bozo, Ben Cooper, 1974, original box, NM.................**$15.00**
Bullwinkle, MIB...**$22.50**
Casper the Friendly Ghost, Collegeville, 1959, glow-in-the-dark mask, original box, EX...............................**$30.00**
Casper the Friendly Ghost, Collegeville, 1970s, MIB...**$15.00**
Cecil, Ben Cooper, EX..**$38.00**
Cinderella, Halco, 1950s, unauthorized Disney, original box, EX...**$27.50**
Cinderella, 1950s, MIB...**$35.00**
Close Encounters Alien, cloth w/plastic mask, marked Ben Cooper, 1978, MIB..**$25.00**
C3PO, Return of the Jedi, Ben Cooper.......................**$15.00**
Dr Strange, 1978...**$30.00**

Farrah Fawcett, Collegeville, 1977, MIB $45.00
Flash Gordon, Collegeville, 1978, MIB $30.00
Hair Bear, Ben Cooper, 1971, MIB $32.50
Huckleberry Hound, Ben Cooper, 1961, MIB.............$28.00
Jed Clampett, Ben Cooper, 1963, MIB......................$150.00
Kiss, 1979, M..$40.00
Land of the Giants, Ben Cooper, 1968, mask & costume
    only, NM...$85.00
Li'l Abner, Ben Cooper, 1957, boxed, EX....................$47.50
Max Headroom, mask, VG $3.50
Miss America, Ben Cooper, EX $10.00
Mummy Universal Monster, Ben Cooper, 1965, MIB ..$125.00
Nancy (Nancy & Sluggo), Ben Cooper, MIB...............$25.00
NASA Astronaut, Ben Cooper, #887, EX.....................$15.00
Olive Oyl, Collegeville, EX...$27.50
Phantom, Collegeville, MIB...$35.00
Psychedelic, Peter Max-type graphics, marked Halco, 1960s,
    boxed, EX...$25.00
Psychedelic Clown, Masquerade, 1969, M $22.50
Raggedy Ann, Ben Cooper, 1973, MIB $22.50
Ricky the Riveter, Collegeville, MIB............................$35.00
Shadow, Collegeville, MIB $38.00
Skeleton, Collegeville, 1960s, MIB $20.00
Smokey the Fireman, Ben Cooper, #807 ....$20.00
Spuds McKenzie, mask, VG...$3.50
Star Wars' Wicket, Ben Cooper, MIB...........................$15.00
Tarzan, 1975, boxed, VG $18.00
Tom & Jerry, Ben Cooper, 1975, M $15.00
Tonto, Kusan, 1960s, boxed, EX....................................$25.00
Tweety, Collegeville, 1950s, original box, EX.............$35.00
Underdog, Collegeville, 1970s, EX................................$30.00
Wolfman, mask, Don Post, 1976, no hair, EX.............$18.00
Wolfman, mask, rubber, Don Post, 1960s, NM...........$50.00
Wolfman, Universal Monsters series, 1980, M on card..$15.00
Yoda, Ben Cooper, 1980, MIB $20.00
Yogi Bear, Ben Cooper, 1961, M $28.00
Zoro, Ben Cooper, 1960s, VG.......................................$50.00

Harker Pottery

Harker was one of the oldest potteries in the country; their history could be traced back to the 1840s. In the thirties, a new plant was built in Chester, West Virginia, and the company began manufacturing kitchen and dinnerware lines, eventually employing as many as three hundred workers.

Several of these lines are popular with collectors today. One of the most easily recognized is Cameoware. It is usually found in pink or blue decorated with white silhouettes of flowers, though other designs were made as well. Colonial Lady, Red Apple, Amy, Mallow, and Pansy are some of their other lines that are fairly easy to find and reassemble into sets.

If you'd like to learn more about Harker, we recommend *The Collector's Encyclopedia of American Dinnerware* by Jo Cunningham and *The Collector's Guide to Harker Pottery* by Neva Colbert.

Amethyst, bean pot...$6.00
Amethyst, custard...$5.00
Amy, server $18.00
Amy, stack set, w/lid, 3-piece......................................$35.00
Basket, creamer..$8.00
Basket, plate..$3.00
Becky, bowl, utility...$20.00

Cameo, casserole, w/lid...$35.00
Cameo, meat platter...$18.00
Cameo, pitcher (lid missing) (illustrated) $30.00
Cameo, plate, 9", Shell Shape $10.00
Chesterton, gravy boat...$15.00
Colonial Lady, bowl, batter $40.00
Colonial Lady, bowl, cereal; tan handles.....................$5.00
Deco Dahlia, pie baker, 9"..$10.00
Deco Dahlia, plate, utility; 12" $15.00
Ivy Vine, plate, 8"..$6.00
Mallow, bowl, utility; 10"..$25.00
Mallow, custard cups, w/lids, in wire rack, set of 4....$40.00
Mallow, lard jar, w/lid $20.00
Modern Tulip, jar, oval, w/lid......................................$30.00
Modern Tulip, spoon..$12.00
Pastel Tulip, cake plate..$18.00
Pastel tulip, gravy boat..$12.00
Petit Point Rose I, pie baker, 9" $20.00
Petit Point Rose II, custard, individual.........................$4.00
Red Apple I, plate, serving..$22.00
Red Apple II, serving spoon $25.00

Rockingham Ware, mug, hound handle, 1960s....$30.00
Rockingham Ware, pitcher, hound handle, 1960s.$50.00
Rose Spray, breakfast plate, 9x9" $8.00
Rose Spray, creamer $12.00
Rose Spray, plate, salad; 7"..$4.00
Ruffled Tulip, plate, serving; 11¾".............................$25.00

Shellridge, sugar bowl $10.00
Slender Leaf, plate, serving $15.00
White Rose, tea tile...$25.00
White Rose, teapot...$27.00

Harlequin Dinnerware

This is another line of solid-color dinnerware made by the Fiesta people, Homer Laughlin. Harlequin was less expensive, designed to cater to the dimestore trade. In fact, it was sold exclusively through the F.W. Woolworth Company. It was introduced to the public in the late 1930s, and records indicate that production continued until near the middle of the 1960s.

Like Fiesta, Harlequin is very Deco in appearance. But in contrast to Fiesta's ring handles, Harlequin's are angular, as are many of its shapes. The band of rings, similar to Fiesta's, is set farther away from its rims. Harlequin isn't nearly as heavy as Fiesta, and it was never marked.

Some of its colors are more desirable to collectors than others, so they're worth more. Two values are given for each item we've listed. The higher values apply to these colors: maroon, gray, medium green, spruce green, chartreuse, dark green, rose, mauve blue, red, and light green. Lower values are for items in turquoise and yellow.

Harlequin animals were made during the forties. There were six: a cat, a fish, a penguin, a duck, a lamb, and a donkey. They were made in maroon, spruce green, mauve blue, and yellow. These were reproduced by other companies; if you find one trimmed in gold, you've probably got a 'maverick.' If you find one in a color not listed, you're very lucky – these are worth twice as much as one in a standard color.

In 1979, complying with a request from the Woolworth company, HLC reissued a line of new Harlequin. It was made in original yellow and turquoise, medium green (slightly different than the original shade), and coral (an altogether new color). Some pieces were restyled, and the line was very limited. If you find a piece with a trademark, you'll know its new.

If you'd like to know more about Harlequin, it's included in *The Collector's Encyclopedia of Fiesta* by Sharon and Bob Huxford.

Animals, mavericks, each $32.00
Animals, non-standard colors, each.........................$158.00
Animals, standard colors $80.00
Ashtray, basketweave, high...$45.00
Ashtray, basketweave, low $30.00
Ashtray, regular, high $42.50
Ashtray, regular, low...$32.00
Bowl, '36s oatmeal; high $17.00
Bowl, '36s oatmeal; low $12.00
Bowl, '36s; high $26.50
Bowl, '36s; low...$17.00
Bowl, cream soup; high $20.00
Bowl, cream soup; low..$16.00

Bowl, fruit; 5½", high..$9.00
Bowl, fruit; 5½", low...$6.00
Bowl, individual salad; high.......................................$28.00
Bowl, individual salad; low $17.00
Bowl, mixing; 10", yellow, Kitchen Kraft $110.00
Bowl, mixing; 6", red or spruce green, Kitchen Kraft .$75.00
Bowl, mixing; 8", mauve blue, Kitchen Kraft............$110.00
Bowl, nappy; 9", high...$26.50
Bowl, nappy:, 9", low...$16.50
Bowl, oval baker, high $25.00
Bowl, oval baker, low $18.00
Butter dish, ½-lb, high $90.00
Butter dish, ½-lb, low $75.00
Candle holders, high, pr...$195.00
Candle holders, low, pr..$162.00
Casserole, w/lid, high $110.00
Casserole, w/lid, low $62.50
Creamer, any color, high lip $75.00
Creamer, individual; high $17.00
Creamer, individual; low $12.50
Creamer, novelty, high $23.00
Creamer, novelty, low $16.00
Creamer, regular, high..$13.50
Creamer, regular, low..$8.00
Cup, demitasse; high $72.50
Cup, demitasse; low..$27.50
Cup, lg, any color..$110.00
Cup, tea; high..$9.50
Cup, tea; low $7.50
Egg cup, double, high $20.00
Egg cup, double, low $14.00
Egg cup, single, high $22.50
Egg cup, single, low $16.50
Gravy boat, high $23.00
Gravy boat, low $17.50
Marmalade, any color...$125.00
Nut dish, basketweave, original color $8.00
Perfume bottle, any color...$75.00

Pitcher, service water; high $65.00
Pitcher, service water; low $37.50
Pitcher, 22-oz jug, high...$46.00

Pitcher, 22-oz jug, low	$28.00
Plate, deep; high	$20.00
Plate, deep; low	$15.00
Plate, 10", high	$24.00
Plate, 10", low	$14.00
Plate, 6", high	$4.50
Plate, 6", low	$3.50
Plate, 7", high	$6.50
Plate, 7", low	$4.50
Plate, 9", high	$12.00
Plate, 9", low	$7.00
Platter, 11", high	$17.50
Platter, 11", low	$12.00
Platter, 13", high	$25.00
Platter, 13", low	$16.50
Salt & pepper shakers, high, pr	$17.50
Salt & pepper shakers, low, pr	$13.00
Saucer, demitasse; high	$13.50
Saucer, demitasse; low	$8.00
Saucer, high	$3.50
Saucer, low	$2.00
Saucer/ashtray, high	$47.00
Saucer/ashtray, ivory	$70.00
Saucer/ashtray, low	$42.50
Sugar bowl, high	$22.50
Sugar bowl, low	$14.00
Syrup, any color	$200.00
Teapot, high	$100.00

Teapot, low	$58.00
Teapot, low	$58.00
Tray relish; mixed colors	$200.00
Tumbler, high	$40.00
Tumbler, low	$30.00

Hartland Plastics, Inc.

The Hartland company was located in Hartland, Wisconsin, where during the fifties and sixties they made several lines of plastic figures: Western and Historic Horsemen, Miniature Western Series, and the Hartland Sport Series of Famous Baseball Stars. Football and bowling figures and religious statues were made as well. The plastic, virgin acetate, was very durable and the figures were hand painted with careful attention to detail. They're often marked.

Alkali Ike, 8", w/horse, VG	$35.00
Babe Ruth, no bat, EX	$185.00
Bill Longley the Texan, 6½x4", hand-painted hard plastic, 1950s, missing accessories & horse, VG	$37.50
Brave Eagle, 9½", w/horse, missing accessories, VG	$75.00
Bret Maverick, 5½", w/horse, M on card	$50.00
Bullet (Roy Roger's dog), 6" long, #700, MIB	$75.00
Cactus Pete, 8", w/horse, MIB	$125.00
Comanche Kid, 8", w/horse, M	$75.00
Dale Evans, empty box for figure & horse, EX	$90.00
General Custer, 9½", w/horse, M	$100.00
General Robert E Lee, 9½", w/horse, MIB	$250.00
Gil Favor, 5½", w/horse, M on card	$50.00
Hoby Gilman, 9½", w/horse, EX	$125.00

Indian chief w/lance, bow & headdress on 8" black & cream horse	$135.00
Jim Hardie, 5½", w/horse, M	$30.00
Jim Hardie, 9½", w/horse, VG	$50.00
Johnny McKay, 9½", w/horse, VG	$100.00
Johnny Yuma, 5½", w/horse, M	$30.00
Lone Ranger, 5½", w/horse, missing hat, VG	$15.00
Lone Ranger, 9½", w/horse, MIB	$275.00
Lucas McCain, 5½", w/horse, missing hat, VG	$15.00
Lucas McCain, 9½", w/horse, EX	$125.00
Matt Dillon, 9½", figure only, NM	$45.00
Matt Dillon, 9½", w/horse & accessories, MIB	$250.00
Matt Dillon's horse, for sm figure, EX	$22.50
Mickey Mantle, 1960s, bat missing, NM	$225.00
Paladin, 9½", w/horse, VG	$50.00
Roy Rogers, 9½", w/horse, missing accessories, VG	$60.00
St Francis, 13"	$55.00
Tonto, 9½", w/horse in original box, EX	$195.00
Tonto, 9½", w/horse, MIB	$275.00
Trigger, for lg figure, M	$60.00
Wyatt Earp, 9½", w/horse, MIB	$200.00

Head Vases

These were mainly imported from Japan, although a few were made by American companies, and sold to florist shops to be filled with flower arrangements. So if there's an old flower shop in your neighborhood, you might start your search with their storerooms.

If you'd like to learn more about them, we recommend *Head Vases, Identification and Values*, by Kathleen Cole.

Baby, 5½", Sampson #313A, brown-haired boy hugging his bottle, big brown eyes, blue sweater, 1957...........**$37.50**

Baby, 5½", unmarked, blond-haired girl w/pink ruffled bonnet & white bow..**$37.50**

Child, 4", Napcoware #C-7094, brown-haired boy wearing brown overalls & red neckerchief..........................**$35.00**

Child, 5", Inarco (paper label), blond-haired boy in fireman's uniform holding hose, black 5 on hat........**$32.50**

Child, 5", Inarco #E778, blond-haired girl praying, red gown w/long sleeves, 1962..**$32.00**

Child, 5½", Enesco (paper label), blond-haired girl hugging kitten, white hairbow w/red polka dots...............**$42.50**

Child, 5½", Inarco #2523, little girl w/2 braids & bangs, light green head scarf & bodice w/white polka dots....**$45.00**

Child, 5½", Japan, girl w/blond bouffant curls & pink bow in her hair, big brown eyes, pink bodice w/ivory ruffled collar..**$47.50**

Child, 5½", Relpo #6744, blond-haired boy wearing blue beret & shirt w/white collar...................................**$45.00**

Child, 7", marked Jean #231, girl in red, black & white plaid dress..**$42.50**

Child, 7", unmarked, boy wearing red, black & white plaid shirt..**$42.50**

Clown, 4¾", Napcoware #1988, brown hair, blue eye makeup, lg green bow tie w/blue polka dots......**$32.50**

Clown, 5½", Inarco #E-6730, red hair, blue & yellow hat w/white ball, yellow & blue ruffled collar............**$20.00**

Clown, 7", Inarco, blond hair, red cone style hat w/blue ball, white ruffled collar w/red trim.....................**$37.50**

Lady, 11", Inarco #E2966, blond hair, pearl earrings & 4-strand necklace..$150.00

Lady, 11", Napcoware #C7498, brown hair, white bodice w/blue collar, blue hat & white bow, pearl necklace & earrings..**$150.00**

Lady, 3", unmarked, short blond hair w/green scarf & bodice, rosy cheeks, eyes closed.........................**$22.50**

Lady, 3½", Inarco #E480, pink rose in blond hair, light pink bodice, eyes closed, hand to face, 1961...............**$28.50**

Lady, 3½", Napcoware #CF6060, blond w/head tilted, ivory bodice w/gold, pearl earrings, eyes closed..........**$25.00**

Lady, 4", unmarked, Oriental lady w/head tilted, ivory turban, green & white bodice, green earrings...........**$25.00**

Lady, 4½", Napcoware #C7471, blond w/head turned, black bodice w/applied leaf & pearls, pearl earrings.....**$27.50**

Lady, 4½", unmarked, black hat & yellow bodice w/ruffled collar, eyes closed w/thick lashes, hand to face...**$22.50**

Lady, 4¼", unmarked, white hair w/gold highlights, black bodice & hat w/gold trim, eyes closed.................**$37.50**

Lady, 5", blond hair, in dark green dress & hat, pearl necklace...$32.50

Lady, 5½", Japan, white banana curls, pink ruffled bodice, eyes closed, hand to chin....................................**$42.50**

Lady, 5½", Lefton #1736, blond wearing yellow hat & bodice, red necklace, 1 hand holds purse, 1 hand to ear, eyes closed..**$37.50**

Lady, 5½", Robens Originals #500, blond in white floral dress & hat w/gold trim, pearl earrings, 1959.......**$42.50**

Lady, 5½", Thames (paper label), pink hat w/applied flowers, pink bodice w/ruffled neckline, eyes closed..**$32.50**

Lady, 6", Napco #C5708, blond banana curls, light green bodice w/ruffled ivory collar, 1962.......................**$45.00**

Lady, 6", Napcoware #C6428 (paper label), blond wearing white bodice w/daisies, gloved hand to cheek, eyes closed..**$47.50**

Lady, 6", Relpo #2055, blond bouffant curls, green bodice w/white collar, pearl earrings & necklace, hand to cheek **$47.50**

Lady, 6½", Glamour Girl, ivory w/gold-painted features & details in hair & on bodice, eyes closed...............**$25.00**

Lady, 6½", Napco #C3141A, gray hair w/lg flower above right ear, pearl necklace & earrings, 1958.............**$52.50**

Lady, 6½", Relpo #K1175L, pink hat w/checked bow & pink ruffled bodice, pearl earrings & necklace, hands under chin...**$55.00**

Lady, 6½", unmarked, white-haired w/gold dangle earrings, pink bodice & white ruffled collar w/gold trim....**$40.00**

Lady, 7", unmarked, wearing lg pink hat.............$42.50

Lady, 7½", Relpo #1694-L, red flipped-up hair w/peach beret & peach shirt, white-gloved hand up....................**$45.00**

Lady, 7½", unmarked, brown flipped-up hair w/pink hair-bow & bodice, pearl jewelry, thick lashes............**$47.50**

Lady, 8½", Parma #A219, blond bouffant hairdo w/pearl earrings & necklace, green bodice **$150.00**

Teen girl, 5½", Inarco #E3548, blond holding black telephone to ear, yellow headband & bodice w/white ruffled collar...**$32.50**

Teen girl, 5½", Parma #A172 (paper label), blond flipped-up hair, gold barrette, black bodice, pearl necklace..**$32.50**

Teen girl, 5½", Relpo #K1694/S, blond flipped-up hair, pink speckled beret & shirt, white-gloved hand up......**$37.50**

Teen girl, 5½", unmarked, blond bouffant curls, ivory bodice & ruffled collar w/green trim, pearl earrings & necklace..**$37.50**

Teen girl, 5¾", #4796, unmarked, blond w/2 braids & lg ivory hairbow & bodice..**$37.50**

Teen girl, 6", Napco #C4072G, blond in graduation cap & gown w/gold highlights, holding diploma, 1959..**$37.50**

Teen girl, 7", Napcoware #C8494 (paper label), blond hair w/green hairbow, green bodice w/white collar, pearl earrings **$75.00**

Teen girl, 7½", unmarked, blond w/ponytails & orange sunglasses on her head **$125.00**

Teen girl, 8½", Relpo #K1931, long straight blond hair w/bangs & black headband, black bodice...........**$95.00**

Heisey Glass

From just before the turn of the century until 1957, the Heisey Glass Company of Newark, Ohio, was one of the largest, most successful manufacturers of quality tableware in the world. Though the market is well established, many pieces are still reasonably priced; and if you're drawn to the lovely patterns and colors that Heisey made, you're investment should be sound.

After 1901, their glassware was marked with their familiar trademark, the 'Diamond H' (an H in a diamond), or a paper label. Blown pieces are often marked on the stem instead of the bowl or foot.

Numbers in the listings are catalog reference numbers assigned by the company to indicate variations in shape or stem style. Collectors use them, especially when they buy and sell by mail, for the same purpose. Many catalog pages (showing these numbers) are contained in *The Collector's Encyclopedia of Heisey Glass* by Neila Bredehoft. This book and *Elegant Glassware of the Depression Era* by Gene Florence are both excellent references for further study.

See also Glass Animals.

Chintz, clear, compote, 7", oval **$40.00**
Chintz, clear, creamer, individual **$12.00**
Chintz, clear, oil, 4-oz...**$60.00**
Chintz, clear, plate, dinner; 10½" square....................**$40.00**
Chintz, clear, stem, sherbet; #3389, 5-oz **$8.00**
Chintz, clear, stem, wine; #3389, 2½-oz **$17.50**
Chintz, clear, tumbler, water; #3389, 10-oz, footed.....**$13.00**
Chintz, clear, vase, 9", dolphin foot............................**$85.00**
Chintz, yellow, creamer, 3 dolphin feet **$45.00**
Chintz, yellow, plate, luncheon; 8" square...................**$22.00**
Chintz, yellow, plate, 12", 2-handled...........................**$45.00**
Chintz, yellow, stem, parfait; #3389, 5-oz....................**$35.00**
Chintz, yellow, tumbler, water; #3389, 10-oz, footed ..**$25.00**
Crystolite, clear, ashtray, 4" dia **$6.00**
Crystolite, clear, bonbon, 7", shell..............................**$17.00**
Crystolite, clear, bowl, dessert; 4½"..............................**$8.00**
Crystolite, clear, bowl, gardenia; 12", shallow **$30.00**
Crystolite, clear, bowl, jelly; 6", oval, 4-footed............**$16.00**
Crystolite, clear, candlestick, 1-light, footed...............**$15.00**
Crystolite, clear, candy box, 7", w/lid..........................**$55.00**
Crystolite, clear, cigarette holder, footed.....................**$17.50**
Crystolite, clear, creamer, individual...........................**$17.00**
Crystolite, clear, cup...**$20.00**
Crystolite, clear, ladle, punch......................................**$25.00**
Crystolite, clear, oil bottle, 3-oz **$40.00**
Crystolite, clear, pitcher, ½-gal, blown......................**$100.00**
Crystolite, clear, plate, salad; 8½" **$15.00**
Crystolite, clear, plate, sandwich; 12" **$35.00**
Crystolite, clear, puff box, 4¾", w/lid..........................**$50.00**
Crystolite, clear, saucer..**$5.00**
Crystolite, clear, stem, oyster cocktail; #5003, 3½-oz, wide optic, blown...**$18.00**
Crystolite, clear, tray, relish; 12", 3-part......................**$25.00**

Crystolite, clear, tumbler, juice; #5003, 5-oz, footed, wide optic, blown $24.00

Crystolite, clear, vase, 6", footed $22.50

Empress, alexandrite, plate, 8" square $65.00

Empress, alexandrite, saucer, square $25.00

Empress, alexandrite, tray, celery; 10" $150.00

Empress, cobalt, plate, 8" $70.00

Empress, green, bowl, individual nut; dolphin-footed ..$32.00

Empress, green, bowl, nappy; 8" $40.00

Empress, green, celery tray, 13" $30.00

Empress, green, creamer, dolphin-footed $42.50

Empress, green, cup $36.00

Empress, green, plate, 12" $65.00

Empress, green, saucer, square $16.00

Empress, green, sugar bowl, individual $40.00

Empress, green, tumbler, tea; 12-oz, ground bottom ..$45.00

Empress, pink, bonbon, 6" $20.00

Empress, pink, bowl, relish; 7", 3-part, center handle..$45.00

Empress, pink, bowl, salad; 10" square, handles.........$40.00

Empress, pink, candy, 6", w/lid, dolphin-footed $120.00

Empress, pink, cup $27.00

Empress, pink, plate, 8" square $18.00

Empress, pink, saucer, square $8.00

Empress, pink, stem, saucer champagne; 4-oz $35.00

Empress, pink, tray, relish; 10", 3-part $25.00

Empress, pink, vase, 8", flared $80.00

Empress, yellow, bowl, cream soup $27.00

Empress, yellow, bowl, dessert; 10", oval, handles $60.00

Empress, yellow, candlestick, low, 4-footed $40.00

Empress, yellow, compote, 6", footed $55.00

Empress, yellow, cup $31.00

Empress, yellow, platter, 14" $40.00

Empress, yellow, saucer, square $14.00

Empress, yellow, stem, sherbet; 4-oz $28.00

Empress, yellow, tray, sandwich; 12", center handle...$57.00

Empress, yellow, tumbler, 8-oz, ground bottom.........$35.00

Greek Key, clear, bowl, banana split; 9", footed $25.00

Greek Key, clear, bowl, jelly; 5", handled $35.00

Greek Key, clear, coaster $12.00

Greek Key, clear, compote, 5" $60.00

Greek Key, clear, pitcher, 1-pt $75.00

Greek Key, clear, plate, 8" $20.00

Greek Key, clear, puff box, #1, w/lid $85.00

Greek Key, clear, stem, cocktail; 3-oz $40.00

Greek Key, clear, tray, celery; 9" oval $40.00

Greek Key, clear, tumbler, 13-oz, straight sides $42.00

Greek Key, clear, tumbler, 5-oz, flared rim...............$20.00

Ipswich, clear, candlestick, 6", 1-light $75.00

Ipswich, clear, oil bottle, 2-oz, footed, #86 stopper $75.00

Ipswich, clear, stem, saucer champagne; 5-oz $20.00

Ipswich, green, plate, 8" square $40.00

Ipswich, green, sherbet, 4-oz $30.00

Ipswich, green, tumbler, 10-oz, straight rim $50.00

Ipswich, pink, plate, 8" square $30.00

Ipswich, pink, sherbet, 4-oz $17.50

Ipswich, pink, tumbler, 5-oz, footed $40.00

Ipswich, yellow, sherbet, 4-oz $22.50

Ipswich, yellow, tumbler, 12-oz, footed $45.00

Lariat, clear, bowl, nappy;, 7" $15.00

Lariat, clear, bowl, salad; 10½" $32.00

Lariat, clear, celery bowl, 13" $22.00

Lariat, clear, coaster, 4" $8.00

Lariat, clear, compote, 10", w/lid $75.00

Lariat, clear, cup $12.00

Lariat, clear, mayonnaise set, 5" bowl, plate & ladle...$55.00

Lariat, clear, plate, salad; 8" $9.00

Lariat, clear, saucer $5.00

Lariat, clear, stem, cocktail; 3½-oz, blown $15.00

Lariat, clear, stem, low sherbet; 6-oz $10.00

Lariat, clear, stem, 10-oz, blown $20.00

Lariat, clear, tumbler, juice; 5-oz, footed, blown $15.00

Lariat, clear, vase, 7", footed fan form $25.00

Lodestar, Dawn, bowl, 8" $45.00

Lodestar, Dawn, celery, 10" $60.00

Lodestar, Dawn, creamer, handled $85.00

Lodestar, Dawn, jar, #1626, 8", w/lid $140.00

Lodestar, Dawn, plate, 14" $85.00

Lodestar, Dawn, relish, 7½", 3-part $55.00

Lodestar, Dawn, sugar bowl, no handles $50.00

Lodestar, Dawn, tumbler, juice; 6-oz $35.00

Lodestar, Dawn (gray), sugar bowl, w/handles....$85.00

Minuet, clear, bowl, #1514, 12", oval $50.00

Minuet, clear, compote, #5010, 5½" $35.00

Minuet, clear, cup $35.00

Minuet, clear, finger bowl, #3309 ....$18.00

Minuet, clear, ice bucket, dolphin-footed $135.00

Minuet, clear, plate, luncheon; 8" $15.00

Minuet, clear, plate, service; 10½" $50.00

Minuet, clear, saucer $10.00

Minuet, clear, stem, claret; #5010, 4-oz $30.00

Minuet, clear, stem, cocktail; #5010, 3½-oz $30.00

Minuet, clear, stem, sherbet; #5010, 6-oz $12.00

Minuet, clear, tray, 15" $60.00

Minuet, clear, tumbler, tea; #5010, 12-oz $40.00

Minuet, clear, vase, #4196, 8" $75.00

New Era, clear, ashtray $30.00

New Era, clear, creamer $35.00

New Era, clear, cup $10.00
New Era, clear, cup, demitasse $50.00
New Era, clear, plate, 9x7", rectangular.......$20.00
New Era, clear, saucer $5.00
New Era, clear, stem, cordial; 1-oz...............$45.00
New Era, clear, stem, goblet; 10-oz...............$15.00
New Era, clear, stem, oyster cocktail; 3½-oz...........$10.00
New Era, clear, sugar bowl $35.00
New Era, clear, tumbler, soda; 12-oz, footed...........$12.50
Octagon, clear, bowl, #500, 6" $14.00
Octagon, clear, bowl, cream soup; handles............$10.00
Octagon, clear, cup.......................................$5.00
Octagon, clear, plate, luncheon; 8".................$6.00
Octagon, clear, platter, 12¾" oval...............$20.00
Octagon, green, bowl, vegetable; 9"..............$30.00
Octagon, green, cup.....................................$20.00
Octagon, green, plate, luncheon; 8" $12.00
Octagon, green, saucer..................................$7.00
Octagon, orchid, bowl, cream soup; 2-handled $40.00
Octagon, orchid, celery tray, 12" $35.00
Octagon, orchid, cup...................................$35.00
Octagon, orchid, plate, 14"...........................$45.00
Octagon, orchid, plate, 6"............................$12.00
Octagon, orchid, saucer..................................$9.00
Octagon, pink, bonbon, #1229, 6", sides up..............$10.00
Octagon, pink, candlestick, 3", 1-light..........$25.00
Octagon, pink, cup.......................................$15.00
Octagon, pink, plate, 10½"............................$25.00
Octagon, pink, saucer.....................................$5.00
Octagon, yellow, bowl, flat soup; 9" $20.00
Octagon, yellow, cup $20.00
Octagon, yellow, plate, sandwich; #1229, 10" $25.00
Octagon, yellow, saucer $6.00
Old Colony, amber, compote, #3368, 7", footed $95.00
Old Colony, amber, finger bowl, #4075 ....$18.00
Old Colony, amber, stem, oyster cocktail; #3380, 4-oz ..$25.00
Old Colony, amber, tumbler, soda; #3380, 8-oz, footed ..$32.50
Old Colony, clear, bowl, 9", 3 handles............$36.00
Old Colony, clear, bowl, cream soup, handles...........$12.00
Old Colony, clear, oil, 4-oz, footed $42.50
Old Colony, clear, stem, claret; #3380, 4-oz.............$20.00
Old Colony, clear, tumbler, soda; #3390, 8-oz, footed ..$10.00
Old Colony, green, bowl, jelly; 6", 2 handles, footed .$32.50
Old Colony, green, cup..................................$38.00
Old Colony, green, plate, 10½".......................$75.00
Old Colony, green, saucer, square $10.00
Old Colony, green, stem, sherbet; #3380, 6-oz............$15.00
Old Colony, green, stem, tall water; #3390, 11-oz........$32.00
Old Colony, pink, bowl, nappy; 8".................$35.00
Old Colony, pink, celery tray, 10" $20.00
Old Colony, pink, creamer, individual $30.00
Old Colony, pink, plate, 10½", square...........$50.00
Old Colony, pink, plate, 8", square $17.00
Old Colony, pink, stem, parfait; #3380, 5-oz $15.00
Old Colony, pink, stem, wine; #3390, 2½-oz.............$20.00
Old Colony, pink, vase, 9", footed..................$130.00
Old Colony, yellow, bowl, mint; 6", dolphin-footed ...$27.50
Old Colony, yellow, cup, demitasse................$35.00

Old Colony, yellow, plate, 12" $70.00
Old Colony, yellow, plate, 8" $22.00
Old Colony, yellow, saucer............................$10.00
Old Colony, yellow, stem, champagne; #3380, 6-oz ...$15.00
Old Colony, yellow, stem, cocktail; #3390, 3-oz.........$20.00
Old Colony, yellow, tray, hors d'oeuvre; 13", handles..$45.00
Old Colony, yellow, tumbler, tea; #3380, 12-oz, footed.$22.00
Old Sandwich, clear, candlestick, 6"..............$35.00

Old Sandwich, clear, creamer & sugar bowl........$60.00
Old Sandwich, clear, plate, 8", square..............$9.00
Old Sandwich, clear, sugar bowl, oval.............$10.00
Old Sandwich, clear, tumbler, iced tea; 12-oz $12.00
Old Sandwich, cobalt, tumbler, bar; 1½-oz.............$95.00
Old Sandwich, green, cigarette holder $65.00
Old Sandwich, green, creamer, oval................$25.00
Old Sandwich, green, plate, 8", square $30.00
Old Sandwich, green, salt & pepper shakers, pr.........$85.00
Old Sandwich, pink, ashtray, individual.........$35.00
Old Sandwich, pink, cup...............................$65.00
Old Sandwich, pink, saucer $15.00
Old Sandwich, pink, tumbler, juice; 5-oz $13.00
Old Sandwich, yellow, compote, 6" $90.00
Old Sandwich, yellow, finger bowl $60.00
Old Sandwich, yellow, plate, 7", square..........$20.00
Old Sandwich, yellow, stem, oyster cocktail; 4-oz $25.00
Orchid, clear, bowl, jelly; 7", footed...............$40.00
Orchid, clear, bowl, relish; 9", 4-part, round $65.00
Orchid, clear, bowl, 11", flared $55.00
Orchid, clear, candy dish, 6", lid w/bow knot
    finial $160.00
Orchid, clear, creamer, footed $25.00
Orchid, clear, plate, dinner; 10½".................$130.00
Orchid, clear, plate, sandwich; 12", handled, round ...$50.00
Orchid, clear, plate, 6"................................$12.50
Orchid, clear, stem, oyster cocktail; #5022, 4-oz $55.00
Orchid, clear, stem, sherbet; #5022 or #5025, 6-oz......$25.00
Orchid, clear, vase, fan; 7", footed $85.00
Plantation, clear, bowl, dressing; 8½", 2-part..........$45.00
Plantation, clear candle holder, 1-light...........$75.00
Plantation, clear candle holder, 2-light..........$50.00
Plantation, clear, celery bowl, 13"................$35.00
Plantation, clear, coaster, 4" $45.00
Plantation, clear, compote, 5" $30.00
Plantation, clear, cup.................................$15.00
Plantation, clear, plate, salad; 8" $20.00
Plantation, clear, plate, sandwich; 14"...........$45.00
Plantation, clear, saucer..............................$5.00
Plantation, clear, stem, claret; 4½-oz, pressed $30.00

Plantation, clear, stem, wine; 3-oz, blown **$50.00**

Plantation, clear, stem, 10-oz, pressed or blown **$25.00**

Plantation, clear, sugar bowl, footed **$25.00**

Plantation, clear, tumbler, juice; 5-oz, footed, pressed or blown **$35.00**

Plantation, clear, vase, 5", footed, flared **$40.00**

Pleat & Panel, clear, bowl, bouillon; 5", handles **$7.00**

Pleat & Panel, clear, cup **$7.00**

Pleat & Panel, clear, plate, sandwich; 14" **$15.00**

Pleat & Panel, green, bowl, jelly; 5", handles **$15.00**

Pleat & Panel, green, cup **$17.50**

Pleat & Panel, green, plate, luncheon; 8" **$15.00**

Pleat & Panel, green, tumbler, tea; 12-oz **$20.00**

Pleat & Panel, pink, bowl, lemon; 5", w/lid **$25.00**

Pleat & Panel, pink, cup **$15.00**

Pleat & Panel, pink, pitcher, 3-pt $130.00

Pleat & Panel, pink, plate, dinner; 10¾" **$40.00**

Pleat & Panel, pink, saucer **$5.00**

Pleat & Panel, pink, stem, 7½-oz, low foot **$15.00**

Provincial, clear, bowl, relish; 10", 4-part **$40.00**

Provincial, clear, cigarette box, w/lid **$45.00**

Provincial, clear, plate, luncheon; 8" **$15.00**

Provincial, clear, stem, wine; 3½-oz **$20.00**

Provincial, clear, tumbler, juice; 5-oz, footed **$12.00**

Provincial, limelight green, bowl, nappy; 4½" **$60.00**

Provincial, limelight green, tumbler, iced tea; footed ..**$75.00**

Provincial, limelight green, tumbler, juice; 5-oz, footed **$50.00**

Provincial, limelight green, vase, violet; 3½" **$85.00**

Queen Ann, clear, ashtray **$30.00**

Queen Ann, clear, bowl, salad; 10", square, handles ..**$30.00**

Queen Ann, clear, candlestick, 6", dolphin-footed **$50.00**

Queen Ann, clear, compote, 6", footed **$25.00**

Queen Ann, clear, cup, bouillon; 2 handles **$16.00**

Queen Ann, clear, plate, 8", square **$10.00**

Queen Ann, clear, stem, oyster cocktail; 2½-oz **$15.00**

Queen Ann, clear, sugar bowl, 3-handle, dolphin foot .**$10.00**

Queen Ann, clear, tray, sandwich; 12", square, w/center handle **$32.50**

Queen Ann, clear, tumbler, iced tea; 12-oz **$18.00**

Ridgeleigh, clear, ashtray, 4" dia **$12.00**

Ridgeleigh, clear, bowl, nappy; 5", square **$6.50**

Ridgeleigh, clear, bowl, punch; 11" **$90.00**

Ridgeleigh, clear, bowl, salad; 9" **$30.00**

Ridgeleigh, clear, candlestick, 2", 1-light **$20.00**

Ridgeleigh, clear, cup **$8.00**

Ridgeleigh, clear, ice tub, handles **$60.00**

Ridgeleigh, clear, oil cruet, 3-oz, w/#103 stopper **$50.00**

Ridgeleigh, clear, plate, sandwich; 13½" **$40.00**

Ridgeleigh, clear, plate, 6", scalloped **$5.00**

Ridgeleigh, clear, salt & pepper shakers, pr **$30.00**

Ridgeleigh, clear, stem, cocktail; 3½-oz, blown **$30.00**

Ridgeleigh, clear, stem, sherbet; pressed **$12.00**

Ridgeleigh, clear, sugar bowl **$20.00**

Ridgeleigh, clear, tumbler, iced tea; 13-oz, blown **$22.00**

Ridgeleigh, clear, tumbler, old-fashioned; pressed **$20.00**

Rose, clear, ashtray, 3" **$37.50**

Rose, clear, bowl, jelly; 6", handles, footed, Queen Anne blank **$42.50**

Rose, clear, bowl, salad; 7", Waverly blank **$55.00**

Rose, clear, butter dish, 6", Waverly blank **$175.00**

Rose, clear, candlestick, 3-light, Waverly blank **$90.00**

Rose, clear, candy dish, 6", low, bow knot finial **$165.00**

Rose, clear, compote, 6½", low foot, Waverly blank ...**$60.00**

Rose, clear, cup, Waverly blank **$65.00**

Rose, clear, ice bucket, dolphin-footed **$275.00**

Rose, clear, plate, dinner; 10½" **$155.00**

Rose, clear, plate, service; 10½", Waverly blank **$75.00**

Rose, clear, stem, sherbet; #5072, 6-oz **$27.50**

Rose, clear, sugar bowl, individual; Waverly blank **$25.00**

Rose, clear, tray, for individual creamer & sugar, Queen Ann blank **$55.00**

Rose, clear, tumbler, juice; #5072, 5-oz, footed **$45.00**

Rose, clear, vase, fan; 7", footed, Waverly blank **$100.00**

Saturn, clear, bowl, fruit; 12", flared rim **$35.00**

Saturn, clear, bowl, pickle; 7" **$15.00**

Saturn, clear, compote, 7" **$30.00**

Saturn, clear, cup **$9.00**

Saturn, clear, pitcher, juice **$40.00**

Saturn, clear, sugar bowl **$12.50**

Saturn, clear, tumbler, luncheon; 9-oz **$12.00**

Saturn, limelight green, cup **$150.00**

Saturn, limelight green, plate, luncheon; 8" **$55.00**

Saturn, limelight green, saucer **$30.00**

Saturn, limelight green, stem, sherbet; 4½-oz **$70.00**

Saturn, limelight green, sugar bowl **$90.00**

Saturn, limelight green, vase, violet **$85.00**

Stanhope, clear, bowl, mint; 6", handles **$15.00**

Stanhope, clear, cup **$15.00**

Stanhope, clear, ice tub, handles **$45.00**

Stanhope, clear, plate, torte; 12", handles **$30.00**

Stanhope, clear, plate, 7" **$7.50**

Stanhope, clear, salt & pepper shakers, #60 top, pr **$45.00**

Stanhope, clear, stem, wine; #4083, 2½-oz **$25.00**

Stanhope, clear, tumbler, soda; #4083, 5-oz **$20.00**

Twist, amber or yellow, bowl, cream soup..................$50.00
Twist, amber or yellow, plate, muffin; 12", handles....$65.00
Twist, amber or yellow, saucer champagne, 5-oz.......$25.00
Twist, clear, bowl, nasturtium; 8", oval......................$25.00
Twist, clear, platter, 12"...$15.00
Twist, clear, tumbler, fruit; 5-oz................................$4.00
Twist, green, candlestick, 2", 1-light.........................$25.00
Twist, green, sugar bowl, zigzag handles, w/lid..........$40.00
Twist, green, tumbler, iced tea; 12-oz.......................$35.00
Twist, pink, bonbon, 6", handles...............................$12.00
Twist, pink, cup, zigzag handle.................................$25.00
Twist, pink, saucer..$5.00
Victorian, clear, butter dish, ¼-lb............................$65.00
Victorian, clear, plate, 8"...$30.00
Victorian, clear, salt & pepper shakers, pr................$40.00
Victorian, clear, stem, wine; 2½-oz..........................$20.00
Victorian, clear, sugar bowl......................................$25.00
Victorian, clear, tumbler, old-fashioned; 8-oz............$30.00
Waverly, clear, bowl, fruit; 9"...................................$20.00
Waverly, clear, candy box, 6", lid w/bow tie finial.....$45.00
Waverly, clear, compote, 6", low foot........................$12.00
Waverly, clear, cup..$12.00
Waverly, clear, plate, dinner; 10½"...........................$45.00
Waverly, clear, plate, sandwich; 14", center handle....$65.00
Waverly, clear, tumbler, juice; 5-oz, footed, blown.....$20.00
Yeoman, amber, bowl, berry; 8½", handles................$50.00
Yeoman, amber, creamer..$28.00
Yeoman, amber, oil cruet, 2-oz.................................$65.00
Yeoman, amber, sugar bowl, w/lid.............................$40.00
Yeoman, clear, bowl, bouillon; handles, footed..........$10.00
Yeoman, clear, compote, 6", low footed, deep...........$20.00
Yeoman, clear, pitcher, 1-qt.....................................$35.00
Yeoman, clear, tumbler, 10-oz, cupped rim................$4.00
Yeoman, green, bowl, cream soup; handles...............$24.00
Yeoman, green, egg cup...$39.00
Yeoman, green, platter, 12", oval..............................$26.00
Yeoman, green, tray, 7x10", rectangular....................$35.00
Yeoman, orchid, bowl, jelly; 5", low, footed..............$30.00
Yeoman, orchid, cup..$30.00
Yeoman, orchid, plate, 10½".....................................$60.00
Yeoman, orchid, stem, oyster cocktail; 2¾-oz, footed...$14.00
Yeoman, pink, bowl, vegetable; 6"............................$10.00
Yeoman, pink, cup...$15.00
Yeoman, pink, plate, 10½".......................................$50.00
Yeoman, yellow, bowl, baker; 9"...............................$35.00
Yeoman, yellow, gravy boat, w/underliner..................$30.00
Yeoman, yellow, plate, 7"...$10.00
Yeoman, yellow, sugar bowl, w/lid............................$30.00

Holly Hobbie and Friends

Back in the late 1960s, Holly Hobbie was a housewife and mother who also happened to be an artist who used her children as models for her drawings. A friend who had long admired her work suggested that she send some of her drawings to the American Greetings Company. What came of that contact is very obvious! Since then, more than 400 items have been licensed. Today there's a Holly Hobbie newsletter and club, whose members are devoted to collecting anything related to or decorated by Holly Hobbie.

Knickerbocker produced dolls in cloth, vinyl, and bisque until they went out of business in 1982. There were four different sizes for Hollie, Heather, Carrie, Amy, and Robby: 9", 16", 27", and 33". You'll often find these at garage sales, but not always in good condition. Should you find one still new in the box, expect to pay $10.00 for the 9" doll and up to $30.00 for the 33" cloth dolls. Played-with, soiled dolls are worth much less, only about one-tenth as much.

Perhaps 95% of all items are signed either HH, H Hobbie, or Holly Hobbie. This trademark will help you identify the genuine Holly Hobbie merchandise. Other companies have put out look-alike items, so beware!

See the Directory for information concerning the Holly Hobbie club and newsletter.

Cake pan, 15x7x2", half figure of Holly Hobbie, Wilton, 1975...$9.00
Candle holder, 3½x3¾" dia, Happiness Is Found in Little Things, Holly w/cat..$8.00
Cup, When Friends Get Together It's Always Fair Weather, 2 girls on beach, footed, 1974.............................$7.00

Doll, 33", Knickerbocker, MIB $30.00
Doll, 9", Knickerbocker, MIB (illustrated) $10.00
Drinking glass, Christmas Is Fun for Everyone, Coke logo, marked 1 of 4, 1977......................................$2.00
Figurine, American Greetings, 1971 & 1974, musical, from $10.00 up to...$20.00
Figurine, American Greetings, 1971 & 1974, non-musical.$6.00
Figurine, girl in blue dress w/nosegay, marked Deluxe HHF 2, 1973..$95.00
Figurine, It's Nice To Hear From Someone Dear, girl on phone, marked 600-HHF-20, 1974.....................$15.00
Figurine, The Perfect Tree, Holly & Robby w/Christmas tree, 1985...$50.00

Figurine, 5½", Holly holds basket in front w/both hands, Summit, 1990, 5½"....................**$18.00**

Lap tray, 8x12", Happiness Is Sharing w/Someone You Love, 1974....................**$6.00**

Plate, 10", A Little Patience..., girl at sewing machine, light green border, 10"....................**$10.00**

Plate, 10", Happy Memories Warm the Heart, Christmas 1972, M....................**$10.00**

Plate, 6", The Time To Be Happy Is Now....................**$6.00**

Plate, 8", Merry Christmas 1979, Holly & Robby string popcorn....................**$10.00**

Plate, 8", Mother's Day 1982, Mother Love Will Stay w/You No Matter Where You Go....................**$10.00**

Purse, 7", Knickerbocker, M (illustrated on page 213)....................**$12.00**

Tile, 5x6", Happy Is the Home That Welcomes a Friend, oval....................**$8.00**

Tile, 6x6", The Time To Be Happy Is Now, 1973, w/wood frame....................**$5.00**

Trinket box, Gather a Bouquet of Nice Things Today, heart form, Made in Brazil, 1975....................**$6.50**

Trinket dish, Put on a Happy Face, egg form, 1973......**$6.50**

Vase, 8½", Happiness Is Having Someone To Care For, girl in big bonnet w/cat, 1973....................**$7.00**

Homer Laughlin China Co.

Since well before the turn of the century, the Homer Laughlin China Company of Newell, West Virginia, has been turning out dinnerware and kitchenware lines in hundreds of styles and patterns. Most of their pieces are marked either 'HLC' or 'Homer Laughlin.' As styles changed over the years, they designed several basic dinnerware shapes that they used as a basis for literally hundreds of different patterns simply by applying various decals and glaze treatments. If you find pieces stamped with names like Virginia Rose, Rhythm, or Nautilus, don't assume it to be the pattern name; it's the shape name. Virginia Rose, for instance, was decorated with many different decals. If you have some you're trying to sell through a mail or a phone contact, it would be a good idea to send the prospective buyer a zerox copy of the pattern.

For more information, we recommend *Homer Laughlin China, An Identification Guide,* by Darlene Nossman and *The Collector's Encyclopedia of Homer Laughlin Pottery* by Joanne Jasper.

See also Fiesta; Harlequin.

Brittany, bowl, 15"....................**$15.00**
Brittany, bowl, 6", deep....................**$10.00**
Brittany, chop plate, 13"....................**$18.00**
Brittany, creamer....................**$8.00**
Brittany, plate, 7"....................**$5.00**
Brittany, sauce boat....................**$12.00**
Cavalier, bowl, vegetable; 9"....................**$10.00**
Cavalier, plate, 7"....................**$4.00**
Cavalier, platter, 11"....................**$10.00**
Cavalier, sauce boat....................**$14.00**
Cavalier, teacup & saucer....................**$5.00**
Century, bowl, oatmeal; 6"....................**$10.00**
Century, bowl, 1-pt, deep....................**$15.00**
Century, bowl, 13", oval well....................**$16.00**
Century, casserole, w/lid....................**$50.00**
Century, coffee cup & saucer....................**$18.00**
Century, cream soup cup & saucer, 11-oz....................**$25.00**
Century, creamer....................**$10.00**
Century, jug, ⅝-pt....................**$25.00**
Century, muffin cover....................**$45.00**
Century, plate, 9"....................**$9.00**
Century, platter, 10"....................**$10.00**
Century, sauce boat underplate....................**$16.00**
Coronet, bowl, 13"....................**$16.00**
Coronet, bowl, 5"....................**$6.00**
Coronet, creamer....................**$9.00**
Coronet, plate, 10"....................**$11.00**
Coronet, plate, 6"....................**$4.00**
Coronet, sauce boat & underplate....................**$26.00**
Craftsman, baker, 9"....................**$14.00**
Craftsman, bowl, vegetable; 10"....................**$16.00**
Craftsman, pickle dish....................**$7.25**
Craftsman, plate, 10"....................**$9.50**
Craftsman, platter, 11"....................**$14.00**
Craftsman, salt & pepper shakers, pr....................**$20.00**
Debutante, bowl, vegetable; 9", Skytone....................**$11.50**
Debutante, casserole, w/lid, colors other than Suntone or Skytone....................**$25.00**
Debutante, casserole, w/lid, Suntone....................**$30.00**
Debutante, chop plate, 15", colors other than Suntone or Skytone....................**$16.00**
Debutante, cup & saucer, after dinner; Suntone....................**$20.00**
Debutante, onion soup, colors other than Suntone or Skytone....................**$6.00**
Debutante, pie server, Skytone....................**$23.00**
Debutante, plate, 10", Suntone....................**$9.50**
Debutante, plate salad; 7", colors other than Suntone or Skytone....................**$5.00**
Debutante, salt & pepper shakers, colors other than Suntone or Skytone, pr....................**$10.00**
Debutante, teacup & saucer, colors other than Suntone or Skytone....................**$5.00**
Duraprint, ashtray....................**$15.00**
Duraprint, bowl, cereal/soup; 5½"....................**$4.00**
Duraprint, creamer, Charm House....................**$7.00**
Duraprint, plate, 7"....................**$4.00**
Duraprint, plate, 9"....................**$6.00**
Duraprint, salt & pepper shakers, Charm House, pr...**$10.00**
Duraprint, sauce boat....................**$8.00**
Duraprint, teacup & saucer, Charm House....................**$5.00**
Eggshell Georgian, baker, 10"....................**$14.00**
Eggshell Georgian, bowl, fruit....................**$3.00**
Eggshell Georgian, cream soup....................**$8.00**
Eggshell Georgian, egg cup, double....................**$12.00**
Eggshell Georgian, plate, 10"....................**$8.00**
Eggshell Georgian, plate, 6"....................**$3.00**
Eggshell Georgian, plate, 8" square....................**$8.00**

Eggshell Georgian, sauce boat **$14.00**
Eggshell Georgian, teacup & saucer **$3.50**
Eggshell Georgian, teapot **$40.00**
Eggshell Nautilus, bowl, vegetable; 9" **$12.00**
Eggshell Nautilus, bowl, 13" **$12.00**
Eggshell Nautilus, bowl, 5" **$6.00**
Eggshell Nautilus, cream soup **$8.00**
Eggshell Nautilus, egg cup, Swing, double **$12.00**
Eggshell Nautilus, pickle dish **$6.00**
Eggshell Nautilus, plate, 6" **$3.00**
Eggshell Nautilus, plate, 8" round or square **$6.00**

Eggshell Nautilus, platter, 13", w/pattern #N-1402 . $18.00
Eggshell Nautilus, rim soup **$6.00**
Eggshell Nautilus, salt & pepper shakers, Swing, pr ... **$12.00**
Eggshell Nautilus, sugar bowl, w/lid **$12.00**
Empress, baker, 10" **$14.00**
Empress, bouillon cup, 6-oz **$15.00**
Empress, bowl, vegetable; 9" **$12.00**
Empress, bowl, 10" **$10.00**
Empress, bowl, 15" **$15.00**
Empress, cream soup **$12.00**
Empress, creamer, 5-oz **$8.00**
Empress, jug, 30s, 18-oz **$22.00**
Empress, ladle **$15.00**
Empress, plate, 10" **$8.00**
Empress, plate, 7" **$5.00**
Empress, sauce boat **$14.00**
Empress, sugar bowl, 4", w/lid **$12.00**
Georgian, baker, 10" **$16.00**
Georgian, bowl, 15" **$18.00**
Georgian, cream soup **$9.00**
Georgian, cup & saucer, after dinner **$16.00**
Georgian, plate, deep (rim soup) **$8.00**
Georgian, plate, 7" **$5.00**
Jade, bowl, fruit **$6.00**
Jade, butter dish, w/lid **$40.00**
Jade, cake plate **$30.00**
Jade, coffee cup & saucer **$25.00**
Jade, cream soup **$12.00**

Jade, creamer **$12.00**
Jade, plate, 6" **$5.00**
Jade, plate, 8" **$7.00**
Kwaker, baker, 9" **$14.00**
Kwaker, bowl, fruit; 6" **$6.00**
Kwaker, bowl, oatmeal; 6" **$6.00**
Kwaker, bowl, 14" **$14.00**
Kwaker, bowl, 9" **$9.00**
Kwaker, butter dish, w/lid **$45.00**
Kwaker, casserole, w/lid **$20.00**
Kwaker, creamer **$10.00**
Kwaker, plate, coupe; 8" **$8.00**
Kwaker, plate, 8" **$6.00**
Kwaker, teacup & saucer **$8.00**
Liberty, bowl, 15" **$14.00**
Liberty, bowl, 5" **$5.00**
Liberty, plate, 10" **$8.00**
Liberty, plate, 6" **$3.00**
Liberty, plate, 8" **$6.00**
Liberty, sauce boat, w/underplate **$22.00**
Liberty, teacup & saucer **$5.00**
Marigold, bowl, fruit **$3.00**
Marigold, bowl, 6" **$8.00**
Marigold, milk pitcher **$25.00**
Marigold, plate, deep (rim soup) **$6.00**
Marigold, plate, 7" **$5.00**
Marigold, plate, 8" square **$8.00**
Marigold, platter, 11" **$12.00**
Marigold, sugar bowl, w/lid **$14.00**
Nautilus, bowl, vegetable; 10" **$14.00**
Nautilus, bowl, 12" **$12.00**
Nautilus, bowl, 5" **$6.00**
Nautilus, coupe soup **$6.00**
Nautilus, cup & saucer, after dinner **$15.00**
Nautilus, plate, 7" **$5.00**
Nautilus, sauce boat, w/underplate **$22.00**
Nautilus, teacup & saucer **$5.50**
Newell, baker, 7" **$8.00**
Newell, bowl, oyster; ¾-pt **$10.00**
Newell, bowl, 15" **$18.00**
Newell, casserole, w/lid **$30.00**
Newell, coffee cup **$10.00**
Newell, pitcher, 4-pt **$30.00**
Newell, plate, coupe; 8" **$6.00**
Newell, plate, 7" **$6.00**
Newell, teapot **$40.00**
Orleans, bowl, 13" **$18.00**
Orleans, bowl, 5" **$6.00**
Orleans, bowl, 9" **$16.00**
Orleans, plate, 10" **$13.00**
Orleans, plate, 7" **$6.00**
Orleans, sauce boat **$18.00**
Orleans, teacup & saucer **$8.00**
Piccadilly, bowl, fruit **$2.00**
Piccadilly, cream soup & saucer **$14.00**
Piccadilly, creamer **$8.00**
Piccadilly, plate, 10" **$8.00**
Piccadilly, platter, 11" **$10.00**

Piccadilly, sugar bowl, w/lid $10.00
Ravenna, bowl, fruit $5.00
Ravenna, casserole, w/lid $30.00
Ravenna, creamer $12.00
Ravenna, plate, 6" $5.00
Ravenna, plate, 9" $10.00
Ravenna, sauce boat, w/underplate $28.00
Red Apple, nappy $15.00

Red Apple, platter, 18" $18.00
Republic, baker, 7" $8.00
Republic, bowl, fruit; 5" $2.00
Republic, bowl, vegetable; 8" $8.00
Republic, bowl, 1⅜-pt, deep $15.00
Republic, bowl, 11" $12.00
Republic, bowl, 13" $14.00
Republic, cake plate, 10½" $16.00
Republic, coffee cup & saucer; after dinner $16.00
Republic, ladle $15.00
Republic, pitcher, 2½-pt $26.00
Republic, plate, 7" $3.00
Republic, plate, 9", deep $8.00
Republic, sauce boat $10.00
Republic, teacup & saucer $3.00
Rhythm, coupe soup $6.00
Rhythm, plate, 10" $8.00
Rhythm, plate, 7" $5.00
Rhythm, platter, 11½" $12.00
Rhythm, sauce boat, w/attached underplate $12.00
Rhythm, sugar bowl, w/lid $10.00
Rhythm, teacup & saucer $5.00
Rhythm, teapot $35.00
Swing, bowl, fruit $2.00
Swing, coffeepot $16.00
Swing, creamer $12.00
Swing, creamer, after dinner $4.00
Swing, plate, 10" $10.00
Swing, plate, 7" $6.00
Swing, platter, 11" $12.00
Swing, salt & pepper shakers, pr $10.00
Swing, soup saucer $5.00
Theme, baker, 9" $15.00

Theme, bowl, fruit $3.00
Theme, cream soup $10.00
Theme, cup & saucer, after dinner $16.00
Theme, pickle dish $6.00
Theme, plate, 7" $5.00
Theme, plate, 9" $7.00
Theme, sauce boat w/attached underplate $14.00
Trellis, baker, 10" $21.00
Trellis, bouillon cup & saucer $24.00
Trellis, bowl, vegetable; 9" $18.00
Trellis, bowl, 10½" $18.00
Trellis, jug, 1-pt $30.00
Trellis, plate, 10" $15.00
Trellis, sugar bowl, w/lid $20.00
Trellis, teacup & saucer $7.50
Virginia Rose, baker, 9" $10.00
Virginia Rose, bowl, fruit $3.50
Virginia Rose, bowl, vegetable; 10" $15.00
Virginia Rose, bowl, 11½" $12.00
Virginia Rose, casserole, w/lid $45.00
Virginia Rose, coffee mug $16.00
Virginia Rose, coupe soup $8.00
Virginia Rose, cream soup & saucer $18.00
Virginia Rose, pickle dish $8.00
Virginia Rose, pitcher, 5" $20.00
Virginia Rose, pitcher, 7½", w/lid $95.00
Virginia Rose, plate, 10" $8.00
Virginia Rose, plate, 7" $4.00
Virginia Rose, salt & pepper shakers, Swing, pr $40.00
Virginia Rose, teacup & saucer $6.00
Wells, bowl, 13" $18.00
Wells, bowl, 6", deep $14.00
Wells, chop plate $18.00
Wells, cream soup $12.00
Wells, cup & saucer, after dinner $16.00
Wells, egg cup, double $12.00
Wells, plate, 10" $12.00
Wells, plate, 6" $4.00
Wells, plate, 8" square $12.50
Wells, sugar bowl, w/lid $14.00
Wells, teapot $40.00
Yellowstone, baker, 10" $12.00
Yellowstone, bowl, fruit $3.00
Yellowstone, bowl, oyster; 5" $12.00
Yellowstone, bowl, vegetable; 10" $16.00
Yellowstone, bowl, 13" $16.00
Yellowstone, butter dish, individual $6.00
Yellowstone, cream soup $8.00
Yellowstone, plate, coupe; 8" $6.00
Yellowstone, plate, 9" $8.00
Yellowstone, platter, 8" $10.00
Yellowstone, sauce boat stand $15.00
Yellowstone, sugar bowl, individual $8.00

Hull

This company operated in Crooksville (near Zanesville), Ohio, from just after the turn of the century until they closed in 1985. From the thirties until the plant was destroyed by fire in 1950, they preferred the soft matt glazes so popular with today's collectors, though a few high gloss lines were made as well. When the plant was rebuilt, modern equipment was installed which they soon found did not lend itself to the duplication of the matt glazes, so they began to concentrate on the production of glossy wares, novelties, and figurines.

During the forties and fifties, they produced a line of kitchenware items modeled after Little Red Riding Hood. Some of this line was sent to Regal China, who decorated Hull's whiteware. (See also Little Red Riding Hood.) All of these pieces are very expensive today.

Hull's Mirror Brown dinnerware line made from about 1960 until they closed in 1985 was very successful for them and was made in large quantities. Its glossy brown glaze was enhanced with a band of ivory foam, and today's collectors are finding its rich colors and basic, strong shapes just as attractive now as it was then. In addition to table service, there are novelty trays shaped like gingerbread men and fish, canisters and cookie jars, covered casseroles with ducks and hens as lids, vases, ashtrays, and mixing bowls. It's easy to find, and though you may have to pay 'near book' prices at co-ops and antique malls, because it's just now 'catching on,' the bargains are out there. It may be marked Hull, Crooksville, O; HPCo; or Crestone.

If you'd like to learn more about this subject, we recommend *The Collector's Encyclopedia of Hull Pottery* by Brenda Roberts and *Collector's Guide to Hull Pottery, The Dinnerware Lines,* by Barbara Loveless Gick-Burke.

Ashtray, Butterfly, 7", raised pastel butterfly & flower motif on ivory, combined matt & gloss, heart shape, 1956, #B3...$35.00
Ashtray, Novelty, 7", brown veiled design on pink, heart shape, glossy, 1955-59, #18...................................$20.00

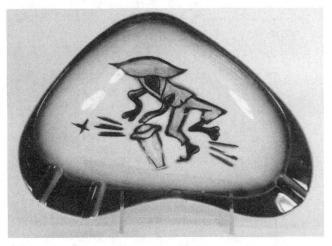

Ashtray, 10", Tropicana, colorful Caribbean figures on white, rare...$300.00
Basket, Bow Knot, 6½", embossed flowers on shaded pastels, matt, bow on handle, 1949-50, #B-25..........$175.00
Basket, Iris, 7", embossed flowers on cream shading to pink, matt, scalloped top, handled, 1940-42, #408.......$200.00

Basket, Mardi Gras/Granada, 8", embossed flowers on white, matt, handled, 1938-46, #32.....................$130.00
Basket, Orchid, 7", embossed flowers on yellow shading to pink, scalloped edge, handled, 1939-41, #305....$340.00
Basket, Parchment & Pine, 16½", embossed pine spray on shaded pastels, glossy, 1951-54, #S-8.................$150.00
Basket, Rosella, 7", embossed flowers on coral, glossy, scalloped edge & handle, 1946, #R-12......................$200.00
Basket, Serenade, 12", embossed bough & chickadee on pink, matt w/glossy interior, 1957, #S14.............$375.00
Basket, Woodland, 8¾", embossed flowers on shaded pastels, matt, handled, 1949-50, #W9.....................$175.00

Basket, 8¼", Tuscany, embossed leaf & grape design on white...$80.00
Bell, Sun-Glow, 6¼", embossed yellow floral decoration on pink, rope handle, unmarked $90.00
Bowl, console; Calla Lily, 10" dia, dusky green & cream, matt, 1938-40, #500/32...$145.00
Bowl, console; Magnolia, 12", embossed flowers on shaded pastels, matt, boat shape, ring handles, #26.......$125.00
Bowl, console; Royal Woodland, 14", white spatter on pink, ribbed, glossy, 1955-57, #W30...............................$70.00
Candle holder, Butterfly, 2½", pastel butterfly & flower motif on ivory, matt & gloss, 3-footed, 1956, #B22, pr ..$75.00
Candle holder, Camellia, 6½", embossed flowers on figural bird, shaded pastels, matt, 1943-44, #117, pr......$200.00
Candle holder, Dogwood, 3¾", embossed flowers on cream, matt, cornucopia form, 1942-43, #512, pr...........$150.00
Candle holder, Woodland, 3½", embossed flower on yellow shading to green, matt, 1950-51, #W30, pr............$80.00
Candle holder/planter, Continental, 4", mountain blue w/contrasting stripes, glossy, 1959-60, #67, ea $28.00
Cornucopia, double; Magnolia, 12", embossed flowers on shaded pastels, matt, 1946-47, #6 ....$130.00
Cornucopia, Novelty, 9", white, matt, 1938, #200........$40.00
Cornucopia, Tokay, 11", embossed leaf & grape decor on white, glossy, 1958, #10.......................................$55.00

Cornucopia, Water Lily, 6½", embossed flowers on pastels, matt w/gold highlights & handle, 1948-49, #L-7 ...**$85.00**

Cornucopia, Wild Flower, 6¼", embossed flowers on pink shading to cream, matt, 1942-43, #58 ....**$95.00**

Ewer, Dogwood, 4¾", embossed flowers on pink shading to blue, matt, 1942-43, #520...**$80.00**

Ewer, Morning Glory, 11", embossed flowers on white, matt, 1938-46, #63 ....**$550.00**

Ewer, Tuscany, 14", embossed leaf & grape design on white, gold trim, glossy, 1958, #21 ....**$165.00**

Figurine, elephant, 5¼", turquoise, glossy, unmarked.**$30.00**

Figurine, monkey, 5½", yellow, glossy, unmarked......**$40.00**

Figurine, rabbit, 6", coral & black, glossy, #968...........**$28.00**

Flower bowl, Tropicana, 15½", colorful Caribbean figure on white, glossy, 1959, #T51 ....**$250.00**

Flowerpot, Bow Knot, 6½", embossed flowers on pastels, matt, attached underplate, 1949-50, #B-6............**$150.00**

Flowerpot, Water Lily, 5¼", embossed flowers on shaded pastels, matt, attached saucer, 1948-49, #L-25.....**$125.00**

Jardiniere, Butterfly, 6", raised pastel butterfly & flower on ivory, combined gloss & matt, 1956, #B5.............**$55.00**

Jardiniere, Camellia, 8¼", embossed flowers on shaded pastels, 1943-44, #114...**$225.00**

Jardiniere, Iris, 5½", embossed flowers on yellow, matt, 1940-42, #413 ....**$140.00**

Jardiniere, Orchid, 6", embossed flowers on cream center shading to blue, matt, sm ear-type handles, 1939-41, #310 ....**$190.00**

Jardiniere, Royal Imperial, 7", white spatter on pink, ribbed, glossy, 1955-57, #75 ....**$45.00**

Jardiniere, Woodland, 5½", embossed flower on ivory, glossy, gold highlights & handles, 1949-50, #W7..**$70.00**

Jardiniere, Woodland, 9½", embossed flowers on cream shading to pink, matt, scalloped edge, ring handles, 1949-50, #W21 ....**$450.00**

Planter, Novelty, 14", figural dachshund, glossy, 1952 ....**$130.00**

Planter, Novelty, 5½", pup w/ball of yarn, yellow & brown w/black facial features, glossy, 1951, #88 ....**$30.00**

Planter, Novelty, 7¾", figural wishing well, brown & cream, glossy, 1951, #101 ....**$35.00**

Planter, Novelty, 8", figural French poodle, wine & dark green, glossy, 1951-54, #114...................................**$40.00**

Planter, Novelty, 8", knight on horseback, shaded pastels w/black highlights, glossy, 1953, #55 ....**$55.00**

Planter, 7½", figural lamb, white w/blue bow, #965 ...**$40.00**

Teapot, Ebb Tide, 6½", chartreuse shading to wine, glossy, shell form w/sea horse finial, 1955, #E-14 ....**$175.00**

Teapot, Parchment & Pine, 6", embossed pine spray on shaded pastels, glossy, 1951-54, #S-11...................**$90.00**

Teapot, Wild Flower, 8", embossed flowers on pink to cream, matt, butterfly motif on lid, 1942-43, #72..............**$385.00**

Urn, Tokay, #5, embossed leaf & grape design on white, glossy, 1958, #5..**$50.00**

Vase, Bow Knot, 5", embossed flowers on shaded pastels, matt, bow at foot, 1949-50, #B-2............................**$90.00**

Vase, Bow Knot, 6½", embossed flowers on cream center shading to blue, matt, fish form, 1949-50, #B-3 ....**$85.00**

Vase, bud; Continental, 9½", persimmon w/contrasting vertical stripes, glossy, 1959-60, #66 ....**$35.00**

Vase, bud; Tulip, 5", embossed flowers on cream shading to blue, matt, ring handles, 1938-41, #117-30............**$80.00**

Vase, Calla Lily, 13", embossed flowers on yellow, matt, angle handles, 1938-40, #560/33........................**$225.00**

Vase, Ebb Tide, 9¼", shrimp & turquoise, glossy, fish form, 1955, #E-6...**$100.00**

Vase, Iris, 10½", embossed flowers on pink shading to blue, matt, scalloped edge, lg handles, 1940-42, #404.**$200.00**

Vase, Medley, 9", persimmon shading to charcoal, glossy, leaf shape, 1952, #100 ....**$35.00**

Vase, Novelty, 11½", figural twin deer at base, shaded pastels w/black highlights, glossy, 1953, #62 ....**$65.00**

Vase, Novelty, 9", figural telephone, pink & charcoal, glossy, 1955-59, #50 ....**$40.00**

Vase, Orchid, 4¾", embossed flowers on pink shading to turquoise, matt, ear-type handles, 1939-41, #303..**$70.00**

Vase, Orchid, 6½", embossed flowers on yellow shading to pink, matt, ruffled top, handles, 1939-41, #307 ..**$120.00**

Vase, Poppy, 8½", embossed flowers on cream shading to pink, matt, sm angle handles, 1943-44, #607 ......**$165.00**

Vase, Rosella, 5", embossed flowers on coral, heart shape, glossy, 1946, #R-1..**$90.00**

Vase, Royal Ebb Tide, 7", white spatter on pink, glossy, brushed charcoal gray on base, shell form, #E1 ...**$35.00**

Vase, Sueno, 5", dusky green to yellow to pink, matt, angle handles, #920-33-1 ....**$35.00**

Vase, Sueno, 9½", yellow, glossy, scalloped edge, sm ring handles, #750-33 ....**$90.00**

Vase, Sun-Glow, 8", embossed flowers on pink, glossy, sm ring handles, 1948-49, #94......................................**$55.00**

Vase, Thistle, 6½", embossed flowers on turquoise shading to pink, matt, angle handles, 1938-41, #52...........**$55.00**

Vase, Tropicana, 8½", colorful Caribbean figure on white, glossy, flat-sided, 1959, #T53 ....**$235.00**

Vase, Tulip, 4", embossed flowers on yellow shading to blue, matt, ear-type handles, 1938-41, #100-33.....**$60.00**

Vase, Water Lily, embossed flower on ivory, glossy, gold highlights & handles, 1949-50, #L-2......................**$35.00**

Vase, 6½", Wild Flower, embossed flowers on pink shading to cream, matt, 1942-43, #W5............$65.00

Wall plaque, Bow Knot, 10" dia, embossed flowers on cream shading to blue, matt, 1949-50, #B-28......**$650.00**

Wall pocket, Novelty, 6", figural goose, dark green & wine, glossy, 1951-54, #67.............................**$40.00**

Wall pocket, Novelty, 6", ribbon shape, yellow shading to pink, glossy, 1951, #71 ....**$40.00**

Wall pocket, Poppy, 9", embossed flowers on cream to pink, matt, cornucopia form, 1943-44, #609 ....**$225.00**

Wall pocket, Sun-Glow, 5½", embossed flowers on pink, glossy, jug form, 1948-49, #81.............................**$70.00**

Wall pocket, Bow Knot, 8¼", whisk broom shape **$150.00**

Window box, Novelty, 12½", pink & charcoal, embossed scroll on sides, glossy, 1955-59, #71 ....**$30.00**

Window box, Serenade, 12½", embossed bough & chickadee on yellow, matt w/glossy interior, 1957, #S9 ....**$60.00**

Window box, Woodland, 10", embossed flower on yellow, glossy, 1952-54, #W14 ....**$55.00**

Dinnerware

Avocado, bowl, soup or salad; 6½", #669 ....**$6.00**

Avocado, dish, divided vegetable; 7¼x10¾", #642......**$10.00**

Avocado, jug, 2-pt, #625...**$22.00**

Avocado, plate, dinner; 10¼", #642 ....**$10.00**

Avocado, teapot, 5-cup, ball form, ivory trim, #649....**$10.00**

Centennial, bowl, cereal; 5¾", brown w/ivory trim, American Bald Eagle imprinted in center, #571.............**$45.00**

Centennial, creamer, 4½", brown w/ivory trim, American Bald Eagle imprinted in center, #581.....................**$45.00**

Country Belle, baker, ivory w/blue flower & bell design in center, tab handles, square, #6568..........................**$16.00**

Country Belle, bowl, 8", ivory w/blue flower & bell design stenciled in center, #6438......................................**$18.00**

Country Belle, mug, ivory w/blue flower & bell design stenciled in center, ear-type handle, footed, #6471.....**$10.00**

Country Belle, plate, salad; ivory w/blue flower & bell design stenciled in center, #6401 ....**$7.50**

Country Belle, platter, ivory w/blue flower & bell design stenciled in center, oval, #6441 ....**$24.00**

Country Squire, bowl, divided vegetable; 7¼x10¾", green agate w/white trim, #142....................................**$20.00**

Country Squire, bowl, fruit; 5¼", green agate w/white trim, #103..**$4.00**

Country Squire, bowl, mixing; 5¼", green agate w/white trim, #105...**$9.00**

Country Squire, ice jug, 2-qt, green agate w/white trim, ball form, handled, #114..**$26.00**

Country Squire, mug, soup; 11-oz, green agate w/white trim, #153..**$7.50**

Country Squire, plate, dinner; 10¼", green agate w/white trim, #100..**$8.00**

Crestone, bowl, fruit; 6", turquoise, #303 ....**$5.00**

Crestone, coffeepot, 60-oz, turquoise, #322.................**$50.00**

Crestone, plate, bread & butter; 6½", turquoise, #304...**$4.50**

Crestone, plate, luncheon; 9", turquoise, #331..............**$8.00**

Crestone, tray, 10¼x14¼x2¼", turquoise, leaf shape w/4 sections, #321 ....**$38.00**

Heartland, bowl, 10", ivory w/buttercup yellow trim, brown stenciled heart pattern in center, #440.................**$25.00**

Heartland, creamer, ivory w/buttercup yellow trim, brown stenciled heart pattern in center, #418..................**$12.00**

Heartland, custard cup, ivory w/buttercup yellow trim, brown stenciled heart pattern in center, #476.........**$7.50**

Heartland, plate, dinner; ivory w/buttercup yellow trim, brown stenciled heart pattern in center, #400......**$10.00**

Heartland, platter, ivory w/buttercup yellow trim, brown stenciled heart pattern in center, #441..................**$24.00**

Mirror Almond, bowl, fruit; 5¼", caramel trim, #803 .....**$5.50**

Mirror Almond, bowl, mixing; 6", caramel trim, #836 .**$12.00**

Mirror Almond, dish, divided vegetable; 7¾x10¾", caramel trim, #842...**$16.00**

Mirror Almond, plate, dinner; 10¼", caramel trim **$10.00**

Mirror Almond, vegetable server, 11x8¾", caramel trim, ring handle, #867 ....**$15.00**

Mirror Brown, baker, 7-pt, rectangular, open, #534 ....**$38.00**

Mirror Brown, bean pot, 2-qt, w/lid, #510 ....**$16.50**

Mirror Brown, bowl, fruit; 6", #533...............................**$4.00**

Mirror Brown, bowl, mixing; 8", #538 ....**$10.00**

Mirror Brown, canister, Sugar, #558............................**$50.00**

Mirror Brown, casserole, 2-qt, w/lid, oval, #548.........**$18.00**

Mirror Brown, casserole, 3-pt, stick handle, w/lid & warmer, #579 ....**$75.00**

Mirror Brown, casserole, 32-oz, w/lid, #507 ....**$14.00**

Mirror Brown, cheese server, #582.............................**$15.00**

Mirror Brown, coffeepot, 8-cup, #522 ....**$20.00**

Mirror Brown, custard cup, 6-oz, #576.........................**$6.50**

Mirror Brown, custard cup, 8-oz, #376.........................**$6.00**

Mirror Brown, dish, divided vegetable; 7x11", #542....**$10.00**

Mirror Brown, gravy boat, #511 ....**$12.00**

Mirror Brown, pie plate, 9½" dia, #566 ....**$20.00**

Mirror Brown, plate, luncheon; 9⅜", #599.....................**$8.00**

Mirror Brown, plate, salad; 6½", #501...........................**$2.50**

Mirror Brown, platter, 11", fish form, #596, rare.........**$35.00**

Mirror Brown, salt & pepper shakers, 3¾", mushroom figurals, #587 & 588, pr...**$16.00**

Mirror Brown, saucer, 5½", #530.......................**$4.00**

Mirror Brown, spoon rest, oval, Spoon Rest imprinted in center, #594 ....**$20.00**

Mirror Brown, stein, 32-oz, #572....................**$30.00**

Mirror Brown, sugar bowl, 12-oz, #519 ....**$4.00**

Mirror Brown, teapot, 5-cup, #549..................**$16.50**

Mirror Brown, tidbit, 2-tiered, #592 ....**$25.00**

Provincial, bean pot, 2-qt, brown w/white lid, #710...**$40.00**

Provincial, bowl, mixing; 5¼", brown w/white trim, #705 ....**$10.00**

Provincial, casserole, individual; 12-oz, brown w/white trim, stick handle, #727 ....**$16.00**

Provincial, sugar bowl, 12-oz, brown w/white trim & lid, #719 ....**$15.00**

Rainbow, mug, 6-oz, butterscotch w/ivory trim, handled, #232RA **$5.00**

Rainbow, plate, salad; butterscotch w/ivory trim...........**$4.50**

Rainbow, saucer, 5½", butterscotch w/ivory trim **$3.50**

Rainbow, tray, 7½x12", butterscotch w/ivory trim, leaf shape, rare, #540 ....**$40.00**

Ridge, creamer, 8-oz, walnut w/ivory trim, #310..........**$8.50**

Ridge, mug, 10-oz, tawny w/ivory trim, #202 ....**$4.00**

Ridge, plate, dinner; 10¼", gray w/ivory trim, #100 .....**$7.50**

Ridge, plate, salad; 7¼", tawny w/ivory trim, #201........**$4.50**

Ridge, plate, salad; 7¼", walnut w/ivory trim, #301 ......**$4.50**

Ridge, saucer, 6", gray w/ivory trim, #105.....................**$4.00**

Tangerine, bean pot, individual; 12-oz, ivory trim **$10.00**

Tangerine, casserole, individual; 12-oz, ivory trim, stick handle, #927 ....**$8.50**

Tangerine, dish, 4¼x7¼", leaf shape, ivory trim, #590 ..**$8.00**

Tangerine, mug, 9-oz, ivory trim, slightly flared rim, handled, #902 ....**$6.00**

Tangerine, pie plate, 9¼" dia, ivory trim, #966...........**$20.00**

Hummels

Hummels have been made in Rodental, (West) Germany since 1935. All have been inspired by the drawings of a Franciscan nun, Sister M. Innocentia. They're commonplace today, both on the retail level and the secondary market. You'll find them in any fine gift shop. In addition to the figurines, a line of collector plates and bells have been made as well.

The figurines have been in demand by collectors for many years, and some are very valuable. It's sometimes difficult to determine what prices you should be paying. Even if the figure is currently in production, the law of supply and demand may cause retail prices to fluctuate as much as 50% in different parts of the country. Several marks have been used over the years, and generally speaking, the older the mark, the more valuable the piece. But if a particular piece happens to be hard to find, scarcity may override the age factor.

Here are some of the marks you'll find: 1) Crown WG – a two-lobed crown over the letters 'W and G,' one superimposed over the other, 1934-1950; 2) full bee – a realistically styled bee within a large 'V,' with variations, 1940-56; 3)

stylized bee – bee (represented by a solid circle having triangular wings) within a large 'V,' with variations, mid-1950s until around 1965; 4) 3-line mark – same stylized bee plus three lines of words to the right: c by/W. Goebel/W. Germany; 5) Goebel bee or last bee – stylized bee in 'V' above and toward the right end of 'Goebel/W. Germany,' 1970-80; 6) missing bee – simple 'Goebel/W. Germany' (no bee), mid-eighties to present.

For further information, we recommend *Hummel Figurines and Plates, A Collector's Identification and Value Guide,* by Carl Luckey.

#10/I, Flower Madonna, white, full bee, 9½".............**$145.00**

#109/0, Happy Traveler, stylized bee, 5".....................**$90.00**

#118, Little Thrifty, last bee, 5"..................................**$120.00**

#12/2/0, Chimney Sweep, full bee, 4" **$90.00**

#123, Max & Moritz, 3-line mark, 5¼" **$135.00**

#128, Baker, stylized bee, 4¾" **$110.00**

#133, Mother's Helper, 3-line mark, 5".....................**$140.00**

#135, Soloist, 3-line mark, 4¾"..................................**$100.00**

#136/I, Friends, full bee, 5" **$250.00**

#141/3/0, Apple Tree Girl, full bee, 4" **$165.00**

#144, Angelic Song, 3-line mark, 4¼"........................**$110.00**

#152/A/0, Umbrella Boy, last bee **$450.00**

#154/I, Waiter, stylized bee, 7" **$200.00**

#16/2/0, Little Hiker, 3-line mark, 4¼" **$80.00**

#171, Little Sweeper, full bee, 4½"............................**$150.00**

#176/0, Happy Birthday, last bee, 5½".......................**$145.00**

#179, Coquettes, stylized bee, 5¼" **$180.00**

#18, Christ Child, last bee, 2x6" **$85.00**

#182, Good Friends, 3-line mark, 4"...........................**$135.00**

#183, Forest Shrine, last bee **$550.00**

#186, Sweet Music, 3-line mark, 5¼" $135.00
#188, Celestial Musician, stylized bee, 7" $175.00
#195/2/0, Barnyard Hero, full bee, 4" $190.00
#2/0, Little Fiddler, 3-line mark, 6" $160.00
#200/0, Little Goat Herder, last bee, 4¾" $145.00
#203/2/0, Signs of Spring, crown mark, 4" $400.00
#21/0, Heavenly Angel, 3-line mark, 4¼" $85.00
#32/0, Little Gabriel, stylized bee, 5" $95.00
#359, Tuneful Angel, 3-line mark, 2¾" $65.00
#36/I, Child w/Flowers, crown mark, 3½x4½" $325.00
#381, Flower Vendor, last bee, 5½" $165.00

#4, Little Fiddler, 3-line mark...............................$125.00
#42/0, Good Shepherd, full bee, 6¼" $250.00
#5, Strolling Along, stylized bee, 4¾" $250.00
#51/3/0, Village Boy, 3-line mark, 4"........................$80.00
#56/B, Out of Danger, full bee, 6¼" $275.00
#57/0, Chick Girl, 3-line mark, 3½" $125.00
#58/0, Playmates, full bee, 4" $190.00
#59, Skier, 3-line mark, 5¼" $185.00
#64, Shepherd's Boy, stylized bee, 5½" $165.00
#7/0, Merry Wanderer, 3-line mark, 6¼" $150.00
#70, Holy Child, full bee, 6¾" $200.00
#74, Little Gardener, 3-line mark, 4¼" $85.00
#80, Little Scholar, full bee, 5½" $225.00
#82/2/0, School Boy, 3-line mark, 4"........................$100.00
#86, Happiness, crown mark, 4¾" $300.00
#89/I, Little Cellist, stylized bee, 6" $180.00
#96, Little Shopper, full bee, 4¾" $200.00
#98/2/0, Sister, last bee, 4¾" $135.00
#99, Eventide, 3-line mark, 4¾" $250.00

Ice Cream Molds

Normally made of pewter (though you might find an aluminum example now and then), these were used on special occasions and holidays to mold ice cream (usually single servings) into a shape that was related somehow to the celebration – bells and snowmen at Christmas time, eggs and flowers at Easter, and cupids and rings for Valentine's Day or weddings, for instance. They were designed with two or three hinged sections, so that the ice cream could be removed with ease.

Apple, E-240 ....$25.00
Asparagus bunch, 3", #333 ....$35.00
Aster, #926, 3" $22.50
Basket, E-1013, octagonal..$35.00
Bell, #605 ....$32.00
Bicyle, K-432, lady rider $60.00
Bunch of grapes, E-278 ....$30.00
Cat w/arched back, E-644 ....$35.00
Champagne bottle in cooler, S-206 ....$65.00
Cherub on Easter Bunny, 4" $28.00
Chrysanthemum, #313 ....$30.00

Cow, #358 ....$65.00
Cupid sits on rose, E-959, full figure $55.00
Diamond playing card, E&Co $55.00
Dutch shoe, 5", #978..$32.00
Easter egg, E-906 ....$22.50
Easter lily, 3-part $60.00
Engagement ring, #376 ....$30.00
Goat, S-346, rearing $80.00
Goose egg, #298 ....$25.00
Gourd, 4" $18.00
Harp, K-361, aluminum, 1940s $32.00
Lion, 4", #618, side view $32.00
Log, E-987 ....$25.00
Melon, E-204 ....$15.00
Mum, E-355 ....$30.00
Orange, 3", #307 ....$25.00
Peach, #152 ....$22.50
Peach half w/stone, #160 ....$25.00
Pears, 4", #942, 3 in mold..$25.00
Penguin, 3½" $40.00
Pond lily, E-318 ....$30.00

Rose, E-295..$30.00
Rose, 4", #939, open, 3 in mold..................$25.00
Shriner emblem, E-1081...........................$30.00
Snowman, 5", #601 ....$95.00
Spade playing card, 4"..............................$60.00
Stork..$35.00
Stork w/baby, E-1151, standing $55.00
Strawberry, E-316 ....$32.00
Tomato, 3", #208 ....$40.00
Tulip, 4¼", E&Co....................................$36.00
Turkey, 4", #364, roasted..........................$38.00
Washington bust, 4", #1084.......................$60.00
Wolf, K-428, 3-part..................................$80.00

Imperial Glass

Organized in 1901 in Bellaire, Ohio, the Imperial Glass Company made carnival glass, stretch glass, a line called NuCut (made in imitation of cut glass), and a limited amount of art glass within the first decade of the century. In the mid-thirties, they designed one of their most famous patterns (and one of their most popular with today's collectors), Candlewick. Within a few years, milk glass had become their leading product.

During the fifties, they reintroduced their NuCut line in crystal as well as colors, marketing it as 'Collector's Crystal.' In the late fifties they bought molds from both Heisey and Cambridge. The glassware they reissued from these old molds was marked 'IG,' one letter superimposed over the other. When Imperial was bought by Lenox in 1973, an 'L' was added to the mark. The company changed hands twice more before closing altogether in 1984.

In addition to tableware, they made a line of animal figures, some of which were made from Heisey's molds. *Glass Animals of the Depression Years* by Lee Garmon and Dick Spencer is a wonderful source of information and can help you determine the value and the manufacturer of your figures.

Numbers in the listings were assigned by the company and appeared on their catalog pages. They were used to indicate differences in shapes and stems, for instance. Collectors still use them. For more information on Imperial in general, we recommend *Imperial Glass* by Margaret and Douglas Archer and *Elegant Glassware of the Depression Era* by Gene Florence.

See also Carnival Glass; Candlewick; Glass Animals.

Ashtray, Cathay Crystal, #5007, plum blossom $25.00
Ashtray, purple slag satin $17.00
Ashtray, 4", Cape Cod, #150/134/1 ....$8.00
Basket, Daisy, milk glass, Doeskin $25.00
Bonbon, 5¾", Mount Vernon, #699, handled..............$14.00
Book stop, Cathay Crystal, #5029, Empress..............$250.00
Bowl, baked apple; Tradition, blue......................$12.00
Bowl, salad; 10", Pillar Flute, blue $45.00
Bowl, 5½", Cape Cod...................................$8.00

Bowl, 7½", Niagara, #L4736B $18.00
Bowl, 8", swan, milk glass, Doeskin...............$35.00
Box, flat iron, w/lid, purple slag..................$100.00
Butter dish, 5", Cape Cod, #160/144 ....$35.00
Cake plate, Cape Cod, #160/220, square, 4-footed.....$90.00
Cake plate, 11", Mount Vernon, #6997D $20.00

Cake plate, 12", Crochet Crystal............................$40.00
Candle base, Cathay Crystal, #5013, pillow.................$50.00
Candlesticks, Pillar Flute, blue, twin, pr.....................$35.00
Celery tray, Pillar Flute, blue, oval.........................$35.00
Cordial, Cape Cod, #1602.....................................$10.00
Creamer & sugar bowl, Cape Cod, #160/30.................$15.00
Cruet, 4-oz, Cape Cod, amber, #160/70, w/stopper $30.00
Cup & saucer, Monticello $6.00
Cup & saucer, Niagara, #L473 ....$16.00
Cup & saucer, Pillar Flute, blue..............................$35.00
Custard, Mount Vernon, #669, handled......................$14.00
Decanter, 24-oz, Cape Cod, #160/212 ....$58.00
Decanter, 31-oz, Niagara, #L473, w/stopper $44.00
Egg cup, #160/225, Cape Cod..................................$27.50
Goblet, water; Cape Cod, Antique Blue, #1602 ....$28.00
Goblet, 10-oz, Niagara, #L473 ....$16.00
Ming jar, Cathay Crystal, #5019.............................$80.00
Mint set, Cathay Crystal, #5008, peach blossom $20.00
Nappy, 10", Niagara, #L4738B................................$20.00
Old-fashioned, 7-oz, Cape Cod, #160 ....$8.00

Owl, blue carnival, head is lid..............................$40.00

Parfait, Cape Cod, #1602 ....**$12.00**
Pitcher, milk; 16-oz, Cape Cod, #160/240 ....**$49.00**
Pitcher, 54-oz, Mount Vernon, #6996 ....**$40.00**
Pitcher, 80-oz, Cape Cod, blown, #160/176...............**$175.00**
Plate, bread & butter; 6", Mount Vernon, #699D **$12.00**
Plate, Coin, Kennedy Series, 1971 ....**$25.00**
Plate, luncheon; Monticello....................................**$5.00**
Plate, torte; 14", Cape Cod **$30.00**
Plate, 12½", Niagara, #L4738D...................................**$24.00**
Plate, 8", Mount Vernon, #6990D................................**$14.00**
Plate, 8½", Pillar Flute, blue **$15.00**
Platter, 12", Cape Cod..**$70.00**
Relish, 8", Cape Cod, 2-part, handles **$35.00**
Salt & pepper shakers, Cape Cod, #160/116, pr.........**$15.00**
Salt & pepper shakers, Stamm House, Dewdrop opalescent, pr...**$30.00**
Sherbet, Mount Vernon, low **$70.00**
Spider, 4½", Cape Cod, #160/180, handled.................**$18.00**
Stein, Cape Cod, milk glass, Doeskin..........................**$35.00**
Stem, cordial, Cape Cod **$8.00**
Sugar bowl, Mount Vernon, #6990, individual, open..**$10.00**
Tidbit, Mount Vernon, #699, 2-tier..............................**$34.00**
Tray, celery; 10½", Mount Vernon, #699 ....**$18.00**
Tray, lunch; 16", Niagara, #L473, center handle **$24.00**
Tray, pastry; 11", Cape Cod, amber.............................**$75.00**

Tumbler, Cape Cod, 16-oz **$17.50**
Tumbler, juice; Cape Cod, #1602, amber **$12.00**
Tumbler, 5", Cape Cod, #160 ....**$12.00**
Tumbler, 9-oz, Pillar Flute, blue **$45.00**
Vase, Mount Vernon, square, pink **$10.00**
Vase, 8", Niagara, blown **$40.00**
Whiskey, 2½-oz, Cape Cod, flat...................................**$14.00**
Wine, Mt Vernon...**$80.00**

Imperial Porcelain

Figurines representing Paul Webb's Blue Ridge Mountain Boys were made by the Imperial Porcelain Corporation of Zanesville, Ohio, from the late 1940s until they closed in 1960. You'll see some knocking on outhouse doors by ash trays, drinking from a jug of 'moonshine' as they sit by washtub planters, or embossed in scenes of mountain-life activity on mugs and pitchers. Imperial also made the Al Capp Dogpatch series and a line of twenty-three miniature animals, 2" tall and under, that they called American Folklore miniatures.

Ashtray, #101, man w/jug & snake.............................**$75.00**
Ashtray, #105, baby, hound dog & frog....................**$110.00**

Ashtray, 8¼", baby knocks on outhouse door $125.00
Cigarette box, #98, dog on top, baby at door...........**$115.00**
Decanter, #100, outhouse, man & bird.......................**$75.00**

Decanter, #102, Pa leans on barrel, chick perched on his knee $120.00
Decanter, #104, Ma leans on stump, w/baby & skunk .**$95.00**
Figurine, #101, man leaning against tree trunk, 5" **$90.00**
Figurine, man on hands & knees, 3" **$95.00**
Miniature, cat, 1½" **$40.00**
Miniature, cow, 1¾"...**$35.00**

Miniature, sow...$30.00
Mug, #94, double baby handle, 4¼"..............$95.00
Mug, #94, man w/blue pants handle, 4¼"......$95.00
Planter, #105, man w/chicken on knee, washtub......$110.00
Planter, #81, man sitting by washtub drinks from jug.$75.00
Salt & pepper shakers, standing pigs, IP mark, 8", pr.$95.00

Indiana Glass Carnival Ware

In the mid-1980s, the Indiana Glass Company produced a line of iridescent 'new carnival' glass, much of which was embossed with grape clusters and detailed leaves reminescent of the old Northwood carnival. It was made in blue, marigold, and green and was evidently a good seller for them, judging from the amount around today. They also produced a line of 'press cut' iridescent glass, some of which can be found in red as well as the other colors mentioned. Collectors always seem to gravitate toward lustre-coated glassware, whether it's old or recently made, and there seems to be a significant amount of interest in this line.

It's a little difficult to evaluate, since you see it in malls and at flea markets with such a wide range of 'asking' prices. On one hand, you'll have sellers who themselves are not exactly sure what it is they have, but since it's 'carnival' assume it should be fairly pricey. On the other hand, you have those who've just 'cleaned house' and want to get rid of it. They may have bought it new themselves and know it's not very old and wasn't expensive to start with. This is what you'll be up against if you decide you want to collect it.

As I mentioned up front, the collectibles market has changed. Nowadays, some shows' criteria regarding the merchandise they allow to be displayed is 'if it's no longer available on the retail market, it's OK.' I suspect that this attitude will become more and more widespread. At any rate, this is one of the newest interests at the flea market/antique mall level, and if you can buy it right (and like its looks), now is the time!

Candy dish, sm, ribbed, open lace rim, w/lid................$8.00
Compote, 8" dia, embossed grapes & leaves, w/lid....$28.00
Covered dish, hen on nest............................$18.00
Creamer & sugar bowl on try, embossed grapes & vines.$15.00
Egg plate, Press Cut design............................$12.00
Goblet, water; embossed grapes....................$8.00
Goblet, water; Press Cut design, red.............$15.00
Pitcher, water; Press Cut design, red.............$40.00
Pitcher, 10", embossed grapes & vines, pedestal foot.$25.00
Punch bowl, embossed around rim only, w/12 hangers &
    cups..$85.00
Tumbler, 5½", embossed grapes & vines, scarce.........$10.00
Vase, 9", Press Cut design, red, footed........................$20.00

Jadite Glassware

For the past few years, jadite has been one of the fastest-moving types of collectible glassware on the market. It was produced by several companies from the 1940s

through the 1965. Many of Anchor Hocking's Fire-King lines were available in the soft opaque green jadite, and Jeannette Glass as well as McKee produced their own versions.

It was always very inexpensive glass, and it was made in abundance. Dinnerware for the home as well as restaurants and a vast array of kitchenware items literally flooded the country for many years. Though a few rare pieces have become fairly expensive, most are still reasonably priced, and there are bargains to be had.

For more information we recommend *Kitchen Glassware of the Depression Years* and *Collectible Glassware of the 40s, 50s, and 60s,* both by Gene Florence.

Batter jug, square, w/spout & handle, Jeannette.........$50.00
Beater bowl, w/beater.................................$30.00
Bowl, cereal; 5", Breakfast Set (Fire-King), Anchor Hocking,
    1954-56 ....$10.00
Bowl, cereal; 5⅞", Swirl line (Fire-King), Anchor Hocking,
    1963-67..$6.00
Bowl, cereal; 8-oz, Restaurant Ware (Fire-King), Anchor
    Hocking, 1948-74 ....$6.00
Bowl, chili; 5", Jane-Ray line (Fire-King), Anchor Hocking,
    1945-63...$3.00
Bowl, dessert; 4⅞", Jane-Ray line (Fire-King), Anchor Hocking, 1945-63 ....$3.00
Bowl, fancy; 8½", Bubble line (Fire-King), Anchor Hocking,
    1930s-60s...$12.00
Bowl, soup; 7⅝", Swirl line (Fire-King), Anchor Hocking,
    1963-67..$8.00
Bowl, vegetable; 8½", Shell line (Fire-King), Anchor Hocking, 1963 ....$7.00
Bowl, vegetable; 8¼", Jane-Ray line (Fire-King), Anchor
    Hocking, 1945-63 ....$10.00
Bowl, vegetable; 8¼", Swirl line (Fire-King), Anchor Hocking, 1963-67...$12.00
Butter dish, 1-lb, rectangular, embossed Butter lettered on
    lid, Jeannette...$35.00
Canister, coffee; square, black floral decoration & lettering,
    flat lid, Jeannette....................................$35.00
Canister, spice; 3", black lettering, Jeannette...............$40.00
Canister, 10-oz, round bowl shape, w/lid..................$15.00

Canister, 3½x5¾" dia, w/lid................................$25.00
Canister, 48-oz, square, black lettering, flat lid...........**$40.00**

Canister, 48-oz, square, black lettering, screw-on metal lid, McKee **$50.00**

Cheese dish, 2-lb, rectangular, McKee..........................**$35.00**

Creamer, Shell line (Fire-King), Anchor Hocking, 1963 ..**$4.00**

Creamer, Swirl line (Fire-King), Anchor Hocking..........**$8.00**

Crock, 40-oz, round, w/lid, Jeannette.......................**$40.00**

Cup, 6½-oz, Sheaf of Wheat line (Fire King), Anchor Hocking, 1957-59 ....**$5.00**

Cup, 8-oz, Alice line (Fire-King), Anchor Hocking........**$5.00**

Cup, 8-oz, Jane-Ray line (Fire-King), Anchor Hocking, 1945-63 ....**$3.00**

Cup, 8-oz, Shell line (Fire-King), Anchor Hocking, 1963 .**$3.00**

Cup, 8-oz, straight sides, Restaurant Ware (Fire-King), Anchor Hocking, 1948-74 ....**$4.00**

Cup, 8-oz, Swirl line (Fire-King), Anchor Hocking........**$4.00**

Cup, 9-oz, Breakfast Set (Fire-King), Anchor Hocking, 1954-56.**$5.00**

Egg cup, double; 5", Breakfast Set (Fire-King), Anchor Hocking, 1954-56 ....**$10.00**

Egg cup, 4", double **$10.00**

Measure, 1-cup, double spout, open handle **$145.00**

Measure, 1-cup, no spout, tab handle, Jeannette.........**$15.00**

Measure, ¼-cup, no spout, tab handle, Jeannette **$8.00**

Measuring pitcher, 2-cup, dark Jadite, sunflower in bottom, Jeannette..**$45.00**

Measuring pitcher, 2-cup, light Jadite, sunflower in bottom, Jeannette..**$15.00**

Measuring pitcher, 2-cup, McKee **$15.00**

Pie plate, 10⅜", juice saver type, Fire-King.................**$70.00**

Pitcher, milk; 20-oz, Breakfast Set (Fire-King), Anchor Hocking, 1954-56 ....**$20.00**

Plate, dinner; Restaurant Ware (Fire-King), Anchor Hocking, 1948-74..**$7.00**

Plate, dinner; 9⅛", Jane-Ray line (Fire-King), Anchor Hocking, 1945-63 ....**$6.00**

Plate, dinner; 9⅛", Swirl line (Fire-King), Anchor Hocking, 1963-67 ....**$8.00**

Plate, luncheon; 8", Restaurant Ware (Fire-King), Anchor Hocking, 1948-74 ....**$6.00**

Plate, salad; 7¼", Shell line (Fire-King), Anchor Hocking, 1963...**$3.00**

Plate, salad; 7¾", Swirl line (Fire-King), Anchor Hocking, 1963-67...**$5.00**

Plate, sandwich; 9¾", oval, Restaurant Ware (Fire-King), Anchor Hocking, 1948-74 ....**$12.00**

Plate, 11½", oval, Restaurant Ware (Fire-King), Anchor Hocking, 1948-74 ....**$12.00**

Plate, 8½", Alice line (Fire-King), Anchor Hocking **$12.00**

Plate, 9", Sheaf of Wheat line (Fire-King), Anchor Hocking, 1957-59 ....**$7.00**

Plate, 9⅛", Breakfast Set (Fire-King), Anchor Hocking, 1954-56 ....**$9.00**

Plate, 9⅝", 3-part, Restaurant Ware (Fire-King), Anchor Hocking, 1948-74 ....**$10.00**

Platter, 9½x13", oval, Shell line (Fire-King), Anchor Hocking, 1963...**$6.00**

Platter, 9x12", oval, Jane-Ray line (Fire-King), Anchor Hocking, 1945-63 ....**$10.00**

Reamer, light Jadite, swirl cone **$22.00**

Refrigerator dish, 10x5", floral on lid, Jeannette **$30.00**

Refrigerator dish, 4½x5¼", w/lid & tab handles, Fire-King, Anchor Hocking..**$8.00**

Refrigerator dish, 4x4", w/lid **$15.00**

Salt box, half-bowl shape w/metal hinged lid, McKee.**$85.00**

Salt box, square w/wood lid, black lettering, Jeannette.**$225.00**

Salt or pepper shaker, round w/grooved lower half, floral decoration & black lettering above, metal lid, Jeannette, each **$15.00**

Salt or pepper shaker, squared w/arched panels, black lettering, metal lid, Jeannette, each...........................**$15.00**

Saucer, 5¾", Jane-Ray line (Fire-King), Anchor Hocking, 1945-63...**$2.00**

Saucer, 5¾", Swirl line (Fire-King), Anchor Hocking.....**$3.00**

Saucer, 5⅞", Alice line (Fire-King), Anchor Hocking.....**$3.00**

Saucer, 5⅞", Breakfast Set (Fire-King), Anchor Hocking...**$3.00**

Saucer, 6", Sheaf of Wheat line (Fire-King), Anchor Hocking, 1957-59 ....**$3.00**

Skillet, 2-spout, Fire-King, Anchor Hocking................**$30.00**

Sugar bowl, w/lid, Shell line (Fire-King), Anchor Hocking, 1963...**$5.00**

Sugar shaker, light Jadite, metal screw lid, Jeannette ..**$55.00**

Jewelry

Though the collectible jewelry frenzy of a few years ago seems to have subsided a bit, better costume jewelry remains a strong area of interest on today's market. Signed pieces are especially good. Check for marks on metal mounts. Some of the better designers are Hobé, Haskell, Monet, Trifari, Weiss, and Eisenberg.

Early plastic pieces (Lucite, Bakelite, and celluloid, for example) are very collectible; some Lucite is used in combination with wood, and the figural designs are especially desirable. The better rhinestone jewelry, especially when it's signed, is a good investment as well.

There are excellent reference books available, if you'd like more information. Lillian Baker has written several: *Art Nouveau and Art Deco Jewelry, An Identification and Value Guide; Twentieth Century Fashionable Plastic Jewelry;* and *50 Years of Collectible Fashion Jewelry.* Other books: *Collecting Rhinestone Colored Jewelry* by Maryanne Dolan and *The Art and Mystique of Shell Cameos* by Ed Aswad and Michael Weinstein.

Bar pin, 14k white gold filigree, tiny blue sapphire, yellow gold back, 1920s **$60.00**

Bar pin, 2½x½", pave set rhinestones, center cabochon stone, open sides **$32.00**

Bracelet, bangle; dark green Peking glass, ca 1930s ...**$55.00**

Bracelet, bangle; 1½" wide, Lanvin Paris, gold-plated metal, geometric black, purple & white designs, hinged...**$40.00**

Bracelet, bangle; ½" wide, amber to clear Bakelite, carved diagonal lines **$35.00**

Bracelet, bangle; ⅜" wide, Whiting & Davis, textured diagonal stripes, hinged...**$40.00**

Bracelet, Beau, sterling, etched & engraved leaves form links, 1940s...**$55.00**

Bracelet, charm; sterling, 5 assorted sm charms w/turquoise stones & blue enameling...**$45.00**

Bracelet, G Jensen, silver, lg beads alternate w/buds, Arts & Crafts type **$275.00**

Bracelet, Kreisler, 5 silver & gold-tone metal open floral plaques **$25.00**

Bracelet, tennis; square blue rhinestones...**$40.00**

Bracelet, 1½" wide, Coro, gold-plated links w/openwork flowers, scalloped edges, oval spacers...**$27.50**

Bracelet, 1¼" wide, gold-filled shell cameo links...**$80.00**

Bracelet, ½" wide, Coro, blue moonstone links w/rhinestones, shapes between...**$27.50**

Bracelet, ½" wide, sterling leaves form links **$35.00**

Bracelet, ¼" wide, sterling log-shaped links w/black onyx beads...... ....**$40.00**

Bracelet, ¾" wide, Weiss, yellow Bakelite w/lg & sm rhinestones...**$95.00**

Bracelet, 5 yellow glass scarabs hang from chain **$37.50**

Bracelet, 6.5-5.0mm cultured pearls, 14k gold clasp.**$150.00**

Bracelet, 7" long, Sorrento, 5 tiger-eye sections w/guard chain **$40.00**

Bracelet & earrings, Trifari, gold-plated w/white enameling & turquoise blue stones, cast mounting...**$35.00**

Brooch, gold filled, lg faux amethyst, Victorian **$100.00**

Brooch, 18k yellow gold w/8mm cultured pearl amid cobalt blue enameling **$180.00**

Cross, sterling, engraved ivy motif, w/chain, ca 1900.**$65.00**

Earrings, Chr Dior (Christian Dior) & Germany, gold-tone metal w/simulated jade & sapphires, 1967, pr......**$65.00**

Earrings, Hollycraft, gold-tone metal w/pastel multicolor & faceted stones, clip, 1960s, pr **$35.00**

Earrings, JKL (Kenneth Jay Lane), simulated coral & emeralds w/seed pearls, 1970, pr **$120.00**

Earrings, Miriam Haskell, prong-set clear & red stones w/red drops, pr...**$100.00**

Earrings, Mosell, hand-painted gold-plated seashell, clip, 1960, pr...**$35.00**

Earrings, sterling & brass parrot, pr **$24.00**

Earrings, Trifari, rhodium flower w/pink enameling & rhinestones, clip, 1945, pr...**$55.00**

Earrings, Trifari, sm gold-tone mounting w/green cabochons & pave-set rhinestones, pr...**$80.00**

Earrings, Weiss, butterfly, simulated gem stones on japanned mounting, 1950s-60s, pr **$85.00**

Earrings, 1", Coro, amber aurora borealis rhinestones, 2 lg round w/2 lg pear-shaped stones, clip, pr **$15.00**

Earrings, 1", Marino, chrome bow, clips, pr...**$10.00**

Earrings, 1¼", gold filled, garnet drops, replaced gold ear wires, pr...**$90.00**

Earrings, 1¼" dia, snowflake, 4 lg marquise rhinestones w/square rhinestone center, clip, pr...**$15.00**

Earrings, 14k yellow gold, ball studs, 7mm, pr...**$20.00**

Earrings, 14k yellow gold, 6mm pearl, pr **$30.00**

Earrings, 2⅜" dia, Boucher, gold-plated flower w/florentine finish, pr...**$35.00**

Earrings, ¾", Marvella, simulated green jade, oval, pr.**$25.00**

Earrings, ¾", Pell, diamond-shaped rhinestone w/baguette border, clip, pr...**$15.00**

Earrings, ¾" dia, knot design, fuchsia Bakelite, pr **$15.00**

Earrings, ⅞", Weiss, flower, rhinestones w/simulated emerald, clip, pr...**$25.00**

Locket, 14k yellow gold, oval w/lovebirds...**$96.00**

Necklace, amber & jet faceted glass beads, Czechoslovakia, ca 1950 ....**$150.00**

Necklace, amber Bohemian glass beads, single strand, ca 1920s...**$75.00**

Necklace, aurora borealis beads, 4 strands, 1960s.....**$135.00**

Necklace, Deco-style pendant w/blue emerald-cut glass stones in white metal mounting w/rhinestone trim on 12" chain...**$80.00**

Necklace, finely faceted Bohemian glass rope of graduated beads, 1930s...**$95.00**

Necklace, Miriam Haskell, pearl choker w/butterfly shaped pendant **$150.00**

Necklace, Sarah Coventry, leaf drop w/5 green stones on gold-tone chain **$8.00**

Necklace, Sarah Coventry, rhodium chain, 1960 ....**$10.00**

Necklace, short, bright red glass faceted beads in graduated sizes **$32.00**

Necklace, short, Castlecliff, snake chain w/frosted gold abstract design, leather trim on bar **$48.00**

Necklace, short, hammered sterling rods hang from chain, bead spacers...**$22.50**

Necklace, short, red & white coral beads, chunky **$40.00**

Necklace, short, 3 strands of red & black cut glass beads, center gold ornate piece set w/multicolor stones.**$55.00**

Necklace, silver filigree pendant on chain, 1930s........**$45.00**

Necklace, sterling heart set w/14 rubies on 9" chain ..**$95.00**

Necklace, Victorian reproduction w/rhinestones & simulated emeralds w/2" blossom-shaped pendant, 1950s.**$145.00**

Necklace, 10½", Faberge, gold-plated snake chain w/tiger-head locket, faceted amber eyes, perfume inside **$35.00**

Necklace, 10½" gold chain w/9 graduated drop chains, each w/lg amber cut glass bead dangles **$35.00**

Necklace, 11", garnet chips **$45.00**

Necklace, 12", red & opaque glass beads, 1920s.........**$32.00**

Necklace, 16", pearls, 1-strand, 8mm...........................**$375.00**

Necklace, 16", rose quartz beads & 2 cultured pearls, sm heart-shaped pendant......................................**$35.00**

Necklace, 16½", Miriam Haskell, lg pearl & clear plastic crystals..**$95.00**

Necklace, 17", black & crystal beads, 6 strands w/drop, 1920s...**$40.00**

Necklace, 22", 2mm wide, 14k gold solid rope **$300.00**

Necklace, 26", brass rope chain w/alternating carnelian glass, cut crystal & brass beads...............................**$55.00**

Necklace, 30", 14k yellow gold beveled-edge herringbone chain **$225.00**

Necklace, 54", can-shaped wooden beads in green & natural tones **$15.00**

Necklace, 6 cut glass beads on sterling 8" chain **$45.00**

Necklace, 9", carved yellow Bakelite rose (1¼" dia) on white metal chain..**$22.50**

Pendant, 1¾", sterling cat, hallmarked, heavy **$85.00**

Pendant, 1¾" dia, sterling, Nouveau openwork w/paisley-type swirl design..**$45.00**

Pendant, ¾", yellow agate glass heart **$15.00**

Pendant, ¾x1¼", cloisonne leaves w/green cabochon stone in brass frame..**$30.00**

Pin, BSK, gold-tone macaw w/faux rubies, 1950s **$30.00**

Pin, Cadoro, gold-tone double bow, 1955 ....**$15.00**

Pin, carved plastic scottie w/rhinestone eyes on square plastic mounting, ca 1930 ....**$95.00**

Pin, Coro, gold-tone flower w/rhinestones, 1960-65 ...**$35.00**

Pin, Emmons, gold-plated crown shape w/multicolor simulated cabochons & rhinestones, ca 1960 ....**$35.00**

Pin, Emmons, gold-tone metal w/aurora borealis stones forming star w/cultured pearl center, 1950s.........**$30.00**

Pin, Lang, sterling ballerina...**$28.00**

Pin, lg, sterling cat & kittens **$26.00**

Pin, lg, Vendome, antiqued copper lustre, prong-set multicolor cut stones, japanned center mount, 1950s **$125.00**

Pin, Marvella, gold-plated fan w/alternating engraved & simulated jade spokes, 1955 ....**$110.00**

Pin, Park Lane, prancing horse, 2-tone florentine & brushed antique finish w/gold-tone accents, 1950-60.........**$35.00**

Pin, Sarah Coventry, stylized flower w/rhinestones & prong-set amber glass, 1950......................................**$85.00**

Pin, sterling kangaroo w/baby in pouch......................**$22.00**

Pin, Trifari, gold-plated dragonfly w/yellow enameling.**$45.00**

Pin, Trifari, gold-plated leaves w/green enameling among cultured pearls, 1965.......................................**$65.00**

Pin, Trifari, leaf, finely cut baguette & pave rhinestones, 1960s...**$55.00**

Pin, Trifari, rhodium fleur-de-lis w/cultured pearls **$75.00**

Pin, Trifari, sterling vermeil elephant, rhinestone accents, 1940s...**$90.00**

Pin, Weiss, gold-plated heart set w/tiny faux rubies ...**$35.00**

Pin, 1½", Beau, sterling horseshoe w/horse's head **$20.00**

Pin, 1½", black Bakelite flying bird, wings trimmed in clear rhinestones...**$25.00**

Pin, 1½", crossed golf clubs w/in twist circle, cultured pearl ball...**$25.00**

Pin, 1½", Danecraft, sterling thistle in open circle.......**$55.00**

Pin, 1½", sterling penguin...**$30.00**

Pin, 1½", Weiss, pink aurora borealis w/lg round marquis in center, 2 matching center drops **$32.00**

Pin, 1½" wide, yellow, red & purple enamel butterfly.**$15.00**

Pin, 1¼x1¼", gold-plated American eagle, EX details .**$25.00**

Pin, 1¾", Capri, gold-tone crescent w/lg & sm green stone cabochons **$15.00**

Pin, 1¾", gold-tone metal w/white glass scottie, multicolor rhinestones...**$27.50**

Pin, 1¾", rhinestone-set windmill, blue w/clear accents, movable arms...**$22.50**

Pin, 1¾", Weisner, gold-plated pleated circle w/rhinestones & baroque pearl center.....................................**$40.00**

Pin, 1¾" dia, Krementz, silverplate, rhinestone flowers .**$20.00**

Pin, 1⅝", Otis, bow w/white stones.............................**$35.00**

Pin, 2", Beau, sterling sea gull....................................**$22.00**

Pin, 2", Beau, sterling stylized horse, Art Moderne.....**$40.00**

Pin, 2", tan & black Bakelite sunflower, black dangles.**$25.00**

Pin, 2", cameo, black on clear Bakelite **$22.00**

Pin, 2", gold wire-work pineapple w/turquoise stones **$22.00**

Pin, 2", gold-plated pearl cat w/red rhinestone eyes...**$15.00**

Pin, 2", gold-plated lovebirds, double hearts locket hangs below **$22.50**

Pin, 2", lady w/umbrella, allover rhinestones of clear & blue w/blue baguette rhinestone accents on skirt **$32.00**

Pin, 2", Trifari, white enamel kite w/tail dangle **$18.00**

Pin, 2½", Avante, silverplated cluster of filigree leaves w/lg marquise rhinestone center **$28.00**

Pin, 2½", diamond shape, unfoiled purple marquise stones, blue center & accents **$32.00**

Pin, 2½", Kim, matt-finished copper stylized cat w/pierced eyes...**$18.00**

Pin, 2½", sterling flower **$16.00**

Pin, 2½x1¼", gold filled, hanging drops w/3 real pearls, Nouveau style **$130.00**

Pin, 2¼", Lang, sterling lamppost................................**$10.00**

Pin, 2¼", Mexican silver flamingo w/turquoise eye.....**$40.00**

Pin, 2¼x1½", copper poodle..**$12.00**

Pin, 2¼x1¾", brass, Nouveau flowers & ribbons, center stone **$50.00**

Pin, 3", wooden leaf w/3 wooden acorn dangles........**$18.00**

Pin, 3¼x2", brass, pink stones in center, 3 hanging brass leaves **$35.00**

Pin, 4", rhinestones (pasted in), very heavy, unmarked, 1930s...**$65.00**

Pin, ⅞" dia, 10k gold circle w/crisscrosses, ca 1910s ..**$45.00**

Pin & earrings, Sarah Coventry, rhodium snowflakes, smokey faceted glass w/rhinestones, 1960s..........**$65.00**

Ring, sterling, marcasites & Swiss lapis (dyed jasper), Deco style, ca 1925..**$185.00**

Ring, sterling, marquise-cut black onyx surrounded by marcasites in openwork design.................................**$65.00**

Ring, sterling, marquise-cut synthetic pink tourmaline surrounded by marcasites.................................**$60.00**

Ring, white gold, European diamond (.56 ct) & 7 square-cut simulated sapphires **$350.00**

Ring, yellow gold, claw-set ruby doublet, 1900s.......**$125.00**

Ring, 10k white gold filigree, sm solitaire diamond in engraved square mounting................................**$120.00**

Ring, 10k yellow gold filigree, sm ruby **$125.00**

Ring, 14k rose gold, oval amethyst 20x14mm, cut-out design on sides, ca 1940s.................................**$165.00**

Ring, 14k white gold, square emerald w/round emerald each side, Deco styling...**$145.00**

Ring, 14k white gold, tiered cluster w/12 rubies & 7 sm diamonds..**$300.00**

Ring, 14k white gold filigree, sm diamond **$125.00**

Ring, 14k yellow gold, ½ carat oval ruby w/6 sm diamonds each side **$250.00**

Ring, 14k yellow gold filigree mounting, 5 graduated marquise blue topaz......................................**$85.00**

Ring, ¾" front, red-orange Bakelite, carved leaves......**$30.00**

Scarf pin, Trifari, gold-tone metal feather, 1960..........**$15.00**

Tie tack, 14k yellow gold front, sm European-cut diamond, white metal backing & stud w/chain rod..............**$35.00**

Tie tack, 14k yellow gold w/6mm cultured pearl........**$35.00**

Watch pendant, Charlo, Swiss made, lady's portrait in filigree frame, seed pearl trim, hanging tassel, 12" chain, working **$50.00**

Jukeboxes

Because so many suppliers are now going to CD players, right now the market is full of jukeboxes from the past twenty-five years that you can usually buy very inexpensively. One as recent as these in good working order should cost you no more than $500.00. Look for one that has a little personality (some from the early seventies are fairly 'funky'), and if you're buying it for your own use and particularly enjoy hearing the 'oldies,' you'll find it to be one of the best investments you've ever made. Look in the Yellow Pages under 'Amusements' or 'Arcade Machines' to locate a supplier in your area.

The older models are another story. They've been appreciated by collectors for a long time, as their prices indicate. The forties was an era of stiff competition among jukebox manufacturers, and as a result many beautiful models were produced. Wurlitzer's 1015 with the bubble tubes (see our listings) is one of the most famous and desirable models ever made. It's being made again today as the 'One More Time.'

Buying a completely restored vintage jukebox will be an expensive move. You're not only paying for parts that are sometimes hard to find but hours upon hours of hard work and professional services involved in refinishing the chrome and paint.

There are several books on the market that offer more information; two that we'd recommend are: *A Blast from the Past! Jukeboxes* by Scott Wood and *An American Premium Guide to Jukeboxes and Slot Machines* by Jerry Ayliffe.

AMI #J200, EX orig.................................**$1,000.00**
Rockola #F-80, EX original.....................**$1,750.00**
Rockola Rocket, EX original....................**$750.00**
Seeburg #VL-200, fully restored..............**$5,800.00**
Seeburg #147 Blond Trashcan, EX original..............**$750.00**
Seeburg A, plays 45s, EX original.............**$850.00**
Seeburg B, restored................................**$2,750.00**
Seeburg Electra Discotheque, EX original.................**$950.00**
Seeburg G, EX original............................**$1,550.00**

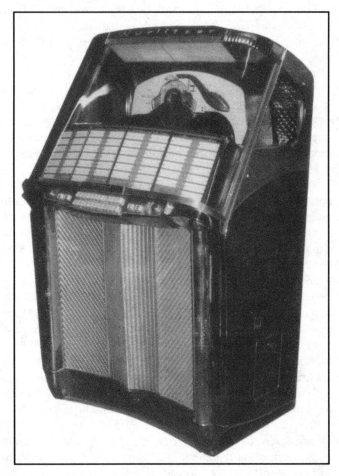

Wurlitzer #1900, 1956, EX **$3,500.00**
Wurlitzer #2000, 1956, EX original **$5,000.00**
Wurlizter, #1650, EX original **$750.00**
Wurlizter #2150, EX original **$1,650.00**
Wurlizter #3800, EX original **$750.00**

Keen Kutter

The E.C. Simmons Company used 'Keen Kutter' as a tradename on an extensive line of tools, knives, and other hardware items made by them from about 1870 until the mid-'30s. The older items are especially collectible, so is advertising material such as catalogs, calendars, and wooden packing boxes.

For more information, we recommend *Keen Kutter*, an illustrated guide by Elaine and Jerry Heuring. See also Knives.

Alligator wrench, KK #40, EX..........$60.00
Auger bit set, KK, 13-piece $132.00
Auger bit set, KK #16, 9-piece, complete..........$115.00
Axe, broad; KK #67..........$78.00
Axe, camp; KK #30 ....$35.00
Axe, freighter's, KK #88 ....$35.00
Brace, bit; KK #110, 10"..........$27.50
Brace, bit; KK #112, 12"..........$28.00
Brace, corner; KK #500..........$110.00
Brace, KK #18, 8" sweep $30.00
Cabinet scraper, KK #212, 6¼"..........$55.00
Can opener..........$28.00
Cold chisel, KK #10, 1", EX..........$12.50
Compass, 8"..........$22.50
Drill, 10½", KK #4, hand type $45.00
Drill, 13½", KK #5, hand type $45.00
Firmer chisel set, KK #8, 8-piece, complete..........$165.00
Garden trowel, KK #2, socket pattern w/bent neck....$15.00
Gauge, shingle; KK #5 ....$28.00
Grinder, meat; KK #112, sliding base & thumbscrew..$35.00
Hammer, brick; KK #15, 24-oz, EX..........$42.50
Hammer, machinist's, 32-oz $28.00
Hammer, nail; KK #11, 20-oz $30.00
Hammer, nail; KK #412, 13-oz $27.50
Hammer, riveting; 4-oz..........$48.00
Hatchet, flooring $32.50
Hatchet, lathing $32.50
Hatchet, rig builder's..........$32.50
Hatchet, shingling; KK #1, EX..........$28.50
Horse clippers, KK #920, EX..........$18.00
Knife, pruning; KK #105, 4⅜", cocobolo handle..........$35.00
Level, KK #104, 12", wooden..........$40.00
Level, KK #13, 12" or 18", non-adjustable, brass plate ..$45.00
Level, KK #30, 30", wooden..........$35.00
Level, KK #624, iron, 24", EX..........$95.00
Mallet, KK #306, EX..........$125.00
Monkey wrench, KK #15..........$45.00
Monkey wrench, KK #6, 6", M..........$55.00
Nail apron..........$70.00
Nippers, cutting; KK #6 ....$32.00
Pinchers, carpenter's, any style $18.00
Plane, block; KK #103, 5½"..........$30.00
Plane, block; KK #17, 7"..........$35.00
Plane, combination; KK #64, 21 cutters, NM..........$350.00
Plane, jack; KK #27, 15", EX..........$45.00
Plane, jointer; KK #8, iron, smooth bottom..........$75.00
Plane, milliner's, KK #51..........$27.50
Plane, rabbet; 13", KK #10 ....$210.00
Plane, smooth; KK #4C, 9"..........$35.00
Pliers, channel lock; KK #507, 5½", EX $40.00
Pliers, lineman's, KK #966..........$28.00
Pliers, long nose, KK #66 ....$30.00
Plumb bob..........$60.00
Pocketknife, KK #882 ....$47.50
Post drill, KK #1902, EX $120.00
Reamer, KK #126, EX..........$12.50
Reamer bit, KK #117 ....$18.00
Rule, KK #312, 12", steel $28.00

Saw, compass; KK #93, M $22.00
Saw, crosscut; KK #2005, VG $40.00
Saw, hand; KK #88, EX..........$22.50

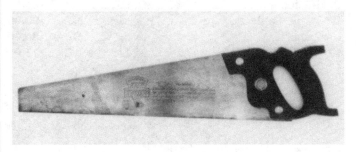

Saw, metal cutting; #K106, 15 teeth per inch $100.00
Saw set, KK #10, VG..........$15.00
Saw set, KK #195, EX..........$27.50
Scissors, 8"..........$20.00
Screwdriver, KK #50, 8" blade, EX..........$17.50
Screwdriver bit, KK #102..........$18.00

Sign, 30x30", metal, white w/blue outlines, red & white emblem..........$125.00
Spoke shave, KK #95..........$30.00
Square, carpenter's, 34"..........$30.00
Square, combination; KK #120, 12" $48.00
Square, takedown; 24"..........$95.00
Square, try; KK #228, 8"..........$30.00
Staple puller, KK #700, EX..........$20.00
Tack puller, KK #5..........$15.00
Tin snips, KK #7, EX..........$27.50
Watch fob (reproduction $10.00), original..........$125.00
Wrench, double end; KK #23..........$22.50

Kentucky Derby Glasses

Since the 1940s, every running of the Kentucky Derby has been commemorated with a drinking glass. Race fans have begun to collect them, and now some of the earlier glasses are worth several hundred dollars.

1940s, aluminum	$165.00
1940s, plastic Beetleware	$300.00
1945, short	$400.00
1945, tall	$175.00

1948	**$65.00**
1950	$175.00
1951	$150.00
1952, Gold Cup	$65.00
1953	$50.00
1954	$45.00
1955	$40.00
1956	$40.00
1957	$35.00
1958, Gold Bar	$45.00
1958, Iron Liege	$50.00
1959	$30.00
1960	$30.00
1961	$25.00
1962-65, each	$22.00
1966	$18.00
1967-68, each	$16.00
1969	$15.00
1970-72, each	$12.00
1973	$10.00
1974	$8.00
1975	$7.00
1976	$6.00
1977-80, each	$5.00

1979	**$5.00**
1981-82, each	$4.00
1983-88, each	$3.00
1989-93, each	$2.00

King's Crown Thumbprint Line

Back in the late 1800s, this pattern was called Thumbprint. It was made by the U.S. Glass Company and by Tiffin, one of the companies who were a part of that conglomerate, through the 1940s. U.S. Glass closed in the late '50s, but Tiffin reopened in 1963 and produced this line again. Indiana Glass bought the molds, made some minor changes, and during the 1970s they made this line. Confusing? To say the least. Gene Florence's *Collectible Glassware of the 40s, 50s, and 60s* explains that originally the thumbprints were oval, but at some point Indiana changed theirs to circles. And Tiffin's tumblers were flared at the top, while Indiana's were straight. Our values are for the later issues of both companies.

Bowl, 3x12½"	$35.00
Bowl, 4", mayonnaise	$15.00
Bowl, 9¼", salad	$45.00
Bud vase, 9"	$25.00
Candle holder, 5½", 2-light	$25.00
Cup & saucer	$15.00

Plate, 10", dinner	**$30.00**
Plate, 9¾", snack, w/indent	$15.00
Punch cup	$8.00
Stem, 4-oz, claret	$12.00
Stem, 9-oz, water goblet	$12.00
Tumbler, 11-oz, iced tea	$15.00
Tumbler, 4-oz, juice, footed	$10.00

Kitchen Appliances

If you've never paid much attention to old kitchen appliances, now is the time to do just that. Check in Grandma's basement – or your mother's kitchen cabinets, for that matter. As styles in home decorating changed, so did the styles of appliances. Some have wonderful Art Deco lines, while others border on the primitive.

Most of those you'll find will still work, and with a thorough cleaning you'll be able to restore them to their original 'like-new' appearance. Missing parts may be impossible to replace, but if it's just the cord that's gone, you can usually find what you need at any hardware store.

Even larger appliances are collectible and are often used to add the finishing touch to a period kitchen.

Baby food warmer, Triangle Lektrick, American Electrical Heater Co, pitcher-like form on heated base **$85.00**
Beater jar, Chicago Electric, jadite bottom **$30.00**
Blender, Knapp Monarch Liquidizer, Art Deco style, 1940s, EX...**$45.00**
Bottle warmer, 12¼", Sunbeam, chrome, ca 1950s....**$235.00**
Broiler, Broil Maid, chromium w/Bakelite handles, 12" dia, EX...**$50.00**
Coffee urn, 12", Manning-Bowman, Bakelite & chrome..**$185.00**
Egg cooker, Hankscraft #599, ceramic w/dome-shaped chrome lid, 1930s..**$42.50**
Fan, Diehl, oscillating, cast iron base, 1930s...............**$50.00**
Fudge sauce warmer, Johnston's, 1920s.....................**$42.50**
Hot plate, Sampson #3345N, Deco style **$18.00**
Iron, Coleman #2, 7½", gas burner, worn nickel, worn paint on handle **$38.00**
Iron, Peerless, fuel burner, red tank on face...............**$75.00**
Iron, Proctor Never-Lift, 9¼", uncommon center prong w/handle release, Deco styling............................**$185.00**
Iron, Sun Manufacturing Co, 7", cylindrical tank, nickel finish w/light wear, EX **$150.00**
Mixer, Dormeyer Mfg, Chicago IL, Pat 1932, on/off knob, 2 beaters **$40.00**
Mixer, Gilbert Polar Cub, 10", gray painted metal, EX ..**$60.00**
Mixer, Sunbeam Mixmaster, white w/black handle & dial, 1930s..**$85.00**
Oven, Griswold Kwik-Bake, portable............................**$90.00**
Popcorn popper, Fire-King, chrome, w/glass lid.........**$35.00**
Teapot, Landers Universal #E-975, EX..........................**$30.00**
Toaster, Delta, chrome & black enamel on steel, 3-slice, ca 1935 ....**$80.00**

Toaster, Electrex, nickel plated w/blue wood knobs, ca 1927, EX..$100.00
Toaster, Knapp Monarch #21-501, chrome, Bakelite handles, 1930s..**$22.50**

Toaster, Universal Double-Quick, chromium & black metal w/Bakelite knob, end loading, 1935.....................**$40.00**
Toaster, Universal E-944, flip-down sides, black Bakelite handles **$55.00**
Toaster/hot plate combination, Breakfaster, Calkins #T-2, 1930s..**$45.00**
Waffle iron, Empress, Fitzgerald Mfg Co Torrington CT, 1928, electric, all original, EX.................................**$75.00**
Waffle iron, Sampson United, chrome w/green handles, EX **$35.00**
Waffle iron, Westinghouse, #WD-4.............................**$35.00**

Kitchen Gadgets

Whether you're buying them to use or to decorate with, you'll find good examples just about anywhere you go at prices that won't wreck your budget. During the 19th century, cast iron apple peelers, cherry pitters, and food choppers were patented by the hundreds, and because they're practically indestructible, they're still around today. Unless parts are missing, they're still usable and most are very efficient at the task they were designed to perform.

A collection of egg beaters can be very interesting, and you'll find specialized gadgets for chores no one today would even dream of doing. Some will probably leave you in doubt as to their intended use.

If this area of collecting interests you, you'll enjoy *300 Years of Kitchen Collectibles* by Linda Campbell and *Kitchen Antiques, 1790-1940,* by Kathryn McNerney.

Apple corer, A&P Eng Co, stainless steel, green wooden handle **$6.50**
Apple corer, tin, T-bar handle....................................**$17.50**
Apple corer/peeler, Morton Salt advertising **$12.00**
Apple peeler, Lockey & Howland, cast iron, patent dated 1856 ....**$65.00**
Apple peeler, Renwal #296, cast iron, Pat'd 1889......**$200.00**
Apple peeler, Sinclair Scott, cast iron, 8-gear.............**$70.00**
Apple peeler, The Union, cast iron, multiple gears, clamp-on style **$85.00**
Apple peeler, White Mountain, cast iron, EX...............**$45.00**
Baster, glass tube w/blue rubber squeeze ball **$4.00**
Bean slicer, cast iron, green wooden crank handle, clamp-on type, Germany...**$60.00**
Bean slicer, 6½", dark japanning on cast iron, clamp-on style, EX...**$55.00**
Butter paddle, NUCO stamped on blade, 8½", 3" wide blade w/curved handle..**$12.50**
Can opener, Jewel..**$5.00**
Can opener, Pet Milk, tin, round **$15.00**
Can opener, tan & brown, marbleized Catalin handle ..**$8.00**
Cheese slicer, Cut-Rite #300, Wagner Ware, aluminum ...**$37.50**
Cherry seeder, New Standard #50, Mt Joy PA, 1870s..**$45.00**
Cherry seeder, Scott, cast iron, 3-legged **$65.00**
Chopper, Dandy, 7½", 4-way knife assembly, Patent Pending...**$12.00**
Chopper, food; Everbright, 1-blade, cast iron handle....**$5.00**

Chopper, food; Franklin, 1-blade, iron handle **$8.00**

Chopper, food; wrought iron 2x8½" blade w/rounded bottom, wooden handle....................**$55.00**

Churn, Anchor Hocking, 2-qt....................**$85.00**

Churn, Elgin, label on glass base, metal lid, wooden paddles, VG....................**$45.00**

Churn, 1-qt, glass, unmarked....................**$210.00**

Churn, 14x12¼" dia, JP Lynott's Patent Triumph Churn, can-shaped tin, 1912....................**$125.00**

Churn, 19½x8½" dia, dark gray tin w/original wooden dasher, VG....................**$225.00**

Clam lifter, twisted wire, spring action w/long handle, net for draining....................**$27.50**

Coffee grinder, A Kendrick & Sons, cast iron, box type, brass hopper....................**$85.00**

Coffee grinder, Arcade #40, cast iron & glass canister .**$85.00**

Coffee grinder, Chicago Double Grinder #60, wood & cast iron, box type, EX....................**$98.00**

Coffee grinder, French style, wood w/ornate cast iron top, raised hopper **$50.00**

Coffee grinder, Landers, Frary & Clark, cast iron & tin, Pat 1905, canister type, VG....................**$70.00**

Coffee grinder, New Model, cast iron w/cast iron drawer, bottom opens on all 4 sides, lap type **$75.00**

Coffee grinder, tin, covered, grind caught in cup underneath, lap type **$55.00**

Coffee grinder, Universal #109, black tin w/green decal, Pat 1905, EX....................**$65.00**

Coffee grinder, 4x4x4", cast iron lap type, octagon base & hopper, cup in base....................**$95.00**

Coffee measure, Dix Coffee Meter, tin can shape **$38.00**

Cookie roller/meat tenderizer, 10" long, maple..........**$50.00**

Cream whip, Fries, 9½", galvanized tin.................$75.00

Cucumber slicer, 9⅝", The Patent Slicer, cast iron, clamp-on type, 1920s-30s....................**$80.00**

Cutter, biscuit; tin, scalloped, green painted wooden handle, 1930s **$6.00**

Cutter, cabbage; Brady, 1 steel blade adjusts, cast iron handle....................**$110.00**

Cutter, doughnut; 2⅞" dia, dark gray tin, smithy made, hand soldered, flat top w/strap handle....................**$18.00**

Cutting board, pine, 15½x9¼"....................**$45.00**

Dish drainer, 4x14x8", wavy wire, 6 sm feet, EX........**$24.00**

Doughnut cutter, wooden, VG **$110.00**

Egg basket, twisted wire, footed, looped top, 10" dia..**$55.00**

Egg beater, AJ Spinnit, Super Center Drive, EX..........**$10.00**

Egg beater, Cyclone, cast iron, 1901....................**$35.00**

Egg beater, Dover, narrow wavy blades at bottom (also called tumbler or drink mixer), dated 1903...........**$48.00**

Egg beater, Handy Andy Auto Cream, EX....................**$50.00**

Egg beater, sm, Baby Bingo....................**$15.00**

Egg beater, Taplin, cast iron, 1908....................**$35.00**

Egg beater, 12", Ram Beater Patent, metal & wire.......**$40.00**

Egg poacher, 3x10¼", Buffalo Steamer-Poacher, tin skillet shape w/5 cups inside....................**$50.00**

Egg separator, T&S Flour....................**$12.50**

Egg slicer, Bloomfield Industries, 4x4", Chicago, aluminum, 1935 ....**$38.00**

Egg whisk, 9", tinned wire, diamond design, 1930s **$8.00**

Food press, Starret's #1, 9½x6½", cast & sheet iron ..**$110.00**

Fruit press, Griswold, 4-qt, cast iron....................**$85.00**

Grater, All in One, Pat Pending, 10½", stainless steel....**$4.00**

Grater, cheese; pine w/gray punched tin front, drawer catches cheese, handle w/hanging hole **$175.00**

Grater, Lorraine Metal Mfg, 8½", revolving type, cast iron, EX green paint **$30.00**

Grater, Norlund Corn, 12", 2 metal-toothed blades, wooden frame....................**$15.00**

Grater, nutmeg; Gilmore, punctured tin....................**$15.00**

Grater, nutmeg; Made in France **$15.00**

Grater, nutmeg; 7¾", turned wood w/brass trim, EX..**$195.00**

Grater, 10½", Ekco, tin & wire **$14.00**

Grinder, food; Enterprise #4....................**$28.00**

Grinder, food; Foley, red handle **$12.50**

Grinder, food; Rollman #11, sm....................**$55.00**

Grinder, spice; black cast iron, wall mount, ca 1890...**$38.00**

Ice cream freezer, Alaska, 9", Made in USA, 1-qt **$65.00**

Ice crusher, Dazey, chrome & black, standing style....**$20.00**

Ice cube breaker, Dandy....................**$10.00**

Ice pick, steel, metal ferrule, square wooden handle....**$5.00**

Ice tongs, 13", hand-wrought iron, double hinged, EX ...**$30.00**

Jar lifter, wooden clothespin type....................**$15.00**

Juicer, Handy Andy, reamer on stand, crank handle...**$30.00**

Juicer, Juice-O-Mat, chrome top & handle, red base...**$16.00**

Juicer, Universal, 10", stamped cast iron & aluminum, side crank....................**$24.00**

Knife, bread; Rumford, green wooden handle **$17.50**

Lemon squeezer, cast iron w/ironstone ball & cup, dated Apr 7, 1868....................**$55.00**

Lemon squeezer, Pearl, cast iron **$28.00**

Lifter, utility; Klever Klaw, 14", 1920s....................**$25.00**

Masher, cast iron w/flat lacy round mashing end........**$25.00**

Masher, 10½", single wire w/red wooden handle **$4.00**

Masher, 11½", 2 zigzag wire mashers, black wooden handle w/fulcrum action....................**$55.00**

Measuring cup, Rumford, tin...$30.00

Meat tenderizer, galvanized tin w/wooden handle, unmarked..$35.00

Meat tenderizer, glazed white ironstone w/turned wooden handle, 1890s...$75.00

Meat tenderizer, wooden mallet type, EX.................$15.00

Meat tenderizer, 7½", cast iron, hammer-like form w/grid, ca 1900..$32.00

Melon baller, 7¾", stainless steel w/red wooden handle, 1940s...$6.00

Noodle cutter, cast iron w/5 different cutters, 1930s...$50.00

Pastry blender, 9½", nickeled iron, green painted handle, ca 1900s..$18.00

Pastry sheet & rolling pin set, sheet: 22x18½", tin.....$475.00

Pea sheller, Acme, 7", galvanized cast iron, clamps on ...$85.00

Peach peeler, Sinclair Scott Co, Baltimore, cast iron $85.00

Pie crimper, Vaughn's, green Catalin handle, 1920s....$17.50

Pie crimper, 8½", wide brass wheel, steel stem, Bakelite handle..$25.00

Pie lifter, 2 wire prongs, wooden Shaker-style handle $40.00

Raisin seeder, Enterprise $55.00

Raisin seeder, Lightning, 7" long, cast iron, table clamp, ca 1895..$78.00

Rice baller, aluminum...$10.00

Ricer, cast iron & tin w/japanned handles..................$10.00

Rolling pin, metal center w/long oval cutouts, wooden handles...$40.00

Rolling pin, wooden, Munsing engraved on end.........$15.00

Rolling pin, 12x2¼" dia, springerle, wooden handles, 12 designs...$165.00

Rolling pin, 15½x2" dia, wooden, 1-piece..................$35.00

Rolling pin, 17", white ironstone, cobalt advertising, ca 1910s..$210.00

Rolling pin, 19½x3½" dia, wooden w/⅛" grooves all the way across, for noodle rolling, EX............................$48.00

Shredder/slaw cutter, Wonder Grater, 8½", 1930s.........$8.00

Sifter, flour; Androck Hand-i-Sift, 5½x5" dia, painted tin w/flowers, wooden squeeze handle, EX..............$60.00

Sifter, flour; Belmont, 7x5" dia, tin rotary type w/black wooden knob on handle................................$35.00

Sifter, flour; Blood's Pat Sept 17, 1861, wooden, EX.$295.00

Sifter, flour; Calumet Baking Powder, 2-cup, tin, EX..$15.00

Sifter, flour; Duplex, double ended, w/lids, EX...........$40.00

Sifter, flour; Kno-Bugs, tin can shape, tall strap handle, w/label & instructions, EX.................................$25.00

Sifter, flour; 1-cup, rotary type w/metal handle & green wooden knob, EX..$8.00

Skimmer, 8" dia, punched tin w/wide round strap handle on side..$48.00

Spice box, Kreamer, tin, oblong w/5 sm containers inside, EX..$75.00

Strainer, fine wire, bowl shaped, for teapot spout......$25.00

Tea strainer, Tetley tea, silverplate, side handle..........$20.00

Teakettle, Revere copper, 5-qt....................................$55.00

Tongs, meat; cast iron, 15", ca 1900..........................$25.00

Waffle iron, Shapleigh #8, cast iron...........................$30.00

Kitchen Glassware

Though there's still lots of this type of glassware around, some harder-to-find items and pieces in the more desirable colors and types of glass often bring unbelievably high prices. We've listed a cross section of values here, but you'll really need to study a good book before you decide to invest. One of the best is *Kitchen Glassware of the Depression Years* by authority Gene Florence.

See also Fry; Jadeite Glassware; Fire King Ovenware; Glass Knives; Reamers; Peach Lustre Glassware.

Batter jug, black opaque w/chrome holder, handle & lid, McKee..$65.00

Batter jug, dark amber, tall & square w/slightly bowed sides, etched band in middle, w/lid, Paden City...........$45.00

Bowl, batter; transparent yellow, plain, w/slick side handle, pour spout, footed, US Glass Co........................$35.00

Bowl, batter; white opaque w/peach & grape design, pour spout & handle, Fire-King, Anchor Hocking.........$15.00

Bowl, batter; yellow opaque, vertically ridged w/flat bottom, pour spout & handle................................$75.00

Bowl, beater; Delphite blue, high sides, w/beater......$50.00

Bowl, beater; 4½" tall, Chalaine blue.........................$45.00

Bowl, mixing; 10" dia, 5-pt, transparent green, vertical panels, pour spout, tab handles, Tufglas, JE Marsden........$40.00

Bowl, mixing; 11½" dia, transparent green round shape w/paneled design on square base, rolled rim, Anchor Hocking..$20.00

Bowl, mixing; 7" dia, transparent green, plain w/rolled rim, short base $12.00

Bowl, mixing; 9" dia, Chalaine blue...........................$80.00

Bowl, mixing; 9" dia, Delphite blue, vertical panels on lower half, Jeannette Glass Co, late 1930s....................$35.00

Bowl, mixing; 9" dia, transparent pink, Hex Optic design w/flat rim..$22.00

Bowl, 10" dia, opaque white w/horizontal ribbing & 3 red rings, Anchor Hocking..**$20.00**

Bowl, 4½" dia, opaque yellow, rolled rim, McKee......**$12.00**

Bowl, 6" dia, dark amber, plain w/thick flat rim.........**$17.50**

Bowl, 7½" dia, Delphite blue, horizontal ribbing on lower part, raised rim band, flat bottom **$45.00**

Bowl, 9¼" dia, transparent blue, horizontal ribbing, cone shape w/flat bottom, rolled rim, LE Smith **$75.00**

Bowls, mixing; Jennyware, ultramarine, Jeannette Co, 3-piece set..$120.00

Butter dish, opaque green, rectangular, high lid w/short vertical hash marks, inverted stair-step base.............**$65.00**

Butter dish, opaque yellow rectangular shape, tab handled base, tall lid w/ribbed design.................................**$65.00**

Butter dish, 1-lb, amber, rectangular w/ribbed design, tab handles, Federal Glass Company..........................**$30.00**

Butter dish, 1-lb, red dots on white, rectangular w/tab handles, McKee, late 1930s-early 1940s.....................**$40.00**

Butter dish, 1-lb, transparent green, Butter Cover embossed on lid, Bottom embossed on tab-handled base.....**$40.00**

Butter dish, 2-lb, transparent green, rectangular, flat lid w/circular design in center, tab handles.............**$150.00**

Cake plate, transparent pink w/snowflake design **$20.00**

Canister, cereal; 48-oz, white square shape w/horizontal black lettering, metal lid, flat bottom, McKee.......**$45.00**

Canister, clear w/painted-on tulip design, cylindrical, knob lid, flat bottom..**$15.00**

Canister, coffee; 40-oz, frosted crystal, square w/diagonal ribbing, Coffee lettered on silver label, metal lid...**$15.00**

Canister, crystal, square w/vertically ribbed corners, Dutch boy decal, pink lid, flat bottom..........................**$20.00**

Canister, flour; 128-oz, crystal, ball shaped w/wide vertical ribbing, metal lid, flat bottom **$35.00**

Canister, sugar; caramel, tall w/4 flat panels rounded at corners, horizontal black lettering, black lid............**$100.00**

Canister, sugar; crystal w/vertical ribs on ovoid, letters on vertical black strip, black lid, Owens-Illinois........**$20.00**

Canister, sugar; crystal, square shape w/fired-on blue checkerboard design & lettering, black lid............**$20.00**

Canister, tea; 20-oz, transparent peacock blue, raised ring around middle, paneled design, metal lid...........**$110.00**

Canister cereal; 5" square, 29-oz, Delphite blue, flat lid, Jeannette Glass Co, late 1930s **$125.00**

Casserole, clambroth white, oval w/lid, Pyrex..........**$125.00**

Casserole, dark amber, dome lid w/open triangular finial, flat rim, Cambridge **$25.00**

Coaster, transparent cobalt blue....................................**$7.50**

Container, transparent green, rectangular shape w/Orasorb embossed on side, metal lid hinged in center **$75.00**

Cookie jar, black w/rings at top & bottom, tab handles, LE Smith...**$60.00**

Creamer & sugar bowl w/plate, transparent green stack set, ear-shaped handles...**$50.00**

Cruet, transparent green, 4 triangular sides, w/stopper...**$85.00**

Cruet, transparent pink, bulbous w/flat bottom, tear-drop stopper, handled...**$30.00**

Custard or gelatine cup, cup shape w/rolled rim **$5.00**

Drip jar, Delphite blue, bowl shape w/horizontal ribbing on lower part, Drippings in black lettering, flat lid....**$65.00**

Drip jar, tulips on custard, round tapered shape w/flat bottom, dome lid w/knob, Fire-King.........................**$12.50**

Dripolator, crystal, 2-piece cylinder w/bottom having pour spout & handle, w/lid..................................**$12.50**

Egg cup, transparent yellow, footed, Hazel Atlas..........**$5.00**

Gelatine mold, transparent green, fluted, tapering toward base, Tufglas...**$15.00**

Horseradish jar, crystal, footed tulip shape w/scalloped rim, lid w/round knob...**$12.50**

Ice bucket, jade green, Fenton.............................$85.00

Ice bucket, light yellow, Fenton (illustrated)......$125.00

Jelly jar, amber, smooth cylinder, ribbed lid...............**$15.00**

Ladle, crystal, lg oval bowl w/short handle.................**$15.00**

Ladle, transparent green, long handle, deep round bowl w/pour spout..**$45.00**

Marmalade, transparent green, footed bowl form w/metal spoon & dome lid...**$25.00**

Measure, ½-cup, Delphite blue, pour spout & tab handle, flat bottom...**$37.50**

Measure, 2-cup, clambroth green, w/pour spout & handle, footed, Anchor Hocking.......................................**$100.00**

Measure, 2-cup, transparent pink, w/pour spout & handle, footed, Anchor Hocking...................................**$35.00**

Measure, 4-cup, Chalaine blue, w/pour spout & handle, footed **$200.00**

Measure, 4-cup, custard, w/pour spout & handle.......**$30.00**

Mug, clambroth green, footed cylinder shape **$30.00**

Mug, transparent cobalt blue, paneled, Cambridge.....**$50.00**

Mustard pot, swirl design of fired-on yellow w/red lid, spoon, Gemco...**$5.00**

Mustard pot, transparent cobalt blue, sm urn shape, w/lid, silver-look spoon & finial.....................................**$25.00**

Napkin holder, black, Party Line, Paden City **$135.00**

Pickle jar, transparent green barrel shape w/banded window pane design, wire & wood bail handle, black metal lid...**$100.00**

Pretzel jar, transparent pink, vertical panel design, Anchor Hocking **$55.00**

Refrigerator dish, transparent green, rectangular w/Vegetable Freshener embossed on lid, tab handles, Anchor Hocking **$125.00**

Refrigerator dish, 4½x5", transparent cobalt, flat lid....**$45.00**

Refrigerator dish, 4x4", transparent pink, vertical ribbing, vegetable embossed on lid (asparagus), Federal Glass Co..**$20.00**

Refrigerator dish, 4x5", Chalaine blue, w/lid **$50.00**

Refrigerator dish, 4x5", Delphite blue, w/flat lid **$25.00**

Refrigerator dish, 4x5", Skokie green (Jadite), McKee Glass Co..**$12.00**

Rolling pin, dark transparent amethyst.....................**$100.00**

Rolling pin, Kardov Flour Famous Self Rising etched in crystal, short knob handles.....................**$45.00**

Rolling pin, white w/wooden handles **$35.00**

Rolling pin, 13½", dark amber, blown.....................**$65.00**

Rolling pin, 18", clear w/tin handles, dated June 18, 1907, EX..**$55.00**

Salad set, spoon & fork; ribbed cobalt blue rod-like handles, clear spoon bowl & fork tines.....................**$45.00**

Salad set, spoon & fork; transparent peacock blue handles w/clear spoon bowl & fork tines.....................**$70.00**

Salt box, crystal, round w/vertical panel design, embossed letters, flat glass lid **$17.50**

Salt box, crystal, round w/vertical zipper design.........**$12.00**

Server, 9⅞" dia, clambroth white, shallow w/flat rim..**$18.00**

Shaker, flour; black, Flour lettered vertically in white, black metal lid.....................**$20.00**

Shaker, flour; opaque white w/3 concentric circles, red letters, flattened front & back, ribbed sides, Anchor Hocking.....................**$10.00**

Shaker, pepper; Delphite blue, square w/black lettering, metal lid.....................**$65.00**

Shaker, salt or pepper; fired-on orange w/black lettering, square w/arched panels, metal lid, McKee **$10.00**

Shaker, salt or pepper; transparent forest green, bulbous shape w/metal dome lid, flat bottom.....................**$9.00**

Shaker, salt or pepper; transparent green, tall square shape w/embossed decorative border around lettering, metal lid.....................**$35.00**

Shaker, salt; transparent ultramarine, footed tumbler shape w/metal lid, lettered paper label, Jennyware........**$22.00**

Shaker, salt; 4½", black, 4-sided, lettering on arched front panel, metal lid, McKee.....................**$15.00**

Shaker, spice; dark amber, 4-sided, ribbed arched panel, embossed lettering on smooth band, metal lid.....**$27.50**

Shaker, spice; crystal w/blue Dutch design, red metal lid.**$9.00**

Shaker, sugar; dark amber, paneled, metal cone top..**$135.00**

Shaker, sugar; fired-on red, chrome lid, Gemco..........**$22.50**

Shaker, sugar; transparent forest green, cylindrical w/band at rim & base, metal cone top, 1950s **$65.00**

Skillet, crystal, round w/glass handle, McKee Range Tec..**$9.00**

Spoon, salad; transparent yellow.....................**$35.00**

Syrup pitcher, black, w/lid, footed, Fenton **$50.00**

Syrup pitcher, crystal, cylindrical tankard shape w/glass top & pour spout, flared double-ring base **$25.00**

Teakettle, crystal, ball-shaped w/horizontal ribbing, flat bottom, glass handle w/red metal clamp, metal cap, Glasbake.....................**$20.00**

Toast rack, crystal, flared paneled base holds 6 slices, decorative center handle **$65.00**

Towel bar, transparent green rod w/metal end caps ..**$30.00**

Tray, dark amber, oval w/well & tree, wide flat rim, 6 ball feet, Fry.....................**$50.00**

Tray, 10⅝" long, clambroth white, rectangular shape w/raised sides, flat rim **$20.00**

Tumbler, clambroth green, footed.....................**$12.00**

Water bottle, 32-oz, crystal, crisscross design, round shouldered, metal lid.....................**$14.00**

Water bottle, 32-oz, transparent green, flat-sided w/vertical ribbing, round shoulders, metal lid **$20.00**

Water bottle, 64-oz, 10", transparent cobalt blue, flattened front & back, ribbed sides, rounded shoulders, metal cap **$60.00**

Water dispenser, opaque white, rectangular w/rounded corners, spigot, McKee **$110.00**

Water or vinegar bottle w/tray, transparent forest green, embossed checkerboard design on square shape, Owens-Illinois **$35.00**

Knives

Knives have been widely collected since the 1960s. The most desirable are those from before WWII, but many made since then have value as well. Don't try to clean or sharpen an old knife, collectors want them as found. Of course, mint unused knives are preferred, and any apparent use or damage greatly reduces their value. Our prices are for those in near mint to mint condition.

For more information, we recommend *Sargent's American Premium Guide to Knives and Razors, Identification and Values,* by Jim Sargent.

Case, #M100, 3¼", 1-blade, XX, all metal **$110.00**

Case, #M1218K, 3", 1-blade, Tested XX, metal handle, 1920-40 ....**$135.00**

Case, #S2LP, 2¼", 2-blade, XX, sterling handle..........**$125.00**

Case, #1101, 4", walnut hawkbill, 1-blade, USA **$38.00**

Case, #1116SP, 3½", bud walnut, 1-blade, USA, 1960s..**$32.00**

Case, #1116SP, 3½", 1-blade, 10 Dot, bud walnut handle, 1970 ....**$35.00**

Case, #1199SHRSS, 4⅛", 1-blade, 10 Dot, walnut handle, 1970 ....**$32.50**

Case, #2138, 5⅝", 1-blade, 10 Dot, black composition handle, 1970 ....**$25.00**

Case, #2217, 3⅞", 2-blade, Tested XX, slick black handle.....................**$260.00**

Case, #2220, 2¾", 2-blade, 10 Dot, slick black handle, 1970, NM **$45.00**

Case, #31048, 4⅛", 1-blade, XX, yellow composition handle, 1940-64 ....**$40.00**

Case, #32024½, 3", 2-blade, USA, yellow composition handle, 1965-69 ....**$35.00**

Case, #4200SS, 5½", citrus or melon tester, 2-blade, sm & lg stamps **$88.00**

Case, #4318HP, 3½", 3-blade, XX, white composition handle, NM **$75.00**

Case, #61011, 4", hawkbill, jigged wood handle, 1-blade, Case XX, 10-Dot **$30.00**

Case, #61048, 4⅛", 1-blade, Tested XX, green bone handle, NM **$160.00**

Case, #61048SSP, 4⅛", Delrin, 1-blade, 10 Dot, stainless, 1970 ....**$2,650.00**

Case, #61049, 4", 1-blade, Tested XX, green bone handle, 1920-40 ....**$320.00**

Case, #6106, 2⅝", 1-blade, Tested XX, green bone handle, 1920-40s **$315.00**

Case, #61093, 5", toothpick, 1-blade, 10 Dot, bone handle, 1970 ....**$88.00**

Case, #6143, 5", Daddy Barlow, 1-blade, USA, bone handle, 1965-69 ....**$40.00**

Case, #62009, 3¾", 2-blade, 10 Dot, bone stag handle, 1970, NM **$35.00**

Case, #62009½, 3¼", 2-blade, XX, red bone handle, 1940-64, NM **$55.00**

Case, #6201, 2⅝", 2-blade, 10 Dot, bone handle, 1970 ..**$32.00**

Case, #62042, 3", 2-blade, 10 Dot, bone handle, 1970 ..**$35.00**

Case, #6207, 3½", 2-blade, XX, rough black handle, 1940-50, NM **$180.00**

Case, #6217, 4", 2-blade, USA, wood handle, 1965-69 ..**$45.00**

Case, #6308, 3¼", 3-blade, XX, red bone handle, 1940-64, NM **$90.00**

Case, #7103SP, 3¼", Tested XX, tortoise handle **$360.00**

Case, 3⅞", Muskrat, 2-blade, USA, bone handle, 1965-69, NM **$50.00**

Keen Kutter, 3", dog-leg pen, 2-blade, black celluloid handle **$42.50**

Keen Kutter, 3½", jack, 2-blade, brown bone handle .**$45.00**

Keen Kutter, 3¾", EC Simmons, swell-end jack, 2-blade, brown bone handle **$78.00**

Keen Kutter, 3⅜", Diamond Edge, equal end jack, 2-blade, mingled brown & yellow celluloid handle **$40.00**

Primble, #4861, 3¾", Belknap, jack, 2-blade, bone handle, NM **$45.00**

Primble, #5380, 3¾", Belknap, stockman's, 3-blade, bone handle **$45.00**

Primble, #703, 3¼", Belknap, 3-blade, Rogers bone handle, NM **$35.00**

Primble, #903, 2⅞", Belknap, simulated peachseed handle, NM **$25.00**

Queen, #11, 4⅛", Queen Steel, 1-blade, winterbottom bone handle **$27.50**

Queen, #139, 3½", Barlow, 2-blade, brown bone handle, NM **$40.00**

Queen, #15, 3½", Congress, 2-blade, Rogers bone handle, NM **$40.00**

Queen, #20, 5", Queen Steel, Texas toothpick, 1-blade, bone handle **$88.00**

Queen, #2175, 3½", whittler, 3-blade, Rogers bone handle, NM **$35.00**

Queen, #24, trapper, 2-blade, steel handle **$35.00**

Queen, #3, 3¼", 2-blade, winterbottom bone handle..**$25.00**

Queen, #33, 3½", Congress, 4-blade, bone handle......**$42.50**

Queen, #36, 4½", lockback, 1-blade, winterbottom handle, NM **$60.00**

Queen, #4, 3⅜", sleeveboard, 2-blade, smoke pearl handle, NM **$75.00**

Queen, #48, 3½", Queen Steel, whittler, 3-blade, winterbottom bone handle **$48.00**

Queen, #5, 2½", Crown & Dots, 2-blade, Rogers bone handle **$40.00**

Queen, #5, 2½", Senator, 2-blade, winterbottom bone handle **$20.00**

Queen, #57, 3⅜", 3-blade, smoked pearl handle........**$75.00**

Queen, #62, 5⅜", Queen Steel, 1-blade, easy opener bone handle **$50.00**

Queen, #8150, 5¼", folding hunter, 2-blade, stag handle..**$55.00**

Queen, #8460, toothpick, 1-blade, green bone handle..**$50.00**

Remington, #RB041, 3⅜", 2-blade, brown bone handle..**$90.00**

Remington, #R1437, 1-blade, lockback, ivory handle....**$140.00**

Remington, #R2093, 3⅛", 2-blade, bone handle **$95.00**

Remington, #R2403, 4⅛", 1-blade, bone handle **$58.00**

Remington, #R31, 3¾", 2-blade, redwood handle........**$90.00**

Remington, #R3352, 3¾", 4-blade, black handle........**$175.00**

Remington, #R3485, 3⅜", equal end, 3-blade, metal handle, NM **$180.00**

Remington, #R3555, 4", stockman, 3-blade, mingled red scale handle **$260.00**

Remington, #R4053, 3⅝", 2-blade, bone handle........**$200.00**

Remington, #R6362, 3½", half whittler, 2-blade, black handle, NM **$130.00**

Remington, #R6573, 3½", sleeveboard, brown bone handle, tip bolsters, 2-blade **$125.00**

Remington, #R693, 4", gunstock, 2-blade, bone handle ..**$150.00**

Remington, #R698, 4", hawkbill, 1-blade, cocobolo handle, NM **$90.00**

Schrade Cutlery, #136, 5¼", lineman's, 1-blade, cocobolo handle **$28.00**

Schrade Cutlery, #151, 4", switchblade, mottled celluloid handle **$100.00**

Schrade Cutlery, #2064 W, 3⅝", 2-blade, ivory celluloid handle **$85.00**

Schrade Cutlery, #708, 2⅜", 2-blade, yellow composition handle **$40.00**

Schrade Cutlery, #7236, 2½", 2-blade, mother-of-pearl handle **$42.50**

Schrade Cutlery, #8564, 3⅜", 3-blade, Christmas tree handle, NM **$220.00**

Schrade Cutlery, #884, 4", 3-blade, stag handle **$135.00**

Winchester, #1922, 3⅜", folding hunter, 1-blade, stag handle, NM **$125.00**

Winchester, #1938, 3⅜", 1-blade, brown bone handle ..**$125.00**

Winchester, #2309, 3", Senator, 2-blade, pearl handle...**$120.00**

Winchester, #2603, 3⅜", jack, 2-blade, cocobolo handle..**$165.00**

Winchester, #2931, 3¼", jack, 2-blade, stag handle ...**$155.00**

Winchester, #3046, 3¼", whittler, 3-blade, celluloid handle, NM **$180.00**

Winchester, #4950, 3⅝", scout's, bone handle **$200.00**

Edwin M. Knowles

This was one of the major chinaware manufacturers that operated in the Newell, West Virginia, area during the first half of the century. You'll find their marks on a variety of wares.

One of their most popular and collectible lines is 'Fruits,' marketed under the tradename of Sequoia Ovenware through Montgomery Ward's in the 1930s. Its shapes are quaintly styled and decorated with decals of a red apple, a yellow pear, and some purple grapes. They made at least three of their own versions of the Mexican-style decaled ware that is so popular today and in the late thirties produced some dinnerware that is distinctly Art Deco.

For more information, we recommend *The Collector's Encyclopedia of American Dinnerware* by Jo Cunningham.

Bench, bowl, vegetable; 9" **$15.00**

Bench, platter, 12" **$18.00**

Border Rim, dish, sm **$3.00**

Fruits, batter pitcher, w/lid **$32.50**

Fruits, plate, serving; tab handles **$15.00**

Fruits, saucer **$3.00**

Fruits, syrup pitcher, w/lid (illustrated) **$27.50**

Fruits, utility plate, tab handles (illustrated) **$20.00**

Golden Wheat, meat platter **$10.00**

Leaf Spray, sugar bowl **$6.00**

Mini Flowers, salt & pepper shakers, on Deanna shape, pr **$18.00**

Pink Pastel, creamer...**$3.00**

Plaid, salt & pepper shakers, on Deanna shape, pr **$16.00**

Rose, plate, 9", on Deanna shape **$6.00**

Sleeping Mexican, plate, 6" **$4.00**

Sleeping Mexican, salt & pepper shakers, pr..............**$16.00**

Stripes, coffee server, on Deanna shape **$37.00**

Tia Juana, plate, serving; tab handles.........................**$20.00**

Tia Juana, refrigerator bowls, 3-piece stack set **$15.00**

Tulip Time, plate, utility; 12"......................................**$14.00**

Tulip Time, dish, sm **$4.00**

Tulip Time, meat platter **$10.00**

Wildflower, creamer..**$6.00**

Wildflower, saucer **$3.00**

Yellow Trim Poppy, plate, 8", on Deanna shape..........**$4.00**

Yorktown, coaster, white...**$8.00**

Yorktown, plate, chop; 10¾".......................................**$18.00**

L. E. Smith Glass

Originating just after the turn of the century, the L.E. Smith company continues to operate in Mt. Pleasant, Pennsylvania, at the present time. In the 1920s they introduced a line of black glass that they are famous for today. Some pieces were decorated with silver overlay or enameling. Using their own original molds, they made a line of bird and animal figures in crystal as well as in colors. The company is currently producing these figures, many in two sizes. They're one of the main producers of the popular Moon and Star pattern which has been featured in their catalogs since the 1960s in a variety of shapes and colors. (See also Moon and Star; Glass Animals.)

If you'd like to learn more about their bird and animal figures, *Glass Animals of the Depression Era* by Lee Garmon and Dick Spencer has a chapter devoted to those made by L.E. Smith. See also Eyewinker.

Bean pot, black w/silver decoration, lid doubles as center-handled tray **$45.00**

Bonbon, 7", Mt Pleasant (Double Shield), cobalt, rolled-up handles **$22.00**

Bowl, 7", #515, black, footed **$18.00**

Cake plate, 9½", Do-Si-Do, handled **$20.00**

Candlesticks, black, 2-light, pr **$40.00**

Candlesticks, Mt Pleasant (Double Shield), black, 1-light, pr...**$26.00**

Cookie jar, amber..**$55.00**

Cordial tray, #381, black..**$10.00**

Creamer & sugar bowl, black.....................................**$35.00**

Flowerpot, 3", black, ca 1930 ....**$12.00**

Plate, Mt Pleasant (Double Shield), black, 3-footed **$20.00**

Saucer, 6½", Mt Pleasant (Double Shield), black **$5.00**
Vase, 6", #49, black **$11.00**
Vase, 6½", #102-4, black **$10.00**
Vase, 7", #433, dancing girls, black **$18.00**
Vase, 7¼", #1900, black **$18.00**
Vase, 7¼", Mt Pleasant (Double Shield), amethyst **$30.00**
Vase, 8½", black amethyst, scalloped rim, footed **$40.00**

Labels

Each one a work of art in miniature, labels of all types appeal to collectors through their colorful lithography and imaginative choice of graphics representative of the product or the producer. Before cardboard boxes became so commonplace, wooden crates were used to transport everything from asparagus to yams. Cigar boxes were labeled both outside and in the lid. Tin cans had wonderful labels with Black children, lucious fruits and vegetables, animals, and birds. Some of the better examples are listed here. Many can be bought at much lower prices.

Can, Belgian Lion Malt Syrup, lions holding coat of arms, 1929 .... **$5.00**
Can, Blue Moon Coffee, smiling man in blue moon ... **$15.00**
Can, Caroga Can Syrup, Black waiter holds tray, 1940 .. **$30.00**
Can, Chevron Sauerkraut, 2 lg cabbages **$6.00**
Can, Defender Brand Tomatoes, sailing ship on white background **$5.00**
Can, Del Monte Beets, whole red beet & logo on green background, 1930s **$3.00**
Can, Delicious Pie Fruits, fox jumping over stream **$4.00**
Can, Della Rocca Cigars, bust of young woman w/gold flowing hair **$12.00**
Can, Easter Peaches, lilies & peaches, 1936 .... **$20.00**
Can, Electric Brand Succotash, black & white image of woman w/light **$4.50**
Can, Emery Apricots, apricots on branch **$7.50**
Can, Gold Bar Hominy, blue lettering & hominy in china dish on gold background **$2.00**
Can, Hawthorn Mixed Fruit, blossoms & vignette of mixed fruits on light blue background **$5.00**
Can, Hi-Gloss Auto Enamel, man paints old car, 1927 .. **$16.50**
Can, Kamo Bird Seed, mallard duck on water, 1923 ..... **$7.50**
Can, Libby's Hawaiian Pineapple **$2.00**
Can, Mayfield Tomatoes, bright red tomato & sunrise over field of flowers **$4.00**
Can, Mi-Boy Sweet Corn, smiling young boy **$3.00**
Can, Morning Star Salmon, ships on open sea **$8.00**
Can, Peacock Lima Beans, peacock & ornate design **$5.00**
Can, Pride of Sharon Green Beans, country scene & bowl of green beans **$3.00**
Can, Purity, embossed cupid in red heart **$4.00**
Can, Roth's Coffee, cup of coffee & flowers **$5.00**
Can, Rowley's Kidney Beans, embossed bowl & gold logo on blue background **$3.00**
Can, Royal Crest Malt Syrup, mountain peak **$4.00**
Can, Sea King Clams, bowl of clams on red & blue **$18.00**

Can, Seminola Cigars, Indian princess in native dress ... **$9.50**
Can, Today's Olives, repeating Deco-style graphic of olives on white background **$3.00**
Cigar box, inner lid; American Kid, 6x9", Indian girl .. **$10.00**
Cigar box, inner lid; Calsetta, 6x9", renaissance lady, gold coins in border **$2.00**
Cigar box, inner lid; Dick Custer, 6x9", cowboy w/pistol, Holds You Up **$8.00**
Cigar box, inner lid; El Tolna, 6x9", woman wearing red dress in tropical setting **$6.00**

Cigar box, inner lid; Flor Fina, 6x10", ca 1910 ..... $12.00
Cigar box, inner lid; Frank Mayo, 6x9", man in profile & theatrical symbols **$5.00**
Cigar box, inner lid; Ideolo, 6x9", Roman man & woman w/coat of arms **$2.00**
Cigar box, inner lid; La Carita, 6x9", lady w/violets **$5.00**
Cigar box, inner lid; Navy Ribbon, 6x9", sailor **$6.00**
Cigar box, inner lid; O'San, 6x9", Egyptian scenes **$3.50**
Cigar box, inner lid; Purple Ribbon, 6x9", plantation scene, purple ribbon on yellow background **$3.00**
Cigar box, inner lid; White Orchid, 6x9", cigar w/lg white orchid above **$5.00**
Cigar box, outer; Affecionada, 5x5", Spanish woman **$1.50**
Cigar box, outer; El Wendo, 5x5", woman, globe & tobacco leaves **$1.00**
Cigar box, outer; Grand Council, 5x5", 3 men in front of lake smoking cigars **$4.00**
Cigar box, outer; Hummer, 5x5", hummingbird at tobacco flower **$6.00**
Cigar box, outer; La Natalia, 5x5", lady wearing crown .. **$7.50**
Cigar box, outer; Michigan, 5x5", fish chasing lure **$4.50**
Cigar box, outer; Red Bloomers, 5x5", red rose on woodgrain background **$2.00**
Cigar box, outer; Regalia de Cuba, 5x5", green cherubs, eagle & globe **$12.50**
Cigar box, outer; Scarlet Crown, 5x5", lion & crown **$4.50**
Cigar box, outer; Wedding Veil, 5x5", bride in wedding gown **$2.00**
Crate, All Year, California lemons, 9x12", palm trees over valley w/purple trees beyond **$4.00**
Crate, Big J, California apples, red & green apples on blue background, yellow Big J logo on blue seal **$2.00**
Crate, Blue Heron, Florida citrus, 9x9", lg blue bird walking in Everglades, red background **$3.00**
Crate, Color-Ful, California pears, 8x11", 3 pears & foilage on black background **$4.00**
Crate, Coon Yams, 9x9", raccoon holding giant yam **$5.00**
Crate, Dainty Maid, Washington apples, dark-haired girl holding apple on blue background, 1950s **$3.00**

Crate, Dixie Delite, Florida citrus, 9x9", dancing couple **$5.00**
Crate, Eureka, Florida citrus, 9x9", Indian plays flute....**$5.00**
Crate, Ev-a-Green Asparagus, 9x10", lg bunch of asparagus w/farms in background **$2.00**
Crate, Florigold, Florida citrus, 9x9", gold medallion portrait of an Indian in profile...**$2.00**
Crate, Index Supreme, California lemons, 9x12", sm hand pointing at lemon crate, 3-D logo, 1951 ....**$6.00**
Crate, Jackie Boy apples, 9x10½", little boy in naval attire w/apple, 1925 ....**$12.00**
Crate, King Pelican lettuce, 7x9", green pelican wearing a crown on black background **$2.00**
Crate, Little Lue yams, 9x9", little girl in field................**$2.00**
Crate, Minerva lemons, 9x12", goddess looking at lemon, 1930...**$3.50**
Crate, Moonbeam, Florida citrus, 9x9", moon over orange groves, white logo slanted upward.......................**$3.00**
Crate, Muckalee Brand peaches, 7x8", lg peach, orchard & river...**$20.00**
Crate, Old Gold, Oregon pears, 8x11", yellow logo & blue panel on red background **$2.00**
Crate, Pacific California lemons, 9x12", lg lemon & map of Pacific showing sea routes **$3.00**
Crate, Piggy pears, 7½x11", pig carrying basket of pears, 1940...**$4.00**
Crate, Prince of Wales, Florida citrus, 9x9", man dressed in purple, 1940...**$2.00**
Crate, River Boy, California pears, 8x11", little boy in straw hat w/fishing pole & bait.....................................**$15.00**
Crate, River Lad asparagus, Dutch boy next to water & windmills, 1930 ....**$4.00**
Crate, Rocky Hill, California oranges, 10x11", bronze Indian on horseback at top of rock **$6.00**
Crate, Safe Hit vegetables, 9x6", baseball player, 1940..**$3.00**
Crate, Sea Cured, California lemons, 9x12", lg ocean liner steaming away from smog bank **$6.00**
Crate, Sea Treat lemons, 9x12", view of ship through porthole, 1930 ....**$7.50**
Crate, Smoky Jim's yams, 9x9", Black man emptying sweet potato crate..**$5.00**
Crate, Snow Crest pears, 7½x11", orchard & ranch house, 1940...**$1.00**
Crate, Snow-Line apples, 9x10½", lg apple, orchard & mountains..**$4.00**
Crate, Solid Gold, California oranges, 10x11", California state seal in gold on red background **$4.00**
Crate, Sunbeam, Spanish citrus, smiling girl..................**$5.00**

Crate, Sunny Heights, California oranges, 10x11", landscape of groves w/mountains in the distance **$5.00**
Crate, Tartan grapefruit, fancy plate w/grapefruit half on green plaid background..**$5.00**

Crate, U-Like-Um Apples, Washington state, 10½x9", Indian on horseback, 1940s **$3.00**
Crate, Woodlake Gold, California oranges, 10x11", silhouette of gnarly tree beside lake, hills & mountains..........**$4.00**
Crate, Yale Brand cranberries, university buildings.......**$6.50**
Lug box, Blue Bird grapes, bluebird in flight & white script logo **$2.00**
Lug box, Embarcadero pears, harbor scene & orchard on blue background **$3.00**
Lug box, Humdinger melons, red script logo on yellow & green shaded background.................................**$2.00**
Lug box, State Pride grapes, poppy wreath around map of California & blue banner on red background **$3.00**
Lug box, White Star tomatoes, white star in blue circle on red background...**$2.00**

Letter Openers

Interesting together or singularly as a decorative accent, old letter openers are easy to find and affordable. They've been made in just about any material you can think of – some very fancy, others almost primitive. If you like advertising, you'll want to add those with product or company names to your collection.

Brass, 6¾", Napoleon figural....................................**$37.50**
Brass, 8¾", folding 2½" knife in handle, 5" ruler blade..**$17.50**
Brass, 9", Indian figural handle **$25.00**
Brass, 9", ship engraved on handle **$22.50**
Bronze, Mechanics Saving Bank, Manchester NH **$18.00**
Celluloid, 9", Railway Express agency on handle, EX ...**$6.00**
Chromed steel, Irwin Auger Bit, Wilmington, auger-shaped handle...**$25.00**
Ebony wood, 12", tribal chieftan in headdress figural...**$8.00**
Metal, AS&W Co, nail figural....................................**$12.50**
Metal, Cyprus Novelty, Brooklyn NY, w/ruler **$15.00**
Metal, Gulf Oil..**$10.00**
Metal, Prudential Life Insurance................................**$15.00**
Plastic, Fuller Brush Man figural **$8.00**
Pot metal w/brass blade, 8", cowboy on rearing horse..**$10.00**
Silverplate, figural horse head handle, Reed & Barton..**$85.00**

License Plates

Some of the early porcelain license plates are valued at more than $500.00. First-year plates issued by each state are especially desirable. Steel plates with the aluminum 'state seal' attached range in value from $150.00 (for those from 1915-20) to $20.00 (for those from the early forties to 1950). Even some modern plates are desirable to collectors who like those with special graphics and messages.

1923, Iowa	$12.50
1924, Pennsylvania	$9.00
1926, New York	$11.00
1927, New Hampshire	$9.00
1928, Maine	$10.00
1928, South Dakota	$17.50
1930, North Dakota	$15.00
1932, Arizona, copper, flaking paint	$68.00
1932, Nebraska	$9.00
1941, Wisconsin	$10.00
1942, Kansas, sunflower	$32.00
1942, Kentucky, repainted	$5.00
1943, Mississippi	$40.00
1948, Illinois, soybean	$11.00
1949, Michigan	$7.50
1953, Tennessee	$20.00
1957, Wyoming	$8.00
1959, Tennessee	$11.00
1962, California, metal tab	$7.00
1964, Maryland	$3.75
1964, Massachusetts	$7.00
1964, Montana	$7.50
1964, South Carolina	$7.00
1968, Nevada	$10.00
1968, Virginia, pr	$15.00
1969, Hawaii	$16.00
1969, Ohio	$2.75
1971, Nebraska	$3.50
1974, Indiana	$3.50
1976, Florida	$6.00
1978, Delaware	$8.50
1978, Idaho	$5.00
1979, Connecticut	$9.00
1981, Hawaii	$6.00
1985, Georgia	$2.50
1988, Florida, Challenger	$42.50
1988, West Virginia, map, blue border	$12.50
1992, South Dakota, Great Faces	$12.50

Liddle Kiddles

These tiny little dolls ranging from ¾" to 4" tall were made by Mattel from 1966 until 1979. They all had posable bodies and rooted hair that could be restyled, and they came with accessories of many types. Some represented storybook characters, some were flowers in perfume bottles, some were made to be worn as jewelry, and there were even spacemen 'Kiddles.' Our prices are for dolls still mint and in their original packaging. If only the package is missing, deduct 25%; if the doll is dressed but has none of the original accessories, deduct 75%.

For more information, we recommend *Modern Collector's Dolls* by Pat Smith.

Alice in Wonderliddle Castle, all original, complete, 1967, minimum value $75.00
Anabelle Autodiddle, 4", all original w/car, 1967, minimum value $45.00
Cherry Blossom Skediddle, 3½", vinyl, brown hair, brown almond-shaped eyes, all original w/trikediddle, minimum value...$50.00
Cinderiddles Palace, complete, 1966, minimum value ..$45.00
Dainty Deer Animiddle, 2", vinyl, orange hair, brown painted eyes, all original, 1967, minimum value ..$35.00
Freezy Sliddle, 3", auburn hair, all original, w/sled & accessories, 1966, minimum value................................$45.00
Frosty Mint Kone, 2", green hair, blue painted eyes, all original, w/cone holder, 1966, minimum value $25.00
Funny Bunny Animiddle, 2", orange hair attached to cap, all original, 1968, minimum value.............................$45.00
Heart Pin Kiddle, 1", vinyl, yellow hair, blue painted eyes, all original w/heart pin, 1966, minimum value.....$25.00
Heather Hiddlehorse Skediddle, 4", vinyl, red hair, blue eyes, all original w/horse, 1967, minimum value .$45.00

Honeysuckle Kologne, 2", yellow hair, blue eyes, 1968, complete w/cologne, minimum value $20.00
Kiddle case, lavender, 1967, M $8.00
Lady Lace Tea Party Kiddle, 3½", vinyl, rooted blond hair, blue eyes, w/cup & saucer, minimum value.......$125.00
Laffy Lemon Kola Kiddle, 2", vinyl, long blond hair, painted features, w/bottle, 1967, minimum value $25.00
Larky Locket, 2", blond hair, blue painted eyes, all original w/locket, 1966, minimum value............................$25.00
Laverne Locket, 2", vinyl, long blond hair, painted eyes, all original w/locket, 1967, minimum value $25.00
Liddle Baby Kiddle-Baby Rockaway, 2½", brown vinyl, all original in rocker, 1969, minimum value..............$60.00

Liddle Biddle Peep, 3", all original, complete, 1966, minimum value $100.00

Liddle Red Riding Hiddle, 3½", vinyl, rooted blond hair, all original, 1966, minimum value......................$100.00

Little Middle Muffet, 3", all original, complete, minimum value $100.00

Lola Locket, 2", blond hair, blue eyes, all original w/locket, minimum value (illustrated on page 240) $25.00

Lolli Lemon, 2", yellow hair, lavender eyes, all original, 1966, minimum value $25.00

Lorelie Bracelet Kiddle, 1", vinyl, lavender hair, blue painted eyes, all original w/bracelet, 1966 ....$25.00

Peter Paniddle, 3", all original, complete, 1966, minimum value $100.00

Santa Kiddle, plastic, M on card........................$8.00

Shirley Skediddle, 4", rooted blond hair, blue painted eyes, plugs into Skiddle machine, minimum value........$50.00

Shirley Strawberry Kola Kiddle, 2", vinyl, long red hair, painted features, all original w/bottle, 1967, minimum value $25.00

Sizzly Friddle, 3", all original, complete w/barbeque set, 1955, minimum value $45.00

Sleeping Biddle, 3", w/chair, 1966, minimum value..$100.00

Sukie Skediddle, 4", vinyl & plastic, rooted blond hair, painted features & socks, all original, 1966, minimum value $30.00

Tessie Tractor Skediddle, 4", vinyl, rooted blond hair, brown painted eyes, freckles, w/tractor, minimum $25.00

Tiny Tiger Animiddle, 2½", all original, 1968, minimum value $45.00

Tracy Skediddle, 4", long blond ponytails, all original w/trikediddle, minimum value..............................$50.00

Violet Kiddle Kolognes, 2½", vinyl, lavender hair, w/cologne bottle, minimum value......................................$25.00

Windy Fiddle, 2", vinyl, rooted blond hair, blue painted eyes, w/airplane, 1966, minimum value...............$50.00

Limited Editions

If you're going to buy any of these items, pick those that you will personally enjoy, because contrary to what you may have heard, investment potential is poor. Values we've listed are retail, but if you sell to a dealer, don't expect to get much more than 20% to 30%.

Bells

Bing & Grondahl, 1984, Christmas Letter $40.00
Bing & Grondahl, 1989, Christmas Anchorage.............$50.00
Bing & Grondahl, 1991, Independence Hall................$35.00
Danbury Mint, 1976, No Swimming.........................$42.50
Danbury Mint, 1977, Puppy Love $38.00
Danbury Mint, 1979, Back to School $28.00
Gorham, 1976, Snow Sculpture..............................$42.00
Gorham, 1981, Sweet Serenade $26.00
Gorham, 1983, Winter Wonderland.........................$16.50

Gorham, 1985, Yuletide Reflections............................$32.50
Lenox, 1984, Dove $57.00
River Shore, 1978, Dressing Up $47.50
River Shore, 1981, Grandpa's Guardian.....................$45.00

Dolls

Bello, 1987, Little Bo Peep.....................................$275.00
Bello, 1989, Miss Muffett $125.00
Effner, 1982, Cleo $245.00
Effner, 1983, Noel $235.00
Gorham, 1981, Christina, 16", S Stone Aiken $450.00
Gorham, 1982, Jeremy, 23" $735.00
Gorham, 1982, Mademoiselle Lucille, 12" $450.00
Gorham, 1985, Amelia, 19"....................................$385.00
Gorham, 1987, Merrie (Christmas), 19" $765.00
Gorham, 1988, Bethany.......................................$1,250.00
Lenox, 1984, Jessica, 20" $1,800.00
Lenox, 1985, Elizabeth, 14" $975.00
Mann, 1985, Christmas Cheer..................................$95.00
Mann, 1987, Rapunzel...$150.00
Mann, 1988, Cissie $120.00
Middleton Dolls, 1988, Christmas Angel....................$150.00
Middleton Dolls, 1990, Angel Locks $145.00

Figurines

Anri, 1974, Tender Moments, 3", Ferrandiz................$365.00
Anri, 1976, Gardener, 6", Ferrandiz $275.00
Anri, 1977, The Blessing, 3", Ferrandiz....................$135.00
Anri, 1984, Watchful Eye, 6", S Kay........................$425.00
Anri, 1986, Always by My Side, 6", S Kay $335.00
Anri, 1988, Winter Memories, 6", Ferrandiz $440.00
Boehm, 1958, Nonpareil Buntings.........................$1,000.00
Boehm, 1969, Verdins.......................................$1,350.00
Boehm, 1979, Avocet $1,100.00
Department 56, 1977, Stone Church........................$550.00
Department 56, 1984, Crowntree Inn $365.00
Department 56, 1984, Dickens' Village Church $300.00
Department 56, 1986, Tuttle's Pub..........................$215.00
Department 56, 1988, C Fletcher Public House.........$525.00
Department 56, 1989, Dorothy's Dress Shop $300.00
Lilliput Lane, 1979, William Shakespeare $140.00
Lilliput Lane, 1983, Troutbeck Farm $265.00
Lilliput Lane, 1986, Bay View.................................$95.00

Lladro, Aggressive Duck, 6"................................$120.00
Lladro, 1969, Flute Player....................................$785.00

Lladro, 1973, Boy w/Donkey $250.00
Lladro, 1986, Boy & His Bunny $150.00
Sarah's Attic, 1988, Betsy Ross $38.00
Sarah's Attic, 1989, St Anne $30.00
Sarah's Attic, 1990, Lucas w/Bibs $85.00
Wee Forest Folk, 1977, Hiker Raccoon $350.00
Wee Forest Folk, 1978, Beaver Wood Cutter ...$215.00
Wee Forest Folk, 1978, Picnic Piggies $195.00

Ornaments

Anri, 1988, Heavenly Drummer $200.00
Bing & Grondahl, 1987, Christmas Eve at White House ..$35.00
Department 56, 1986, Apothecary Shop, lights up $15.00
Department 56, 1986, Poulterer $14.00
Department 56, 1986, Snowbaby, sitting, lights up $30.00
Gorham, 1979, snowflake, sterling $60.00
Gorham, 1982, snowflake, sterling $70.00
Lenox, 1984, deeply cut ball $40.00
Lenox, 1988, Christmas annual $40.00
Reed & Barton, 1978, sterling...............................$48.00
Reed & Barton, 1983, Partridge in a Pear Tree $18.00
Towle, 1979, Nine Ladies Dancing $45.00
Towle, 1984, Let It Snow..$45.00
Wallace, 1982, Train $12.50
Wallace, 1983, Cinnamon Candy Cane.....................$42.50
Wallace, 1987, Snowbird $10.00

Plates

Bing & Grondahl, 1928, Eskimos..................................$60.00
Bing & Grondahl, 1951, Jens Bang..............................$90.00
Bing & Grondahl, 1959, Christmas Eve $115.00
Bing & Grondahl, 1971, Christmas at Home $19.00
Bing & Grondahl, 1978, A Christmas Tale....................$19.00
Bing & Grondahl, 1981, Christmas Peace.....................$24.00
Edwin M Knowles, 1981, Rhett.................................$70.00
Edwin M Knowles, 1985, Sarah & Isaac $50.00
Edwin M Knowles, 1988, Bald Eagle $42.50
Edwin M Knowles, 1990, Lazy Morning $37.50
Edwin M Knowles, 1990, Singin' in the Rain $36.00
Gorham, 1974, Tiny Tim, Rockwell $32.00
Gorham, 1976, A Scout Is Loyal, Rockwell $50.00
Gorham, 1976, Cavalry Officer................................$72.50
Gorham, 1983, Christmas Dancers, Rockwell $32.00
Gorham, 1983, Winter Trail.....................................$60.00
Lenox, 1970, Wood Thrush.....................................$120.00
Lenox, 1977, Robins..$50.00
Lenox, 1981, Colonial Virginia, Christmas wreath $70.00
MI Hummel, 1972, Hear Ye, Hear Ye.........................$50.00
MI Hummel, 1974, Goose Girl $50.00
MI Hummel, 1976, Apple Tree Girl $50.00
MI Hummel, 1980, School Girl.................................$40.00
Reed & Barton, 1971, Red-Shouldered Hawk $70.00
Reed & Barton, 1973, Red Cardinal $65.00
River Shore, 1979, Spring Flowers $125.00
River Shore, 1982, Freedom of Speech, Rockwell $75.00
Rockwell Society, 1976, Golden Christmas $30.00

Rockwell Society, 1980, Ship Builder $25.00
Rockwell Society, 1984, Waiting on the Shore............$25.00
Rockwell Society, 1990, Back to School.....................$32.50
Rockwell Society, 1990, Christmas Prayer $38.00
Rosenthal, 1950, Christmas in the Forest....................$175.00
Rosenthal, 1958, Christmas Eve $185.00
Rosenthal, 1963, Silent Night...................................$190.00
Rosenthal, 1974, Christmas in Wurzburg....................$98.00
Royal Copenhagen, 1912, Christmas Tree.................$160.00
Royal Copenhagen, 1931, Mother & Child...............$115.00
Royal Copenhagen, 1939, Greenland Pack Ice.........$375.00
Royal Copenhagen, 1952, Christmas in the Forest $135.00

Royal Copenhagen, 1959, Christmas Night $125.00
Royal Copenhagen, 1960, Stag...............................$145.00
Royal Copenhagen, 1972, In the Desert....................$24.00
Royal Copenhagen, 1979, Choosing the Tree.............$45.00
Royal Copenhagen, 1982, Waiting for Christmas.........$45.00
Royal Worcester, 1973, Paul Revere, PW Baston.......$265.00
Royal Worcester, 1985, Purrfect Treasure...................$30.00
Royal Worcester, 1987, Fishful Thing (cat)..................$52.50
WS George, 1988, Scarlett & Her Suitors....................$85.00
WS George, 1990, Cherished Moment........................$45.00
WS George, 1990, Silent Night.................................$45.00

Little Golden Books

Everyone has had a few of these books in their lifetime, some we've read to our own children so many times that we still know them word for word. Today they're appearing in antique malls and shops everywhere, and when they're found in good condition, dust jacket intact, first editions from the 1940s may go as high as $30.00.

The first were printed in 1942; these are recognizable by their blue paper spines (later ones had gold foil).

Until the early 1970s, they were numbered consecutively; after that they were unnumbered.

First editions of the titles having a 25¢ or 29¢ cover price can be identified by either a notation on the first or second pages, or a letter on the bottom right corner of the last page (A for 1, B for 2, etc.). If these are absent, you probably have a first edition.

Condition is extremely important. Our prices are for books that are in mint condition – just as they looked the day they were purchased. Obviously, you won't find many in this shape. If your book is just lightly soiled, the cover has no tears or scrapes, the inside pages have only small creases or folded corners, and the spine is still strong (though the cover may be missing), it will be worth about half of its suggested value. Additional damage would of course lessen the value even more.

For more information, we recommend *Collecting Little Golden Books* by Steve Santi.

Alice in Wonderland Meets the White Rabbit, Jane Werner, #D19, Walt Disney Studios, 1951, 1st edition, M...**$10.00**

Animal Daddies & My Daddy, Barbara Shook Hazen, #576, 1968, 3rd edition, M.....................................**$4.00**

Animals of Farmer Jones, Leah Gale, #11, blue binding, 1942, 7th edition, M...................................**$10.00**

Annie Oakley Sharpshooter, Charles Spain Verral, #275, 1956, 1st edition, M...................................**$12.00**

Boats, Ruth Mabee, #125, 1951, 1st edition, M.............**$7.00**

Brave Eagle, Charles Verral, #394, 1957, 1st edition, M..**$10.00**

Brave Little Tailor, Brothers Grimm, #176, 1953, 2nd edition, NM...**$3.00**

Child's Garden of Verses, Robert Louis Stevenson, #289, 1957, 1st edition, NM...............................**$10.00**

Christmas Carols, Marjorie Wyckoff, #26, 1946, 10th edition, M..**$7.00**

Christmas in the Country, Benjamin Colman, #95, 1950, 1st edition, 28 pages, NM..............................**$15.00**

Cinderella, #D114, Walt Disney Studios, 1950, 34th edition, M...**$3.00**

Daniel Boone, Irwin Shapiro, #256, 1956, 1st edition, NM..**$9.00**

Donald Duck & Santa Claus, #D27, Walt Disney Studios illustrations, 1952, 3rd edition, Mickey Mouse Club Book, VG..**$7.50**

Donald Duck Adventure, #D4, Walt Disney Studios, Campbell Grant illustrator, 1950, 1st edition, M.............**$10.00**

Dragon in the Wagon, Janette Rainwater, #565, 1966, 2nd edition, M...**$4.50**

Dumbo, #D3, Walt Disney, 1947, 36th edition, M.........**$2.00**

Emerald City of Oz, ca 1952, 28 pages, EX................**$28.50**

First Little Golden Book of Fairy Tales, #9, 1948, 6th edition, VG...**$9.50**

Gingerbread Shop, PL Travers, #126, '52, 1st edition, M..**$8.00**

Gingham's Backyard Picnic, Joan Chase Bowden, #148, 1976, 2nd edition, M.....................................**$2.50**

Golden Book of Birds, Hazel Lockwood, #13, 1943, 4th edition, M...**$8.00**

Hansel & Gretel, Brothers Grimm, #491, 1954, 16th edition, M...**$2.00**

Heidi, Johanna Spyri, #470, 1954, 9th edition, M..........**$2.50**

Heidi, Johanna Sypri, #258, 1954, 3rd edition, M..........**$5.00**

How Big, Corinne Malvern, #83, 1949, 4th edition, M..**$10.00**

Howdy Doody's Circus, Don Gormley, #99, copyright Robert E (Bob) Smith, 1950, 2nd edition, EX........**$12.00**

I Can Fly, Ruth Krauss, #92, 1950, 1st edition, M **$12.00**

Lady, Samuel Armstrong, #D103, Walt Disney Studios, 1954, 9th edition, M **$3.00**

Lady, Samuel Armstrong, #D42, Walt Disney Studios, 1954, 4th edition, M **$8.00**

Life & Legend of Wyatt Earp, Monica Hill, #315, copyright Wyatt Earp Enterprises, 1958, 1st edition, EX **$9.00**

Little Cottontail, Carl Memling, #414, '60, 4th edition, NM..**$4.00**

Little Golden Book of Hymns, Elsa Jane Werner, #34, 1947, 8th edition, VG.....................................**$6.00**

Little Pond in the Woods, Muriel Ward, #43, 1948, 2nd edition, NM...**$9.00**

Little Red Hen, Folk Tale, #209, 1954, 2nd edition, M...**$4.00**

Little Trapper, Kathryn & Byron Jackson, #79, 1964, 2nd edition, EX...**$7.00**

Magilla Gorilla, BR Carrick, #547, 1964, 1st edition, EX..**$4.00**

Mickey Mouse & Pluto Pup, Elizabeth Beecher, #D76, Walt Disney Studios, 1953, 10th edition, EX....................**$3.50**

Mickey Mouse Picnic, Jane Werner, #D15, Walt Disney Studios, 1950, 13th editiion, M **$7.00**

Night Before Christmas, Clement Clarke Moore, #20, 1946, 4th edition, 42 pages, NM **$15.00**

Noah's Ark, Annie North Bedford, #D26, Walt Disney Studios, 1952, 1st edition, NM.............................**$9.00**

Peter & the Wolf, Serfe Prokofieffi, #D56, Walt Disney Studios, 1946, 3rd edition, M.............................**$3.50**

Pinocchio, #D100, Walt Disney Studios, 1948, 22nd edition, M **$8.00**

Poky Little Puppy, Janet Sepring Lowrey, #506, 1942, 41st edition, M...**$2.50**

Robin Hood, #D126, Walt Disney Studios, 1973, 2nd edition, M **$6.00**

Robin Hood & the Daring Mouse, #D128, Walt Disney Studios, 1974, 2nd edition, M.............................**$4.00**

Rootie Kazootie Baseball Star, #190, 1954, VG........$7.50

Scuffy the Tugboat, Gertrude Crampton, #363, 1946, 7th edition, VG **$2.50**

Sleeping Beauty & the Good Fairies, Annie North Bedford, #D71, Walt Disney Studios, 1952, 2nd edition, M...**$8.00**

Story of Jesus, Beatrice Alexander, #27, 1946, 1st edition, 42 pages, NM...**$20.00**

Surprise for Mickey Mouse, #D105, Walt Disney Studios, 1971, 2nd edition, M **$7.50**

Three Bears, Feodor Rojankovsky, #47, 1948, 38th edition, M **$8.00**

Through the Picture Frame, Robert Edmonds, #D1, Walt Disney Studios, 1944, 2nd edition, M.....................**$30.00**

Toby Tyler, Carl Memling, #D87, Walt Disney Studios, 1960, 1st edition, M.......................................**$10.00**

Tootle, Gertrude Crampton, #21, 1946, 11th edition (1949), 42 pages, EX...**$8.00**

When You Were a Baby, Rita Eng, #70, 1949, 2nd edition, M..**$10.00**

Wonderful House, Margaret Wise, #76, '40, 1st edition, M..**$12.00**

Woody Woodpecker, Annie North Bedford, #330, 1952, 4th edition, VG **$5.00**

Little Red Riding Hood

This line of novelty cookie jars, canisters, mugs, teapots, and other kitchenware items was made by both Regal China and Hull. Any piece today is expensive. There are several variations of the cookie jars. The Regal jar with the open basket marked 'Little Red Riding Hood Pat. Design 135889' is worth about $250.00. The same with the closed basket goes for about $25.00 more. An unmarked Regal variation with a closed basket, full skirt, and no apron books at $600.00. The Hull jars are valued higher, about $350.00 unless they're heavily decorated with decals and gold trim, which can add as much as $250.00 to the basic value.

A companion piece, the wolf on the basketweave jar is valued at $950.00; it was also made by Regal.

The complete line is covered in *The Collector's Encyclopedia of Cookie Jars* by Joyce and Fred Roerig.

Butter dish...**$350.00**
Canister, salt..**$1,100.00**
Canister, spice..**$650.00**
Cookie canister **$2,500.00**
Cracker jar, 8½", skirt held wide.................**$550.00**
Creamer, tab handle **$225.00**
Creamer & sugar bowl, head pour, w/lid **$700.00**
Creamer & sugar bowl, side spout **$300.00**
Match holder, wall hanging **$800.00**
Mug, decoration...**$2,000.00**
Pitcher, milk; 8", standing **$250.00**
Pitcher, milk; 8½", ruffled skirt, w/apron, rare **$3,000.00**
Planter, standing, wall hanging...................**$475.00**
Salt & pepper shakers, 3¼", standing, pr **$50.00**
Salt & pepper shakers, 4½", standing, rare, pr..........**$850.00**
Salt & pepper shakers, 5 /14", standing, pr................**$150.00**
Sugar bowl, crawling....................................**$225.00**

Teapot **$350.00**

Lu Ray Pastels

This was one of Taylor, Smith, and Taylor's most popular lines of dinnerware. It was made from the late 1930s until sometime in the early '50s in five pastel colors: Windsor Blue, Persian Cream, Sharon Pink, Surf Green, and Chatham Gray.

If you'd like more information, we recommend *The Collector's Encyclopedia of American Dinnerware* by Jo Cunningham.

Bowl, cream soup.......................................**$24.00**
Bowl, soup; 8"..**$10.00**
Bowl, vegetable; oval **$12.50**
Butter dish, ¼-lb, w/lid..............................**$25.00**
Cake plate..**$25.00**
Creamer **$5.00**

Creamer, demitasse; ovoid shape...........................**$22.00**
Cup & saucer...**$7.50**
Nut dish..**$22.50**
Pitcher, bulbous w/flat bottom **$40.00**

Pitcher, footed	$45.00
Pitcher, syrup	$40.00
Plate, divided	$25.00
Plate, grill	$15.00
Plate, 7"	$5.00
Platter, oval, 12"	$9.00
Salt & pepper shakers, pr	$8.50

Sugar bowl, demitasse; ovoid, w/lid (illustrated on page 244) $24.00

Teapot, w/lid, curved spout	$40.00
Tray, pickle	$15.00
Tumbler, juice	$22.50

Lunch Boxes

Character lunch boxes made of metal have been very collectible for several years, but now even those made of plastic and vinyl are coming into their own.

The first lunch box of this type ever produced featured Hopalong Cassidy. Made by the Aladdin company, it was constructed of steel and decorated with decals. But the first fully lithographed steel lunch box and matching thermos bottle was made a few years later (in 1953) by American Thermos. Roy Rogers was its featured character.

Hundreds have been made, and just as is true in other areas of character-related collectibles, the more desirable lunch boxes are those with easily recognized, well-known subjects – western heroes; TV, Disney, and cartoon characters; and famous entertainers.

Values given in our listings are for boxes in excellent condition. For metal boxes this means that you will notice only very minor defects and less than normal wear. Plastic boxes may have a few scratches and some minor wear on the sides, but the graphics are completely undamaged. If the box you're trying to evaluate is in any worse condition than we've described, to be realistic, you must cut these prices rather drastically. Values are given for boxes without matching thermoses; they're priced separately. If you'd like to learn more, we recommend *A Pictorial Price Guide to Metal Lunch Boxes and Thermoses* by Larry Aikins, who recently has written a second book on plastic and vinyl lunch boxes.

Metal

Addams Family, King Seeley, 1974	$80.00
Annie Oakley & Tagg, Aladdin, 1955	$250.00
Battle of the Planets, King Seeley, 1979	$45.00
Bee Gees (Barry), King Seeley, 1978	$40.00
Bionic Woman, Aladdin, w/car, 1977	$35.00
Bonanza, Aladdin, green, 1963	$110.00
Brave Eagle, American Thermos, 1957 (matching steel thermos, $120.00)	$220.00
Care Bears, Aladdin, 1984	$7.50
Casey Jones, Universal, dome top, 1960	$475.00
Close Encounters, King Seeley, 1978	$45.00
Colonial Bread Van, 1984	$60.00

Daniel Boone, Aladdin, 1965	$120.00
Disco Fever, Aladdin, 1980	$45.00
Disney School Bus, Aladdin, dome top, orange, 1961	$60.00

Doctor Dolittle, Aladdin, 1968 ....$80.00

Double Decker, Aladdin, 1970	$60.00
Emergency, Aladdin, 1973	$40.00
Empire Strikes Back, King Seeley, 1980	$15.00
Flintstones, Aladdin, 1964	$110.00
Fraggle Rock, King Seeley, 1984	$12.00
Globetrotters, purple uniforms, King Seeley, 1971	$45.00
Green Hornet, King Seeley, 1967	$310.00
Happy Days, American Thermos, 1978	$40.00
Hee Haw, King Seeley, 1971	$70.00
Holly Hobbie, Aladdin, 1979	$5.00
Hopalong Cassidy, Aladdin, 1954	$210.00
Huckleberry Hound, Aladdin, 1961	$110.00
Joe Palooka, Continental Can, 1949	$85.00

Kiss, King Seeley, 1977 (matching plastic thermos, $30.00) $65.00

Land of the Lost, Aladdin, 1975	$80.00
Lone Ranger, Aladdin, 1980	$35.00
Lost In Space, King Seeley, dome-top, 1967	$350.00
Mary Poppins, Aladdin, 1965	$60.00

Mickey Mouse Club, Aladdin, yellow, 1963 .... $50.00
Miss America, Aladdin, 1972 .... $50.00
Muppets (Fozzie Bear), King Seeley, 1976 .... $10.00
Peanuts, King Seeley, red band, 1980 .... $10.00
Pebbles & Bamm Bamm, Aladdin, 1971 .... $70.00
Plaid Tweed, American Thermos, green band, 1960 ... $65.00
Popeye, King Seeley, 1964 .... $90.00
Road Runner, King Seeley, lavender, 1970 .... $60.00
Scooby Doo, King Seeley, orange rim, 1973 .... $45.00
Smurfs, King Seeley, 1983 .... $160.00
Snoopy, King Seeley, dome top, 1968 .... $40.00
Strawberry Shortcake, Aladdin, 1980 .... $12.00
Superman, Aladdin, 1978 .... $35.00
US Mail, Aladdin, dome top, 1969 .... $60.00
Walton's, Aladdin, 1973 .... $45.00
Wild Wild West, Aladdin, 1969 .... $160.00
Yogi Bear & Friends, Aladdin, 1961 .... $140.00

Plastic

Back to the Future, Thermos, 1989 .... $20.00
Batman, Taiwan, black, 1989 .... $30.00
Beach Party, Deka, pink or blue, 1988 .... $15.00
Beauty & the Beast, Aladdin, 1991 .... $10.00
Chipmunks, Thermos, 1983 .... $25.00
Days of Thunder, Thermos, 1988 .... $20.00
Dukes of Hazzard, Aladdin, dome top, 1981 .... $20.00
Flash Gordon, Aladdin, dome top, 1979 .... $75.00
Goonies, Aladdin, 1985 .... $25.00
Hello Kitty, Japan, dome top, 1984 .... $40.00
Kermit's Scout Van, Superseal, 1989 .... $18.00
Looney Tunes Dancing, Thermos, 1977 .... $25.00
Marvel Super Heroes, Thermos, 1990 .... $10.00
Mickey & Minnie, Aladdin, pink car, 1988 .... $15.00
Muppets, Thermos, blue, 1982 .... $12.00
Peter Pan, Taiwan, 1984 .... $65.00
Popeye, Aladdin, dome top, 1979 .... $35.00
Scooby-Doo, Thermos, 1973 .... $35.00
Snow White, Aladdin, 1980 .... $35.00
Superman II, Aladdin, dome top, 1986 .... $40.00
Transformers, Aladdin, Canada, dome top, 1985 ...... $35.00
Wizard of Oz, Aladdin, 1989 .... $40.00
Wuzzles, Aladdin, 1985 .... $15.00
101 Dalmations, Aladdin, 1990 .... $10.00
Alice in Wonderland, Aladdin, 1974 .... $230.00
All Dressed Up, Bayville, 1970s $90.00
Barbie & Midge, King Seeley, dome top, 1964 .... $375.00
Barbie & Midge, King Seeley, 1965 .... $90.00
Betsy Clark, King Seeley, 1977 .... $140.00
Buick 1910, Bayville, 1974 .... $140.00
Care Bears, Mexico, 1980s $95.00
Donny & Marie, Aladdin, 1976 .... $110.00
GI Joe, King Seeley, 1989 .... $55.00
Kodak Gold, Aladdin, 1970s $85.00
Mary Poppins, Aladdin, 1973 .... $140.00
Peanuts, King Seeley, red, 1967 .... $90.00
Penelope & Penny, Gary, 1970s $120.00
Pink Panther, Aladdin, 1980 .... $95.00

Psychedelic, King Seeley, blue, 1970 .... $70.00
Quilt Work, unknown manufacturer, dome top $145.00
Roy Rogers, King Seeley, brown, 1960 .... $200.00

Roy Rogers Saddlebag, King Seeley, 1960 .... $200.00
Sesame Street, Aladdin, 1979 .... $85.00
Speedy Petey & Pals, Gary $140.00
Strawberry Shortcake, Aladdin, 1980 .... $40.00
Tic Tac Toe, unknown manufacturer, blue $50.00
Twiggy, Aladdin, 1967 .... $195.00
Wonder Woman, Aladdin, blue, 1977 .... $150.00

Thermoses

Action Jackson, Okay Industries, steel, 1973 .... $140.00
Addams Family, King Seeley, plastic, 1974 .... $30.00
Alice in Wonderland, Aladdin, plastic, 1974 .... $40.00
Alvin, King Seeley, plastic, 1963 .... $120.00
Annie Oakley & Tagg, Aladdin, steel, 1955 .... $95.00
Back to the Future, Thermos, plastic, 1989 .... $8.00
Barbie & Midge, King Seeley, steel & glass, 1964 ..... $80.00
Battle Star Galactica, Aladdin, plastic, 1978 .... $20.00
Beauty & the Beast, Aladdin, plastic, 1991 .... $5.00
Bee Gees (Barry), King Seeley, plastic, 1978 .... $30.00
Betsy Clark, King Seeley, plastic, 1977 .... $15.00
Bobby Sherman, King Seeley, steel, 1972 .... $50.00
Buick 1910, Bayville, styrofoam, 1974 .... $12.00
Care Bears, Aladdin, plastic, 1984 .... $5.00
Chipmunks, Thermos, plastic, 1983 .... $10.00
Cracker Jack, Aladdin, plastic, 1969 .... $25.00
Daniel Boone, Aladdin, steel, 1965 .... $90.00
Days of Thunder, Thermos, plastic, 1988 .... $8.00
Disney School Bus, Aladdin, steel, orange, 1961 ...... $30.00
Donny & Marie, Aladdin, plastic, 1976 .... $20.00
Dr Seuss, Aladdin, plastic, 1970 .... $40.00
Dunkin Munchkins, Thermos, plastic, 1972 .... $25.00
Emergency, Aladdin, plastic, 1973 .... $30.00
Family Affair, King Seeley, steel, 1969 .... $35.00
Flash Gordon, Aladdin, plastic, 1979 .... $40.00
Fraggle Rock, King Seeley, plastic, 1984 .... $8.00
Ghostbusters, Deka, plastic, 1986 .... $10.00
GI Joe, King Seeley, plastic, 1989 .... $10.00
Green Hornet, King Seeley, steel, 1967 .... $130.00
Grizzly Adams, Aladdin, plastic, 1977 .... $40.00
Hair Bear Bunch, King Seeley, steel, 1971 .... $45.00
Hee Haw, King Seeley, steel, 1971 .... $50.00
Hello Kitty, Japan, plastic, 1984 .... $10.00
Hot Wheels, King Seeley, steel, 1969 .... $25.00
Huckleberry Hound, Aladdin, steel, 1961 .... $60.00

It's a Small World, Aladdin, steel & glass, 1968 ....$50.00
Keebler, Taiwan, plastic, 1978 ....$20.00
Kung Fu, King Seeley, plastic, 1974............................$35.00
Lassie, Ardee, styrofoam, 1960s $12.00
Lone Ranger, Aladdin, plastic, 1980............................$20.00
Lucy's Luncheonette, Thermos, plastic, 1981 ....$8.00
Marvel Super Heroes, Thermos, plastic, 1990 ....$5.00
Mary Poppins, Aladdin, plastic, 1973...........................$50.00
Mickey & Minnie, Aladdin, plastic, 1988 ....$10.00
Miss America, Aladdin, plastic, 1972............................$40.00
Nestles Quik, Taiwan, plastic, 1980 ....$20.00
NFL Quarterback, Aladdin, steel, 1964 ....$60.00
Peanuts, King Seeley, steel & glass, red, 1967 ....$25.00
Pebbles & Bamm Bamm, Aladdin, plastic, 1971 ....$45.00
Peter Pan, Taiwan, plastic, 1984 ....$25.00
Pink Panther, Aladdin, plastic, 1980 ....$20.00
Plaid Tweed, American Thermos, steel, 1960 ....$35.00
Planet of the Apes, Aladdin, plastic, 1974....................$45.00
Psychedelic, King Seeley, steel & glass, blue, 1970.....$30.00
Raggedy Ann & Andy, Aladdin, plastic, 1988.............$15.00
Road Runner, King Seeley, steel, lavender, 1970........$50.00
Scooby Doo, King Seeley, plastic, orange rim, 1973...$30.00
Sesame Street, Aladdin, plastic, 1979..........................$15.00
Six Million Dollar Man, Aladdin, plastic, 1974 ....$25.00
Smurfette, Thermos, plastic, 1984 ....$8.00
Smurfs Fishing, Thermos, plastic, 1984........................$8.00
Snow White, Aladdin, plastic, 1980 ....$15.00
Stars & Stripes, Aladdin, plastic, 1970.........................$30.00
Strawberry Shortcake, Aladdin, plastic, 1980 ....$15.00
Superman II, Aladdin, plastic, 1986 ....$20.00
Tommy Teaddy, Taiwan, plastic, pink or blue, 1987 ....$8.00
Transformers, Aladdin, plastic, 1986............................$6.50
US Mail, Aladdin, plastic, 1969....................................$25.00
Walton's, Aladdin, plastic, 1973 ....$20.00
Wizard of Oz, Aladdin, plastic, 1989 ....$20.00
Wonder Woman, Aladdin, plastic, blue, 1977..............$25.00
Woody Woodpecker, Aladdin, plastic, 1972.................$60.00
Wuzzles, Aladdin, plastic, 1985....................................$10.00
Yosemite Sam, King Seeley, steel & glass, 1971 ....$85.00
101 Dalmations, Aladdin, plastic, 1990.........................$5.00

Maddux of California

Founded in Los Angeles in 1938, Maddux not only produced ceramics but imported and distributed them as well. They supplied chainstores nationwide with well-designed figural planters, TV lamps, novelty and giftware items, and during the mid-1960s their merchandise was listed in every major stamp catalog. Because of an increasing amount of foreign imports and a sluggish national economy, the company was forced to sell out in 1976. Under the new management, manufacturing was abandoned, and the company was converted solely to distribution. Collectors have only recently discovered this line, and prices right now are affordable though increasing.

Console bowl set, 11½", swan, white porcelain, #1019..$20.00
Cookie jar, Humpty Dumpty, #2113.....................$200.00
Cookie jar, Raggedy Andy, #2108........................$200.00
Figurine, 11", flying flamingo, #970 ....$25.00
Figurines, horses, rearing or charging, #925 & #926, pr ..$20.00
Figurines, 10½", swan, black matt, #923, pr............$25.00
Figurines, 14½", Early Birds, black & tangerine, #969, pr....$25.00
Figurines, 9½", mallards, natural pose, male #928/female
    #929, pr..$30.00
Planter, 10x7½", rearing horse $22.00
TV lamp, 10½", Colonial ship, #892........................$20.00
TV lamp, 11½", Persian Glory (horse head), #887.......$15.00

TV lamp, 12½", basset hound, #896 ....$35.00
TV lamp, 13", shell, Pearltone, #808......................$20.00
TV lamp, 3-D planter, head of Christ, #841 ....$25.00

Magazines

There are lots of magazines around today, but unless they're in fine condition (clean, no missing or clipped pages, and very little other damage); have interesting features (cover illustrations, good advertising, or special-interest stories); or deal with sports greats, famous entertainers, or world-reknowned personalities, they're worth very little, no matter how old they are. Address labels on the front are acceptable, but if you find one with no label, it will be worth about 25% more than our listed values. See also Movie Stars, Magazines; TV Guides.

After Dark, 1981, Marilyn Monroe cover, M...................$8.00
American Cinematographer, 1979, January, NM..........$30.00
Architectural Digest Magazine, 1977, October, NM $10.00
Argosy, 1942, March 7, Dorothy Lamour cover, EX.....$15.00
Bananas, Kiss cover, 1978, 40-page, NM.......................$2.50
Baseball Magazine, 1938, May, Joe DiMaggio cover,
    NM $60.00
Baseball Magazine, 1944, July, Jimmie Foxx cover, NM ..$20.00
Camera Craft, 1925, July, EX $15.00

Colliers, 1948, April 4, VG **$5.00**
Collier's, 1955, April, Rocky Marciano, VG....................**$5.00**
Collier's, 1956, March 2, Grace Kelly & Prince Rainier cover, VG...**$14.00**
Colliers, 1948, September 11, VG...............................**$5.00**
Colliers, 1950, April 8, Harry Truman cover, G..............**$7.50**
Confidential, 1957, July, Liberace cover, EX..................**$5.00**
Confidential, 1957, May, Marilyn Monroe cover, EX ...**$12.50**
Confidential, 1961, April, Perry Mason cover, VG **$3.00**
Cosmopolitan, 1952, October, Queen Elizabeth II on cover, VG...**$20.00**
Cosmopolitan, 1953, May, Marilyn Monroe cover, VG..**$25.00**
Cosmopolitan, 1969, August, Elizabeth Taylor cover, VG..**$6.00**
Dare-Devil Aces, 1935, April, NM **$12.50**
Disney Channel Magazine, 1986, December, Mary Poppins cover, M...**$8.00**
Disneyland Holiday Magazine, 1957-58, Winter, M.....**$35.00**
Down Beat, 1941, January 15, Duke Ellington cover, NM..**$22.50**
Down Beat, 1942, March 15, Dinah Shore & Gene Krupa cover, EX **$22.50**
Escapade, 1956, Marilyn Monroe centerfold, December, VG ..**$15.00**
Esquire, 1941, November, Vargas & Petty illustrations, VG ..**$18.00**
Esquire, 1943, May, Vargas illustrations, VG **$15.00**
Esquire, 1951, April, Al Morre gatefold, EX...................**$3.00**
Esquire, 1951, October, special TV edition, VG...........**$15.00**
Esquire, 1951, September, Marilyn Monroe fold-out, VG ..**$25.00**
Esquire, 1958, October, Silver Anniversary issue, original shipping box, VG..**$25.00**
Family Circle, 1934, January 26, EX.............................**$12.50**
Family Circle, 1944, July 4, Judy Garland cover, VG **$5.00**
Family Circle, 1946, January 25, Bob Hope cover, M.**$10.00**
Fortune, 1940, November, White House cover, VG **$12.00**
Gent, 1964, August, Elke Sommer cover, VG.................**$7.50**
Good Housekeeping, 1935, May, Golden Anniversary issue, VG **$10.00**
Good Housekeeping, 1945, August, baby cover, EX.....**$6.50**
Good Housekeeping, 1959, July, Ingrid Bergman cover, NM **$8.00**
Good Housekeeping, 1967, March, Grace Kelly cover, VG..**$3.00**
Good Housekeeping, 1972, May, Sonny & Cher cover, VG ..**$4.00**
High Times, 1976, December, Santa cover, NM...........**$17.50**
Holiday, 1949, October, Pittsburgh photo cover, VG **$5.00**
Interview, 1987, July, Pee-Wee Herman cover, VG **$20.00**
Ladies' Home Journal, 1938, October, VG **$45.00**
Ladies' Home Journal, 1957, April, America's 10 Richest Men, G **$3.00**
Ladies' Home Journal, 1957, August, Motherhood Possible for Many Women, VG..**$4.00**
Ladies' Home Journal, 1958, April, I Was Churchill's Secretary, VG...**$4.00**
Ladies' Home Journal, 1958, August, Billy Graham cover, EX **$5.00**
Ladies' Home Journal, 1958, January, Greengage Summer: A New Serial, VG...**$4.00**
Ladies' Home Journal, 1958, July, America's Most Fabulous Jewels, VG...**$4.00**
Ladies' Home Journal, 1960, December, Jacqueline Kennedy, VG **$3.00**

Ladies' Home Journal, 1961, April, Jacqueline Kennedy, VG...**$7.00**
Ladies' Home Journal, 1961, November, VG.................**$2.00**
Ladies' Home Journal, 1962, June, Bette Davis cover, EX..**$5.00**
Ladies' Home Journal, 1966, March, Sophia Loren, VG..**$4.00**
Ladies' Home Journal, 1967, May, Mia Farrow's Swinging Life, VG...**$4.00**
Ladies' Home Journal, 1968, August, Mia Farrow cover, NM..**$6.00**
Ladies' Home Journal, 1968, February, That Bonnie & Clyde Girl Faye Dunaway, VG...**$4.00**
Ladies' Home Journal, 1968, May, My Father, Dr Spock, G..**$3.00**
Ladies' Home Journal, 1969, November, LBJ's Own Story-The Day Kennedy Was Shot, VG...........................**$4.00**
Laff, 1940, July, Three Stooges article, EX...................**$30.00**
Laff, 1946, February, Ava Gardner cover, VG **$7.50**
Liberty, 1936, May, Greta Garbo cover, EX.................**$12.50**
Liberty, 1938, April, Snow White & Dopey cover, EX..**$25.00**
Life, 1942, Roy Rogers & Trigger cover, EX **$40.00**
Life, 1944, October 16, Lauren Bacall cover, EX.........**$17.50**
Life, 1947, April 28, Alice in Wonderland cover, G **$7.50**
Life, 1953, July, Mickey Mantle cover, EX **$12.00**
Life, 1954, April 25, Grace Kelly cover, NM **$20.00**
Life, 1954, May 31, William Holden cover, VG **$8.50**
Life, 1955, October 2, Rock Hudson cover, NM **$20.00**
Life, 1958, January 20, Lyndon Johnson cover, G.........**$6.50**

Life, 1961, June 9, Kennedy in Paris cover, VG $6.50
Life, 1962, January 5, Lucille Ball cover, NM................**$15.00**
Life, 1965, August 13, Lady Bird Johnson cover, G **$3.50**
Life, 1965, February, Dr Schwietzer cover, EX..............**$7.50**
Life, 1965, May 7, John Wayne cover, EX **$32.00**
Life, 1966, August, Gemini 10 cover, NM.....................**$7.50**
Life, 1966, July, Claudia Cardinale cover, EX................**$5.00**
Life, 1966, May, Jackie Kennedy cover, NM................**$10.00**
Life, 1968, June, Robert Kennedy cover, VG.................**$5.00**
Life, 1968, March 15, Boris Karloff cover, M...............**$15.00**
Life, 1968, September 13, Beatles cover, VG...............**$20.00**
Life, 1969, July, Neil Armstrong cover, NM **$8.00**
Life, 1971, October 15, Disney World Opens, M.........**$18.00**

Life, 1972, September 8, Marilyn Monroe cover, EX....**$10.00**
Look, 1940, July, Linda Darnell cover, EX......................**$7.50**
Look, 1941, June 5, Winston Churchill cover, G..........**$10.00**
Look, 1941, May 20, Gale Storm cover, VG **$7.50**
Look, 1949, August, Ginger Rogers cover, NM **$8.00**
Look, 1955, July 26, Walt Disney & Fess Parker as Davy
    Crockett cover, M..**$28.00**
Look, 1956, Lucille Ball cover, EX **$10.00**
Look, 1956, November, James Dean cover, EX **$15.00**
Look, 1957, Frank Sinatra cover, EX.............................**$5.00**
Look, 1957, Queen Elizabeth cover, EX **$5.00**
Look, 1958, May, Bing Crosby cover, EX **$6.50**
Look, 1961, January 31, Clark Gable cover, VG **$17.50**
Look, 1962, June 5, Jackie Kennedy cover, VG **$5.00**
Look, 1968, January 9, John Lennon cover, M............**$25.00**

Love Story, 1927, Street & Smith Publishing, G......$7.00
Mad, 1972, October, G **$2.00**
Mad, 1977, April, VG **$2.50**
McCall's, 1942, June, VG...**$9.00**
McCall's, 1946, January, VG..**$9.00**
McCall's, 1968, August, children's fall fashions, VG.......**$5.00**
McCall's, 1968, June, Jacqueline Kennedy cover, VG....**$5.00**
Mickey Mouse Club Magazine, 1956, Summer, Fess Parker &
    Annette cover, M..**$25.00**
Mickey Mouse Magazine, 1938, Volume 4, No 3, Ferdinand
    the Bull cover, NM..**$65.00**
Modern Priscilla, September 1923, VG **$10.00**
Monster Magazine, #5, EX **$3.00**
National Geographic, 1930-1950, EX, from $6.00 up to ..**$8.00**
National Geographic, 1950-60, EX, from $5.00 up to **$6.00**
National Geographic, 1960-70, EX, from $4.00 up to **$5.00**
National Geographic, 1970-80, EX, from $3.00 up to **$4.00**
National Geographic, 1980-90s, from $1.00 up to **$2.00**
Needlecraft, The Home Arts Magazine; 1933, January,
    EX **$16.00**
Nevada, 1971, Summer, Bonanza cover, M..................**$17.50**
Nevada, 1974, Summer, John Wayne color cover..........**$8.50**
Newsweek, December 14, 1981, M..............................**$5.00**

Newsweek, 1972, January 10, Who Can Beat Nixon?,
    VG...**$10.00**
Newsweek, 1973, June 11, Secretariat, VG....................**$3.00**
Newsweek, 1974, October 28, Stevie Wonder, VG........**$3.00**
Newsweek, 1978, Woody Allen cover, EX.....................**$5.00**
Newsweek, 1987, August, Elvis Presley, VG **$25.00**
Newsweek, 1989, April 3, Sorcerer Mickey Mouse cover,
    M...**$12.00**
Newsweek, 1989, June 26, Batman, VG **$5.00**
Penthouse, 1978, September, VG...................................**$3.00**
People Weekly, 1976, December 20, Led Zeppelin cover ..**$5.00**
People Weekly, 1976, January 13, Elvis Is 40, M **$7.50**
People Weekly, 1976, July 7, Paul McCartney cover **$5.00**
People Weekly, 1976, September 6, David Bowie cover,
    M...**$3.50**
People Weekly, 1977, June 27, Peter Framton cover, NM ..**$3.50**
People Weekly, 1977, June 6, Fleetwood Mac cover, M ..**$3.50**
People Weekly, 1977, May 2, Bianca Jagger cover, M...**$3.50**
Photographic Magazine, 1987, September, John Wayne color
    cover **$5.00**

**Playboy, 1953, December, Marilyn Monroe cover,
    VG..$1,500.00**
Playboy, 1955, February, Jayne Mansfield, centerfold, VG ..**$150.00**
Playboy, 1957, December, Linda Vargas, VG..............**$34.00**
Playboy, 1959, November, Donna Lynn centerfold, VG ..**$17.00**
Playboy, 1962, August, Jan Roberts centerfold, VG.....**$23.00**
Playboy, 1964, August, China Lee centerfold, VG **$20.00**
Playboy, 1964, January, Marilyn Monroe nude photo, VG ..**$30.00**
Playboy, 1964, June, Mami Van Doren cover, M........**$17.50**
Playboy, 1966, October, Linda Moon centerfold, VG..**$15.00**
Playboy, 1969, May, Sally Sheffield centerfold, VG **$13.00**

Playboy, 1971, September, Crystal Smith centerfold, VG..**$13.00**

Playboy, 1973, February, Cyndi Wood centerfold, VG **$12.00**

Playboy, 1975, May, Bridgett Rollins centerfold, VG **$4.00**

Playboy, 1977, November, Rita Lee centerfold, VG **$5.00**

Playboy, 1982, February, Anne Fox centerfold, VG.......**$5.00**

Playboy, 1983, November, Kenny Rogers cover, VG.....**$3.00**

Playboy, 1985, March, Donna Smith centerfold, VG......**$4.00**

Playboy, 1988, May, Diana Lee centerfold, VG..............**$4.00**

Playboy, 1989, October, Karen Foster centerfold, VG...**$3.00**

Playboy, 1990, December, Morgan Fox centerfold, VG ..**$5.00**

Playboy, 1992, May, Vicki Smith centerfold, VG............**$2.00**

Popular Mechanics, 1942, April, Call to Battle Stations cover, EX..**$6.00**

Popular Mechanics, 1942, Frozen Billions, VG **$8.00**

Popular Mechanics, 1942, June, Dogs of War, VG.........**$8.00**

Popular Mechanics, 1942, March, The Emergency Patrol, VG **$8.00**

Popular Mechanics, 1942, November, Miracle on Wheels cover, EX **$6.50**

Popular Mechanics, 1942, September, Planes of Tomorrow, VG **$8.00**

Popular Mechanics, 1943, October, Planes of 1953, VG..**$8.00**

Popular Mechanics, 1957, June, G **$3.00**

Popular Mechanics, 1960, December, World of Models issue, G **$3.50**

Popular Science, 1954, December, G.............................**$5.00**

Post, 1961, April 22, Shirley Maclaine cover, M.............**$4.00**

Post, 1966, November 19, Mary Tyler Moore, EX..........**$3.00**

Radio & TV Mirror, 1940, August, Barbara Stanwick cover, NM..**$9.00**

Radio & TV Mirror, 1941, June, Ginger Rogers cover, EX ..**$10.00**

Radio Mirror, 1942, Marjorie Bell cover, EX..................**$7.50**

Radio Mirror, 1943, September, Cheryl Walker cover, NM ..**$10.00**

Radio Mirror, 1944, February, Dinah Shore cover, EX...**$7.50**

Radio Stars, 1938, May, Eddie Cantor cover, NM.........**$15.00**

Ramparts, 1967, May, Bertrand Russell by Norman Rockwell cover, NM..**$35.00**

Real Confessions, 1967, January, Divorced But I Still Have That Urge, EX **$2.50**

Real Story, 1945, December, I Clung to Heartbreak, EX ..**$5.00**

Real Story, 1945, October, Journey to Paradise, NM......**$7.00**

Remember When, 1972, John Wayne cover, M **$7.50**

Rolling Stone, 1982, October 14, John Lennon & Yoko Ono cover, VG...**$4.00**

Rolling Stone, 1985, May 9, Madonna cover, M.............**$4.00**

Rolling Stone, 1990, August 9, Warren Beatty cover, M ..**$3.50**

Rolling Stone, 1991, December 12, Yearbook, M **$4.00**

Saturday Evening Post, 1053, December 29, Norman Rockwell cover, VG **$30.00**

Saturday Evening Post, 1942, June 27, Norman Rockwell cover, VG..**$15.00**

Saturday Evening Post, 1943, May 29, Norman Rockwell cover: Rosie the Riveter, VG **$15.00**

Saturday Evening Post, 1944, June 17, VG **$5.00**

Saturday Evening Post, 1958, August 16, VG **$5.00**

Saturday Evening Post, 1958, March 15, Norman Rockwell cover: Boy in Doctor's Office, VG **$12.00**

Saturday Evening Post, 1962, baseball cover, EX...........**$4.00**

Saturday Evening Post, 1963, April, Norman Rockwell cover of Kennedy, VG **$3.00**

Saturday Evening Post, 1963, February 2, Beverly Hillbillies (as American Gothic) cover, VG+.........................**$35.00**

Saturday Evening Post, 1964, March 21, The Beatles cover, VG **$90.00**

Saturday Evening Post, 1965, December 4, Cast of Bonanza (Hoss, Ben & Little Joe) cover, VG **$10.00**

Saturday Evening Post, 1965, May, Brigitte Bardot cover, EX...**$6.00**

Saturday Evening Post, 1985, August, Elvis Presley, VG..**$25.00**

See, 1946, May, Jane Russell cover, NM.......................**$12.50**

Seventeen, 1948, November, Your Parents & You, EX..**$3.00**

Seventeen, 1965, July, Give a Party, EX........................**$3.00**

Smokehouse Monthly, 1931, December, EX **$12.00**

Sports Illustrated, 1957, May 13, Wally Moon cover, NM ..**$12.00**

Sports Illustrated, 1961, March 6, Spring Training issue, M **$10.00**

Sports Illustrated, 1961, October 2, Roger Maris cover, NM **$22.50**

Sports Illustrated, 1964, August 10, Brooks Robinson cover, NM **$10.00**

Sports Illustrated, 1965, December 20, Sandy Koufax cover, M **$15.00**

Sports Illustrated, 1969, October 20, World Series issue, M **$10.00**

Time, 1962, August 10, Reaching for the Moon cover, M ..**$2.50**

Time, 1962, September 28, Ted Kennedy cover, M.......**$2.50**

Time, 1963, May 17, James Baldwin cover, NM $35.00

Time, 1968, June 28, Aretha Franklin cover, G **$3.50**

Time, 1969, February 7, Dustin Hoffman & Mia Farrow cover, G..**$4.00**
Time, 1970, August 10, Bill Rogers cover, VG **$2.00**
Time, 1970, July 6, VG...**$2.00**
Time, 1970, November 23, Sesame Street cover, VG.....**$5.00**
Time, 1970, October 5, Richard Nixon cover, VG **$3.00**
Time, 1971, June 7, Dick Cavett cover, EX.....................**$2.00**
Time, 1973, January 22, Marlon Brando cover, VG **$3.50**
Time, 1974, August 19, Gerald Ford Cover, VG.............**$2.50**
Time, 1975, August 25, Henry Kissinger cover, VG.......**$2.50**
Time, 1978, January 9, Burt Reynolds cover, VG...........**$2.50**
Town & Country, 1954, March, VG.................................**$7.50**
True, 1963, July, EX **$3.50**
True, 1967, Secret Nazi Surrender, M **$5.00**
True Confessions, 1947, December, I Passed As White, EX..**$7.00**
True Confessions, 1951, September, I Was a Narcotics Girl, NM...**$6.00**
True Romance, 1955, August, Love From a Stranger, NM..**$8.00**
True Story, 1940, May, Susan Hayward cover, NM......**$10.00**
True Story, 1949, October, Complete Home Beauty Plan, EX...**$4.50**
True Story, 1953, June, Love Before Marriage, EX.........**$4.00**
True Story, 1965, April, College Men Are Not the Best Lovers, EX...**$3.00**
True Story, 1972, March, Daddy Are You Our Mommy Now?, M..**$2.00**
Whisper, 1969, December, Mia Farrow cover, NM........**$5.00**
Wisdom, 1956, April, Albert Schweitzer cover, M........**$17.50**
Wisdom, 1956, August, Volume 1, #7, Helen Keller cover, EX..**$17.50**
Woman's Day, 1983, June 7, EX.......................................**$1.50**
Woman's Home Companion, July 1943, VG **$5.00**
Woman's Home Companion, 1955, February, Joan Crawford cover, NM **$6.00**

Majolica

Vast amounts of majolica were made by potters both here and abroad from the Victorian era until the early 1900s, so it has roots in a much earlier time period than we generally deal with in this publication, but there are many examples of it still around today, and because it is such an interesting field, we want to at least touch on it.

Broadly defined, majolica is a lead-glazed pottery with relief designs taken from nature. Colors are nearly always vivid. Figural pieces are common. Much of it is unmarked, but items that are will be stamped with names like Winton, George Jones, Sarreguemines, Griffin Smith and Hill (Etruscan), Wedgwood, and Fielding. Of course, if a mark is present, the design very detailed, and the color good, majolica can be very expensive. But many of the smaller pieces are very beautiful and can sometimes still be picked up at reasonable prices.

For more information, we recommend *The Collector's Encyclopedia of Majolica* by Mariann Katz-Marks.

Basket, Bamboo & Basketweave, Banks & Thorley, pink interior **$250.00**

Basket, Bird's Nest, 9x8½", brown background, pink interior **$285.00**
Bowl, Begonia Leaf, 5"...**$115.00**
Bowl, Picket Fence, 9", turquoise interior..................**$180.00**
Bowl, Pond Lily, 8" **$250.00**
Bowl, vegetable; Bird & Fan, 10" long, Wardle **$280.00**
Bowl, waste; Leaf & Berry, 5".......................................**$120.00**
Butter pat, Astor, Wedgwood..**$45.00**
Butter pat, Butterfly, Fielding.......................................**$40.00**
Butter pat, Geranium Leaf, later style, Griffin Smith & Hill, NM **$40.00**
Butter pat, green leaf form **$25.00**
Butter pat, Pansy, Etruscan...**$55.00**
Butter pat, Shell & Seaweed, Etruscan **$190.00**
Cheese keeper, 6½x10" dia, Wedgwood, yellow flowers on red background, repair to underplate **$500.00**
Cup & saucer, Bamboo, 6", Etruscan.........................**$275.00**
Cup & saucer, Bamboo & Floral, 6", turquoise w/pink interior **$235.00**
Cup & saucer, Pineapple..**$175.00**
Humidor, 9", Black man playing accordion while seated on barrel, figural..**$375.00**
Jar, 5", bison head, figural...**$120.00**
Match holder & striker, 7", Black man w/basket seated on log, figural, repaired **$275.00**

Mug, Picket Fence & Floral, 3¾", leaves & white blossom on wood-grain, blue interior, yellow handle.$145.00
Mustache cup, floral decor on white background, pink interior **$100.00**
Pitcher, Bamboo & Bow, 5", pewter top...................**$165.00**
Pitcher, Bamboo & Floral, 4½", white w/gold trim ...**$100.00**
Pitcher, Butterfly & Bamboo, 3", lavender interior....**$150.00**
Pitcher, Chicken w/Sheaf of Wheat, 8½", minor roughness **$300.00**
Pitcher, Cobalt & Floral, 5½", aqua bands top and bottom, yellow & white mums on cobalt, branch handle .**$145.00**
Pitcher, Corn, 4½"...**$150.00**
Pitcher, Corn, 9"...**$300.00**
Pitcher, flowers on white background, sm.................**$50.00**
Pitcher, Fruit, 6½", white background, brown handle ...**$145.00**
Pitcher, parrot figural, 11½" **$275.00**

Pitcher, Stork in Lily Pads, 8½", owl handle **$400.00**
Pitcher, syrup; Bow & Floral, 8¼".....................**$180.00**
Pitcher, syrup; Sunflower, Etruscan, yellow & brown flower on white background, minor wear......................**$275.00**
Pitcher, Water Lily, 4½", Holdcroft type, turquoise & green on brown background, turquoise interior..........**$150.00**
Pitcher, Wild Rose on Tree Bark, 6½", brown background..**$135.00**
Plate, Bow on Basketweave, 6" **$100.00**
Plate, Fish & Daisy, 9", Holdcroft, cobalt background..**$150.00**
Plate, Overlapping Begonia Leaf, 8¼", green, white & pink **$85.00**
Plate, oyster; 9", Minton design of alternating pink & white wells w/green center well....................................**$275.00**
Plate, Pond Lily, 9¼", EX color & glaze.....................**$175.00**
Plate, Running Stag & Dog, 8", fancy embossed rim....**$110.00**
Plate, Strawberry, 9", Etruscan, blue background......**$225.00**
Platter, Begonia Leaf on Bark, 12¼x9".......................**$175.00**
Platter, Bird & Fan, 14" long **$235.00**
Platter, Dog & Doghouse, 11"....................**$215.00**
Platter, Grapevine, 13" dia, multicolor leaves...........**$225.00**
Platter, Leaf & Floral, 15" long, turquoise **$175.00**
Platter, Pond Lily, 12" dia, green leaves on brown background **$225.00**
Platter, Rose on Basketweave, 13" dia......................**$225.00**
Relish tray, Onion & Pickle, 8", Wedgwood, diamond shape **$180.00**
Sugar bowl, Basket & Blackberry, mottled **$150.00**
Sugar bowl, Floral...**$120.00**
Teapot, Chick on Nest, 6" **$245.00**
Toothbrush holder, Leaf on Fence & Basket, 4½", turquoise & yellow background **$250.00**
Tray, bread; Corn, 12" **$225.00**
Tray, bread; Pineapple, 13", Wardle **$225.00**

Male Action Figures and Accessories

Just as the generations before them enjoyed playing with lead soldiers and munitions of war, since the sixties, boys have engaged in 'battle' with combat-ready warriors dressed in camouflage fatigues, trained with would-be pilots in orange jumpsuits, and explored the universe with spacemen in suits made of the same silver fabric used to clothe real US Astronauts.

GI Joe is the most famous of these action figures. He has been made in hundreds of variations by Hasbro from 1964 to the present. They also made vehicles for all types of terrains and situations, accessories such as bunk beds and footlockers, and even buildings. Action figures were so successful here that companies overseas obtained the rights and became licensed to produce their own versions. Eventually they were made in Japan, England, Australia, Spain, Brazil, and Germany.

If you'd like to learn more about them, we recommend *Collectible Male Action Figures* by Susan and Paris Manos.

Our listings are for figures in mint condition and in their original boxes. 'Played-with' figures in very good condition may be worth from 60% to 75% less.

Action Man, accessory pack, Palitoy of England, M on card, minimum value **$30.00**
Action Man, basic figure, Palitoy of England, MIB, minimum value **$85.00**
Action Man, British Infantryman, Palitoy of England, MIB, minimum value **$60.00**
Action Man, German Pilot Outfit, Palitoy of England, w/accessories, M in package, minimum value......**$65.00**
Action Man, Indian Brave Outfit, Palitoy of England, M on card, minimum value..**$85.00**
Action Man, Transport Command Armoured Jeep, Palitoy of England, w/machine guns & net, MIB, minimum value.**$150.00**
Action Super Team, Hard Rock figure, Schildkrot of Germany, dressed, MIB, minimum value.................**$120.00**
Action Team, Action Girl Ski Racing Outfit, Schildkrot of Germany, MIB, minimum value............................**$65.00**
Captain Action, Action Cave carrying case, Ideal, ca 1967, M, minimum value **$120.00**
Captain Action, Aqua Lad disguise (no figure), Ideal, ca 1966-68, missing spear..**$120.00**

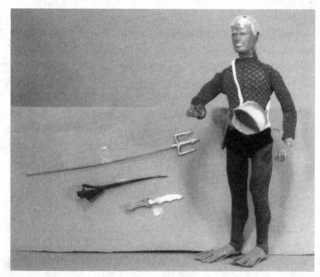

Captain Action, Aquaman disguise (no figure), Ideal, ca 1966-68, M, minimum value $120.00
Captain Action, basic figure, 11½", Ideal, MIB, minimum value **$240.00**
Captain Action, Batman disguise (no figure), Ideal, ca 1966-68, M, minimum value......................................**$135.00**
Captain Action, Dr Evil figure, Ideal, in suit only, ca 1966-68, M, minimum value......................................**$200.00**
Captain Action, Phantom disguise (alone), Ideal, 1966, M, minimum value **$120.00**
Combat Joe, Real Action Figure, Small Arms Accessory Pack, Takara of Japan, M on card, minimum value........**$25.00**
Combat Joe, Real Action Figure, Takara of Japan, #1, dressed as American soldier, MIB, minimum value.................**$120.00**
Combat Joe, Real Action Figure, Takara of Japan, #3, basic figure, brown hair, MIB, minimum value.............**$60.00**

Combat Man, German Soldier, Tsukuda of Japan, full uniform, w/accessories, MIB, minimum value **$115.00**

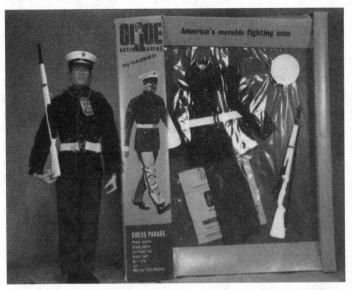

GI Joe, Action Marine Dress Parade Set, #7710, Hasbro, dress blues, cap & M-1 rifle, MIB $150.00

GI Joe, Action Marine Medic Set, #7719, Hasbro, stretcher, crutch, satchel, armbands, flag...; 11 pieces, MIB......**$125.00**

GI Joe, Action Marine Weapons Rack, #7727, Hasbro, 4-piece set, MIB, minimum value **$70.00**

GI Joe, Action Pilot Coloring Book, Watkins & Strathmore Company, 300-page, M, minimum value...............**$18.00**

GI Joe, Action Pilot Scramble Set, #7807, Hasbro, flight suit, life vest, pistol, holster, etc; 8 pieces, MIB...........**$175.00**

GI Joe, Action Sailor Deck Commander Set, #7621, Hasbro, jumpsuit, helmet, goggles, binoculars, etc; 9 pieces, MIB **$150.00**

GI Joe, Action Soldier, #7500, Hasbro, realistic fatigues, dog tag & insignias, MIB..**$175.00**

GI Joe, Action Soldier, Hasbro of Canada, dressed, w/manual, MIB, minimum value......................................**$225.00**

GI Joe, Action Soldier Coloring Book, Watkins & Strathmore Company, M, minimum value................................**$12.50**

GI Joe, Action Soldier Military Police Set, #7521, Hasbro, Ike jacket, trousers, white belt, etc; 10 pieces, MIB..**$150.00**

GI Joe, Adventure Team Book & Record Set, Secret of the Mummy's Tomb, M, minimum value.....................**$12.50**

GI Joe, Adventure Team Foot Locker & Interior, Hasbro, hard plastic, M, minimum value............................**$30.00**

GI Joe, Adventure Team Hidden Treasure Outfit, Hasbro, M in package **$15.00**

GI Joe, Adventure Team Jungle Survival Outfit, Hasbro, w/accessories, M in package..................................**$50.00**

GI Joe, Adventure Team Secret Mission Outfit, Hasbro, M in package **$15.00**

GI Joe, Adventure Team Smoke Jumper Outfit, Hasbro, w/accessories, M in package..................................**$42.50**

GI Joe, Adventure Team Underwater Demolition Accessories, Hasbro, 4-piece set, M in package.............**$18.00**

GI Joe, Coloring Book, Whitman, M, minimum value ..**$18.00**

GI Joe, Combat & Adventure Team All-Terrain Vehicle Play

Set, #7450, Hasbro, MIB, minimum value...........**$120.00**

GI Joe, Combat & Adventure Team Canteen, Hasbro, child size, minimum value..**$20.00**

GI Joe, Combat & Adventure Team Equipment Case, M $25.00

GI Joe, Combat & Adventure Team Flare Gun, Hasbro, child size, minimum value..**$20.00**

GI Joe, Combat & Adventure Team Foot Locker, Hasbro, painted wood, M..**$60.00**

GI Joe, Combat & Adventure Team Helicopter, Hasbro, M **$75.00**

GI Joe, Combat & Adventure Team Motorcycle & Side Car, Hasbro, minimum value **$125.00**

GI Joe, Combat & Adventure Team Walkie Talkie Set, Hasbro, child size, minimum value.............................**$24.00**

GI Joe, Combat & Adventure Team 5-Star Jeep, #7000, Hasbro, minimum value **$155.00**

GI Joe, Electric Drawing Set, #8266, Hasbro, MIB, minimum value **$30.00**

GI Joe, Fighting Men, British Commando Accessories, canteen, case, cartridge belt, gas mask, etc; 7 pieces, 1966, MIB **$100.00**

GI Joe, Fighting Men, Japanese Imperial Soldier Accessories, cartridge belt, rifle, pistol, medal, etc; 7 pieces, MIB **$120.00**

GI Joe, Fighting Men, Russian Infantry Man, 1966, MIB..**$300.00**

GI Joe, Green Beret, Hasbro, dressed figure, w/8-piece accessory set, any eye or hair color, 1969, MIB..**$325.00**

GI Joe, Jigsaw Puzzle, 14x18", Whitman, 150-piece, MIB, minimum value **$12.00**

GI Joe, Pencil Case, Hasbro, color decal on rectangular plastic box, M, minimum value **$35.00**

GI Joe, Super Joe, basic figure, Hasbro, 1977, MIB.....**$40.00**

GI Joe, Super Joe Command Center, Hasbro, 1977, minimum value...**$30.00**

GI Joe, Super Joe Paths of Danger Playset, Hasbro, M....**$25.00**

GI Joe, Talking Action Sailor, Hasbro, realistic fatigues, hat, dog tag & insignias, MIB **$225.00**

GI Joe, Talking Action Soldier, Hasbro, fatigues, hat, dog tag & insignias, 1967, MIB..**$225.00**

Ken, Army & Airforce, #797, Mattel, uniformed w/accessories, ca early 1970s, M.......................................**$125.00**

Marbles

Antique marbles can be very expensive (some are worth more than $1,500.00) and variations are endless. In his books *Antique and Collectible Marbles, Machine-Made and Contemporary Marbles,* and *Everett Grist's Big Book of Marbles,* author Everett Grist thoroughly describes and pictures each type. These books are a must if you plan on doing much in the way of buying or selling marbles.

Mr. Grist divides antique marbles into several classes: 1) Transparent Swirls, of which he lists six types (Solid Core, Latticinio Core, Divided Core, Ribbon Core, Lobed Core, and Coreless); 2) Lutz or Lutz-type, having bands containing copper flecks which alternate with colored or clear bands; 3) Peppermint Swirl, made with red, white, and blue opaque glass; 4) Indian Swirl, made of black glass with multicolored surface swirls; 5) Banded Swirl, opaque or transparent, having wide swirling bands; 6) Onionskin, given an overall mottled appearance by its spotted swirling lines or lobes; 7) End of Day, single pontil, allover spots, 2-colored or multicolored; 8) Clambroth, evenly spaced, swirled lines on opaque glass; 9) Mica, transparent color with mica flakes added; 10) Sulphide, usually made of clear glass (though colored examples may be found) containing figures

In addition to the glass marbles, there were those made of clay, pottery, china, steel, and various types of semiprecious stones.

Then come the machine-made marbles! Most of these defy description. Many are worth no more than 50¢, but some of the harder-to-find colors and those with well-defined color placement may run from $10.00 up to $20.00. Guineas (Christensen agates with small multicolored specks instead of swirls) go for as much as $200.00, and the comic character marbles made by Peltier range from $60.00 to $80.00, except for Betty Boop and Kayo which are worth $100.00 to $150.00 each.

As for condition, it is all-important. An absolutely mint marble is very rare and may be worth as much as three to five times more than one in near-mint condition. Marbles in only 'good' condition, having large chips and cracks, may be worth half (or less) of near-mint values. The same is true of one that has been polished, regardless of the improvement the polishing makes. Our values are for marbles in at least excellent condition.

Banded Opaque Swirl, ⅝" **$75.00**
Banded Transparent Swirl, ⅝", amber w/yellow band ..**$50.00**
Blue Lace Agate, ⅞" **$25.00**
Clay, 1¾", brown & blue **$20.00**
Clay, ⅝", Line Crockery, white w/zigzag lines of blue & green **$10.00**
Comic, ⅝", Andy **$75.00**
Comic, ⅝", Annie **$80.00**
Flame Swirl, ⅝", opaque white base w/black lines, Christensen Agate Co **$35.00**

Indian Swirl, ⅝", black glass w/colored bands applied to surface **$95.00**
Lutz, ⅝", colored transparent swirl, blue, green, or yellow **$100.00**
Lutz, ⅝", ribbon core, gold-colored flakes & outlined w/ threads of white glass **$250.00**
Lutz-type Indian swirl, ⅝", w/gold-colored flakes **$400.00**
Machine made, ¾", crackle glass, any color, 1940s **$2.00**
Machine made, ⅝", multicolor swirls **$5.00**
Machine-made, ¹¹⁄₁₆", Cub Scout, yellow & blue **$5.00**
Machine-made, ¹¹⁄₁₆", 3-color opaque corkscrew, Akro Agate **$15.00**
Machine-made, ¾", green, brown, blue & purple slag, Akro Agate **$8.00**
Machine-made, ⅝", lemonade corkscrew, Akro Agate ..**$12.00**
Machine-made, ⅞", carnelian, Akro Agate **$15.00**
Machine-made, ⁹⁄₁₆", tiger, orange & black **$10.00**
Machine-made slag, ¾", green, brown, blue, & purple, Akro Agate **$8.00**
Onionskin, ⅝", w/mica **$85.00**
Onionskin Lutz, ⅝", w/gold-colored flakes **$175.00**
Opaque Swirl, ⅝", light blue base w/mustard yellow swirls, Christensen Agate Co **$20.00**

Open Core Swirl & Multicolored Ribbon Swirl, 1" to 1⅛", any as shown **$85.00**
Peppermint Swirl, ⅝", opaque, red, white, & blue **$90.00**
Slag, ¾", orange, Christensen Agate Co **$12.50**
Slag-type, ⅝", opaque yellow, ground pontil transition ..**$45.00**
Solid Core Swirl, 1½", white core w/red, green & blue strands, yellow outer strands **$125.00**
Solid Core Swirl, 1¾", red, green & yellow core w/white outer strands **$150.00**
Solid Opaque, ⅝", black, white, blue, green or pink, 1 or 2 pontil marks **$50.00**
Sulphide, 1½", feeding lamb on a grass mound **$125.00**

Sulphide, 1¼", elephant **$135.00**
Sulphide, 1¼", seated cat on mound **$175.00**

Sulphide, 1¾", male lion standing on a grass mound ..**$150.00**

Sulphide, 1⅜", hen seated on a nest **$175.00**

Swirl, ⅝", black base w/yellow swirls, Christensen Agate Co...**$35.00**

Transparent glass w/mica flakes, ⅝", blue, green, amber or clear **$25.00**

Transparent Swirl, 1¾", solid core **$175.00**

Transparent Swirl, ⅝", coreless swirl **$15.00**

Transparent Swirl, ⅝", latticino core, yellow or white **$10.00**

Transparent Swirl, ⅝", lobed core swirl, transparent glass..**$35.00**

Match Covers

Only two or three match covers out of a hundred have any value to a collector. Of that small percentage, most will be worth considerably less than $10.00. What makes a match cover collectible? First of all, it must be in mint condition. Collectors prefer to remove the staples and the matchsticks and to store them in special albums for protection. Secondly, those with the striker on the front are preferred. These pre-date the mid-1970s, when new laws were passed that resulted in the striker being moved to the back cover.

General categories include restaurants, hotels and motels, political, girlies, and sports stars and events.

The American Match Cover Association publishes a book with information on both pricing and identification. See the Directory under Newsletters for the address of the Front Striker Bulletin.

Charlie Low's Forbidden City, a nightclub in San Francisco's China Town, ca 1930s...**$8.50**

Democratic National Convention, 1940, Chicago Welcomes You, red, white & blue, Superior Match Co $6.00

Down Argentine Way, film scene featuring Betty Grable, ca 1940s..**$10.00**

Drink Coca-Cola, 1930s **$5.00**

Icy Point Salmon, features salmon, Packed In Alaska for Skinner & Eddy Core, Seattle, Washington **$3.50**

Joe Di Maggio, New York Yankees & Joe Di Maggio's Grotto, San Francisco, Joe in batting pose, blue & white, ca 1939, EX...**$12.50**

Playland at the Beach, San Francisco **$3.50**

World's Fair, features Wrigley's Spearmint Gum advertising, Come & Enjoy...A Delicious Treat..., 1939, EX........**$5.00**

McCoy Pottery

This is probably the best-known of all American potteries, due to the wide variety of goods they produced from 1910 until the pottery finally closed only a few years ago.

They were located in Roseville, Ohio, the pottery center of the United States during the first half of the century. They're most famous for their cookie jars, of which were made several hundred styles and variations. Some of the rarer, more desirable jars are 'Mammy with Cauliflowers,' 'Leprechaun,' and 'Hillbilly Bear,' any one of which is worth at least $1,000.00. Many are in the $200.00 to $400.00 range, and even the most common jars generally bring $30.00 to $40.00. Condition is important, not only in regard to hairlines and chips, but paint as well. Many of the early jars were painted over the glaze with 'cold' (unfired) paint which over the years tends to wear off. Be sure to evaluate the amount of remaining 'cold' paint when you buy or sell.

In addition to the cookie jars, McCoy is well-known for their figural planters, novelty kitchenware, and dinnerware. A line introduced in the late 1970s is beginning to attract collectors — a glossy brown stoneware-type dinnerware with frothy white decoration around the rims. Similar lines of brown stoneware was made by many other companies, Hull and Pfaltzgraff among them. See Hull and/or Pfaltzgraff for values that will also apply to McCoy's line.

They used a variety of marks over the years, but with little consistency, since it was a common practice to discontinue an item for awhile and then bring it out again decorated in a manner that would be compatible with current tastes. All of McCoy's marks were 'in the mold.' None were ink stamped, so very often the in-mold mark remained as it was when the mold was originally created. Most marks contain the McCoy name, though some of the early pieces were simply signed 'NM' for Nelson McCoy (Sanitary and Stoneware Company, the company's original title). Early stoneware pieces were sometimes impressed with a shield containing a number. If you have a piece with the Lancaster Colony Company mark (three curved lines — the left one beginning as a vertical and terminating as a horizontal, the other two formed as 'C's contained in the curve of the first), you'll know that your piece was made after the mid-70s when McCoy was owned by that group. Today even these later pieces are becoming collectible.

If you'd like to learn more about this company, we recommend *The Collector's Encyclopedia of McCoy Pottery* by Sharon and Bob Huxford.

Beware of *new* cookie jars marked McCoy. It seems that McCoy never registered their trademark, and it is now legally used by a small company in Rockwood, Tennessee.

Not only do they use the original mark, but they are reproducing some of the original jars as well. If you're not an experienced collector, you may have trouble distinguishing the new from the old. Some (but not all) are dated #93, but there are differences to watch for. The new ones are slightly smaller in size, and the finish is often flawed. He is also using the McCoy mark on jars never produced by the original company, such as Little Red Riding Hood and the Luzianne mammy.

Basket, oak leaves & acorns embossed overall, marked ..**$35.00**
Bean pot, bright flowers on black, round handles......**$22.00**
Bean pot, yellow 'hammered' pot w/3 legs, marked USA, individual size **$9.00**
Beverage jug, Sunburst Gold, w/lid, marked...............**$50.00**
Bookend, rearing horse, white.....................................**$20.00**
Bookends, swallow embossed on side, marked, pr....**$60.00**
Bowl, shouldered type, green w/embossed rings, lg, marked...**$30.00**
Bowl, shouldered type, pink & blue bands, lg, marked USA..**$25.00**
Cache pot, double; 2 flower forms w/bird between, marked **$20.00**
Cookie jar, American Eagle, embossed eagle on front of woven basket shape, unmarked **$40.00**
Cookie jar, Animal Crackers, multicolor embossed animal shapes on sides, clown head finial, marked **$95.00**

Cookie jar, Apollo, silver lunar module, w/all original labels, minimum value.................................$800.00
Cookie jar, Apple, green w/pink blush, leaf finial, marked **$50.00**
Cookie jar, Apple on Basketweave, multicolor details on tan, marked **$50.00**
Cookie jar, Bananas, yellow bunch w/brown stem finial, marked...**$90.00**
Cookie jar, Barnum's Animals (also known as Nabisco Wagon), clown head finial............................**$275.00**

Cookie jar, Bear, multicolor paint on tan, no 'Cookies' on front, marked...**$60.00**
Cookie jar, Betsy Baker, figure in style of 'Pillsbury Dough Boy,' marked...**$200.00**
Cookie jar, Black Kettle, yellow & white flowers on black, immovable bail handle on lid, marked..................**$35.00**
Cookie jar, Bobby Baker **$6.50**
Cookie jar, Brown Milk Can, marked **$25.00**
Cookie jar, Caboose, multicolor details on tan, 'Cookie Special' on front, marked **$165.00**
Cookie jar, Chef, mustached man' head, 'Cookies' on hat, marked...**$110.00**
Cookie jar, Chipmunk, figure eating nut, brown & green on tan, black eyes & nose, marked..........................**$100.00**
Cookie jar, Christmas tree, star finial, marked, minimum value **$550.00**
Cookie jar, Churn, brown form w/embossed bands, unmarked **$35.00**
Cookie jar, Circus Horse, black w/red & white details, marked...**$175.00**
Cookie jar, Clown (bust), multicolor details on tan, marked...**$75.00**
Cookie jar, Clown in Barrel, red, black & yellow details on clown, green barrel, marked................................**$120.00**
Cookie jar, Coalby Cat, black w/multicolor details, marked...**$350.00**
Cookie jar, Coffee Grinder, brown & black on tan w/'Cookies' in red on front, marked..................................**$35.00**
Cookie jar, Colonial Fireplace, hearth embossed on front of rectangular shape, clock finial, marked USA............**$90.00**
Cookie jar, Cookie Barrel, brown embossed staves & bands on barrel form, 'Cookies' on front, ball finial........**$30.00**
Cookie jar, Cookie Boy, half-figure, tan, marked......**$160.00**
Cookie jar, Cookie Cabin, log cabin shape, roof removes, marked...**$80.00**
Cookie jar, Cookie Jug, brown top w/tan woven 'rope' base, marked...**$30.00**
Cookie jar, Cookie Log, brown tree trunk w/squirrel finial, 'Cookie Log' embossed in knothole, unmarked **$35.00**
Cookie jar, Cookie Safe, black safe form, marked USA on leg **$65.00**
Cookie jar, Corn, yellow ear w/green leaves at base, marked **$125.00**
Cookie jar, Country Stove (also known as Potbellied Stove), black w/red & gold details, marked **$35.00**
Cookie jar, Covered Wagon, Conestoga-type wagon, cream w/yellow & brown details, marked....................**$100.00**
Cookie jar, Dog on Basketweave, multicolor details on tan, marked...**$55.00**
Cookie jar, Drum, red w/a black band at top & bottom, sm drum finial, marked **$65.00**
Cookie jar, Duck on Basketweave, multicolor details on yellow, marked...**$55.00**
Cookie jar, Dutch Boy, multicolored embossed figure on white, pink at rim & base, marked......................**$45.00**
Cookie jar, Dutch Treat Barn, tall brown barn w/yellow details, 'Dutch Treat' on front, unmarked **$60.00**

Cookie jar, Early American (also known as Frontier Family), embossed scenic reserve w/brown on cream, unmarked **$50.00**

Cookie jar, Early American Chest (also known as Chiffionier), brown form w/'Cookies' on front, marked....**$75.00**

Cookie jar, Elephant, tan w/red & black details, wearing vest, trunk curled..**$130.00**

Cookie jar, Engine, black locomotive engine w/red & yellow details, marked..**$140.00**

Cookie Jar, Flowerpot, creamy white pot w/plastic flower top, unmarked, minimum value **$500.00**

Cookie jar, Fortune Cookie, Chinese lantern form, red, white & black, marked..**$60.00**

Cookie jar, Fox Squirrel, marked, very rare, minimum value $700.00

Cookie jar, Freddy Gleep, green comic figure hugging knees, black details, unmarked............................**$500.00**

Cookie jar, Gingerbread Boy, embossed figure in reserve w/multicolor cookie shapes, marked **$50.00**

Cookie jar, Globe, airplane finial, hand-decorated countries, marked...**$225.00**

Cookie jar, Grandfather Clock, brown, marked USA **$85.00**

Cookie jar, Granny, lady w/glasses & hands folded, hair bun forms lid, marked USA..**$80.00**

Cookie jar, Hen on Nest, 'Cookies' in red along base, marked USA **$85.00**

Cookie jar, Hexagon, bright red flowers on cream, square handles, 'W' finial, marked......................................**$45.00**

Cookie jar, Hillbilly Bear, sitting on stump, multicolor paint, marked, minimum value **$1,000.00**

Cookie jar, Hobby Horse, brown, red & green details, yellow rockers, marked..**$120.00**

Cookie jar, Honey Bear, brown & green on tan, mushroom finial, marked **$75.00**

Cookie jar, House, brown & green on tan, half of roof forms lid, marked..**$110.00**

Cookie jar, Humpty Dumpty decal on cylindrical shape, gold trim, unmarked...**$65.00**

Cookie jar, Indian, head figural in brown shades, 'Cookies' at base, marked..**$300.00**

Cookie jar, Jug, brown top over tan base (to resemble Albany slip over salt glaze), marked.....................**$22.00**

Cookie jar, Kettle, brown, movable bail handle, jumbo size, marked..**$40.00**

Cookie jar, Kittens on Ball of Yarn, 3 kittens on top form lid of red ball form, 'Cookies' embossed on side, marked **$110.00**

Cookie jar, Kookie Kettle, kettle form w/movable bail handle, 'Kookie Kettle' in gold on black, marked **$25.00**

Cookie jar, Lazy Pig, marked 201 McCoy USA, white w/black facial features, 1978-79.............................**$35.00**

Cookie jar, Liberty Bell, bronze bell w/crack' embossed on front, marked...**$40.00**

Cookie jar, Little Clown, red & black details on tan, marked **$65.00**

Cookie jar, Lollipops, multicolored lollipops on sides, lollipops form finial, marked.....................................**$55.00**

Cookie jar, Love Birds (also known as Kissing Penguins), red & black details, marked **$80.00**

Cookie jar, Mac Dog, raised paw, head & shoulders form lid, marked USA..**$85.00**

Cookie jar, Mammy, 'Cookies' embossed on skirt, red & white checked apron, marked **$190.00**

Cookie jar, Mammy w/Cauliflowers, multicolor paint, marked, minimum value.................................**$1,100.00**

Cookie jar, Modern, stylized futuristic shape w/'Cookies' in red on tan, marked..**$40.00**

Cookie jar, Monk, 'Thou Shalt Not Steal' on brown robe, unmarked **$40.00**

Cookie Jar, Mother Goose, tan w/yellow & green details, marked..**$120.00**

Cookie jar, Mr & Mrs Owl, couple in hats sit among pine cones, 'Cookies' on base, marked.........................**$95.00**

Cookie jar, multicolor fruit on blue concave shape.....**$30.00**

Cookie jar, Mushrooms on Stump, marked 214 McCoy USA, 1972 ....**$30.00**

Cookie jar, Oaken Bucket, embossed staves & bands on brown bucket form, rope finial, marked USA.......**$25.00**

Cookie jar, Old Fashioned Auto (also known as Touring Car), marked...**$85.00**

Cookie jar, Penguin, green figural, marked **$150.00**

Cookie jar, Picnic Basket, 'Cookies' on side, handles form lid, marked USA **$70.00**

Cookie jar, Pineapple, leaves finial, marked...............**$65.00**

Cookie jar, Pirates Chest, brown on tan, unmarked....**$70.00**

Cookie jar, Pitcher, harvesting couple painted in multicolor on green pitcher form, marked...........................**$50.00**

Cookie jar, Pitcher, ivory form w/ornate handle **$25.00**

Cookie jar, Pumpkin, smiling jack-o'-lantern face, marked, minimum value **$500.00**

Cookie jar, Quaker Oats, Quaker man in reserve, cylindrical, marked USA, minimum value **$350.00**

Cookie jar, Red Bean Pot, bail handle, unmarked.......**$28.00**

Cookie jar, Rocking Chair, Dalmations; many spotted dogs in black rocker, 'Cookies' on front of chair, marked **$350.00**

Cookie jar, Spaceship, 'Friendship' in white & '7' in red on black space capsule form.................................$165.00

Cookie jar, Strawberry, bright round red body w/green cap lid, marked $38.00

Cookie jar, Teapot, 'Cookies' embossed on side, marked..$190.00

Cookie jar, Tepee, Indian in doorway, multicolor, straight top, marked...$235.00

Cookie jar, Tomato, bright red w/green stem finial, marked $35.00

Cookie jar, Turkey, tail spread, head & neck form lid, natural colors, marked...$185.00

Cookie jar, Turkey, tail spread, head & neck form lid, green, rare color, marked...$250.00

Cookie jar, Uncle Sam's Hat, red, white & blue upturned hat w/stars & stripes, marked USA $210.00

Cookie jar, WC Fields, head figural, hat forms lid, marked USA $175.00

Cookie jar, white ball shape w/rooster finial, gold trim, marked $80.00

Cookie jar, White Rooster, red comb & waddle, yellow beak $55.00

Cookie jar, Windmill, blue w/pink bud finial, marked..$100.00

Cookie jar, Wishing Well, 'Wish I Had a Cookie' on front, marked $40.00

Cookie jar, Woodsy Owl, figure w/green hat & pants plays guitar, marked USA..$200.00

Cookie jar, Wren House, brown & green on tan, half of roof removes, bird finial, marked $115.00

Creamer, dog figural, tail handle, marked...................$35.00

Creamer, embossed water lily on brown, unmarked......$25.00

Cuspidor, embossed grapes on green, flared rim, unmarked $30.00

Custard cup, cobalt w/embossed ribs...........................$4.00

Custard cup, plain cylinder w/sm scalloped band at top on golden tan...$8.00

Dripolator, ivory 6-sided shape, marked.....................$25.00

Flowerpot, embossed floral band at rim & on matching saucer, unmarked...$20.00

French casserole, brown & yellow mottle, stick handle, marked $12.00

Grease jar, cabbage form, green w/red base, marked..$40.00

Jardiniere, embossed flying birds on light green, unmarked $15.00

Jardiniere, embossed holly on green, unmarked.........$28.00

Jardiniere, fruit-filled branches & basketweave embossed on creamy salmon, 10½", marked.............................$65.00

Lamp base, black panther on log $35.00

Lamp base, boots, cowboy style, lg, marked.............$100.00

Lamp base, mermaid w/seashell, black & white $85.00

Mug, buccaneer embossed on green, marked.............$22.00

Mug, Campbell Kids decoration on white, marked USA ..$15.00

Mug, embossed grapes medallion on green, unmarked..$20.00

Novelty, duck on base, head down, white, unmarked..$12.00

Novelty, fawn on base, head up, white, unmarked $12.00

Novelty, Hillbilly, figure holding knees, green, marked USA $22.00

Novelty, Madonna, head & shoulders, white, unmarked..$15.00

Novelty, pigeon, chest puffed up, pink, marked USA..$12.00

Pencil holder, brown cowboy boot form.....................$20.00

Pitcher, Antique Rose, pink roses on white jug form, gold trim, marked...$18.00

Pitcher, bright flowers on black, tilt type, unmarked ..$28.00

Pitcher, elephant figural, golden tan, marked.............$45.00

Pitcher, embossed bird & cherries on light green, unmarked $28.00

Pitcher, embossed water lilies on green, fish handle, unmarked $45.00

Pitcher, embossed water lily decoration on ivory, sm, unmarked $18.00

Pitcher, fish figural, open mouth forms spout, marked...$45.00

Planter, alligator figural, green, marked.....................$20.00

Planter, butterfly figural, green, unmarked $25.00

Planter, Calypso Banana Boat, 1959 ....$50.00

Planter, cat figural, brown w/green bow, unmarked ..$15.00

Planter, conch shell form, pink shaded to ivory, unmarked $12.00

Planter, cowboy roping steer embossed on front, marked..$50.00

Planter, cradle form, pink, holes on hood to hold ribbon, unmarked $10.00

Planter, dachshund done in 'stretch' style, green, unmarked $15.00

Planter, dog w/cart figural, marked...........................$15.00

Planter, fish figural, pink & green on white, marked..$45.00

Planter, frog figural, lg, 1967 reissue, marked.............$15.00

Planter, Grecian, garland swags on veined background, rectangular, marked..$18.00

Planter, hand figural, opening in palm, green, marked USA $18.00

Planter, lamb figural, white w/curly wool & blue bow, marked...$15.00

Planter, lion figural, white, marked $20.00

Planter, parrot beside planter, green $15.00

Planter, pig figural, white, unmarked.........................$12.00

Planter, poodle w/head up figural, marked.................$15.00

Planter, 'Pussy at the Well' on front...........................$20.00

Planter, rocking chair form, black, marked.................$25.00

Planter, rooster figural, gray w/red comb, marked......$15.00

Planter, squirrel w/nut figural, brown, marked $15.00

Planter, stork stands beside basket, marked $15.00

Planter, swan w/wings up, white, unmarked $15.00

Planter, turtle figural, green, open back, marked $20.00

Salt box, embossed butterflies on dark brown, unmarked $50.00

Spoon rest, butterfly figural, marked $40.00

Spoon rest, penguin figural, marked $45.00

Sugar bowl, Sunburst Gold, w/lid, marked.................$22.00

Tankard, brown staved barrel shape w/embossed bands, marked...$40.00

Tankard, embossed buccaneer on green, unmarked ..$75.00

Tankard, willow branch & basketweave embossed on green, rope handle..$75.00

Tea set, Pine Cone, embossed pine cones, green w/brown wash, marked, 3-piece set....................................$65.00

Teapot, cat figural, black & white, paw spout, tail handle, head forms lid...$60.00

Teapot, embossed cherries & leaves on ball form, blue, unmarked..$45.00

Teapot, Sunburst Gold, marked....................................$45.00

Vase, applied pine cones on 6-sided shape, marked ..$35.00

Vase, bud; lily figural, white w/green leaves, marked ..$22.00

Vase, cornucopia; embossed florals at base, green, lg, unmarked $20.00

Vase, embossed flower decoration on blue Onyx, ball form, unmarked $35.00

Vase, embossed water lily motif on green bulbous shape w/lizard handles, unmarked................................$40.00

Vase, embossed wheat on green 6-sided shape, handles, marked...$15.00

Vase, stylized black cat figural, marked $35.00

Vase, Uncle Sam's head figural, yellow, marked.........$40.00

Wall pocket, basketweave, marked $25.00

Wall pocket, bellows w/red flowers, marked..............$40.00

Wall pocket, bird perched on lg flower, marked $30.00

Wall pocket, bunch of bananas amid green leaves $40.00

Wall pocket, lady's fan, Sunburst Gold, marked..........$35.00

Wall pocket, orange resting on green leaves...............$35.00

Wall pocket, red berries & green holly-like leaves..........$40.00

Wall pocket, umbrella, yellow w/green handle, marked..$22.00

Wall pocket, violin, marked $32.00

Metlox Pottery

Founded in the late 1920s in Manhattan Beach, California, this company initially produced tile and commercial advertising signs. By the early thirties their business in these areas had dwindled, and they began to concentrate their efforts on the manufacture of dinnerware, figurines, and kitchenware.

Carl Romanelli was the designer responsible for modeling many of the figural pieces they made during the late thirties and early forties. These items are usually imprinted with his signature and are very collectible today.

Poppytrail was the tradename for their kitchen and dinnerware lines. Among their more popular patterns were California Ivy, Red Rooster, Homestead Provincial,

and the later embossed patterns, Sculptured Grape, Sculptured Zinnia, and Sculptured Daisy.

Some of their lines can be confusing. There are two 'rooster' lines, Red Rooster (red, orange, and brown) and California Provincial (this one is in dark green and burgundy), and two 'homestead' lines, Colonial Homestead (red, orange, and brown like the Red Rooster line) and Homestead Provincial (dark green and burgundy). If you'd like to learn more about this pottery, we recommend *The Collector's Encyclopedia of California Pottery* by Jack Chipman.

Ashtray, Homestead Provincial $12.00

Bowl, cereal; 7", California Ivy.....................................$8.50

Bowl, cereal; 7½", Antique Grape................................$6.00

Bowl, divided vegetable; California Ivy.................$20.00

Bowl, fruit; Pepper Tree...$6.00

Bowl, lug soup; 5", Provincial Fruit $7.00

Bowl, salad; 11", Homestead Provincial.....................$22.00

Bowl, salad; 7", California Ivy.....................................$12.00

Bowl, serving; Geranium, 16" oval, divided................$22.00

Bowl, soup; 8½", Red Rooster Provincial $8.00

Bowl, vegetable; 10", Geranium $15.00

Bowl, vegetable; 9" square, California Ivy $15.00

Bowl, 10", Provincial Fruit...$18.00

Bowl, 5¾", Geranium..$6.00

Bowl, 6", California Ivy...$6.50

Bowl, 6", Provincial Fruit...$6.00

Bowl, 7", Provincial Fruit, deep $8.00

Bowl, 7", Sculptured Daisy, deep $8.00

Bowl, 7½", Della Robbia, deep $8.00

Bowl, 8", Homestead Provincial..................................$12.00

Butter dish, Geranium $18.00

Butter dish, Provincial Fruit...$25.00

Canister, flour; California Provincial, wooden lid..........$75.00

Carafe, Poppytrail, orange, w/lid.................................$27.00

Casserole, 8½", Pepper Tree, w/lid.............................$28.00

Casserole, 9½", California Ivy, w/lid............................$35.00

Coffee server, Geranium...$15.00

Compote, Navajo, divided...$15.00

Cookie jar, Beaver, brown tones, holds flowers, eyes closed, unmarked $85.00

Cookie jar, Clown, white costume w/black details, Made in Poppytrail, Calif $125.00

Cookie jar, clown, yellow suit, marked Made in Poppytrail Calif...**$85.00**

Cookie jar, Dino, blue dinosaur, Metlox Calif USA copyright '87 by Vincent **$115.00**

Cookie jar, Drum, bisque, brown w/figures in relief along sides, Made in Poppytrail, Calif.................**$40.00**

Cookie jar, Mrs Rabbit, white w/blue details, holding carrot in left hand, Metlox Calif USA...............**$70.00**

Cookie Jar, Raggedy Andy, blue shirt & bow tie, Made in Poppytrail, Calif **$165.00**

Cookie jar, Sir Francis Drake, white duck w/yellow beak & feet, unmarked..**$65.00**

Cookie jar, The Bandit, raccoon holding red apples $135.00

Creamer, Antique Grape..**$10.00**

Creamer, California Ivy **$6.00**

Creamer, Provincial Fruit **$7.00**

Creamer & sugar bowl, Geranium **$15.00**

Creamer & sugar bowl, Homestead Provincial, w/lid ..**$18.00**

Cruet, Homestead Provincial..**$25.00**

Cruet, Navajo...**$12.00**

Cup, Della Robbia..**$8.00**

Cup & saucer, Antique Grape **$7.00**

Cup & saucer, Della Robbia **$10.00**

Cup & saucer, Geranium **$8.00**

Cup & saucer, Homestead Provincial **$10.00**

Cup & saucer, Pepper Tree **$8.00**

Cup & saucer, Provincial Fruit **$10.00**

Cup & saucer, Sculptured Grape **$12.00**

Cup & saucer, Woodland Gold **$7.00**

Gravy boat, California Ivy **$22.00**

Gravy boat, Golden Fruit, 2-spout **$18.00**

Gravy boat, Luau, w/ladle..**$20.00**

Gravy boat, Sculptured Daisy......................................**$25.00**

Gravy boat & ladle, Geranium **$22.50**

Jug, 1½-qt, Red Rooster Provincial...............................**$8.00**

Lazy susan, Ivy, 7-piece...**$150.00**

Mustard, Homestead Provincial...................................**$20.00**

Pitcher, 1-qt, Antique Grape.......................................**$15.00**

Pitcher, ½-gal, Poppytrail, glossy green, ice lip **$30.00**

Plate, dinner; Della Robbia..**$12.00**

Plate, dinner; Luau **$10.00**

Plate, dinner; Pepper Tree **$8.00**

Plate, dinner; Tropicana **$10.00**

Plate, dinner; Woodland Gold..**$8.00**

Plate, salad; Della Robbia..**$8.00**

Plate, salad; Pepper Tree **$7.00**

Plate, 10", California Ivy **$10.00**

Plate, 10½", Antique Grape **$8.50**

Plate, 10½", Geranium **$8.00**

Plate, 10½", Provincial Fruit **$10.00**

Plate, 10⅛", Ivy..**$12.00**

Plate, 6½", Provincial Fruit **$6.50**

Plate, 7½", Happy Time **$7.00**

Plate, 7½", Provincial Fruit **$8.00**

Plate, 7½", Red Rooster Provincial **$6.50**

Platter, 13", California Ivy..**$22.00**

Platter, 13", Homestead Provincial...............................**$20.00**

Platter, 13", Tropicana...**$25.00**

Platter, 13", Woodland Gold...**$14.00**

Platter, 14", Provincial Fruit **$20.00**

Salt & pepper shakers, Antique Grape, pr **$10.00**

Salt & pepper shakers, Geranium, pr..........................**$10.00**

Sugar bowl, Della Robbia, w/lid..................................**$10.00**

Sugar bowl, Provincial Fruit, open................................**$4.00**

Teapot, Sculptured Daisy **$40.00**

Tray, bread; Pepper Tree..**$25.00**

Tray, 7¾", California Provincial, metal...........................**$8.00**

Wall pocket vase, Homestead Provincial **$42.00**

Military Awards

These items are being sought out by a growing number of passionate collectors, and many are beginning to appreciate at an unbelievable pace. There are hundreds of types to look for. Check boxes of memorabilia at estate sales and auctions and attend specialized militaria shows. There is no shortage of these as yet, and you should be able to put together a very interesting collection for a modest investment.

Air Force Good Conduct Medal, full size **$12.50**
Airman's Medal, full size..**$35.00**
American Campaign Medal, full size **$15.00**
Army Achievement Medal, full size **$15.00**
Army Achievement Medal, full size, w/lapel pin & ribbon bar in case **$20.00**
Army Commendation Medal, full size **$20.00**
Army Meritorious Civilian Service Medal, full size.......**$45.00**
Coast Guard Distinguished Service Medal, full size.....**$90.00**
Coast Guard Expert Pistol Shot Award, full size **$25.00**
Coast Guard Medal, miniature **$12.50**
Coast Guard Sea Service Ribbon....................................**$1.50**
Legion of Merit Officer Medal, full size **$50.00**
Marine Corps Expeditionary Service Medal, full size...**$22.50**
Marine Corps WWII Occupation Service Medal, full size ..**$20.00**
National Guard Reserve Medal, full size.......................**$15.00**
Navy 'E' Ribbon w/'E'...**$2.50**
Navy Good Conduct Medal, full size **$15.00**
Navy Marine Distinguished Service Medal, miniature ..**$17.50**
Navy Reserve Meritorious Service Award, full size......**$30.00**
Navy Reserve Sea Service Ribbon..................................**$1.50**
Navy Unit Commendation Ribbon **$1.50**
US Armed Forces Asiatic Pacific Campaign Medal, miniature...**$6.50**
US Armed Forces Defense Meritorious Service Award, full size **$30.00**
US Armed Forces Soldier's Medal, full size, w/lapel pin & ribbon bar in case **$35.00**
US Armed Forces WWII Philippine Liberation Medal, full size **$20.00**
Vietnam War Campaign Medal w/60 bar, full size **$12.50**
Vietnam War Wound Medal, full size..........................**$20.00**

Moon and Star

Moon and Star (originally called Palace) was first produced in the 1880s by John Adams & Company of Pittsburgh. But because the glassware was so heavy to transport, it was made for only a few years. In the 1960s, Joseph Weishar of Wheeling, West Virgina, owner of Island Mould & Machine Company, reproduced some of the original molds and incorporated the pattern into approximately forty new and different items. Two of the largest distributors of this line were L.E. Smith of Mt. Pleasant, Pennsylvania, who pressed their own glass, and L.G. Wright of New Martinsville, West Virginia, who had theirs pressed by Fostoria, Fenton, and Westmoreland. Both companies carried a large and varied assortment of shapes and colors. Several other companies were involved in its manufacture as well, especially of the smaller items. All in all, there may be as many as one hundred different pieces, plenty to keep you involved and excited as you do your searching.

The glassware is beautiful and is being actively collected today, even though it is still being made on a limited basis. Colors you'll see most often are amberina (yellow shading to orange-red), green, amber, crystal, light blue, and ruby. Pieces in ruby and light blue are most collectible and harder to find than the other colors, which seem to be abundant. Purple, pink, cobalt, amethyst, tan slag, and light green and blue opalescent were made, too, but on a lesser scale.

Current L.E. Smith catalogs contain a dozen or so pieces that are still available in crystal, pink, cobalt (lighter than the old shade), and these colors with an iridized finish. A new color was introduced in 1992, teal green, and at least the water set in sapphire blue opalescent was pressed in 1993 for a small Ohio-based company who specializes in reproductions.

Our values are given for ruby and light blue. For amberina, green, and amber, deduct 30%. These colors are less in demand and unless your prices are reasonable, you may find them harder to sell.

Ashtray, 5½", patterned 'moons' at rim, 'star' in base, 6-sided shape **$12.00**
Butter dish, 6x5½" dia, allover pattern, scalloped foot, patterned lid & finial..**$45.00**
Cake salver, 5x12", allover pattern w/scalloped rim, raised foot w/scalloped edge...**$45.00**
Candle holders, 6", allover pattern, flared foot w/scalloped edge, pr **$30.00**
Compote, 10x8", allover pattern, raised foot on stem, w/patterned lid & finial...**$45.00**
Compote, 12x8", allover pattern, raised foot on stem, w/patterned lid & finial...**$65.00**
Compote, 5½x8", allover pattern, footed, scalloped rim..**$30.00**
Compote, 5x6½", allover pattern, footed, scalloped rim..**$15.00**
Compote, 7½x6", allover pattern, raised foot, w/patterned lid & finial..**$35.00**
Compote, 7x10", allover pattern, footed, scalloped rim...**$40.00**
Compote, 8x4" dia, allover pattern, scalloped foot on stem, w/patterned lid & finial **$30.00**
Console bowl, 8" dia, allover pattern, scalloped rim, flared foot w/flat (not scalloped) edge **$25.00**
Creamer, 5¾x3", allover pattern, raised foot w/scalloped edge **$30.00**
Creamer & sugar bowl, sm, open, disk foot **$25.00**
Decanter, 32-oz, 12", bulbous body w/allover pattern, plain neck, foot ring, original patterned stopper **$50.00**

Goblet, water; 5¾", plain rim & foot.....................**$12.00**
Goblet, wine; 4½", plain rim & foot...........................**$9.00**

Jelly dish, 10½", allover pattern, stemmed foot, w/patterned lid & finial...**$45.00**

Jelly dish, 6¾x3½" dia, patterned body w/plain flat rim & disk foot, w/patterned lid & finial **$30.00**

Jelly dish, 8½", allover pattern, stem foot, w/patterned lid & finial..**$35.00**

Nappy, 2¾x6" dia, allover pattern, crimped rim..........**$18.00**

Pitcher, water; 1-qt, 7½", patterned body, straight sides, plain disk foot (illustrated on page 261) $65.00

Relish bowl, 1½x8" dia, 6 lg scallops form allover pattern **$16.00**

Relish dish, 2x8" dia, allover pattern, 1 plain handle ..**$18.00**

Relish tray, 8" long, patterned 'moons' form scalloped rim, 'star' in base, rectangular....................................**$18.00**

Salt & pepper shakers, 4x2" dia, allover pattern, metal tops, pr...**$25.00**

Salt cellar, allover pattern, scalloped rim, sm flat foot...**$7.00**

Sherbet, 4¼x3¾", patterned body & foot w/plain rim & stem **$12.00**

Soap dish, 2x6", allover pattern, oval shape **$12.00**

Spooner, 5¼x4" dia, allover pattern, scalloped rim, straight sides, raised foot **$30.00**

Sugar bowl, 5¼x4" dia, allover pattern, sm flat foot, patterned lid & finial...**$30.00**

Sugar bowl, 8x4½", allover pattern, straight sides, scalloped foot, w/patterned lid & finial **$35.00**

Sugar shaker, 4½x3½" dia, allover pattern, metal top ..**$25.00**

Syrup, 4½x3½", allover pattern, metal top **$25.00**

Toothpick holder, allover pattern, scalloped rim, sm flat foot..**$9.00**

Tumbler, iced tea; 11-oz, 5½", no pattern at flat rim or on disk foot...**$14.00**

Tumbler, juice; 5-oz, 3½", no pattern at rim or on disk foot **$10.00**

Tumbler, 7-oz, 4¼", no pattern at rim or on disk foot (illustrated on page 261).................................$12.00

Mortens Studios

During the 1940s, a Swedish sculptor by the name of Oscar Mortens left his native country and moved to the United States, settling in Arizona. Along with his partner, Gunnar Thelin, they founded the Mortens Studios, a firm that specialized in the manufacture of animal figurines. Though he preferred dogs of all breeds, horses, cats, and wild animals were made, too, but on a much smaller scale.

The material he used was a plaster-like composition molded over a wire framework for support and reinforcement. Crazing is common, and our values reflect pieces with a moderate amount, but be sure to check for more serious damage before you buy. Most pieces are marked with either an ink stamp or a paper label.

Beagle, recumbent...**$48.00**
Beagle, 4½x4½", standing...**$60.00**
Boxer, 8" long, recumbent **$60.00**
Bulldog, 5x6½", standing..**$85.00**

Chihuahua, 4½" long, standing **$90.00**
Collie, 6", seated **$90.00**

Dalmation family, sizes range from 2" up to 5½" tall, for the 4-piece set..$300.00
Doberman, 6½x6", sitting **$90.00**
English Spaniel, 5½x6½", ivory w/black, standing **$80.00**
German Shepherd pup, 3½x3½", sitting.......................**$40.00**
Great Dane, 7½x6½", sitting...**$80.00**
Horse, lg, #701D **$68.00**

Horse, 9", rearing...$70.00
Lion, 4x6", recumbent...**$135.00**
Lynx..**$175.00**
Persian cat...**$48.00**
Pomeranian, 4½", standing..**$70.00**
Pug pup, 2½x4", recumbent...**$45.00**
Siamese, 5", seated..**$68.00**
Springer Spaniel, 5"..**$65.00**
Wire-Haired Terrier, 4", begging.................................**$58.00**

Morton Pottery

Morton, Illinois, was the location for six potteries that operated there at various times over the course of nearly a hundred years. The first was established by six brothers by the name of Rapp, who immigrated to America from Germany. Second- and third-generation Rapps followed in the tradition that had been established by their elders in the late 1870s.

The original company was titled Morton Pottery Works and was later renamed Morton Earthenware Co. It was in business from 1877 until 1917. The next to be established was Cliftwood Art Potteries, Inc. (1920-1940). The Morton Pottery Company opened in 1922 and became the longest running of the six, having operated for more than fifty-four years by the time Midwest Potteries, Inc., incorporated in 1940. They were in business for only four years. The last to open was the American Art Potteries who operated from 1947 until 1961. Various types of pottery was made by each — Rockingham and yellow ware in the early years, novelties and giftware from the 1920s on.

To learn more about these companies, we recommend *Morton's Potteries: 99 Years,* by Doris and Burdell Hall.

American Art Potteries

Bottle, 2x6x4", crown, gray w/pink spray....................$15.00
Figurine, 4½", hen & rooster, mauve w/white spray...$18.00
Figurine, 5½", hog, white w/gray spots........................$35.00
Figurine, 6", elephant, gray & white spray..................$20.00
Figurine, 9", quail, multicolored spray..........................$30.00
Flower bowl, 3½x12", bullet form, black & gray spray ..$12.00
Flower bowl & plate, 3x8½", scalloped oval, purple & yellow spray $14.00
Lamp, 12", Driftwood, brown spray on green $22.00
Lamp, 16", pillar of 8 flat squares on lg square base, white & gold...$30.00
Lamp, 6x14x8", Art Deco, rectangular, dark green......$30.00
Planter, 2x4", diaper w/safety pin, pink or blue..........$10.00
Planter, 3½", Grecian urn, brown & green spray...........$5.00
Planter, 5", cowboy boot, yellow & gray spray $12.00
Planter, 5½", duck, dark green w/yellow spray, paper label $10.00
Vase, 10½", double cornucopia, blue & rose spray.....$20.00
Vase, 11", swan w/long neck, green & yellow spray w/gold...$20.00

Cliftwood Art Potteries, Inc.

Bean pot, individual, old rose....................................$10.00
Bowl, console; 3¾x7½x6¼", tree trunk form w/brown drip glaze..$30.00
Candlestick, 3x3x2", tree trunk form w/brown drip glaze, pr...$36.00
Card holder, 4x6", elephant w/side boxes, brown drip glaze $69.00
Figurine, 6¼", cat, reclining, blue w/gray drip glaze...$35.00
Figurine, 8", German shepherd, recumbent, jade green ..$75.00
Figurine, 5", German shepherd, recumbent, white matt glaze..$50.00
Flower frog, 3¾", tree trunk form, brown drip glaze ..$18.00
Lamp, 7x24", spherical, jade green $38.00

Planter, 6½", crane, open back, turquoise matt glaze .$18.00

Vase, 18", cobalt glaze, fish & snake handles......$125.00
Vase, 18", cone shape, brown chocolate drip glaze....$75.00
Vase, 8", ewer form, turquoise matt glaze...................$25.00
Wine, swirl decoration w/blue mulberry drip glaze....$12.00

Midwest Potteries, Inc.

Ashtray/ring holder, flat tray w/attached hand, white w/gold..$20.00
Bowl, flower; 6½", nest w/attached bird, blue spray ..$15.00
Creamer, standing cow, white w/gold $25.00
Figurine, Oriental boy & girl shelf sitters, black, white & gold..$22.00
Figurine, 3x6½", ducks, 3 in a row, white...................$10.00
Figurine, 6", pigeon, yellow & green drip glaze $18.00
Figurine, 6", spaniel, white w/gold.............................$25.00
Planter, 3½x5½", lion, yellow....................................$12.00
Planter, 3½x5½", lioness, green $10.00
Planter, 4x3", fox, yellow matt glaze $8.00
Planter, 4x5", dog w/bow tie, white $8.00
Planter, 4x6", rabbit, white w/pink ears......................$16.00
Plaque, head sculpture, Elizabethan Friar, green.........$20.00
Plaque, head sculpture, Sad Monk, yellow $20.00
Plaque, head sculpture, Winking Gigalo, blue $20.00
Vase, bud; 4¾", hand form, green $12.00
Vase, bud; 5¾", hand form, Fawn matt glaze $14.00

Morton Pottery Company

Amish Pantry Ware, cereal jar, 3-qt, green..................$30.00
Amish Pantry Ware, jar, 5-qt, green, w/lid..................$40.00
Amish Pantry Ware, milk jug, 3-pt, Pilgrim Blue $25.00
Amish Pantry Ware, water jug, 3-pt, Pigrim Blue $35.00
Bank, 7x6", yellow shoe w/red roof figural $30.00
Basket, hanging; 7½", embossed bird design, unglazed.$25.00
Bookends, bald eagle, brown & white, pr $30.00

Bookends, parrot planters, multicolored, pr **$25.00**
Bowls, nesters, straight sides, pastel, set of 5 ....**$45.00**
Cookie jar, harlequin embossed on square form, green..**$25.00**
Cookie jar, panda, marked AFK Industries **$30.00**
Dresser tray, lady's pink collar w/hand-painted brooch..**$12.00**
Dresser tray, man's white collar w/black bow tie **$14.00**
Figurine, 3½", praying boy, blue sleeper......................**$7.50**
Figurine, 6", seeing-eye dog, black............................**$16.00**
Mug, milk; cow & calf, Sunshine Dairy Products **$25.00**
Planter, touring car, top down, brown **$16.00**
Vase, 14½", bamboo w/embossed heron decoration, white..**$35.00**
Wall pocket, birdhouse, white w/multicolored bird....**$15.00**
Wall pocket, multicolored lovebirds on nest **$18.00**
Wall pocket, rooster, multicolored **$20.00**
Wall pocket, teapot, white w/hand-painted cherries ..**$14.00**
Wall pocket, violin, white w/hand-painted forget-me-nots...**$16.00**

Morton Pottery Works-Morton Earthenware Co.

Bowl, 10¼", #9s, yellow ware w/wide center white band..**$65.00**
Coffeepot, ¾-qt, individual, brown Rockingham.........**$25.00**
Crock, 1-gal, brown Rockingham, reversed N&S in mark ..**$65.00**
Milk boiler, 2½-pt, bulbous form, brown Rockingham..**$50.00**
Milk jug, 2¾-pt, brown Rockingham **$75.00**
Pie baker, 10", yellow ware......................................**$85.00**
Pie baker, 9¼" dia, yellow ware **$75.00**
Rice nappy, 6½", fluted, yellow ware.........................**$40.00**
Teapot, 1½-cup, individual, brown Rockingham.........**$25.00**
Teapot, 2½-pt, Rebecca at the Well, brown Rockingham...**$60.00**

Motion Lamps

Though some were made as early as 1920 and as late as the '70s, motion lamps were most popular during the '50s. Most are cylindrical with scenes such as waterfalls and forest fires and attain a sense of motion through the action of an inner cylinder that rotates with the heat of the bulb. Linda and Bill Montgomery have written a book called *Motion Lamps, 1920s to the Present,* containing full-page color photographs and lots of good information if you'd like to learn more about these lamps.

Antique Car, plastic, Econolite, Los Angeles, 1957, 11" ...**$50.00**
Boy & Girl Scouts, plastic, Econolite (Roto-Vue Jr), Los Angeles, 1950, 10", minimum value......................**$200.00**
Butterflies, plastic, Econolite, Los Angeles, 1954, 11" **$50.00**
Christmas Tree, paper, red, Econolite, Los Angeles, 1952, 10"..**$40.00**
Clock w/fish, wood, United Clock Corp, 1950s, 11" ...**$50.00**
Disneyland, plastic & tin litho, Econolite, Los Angeles, 1955, 11", minimum value..**$200.00**
Forest Fire, plastic, Econolite (Roto-Vue Jr), Los Angeles, 1949, 10"...**$40.00**
Hawaiian Scene, plastic, Econolite, Los Angeles, 1959, 11" ..**$50.00**

Hopalong Cassidy, plastic, Econolite (Roto-Vue Jr), Los Angeles, 1949, 10", minimum value....................**$250.00**
Merry Go Round, plastic, Econolite, Los Angeles, 1948, 11"..**$50.00**
Miss Liberty, plastic, Econolite, Los Angeles, 1957, 11" ...**$65.00**
Mother Goose, plastic & paper litho, Econolite, Los Angeles, 1948, 11"...**$70.00**
Niagara Falls, plastic, Econolite (Roto-Vue Jr), Los Angeles, 1950, 10" **$40.00**
Snow Scene Church, plastic, Econolite, Los Angeles, 1957, 11"...**$55.00**
Totville Train, plastic & paper litho, Econolite, Los Angeles, 1948, 11"...**$85.00**

Movie Stars

Americans have been fans of the silver screen stars since the early days of movies. Cashing in on their popularity, manufacturers took full advantage of the moment by filling stores with merchandise of all types — coloring books, paper dolls, games, and toys for the children; calendars, books, magazines, and pin-up posters for more mature fans. The movies themselves generated lobby cards (11x14" scenes on cardboard, usually issued in sets of eight), press books (given to theatre owners, containing photos of posters and other types of promotional items available to them), and posters (the most common of which are the 1-sheet, measuring 41" x 27"), all of which are very collectible today. Be sure an item is authentic before you invest much money in it; there are many reproductions around.

See also Autographs; Magazines; Paper Dolls; Posters; Puzzles; Sheet Music; Shirley Temple; Western Heroes.

Abbott & Costello, film, 8mm, Fun on the Run, VG in original box..**$10.00**
Abbott & Costello, sheet music, 9x12", Boogie Woogie Bugle Boy, w/Andrew Sisters, Universal Pictures, 1941, EX...**$20.00**
Al Pacino, lobby card, 11x14", Panic in Needle Park, color, EX...**$8.00**
Al Pacino, lobby card, 11x14", Scarface, color, 1983, M..**$2.00**
Alan Alda, lobby card, 11x14", Mephisto Waltz, color, 1971, EX...**$5.00**
Andy Griffith, press book, 9x14", Angel in My Pocket..**$3.00**
Audrey Hepburn, song sheet, Moon River, ca 1961, EX ..**$2.50**
Autie Murphy, press book, Showdown **$3.00**
Barry Bostwick, press kit, Megaforce, 1982 ....**$10.00**
Bette Davis, book, The Lonely Life, GP Putnam's Sons, hardcover, 1962, w/dust jacket, VG **$20.00**
Bette Midler, postcard, 3½x5½", color photo, M...........**$1.00**
Betty Grable, coloring book, dated 1951, M **$45.00**
Betty Grable, match book, scene from Down Argentine Way, 1940s, M **$10.00**
Betty Grable, tablet, 8x10", M **$20.00**
Bill Cosby, pillow, inflatable, 1970s, NM....................**$10.00**
Bing Crosby, coloring book, Saalfield, #1295, 1950, NM ..**$15.00**

Bing Crosby, still, Road to Hong Kong, w/Bob Hope, 1962 ....**$7.50**

Bob Hope, Bing Crosby & Dorothy Lamour; lobby card, 11x14", Road to Bali, VG......................**$27.50**

Bob Hope, press book, 13x18", Cancel My Reservation ..**$3.00**

Bob Hope, still, 8x10", from Eight on the Lam, 1967 ....**$5.00**

Brooke Shields, credit sheet, The Blue Lagoon, 1980 ...**$1.00**

Bruce Bennett, lobby card, 11x14", Flaming Frontier, 1958, EX...**$5.00**

Buck Jones, lobby card, 11x14", Outlawed Guns........**$20.00**

Burt Lancaster, tablet, 8x10", color photo cover, 1950s, EX...**$8.00**

Buster Crabb, postcard, dressed as cowboy, NM..........**$4.50**

Candice Bergen, still, 8x10", Getting Straight, color **$3.00**

Charlie Chaplin, coloring book, The Great Dictator, Saalfield, 1941, EX..**$32.50**

Chuck Conners, 8x10" black & white signed photograph as the Rifleman $65.00

Clark Gable, lobby card, 11x14", Boomtown, color, 1938, NM **$40.00**

Clark Gable, press book, Magambo, NM **$40.00**

Clint Eastwood, book, Signet, 16 pages of photos, 1977, NM **$12.50**

Clint Eastwood, press book, Play Misty for Me.............**$6.00**

Dana Andrews, lobby card, 11x14", Comanche, 1956, G ..**$3.00**

David Niven, tobacco card, 3x2½", Bachelor Mother, black & white **$3.50**

Dean Martin, press book, Career, 1959 ....**$6.00**

Debbie Reynolds, coloring book, 1953, EX **$22.50**

Deborah Kerr, lobby card, 11x14", Julius Caesar, 1953, NM **$28.00**

Dolly Parton, postcard, 3½x5½", color photo, M...........**$1.00**

Dolly Parton, wristwatch, photo on dial, silver expansion band, ca 1970s, MIB.......................................**$25.00**

Don Ameche, tobacco card, 3x2½", Hollywood Cavalcade, color..**$5.00**

Don Barry, lobby card, 11x14", Gunfire, 1950, M..........**$7.50**

Don Knox, press book, The Ghost & Mr Chicken........**$4.00**

Doris Day, coloring book, 1958, EX.............................**$15.00**

Eddie Dean, lobby card, 11x14", West to Glory, EX......**$8.50**

Edgar Bergen & Charlie McCarthy w/Fibber McGee & Molly, lobby card, 11x14", Here We Go Again, 1942, M $40.00

Edward G Robinson, tobacco card, 1⅜x2⅝", A Slight Case of Murder, black & white....................................**$2.50**

Elizabeth Taylor, still, 8x10", Ivanhoe, black & white, 1962, EX...**$7.50**

Ernest Borgnine, lobby card, 11x14", Pay or Die, color, 1960, NM...**$5.00**

Errol Flynn, still, 8x10", The Master of Ballantrae, black & white, 1952, NM **$3.00**

Ethel Merman, coaster, Piel's Beer, black & white photo, EX **$10.00**

Farrah Fawcett, play set, 9x4x9", Glamour Center, figural bust w/life-like hair for styling, Mego, 1977, EX...**$37.50**

Faye Dunaway, still, 8x10", Bonnie & Clyde, 1967........**$2.00**

Frank Sinatra, pillow, inflatable, 1970s, NM.................**$10.00**

Frank Sinatra, record, 33⅓ rpm, Pal Joey soundtrack, EX...**$7.50**

Fred Astaire, still, 8x10", Finian's Rainbow, color, 1968, EX...**$2.00**

Freddy Kreuger, Freddy's Dead coffin, 8", promotional item...**$25.00**

Fredric March, coin, aluminum, Popsicle premium, ca early 1930s, M..**$8.00**

Gary Cooper, coin, aluminum, Popsicle premium, ca early 1930s, M..**$8.00**

Gary Cooper, lobby card, 11x14", Good Sam, 1948, EX..**$10.00**

George Montgomery, lobby card, 11x14", Davy Crockett Indian Fighter, 1955, VG.....................................**$5.00**

George O'Brien, lobby card, 11x14", Whispering Smith Speaks, 1935, VG **$12.00**

George Reed, tobacco card, 4x2¾", The Women, black & white **$3.50**

Ginger Rogers, postcard, view of home, M...................**$5.00**

Goldie Hawn, press book, Foul Play.............................**$7.50**

Gordon MacRae, press book, The Best Things in Life Are Free, 1956...**$2.00**

Grace Kelly, coloring book, 1956 ....**$30.00**

Greta Garbo, tobacco card, 1⅜x2⅝", Anna Karenina, black & white $3.00

Groucho Marx, dinner napkins, set of 4, MIB $15.00

Haley Mills, still, 8x10", The Chalk Garden, color $4.00

Harold Lloyd, sheet music, Freshie, Robbins-Engel Inc, color photo cover, VG.....................................$25.00

Harpo Marx, record, 33⅓ rpm, Harpo at Work, color photo sleeve, 1950s, NM $32.50

Henry Fonda, badge, Texas Ranger Sheriff's Deputy, 1951, M .$80.00

Henry Fonda, tobacco card, 4x2¾", Jesse James, color.$5.00

Jack Nicholson, press book, Shooting $5.00

Jackie Gleason, lobby card, 11x14", Don't Drink the Water, color, 1967, NM $5.00

Jackie Gleason, still, 8x10", Papa's Delicate Condition, color, 1963...$3.00

James Cagney, still, 8x10", White Heat, 1956, NM $5.00

James Craig, window card, 14x22", Four Fast Guns, 1960, EX..$10.00

James Dean, doll, marked Dakin, MIB $225.00

James Dean, pressbook, 11x17", Rebel w/out a Cause, 20-page, complete, original issue, ca 1955, M $150.00

James Dean, token, 1½", I Am a Lifetime Member of James Dean Memory Ring Around the World & portrait on wood, EX..$20.00

Jane Powell, lobby card, 11x14", 7 Brides for 7 Brothers, 1954, NM $10.00

Jane Russell, puzzle, Esquire magazine premium, in original mailing envelope, M $75.00

Jane Russell, song sheet, Underwater, ca 1950, 6-page, EX..$2.50

Jane Wyman, pencil tablet, EX.................................$20.00

Jean Harlow, Dixie Cup lid, 2¼", M..........................$6.00

Jean Tierney, lobby card, 11x14", The Mating Season, 1951, EX..$7.50

Jerry Lewis, still, 8x10", Pardners, color, 1956, NM........$3.00

Jimmy Durante, mask, painted rubber, marked Topstone Toys, 1940s, VG $20.00

Joan Carroll, coloring book, Saalfield, 1942 ....$17.50

John Wayne, change purse, 3", The Duke 1907-1979 in gold on leather, M $6.50

John Wayne, coin, 1¼", memorial, issued in 1980, M ...$8.50

John Wayne, decanter, Mike Wayne Distillery Co $65.00

John Wayne, movie announcement card, 5½x8½", photo & black ink on color paper, M...................................$2.50

John Wayne, note card, 4x7", black & white photo, 1963, M...$5.00

John Wayne, playing cards, 1970s, MIB $17.50

John Wayne, pocket mirror, 2x3", color photo in Western outfit, promotional item for film, M $5.00

John Wayne, postcard, 3½x5½", birthplace in Winterset, Iowa, M..$1.50

John Wayne, postcard, 4x6", color photo in civilian clothes, M...$2.50

John Wayne, spoon, color bust photo w/name, M $10.00

John Wayne, still, 8x10", Donovan's Reef, 1963, color..$5.00

Jose Ferrer, program, Cyrano de Bergerac play, 1947, VG...$22.50

Judy Garland, concert program, 9x12", black & white photos, 1960s, 20-page, VG......................................$25.00

Judy Garland, song sheet, Meet Me in St Louis, Louis; w/ Margaret O'Brien on cover, 6-page, complete, VG..$2.50

Katharine Hepburn, program, As You Like It, includes photos & information on play, 1950, EX.....................$25.00

Katherine Hepburn, lobby card, 11x14", Pat & Mike, 1952, EX..$10.00

Kenny Rogers, postcard, 3½x5½", color photo, M.........$1.00

Kim Novak, lobby card, 11x14", The Great Train Robbery, 1969, EX...$5.00

Kris Kristofferson, press book, Convoy, NM $5.00

Lana Turner, paint book, Whitman, 1947.....................$22.50

Laurel & Hardy, lobby card, Big Parade of Comedy, 1964, M...$12.00

Lauren Bacall, lobby card, 11x14", Flame Over India, color, 1960, EX...$5.00

Leslie Caron, lobby card, 11x14", The Glass Slipper, 1955, set of 8, NM..$28.00

Louie Armstrong, still, 8x10", When the Boys Meet the Girls, 1965, M...$3.00

Lucille Ball, still, 8x10", The Long, Long Trailer, 1963, NM $10.00

Macdonald Carey, press book, Man or Gun, 1958.........$5.00

Mamie Van Doren, lobby card, 11x14", Big Operator, 1959, EX..$5.00

Margaret O'Brien, coloring book, 1943, EX $20.00

Marie Dressler, coin, aluminim, Popsicle premium, ca early 1930s, EX...$6.00

Marilyn Monroe, book, Diary of a Lover of Marilyn Monroe, paperback, Bantam, 1979, VG...............................$6.00

Marilyn Monroe, calendar, 11x17", nude photos, 1955, complete, M..$75.00

Marilyn Monroe, lobby card, 11x14", Bus Stop, color, 1956, M...$50.00

Marilyn Monroe, lobby card, 14x11", Gentlemen Prefer Blonds, G..$50.00

Marilyn Monroe, playing cards, 1956, original issue, EX original box, NM..$17.50

Marilyn Monroe, pocketknife, Golden Dreams pose, 1970s, M...$8.00

Marilyn Monroe, postcard, 3½x5½", black & white scene from Let's Make Love, 1960, M...............................$1.50

Marilyn Monroe, title lobby card, 14x11", The Seven Year Itch, 1955, G.................$225.00

Mark Damon, lobby card, 11x14", The House of Usher, color, 1960, EX.................$7.50

Marlene Dietrich, tobacco card, 4x2¾", The Scarlet Empress, black & white $5.00

Mell Brooks, press book, 12x18", Blazing Saddles $7.00

Mickey Rooney, paint book, 1940, EX $30.00

Monte Hale, lobby card, 11x14", Outcasts of the Trail, 1949, EX.................$5.00

Morgan Fairchild, lobby cards, 11x14", The Seduction, 1981, set of 5, M.................$12.50

Movie, 34x14", Bette Davis, Pocket Full of Miracles, 1962, VG.................$15.00

Neville Brand, window card, 14x22", Three Guns to Texas, 1968, NM $10.00

Oliver Hardy, hand puppet, 10½", vinyl head w/fabric body, marked Knickerbocker, 1966 copyright, original tag, EX.................$37.50

Our Gang, ink blotter, marked Majestic Radios, ca 1930s, EX.................$35.00

Paul Newmun, lobby card, 11x14", Sometimes a Great Notion, 1971, set of 8, NM.................$20.00

Peter & Gordon, lobby card, 11x14", Disk-O-Tek Holiday, color, 1966, M.................$15.00

Peter Fonda, lobby card, 11x14", The Trip, color, 1967, M.................$15.00

Peter Sellers, press book, The Pink Panther Strikes Again $3.00

Ray Charles, lobby cards, 14x11", Blues for Lovers, black & white photos, 20th Century, 1966, set of 4, EX.....$27.50

Ray Milland, tobacco card, 3x2½", Untamed, color $3.50

Richard Burton, program, Camelot play, 1970s, EX.....$10.00

Richard Pryor, press kit, Blue Collar, M $20.00

Robert Blake, lobby card, 11x14", In Cold Blood, black & white, 1968, NM.................$4.00

Rock Hudson, tablet, 8x10", color photo cover, 1950s, M..$8.00

Ronald Coleman, tobacco card, 3x2½", Lost Horizon, black & white $3.50

Ronald Reagan, lobby cards, 14x11", The Winning Team, color photos, Warner Brothers, 1952, set of 8, VG...........$90.00

Rosalind Russell, tobacco card, 3x2½", black & white ..$3.50

Roy Rogers, Bob Hope & Jane Russell, window card, 14x22", Son of Paleface, 1952, G $60.00

Rudolph Valentino, cigar box label, 2½x5", full color, 1920s, NM.................$17.50

Sal Mineo, sheet music, Start Movin', 1957, M.................$15.00

Sandra Dee, press book, I'd Rather Be Rich $4.00

Sean Connery, movie stills, as James Bond in Dr No, 1962, set of 8, VG $30.00

Sean Connery, sheet music, as James Bond in Casino Royal on cover w/psychedelic nude, 1967, NM.................$15.00

Sean Connery, still, 8x10", From Russia w/Love, EX $3.00

Sidney Portier, lobby card, 11x14", To Sir w/Love, 1967, NM.................$5.00

Sophia Loren, still, 8x10", Arabesque, color, 1966, EX..$4.00

Spencer Tracy, tobacco card, 3x2½", Big City, black & white $3.50

Steve Reeves, lobby card, 11x14", Hercules Unchained, 1960, set of 8, NM.................$22.50

Sylvester Stallone, stamp, bust figural, dated 1985, M on original card.................$6.00

Tex Ritter, song sheet, Green Grows the Lilacs, ca 1945, 4-page, EX $4.00

Three Stooges, cancelled check, signed Curly Joe Derita..$15.00

Three Stooges, colorform kit, dated 1959, VG.................$35.00

Three Stooges, fan club kit, facsimile signed photo, letter, fan cards & stamp sheet, original envelope, NM...........$87.50

Three Stooges, lobby card, 11x14", Three Stooges in Orbit, M.................$10.00

Three Stooges, magazine, Laf, 13½x10½", article & photos, July 1940, EX.................$28.00

Three Stooges, pressbook, Around the World in a Daze, VG.................$25.00

Three Stooges, record, 33⅓ rpm, The Three Stooges Sing for Kids, in original sleeve, M.................$35.00

Three Stooges, record, 45 rpm, Three Stooges Come to Your House & Make a Record, in picture sleeve, NM.......$25.00

Three Stooges, stills, 8x10", The Three Stooges Meet Hercules, black & white, set of 15, original bag, EX.................$35.00

Three Stooges, trick cane, marked Empire Plastic Corporation, 1959, EX.................$80.00

Three Stooges, 16mm home movie film, Heavy Gunners, black & white, ca 1930s, EX in 4x4x1" box.................$62.50

Three Stooges, 8mm film, Studio Stoops, for home viewing, MIB $20.00

Van Johnson, press book, Subway in the Sky, 1959......$3.00

Virginia Mayo, still, 8x10", South Sea Women, 1953, EX ...$5.00

WC Fields, liquor bottle, ceramic, Paul Lux, NM.................$10.00

Magazines

Before the late 1930s, the covers of many movie magazines were often illustrated with portraits of the stars by such well-known artists as James Montgomery Flagg, Rolf Armstrong, Earl Chandler Christie, and many others. But when *Photoplay* broke tradition by featuring a photograph of Ginger Rogers in 1937, a new era began. There were scores of different magazines, each contained stories about a top Hollywood personality. Some of these features were explicit and often exaggerated. The ads they contained portrayed the stars plugging their favorite products — cigarettes, a particular brand of liquor, etc. Some factors to consider when evaluating a vintage movie magazine are who is on the cover, who the articles are about and their content, the photos the magazine contains, and of course, condition.

American Film, 1985, May, Rip Torn cover, VG.............$4.00

American Film, 1985, November, Ally Sheedy cover, EX...$3.00

American Film, 1987, June, Kevin Costner cover, NM...$4.00

American Film, 1987, March, Mia Farrow cover, NM.....$3.00

Hollywood, 1938, October, Sonja Henie cover, G.......$10.00

Hollywood, 1942, Hedy Lamarr cover, NM.................$20.00

Modern Movies, 1968, Lennon Sisters cover, VG...........$4.00

Modern Screen, 1940, May, Ginger Rogers cover, M...$15.00

Modern Screen, 1936, Howard Chandler Christy cover **$7.50**

Modern Screen, 1949, Betty Grable cover, NM **$15.00**

Modern Screen, 1955, Ann Blyth cover, EX **$10.00**

Modern Screen, 1956, June, Jane Powell cover, VG **$15.00**

Modern Screen, 1964, January, Liz Taylor & Richard Burton cover, NM **$10.00**

Modern Screen, 1964, January, Liz Taylor cover, NM .. **$10.00**

Modern Screen, 1968, Jackie Kennedy cover, NM **$5.00**

Modern Screen, 1972, June, Cast of All in the Family cover, VG **$10.00**

Modern Screen, 1973, July, Marlon Brando & Maria Schneider cover, VG **$10.00**

Modern Screen, 1974, November, Barbra Streisand cover, EX **$8.00**

Motion Picture, 1951, Janet Leigh cover, EX **$15.00**

Motion Picture, 1953, December, VG **$4.00**

Motion Picture, 1955, March, June Allison cover, NM .. **$15.00**

Motion Picture, 1956, August, Kim Novak cover, NM .. **$15.00**

Motion Picture, 1959, March, Dick Clark Family cover, NM **$10.00**

Motion Picture, 1960, June, Pat Boone & Daughters cover, VG **$8.00**

Motion Picture, 1960, March, Debbie Reynolds cover, NM **$10.00**

Motion Picture, 1961, October, Doris Day cover, G+ **$8.00**

Motion Picture, 1962, October, Sandra Dee cover, EX .. **$10.00**

Motion Picture, 1963, January, Vince Edwards cover, EX+ **$10.00**

Motion Picture, 1966, February, Hayley Mills cover, VG ... **$7.00**

Motion Picture, 1966, October, John Wayne cover, NM .. **$10.00**

Motion Picture, 1966, September, Sophia Loren cover, NM **$10.00**

Motion Picture, 1967, August, Lennon Sisters cover, EX .. **$10.00**

Motion Picture, 1967, June, Dorothy Malone cover, EX .. **$8.00**

Motion Picture, 1968, August, Sidney Poitier & Kate Houghton, EX **$8.00**

Motion Picture, 1968, September, Ted Kennedy cover, EX **$7.00**

Motion Picture, 1969, August, Glen Campbell & wife cover, VG+ **$6.00**

Motion Picture, 1970, March, Dean Martin cover, EX+ .. **$7.00**

Motion Picture, 1970, November, Taylor & Burton cover, NM **$10.00**

Motion Picture, 1971, March, Ali McGraw cover, NM **$7.00**

Motion Picture, 1971, September, Andy Williams cover, NM **$10.00**

Motion Picture, 1972, March, Lucy & children cover, EX ... **$8.00**

Motion Picture, 1973, February, Dean Martin cover, NM .. **$10.00**

Motion Picture, 1973, September, Cher cover, NM **$12.50**

Motion Picture, 1974, October, Jean Harlow cover, EX .. **$8.00**

Motion Picture, 1975, September, Raquel Welch cover, NM **$6.00**

Motion Picture, 1976, October, Robert Blake cover, NM ... **$5.00**

Motion Picture, 1977, February, Raquel Welch cover, NM .. **$10.00**

Motion Picture, 1977, March, Robert DeNiro cover, NM .. **$5.00**

Motion Picture, 1978, January, Natalie Wood cover, M .. **$9.00**

Movie Illustrated, 1965, August, Elizabeth Taylor & Richard Burton cover, EX **$10.00**

Movie Illustrated, 1965, November, Frank Sinatra cover, EX **$10.00**

Movie Life, 1960, Cary Grant & Connie Stevens cover, EX .. **$5.00**

Movie Mirror, 1932, June, Norma Shearer cover, EX ... **$25.00**

Movie Mirror, 1961, November, Sandra Dee cover, NM .. **$10.00**

Movie Mirror, 1963, August, Liz Taylor & Richard Burton cover, NM **$10.00**

Movie Mirror, 1967, November, John Wayne cover, NM .. **$10.00**

Movie Mirror, 1971, February, Lucy & kids on cover, G+ .. **$4.00**

Movie Mirror, 1971, July, Ali McGraw & Bob Evans cover, EX **$6.00**

Movie Mirror, 1972, July, Burt Reynolds & Dinah Shore cover, NM **$7.00**

Movie Play, 1956, January, Kim Novak cover, NM **$12.50**

Movie Screen, 1954, December, Grace Kelly cover, G .. **$8.00**

Movie Screen, 1962, January, Jackie Kennedy cover, NM .. **$12.00**

Movie Screen, 1964, October, Liz Taylor & Richard Burton cover, G+ **$8.00**

Movie Stars, 1960, June, Troy Donahue & Sophia Loren cover, VG **$10.00**

Movie Stars, 1966, July, Annette Funicello cover, M **$10.00**

Movie Stars, 1967, July, Sinatra family cover, EX **$7.50**

Movie Stars, 1969, November, Jackie & Aristotle Onassis cover, M **$12.00**

Movie Stars, 1971, January, Lennon Sisters cover, EX ... **$8.00**

Movie Stars, 1972, June, Liz Taylor cover, VG **$7.00**

Movie Stars' Parade, 1944, September, Susan Hayward cover, EX **$17.50**

Movie Story, 1937, July, Frances Dee & Gary Cooper cover, VG **$17.50**

Movie Story, 1940, September, Judy Garland & Mickey Rooney cover, NM **$45.00**

Movie Story, 1947, August, Shirley Temple & Cary Grant cover, VG **$16.00**

Movie Story, 1950, May, Richard Widmark & Jean Tierney cover, NM **$17.50**

Movie Teen Illustrated, 1960, March, Sandra Dee & Troy Donahue cover, NM......................................$15.00

Movie Teen Illustrated, 1964, January, Elvis Presley cover, EX...$19.00

Movie World, 1967, September, Barbara Parkins, VG ...$5.00

Movieland, 1947, July, Lana Turner cover, EX.............$20.00

Movies Illustrated, 1964, August, Carroll Baker cover, EX ..$7.50

Photoplay, 1937, January, Ginger Rogers cover, EX....$27.50

Photoplay, 1939, April, Norma Shearer cover, VG $20.00

Photoplay, 1949, November, June Haver cover, VG ...$12.50

Photoplay, 1954, March, Debbie Reynolds cover, EX .$14.00

Photoplay, 1955, January, Janet Leigh cover, EX.........$15.00

Photoplay, 1956, May, Mitzi Gayner cover, EX............$14.00

Photoplay, 1960, December, Debbie Reynolds cover, VG..$5.00

Photoplay, 1961, August, Jackie Kennedy cover, EX...$10.00

Photoplay, 1963, January, Natalie Woods & Warren Beatty cover, NM $10.00

Photoplay, 1965, September, Sean Connery vs Robert Vaughn cover, M...$6.00

Photoplay, 1970, April, Lennon Sisters cover, EX........$10.00

Photoplay, 1971, September, Dean Martin & Frank Sinatra cover, M..$10.00

Photoplay, 1972, September, Sonny & Cher cover, M.$12.00

Photoplay, 1973, December, Dean & Cathy Martin cover, VG $5.00

Photoplay, 1974, November, 20th Year Show Business cover, many pictures, G............................$7.00

Photoplay, 1975, August, Burt Reynolds cover, NM $7.50

Photoplay, 1976, July, Jack Nicholson cover, VG $7.00

Photoplay, 1977, January, Henry Winkler cover, NM....$7.00

Photoplay, 1978, August, Elvis Presley cover, EX........$10.00

Photoplay, 1978, March, Penny Marshall & Cindy Williams cover, EX $5.00

Photoplay, 1978, May, John Travolta cover, EX.............$8.00

Photoplay, 1979, December, Dolly Parton cover, M......$8.00

Pic, 1942, January, Gene Tierney cover, EX...................$7.50

Pic, 1944, October 24, Lucille Ball cover, VG $20.00

Picture Play, 1940, December, Martha Scott cover, NM ..$17.00

Screen Album, 1943, Alan Ladd cover, NM..................$12.00

Screen Album, 1948, Elizabeth Taylor cover, EX.........$10.00

Screen Album, 1961, July, Connie Stevens cover, EX..$12.50

Screen Guide, 1951, Janet Leigh cover, NM................$17.50

Screen Romances, 1939, July, Tyrone Power cover, NM ..$22.50

Screen Romances, 1940, September, Ginger Rogers & Ronald Coleman, EX.................................$20.00

Screen Romances, 1945, January, Van Johnson cover, VG...$10.00

Screen Stories, 1952, March, Jane Powell cover, NM...$10.00

Screen Stories, 1967, August, Jane Fonda cover, VG...$10.00

Screen Stories, 1967, November, Julie Christie cover, NM ..$6.00

Screenland, 1946, May, Betty Hutton cover, VG............$7.50

Screenplay, 1932, February, Dolores Del Rio cover, M ...$30.00

Silver Screen, 1940, July, Loretta Young cover, EX......$12.50

Silver Screen, 1948, Maureen O'Hara cover, EX $10.00

Silver Screen, 1958, June, Mitzi Gaynor cover, VG+....$13.00

Silver Screen, 1959, June, Sophia Loren cover, EX+ $15.00

Silver Screen, 1960, December, Tuesday Weld cover, EX+ $12.00

Silver Screen, 1964, August, Paul McCartney, Break Up? cover, NM $15.00

Silver Screen, 1965, June, Hayley Mills cover, NM $13.00

Silver Screen, 1966, June, Batman & Robin cover, EX+ ...$10.00

Silver Screen, 1968, August, Paul Newman cover, EX+ ..$8.00

Silver Screen, 1968, February, Connie Stevens cover, VG..$6.00

Silver Screen, 1968, November, Lawrence Welk & Lennon Sisters cover, NM.................................$10.00

Silver Screen, 1969, June, Ethel & Bobby Kennedy cover, NM $10.00

Silver Screen, 1970, August, Johnny Cash & wife cover, NM $8.00

Silver Screen, 1970, December, Jackie Onassis cover, NM ..$8.00

Silver Screen, 1970, March, Carol Burnett & kids on cover, NM..$8.00

Silver Screen, 1971, June, Ryan O'Neil & Barbara Streisand cover, EX $6.00

Silver Screen, 1971, May, Chuck Conners & Chad Everett cover, NM $8.00

Silver Screen, 1972, December, Sonny & Cher cover, EX..$8.00

Silver Screen, 1972, May, James Brolin & Chad Everett cover, VG $5.00

Silver Screen, 1973, August, The Waltons cover, NM $8.00

Silver Screen, 1973, July, Maude stars, Bea Arthur w/cast cover, NM $8.00

Silver Screen, 1973, March, Ryan O'Neil & Goldie Hawn cover, NM $8.00

Silver Screen, 1974, July, Sonny & Cher cover, NM.......$8.00

Silver Screen, 1976, July, Robert Redford cover, NM.....$5.00

Starland, 1955, Fess Parker cover, VG $15.00

TV Star Parade, 1952, October, Red Skelton cover, M ..$12.50

TV Star Parade, 1959, September, James Garner cover, VG...$6.00

TV Star Parade, 1971, April, Nancy Sinatra wedding cover, EX $8.00

TV Star Parade, 1973, March, Lawrence Welk cover, EX...$7.50

TV World, 1959, June, Dick Clark cover, VG $6.00

New Martinsville Glass

Located in a West Virginia town by the same name, the New Martinsville Glass Company was founded in 1901 and until it was purchased by Viking in 1944 produced quality tableware in various patterns and colors that collectors admire today. They also made a line of glass animals which Viking continued to produce until they closed in 1986. In 1987 the factory was bought by Mr. Kenneth Dalzell who reopened the company under the title Dalzell-Viking. He used the old molds to reissue his own line of animals, which he marked 'Dalzell' with an acid stamp. These are usually priced in the $50.00 to $60.00 range. Examples marked 'V' were made by Viking for another company, Mirror Images. They're valued at $15.00 to $35.00.

See also Glass Animals.

Geneva, perfume bottle, w/black stopper $32.00

Georgian, cordial, ruby...$12.50

Georgian, goblet, 5⅝", ruby $15.00
Janice, basket, 8¼", cobalt or ruby, each $110.00
Janice, bonbon, rolled-up handles............................$16.00
Janice, bowl, 11", etched, dolphin foot $35.00
Janice, cup & saucer, light blue $13.00
Janice, plate, 13½", Canterbury etching.....................$36.00
Janice, relish, 6", silver overlay, 2-part $20.00
Moondrops, ashtray, 3", green $12.00
Moondrops, bowl, 8½", amber, concave, footed........$24.00
Moondrops, candlesticks, 8½", amethyst or crystal, metal
    stem, pr...$27.50
Moondrops, candy dish, 8", dark green, ruffled rim....$19.00
Moondrops, cordial, amber.......................................$22.50
Moondrops, creamer & sugar bowl, amber.................$22.00
Moondrops, creamer & sugar bowl, miniature, red.....$35.00
Moondrops, cup, red or blue $15.00
Moondrops, cup & saucer, amber $10.00
Moondrops, goblet, 4¾", red or blue..........................$22.50
Moondrops, plate, 6", amber.......................................$4.00
Moondrops, plate, 9", amber.....................................$10.00
Moondrops, plate, 9¼", emerald green $18.00
Moondrops, platter, 12", amber $15.00
Moondrops, relish, red, 3-compartment, footed.........$50.00
Moondrops, shot, 2-oz, amber $9.00
Moondrops, tumbler, 4½", amethyst...........................$15.00
Moondrops, tumbler, 5⅛", pink or green....................$13.00
Moondrops, tumbler, 5-oz, cobalt..............................$15.00
Mt Vernon, sherbet, 4", amber, footed $5.00
Oscar, tumbler, amber, platinum trim...........................$5.00

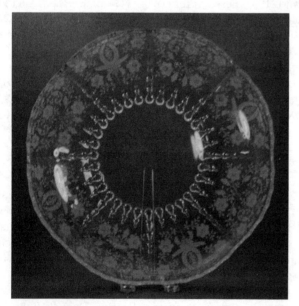

Prelude, bowl, 13", shallow....................................$52.00
Radiance, bowl, pickle; 7", amber $11.00
Radiance, bowl, 7", amber or crystal, 2-part $12.00
Radiance, candlesticks, 6", blue or red, ruffled, pr....$105.00
Radiance, cruet, red or blue, individual $47.50
Radiance, cup, punch; amber.....................................$6.00
Radiance, cup, red $16.00
Radiance, plate, 8", ice blue or crystal.........................$9.00
Radiance, punch ladle, amber...................................$95.00

Radiance, salt & pepper shakers, amber, pr $45.00
Radiance, tumbler, 9-oz, amber.................................$16.00
Radiance, vase, 12", red or cobalt, crimped rim $65.00

Newspapers

Papers that cover specific events, whether historical, regarding well-known political or entertainment figures, natural disasters of unusually large proportions, or catastropic events of any nature, are just the type that people tend to keep, and they're also the most collectible. Those that carry first-report accounts are more valuable than those with subsequent reporting. Other factors that bear on value are where the article appears (front page is best), how visual it is (are there photographs or a large headline), and whether it is from a small town or city paper.

An authentic copy of The New York Herald's April 15, 1865, 10 AM edition, reporting the assassination of Lincoln is rare and expensive, valued at about $2,000.00. There are thousands of reprints around today, so beware!

Historical content has much more bearing on the value of a newspaper than age. Condition is extremely important. Even if yours is historically significant, if it's fragile and stained, don't expect to get more than a few dollars for it. In fact, a collector may not be interested in buying it at all.

1930, March 4, 'Cittandiro Aide Arrested' headline, St Paul
    Dispatch, complete front section $7.50
1932, March 2, 'Lindbergh To Pay Ransom' headline, Lind-
    bergh baby photo w/nurse, St Paul Dispatch, EX ..$12.00
1933, February 16, Roosevelt assassination attempt report on
    front page, St Paul Pioneer, VG $5.00
1934, April 23, 'Dillinger Shoots US Aids!' headline, Extra
    edition, San Francisco Chronicle, EX....................$50.00
1934, October 23, 'Pretty Boy Floyd Slain As He Flees' head-
    line, New York Times, EX.....................................$32.00
1936, December 10, 'King Abdicates' headline, New York
    Daily Mirror, EX $32.00
1936, November 4, 'Roosevelt Sweeps US' headline, Milwau-
    kee Sentinel, EX $8.00
1937, May 7, 'Two Nations Join To Probe Zep Tragedy'
    headline, Stockton Democrat Record, front page only,
    EX...$45.00
1939, February 12, Wilentz calls for Hauptmann's death, St
    Paul Dispatch, front page section, EX $6.00
1939, September 1, 'Undeclared War On: Nazis Bomb Warsaw'
    headlines, Cincinnati Post Extra, complete, EX $10.00
1940, April 9, 'Hitler Troops Seize Norway' headline, Min-
    neapolis Times-Tribune, edge wear, EX.................$6.00
1941, December 16, 'Japan Sought Peace After Raid, FDR
    Reveals' headline, Honolulu Advertiser, NM........$26.50
1943, January 27, 'FDR Flies to Africa; Lays Out Victory
    Plans w/Churchill' headline, St Paul Pioneer, complete,
    EX...$12.00
1944, June 6, 'Invasion Land in France' headline, w/English
    Channel map, San Francisco Call Bulletin, EX......$25.00

1945, April 13, 'Roosevelt Mourned' headline, Oakland Post Enquirer, EX...**$22.50**

1945, August 16, 'Surrender Parley Stalled by Hirohito' headline, San Francisco Call Bulletin, EX......................**$12.50**

1945, August 6, 'Mighty Atomic Bomb Rips Nips' headline, San Francisco Call Bulletin, front section, EX.......**$24.00**

1945, July 27, 'British Oust Churchill' headline, Stars & Stripes, EX...**$4.00**

1945, March 8, 'Yanks Cross Rhine' headline, photo of Iwo Jima, St Paul Dispatch 1st section, EX **$5.00**

1945, May, 'Adolf Hitler Dead' headline, Hitler photo, San Francisco News, NM **$40.00**

1945, May 15, 'Planes Blast Japan' headline, Honolulu Advertiser, VG **$5.00**

1953, June 20, 'Rosenbergs Electrocuted! Both Calm, Refuse To Talk' headline, San Francisco Examiner, 1st section only..**$15.00**

1955, April 6, 'Churchill Resigns as Prime Minister' headline, Los Angeles Times, front page only........................**$8.00**

1956, April 15, 'Fifty Years After the Fire' headline, San Francisco Examiner, EX **$15.00**

1956, November 7, 'Adlai Concedes' headline, San Francisco Examiner Election Extra, first section, EX.............**$15.00**

1959, December 17, 'Terrible Toohy Slain' headline, Arizona Republic, 1st section only....................................**$22.50**

1963, November 22, 'President Slain by Assassin' headline, Philadelphia Daily News, EX..................................**$27.50**

1963, November 23, 'Johnson at Helm as US Mourns Kennedy' headline, Los Angeles Herald Examiner, 1st section, EX...**$12.50**

1963, November 25, 'John Kennedy Rests in Arlington' headline, Minneapolis Star, EX..................................**$6.00**

1963, November 25, 'Oswald Murdered' headline, Chicago Tribune, VG..**$7.50**

1964, April 6, 'Gen MacArthur Succumbs at 84' headline, photo on front page, Washington Daily Chronical, EX **$12.00**

1964, November 4, 'LBJ Landslide' headline, Johnson photo on front page, San Francisco Examiner, EX..........**$15.00**

1966, March 16, 'Great Gemini Space Chase Is On' headline, California paper, 1st section only, EX....................**$10.00**

1968, April 5, 'Dr King Murdered' headline, photo on front page, San Jose Mercury, Extra edition, 1st section only..**$22.50**

1969, July 16, 'Off to the Moon!' headline, Los Angeles Herald Examiner, 1st section only, NM **$17.50**

1969, March 28, 'Eisenhower Is Dead' headline, Vallejo News Chronical, EX...**$20.00**

1972, December 26, news of Truman's death, photo of him w/'Dewey Defeats Truman' newspaper, Las Vegas Review Journal, EX **$12.50**

1972, November 8, 'Landslide Victory for Nixon' headline, Los Angeles Times, NM **$15.00**

1973, 'Peace Pact' headline, much inside material on LBJ funeral, Torrance Daily Breeze, EX **$10.00**

1974, August 8, 'Nixon Quits' headline, lg Nixon photo on front page, Los Angeles Times Extra, 1st section only **$15.00**

1974, August 9, 'Ford Says Nightmare Over' headline, Tucson Democrat Citizen, EX.....................................**$12.00**

1974, August 9, 'Nixon Resigns' headline, San Francisco Chronicle, 1st section only, EX **$15.00**

1976, April 6, 'Howard Hughes Dies' headline, Hughes photo on front page, Los Angeles Herald Examiner, 2 sections **$15.00**

1976, July 4, 'Happy Birthday America Let Freedom Ring' headline, Los Angeles Herald Examiner, bicentennial sections **$10.00**

1977, August 16, 'Elvis Presley Dies' headline, Los Angeles Herald Examiner, 2 sections only, EX **$12.50**

1984, April 24, Ansel Adams death reported, photo on front page, San Francisco Chronicle, front section only..**$10.00**

1984, August 6, 'Richard Burton Dies' headline, sm photo, San Francisco Chronicle, 2 sections.....................**$12.50**

Niloak Pottery

This company operated in the Little Rock area of Arkansas from the turn of the century until 1947 (when it was converted to a tile company which is still in existence). It was founded by Charles Hyten, whose partner was a former Rookwood potter, Arthur Dovey. It was originally known as the Hyten Pottery, renamed Eagle Pottery soon after that, and finally was incorporated in 1911 as the Niloak Pottery Company. Niloak (the backwards spelling of kaolin, a type of clay) is best known today for their Mission Ware line, characterized by swirled colors of natural and artificially dyed clay. Though other companies made swirled pottery, none were as successful as Hyten, who received a patent for his process in 1928. Except for a few rare examples, Mission Ware was glazed only on the inside.

Facing financial difficulties at the onset of the Depression, the company changed ownership and began to manufacture a more extensive line of molded wares, including figural planters, vases, jardinieres, clocks, and some tile.

Several marks were used, all of which include the company name, and paper labels were used as well.

Ashtray, advertising, 3½x5¾", Crow-Burlington Co Parts & Equipment in white lettering on brown **$70.00**

Ashtray, 1¼x3¼" dia, Mission Ware, swirled colors.....**$70.00**

Basket, 6½", tan w/blue overspray, handled **$75.00**

Bowl, 4", peacock blue, scalloped rim.........................**$50.00**

Candlestick, 10¼", Mission Ware, swirled colors.......**$235.00**

Candlestick, 3¼", Mission Ware, swirled colors.........**$185.00**

Chamber stick, 5", Mission Ware, swirled colors, flared bottom, handled **$200.00**

Creamer, 4¼", pink w/blue overspray.........................**$25.00**

Ewer, 10", eagle & stars in relief, celery green & caramel mottle **$35.00**

Ewer, 8", pink w/blue overspray **$25.00**

Figurine, 10", Southern Belle, cobalt **$110.00**

Figurine, 3½", donkey, red, 1935.................................**$40.00**

Flower bowl, 4¾x4½", Mission Ware, swirled colors, ball form **$170.00**

Pitcher, 3¼", burgundy w/high gloss finish, barrel shape, ear-type handle **$20.00**

Pitcher, 7½", light green, ball form $35.00
Planter, 3½", rabbit figural, white w/high gloss finish..$25.00
Planter, 3½", Scottie dog figural, cobalt........................$35.00
Planter, 3¾", swan figural, yellow, high gloss $25.00
Planter, 3¾x10", peacock blue Lewis glaze, hills & trees in
  relief, unmarked..$70.00
Planter, 4", frog on lily pad, light teal w/high gloss finish,
  Dicky Clay in relief on pad, unmarked $30.00
Planter, 6", circus elephant figural, pink w/blue over-
  spray...$40.00
Plate, dinner; 10", peacock blue w/embossed petal
  design...$50.00
Tumbler, 5", Mission Ware, swirled colors, slightly flared
  rim...$135.00
Tumbler, 5", peacock blue, unmarked $60.00
Vase, 10¼", Mission Ware, swirled colors, bulbous w/flared
  rim...$235.00
Vase, 2", Mission Ware, swirled colors, cone shape,
  unmarked $85.00
Vase, 4½", Mission Ware, swirled colors, hourglass
  shape...$75.00
Vase, 5½", Mission Ware, swirled colored, bulbous, black
  ink stamp $85.00
Vase, 5½", pink w/blue overspray, Lewis glaze, bulbous,
  unmarked $35.00
Vase, 5¾", peacock blue, bulbous w/slightly flared rim,
  applied handles..$50.00
Vase, 6", pink shading to blue, ruffled rim.....................$35.00
Vase, 7", cobalt, ruffled top, ear-type handles $35.00
Vase, 7¼", Mission Ware, swirled colors, fan form on round
  base $245.00
Vase, 8", Mission Ware, swirled colors, cone shape, black
  ink stamp...$200.00
Vase, 8¼", Mission Ware, swirled colors, cylinder form
  w/slightly flared base $170.00

Vase, 9", Mission Ware, swirled colors **$175.00**
Wall pocket, 5¼", cup & saucer, yellow w/bouquet pattern
  & high gloss finish $40.00

Nippon

In 1890 the McKinley Tariff Act was passed by Congress, requiring that all items of foreign manufacture be marked in 'legible English' with the name of the country of origin. In compliance, items imported from Japan were marked 'Nippon,' the Japanese word for their homeland. For many years this was acceptable. In 1921, however, the United States government reversed its position and instructed their custom agents to deny entry to imported items bearing only the Nippon mark and in so doing forced the Japanese to add or substitute the English word 'Japan' in their trademarks.

This was an era of prosperity in our country, a time when even laboring families had money to spend on little niceties. The import business was booming. Japanese-made porcelain was much more inexpensive than similar items from Germany and Austria, and as a result, it was imported in vast quantities. It was sold at fairs, through gift stores, five and ten cent stores, Sears and Roebuck, and Montgomery Wards.

Today Nippon is an active area of buying and selling among collectors. Quality varies from piece to piece. The more desirable pieces are those with fine art work and lavish gold overlay. The term moriage used in the descriptions that follow refers to a decorating method where soft clay is piped on with a squeeze bag, similar to decorating a cake with icing. Items with animals in relief, children's dinnerware, unusual forms (such as hanging hatpin holders, for instance), and those with out-of-the-ordinary decorative themes are good to invest in.

If you'd like to learn more about this subject, we recommend *The Collector's Encyclopedia of Nippon Porcelain* (there are three volumes) by Joan F. Van Patten.

Ashtray, 4¾", steam engine & buildings, marked.$125.00
Ashtray, 5" square, pipe & matches on brown shaded back-
  ground, green mark...$135.00
Bottle, cologne; 5¼", white w/gold bands, 6-sided base,
  flowers on stopper, green mark..........................$95.00
Bowl, chestnuts in relief along sides, brown & cream tones,
  handles, green mark...$150.00
Bowl, fruit; 5½", Doll Face pattern, Morimura,
  child's $75.00
Bowl, 7" dia, fruit on brown to cream shaded background,
  folded rim, blue mark...$85.00
Bowl, 7½" dia, yellow roses inside & out, gold rim, tub handles, green mark $200.00

Bowl, 7¼" dia, flower interior, gold reticulated rim, 3-legged, green mark $95.00

Box, cigarette; 4½" long, camel rider in desert, rectangular, green mark $250.00

Candlestick, 6¼", river scene, earth tones, green M-in-wreath mark $135.00

Celery dish, 12", lg florals on white, handles, oval, green mark $75.00

Chamberstick, 6" dia, sm red flowers on white, much red & gold trim, green mark, pr $220.00

Cinnamon stick holder, 4½", river scene, gold top & foot, blue mark $225.00

Coaster, 3¾" dia, sampan scene, gold trim, green mark ..$30.00

Compote, 3½x6½", woodland scene, scalloped rim, M-in-wreath mark $175.00

Condensed milk holder, 6", gold overlay on white, RC mark, w/tray $115.00

Cookie jar, 9½" dia, floral on tan, cobalt rim & foot, unmarked $200.00

Cup & saucer, Deco style yellow & blue border on white, green mark $35.00

Cup & saucer, lacy gold on cobalt, unmarked............$80.00

Cup & saucer, pink roses w/much gold trim, blue mark ..$50.00

Egg cup, 3½", Doll Face pattern, Morimura sticker $75.00

Ferner, 7" long, river scene, footed, green mark $200.00

Ferner, 7¼", yellow roses on green, gold scalloped rim, footed, Maple Leaf mark $200.00

Hair receiver, 4½" wide, white w/much gold overlay, green mark $70.00

Humidor, 5½", elk at sunset, earth tones, green mark ..$350.00

Humidor, 6¾", sampan scene in earth tones, blue mark..$350.00

Incense burner, 3¼", blue w/gold overlay, footed, red mark $150.00

Jam jar, 6", flower medallions w/much gold trim, w/underplate, blue mark $225.00

Jar, 5½", pastoral band on green w/gold trim, shouldered shape, M-in-wreath mark $125.00

Lemon dish, 5½" dia, blue birds on white, sm handles, gold rim, blue mark....................$30.00

Matchbox holder, 4½", white w/flowers & gold trim, hanging, green mark $125.00

Mug, 4¾", camel rider in desert, moriage trim, green mark $250.00

Nut dish, 5½", American Indian in canoe, handles, 6-sided, M-in-wreath mark $150.00

Pin box, 2½x2" dia, Capitol Building in Washington DC in center reserve on lid, green mark...........$75.00

Pitcher, lemonade; 6", pink & yellow roses on cream background, gold scalloped rim, blue mark...........$210.00

Plaque, 7¾", pastoral scene w/moriage florals at side, M-in-wreath mark $185.00

Plaque, 7¾", river landscape, earth tones, blue mark ..$250.00

Relish dish, 9½" long, floral reserves on white w/gold trim, gondola shape w/handles, blue mark $65.00

Salt & pepper shakers, blue floral band on white, blue mark, pr...................................$35.00

Snack set, Deco-style border w/birds & flowers on white w/much gold trim, cup on matching tray, blue mark...$70.00

Sugar shaker, 4", red roses on white w/gold trim, green mark...................................$135.00

Tankard, 13", coralene flowers on green, gold trim, marked $500.00

Tea tile, 5½", windmill scene, octagonal, M-in-wreath mark...................................$65.00

Teapot, 5¼", white w/much gold overlay, blue mark, +creamer & sugar bowl...................................$150.00

Vase, 12x5½", poppies on lavender shaded, gold trim, Royal mark...................................$130.00

Vase, 5½", inscribed Toronto Exhibition 1919 on front, blue butterflies on white, gold trim, angle handles, blue mark.....$65.00

Vase, 6", moriage dragon, angle handles, 3-footed, green mark...................................$160.00

Vase, 7½", river scene, heavy gold overlay, long handles, green mark...................................$275.00

Vase, 8", scenic reserve, heavy gold trim & beading, dolphin handles, blue mark $325.00

Vase, 8½", lg pink stemmed roses on tan, gold trim, sm foot, Maple Leaf mark $180.00

Vase, 8½", winter scene, gold overlay, footed, handles, blue mark...**$225.00**
Vase, 9½", floral on green w/gold trim, upturned handles, green mark..**$335.00**
Vase, 9½", open roses on cream shaded ground, gold trim, cylindrical, green mark...**$225.00**
Vase, 9½", swan reserve, much gold overlay on cobalt, blue mark...**$500.00**

Noritake

Before the government restricted the use of the Nippon mark in 1921, all porcelain exported from Japan (even that made by the Noritake Company) carried the Nippon mark. The company that became Noritake had its beginning in 1904, and over the years experienced several changes in name and organization. Until 1941 (at the onset of WWII) they continued to import large amounts of their products to America. (During the occupation, when chinaware production was resumed, all imports were marked 'Occupied Japan.')

Many variations will be found in their marks, but nearly all contain the Noritake name. If you'd like to learn more about this subject, we recommend *The Collector's Encyclopedia of Noritake* (there are two in the series) by Joan Van Patten.

Ashtray, 4¼", dog scene, 3 rests, M-in-wreath mark....**$70.00**
Ashtray, 5", Egyptian portrait, green mark **$95.00**
Bowl, 6" wide, floral w/much gold, 4 lobes, marked..**$35.00**
Bowl, 6¼", flower form, arched handle, footed, red mark.**$80.00**
Cake plate, 8", pheasants in lg medallion, pink & gold trim, M-in-wreath mark **$48.00**
Candlestick, 5½", blue butterfly at orange lustre base, M-in-wreath mark **$80.00**
Coaster, 4", sailboat scene, orange & blue lustre.........**$14.00**
Cookie jar, 8", lavender roses on gray tones, footed, green mark...**$80.00**
Egg cup, 3½", windmill scene, gold rim, green mark .**$25.00**
Inkwell, 4", boy in pointed hat figural, M-in-wreath mark **$265.00**
Jam jar, 3½", strawberries on lid, w/ladle, green mark ..**$70.00**
Nappy, 6½", floral w/gold scalloped rim, handle, M-in-wreath mark **$35.00**

Nappy, 6½", red & blue poppies on white w/gold trim, marked $40.00
Plaque, 10", steamship, gold trim, Komaru mark **$175.00**

Plaque, 10" dia, tree at lake side, green mark.....$145.00
Punch cup, 2¾", scenic w/gold rim & foot, cream interior, M-in-wreath mark...**$35.00**
Spooner, 8", river scene, angle handles, red mark......**$40.00**
Sugar bowl, 3¼", parrots on red, gold trim, M-in-wreath mark...**$25.00**
Toast rack, 5½" long, bird finial, green mark..............**$85.00**
Tray, 11", Deco fruit border, gold handles, red mark..**$90.00**
Tray, 13", river reserves, much gold, canted corners, Komaru mark **$70.00**
Trinket box, 3", Deco lady & whippet on cream, footed, green mark **$50.00**
Vase, 2½", man on camel scene, gold trim, squat, Komaru mark...**$110.00**
Vase, 5½", red ruffled basket form w/gold handle & interior **$120.00**
Vase, 5½", tulip figural, lavender & green, red mark .**$175.00**
Vase, 8½", multicolored roses on white, gold at top, upright handles, M-in-wreath mark **$120.00**
Wall pocket, 8", swan scenic band, orange lustre trim, M-in-wreath mark **$95.00**
Wall pocket, 8¼", applied butterfly & bee, red mark..**$90.00**

North Dakota School of Mines

The University of North Dakota School of Mines' professor Earle J. Babcock had an interest in the state's natural resources. Before the turn of the century, he had discovered clay deposits suitable for pottery production. He shipped some of this clay to a company in the east who used it to make vases for him. At first they decorated the vases as well, but eventually some were shipped back to the University to be decorated by the students. By 1909 the work had progressed to where the students themselves were making tile, brick, and other utilitarian items. Then in 1901 a ceramic department was established under the direction of Margaret Kelly Cable. Under her supervision, the students learned to produce fine art ware, usually decorated with animals, birds, flowers, and other subjects representative of North Dakota. Until she retired in 1949, the pottery the students made was distributed throughout the state in fine gift stores and souvenir shops. Much of the ware was marked with their official seal – 'Made at School of Mines, N.D. Clay, University of North Dakota, Grand Forks, N.D.,' and most are signed by the artist. Though some pieces are simply thrown and glazed, the more desirable examples are hand decorated.

Bowl, 5½", brown high glaze, Julia Mattson **$135.00**
Coaster, 3½" dia, fawn outlined in buff clay in light blue..**$95.00**
Cup, 3x4", tooled lineation, green gloss, brown body ..**$195.00**
Paperweight, Rebekka, green gloss, signed **$65.00**

Teapot, Scorbio, Peterson, late line **$150.00**
Vase, 9½", aqua, 3 deep vertical ribs, Julia Mattson ..**$165.00**
Vase, 4", green matt, incised curvilinear design, Huc....**$135.00**
Vase, 4x5", Indian motif carved on green & brown matt, M
   Heith, ...**$325.00**

Novelty Clocks

The largest producers of these small clocks were Lux, Keebler, Westclox, and Columbia Time. Some had moving parts, others a small pendulette. They were made of wood, china, Syroco (a pressed wood product), and eventually plastic. Until the late 1940s when electric-powered novelties were made by the Mastercrofter Company, they were all wind-ups. The last Lux clocks were made in the mid-1950s.

Barbie, wind-up, NM **$125.00**
Batman, talking, battery operated, 1974, NM **$35.00**
Bird's nest, top bird faces right, pendulette **$25.00**
Black shoeshine boy, Lux **$250.00**
Bluebird, pressed wood, pendulette **$75.00**
Bobbing Dove (bird), 10", plastic, pendulette **$45.00**
Cat, 7½x4½", moving eyes & tail, pendulette **$150.00**
Doghouse, Scotty dog's head moves, pendulette,
   4½x7" **$350.00**
Dog looks out of his house, sunflower atop, Waterbury..**$70.00**
Enchanted forest, animated, pendulette **$125.00**

Fireplace, log lights up, United, electric....................**$17.50**
Sailor, animated, pendulette.......................................**$125.00**
Spinning wheel, alarm, Lux, MIB..............................**$165.00**
Woody Woodpecker, animated, pendulette **$225.00**

Occupied Japan Collectibles

Some items produced in Japan during the period from the end of WWII until the occupation ended in 1952 were marked Occupied Japan. No doubt much of the ware from this era was marked simply Japan, since obviously the 'Occupied' term caused considerable resentment among the Japanese people, and they were understandably reluctant to use the mark. So even though you may find identical items marked simply Japan or Made in Japan, only those with the more limited Occupied Japan mark are evaluated here.

Assume that the items described below are ceramic unless another material is mentioned. For more information, we recommend *The Collector's Encyclopedia of Occupied Japan* (there are five in the series) by Gene Florence.

Ashtray, fielder's glove form, metal **$12.00**
Ashtray, Louisiana souvenir, 2 lobes, embossed metal..**$5.00**
Ashtray, sm, peacock embossed on metal **$4.00**
Ashtray, 2½" square, Wedgwood type..........................**$6.50**
Ashtray, 3⅝", flowers on green & white **$4.00**
Bookends, 4", penguins, pr......................................**$36.00**
Bowl, salad; 10", wooden...**$20.00**
Candlestick, 5", silver-toned metal, pr........................**$24.00**
Child's tea set, 9-piece, florals, serves 2 ....**$45.00**
Cigarette box, pink roses applied to lid **$24.00**
Cigarette lighter, camel figural, metal........................**$17.50**
Cigarette lighter, golf ball form, metal........................**$15.00**
Cigarette lighter, horse's head figural, embossed NY Silver
   Plate **$15.00**
Cigarette lighter, peacock figural, metal.....................**$12.50**
Cigarette lighter, piano form, celluloid........................**$25.00**
Creamer, 1½", floral w/lustre trim...............................**$7.50**
Creamer, 2½x2⅞", cow figural, multicolor paint..........**$18.00**
Creamer, 4", Collie dog figural, Ucagco **$32.50**
Creamer & sugar bowl, lobster on leaves figural, Royal
   Bayreuth type, w/lid..**$50.00**
Crumb butler, 5x6", metal **$10.00**
Cup & saucer, blue border, floral interior, Merit China ...**$12.50**
Cup & saucer, blue floral, marked Gold China............**$16.00**
Cup & saucer, demitasse; multicolor flowers on white
   w/much gold trim, egg shell porcelain....................**$9.00**
Cup & saucer, demitasse; yellow w/gold trim, floral on
   white interior...**$12.50**
Cup & saucer, flow blue, marked Trimont China........**$14.00**
Cup & saucer, flow blue, Maruta China **$20.00**
Cup & saucer, flowers & swags on white, Ucagco......**$12.50**
Cup & saucer, multicolor Deco-style flowers on black,
   faintly scalloped rims w/gold trim **$17.50**
Cup & saucer, Phoenix Bird, blue on white **$25.00**
Cup & saucer, pink oversize flowers on black, Merit-in-
   wreath mark **$17.50**

Cup & saucer, roses on pale blue w/gold trim, Diamond China..**$12.50**

Cup & saucer, rust floral on white, Hudson **$12.50**

Cup & saucer, tulips on white, Aladdin Fine China **$12.50**

Cup & saucer, 1⅛", 2½", pink flowers on white w/blue scalloped border **$17.50**

Cup & saucer, 1⅛", 2½", pink flowers on white w/gold trim **$16.00**

Cup & saucer, 1⅞", 3⅞", house w/red roof & black picket fence, yellow lustre ware trim................................**$17.50**

Doll, 4½x3", 2 babies in red basket, celluloid............**$50.00**

Doll, 4¾", celluloid, molded hat, nude....................**$15.00**

Doll, 6", football player, celluloid..........................**$17.50**

Doll, 8", Betty Boop type, celluloid, embossed leaf on back **$50.00**

Doll, 8⅝", Dutch girl, celluloid..............................**$50.00**

Egg cup, 2¾x2½", Blue Willow..............................**$17.50**

Figurine, 4", cat w/girl holding basket and sitting on fence, Hummel type..$25.00

Figurine, 10", cherub pulling cart **$220.00**

Figurine, 10", lady, aqua hat & scarf.......................**$22.00**

Figurine, 10¼", horse w/rider, signed Andrea, hand painted **$175.00**

Figurine, 10¼", man w/flower, bisque **$55.00**

Figurine, 10⅛", Colonial couple, multicolor w/gold trim, Orion China, pr..**$85.00**

Figurine, 2½", girl w/doll buggy, multicolor **$4.00**

Figurine, 2¼x2", piano, brown w/black & white keys & music...**$7.50**

Figurine, 2⅛", angel seated w/musical instrument **$5.00**

Figurine, 2¾x4", cow, black & white........................**$10.00**

Figurine, 2⅝", angel playing mandolin.....................**$5.00**

Figurine, 3", Eskimo..**$15.00**

Figurine, 3", poodle **$14.00**

Figurine, 3½", boy skier, multicolor.........................**$12.50**

Figurine, 3½", Colonial lady, red shawl.....................**$5.00**

Figurine, 3½", dog, brown & white terrier **$16.00**

Figurine, 3½", rooster, white w/red & black details **$10.00**

Figurine, 3¼", lady dancer, flowing orange skirt **$6.00**

Figurine, 3⅛", monkey w/cello, dressed in blue pants, red jacket, black hat & shoes.................................**$15.00**

Figurine, 3¾", boy w/duck....................................**$27.50**

Figurine, 3¾", girl w/'Betty Boop' doll, red cross in cloverleaf **$22.50**

Figurine, 3¾", girl w/book & basket, multicolor...........**$6.00**

Figurine, 3¾", horse, prancing pose, on green base ...**$22.00**

Figurine, 3⅝", ballerina, gold trim, Ucagco China **$20.00**

Figurine, 4", bellhop w/2 suitcases, Hummel type......**$32.00**

Figurine, 4", boy hiker, Hummel type **$18.00**

Figurine, 4", boy w/basket, Hummel type **$25.00**

Figurine, 4", bride & groom, bisque, pr **$42.50**

Figurine, 4", couple at piano.................................**$22.50**

Figurine, 4", Dutch water girl................................**$12.50**

Figurine, 4", girl w/chicks in basket........................**$16.00**

Figurine, 4", Oriental musician..............................**$6.50**

Figurine, 4½", boy drummer, Hummel type...............**$15.00**

Figurine, 4½", Dutch girl w/basket.........................**$15.00**

Figurine, 4½", Indian lady **$12.50**

Figurine, 4¼", lady dancer, holds skirt wide, red hat, blue trim...**$12.50**

Figurine, 4⅛", girl w/dog, Hummel type....................**$10.00**

Figurine, 4⅛", pride of lions, male & female w/2 cubs.**$45.00**

Figurine, 4⅝", Oriental lady w/fan, bisque **$12.50**

Figurine, 5", Black fiddler.....................................**$40.00**

Figurine, 5", boy w/begging dog, Hummel type **$30.00**

Figurine, 5", cat musician, bisque **$48.00**

Figurine, 5", cherub, holding bouquet of flowers........**$12.00**

Figurine, 5½", Colonial couple, arms up, dog at feet, pr..**$25.00**

Figurine, 5⅛", cowboy w/rope in hand, multicolor.....**$10.00**

Figurine, 5¾", ballerina, pastel colors, gold trim **$35.00**

Figurine, 5¾", Colonial lady w/basket.........................**$10.00**

Figurine, 5⅜", dancer, Delft type, ruffled dress **$22.50**

Figurine, 6½", Colonial couple, he w/instrument, she listens, pr $35.00

Figurine, 6¼", clown, short jacket, pointed hat, lg tummy, puffy pants **$25.00**

Figurine, 6¼", clown w/ruffle at neck, long coat & full pants **$25.00**

Figurine, 7", peacock perched on floral branch..........**$28.00**

Figurine, 7¼", Mexican girl, wide skirt, oversize sombrero, marked Ucagco **$36.00**

Figurine, 7⅛", cowboy, red bandana, brown holster & gun...**$37.50**

Figurine, 7⅝", Oriental couple praying, pr...................**$68.00**

Figurine, 7⅞", bird, multicolored on brown branch **$30.00**

Figurine, 8", boy w/dog, Hummel type, bright colors.**$48.00**

Figurine, 8", Colonial lady w/flower basket, multicolor paint, gold trim..**$35.00**

Figurine, 8", Oriental lady w/muff...............................**$25.00**

Figurine, 8¼", Oriental couple, lady w/fan, man w/dagger, pr..**$35.00**

Furniture, 1¾", piano...**$7.50**

Furniture, 3", couch, applied flowers **$10.00**

Incense burner, 3¾", American Indian figural, seated w/legs crossed...**$37.50**

Incense burner, 4¼", East Indian lady figural **$20.00**

Lamp base, 10", lady's head, Cordey type....................**$55.00**

Lamp base, 10½", Colonial man, metal base................**$27.50**

Lighter, 2", gun form, metal...**$17.50**

Match holder, 3½", bald fat man w/fly on upper lip...**$25.00**

Mug, Santa's head figural **$35.00**

Mug, 3¼", lilacs & gold, 'Little Shaver' in gold, Rossetti Chicago USA mark...**$50.00**

Mug, 4¼", grapes embossed on front of barrel shape on white..**$16.00**

Planter, 2½x5½x3½", window box form, flowers & blue scallops..**$15.00**

Planter, 2¾", Dutch girl pushing cart figural **$9.00**

Planter, 3", bird beside house figural............................**$8.00**

Planter, 3", elephant figural, trunk up, multicolor garland surrounds base..**$7.50**

Planter, 4¼x5", shoe house form, rooster on toe.........**$17.50**

Planter, 4⅛", Oriental boy beside bamboo tree..........**$10.00**

Planter, 5¼", baby buggy form, blue **$10.00**

Planter, 6", Oriental lady w/fan figural.......................**$15.00**

Plaque, 6¼", Colonial couple, multicolor, gold trim,...**$30.00**

Plaque, 7x4½", Colonial couple swing, oval, pr **$60.00**

Plate, 6", floral center, lattice rim, Rosetti..................**$25.00**

Plate, 6", lady's portrait, signed Andrea, SGK China....**$20.00**

Plate, 6", raspberries on white, plain gold rim, Ohata China **$15.00**

Plate, 7", multicolor roses, plain gold rim, Gold China ..**$35.00**

Salt & pepper shakers, comic baseball players, pr **$25.00**

Salt & pepper shakers, geisha girls, pr **$22.50**

Salt & pepper shakers, 2½x4", frogs on lily pad, pr **$22.50**

Salt & pepper shakers, 3¼x4⅛", cabbages, pr **$16.00**

Salt & pepper shakers, 3¾", strawberries, pr **$20.00**

Salt & pepper shakers, 4", boy & girl, Hummel type, pr ..**$36.00**

Shelf sitter, 3", girl w/bucket......................................**$12.50**

Shelf sitter, 6¼", ballerina, pink & blue dress, gold slippers, porcelain, Ucagco mark...**$42.00**

Shelf sitters, 4", boy & girl seated on 6¾" long wooden bench...**$48.00**

Teapot, 2x4", tomato form..**$25.00**

Toby mug, 2", devil bust **$25.00**

Toothpick holder, man sits & holds top hat, red trim..**$10.00**

Tray, 5½", leaf form, metal **$6.00**

Umbrella, 18", paper..**$27.50**

Vase, 2¾", multicolor florals on green, maroon trim.....**$8.00**

Vase, 3¾", fruit relief, cobalt on black w/gold............**$14.00**

Vase, 5½", snake charmer couple figural **$22.50**

Vase, 6⅛", Wedgwood type **$32.00**

Vase, 7¼", white matt w/heavy gold floral overlay flowers, marked Ucagco **$42.50**

Old MacDonald's Farm

This is a wonderful line of novelty kitchenware items fashioned as the family and the animals that live on Old MacDonald's Farm. It's been popular with collectors for quite some time, and over the past year or so, prices have become astronomical. But I've found shakers at a garage sales and spice jars that were way underpriced at a small flea market, and at these prices, just one good find can make your day.

These things were made by the Regal China Company, who also made some of the Little Red Riding Hood items that are so collectible, as well as figural cookie jars, 'hugger' salt and pepper shakers, and decanters. The Roerigs devote a chapter to Regal in their book *The Collector's Encyclopedia of Cookie Jars* and, in fact, show the entire Old MacDonald's Farm line.

Butter dish, cow's head..**$235.00**

Canister, Cookies, lg...**$350.00**

Canister, flour, cereal, coffee or cookie; med, each..**$235.00**

Canister, pretzels, peanuts, popcorn, chips, tidbits; lg, each...**$350.00**

Canister, salt, sugar, or tea; med, each......................**$235.00**

Canister, soap; lg **$350.00**

Cookie jar, barn...**$275.00**

Creamer, rooster **$110.00**

Grease jar, pig...**$185.00**

Jar, spice; sm, any...**$125.00**

Pitcher, milk..**$395.00**

Salt & pepper shakers, boy & girl, pr **$80.00**

Salt & pepper shakers, churn, pr **$80.00**

Salt & pepper shakers, feed sacks w/sheep, pr.........$165.00
Sugar bowl, hen..$125.00
Teapot, duck's head $275.00

Olympic Memorabilia

The 1974 Los Angeles Olympiad had a very positive effect on collectors of Olympic material. Many corporate sponsors issued commemorative pins, singly and in sets, causing a renewed interest in the older pins as well as all other types of official souvenirs that have been issued through the years since the 1896 games.

Autograph, any other than Jesse Owens or Jim Thorpe (these 2 are at least $100.00 each), from $10 up to..........$25.00
Blotter, Sonja Henie photo & One in a Million, EX.....$30.00
Cigarette card, Mecca, any athlete's photo, ca 1910, from $1 up to $10.00
Doll, 11½", Florence Griffith Joyner, 1989, MIB..........$20.00
Doll, 12", Dorothy Hamill, marked Ideal, 1970s, MIB ..$80.00
Postcard, post-1948, from $5 up to..............................$15.00
Program, 1936, Berlin $35.00
Tray, 8½x11" oval, 1984 Olympic & McDonald's logos w/ female gymnast on lithographed tin, full-color, EX..$15.00

Tumbler, Olympic Games (not from a series), from
$2.00 up to $5.00
Tumbler, 5½", 1984 Olympic & Coca-Cola logos in red, white & blue on clear glass, stylized athletes on band at top...$9.00

Opalescent Glass

Opalescent glass was press molded in many patterns and colors, but the characteristic common to all of it is its white (or opalescent) rims, developed through the application of a strong acid to those areas. It was made early in the century by many American glasshouses, and it isn't at all uncommon to find a piece from time to time at estate sales, flea markets, or even garage sales, for that matter. Colors are more valuable than clear, and examples of major patterns are usually worth more than those with few or no matching pieces.

If you'd like to learn more about the subject, we recommend *The Standard Opalescent Glass Price Guide* by Bill Edwards.

Alaska, salt & pepper shakers, white, pr.....................$65.00
Alaska, sauce bowl, canary $45.00
Alaska, spooner, blue $75.00
Alaska, tumbler, emerald gr $70.00
Alaska, tumbler, white...$56.00
Arabian Nights, tumbler, white $40.00
Argonaut Shell, bowl, master; blue..............................$100.00
Argonaut Shell, tumbler, white....................................$70.00
Beaded Drapes, bowl, canary, footed $40.00
Beaded Ovals in Sand, creamer, green $70.00
Beaded Ovals in Sand, salt & pepper shakers, green, pr ..$80.00
Beaded Ovals in Sand, tumbler, blue $80.00
Beaded Shell, cruet, white $340.00
Beaded Shell, spooner, green $85.00
Beaded Shell, tumbler, blue $75.00
Beatty Honeycomb, butter dish, white.........................$150.00
Beatty Honeycomb, mug, white $32.00
Beatty Honeycomb, spooner, blue $50.00
Beatty Honeycomb, toothpick holder, blue..............$240.00
Beatty Rib, celery vase, white $60.00
Beatty Rib, finger bowl, white $20.00
Beatty Rib, salt cellar, blue..$50.00
Beatty Rib, sugar bowl, white $70.00
Beatty Swirl, mug, blue $50.00
Beatty Swirl, spooner, white $50.00
Beatty Swirl, tumbler, canary $45.00
Blown Drape, barber bottle, green..............................$105.00
Blown Drape, tumbler, cranberry $38.00
Blown Twist, sugar shaker, green.................................$75.00
Blown Twist, tumbler, canary $40.00
Bubble Lattice, butter dish, white..............................$140.00
Bubble Lattice, celery vase, cranberry.........................$100.00
Bubble Lattice, sauce bowl, green................................$20.00
Bubble Lattice, sugar shaker, blue..............................$180.00

Chick w/Leaf & Scroll Border, plate, 7", blue, late .$100.00
Chrysanthemum Base Swirl, creamer, white...............$65.00

Chrysanthemum Base Swirl, cruet, cranberry $450.00
Chrysanthemum Base Swirl, tumbler, blue $80.00
Circle Scroll, spooner, white $50.00
Circle Scroll, sugar bowl, green $210.00

Coin Spot, pitcher, water; white $90.00
Coin Spot, sauce bowl, green $26.00
Coin Spot, toothpick holder, green $240.00
Consolidated Crisscross, celery vase, white $120.00
Consolidated Crisscross, cruet, cranberry $750.00
Consolidated Crisscross, spooner, white $205.00
Daisy & Fern, creamer, green $70.00
Daisy & Fern, perfume bottle, white $100.00
Daisy & Fern, rose bowl, cranberry $95.00
Daisy & Fern, sauce bowl, cranberry $42.00
Daisy & Fern, spooner, white $40.00
Daisy & Fern, tumbler, blue $40.00
Diamond Spearhead, bowl, master; white $40.00
Diamond Spearhead, cup & saucer, cobalt...............$125.00
Diamond Spearhead, goblet, green $90.00
Diamond Spearhead, salt & pepper shakers, blue, pr..$80.00
Diamond Spearhead, tumbler, white..........................$45.00
Dolly Madison, spooner, blue.....................................$70.00
Dolly Madison, tumbler, white....................................$55.00

Dolphins, compote, blue...$75.00
Double Greek Key, celery vase, white......................$100.00
Double Greek Key, creamer, blue.................................$70.00
Double Greek Key, tumbler, white $40.00
Drapery (Northwood), spooner, white........................$60.00
Drapery (Northwood), tumbler, blue $35.00
Duchess (English), butter dish, white.........................$130.00

Duchess (English), toothpick holder, white...............$110.00
Everglades, butter dish, blue.....................................$230.00
Everglades, creamer, canary......................................$90.00
Fan, gravy boat, green...$35.00
Fan, spooner, blue...$75.00
Fan, tumbler, white...$18.00
Fern, creamer, blue..$110.00
Fern, mustard pot, white..$110.00
Fern, sugar bowl, blue $180.00
Fern, tumbler, cranberry..$90.00
Flora, celery vase, blue..$115.00
Flora, sauce bowl, white $20.00
Flora, sugar bowl, blue...$120.00
Flora, tumbler, canary..$70.00
Fluted Scrolls, salt & pepper shakers, canary, pr........$75.00
Fluted Scrolls, spooner, blue......................................$50.00
Fluted Scrolls, tumbler, white....................................$30.00
Gonterman (Adonis) Swirl, spooner, blue $80.00
Gonterman (Adonis) Swirl, tumbler, amber................$75.00
Hobnail (Hobbs), celery vase, blue............................$160.00
Hobnail (Hobbs), sauce bowl, canary, square............$30.00
Hobnail (Hobbs), sugar bowl, white...........................$130.00
Hobnail (Hobbs), tumbler, cranberry $85.00
Hobnail (Northwood), sugar bowl, white $95.00
Hobnail (4-footed), spooner, canary $75.00
Hobnail & Panelled Thumbprint, pitcher, white.......$150.00
Hobnail & Panelled Thumbprint, spooner, white.......$65.00
Hobnail in Square (Vesta), salt & pepper shakers,
   pr $85.00
Hobnail in Square (Vesta), sugar bowl, white $120.00
Honeycomb, cracker jar, cranberry $285.00
Honeycomb, tumbler, amber $70.00
Honeycomb, tumbler, white..$30.00
Honeycomb & Clover, butter dish, green $300.00
Honeycomb & Clover, sauce bowl, blue.....................$30.00
Idyll, creamer, green..$85.00
Idyll, cruet, white..$160.00
Idyll, tumbler, blue $80.00
Inside Ribbing, jelly compote, white $20.00
Inside Ribbing, pitcher, blue......................................$250.00
Intaglio, creamer, blue...$60.00
Intaglio, cruet, white...$125.00

Intaglio, pitcher, water; blue...............................$150.00
Intaglio, salt & pepper shakers, blue, pr....................$85.00

Intaglio, tumbler, white $50.00
Inverted Fan & Feather, creamer, blue................$140.00
Inverted Fan & Feather, tumbler, white $50.00
Iris w/Meander, plate, white $110.00
Iris w/Meander, salt & pepper shakers, green, pr $185.00
Iris w/Meander, spooner, canary $85.00
Iris w/Meander, tumbler, green $70.00
Iris w/Meander, vase, blue, tall $50.00
Jackson, creamer, white $55.00
Jackson, epergne, blue, sm $150.00
Jackson, sauce bowl, canary $25.00
Jackson, tumbler, blue $75.00
Jewel & Flower, sauce bowl, blue $30.00
Jewel & Flower, spooner, canary $120.00
Jewel & Flower, tumbler, white $55.00
Jewelled Heart, novelty bowl, white $20.00
Jewelled Heart, spooner, blue $110.00
Jewelled Heart, tumbler, green $55.00
Leaf Mold, sauce bowl, cranberry $40.00
Leaf Mold, toothpick holder, cranberry $450.00
Leaf Mold, tumbler, cranberry $90.00
Lustre Flute, creamer, white $55.00
Lustre Flute, custard cup, white $16.00
Lustre Flute, tumbler, blue $65.00
Northern Star, plate, blue $90.00
Northwood Block, celery vase, white $36.00
Over-All Hob, creamer, white $40.00
Over-All Hob, toothpick holder, blue $18.00
Over-All Hob, tumbler, white $25.00
Palm Beach, creamer, canary $120.00
Palm Beach, jelly compote, blue $120.00
Palm Beach, tumbler, blue $85.00
Panelled Holly, bowl, master; white $40.00
Panelled Holly, sugar bowl, blue $225.00
Picadilly (English), basket, green, sm $60.00
Poinsettia, syrup, white $200.00
Polka Dot, salt & pepper shakers, white, pr $40.00
Polka Dot, sugar shaker, cranberry $200.00
Polka Dot, syrup, blue $200.00
Prince William (English), pitcher, blue $90.00
Princess Diana (English), pitcher, canary $90.00
Princess Diana (English), sugar bowl, blue, open $60.00
Princess Diana (English), water tray, canary $40.00
Regal (Northwood), butter dish, green $235.00
Regal (Northwood), celery vase, blue $165.00
Regal (Northwood), creamer, white $80.00
Regal (Northwood), sauce bowl, blue $25.00
Reverse Swirl, custard cup, blue $45.00
Reverse Swirl, mustard, white $40.00
Reverse Swirl, sauce bowl, blue $25.00
Reverse Swirl, sugar bowl, cranberry $210.00
Reverse Swirl, tumbler, blue $40.00
Reverse Swirl, water bottle, cranberry $180.00
Ribbed Spiral, jelly compote, white $25.00
Ribbed Spiral, plate, blue $35.00
Ribbed Spiral, salt & pepper shakers, white, pr $110.00
Ribbed Spiral, sugar bowl, white $125.00
Richelieu (English), creamer, canary $52.00

Scroll w/Acanthus, jelly compote, green $40.00
Scroll w/Acanthus, spooner, blue $65.00
Scroll w/Acanthus, tumbler, canary $70.00
Seaweed, celery vase, white $115.00
Seaweed, creamer, white $85.00
Seaweed, sauce bowl, blue $20.00
Seaweed, syrup, cranberry $175.00
Spanish Lace, perfume bottle, cranberry $250.00
Spanish Lace, salt & pepper shakers, white, pr $60.00
Spanish Lace, spooner, canary $125.00
Spanish Lace, syrup, blue $230.00
Spanish Lace, tumbler, white $30.00
Spanish Lace, water bottle, cranberry $395.00
Stripe, salt & peppers shakers, white, pr $60.00
Stripe, syrup, blue $250.00
Stripe (Wide), sugar shaker, cranberry $190.00
Stripe (Wide), tumbler, white $30.00
Sunburst on Shield, sauce bowl, canary $224.00
Sunburst on Shield, sugar bowl, blue $175.00
Swag w/Brackets, jelly compote, blue $48.00
Swag w/Brackets, sugar bowl, green $125.00
Swag w/Brackets, toothpick holder, canary $285.00
Swastika, pitcher, white $175.00
Swirl, celery vase, blue $70.00
Swirl, custard cup, green $45.00
Swirl, finger bowl, cranberry $75.00
Swirl, sauce bowl, blue $18.00
Swirl, sugar bowl, white $44.00
Swirling Maze, tumbler, green $40.00
Thousand Eye, creamer, white $65.00
Thousand Eye, tumbler, white $20.00
Tokyo, plate, blue $55.00
Tokyo, toothpick holder, green $180.00
Tokyo, tumbler, green $60.00
Tokyo, vase, white $30.00
Twig, vase, blue, sm $50.00
Waterlily & Cattails, creamer, amethyst $55.00
Waterlily & Cattails, relish, blue, handles $80.00
Waterlily & Cattails, sauce bowl, amethyst $30.00
Waterlily & Cattails, spooner, green $42.00
Waterlily & Cattails, tumbler, white $20.00
Wild Bouquet, jelly compote, white $60.00
Wild Bouquet, sauce bowl, green $30.00
Wild Bouquet, tumbler, green $65.00
Wild Bouquet, tumbler, white $22.00
Windows (Plain), finger bowl, white $38.00
Windows (Plain), tumbler, blue $40.00
Windows (Swirled), barber bottle, cranberry $275.00
Windows (Swirled), celery vase, cranberry $140.00
Windows (Swirled), sauce bowl, blue $25.00
Windows (Swirled), spooner, cranberry $150.00
Windows (Swirled), sugar shaker, blue $135.00
Windows (Swirled), tumbler, white $50.00
Wreath & Shell, cracker jar, white $410.00
Wreath & Shell, creamer, white $60.00
Wreath & Shell, rose bowl, blue $80.00
Wreath & Shell, tumbler, cranberry, flat or footed $80.00
Wreath & Shell, tumbler, white, flat or footed $35.00

Pacific Clay Products

This company was formed by the consolidation of several small California potteries. In the early twenties, they produced stoneware staples from local clay taken from their own mines. Their business, along with many others, suffered at the onset of the Depression, and taking note of Bauer's success, they initiated the production of earthenware dishes which they marketed under the tradename Hostess Ware. During the next decade they developed several dinnerware lines in both vivid colors and pastel glazes as well as artware such as vases, figurines, flowerpots, and large architectural sand jars and birdbaths. 1942 saw the end of all pottery manufacture, due to the company's committment to full-time defense work. Today they are located in Corona, California, where they specialize in the production of roof tile.

If you're interested in learning more about this company, we recommend *The Collector's Encyclopedia of California Pottery* by Jack Chipman.

Bean pot, 6¼", no rings, 1 handle $30.00
Bowl, 8½", Ring-style...$22.00
Carafe, Ring-style, w/lid $30.00
Chop plate, 12", Ring-style...$30.00
Cup & saucer, demitasse; Ring-style............................$25.00
Figurine, 15½", nude holds feather.............................$55.00
Pitcher, tilt-type jug w/ice lip......................................$50.00
Plate, 11", Ring-style $10.00

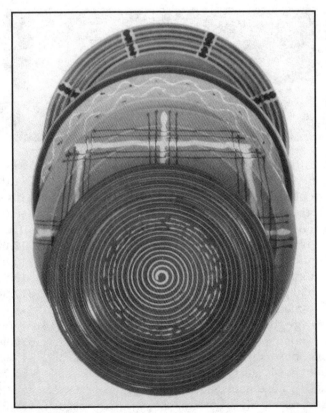

Plates, various hand-painted designs available on Pacific Ware from the mid-thirties, each........$25.00

Relish tray, Ring-style, 4-part, wood handle.................$40.00
Syrup pitcher, Ring-style...$36.00
Teapot, Ring-style, sm, squat form, dark blue $55.00
Vase, 4", #417, green $15.00
Vase, 7", Art Deco, blue $45.00
Vase, 8", slender, green..$35.00

Paden City Glass

Operating in this West Virginia City from 1916 until 1951, this company is best known to collectors for their many handmade lines of colored dinnerware such as we have listed here. They almost never marked their glass, making it very difficult to identify.

A line of glass animals and birds was also made here; see also Glass Animals.

Ardith, cake plate, 10", footed.......................................$65.00
Ardith, compote, yellow w/cherry etching, high standard ..$57.50
Ardith, sandwich plate, 9½", green, center handle $60.00
Black Forest, bowl, pink, rolled edge, w/3" candle set ..**$255.00**

Black Forest, plate, 8", black $30.00

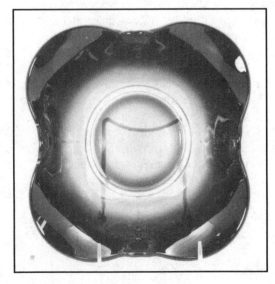

Crow's Foot, bowl, 8", ruby $50.00

Crow's Foot, plate, 6", amber.....................................$3.00
Crow's Foot, tumbler, amber...................................$38.00
Cupid, bowl, 9¼", green or pink........................$135.00
Cupid, candy dish, 5¼", green or pink, footed.........$150.00
Cupid, creamer, 5", green or pink, footed.................$75.00
Cupid, tray, 10⅞", green or pink, oval, footed.........$100.00
Gadroon, candle holders, 5½", blue, pr.....................$120.00
Gothic Garden, bowl, yellow, square..........................$40.00
Lela Bird, candlestick, 5", pink, rolled edge, Archaic shape...$60.00
Lela Bird, vase, 12", green.......................................$100.00
Lucy, cup & saucer, ruby..$20.00
Mrs B, server, amber, center handle..........................$24.00
Nora Bird, candlesticks, pink or green, pr..................$65.00
Nora Bird, creamer, 4½", pink or green, round handle...$40.00
Nora Bird, cup & saucer, pink or green.....................$60.00
Nora Bird, ice tub, 6", pink or green.........................$95.00
Nora Bird, mayonnaise liner, pink.............................$25.00
Nora Bird, tumbler, 4", pink or green........................$45.00
Orchid, bowl, 11" square, ruby or cobalt...................$67.50
Orchid, bowl, 4½" square, yellow, amber or pink.....$15.00
Orchid, creamer, yellow or green...............................$25.00
Orchid, ice bucket, 6", black or ruby.......................$100.00
Orchid, sugar bowl, amber or pink.............................$25.00
Orchid, vase, 10", cobalt or ruby..............................$95.00
Party Line, cocktail shaker, ruby...............................$20.00
Party Line, ice tub, pink...$22.50
Party Line, salt & pepper shakers, amber, pr..............$8.50
Party Line, salt & pepper shakers, ruby, pr...............$45.00
Pea & Rose, sandwich plate, 9½", green, center handle..$85.00
Peacock & Wild Rose, bowl, 10½", any color.............$80.00
Peacock & Wild Rose, bowl, 8½", any color, oval, footed$75.00
Peacock & Wild Rose, bowl, 9½", any color, footed...$65.00
Peacock & Wild Rose, candlesticks, 5", any color, pr..$100.00
Peacock & Wild Rose, compote, green, footed..........$75.00
Peacock & Wild Rose, pitcher, 5", any color.............$100.00
Peacock & Wild Rose, vase, 8¼", any color, elliptical..$125.00
Peacock Reverse, bowl, 4⅞" square, any color............$30.00
Peacock Reverse, creamer, 2¾", any color, flat...........$75.00
Peacock Reverse, plate, 5¾", any color.......................$20.00
Peacock Reverse, sherbet, 4⅝", any color...................$40.00
Peacock Reverse, tumbler, 4", any color, flat..............$55.00
Peacock Reverse, vase, 10", any color........................$85.00
Penny Line, creamer, ruby...$12.00
Penny Line, cup & saucer, ruby.................................$10.00
Penny Line, goblet, cordial; green..............................$18.00
Penny Line, goblet, 6", ruby.....................................$20.00
Popeye & Olive, sherbet, 3¼", ruby..........................$12.50
Popeye & Olive, tumbler, 5-oz, ruby, flat..................$12.00
Popeye & Olive, vase, 7", ruby, ruffled......................$42.50
Utopia, vase, 10½", black amethyst, panelled...........$175.00
Wotta Line, cup & saucer, ruby.................................$20.00
Wotta Line, plate, ruby, 9½".......................................$8.00

Paden City Pottery

Founded in 1907, this company produced many dinnerware and kitchenware lines until they closed in the 1950s.

Many were decaled; in fact, this company is credited with originating the underglaze decal process.

One of their most collectible lines is called Caliente. It was Paden City's version of the solid-color dinnerware lines that became so popular in the thirties and forties. Caliente's shapes were simple and round, but its shell-like finials, handles, and feet did little to accentuate its Art Deco possibilities, which the public seemed to prefer at that time. As a result, it never sold in volume comparable to Fiesta or Bauer's Ring, but you should be able to rebuild a set eventually, and your efforts would be well worthwhile. If you'd like to see photographs of this line and many others produced by Paden City, see *The Collector's Encyclopedia of American Dinnerware* by Jo Cunningham.

American Beauty, cup & saucer, Minion shape...........$15.00
American Beauty, plate, serving; Minion shape...........$12.00
Caliente, candle holder...$17.00
Caliente, casserole, w/lid...$32.00
Caliente, creamer...$15.00
Caliente, cup & saucer...$17.00
Caliente, plate, dessert...$8.00
Caliente, plate, dinner...$10.00
Caliente, salt & pepper shakers, pr............................$16.00
Caliente, saucer...$3.00
Caliente, sugar bowl, w/lid...$20.00
Calinete, teapot...$45.00
Far East, plate, salad; Shell-Crest shape......................$6.00
Jonquil, plate, salad; Regina shape.............................$6.00

Morning Glory, creamer, Shenandoah Ware..........$8.00
Morning Glory, plate, 7", Shenandoah Ware.................$4.00
Morning Glory, sugar bowl, Shenandoah Ware (illustrated)..$8.00
Morning Glory, teapot, Shenandoah Ware (illustrated)..$32.00
Narturtium, creamer, Shell-Crest shape......................$10.00
Nasturtium, creamer, Shell-Crest shape......................$10.00
Nasturtium, lg creamer or gravy boat, Shell-Crest shape.$17.00
Nasturtium, sugar bowl, Shell-Crest shape.................$14.00
Orange Blossom, casserole, in Manning Bowman frame..$30.00
Patio, bowl, oval, Shell-Crest shape...........................$17.00
Patio, bowl, sauce; Shell-Crest shape...........................$6.00
Patio, plate, dinner; Shell-Crest shape.........................$8.00
Patio, platter, Shell-Crest shape..................................$17.00
Springblossom, cup, Regina shape................................$6.00
Springblossom, plate, dinner; Regina shape................$10.00
Touch of Black, cup, Regina shape...............................$6.00

Touch of Black, plate, dinner; Regina shape $6.00

Paper Dolls

One of the earliest producers of paper dolls was Raphael Tuck of England, who distributed many of their dolls in the United States in the late 1800s. Advertising companies used them to promote their products, and some were often included in the pages of leading ladies' magazines.

But over the years, the most common paper dolls are those printed on the cover of a book that contains their clothes on the inside pages. These were initiated during the 1920s and, because they were inexpensive, retained their popularity even during the Depression years. They peaked in the 1940s, but with the advent of television in the fifties, children began to loose interest. Be sure to check old boxes and trunks in your attic, you may find some waiting for you.

But what's really exciting right now are those from more recent years – celebrity dolls from television shows like 'The Brady Bunch' or 'The Waltons,' the skinny English model Twiggy, and movie stars like Rock Hudson and Debbie Reynolds. Just remember that cut sets (even if all original components are still there) are worth only about half the price of dolls in mint, uncut, original condition.

If you'd like to learn more about them, we recommend *Collector's Guide to Paper Dolls* (there are two in the series) and *Collector's Guide to Magazine Paper Dolls,* all by Mary Young. Other references: *Collecting Toys #6* by Richard O'Brien and *Toys, Antique and Collectible,* by David Longest.

Alice in Wonderland, Whitman, #1948, 1976, M..........**$28.00**
American Beauties, Reuben Lilja & Company, #917, 1942, M **$25.00**
American Beauty White House First Ladies 1789-1951, Merrill, #154815, 1951, M **$40.00**
American Family Paper-Doll Book, Grinnel, #C1002, M..**$75.00**

Animal Paper Dolls To Dress, Saalfield, #2598, 1950, M ..**$20.00**
Ann Blythe, Merrill, #2250-25, 1952, M.......................**$90.00**
Archie, Whitman, 1969, NM **$22.50**
Archie Bunker, 1969, original box, EX **$37.50**

Arlene Dahl, Saalfield #4311, 1953, EX..................$50.00
Army Nurse & Doctor Paper Dolls, Merrill, #3425, 1942, M **$75.00**
Ava Gardner, Merrill, 1942, EX **$45.00**
Baby Sitter Paper Dolls, Lowe, #945, M **$40.00**
Baby Sparkle Plenty, Saalfield, #1510, M...................**$70.00**
Barbara Britton w/Magic Stay-On Costumes, Saalfield, #5190, 1954, MIB.......................**$60.00**
Barbie & Skipper, Whitman, #1957, 1964, M **$18.00**
Barbie Boutique, Whitman, #1954, 1973, M................**$18.00**
Bell of the Ball, Saalfield, #2702, 1948, M **$40.00**
Betsy McCall, Whitman, #4744, 1971, M.....................**$15.00**
Betsy Ross & Her Friends, Platt & Munk, #224B, 1963, MIB **$20.00**
Bette Davis, Merrill, 1942, EX.......................**$45.00**
Betty Grable, Merrill, #1558, 1951, M **$95.00**
Beverly Hillbillies, Whitman, #1955, 1964, M..............**$35.00**
Bonnie Braids, Saalfield, #2724, 1951, M...................**$50.00**
Book of Paper Doll Cutouts, Saalfield, #2051, 1927, M ...**$75.00**
Brady Bunch, Whitman, #1976, 1973, M **$40.00**
Bridal Party, Whitman, #1187, 1950, M.......................**$25.00**
Bride & Groom, Merrill, #1555, 1949, M.....................**$75.00**
Charmin' Chatty, Whitman, #1959, 1964, M **$15.00**
Chatty Cathy, Whitman, 1963, MIP **$15.00**
Claudette Colbert, Saalfield, 1943, EX.......................**$40.00**
College-Style Paper Dolls, Merrill, #3400, 1941, M **$75.00**
Connie Francis, Whitman, #1956, 1963, M **$60.00**
Cowgirl Jill & Cowboy Joe, Merrill, #3459, M **$45.00**
Daisy Mae & Li'l Abner, Saalfield, #2360, 1941, M.......**$90.00**
Daisy Mae & Li'l Abner, Saalfield, #280, 1942, NM......**$70.00**
Deanna Durbin, 1941, M.......................**$180.00**
Diana Lynn Paper Dolls, Saalfield, #157910, 1953, M..**$65.00**
Donna Reed, dated 1964, M.......................**$75.00**
Doris Day, Whitman, #210325, 1952, M **$65.00**
Dr Kildare, marked Lowe, 1962, NM.......................**$25.00**
Dress Up for the New York World's Fair, Spertus, #700, 1963, M **$15.00**

Dress-Up Paper Doll Cutouts, Reuben Lilja & Co, 1947, M ..**$25.00**
Dyna-Mite, marked Mego, M...**$30.00**
Elizabeth Taylor, Whitman, 1949, EX **$65.00**
Fabulous High Fashion Models, Bonnie Brooks & Child
    Craft, #2776, 1958, M **$15.00**
Family of Paper Dolls, Saalfield, #2564, 1947, M.........**$40.00**
Flying Nun, Artcraft, #4417, 1969, M **$30.00**
Four Sisters Paper Dolls, Saalfield, #269, 1943, M **$25.00**
Girl Friend-Boy Friend Paper Dolls, Saalfield, #1605, 1955,
    M **$20.00**
Gloria Jean, Saalfield, 1940, VG **$37.50**

Gloria Jean, Saalfield #1666, 1941, EX.....................$45.00
Gone w/the Wind, Merrill Publishing, 1940, EX........**$150.00**
Good Neighbor Paper Dolls, Saalfield, #2487, 1944, M ..**$25.00**
Heidi & Peter, Saalfield, #1355, ca 1970, M.................**$15.00**
Here's the Bride, Whitman, #1209, 1953, NM **$27.50**
Holiday Paper Dolls, Saalfield, #1742, 1950s, M.........**$12.00**
Jack & Jill, Merrill, #1561, 1962, M.............................**$25.00**
John Wayne, marked Tierney, ca early 1980s, M..........**$8.50**
Julia, Artcraft, #5140, M...**$35.00**
Julia, Saalfield, NM...**$48.00**
Little Friends Paper Dolls, Saalfield, #1746, 1950s, M..**$15.00**
Little Lulu, Whitman, 1970, NM................................**$15.00**
Little Women, Artcraft, #5127, ca 1970, M...................**$18.00**
Lori Martin in National Velvet, Whitman, #4612, 1962,
    boxed, M **$22.00**
Lucille Ball, Saalfield, 1945, EX **$50.00**

Marie Osmond, Saalfield #5255, NM......................$30.00
Mary Poppins, marked Walt Disney, 1960s, NM.........**$25.00**
Mary Poppins, Whitman, #1977, 1973, M....................**$28.00**
Modern Miss in Paper Dolls, Saalfield, #2397, 1942, M..**$45.00**

Mouseketeer Cutouts, Whitman, #1974, 1957, M.........**$50.00**
Movie Starlets Paper Dolls, Stephens Publishing, #178, ca
    1949, M...**$28.00**
Mrs Beasley, Whitman, 1972, M.................................**$30.00**
My Fair Lady, Ottenheimer Publishers, #2960-2, 1965, M..**$40.00**
My Very First Paper Doll Book, A Bonnie Book, Samuel
    Lowe, #4732, 1957, M...**$12.00**
National Velvet, Whitman, #1958, 1951, M.................**$35.00**
On Guard, Lowe, #L535, 1942, M **$50.00**
Our Soldier Jim, Whitman, #3980, 1943, M **$40.00**
Outdoor Paper Dolls, Saalfield, #1958, 1941, M.........**$18.00**
Paper Dolls Julie & Maria, Saalfield, #1530, 1958, NM ..**$22.50**
Partridge Family, Artcraft, #5143, 1972, M................**$25.00**
Patsy, Children's Press, #30002, 1946, M...................**$30.00**
Pebbles & Bamm-Bamm, Whitman, 1965, M **$42.50**
Peter & Peggy, Whitman, #99210, 1950, M.................**$15.00**
Playhouse Dolls, Stephens Publishing, #1965, 1949, M ..**$15.00**
Pollyana, dated 1960, EX..**$15.00**
Pre-Teen Paper Dolls, Saalfield, #1366, ca 1960s, M ...**$12.00**
Rhonda Fleming, Saalfield, 1954, EX **$30.00**
Rita Hayworth, as Carmen, Saalfield, 1948, EX...........**$25.00**
Rock Hudson, Whitman, #2087, M **$75.00**
Rowan & Martin's Laugh-In Punch-Out Paper Doll Book,
    Saalfield, #1325, 1969, M **$35.00**
Roy Rogers Cut-Out Dolls, Whitman, #995, 1948, NM ..**$85.00**
Sabrina, 1971, NM...**$22.50**
Sandy & Sue, Whitman, #1956, 1963, M.....................**$18.00**

Shirley Temple, Saalfield #2122, 1934, EX $60.00
Skating Stars, Whitman, #2105, 1954, M **$18.00**
Snow White & the 7 Dwarfs, original box, 1938, NM ..**$80.00**
Sports Time, Whitman, #210525, 1952, M **$12.00**
Square Dance Paper Dolls, Lowe, #968-10, M **$18.00**
Style Shop Paper Dolls, Saalfield, #1516, 1943, M **$30.00**
Sunbonnet Sue, Whitman, #2062-29, 1951, M.............**$18.00**
Susan Dey as Laurie, Artcraft, 1972, M **$35.00**
That Girl Marlo Thomas, Saalfield, #1351, 1967, M **$40.00**

Tiny Chatty Twins Paper Dolls, Whitman, #1985, 1963, M..**$15.00**
Top Notch Paper Dolls, Saalfield, #1504, 1948, M.......**$35.00**
Trudy Phillips & Her Crowd, Whitman, #2104, 1954, M..**$25.00**
Twiggy, Whitman, 1967, M..............**$60.00**
Uncle Sam's Little Helpers, Saalfield, #2450, 1943, M..**$45.00**
Virginia Mayo, Saalfield, #4422, 1957, M **$55.00**
Walt Disney's Mary Poppins, Whitman, #1982, 1964, M..**$35.00**
Wedding Paper Dolls, Whitman, #1970, 1970, M **$15.00**
Welcome Back Kotter, NM..............**$15.00**
White House Party Dresses, Merrill, #1550, 1961, M ...**$40.00**

Paperback Books

Here is a field that you can really have some fun with. These are easy to find, but you may have to spend some time going through many to find some really good ones. Most collectors prefer those that were printed from around 1940 until the late 1950s. Obviously you could buy thousands, so you may prefer to limit your collection to a particular author, genre, publisher, or illustrator. Be particular about the condition of the books you buy. For more information, refer to *Huxford's Paperback Value Guide* by Bob and Sharon Huxford.

Abyss, Orson Scott Card, Pocket #6725, 2nd printing, VG....................**$4.00**
Adventure of the Ectoplastic Man, Daniel Stashower, Penguin #8343, 1986, NM **$5.00**
Agatha Cristie Quizbook, Andy East, Pocket #80335, 1976, VG....................**$4.00**
And When She Was Bad She Was Murdered, Richard Starnes, Pocket #779, 1951, VG.............**$9.00**
Bachelors of Broken Hill, Arthur W Upfield, Pan G-424, 1961, VG................**$7.50**
Beatles the Real Story, Julius Fast, Berkley S-1653, 1968, VG....................**$10.00**
Bessie Cotter, Smith, Berkley G-21, 1956, VG...............**$9.00**
Big Book of Science Fiction, Groff Conklin, Berkley G-53, 1957, VG....................**$5.50**
Big Sin, Jack Webb, Signet #1076, 1953, VG.................**$8.50**
Blackboard Jungle, Evan Hunter, Dell #0579, 1966, VG ..**$8.00**
Blade of Conan, L Sprague De Camp, Ace #11670, 1979, M, VG....................**$5.00**

Blondie & Dagwood in Footlight Folly, Chic Young, Dell (no number), 1947, VG+..........................$55.00

Bloody Medallion, Richard Telfair, Gold Medal D-1665, 1966, 2nd printing, VG **$5.00**
Booby Trap, William Stevenson, Zebra #2571, 1979, VG ..**$4.00**
Boys in the Band, Crowley, Dell #0773, 1970, VG **$6.50**
Brand New World, Ray Cummings, Ace F-313, 1964, M..**$12.00**
Bride Wore Black, Cornell Woolrich, Ace G-699, 1968, VG....................**$6.00**
Bring Back Yesterday, A Bertram Chandler, Ace D-517, 1961, M....................**$16.00**
Brothers of Earth, CJ Cherryh, Daw UE1869, 5th printing, M....................**$4.00**
Butch Cassidy & the Sundance Kid, William Goldman, Bantam S-4623, 1969, VG....................**$3.50**
Cat From Outer Space, Ted Key, Disney, Pocket Arch #56106, 6th printing, VG....................**$4.00**
Chitty Chitty Bang Bang, Ian Fleming, Scholastic TK-1365, 1966, VG....................**$4.50**
Circle of Sin, Mark, Lancer #73-620, 1967, VG.............**$5.00**
City Outside the World, Lin Carter, Berkley #3549, 1977, VG....................**$3.50**

City Streets, Gene Harvey, DeSoto cover, Original Digest Reprint, EX $70.00

Creation, Gore Vidal, Ballantine #30007, 1982, VG **$3.50**
Crystal Cave, Mary Stewart, Hodder #15133, 1973, VG ..**$3.50**
Curiosity Didn't Kill the Cat, MK Wren, Ballantine #35002, 1988, VG....................**$3.50**
Cycle of Fire, Hal Clement, Ballantine #24368, 1975, 4th printing, G....................**$2.75**
Danse Macabre, Stephen King, Signet #08110, 1985, 13th printing, VG....................**$4.00**
Dark Watch, Genevieve St John, Belmont #B-50-667, 1966, VG....................**$5.50**
Day of the Giants, Lester Del Ray, Airmont, 1976, VG..**$3.50**
Death of a Dude, Rex Stout, Fontana #3661, 1976, 3rd printing, VG....................**$4.00**
Diary of a Young Girl, Anne Frank, Cardinal C-317, 1959, 12th printing, VG....................**$5.00**
Doctor Who, Destiny of the Daleks; Terrance Dicks, Target #20096, 1983, 4th printing, VG....................**$4.50**

Domino, Phyllis A Whitney, Crest #2-4350, 1980, VG ...**$2.75**

East Wind Coming, Arthur Byron Cover, Berkley #04439, 1978, VG **$7.50**

French Kiss, Erick Van Lustrader, Chest #21849, 1990, VG **$5.00**

Fugitive Trail, Zane Grey, Cardinal C-441, 1963, NM **$7.00**

Full Cry, Teona Tone, Gold Medal #12747, 1985, VG ...**$3.50**

Gallows on the Sand, Morris L West, Bantam #24248, 1984, VG **$3.50**

Glass Cage, Colin Wilson, Bantam Q-7636, 1973, VG ...**$3.25**

Golden Spiders, Rex Stout, Bantam #1387, 1955, G **$6.00**

Good, Bad, & Ugly; Joe Millard, Award A-274X, 1967, VG ..**$3.50**

Green Ribbon, Edgar Wallace, Arrow #909570, 1974, VG ..**$4.00**

Guys & Dolls, Damon Runyon, Pocket #1098, 1955, 3rd printing, VG **$6.50**

Holocaust, Gerald Green, Bantam #13564, 1978, 13th printing, VG **$4.50**

Honey I'm Home, Marione R Nickles, Bantam #1364, 1955, VG **$8.00**

Honeymoon Hotel, Maxwell, Domino #72-924, 1954, M..**$12.00**

House of Soldiers, Garve, Lancer #72-674, 1963, VG **$6.00**

I Kid You Not, Jack Paar, Cardinal GC-103, 1961, VG ..**$6.50**

Key to Rebecca, Ken Follet, Signet AE3509, 17th printing, VG **$4.00**

Last Cop Out, Mickey Spillane, Corgi #9577, 1974, VG..**$4.00**

Leather Boys, Gillian Freeman, Ballantine U5065, 1967, NM **$15.00**

Lest Darkness Fall, L Sprague De Camp, Del Ray #28285, 1979, 3rd printing, VG **$3.00**

Lonesome River, Frank Gruber, Bantam #1742, 1958, VG..**$7.50**

Lonesome Road, Patricia Wentworth, Coronet #28645, 1982, VG **$4.00**

Mad Look at TV, Dick De Bartolo, Warner #75-034, 1974, VG **$3.50**

Maid of Thuro, John Lane, Curtis (British), paperback original, 1952, VG+ $65.00

Man at the Carlton, Wallace, Hodder & Stoughton Yellowjacket C-170, 1954, VG...................................**$10.00**

Man w/the Miracle Cure, Ross, MacFadden #75-156, 1965, VG...**$4.00**

Marilyn, Norman Mailer, Warner #71-850, 1974, VG **$5.00**

Mercenaries, White, Major #3248, 1979, VG..................**$3.50**

Money Harvest, Ross Thomas, Perennial P-831, 1986, VG...**$3.50**

Moonspin, Elmer J Carpenter, Flagship #715, 1967, G..**$10.00**

My Cousin Rachel, Daphne Du Maurier, Pan #24141, 1979, 10th printing, VG...**$3.50**

Night Stop, Elleston Trevor, Ballantine #25057, 1976, VG ..**$3.50**

Night Walk, Elizabeth Daly, Dell #16609, 1982, VG **$3.50**

No Blade of Grass, John Christopher, Avon S-288, 1967, G...**$3.50**

One Lonely Night, Mickey Spillane, Signet #888, 1951, VG..**$7.00**

Outcasts of Poker Flat, Bret Harte, Avon #446, 1952, VG..**$6.00**

Park Avenue Nurse, Humphries, Hillman #35-100, 1961, VG...**$4.50**

Power of Negative Thinking, Charles Preston, Ballantine #115, 1955, 2nd printing, VG...**$5.00**

Prelude to Space, Arthur C Clark, Ballantine #68, 1954, VG...**$8.50**

Rawhiders, Ray Gogan, Signet AEA-3492, 1986, VG......**$2.50**

Red River Road, Echols, MacFadden #50-460, 1968, VG..**$4.00**

Rising Storm, Dennis Wheatley, Arrow #627, 1963, 2nd printing, VG...**$5.00**

Rock Pine, Muskett, Hodder #509, 1962, VG **$4.00**

Rogue Slave, Webb, Lancer #75-061, 1959, M................**$6.00**

Romance of Atlantis, Taylor Caldwell w/Jess Stearn, Crest X2748, 1976, VG...**$3.50**

Runaway Wife, Savage, Beacon #442F, 1961, M..........**$14.50**

Sex & the Starlet, Balke, Merit Book #7MB13, 1965, VG ..**$8.00**

Smooth Face of Evil, Margaret Yorke, Arrow #944200, 1985, VG...**$4.00**

Stones of Satan, Robert Wallace, Corinth CR-119, 1966, M..**$20.00**

Strange Love, Morrison (editor), Lancer #73-418, 1963, VG...**$3.75**

Strangers in the Dark, Gaddis, Carnival #953, 1957, VG..**$18.50**

Tarnished, Furlough, Beacon #721X, 1964, M **$18.00**

Taxi Dancers, Linkletter, Fabian Z-120, 1959, 3rd printing, M...**$17.50**

Thunder on the Right, Mary Stewart, Crest D-609, 1965, 45th printing, M...**$9.00**

Toff & the Spider, Creasey, Hodder #2924, 1968, VG ...**$5.00**

Too Many Women, Rex Stout, Bantam #1395, 1955, 2nd printing, NM...**$10.00**

Tower at the Edge of Time, Lin Carter, Belmont B-40-804, 1968, M...**$10.00**

Vermilion, Phyllis A Whitney, Crest #24555, 1982, VG..**$3.50**

Wilderness Trek, Zane Grey, Pocket #50203, 1965, NM..**$6.50**

Winter Hawk, Craig Thomas, Avon #70389, 1988, VG..**$4.50**

2001 a Space Odyssey, Arthur C Clark, Signet Q-3580, 4th printing, VG...**$3.25**

Paperweights

The most collectible weights on the market today are the antique weights, those made from 1845 to 1870, and those made by contemporary artists like Rick Ayotte and Paul Ysart. There are many types – millefiori, sulphides, and those that contain fruit and animals. These are usually very expensive. Among the lower priced-weights are those that were sold through gift stores, made in American glasshouses and studios, China, Murano, Italy, and Scotland.

Ayotte, Rick; 3¼", 5 crab apples w/3 blossoms, 4 buds & foliage......$850.00

Ayotte, Rick; 3¾", Paradisea butterfly over cosmos bouquet......$750.00

Baccarat, 3⅛", pink flower w/3 buds on blue ground, 1972......$400.00

Banford, Bob; 3"-4", white latticinio pieces form balanced design w/cherries on branch......$600.00

Banford, Bob; 3"-4", 2 pears on branch w/veined leaves on latticinio ground......$600.00

Banford, Bob; 3"-4", 3 pears on branch w/veined green leaves over star-cut opaque white bottom, faceted 6 & 1.....$750.00

Banford, Bob; 3¼", 6 cherries & leaves on branch, horizontal latticinio......$600.00

Banford, Bob; 3⅛", 4 pears & 5 cherries w/leaves on muslin ground, blue, green & white torsade......$800.00

Banford, Bobby; 3"-4", 2 turquoise flowers, yellow buds & knotweed......$600.00

Banford, Bobby; 3"-4", 3 amethyst & yellow flowers w/black stamens, buds & knotweed......$600.00

Banford, Ray; 3"-4", amethyst iris in diamond-cut base, magnum......$800.00

Banford, Ray; 3"-4", 3 orange-yellow iris & buds w/variegated green leaves on black background......$700.00

Banford, Ray; 3"-4", 3 yellow iris & buds w/variegated green leaves......$700.00

Banford, Ray; 3¼", 5 blue & white iris & buds in green & white overlay basket, cut......$1,400.00

Deacons, John; 2½", pink 5-petal flower w/pink, blue & white torsade w/in garland of red & white star canes on blue......$250.00

Deacons, John; 2½", purple dragonfly w/latticinio wings in red & white star cane garland, signed w/J cane.$240.00

Deacons, John; 2⅝", red 6-petal flower & bud w/red & white garland......$250.00

Deacons, John; 3", clematis on stem on bed of latticinio, light blue & white garland, signed w/JD cane....$240.00

Donofrio, Jim; 3½", salamander & blooming yucca plant w/shards of pot......$1,000.00

Grubb, Randall; purple dahlia, 1987......$375.00

Grubb, Randall; 3¼", cluster of grapes, 1991......$250.00

Grubb, Randall; 3⅜", compound, 3 clusters of green grapes w/dark bark & green leaves......$375.00

Lundberg, Stephen; 3¼", nasturtium w/bud & leaves on stem, blue & white ground......$320.00

Lundberg, Steven; 3¼", cherry dahlia w/green stems & leaves on blue ground......$290.00

Lundberg, Steven; 3¼", pink water hyacinth floating among lily pads......$290.00

Lundberg, Steven; 3¼", red azalea......$290.00

Lundberg Studios, 3¼", Royal Zinnia......$320.00

Parabelle, 2¾", Clichy-type rose on lime green ground w/circles of canes, 1991......$165.00

Parabelle, 3", 4 red pansies in center of floral pattern within millefiori garland, white latticinio ground......$450.00

Parabelle, 3⅜", green Clichy-type rose in blue & white stave basket, multicolor heart & pansy canes, 1988......$335.00

Perthshire, penguin in hollow weight, blue overlay, faceted......$450.00

Perthshire, 2½", faceted strawberry, 1986......$400.00

Perthshire, 3⅛", multicolor butterfly silhouette cane centers millefiori......$95.00

Rosenfeld, Ken; 3½", orange & green flower w/2 blue & white striped flowers w/red edging......$475.00

Rosenfeld, Ken; 3½", rattlesnake among rocks & desert flowers on sand ground, 1993......$700.00

Rosenfeld, Ken; 3½", yellow & blue flowers amid smaller lavender flowers......$550.00

Rosenfeld, Ken; 3½", 4 ripe tomatoes & 1 green tomato..$400.00

Rosenfeld, Ken; 3¼", 2 yellow orchids......$350.00

Rosenfeld, Ken; 3¼", 3 pumpkins w/vines & leaves..$350.00

Rosenfeld, Ken; 3⅝" dia, coleus bouquet w/yellow & blue flowers......$500.00

Salazar, Daniel (of Lundberg Studios); 2½", white crane in blue sky......$240.00

Salazar, Daniel (of Lundberg Studios); 3¼", lady slipper flower on blue background......$270.00

Salazar, Daniel (of Lundberg Studios); 3¼", multicolored hydrangeas in basket, frosted surface......$350.00

Salazar, Daniel (of Lundberg Studios); 3¼", yellow Peace rose w/ruffled petals & green leaves......$290.00

Smith, Gordon; 1 green & 4 ripe strawberries w/1 blossom, green stems & leaves on dark blue ground......$800.00

Smith, Gordon; 3¼", Bird of Paradise flower on dark blue translucent ground......$500.00

Smith, Gordon; 3⅛x1¾", plaque type, Regal Tang swims among white & blue coral w/blue background..$800.00

Stankard, Paul; prickly pear in full bloom w/root system, 1983, 3⅞"......$2,000.00

Trabucco, David & Jon; 3", pink rose & 4 buds amid 5 light blue blossoms **$300.00**

Trabucco, David & Jon; 3½", 3 raspberries & blossoms in clear **$400.00**

Trabucco, Victor; 3⅛", pink & white citron flower w/2 pink buds & 3 smaller brown buds.............................**$600.00**

Trabucco, Victor; 3⅜", yellow rose & buds on cobalt ground..**$600.00**

Trabucco, Victor; 4", blueberry Hawthorn **$950.00**

Val Saint Lambert, 4" dia, red, white & blue marble swirl...**$250.00**

Peach Lustre Glassware

Fire-King made several lines of peach lustre glassware that have been causing lots of excitement among today's collectors. Peach lustre was their white glassware with a fired-on iridescent gold finish (called 'copper-tint' when applied to their ovenware line).

Their first line, introduced in 1952, was ('laurel leaf') Peach Lustre. It consisted of a cup and saucer, creamer, sugar bowl, vegetable bowl, dessert bowl, soup bowl, dinner and salad plates, and an 11" serving plate. It was made until about 1965.

Lustre Shell was introduced in the late 1960s. By this time, the term Peach Lustre was used to describe the finish of the glassware rather than a particular pattern. Lustre Shell, as the name suggests, was a swirled design. In addition to the pieces mentioned above, a 13" platter and a demitasse cup and saucer were added to the assortment. A set of nested mixing bowls were also available.

You'll find baking dishes, bowls and mugs in other styles, vases, and miscellaneous items in this glassware, too; all are collectible and at this point, at least, none are very expensive. If you'd like to learn more about Peach Lustre, we recommend *Collectible Glassware from the 40s, 50s, and 60s* by Gene Florence.

Bowl, dessert; 4¾", Lustre Shell, 1965-76 ....**$3.00**

Bowl, dessert; 4⅞", Peach Lustre (laurel design), 1951-65 ....**$4.00**

Bowl, mixing; 6", Beaded Rim, 1950-64 ....**$6.00**

Bowl, mixing; 8½", Colonial Rim, 1960-71 ....**$10.00**

Bowl, mixing; 9", Swirl, 1949-72 ....**$12.00**

Bowl, soup; 6⅜", Lustre Shell, 1965-76..........................**$5.00**

Bowl, vegetable; 8½", Royal Lustre (ribbed w/scalloped edge), 1976 ....**$6.00**

Bowl, vegetable; 8¼", Peach Lustre (laurel design), 1951-1965 ....**$8.00**

Creamer, footed, Peach Lustre (laurel design), 1951-65 ..**$4.00**

Creamer, Lustre Shell **$4.00**

Cup, demitasse; 3½-oz, Lustre Shell, 1965-76................**$3.00**

Cup, demitasse; 3¼-oz, Royal Lustre (ribbed w/scalloped edge), 1976 ....**$3.00**

Cup, 8-oz, Peach Lustre (laurel design), 1951-65...........**$3.00**

Cup, 8-oz, Royal Lustre (ribbed), 1976 ....**$2.00**

Cup, 8-oz, Three Bands, 1950s.............................**$3.00**

Plate, dinner; 10", Lustre Shell, 1965-76..........................**$5.00**

Plate, dinner; 9⅛", Peach Lustre (laurel design), 1951-65 ..**$6.00**

Plate, salad; 3¼", Royal Lustre (ribbed w/scalloped edge), 1976..**$3.00**

Platter, 9½x13", oval, Lustre Shell, 1965-76 ....**$6.00**

Platter, 9½x13", oval, Royal Lustre (ribbed w/scalloped edge), 1976 ....**$6.00**

Platter, 9x12", oval, Three Bands, 1950s....................**$7.00**

Saucer, demitasse; 4¾", Royal Lustre (ribbed w/scalloped edge), 1976 ....**$2.00**

Saucer, 5¾", Three Bands, 1950s **$2.00**

Saucer, 5⅞", Peach Lustre (laurel design), 1951-65.......**$2.00**

Saucer, 8¾", Lustre Shell, 1965-76..........................**$2.00**

Sugar bowl, footed, open, Peach Lustre (laurel design), 1951-65...**$4.00**

Peanuts Collectibles

Charles M. Schultz first introduced the world to the *Peanuts* cartoon strip in 1950. Today it appears in more than 2,000 newspapers across the United States. Its popularity naturally resulted in the manufacture of hundreds of items, each a potential collectible. Books, toys, movies, and theme parks have been devoted to entertaining children and adults alike through the characters of this cartoon – Linus, Snoopy, Lucy, and Charlie Brown.

If you're going to collect *Peanuts* items, be sure to look for the United Features Syndicate logo and copyright date. Only these are authentic. The copyright date (in most cases) relates not to when an item was made but to when the character and the pose in which he is depicted first appeared in the strip.

If you'd like to learn more about this subject, we recommend *The Official Price Guide to Peanuts Collectibles* by Freddi Margolin and Andrea Podey.

Bank, 3", Snoopy & Woodstock ceramic figural, Determined, 1976, M **$17.00**

Banner, All Systems Go & Snoopy as astronaut, Determined, 1970, M **$20.00**

Bell, Snoopy on doghouse w/Woodstock in Santa outfit on nose, ceramic, Schmid, 1975, MIB **$35.00**

Book, All About Friendship, Snoopy & Woodstock on doghouse, Hallmark, #100HEK 4-3, 1971, M **$8.00**

Book, The Gospel According to Peanuts, Charlie Brown & Snoopy cover, John Knox Press, 1964, EX.............**$3.50**

Bracelet, 5 enameled figural charms on heavy links w/closure, Aviva, 1969, M...**$30.00**

Cake decoration set, Snoopy Flying Ace, 6 Woodstocks, 10 holders & Happy Birthday, Hallmark, mid-1970s, M in package **$15.00**

Candle, 7", Charlie Brown figural in traditional dress, Hallmark, late 1970s, sealed in plastic, M **$15.00**

Coloring book, Charlie Brown & Snoopy in baby carriage, Saalfield, #5695, 1960s, NM **$27.50**

Doll, 14", Snoopy as astronaut, rag type, Ideal, #1441-5, 1977, MIB **$140.00**

Doll, 15", Snoopy, stuffed plush w/felt eyes, eyebrows & nose, red plastic tag, Determined, #833, 1971, MIB **$30.00**

Doll, 8½", Lucy, painted plastic figural, marked Hungerford Plastics, 1958, G **$20.00**

Fan, 8¾x9¼", Snoopy rides wave w/Surf's Up! caption, cardboard w/stick handle, Springbock, 1974, M..........**$15.00**

Greeting card, pop-up characters at piano & Happy Birthday, Hallmark, mid-1960s, M....................................**$6.00**

Jack-in-the-box, double popping action, Snoopy through door & Woodstock through nest, Hasbro, #818, 1980, MIB **$25.00**

Lobby card, 14x11", Race for Your Life Charlie Brown, Paramount Pictures, set of 8, M **$40.00**

Mug, 3¼", Snoopy kicking green football, ceramic, Determined, mid-1970s, M **$12.00**

Needlework kit, 12x16", No One Understands My Generation, crewel, Malina, mid-1970s, MIB **$15.00**

Nodder, Linus, 5½", made by Lego, Japan sticker, 1959 .$75.00

Paint-by-number set, 12x16", Craft House, early 1980s, MIB **$20.00**

Paperweight, 3½", Snoopy sits at yellow & blue typewriter, heart-shaped base, ceramic, Butterfly, 1970s, MIB **$25.00**

Patch, 3" dia, Snoopy in ski outfit & To the Bunny Slope, Determined, #730, 1970, M in package **$4.00**

Phonograph, characters at disco party pictured inside lid, solid state, Vanity Fair, #66, 1979, EX....................**$55.00**

Pin, Snoopy cloisonne figure holding flag of 13 colonies, Aviva, 1976, M in package **$15.00**

Push puppet, Lucy dressed as nurse, plastic, Ideal, dated 1977, EX...**$30.00**

Scissors, Snoopy Snippers, figural plastic w/blades in mouth, Mattel, #7410, 1975, MIB **$45.00**

Stationery, main characters on notes, Snoopy in mailbox on envelope flap, w/pen, Hallmark, late 1960s, MIB ..**$15.00**

Switchplate, Pigpen surrounded by dust w/Cleanliness Is Next to Impossible, plastic, Hallmark, ca 1975, NM..........**$7.50**

Tile, 5¾x5¾", Merry Christmas 1978, Snoopy reads list of Good Boys & Girls, Determined, 1978, MIB........**$35.00**

Toothbrush, doghouse holds brushes & batteries, figural Snoopy brush handle, plastic, Kenner, #30301, 1972, MIB **$45.00**

Trophy, 2", Snoopy in disco jacket ceramic figural, Saturday Night Beagle, Aviva, 1974, EX................................**$3.00**

Walker, 3", Joe Cool, figural plastic wind-up, Aviva, ca 1975-82, M in package...**$3.00**

Walker, 3½", Woodstock wearing red nightcap, plastic wind-up, Aviva, 1975, M in package **$6.00**

Wastebasket, 13", Snoopy the Flying Ace, lithographed metal, Chein Company, early 1970s, NM..............**$22.50**

Wind chime, Snoopy in headphones, Woodstock & music notes, ceramic, Quantasia, #124001, 1984, M **$25.00**

Pennsbury Pottery

From the 1950s throughout the '60s, this pottery was sold in gift stores and souvenir shops up and down the Pennsylvania Turnpike. It was produced in Morrisville, Pennsylvania, by Henry and Lee Below. Much of the ware was hand painted in multicolor on caramel backgrounds, though some pieces were made in blue and white. Most of the time, themes centered around Amish people, barber shop singers, roosters, hex signs, and folksy mottos.

Much of the ware is marked, and if you're in the Pennsylvania/New Jersey area, you'll find lots of it. It's prevalent in the Midwest as well and can still sometimes be found at bargain prices. If you'd like to learn more about this pottery, we recommend *Pennsbury Pottery Video Book* by Shirley Graff and B A Wellman.

Ashtray, 2 Amish people **$18.00**
Bird, 3", wren...**$100.00**
Bird, 4", hummingbird..**$145.00**

Bowl, pretzel; Gay Nineties **$85.00**

Bowl, 5½", Folk Art...$20.00
Bowl, 5½", Red Rooster, deep..............................$20.00
Bowl, 7", Fidelity Mutual, gray..............................$40.00
Butter dish, Red Rooster.......................................$35.00

Candle holder, 3½", rooster & hen figures, pr ...$125.00
Candlestick, Red Rooster.......................................$30.00
Candlesticks, 5", hummingbird on flower, pr...........$145.00
Coaster, Olson...$15.00
Creamer, 2", Folk Art..$20.00
Cruets, Gay Nineties, pr $150.00
Cup & Saucer, Black Rooster................................$25.00
Cup & saucer, Pennsylvania Hex...........................$25.00
Cup & saucer, Red Rooster...................................$25.00
Desk basket, Eagle..$25.00
Hot plate, Red Rooster, EX working condition, w/cord ..$75.00
Mug, beer; Amish couple $30.00
Mug, beer; fisherman...$25.00
Mug, beer; Sweet Adeline $30.00
Pitcher, 1-pt, 5", Folkart..$25.00
Pitcher, 2", Amish man at fence.............................$20.00
Pitcher, 4", Amish woman $20.00
Pitcher, 4", Pennsylvania Hex $20.00
Pitcher, 4", Red Rooster $20.00
Pitcher, 4", Tulip $20.00
Pitcher, 7¼", Red Rooster $50.00
Plaque, 4" dia, What Giffs $32.00
Plaque, 5" dia, Washington Crossing Delaware.........$20.00
Plaque, 7x5", Red Rooster $25.00
Plaque, 7x5", 2 birds over heart.............................$25.00
Plate, Angel, Stumar..$30.00
Plate, bread & butter; Hex.....................................$10.00
Plate, 10", Hex..$20.00
Plate, 10", Red Rooster..$20.00
Plate, 13½", Red Rooster.......................................$100.00
Platter, 10½", Folk Art, oval...................................$25.00
Salt & pepper shakers, Amish heads, pr.....................$55.00
Salt & pepper shakers, Red Rooster, shaped like pitchers,
    pr...$20.00
Sugar bowl, 4", Amish man & woman..........................$25.00
Sugar bowl, 4", Red Rooster, w/lid.........................$25.00
Tray, 5x3", octagonal, crested birds.......................$20.00
Wall pocket, sailboats, brown border.......................$45.00
Wall pocket, 6½x6½", blue flowers & leaves, green bor-
    der..$40.00

Pepsi-Cola

People have been enjoying Pepsi-Cola since before the turn of the century. Various logos have been registered over the years; the familiar oval was first used in the early 1940s. At about the same time, the two 'dots' between the words Pepsi and Cola became one, though more recent items may carry the double-dot logo (indicated by '=' in our descriptions), especially when they're designed to be reminiscent of the old ones. The bottle cap logo came along in 1943, and with variations was used through the early sixties.

Though there are expensive rarities, most items are still reasonable, since collectors are just now beginning to discover how fascinating this line of advertising memorabilia can be. There are three books in the series called *Pepsi-Cola Collectibles* written by Bill Vehling and Michael Hunt, which we highly recommend. Another good reference is *Introduction to Pepsi Collecting* by Bob Stoddard.

Bank, 3¾x3", composition cooler form, Pepsi-Cola Ice Cold
    Sold Here, G..$65.00
Blotter, 1945, Pepsi=Cola bottle cap at right of girl serving
    2 bottles of Pepsi w/Tempty & ...Tasty flanking head,
    NM $85.00
Bottle, 12-oz, painted label, Pepsi-Cola, NM.................$6.00
Bottle, 8-oz, painted label, Pepsi=Cola, full, NM.........$10.00

Bottle carrier, 1930s, 12-pack, metal, EX $150.00
Bottle carrier, 1960s, 6-pack, cardboard, some wear, VG ..$4.00
Calendar, 1955, 16x13", paper w/cardboard frame, easel
    back, NM $40.00
Checkers game, 1970s, 14x14", wood, features Pepsi &
    Mountain Dew cans on checkerboard, NMIB.....$100.00
Clock, 1950s, white plastic bottle cap w/Drink Pepsi-Cola
    Ice Cold surrounded by numbers, light-up, 12" dia,
    VG+..$145.00
Clock, 1970s, 14" dia, plastic, EX.........................$50.00
Fan, 1940s, paper w/wood handle, 2-sided, Pepsi logo on
    front, comic scene on back, EX........................$45.00
Folding chair, 1954, padded back, Relax, Have a Pepsi, the
    Light Refreshment, VG......................................$75.00
Ice pick, square wood handle, EX.............................$4.00

Kaleidoscope, 1970s, can form, EX..............................$25.00

Menu board, 1950s, 30x19", Have a Pepsi in script at left of slanted Pepsi-Cola bottle cap on striped background, EX...$90.00

Mirror sign, 1960, girl looking in mirror to left of angled bottle cap, G+..$30.00

Music box, 1982, stuffed Pepsi & Pete figures, plays original Pepsi radio jingle, NM in original package $70.00

Picnic cooler, 1951, 18x18", metal, VG+.....................$55.00

Playing cards, 1945, Pepsi=Cola, complete w/box.....$75.00

Pocket lighter, 1950s, applied bottle cap logo on front, Zippo brand, EX...$40.00

Push bar, 30" long, steel plate over wire bar w/diamond design, Pepsi on bottle cap flanked by Say... & Please, G+ $45.00

Push plate, 1930s, Come in for That Big Big Bottle..., tin, EX...$125.00

Radio, 1970s, 5", can form, NM in original box $35.00

Radio, 1970s, 8½", bottle form w/oval Pepsi-Cola label, NM $35.00

Shot glass, 1989, Happy New Year, EX.........................$3.00

Sign, 1910-15, 13½x5", embossed tin, Drink Pepsi=Cola... Delicious Delightful on green ground bordered in red, M........$250.00

Sign, 1940s, 26x18", cardboard, couple on bank after swimming & several bottles on tray, Hits the Spot logo, G......$150.00

Sign, 1950s, 20", cardboard stand-up, Santa w/bottle standing against snow, Pepsi-Cola Greetings bottle cap, EX...$60.00

String holder, 1940s, 16x12", metal, 2-sided, Join the Swing to above Pepsi=Cola on wavy band, Bigger & Better 5¢, EX $475.00

Thermometer, 1973, 28", metal w/square corners, Pepsi lettered over bottle cap top & bottom, NM.............$30.00

Thermomter, 1954, 27", tin, embossed bottle cap above, The Light Refreshment lettered below, rounded corners, EX $95.00

Tip tray, 1950s, 5x7", black w/floral decoration, advertising on back, G+...$30.00

Toy syrup dispenser, 1950s, plastic, white soda fountain type w/slanted bottle cap & Pepsi-Cola in print, NMIB $110.00

Toy truck, 1958, 16", tin, Ny-Lint, various logos on cargo bed, enclosed top & back, open sides, VG+ $100.00

Toy truck, 1960s, 4", plastic & tin, red w/Fresh Drink bottle & round 1950s logo on enclosed cargo bed, NM..$80.00

Tray, 1950s, 14x11", Everess in snow-capped letters above Sparkling Water lettered over mountains, It's Good for You, VG..$60.00

Trolly sign, 1950s, 11x28", cardboard, party couple w/ bottles of Pepsi, Wonderful w/Snacks, More Bounce..., EX $60.00

Perfume Bottles

Here's an area of bottle collecting that is right now coming into its own. Commercial bottles, as you can see from our listings, are very popular. Their values are based on condition: is it sealed or full, does it have its original label, and is the original package or box present.

Figural bottles are interesting, especially the ceramic ones with tiny regal crowns as their stoppers.

Blown, cobalt, 6⅛", 12-sided, flared mouth, smooth base..$75.00

Blown, 2", doughnut form w/cut design......................$55.00

Blown, 4½", citron, waisted hexagon shape w/matching stopper..$450.00

Ceramic, 2¾", flat medallion form w/picture of jockey on horseback, metal crown stopper, Germany $38.50

Commercial, A Biento, Lenteric, 1-oz, 1930s................$65.00

Commercial, A'Suma, Coty, spherical shape, floral stopper, in 3" box..$225.00

Commercial, Air de France, 1⅜", gold & black label, sealed..$6.00

Commercial, Apple Blossom, Helena Rubenstein, 2⅞", 3-sectioned cylindrical form, light wear on label....$45.00

Commercial, April Showers, Cheramy, paper label, green Bakelite screw top w/tassel, 1930s, EX $42.50

Commercial, Ave Marie, Prince Matchabelli, 1¾", gold & black enameling, glass stopper $48.00

Commercial, Baghari, Robert Puguet, 2¼", crystal, black label, paneled stopper $40.00

Commercial, Balalaika, Lucien Lelong, 4-oz, 4½", wings design, gold metal ball cap $25.00

Commercial, Beau Catcher, Vigney, 5¾", labels, ground glass stopper...$90.00

Commercial, Bellodgia, Caron, 2½", empty in box......$50.00

Commercial, Blue Grass, Elizabeth Arden, 5¼", frosted horses, blue cord & bulb, gold metal parts, in 6" box........$28.00

Commercial, Blue Grass Flower Mist, Elizabeth Arden, 5", MIB $42.50

Commercial, Blue Waltz, 5-piece set, all sealed, MIB .. $98.00

Commercial, Breathless, Charbert, drum shape $22.50

Commercial, Cabochard, Gres, 2", gray bow, black enamel label $15.00

Commercial, Cabochard, Gres, 3¼", sealed, MIB........ $50.00

Commercial, Caprice d'Avril, 1⅜", gold & black label, sealed $5.00

Commercial, Caravan de France, 2¾", clear flat oval, MIB .. $35.00

Commercial, Chanel No 5, ¼-oz, 2", marked Made in France, ground stopper... $25.00

Commercial, Chantilly, Houbigant, 2-oz, 4¾", white screw cap, 1941 .... $15.00

Commercial, Chantilly, Houbigant, 4", labels, plastic screw top... $20.00

Commercial, Chi Chi, Renoir, 3", heavy crystal, clear & frosted, brass cap $55.00

Commercial, Chloe, 2½", frosted lily stopper.............. $12.00

Commercial, Citana, 1½", gray & gold label, sealed $7.50

Commercial, Crepe de Chine, Millot, 2¾", heavy crystal w/foil label, Lucite cap $32.50

Commercial, Crown, Prince Matchabelli, 3", green enameling w/gold, MIB.. $160.00

Commercial, Danger, Ciro, 3", stacked rectangles, black Bakelite cap.. $60.00

Commercial, Dans le Nuit, Worth, ½-oz, signed Lalique, lavender-blue, sealed... $55.00

Commercial, Dioressence, Christian Dior, 4", heavy crystal, gold at shoulders & neck, white enamel labels $37.50

Commercial, Dreamy, Luzier, 2½", black cap w/gold & clear plastic flame, gold label on bottom $17.50

Commercial, Eau de Caron, Caron, 4¾", heavy crystal, MIB $48.00

Commercial, Emeraude, Coty, 2½", clear w/gold label, glass stopper, sm stain.. $22.00

Commercial, Entendu, 1½", gold & brown label, sealed .. $10.00

Commercial, Epres, Max Factor, 1¾", paper label, sealed .. $10.00

Commercial, Essence Imperial Russe, Lengyel, 3¾", green collar on crown shape, glass & cork stopper........ $12.00

Commercial, Essence Rare, Houbigant, 6¾", textured surface, silver metal cap $18.00

Commercial, Eve, Eve of Roma, 2¼", cross-shaped stopper, NM $20.00

Commercial, Evening in Paris, Bourjois, purse size, cobalt, lipstick shape.. $45.00

Commercial, Evening in Paris, Bourjois, 5½", cobalt, worn label $12.50

Commercial, Fleurs de Rocaille, Caron, flat urn-shaped bottle, in original inner & outer boxes, original paper wrapping $75.00

Commercial, Flora Danica, Swank, 3¼", blue morning-glories on clear, black enameling on back........ $22.50

Commercial, Florient, Colgate & Co, 7", frosted stopper .. $27.50

Commercial, Flowers of Devonshire, Mary Dunhill, spherical w/8 ridged sections, label around neck, bottom of box missing $85.00

Commercial, Friendship Garden, Shulton, 3⅛", wear on labels $22.50

Commercial, Frimousse d'Or, Lorenzy-Palanca, 5¾", cobalt, NM label, light blue cap $38.00

Commercial, Gamin, Gragonard, 2⅜", gold-covered urn form $88.00

Commercial, Gardenia, Chanel, 2⅜", crystal, marked France on bottom, ground stopper $7.50

Commercial, Gardenia, Lander, 5¼", colorful label, green ribbed cap $12.50

Commercial, Harade, 1½", black & gold label, empty $6.00

Commercial, Ideal, Houbigant, 2¾", gold enamel labels, bronze metal cap $14.00

Commercial, Incognito, Noxell, 1½", frosted, green enameled label, green 'marble' cap, full...................... $10.00

Commercial, Indescret, Lucien Lelong, 7¾", gold & black foil label, pink cap $12.00

Commercial, Intoxication, D'Orsay, 3¾", blown glass stopper $42.50

Commercial, It's You, Elizabeth Arden, Baccarat, 7½", clear & frosted, 1939.. $600.00

Commercial, Jasmine, Rallet, 8", paneled shape w/glass stopper $42.50

Commercial, Joy, Jean Patou, Baccarat, 1⅞", gold enamel label w/much wear $22.50

Commercial, Joy, Jean Patou, 2¼", black crystal w/gold label, long dauber w/red button stopper, wear on label $25.00

Commercial, Khadine, Yardley, 6-oz, MIB $37.50

Commercial, L'Aimont, Coty, 1¾", crystal, 2 EX labels, ground stopper.. $32.50

Commercial, L'Air du Temps, Nina Ricci, 3½", Lalique dove stopper, M in yellow box $100.00

Commercial, L'Interdit, Givenchy, 3¼", heavy crystal, gold foil label, in red & gold silk box........................... $42.50

Commercial, L'Origan, Coty, 1½", blue paper label, white screw cap, sample type $20.00

Commercial, lady's head figural, Hattie Carnegie, Wheaton, 1938 .... $185.00

Commercial, Lea, Ethyl Leanore, 2", 2 purple paper labels, metal screw cap w/red 'jewel,' stain...................... $12.00

Commercial, Lilac, Lander, 2¼", ball shape w/labels, red tassel $70.00

Commercial, Lily of the Valley, Melba, 7½", w/label, glass stopper $22.50

Commercial, Lumiere, Rochas, 2¼", amethyst plastic jewel top... $17.50

Commercial, Meracle, Lentheric, 3⅛", 10-sided, paper label, gold Bakelite cap $8.50

Commercial, Midnight Cologne, Tussy, 4½", square shape, EX label, metal top, 1950s $22.50

Commercial, Miss Dior, Dior, 2⅞", white enamel label, glass stopper, paper label on bottom $18.00

Commercial, Moment Supreme, Jean Patou, 4", heavy crystal w/2 labels, ground stopper $32.00

Commercial, My Sin, Lanvin, black glass, spray type, 1960s.. $22.50

Commercial, Narcisse, Lioret, 4", flat shape, ground stopper w/cork **$12.00**

Commercial, Narcissus, Brown of NY, 7", gold metal stopper w/company name, in box **$35.00**

Commercial, New Horizons, Ciro, 2¾", blue enameling, eagle figural cap..**$45.00**

Commercial, Night of Delight, Roger et Gallet, 6", gold label, ivory plastic cap **$27.50**

Commercial, Nuit de Noel, Caron, 3", black glass w/gold label, glass stopper **$37.50**

Commercial, Old Fashioned Garden, Ybry, 6⅛", no labels, 1930s..**$50.00**

Commercial, Ombre Rose, Brosseau, 4¼", clear & frosted, clear stopper..**$16.00**

Commercial, Orange Blossom, Bo-Kay, 2⅜", orange & green paper label, orange cap, in box **$24.00**

Commercial, Pois de Senteur de Chez Moi, Caron, 6", crystal, pedestal base, paper label, green enameling on stopper..**$65.00**

Commercial, Poison, Christian Dior, 3⅝", purple w/gold enamel label, clear stopper **$8.00**

Commercial, Possession, Corday, 5¼", cylindrical, silver labels, red leather cap cover, sealed....................**$22.50**

Commercial, Private Collection, 5-oz, 3¼", frosted bottle, in leather purse w/drawstrings **$14.00**

Commercial, Quelques Fleurs, Houbigant, 3⅛", no labels, marked France on base, ground stopper **$12.50**

Commercial, Replique, Raphael, 2", stain on label **$12.00**

Commercial, Rosee d'Arabie, Alain Steven, 2", green paper label, glass stopper, full, in box **$25.00**

Commercial, Royal Command, Imperial Formula, 2", gold enamel label **$5.00**

Commercial, Scoundrel, 1¼", sealed, on black plastic stand, M **$17.50**

Commercial, Sentinel, Mary Dunhill, gold plated, no label, w/stopper, EX **$55.00**

Commercial, Shalimar, Guerlain, 3¼", light wear on label, w/neck cord..**$37.50**

Commercial, Shocking, Shiaparelli, 4¾", gold-plated glass stopper..**$195.00**

Commercial, Shocking, Shiaparelli, 6", gold-plated glass stopper..**$265.00**

Commercial, Singapore Nights, Duchess, 1⅝", no labels..**$22.50**

Commercial, Sirocco, Lucien Lelong, 1¾", gold label & cap..**$22.00**

Commercial, Snob, Le Galion, 2", column shape, gold labels, in box **$22.00**

Commercial, Soir de Paris, Bourjois, lg, cobalt, 1930s.**$30.00**

Commercial, Sophia, 2⅜", round shape w/gold neck cord & gold & red metal neck tag..............................**$15.00**

Commercial, Sortilege, Le Galion, 2½", 12-sided, marked Made in France..**$42.50**

Commercial, Strategy, Mary Chess, 3", chess castle shape, empty, original inner & outer boxes....................**$70.00**

Commercial, Surrender, Ciro, 5", wear on labels **$65.00**

Commercial, Sweet Pea, Renaud, 2⅜", green crystal, cylindrical, brass cap, in original box **$75.00**

Commercial, Tabu, Dana, ½-oz, 2¾", w/label, black crystal stopper..**$7.50**

Commercial, Tamoure, 1½", blue & gold label, sealed..**$7.50**

Commercial, Tempest, Lucien Lelong, 3¾", prismatic, gold label, sealed, w/gold cord..................................**$95.00**

Commercial, Tornade, Revillon, 2¾", scalloped side, gold label, MIB..**$45.00**

Commercial, Tourjours Fidele, D'Orsay, 3½", pillow form w/crystal bulldog stopper **$265.00**

Commercial, Via, Lanvin, 1⅝", green marble-look top, sealed..**$8.50**

Commercial, Vivons, Merle Norman, 4", rectangular, empty in box **$45.00**

Commercial, White Shoulders, Evyan, 3", gold enamel label, gold-plated glass stopper..............................**$12.00**

Commercial, Windsong, Prince Matchabelli, w/labels, gold screw top..**$27.50**

Commercial, Yankee Clover Toilet Water, Richard Hudnut, EX label, metal stopper **$27.50**

Commercial, Youth Dew, Estee Lauder, 2⅛", frosted, plastic sleeve on stopper..**$20.00**

Cut glass, 6x3", green to clear, prism & mirror cuttings, faceted stopper **$135.00**

Cut glass, 7x3¾", ruby cut panels w/gold, fancy stopper..**$150.00**

Figural, angel, 2½", Helena Rubenstein, Heaven Scent, frosted glass, gold cap, label on bottom **$55.00**

Figural, dachshund, 3", ceramic w/metal crown stopper, red-orange paint, Goebel crown mark **$82.50**

Figural, duckling, 3", ceramic w/metal crown stopper, yellow & orange paint, Goebel crown mark **$50.00**

Figural, Dutch lady, 3¼", ceramic w/metal crown stopper, realistic paint details, Germany **$75.00**

Figural, lady in ballgown w/bouquet & fan, 3¼", ceramic w/ metal crown stopper, multicolored paint, Germany..**$90.00**

Figural, Mexican w/sombrero (seated), 1¼", mk sterling Mexico, w/funnel, MIB..................................**$120.00**

Figural, Scot w/tam-o'-shanter, 2¼", Palmyra, Heather, clear glass, w/painted wooden cap, M in plaid box w/ window **$25.00**

Figural, sea horse, 3½", light aqua w/white loopings & applied rigaree **$165.00**

Milk glass, 8", vertical ribs w/swirling stars................**$22.50**

Porcelain, 5¼", floral reserve on pink w/much gold trim, marked Made in France..................................**$105.00**

Pez Candy Dispensers

Though Pez candy has been around since the late 1920s, the dispensers that we all remember as children weren't introduced until the 1950s. Each had the head of a certain character – a Mexican, a doctor, Santa Claus, an animal, or perhaps a comic book hero. It's hard to determine the age of some of these, but if yours have tabs or 'feet' on the bottom so they can stand up, they were made in the last ten years. Though early on, collectors focused on this feature to evaluate their finds, now it's simply the character's head that's important to them. Some have variations in color and design, both of which can greatly affect value. For instance, Batman may have a blue hood and a black mask, or both his mask and his hood may match; sometimes they're both black and sometimes they're blue. (The first one is the most valuable, but not much more than the all-black variation.)

Condition is important; watch out for broken or missing parts. If a Pez is not in mint condition, most are worthless. Original packaging can sometimes add to the value, especially if the figure in question came out on a blister card. If the card has special graphics or information, this is especially true. Early figures were sometimes sold in boxes, but these are hard to find. Nowadays you'll see them offered 'mint in package,' sometimes at premium prices. But most intense Pez collectors say that those cellophane bags add very little if any to the value.

For more information, refer to *A Pictorial Guide to Plastic Candy Dispensers Featuring Pez* by David Welch and *Collecting Toys #6* by Richard O'Brien.

Air Spirit, wine-red & red on pink stem, no feet..$75.00
Batgirl, no feet, MIB..$42.50
Batman, blue hood, black mask, no feet $32.50
Batman, blue hood & mask, w/feet, M on card............$5.00
Big Top Elephant, orange w/blue hat..........................$25.00
Boy w/brown hair, red stem, w/feet $3.00
Chick in Egg, (no hat), marked Made in Austria $37.50
Clown, no feet, marked Pez on hat & Made in Hong Kong, EX...$32.00
Clown w/long chin..$20.00
Cockatoo, blue...$22.00
Daffy Duck, blue stem, w/feet, M on card....................$5.00
Diabolic, orange & black, orange stem, no feet (illustrated)..$75.00
Donald Duck, blue & white head on blue stem, no feet, marked Austria, NM $12.50
Donald Duck, sm yellow bill, blue stem, w/feet..........$2.00

Elephant, no feet, marked Made in Austria..................$30.00
Garfield w/green hat, orange stem, no feet, M on card..$5.00
Girl w/pigtails, red stem, w/feet..................................$10.00
Lamb, w/pink stem, no feet...$10.00
Miss Piggy, purple stem, w/feet, M on card..................$5.00
Papa Smurf, red stem, w/feet, M on card......................$5.00
Pony, orange, blue, green & white head on blue stem, marked Austria, no feet, NM $22.50
Popeye, red w/white cap, no feet, M...........................$30.00
Rabbit w/pink face & long ears, blue stem, w/feet.......$2.00
Road Runner, no feet, painted eyes, M $15.00
Rooster, yellow $18.00
Scrooge McDuck...$10.00
Snowman, black stem, no feet, M on card...................$10.00
Spiderman, red stem, no feet $8.00
Truck, yellow cab, green stem, w/feet, M on card........$5.00
Tweety Bird, blue stem, no feet...................................$10.00
Uncle Sam, no feet, marked Made in Austria..............$35.00
Witch w/green face, red stem, w/feet............................$2.00
Woodstock, yellow stem, w/feet, M on card $5.00

Pfaltzgraff Pottery

Pfaltzgraff has operated in Pennsylvania since the early 1800s making redware at first, then stoneware crocks and jugs, yellowware and spongeware in the twenties, artware and kitchenware in the thirties, and stoneware kitchen items through the hard years of the forties. In 1950 they developed their first line of dinnerware, called Gourmet Royal (known in later years as simply Gourmet). It was a high-gloss line of solid color accented at the rims with a band of frothy white, similar to lines made later by McCoy, Hull, Harker and many other companies. Although it also came in pink, it was the dark brown that became so popular. Today these brown stoneware lines are one of the newest interests of young collectors.

The success of Gourmet was the inspiration the company needed to initiate the production of the many dinnerware lines that have become the backbone of the Pfaltzgraff company.

A giftware line called Muggsy was designed in the late 1940s. It consisted of comic character mugs, ashtrays, bottle stoppers, children's dishes, a pretzel jar, a cookie jar, etc. All of the characters were given names. It was very successful and continued in production until 1960. The older versions have protruding features, while the features of later ones were simply painted on.

For further information, we recommend *Pfaltzgraff, America's Potter,* by David A. Walsh and Polly Stetler, published in conjunction with the Historical Society of York County, York, Pennsylvania.

Gourmet Royal, cruets, 5", 4¾" from handle to spout, coffeepot shape, fill by spout, pr..................................$30.00
Gourmet Royale, bowl, mixing; 5⅜x9¾"......................$12.00
Gourmet Royale, bowl, soup; 2¼x7¼" $5.00

Gourmet Royale, chafing dish, 8" tall on stand, w/lid, 9" dia, w/handles **$30.00**

Gourmet Royale, cheese shaker, 6¾", bulbous **$15.00**

Gourmet Royale, coffee server, 10¾" on metal & wood stand, from $80.00 up to **$100.00**

Gourmet Royale, flour scoop, 7½" long, 2½" wide, tapers down to open end **$12.00**

Gourmet Royale, ladle, 3½" dia w/11" handle **$8.00**

Gourmet Royale, meat platter, 13¾x9⅝" **$25.00**

Gourmet Royale, mug, coffee; 4x5", bulbous **$4.00**

Gourmet Royale, plate, dinner; 10" **$10.00**

Gourmet Royale, souffle dish, 4x8¼" dia, ribbed exterior ..**$20.00**

Muggsy, ashtray, Burnie **$125.00**

Muggsy, canape holder, Carrie, face jar w/lift-off hat pierced for toothpicks **$95.00**

Muggsy, cookie jar, character face, minimum value .$250.00

Muggsy, jar, utility; Handy Harry, flat lid is hat w/short bill **$165.00**

Muggsy, mug, action-type figure (golfer, fisherman, etc), any, from $65.00 up to **$80.00**

Muggsy, mug, Black action-type figure **$125.00**

Muggsy, mug, character face, any, from $35.00 up to .**$40.00**

Muggsy, shot mug, character face, from $45.00 up to ..**$50.00**

Muggsy, tumbler **$60.00**

Phoenix Bird Pottery

This is a type of blue and white porcelain dinnerware that has been imported from Japan since the early 1900s. It is decorated with the bird of paradise and stylized sprigs of Chinese grass. You'll find several marks on the older pieces. The newer ones, if marked at all, carry a paper label; backgrounds are whiter and the blue more harsh.

For more information, we recommend _Phoenix Bird China_ by Joan Collett Oates.

Bowl, cereal; 6" **$15.00**

Bowl, 4¾" **$7.00**

Bowl, 7¾x6" oval, M-in-wreath mark **$20.00**

Butter pat, old **$12.00**

Candy or nut tub, 2", handled **$25.00**

Creamer, hotel size **$10.00**

Creamer & sugar bowl, 3", 4", marked Nippon, pr **$45.00**

Creamer & sugar bowl (open), M-in-wreath mark, Made in Japan **$30.00**

Cup & saucer, demitasse; no mark **$16.00**

Cup & saucer, design also on inside edge, Made in Japan in circle **$12.00**

Cup & saucer, thin, Made in Japan on saucer only **$12.00**

Custard cup, inside border design **$15.00**

Egg cup, 2¼", single **$12.00**

Plate, 6", M-in-wreath mark **$5.00**

Plate, 6", Made in Japan **$4.50**

Plate, 7¼" **$7.00**

Plate, 7¼", Made in Japan **$9.00**

Plate, 8½", M-in-wreath mark **$22.00**

Platter, 10", M-in-wreath mark, Made in Japan **$22.00**

Salt & pepper shakers, 3", self tops, pr **$20.00**

Sugar bowl, 3½", w/lid, no mark **$13.00**

Phoenix Glass

Though this company has operated in Monaca, Pennsylvania, from 1880 until the present (it's now a division of the Newell Group), collectors are primarily interested in the sculptured glassware lines they made during the thirties and forties. These quality artware items were usually made in milk glass or crystal with various color treatments or with a satin finish. Most of the time, the backgrounds were colored and the relief designs left plain. The glassware was never signed, instead the company used paper labels in the shape of a phoenix bird.

For more information, refer to _Phoenix and Consolidated Art Glass_ by Jack D. Wilson.

Ashtray, 5½" long, coral background, mother-of-pearl flowers on milk glass **$65.00**

Banana server, 11", Lace Dew Drop, pink on milk glass, footed **$50.00**

Bowl, 8" square, Lace Dew Drop, pink on milk glass ..**$40.00**

Candle holders, 4¾", Water Lily, green on crystal, pr ..**$125.00**

Celery vase, 7¾", Ivy & Snow, crystal **$25.00**

Compote, 8" dia, Moon & Star, pearl lustre on milk glass ..**$40.00**

Jell-O mold, Queen Anne, star shape, crystal **$3.00**

Plate, 13¾", Tiger Lily, cream satin flowers on blue background **$160.00**

Server, 11¼", Moon & Star, pearl lustre on milk glass, footed **$38.00**

Shade, 10" dia, Electro, #6608, etched floral on crystal ..**$45.00**

Shade, 5", crystal w/acid-etched design, 2" fitter **$20.00**

Shade, 8", #5809, Phoenix Rich Cut Electric Ball, crystal ..**$135.00**

Vase, Reuben line, Wild Geese, amber on crystal, satin pattern, label **$200.00**

Vase, 10", Madonna, blue background on milk glass, white profile portrait **$225.00**

Vase, 10", Reuben Line, Dogwood, sea green on crystal satin **$150.00**

Vase, 10½", Wild Rose, mother-of-pearl flowers on milk glass, light blue background.............................**$130.00**

Vase, 10½", Wild Rose, taupe background on milk glass, shaded pattern.............................**$150.00**

Vase, 12", Dancing Girl, satin figures, green background on milk glass.............................**$365.00**

Vase, 5", Jewel, mother-of-pearl pattern on milk glass, light blue background.............................**$70.00**

Vase, 7", Aster, yellow flowers & green leaves on white satin background.............................**$75.00**

Vase, 7", Fern, mother-of-pearl fronds on milk glass, chartreuse background, 1976.............................**$35.00**

Vase, 7", Fern, pink ferns & green grass, pale blue background on milk glass.............................**$90.00**

Vase, 7", Reuben Line, Catalonian, amber on crystal, cylindrical.............................**$60.00**

Vase, 7½", Cosmos, white flowers on crystal, aqua background.............................**$125.00**

Vase, 8", Freesia, crystal satin on sea green background, flared.............................**$95.00**

Vase, 8", Lily, orchid background on crystal satin, cylindrical.............................**$130.00**

Vase, 8¾", Primrose, cedar rose on crystal.............................**$275.00**

Pie Birds

Popular since Victorian times, a pie bird is a hollow figure used in the middle of the pie to allow steam to vent through the top crust. They're glazed inside and out and were made as various types of birds, as elephants, and sometimes as chefs and bakers. At least one hundred 'new' pie birds are on the market today, and the number is growing. Many of these are more expensive than the old ones. As far as we know, though, the new designs are all original.

Bennie the Baker, Cardinal China.............................**$68.00**

Blackbird, dark gray, England.............................**$22.00**

Blackbird, Royal Worcester, 2-piece.............................**$32.00**

Blackbird on log, England.............................**$30.00**

Bluebird w/babies on nest, 5", marked w/a circled C stamp, 1950s, rare $75.00

Chick, yellow, w/bonnet, Josef Original.............................**$21.50**

Crow, dark brown.............................**$20.00**

Dragon, copper lustre or gray.............................**$56.00**

Duck, rose & charcoal gray.............................**$12.00**

Elephant, ceramic, light nut brown.............................**$60.00**

Funnel, plain white, English.............................**$15.00**

Patch Bird, Morton Pottery.............................**$28.00**

Pillsbury Chick, pink or blue base.............................**$18.00**

Rooster, 5", multicolored, Cleminsons.............................**$22.50**

Howard Pierce

Mr. Pierce was a potter who had his own studio in Claremont, California, where from the 1940s until he died a few years ago he designed distinctively styled sculptures of animals, birds, and human figures that were sold in gift shops and department stores nationwide. Many of his animal 'families' were sold in pairs or three-piece sets.

You may also find examples of vases and lamps with openings containing small animals or plant forms. Most of his work, except for some of the smaller animals, was marked.

If you'd like to learn more about Howard Pierce and his work, *The Collector's Encyclopedia of California Pottery* by Jack Chipman contains a chapter devoted to him.

Antelope's head, 16½".............................**$48.00**

Bear, 5½", brown, 1950s.............................**$30.00**

Bobwhite hen, standing.............................**$22.50**

Eagle, black, 1960s.............................**$35.00**

Flower frog, 12x7", St Francis.............................**$50.00**

Flower frog, 6½", quail w/2 young.............................**$35.00**

Gander & 2 geese, brown & white, 3-piece set.............................**$50.00**

Geese, white, 1950s-60s, pr.............................**$35.00**

Hippo, 6", lava-type brown glaze, recent.............................**$22.00**

Monkey, 9½", seated, gray, rare.............................**$65.00**

Planter, 8", rectangular, deer in central opening, green gloss glaze.............................**$62.50**

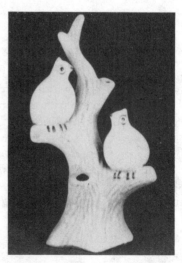

Quail pr in tree, 7", black detailing on gray, 1970s..$50.00

Rabbit, 10½", long ears, brown agate.............................**$36.00**

Rooster & hen, 9¼", 7¼, brown & white, 1950s **$45.00**
Vase, 8", creche style w/fish insert, green...................**$35.00**

Pin-Back Buttons

Literally hundreds of thousands of pin-back buttons are available; pick a category and have fun! Most fall into one of three fields – advertising, political, and personality related, but within these three broad areas are many more specialized groups. Just make sure you buy only those that are undamaged, are still bright and unfaded, and have well-centered designs and properly aligned printing. The older buttons (those from before the 1920s) may be made of celluloid and the cardboard backing printed with the name of a company or a product.

See also Political.

ABC News Elections '76 Guest, 2½", Ford & Carter photos against stylized flag, EX **$20.00**
Archie's Official Fan Club, 1½", 1968, M **$6.00**
Babe Ruth Baseball Club, 1½", 1970s, M......................**$6.00**
Batman & Robin Society, 1966, M on card....................**$5.00**
Batman Club, 2¼", 1970s, M......................................**$5.00**
Boris & Natasha, EX...**$2.50**
Bruce Juice, 2¼x1¼", can form w/black & white Bruce Springsteen photo, red & black, 1970s, M..............**$3.50**
Buck Jones for US Marshal, red, black & white, M........**$8.00**
Bugs Bunny, Help Crippled Children; 1¼", M **$6.00**
Buy American, ⅞", American flag on blue & white ground, 1930s, EX...**$20.00**
California State Park System, She's a Bear; ⅞", brown & yellow, ca 1930s, EX..**$6.00**

Charles Starrett Famous Cowboy Series, 1¼", black & white photo on purple background................$10.00
Chicago White Sox American League Champs 1959, red, white & blue..**$30.00**
Detroit Where Life Is Worth Living, 1¾", lighthouse against ships at sea, colorful, early 1900s, EX...................**$50.00**
Dixie Cups, 1¾", Save Your...the South Will Rise Again, ice, ice cream cup in center, 1960s, EX........................**$18.00**

Don't Forget the Homeless Children, Native Sons of the Golden West, ⅝", celluloid, ca 1914, EX **$20.00**
Donald Duck, 3½", marked Disney, 1960s, M...............**$5.00**
Down in Dixie, 1¼", Black youths eating watermelon slice, South Carolina...West Indian Exposition, dated 1902, EX **$125.00**
Elks Jubilee Carnival, 1¾", clown w/rabbit on back, black letters, colorful, dated 1902, EX **$50.00**
Elsie the Cow for President, 3", red, white & blue, 1960s ..**$25.00**
Evel Knievel Snake River Canyon, September 3, 1974, M...**$2.00**
Gabby Hayes Famous Cowboy Series, black & white, M..**$10.00**
Gene Autry Famous Cowboy Series, 1¼", black & white photo on red background, M (illustrated)......$12.00
Greatful Dead, August 31, 1981, 2", black & red, M......**$1.50**
Green Hornet Agent, 4", Green Hornet in car, 1960s, EX..**$15.00**
Happy Birthday Donald Duck 1934-1984, 2½" **$7.00**
Happy Birthday Mickey WDW 50th, 3½", M.................**$7.00**
Heinz Ketchup, 1¼", ...the People's Choice & bottle, 1930s, EX...**$28.00**
Holsum Bread, 1¼", Junior Police Club Safety Patrolman, yellow & black, 1940 copyright, EX.......................**$20.00**
Howard Hughes Around the World in 4 Days, 1¼", black & white photo, red, white & blue rim, ca 1938, EX ..**$25.00**
Hubie Baby, 1½", white stylized letters on red ground, 1968, EX...**$12.50**
I Build Buicks, 1½", red letters on white ground, ca 1940, EX...**$32.50**
I Conquered Space Mountain Disneyland 1977, 2½", M ..**$7.00**
I Love Lucy 1911-1989, 3½", portrait in center, EX........**$7.50**
I'm a Booster 4U Drink, 1¾", lady dressed as belle, red white & blue, 1930s, EX..**$25.00**
I'm Looking Over Estes Kefauver, 1¼", blue letters on cream, 1952, EX...**$12.50**
It's Howdy Doody Time, 2¼", 1980s, M **$5.00**
Jews Look to America for Help, ⅞", man holds baby & bag, Hebrew Relief Ball 1916 on back, EX....................**$20.00**
Jim Hendrik, 1⅛", black & white, ca 1970s, M..............**$2.50**
Joe DiMaggio, 3", Happy Birthday, Resorts Casino, M ..**$6.50**
John Wayne Western Saddle Kings Series, 1¾", black & green, M...**$12.00**
Johnston Fudge Sundae, 2¼", red, white & blue, 1940s, EX **$20.00**
Kool Cigarettes, 1", trademark mascot w/donkey & elephant, In Either Case Keep Kool, 1930s, NM....................**$35.00**
Lash Larue Famous Cowboy Series, 1¼", black & white photo on teal background (illustrated) $10.00
Led Zeppelin, 1½", blue, black & white, ca 1970s, M....**$2.50**
Lee Jeans, 3", blue on white, M **$4.00**
Life Bread Radio Club, 1", loaf of bread by radio microphone, yellow, red & blue, 1930s.........................**$20.00**
Little King, 1", marked King Features, M......................**$5.00**
M*A*S*H, original, M...**$5.00**
Maggie & Jiggs, 1", marked King Features, M................**$4.00**
Member NAACP 1961, ¾", blue & white, 1961, EX **$15.00**
Metropolitan Life Insurance Co, 1", insurance building on blue, Happiness League..on yellow rim, EX...........**$6.00**
Mickey Mantle, ⅞", 1969, M......................................**$6.00**

Mickey Mouse Club, 3", 1960s, M $8.00

Miller Beer, ⅞", lady on crescent moon, ...High Life Beer below, colorful, ca 1935, EX $15.00

Mohammad Temple 1905, 1¾", lady seated on camel, red letters, colorful $50.00

National Rifle Association Consumer, ⅞", letters on red, white & blue ground $20.00

New York Hunting & Fishing License, 1¾", Citizen Resident in light blue, black & white, dated 1940, EX........$12.50

Oscar Mayer, 1¼", ...Approved Meat Products on center logo seal, 1920s-30s.....................................$16.50

Peace Equality, 1", peace dove, black & white, 1960s, EX $15.00

Philadelphia Phillies 1950 Champs, 1¾", M....................$8.00

Popeye, ¾", Kellogg's Pep Comic series, ca 1945-47, 1 of set of 86..$12.00

Remember Pearl Harbor, 1¼", flying American flag, red, white & blue, EX-.....................................$20.00

Rolling Stones, 1½", tongue logo, black, red & yellow, ca 1970s, M...$2.50

Snuffy Smith, 1", marked King Features, M...................$5.00

Springsteen: The Boss, 2¼", color photo, 1970s, M.......$2.50

Star Tours Disneyland, on black ground, 3"................$6.00

Star Tours MGM Studios, 3", glow-in-the-dark, 1980s, M $5.00

Sunbeam Bread Presents the Gene Autry Show, 3½", white letters on red ground, early 1950s $35.00

Super Bowl XXII Redskins & Broncos, 2¼", M.............$6.00

Ted Williams Boston Red Sox, 1¼", M $4.00

Tex Ritter Famous Cowboy Series, black & white, M....$5.00

Tom & Jerry, 1¼", Sunbeam Bread premium, 1960s, M $6.00

Tom Mix & Tony, 2", brass, EX................................$35.00

Welcome Home 363rd & 347th Heroes of the Aragonne, 1¼", 1919, EX $22.50

With Honor, 1¾", red letters & peace dove on blue ground, 1960s..$15.00

1st American in Orbit, 1¾", John H Glenn Jr black & white photo, red, white & blue rim, 1962, EX................$20.00

Pinup Art

Some of the more well-known artists in this field are Vargas, Petty, Ballantyne, Armstrong, and Phillips, and some enthusiasts pick a favorite and concentrate their collections on just his work. From the mid-thirties until well into the fifties, pinup art was extremely popular. Female movie stars from this era were ultra-glamorous, voluptuous, and very sensual creatures, and this type of media influence naturally impacted the social and cultural attitudes of the period. As the adage goes, 'Sex sells.' And well it did. You'll find calendars, playing cards, magazines, advertising, and merchandise of all types that depict these unrealistically perfect ladies. Though not all will be signed, most of these artist have a distinctive, easily identifiable style that you'll soon be able to recognize.

Ad for Gainsborough Hair Nets, redhead in yellow satin holds mirror, Rolf Armstrong, Ladies' Home Journal, November 1923, M..................................$10.00

Ad for Jantzen Bathing Suits, This Way to the Beach, features couple at the beach, ca 1940s, EX+..............$9.00

Ad for Jergens' Face Powder, 11x9", black-haired girl on tummy holding medal, Vargas, 1943, M................$10.00

Blotter, postcard front, man looking out window at man looking back at girl, ca 1940, unused.....................$9.00

Blotter, 3½x6¼", salesman's sample, blond in black gown & pink gloves & shoes, blue & red borders, D'Ancona, NM...$8.00

Blotter, 3⅜x6⅛", Jewel Flowers in halter & shorts, Brown & Bigelow Co, Rolf Armstrong, ca 1934, EX............$15.00

Book, Vargas, by Reid Austin & Alberto Vargas, Bell Publishing Co, 1984 edition, out of print, 128 pages, NM+...$55.00

Booklet, 4¼x5¼", Pinups by Zoe Mozert, Brown & Bigelow, ca early 1940s, 11 pages, EX...........................$100.00

Calendar, a takeout removed from a January holiday issue of Esquire, Vargas, 1944, pages unattached, EX+......$60.00

Calendar, 10x4⅝", It's the New Look, blond on phone in short jacket & heels, full pad, Mac Pherson, ca 1956, EX..$12.00

Calendar, 15½x11", Lucky Dog, Zoe Mozert brunette holding little white dog next to her face, full pad, 1942, EX...$45.00

Calendar, 8½x12", The Vargas Girl 1948, spiral-bound wall type, full-color art & verse each month, EX........$100.00

Calendar, 8x12½", 1971 Playboy Playmate, spiral-bound wall type, full-color Playmate photo for each month, EX..$37.50

Calendar (w/Al Moore gatefold), 11x8½", date sheets signed by various artists, plastic spiral, w/envelope, 1953.......$30.00

Calendar print, 12x16½", Reflections, elegant nude wearing net stockings in front of mirror, 1944, NM...........$45.00

Cartoon, Talk About Gratitude, George Petty, Esquire, February 1939, EX................................$10.00

Cartoon, This Is His Secretary Speaking, blond girl on sofa w/phone, Petty, Esquire, September 1935, M.......$14.00

Fan, 9x8", Queen of the Ball, redhead in green hat looking over shoulder, stapled wooden handle, Rolf Armstrong, 1925 ....$25.00

Gatefold, blond sitting in white teddy holding phone, George Petty, Esquire, December 1941, M...........$30.00

Gatefold, Patriotism Minus, dark-haired girl in tight silver gown, Petty, Esquire, November 1941, VG.......................$22.00

Gatefold, redheaded Irish girl in green pants, jacket & top, George Petty, True, EX.................................$10.00

Gatefold, V Mail for a Soldier, pretty blond in blue & white ruffles, Vargas, Esquire, 1943, EX+ $30.00

Magazine, True, features Miss Marilyn Waltz, has Vargas beauties, April 1957, VG...............................$30.00

Magazine cover, 11x8½", blond blue-eyed Madeline Carrol type w/hands on chin, True Confessions, October, ca 1940s, M...$6.00

Mutoscope card, A Run on Sugar, blond in black lingerie & stockings, Zoe Mozert, M.................................$6.00

Print, advertising Acme Brewing Co, George Petty, framed under glass, 12x25" $125.00

Print, 10½x8", A Good Deal, pictures girl holding cards marked ZM, EX.......................................$20.00

Print, 10½x8", Lovely, woman in evening gown, corsage & white fur, ca 1940s, EX..............................$17.00

Print, 10½x8½", Here's Looking at You, blond in green gown lifting glass & gown, Earl Moran $15.00

Print, 11x14", A Pleasing Discovery, nude standing on scales while dog steps on, Gil Elvgren, VG $22.00

Print, 12x9½", Suntan Girl, topless bathing beauty rubbing suntan lotion on shoulder, signed Mac Pherson, 1949, EX...$55.00

Print, 20x12", brown-haired girl in white shorts & pink top leaning against ship's rail, blue sky & gulls, Erbit, NM $15.00

Print, 7x5", redhead in light green halter-top evening gown, white fur trim, black background, De Vorss, ca 1939, VG...$10.00

Print, 9¾x7¾", Stepping Out, blond in strapless pink gown holding roses, signed Earl Moran, ca 1959, EX.....$16.00

Punchboard, 8½x3½x1", 26 girls on stand-up base, used in bars, ca 1940s, NM..$30.00

Puzzle, #AP 118, Avis Miller, sm can............................$15.00

Puzzle, #AP 131, Carol O'Neal, sm can $15.00

Record cover, The Cars Candy-O, leggy redhead laying on hood of car, EX...$15.00

Tumbler, 4½", full-color illusion decal on glass, by Petty, 1940s..$15.00

Planters Peanuts

The personification of the Planters Company, Mr. Peanut has been around since 1916, adding a bit of class and dash to all their advertising efforts. Until the company was sold in 1961, he was a common sight on their product containers and at special promotional events. He was modeled as salt and pepper shakers, mugs, whistles, and paperweights. His image decorated neckties, playing cards, beach towels, and T-shirts. Today he has his own fan club, a collectors' organization for those who especially enjoy this area of advertising memorabilia.

Just about everyone remembers the Planters Peanut jars, though they're becoming very scarce today. There are more than fifteen different styles and shapes, and some have been reproduced. The earliest, introduced in 1926, was the 'pennant' jar. It was octagonal, and the back panel was embossed with this message: 'Sold Only in Printed Planters Red Pennant Bags.' A second octagonal style carried a paper label instead. Pennant jars marked 'Made in Italy' are reproductions, beware!

Ashtray, metal Mr Peanut figure, 1956, EX...................$18.00

Bag for roasted peanuts, 24x7½", Mr Peanut against diamond graphics w/peanut shape lettered The Peanut Store, NM..$17.00

Bag for salted nuts, 6x3", Planters in script above Mr Peanut holding flag lettered Pennant, The Nickel Lunch, NM..$6.00

Bank, 8½", plastic Mr Peanut figure.......................$20.00

Beach ball, blue & yellow plastic w/Mr Peanut...........$15.00

Can, 3x2½", Mixed Nuts, metal, Mr Peanut on sides & top $28.00

Case cutter, holds razor blade to open cartons, Mr Peanut & lettering on yellow label, EX.................................$10.00

Coasters, silver-tone metal, features Mr Peanut & the 1980 Winter Olympics logo, set of 4 ....$45.00

Coin, silver-tone metal, Mr Peanut, commemorates 1980 Olympics, EX...$14.00

Coloring book, 8½x5½", features the 12 months...........$8.00

Doll, 19", stuffed cloth Mr Peanut, premium, M $20.00

Doll, 8", Planters plush Honey Bear, mail-away premium, ca 1970s, EX..$25.00

Frisbee, 10" dia, foam, Mr Peanut, EX..........................$12.00

Golf balls, Spalding brand featuring Mr Peanut, MIB..$20.00

Iron-on transfer, 8½", Mr Peanut, EX............................$6.00

Jar, Fish Bowl, square paper label...............................$150.00

Jar, hexagon, printed square label................................$60.00

Jar, octagon, pennant 5¢, 7 sides embossed..............$250.00

Jar, square, peanut finial, Planters embossed each side..$150.00

Jar, 4½-oz, for mixed nuts w/full-color label, 1944, EX...$60.00

Knapsack, 14x14", cloth, features Mr Peanut, EX $15.00

Lunch tote, 9x10", full-color vinyl, 1979, EX...............$25.00

Mechanical pencil, floating Mr Peanut, EX..........$22.00

Mug, 4", hard plastic, Mr Peanut head figure..........$12.00
Nut dish, plastic, Mr Peanut shape in bottom.............$12.50
Optical illusion card, 4x3", Mr Peanut in dark circle labeled
    Spooky Picture, directions & advertising below, EX...$8.00
Pencil, Mr Peanut figure, 1950s, 5½", EX.....................$10.00
Pin-back button, 1¼" dia, Mr Peanut, 1930s, EX.........$15.00
Poster, 18x26", features the history of the Winter Olympics,
    1980...$7.50

Salt & pepper shakers, 3", plastic Mr Peanut figures, EX..$12.00
Store jar, glass fish bowl shape w/Planters embossed on
    base, top missing, EX...$20.00
Straw, white plastic w/tan Mr Peanut figure atop, EX...$8.00
T-shirt, man's lg, features Planters potato chips..........$15.00
Thermometer, 16", Mr Peanut figure, EX.....................$55.00
Thermos, 11", features Mr Peanut w/Planters lettered below,
    Aladdin, EX...$40.00
Tin, 14x9¼", Peanut Oil, Mr Peanut on all sides, screw lid &
    wire handle, w/original box.....................................$60.00
Tote bag, 18x12", lg Mr Peanut figure in black, yellow &
    white on blue, M...$15.00

Plastics

Early plastics such as Bakelite, Catalin, gutta percha, and celluloid are not new to collectors, and most of us realize the value of the wonderful radios and jewelry items, but did you know that even plastics from after WWII are becoming collectible as well? The market is not yet well established, and here's an area where you will be able to make some good buys well before the public in general. Prices are still low, and besides, it's fun.

Because plastic was such an inexpensive material, manufacturers produced literally thousands of household items with the intent of very short-term appeal. Their theory was simple: replace existing models with those that varied just enough to promote sales. Buyers would be willing to throw out the old and replace with the new, since most items were very cheap. As a result, new colors, new styles, new looks epitomized the public's fascinations and fads. Pop beads, flying saucer lamps, and kitchenware items in streamlined shapes all had their time in the spotlight.

Items that you may want to buy are interesting pieces of jewelry, well-designed kitchenware and appliances, and things that relate to celebrities, Disney characters, advertising, or special holidays. Whatever aspect of plastic collecting you personally enjoy should afford you good shopping and lots of satisfaction.

Barometer, 4", amber & dark green Catalin, Taylor, rectangular..$40.00
Bracelet, bangle; Catalin, cellulose acetate chain, 7 carved
    figural charms..$250.00
Bracelet, bangle; Catalin, deep carving, w/rhinestones...$80.00
Bracelet, bangle; Catalin, light geometric carving, narrow...$28.00
Bracelet, bangle; Catalin, light geometric carving, wide..$45.00
Bracelet, bangle; Catalin, scratch carved, narrow........$18.00
Bracelet, bangle; Catalin, scratch carved, wide...........$25.00
Bracelet, bangle; Catalin, uncarved, narrow..................$6.00
Bracelet, bangle; Catalin, 3-color stripes.....................$90.00
Bracelet, celluloid (resembles tortoise) w/inlaid rhinestones..$40.00
Bracelet, clamper; Catalin, stylized floral carving........$52.00
Bracelet, stretch; Catalin, deeply carved, original elastic..$60.00
Bracelet, stretch; clear lucite, back-carved, original elastic..$25.00

Bread box, red Lustro-Ware, rectangular, hinged white lid......$30.00

Bridge marker, painted ivoroid animal or figure, France..$20.00

Buckle, Catalin, latch type, multicolor, stylized floral carving......$40.00

Buckle, Catalin, latch type, single color, uncarved......$5.00

Buckle, Catalin, slide type, single color, stylized floral or geometric carving......$8.00

Buttonhook, 5⅝", plain ivory, unmarked, EX......$5.00

Buttons, 1" dia, Catalin, amber, octagonal, uncarved, 6 on card......$10.00

Buttons, 1½" rod, Catalin, red or black laminated, 6 on card......$18.00

Buttons, ¾" dia, ivoroid or pearlescent, 6 on card......$8.00

Canister set, red Lustro-Ware, white flowers, set of 4..$16.00

Carving set, Catalin, 3-piece, w/wood wall rack......$40.00

Cheese slicer, Catalin scotty dog handle, wood & chrome base......$15.00

Cigarette box, 5½x3¾", light green Catalin w/wooden bottom, rectangular......$30.00

Cigarette lighter, Catalin, multicolor stripes or inlay....$45.00

Clock, black or dark brown Bakelite, electric alarm type w/Art Deco design......$65.00

Clock, ivoroid, Greek temple facade, wind-up alarm type......$45.00

Clothesline, Jigger, Catalin, red anchors, 10 pins, metal box......$10.00

Corkscrew, chrome w/red, green or amber Catalin handle......$12.50

Crib toy, Tykie Toy, elephant, laolin head & Catalin body......$60.00

Crib toy, Tykie Toy, 11 multicolor Catalin spools on string, 1940s......$50.00

Cup & saucer, angle handle, Beetleware, plain......$6.00

Dice, 2½", ivory or red Catalin, pr......$15.00

Dice, ¾", ivory or red Catalin, pr......$2.00

Drawer pull, Catalin, 1-color, painted inlay stripe......$2.00

Dress clip, Catalin, stylized floral carving......$20.00

Dress clip, Catalin novelty, animal or vegetable form..$50.00

Dresser set, ivory pearlescent or amberoid, 5-piece set..$50.00

Dresser set, ivory w/amber trim, marked Pyralin Mayflower, 6-piece set, VG......$20.00

Earrings, Catalin, uncarved disks, pr......$6.00

Earrings, Catalin novelty, figure or animal, pr......$35.00

Figurine, 2¼x3½", elephant, dark gray w/white tusks, marked Putz & Made in USA, NM......$22.50

Figurine, 3¼x4½", ram figural, ivory & gray, marked Putz & Made in USA, VG......$5.00

Flatware, chrome plate, Catalin handle, 3-piece matched place setting......$6.00

Flatware, ivoroid handle, table knife, fork or spoon, each piece......$1.00

Flatware, stainless steel, 1-color Catalin handle, each piece......$2.00

Flatware, stainless steel, 2-color Catalin handle, 3-piece matched place setting......$12.00

Flatware, stainless steel, 2-color Catalin handle, 36-piece set in wooden box......$225.00

Flatware set, red & yellow Catalin, marked Hull Stainless 18/8, 6 4-piece place settings, EX......$105.00

Flour sifter, white w/red handle, painted flower decoration on side......$6.50

Foam scraper, celluloid stick w/beer advertising......$12.50

Hairbrush, baby's; hand-painted florals on ivory, VG...$6.00

Inkwell, amber Catalin, Carvacraft Great Britain, single well......$70.00

Inkwell, black Bakelite, streamlined, w/lid......$25.00

Letter opener, chrome & Catalin, Art Deco design......$14.00

Manicure set, 4 mini-tools in coral-color celluloid tube, Germany......$22.00

Mirror, dresser; 8", ivoroid, cut-out handle, beveled glass......$18.00

Mug, Lefty Lemon figural, marked F&F Mold & Die Works, ca 1969-74, EX......$7.50

Nail brush, 2" dia, Masso, amber Catalin octagon......$8.00

Nail buffer, 6", plain ivory, marked French ivory, VG...$4.00

Nail file, 7½", plain ivory, unmarked, EX......$3.50

Necklace, Catalin, cellulose acetate chain, Deco-style dangling pieces......$175.00

Pencil sharpener, Catalin gun, tank or plane shape w/ decal......$30.00

Pencil sharpener, yellow Catalin, scotty silhouette......$20.00

Pencil sharpener, ¾x1", red Catalin w/Mickey Mouse decal......$30.00

Penholder, red Catalin scotty dog w/black base......$45.00

Picture frame, 2" dia, ivoroid, easel back......$12.00

Picture frame, 5" square, clear lucite, Art Deco style...$14.00

Picture frame, 6" square, Catalin, red, green or amber..$35.00

Pin, lg, 1-color Catalin, patriotic figural......$95.00

Pin, sm, Catalin, animal shape, resin wash w/glass eye ..$75.00

Pin, sm, Catalin, stylized floral carving......$32.00

Pin, sm, 1-color Catalin, animal or vegetable form......$60.00

Pipe, amber & green Catalin, bowl lined w/clay......$28.00

Plate, picnic; molded sections, 3 compartments for food, 1 for tumbler......$1.75

Poker chip rack, Catalin, 4", rectangular, w/200 chips..$120.00

Powder box, 3x2½" dia, ivory w/hand-painted floral design on lid, unmarked, w/fancy puff, EX......$12.50

Rabbit, 6", thin plastic figure marked Knickerbocker Plastics Co California $12.00

Ring, 1-color Catalin, stylized floral carving................$35.00
Safety razor, amber Catalin handle, Schick Injector.....$12.00
Salad server, chrome w/red or amber Catalin handles, pr..$12.00
Salt & pepper shakers, 3¼", Catalin, Washington Monument form, pr...$25.00
Shaving brush, red, green or amber Catalin, w/holder ..$30.00

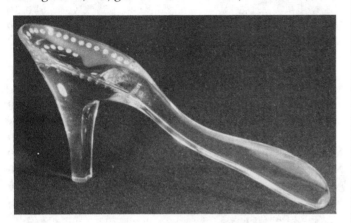

Shoe horn, lucite w/rhinestones, marked Your Boudoir Shoe Horn US Patent, ca 1950s, in plastic box...$40.00

Spoon, slotted type, stainless w/red or green Catalin handle...$4.50
Steering wheel knob, Catalin w/chrome clamp...........$18.00
Stirrer, iced tea; shovel blade, Catalin handle, 6-piece set..$36.00
Strainer, red, green or amber Catalin handle, 5" dia......$6.00
Swizzle sticks, Zulu-Lulu, set of 6, M on card.............$12.00
Watch, lady's handbag; 2¾" dia, black Bakelite, Westclox...$70.00

Playing Cards

Here is another collectible that is inexpensive, easy to display (especially single cards), and very diversified. The backs are printed with reproductions of famous paintings and pinup art, carry advertising of all types, and picture tourist attractions and world's fair scenes. Early decks are scarce, but those from the forties on are usually more attractive anyway, so pick an area that interests you most and have fun! Though they're usually not dated, you may find some clues that will assist you in determining an approximate date. Telephone numbers, zip codes, advertising slogans, and patriotic messages are always helpful.

Everett Grist has written an informative book, *Advertising Playing Cards*, which we highly recommend to anyone interested in playing cards with any type of advertising.

Advertising

Dallas Cowboys Cheerleaders, wide, 1982 issue, M in sealed box...$5.00
Fitzgerald's Casino, Sparks NV, wide, 1977, 52+Joker, EX in box...$5.00

Florsheim Shoes, wide, 1935, special Ace of Spades & Joker, 52+logo Joker & logo score card, MIB $3.00
Gaiety Brand, no date, 54 nude models on backs, MIB..$3.50
Moron Motor Oil, can shape, 52 complete, EX in box..$5.00
Old Gold Lights, no date, EX in box $2.00

On the Spot, C James for Better Plumbing, Saturday Evening Post, double deck, EX $20.00

Patent Cereals Co, Old Man Rex back, wide, special Ace of Spades, 52 complete, NM in box $20.00
Petoskey Cement, 1935, special courts, gold edges, MIB..$18.00
Royal Crown Cola, 1945, 52+Joker, VG in torn box....$22.00
Schering Medical II, ChlorTrimeton ad on back, nonstandard size, 52+2 Jokers complete, MIB $15.00
Springmaid Fabrics, double deck, 1956, special Queens & Aces, colored Jokers, M, sealed $40.00
Time Magazine, 1962, lovely courts & Jokers, 52+Joker +extra card, MIB...$60.00
University of Michigan, 1928, blue w/gold logo center, gold edges, sealed, MIB...$30.00
Virginia Slims, no date, MIB...$2.00
Vulcan Iron Works, double deck, 1949, locomotive backs, sealed, MIB...$20.00

Games, Tarot, Magic and Miscellaneous

Baseball, Whitman #3923, 1938, 54 complete+instructions, VG in broken box..$24.00
Bond 007 Tarot, 1973, Hall, 78+2 extra cards+booklet, NM in box $20.00
Carreras, ca 1926, Dondorf type, 36 complete, EX......$17.50
Cowboy Slap Jack, no date, child's, EX in original box ..$2.50
Fortune Telling, 1934, Jan Eric, 44 complete, missing instructions, EX $24.00
Fortune Telling Playing Cards, Whitman #3013, 1936, 45 complete+instructions, NM in box......................$22.00
Ingall's Zodiac Fortune Telling Cards, Zodiac backs, 30 complete+instructions, EX in taped box.........................$6.00
Jungle Book, 1981, Walt Disney, Binney & Smith, MIB.$3.00
Laurel & Hardy, 1972, Edu-Cards, MIB..........................$4.50
Lie, 1988, Fun Games, 52+2 Jokers+instructions, M in plastic box...$3.00
Old Gypsy, 1940, Whitman, complete w/instructions, MIB..$6.00

Petit Lenormand, 1975, Grimaud, 36+instructions, NM in box..**$5.00**
Snow White & 7 Dwarfs, 1965, Disney, Russel Mfg, MIB..**$12.00**
Zolar's Astrological Fortune Telling Horoscope Cards, 1943, MIB...**$6.50**

Modern Decks

Cheer-Up, 1963, wide, hospital cartoons on backs, 52+2 Jokers, EX in box...**$4.00**
Degas, double deck, Danseuses in Bleu/La Classe de Danse (Dancers in Blue/The Dance Class), complete, NM in box..**$25.00**
Kennedy Cards, 1963, Kennedy family members on courts, NM in box..**$16.00**
Politicards, 1971, Nixon administration characters on each card, sealed, M...**$8.00**
Texas Whitehouse, wide, 1966, square corners, tourist information on each card, complete, MIB...................**$15.00**
Victory, non-standard, 1945, Kings are Uncle Sam, Queens are Staute of Liberty, etc, complete, NM in box....**$45.00**
Worshipful, double deck, 1975, American Bicentenary, 52+2 Jokers+booklet, NM in box...............................**$85.00**

Pinups

American Girls, nudes, 54 color photos, MIB..............**$10.00**
Elvgren, A Number To Remember, advertising at bottom, 52+Joker, NM in box...**$18.00**
Elvgren, Charmaine, pretty blond in blue sheer teddy, full deck, no jokers, no box, used, EX........................**$20.00**
Elvgren, 52 different pinups on faces, Special Joker+52+Joker+bio card, MIB...**$65.00**
Esquire, double deck, 1943, blond on black background, redhead on blue background, gold edges, EX in box...**$35.00**
Models of All Nations, 1950s, nudes w/accessories from other nations, VG in torn box............................**$10.00**
Naked Truth, no date, 5x7" king-size deck, M...............**$5.00**
Petty, Sailor Girl w/Ship's Wheel, complete, EX in box..**$10.00**
Vargas, redhead sitting in blue flowers viewed from bare backside, single card, VG+.......................................**$2.00**
Vargas, 1953, 52 different pinups on faces, MIB.......**$115.00**

Souvenir

Black Hills, 1930s, narrow, 53 photos, NM in torn box...**$25.00**
Brown Derby City of Hope, Aces are photos w/caricatures on 44 cards, EX, no box...**$20.00**
Century of Progress, 1933, narrow, maroon backs, EX, no box...**$9.00**
Connecticut, 1950s, double deck, 54 photo scenic backs, complete, NM in box..**$18.00**
Detroit, 1951, double deck, 54 photo scenic backs, 250th birthday, complete, VG in replaced box...............**$10.00**
Hawaiian scenes, ca 1950s, double deck, VG.............**$10.00**
Republican Convention, 1984, double deck, MIB.........**$5.00**
Rocky Mountains, 1940, scenic backs w/gold edges, MIB...**$22.50**

Seashore Trolley Museum, Kennebunkport ME, EX in box..**$1.50**
Washington DC, 1925, Goddess of Justice backs, 52+cherry tree Joker+ad card+fact card, MIB..........**$25.00**
Yellowstone, 1925, wide, blue rays, white border, gold edges, M in broken box......................................**$25.00**
Yellowstone, 1929, narrow, standard faces, Old Faithful backs, complete, VG in box................................**$5.00**

Transportation

Air Canada, 1966, gold logo on black background, MIB...**$5.00**
America West, pink logo on maroon w/gold lettering, MIB...**$5.00**
American Air, 1962, light blue background, complete, EX in box..**$7.00**
American Airlines, 1955, DC-7, wings & logo on gold, sealed, MIB...**$20.00**
British Air, 1988, 'Club' reversed on dark blue background, MIB...**$7.00**
Canadian Pacific Railway & Royal Mail Steamship Line, 1900, complete, MIB..**$25.00**
Delta Airlines, 1979, 50th Anniversary, EX in box.........**$2.00**
Great Northern Railroad, 1935, green & silver, MIB....**$35.00**
Missouri Pacific RR, 1930, Sunshine Special, EX in box...**$80.00**
Monarch Charter Airline, B-757 backs, MIB..................**$5.00**
Ozark World's Fair, 1984, white print, MIB....................**$7.00**
Pan-Am, World Series USA back, MIB............................**$5.00**
Pullman, logo on ace of Spades, 52+Joker+extra card, EX in original case...**$24.00**
Rio Grande RR, 1955, Glenwood Springs, complete, NM in box..**$20.00**
Sante Fe RR, 1952, train in the desert backs, MIB.......**$18.00**
Swissair, 1940s, red background, EX in box..................**$8.00**
Trans Caribbean, 1960s, purple-toned photo of DC-8, EX in box..**$17.50**
United Airlines, no date, logo on red backs, MIB..........**$2.00**

Political Memorabilia

From 1840 until 1896 when celluloid (cellos) buttons appeared, American voters showed support for presidential candidates and their platforms by wearing sulphide brooches, ferrotype pins, mechanical badges, silk ribbons and other lapel devices. Today some of these are valued at thousands of dollars. Celluloid pin-backs were made until the 1920s; many are attractively and colorfully designed, and their values hinge on scarcity, historical significance, and of course condition. Most (but not all) buttons since then have been produced by lithography directly on metal disks (lithos). Jugates are those that feature both the presidential and the vice-presidential candidates and are generally preferred by collectors, but there are several specialty areas that are also desirable such as state and local, third party, and 'cause' types.

Many buttons have been reproduced, but because of a bill passed by Nixon called 'The Hobby Protection Act,' they are all marked. A set distributed by the American Oil company in 1972 can be confusing, however; look on the edge of the button for this mark: 'A-O-1972.' Don't buy buttons that have been tampered with, because unscrupulous dealers sometimes try to scratch off or paint over the 'Reproduction' mark. When these marks are on the paper backing, they may paint that too, so beware.

Besides buttons, look for pamphlets, leaflets, flyers, tickets, electoral ballots, and hand cards used to promote candidates to the presidency. Even memorabilia from the past few decades is something you'll want to hang on to, especially items dealing with Kennedy, Nixon (Watergate) – and, who knows, maybe even Perot.

Ashtray, ceramic, Nixon for President, elephant & GOP in relief in bottom, 2 cigarette rests on octagonal shape **$40.00**

Bank, 5x3½" dia, Support WPA National Job March to Washington, beige & orange paper label on cardboard & tin ..**$37.50**

Belt buckle, Spanish American War, shows Uncle Sam kicking a Spaniard off the Earth, rare, EX **$160.00**

Bumper sticker, Ike & Dick, both portraits in center, names in lg print on sides, EX $17.00

Campaign flyer, 3½x8½", Nixon & Agnew, w/photos, 6-page, EX **$5.00**

Comic book, Lyndon B Johnson's Complete Life Story, marked Dell Comics, copyright 1964, NM............**$15.00**

Dog tag, 2", black peace symbol over American flag on aluminum, marked 1969 Peacestix, EX......................**$20.00**

Doll, 5½", LBJ Himself...by Remco, vinyl w/campaign button on chest, 1964, MIB **$50.00**

Election card, 2½x4½", Vote for Candidates of Roosevelt Democracy in Pennsylvania, cardboard, 1934, EX **$20.00**

Key case, leather, It's a Fair Deal w/Harry, EX............**$35.00**

License plate, Nixon-Agnew, white w/blue print & border, EX...**$20.00**

License plate, Wallace Country, rebel flag w/Wallace & Mrs Wallace in center, EX **$100.00**

License plate, We Want Willkie, portrait over 2 flags, red, white & blue, EX...**$295.00**

License plate, 2½x4", California/JFK 464 in raised yellow letters on black painted metal, M............................**$37.50**

Lyndon B Johnson, convention hat, plastic straw w/paper band, EX..**$25.00**

Matchbook cover, Let Us Now Close Ranks, Reagan & Ford portraits, blue & red on white, NM.........................**$6.00**

Mechanical pencil, MacArthur portrait in blue, 2 flags on white band, unusual, EX **$65.00**

Membership card, Truman & Barkley, 1948.................**$45.00**

Paperweight, FDR bust, A New Deal, heavy metal, EX...**$55.00**

Pencil, mechanical; 5½", Kennedy for President on gray plastic, PT 109 boat floats in clear section, metal clip, EX...**$35.00**

Penknife, Reagan-Bush, 1980, elephant symbol, plastic handle, EX **$14.00**

Photo, 5½x8", Herbert Humphrey sepia portrait, inscribed w/Best Wishes..., framed, ca 1950, EX...............**$100.00**

Pin, IKE, die-cut silver-colored metal outlined in rhinestones, EX..**$20.00**

Pin-back button, 1¼", Wallace & LeMay, letters in red, white & blue, 1968, EX **$2.50**

Pin-back button, 1", John F Kennedy purple image in center, red & white rim, Vote Democratic, 1960, EX..**$87.50** Pin back button, 1½", Come Home America, McGovern & Shriver 72, red & white letters on dark blue, EX ..**$12.50**

Pin-back button, 1½", Confidentially I'm for Ike, yellow & black **$20.00**

Pin-back button, 1½", Go Go Spiro, stylized letters, 2-color...**$4.50**

Pin-back button, 1½", Keep Jerry Ford in the White House, blue letters over images of Ford & US Capitol, EX...**$12.50**

Pin-back button, 1½", McCarthy & portrait, red, white & blue, faded..**$3.00**

Pin-back button, 1½", To Hell w/Hitler, yellow letters on blue, EX...**$25.00**

Pin-back button, 1½", Udall, black lettering & red arrow on yellow background **$3.50**

Pin-back button, 1½", USA Likes LBS, portrait in outline of US, red, white & blue **$4.50**

Pin-back button, 1¼", Allen Ginsberg for President surrounding portrait, ca 1960s, EX..............................**$7.50**

Pin-back button, 1¼", Cambodia Love It or Leave It, black letters on white ground, EX **$12.50**

Pin-back button, 1¼", Jimmy No HHH Yes, 1976.......**$12.50**

Pin-back button, 1¼", Re-Elect Mr Peanut in green letters, black & red caricature of Carter on red, EX.........**$10.00**

Pin-back button, 1¼", All the Way w/LBJ, red, white & blue, EX...**$3.50**

Pin-back button, 1", Wallace & LeMay in white letters on red & blue **$2.50**

Pin-back button, 1⅛", Harry S Truman lettered below brown & white photo, EX **$30.00**

Pin-back button, 1¾", Cleaver for President, photo at side on black & gold ground, EX **$20.00**

Pin-back button, 1¾", Nancy Reagan for First Lady in red letters, black & white tinted photo, EX...................**$8.00**

Pin-back button, 1⅜", Peace Jobs McGovern 72, red, white & blue, EX..**$12.50**

Pin-back button, 2", Humphrey for President, portrait, red, white & black, 1960 ....**$8.50**

Pin-back button, 2½", Nixon-Agnew flasher................**$15.00**

Pin-back button, 2¼", Gerald Ford Whip Inflation Now, EX...**$2.00**

Pin-back button, 3", Anderson for President, portrait w/flag in background, red, white, blue & black................**$4.00**

Pin-back button, 3", I Hate Barry (anti-Goldwater), 2-color...**$7.50**

Pin-back button, 3", If I Were 21 I'd Vote for Nixon.....**$7.50**

Pin-back button, 3", Reagan & Bush Ethnic Voters, black & yellow $4.50

Pin-back button, 3", Vote Republican for Dewey & Warren, portraits on red, white & blue....................$55.00

Pin-back button, 3½", Eisenhower, Man of the Hour, black & white portrait on red, white & blue ground, 1952, EX..$30.00

Pin-back button, 3½", There's a Better Way Than LBJ, bright yellow & dark green w/peace symbol, ca 1965, EX $32.00

Pin-back button, 4", Carter & Mondale in '76, portraits, multicolor $5.50

Pin-back button, ⅝", Keep Coolidge, black & white portrait, EX...$30.00

Pin-back button, ⅞", Democrats for Willkie, red, white & blue, EX $9.00

Pin-back button, ⅞", No Third Term in white letters on blue ground, 1940, EX $12.50

Pin-back button, 1⅜", Union Women United for Lyndon B Johnson & H Humphrey, blue, white & gold, EX...$7.50

Plate, 10½", Jimmy Carter color portrait w/eagle below, past president portraits around rim, unmarked, EX......$20.00

Postcard, Don't Hesitate To Vote for Wilson for President, portrait & pennant $27.50

Poster, 11x14½", Kennedy for President, Leadership for the '60s, w/8-page flyer, NM $40.00

Poster stamp, GOP elephant, 1956, M............................$4.00

Snowdome, Douglas MacArthur, 1940s, NM................$38.00

Stickpin, 1½", JF Kennedy in die-cut silver metal........$20.00

Straight razor, etched jugate of Wilson-Marshall, Miss Liberty & flag on blade, EX $200.00

Tin sign, T-R Cigars, Worthy of the Name, Teddy's portrait, blue w/white & yellow print, EX........................$375.00

Toy, 4½", Jimmy Carter figural peanut caricature, colorful plastic, key wind-up, ca 1980, MIB......................$25.00

Tumbler, 5½", Kennedy commemorative, 1917-1963. $12.00

Postcards

Postcards are generally inexpensive, historically interesting, graphically pleasing, easy to store, and very easy to find. They were first printed in Austria in 1886, where they were very well accepted. In this country, souvenir cards were printed for the Columbian Exposition in 1892, and postcards became the rage.

Until WWI they remained very collectible, with many being preserved in special postcard albums. Even today postcards rank near the top of paper collectibles, second only to stamps.

Today's postcard collectors often specialize. Themes that are particularly worth investing in are advertising, industry, transportation, and entertainment. Other popular cards deal with certain holidays, Black Americana, and patriotism. Some prefer the work of a particular illustrator such as Ellen Clapsaddle, Frances Brundage, Rose O'Neill, Raphael Tuck, Charles Dana Gibson, and Philip Boileau. Don't forget how important condition is with any type of paper collectible. Even though many of these cards are sixty to ninety years old, they must be in excellent shape to have value, whether used or unused.

There are several books available for further study; we recommend *The Collector's Guide to Postcards* by Jane Wood and *Postcards, Mail Memories,* by John M. Kaduck.

Advertising, Happy Thought Tobacco, woman greeting husband w/lₓ box of tobacco, The Secret of a Wife's..., EX...$6.50

Advertising, Heinz 57, bank of London w/carriage in front, multicolored, M $5.00

Advertising, Hyklas Ginger Ale, woman w/bottle & glass, photographic fade-away style, hand-colored, English $75.00

Advertising, Kellogg's Frosted Flakes, sm, little girl & elephant, I Eat It by the Trunk-Full Too....................................$30.00

Advertising, Nestlé Baby Meal, pictures naked baby, chromolitho $35.00

Animal, bear swinging golf club, EX $4.00

Animal, bulldog smoking a pipe, EX............................$3.50

Animal, cat playing mandolin & kittens singing, heavily embossed chromolitho, G $4.00

Animal, First Lesson in Art, little girl reading book to her dachshunds, EX..$6.00

Animal, I Wonder If You Love Me, kitten pulling petals off a daisy, EX..$10.00

Animal, kitten pouring water out of fish bowl, EX........$2.50

Birthday Greetings, embossed flowers, chromolitho, Germany, VG $4.00

Black theme, Oh Boy Can You Throw It $10.00

Fantasy, naked baby seated on bouquet of dandelions reaching for a butterfly, EX $4.00

Fantasy, Oh You Chicken, woman's head on chicken's body, EX $5.00

Hold-to-light, Absecom Light House & US Life Saving Station, Atlantic City NJ, multicolored, EX $30.00

Hold-to-light, Loves Token, bride & groom in heart shape inset w/flowers & hearts above, EX $38.00

Holiday, A Glorious Fourth, eagle on branch atop bell, EX $3.50

Holiday, A Happy Christmas, Santa looking through window at children in bed, EX $5.50

Holiday, A Happy New Year, naked baby talking on telephone, EX.................$1.50

Holiday, A Merry Christmas, little girl w/her arms full of toys, Frances Brundage, EX.................$9.50

Holiday, Easter, village scene w/dogwood, silk, Germany, EX.................$4.00

Holiday, Easter Greetings, baby chick w/umbrella, Ellen Clapsaddle, EX $2.50

Holiday, Easter Greetings, silk pussy willows in pink egg, gold lettering & border, satin, heavily embossed, Germany, VG.................$6.00

Holiday, Merry Christmas, signed Mrs Rodenberg, EX.................$8.00

Holiday, Merry Christmas, sleeping kitten, May Every True Friend Cling To Thee..., Ellen Clapsaddle, EX $6.50

Holiday, Merry Christmas To You, Santa holding sm Christmas tree, EX $5.00

Holiday, Thanksgiving, Pilgrim lady serving cider & donuts, embossed, #132, Frances Brundage, VG $5.00

Holiday, Thanksgiving, Uncle Sam & turkey, Ruler of the Day, green & red, G.................$4.00

Holiday, Thanksgiving 1909, lg turkey, embossed, Ellen Clapsaddle, G $4.00

Holiday, To My Valentine, child holding rose, I Love My Love Because I Know My Love..., Ellen Clapsaddle, EX.......$4.50

Holiday, Valentine Greetings, man holding bowling ball, The Bowler has a Record Fine, The Ball Goes Rolling..., EX .$2.50

Holiday, With Best New Year Wishes, barn & river scene, silk, Germany, VG.................$7.50

Holiday, 4th of July, eagle atop shield, stars around border, Liberty & Union Now & Forever, Ellen Clapsaddle, EX.................$4.00

Katherine Gassaway, little girl mailing letter, I Send My Love by Mail, EX $5.50

Katherine Gassaway, little girl standing behind fence, Howdy, EX $5.50

Kentucky Derby, winner Citation, 1948.................$10.00

Patriotic, colorful flag, shield & eagle, copyright 1907 by Illustrated Postal Card, G $4.00

Patriotic, flag, eagle & Connecticut State Capitol, embossed, Langsdorf, EX $4.00

Political, birthplace of Woodrow Wilson, Staunton VA, shows house & picture, Kaufmann, EX $4.00

Political, black & white medallion photos of Alice Roosevelt & Nickolas Longworth, copyright 1904 Pack Brothers, VG $4.00

Political, bust portrait of Abraham Lincoln in oval inset, lettering below, EX.................$3.50

Political, Eisenhower's birthplace, Denison TX, multicolored, M $4.00

Political, Temple of Music, Buffalo NY, where McKinley was shot, PSC Co, G.................$5.00

Political, Washington Birthday Series #1, Washington taking oath of office, gold, embossed, VG.................$7.00

Souvenir, Boston, 2 teddy bears carrying pot of baked beans, copyright 1907, VG $12.50

Sports, Golfer's Award, humorous image of man smoking pipe, EX.................$4.00

Transportation, Brockton Massachusetts Train Station, mobs of people & early touring cars, multicolored, VG...$4.00

Transportation, Continental Trailways, full view of bus, multicolored, M $4.00

Transportation, West Philadelphia Train Station, train pulling out of station, multicolored, EX $3.00

Posters

Posters are popular among many collectors, not only as an alternative to more expensive art forms but also because they seem to be appreciating very quickly.

Though you may not find a Cheret or a Lautrec, there are many kinds of contemporary posters that are well worth your attention. Hundreds of movie posters can be bought for less than $100.00, many for less than $25.00. Of course, those featuring the Hollywood legends like Marilyn Monroe or James Dean are bringing thousands of dollars at auction. Early monster movies are hot as well, and some of those posters are estimated to be worth tens of thousands of dollars! The most available size is about 41" x 27"; collectors refer to them as 1-sheets.

Though not as easy to find, posters from the WWII era are well worth looking for. They will vary in price from about $20.00 up to several hundred or more. Look for fine graphics, artists' signatures, interesting subject matter, and, of course, good condition.

Advertising, 19x16", close-up of gent smoking pipe & enjoying a mug of Wiedeman's beer, VG+ **$75.00**
Advertising, 20½x27½", shows double-horse carousel w/CW Parker advertising on canopy, vignettes in sky, NM **$225.00**

Advertising, 47x6", Fap' Anis, Celui Des Connaisseurs, printed by Publicite Wall, Paris, EX $700.00
Circus, 28x42", Ringling Brothers & Barnum & Bailey, clown portrait, EX **$125.00**
Magic, 30x20", Carter the Great, Ackermann-Quigley, 1930, EX **$350.00**
Movie, 1-sheet, Angel Alley, Bowery Boys, 1948, G ...**$75.00**
Movie, 1-sheet, April Fools, Jack Lemmon, 1969, NM.**$15.00**
Movie, 1-sheet, Ashanti, Michael Caine, 1979.............**$10.00**
Movie, 1-sheet, Back to the Future 3, EX.....................**$12.50**
Movie, 1-sheet, Bandits of the West, Allen Rocky Lane, 1953, EX...**$25.00**
Movie, 1-sheet, Boy Did I Get a Wrong Number, Bob Hope, Elke Sommer, Phyllis Diller, 1966, EX **$8.50**
Movie, 1-sheet, Boy's Night Out, Kim Novak, James Garner, Tony Randall, Patti Page, Metro-Goldwyn-Mayer, 1962, VG **$7.50**
Movie, 1-sheet, Breaking Away, Dennis Quaid, EX **$10.00**
Movie, 1-sheet, Coming to America, Eddie Murphy, color ..**$5.00**
Movie, 1-sheet, Gidget Goes Hawaiian, James Darren, Deborah Walley, Columbia Pictures, 1961, VG **$6.00**
Movie, 1-sheet, Hiawatha, Vince Edwards in full-color scenes, marked Walter Mirisch Production, 1953, EX **$37.50**
Movie, 1-sheet, Louisa, Ronald Reagan in bathrobe, 1950, VG..**$200.00**

Movie, 1-sheet, Luna, Jill Clayburgh, 1979, EX..............**$8.00**

Movie, 1-sheet, Mad Max Beyond Thunderdome, Mel Gibson, Warner Brothers, 1985, NM $25.00
Movie, 1-sheet, Massacre at Central High, Andrew Stevens, 1976..**$8.50**
Movie, 1-sheet, On the Beach, Gregory Peck, Ava Gardner, Fred Astaire & Anthony Perkins, United Artists, 1959, VG...**$12.00**
Movie, 1-sheet, Paris Blues, Paul Newman, Joanne Woodward, Sidney Poitier & Diahann Carroll, 1961, G ..**$22.50**
Movie, 1-sheet, Prudence & the Pill, Deborah Kerr & David Niven, 20th Century-Fox, 1968, EX.........................**$6.00**

Movie, 1-sheet, Psycho III, Anthony Perkins, NM .$20.00
Movie, 1-sheet, Rambo III, Sylvester Stallone.................**$5.00**
Movie, 1-sheet, Red Hot Wheels, Clark Gable, '62, NM.**$25.00**
Movie, 1-sheet, Reflections in a Golden Eye, Elizabeth Taylor & Marlon Brando, Warner Brothers, 1967, VG.............**$25.00**
Movie, 1-sheet, Shadows of Tombstone, Rex Allen.....**$30.00**
Movie, 1-sheet, The Green Hornet, Green Hornet & Kato, 1974, NM **$28.00**
Movie, 1-sheet, The Long Ships, Richard Widmark & Sidney Poitier, Columbia Pictures, 1964, EX........................**$8.50**
Movie, 1-sheet, The Naked Ape, Victoria Principal, 1973, EX...**$8.00**
Movie, 1-sheet, The Outlaw Is Coming, Three Stooges, NM **$40.00**
Movie, 1-sheet, The Secret War of Harry Frig, Paul Newman & Sylvia Koscina, Universal Pictures, 1968, EX.....**$12.00**

Movie, 1-sheet, The Swimmer, Burt Lancaster, Janice Rule & Janet Landard, Columbia Pictures, 1968, EX............**$7.00**

Movie, 1-sheet, The Thomas Crown Affair, Steve McQueen & Faye Dunaway, United Artists, 1968, VG..........**$12.00**

Movie, 1-sheet, Warning Shot, David Jansen, 1966, VG..**$5.00**

Movie, 1-sheet, 40 Pounds of Trouble, Tony Curtis, 1963.......................**$12.00**

Movie, 11x14", Gay Ranchero, Roy Rogers, 1948 ....**$37.50**

Movie, 21x27" (half-sheet), Stowaway, Shirley Temple, Robert Young, & Alice Faye, 20th Century Fox, 1936, creases $500.00

Movie, 22x28", Airport, Charlton Heston, 1974, NM...............................**$10.00**

Movie, 63x47", From Russia w/Love, French, 1963 ...**$350.00**

Movie, 79x41", Buffalo Bill Rides Again, Richard Arlen & Jennifer Holt full-color portraits, ca 1947, EX **$62.50**

Movie, 81x81", Old Spanish Trail, Roy Rogers, '47, VG.....**$120.00**

Political, 28x22", I Am a Man, used in Memphis strike by Martin L King supporters before his death, 1968, EX **$65.00**

Theater, 26x18½", The Convict's Daughter, scene w/convict being waited on by daughter, National Engraving Co, VG.................................**$50.00**

Theater, 27¾x18", Dr Jekyll & Mr Hyde, 2 gents wearing top hats in garden, Donaldson Litho Co, VG.................**$70.00**

Theater, 27x36¾", In Old Kentucky, depicts victory of the thoroughbred Queen Bess at Lexington track, G **$300.00**

Theater, 30x20", Uncle Tom's Cabin, Uncle Tom & Little Eva, Ackermann-Quigley, EX **$75.00**

Theater, 81x41", Ashes, lady on bed covered w/sheet, NY Shakespeare Festival, 1977, VG **$125.00**

Theater, 81x41", Frankenstein, hand & word Frankenstein, red & white on black, 1970s, EX **$125.00**

Travel, 40x24", Ireland Invites You, Irish scene, 1955 ....**$95.00**

Travel, 40x30", American Airlines, snowman, E McKnight Kauffer, G **$150.00**

Travel, 42½x29¾", features French hillside resort town of Digne by Chanteau, L'Eclaideur litho, 1935, EX **$220.00**

WWII, 28x20", Care Is Costly, GI sits against wall, Treidler, 1945, EX.................................**$55.00**

WWII, 28x20", Join Women's Land Army, ladies in farm clothes, 1943, EX.................................**$130.00**

WWII, 28x22", Attack, Attack, Attack; soldiers w/bayonets, Warren, 1942, VG.................................**$45.00**

WWII, 29x39", Victory Liberty Loan, U-boat in choppy waters surrendering to Allied gunboat, marked WF Powers Co, EX **$150.00**

WWII, 30x40", America's Answer! Production; hand holding wrench, 1942, VG **$275.00**

WWII, 40x28", Battle-Wise Infantryman Is Careful..., soldier w/rifle, 1944, EX **$45.00**

WWII, 40x28", Put Them Across, soldiers walk up gang-plank, Falter, 1943, G **$100.00**

WWII, 40x28", Save Rubber Check Your Tires Now, 1942, VG **$80.00**

WWII, 40x28", She's a Swell Plane Give Us More, pilot, 1944, VG **$95.00**

WWII, 40x29", Let 'Em Have It, soldier throws grenade, Perlin, 1943, EX.................................**$100.00**

WWII, 41x27", Help China, Uncle Sam w/war refugees, Flagg, VG.................................**$185.00**

WWII, 41x29", They Did Their Part, Sullivan brothers illustration, 1943, EX.................................**$100.00**

WWII, 58x40", Triumph Over Tyranny, woman's head among artillery projectiles, VG...........................**$100.00**

Precious Moments

These modern collectibles are designed by Samuel J. Butcher and produced in the Orient by the Enesco company. You'll see them in gift stores and card shops all across the nation. They were introduced less than fifteen years ago, and already some are selling on the secondary market for as much as five or six times their original retail price. Each piece is marked, and like the Hummel figures to which they're sometimes compared, the older retired items are the most valuable. Their figurines, bells, ornaments, and plates all portray children actively engaged in a particular pursuit, and many have an inspirational message.

If you'd like to learn more, we recommend *Precious Moments Secondary Market Price Guide* by Rosie Wells.

Bell, Jesus Is Born, boy shepherd w/staff, #E5623, no mark, 1980 ....**$40.00**

Container, Jesus Loves Me, girl w/bunny, #E-9281, Hourglass mark, 1982.................................**$35.00**

Container, Our Love Is Heaven-Scent, skunk, #E-9266, Fish mark, 1983.................................**$25.00**

Container, The Lord Bless You & Keep You, bride & groom on heart-shaped box, Hourglass mark, 1982.........**$30.00**

Doll, Angie the Angel of Mercy, nurse, #12491, Cedar Tree mark, 1987.................................**$160.00**

Doll, Timmy, dressed in jogging clothes, #E-5397, Cross mark, 1984.................................**$150.00**

Figurine, bride, 7th in Bridal Party series, #E-2846, Cedar Tree mark, 1987.................................**$22.00**

Figurine, Cheers to the Leader, girl cheerleader, #104035, Cedar Tree mark, 1987 ....**$35.00**

Figurine, Friends Never Drift Apart, children in boat, #100250, Dove mark, 1985..............................$60.00

Figurine, God Understands, boy & dog w/report card, #E-1379B, no mark, 1978.....................$95.00

Figurine, groom w/no hands #E-2837, Olive Branch mark, 1986 ....$40.00

Figurine, I Would Be Sunk w/out You, little boy w/sinking boat in round tub, Flame mark, 1990 ....$19.00

Figurine, Love Is Kind, boy w/turtle on knee, from Original 21, #E-1379A, Cross mark, 1984.............................$70.00

Figurine, O How I Love Jesus, Indian boy & little dog, part of Original 21, #E-1380B, no mark, 1977 ....$105.00

Figurine, Sharing Begins in the Heart, girl w/slate, #520861, Flower mark, 1988 ....$70.00

Figurine, Tell Me a Story, little boy sitting, 1st in Christmas Scene series, #15792, Dove mark, 1985................$18.00

Figurine, The Lord Bless You & Keep You, boy in graduation cap & gown, #E-4720, no mark, 1980............$50.00

Figurine, There Is Joy in Serving Jesus, waitress, #E-7157, Hourglass mark, 1982 ....$50.00

Figurine, Yield Not to Temptation, girl w/apple, #521310, Bow 'n Arrow mark, 1989 ....$35.00

Frame, Loving You, boy holding heart, #12017, Cross mark, 1984 ....$45.00

Ornament, Baby's First Christmas, boy w/block, #E-2372, Hourglass mark, 1982 ....$25.00

Ornament, Dropping Over for Christmas, girl w/pie, #E-2376, Hourglass mark, 1982, ...$75.00

Ornament, Jesus Is the Light That Shines, boy in nightcap w/candle, #E-0537, Fish mark, 1983 ....$40.00

Ornament, O Come All Ye Faithful, boy caroler, #E-0531, Dove mark, 1985...$30.00

Ornament, Peace on Earth, boy on globe, #E-2804, Cross mark, 1984..$90.00

Ornament, rocking horse, #102474, Olive Branch mark, 1986 ....$22.00

Ornament, Surrounded w/Joy, boy w/wreath, E-0506, Fish mark, 1983..$70.00

Ornament, The First Noel, angel, E-2368, Fish mark, 1983 .$35.00

Ornament, Unicorn, #E-2371, no mark, 1982...............$50.00

Plate, Come Let Us Adore Him, Nativity scene, 1st in Christmas Collection series, #E-5646, no mark, 1980.....$45.00

Plate, I'll Play My Drum for Him, boy playing drum, from Joy of Christmas series, #E2357, no mark, 1982....$65.00

Plate, Jesus Loves Me, boy w/teddy bear, #E-9275, Fish mark, 1983...$30.00

Plate, Mother Sew Dear, mother doing needlepoint, 1st edition of Mother's Love, #E5217, no mark, 1981......$45.00

Plate, Summer's Joy, girl holding rose, 2nd in Four Seasons series, #12114, Dove mark, 1985............................$55.00

Plate, The Wonder of Christmas, boy & girl w/sled, 3rd in Joy of Christmas series, #E5396, Cross mark, 1984........$40.00

Plate, Wee Three Kings, #E-0538, Olive Branch mark, 1986 ....$60.00

Thimble, Mother Sew Dear, a mother sewing, #13293, Dove mark, 1985...$10.00

Thimble, The Purr-fect Grandma, a grandma in a rocking chair, #13307, Cedar Tree mark, 1987 ....$8.00

Purinton Pottery

The Purinton Pottery Company moved from Ohio to Shippenville, Pennsylvania, in 1941 and began producing several lines of dinnerware and kitchen items hand painted with fruits, ivy vines, and trees in bold brush strokes of color on a background reminiscent of old yellowware pieces. The company closed in 1959 due to economic reasons.

Purinton has a style that's popular today with collectors who like the country look. It isn't always marked, but you'll soon recognize its distinct appearance. Some of the rarer designs are Palm Tree and Peasant Lady, and examples of these lines are considerably higher than the more common ones. You'll see more Apple and Apple and Pear pieces than any, and in more diversified shapes.

Apple, creamer & sugar bowl, w/lid $25.00
Apple, drip jar, w/lid $20.00
Apple, pitcher, lg $40.00
Apple, relish, 3-part $30.00
Apple, sugar bowl, w/lid...$10.00

Apple & Pear, cookie jar......................................$50.00
Apple & Pear, salt & pepper shakers, range size, pr...$20.00
Chartreuse, bowl, friut; 12" $18.00
Chartreuse, canister, coffee $35.00
Chartreuse, plate, salad..$8.00
Intaglio, jug, 5-pt...$35.00
Intaglio, platter, 11" $28.00
Intaglio, relish, 3-part, center handle.......................$28.00
Intaglio, teapot, 2-cup $20.00
Ivy, cup & saucer...$12.50
Ivy, salt & pepper shakers, range size, pr..................$20.00
Ivy, sugar bowl, w/lid $10.00
Maywood, creamer & sugar bowl.............................$35.00
Maywood, jug, 5-pt..$50.00
Maywood, salt & pepper shakers, jug form, pr $25.00
Maywood, teapot, 2-cup...$24.00
Palm Tree, salt & pepper shakers, range size, pr $42.50
Pennsylvania Dutch, canisters, 4-piece set.................$175.00
Plaid, bowl, soup or cereal.......................................$8.00
Plaid, bowl, vegetable; 8" $12.50
Plaid, cookie jar $50.00
Plaid, creamer $10.00
Plaid, cup & saucer..$12.50
Plaid, plate, 6¾" $8.00
Plaid, teapot, 2-cup..$15.00
Rose, bowl, cereal...$8.00
Rose, creamer..$12.50
Rose, cup & saucer $15.00

Purses

Purses from the late 1800s through the '20s and '30s have long been collectible, but they're not as scarce as you might think. You'll still be able to find some nice examples at many flea markets and antique malls. Some of the very early purses were covered allover with fine glass or cut steel beads. Flowers, birds, scenics or geometric designs were popular. By the turn of the century, the design was stylized and Victorian, like you see in stained glass windows and lamp shades from that period. Instead of beads, mesh became the material of preference. Some mesh purses were simply left plain to reflect the beauty of the metal itself, but many featured enameling. Sometimes the framework was sterling silver, and small semiprecious stones were added. Whiting and Davis was one of the larger manufacturers; Mandalian was another. Most purses with the mark of either of these companies is worth $150.00 at a very minimum. During the '50s, purses made of Lucite or some other plastic became popular. Nowadays these are often priced from $40.00 on up, depending upon style, color, condition, and whether or not the label of the manufacturer is present.

For more information, we suggest *Antique Purses, A History, Identification, and Value Guide*, Second Edition, by Richard Holiner.

Bakelite top, handle & snap w/rose in center, EX $70.00
Beaded, 2¾" dia tam-o'-shanter style, silver w/silverplated
    lid w/classic profile..$48.00
Beaded, 4x2¾", silver on beige crochet body, leather lining,
    EX $35.00

Beaded, 6x5", brown w/red, blue & green devices .$100.00
Beaded, 7x9", green & black check on white, black & white
    fringe, Czechoslovakia..$70.00
Beaded, 8½x6", silvery clear beads in swag design, clusters
    of fringes, beaded handles $75.00
Beaded, 8x5½", black & white on beige fabric w/beige tas-
    sel, 18½" chain handle..$98.00
Beaded clutch, amber, beaded strap $35.00
Beaded reticule, 8x11", floral pattern, M $75.00
Crochet, 6½x8¼", ecru w/rust lining, heavily embossed
    frame..$65.00
Enamel mesh, 5x3", brown squares on white ground, Whiting-
    Davis oval frame w/leaves, chain handle...............$125.00
Enameled mesh, 7x5", Art Deco multicolor design on white,
    Whiting-Davis flowered frame, w/14" chain handle..$150.00
Leather, alligator, 12x8x4" $65.00
Leather, 5¾x7¾", alligator paw, square metal frame ...$50.00
Leather, 6x5", hand tooled & stitched, Morocco, 1950s,
    EX $25.00

Leather, 9x4½", light brown snakeskin, clutch style, EX..**$50.00**
Lucite, clutch style w/rhinestones, 1950s, EX **$40.00**

Lucite, hat box shape, gray pearl **$40.00**
Lucite, rectangular, rusty-red, clear lid w/intaglio flower ..**$65.00**
Lucite, trapezoid, pearl sides, clear bottom & handle, intaglio flower in clear lid, marked, M, unused....**$75.00**
Rhinestones, sm, hand set, Czechoslovakia **$55.00**
Satin, brown clutch type, coin purse & mirror inside .**$24.00**
Satin, clutch style, black w/pearl clasp, EX.................**$30.00**
Velvet, 7x4", black w/ornate brocade design, chain handle, India...**$30.00**

Puzzles

The first children's puzzle was actually developed as a learning aid by an English map maker, trying to encourage the study of geography. Most 19th-century puzzles were made of wood, rather boring, and very expensive. But by the Victorian era, nursery rhymes and other light-hearted themes became popular. The industrial revolution and the inception of color lithography combined to produce a stunning variety of themes ranging from technical advancements, historical scenarios, and fairy tales. Power saws made production more cost effective, and wood was replaced with less expensive cardboard.

As early as the twenties and thirties, American manufacturers began to favor character-related puzzles, the market already influenced by radio and the movies. Some of these were advertising premiums. Die-cutters had replaced jigsaws, cardboard became thinner, and now everyone could afford puzzles. During the Depression they were a cheap form of entertainment, and no family get-together was complete without a puzzle spread out on the card table for all to enjoy.

Television and movies caused a lull in puzzle making during the fifties, but advancements in printing and improvements in quality brought them back strongly in the sixties. Unusual shapes, the use of fine art prints, and more challenging designs caused sales to increase.

If you're going to collect puzzles, you'll need to remember that unless all the pieces are there, they're not of much value, especially those from the 20th century. The condition of the box is important as well. Right now there's lots of interest in puzzles from the fifties through the seventies that feature popular TV shows and characters from that era.

To learn more about the subject, we recommend *Character Toys and Collectibles* and *Toys, Antique and Collectible*, both by David Longest, and *Toys of the Sixties, A Pictorial Guide*, by Bill Bruegman.

All My Children, jigsaw type, M..................................**$12.50**
Alvin & Chipmunks, Saalfield, frame tray, 1962, EX....**$18.00**
American soldiers w/Japanese planes, Whitman, ca 1940s, in original box, VG..**$17.50**
Archie, Betty & Veronica, Jaymar, jigsaw type, 1960s, NM **$9.00**
Atom Ant, Milton Bradley, 1980, frame tray, NM..........**$8.00**
Atom Ant, Whitman, 1967, EX **$30.00**
Banana Splits, Whitman, #4534, 1969, frame tray, NM.**$32.50**
Barbie & Ken, 1960s, EX..**$15.00**
Batman, sliding tile type, 1977, M on card..................**$17.50**
Bozo the Clown, Whitman, frame tray, 1966, EX **$15.00**
Brady Bunch, Whitman, 1972, frame tray, EX.............**$22.50**

Brownies, 12x10", copyright Palmer Cox, wooden jigsaw type, 1891, EX...$150.00
Bugs Bunny, pocket type, marked Gordy, 1980, set of 2, M on card..**$5.00**
Bugs Bunny, Whitman, 1979, frame tray, M..................**$5.00**
Bugs Bunny, 15x11", Whitman, jigsaw type, 1964, EX..**$7.50**
Charmin' Chatty, 1963, frame tray, EX.......................**$12.50**
Chitty Chitty Bang Bang, dated 1968, frame tray, EX..**$18.00**
Daniel Boone, Indian Warfare, Jaymar, 1964, 100-piece, EX **$22.50**
Dennis the Menace, Whitman, 1960, frame tray, EX **$8.00**
Dick Tracy, Jaymar, frame tray, EX..............................**$25.00**
Dick Tracy & the Bank Lineup, jigsaw, ca early 1960s, original box, EX...**$30.00**
Dick Tracy Crime Does Not Pay, ca early 1950s, MIB ..**$30.00**
Dr Doolittle, Whitman, frame tray, 1967, EX................**$15.00**
Dudley Do-Right, Whitman, EX **$30.00**

Eight Is Enough, cast photo, Associated Pictures, 1978, MIB **$15.00**

Elly May, Jaymar, 1963, frame tray, NM **$22.50**

Family Affair, 20" dia, Whitman, jigsaw type, 1970, 125-piece, M **$17.50**

Famous Airplanes, Saalfield, #1826, set of 3, MIB **$75.00**

Flash Gordon, Milton Bradley, set of 3, boxed, EX **$30.00**

Flintstones, Warren, pictures Fred on mammoth, jigsaw type, 1978, EX **$5.00**

Flintstones, Whitman, Fred at piano, 1962, NM **$30.00**

Flintstones, 5x5" square, sliding tile type, 1983, M in package **$6.00**

Flipper, jigsaw type, set of 3, MIB **$10.00**

Fury, Whitman, pictures boys on Fury's back, jigsaw type, 1955, NM...**$7.50**

General Hospital, MIB **$12.00**

Green Hornet, Whitman, 1966, frame tray, set of 4, MIB ..**$125.00**

Gumby & Pokey, Whitman, 1968, frame tray, EX........**$28.00**

Gunsmoke, Whitman, Matt Dillon facing lynch mob, 1969, EX...**$25.00**

Happy Days, 14x10", H-G toys, featuring The Fonz, 150-piece, VG **$7.50**

Heckle & Jeckle, Jaymar, characters build doghouse, jigsaw type, 1960s, NM...**$17.50**

Herculoids, Whitman, 1967, frame tray, EX **$70.00**

Hippity Hopper, Whitman, jigsaw type, 1965, NM......**$37.50**

Howdy Doody, Whitman, Howdy's One-Man Band, jigsaw type, 1954, NM...**$17.50**

Huckleberry Hound, 15x11", 1960s, frame tray, EX **$12.50**

Jetsons, Whitman, jigsaw type, 1962, 70-piece, EX......**$25.00**

Just Kids, Saalfield, 1932, set of 4, boxed, NM............**$60.00**

Katzenjammer Kids, 1920s, set of 4, boxed, EX...........**$75.00**

Little Lulu, Whitman, 1950s, EX **$35.00**

Little Orphan Annie, Jaymar, 1960s, MIB **$17.50**

Little Tots Scroll Puzzle, Milton Bradley, 1900s, EX.....**$95.00**

Magilla Gorilla, sliding tile type, 1960s, EX................**$30.00**

Man from UNCLE, Jaymar, 1965, frame tray, EX.........**$28.00**

Mary Poppins, Whitman, frame tray, 1964, EX **$15.00**

Maverick, Whitman, 1958, in original box, EX............**$20.00**

Mean Joe Green, 10x12", licensed by Pittsburgh Steelers, 1980, frame tray, M **$15.00**

Mighty Heroes, Whitman, 1967, frame tray, EX..........**$42.50**

Mr Smith (Lost in Space), sliding tile type, dated 1983, M on card **$5.00**

Munsters, 14x18", Whitman, jigsaw type, 1965, 100-piece, NM **$45.00**

Paula Abdul, MIB...**$15.00**

Popeye, Jaymar, #179, 1960s, EX **$12.50**

Popeye, Jaymar, 1952, MIB **$35.00**

Popeye, Roalex, sliding tile type, M on card................**$48.00**

Popeye, 22x17", Jaymar, jigsaw type, EX **$22.00**

Rifleman, Whitman, 1958, frame tray, NM...................**$45.00**

Road Runner, 1970s, NM..**$12.00**

Roger Ramjet, Whitman, 1966, frame tray, EX-............**$32.00**

Ronald McDonald, Whitman, 1984, jigsaw type, 100-piece, MIB **$25.00**

Rubik's Cube, Ideal Toys, MIB..................................**$10.00**

Scooby Doo, Playskool, VG **$2.00**

Sergeant Preston, Milton Bradley, 1950s, M **$25.00**

Shazam, Whitman, 1967, NM **$28.00**

Skippy, marked Skippy Incorporated, jigsaw type, dated 1933, EX..**$28.00**

Sleeping Beauty, Whitman, 1959, frame tray, EX **$10.00**

Snow White & Seven Dwarfs, Jaymar, frame tray, 1952, VG...$15.00

Space Ghost, Whitman, 1967, frame tray, EX..............**$48.00**

Space Kidettes, Whitman, 1967, frame tray, EX **$25.00**

Space 1999, jigsaw type, 1970s, EX............................**$7.50**

Superman Versus Brainstorm, Whitman, 1966, EX......**$28.00**

Tarzan, 14x18", Whitman, jigsaw type, 1968, 100-piece, NM **$22.50**

Terry & the Pirates, 7x10", Jaymar, 1946, EX **$30.00**

Three Little Pigs, Jaymar, 1940s, EX............................**$15.00**

Tom Mix, Rexall Drugs premium, 1930s, EX **$40.00**

Welcome Back Kotter, 1970s, NM..............................**$7.50**

Wild Bill Hickok, Built-Rite, 1965, in original box, EX..**$20.00**

Woody Woodpecker, Whitman, Woody & bulldog, 1964, frame tray, EX..**$7.50**

Yogi Bear, Whitman #4435, frame tray, 1963, M **$25.00**

Zorro, Whitman, Guy Williams fencing w/guard, frame tray, 1957, EX...**$15.00**

Quilts

Early quilts were considered basic homemaking necessities. They were used not only on the bed for warmth but also to hang over the windows and walls for extra insulation from gusty winter winds and on the floor as mattresses for overnight guests. Even into the thirties and forties they were made primarily to be used. But most of the contemporary quilts, of course (though they may be displayed with care as a bed covering), are designed and made as show pieces, some of them requiring several months of steady work to complete. Quilts from any circa are collectible and should be judged on condition, craftsmanship, intricacy of design, and color composition.

Though modern quilt artists sometimes devise some very unique methods of dying, printing, and construction, basically there are four types of quilts: 1) crazy – made up of scraps and pieces of various types of materials and sometimes ribbons sewn together in no specific design; 2) pieced – having intricate patterns put together with pieces that have been cut into specific shapes; 3) appliqued – made by applying a cut-out design (sometimes of one piece, sometimes pieced) to background material that is basically the size of the finished quilt; 4) trapunto – having a one-piece top lined with a second layer of loosely woven fabric through which padding is inserted to enhance the stitched pattern.

Nowadays you can't go to any retail flea market, or department store, for that matter, without seeing new quilts that have been imported from China. At retail these are priced as low as $50.00 up to $200.00 in the more exclusive outlets. Upon examination you'll see poor workmanship and large, careless quilting stitches that are in sharp contrast to the fine sewing done by an accomplished quilter.

If you like quilts, you'll want to get these books: *Collecting Quilts* by Cathy Gaines Florence and *Gallery of American Quilts, 1849–1988,* and *Arkansas Quilts,* both published by The American Quilter's Society.

Appliqued, Acorn & Leaf, 80x98", 12 multicolor blocks, green border, lightweight, EX..............................**$450.00**

Appliqued, Apple Blossom, 68x83", 1930s, pink flowers, green leaves, brown stems on white, some fading, diamond quilting..............................**$200.00**

Appliqued, Butterfly, 50x72", 1930s prints form butterflies on white, pink & white border, M......................**$275.00**

Appliqued, Dogwood, 75x90", pink flowers w/green leaves & brown stems on white, NM..............................**$300.00**

Appliqued, English Flowerpot, 74x76", pink & yellow w/green on white, pink border, machine bound, EX quilting, EX..**$285.00**

Appliqued, Fleur-de-lis, 80x80", primitive, EX...........**$400.00**

Appliqued, flowers, 82x90", many colorful flowers on field of polished cotton, EX quilting, NM....................**$500.00**

Appliqued, plumes & stars in swag border, w/diamond & parallel line quilting, 1800s, 82x84".........$600.00

Appliqued, Rose, 84x100", 1930s pink flowers on white muslin, 1" diamond quilting, M..............................**$425.00**

Appliqued, Snowflake Medallion, 72x74", red on white w/9 repeats, EX..............................**$365.00**

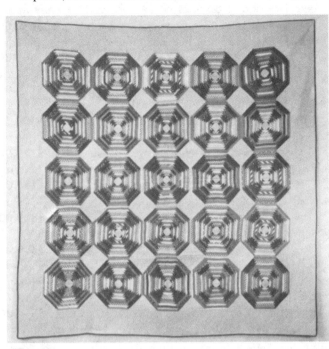

Appliqued & pieced, geometrics on pink ground, light wear, 84x84" **$300.00**

Pieced, Amish Shadows, full size, 1983, machine made from kit, machine quilted, M........................**$300.00**

Pieced, Arrows, 64x88", ca 1900, prints & ginghams, heavy, EX quilting, M..............................**$325.00**

Pieced, Bear Paw, 70x86", multicolor prints, red binding, sawtooth border................................**$365.00**

Pieced, Bow Tie, 70x84", 1930s, dark & light ginghams, pink & white binding, EX quilting, EX........................**$325.00**

Pieced, Broken Dishes, 78x82", 1930s, cotton prints & solids, pink border, EX **$385.00**

Pieced, Broken Star, 75x77", 1930s, multicolor pastels on white, shell & feather quilting, VG **$150.00**

Pieced, Broken Star, 78x92", 1930s, solids on white background, blue lining & binding, EX quilting, M ...**$400.00**

Pieced, Broken Sugar Bowl, 69x77", 1930s, blue & white, square quilting, frayed binding..........................**$250.00**

Pieced, Butterflies, full size, 1930s, bright pink on white background, NM **$365.00**

Pieced, Cactus Basket, 64x82", 1930s, blue & pink prints on white, EX quilting, EX **$285.00**

Pieced, Carpenter's Square, 1930s, lavender & pink, medallion quilting, EX **$275.00**

Pieced, Corn & Beans, 70x82", 1930s, indigo & red mini prints on white, straight quilting, EX..................**$265.00**

Pieced, Crazy, 75x86", 1920, chambrays & ginghams, hand sewn, unused, M..................................**$300.00**

Pieced, Diamond in Squares, 79x79", multicolor calicos, sawtooth border, EX..............................**$800.00**

Pieced, Double Irish Chain, 70x81", cotton solids & prints w/white cotton muslin, fine quilting, EX **$335.00**

Pieced, Double Wedding Ring, 72x90", 1920s, pink & blue, hand sewn, EX quilting, NM **$425.00**

Pieced, Double Wedding Ring, 84x87", 1930, prints & solids on white muslin, green scalloped edge, EX........**$295.00**

Pieced, Dresden Plate, 88x105", old material, recently made, EX quilting, NM.............................**$450.00**

Pieced, Drunkard's Path, 76x86", red & white, close quilting, M.............................**$500.00**

Pieced, Drunkard's Path, 81x68", pink & creamy white, hand sewn, rebound, sm stain on back.................**$175.00**

Pieced, embroidered yellow & white blocks, 74x90", EX quiltings w/designs in border & sashing, M........**$300.00**

Pieced, Fannie's Fan, 71x88", 1930s, multicolor prints & solids, w/green border, light wear, fading, VG ..**$175.00**

Pieced, Fans, full size, ca 1930s, pink calicos, fine quilting, EX **$345.00**

Pieced, Field of Diamonds, 80x88", 1930, prints & solids, green border, M **$325.00**

Pieced, Flower Garden, 66x90", 1930s, pastels & solids, yellow border of hexagons, lining & binding, M **$300.00**

Pieced, Flower Garden, 84x84", multicolor pastels & solids, pink binding, EX quilting, NM **$400.00**

Pieced, Friendship Star, 72x82", 1950, multicolor prints & solids, EX.............................**$350.00**

Pieced, Goblet, 72x82", red & white, triple line quilting, VG.............................**$300.00**

Pieced, Grandmother's Fan, 85x88", old top, newly quilted, EX **$385.00**

Pieced, Grandmother's Flower Garden, 74x86", 1930s, multicolor prints, EX **$365.00**

Pieced, Laced Star, 60x73", 1983, multicolor stars on white, blue border, EX quilting, NM **$425.00**

Pieced, Little Boy's Breeches, 67x83", 1940s, red, white, blue & yellow, outline quilting, VG **$200.00**

Pieced, Log Cabin, 68x70", ca 1900, satins, silk & velvets, velvet binding, not heavily quilted, NM **$300.00**

Pieced, Log Cabin, 68x70", earth shades & blue, sm frayed spot **$275.00**

Pieced, London Roads, 64x79", old calico, fan quilting, EX **$300.00**

Pieced, Lone Star, 69x81", 1930s, cotton prints & solids, feather quilting, machine bound, EX **$295.00**

Pieced, Lone Star, 71x72", 1935, multicolor prints & solids on white, shell quilting in corners, outline elsewhere, EX **$450.00**

Pieced, Lone Star, 72x80", red & white, red sawtooth border, EX quilting, EX.............................**$300.00**

Pieced, Lone Star, 84x94", 1930s, pastels & solids, peach binding, detailed quilting, M **$400.00**

Pieced, Maple Leaf, 72x88", 1940s, prints & solids, appliqued stems, EX quilting, NM **$325.00**

Pieced, Missouri Daisy, 68x80", 1930s, prints & solids, yellow border, EX quilting, unused, M **$300.00**

Pieced, Monkey Wrench, 68x84", 1920s, blue & white gingham w/chambray, EX quilting, NM **$300.00**

Pieced, Nine Patch, 72x86", multicolor prints, ginghams & solids, green border, hand sewn, EX quilting, lightweight.............................**$135.00**

Pieced, Ocean Wave, 68x84", blue & white, EX quilting, unused **$400.00**

Pieced, Open Windows, full size, red, blue & green, EX quilting, EX.............................**$300.00**

Pieced, patchwork, full size, 1930s, multicolor prints on white, fine quilting, EX.............................**$225.00**

Pieced, Pineapple, 86x106", 1976, green, blue & cream w/contrasting detailed quilting, NM **$450.00**

Pieced, Pinwheel, 66x74", blue ginghams on white background, EX **$425.00**

Pieced, Pinwheel, 68x84", 1930s, red, white & blue cottons, red & blue border, machine-sewn binding, EX ..**$300.00**

Pieced, Pinwheel, 74x86", 1920s multicolor ginghams, dark & light blocks alternate, unused **$300.00**

Pieced, Radiating Star, indigo sprigged cotton on wht, fine princess feather quilting, zigzag border, 1875 ....$800.00

Pieced, Rising Star, 69x82", 1958, red, white & blue, outline quilting, NM **$325.00**

Pieced, Rising Stars, 78x95", 1940s, multicolor stars on white, medallion & leaf quilting, EX.................**$350.00**

Pieced, Sawtooth, ca 1933, pink & white, fine detailed quilting, EX.............................**$750.00**

Pieced, Sawtooth, 78x80", ca 1940, blue & white, diamond & tulip quilting, EX.............................**$900.00**

Pieced, Schoolhouse, full size, 1940s, red, white & blue, unused.............................**$625.00**

Pieced, Smoothing Iron, 60x76", pumpkin & reds, fair quilting, EX.............................**$250.00**

Pieced, Snail's Trail, 66x72", 1930, lavender & bleached muslin, machine-sewn binding, EX **$285.00**

Pieced, Snowball, 62x80", 1930s, prints & solids, yellow border, EX.............................**$235.00**

Pieced, Spider Web, 74x88", 1930s, multicolor prints on white, EX quilting, EX **$325.00**

Pieced, Star, queen size, blues & browns, machine sewn in 8" blocks, lightweight **$125.00**

Pieced, Stars, 74x76", 25 stars in colored stripes on gray-green calico, EX.............................**$325.00**

Pieced, Sunbonnet Sue, 68x92", ca 1910, fine quilting, EX **$350.00**

Pieced, Sunbonnet Sue, 76x98", 1930s, pastel prints & solids, med green border, fine quilting, NM.................**$425.00**

Pieced, Sunburst, 84x94", 1930s, prints & solids form rays, close quilting, unused...**$325.00**

Pieced, Texas Stars, 66x82", 1930s, black, wine, blue & multicolored prints on white, scalloped edge, M......**$275.00**

Pieced, Turkey Tracks Variation, 72x98", 1964, red & white, straight line & medallion quilting, NM **$850.00**

Pieced, Union Star, 76x80", 1930s, prints & ginghams, red sashing, heart quilting, NM **$300.00**

Pieced, Wedding Ring, 66x80", 1930s, pastels & prints, pink binding, EX quilting, NM......................................**$300.00**

Pieced, Wedding Ring, 72x90", peach & white, scalloped border, white binding, unused **$300.00**

Pieced, Wedding Ring, 72x90", 1930s, pink & lavender prints, unused **$300.00**

Pieced, Windmill, 72x82", 1940s, pastel prints & solids, hand sewn, EX quilting, NM..**$225.00**

Pieced, Yo-Yo, 88x88", 1930s, unlined, EX...............**$185.00**

Pieced, 4-Point Star, 76x88", red & blue on white, hand sewn, recent, M...**$300.00**

Pieced, 9-Patch variation, 72x84", red, black & white ginghams, EX quilting, EX..**$350.00**

Pieced & appliqued, Dahlia, 78x88", 1950s, multicolor stars on white, yellow border, EX quilting, EX **$200.00**

Pieced & appliqued, Fancy Dresden Plate, 1933, blue & pastels on white, scalloped edge, EX........................**$125.00**

Pieced & embroidered, Basket of Tulips, 80x82", ca 1930s, blue & white w/multicolor flower baskets, green border, EX...**$350.00**

Pieced & embroidered, birds, 81x81", 1930s, bright embroidered birds on white w/green lattice 'frames,' EX quilting, EX...**$900.00**

Quimper

This is a type of enamel-glazed earthenware that has been made in Quimper, France, since the 1600s. They still operate there today, so some of their production falls into the time period we're interested in. Since its inception, the company has undergone several management and name changes, and since 1983 it has been owned by Americans.

Most of the ware you'll see is decorated by hand with colorful depictions of peasant men and women on a yellowware background. Besides dinnerware, they also made vases, figurines, tiles, and bookends.

If you'd like to learn more about the subject, we recommend *Quimper Pottery: A French Folk Art Faience* by Sandra V. Bondhus.

Ashtray, shell, Breton man & flowers, scalloped, footed, marked HR **$32.00**

Bowl, 3¼x9½", Panier aux Fleurs (flower basket), marked HBQ, EX **$50.00**

Bowl, 7½", peasant man, 6-sided, HBQ **$90.00**

Butter pat, Eskimos on green ground, scalloped, HR .**$30.00**

Candle holder, 8¾", Deco-style figure w/polka dots & stripes, HBQF...**$98.00**

Cup & saucer, Breton lady w/floral garland, trefoil shape, marked AP...**$130.00**

Dinner bell, 4", lg blue rose & red buds, unmarked ...**$25.00**

Inkwell, peasant man & geometrics, blue, square, marked, HR..**$145.00**

Nut dish, 4x5½", Breton man, trefoil form, handled, marked HQ **$80.00**

Pitcher, 5", man w/pipe, 4-lobed, marked HBQ..........**$95.00**

Pitcher, 8x7", Deco portrait, w/blue & black bands, marked HBQ **$55.00**

Plate, 6", peasant man & lady on yellow, HB.............**$30.00**

Plate, 8", exotic bird on branch, multicolored, marked HQ, restored...**$25.00**

Plate, 9½", multicolored floral pattern w/multicolored banded rim...**$125.00**

Porringer, 7", Breton lady, HRQ...................................**$32.00**

Salt cellar, 3½x3½", man & lady, double swan form, marked HQF **$50.00**

Teacup & saucer, 2½", man w/walking stick & pipe, marked HBQ..**$55.00**

Teapot, 8", Breton lady, marked Henriot............$235.00

Tile, 6¼", Breton man, unglazed bottom cuff, marked QF/Macy star...**$110.00**

Tureen, 5¼x8", child size, multicolored flowers, marked HBQ **$75.00**

Vase, 6½x6", Deco-style lady, jug form, HBQ **$115.00**

Vase, 8½", Breton man's portrait, bulbous form, artist signed, marked HBQ...**$145.00**

Wall pocket, 10¾", Breton lady, cornucopia shape, marked HQF **$135.00**

Radios

Vintage radios are those made from 1920 through the fifties. The most desirable and those whose values have been increasing the most consistently are the streamlined Deco styles, novelties, and of course the harder-to-find sets.

But experts tell us that as the older sets become more scarce and expensive, even some transistors are beginning to attract radio collectors.

There are several basic types: 1) breadboard – having exposed tubes and other components that are simply attached to a rectangular board; 2) cathedral – vertical shape with a rounded or peaked top; 3) console – floor model consisting of a cabinet on legs or a tall rectangular case; 4) portable – smaller set made to be used at any location; 5) table – general term referring to sets of all shapes and sizes designed to be used atop a table; 6) novelty – having an unusual case such as a bottle or a camera, or one depicting a well-known character.

The primary factor to consider when evaluating a radio is condition. Whether or not it plays, be sure that all parts are present. Cabinet condition is important as well, and even though it is unrealistic not to expect a few nicks and scratches, be sure there are no cracks, chips, or other highly visible signs of damage. These are the criteria our evaluations are based on.

If you'd like to learn more, we recommend *The Collector's Guide to Antique Radios, Vols 1 and 2*, and *Collector's Guide to Transistor Radios*, all by Sue and Marty Bunis. Also refer to *Collecting Transistor Novelty Radios, A Value Guide*, by Robert F. Breed.

Admiral, #218, portable w/leatherette case, metal perforated grill w/logo, right front dial, 2 knobs, 1958 .... **$40.00**

Admiral, #4207-A10, walnut console w/double doors, pull-out phonograph, front dial, AC, 1941 .... **$125.00**

Admiral, #4922, red portable transister, perforated grill w/right dial, thumbwheel knob, AM, 1957 .... **$40.00**

Admiral, #5J21, plastic table model, left horizontal openings w/right trapezoid dial, 2 knobs, AC/DC, 1951 ...... **$40.00**

Admiral, #6C22AN, plastic table model w/lg center gold dial over cloth grill, center knob, footed, 1954 .... **$45.00**

Admiral, #6T06, wooden table model, grill w/circular cutouts, slide rule dial, 2 knobs, battery, 1946 ...... **$45.00**

Admiral, #7T01C-N, plastic table model w/upper horizontal louvers & lower slide rule dial, 2 knobs, 1948 ..... **$35.00**

Admiral, #7T10E-N, plastic, right front square dial, left horizontal louvers, 2 knobs, BC, AD/DC, 1947 . $35.00

Admiral, #757, portable transistor w/tan leather case, lattice grill, right front dial, handle, battery, 1960 .... **$30.00**

Air Castle, #472.254, wood console w/double doors, pull-out phonograph, inner right slide rule dial, 4 knobs, AC, 1953 .... **$50.00**

Air Castle, #5050, table model, square cloth grill, right front dial, 2 knobs, AC/DC, 1948 .... **$30.00**

Air Castle, #9151-W, plastic table model, perforated center grill, alarm clark on left, half-moon dial, 1951 ...... **$30.00**

Airline, #GTM-1201A, portable transistor, lower round dial over horizontal bars, swing handle, AM, 1960 ...... **$25.00**

Airline, #25BR-1542A, plastic table model, upper lattice grill, lower slide rule dial, 4 knobs, AC/DC, 1953 .... **$45.00**

Airline, #25GSE-1555A, plastic table model, right front dial over lg woven grill w/logo, 2 knobs, 1952 .... **$30.00**

Airline, #74BR-1055A, portable, lower lattice grill w/upper slide rule dial, 2 knobs, AC/DC or battery, 1948 .. **$30.00**

Airline, #84WG-2506B, 2-tone wood console, cloth grill w/bars, slide rule dial, 4 knobs, FM, AC, 1949 ..... **$75.00**

American Bosch, #5A, wood table model, round grill w/cutouts, right window dial, 2 knobs, gold pin striping, AC, 1931 .... **$75.00**

American Bosch, #680, 2-tone wood console, lower cloth grill w/vertical bars, black dial, 5 knobs, 1934 ... **$150.00**

Arvin, #2598, leatherette portable transistor, horizontal grill bars, thumbwheel dial, AM, battery, 1959 .... **$35.00**

Arvin, #2598, portable transistor, lg center dial over horizontal grill bars, AM, battery, 1960 .... **$25.00**

Arvin, #522A, table model, ivory metal, midget size, left horizontal louvers, right front square dial, 2 knobs, AC, 1941 .... **$75.00**

Arvin, #60R23, red plastic portable transistor w/lg right round dial over vertical bars, 1960 .... **$25.00**

Arvin, #840T, metal table model, right round plastic dial knob over vertical bars, plastic knob, 1954 .... **$65.00**

Arvin, midget, right front dial, rounded corners, horizontal louvres, 2 knobs, BC, AC/DC, 1946 ...... $80.00

Automatic, #PTR-15B, portable transistor, leather case, lattice grill cutouts, right front dial knob, handle, 1958 .... **$25.00**

Automatic, #1975, wood table model, left horizontal wraparound louvers, right front slide rule dial, 3 knobs, 1935 .... **$50.00**

Belmont, #5D110, wood table model, inner phonograph, cloth grill, front slide rule dial, 2 knobs, ¾ lift top, AC, 1947 ....**$30.00**

Bendix, #0516A, plastic Deco table model, vertical louvers, upper slide rule dial, 2 knobs, AC/DC **$65.00**

Bendix, #115, ivory & burgundy plastic table model, wraparound grill bars, slide rule dial, 2 knobs, AC/DC, 1948 ....**$275.00**

Bendix, #55P3U, walnut plastic table model, wood-grained grill, slide rule dial, AC/DC, 1949 ....**$45.00**

Brunswick, #D-1000, wood console, pull-out phonograph, inner slide rule dial, 4 knobs, FM, AC, 1949 ......**$100.00**

Bulova, #120, plastic table model, step-down top, right front grill, left dial & clock, footed, AC **$40.00**

Bulova, #250, portable plastic transistor, lower perforated grill, upper right round dial, battery....................**$250.00**

Capehart, #75C56, table model, center front square alarm clock over recessed grill, dial knob on right side, AC, 1956 ....**$25.00**

Channel Master, #6509, red plastic portable transistor, center perforated grill, upper window dial, 1960.............**$35.00**

Channel Master, #6511, plastic transistor table model, left horizontal bars, slide rule dial, footed, 1960 ....**$40.00**

Clarion, #AC-60 Jr, Cathedral, walnut w/off-center window dial, upper scalloped cloth grill w/cutouts, 3 knobs, 1932...$175.00

Clarion, #C103, plastic table model, cloth grill w/horizontal bars, upper slide rule dial, 4 knobs, AC, 1946..**$40.00**

Continental, #C-45, plastic table model, right circular louvers, round center dial knob, alarm clock on left side, AC, 1957 ....**$30.00**

Continental, #TR-300, portable transistor, perforated grill, slide rule dial, thumbwheel knobs, AM, 1960.......**$25.00**

Coronado, #35RA4-43-9856A, portable, center front dial over crisscross grill, 2 knobs, handle, 1953, AC/DC/battery, 1953 ....**$30.00**

Coronado, #43-8354, plastic table model, cloth grill w/2 bars, slide rule dial, 2 knobs, 5 push buttons, AC/DC, 1947 ....**$45.00**

Crosley, #E-10BE, plastic table model, lg front dial w/center pointer & inner crisscross dial, 2 knobs, 1953 ......**$85.00**

Crosley, #E-90BK, plastic table model, left front grill, left alarm clock, right side dial knob, AC, 1953 ....**$30.00**

Crosley, #10-136E, plastic table model, center front dial w/inner perforated grill, 2 knobs, 1950..............**$100.00**

Crosley, #167, wood cathedral table model, upper grill w/cutouts, center window dial, 3 knobs, 5 tubes, AC, 1936 ....**$210.00**

Crosley, #25AY, walnut console, lower vertical grill bars, upper slanted dial, push buttons, broadcast/shortwave, 1940 ....**$135.00**

Crosley, #58TW, plastic table model, wraparound louvers, slide rule dial, 2 knobs, AC/DC, 1948 ....**$55.00**

Delco, #R-1251, wood console, left pull-out phonograph, lower grill w/cutouts, inner right dial, w/shortwave, 1947 ....**$80.00**

Delco, #1102, wood tombstone table model, upper grill w/vertical bars, center dial, 4 knobs, 1935..........**$110.00**

Detrola, #611-A, wood table model, 2 horizontal grill bars, right front dial, 4 knobs, rounded corners, 4 knobs, 1948.**$35.00**

Dewald, #E-520, plastic table model, horizontal louvers, upper front slide rule, w/shortwave, 1955 ....**$40.00**

Dewald, #L-703, portable transistor, leather case, front brick cutouts, handle, AM, battery, 1959.........................**$35.00**

Emerson, #AU-190, tombstone, Catalin, lower scalloped gold dial, 3 upper vertical sections, cloth-covered grill, 3 knobs, 1938........................$1,000.00

Emerson, #BL-200, plastic table model, left horizontal louvers, 2 knobs, decorative lines, AC, 1938..............**$55.00**

Emerson, #DM-331, 2-tone wood table model, 2-section grill w/vertical bars, right front dial, 3 knobs, 1939 .....**$40.00**

Emerson, #380, portable pocket-size, front vertical grill bars, slide rule dial & knobs, handle, battery, 1940.......**$45.00**

Emerson, #45, walnut tombstone table model, upper grill w/cutouts, airplane dial, 3 knobs, AC, 1934 ....**$100.00**

Emerson, #522, plastic table model, Deco grill, right front black dial, 2 knobs, footed, AC/DC, 1946.............**$50.00**

Emerson, #640, red plastic portable, flip-out front, horizontal louvers, inner slide rule dial, 2 knobs, 1950 ....**$45.00**

Emerson, #811, plastic table model, half-round dial over horizontal grill bars, side knob, footed, 1955........**$40.00**

Emerson, #852, green plastic series B table model, lg recessed checkered grill, lower left window dial, AC/DC, 1957....................**$30.00**

Emerson, #888, red plastic transistor Vanguard model, randomly patterned grill, upper dial, swing handle, AM, 1955 ....**$55.00**

Espy, #6613, wood table model, lower horizontal louvers, slanted slide rule dial, 4 knobs, AC/DC, 1947.......**$40.00**

Esquire, #65-4, plastic table model, left horizontal louvers, right half-moon dial, 2 knobs, AC/DC, 1947.........**$55.00**

Fada, #P111, plastic portable, lattice grill w/inner right round dial, flip-up front, AC/DC/battery, 1952 .....**$45.00**

Fada, #60W, plastic table model, left grill w/Deco cutouts, right square dial, 3 knobs, footed..........................**$85.00**

Fairbanks-Morse, #7014, wood Deco tombstone model, upper wrap-over vertical grill bars, lower front round dial, 1934 ....**$150.00**

Farnsworth, #BT-1010, wood table model, left horizontal louvers, right slide rule dial w/plastic escutcheon, 4 knobs **$50.00**

Farnsworth, #EK-264, wood console w/phonograph, crisscross dial, lift top w/dial & 3 knobs, AC, 1946 ....**$125.00**

Firestone, #4-A-163, plastic table model, left checkered grill, knob dial over patterned grill, AC/DC, 1957.........**$20.00**

Firestone, #4-A-26, plastic Newscaster table model, lower horizontal louvers, slanted slide rule dial, 1948....**$45.00**

Firestone, #4-C-36, portable transistor, horizontal front bars, thumbwheel dial, AM, battery, 1959 ....**$25.00**

Freed-Eisemann, #29-D, walnut table model, left grill w/horizontal bars, tuning eye, w/shortwave, 1937.........**$65.00**

Garod, #11FMP, wood console w/pull-out phonograph, slide rule dial, w/shortwave, FM, AC, 1948...........**$80.00**

General Electric, #K-126, lower grill w/cutouts, upper window dial, 6 legs, 12 tubes, shortwave, AC, 1933....................**$175.00**

General Electric, #P-791B, turquoise & white portable transister, left grill w/ cutouts, right dial, AM, 1960 ....**$30.00**

General Electric, #P-796A, blue leatherette portable w/front lattice grill, right knob dial, AM, battery, 1958......**$35.00**

General Electric, #T-129C, turquoise plastic table model, lattice grill, right dial, left knob, footed, 1959...........**$25.00**

General Electric, #203, wood table model, upper metal woven grill, lower black rectangular dial, 2 knobs, AC/DC, 1946....................**$45.00**

General Electric, #42 8, plastic table model, vertical front bars, raised center half-moon dial, 2 knobs, AC/DC, 1955 ....**$30.00**

General Electric, #50, plastic table model, left square clock, upper checkered grill, lower right dial, 1946........**$45.00**

General Electric, #515F, plastic, upper thumbwheel dial, left alarm clock, right vertical grill bars, BC, AC, 1951....................$25.00

General Electric, #54, plastic Deco table model, left round grill, horizontal bars, right slide rule dial, 1940.....**$85.00**

Gilfillan, #68048, wood console w/left pull-out phonograph, inner right slide rule dial, 4 knobs, AC, 1949........**$70.00**

Globe, #85, wood table model w/lg electric clock, right thumbwheel dial, thumbwheel knob, AC, 1948....**$65.00**

Hallicrafters, #5R60, mahogany plastic table model, right checkered grill, left front round dial, 2 knobs, footed, 1955 ....**$35.00**

Hoffman, #C-514, wood console w/phonograph, lift top, inner right slide rule dial, push buttons, 5 knobs, FM, AC, 1948 ....**$125.00**

Howard, #780, 2-tone wood table model, crisscross grill, slide rule dial, 6 knobs, shortwave, AC, 1941.......**$50.00**

Kadette, #5947, red plastic table model, Deco pocket-size Kadette Jr, grill cutouts, thumbwheel dial, 1933....................**$300.00**

Knight, #5H-605, plastic table model, upper square clock, right dial knob over horizontal bars, AC, 1951 .....**$45.00**

Lafayette, #FS-200, portable transistor, left perforated grill w/logo, thumbwheel dial, AM, battery, 1960........**$20.00**

Magnavox, #AM 23, plastic portable transistor, perforated grill, telescoping antenna, AM, battery, 1960 ....**$25.00**

Magnavox, #155B, Regency Symphony wood console w/phonograph, left lift top, inner dial, 5 knobs, push buttons, 1947....................**$95.00**

Majestic, #211, Whitehall wood console, Jacobean design, upper grill w/cutouts, quarter-round dial, 1932..**$175.00**

Mantola, #R-7543, plastic table model, left horizontal louvers, right square dial, 2 knobs, AC/DC, 1947......**$65.00**

Meck, #EF-730, plastic Deco table model, horizontal wraparound louvers, right 'sunrise' dial, 2 knobs, AC/DC, 1950....................**$65.00**

Motorola, #45P2, Pixie plastic portable, vertical grill bars, right metal dial plate, 2 thumbwheel knobs, handle, 1956 ....**$40.00**

Motorola, #5T22Y, plastic table model, horizontal front grill bars, lg lower right dial, left knob, AC/DC, 1957..**$30.00**

Motorola, #68L11, plastic-coated cloth portable, dial moves inside handle, 4 thumbwheel knobs on each corner, 1948 ....**$70.00**

Motorola, #76T2, brown portable transistor, lg metal perforated grill, right dial, left knob, AM, 1957 ....**$35.00**

Olympia, #6-606-A, luggage-style portable w/plastic escutcheon grill, slide-rule dial, 2 knobs, AC/DC, battery, 1947 ....**$35.00**

Olympic, #FM-15, plastic table model, trapezoid case w/slide rule dial over checkered grill, 3 knobs, AM/FM, 1960 ....**$25.00**

Packard-Bell, #5R, plastic table model, dial numerals over lg checkered grill area, 2 knobs, AC/DC, 1957 ....**$35.00**

Packard-Bell, #551, plastic table model, lower vertical grill bars, upper curved slide-rule dial, AC, 1946.........**$65.00**

Philco, #F-673-124, portable, leather case, metal perforated grill, right half-moon dial, left side knob, 1957.....**$25.00**

Philco, #37-62, 2-tone wood, right front round dial, left cloth grill w/Deco cutouts, 3 knobs, 1937 ......$75.00

Philco, #49-503, plastic Transitone table model, modern checkerboard grill design, curved sides, 2 knobs, AC/DC, 1949...**$75.00**

Philco, #52-544-I, plastic Transitone table model, horizontal grill bars, left clock below thumbwheel dial, 1952 ....**$45.00**

Raytheon, #8TP4, red leatherette portable transistor w/metal perforated grill, top knobs, AM, battery, 1955 ....**$140.00**

RCA, #BX6, leatherette & aluminum portable Globe Trotter slide rule dial, 2 thumbwheel knobs, 1950 ....**$40.00**

RCA, #128, wood tombstone table model w/shouldered rounded top, grill cutouts above front round dial, 1934 ....**$275.00**

RCA, #5X, wood table model, top louvers, center dial, 3 knobs, finished front & back, rounded sides, footed, AC, 1936 ....**$100.00**

RCA, #6-X-7, plastic table model, right front dial over lattice grill, left Nipper logo, footed, AC/DC, 1956.........**$25.00**

RCA, #66X12, ivory plastic table model, rectangular grill cutouts below slanted slide rule dial, 3 knobs, AC/DC, 1947 ....**$50.00**

RCA, #96-X-1, plastic Deco table model, left side curved w/wraparound louvers, right dial, raised top, 3 knobs, 1939 ....**$175.00**

Remler, #54, plastic table model, 'Venetian blind' louvered grill, right front dial, 2 knobs, 5 tubes, AC, 1938..**$55.00**

Roland, #10TF-1, wood table model, upper grill, lower front slide rule dial, 4 knobs, AM/FM, AC, 1954............**$25.00**

Sentinel, #1U-363, plastic table model, center front recessed horizontal grill bars, right side dial, AC/DC, 1956 .**$25.00**

Silvertone, #1, brown metal table model, horizontal grill bars, right round ivory-colored dial, 2 knobs, AC/DC, 1950 ....**$75.00**

Silvertone, #101.585, wood table model, rounded base, grill 'X' cutouts, step-down top, & 4 push buttons **$130.00**

Silvertone, #1660, cathedral, wood, window dial w/escutcheon, upper grill w/cutouts, 5 tubes, 3 knobs...**$185.00**

Silvertone, #2005, red plastic table model, checkerboard grill, slide rule dial, 2 knobs, AC/DC, 1953...........**$30.00**

Sonora, #WAU-243, plastic Deco table model, lg round dial on top, 4 push buttons, AC/DC, 1947 ....**$125.00**

Sony, #TR-63, plastic portable transistor, lower perforated grill, left front dial, AM, battery, 1958.................**$150.00**

Sparton, #132, dark red plastic table model w/footed oval case, metal perforated grill, half-moon dial, 2 knobs, 1950 ....**$60.00**

Sparton, #141XX, wood table model, lg upper grill, lower front slide rule dial, 4 knobs, AM/FM, AC, 1951...**$40.00**

Stewart-Warner, #07-51H, plastic streamline table model w/ wraparound louvers, right front dial, 1940............**$85.00**

Stewart-Warner, #9001-F, wood end table model, fold-down front, 4-legged base, inner slide rule dial, push buttons, 1946 ....**$135.00**

Stewart-Warner, #91-513, wood table model, triangular case, grills on all 4 sides, slide rule dial, push buttons, 1938 ....**$185.00**

Stromberg-Carlson, #1105, cloth-covered portable, Deco grill design, window dial, 2 knobs, handle, AC/DC/battery, 1947 ....**$45.00**

Stromberg-Carlson, plastic table model, center checkered pane, left alarm clock, right front dial, AC, 1951 ..**$40.00**

Tele-Tone, #206, plastic table model, upper vertical grill, lower slide rule dial, 2 knobs, AM/FM, AC, 1951 .**$30.00**

Toshiba, #8TM-294, portable transistor, lg front lattice grill, top wrap-over dial, side knobs, AM, battery.........**$50.00**

Trav-Ler, #5008, 2-tone wood table model, lower cloth grill, slanted slide rule dial, 3 knobs, AC/DC, 1946.......**$40.00**

Trav-Ler, #5028-A, portable, 'snakeskin' case, left plastic grill bars, right dial, 3 knobs, AC/DC/battery, 1947 .....**$45.00**

Trav-Ler, plastic table model, 'steering wheel' dial over recessed horizontal bars, AC/DC, 1959 ....**$40.00**

Truetone, #DC2980A, plastic table model, left lattice grill, right center front round dial, AC/DC, 1959...........**$15.00**

Truetone, #D2624, wood table model, metal crisscross grill, upper slide rule dial, 3 knobs, w/shortwave, AC/DC, 1946 ....**$40.00**

Westinghouse, #H-188, plastic table model, Oriental design, left grill w/cutouts, right dial, AC/DC, 1948..........**$80.00**

Westinghouse, #H-503T5A, plastic table model, right front knob dial, plaid metal perforated grill, AC/DC.....**$30.00**

Westinghouse, #H769P7A, portable transistor w/leather case, left checkered grill, right round dial, 1960 ....**$25.00**

Westinghouse, #WR-368, wood console, vertical grill, slide rule dial, push buttons, tuning eye, 4 knobs, 10 tubes, 1938 ....**$165.00**

Zenith, #M510-R, plastic table model, oblong case, checkered grill, right round dial, left volume control, AC/DC, 1955 ....**$40.00**

Zenith, #Royal 500D, plastic portable transistor, lower round grill, upper 'owl-eye' knobs, AM, 1959................**$60.00**

Zenith, #5-R-312, plastic table model, rounded raised left side w/horizontal louvers, right dial, knobs, push buttons **$150.00**

Zenith, #7-S-635, wood table model, wraparound grill w/horizontal bars, black dial, 2 knobs, push buttons, 1942 ....**$75.00**

Novelty

A Team, 5x4¾", white plastic w/red label featuring BA Baracus, 1983 Cannell Productions, Hong Kong..........**$25.00**

Cabbage Patch Girl, 5½x6¼", girl w/headset leaning on pillow, green base, Playtime Products 1985..............**$25.00**

Charlie the Tuna, 3¼x5¼", clamps onto bicycle handlebars, Starkist, Hong Kong, 1973 ....$50.00

Cookie, 1¾x6" dia, bite taken from Oreo-type cookie w/Amico in raised letters in center, strap handle.**$30.00**

Elvis Presley, 10x5", figure in white w/gold trim, holding mike, on lettered base, from memorial series.......**$50.00**

Fire Chief Volkswagen Bug, 4x6", red & white plastic w/red light & siren, light tunes radio, Hong Kong **$35.00**

Fred Flinstone, 6½x7", outlined head, marked TM Columbia Pictures, 1972 Hanna Barbera, Hong Kong...........**$40.00**

Gas pump, 9½x3⅛" dia, red plastic 1930s style, Standard Oil, AM/FM, distributed by Synanon, made in China...**$25.00**

Globe, 5⅝x8½", wood Old World type w/knobs on footed base..**$30.00**

Holly Hobbie, 7½x4" dia, Holly Hobbie in rocking chair, round base w/controls, American Greetings Corp .**$40.00**

Horse w/saddle, metal, Abbotwares #Z477.........$285.00

Hot dog w/mustard, 2½x8¼", strap handle, box reads Hot & Spicy Sound, distributed by Amico, Hong Kong ..**$35.00**

Ice cream cone, 7", pink ice cream in pointed cone w/thumbwheel controls, distributed by Amico 1977, Hong Kong..**$35.00**

John Lennon, 10x5", figure holding mike on lettered base, from memorial series, Hong Kong.........................**$35.00**

John Wayne, 10x5", figure in cowboy hat & clothing on lettered base, from memorial series, Hong Kong **$50.00**

Jukebox featuring the Fonz, 6x4½", plastic dome top w/2 knobs, 1977 Paramount Pictures, Hong Kong **$30.00**

Knight 2000 car, 2½x9½", black Trans Am, based on the Knight Rider TV series, distributed by Royal Condor 1984 ....**$25.00**

Life preserver, 10½" dia, clock radio model #BCR 1300, distributed by Aimor Corp, made in Japan **$30.00**

Little Sprout (Green Giant's son), 8¼x4⅜", green plastic 2-D figure outlined in black, white eyes, Hong Kong.**$45.00**

Locomotive (The General), 7x9¼", blue & orange plastic, made in Japan, distributed by General Electric.....**$35.00**

Marlboro cigarette soft pack, 4⅛x2½", strap handle....**$35.00**

Michael Jackson, 5¾x2¾", red rectangular case w/paper decal of Michael & signature, 1984 MJ Products ..**$20.00**

Mickey Mouse, 5½x6", Mickey's head in 2-D resting on chin & nose, distributed by Philgee International, ...**$50.00**

Mickey Mouse, 7¾x7½", Mickey figural w/'pie eyes' (against yellow case) pointing at red numbers **$40.00**

Model T (ca 1912), 6x9¾", Japanese metal body, plastic trim, controls in rumble seat, distributed by Waco **$45.00**

Mork's Eggship, Concept 2000, AM, 1970s, MIB.........**$35.00**

Parkay Margarine, 4½x4½", 1-lb box of margarine sticks from Kraft, strap handle, Hong Kong **$35.00**

Pinocchio, 6¾x6", head in 2-D, Hong Kong **$50.00**

Playing cards, 3½x2½", features King of Hearts & Ace of Spades, marked Golden Sky Playing Card Radio..**$20.00**

Popeye, 6½x7", head in 2-D, w/pipe, King Features Syndicate, distributed by Philgee International **$45.00**

Raggedy Ann & Andy, 4x4¾", heart-shaped 2-D case w/paper decal, 1974, Bobbs Merrill Co **$25.00**

Riverboat (the Mark Twain), 7¼x12", plastic hull w/metal trim, knobs on top deck, made in Japan...............**$45.00**

Rolls Royce (ca 1912), 5x9", plastic w/convertible roof, license plate #SD8451, Hong Kong........................**$35.00**

Sesame Street, 6x6", features Bert in tub w/yellow duck, Sesame Street logo on side of tub, Muppets Inc...**$45.00**

Snoopy, 6½x5", 2-D sitting Snoopy in black outline, 1958-74 United Features Syndicate, Hong Kong.................**$20.00**

Spiderman, 5¼x3¼", head form, thumbwheel controls, 1978 by Marvel Comics Group, distributed by Amico...**$45.00**

Stage Coach (Overland Stage Express), 5x7¼", brown plastic w/gold & red details, US Mail on metal **$50.00**

Thunderbird car (ca 1965), 3x8", model #NT-11, marked Philco Corp Division Ford Motor Co, made in Hong Kong **$45.00**

Tony the Tiger, 7x4", green & orange plastic 2-D figure on base lettered Tony, #993394, Hong Kong **$35.00**

Tune-A-Frog, 4½x6¾", green plastic w/white stomach, resting on side...**$18.00**

TWA 747 jet, 12½" wing span, 13" long, white plastic w/red & gray, distributed through Windsor, made in Hong Kong **$45.00**

Railroad Collectibles

Prices continue to rise as this hobby gains in popularity. It is estimated that almost two hundred different railway companies once operated in this country, so to try to collect just one item representative of each would be a real challenge. Supply and demand is the rule governing all pricing, so naturally an item with a mark from a long-defunct, less-prominent railroad generally carries the higher price tag.

Railroadiana is basically divided into two main categories, paper and hardware, with both having many subdivisions. Some collectors tend to specialize in only one area – locks, lanterns, ticket punches, dinnerware, or timetables, for example. Many times estate sales and garage sales are good sources for finding these items, since retired railroad employees often kept such memorabilia as keepsakes. Because many of these items are very unique, you need to

get to know as much as possible about railroad artifacts in order to be able to recognize and evaluate a good piece. For more information, we recommend *Railroad Collectibles, 4th Edition,* by Stanley L. Baker.

Airhorn, diesel; Westinghouse, 1-chime, steel, EX **$115.00**

Badge, breast; Pennsylvania RR Police, pie-plate style w/state seal, EX..**$150.00**

Badge, cap; 1¾x3", Amtrak Assistant Conductor, black lettering w/red & blue logo on gold finish...................**$28.00**

Badge, cap; 1x3", Long Island, silver w/black LIRR lettered over Conductor, older style, VG **$65.00**

Badge, 1¼x4", Great Northern Railway Conductor, nickel finish, curved top **$65.00**

Badge, 1⅛x3⅝", Boston & Maine Trainman, nickel finish, curved top **$40.00**

Badge, 1x3⅞", Lackawanna Railroad Baggageman embossed on silver pebbled finish...................................**$45.00**

Baggage check, 1½x2½", Baltimore & Ohio Local 39590, B&O capitol dome logo......................................**$45.00**

Bell box, 6½x5", dovetailed, original paint, EX **$45.00**

Blotter, 4x9", Great Northern, Indian Chief Little Plume at left, schedules in green on tan, dated 3-31 ....**$12.00**

Book, 9½x4", Chicago Burlington & Quincy Freight-Car Diagrams, 1956, EX..**$40.00**

Button, sm, Quebec Central Railway, gold-tone **$6.00**

Calendar, on slanted 3½x6¼" wooden base, Missouri Kansas & Texas Railway, EX.......................................**$10.00**

Clothes hanger, Pullman, wood, both sides marked Pullman Travel & Sleep in Safety & Comfort.....................**$22.00**

Compass, 1⅛", Missouri Pacific, copper-looking metal w/loop for chain, NM...**$22.50**

Directory, Wells Fargo Express Official, 1916, 304 pages, EX **$115.00**

Headrest cover, Santa Fe, blue on brown cloth, cross logo, EX **$15.00**

Insulator, 4x3", Baltimore & Ohio, aqua **$10.00**

Key, coach; 3½", Pennsylvania RR, brass, Marked PRR 31, some wear..**$20.00**

Key, switch; Boston & Maine, brass, marked B&MRR, S & 26486 on reverse, minor wear..............................**$24.00**

Key, switch; Delaware & Hudson, brass, marked D&H, FRAIM on reverse, minor wear **$28.00**

Key, switch; L&NRR, Slaymaker, worn......................**$18.00**

Lamp, berth; Pullman, aluminum w/milk glass shade, 1950s, EX..**$50.00**

Lamp, caboose; 16", Southern Pacific Co, wall type, worn silver paint, some pitting, G **$20.00**

Lamp, inspector's; Southern Pacific Co, Dietz Acme, glass reflector, sm dents, VG..**$40.00**

Lamp, marker; 14", Pennsylvania RR, Dressel, yellow w/1 red lens, oil font & burner......................................**$75.00**

Lantern, Boston & Maine, Adlake Reliable, 5⅜" clear globe, cast B&MRR, top marked B&M **$95.00**

Lantern, Chesapeake & Ohio, Adlake, marked clear cast globe, single wire guard, insert pot, solid frame ..**$80.00**

Lantern, New York Central, Dietz #6, 5⅞" globe clear cast B&A, top marked New York Central...................**$125.00**

Lantern, Pennsylvania RR, Casey, clear globe, extended base, single wire guard......................................**$60.00**

Lighter, Santa Fe, Chico Indian boy holding logo, Santa Fe All the Way, blue on chromium, Zippo................**$20.00**

Lock, signal; Baltimore & Ohio, steel, sm, early, EX...**$15.00**

Lock, signal; Union Pacific, Eagle, brass, round shape, w/chain & key, NM.....................................**$50.00**

Lock, signal; 3½x2½", Rutland RR, Yale, shackle marked RRR Co, no key...**$65.00**

Lock, switch; Missouri Pacific, brass, heart-shaped, raised letters **$90.00**

Lock, switch; Pennsylvania RR, steel, sm letters **$15.00**

Lock, switch; StP&P RR, brass heart shape w/cast & stamped letters, Union Brass Co, 1870s, rare .$300.00

Matchbook, depicts Pennsylvania Railroad's 100 Year emblem, 1846-1946, gold on maroon.....................**$3.00**

Oil can, Eagle, for bench use, NM.............................**$22.00**

Paperweight, Chicago Union Station, glass, 1918, EX.**$24.00**

Pass, annual; L&N RR, 1917 ....**$10.00**

Pass, employee trip; Missouri Pacific, 1899............$8.50

Pin, lapel; Brotherhood of Railroad Trainmen, 20-yr, 10k gold.**$10.00**

Pin-back button, 1¼" wide, Spokane Portland & Seattle Railway, oval, red & white logo on tin, EX...................**$6.00**

Playing cards, Missouri Pacific RR, depicts diesel train, full deck w/1948 score pad, MIB **$22.00**

Poster, 40x30", Pennsylvania RR, litho, Washington the City Beautiful, buildings, people, trees & locomotive, ca 1930s...**$60.00**

Rubber stamp, Half Fare...**$3.00**

Rubber stamp, 3¾", stamps Chicago, Burlington & Quincy Railroad Company.................................**$18.00**

Ruler, 6", Alton & Southern RR, aluminum w/black lettering, reverse has 1937 calendar months, scarce............**$12.00**

Scratch pad & holder, 5x7", 9x5½", Burlington Northern logo, white plastic holder w/green lettering, M....**$10.00**

Sewing kit, 2¾x2¾", Union Pacific souvenir, NM........**$15.00**

Sign, 3¼x21", passenger coach entrance, Watch Your Step in white lettering on black................................**$40.00**

Spittoon, 3x8" dia, Pullman, nickel-plated brass, bottom marked..**$90.00**

Stationery, envelope; 5x11½", goat logo above Great Northern Railway Co **$4.00**

Stationery, sheet; 11x8½", Chicago, Rock Island & Pacific Railroad Company in black lettering.....................**$1.50**

Stepbox, Texas & Pacific, Morton, VG original paint.**$175.00**

Tallow pot, 5x5x7¼", Atchison Topeka & Santa Fe Railway, teapot style, goose-neck spout, screw filler cap ...**$33.00**

Ticket dater, imprints Great Northern Railway, Pekin ND, Hill's Model A Centennial, dates 1946-1957.......**$130.00**

Ticket punch, Chicago Great Western, punches 'L,' diagonal spring w/finger loop handle, LO Crocker, E Braintree, Mass **$35.00**

Timetable, employee; Boston & Maine, April 25, 1948, #46, G **$10.00**

Timetable, public; Atlantic Coast Line, April 26, 1964 ...**$8.00**

Timetable, public; Baltimore & Ohio, Nov 1927, EX.....**$7.50**

Timetable, public; Missouri Pacific Lines, January 15, 1939, black & white trains on black cover w/red logo ..**$18.00**

Token, Union Pacific, Pullman & Alcoa, Lucky Piece, aluminum, 1934, M **$3.50**

Torch, 7x4½", Chicago Milwaukee & St Paul, teapot style w/front spout, grip handle, screw-on filler cap **$40.00**

Towel, Reading RR, blue stripe on white cloth, EX.....**$12.50**

Watch fob, Canadian National, brass, hinged, 2-piece **$60.00**

Wax sealer, For Public Use, Arkansas, EX...................**$60.00**

Dining Car Collectibles

Ashtray, round, Chesapeake & Ohio, Chessie in center, some wear **$65.00**

Ashtray, 3½x3½", Soo Line, glass, 2 corner rests, red & white logo on clear bottom **$15.00**

Ashtray, 5¼" dia, Southern Railway System, copper, Southern Serves the South impressed at border..........**$280.00**

Ashtray w/match stand, Canadian National, blue-green Rupert pattern, gold trim, 1923-29, M..................**$125.00**

Bowl, baker; 4x6", Baltimore & Ohio, Derby pattern, bottom stamped **$38.00**

Bowl, berry; Pennsylvania RR, Purple Laurel pattern, bottom stamped **$45.00**

Bowl, bouillon; 7", Chateau Champlain pattern, w/saucer, M...**$25.00**

Bowl, fruit; 5¾" dia, Canadian National, Rupert pattern, some wear..**$18.00**

Bowl, ice cream; Canadian National, Quetico pattern.**$40.00**

Bowl, oatmeal; 5¼", Southern Railway, Peach Blossom pattern, no rim, G..**$100.00**

Bowl, soup; 7½", Milwaukee, pink Traveler pattern, dated 1945, EX...**$48.00**

Bowl, soup; 9", Union Pacific, Desert Flower pattern, bottom stamped...**$55.00**

Bowl, vegetable; 4½", Milwaukee, Peacock pattern, dated 1953, EX...**$42.00**

Bowl, vegetable; 5½", Norfolk & Western, Cavalier pattern, intertwined logo on top, EX............................**$40.00**

Bowl, 7" dia, Baltimore & Ohio, footed, Thomas Viaduct 1835, blue transfer, Shenango China $95.00

Butter pat, California Poppy pattern.............................**$40.00**

Butter pat, Pennsylvania RR, Purple Laurel pattern, bottom stamped..**$48.00**

Butter pat, 3¼", Burlington, Violets & Daisies, EX......**$35.00**

Celery dish, 9¾", Milwaukee, pink Traveler pattern, dated 1945, EX...**$48.00**

Cocktail, 4¼x2½" dia, Great Northern, side marked, frosted intertwined GN logo, knob stem..........................**$22.00**

Coffeepot, 14-oz, Burlington, silverplate, side mark....**$57.50**

Coffeepot, 6", Pennsylvania RR, International Silver, side marked PRR in keystone, G.................................**$110.00**

Cordial, 3¾", Northern Pacific Railway, Yellowstone Park logo...**$30.00**

Corn holders, Pullman, silverplate, bottom mark, pr...**$45.00**

Creamer, 3", Illinois Central, Shenango, handled......**$130.00**

Creamer, 3¼", Florida East Coast Railway, Sea Horse pattern, no handles, no bottom stamp............................**$30.00**

Creamer, 5", CB&QRR, silverplate, side marked BR (Burlington Route), VG...**$85.00**

Cup, bouillon; Burlington, Violets & Daisies pattern, bottom stamped CB&QRR, EX...............................**$85.00**

Cup & saucer, Canadian National, Ottawa logo w/maple leaf & box, NM..**$65.00**

Cup & saucer, demitasse; Norfolk & Western, Dogwood pattern, EX...**$60.00**

Egg cup, double; lg, Florida East Coast Railway, Mistic pattern...**$35.00**

Finger bowl, Great Northern, silverplate, pierced side, bottom stamped, 1946..**$45.00**

Fork, Atlantic Coastline, Zephyr pattern.....................**$12.00**

Fork, cocktail; Union Pacific, Zephyr pattern, VG.......**$12.00**

Gravy boat, Union Pacific, Blue & Gold pattern, no bottom stamp...**$30.00**

Knife, butter; Great Northern, Hutton pattern, top marked w/intertwined GN, VG................................**$20.00**

Knife, butter; Santa Fe, Cromwell pattern, VG............**$15.00**

Knife, fruit; Alaska RR, Greene-Winkler, 1917, EX......**$27.50**

Knife, Santa Fe, Albany pattern, M.............................**$18.00**

Menu, California Zephyr, 1950....................................**$12.00**

Menu, Union Pacific, Portland Rose, 1954....................**$25.00**

Mustard pot, 3", Chicago & Northwestern, silverplate, Flambeau pattern, w/lid, no back stamp...................**$52.00**

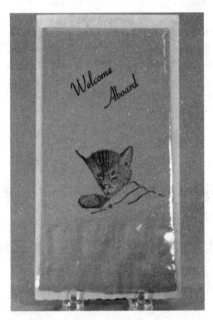

Napkin, Chessie on yellow, paper, M.....................$10.00

Napkin, 17x18", Amtrak, cloth, stamped letters, EX......**$5.00**

Napkin, 18x18", Milwaukee, white on white cloth w/center logo, EX...**$8.50**

Pitcher, 6½", Canadian Pacific, silverplate, Bows & Leaves pattern, bottom stamped.................................**$75.00**

Pitcher, 64-oz, Union Pacific, silverplate, winged ball finial, bottom stamped, EX...............................**$18.00**

Plate, bread & butter; 5½", Burlington Northern, Gold Key pattern, EX...**$20.00**

Plate, bread & butter; 5½", Great Northern, Monad pattern, top logo, EX...**$85.00**

Plate, bread & butter; 6", Great Northern, Glory of the West pattern, full backstamp, EX...............................**$75.00**

Plate, dinner; 9", Bangor & Aroostook, Aroostook pattern, some wear...**$25.00**

Plate, dinner; 9", Missouri Pacific, Eagle pattern, top marked, G...**$95.00**

Plate, dinner; 9¾", Burlington Northern, Gold Key pattern, VG...**$40.00**

Plate, luncheon; 8½", Missouri Pacific, Eagle pattern, top marked, G...**$55.00**

Plate, salad; Canadian Pacific, Green Band pattern, EX .**$25.00**

Plate, salad; 7¼", Great Northern, Mountains & Flowers pattern, backstamped Yellow Flowers, EX.................**$85.00**

Plate, salad; 7¼", Southern Pacific, Prairie Mountain Wildflower pattern, EX....................................**$75.00**

Plate, 5¾", Canadian Pacific, Tremblant pattern, EX ...**$30.00**

Plate, 6½", Canadian Pacific, Royal York pattern, kidney-shaped, EX **$12.00**

Plate, 9", Canadian Pacific, Maple Leaf pattern, EX.....**$45.00**

Platter, 11½", Bangor & Aroostook, Aroostook pattern, 1946, EX..**$35.00**

Platter, 8½x6", Pennsylvania, Broadway pattern, no bottom stamp **$45.00**

Relish dish, 7½x4", L&N RR, Green Leaf pattern, no bottom stamp **$32.00**

Sauce dish, 5½", Santa Fe, Mimbreno pattern, G.........**$40.00**

Sherbet, 2½x3¾" dia, no bottom stamp, Scammell......**$35.00**

Shot glass, 2½", Union Pacific, frosted shield logo & white stripe **$10.00**

Spoon, cheese; Union Pacific, Reed & Barton, bottom marked **$17.50**

Spoon, dessert; Canadian National, Puritan #114 pattern, VG..**$8.00**

Spoon, iced tea; California Zephyr, VG.....................**$15.00**

Spoon, serving; Burlington Rte, Belmont pattern, VG.**$18.00**

Spoon, soup; Canadian Pacific, Waverly #158 pattern, oval, worn...**$8.00**

Spoon, soup; Milwaukee, Ambassador pattern, bottom marked, M **$12.00**

Sugar bowl, Atlantic Coast, silverplate, w/lid, bottom marked..**$50.00**

Sugar bowl, New Haven RR, Reed & Barton, silver hollow ware, fluted, bottom marked NYNY&HRR...........**$45.00**

Sugar tongs, Union Pacific, Winged Streamliner pattern, top marked...**$20.00**

Tablecloth, 33x44", Rock Island, white linen, logo in center w/oak leaf design around border.........................**$35.00**

Tablecloth, 44x48", Canadian National, white w/maple leaf logo, EX **$10.00**

Teapot, Union Pacific, Winged Streamliner pattern, Clinton style, w/lid, M **$125.00**

Teapot, ½-pt, Canadian National, stainless steel, Hall, marked CN..**$8.00**

Teaspoon, Canadian & Pacific, Windsor #160 pattern, Canadian Pacific in belt logo w/flag, EX **$25.00**

Tumbler, juice; 3¾", Northern Pacific, side marked, black & red enamel Monad logo at top, ribbed bottom.....**$28.00**

Tumbler, water; 4", Santa Fe lettered in white on top & side, set of 4...**$20.00**

Tumbler, water; 5¼", New York Central, heavy base....**$8.00**

Tumbler, 5", Illinois Central, white diamond w/Illinois Central & white pin stripe around glass, EX...............**$24.00**

Razors

One of the factors that should be considered when determining the worth of an old straight razor is the handle material. Ivory is preferred over celluloid, and the more decorative, the better. Plain celluloid-handled razors, unless their blades are well marked, are really worth very little. But when embellished with an animal, a nude, an automobile, etc., they often go for prices in the $30 to $50 and up range. Other materials that were used to make handles were bone, buffalo horn, mother-of-pearl, wood, aluminum, and sterling silver.

After 1880, hollow-ground blades (concave in cross-section) took the place of the older, wedge-shaped blades. This will sometimes help you determine the age of your razor.

If you'd like to learn more about them, we recommend *Sargent's American Premium Guide to Knives and Razors, Identification and Values,* by Jim Sargent.

AJ Case's Shoo-Fly Union Cutlery, round point blade, tiger eye handle w/impressed 'Shoo-Fly,' rare, EX **$125.00**

Case, Ringleader, axe point blade, red & brown handle, rare, EX..**$150.00**

Case Brothers, square point blade, butter & molasses handle, EX **$125.00**

Case Brothers Cutlery, square point blade w/worked tang, cream-colored handle w/beaded border, EX......**$150.00**

Case Mfg, square point blade, inlaid black tang w/matching handle, EX..**$260.00**

Cattaraugus Cutlery, square point blade, blue handle w/white lines, EX **$25.00**

Clements, Sheffield, hollow ground blade, ivory handle, EX **$35.00**

Fair & Square, plain blade, faux ivory handle w/wrapped rope design, EX..**$27.50**

JBF Champlin & Sons, square point blade, streaky brown celluloid handle, EX..............................**$85.00**

Kane, hollow point blade, cream & rust rope twist handle, EX...**$40.00**

Kane, hollow point blade, worked tang, transparent red handle, EX..**$35.00**

Rogers, etched blade, black composition handle w/inlaid bird, Germany, EX.......................................**$40.00**

Standard Knife, square point blade, slick black handle, EX...**$100.00**

Warranted Cutlery, gold eagle etched in blade, horn handle, EX..**$22.50**

Western Bros, buffalo horn handle, marked Made in Germany...**$25.00**

Wm Greaves & Sons Sheaf Works, steel blade, bone handle, 1840s, EX **$35.00**

Yankee Cutlery, magnetized blade, bamboo pattern handle, EX...**$25.00**

Reamers

Reamers have been around since the mid-1700s. They've been made in silver, fine china, wood, pottery, and glass, in plain basic styles, patented models with hand-cranks, and as unusual figurals. Before soda pop became such a convenience, fruit juices were routinely served at social gatherings. Sunkist reamers were introduced around 1915 and until the sixties were turned out in hundreds of styles and color variations. Many other companies followed suit, and novelty reamers were imported from Japan and Germany as well. Then came the age of convenience foods and the demise of the reamer.

Today some of the rarer reamers are worth hundreds of dollars. We've listed some of those you're more apt to find here; but if you'd like to know more about them, we recommend that you read *Kitchen Glassware of the Depression Years* by Gene Florence.

Anchor Hocking Glass Co, clambroth green, pointed cone, tab handle **$115.00**
Anchor Hocking Glass Co, crystal 2-cup pitcher set w/ribbed design, ear-shaped handle, footed **$22.50**
Anchor Hocking Glass Co, transparent green 4-cup pitcher set, ear-shaped handle, footed..............................**$35.00**
Anchor Hocking Glass Co, Vitrock white, pointed cone, loop handle, footed **$20.00**
Cambridge, opaque Seville yellow, for grapefruit, straight-sided, squared loop handle..................................**$210.00**
Cambridge, sm, crystal, side tab handle, footed **$15.00**
Cambridge, transparent dark green, fancy handle.....**$125.00**
Cambridge, transparent green, straight-sided, pointed loop handle, footed **$200.00**
Federal Glass Co, green, pointed cone, tab handle.....**$15.00**
Federal Glass Co, pink, vertically ribbed, loop handle, footed..**$25.00**
Fenton, emerald green, straight-sided w/vertical panel design **$30.00**
Fleur-de-Lis, embossed on opaque white, straight-sided, loop handle **$85.00**
Foreign, transparent green octagon shape, vertically ribbed corners, round tab handle, marked Argentina **$150.00**
Foreign, transparent pink, flared vertically ribbed bowl w/pointed cone, straight base, tab handle, Czechoslovakia **$50.00**
Fry, rose pink, tall sides w/vertical 'finger' design, side tab handle, flat bottom..**$55.00**
Fry, translucent pearl, fluted sides, loop handle..........**$35.00**
Hazel Atlas Glass Co, crystal pitcher set, marked A&J & Pat Applied For, ear-shaped handle..............................**$20.00**
Hazel Atlas Glass Co, lg, cobalt blue, Crisscross design, loop handle, tall slightly bowed base **$250.00**
Hazel Atlas Glass Co, lg, transparent green, Crisscross design, loop handle, footed **$12.00**
Hazel Atlas Glass Co, white decorated 2-cup pitcher set, loop handle, footed **$35.00**
Hazel Atlas Glass Co, white 4-cup pitcher set w/decorative trim, ear-shaped handle, footed............................**$35.00**

Indiana Glass Co, crystal, panel design, tab handle....**$12.50**
Jeannette Glass Co, Delphite, swirled pointed cone, pointed loop handle, footed **$65.00**
Jeannette Glass Co, Jennyware, crystal, fluted boat shape, fancy loop handle, footed **$75.00**
Jeannette Glass Co, light Jadite 2-cup pitcher set, ear-shaped handle..**$20.00**
Jeannette Glass Co, transparent green bucket reamer, Hex Optic design, footed metal holder **$40.00**
Jeannette Glass Co, 5", transparent green, horizontally ribbed, side tab handle..**$15.00**
McKee, crystal, Glasbake, high sides w/vertical 'finger' design, tab handle, flat bottom **$125.00**
McKee, opaque Chalaine blue, embossed Sunkist, straight-sided, squared loop handle..............................**$175.00**
McKee, opaque ivory, embossed Sunkist, straight-sided, squared loop handle..**$150.00**
McKee, transparent pink, embossed Sunkist, squared loop handle..**$50.00**
McKee, white, embossed McK, pointed loop handle..**$20.00**
McKee, 5¼", opaque Skokie green, pointed cone, pointed loop handle, footed **$55.00**
Tufglas, crystal, smooth straight sides, slick handle **$75.00**
US Glass Co, dark transparent pink 2-cup pitcher set, thick ear-shaped handle, footed....................................**$40.00**
US Glass Co, transparent pink, smooth straight sides, slick handle..**$100.00**
US Glass Co, opaque white, smooth straight sides, slick handle..**$60.00**

Valencia, transparent pink, embossed letters, squared handle..$200.00
Westmoreland, transparent pink, embossed orange & lemon, ear-shaped handle, footed......................**$150.00**
Westmoreland, transparent pink, vertical panel design, fancy ear-shaped handle..**$85.00**

Records

Records are still plentiful at flea markets and some antique malls, though not to the degree they were a year or so ago. Garage sales are sometimes a great place to buy old records, since most of what you'll find there have been stored more carefully by their original owners.

There are two schools of thought concerning what is a collectible record. While some collectors prefer the rarities –

those made in limited quantities, by an unknown who later became famous, or those aimed at a specific segment of music lovers – others like the vintage Top-10 recordings. Now that they're so often being replaced with CDs, we realize that even though we take them for granted, the possibilty of their becoming a thing of the past may be reality tomorrow.

Whatever the slant your collection takes, learn to visually inspect records before you buy them. Condition is one of the most important factors to consider when assessing value. To be judged as mint, a record may have been played but must have no visual or audible deterioration – no loss of gloss to the finish, no stickers or writing on the label, no holes, no skips when it is played. If any of these are apparent, at best it is considered to be excellent and its value is at least 50% lower. Many of the records you'll find that seem to you to be in wonderful shape would be judged only very good, excellent at the most, by a knowledgeable dealer. Sleeves with no tape, stickers, tears, or obvious damage at best would be excellent; mint condition sleeves are impossible to find unless you've found old store stock.

It's not too uncommon to find old radio station discards. These records will say either 'Not for Sale' or 'Audition Copy' and may be worth more than their commercial counterparts.

If you'd like more information, we recommend *American Premium Record Guide* by L.R. Docks.

Records, 45 rpm

Abba, Take a Chance on Me, Atlantic 3457, EX............**$3.50**

Adams, Arthur; Can't Wait To See You, Chisa 8011, NM **$4.00**

Akers, Doris; Trouble, RCA 6987, EX............................**$4.50**

Alabama, Roll On, RCA 13716, EX................................**$3.00**

Alan, Buddy; Big Mama's Medicine Show, Capitol 4903, M **$4.00**

Alexander, Harold; Sandy's Love, Atlantic 3212, VG **$4.00**

Allen, Rex; Dodie Ann, Buena Vista 370, VG..................**$6.00**

Alpert, Dore; Fallout Shelter, Dot 16396, NM................**$6.00**

Ambrosia, No Big Deal, Warner Brothers 49590, NM....**$3.25**

Anderson, Bill; Something To Believe In, Decca 32077, EX..**$3.00**

Angel, Robin; I'll Be Loving You Forever, CBS 07105, NM **$3.25**

Anka, Paul; My Home Town, ABCP 10106, VG............**$7.50**

Anthony, Ray; Calypso Dance, Capitol 3646, VG **$5.00**

Armstrong, Louie; I Still Get Jealous, Kapp 597, VG **$5.00**

Atlanta Rhythm Section, It Must Be Love, Decca 33051, VG..**$3.00**

Bachelors, Punky's Dilemma, London 20051, w/dust jacket, VG..**$4.00**

Bailey, Pearl; My Man, Mercury 35, w/dust jacket, VG..**$7.50**

Baldwin, Bill; Who's Been Sleeping in My Bed, Epic 50836, w/dust jacket, M...**$3.25**

Barlow, Randy; Willow Run, Paid 110, EX....................**$3.00**

Bassey, Shirley; This Is My Life, UA 1303, VG **$4.00**

Bay City Rollers, Marlina, Arista A50149, in sleeve, VG **$4.00**

Beach Boys, Heroes & Villians, Brother 1001, VG........**$5.00**

Beatles, Long & Winding Road, Capitol 2832, M..........**$3.25**

Beckham, Bob; I Cry Like a Baby, Decca 31391, VG....**$3.00**

Bee Gees, Don't Wanna Live Inside Myself, Atco 6847, VG **$4.00**

Bellamy Brothers, Crossfire, Warner Brothers 8350, EX.**$3.00**

Bennett, Tony; Baby Dream Your Dream, Columbia 43508, EX..**$3.50**

Betts, Dickey; Nothing You Can Do, Arista 0255, EX....**$4.50**

Boone, Pat; New Lovers, Dot 16048, VG.......................**$5.00**

Bowan, Don; Little Leroy, RCA 9290, VG **$5.00**

Brothers Four, Slowly Slowly, Columbia 42391, EX **$5.50**

Bruno, Bruce; Hey Little One, Roulette 4386, VG **$15.00**

Burton, Jenny; You'll Never Come Again, Atlantic 89683, VG..**$2.50**

Campbell, Archie; Twelfth Rose, RCA 7757, VG...........**$4.00**

Caswell, Quentin; You'll Never Belong To Me, Jada 1213, EX..**$3.50**

Charles, Ray; Come Rain or Come Shine, Atlantic 2470, VG..**$7.50**

Chicago, Old Days, Columbia 10131, EX **$3.00**

Commodores, Wonderland, Motown 1479, EX..............**$3.00**

Corey, Jill; Should I Tell, Columbia 40188, EX..............**$4.50**

Crosby, Bing; Adeste Fideles, MCA 65021, EX..............**$3.00**

Dale, Kenny; Two Will Be One, Axbar 6058, M............**$3.25**

Damone, Vic; You're Just Another Pretty Face, Capitol 4947, M..**$3.25**

Darin, Bobby; Plain Jane, Atco 6133, VG......................**$3.00**

Dee, Lola; My Adobe Hacienda, Bally 1046, VG...........**$7.50**

Denver, John; What's on Your Mind, RCA 11535, EX ...**$3.00**

Detroit Road Runners, New Kind of Love, ABC 1117, VG.**$3.00**

Diamond, Neil; This Time, Columbia 08514, EX...........**$3.00**

Domino, Fats; Wait & See, Imperial 5467, EX..............**$13.50**

Dr Hook, Mountain Mary, Capitol 4785........................**$3.00**

Drennon, Eddie; Disco Jam, Casablanca 942, EX **$3.00**

Duncan, Johnny; Talkin' w/My Lady, Columbia 45917, w/dust jacket, EX...**$3.00**

Duran Duran, Is There Something I Should Know?, Capitol 5233, VG $2.50

Dylan, Bob; Tangled Up in Blue, Columbia 10106, VG .$9.00

Eagles, One of These Nights, Asylum 45077, NM..........$3.25

Earl, Robert; Boulevard of Broken Dreams, Columbia 41390, EX...$4.50

Earth, Wind & Fire; Shining Star, Columbia 33335, EX..$3.00

Eddy, Duane; Detour, Jamie 1117, VG $3.75

Elledge, Jimmy; Golden Tear, RCA 8081, VG.................$6.00

Ellington, Duke; Satin Doll, RCA 0337, M $3.25

Elliott, Shawn; Child Is Father to the Man, London 161, EX...$3.00

Emotions, Whole Lot of Shakin', Columbia 10828, EX..$3.00

Esquivel, That Ol' Black Magic, RCA 7316, NM $4.00

Exile, Hang on to Your Heart, Epic 05580, VG..............$2.50

Fargo, Donna; Don't Be Angry, Dot 17660, EX.............$3.00

Feliciano, Jose; I Want To Learn a Love Song, RCA 0140, VG...$3.00

Fender, Freddy; Squeeze Box, Starflite 4904, NM..........$3.25

Fifth Dimension, Love Like Ours, Bell 134, VG..............$2.50

Fisher, Eddie; Just One More Time, RCA 6071, EX........$3.50

Flack, Roberta; Will You Still Love Me Tomorrow, Atlantic 2851, VG $1.50

Floyd, Eddie; Somebody Touch Me, Malaco 1032, VG .$4.00

Forester Sisters, Mama's Never Seen Those Eyes, Warner Bros 21965, M...$3.25

Fountain, Pete; Honey-Wind, Coral 62427, VG..............$3.00

Four Preps, I'll Set My Love to Music, Capitol 5351, NM.$6.00

Francis, Connie; Don't Break the Heart That Loves You, MGM 13059, EX...$5.50

Franklin, Aretha; Jumpin' Jack Flash, Arista 9528, EX....$3.50

Fricks, Janie; Pride, Columbia 06509, NM $3.25

Gaines, Lenny; Banana Man, Columbia 44120, NM.......$3.25

Garfunkel, Art; So Much in Love, Columbia 07711, VG .$3.00

Gaye, Marvin; Take This Heart of Mine, Tamla 54132, M.$5.00

Gentry, Bobbie; Sweet Peony, Capitol 2295, EX...........$3.00

Gibson, Don; Look Who's Blue, RCA 7330, VG.............$5.00

Gilley, Mickey; Too Good To Stop Now, Epic 04563, EX.$3.00

Glaser, Jim; She's Free But She's Not Easy, MCA 40636, VG...$2.50

Goldsboro, Bobby; Black Fool's Gold, Epic 50535, EX.$3.00

Goodman, Al; Students March Song, RCA 0003, VG $3.00

Goulet, Robert; I'm Just Taking My Time, Columbia 42249, EX...$3.00

Grand Funk, Shinin' On, Capitol 3917, EX....................$3.00

Gray, Dobie; Loving Arms, MCA 40100, EX..................$3.50

Green, Larry; Bright Eyes, RCA 3214, NM $3.25

Greene, Jack; Your Favorite Fool, Decca 32352, EX......$3.00

Griffin, Ken; Ain't She Sweet, Columbia 40569, VG $2.50

Guitar, Bonnie; If You See My Love Dancing, Dot 15587, EX...$7.25

Hagar, Sammy; The Winner Takes It All, Columbia 06647, EX...$3.00

Hall & Oates, How Does It Feel To Be Back, RCA 12048, EX...$3.00

Hamilton, Roy; Ebb Tide, Epic 9068, VG $6.00

Harden, Arleen; I Could Almost Say Goodbye, Capitol 4014, VG...$4.00

Harris, Emmylou; Sweet Dreams, Reprise 1371, VG......$4.00

Harrison, George; Got My Mind Set on You, Dark Horse 28178, EX...$3.00

Hart, Freddie; I'd Like To Sleep Sleep Til I Get Over You, Capitol 4031, NM...$4.00

Hayes, Isaac; Rock Me Easy Baby, ABC 12176, EX $3.00

Heart, I Want You So Bad, Capitol 44116, VG...............$3.00

Helms, Bobby; I'm Drinking It Over, Black Rose 82710, NM $3.25

Henderson, Joe; The Searching Is Over, Todd 1079, EX.$5.50

Highway 101, Cry Cry Cry, Warner Brothers 28106, EX.$3.00

Hill, Jim; Old Circuit Rider, Decca 30312, VG...............$5.00

Hilltoppers, You Sure Look Good to Me, Dot 15712, VG .$7.50

Hirt, Al; Janine, RCA 7854, EX.....................................$3.50

Hodge, Chris; We're on Our Way, Apple 1850, EX.......$7.25

Hollies, Long Dark Road, Epic 10920, VG.....................$4.00

Honeycombs, Have I The Right, Interphon 7707, VG...$6.00

Horne, Lena; Come On Strong, RCA 8092, EX...............$5.50

Horton, Jimmy; North to Alaska, Columbia 41782, VG .$5.00

Howard, Bill; I Rode Into Reno, Decca 32172, VG........$4.00

Humperdinck, Engelbert; I Believe in Miracles, Epic 50365, EX...$3.00

Hunter, Ivory Joe; Since I Met You Baby, Atlantic 1111, VG...$6.00

Husky, Ferlin; Wings of a Dove, Capitol 4406, VG........$5.00

Hyman, Dick; Look Up, MGM 12476, VG $3.00

Impressions, Fool for You, Custom 1932, EX.................$3.50

Ingram, Luther; My Honey & Me, KoKo 2104, NM........$4.00

Intruders, Pray for Me, Gamble 4014, EX.....................$3.50

Irish Rovers, Rhyme & Reasons, Decca 32616, VG........$5.00

Ives, Burl; Harlem Man, Decca 29910, EX.....................$5.50

Jackson, Michael; Get on the Floor, Epic 50871, EX......$3.00

Jackson, Stonewall; This World Holds Nothing, Columbia 44283, VG $5.00

Jackson 5, Maybe Tomorrow, Motown 1186, VG $4.00

James, Joni; I Still Get Jealous, MGM 12807, VG $7.50

James, Rick; Cold Blooded, Gordy 1687, EX.................$3.00

James, Sonny; She Believes in Me, Capitol 3653, EX.....$3.50

Jameson, Nick; Weatherman, Motown 1853, EX............$3.00

Janis, Johnny; Distant Drums, Monument 1205, VG $4.00

Jefferson Starship, Miracles, Grunt 10367, EX $3.00

Jennings, Waylon; Mental Revenge, RCA 9146, EX........$3.00

John, Elton; Victim of Love, MCA 41126, VG $5.00

Johnson, Betty; I'm Beginning To Wonder, Bally 1041, NM $6.00

Jones, George; She's My Rock, Epic 04609, EX.............$3.00

Jones, Jack; Strangers in the Night, MCA 60049, VG $2.50

Jones, Tamiko; Touch Me Baby, Atlantic 715, VG.........$4.00

Kaempfert, Bert; Night Dreams, Decca 32159, EX........$4.50

Kansas, Dust in the Wind, Kirshner 4274, VG $2.50

Kelly Brothers, Can't Stand It No Longer, Sims 293, M..$8.00

Kendricks, Eddie; Surprise Attack, Cornerstone 1001, EX .$3.00

Kid Brother, It Was Fun While It Lasted, MCA 41193, EX $3.00

King, BB; When I'm Wrong, ABC 12158, EX $5.50

King, Wayne; Joey's Song, Decca 30505, EX.................$3.50

Kingston Trio, One More Town, Capitol 4842, VG........$4.00

Kirby, Dave; Charleston Cotton Mill, Dot 17416, NM....$4.00

Kool & the Gang, Rhyme Tyme People, De-Lite 1563, EX **$3.00**

LaBelle, Patti; Messin' w/My Mind, Epic 50140, VG **$2.50**

Laine, Frankie; Go On w/Your Dancing, Capitol 5299, EX **$3.50**

Lane, Jerry; She Lives in Your World, Chart 1034, VG ..**$4.00**

LaRosa, Julius; Cryin' My Heart Out for You, RCA 6923, EX..**$3.00**

Lawrence, Steve; Don't Be Afraid, Columbia 42699, EX.**$3.50**

Led Zeppelin, Good Times Bad Times, Atlantic 2613, EX **$4.50**

Lee, Brenda; Too Many Rivers, Atlantic 2613, EX.........**$4.50**

Lee, Johnny; When You Fall in Love, Epic 47444, VG ..**$2.50**

Lee, Peggy; Sweetest Sound, Capitol 4750, VG.............**$5.00**

Lennon, John; Whatever Gets You Thru the Night, Apple 1874, NM..**$6.00**

Leonetti, Tommy; Moonlight Serenade, RCA 7455, EX..**$3.50**

Lewis, Jerry Lee; Closest Thing to You, Mercury 73872, EX..**$3.00**

Lightfoot, Gordon; Wreck of the Edmund Fitzgerald, Reprise 0121, EX **$3.00**

Little Richard, Girl Can't Help It, Specialty 591, VG.......**$7.50**

Little River Band, Take It Easy on Me, Capitol 5057, EX.**$3.00**

Loco, Joe; Yumbambe, Columbia 40636, VG **$4.00**

Lopez, Trini; Takin' the Back Roads, Reprise 0536, EX.**$4.50**

Loverboy, Turn Me Loose, Columbia 03108, EX............**$3.00**

Lowe, Jim; Slow Train, Dot 15611, EX.........................**$5.50**

Lulu, Take Your Mama for a Ride, Chelsea 3011, EX....**$4.50**

Lynn, Loretta; What's the Bottle Done to My Baby, Decca 32693, NM..**$4.00**

Maddox, Johnny; There's a Star Spangled Banner, Dot 15128, EX...**$3.50**

Marx, Bill; Moon Tune, Vee Jay 617, VG.....................**$4.00**

Mathis, Johnny; Call Me, Columbia 41253, VG **$2.50**

McCartney, Paul; Jet, Apple 1871, NM.........................**$30.00**

McCoy, Rosemarie; I Do the Best I Can w/What I Can, Brunswick 55541, NM...**$4.00**

McDowell, Ronnie; Older Woman, Epic 02129, EX.......**$3.00**

McEntire, Reba; Let the Music Lift You Up, MCA 52990, EX..**$3.00**

Mellencamp, John Cougar; Check It Out, Mercury 870126, EX..**$3.00**

Miami Sound Machine, Falling in Love, Epic 06352, EX.**$3.00**

Miller, Jody; Be My Baby, Epic 10835, EX....................**$3.00**

Miller, Steve; Living in the USA, Cap Star 6235, EX.......**$3.00**

Mitchell, Joni; Be Cool, Geffen 29757, EX....................**$3.00**

Monroe, Vaughn; If You Gotta Make a Fool of Somebody, Dot 16308, EX...**$4.50**

Montenegro, Hugo; Happy Together, RCA 0160, EX.....**$3.50**

Moore, Melba; Long Winding Road, Buddah 568, VG ..**$3.00**

Morrison, Van; Call Me Up in Dreamland, Warner Bros 7462, VG **$5.00**

Murdock, Shirley; As We Lay, Elektra 69518, EX...........**$3.00**

Murphy, Chuck; Lay Somethin' on the Bar, Coral 61785, VG **$4.00**

Nelson, Ricky; Lonely Corner, Decca 31656, VG..........**$5.00**

Nelson, Willie; Twilight Time, Columbia 08541, EX......**$3.00**

Nero, Peter; If You've Got a Heart, RCA 8503, EX **$3.50**

New Colony Six, I Could Never Lie to You, Mercury 72920, NM..**$5.00**

New Seekers, When There's No Love Left, Elektra 45710, EX **$4.50**

Newton, Wayne; You Just Don't Know, Capitol 5578, EX.**$3.50**

Nita, Rita & Ruby, Give Me Love, RCA 6124, VG..........**$6.00**

Nitty Gritty Dirt Band, I've Been Lookin', Warner Bros 27750, EX..**$3.00**

Nutter, Mayf; Never Had a Doubt, Capitol 6351, EX **$3.00**

Oak Ridge Boys, Love Song, MCA 52224, EX...............**$3.00**

Ohio Players, Here Today & Gone Tomorrow, Capitol 2385, w/dust jacket, EX..**$4.50**

Orbison, Roy; Wondering, MGM 13386, VG **$7.50**

Osborne Brothers, Don't Even Look at Me, Decca 31546, EX...**$3.50**

Paper Lace, Black-Eyed Boys, Mercury 73620, VG........**$4.00**

Parton, Dolly; Try Being Lonely, RCA 9657, EX............**$3.00**

Pennington, Ray; My Heart's Gonna Rise Again, Capitol 5909, EX...**$3.50**

Perkins, Howard; Johnny Overload, Juke 2012, NM **$3.25**

Peterson, Ray; Tell Laura I Love Her, RCA 11758, M.....**$3.25**

Pickett, Wilson; Soul Dance No. 3, Atlantic 2412, M **$4.00**

Pierce, Webb; Let Me Live a Little, Decca 31737, EX.....**$4.50**

Platters, Magic Touch, Mercury 70819, VG....................**$7.50**

Poco, Break of Hearts, Atlantic 89851, VG....................**$2.50**

Pointer Sisters, Baby Come & Get It, Planet 14041, EX.**$3.00**

Presley, Elvis; Good Luck Charm, RCA 447-0636, M **$4.00**

Presley, Elvis; Return to Sender, RCA 47-8100, VG........**$7.50**

Preston, Billy; Struttin', A&M 1644, VG.......................**$2.50**

Pretenders, My Baby, Sire 28496, NM..........................**$3.25**

Price, Ray; Crazy Arms, Columbia 21510, VG **$2.50**

Prince, When Doves Cry, Warner Brothers, EX............**$3.00**

Pruett, Jeanne; Your Memory's Comin' On, MCA 40116, VG **$2.50**

Rabbit, Eddie; Hearts on Fire, Elektra 45461, VG **$2.50**

Randall, Frankie; Girls in Summer Dresses, RCA 8380, EX **$3.50**

Randolph, Boots; Sanford & Son Theme, Monument 8634, EX...**$3.50**

Rawls, Lou; You've Made Me So Very Happy, Capitol 2734, VG **$3.00**

Ray, Johnnie; Papa Loves Mambo, Columbia 40324, VG.**$5.00**

Redding, Otis; Free Me, Atco 6700, VG **$5.00**

Reddy, Helen; What Would They Say, Capitol 3527, NM.**$3.25**

Reed, Jerry; There's Better Things in Life, RCA 0124, VG.**$2.50**

REO Speedwagon, Can't Fight This Feeling, Epic 04713, EX...**$3.00**

Rich, Charlie; Very Special Love Song, Epic 11091, EX.**$3.00**

Righteous Brothers, Fannie Mae, Moonglow 238, VG ...**$3.00**

Robinson, Smokey; What's Too Much, Motown 1911, VG .**$2.50**

Rodriquez, Johnny; Too Late To Go Home, Epic 04336, EX...**$3.00**

Rogers, Kenny; This Woman, RCA 13710, VG **$2.50**

Ronstadt, Linda; Silver Thread & Golden Needles, Asylum 11032, EX..**$3.00**

Rose Royce, First Come, First Served, Whitfield 8789, EX **$3.00**

Ross, Diana; Smile, Motown 1398, VG **$2.50**

Ruffin, David; I Pray Everyday You Won't Regret Loving Me, Motown 1158, VG **$3.00**

Russell, Johnny; Falsely Accused, Mercury 57016, VG ..**$2.50**

Sam the Sham & Pharoahs, Red Hot, MGM 13452, VG .**$4.00**

Sayer, Leo; More Than I Can Say, Warner Brothers 0405, EX **$3.00**

Seals & Crofts, You're the Love, Warner Brothers 8551, EX **$3.00**

Sedaka, Neil; Calendar Girl, RCA 7829, VG **$3.00**

Shangri-Las, I Can Never Go Home Anymore, Trip 76, VG **$2.50**

Shaw, Georgie; Honeycomb, Decca 28937, VG.............**$3.00**

Shepard, Jean; We Go Good Together, Capitol 3315, VG.**$3.00**

Simon, Joe; Pool of Bad Luck, Spring 124, VG **$3.00**

Simon, Paul; American Tune, Columbia 45900, EX **$3.50**

Sinatra, Frank; Chicago, Capitol 3793, VG....................**$7.50**

Sister Sledge, All American Girls, Cotillion 46007, VG ..**$2.50**

Smith, Carl; Walking the Slow Walk, Columbia 41243, VG.**$3.00**

Smith, Connie; Senses, RCA 8551, VG **$3.00**

Snow, Hank; Hijack, RCA 10338, EX **$3.00**

Sonny & Cher, Cowboys Work Is Never Done, Kapp 2163, VG **$4.00**

Sovine, Red; Best Years of Your Life, Decca 30018, VG .**$4.00**

Spinners, Rubberband Man, Atlantic 3355, VG **$2.50**

Squier, Billy; Rock Me Tonight, Capitol 5370, VG **$2.50**

Stampley, Joe; Double Shot of My Baby's Life, Epic 04173, EX **$3.00**

Starr, Kay; Four Walls, Capitol 4835, VG **$5.00**

Statler Brothers, Do You Know You Are My Sunshine, Mercury 55022, M **$3.25**

Steel Breeze, Dreamin' Is Easy, RCA 13427, EX............**$3.00**

Steppenwolf, Rock Me, Dunhill 4182, EX.......................**$4.50**

Stevens, Ray; Losing Streak, Barnaby 2065, VG **$3.00**

Stewart, Gary; Sweet-Tator & Cisco, Kapp 2008, EX **$3.50**

Stewart, Rod; Da Ya Think I'm Sexy, Warner Brothers 0382, M **$3.25**

Stewart, Wynn; New Love, Capitol 3651, EX.................**$5.50**

Stoloff, Morris; Half of My Heart, Decca 30388, VG **$3.00**

Storm, Gale; Why Do Fools Fall in Love, Dot 15448, VG.**$5.00**

Strait, George; If You Ain't Lovin', MCA 53400, EX **$3.00**

Streisand, Barbra; Kiss Me in the Rain, Columbia 11179, VG **$2.50**

Styx, Babe, A&M 2188, EX...**$3.00**

Summer, Donna; I Feel Love, Casablanca 884, VG........**$2.50**

Sunshine Kids, Love One Another, Decca 30169, VG ...**$6.00**

Supremes, Someday We'll Be Together, Motown 1156, VG **$2.00**

Swan, Billy; Do I Have To Draw a Picture, Epic 51000, VG **$2.50**

Sylvers, High School Dance, Capitol 4405, EX..............**$3.00**

Tavares, Goodnight My Love, Capitol 4453, EX.............**$3.00**

Taylor, James; Your Smiling Face, Columbia 10602, VG.**$2.50**

Taylor, Ted; Somebody's Gettin' It, Alarm 112, VG.......**$3.00**

Temptations, Please Return Your Love to Me, Gordy 7074, VG **$5.00**

Terry, Gordon; Whipping Post, Epic 9855, VG.............**$3.00**

Thomas, BJ; Another Somebody Done Somebody Wrong, ABC 12054, EX **$3.50**

Thompson, Hank; Anybody's Girl, Capitol 4182, VG **$5.00**

Thompson Twins, Nothing in Common, Arista 9511, VG...**$2.50**

Three Suns, Ecstasy Tango, RCA 5185, VG **$3.00**

Tillis, Mel; Ain't No California, MCA 40946, EX **$3.00**

Tillotson, Johnny; Worried Guy, MGM 13193, VG.........**$4.00**

Tompall & Glaser Brothers, Drinking Them Beers, ABC 12329, VG **$2.50**

Toto, Make Believe, Columbia 03143, VG.....................**$2.50**

Travis, Randy; Forever Together, Warner Brothers 19158, EX **$3.00**

Tubb, Ernest; Blue Christmas, Decca 46186, VG **$2.50**

Tucker, Tanya; Call on Me, Capitol 44348, NM.............**$3.25**

Twisted Sister, We're Not Gonna Take It, Atlantic 89641, NM...**$3.25**

Twitty, Conway; Saturday Night Special, MCA 53373, VG .**$2.50**

Uggams, Leslie; My Own Morning, Atlantic 2397, EX ...**$3.50**

Vale, Jerry; For Mama, Columbia 43232, EX **$3.00**

Valli, Frankie; Save Me, Save Me, Warner Brothers 8670, EX **$3.00**

Vaughan, Sarah; Padre, Mercury 71303, EX **$4.50**

Vee, Bobby; Beautiful People, Liberty 56009, VG **$4.00**

Village Stompers, Sweet Water Boy, Epic 9824, EX.......**$3.00**

Vinton, Bobby; College Town, Epic 10168, VG.............**$2.50**

Vogues, Earth Angel, Reprise 0820, VG.......................**$3.00**

Wagoner, Porter; When You're Hot You're Hot, RCA 0267, VG **$2.50**

Walker, Billy; Willie the Weeper, Columbia 42492, VG **$4.00**

Walker, Charlie; Honky-Tonk Season, Epic 10426, VG .**$3.00**

Wallace, Jerry; To Get to You, Decca 32914, VG **$3.00**

Wariner, Steve; Baby I'm Yours, MCA 53287, EX **$3.00**

Warwick, Dionne; Whisper in the Dark, Arista 9460, VG .**$2.50**

Washington, Dinah; Unforgettable, Mercury 71508, VG.**$3.00**

Wayne, Bobby; Harold's Super Service, Capitol 3025, VG.**$3.00**

Welk, Lawrence; Last Date, Dot 16145, VG...................**$3.00**

Wells, Kitty; Memory Of Love, Decca 31065, VG **$3.00**

Wells, Mary; Mister Tough, Jubilee 5718, VG................**$3.00**

West, Dottie; You're The Only World I Know, RCA 8770, VG **$2.50**

Weston, Paul; Chance at Love, Columbia 40561, VG **$3.00**

Wham, Everything She Wants, Columbia 04840, EX **$3.00**

Whispers, I Can Make It Better, Solar 12232, VG **$2.50**

White, Karyn; Way You Love Me, Warner Brothers 27773, EX..**$3.00**

Whiting, Margaret; Only Love Can Break a Heart, London 108, VG **$3.00**

Whitman, Slim; North Wind, Imperial 66248, VG **$3.00**

Wilburn Brothers, Flame's Still Burning, Decca 31214, VG **$4.00**

Williams, Andy; Summertime, Columbia 42523, VG......**$2.50**

Williams, Dick; Don't Look Now, Decca 30476, VG......**$4.00**

Williams, Hank Jr; Happy Kind of Sadness, MGM 14277, EX **$4.50**

Williams, Roger; Moonlight Love, Kapp 186, NM **$4.00**

Wills, David; Queen of the Starlight Ballroom, Epic 50188, EX **$3.00**

Wilson, Nancy; Seventh Son, Capitol 4509, VG **$3.00**

Winwood, Steve; Finer Things, Island 28498, EX **$3.00**

Wonder, Stevie; Yester-Me, Yester-You, Yesterday, Tamla 54188, VG **$2.50**

Wright, Betty; Girls Can't Do What the Guys Do, Atlantic 13102, EX...**$3.00**

Wynette, Tammy; They Call It Making Love, Epic 50661, EX...**$3.00**

Young, Faron; Turn Her Down, Capitol 3549, VG **$6.00**

Albums

Beatles, The Beatles 1967-70, 2 records w/album insert sheet, NM..**$14.00**

Cash, Johnny; Best Of-Ring of Fire, Columbia CS-8853, EX...**$8.00**

Chipmunks, Let's All Sing w/the Chipmunks, Liberty LST-7132, NM **$12.00**

Cramer, Floyd; On the Rebound, RCA LSP-2359, NM....**$8.00**

Creedence Clearwater, Green River, Fan 8393, EX........**$8.00**

Domino, Fats; When I'm Walking, Columbia, NM.......**$15.00**

Laine, Frankie; Golden Hits, Mercury, SR 60587, NM....**$9.50**

Lennon Sisters, Christmas w/Lennon Sisters, Dot DLP 25-343, VG **$8.00**

Love Generation, Generation of Love, Imperial LP 9364, EX...**$9.50**

Presley, Elvis; GI Blues, RCA LSP-2256, NM.................**$20.00**

Presley, Elvis; His Hand in Mine, RCA LSP-2328, EX...**$12.00**

Presley, Elvis; How Great Thou Art, RCA LSP-3758, NM..**$24.00**

Presley, Elvis; I Got Lucky, RCA-Camden CAL-2533, NM **$20.00**

Extended Play

Ames Brothers, Tammy/That's the Way Love Goes, RCA 4096, VG **$5.00**

Armstrong, Louie; Pennies From Heaven/Long Long Journey, RCA 1443, VG **$7.50**

August, Jan; I Wonder Who's Kissing Her Now/Alice Blue Gown, Mercury 3032, VG **$4.00**

Belafonte, Harry; Haiti Cherie/Lucy's Door, RCA 1-1505, w/cover, EX...**$5.50**

Bennett, Tony; These Foolish Things/Boulevard of Broken Dreams, Columbia 9382, EX.....................**$6.50**

Boone, Pat; The Lord's Prayer/Ave Maria, Dot DEP 1068, NM **$6.00**

Boston Pops, Zampa Overture/Gypsy Baron Overture, RCA 23, w/cover, EX.......................................**$4.00**

Carle, Frankie; American Patrol/Loch Lomond, RCA 1-1499, w/cover, VG **$5.00**

Como, Perry; Wanted/Pa-Paya, RCA 563, VG **$4.50**

Darin, Bobby; Clemintine/Guys & Dolls, Atco 4508, VG **$6.50**

Dee, Lenny; Delicious/Stompin' at the Savoy, Decca 2345, VG **$3.75**

Elgart, Les; Who Cares/Boy Next Door, Columbia 10081, w/cover, VG **$7.50**

Flanagan, Ralph; My Hero/Penthouse Serenade, RCA 308, w/cover, EX..**$4.50**

Ford, Tennessee Ernie; Take My Hand Precious Lord/When God Dips His Love, Capitol 3-818, w/cover, VG **$4.50**

Garland, Judy; Life Is Just a Bowl of Cherries/Just Imagine, Capitol 734, w/cover, EX..............................**$5.00**

Goodman, Al; My Heart Stood Still/Love Nest, Camden 349, w/cover, VG **$4.50**

Hampton, Lionel; On the Sunny Side of the Street/Shoe Shiners Drag, RCA 27, EX....................................**$2.00**

Hayman, Richard; Limelight/Eyes of Blue, Mercury 3081, w/cover, EX..**$3.00**

Ives, Burl; Pretty Little Miss/Liza Jane, Decca 91088, EX...**$4.50**

James, Sonny; I Wish I Knew/I'll Always Wonder, Capitol 2-779, w/cover, VG **$4.50**

Kenton, Stan; September Song/Laura, Capitol 1-421, w/cover, VG **$3.50**

Kingston Trio, Raspberries, Strawberries/Sally, Capitol 1-1182, w/cover, EX...**$10.50**

Lombardo, Guy; South Rampart Street Parade/Twelfth Street Rag, Capitol 892, VG **$3.75**

Mariners, Lead Kindly Light/Abide w/Me, Columbia 217, EX...**$2.50**

Miller, Glenn; Boulder Buff/Sliphorn Jive, RCA 0118, EX **$4.50**

Morgan, Jane; Fascination/My Heart Reminds Me, Kapp 747, VG **$1.50**

Page, Patti; Once Upon a Dream/Indian Giver, Mercury 3346, VG **$4.00**

Presley, Elvis; I Need You So/Blueberry Hill, RCA EPA 4041, EX...**$18.00**

Presley, Elvis; Shake Rattle & Roll/Blue Moon, RCA EPA 830, EX...**$18.00**

Rene, Henri; Serenade/Love in Bloom, RCA 730, VG **$6.00**

Royal Military Band, Grand Duke of Baden/March of Van Heutz, Decca 2405, w/cover, EX.......................**$3.50**

Schumann, Walter; Stand Up & Cheer/Hanover Winter Song, Capitol 1-285, EX..**$2.50**

Sherwood, Roberta; I Gotta Right To Sing the Blues/Georgia On My Mind, Decca 2539, VG **$1.50**

Sinatra, Frank; Hey Jealous Lover/I Believe, Capitol 982, w/cover, VG **$15.00**

Sinatra, Frank; That Old Black Magic/American Beauty Rose, Capitol 1594, VG **$11.00**

Three Suns, Donkey Serenade/Serenade in the Night, RCA 241, w/cover, VG **$4.50**

Welk, Lawrence; Girl Friend/Marie, Coral 81101, w/cover, NM..**$8.50**

Weston, Paul; Among My Souvenirs/My Silent Love, Columbia 1661, w/cover, VG **$6.00**

Williams, Roger; Beyond the Sea/Big Town, Kapp 712, EX...**$3.50**

Young, Victor; Cornish Rhapsody/Pearls on Velvet, Decca 2013, w/cover, VG **$4.50**

Picture Sleeves

Air Supply, One That You Love, Arista 0504, VG.........**$1.50**

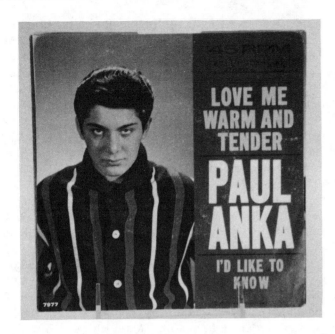

Anka, Paul; Love Me Warm & Tender, RCA 47-7977, EX **$9.50**

Anka, Paul; Put Your Head on My Shoulder, Eric 203, VG.**$3.00**

Beach Boys, Getcha Back, Caribou 04913, EX..............**$4.50**

Beatles, Got To Get You Into My Life, Capitol 4274, EX .**$5.50**

Bowie, David; Ashes to Ashes, RCA 12078, NM **$9.50**

Carpenters, Rainy Days & Mondays, A&M 1260, VG.....**$5.00**

Collins, Phil; Two Hearts, Atlantic 88980, EX.................**$1.75**

Crosby, Stills & Nash, Wasted on the Way, Atlantic 4058, EX...**$3.50**

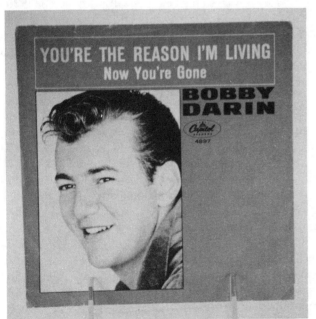

Darin, Bobby; You're the Reason I'm Living, Capitol 4897, EX..**$11.50**

Diamond, Neil; Heartlight, Columbia 03219, NM...........**$2.00**

Everly Brothers, Crying in the Rain, Warner Brothers 5250, VG..**$15.00**

Francis, Connie; Don't Break the Heart, MGM 13059, EX.**$9.50**

Go-Go's, Vacation, IRS 9907, NM...................................**$4.00**

Grand Funk, Shinin' On, Capitol 3917, VG **$4.00**

Houston, David; Sammy, Epic 9884, EX.........................**$4.50**

Huey Lewis & the News, Walking on a Thin Line, Chrysalis 42825, NM...**$2.00**

Jackson, Michael; Wanna Be Startin' Somethin', Epic 03914.**$4.00**

James, Sonny; My Love, Capitol 2782, VG **$5.00**

Joel, Billy; Back in the USSR, Columbia 07626, EX.......**$1.75**

Journey, Open Arms, Columbia 02687, VG...................**$1.50**

Lee, Brenda; My Dreams, Decca 31628, VG **$10.50**

Lennon, John; Woman, Geffen 49644, EX......................**$3.50**

Mancini, Henry; Moon River, RCA 7916, EX **$9.50**

McCartney, Paul; Listen to What the Man Said, Capitol 4091, VG **$5.00**

Mellencamp, John Cougar; Cherry Bomb, Mercury 888 934 .**$2.00**

Murray, Anne; Are You Still in Love w/Me?, Capitol 44005, EX..**$1.75**

Oak Ridge Boys, Little Things, MCA 52556, NM............**$2.00**

Presley, Elvis; Tell Me Why, RCA 47-8740, VG **$15.00**

Presley, Elvis; Way Down, RCA PB-10998, EX...............**$9.50**

Queen, Play the Game, Elektra 46652, VG.....................**$3.00**

Richie, Lionel; Love Will Conquer All, Motown 1866, EX .**$1.75**

Rogers, Kenny; This Woman, RCA 13710, NM...............**$2.00**

Sherman, Bobby; Together Again, Metromedia 240, VG.**$4.00**

Simon, Carly; Let the River Run, Arista 7822, NM..........**$2.00**

Springsteen, Bruce; I'm Goin' Down, Columbia 05603, EX...**$1.75**

Starr, Ringo; Photograph, Apple 1865, VG **$5.00**

Supertramp, Cannonball, A&M 2731, NM.......................**$2.00**

Thirty-Eight Special, Like No Other Night, A&M 2831, NM **$2.00**

Twitty, Conway; Clown, Elektra 47302, VG **$1.50**

Vannelli, Gino; Living Inside Myself, Arista 0588, NM...**$4.00**

Vinton, Bobby; Just As Much As Ever, Epic 10266, EX .**$4.50**

Williams, Hank Jr; Long Gone Lonesome Blues, MGM 13208, VG **$7.50**

Wonder, Stevie; Send One Your Love, Tamla 54303, NM.**$5.00**

Records, 78 rpm

Values are for records in excellent condition.

Alabama Four, Queen Street Rag, Victor 21136...........**$35.00**

Alabama Harmony Boys, My Gal Sal, Decca 7000 ......**$15.00**

Allen Brothers, Reckless Night Blues, Bluebird 5224 ..**$12.50**

Arcadian Serenaders, Fidgety Feet, Okeh 40272..........**$35.00**

Bailey Swing Group, Eccentric Rag, Juke Box 506........**$6.00**

Baker, Buddy; Box Car Blues, Victor 21549.................**$12.50**

Banta, Frank; My Sugar, Victor 19705.........................**$7.50**

Beaman, Lottie; Honey Blues, Paramount 12201.........**$30.00**

Bernard, Al; St Louis Blues, Banner 1211.....................**$8.00**

Blue Boy, Back-Biter Blues, Varsity 6052....................**$12.50**

Boots & His Buddies, Swanee River Blues, Bluebird 6921 ....**$12.50**

Calloway, Ermine; Good Little, Bad Little You, Edison 52519 ....**$16.00**

Carolina Buddies, Otto Wood the Bandit, Columbia 15652-D **$15.00**

Cherwin, Dick & His Orchestra; Birmingham Bertha, Banner 6497 ....$8.00

Cotton Club Orchestra, Down & Out Blues, Columbia 287-D $35.00

Country Jim, Rainy Morning Blues, Imperial 5062 ....$8.50

Davis, Walter; Sloppy Drunk Again, Bluebird 5879 .....$35.00

Dixie Daisies, St Louis Blues, Banner 0839 ....$10.00

Dixie Stompers, Alamama Stomp, Harmony 283-H $12.00

Down Home Boys, You Do It, Bluebird 6331 ....$35.00

Earl & Bill, On the Oregon Trail, Vocalion 15014 ....$8.00

Eckstein, Willie; Maple Leaf Rag, Okeh 40018 ....$10.00

Eddie Kelly's Washboard Band, Shim Shaming, Bluebird 7148 ....$14.00

Erby, Jack; Hot Peter, Columbia 14570-D $45.00

Fox, Curley; Tennessee Roll, Decca 5169....................$8.50

Franklin, Emery; Lonesome Day, Cava-Tone 251 ....$12.50

Fuller, Bob; Crossword Puzzle Blues, Ajax 17088 ....$20.00

Golden Gate Serenaders, On! Baby, Gennett 6487.....$12.50

Gordon, Alex; A Message From Home Sweet Home, Conquerer 7269 ....$12.50

Hall, James; My Jivin' Woman, Vocalion 04231 ....$12.50

Harlem Trio, Bass Clarinet Blues, Okeh 8189 ....$50.00

Harris, Alfoncy; All Alone Blues, Vocalion 02902........$90.00

Harris, Sim; Pass Around the Bottle, Oriole 916 ....$10.00

Hunter, Lee; Lees Boogie, Gold Star 651....................$15.00

Imperial Dance Orchestra, Let's Do It, Banner 6245 .....$8.00

Jelly-Roll Morton & His Red Hot Peppers, Stroking Away, ca 1930..$80.00

Johnson, Gene; TB Blues, Timely Tunes 1550............$65.00

Johnson, Lil; My Stove's in Good Condition, Vocalion 03251 ....$18.00

Jones, Sonny; Dough Roller, Vocalion 05056..............$25.00

Kaufman, Irving; Let Me Sing & I'm Happy, Okeh 41412 ....$12.00

Kincaid, Bradley; Death of Jimmie Rodgers, Bluebird 5377 ....$12.50

La Palina Broadcasters, Little by Little, Domino 4405....$8.00

Lane, Duke; Blue Yodel No 4, Supertone 9425 ....$12.00

Liston, Virginia; Bed Time Blues, Okeh 8092 ....$16.50

Markham Brothers, I Am Resolved, Challenge 399........$8.00

Martin, Sara; Squabbling Blues, Okeh 8108 ....$50.00

Marvin, Johnny; Memphis Blues, Edison 51709...........$12.50

Memphis Melody Boys, Washboard Blues, Buddy 8005.$95.00

Mills, Violet; Worried Blues, Domino 437 ....$12.50

Neal, David; Good Old Turnip Greens, Supertone 9184 .$12.00

New Orleans Jazz Band, Some of These Days, Banner 1544 ....$12.50

Nixon, Elmore; Playboy Blues, Mercury 70061 ....$8.00

Noble, Ray & His Orchestra; Crazy Rhythm, Brunswick 8098..$8.00

Oaks, Charlie; Fatal Wedding, Vocalion 5076 ....$8.00

Okeh Syncopators, Birmingham Papa, Okeh 40316......$8.00

Original Indiana Five, Struttin' Jerry, Banner 6023........$8.50

Palmer, Sylvester; Lonesome Man Blues, Columbia 14492-D $65.00

Park Lane Orchestra, You Can't Cry Over My Shoulder, Brunswick 3513...$10.00

Potter, Nettie; A Good Man Is Hard To Find, Banner 1483 ....$12.50

Prairie Ramblers, Blue River, Bluebird 5302 ....$25.00

Quinn, Frank; Pop Goes the Weasel, Okeh 45030......$10.00

Ramona & Her Gang, What Have We Got To Lose?, Victor 24268..$15.00

Red Devils, Tiger Rag, Columbia 14586 ....$65.00

Renfro Valley Boys, Twenty-One Years, Paramount 3311.$20.00

Rolling Stones, Down by the Old Rio Grande, Victor V40316..$20.00

Ross, Lucy; West End Blues, Champion 15715.........$125.00

Roy Carlson's Dance Orchestra, Smile the Blues Away, Banner 0729 ....$8.50

Royal Troubadours, Highways Are Happy Ways, Harmony 498-H $10.00

Seven Little Polar Bears, Someone Is Losin' Susan, Cameo 915..$8.00

Six Black Diamonds, Dixie Flyer Sam, Banner 1428 ...$12.50

Smith, Clara; 31st Street Blues, Columbia 14009-D......$25.00

Smoky Mountain Fiddler Trio, Bonaparte's Retreat, Bluebird 6387..$8.00

Sparton Syncopators, My Mad Moment, Parlophone PNY34071 ....$20.00

Speckled Red, Welfare Blues, Bluebird 8069 ....$12.50

Tennessee Ten, Down Hearted Blues, Victor 19094......$8.00

Texas Drifter, Yodeling Teacher, Decca 5020.............$12.00

Texas Red & Jimmy, Black Snake Blues, Viceroy 3333 ....$18.00

Thomas, Hociel; I Can't Feel Frisky w/out My Liquor, Gennett 3004..$85.00

Thomas, Rufus; Night Walkin' Blues, Chess 1466........$20.00

Three Monkey Chasers, Corn Bread Wiggle, Harmony 23-H $10.00

Uncle Bud & His Plowboys, Five Cent Cotton, Oriole 8170 ....$8.00

Uncle Skipper, Cutting My ABC's, Decca 7353 ....**$25.00**
University Orchestra, Button Up Your Overcoat, Gennett 6815 ....**$14.00**
Van Loan, Paul & His Orchestra; Deep Elm, Cameo 820 .**$7.50**
Vassar, Callie; All Night Blues, Gennett 5172...............**$65.00**
Walter Family, Too Young To Get Married, Champion 16595 ....**$50.00**
Walters, Eddie; Singin' in the Bathtub, Columbia 2035-D .**$10.00**
Washboard Serenaders, Teddy's Blues, Victor V38610 .**$125.00**
West, CA; A Mother's Advice, Gennett 7098 ....**$15.00**
White, Georgia; Honey Dripper Blues, Decca 7122 ....**$12.50**
Yancey, Jimmy; Death Letter Blues, Bluebird 8630 .....**$15.00**
Yankee Six, Oh! Those Eyes, Okeh 40335 ....**$40.00**
Yas Yas Girl, Worried Heart Blues, Okeh 05870 ....**$8.00**
Yellow Jackets, Heel & Toe Polka, Champion 16070 ..**$12.50**

Red Wing Potteries, Inc.

For almost a century, Red Wing, Minnesota, was the center of a great pottery industry. In the early 1900s, several local companies merged to form the Red Wing Stoneware Company. Until they introduced their dinnerware lines in 1935, most of their production centered around stoneware jugs, crocks, flowerpots, and other utilitarian items. To reflect the changes made in '35, the name was changed to Red Wing Potteries, Inc. In addition to scores of lovely dinnerware lines, they also made vases, planters, flowerpots, etc., some with exceptional shapes and decoration.

Some of their more recognizable lines of dinnerware and those you'll most often find are Bob White (decorated in blue and brown brushstrokes with quail), Tampico (featuring a collage of fruit including watermelon), Random Harvest (simple pink and brown leaves and flowers), and Village Green (or Brown, solid color pieces introduced in the fifties). Often you'll find complete or nearly complete sets, and when you do, the lot price is usually a real bargain.

If you'd like to learn more about the subject, we recommend *Red Wing Stoneware, An Identification and Value Guide,* and *Red Wing Collectibles,* both by Dan and Gail DePasquale and Larry Peterson.

Art Ware

Ash receiver, 5", donkey figural.....................................**$50.00**
Ashtray, red wing form, embossed feathers.................**$35.00**
Bowl, 13½", floral relief on gun-metal brown, lime interior **$25.00**
Candlesticks, #1226, magnolia, white, pr **$28.00**
Figurine, 10", lady w/tambourine, cinnamon............**$175.00**
Planter, 12" long, #1561, glossy speckled gold, fluted .**$12.00**
Trivet, yellow, 1858-1958...**$65.00**
Urn, 9", #159, Grecian motif.......................................**$45.00**
Vase, 10", orange w/pelican handles, ca 1930s **$50.00**
Vase, 6", light green semigloss, ribbed flared top, bulbous bottom......................................**$8.00**

Wall clock, Mammy **$125.00**
Wall pocket, #1004, tan, Red Wing Potteries **$20.00**

Cookie Jars

Bob White, unmarked **$80.00**
Crock, white **$25.00**
Dutch Girl, yellow w/brown trim **$60.00**
Friar Tuck, cream w/brown trim, marked....................**$60.00**
Friar Tuck, yellow, unmarked......................................**$60.00**
Grapes **$70.00**
Grapes, cobalt or dark purple, each............................**$80.00**

Jack Frost, unmarked, minimum value...............**$600.00**
King of Tarts, marked Red Wing USA, pink w/black crown **$350.00**
Peasant design, embossed & painted on brown..........**$60.00**
Pierre (chef), brown, unmarked **$60.00**
Pierre (chef), green, unmarked..................................**$200.00**
Pineapple **$100.00**

Dinnerware

Blossomtime, cup......................................**$6.00**
Bob White, bowl, vegetable; divided **$25.00**
Bob White, casserole, 2-qt..**$25.00**
Bob White, cup & saucer **$16.00**

Bob White, gravy boat w/lid......................................**$47.50**
Bob White, hors d'oeuvres bird **$45.00**
Bob White, pitcher, water; 60-oz **$35.00**
Bob White, plate, dinner size......................................**$12.00**
Bob White, relish, 12", 3-part......................................**$22.00**

Bob White, salt & pepper shakers, tall, pr $20.00
Brittany, plate, dinner $7.50
Brittany, salt & pepper shakers, pr $10.00
Capistrano, plate, dinner; 10" $10.00
Capistrano, platter, 13½" $13.00
Country Garden, gravy boat $22.00
Country Garden, plate, 10½" $15.00
Country Garden, sauce dish $10.00
Driftwood, bowl, divided vegetable $12.00
Driftwood, plate, bread & butter $5.00
Driftwood, plate, salad $7.00
Fantasy, plate, 10½" $10.00
Frontenac, creamer $7.50
Frontenac, plate, dinner $7.50
Frontenac, saucer $2.50
Lotus, creamer $8.00
Lotus, plate, 10½" $8.00
Lotus, plate, 6" $3.50
Lotus, relish, 3-part $17.50
Lute Song, bowl, cereal; 6¾" $7.50
Lute Song, bowl, vegetable; 8" $15.00
Lute Song, butter dish $20.00
Lute Song, creamer $10.00
Lute Song, cup & saucer $10.00
Lute Song, plate, dinner; 10½" $10.00
Lute Song, plate, 7" $7.00
Lute Song, platter, 13" $20.00
Magnolia, cup & saucer $8.00
Magnolia, plate, 10" $10.00
Morning-Glory, cup & saucer $6.00
Morning-Glory, plate, 10¼" $8.00
Pepe, cup & saucer $10.00
Pompeii, creamer $6.00
Pompeii, cup & saucer $8.00
Pompeii, plate, 10" $8.00
Pompeii, plate, 7½" $5.00
Random Harvest, casserole, w/lid $25.00
Random Harvest, coffeepot, tall $25.00
Random Harvest, cup & saucer $8.00
Random Harvest, platter, 13" $12.50
Round-Up, cup & saucer $40.00
Round-Up, plate, 6" $16.00
Tampico, bowl, rim soup $15.00
Tampico, creamer & sugar bowl $30.00
Tampico, cup & saucer $12.00

Tampico, plate, dinner size, 10½" $10.00
Tampico, plate, 7" $5.00
Tampico, platter, 13" $25.00
Village Green, casserole stand, 10" $18.00
Village Green, warmer $18.00
Zinnia, chop plate, 12½x11" $6.00
Zinnia, plate, 10" $8.00

Stoneware

Bean pot, ½-gal, Boston style, brown Albany slip, marked
RW $135.00
Bowl, 12", blue bands on salt glaze, marked RW $78.00
Butter crock, 5-lb, brown Albany slip, low style, marked
RW $45.00
Churn, 3-gal, red wing & #3 stenciled on salt glaze,
marked RWUS $145.00
Crock, 12", red wing & #12 on white, marked RWUS .$70.00
Crock, 2-gal, double 'P' & #2 stenciled on salt glaze, marked
MN $90.00
Cuspidor, 10" dia, molded seam, blue sponging $350.00
Custard cup, blue to white shaded, unmarked $50.00
Flowerpot, 7", brown Albany slip, marked MN $225.00
Jug, 1-gal, bailed, white, marked RWUS, ca 1930 ......$90.00
Jug, 1-gal, common type, brown Albany slip, ball top,
marked MN $50.00
Jug, 1-gal, molded seam, blue mottle, bail handle, marked
MN $100.00
Jug, 1-qt, fancy, brown & white, marked RW $90.00
Jug, ½-gal, shouldered cone top, white, marked RW .$90.00
Jug, ½-gal, shouldered dome top, brown & salt glaze,
marked MN $125.00
Jug, 2-gal, shouldered funnel type, white, marked MN .$60.00
Pan, milk; 7", blue, marked RW $120.00
Pie plate, brown, marked RW $110.00
Pie plate, salt glaze & brown, marked MN $175.00
Pitcher, lg, embossed iris on brown Albany slip, marked
RWP $85.00
Pitcher, lg, Saffron, marked RWUS $85.00
Pitcher, mustard; 1-qt, salt glaze, marked MN $85.00

Tampico, gravy boat & undertray $35.00

Pitcher, Spongeband, w/advertising & date $250.00

Spittoon, salt glaze, unmarked.........................$165.00
Wax sealer, 1-qt, brown Albany slip, straight sides, marked
    RW $170.00

Riviera Dinnerware

A sister to the Fiesta line, Riviera was made by The Homer Laughlin China Company from 1938 until just before 1950. It was a thinner line, unmarked, and inexpensive. Their major marketing outlet was the Murphy Company chain of dime stores. Its pieces are squared with shaped rounded corners. Colors are mauve blue, red, yellow, light green, and ivory.

If you'd like to learn more about Riviera, we recommend *The Collector's Encyclopedia of Fiesta* by Sharon and Bob Huxford.

Batter set, ivory, w/decals........................$145.00
Bowl, baker; 9" $18.00
Bowl, cream soup; w/liner, ivory $65.00
Bowl, fruit; 5½" $9.00
Bowl, nappy; 9¼" $18.00
Bowl, oatmeal; 6".....................................$25.00
Butter dish, ½-lb $85.00
Butter dish, ¼-lb, all colors except cobalt & turquoise .$95.00
Butter dish, ¼-lb, cobalt...........................$200.00
Butter dish, ¼-lb, turquoise.......................$185.00
Casserole $80.00
Creamer $8.00
Cup & saucer, demitasse; ivory..................$50.00
Jug, w/lid...$95.00
Pitcher, juice; mauve blue.........................$170.00
Plate, deep...$16.00
Plate, 10"...$30.00
Plate, 6"..$6.00
Plate, 7"..$7.50
Plate, 9"..$12.50
Platter, 11½" $14.00

Platter, 11¼", w/closed handles $17.50
Platter, 12", cobalt...................................$45.00

Salt & pepper shakers, pr............................$15.00
Sauce boat $16.50
Saucer $3.00
Sugar bowl $16.00
Syrup, w/lid...$105.00
Teacup $8.00
Teapot..$95.00
Tidbit, 2-tier, ivory $70.00
Tumbler, handled......................................$55.00
Tumbler, juice...$40.00

Rock 'n Roll Memorabilia

Buy these items with an eye to the future! Already some of the large auction houses in the East have had rock 'n roll celebrity auctions, and some of the one-of-a-kind examples they've sold have brought high dollar results.

See also Beatles Collectibles; Elvis Presley Memorabilia; Magazines; Pin-Back Buttons.

Andy Gibb, doll, 8", Ideal, 1979, MIB $37.50
Bobby Sherman, paint & color book, 10x12½", marked Art
    Craft & Columbia Pictures, 1971, 32-page, EX **$20.00**
Book, Color & Re-Color Book, 6x13½", over 400 rock star
    combination figures to color, Magic Wand Corp, 1967,
    EX..**$45.00**
Cher, doll, 12", in bathing suit, Mego, 1970s, MIB......**$40.00**
Chubby Checker, lobby cards, 11x14", Don't Knock the
    Twist, 1962, set of 5, M.........................**$40.00**
Dave Clark Five, doll set, 4½" & 3", painted vinyl, Remco,
    1964, set of 5, MIB..............................**$50.00**
Dave Clark Five, souvenir booklet, 9x12½", black & white
    photos, 1960s, NM **$17.50**
Donnie & Marie, guitar, 1977, purple plastic, NM **$55.00**
Donnie & Marie, record player, marked Sing Along Radio
    Record Player, MIB...............................**$50.00**

Elton John, concert program, 12x12", photos included, soft-cover, early 1970s, 20-page, EX $22.50

Fats Domino, sheet music, I'm Walkin', photo cover, 1957, EX..$15.00

Jackson Five, game, 10½x12½x1", Jackson Five Action Game, marked Motown Record Corp & Shindana Toys, 1972, EX...$30.00

Kiss, alarm clock, marked Westclox, M.......................$75.00

Kiss, Colorforms, 1979, M...$45.00

Kiss, dolls, 13", vinyl w/rooted hair, Mego & Aucoin Management Inc, 1978, set of 4, EX $250.00

Kiss, model, Chevy van, marked AMT, MIB $75.00

Kiss, patches, 1970s, set of 4, M $20.00

Kiss, pencil, graphite & painted wood, set of 4, M $60.00

Led Zeppelin, song book, 48-page, WB Music, NM....$16.00

Linda Ronstadt, postcard, 3½x5½", color photo, M $1.50

Madonna, sheet music, Like a Virgin, M $17.50

Marie Osmond, dress pattern, MIP $6.00

Michael Jackson, Colorforms, deluxe set, M $10.00

Monkees, book, Who's Got the Button, Whitman, 1968, 208-page, NM..$16.00

Monkees, bracelet, photo charms, 1967, M on card....$37.50

Monkees, clothes hanger, die-cut cardboard, marked Reybert Products, 1967, missing plastic hanger, VG...$45.00

Monkees, Files Magazine, group photo on cover, NM.$10.00

Monkees, finger puppet, Mike Nesmith figure w/boots, marked Remco, 1970, NM $32.50

Monkees, flip book, ca 1967, M..................................$5.00

Monkees, guitar, 13x5x1½", hard black plastic w/full-color paper label, Raybert Productions, 1966, EX..........$37.50

Monkees, postcard, 5½x8", group photo w/fan club information, 1966, M..$5.00

Monkees, ring, flasher type, 1967, EX $20.00

Partridge Family, coloring book, Artcraft, 1970, NM ...$20.00

Partridge Family, David Cassidy Colorforms, 1972, NM.$20.00

Partridge Family, View-Master pack, 1971, M, sealed..$10.00

Pat Boone, comic book, 1959, EX $27.50

Pat Boone, song sheet, Sugar Moon, 1958, 4-page, EX.$15.00

Peter, Paul & Mary; song book, A Song Will Rise, ca 1968, 20-page, EX $15.00

Rolling Stones, table cover, paper, w/logo, M..............$7.00

Scott Joplin, tumbler, 6½", photo & song in tan & cream, Anchor Hocking, 1970s, set of 4, M in package ...$12.50

Sonny & Cher, lobby card, 11x14", Wild on the Beach, color, 1965, NM...$15.00

Sonny Bono, doll, 12", Mego, 1976, MIB $45.00

Stevie Wonder, postcard, 3½x5½", color photo, marked Printed in Italy, dated 1975, NM.............................$1.50

Three Dog Night, concert poster, 14x22", NM $20.00

Rookwood

Although this company was established in 1879, it continued to produce commercial artware until it closed in 1967. Located in Cincinnati, Ohio, Rookwood is recognized today as the largest producer of high-quality art pottery ever to operate in the United States.

Most of the pieces listed here are from the later years of production, but we've included a few early pieces as well. With few exceptions, all of these early art pottery companies produced an artist decorated brown-glaze line – Rookwood's was called Standard. Other early lines were Sea Green, Iris, Jewel Porcelain, Wax Matt, and Vellum.

Virtually all of Rookwood's pieces are marked. The most familiar is the 'reverse R'-P monogram. It was first used in 1886, and until 1900 a flame point was added above it to represent each passing year. After the turn of the century, a Roman numeral below the monogram indicated the current year. In addition to the dating mark, a die-stamped number was used to identify the shape.

The Cincinnati Art Galleries held two large and important cataloged auctions in 1991. The full-color catalogs contain a comprehensive history of the company, list known artists and designers with their monograms (as well as company codes and trademarks), and describe each lot thoroughly. Collectors now regard them as an excellent source for information and study.

Bookends, 4x6", #2846, green glossy w/molded floral deisgn, 1945, MIB $370.00

Bowl, 2x4", #2133, green crystalline, Arts & Crafts panel design, 1926 ....$80.00

Bowl, 3x5", #974C, pink matt w/green, 1916..............$70.00

Bowl, 3x6", #2256D, blue glossy w/green glossy interior, 1921 ....$50.00

Bowl, 3x7", #2760, green crystalline, 3 handles around top, 1924 ....$100.00

Box, 2x5", #6856, white matt w/molded florals on lid, 1944, sm hairline in lid...$100.00

Bust, 8x8", #2026, Beatrice, white matt, 1925, EX........$60.00

Figurine, 5", #6483, boxer dog, brown glossy w/blue traces, paper label, 1934 ....$350.00

Figurine, 6x6", #2778, Collie, butterscotch & brown matt, 1927 ....$400.00

Flower frog & bowl, 3x6", #1621E & #1877, purple matt, 1923 ....**$140.00**

Humidor, 5", #1896, yellow glossy w/band of sailing ships, porcelain, 1916..**$350.00**

Paperweight, 4x5", #1855, pr of swans, white, 1929 .**$200.00**

Paperweight, 5x4", #6521, seated nude w/frog, white matt, 1935 ....**$290.00**

Pitcher, 4", #259E, incised geometric design on red matt, tri-corner shape, 1904, glaze miss on handle **$90.00**

Pitcher, 6¼", #551W, floral spray on burnt sienna to burnt umber (Standard), artist signed..........$325.00

Sugar bowl, 5x5", #2663, gray, brown & white glossy, handles, twig finial..**$40.00**

Trivet, 6" dia, #3091, star shape, light blue border, purple berries & green leaves on cream, 1922 ....**$140.00**

Trivet, 6" square, #3077, pink & gray parrot on tan w/flowers, 1921 ....**$100.00**

Vase, 10", #2414, green matt, leafy Arts & Crafts decoration, 1928 ....**$300.00**

Vase, 10", #903B, standard, Indian portrait, light green, orange to light ground, bronze band at top, S Lawrence, 1900..**$2,800.00**

Vase, 11", #198B, Z glaze, green matt, geometric Arts & Crafts linear design at top, 1904 ....**$350.00**

Vase, 13", vellum glaze w/ocean scene & gulls, signed ET Hurley, dated 1908 ....$1,100.00

Vase, 3", #6352, light & dark blue crystalline w/molded clover & berries, 1936..............................**$80.00**

Vase, 5", #162D, Standard, orange poppies on dark ground, C Schmidt, 1897 ....**$400.00**

Vase, 5", #2088, yellow & green matt w/molded leaves & berries **$100.00**

Vase, 5", #2557, pink matt w/green, handles, 1929 .....**$75.00**

Vase, 5", #6094, blue matt w/molded floral band at neck, 1929 ....**$100.00**

Vase, 5", #642, light blue matt w/molded floral decoration, square form, 1952 ....**$100.00**

Vase, 5", #861, vellum, gray-blue to yellow w/red holly berries & green leaves, CC Lindeman, 1903........**$325.00**

Vase, 6", #1902, green crystalline w/molded peacock feather panels **$100.00**

Vase, 6" wide, #256F, pink to lavender matt, 1927......**$80.00**

Vase, 6x7", #1848, light blue & brown wax matt w/pink & green flowers on brown branches, Harris, 1928.**$550.00**

Vase, 7", #1833, yellow w/multicolor flowers, geometric band at bottom, brown interior, Sara Sax, 1924 .**$650.00**

Vase, 7", #2435, light blue w/brown at top, molded Arts & Crafts-type floral design, 1929............................**$110.00**

Vase, 7", #6049, black, yellow & red drip on cream, butterfat glaze, 10-sided, L Eppley, 1930........................**$400.00**

Vase, 7x6", #6818, bold blue-greens & brown, green interior, molded leaf design w/pointed top edge, HE, 1946, hairline **$80.00**

Vase, 8", #916C, Standard, brown to yellow ground w/yellow flowers on olive green, signed LES, 1902 ....**$350.00**

Vase, 8", #952E, vellum, lake scene in earth tones, brown band at top, L Asbury, 1915............................**$1,100.00**

Vase, 8x6", #2302, oxblood, 1928..........................**$375.00**

Vase, 9", #1369D, vellum, navy w/pink flowers & green leaves in separate groupings, Hentschel, 1916, paper label **$650.00**

Vase, 9", #689X, blue glossy w/molded flowers, 1949 ....**$200.00**

Vase, 9", #951D, vellum, gray, yellow to blue background w/yellow roses, buds & foliage, Ed Diers, 1907 .**$850.00**

Roselane Pottery

Beginning as a husband and wife operation in the late 1930s, the Roselane Pottery Company of Pasadena, California, expanded their inventory from the figurines they originally sold to local florists to include a complete line of decorative items that eventually were shipped to Alaska, South America, and all parts of the United States.

One of their lines was the Roselane Sparklers. Popular in the fifties, these small animal and bird figures were airbrush decorated and had rhinestone eyes. They're fun to look for and not at all expensive.

If you'd like to learn more, there's a chapter on Roselane in *The Collector's Encyclopedia of California Pottery* by Jack Chipman.

Deer, 4½" **$9.00**

Elephant, 6" **$14.00**

Figurine, boy w/dog, 5½"................................**$10.00**

Figurine, cat, 6¾", sitting, blue jewels in eyes, amber jewels in collar, Calif USA **$6.00**

Figurine, deer, 5½", standing, pink jewels in eyes, no mark **$5.00**

Figurine, elephant, 5½", blue jewels in eyes, pink & amber jewels on head **$8.00**

Figurine, elephant, 8", brown lustre, modernistic style, wooden base **$100.00**

Figurine, whippet dog, 7½", sitting, amber jewels in eyes, marked Calif USA **$8.00**

Fish, 7" **$12.00**

Rosemeade

The Wahpeton Pottery Company of Wahpeton, North Dakota, chose the tradename Rosemeade for a line of bird and animal figurines, novelty salt and pepper shakers, bells, and miscellaneous items which were sold from the 1940s to the '60s through gift stores and souvenir shops in that part of the country. They were marked with either a paper label or an ink stamp; the name Prairie Rose was also used.

Bank, hippo, bl, w/label **$95.00**

Basket, pink, twisted handle, sm **$30.00**

Bell, 5", peacock, w/sticker **$160.00**

Creamer & sugar bowl, corn, sm **$45.00**

Creamer & sugar bowl w/tray, grapes, chartreuse **$120.00**

Figurine, bear, dark rust, lg **$275.00**

Figurine, buffalo, head turned, lg **$300.00**

Figurine, kangaroo, lg **$90.00**

Figurine, pheasant, 14" **$400.00**

Figurines, penguins, miniature, set of 3 ....**$40.00**

Figurines, seals, miniature, set of 3 ....**$40.00**

Flower frog, doe, spotted back, tan & light blue **$35.00**

Flower frog, heron **$25.00**

Pitcher, ball type, novelty **$25.00**

Planter, bird, pink & cream **$25.00**

Planter, grape design, light green **$75.00**

Planter, swan **$17.50**

Rose bowl, tulip type, rose **$20.00**

Salt & pepper shakers, bears, resting, tan faces, miniature, pr **$50.00**

Salt & pepper shakers, chickens, tan, rose & green, pr .**$60.00**

Salt & pepper shakers, corn, sm, pr **$35.00**

Salt & pepper shakers, deer, tan, pr **$60.00**

Salt & pepper shakers, ducklings, pr **$45.00**

Salt & pepper shakers, Dutch mills, blue, pr **$65.00**

Salt & pepper shakers, flamingos, pr **$145.00**

Salt & pepper shakers, mice, gray, pr **$30.00**

Salt & pepper shakers, pekingese, pr **$45.00**

Salt & pepper shakers, running rabbits, pr **$75.00**

Salt & pepper shakers, Scottie dogs, black, pr **$30.00**

Salt & pepper shakers, setters, tan & white, pr **$40.00**

Salt & pepper shakers, tulip design, rose & green, pr.**$35.00**

Shakers, cats, Siamese, pr **$40.00**

Spoon rest, horse, bl **$45.00**

Spoon rest, pansy **$45.00**

Spoon rest, pheasant **$65.00**

Spoon rest, water lily **$25.00**

Vase, bud; chartreuse, 7½" **$20.00**

Vase, lovebird, cream & green **$30.00**

Wall pockets, crescent, pr **$55.00**

Wall pockets, does, rose & blue, pr **$75.00**

Watering can, rabbit form, tan **$75.00**

Roseville Pottery

This company took its name from the city in Ohio where they operated for a few years before moving to Zanesville in the late 1890s. They're recognized as one of the giants in the industry, having produced many lines of the finest in art pottery from the beginning to the end of their production days. Even when machinery took over many of the procedures once carefully done by hand, the pottery they produced continued to reflect the artistic merit and high standards of quality the company had always insisted upon.

Several marks were used over the years as well as some paper labels. The very early art lines often carried an applied ceramic seal with the name of the line (Royal, Egypto, Mongol, Mara, or Woodland) under a circle containing the words Rozane Ware. From 1910 until 1928, an Rv mark was used, the 'v' being contained in the upper loop of the 'R.' Paper labels were common from 1914 until 1937. From 1932 until they closed in 1952, the mark was Roseville in script, or R USA. Pieces marked RRP Co Roseville, Ohio, were not made by the Roseville Pottery but by Robinson Ransbottom of Roseville, Ohio. Don't be confused. There are many jardinieres and pedestals in a brown and green blended glaze that are being sold at flea markets and antique malls as Roseville that were actually made by Robinson Ransbottom as late as the 1970s and '80s. That isn't to say they don't have some worth of their own, but don't buy them for old Roseville.

Most of the listings here are for items produced from the 1930s on – things you'll be more likely to encounter today. If you'd like to learn more about the subject, we recommend *The Collector's Encyclopedia of Roseville Pottery, Vols 1* and *2,* and *The Catalog of Early Roseville,* all by Sharon and Bob Huxford.

Apple Blossom, cornucopia, 6", flowering branch design on green, #381, relief mark.............................**$50.00**

Apple Blossom, jardiniere, 6", flowering branch design on round bowl shape, twig handles, #342-6 ....**$110.00**

Apple Blossom, vase, 10", flowering branch design on trumpet-shaped body w/slighty domed base, twig handles, #388-10 ....**$135.00**

Apple Blossom, vase, 7", flowering branch design on green, tapers to flared bottom, twig handle, #382 ....**$60.00**

Artwood, planter, 7x9½", green & brown, berry spray in hollow center of rectangular shape, #1005-9..............**$70.00**

Baneda, bowl, 3½x10", leaf & pod design on low elongated shape, flared base, handled **$200.00**

Baneda, candle holder, 5½", leaf & pod design on mottled rose, handled, silver label **$150.00**

Baneda, vase, 7", leaf & pod design on round green jar shape, flared base, sm rim handles **$250.00**

Bittersweet, double vase, 4", berry & leaf on white & rose cornucopia shapes connected by twig handle, rectangular base, #858 ....**$55.00**

Bittersweet, planter, 11½", berry & leaf on green oval shape w/rim rising on sides, twig handles, #827-8..........**$65.00**

Bittersweet, urn 7", berry & leaf on white & rose, angled handles, #842-7 ....**$90.00**

Bittersweet, vase, 5", berry & leaf on white & rose, twig handles, #972 ....**$45.00**

Blackberry, jug, 5", embossed blackberry design on green sm lip rim, black paper label **$225.00**

Blackberry, 4", embossed blackberry design on round green bowl shape, sm handles...................................**$175.00**

Bleeding Heart, vase, 4", floral on bulbous tan body, straight neck w/flared scalloped rim, handled, #138.........**$50.00**

Bleeding Heart, vase, 6½", floral on blue, fancy rim w/U-shaped cut-outs, handled, #964-6 ....**$95.00**

Bushberry, bowl, 3", berry & leaf on round blue shape tapering to slightly flared base, lip rim, closed handles, #657 ....**$40.00**

Bushberry, planter, 6½", berry & leaf on rectangular orange shape w/raised twig motif on rim, #383-6 ....**$100.00**

Bushberry, urn, 6", berry & leaf on round blue bowl shape w/irregular rim, twig handles, #411-6.................**$100.00**

Bushberry, vase, 7", berry & leaf on tall orange body w/flared flat bottom, flared rim, short pedestal base, #32-7 ....**$95.00**

Bushberry, wall pocket, 8", berry & leaf on blue V-shape flaring to fan-shaped rim, twig handles, #1291, relief mark...**$200.00**

Capri, ashtray, 9", green round outer shape w/impressed inner shell, flat partially fluted rim, #598-9...........**$35.00**

Capri, basket, 7", mottled blue & white leaf figural bowl w/irregular handle, #508-7, relief mark.................**$90.00**

Capri, basket, 9", green oval shape w/vine handle, oval base, #510-10..**$95.00**

Capri, bowl, 13½", green shell shape, #582-9..............**$45.00**

Carnelian, flower holder, 6", blue drip glaze on fan-shaped body, pedestal base, plain rim, handled **$35.00**

Carnelian, vase, 7", green drip on heavily textured rose & tan urn shape, handled..**$100.00**

Carnelian I, wall pocket, 8", blue drip glaze on cone shape w/ribbed band, flared rim, handled, ink stamp...**$100.00**

Carnelian II, wall pocket, 8", red & yellow mottled glaze on cone shape, handled, black paper label **$125.00**

Clemana, bowl, 4½", floral on blue, flared rim, angled handles, #281-5, impressed mark....................**$100.00**

Clemana, vase, 6½", white & green floral on tan, round base, angled handles, #750-6, impressed mark...**$120.00**

Clematis, bowl, 4", floral on round blue-green shape w/straight rim, closed angled handles, #445........**$40.00**

Clematis, flowerpot, 5½", floral on tan & brown, saucer base, #668-5, relief mark **$50.00**

Clematis, wall pocket, 8", floral on tan & green V-shape w/straight neck, angled handles, #1295.............**$110.00**

Columbine, bowl, 6", floral on blue angled round shape tapering to flat bottom, plain rim, sharply angled handles, #401...**$40.00**

Columbine, candle holder, 5", floral on tall blue cup, lg round base, handled, #1146-4 ½ **$65.00**

Corinthian, compote, 5x10", deeply ribbed bottom in green & cream w/braided & floral band, short cream pedestal base...**$90.00**

Corinthian, jardiniere, 7", deeply ribbed bottom in green & cream w/braided & floral band on cream...........**$100.00**

Corinthian, wall pocket, 8", deeply ribbed V-shape in green & cream w/braided & floral band on cream.......**$150.00**

Cornelian, pitcher, 5", mottled tan **$55.00**

Cornelian, soap dish, 4", mottled tan, handled lid.......**$85.00**

Cosmos, candle holder, 2½", white floral on tall blue cup w/fancy rim, flared base, handled.....................**$110.00**

Cosmos, flower frog, 3½", floral on blue round shape, round base, slanted top handle................................**$50.00**

Cosmos, vase, 6½", floral on deep yellow, bulbous lower body w/long straight neck, fancy rim, handled....**$75.00**

Cosmos, wall pocket, 8½", floral on fancy blue V-shape, #1286-8, silver paper label **$150.00**

Dawn, vase, 12", spider mum on green cylinder, square base & handles, #318-14...................................**$150.00**

Dawn, vase, 6", spider mum on pale yellow cylinder, square base & handles, plain rim, #826...........................**$90.00**

Dogwood II, basket, 8", floral on round green bowl shape w/flat bottom, irregular rim, plain handle...........**$115.00**

Dogwood II, bud vase, 9", floral on tall green tubular-like body w/flared flat bottom **$60.00**

Dogwood II, 9", floral design connects 2 flared tubular shapes tapering at bottom...................................**$150.00**

Donatello, ashtray, 3", banded cherub design w/flared & fluted top **$75.00**

Donatello, basket, 7½", banded cherub design w/fluted top & bottom, handled...**$130.00**

Donatello, jardiniere, 6", banded cherub design w/fluted top & bottom **$110.00**

Donatello, vase, 8", banded cherub w/flared & fluted top & bottom **$50.00**

Donatello, wall pocket, 9", banded cherub design on fluted cone shape, high fluted back...............................**$125.00**

Earlam, candlestick, 4", blue matte on elongated cup w/rolled rim, sits in shallow tray, loop handle...**$150.00**

Earlam, planter, 5½x10½", blue matte long sides rise in middle, angled handles..**$150.00**

Earlam, wall pocket, 6½", blue matte on wide U-shape, ribbed band in middle, black paper label...........**$225.00**

Falline, bowl, 11", pea pod design on tan, low, handled **$150.00**

Falline, vase, 7½", pea pod design on tan urn shape shape, straight rim, high loop handles, silver label........**$250.00**

Ferella, candlestick, 4½", wine mottled glaze, elongated cup, flared base...**$200.00**

Ferella, urn, 6", light brown mottled glaze w/cut-out shell-like design on rim & base, angled handles.........**$250.00**

Florentine (Ivory), wall pocket, 8½", decorative panels on ivory V-shape...**$110.00**

Foxglove, basket, 10", floral on blue, #314.........$175.00

Foxglove, cornucopia, 8", white floral on green, #659, relief mark...**$55.00**

Foxglove, vase, 3", floral on blue cup shape tapering to short, plain rim, angled handles, #659 ....**$30.00**

Foxglove, vase, 8½", floral on green & red fan shape w/3-tiered rim, handled, #47-8, relief mark..............**$150.00**

Freesia, bookends, white floral on green open-book shape, #15, relief mark, pr **$125.00**

Freesia, bowl, 8½", floral design on Delft Blue, low elongated shape on straight base, handled, #464-6, relief mark.**$60.00**

Freesia, bud vase, 7", floral on green, w/long neck flaring slightly at rim, handled, #195 ....**$50.00**

Freesia, flowerpot/saucer, 7", floral design on tan & green, flared rim, #119-7, relief mark...............................**$85.00**

Freesia, vase, 7", white floral on blue ovoid bulbous body tapering to plain rim, flared base, handled, #120.**$75.00**

Fuchsia, vase, 7", floral on blue, bulbous, plain rim, handled, #895, impressed mark **$140.00**

Fuchsia, vase, 8", floral on blue, bulbous lower body w/straight upper body, slightly flared rim, handled, #898-8 ....**$65.00**

Futura, jardiniere, 6", white geometric floral on tan, squared handles **$200.00**

Futura, vase, 6", gray & green geometric design on trapezoid tapering at bottom then flaring slightly.......**$150.00**

Gardenia, vase, 8", floral on tan & brown, handled, #683-8, relief mark **$75.00**

Gardenia, basket, 8", white floral on flared green body w/scalloped rim, short round pedestal base, handled, #608 ....**$100.00**

Gardenia, bowl, 4", white floral on tan & brown round shape, lip rim, closed handles, #600....................**$40.00**

Holland, mug, 4", Dutch girl $45.00

Holland, powder jar, 3", figure in boat, w/lid..............**$95.00**

Imperial I, bud vase, 12", leaf & loop design on green textured body flaring at bottom, handled **$135.00**

Imperial II, vase, 8½", green 'moss' on rust........$185.00

Iris, basket, 8", white floral on rose & green bowl shape, plain rim, handled, #354, impressed mark.........**$200.00**

Iris, vase, 4", white floral on blue, flaring at top & tapering at bottom, handled, #914....................................**$60.00**

Iris, vase, 5", florals on rose & green, inverted teardrop shape on round base, angled handles, #915-5, impressed mark....................................**$60.00**

Iris, vase, 7½", florals on rose & green, bulbous w/flared rim, handled, #920-7, impressed mark **$125.00**

Iris, vase, 8", florals on blue, cup shape w/flared rim & bottom, pedestal base, angled handles, #923-8, impressed mark.**$135.00**

Ivory II, jardiniere, 6", satin ivory on graduated bowl shape w/4 decorative buttresses, banded rim..................**$50.00**

Ivory II, urn, 6½", satin ivory on bowl shape, handled, #271-6, impressed mark....................................**$55.00**

Ixia, bowl, 4", floral on rose & green, round, plain rim, stand-up handles, #326....................................**$45.00**

Ixia, hanging basket, 7", floral design on pink..........**$200.00**

Ixia, vase, 8½", floral design on yellow U-shape w/fancy rim, handles attached to oval base, #858-8 ....**$80.00**

Jonquil, bud vase, 7", white & green floral on tan, tall neck w/flared rim & bulbous body, handled................**$65.00**

Jonquil, candlestick, 4", floral on dark tan short-stemmed cup on domed base...**$100.00**

Jonquil, urn, 4", floral on dark tan, handled..............**$125.00**

Jonquil, vase, 7", floral on dark tan, flared rim, handles droop downward to flared base **$150.00**

La Rose, wall pocket, 12", swag floral design on ivory V-shape, fancy rim, ink stamp **$135.00**

Laurel, bowl, 7" dia, flowering branches on blue-green, round shape tapering to flat bottom, plain rim ..**$100.00**

Laurel, urn, 6½", floral on reddish-brown bulbous shape w/3-tiered rim, closed handles, sm round base..**$150.00**

Laurel, vase, 9½", floral on tan bowl shape w/2-tiered neck, closed handles, silver paper label......................**$175.00**

Light Rozane, bowl, 3", floral, w/handles, signed MT .**$175.00**

Light Rozane, jardiniere, 5", floral, footed **$150.00**

Light Rozane, sugar bowl, 4½", floral, handled lid, 2 side handles **$200.00**

Lombardy, wall pocket, 8", ribbed blue V-shape **$200.00**

Lotus, pillow vase, 10½", vertical rows of yellow lotus leaves on rectangular blue shape, #L4-10, relief mark...**$135.00**

Lotus, planter, 3½x4", vertical rows of yellow lotus leaves on square green shape, #L9-4, relief mark............**$60.00**

Luffa, vase, 8½", white floral & lg leaf design on horizontally ridged tan bowl, angled handles $135.00

Magnolia, ashtray, 7", floral design on blue, straight rim w/cigarette rests, angled handles, #28.................**$60.00**

Magnolia, bowl, 3", white floral on round green shape tapering to flat bottom, angled handles, #665.......**$40.00**

Magnolia, planter, 6", floral design on blue horizontal comma-shaped bowl on rectangular base, angled handles, #183-6 ....**$60.00**

Magnolia, planter, 8", flowering branches on rectangular blue shape w/lip rim, straight base, angled handles, #389 ....**$100.00**

Magnolia, vase, 8", floral design on green, bulbous lower body w/short neck, angled handles, #91-8.........**$135.00**

Matt Green, wall pocket, 11", floral design on cone shape w/cut-outs on high back **$150.00**

Mayfair, bowl, 4", embossed modernistic floral design on cream cup shape, plain rim, #1110, relief mark....**$25.00**

Mayfair, jardiniere, 7½", square green shape w/yellow interior, 4-footed, #90-4, relief mark **$35.00**

Mayfair, pot, 4½", yellow, 3 horizontal wavy ridges on round shape tapering at bottom, #71-4 ....**$40.00**

Mayfair, teapot, 5", yellow, #1121.............................**$45.00**

Ming Tree, ashtray, 6", ming tree design on green square, cigarette rests at corners, #599, relief mark..........**$45.00**

Ming Tree, basket, 13", ming tree design on blue, tulip shape w/flared irregular base, #509-12 ....**$200.00**

Ming Tree, conch shell, 8½", blue w/cream interior, #563, relief mark **$45.00**

Ming Tree, window box, 4x11", ming tree design on blue rectangle, #569-10, relief mark................................**$75.00**

Mock Orange, bowl, floral on yellow, short flat base, lip rim, closed handles, #900, relief mark..................**$35.00**

Mock Orange, pillow vase, floral on rose, tulip shape w/fancy rim, footed, #930-8 ....**$60.00**

Mock Orange, vase, 8½x4½", floral on rectangular green shape w/flared fancy rim, footed, #956-8.............**$50.00**

Moderne, comport, 5", embossed stylized floral design on round cup, flared foot w/cut-out stem, #295, impressed mark...**$125.00**

Moderne, urn, 6½", stylized embossed florals on bowl shape, beige tones, #299, impressed mark **$100.00**

Monticello, vase, 7", decorated band on tan, bulbous body w/flat bottom, plain rim, handled.........................**$175.00**

Morning Glory, bowl, 5", allover embossed morning-glory design on green flared rim, angled handles.......**$225.00**

Moss, pillow vase, 8", moss-like design on blue-green & cream, angled handles, 6-sided base, #781-8, impressed mark...**$150.00**

Moss, wall pocket, 8", moss-like design on inverted V-shape w/rounded bottom, handled, #1278-8.................**$175.00**

Orian, bowl, 6", blue glaze, slightly flared round base, plain rim, handled, gold paper label **$100.00**

Orian, candle holder, 4½", tall cylindrical cup on flared base, handled **$55.00**

Orian, comport, 4½x10½", flared blue bowl w/pink interior, flared foot, handled, #272-10, impressed mark.....**$75.00**

Pasadena, flowerpot, 4", white drip glaze on square pink shape w/rounded corners, round footed metal base, #L36..**$40.00**

Pasadena, planter, 4", yellow-green drip glaze on square shape that tapers at bottom, footed, #1510 ....**$30.00**

Peony, basket, 7", floral on tan & green, round shape on flared base, plain rim rising on 1 side, angled handle, #376 ....**$90.00**

Peony, bowl, 4", floral on tan & green, round shape w/lip rim & right-angled handles, #427, relief mark.......**$45.00**

Peony, pitcher, 7½", floral & ribbed design on tan, plain rim & spout, slightly angled handle, #1326 ....**$150.00**

Peony, planter, 10", white flowers on ribbed blue rectangular bowl, angled handles, fancy rim, #387-8 ....**$75.00**

Peony, vase, 4", floral on light tan, cup shape slightly flaring at rim & base, handles angling downward, #57....**$35.00**

Peony, wall pocket, 8", floral on tan V-shape, ruffled rim, handled, low back, #1293-8, relief mark **$150.00**

Pine Cone, bowl, 4½", pine cone design on blue, twig handles, #320-5, impressed mark................**$100.00**

Pine Cone, bud vase, 7", tall tan slightly bulbous body on green flared base, pine cone handle, #478 ....**$100.00**

Pine Cone, candlestick, 2½", embossed pine cone cup on flared base, 1 leaf & 1 twig handle, #122-3, impressed mark....................**$70.00**

Pine Cone, cornucopia, 6", blue w/cream interior, pine cone decoration at oval base, #126....................**$90.00**

Pine Cone, mug, 4", pine cone design on blue, twig handle, flared base, #960-4, impressed mark **$150.00**

Pine Cone, pillow vase, 8", pine cone design on blue, twig handles, #845-8, impressed mark........................**$250.00**

Pine Cone, urn, 5", pine cone design on round blue bowl shape, plain rim, twig handle, sm flared base **$200.00**

Poppy, jardiniere, 5", embossed floral design on round bowl, round base, sm high handles, #642-4, impressed mark....................**$75.00**

Poppy, vase, 6½", floral on tan, urn shape on short round base, high round handles, impressed mark........**$125.00**

Poppy, vase, 7½", embossed yellow & green floral design on shaded green, fancy rim, handled, #869-7, impressed mark....................**$125.00**

Primrose, bowl, 4", white floral on golden tan, round shape w/plain rim, round base, angled handles, impressed mark....................**$75.00**

Primrose, vase, 7", white & green florals on green urn shape, tapered bottom, angled handles, #760-6 ....**$100.00**

Primrose, vase, 8", white floral on turquoise, bulbous urn shape, angled handles, #767 ....**$125.00**

Raymor, cruet, 5½", Contemporary White, bulbous shape w/round knob stopper, relief mark **$25.00**

Raymor, individual casserole, 7½", Autumn Brown, handled round bowl & lid, #199, relief mark **$30.00**

Raymor, salad bowl, 11½", irregular shape in Beach Gray, #161, relief mark **$25.00**

Raymor, salt & pepper shakers, 3½", Contemporary White, relief mark **$30.00**

Raymor, water pitcher, 10", Contemporary White, modernistic bulbous shape, #189, relief mark...........**$100.00**

Raymor Modern Artware, bowl, 3x7", mottled yellow glaze, #41-6 ....**$75.00**

Raymor Modern Artware, wall pocket, 10½", coach lamp shape in white, #711............................**$150.00**

Rosecraft Black, wall pocket, 9", black gloss glaze on cone shape, pointed rim, high back, paper label........**$150.00**

Rozane, bud vase, 7½", floral on brown, tall thin neck w/flared top, squatty bulbous body #841/3........**$140.00**

Rozane, candlestick, 9", floral on brown, flared top & bottom, Rozane Ware seal, signed J Imlay **$175.00**

Rozane, ewer, 7½", floral on brown, thin neck w/ruffled rim, flared bottom, on round base, #857/x **$175.00**

Rozane, vase, 7", floral on brown, pear shape on round base, Rozane Ware seal....................**$175.00**

Russco, triple cornucopia, 8x12½", shades of yellow & green, silver paper label......................**$90.00**

Russco, vase, 6½", vertical line decoration on blue bowl shape, closed handles....................**$60.00**

Silhouette, box, 4½", tan, incised design on lid, #740, relief mark....................**$50.00**

Silhouette, cornucopia, 8", carved leaf design on white, #721, relief mark....................**$35.00**

Silhouette, ewer, 6½", incised design on white, thin neck, bulbous bottom, angled handle, #716-6 ....**$45.00**

Silhouette, vase, 6", incised design on dark tan, tall, irregular rim, bulbous bottom, handled, #780-6 ....**$45.00**

Snowberry, ashtray, round plate shape w/berry & leaf design on rose, relief mark....................**$45.00**

Snowberry, bud vase, 7", berry & leaf design on blue, tubular shape flaring at bottom, wavy rim, 1 angled handle, #1BV **$40.00**

Snowberry, flowerpot, 5½", berry, leaf & twig design on rose pink, saucer base, #1PS-5, relief mark...........**$90.00**

Snowberry, vase, 7½", berry & leaf on blue, lower bulbous body, tall straight neck, flared rim, #1V1-7 ....**$60.00**

Snowberry, vase, 8½", berry & leaf on blue, bulbous body on pedestal base, flared rim, handled, #1UR-8, relief mark....................**$110.00**

Sunflower, candlestick, 4", sunflower design on green, tall flared cup w/handles extending to flared base ..**$165.00**

Sunflower, vase, 6", sunflower design on green & tan, cylindrical body, angled handles **$175.00**

Sunflower, vase, 8", sunflower design on green & tan, bulbous base $235.00

Sunflower, vase 6", sunflower design on green & tan, wide round neck flares to bulbous body $175.00

Teasel, vase, 5", embossed teasel design on blue, squatty bulbous body w/straight rim, handled $50.00

Teasel, vase, 6", embossed teasel design on shades of yellow, fancy rim, closed handles, #881-6 ....$60.00

Thornapple, cornucopia, 6", white thistle & floral on rose & green..$50.00

Thornapple, double bud vase, 5½", 2 vases on single base w/floral & leaf design, #1119, impressed mark.....$75.00

Thornapple, planter, 5", floral & leaf on tan, round bowl shape, lip rim, short round flared base, angled handles, #262 ....$60.00

Topeo, vase, 6", vertical tapered bead design on round bowl shape, red, silver paper label $165.00

Topeo, vase, 7", vertical tapered bead design on blue carafe shape, flat bottom, plain rim, paper label..........$150.00

Topeo, vase, 9", vertical tapered bead design on angled pear shape, light blue...................................$150.00

Tourmaline, bowl, 5", blue streaked glaze, round shape w/horizontal ribbed panels, straight round base, straight rim...$60.00

Tourmaline, candlestick, 5", blue, flared ribbed cup & bottom, silver paper label..$50.00

Tourmaline, cornucopia, 7", blue, flared scalloped base, silver paper label..$45.00

Tourmaline, vase, 8", blue streaked glaze, cylinder shape w/concave sides on short round pedestal base, paper label $70.00

Tuscany, wall pocket, 7", light blue on V-shape, ribbed below flared & flat rim, handled, low back $120.00

Velmoss, vase, 9½", berry & leaf design on med blue, angled handles $80.00

Velmoss II, vase, 7", leaf design on green, slightly bulbous body flares upward to plain rim, round base, angled handles $60.00

Water Lily, bowl, 3", floral on tan & green, bulbous lower body, angled handles, #663........................$40.00

Water Lily, vase, 6", floral on blue cruet shape w/handles angling downward, #73 ....$50.00

Water Lily, vase, 9", floral design on Walnut Brown, handles, #78-9 ....$125.00

White Rose, bowl, 3", white floral on blue, round shape on short straight base, straight rim w/U-shaped cutouts, #653 ....$40.00

White Rose, cornucopia, 8", white floral on rose & green, #144, relief mark $50.00

White Rose, double candle holder, 4", floral on rose & green, tall flared cups on connected round bases, handled, #1143 ....$90.00

White Rose, vase, 8", floral on rose & green, 6-sided base, sharply angled handles, #984-8........................$125.00

White Rose, 4½", floral on rose & green, flared cup & base, handled, #1142-4½......................................$55.00

Wincraft, candle holders, short angled cups on square bases in mottled blue glaze, #2CS, relief mark, pr.........$40.00

Wincraft, cornucopia, 7", floral on mottled apricot, rectangular base, #274-7, relief mark $45.00

Wincraft, vase, 7", design on mottled yellow & brown, tall square shape, paneled sides, round base, #274-7, relief mark..$75.00

Windsor, vase, 6", blue urn shape tapers at bottom, high handles attached to straight rim..........................$125.00

Wisteria, vase, 6", floral on textured tan & green, bulbous body w/plain rim, flat bottom, silver label..$225.00

Zephyr Lily, ashtray, 4 white lily petals & 4 pointed green leaves, circular..$40.00

Zephyr Lily, bowl, 4", floral on tan & green, bulbous body, handled, #671, relief mark....................................$50.00

Zephyr Lily, bud vase, 7½", floral on blue, tall body, slightly flared rim & base, handled, #201-7, relief mark....$50.00

Zephyr Lily, cornucopia, 8½", floral on blue, #204-8, relief mark...$60.00

Zephyr Lily, vase, 9½", floral on green, flares at top & bottom, wavy rim, round base, handled, #133-8........$80.00

Royal Copenhagen Figurines

The Royal Copenhagen Manufactory was established in Denmark in the late 1800s and since that time has produced quality china dinnerware, vases, collector plates, and the figurines such as we've listed here. They're very appealing, high in quality, and extremely collectible.

Boy seated on rock rolling up pants legs, 8" $185.00
Boy w/sailboat, 5½", kneeling, #01245 ....$375.00
Boy w/teddy bear, 8½"..$195.00
Cat playing w/tail, 7½", gray tabby..............................$140.00
Dachshund puppy, recumbent, #856 ....$275.00
Dancing girl, 8¼", #2444 ....$285.00
Duck & drake, 6", #2128 ....$65.00
Elephant, 4½", gray, #2998..$175.00
Ermine on log, #01121, 9½"..$250.00

Geese, 9", #2068..**$300.00**	
Girl seated, 4", Tylland **$375.00**	
Girl w/rabbit, ca 1980, #5653.....................**$165.00**	
Jaguar cub, #5649 ....**$385.00**	
Kangaroo, 6", #05154..................................**$325.00**	
Kaola bear, 7", ca 1980................................**$525.00**	
Lady fishmonger sitting behind basket of fish, 9"......**$265.00**	
Lioness, 6½x12½", recumbent, #804 ....**$395.00**	
Man seated wearing Tam-o'-shanter, 8" **$295.00**	
Mare & foal, 7", #4698, ...**$415.00**	
Milkmaid, 11½", #899 ....**$450.00**	
Pan on column, #1020/433 ....**$295.00**	
Partridge, 4x8", ca 1975, #02261 ....**$185.00**	
Pekingese, 5", standing, #11337..................**$175.00**	
Polar bear, 11", hunting...............................**$235.00**	
Robin, #2266..**$50.00**	
Rooster, 3½" **$70.00**	
Sandman, 6½", #1145...................................**$195.00**	
Seated dog, 8", #259 ....**$250.00**	
Snowman, 5", #5658 ....**$125.00**	
Swan, #606 ....**$125.00**	
Thumbelina, 4¾", #4374 ....**$185.00**	
Turkey, 3", #4794, 3".....................................**$100.00**	
Two old ladies going to market, 11½" **$295.00**	
Wirehair fox terrier, 8½", standing, #11009..............**$150.00**	

Royal Copley

This is a line of planters, wall pockets, vases, and other novelty items, most of which are modeled as appealing animals, birds, or human figures. They were made by the Spaulding China Company of Sebring, Ohio, from 1942 until 1957. The decoration is underglazed and airbrushed, and some pieces are trimmed in gold (which can add 25% to 50% to their values). Not every piece is marked, but they have a style that is distinctive. Some items are ink stamped; others have (or have had) labels.

Examples are readily found, and prices are still low. Unmarked items may often be found at a bargain. Some

people choose a particular animal to collect. For instance, if you're a cat lover, they were made in an extensive assortment of styles and sizes. Teddy bears are also popular; you'll find them licking a lollipop, playing a mandolin, or modeled as a bank, for instance. Wildlife lovers can collect deer, pheasants, fish, and gazelles, and there's a wide array of songbirds to be had as well.

If you'd like more information, we recommend *Royal Copley* written by Leslie Wolfe, edited by Joe Devine.

Ashtray, 5" dia, rose-colored straw hat shape w/blue bow, raised letters on bottom...**$12.00**	
Ashtray, 5" long, leaf shape w/embossed flower at end, blue & cream, green stamp on bottom **$6.00**	
Bank, 5½", farmer pig figural, pink bibs w/blue neckerchief, paper label only..**$34.00**	
Bank, 7½", pig in cream shirt w/blue bow tie, For My Cadillac in black on shirt, green stamp on bottom **$30.00**	
Bank, 7½", teddy bear figural, black & white w/pink bow, paper label only..**$60.00**	
Figurine, 4½", nuthatch, gray body w/green tail, paper label only **$14.00**	
Figurine, 5", dove w/wings spread on tree stump, any color variation, paper label only, each............................**$14.00**	
Figurine, 5", warbler on tree stump, any color variation, green stamp or raised letters on bottom, each......**$12.00**	
Figurine, 5", open-beak sparrow on a tree stump, paper label only..**$12.50**	
Figurine, 5½", blue sparrow on a tree stump, paper label only **$28.00**	
Figurine, 6½", full-bodied skylark on tree stump, any color variation, paper label only, each............................**$15.00**	
Figurine, 6½", full-bodied thrush on tree stump, any color variation, paper label only, each............................**$15.00**	
Figurine, 6½", seated Airedale, paper label only **$18.00**	
Figurine, 6¼", full-bodied wren on tree stump, any color variation, paper label only, each............................**$15.00**	
Figurine, 7", swallow w/extended wings, any color variation, paper label only, each **$34.00**	

Figurine, 7½", hen, blue, red & yellow..................$22.00

Figurine, 7½", Oriental boy or girl, any color variation, paper label only, each...**$14.00**

Figurine, 7¼", full-bodied cockatoo w/wings spread, blue, paper label only...**$28.00**

Figurine, 8", black cat facing right, pink bow, paper label only...**$28.00**

Figurine, 8", dancing lady, blue & rose dress & hat...**$35.00**

Figurine, 8", full-bodied titmouse on tree stump, any color variation, paper label only, each...........................**$18.00**

Figurine, 8", seated cocker spaniel, paper label only..**$18.00**

Pitcher, 6", floral decal on white, ear-type handle, gold stamp on bottom..**$10.00**

Pitcher, 8", embossed daffodils, pink & yellow, ear-type handle, green stamp on bottom...........................**$25.00**

Pitcher, 8", Floral Beauty, pink flowers embossed on yellow, green stamp or raised letters on bottom...............**$25.00**

Planter, 2½x6¼", chartreuse & brown w/3 sections, raised letters on bottom.......................................**$10.00**

Planter, 3", lg yellow blossom on green background, green stamp on bottom..**$10.00**

Planter, 3½", brown specks on turquoise background, boat shape, paper label only......................................**$10.00**

Planter, 3½", ribbed, rose, raised letters on bottom.......**$7.50**

Planter, 3½x7½", Oriental boy beside bamboo planter, paper label only...**$24.00**

Planter, 3¼", coach shape, rose, paper label only.......**$15.00**

Planter, 4¼", ivy decoration on cream, footed, paper label only...**$8.00**

Planter, 4¾", Oriental child w/big vase, cream, rose & blue, paper label only...**$10.00**

Planter, 4x7¼", embossed philodendron on cream, footed, paper label only...**$12.00**

Planter, 5", duck eating grass, paper label only...........**$10.00**

Planter, 5½", cocker spaniel w/basket, brown & green, paper label only...**$15.00**

Planter, 5½", dog, Stuffed Animal series, white w/rose spoots, paper label only...................................**$20.00**

Planter, 5½", teddy bear beside open tree stump, paper label only...**$20.00**

Planter, 5½" dia, hat shape w/embossed flowers & bow, raised letters on back, each...................................**$18.00**

Planter, 5¼", black cat leaning on yellow tub, paper label only...**$16.00**

Planter, 5¾", bamboo shoots & green leaves embossed on yellow, paper label only, oval...............................**$12.00**

Planter, 5¾", pouter pigeon figural, brown & rose, paper label only...**$15.00**

Planter, 6", Dutch girl or boy w/bucket, paper label only, each **$15.00**

Planter, 6", elf beside stump, dark green clothing w/red hat, paper label only...**$18.00**

Planter, 6", embossed deer & fawn on white, paper label only, footed, rectangular **$200.00**

Planter, 6", running gazelles embossed on square, light green on dark green w/gold trim, paper label **$20.00**

Planter, 6", teddy bear w/basket on shoulders.....$35.00

Planter, 6½", elephant figural, Stuffed Animal series, cream w/green polka dots, paper label only **$28.00**

Planter, 6½", fighting cock figural, paper label only ...**$18.00**

Planter, 6½x8½", resting poodle figural, cream, paper label only...**$30.00**

Planter, 6¼", little girl leaning on barrel, green & rose clothing, paper label only..**$14.00**

Planter, 6¼", praying angel figural, rose & blue w/gold highlights **$30.00**

Planter, 6¼", teddy bear figural, black & white w/pink bow, paper label only...**$38.00**

Planter, 6¼", woodpecker beside stump, any color variation, green stamp or raised letters on bottom, each......**$15.00**

Planter, 6¼", wren on tree stump, paper label only....**$16.00**

Planter, 6¾", teddy bear w/mandolin, paper label **$32.00**

Planter, 7", girl sitting on wheelbarrow, light green dress & red hat, dark green wheelbarrow, paper label **$16.00**

Planter, 7", pup in basket, pink & green w/gold.........**$16.00**

Planter, 7¾", mallard duck figural, paper label only ...**$14.00**

Planter, 8", birdhouse w/bird on roof, paper label......**$42.00**

Planter, 8", Colonial old woman or man, signed w/raised letters on back, each...**$28.00**

Planter, 8", kitten in picnic basket, paper label only...**$48.00**

Planter, 8", pirate head figural, any color variation, signed w/raised letters on back, each **$30.00**

Planter, 8", rooster & wheelbarrow, paper label only.**$45.00**

Planter, 8½", black & white dog beside mailbox, paper label only...**$42.00**

Planter, 8¼", bear cub clinging to tree stump, paper label only...**$24.00**

Planter, 8¼", kitten w/yellow ball of yarn, green bow around neck, paper label only.............................**$18.00**

Planter, 9", Siamese cats figural w/basketweave planter at rear, paper label only **$55.00**

Planter/wall pocket, 7½", Chinese boy w/wide-brimmed hat, rose & blue, signed w/raised letters on back........**$20.00**

Planter/wall pocket, 8", Blackamoor Prince figural, white turban, signed w/raised letters on back **$28.00**

Vase, 5½", embossed dragon on side, footed, paper label only **$10.00**

Vase, 5½", stylized leaves, rose on beige, paper label ..**$8.50**

Vase, 5½", stylized leaves embossed on yellow, paper label only **$10.00**

Vase, 5¾", embossed fish beside round center opening, blue & cream w/gold highlights, paper label only **$20.00**

Vase, 6½", black floral leaf & stem on coral tone, paper label only **$12.00**

Vase, 6½", embossed bow & ribbon, any color variation, paper label only, each **$10.00**

Vase, 6¼", floral decal on white, bulbous w/slightly flared rim, ear-type handles, footed, gold stamp.............**$10.00**

Vase, 6¼", green ivy on ivory background, footed, paper label only **$12.00**

Vase, 6¼", horse head figural, paper label..................**$15.00**

Vase, 7¼", embossed bird in flight beside round center opening, paper label only **$20.00**

Vase, 8", ivy decor on cream, footed, paper label only .**$12.00**

Vase, 8", Thinking of You lettered on floral decal, green background, cylinder form, #336 ....**$28.00**

Vase/candle holder, 6¾", praying angel embossed on yellow star shape, paper label only, rare **$20.00**

Window box, 3½", black floral leaf & stem on coral, paper label only **$12.00**

Royal Doulton

Probably the best-known producers of figurines, character jugs, and series ware ever to exist, the Royal Doulton Company was established in 1815 and continues today to make quality items that are sold through fine gift stores and distributors worldwide.

Kingsware (1899-1946) was a brown-glazed line decorated with drinking scenes. A popular line of collector plates, twenty-four in all, was called the Gibson Girl series. Made from 1901 until sometime in the forties, it was decorated in blue and white with scenes that portrayed a day in the life of 'The Widow and Her Friends.' From 1908 until the early 1940s, they produced Dickensware, decorated with illustrations from Charles Dickens. Robin Hood and Shakespeare were both introduced around 1914, and their Bunnykin series has been made since 1933.

The first character figures were made in 1913 and have remained very popular with collectors ever since. They are not only marked, but each character (and variation) is assigned an identifying number which is printed on the base following the prefix letters 'HN.' Factors that bear on the value of a figurine are age, detail, color, and availability. The presence of an artist's signature or a 'Potted' (pre-1939) mark adds to it as well.

Many collectors favor the bird and animal figures. They were made in a full-size line (having 'HN' prefixes) as well as miniatures (which have a 'K' prefix). Popular domestic breeds are usually valued higher than the more generic animals.

Toby and character jugs were introduced in the 1930s. Both styles are marked with numbers in a 'D' series; the character jugs are made in three sizes (large, small, and miniature). Occasionally you may find a jug with an 'A' mark which, though apparently used for only factory identification purposes, usually boosts its value to some extent. Dates found on the bottom of some jugs are merely copyright dates, not necessarily production dates.

Animal, Airedale, med, #1023 ....**$150.00**

Animal, bear, Titanian Ware, #170............................**$450.00**

Animal, bulldog, sm, white, #1074 ....**$150.00**

Animal, Cairn, med, #1034 ....**$250.00**

Animal, Cocker Spaniel & pheasant, #1028 ....**$130.00**

Animal, Dalmatian, med, #1113 ....**$180.00**

Animal, elephant w/her young, flambe, #3548...........**$90.00**

Animal, German shepherd, lg, #1115 ....**$1,100.00**

Animal, hare, sm, recumbent, #2594 ....**$60.00**

Animal, hare, 2¾", flambe, #1157 ....**$95.00**

Animal, Irish Setter, med, #1055 ....**$160.00**

Animal, Pekingese, sm, #1012...................................**$120.00**

Animal, Persian cat, black, #999 ....**$225.00**

Animal, Scottish Terrier, sm, #1016 ....**$140.00**

Animal, Sealyham, med, #1031 ....**$265.00**

Animal, tiger, flambe, #809 ....**$450.00**

Bunnykins, figurine, Cooling Off, ca 1972-87 ....**$50.00**

Bunnykins, figurine, Family Photograph....................**$48.00**

Bunnykins, figurine, Oompah Band Drummer, dated Golden Jubilee, 1984 ....**$60.00**

Bunnykins, hug-a-mug, Windy Day, 1-handled, 1984.**$27.50**

Bunnykins, oatmeal/cereal bowl, Mr Piggly's Stores, signed Barbara Vernon, ca 1952 ....**$60.00**

Bunnykins, plate, baby's, Greetings, signed Barbara Vernon, w/A mark, ca 1937..**$135.00**

Bunnykins, plate, baby's, See-Saw, ca 1979.................**$18.00**

Bunnykins, plate, 7½", Ring-a-Ring o'Roses, ca 1954 ..**$32.50**

Bunnykins, plate, 7½", Watering the Flowers, signed Barbara Vernon...**$75.00**

Bunnykins, plate, 8", Mr Piggly Stores, ca 1968..........**$17.50**

Bunnykins, plate, 8", See-Saw, ca 1952 ....**$17.50**

Bunnykins, saucer, Feeding the Baby, signed Barbara Vernon, ca 1937, light wear **$60.00**

Bunnykins, teacup, Row Boat/Nipped by a Crab, signed Barbara Vernon, ca 1952 ....**$60.00**

Character jug, 'Ard of 'Earing, D6591, sm **$800.00**

Character jug, Ann Boleyn, sm, D6650........................**$55.00**

Character jug, 'Arriet, sm, D6236 ....**$95.00**

Character jug, Bacchus, lg, D6499 ....**$95.00**

Character jug, Bootmaker, lg, D6572..........................**$125.00**

Character jug, Cap'n Cuttle, sm, D5842.....................**$120.00**

Character jug, Captain Henry Morgan, mini, D6510....**$45.00**

Character jug, Cavalier, lg, D6614...............................**$175.00**

Character jug, Dick Turpin, mini, 1st version, D6128..**$60.00**

Character jug, Drake, lg, later version w/hat, D6115 .**$155.00**

Character jug, Fat Boy, mini, D6139............................**$80.00**

Character jug, Fortune Teller, mini, D6523 ....**$300.00**

Character jug, Friar Tuck, lg, D6321............................**$445.00**

Character jug, Gaoler, sm, D6577 ....**$65.00**

Character jug, Granny, mini, D6520 ....**$55.00**

Character jug, Grant & Lee, lg, D6698, 2-faced jug, 1983 limited edition **$265.00**

Character jug, Guardsman of Williamsburg, lg, D6568 .**$110.00**

Character jug, Jester, sm, D5556 ....**$120.00**

Character jug, London Bobby, sm, D6762 ....**$100.00**

Character jug, Lumberjack, sm, D6613 ....**$65.00**

Character jug, Mikado, mini, D6525 ....**$350.00**

Character jug, Monty, lg, D6202, 1946-91 ....**$100.00**

Character jug, Mr Pickwick, lg, D6060 ....**$165.00**

Character jug, Night Watchman, sm, D6576................**$78.00**

Character jug, Old Charley, tiny, D6144....................**$120.00**

Character jug, Paddy, lg, D5753..............................**$155.00**

Character jug, Parson Brown, lg, D5486 ....**$155.00**

Character jug, Parson Brown, sm, D5529....................**$70.00**

Character jug, Pied Piper, sm, D6462 ....**$70.00**

Character jug, Regency Beau, sm, D6562.................**$575.00**

Character jug, Robinson Crusoe, lg, D6532................**$115.00**

Character jug, Sam Weller, mini, D6140 ....**$55.00**

Character jug, Samuel Johnson, sm, D6296 ....**$200.00**

Character jug, Scaramouche, mini, D6564................**$425.00**

Character jug, Tam O'Shanter, sm, D6636..................**$55.00**

Character jug, Town Crier, lg, D6530 ....**$215.00**

Character jug, Trapper, lg, D6609 ....$110.00

Character jug, Trapper, sm, D6612 ....**$60.00**

Character jug, Viking, sm, D6502 ....**$110.00**

Character jug, Yachtsman, lg, D6622........................**$120.00**

Dewars whiskey flask, John Dewars & Son..............**$180.00**

Dewars whiskey flask, Jovial Monk..........................**$255.00**

Dewars whiskey flask, Tony Weller..........................**$200.00**

Figurine, Alexandra, 7¾", HN2398.............................**$165.00**

Figurine, Apple Maid, 7", HN2160....................$400.00

Figurine, Autumn Breezes, 7½", HN1913, green skirt .**$250.00**

Figurine, Balloon Man, 7¼", HN1954 ....**$250.00**

Figurine, Bess, 7¼", HN2002...................................**$225.00**

Figurine, Blacksmith, 9", HN2782 ....**$160.00**

Figurine, Bon Appetit, 6", matt, HN2444..................**$195.00**

Figurine, Bon Jour, 6¾", HN1879.............................**$875.00**

Figurine, Bride, 8", 4th version, HN2873, gold trim ..**$200.00**

Figurine, Bridget, 8¾", HN2070 ....**$325.00**

Figurine, Bunny, 5", HN2214 ....**$165.00**

Figurine, Captain Cook, 8", HN2889.........................**$300.00**

Figurine, Charlotte, 6½", HN2421 ....**$150.00**

Figurine, Chloe, 5¾", HN1470..................................**$275.00**

Figurine, Cissie, 5", HN1809, red dress....................**$125.00**

Figurine, Clockmaker, 7¼", HN2279.........................**$250.00**

Figurine, Collinette, 7¼", red cloak, HN1999............**$550.00**

Figurine, Darling, 5¼", 2nd version, HN1985.............**$95.00**

Figurine, Debbie, 5¾", 1st version, HN2385 ....**$115.00**

Figurine, Delight, 6¾", 1st version, HN1772 ....**$155.00**

Figurine, Dulcie, 7¼", HN2305................................**$175.00**

Figurine, Elegance, 7½", HN2264.............................**$150.00**

Figurine, Fair Lady, 7¾", HN2193 ....**$145.00**

Figurine, Farmer's Wife, 9", HN2069 ....**$475.00**

Figurine, Favourite, 7¼", HN2249...........................**$185.00**

Figurine, Fragrance, 7¾", HN2334 ....$225.00

Figurine, Genevieve, 7", HN1962.............................**$250.00**

Figurine, Georgina, 5¾", Kate Greenaway, HN2377..**$125.00**

Figurine, Gillian, 5¼", HN3042................................**$150.00**

Figurine, Good Friends, 9", HN2783.........................**$165.00**

Figurine, Goody Two Shoes, 5¼", HN2307................**$125.00**

Figurine, Happy Anniversary, 6½", HN3097..............**$160.00**

Figurine, Harmony, 8", HN2824...............................**$180.00**

Figurine, Home Again, 3½", HN2167........................**$145.00**

Figurine, Huntsman, 7½", 3rd version, HN2492.........**$200.00**

Figurine, Ivy, 4¾", blue dress, HN1768 ....**$95.00**

Figurine, Jane, 8", HN2806......................................**$155.00**

Figurine, Janice, 7¼", dark green dress, HN2165....**$450.00**

Figurine, Judith, 6⅞", HN2089................................**$300.00**

Figurine, Kathy, 4¾", Kate Greenaway, HN2346 ....**$150.00**

Figurine, Lady Charmian, 8", HN1948 ....**$295.00**

Figurine, Lady Pamela, 8", HN2718 ....**$150.00**

Figurine, Lavinia, 5", HN1955.................................$120.00
Figurine, Lights Out, 5", boy in pajamas, HN2262.....**$245.00**
Figurine, Lynne, 7", HN2329 ....$160.00
Figurine, Mary Had a Little Lamb, 3⅝", HN2048........**$155.00**
Figurine, Mary Mary, 5", HN2044....................................$170.00
Figurine, Maureen, 7½", 1st version, HN1770 ....$295.00
Figurine, Mendicant, 8¼", later version, HN1365.......**$275.00**
Figurine, Midinette, 7¼", HN2090 ....$295.00
Figurine, Morning Ma'am, 9", HN2895 ....$130.00
Figurine, Mother's Help, 5", HN2151 ....$195.00
Figurine, My Love, 6¼", HN2339 ....$195.00
Figurine, Nanny, 5⅝", HN2221......................................$185.00
Figurine, News Vendor, 8¼", HN2891 ....$180.00
Figurine, Orange Lady, 8¾", HN1759 ....$235.00
Figurine, Paisley Shawl, 6¼", 2nd version, HN1988 ..**$165.00**
Figurine, Pillow Fight, 5¼", HN2270..........................$215.00
Figurine, Polka, 7½", HN2156 ....$335.00
Figurine, Professor, 7¼", HN2281 ....$215.00
Figurine, Rag Doll, 4¾", HN2142 ....$95.00
Figurine, Rose, 4⅝", HN1368..$80.00
Figurine, Sharon, 4¾", HN3047 ....$125.00
Figurine, Simone, 7¼", HN2378 ....$145.00
Figurine, Spring Flowers, 7¼", HN1807....................$300.00
Figurine, Spring Morning, 7½", HN1922....................$245.00
Figurine, Summer, 7¼", 2nd version, HN2086..........$445.00
Figurine, Sunday Best, 7½", HN2698 ....$125.00
Figurine, Teatime, 7¼", HN2255 ....$155.00
Figurine, Tess, 5¾", HN2865 ....$165.00
Figurine, To Bed, 6", HN1805 ....$155.00
Figurine, Tuppence a Bag, 5½", HN2320 ....$180.00
Figurine, Winter, 6¼", HN2088 ....$450.00
Flambe, Genie, #2999...$150.00
Flambe, ink holder, desert scene w/palms $145.00
Flambe, vase, country house $215.00
Flambe, vase, pear shape, mottled $185.00
Flambe, vase, 6½", plowing scene, 1930s $125.00
Flambe, vase, 7", Veined Sung, woodcut, #1603 ....$185.00
Flambe, Wizard, #3121...$119.00
Series Ware, biscuit jar, 8", Royal Mail Coach............$195.00
Series Ware, bowl, salad; 6", Bayeux Tapestry, Battle of
    Hastings $95.00
Series Ware, bowl, 9", Babes in the Woods, May Day Chil-
    dren's Procession $230.00
Series Ware, candlestick, 6½", King Arthur's Knights, multi-
    color, dated 1924 ....$110.00
Series Ware, cheese dish, Coaching Days.................$375.00
Series Ware, cup & saucer, Australia, Gum Trees w/House,
    multicolor, D5506...$72.50
Series Ware, demitasse cup & saucer, Dickensware....$65.00
Series Ware, jug, Eglington Tournament, D2792 ....$500.00
Series Ware, jug, 2x1¾", Dutch People, ladies & boy, black
    transfer $95.00
Series Ware, jug, 4¾x4", Moorish Gate, 2 Arabs..........$95.00
Series Ware, jug, 7½", Dickensware, Alfred Jungle ...$135.00
Series Ware, jug, 7½", Jacobean, Ye Little Bottel, multicolor,
    D1011..$350.00
Series Ware, mug, 5½", King Arthur's Knights,
    D2961 ....$245.00

Series Ware, plate, 10", American Buildings, US Capitol
    Washington DC...$230.00
Series Ware, plate, 10", Coaching Days, Wm Ye Driver.$125.00
Series Ware, plate, 10", Town Officials, night watchman
    w/pike & lantern..$65.00
Series Ware, plate, 10½", Canadian Views, Niagara Falls,
    D6476..$70.00
Series Ware, plate, 10½", Gibson, Widow & Friends, She
    Finds Consolation in Her Mirror, dated 1902......$120.00

Series Ware, plate, 10½", The Mayor......................$85.00
Series Ware, plate, 10⅜", Australia, Gum Brees, D6309 .**$98.00**
Series Ware, plate, 10⅜", Flower Garden, From the Poet's
    Garden..$125.00
Series Ware, plate, 10⅜", Porfessionals, Doctor...........$80.00
Series Ware, plate, 10⅜", Ports of Call, New Orleans Royal
    Street..$125.00
Series Ware, plate, 13", Home Waters, Inside a Stone Har-
    bour, D6434..$65.00
Series Ware, plate, 7", Nursery Rhymes, Old Woman .$75.00
Series Ware, sandwich tray, 7½x17½", Dickens Ware, Dick
    Swiveler, signed Noke, D2973 ....$355.00
Series Ware, stein, Night Watchman, 5", D4746..........$88.00

Series Ware, stein, 6", Oliver Twist.....................$135.00

Series Ware, teapot stand, 6½" dia, Old Moreton Hall, acanthus leaf borders, D3858..........................**$75.00**

Series Ware, vase, Dunolly Castle, 4½x2¾", marked.**$185.00**

Series Ware, vase, Shakespeare, 6½x4", Ophelia in pink, handled..........................**$150.00**

Series Ware, vase, 6⅜", Babes in the Woods, flow blue w/gold trim **$260.00**

Stoneware, creamer & sugar bowl, Slater's Patent.....**$115.00**

Stoneware, humidor, 5x4¼", figures in relief, brown to tan, marked..........................**$175.00**

Stoneware, jug, utility; 5¼", yellow & beige panels on salt glaze, ca 1858-90..........................**$100.00**

Stoneware, jug, 7", hunt scene, brown & tan panels, salt glaze, sterling rim, 1922-31..........................**$485.00**

Stoneware, pitcher, 7", pate-sur-pate birds & leaves, FE Barlow..........................**$465.00**

Stoneware, ring dish, 4x3¼", brown & tan figural owl .**$165.00**

Stoneware, teapot, 5x4½", floral tapestry, marked **$145.00**

Stoneware, vase, mini, hunting scene, Coleman..........**$40.00**

Stoneware, vase, 10½", floral design, signed F Roberts, Lambeth..........................**$250.00**

Stoneware, vases, 5½", purple, green & brown banded Deco design, signed BN, pr **$125.00**

Toby jug, Best Is None Too Good, D6107..............**$325.00**

Toby jug, Cliff Cornell, lg, blue **$300.00**

Toby jug, Double XX (Man on the Barrel), lg, D6088 .**$300.00**

Toby jug, Falstaff, sm, D6063..........................**$75.00**

Toby jug, Happy John, sm, D6070 ....**$75.00**

Toby jug, Honest Measure, 4½", D6108 ....**$85.00**

Toby jug, Jolly Toby, 6½", D6109 ....**$90.00**

Toby jug, Mr Micawber, D6262..........................**$180.00**

Toby jug, Mr Pickwick, D6261 ....**$180.00**

Toby jug, Old Charley, seated, sm **$175.00**

Toby jug, Sairy Gamp, D6263 ....**$180.00**

Toby jug, Sherlock Holmes, 8¾", D6661 ....**$145.00**

Toby jug, Sir Winston Churchill, lg, D6171..............**$120.00**

Toby jug, Squire, D6319..........................**$265.00**

Ruby Glass

Red glassware has always appealed to the buying public, and today there are lots of collectors who look for it. It's been made for more than one hundred years by literally every glasshouse in the country, but most of what's out there today was made during the Depression era through the decade of the seventies. Anchor Hocking made lots of it; they called their line 'Royal Ruby.'

If you like this type of glassware, we recommend you read *Ruby Glass of the 20th Century* by Naomi Over. See also Eyewinker; Moon and Star.

Ashtray, Royal Ruby, 4½" leaf **$4.50**

Bowl, Royal Ruby, 11½" **$30.00**

Bowl, 10", double crimped..........................**$65.00**

Bowl, 3¼" high, Blenko, ruffled rim..........................**$17.50**

Bowl, 4", Rock Crystal, McKee..........................**$30.00**

Candy dish, Rock Crystal, McKee, round, w/lid........**$150.00**

Candy dish, 3¾", Sweetheart, LG Wright, 1974............**$22.00**

Cup, measuring; 16-oz, unknown manufacturer..........**$26.00**

Cup, Royal Ruby, round **$5.00**

Cup & saucer, Royal Ruby, square..........................**$7.50**

Goblet, Royal Ruby, ball stem..........................**$9.50**

Goblet, wine; Plymouth, Fenton..........................**$18.00**

Lamp, oil; 9", Viking, 1976 ....**$27.50**

Mayonnaise & plate **$40.00**

Mustard jar, 3-pc **$30.00**

Pitcher, Royal Ruby, 8" **$40.00**

Pitcher, 6¾", bulbous, applied red handle, Blenko **$32.50**

Plate, Royal Ruby, 8"..........................**$7.50**

Sherbet, Royal Ruby..........................**$7.00**

Sugar bowl, Royal Ruby, footed..........................**$8.00**

Tumbler, Georgian, juice size **$10.00**

Tumbler, Georgian, water size..........................**$12.00**

Tumbler, Georgian, 4½", scalloped base..........................**$10.00**

Tumbler, Royal Ruby, iced tea, 14-oz..........................**$13.00**

Tumbler, Royal Ruby, 4¼"..........................**$4.00**

Tumbler, Royal Ruby, 5-oz, footed **$8.00**

Vase, 10", Rachel, Anchor Hocking, 1940s..........**$42.50**

Vase, 11x8¼", Blenko, shaped rim **$58.00**

Vase, 8", double crimped **$65.00**

Ruby-Stained Souvenirs

These were popular at fairs around the turn of the century up until the 1920s, and even today they're not at all hard to find. You'll find them with names, dates, and sometimes an inscription, all etched onto the ruby-flashed pattern glass at the direction of the souvenir buyer.

Coal bucket, 2¾", town's name, no date..........**$20.00**

Cordial, Button Arches, 3⅜", Rochester Fair, 1909......**$25.00**

Creamer, Button Arches, 2½", loving inscription, 1907 .**$22.50**

Creamer, Heart Band, 4", Souvenir of Union City **$20.00**

Creamer, Scalloped Daisy, 2½", names, 1911 ....$25.00
Creamer, unknown pattern, 4½", name, Dallas 1905 ..$27.50
Mug, Button Arches, 3", name, dated 1921 ....$20.00
Mug, Heart Band, 2¾", name, dated 1911 ....$20.00
Mug, Sunk Honeycomb, 3", name $20.00
Pitcher, Plume, 5½", 1893 World's Fair......................$55.00
Punch cup, Button Arches, 3", 1904 World's Fair........$22.50
Salt & pepper shakers, Punty Band, 3", name, 1902 ...$55.00

Salt shaker, 3", inscribed Mother, Christmas 1898 .$12.00
Spooner, Button Arches, 4", name, dated 1902............$25.00
Toothpick holder, Beaded Swag, 2", name, 1908........$25.00
Toothpick holder, Punty Band, 2¼", name, 1901 ....$27.50
Toothpick holder, Red Shield, 2½", 1927 State Fair.....$20.00
Toothpick holder, 2½", World's Fair, 1893 (illustrated)..$32.00
Tumbler, Button Arches, 4", Atlantic City, 1906...........$22.50
Wine, Button Arches, 4", 1921 ....$22.50

Russel Wright Designs

One of the country's foremost industrial designers, Russel Wright, was also responsible for several dinnerware lines, glassware, and aluminum that have become very collectible. American Modern, produced by the Steubenville Pottery Company (1939-1959) is his best known and most popular line today. It had simple, sweeping lines that appealed to tastes of that period, and it was made in a variety of solid colors.

Iroquois China made his Casual line, and because it was so serviceable, it's relatively easy to find today. It will be marked with both Wright's signature and 'China by Iroquois.' (To price Brick Red and Aqua Casual, double our values; for Avocado Yellow, reduce them by half.)

Wright's aluminum ware is highly valued by today's collectors, even though it wasn't so well accepted in its day, due to the fact that it was so easily damaged.

If you'd like to learn more about the subject, we recommend *The Collector's Encyclopedia of Russel Wright Designs* by Ann Kerr.

American Modern

Bowl, child's; Chartreuse...$70.00
Bowl, divided vegetable; Chartreuse $75.00

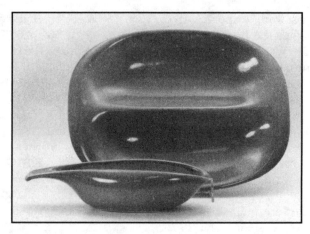

Bowl, divided vegetable; Coral or Gray $77.50
Bowl, vegetable; 12", Coral or Gray, w/lid $42.50
Butter dish, Canteloupe, Glacier Blue, or White $325.00
Butter dish, Chartreuse $155.00
Butter dish, Coral or Gray $160.00
Carafe, Cedar, Black Chutney or Seafoam $165.00
Celery dish, Canteloupe, Glacier Blue, or White $50.00
Celery dish, Chartreuse $23.00
Chop plate, Chartreuse $25.00
Chop plate, Coral or Gray $27.50
Coaster ashtray, Chartreuse $13.00
Coaster ashtray, Coral or Gray $14.00
Coffeecup cover, Chartreuse......................................$100.00
Coffeepot, AD; Cedar, Black Chutney or Seafoam $65.00
Coffeepot, AD; Chartreuse..$55.00
Coffeepot, AD; Coral or Gray..$60.00
Cup & saucer, Canteloupe, Glacier Blue, Bean Brown or White $30.00
Cup & saucer, Cedar, Black Chutney or Seafoam........$12.00
Cup & saucer, Chartreuse...$10.00
Gravy boat, 10½", Canteloupe, Glacier Blue, Bean Brown or White (illustrated) $40.00
Gravy boat, 10½", Chartreuse.......................................$18.00
Ice box jar, Cedar, Black Chutney or Seafoam $165.00
Lug soup, Cedar, Black Chutney or Seafoam...............$15.00
Lug soup, Chartreuse..$12.00
Pickle dish, Cedar, Coral, Gray, or White....................$16.00
Pickle dish, Chartreuse...$15.00
Plate, 10", Canteloupe, Glacier Blue, or White $24.00
Plate, 10", Charteuse $8.00
Plate, 10", Coral or Gray $9.00
Plate, 6¼", Cedar, Black Chutney or Seafoam.............$10.00
Plate, 6¼", Chartreuse...$3.50
Plate, 8", Canteloupe, Glacier Blue, or White $24.00
Plate, 8", Cedar, Black Chutney or Seafoam................$12.00
Platter, 13¼", Cedar, Black Chutney or Seafoam $25.00
Relish, Coral or Gray, divided................................$160.00
Relish rosette, Chartreuse $125.00
Relish rosette, Coral or Gray $140.00
Salt & pepper shakers, any color, pr $15.00
Sauce boat, 8¾", Coral or Gray $27.50
Sugar bowl, Canteloupe, Bean Brown or White, w/lid.$28.00
Sugar bowl, Coral or Gray, w/lid.................................$13.00
Teapot, 6", Canteloupe, Bean Brown or White $150.00

Teapot, 6x10", Coral or Gray..................................**$70.00**
Tumbler, child's, Canteloupe, Glacier Blue, Bean Brown or
    White **$120.00**

Casual

Bowl, cereal; 5", Avocado **$7.00**
Bowl, cereal; 5", early foam glaze **$12.00**
Bowl, fruit; 5½", Aqua or Brick Red..................**$16.00**
Bowl, fruit; 5½", Canteloupe, Oyster or Charcoal........**$12.00**
Bowl, soup; 18-oz, Aqua or Brick Red, restyled..........**$40.00**
Bowl, soup; 18-oz, Avocado, restyled **$18.00**
Butter dish, ½ -lb, Avocado..................................**$60.00**
Casserole, 10", Aqua or Brick Red **$50.00**
Casserole, 10", Avocado **$45.00**
Casserole, 2-qt, Aqua or Brick Red..................**$60.00**
Casserole, 3-qt, Avocado **$80.00**
Casserole, 3-qt, early foam glaze **$130.00**
Casserole, 6-qt, Aqua or Brick Red..................**$200.00**
Coffeepot, AD; 4½", Oyster or Charcoal..................**$100.00**
Creamer, lg family size, Aqua or Brick Red **$60.00**
Cup & saucer, AD; Aqua or Brick Red..................**$170.00**
Cup & saucer, AD; Canteloupe, Oyster or Charcoal .**$125.00**
Dutch oven, Avocado..................................**$95.00**
Gravy bowl, 5¼", Avocado..................................**$10.00**
Gravy bowl, 5¼", early foam glaze..................**$18.00**
Gravy stand, 7½", Aqua or Brick Red..................**$30.00**
Gravy stand, 7½", Canteloupe, Oyster or Charcoal **$22.50**
Mug, 9-oz, Aqua or Brick Red, restyled **$115.00**
Mug, 9-oz, Avocado, restyled..................................**$70.00**
Pitcher, water; 5¼", Avocado **$65.00**
Plate, 10", Aqua or Brick Red..................................**$20.00**
Plate, 10", early foam glaze **$15.00**
Platter, 12¾", Avocado..................................**$20.00**
Platter, 12¾", Canteloupe, Oyster or Charcoal, oval....**$37.50**
Salt & pepper shakers, Brick Red, stacking, pr..........**$24.00**
Sauce pan, Aqua or Brick Red, w/lid..................**$230.00**
Sugar bowl, Canteloupe, Oyster or Charcoal, restyled.**$30.00**

Glassware

American Modern, cordial, 2", Smoke or Crystal **$35.00**

American Modern, dessert dish, Smoke or Crystal.$35.00
American Modern, double old-fashioned, Coral..........**$45.00**

American Modern, tumbler, 5", Smoke or Crystal.......**$25.00**
American Modern, tumbler, juice; 4", Coral or Seafoam .**$30.00**
Imperial Flair, tumbler, juice **$50.00**
Imperial Flair, tumbler, water..................................**$65.00**
Iroquois Pinch, tumbler, iced tea; any color but Red or Can-
    teloupe..**$35.00**
Iroquois Pinch, tumbler, iced tea; Red or Canteloupe .**$115.00**
Snow Glass, candle holders, pr **$150.00**
Snow Glass, tumbler, 10-oz..................................**$90.00**
Snow Glass, tumbler, 14-oz..................................**$90.00**
Snow Glass, tumbler, 5-oz..................................**$90.00**
Tumbler, iced tea; 5", Smoke or Crystal..................**$25.00**

Highlight

Butter dish, Citron or Nutmeg..................................**$100.00**
Butter dish, Green **$125.00**
Creamer, Citron or Nutmeg **$25.00**
Creamer, high gloss **$24.00**
Gravy boat, White, Pepper or Blueberry..................**$35.00**
Mug, Citron or Nutmeg **$30.00**
Plate, dinner; Citron or Nutmeg..................................**$25.00**
Plate, dinner; White, Pepper or Blueberry **$30.00**
Salt & pepper shakers, Citron or Nutmeg, any size, pr.**$45.00**
Salt & pepper shakers, White, Pepper or Blueberry, any
    size, pr **$50.00**
Sugar bowl, White, Pepper or Blueberry **$30.00**
Teapot, Citron or Nutmeg **$95.00**
Teapot, Green **$100.00**

Knowles

Bowl, serving; 9¼" **$22.00**
Bowl, 6¼" **$10.00**
Creamer **$14.00**
Cup & saucer..**$14.00**
Pitcher, 2-qt **$70.00**
Plate, 10¾"..**$15.00**
Platter, 13", oval **$18.00**
Platter, 14¼", oval **$22.00**
Platter, 16", oval **$30.00**
Sauce boat **$30.00**
Sugar bowl, w/lid **$20.00**
Teapot **$125.00**

Plastic

Black Velvet, bowl, divided vegetable **$22.50**
Black Velvet, creamer..................................**$12.50**
Black Velvet, cup & saucer **$16.00**
Copper Penny, plate, salad or dinner..................**$12.50**
Copper Penny, platter..................................**$22.50**
Copper Penny, tumbler **$17.50**
Flair, bowl, fruit **$13.00**
Flair, bowl, vegetable; oval, deep..................**$13.00**
Home Decorator, bowl, vegetable; oval, shallow........**$12.00**
Home Decorator, plate, salad or dinner..................**$5.00**
Home Decorator, tumbler **$15.00**
Meladur, bowl, fruit; 6-oz..................................**$8.00**

Meladur, bowl, soup; 12-oz..................................$9.00
Meladur, cup & saucer..$11.00
Meladur, plate, 10"..$10.00
Meladur, plate, 6¼"..$5.00
Meladur, plate, 9"...$8.00
Residential, bowl, vegetable; w/lid....................$30.00
Residential, cup & saucer....................................$9.00
Residential, lug soup...$12.00
Residential, platter...$18.00

Residential, tumbler, either style..........**$15.00**

Spun Aluminum

Beverage set...$400.00
Bowl...$75.00
Candelabra...$200.00
Casserole..$85.00
Cheese board..$85.00
Flower ring..$125.00
Flowerpot, sm...$85.00
Ice bucket...$75.00
Relish rosette..$125.00
Sherry pitcher...$250.00
Spaghetti set...$400.00
Tidbit tray...$85.00
Vase, 12"...$110.00
Waste basket...$110.00

Sterling

Ashtray..$75.00
Bowl, fruit; 5"...$7.00
Bowl, 6½"...$15.00
Bowl, 7½"...$12.00
Creamer, 3-oz...$12.00
Creamer, 9-oz...$12.00
Cup, 7-oz...$10.00
Onion soup, 10-oz...$20.00
Pitcher, water; restyled......................................$60.00
Pitcher, water; 2-qt..$55.00
Plate, 11½"..$15.00
Plate, 6¼"...$5.00
Plate, 9"...$7.00

Platter, 13⅝"..$20.00
Relish, 16½", divided..$55.00
Sugar bowl, 10-oz, w/lid......................................$17.00
Teapot, 10-oz...$65.00

White Clover (for Harker)

Ashtray, clover decoration...................................$30.00
Bowl, vegetable; 7½"..$20.00
Bowl, vegetable; 8¼", w/lid.................................$45.00
Clock, General Electric..$50.00
Gravy boat, clover decoration.............................$25.00
Pitcher, 2-qt, clover decoration, w/lid................$65.00
Plate, 10", clover decoration...............................$16.00
Plate, 11", clover decoration...............................$20.00
Plate, 7⅝", color only...$9.00
Salt & pepper shakers, either size, pr................$25.00
Sugar bowl, w/lid...$20.00
Tea cup & saucer...$14.00

Salem China

This company operated in Salem, Ohio, from 1920 until the fifties, producing various lines of dinnerware, most of it marked with some form of the company name and various logos. The pattern name was often included in the mark. Styles naturally changed from decade to decade and ranged from very formal lines heavily encrusted with gold to simple geometric shapes glazed in solid colors.

For more information, we recommend *The Collector's Encyclopedia of American Dinnerware* by Jo Cunningham.

Goldtrim, plate, 6", Briar Rose shape..................$3.00
June, plate, 7", Briar Rose shape.........................$3.00
Mandarin Red, cup, Streamline shape..................$5.00
Northstar, bowl, 5¼"..$3.00
Northstar, plate, bread & butter...........................$2.00
Northstar, plate, 10"..$5.00
Petit Point Basket, bowl, 6", pink rim...................$5.00

Petit Point Basket, plate, 7".............................**$3.00**
Petit Point Basket, plate, 9", Victory shape (illustrated)..**$5.00**
Petit Point Basket, salt shaker, (illustrated)......**$6.00**
Rust Tulip, platter, Victory shape.........................$6.00
Sailing, bowl, Tricorne shape...............................$6.00

Tulip, creamer, Streamline shape..................................**$10.00**
Tulip, cup & saucer, Streamline shape **$6.00**
Tulip, plate, dinner **$3.00**
Tulip, sugar bowl, Streamline shape **$10.00**

Salt Shakers

Probably the most common type of souvenir shop merchandise from the twenties through the sixties, salt and pepper shaker sets can be spotted at any antique mall or flea market today by the dozens. Most were made in Japan and imported by various companies, though American manufacturers made their fair share as well. There is a states series called 'America,' made in the U.S. by Parkcraft. Each set is made up of one shaker in the shape of a state with the other modeled as an object that represents it – an ear of corn for Iowa or a cactus for Arizona, for instance.

'Miniature shakers' are hard to find and their prices have risen faster than any others. They were made by Arcadia Ceramics (probably an American company). They're under 1½ " tall, some so small they had no space to accommodate a cork. Instead they came with instructions to 'use Scotch tape to cover the hole.'

Advertising sets and premiums are always good, since they appeal to a cross section of collectors. If you have a chance to buy them on the primary market, do so. The F&F Mold & Die Works of Dayton, Ohio, made plastic shakers (as well as other kitchenware items) with painted details for such companies as Quaker Oats, Kool Cigarettes, and Ken-L Ration Pet Food. You'll find Aunt Jemima and Uncle Mose, Willie and Millie Penguin, and Fido and Fifi with the F&F mark. The Black couples (there are two sizes) will range in value from $50.00 to $65.00, the others are about $12.00 per pair. F&F also made Luzianne Mammy shakers (so marked) for the tea company – they're worth about $175.00 (the green-skirted version) – and a set representing the Campbell Kids that usually go for about $50.00.

There are several good books on the market. We recommend *Salt and Pepper Shakers, Identification and Values, Vols I, II, and III,* by Helene Guarnaccia; and *The Collector's Encyclopedia of Salt and Pepper Shakers, Figural and Novelty, First and Second Series,* by Melva Davern.

Advertising

Blue Nun Wine, nuns in blue habits w/baskets of grapes on white bases lettered in blue, 1980s, rare, pr **$75.00**
Bromo Seltzer bottles, cobalt blue glass w/black plastic tops, product name is embossed on bottles, 1970s, pr..**$12.00**
Burton's Whiskey bottles, glass w/metal lids, painted labels, pr...**$8.00**
Campbell's cans, lettered Campbell's Condensed Barbeque USA Salt & Pepper, 1980s, pr.................................**$12.00**
Coca-Cola cans, metal, red & white early '80s logo, pr.**$8.00**
Exxon's tiger, plastic, promotes the Tiger in Your Tank campaign, ca 1970s by Whirley Industries, Warren, PA, 1-piece **$15.00**

General Electric, plastic, early television on spindle legs, screen features GE ad, 1-piece..............................**$15.00**
Heinz, glass w/red painted Heinz label, chrome shaker tops, ca 1987, pr...**$6.00**
Hershey, ceramic, paint can & paint brush, decal featuring Hershey 50th Anniversary on can, mini, pr..........**$18.00**
Kentucky Fried Chicken's Colonel Sanders, plastic, white figurals, 1 has red base, dated 1971, pr................**$50.00**
Lenny Lennox for Lennox furnaces, ceramic, whimsical characters in shouting pose, blue shirts & gray pants, 1950, pr..**$100.00**
Northwest Airlines, 1 red & 1 blue cylinder shape w/Northwest logo & marked Salt & Pepper, mini, pr **$10.00**
RCA Victor, metal, features Nipper the dog & a table-top Victrola, ca 1950s, w/box, pr **$30.00**
Schlitz beer cans, metal, features the brown & cream logo, pr...**$9.00**
Sinclair gas pumps, plastic, white fronts w/labels, red sides, pr...**$30.00**
Stanley Precision Sweepers, plastic, 1 red & 1 white, in blue striped box, A Gift For You, 1940s-50s, pr...........**$15.00**
Stokley's Kissin' Strawberries, red plastic, 1 has eyes open, 1 has eyes closed, w/box, 1940s-50s, pr **$10.00**
Tappan, plastic, gold range, salt & pepper pour from sides, dated 1976, rare, 1-piece **$25.00**
TWA, plastic, cone shape w/flat top, 1 white w/turquoise logo, 1 turquoise w/lighter logo, mini, pr..............**$8.00**

Westinghouse washer & dryer, plastic, pr............$25.00

Animals, Birds and Fish

Alligator, ceramic, animated fellow in airbrushed shades of pink, yellow & white on belly, 1-piece.................**$30.00**
Bears, ceramic, brown mamma bear w/flesh-tone face & pink ears carries baby bear on her back, glossy, 2-piece set..**$25.00**
Bears, silver-colored metal, natural looking in seated pose, Japan, pr...**$10.00**
Birds, bone china, chubby bluebirds w/a hint of pink on white breasts, pr...**$8.00**
Birds, ceramic, animated bluebird couple on white bases, he in black top hat & bow tie, she in yellow bonnet, pr...**$10.00**

Birds, ceramic, cardinals perched on snowy branches, Japan, pr...$12.00

Bulls, china, white w/gray airbrushing, gold horns, bells & hooves, boisterous stance, Japan, 1950s-60s, pr...$10.00

Bunnies, huggers, green w/black & rust accents, marked Van Tellingen, pr................................$22.00

Butterflies, ceramic, pink edged in black, on yellow flowers w/green leaves, pr.................................$18.00

Cat hugging ball of yarn, ceramic, cat is yellow w/white face, yarn is pink, Japan, 1960s-70s, 2-piece set...$12.00

Cats, ceramic, brown cats w/pink ears & bow ties perched on top of the 8-ball, Japan, 1950-60, pr.................$10.00

Cats, ceramic, very elongated bodies, 1 gray & 1 tan w/gray spots, Japan, pr..$15.00

Cats, ceramic, winking felines w/a rhinestone eye, he is gray in plaid vest, she is shaded blue, Japan, 1950-60, pr...$12.00

Chicken, ceramic, white chicken w/red comb & waddle sitting on dark green nest, 2-piece set.....................$12.00

Chickens, pot metal, 1 white & 1 black w/red combs & green feathers, yellow eyes, pr.............................$12.00

Chicks, ceramic, yellow chicks nesting in broken egg shells on yellow bases, pr...................................$10.00

Cow & bull, ceramic, kissing couple attached at side, white, she in blue bow, he has blue topknot, 1-piece....$15.00

Cow & bull, ceramic, wedding couple, he is gray in black top hat, gold trim, she is white, gold trim, 1950s-60s, pr.$10.00

Cows, ceramic, clothed, sitting, oversized heads w/smiling faces looking up, clear glazed w/accents, pr..........$8.00

Cows, ceramic, mother cow in light pink dress w/blue collar holds calf, 2-piece set................................$30.00

Crows, ceramic, dressed for a good time, she in yellow cape, he in wine-colored hat & vest, pr................$15.00

Deer, ceramic, stylized fawns w/shaker heads & bodies marked V & O (vinegar & oil), brown airbrushing, glossy, pr...$50.00

Dog & hydrant, ceramic, shaggy pooch, red fire hydrant w/eyes, nose & mouth in black, 2-piece set.........$12.00

Dogs, ceramic, comical looking, tongues hanging out, pink bodies w/red & green dots, 1 winking, pr..............$9.00

Donkeys, ceramic, 1 w/white body, 1 w/gray body, both w/black spots & red scarves w/white dots, pr......$15.00

Duck nodders, hand-painted porcelain, ducks on white base w/pink roses, Salt & Pepper in gold, gold trim, 3-piece set...$35.00

Ducks, ceramic, mallards in flight attached to white containers w/painted cattails, pr.........................$12.00

Ducks, clay, handmade, stylized ochre bodies w/slightly turned heads, yellow bills & colorful feathers, Mexico, pr...$6.00

Elephant heads, bone china, 1 black, 1 white, ears back & trunks up, pr..$8.00

Elephants, ceramic, gray airbrushed bodies dressed in royal blue overalls, red bow ties & black hats, pr.........$12.00

Fish, ceramic, blue-gray rounded bodies on wavy bases, pink shading on tails, glossy, Japan, pr...................$8.00

Fish, chalkware, 3 fish molded together standing upright, gold w/black fins, red mouths, pr...........................$6.00

Fish, silver-colored metal, natural looking w/rounded bodies, resting on bottom fins, Japan, pr....................$10.00

Fish, wood, cut & incised, natural wood-tone, pr.........$7.00

Fish nodders, hand-painted porcelain, fish in shades of brown & red on white base w/pink roses, 3-piece............$40.00

Flamingos, ceramic, dark pink on dark green leafy bases, 1 w/wings spread, Occupied Japan, pr....................$25.00

Frogs, ceramic, green serenading duo sitting on leaf dish, 1 playing accordion, Occupied Japan, 3-piece set...$18.00

Frogs, porcelain, gray bodies dressed in green jackets, sitting Indian style, pr....................................$15.00

Giraffes, ceramic, dapper gents dressed in blue jackets, ties, & black trousers w/briefcases under arms, pr......$20.00

Grasshoppers, ceramic, yellowish-green w/black eyes, eyebrows, nose & mouth, pr......................................$12.00

Greyhounds, ceramic, in realistic-looking racing position, gray airbrushing w/lighter underbodies, pr..........$18.00

Hippos, ceramic, sitting upright w/endearing expressions, nostrils are white spirals, brown glaze, pr...........$10.00

Horse heads, ceramic, Trojan Horse style, black matt heads & black & white manes w/the mosaic look, 1950s-60s, pr...$7.00

Horse nester, ceramic, horse on back seems to have fallen into water trough, 2-piece set.........................$15.00

Horses, ceramic, playing accordions, wearing blue trousers & shirts, glossy, pr....................................$30.00

Kangaroos, ceramic, smiling baby emerges from mom's pouch, brown airbrushing, pink ears, 2-piece......$20.00

Killer whales, ceramic, realistic style, resting on bottom fins, Japan, pr...$15.00

Kittens, ceramic, playful kittens popping out of black boots w/pink lining, Japan, 1950-60, pr.....................$10.00

Kittens, ceramic, white w/oversized heads, pink pointed ears shaded in black, black tails, Japan, pr.............$9.00

Ladybugs, ceramic, red w/lg black dots, Japan, pr......$12.00

Lion, ceramic, fiercely roaring, elongated body w/yellow airbrushing, reddish-brown sponging, 1-piece.........$30.00

Lobsters, ceramic, red, upright on green bases, claws attached to wire springs, pr...............................$25.00

Moose, ceramic, comical critters in gold-brown glaze, sitting w/heads cocked, plastic free-moving eyes, pr **$10.00**

Mouse & cheese, ceramic, sm gray mouse emerging from wedge of yellow cheese, 2-piece set...................**$12.00**

Owls, ceramic, green w/lg yellow eyes, Lefton Co, pr..**$8.00**

Owls, red clay, perched on round bases, black w/white eyes, glossy, pr..**$9.00**

Pelicans, ceramic, squatting, white w/yellow beaks, black eyes & brown dry-brushed feathers, pr.................**$10.00**

Penguins, ceramic, she in yellow scarf w/black dots & holding closed umbrella, he in top hat & yellow bow tie, pr **$15.00**

Piglets, ceramic, resting on each other, white w/black eyes, Fitz & Floyd, 1970s-present, pr **$18.00**

Pigs, ceramic, chef couple in clear glaze w/light air-brushing, 1 holds red cookbook, 1 holds yellow spoon, pr **$10.00**

Pigs, clay, handmade, rounded stylized form, ochre bodies w/green snub noses & leaf design, Mexico, pr.......**$6.00**

Pigs, wood, barrel-shaped bodies w/peg legs & ears in natural wood tone, pr **$7.00**

Poodle, ceramic, white elongated body w/gray topknot, ears & tail, pink plaid bow & design on side of body, 1-piece **$30.00**

Quail, bone china, realistic form of male & female in white glaze, pr...**$6.00**

Rabbit & mushroom, ceramic, brown bunny sleeping under mushroom, pr..**$10.00**

Rabbits, ceramic, white rabbits w/dark red ears emerging from orange carrots w/green tops, pr **$10.00**

Rabbits, porcelain, yellow bulbous shape w/royal blue collars, gold eyes & noses, ca 1940s, pr.....................**$12.00**

Raccoons, ceramic, round jolly characters in brown matt & metallic glaze, black masks & red bow ties, pr.....**$10.00**

Sea horses, gold-toned, on oval bases, pr...................**$15.00**

Seals, ceramic, circus type w/brown airbrushing on white, wearing red collars, balancing red balls, pr **$10.00**

Skunks, ceramic, animated, smiling white faces & red noses, black & white bodies, pr **$7.00**

Snails, bone china, naturalistic form, white glaze, pr **$8.00**

Squirrels, ceramic, animated couple ready for a game of tennis, she in yellow, he in green, pr.........................**$10.00**

Squirrels on tree stumps, silver-colored metal, natural looking, Japan, pr...**$10.00**

Swans, silver-colored metal, natural looking, bills resting on breasts, Japan, pr **$10.00**

Tigers, ceramic, circus type on red, white & blue balls, Japan, late 1940s-50, pr **$20.00**

Turkey nodders, hand-painted porcelain, turkey couple on white base w/red flowers, yellow-green leaves, 3-piece set..**$50.00**

Turkeys, red clay, black w/white, red & yellow accents, tom is larger w/fanned tail, pr...**$12.00**

Turtles, ceramic, 1 sitting upright, 1 lying on its back, light tan w/brown sponging on backs, pr.....................**$12.00**

Zebras, ceramic, black & white striped w/a stuffed animal appearance, red collars, black feet, pr...................**$9.00**

Characters

Cat & the Fiddle, ceramic, smiling gray cat holding over-sized fiddle, 2-piece set...**$20.00**

Cow & the Moon, ceramic, upright black & white cow peering over smiling yellow crescent moon trimmed in gold, pr...**$12.00**

Donald Duck, ceramic, stands on round base marked Donald Duck, appears to be quacking, bright colors, Dan Brechner, pr $100.00

Dumbo, chalkware, pink Dumbo sitting, looking up, black eyes & toes, pr **$12.00**

Goose & Golden Egg, ceramic, white goose w/yellow & gold accents, gold egg, pr **$12.00**

Humpty Dumpty, plastic, black w/white hats, many color variations, pr...**$15.00**

Oswald & Willy, ceramic, characters on marked bases hold white shakers w/silver tops, Walter Lantz, 1958, pr.**$150.00**

Paul Bunyan, ceramic, standing by tree trunk holding ax, red shirt, blue pants, brown tree trunk, 2-piece ...**$35.00**

Pebbles & Bam Bam, ceramic, flanking a blue Dino toothpick holder, green base, mid-1980s, 3-piece set...**$50.00**

Popeye & Olive Oyl, ceramic, stern Popeye, demure Olive Oyl, Vandor, 1980, pr (illustrated) $50.00

Raggedy Ann & Andy, lightweight ceramic, strong colors in blue, green & pink, red hair, Japan, 1970s, pr......**$22.00**

Rock-a-bye Baby, ceramic, baby in yellow diaper lying on white cradle trimmed in dark red, 2-piece set **$50.00**

Snoopy & Woodstock, ceramic, white chef Snoopy w/black ears & features, chef Woodstock on white garbage pail, pr **$45.00**

Snow White & Dopey, ceramic, smiling Dopey in green, kneeling Snow White in yellow, pr.....................**$125.00**

Sylvester the Cat, ceramic, patting cheek w/hand, red nose & smiling red mouth, marked Warner Brothers, 1970s, pr...**$85.00**

Three Men in a Tub, ceramic, center man attached to lid of sugar bowl tub, others are shakers, 4-piece set....**$50.00**

Fruit, Vegetables and Other Food

Apples, ceramic, bright red apples on white tray, center handle (heart-shape top) gold trim, Occupied Japan, 3-piece set..**$18.00**

Apples, ceramic, realistic looking w/red tops graduating to yellow bottoms, sm stems, pr...................**$7.00**

Asparagus spears, ceramic, resting on sides, white w/green tops, pr...................**$5.00**

Banana split, ceramic, vanilla, chocolate, & strawberry ice cream w/cherry in white fluted dish, 2-piece set .**$25.00**

Bananas, ceramic, resting on sides, warm yellow w/brown & green, pr...................**$7.00**

Crackers, ceramic, saltine-type crackers in stacks, produced by Medelman, Italy, pr...................**$20.00**

Donut & coffee cup, ceramic, light brown donut w/light blue cup, 2-piece set...................**$10.00**

Egg in skillet, ceramic, sunny-side-up egg in light brown skillet, 2-piece set...................**$10.00**

Hamburgers, ceramic, meat between buns (no condiments), pr...................**$8.00**

Ice cream cones, ceramic, chocolate-coated cones resting on sides, glossy, pr...................**$10.00**

Ice cream in dish, ceramic, pink ice cream in light blue dish, 2-piece set...................**$25.00**

Mushrooms, ceramic, brown tops w/white dots, yellow stems w/smiling faces, 1 has eyes closed, pr........**$12.00**

Peaches, ceramic, realistic looking, yellow w/pink blushing, pr...................**$7.00**

Pears, ceramic, realistic looking in upright position, yellow w/brown flecks, sm brown stems, pr...................**$7.00**

Pie a la mode, ceramic, scoop of vanilla ice cream on top of lg wedge of pie, 2-piece set...................**$15.00**

Pineapples, gold-toned metal, realistic form, pr...................**$8.00**

Popcorn & pop, ceramic, brown box of popcorn & yellow pop bottle, 2-piece set...................**$22.00**

Potatoes, ceramic, very realistic rendition in brown-shaded matt finish, pr...................**$7.00**

Red peppers, ceramic, lg red peppers resting on green leafy stem side, pr...................**$25.00**

Strawberries, ceramic, lg red berries resting on leafy stem side, yellow ends & seeds, Occupied Japan, pr....**$25.00**

Strawberries on leaf dish, ceramic, red w/white painted seeds, sitting upright on green dish, 3-piece set...**$12.00**

Strawberry & orange chefs, ceramic, happy strawberry in green shirt, sad orange in pink shirt, pr...............**$35.00**

Tomatoes, ceramic, red, on yellow & green leaf dish w/brown center handle, Occupied Japan, 3-piece.**$18.00**

Washing machines, metal, early 3-legged wringer type, 1 black & 1 white, painted details, larger pr...........**$18.00**

Watermelon slices, ceramic, realistic looking in red w/green & white rind, black seeds, pr...................**$8.00**

Household Items

Couch & chair, ceramic, blue sofa, yellow chair w/tuffted backs, black trim, pr...................**$25.00**

Fireplace & logs, ceramic, light brown airbrushed logs rest-. ing on top of white brick fireplace, 2-piece set....**$15.00**

Grandfather clocks, pot metal, 1 black & 1 white, painted details, pointed tops, pr...................**$12.00**

Hammer & nail, ceramic, gray nail w/label, brown & black hammer, pr...................**$15.00**

Lawnmower, plastic, shakers sit atop red mower, in original box **$25.00**

Lock & key, ceramic, blue-gray lock marked Salt Lock, yellow key, gold trim, pr...................**$15.00**

Lunch bucket & thermos, ceramic, brown w/red thermos top, pr...................**$12.00**

Oil lamp, ceramic, globe rests on base w/handle, white w/pink floral details, gold trim, 2-piece set.........**$10.00**

Potbellied stove & bucket of coal, ceramic, shades of brown & black, pr...................**$10.00**

Table & chairs, ceramic, side chairs w/rolled backs on blue base w/table in center, yellow accents, 3-piece ...**$30.00**

Telephone & directory, ceramic, early black desk phone w/brown base, gold trim, red directory, pr...........**$15.00**

Television, ceramic, early upright console type w/viewing screen resting on speaker, 2-piece set...................**$15.00**

Televisions, wood, early upright console type, natural wood-tone w/picture, pr...................**$7.00**

Thimble & spool of thread, ceramic, white thimble w/silver-colored band, white spool w/black thread, pr.....**$12.00**

Tire pump & flat tire, ceramic, pr...................**$25.00**

Toaster, plastic, black & white w/slices of black & white bread, ca 1950s, 2-piece set...................**$12.00**

Toothbrush & tube of toothpaste, ceramic, yellow tube w/black cap & end, green brush, pr...................**$15.00**

Miniatures

Easy chair & grandfather clock, brown clock, brown flecking on chair, pr...................**$40.00**

Giraffes, china, in playful wide stance, heads reared back & pink ears straight out, yellow w/black spots, pr...**$12.00**

Ink bottle & glob of ink, ceramic, pr...................**$35.00**

Lobster & oyster shell w/pearl, ceramic, red lobster, dark metallic shell, pr...................**$40.00**

Monks, plastic, portly gents in shades of brown, Hong Kong, very sm, pr...................**$8.00**

Pixies, china, sitting, 1 w/wide-spread legs, 1 holding knee w/other leg out, green suits, red hats, pr.............**$12.00**

Potbellied stove & bucket of coal, ceramic, brown bucket, white stove, pr...................**$18.00**

Raccoons, china, sitting w/legs apart, in wine-colored shirts & dark blue pants, yellow hats, bandit faces, pr **$12.00**

Thimble & spool of thread, ceramic, gold thimble, cream-colored spool w/gold thread, Arcadia, pr **$18.00**

Washer & basket of laundry, ceramic, pr **$30.00**

Water pump & bucket of water, ceramic, gray pump, brown bucket, pr **$20.00**

Zebras, china, animated, 1 balking & 1 w/front leg bent, white w/black stripes, manes & hooves, pr **$12.00**

Miscellaneous

Barn & silo huggers, ceramic, red w/black roofs, black-outlined windows on barn, 2-piece set **$10.00**

Barrels, wood, keg-type w/floral around middle, pr **$7.00**

Books, ceramic, white w/1 marked Peppery Tales & 1 marked Salty Stories, gold trimmed, pr **$12.00**

Bowling ball & pins, plastic, black ball sugar bowl flanked by cream-colored pins on black base, 3-piece set.**$12.00**

Broken heart, ceramic, pale yellow heart in 2 pieces w/gold arrow, pr...**$12.00**

Candles, wood, bright red flames atop natural wood candles w/a bit of bark, marked S&P, pr **$7.00**

Cannons, pot metal, 1 white & 1 black, red trim, pr...**$15.00**

Cars, ceramic, early touring cars in black w/pink details, glossy, pr **$10.00**

Gavels, silver-colored metal, pr **$12.00**

Happy feet, ceramic, flesh-tone w/smiling faces, pr ...**$10.00**

Italian wine bottles, porcelain, bottles marked Salt & Pepper, sitting in handled baskets on yellow tray, 3-piece set..**$10.00**

Musical notes, plastic, red & yellow quarter notes, black treble cleff on metal music bar, black base, 3-piece.**$15.00**

Oriental sandals, porcelain, red & white decor, pr......**$12.00**

Palm tree & flamingo, ceramic, delicate light pink flamingo next to palm tree on sandy base marked Florida, 1-piece **$25.00**

Pearls in oyster shell, plastic, 2 white pearl shakers in blue shell, 3-piece set...**$18.00**

Rocking horses, pot metal, 1 white & 1 black, colorful details, pr..**$15.00**

S & P, ceramic, white S & P form w/gold trim, pr.......**$12.00**

Sailboat nodders, porcelain, red sailboats on white base w/red roses, silver Salt & Pepper & trim, pr **$50.00**

Sailing ships, ceramic, Columbus-type ships w/billowing sails, white w/blue details, pr **$8.00**

Skull nodders, porcelain, gray skulls sitting on white base w/silver trim, 3-piece set **$50.00**

Stagecoach, ceramic, white coach sits on brown wheels, 2-piece set...**$15.00**

Stagecoach, wood, w/driver & horse, shakers marked S&P sit in coach, marked Black Hills, 3-piece set.........**$10.00**

Tankards, ceramic, colorful mugs in blues & golds w/hinged lids, pr..**$7.00**

Train engine & coal car, ceramic, in black, red & yellow, 1-piece **$25.00**

Trolley cars, ceramic, Desire embossed on each end, in green, yellow & brown glazes, pr..........................**$10.00**

Umbrellas, plastic & metal, yellow plastic umbrellas w/black S & P handles in black metal holder, 3-piece set .**$10.00**

Union & Confederate officer's hats, ceramic, Confederate hat is blue w/yellow trim, other is dark blue, pr **$12.00**

Violin & case, ceramic, med brown glossy glaze, pr...**$12.00**

People

Angels, ceramic, both in green dresses w/black dots, 1 w/blue cup in hand, 1 playing accordion, pr **$12.00**

Angels, ceramic, praying, white wings w/blue wash over hair & gowns, dated 1949, pr **$12.00**

Bellhop, china, in yellow jacket & red pants carrying yellow suitcases, 1-piece..**$25.00**

Boy & girl in winter dress, china, he in green cap, maroon jacket & blue pants, she in blue-green, Occupied Japan, pr..**$15.00**

Boy & girl nodders, porcelain, strolling, he in black hat, green airbrushed jacket & black pants, she in pink, pr...**$165.00**

Boy & girl reading, ceramic, sitting w/books on laps, he in red jacket, she in blue jacket, Occupied Japan, pr..**$15.00**

Boys playing baseball, ceramic, 1 batting & 1 pitching, both in brown caps & blue underwear, no shirts, pr....**$25.00**

Boys playing flutes, ceramic, yellow hair w/blue caps, jackets & shoes, white pants, dated 1949, pr..............**$10.00**

Chef, ceramic, stylized, chef's hat fits on flat head, looking up, white, red bow tie, yellow utensils, 2-piece...**$12.00**

Chef couple, china, he in white & black marked I'm Salt, she in white w/red scarf marked I'm Pepper, pr..**$23.00**

Chef standing at stove, ceramic, gray stove is mustard, gray pots are shakers, black trim, Occupied Japan, 3-piece set...**$70.00**

Children, bisque, boy & girl seated w/legs spread, 1 in blue & 1 in pink pajamas, Holt-Howard, pr **$18.00**

Christmas angels, ceramic, looking down, in white w/gold trim, 1 w/red bells & 1 w/hands in muff, pr.........**$15.00**

Civil War soldiers, wood, stylized rounded form, 1 gray & 1 blue, marked North & South, pr **$15.00**

Dapper gents, wood, egg-shaped bodies on round bases w/heads & arms, 1 red (yellow hat) & 1 blue (red hat) pr..**$12.00**

Dutch children, ceramic, stylized form, he in blue cap, gold shirt & brown pants, she in blue & white, pr **$9.00**

Dutch couple, ceramic, standing, he w/hands in pockets, she calling out, white w/gold trim, black shoes, pr.....**$10.00**

Dutch kissing couple, ceramic, sitting on wooden bench, he in black hat, brown jacket & blue pants, she in yellow, pr..**$12.00**

Eskimo children, both dressed in all white, black hair, dated 1949 on base, pr **$10.00**

Genie couple, ceramic, sitting Indian style, both in turbans, pastel colors & gold trim, Occupied Japan, pr......**$18.00**

Hillbilly couple, ceramic, he in yellow hat & gray beard & she w/broom coming from barrels marked Salt & Pepper, pr...**$12.00**

Indian children, ceramic, kissing couple in tan buckskin clothing, she has black braids, he wears full headdress, pr..**$25.00**

Indian couple, chalkware, she in red dress & white cape, he in blue pants & white tunic, pr **$12.00**

Indian nodders, porcelain, humorous duo on round yellow container w/Indian design, 3-piece set **$40.00**

Lady in rocking chair, pot metal, lady in white night cap & blue robe, red rocking chair, 2-piece **$18.00**

Man & woman, ceramic, couple w/happy side & mad side, he in blue pants & tan hat, she in pink w/hair in bun, pr...**$15.00**

Man on horse, pot metal, man in black & red on brown horse, pr **$18.00**

Man pushing wheelbarrow, ceramic, red shirt & black overalls, red wheelbarrow w/black dirt, floral trim, 2-piece **$18.00**

Mexican kissing couple, ceramic, sitting on wooden bench, black hair, both in white, w/red trim, he wears blue pants, pr...**$12.00**

Nineteenth-century couple, wood, stylized forms in natural finish, pr...**$7.00**

Oriental couple, ceramic, he in yellow top & blue pants, she in blue top & yellow pants, both w/black hats, pr **$15.00**

Oriental couple, china, stylized rounded heads & bodies, he white in black & brown, she white in black, gold trim, pr...**$9.00**

Oriental girl, china, delicate looking in red apron w/white beaded dots, black hair, 1-piece **$25.00**

Pilgrim children, ceramic, boy in black holding gun, girl in red waving, pr..**$12.00**

Pixie chef heads, ceramic, smiling faces w/rosy cheeks & red lips, chef's hats & green leafy collars, pr........**$10.00**

Pixies, ceramic, 1 sitting Indian style & 1 sitting casually on mushrooms, black hats & tops, yellow tights, pr....**$8.00**

Sailor & lady, ceramic, in white w/gold trim, she wearing glasses & holding grapes, he has pipe, pr **$15.00**

Santa & Mrs Claus, ceramic, waving, he in red w/green gloves, she in green w/white apron & red gloves, pr.........**$15.00**

Scarecrow kissing couple, ceramic, sitting on wooden bench, both in yellow straw hats & blue tattered clothes, pr...**$15.00**

Swiss kissing couple, ceramic, Sweethearts of all Nations series, he in black & brown, she in pale pink, NAPCO, pr...**$25.00**

Winking heads, wood, stylized head forms, natural finish, smiling & winking faces, gray hats, pr....................**$7.00**

Wrestlers, ceramic, wrestler in red trunks holds wrestler in black trunks up over his head, pr..........................**$30.00**

Hedi Schoop

One of the most successful California ceramic studios was founded in Hollywood by Hedi Schoop, who had been educated in the arts in Berlin and Germany. She had studied not only painting but sculpture, architecture, and fashion design as well. Fleeing Nazi Germany with her husband, the famous composer Frederick Holander, Hedi settled in California in 1933 and only a few years later became involved in producing a line of novelty giftware items so popular that it was soon widely copied by other California companies. She designed many animated human figures, some in matched pairs, some that doubled as flower containers. All were hand painted and many were decorated with applied ribbons, sgraffito work, and gold trim. To a lesser extent, she modeled animal figures as well. Until fire leveled the plant in 1958, the business was very productive. Nearly everything she made was marked.

If you'd like to learn more about her work, we recommend *The Collector's Encyclopedia of California Pottery* by Jack Chipman.

Bowl, 12", shell shape, pink w/gold trim.....................**$30.00**

Candle holder, 13½", mermaid holds 2 shell holders above head, blue & white, stamped mark, ca 1950......**$150.00**

Figurine, Repose, lady kneeling w/bowl in lap, tinted bisque w/high glaze, stamped mark, 1949............**$65.00**

Figurine, seated cat wearing bow w/applied bell **$50.00**

Figurine, 10", lady w/basket leads lg poodle..............**$70.00**

Figurine, 11", boy w/horn, pink & blue **$75.00**

Figurine, 12½", clown playing cello, overglaze platinum, ca 1943 ....**$85.00**

Figurine, 12½", Southern Belle....................................**$50.00**

Figurine, 13", Josephine, wearing blue sarong w/bowl at hip, stamped mark, ca 1943 ....**$75.00**

Figurine, 13", lady holds shell-like bowl above her. $45.00

Figurines, 10", Chinese couple, black & white, pr.......**$95.00**

Figurines, 14", Siamese dancers, tinted bisque w/high glaze & overglaze gold, stamped mark, ca 1947, pr **$100.00**

Flower holder & lamp base, 11½", Colbert, lady w/2 coil baskets, underglaze painted mark, ca 1940..........**$60.00**

Planter, geisha girl w/umbrella, blue, #223.................**$50.00**

Planter, 5", hobby horse **$45.00**

Vase, 12", crowing cock, tinted clay body w/transparent high glaze & overglaze gold, ca 1949 .... **$55.00**

Scottie Dog Collectibles

Collectors of Scottie dog memorabilia have banded together to form a club called Wee Scots, who hold regional and national shows each year. There's also a quarterly newsletter called the *Scottie Sampler* that includes historical data, current market prices, photographs, ads, and feature articles. They're interested in anything showing Scottie dogs – advertising items, magazine covers, postcards, glassware, ceramic figures, and household items.

Bed cover, chenille, 2 pink Scotties in center, crib size .**$42.50**
Bottle, white Scottie, Avon **$6.00**
Candy container, clear glass Scottie figural, open top.**$16.00**
Cookie jar, standing Scottie, ceramic, black, signed by maker, not old, EX details....................................**$55.00**

Crumb brush w/figural Scottie holder, 4¾", black composition dog **$16.00**
Figure, 3" Scottie w/lg ears, painted cast iron................**$8.00**
Figurine, 5½ ", ceramic Scottie, white w/black bow & nose, Japan **$8.50**
Jewelry set, early plastic Scottie bracelet, ring & pin, child size **$30.00**
Pin, early plastic Scottie in doghouse, jewel eye **$65.00**
Pin, 2", black Bakelite Scottie.....................................**$65.00**
Pin, 3", wooden carved Scottie, 1920s........................**$35.00**
Pipe holder, 2 pressed wood Scotties, holds 3 pipes ..**$22.50**
Planter, 2¾ ", Scottie holding double basket, marked Made in Japan..**$8.00**
Planter, 5", dog figural, marked Japan w/horseshoe ...**$12.00**
Playing card holder, pressed wood Scottie looking over fence **$12.50**
Tie rack, 6x6" cut-out wooden Scottie shape.................**$8.00**
Vase, 6", ceramic black & white Scotties in relief around vase, Ben-da Daisy Brand, Made in Japan **$20.00**

Sebastians

These tiny figures were first made in 1938 by Preston W. Baston and sold through gift stores, primarily in the New England area. When he retired in 1976, the Lance Corporation chose one hundred designs which they continued to produce under Baston's supervision. Since then, the discontinued figures have become very collectible.

Baston died in 1984, but his son, P.W. Baston, Jr., continues the tradition.

The figures are marked with an imprinted signature and a paper label. Early labels (before 1977) were green and silver foil shaped like an artist's palette; these are referred to as 'Marblehead' labels (Marblehead, Massachusetts, being the location of the factory), and figures that carry one of these are becoming hard to find and are highly valued by collectors.

Aunt Polly...**$55.00**

Colonial Watchman **$75.00**
Davy Crockett, 1955 ....**$230.00**
Down East..**$135.00**
Dutchman's Pipe..**$195.00**
Fiorello LaGuardia **$135.00**
Gardener Women **$265.00**
Gathering Tulips **$200.00**
George Washington **$45.00**
Henry Hudson, 1959...**$130.00**
John Smith..**$135.00**
Juliet..**$45.00**
Nathaniel Hawthorne...**$160.00**
National Diaper Service **$215.00**
Paul Bunyan...**$245.00**
Peggotty..**$45.00**
Pilgrims, 1947 (illustrated)...................................**$125.00**
Perplexed Husband, Jell-O..**$275.00**
Princess Elizabeth, 1947 ....**$235.00**
Sam Houston..**$110.00**
Sarah Henry...**$75.00**
Scrooge..**$50.00**
Sir Francis Drake...**$265.00**

State Street Bank Globe..$280.00
Swedish Boy..$215.00
Town Crier $50.00

Sewing Collectibles

Once regarded simply as a necessary day-to-day chore, sewing evolved into an art form that the ladies of the 1800s took much pride in. Sewing circles and quilting bees became popular social functions, and it was a common practice to take sewing projects along when paying a visit. As this evolution took place, sewing tools became more decorative and were often counted among a lady's most prized possessions.

Of course, 19th-century notions have long been collectible, but there are lots of interesting items from this century as well. When machine-made clothing became more readily available after the 1920s, ladies began to lose interest in home sewing, and the market for sewing tools began to drop off. As a result, manufacturers tried to boost lagging sales with novelty tape measures, figural pincushions, and a variety of other tools that you may find hard to resist.

Retail companies often distributed sewing notions with imprinted advertising messages; these appeal to collectors of advertising memorabila as well. You'll see ads for household appliances, remedies for ladies' ills, grocery stores, and even John Deere tractors.

Darner, child's, 4½ ", black egg form w/sterling repousse
    handle $50.00
Darner, girl figural, ceramic, marked Darn-It..............$22.50
Darner, 5", dark green blown glass $65.00
Darner, 5¾ ", maple, 1" ball-shaped working end.......$20.00
Darner, 6", milk glass, blown into fat ball shape w/ridged
    handle $65.00
Emery, rabbit, 1½ x2", sterling silver w/glass eyes, velvet
    pincushion...$125.00
Emery, red strawberry w/sterling leaf top....................$65.00
Hem measure, 3", Webster sterling...............................$55.00
Measure, bear figural, celluloid, Japan $65.00
Measure, deer figural, 2", plastic, multicolored paint ..$45.00
Measure, drum form, 2", metal, red, white & blue paint, 1
    side w/mirror, 1 w/farm scene..............................$55.00
Measure, duck figural, 2", china, yellow w/blue wings..$50.00
Measure, fruit basket form, 1", celluloid......................$57.50
Measure, gold walnut form, 1½ ", w/squirrel pull $40.00
Measure, log form, 2", celluloid, green........................$65.00
Measure, parrot's head figural, 1¾ ", celluloid, multicolored
    paint, Germany $125.00
Measure, pig figural, 2", celluloid, fat shape w/1 ear up &
    winking eye, painted flowers on side $45.00
Measure, teapot form, 1½ " dia, brass, fancy scalloped handle..$195.00
Measure, 2-story house form, 2", celluloid, multicolored
    paint..$60.00
Needle case, umbrella form, ivory, originally w/Stanhope
    (now missing) $60.00

Needle case, 2¼ ", sterling, flat tubular shape w/pull-off cap,
    engraved on 1 side $50.00
Needle case, 2¼ ", sterling w/engraved design, flat form
    w/pull-off cap $45.00
Needle case, 3¼ ", sterling w/vermeil, France $65.00

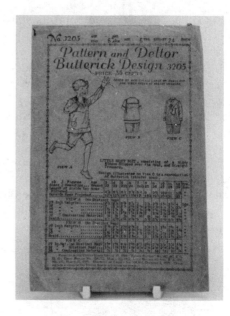

Pattern, Butterick, Boy's Sailor Suit, 1919...............$6.00
Pin box, 1½ " dia, sycamore wood, early Fernware design
    on lid, pull-off cap $62.50
Pin box, 2x2¼ ", brass, embossed decoration, 4 sm feet, red
    lining..$90.00
Pin cube, 1¼ " square, cardboard, glass head pins, cupid
    scrap $24.00
Pincushion, bootie form, 2¾ x1¾ ", gilt metal, old......$45.00
Pincushion, canoe form, 7", celluloid, silk in top........$68.00
Pincushion, egg form, 4½ x3", composition, ball feet .$55.00
Pincushion, heart form, 1½ ", stuffed fabric w/beveled edge
    mirror...$85.00
Pincushion, lady's shoe, leather w/beading trim.........$40.00
Pincushion, swan figural, silverplated, padded top.....$36.00
Pincushion, turtle nodder, 3½ ", red velvet top, marked Florenza $55.00

**Pincushion, velvet w/metal mounts & base, embossed
New Orleans, Rex Carnival, 1906....................$50.00**
Quilting clamp, 4", cast iron, matching pr...................$20.00

Scissors, 10¾ ", mother-of-pearl handles in dolphin shape, chrome blades, minor wear $130.00
Scissors, 2¼ ", mother-of-pearl, folding type...............$85.00

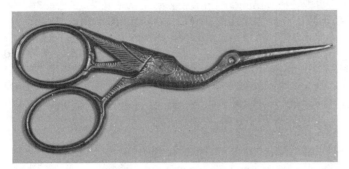

Scissors, 3¼ ", stork handles, Made in Germany ..$20.00
Scissors, 4", cut steel, engraving on shanks, early.......$50.00
Seam ripper, steel blade w/5" wooden handle, NM in box marked It's a Ripper $25.00
Shuttle, iridescent mussel shell, aluminum post $68.00
Shuttle, Tartan ware, slim form, minor wear...............$68.00
Shuttle, 2½ x¾", mother-of-pearl, EX........................$110.00
Spool holder, sterling, American hallmark, exit hole for thread................................$77.50
Thimble case, acorn form, mahogany w/turned grooves around pull-off cap $65.00
Thimble case, acorn form, 1½ ", vegetable ivory, EX..$80.00
Thimble case, acorn form, 2¾", wooden w/turned grooves around pull-off cap................................$68.00
Thimble case, barrel form, 2", treen ware, Falls at Rumbling Bridge scene................................$68.00

Shawnee Pottery

In 1937, a company was formed in Zanesville, Ohio, on the suspected site of a Shawnee Indian village. They took the tribe's name to represent their company, recognizing the Indians to be the first to use the rich clay from the banks of the Muskingum River to make pottery there. Their venture was very successful, and until they closed in 1961, they produced many lines of kitchenware, planters, vases, lamps, and cookie jars that are very collectible today.

They specialized in figural items. There were 'Winnie' and 'Smiley' pig cookie jars and salt and pepper shakers; 'Bo Peep,' 'Puss 'n Boots,' 'Boy Blue,' and 'Charlie Chicken' pitchers; Dutch children; lobsters; and two lines of dinnerware modeled as ears of corn.

Values sometimes hinge on the extent of an item's decoration. For instance, a 'Smiley' pig cookie jar with no decoration is valued at $50.00, while one with a painted neckerchief and a few scattered flowers or cloverleaves may be worth $150.00. Add brown trousers and gold trim and the value zooms to $300.00. And while a 'Bo Peep' pitcher is basically worth $90.00, the addition of some decals and gold adds about 75% more. Most items will increase by 50% to 200% when heavily decorated and gold trimmed.

Not all of their ware was marked Shawnee; many pieces were simply marked USA with a three- or four-digit mold num-ber. If you'd like to learn more about this subject, we recommend *The Collector's Guide to Shawnee Pottery* by Duane and Janice Vanderbilt, and *Collecting Shawnee Pottery* by Mark E. Supnick.

Bank, bulldog, white w/deep rose & blue accents $95.00
Bank, Howdy Doody (on pig), white w/rose & blue air-brushing................................$310.00
Bank, Tumbling Bear, white w/rose & blue accents ...$90.00
Bank, Winnie the Pig, chocolate brown bottom, marked Shawnee Winnie 61, minimum value.................$200.00
Bowl, fruit; Corn, #92 ....$40.00
Bowl, mixing; 8", Corn, marked Shawnee #8 ....$35.00
Bowl, vegetable; Corn, marked #95............................$35.00

Butter dish, Corn, marked #72................................$50.00
Butter dish, white lid w/red lobster handle on black bottom, marked #927................................$65.00
Casserole, Fruit, marked Shawnee #83.........................$55.00
Casserole, lg, white w/red lobster handle on lid, stick handle on bowl, marked #904 ....$65.00
Casserole, sm, Corn, marked #73................................$50.00
Cookie jar, Corn, marked #66 ....$145.00
Cookie jar, Drum Major, gold trim, marked USA #10, minimum value $300.00
Cookie jar, Dutch Boy, solid light-blue pants, marked USA, minimum value $80.00
Cookie jar, Dutch Boy, yellow pants w/allover floral decals, gold trim, marked USA, minimum value.............$200.00
Cookie jar, Dutch Girl, plain white upper body w/yellow skirt, marked USA, minimum value $50.00
Cookie jar, Dutch Girl, white w/blue trim, marked Great Northern #1026, minimum value $175.00
Cookie jar, Fruit Basket, airbrushed fruit on yellow basket, marked Shawnee #84, minimum value $125.00
Cookie jar, Fruit Basket, airbrushed fruit on yellow basket, gold trim, Shawnee #84, minimum value.............$200.00
Cookie jar, Hexagon, white basketweave design w/floral decals & gold trim, USA, minimum value $100.00
Cookie jar, Hexagon, yellow basketweave design, marked USA, minimum value................................$50.00
Cookie jar, Jo Jo the Clown, gold trim, marked Shawnee #12, minimum value $300.00
Cookie jar, Jo Jo the Clown, marked Shawnee #12, minimum value $200.00
Cookie jar, jug, Pennsylvania Dutch design on white, marked USA, minimum value $150.00

Cookie jar, Little Chef, 4-sided, cream w/Cookies lettered diagonally in blue, embossed chef, marked USA, minimum value **$800.00**

Cookie jar, Muggsy, plain white w/blue scarf tied around jaw, marked USA, minimum value **$200.00**

Cookie jar, Octagon, light blue Fernware, marked USA, minimum value..**$75.00**

Cookie jar, Owl, white body w/hand-painted accents, marked USA, minimum value **$125.00**

Cookie jar, Puss 'n Boots, tail behind foot, hand-painted accents w/gold outlined bow & trim, marked, minimum value **$250.00**

Cookie jar, Puss 'n Boots, tail over foot, rose bow, blue trim, marked Pat Puss 'n Boots, minimum value.........**$160.00**

Cookie jar, Sailor Boy, plain white, marked USA, minimum value **$100.00**

Cookie jar, Sailor Boy, white w/decals & gold trim, marked USA, minimum value..**$450.00**

Cookie jar, Sitting Elephant, white w/gold trim & decals, marked USA, minimum value **$200.00**

Cookie jar, Sitting Elephant, white w/red cold-painted bow tie, minimum value.................................$75.00

Cookie jar, Smiley the Pig, allover clover bud design, marked Pat Smiley USA, minimum value............**$175.00**

Cookie jar, Smiley the Pig, gold w/decals, marked USA, minimum value..$275.00

Cookie jar, Smiley the Pig, plain white, marked USA, minimum value..**$50.00**

Cookie jar, Smiley the Pig, red cold-painted bib, marked USA, minimum value..**$50.00**

Cookie jar, Winnie the Pig, green collar w/clover buds, gold trim, marked Pat Winnie USA, minimum value **$400.00**

Cookie jar, Winnie the Pig, peach collar, marked Pat Winnie USA, minimum value..**$175.00**

Cookie jar, 4-sided, yellow w/hand-painted top hat, cane & cigarette motif, gold floral trim, marked USA, minimum value **$60.00**

Creamer, Elephant, white w/gold trim, red mouth, marked Pat USA..**$85.00**

Creamer, Flower & Fern, light blue, marked USA **$17.00**

Creamer, Pennsylvania Dutch ball jug, USA #12 ....**$50.00**

Creamer, Pennsylvania Dutch tilt style, USA #10........**$60.00**

Creamer, Puss 'n Boots, green, yellow & rose shading, marked Shawnee #85.....................................**$45.00**

Creamer, Puss 'n Boots, plain white...........................**$50.00**

Creamer, Puss 'n Boots, white w/red around ears & mouth, gold-trimmed bow & scallops **$70.00**

Creamer, Smiley the Pig, white w/clover & bud design, marked Pat Smiley **$60.00**

Creamer, Smiley the Pig, yellow w/blue scarf, marked Shawnee #86 ....**$50.00**

Creamer, Snowflake, yellow, marked USA...................**$17.00**

Creamer, tilt style w/gold-trimmed embossed flower, blue & rose shading, marked USA #40 ....**$27.00**

Figurine, deer, white w/blue & brown accents **$70.00**

Figurine, puppy dog, white w/floral decals & gilt.......**$80.00**

Figurine, rabbit, white w/pink & blue accents **$40.00**

Figurine, squirrel, white w/floral decals & gold trim...**$80.00**

Figurine, Victorian lady, white w/blue accents on dress, light brown embossed design on base.................**$35.00**

Figurine, white w/blue & brown accents.....................**$40.00**

Figurines, lg or sm, Orientals playing mandolins, green tones on yellow bases, pr....................................**$40.00**

Figurines, Spanish dancers, pr **$40.00**

Match holder, Fernware, yellow, marked USA **$25.00**

Mug, lg, Corn Line, marked #69.................................**$45.00**

Mug, white w/red lobster handle, marked #911.........**$40.00**

Pie bird, white w/pastel accents **$30.00**

Pitcher, Bo Peep, sm, yellow, rose & blue shading, marked Shawnee #47 ....$80.00

Pitcher, Bo Peep, white w/blue & honey trim, marked Pat Bo Peep **$90.00**

Pitcher, Bo Peep, white w/floral decals & gold trim, marked Pat Bo Peep **$155.00**

Pitcher, Boy Blue, blue hat & jacket, deep rose pants, yellow bow, marked Shawnee #46 ....**$90.00**

Pitcher, Charlie Chicken, white w/gold trim, marked Charlicleer **$155.00**

Pitcher, Charlie Chicken, white w/rose & gray trim, marked Pat Charlicleer **$70.00**

Pitcher, Elephant, white w/big red ears, blue floral decals & gold trim, marked Pat USA **$145.00**

Pitcher, Flower & Fern ball jug, med aqua blue **$50.00**

Pitcher, Fruit ball jug, airbrushing on embossed fruit, marked Shawnee #80 ....**$70.00**

Pitcher, Pennsylvania Dutch ball jug, USA #64 ....**$95.00**

Pitcher, Smiley the Pig, white w/peach flower between 2 blue flowers, marked Pat Smiley **$90.00**

Pitcher, Smiley the Pig, white w/rose scarf & apple motif, marked Pat Smiley USA **$105.00**

Pitcher, Sunflower ball jug, marked USA **$80.00**

Pitcher, tall, White Corn Line, marked USA **$70.00**

Planter, black elephant on lg pink leaf base, marked Shawnee USA **$50.00**

Planter, blue conch shell shape, footed, USA #665 .....**$10.00**

Planter, boy leaning on gate yellow & blue w/gilt **$12.00**

Planter, butterfly & flowers on log **$11.50**

Planter, canopy bed, marked Shawnee #734 ....**$45.00**

Planter, coal bucket, white w/embossed flower, blue handle, marked USA **$15.00**

Planter, dog in row boat, marked Shawnee #736 ....**$18.00**

Planter, duck pulling cart, wearing scarf & ruffled collar, lime green, marked Shawnee #752 ....**$20.00**

Planter, Dutch boy & girl at well in shades of blue & green w/gold trim, on base, marked Shawnee #710 ....**$22.00**

Planter, elf on shoe, green shoe w/elf in yellow & blue, marked Shawnee #765 ....**$10.00**

Planter, fish, rounded body w/embossed scales, black & rose shading w/gold trim, marked USA #717 ....**$60.00**

Planter, flying goose on framed square shape w/vertical ribs, footed, marked Shawnee #820 ....**$18.00**

Planter, globe in shades of blue & yellow on pedestal base, marked Shawnee USA **$20.00**

Planter, highchair, pink w/blue trim, USA #727 ....**$50.00**

Planter, horse, reddish brown w/white & black mane, marked Shawnee #506 ....**$35.00**

Planter, hound dog w/head down, light yellow, marked USA **$9.00**

Planter, lg watering can w/embossed basketweave & floral design, marked USA **$14.00**

Planter, lovebirds chest-to-chest on tree stump, blue, marked USA **$8.00**

Planter, open-mouth fish w/tail up & rests on fins, blue .**$7.00**

Planter, Oriental lady w/parasol standing next to urn, blues, rose & yellow, gold trim, USA #701 ....**$18.00**

Planter, Oriental pulling rickshaw, green w/gold trim, marked USA #539 ....**$8.00**

Planter, piano, lime green, marked USA #528 ....**$25.00**

Planter, Polynesian girl, bust, marked Shawnee #896 .**$10.00**

Planter, potbellied stove, white w/blue & brown trim, marked USA **$14.00**

Planter, rocking horse, blue w/cold-painted red saddle, black mane & tail, marked USA #526 ....**$24.00**

Planter, tulip shape on scalloped drip tray, light rose, marked Shawnee USA #466 ....**$10.00**

Planter, wheelbarrow, stylized, white w/embossed flower & blue trim, marked USA **$12.00**

Planter, windmill in green & white w/gold trim, marked Shawnee #715 ....**$26.00**

Planter, 6 shells form dish, blue or gold, marked Shawnee #154 ....**$8.00**

Plate, Corn, marked #93 ....**$25.00**

Platter, 10", Corn, marked #68 ....**$30.00**

Platter, 12", Corn **$45.00**

Salt & pepper shakers, lg, blue jug, pr **$30.00**

Salt & pepper shakers, lg, Charlie Chicken, colorful hand-painting w/gold trim, pr **$60.00**

Salt & pepper shakers, lg, Corn, pr **$25.00**

Salt & pepper shakers, lg, floral decals & gold trim, pr..**$90.00**

Salt & pepper shakers, lg, Flower & Fern, 4-sided, yellow, pr.**$25.00**

Salt & pepper shakers, lg, fruit, gold trim (1 shown in right of photo), pr **$55.00**

Salt & pepper shakers, lg, fruit, marked USA, pr (1 shown at left) **$30.00**

Salt & pepper shakers, lg, Smiley Pig, green bibs, pr..**$60.00**

Salt & pepper shakers, lg, Sunflower, pr......................**$50.00**

Salt & pepper shakers, lg, Swiss Boy & Girl, airbrushed colors w/gold trim, pr...**$50.00**

Salt & pepper shakers, lg, Winnie & Smiley, Clover & Bud design, pr...**$85.00**

Salt & pepper shakers, lg, Winnie & Smiley, w/heart motif, pr..**$70.00**

Salt & pepper shakers, sm, Bo Peep & Sailor Boy, gold trim, pr..**$40.00**

Salt & pepper shakers, sm, Bo Peep & Sailor Boy, white w/blue & rose accents, pr **$20.00**

Salt & pepper shakers, sm, Charlie Chicken, colorful dry-brushing w/gold trim, pr...**$40.00**

Salt & pepper shakers, sm, Charlie Chicken, white w/green accents, pr **$20.00**

Salt & pepper shakers, sm, Chef S&P, gold trim, pr....**$30.00**

Salt & pepper shakers, sm, Chef S&P, rose airbrushing w/blue accents, pr **$15.00**

Salt & pepper shakers, sm, cottage, USA #9, pr..........**$85.00**

Salt & pepper shakers, sm, farmer, white w/blue & gold trim, pr...**$47.00**

Salt & pepper shakers, sm, Flower & Fern, blue, pr ...**$15.00**

Salt & pepper shakers, sm, flowerpot, rose pots w/blue flowers, pr **$15.00**

Salt & pepper shakers, sm, flowers, rose & yellow w/gold trim, pr...**$30.00**

Salt & pepper shakers, sm, fruit, airbrushed (1 shown on right of photo, illustrated on page 363), pr $15.00

Salt & pepper shakers, sm, milk can, white w/floral decal & gold trim, pr **$40.00**

Salt & pepper shakers, sm, Muggsy, white w/dry-brushed black accents, blue scarf, gold trim, pr...................**$60.00**

Salt & pepper shakers, sm, owl, dry-brushed colors & gold trim, pr...**$40.00**

Salt & pepper shakers, sm, owl, white w/peach & brown accents, pr **$23.00**

Salt & pepper shakers, sm, Puss 'n Boots, white w/rose & gold trim, pr **$60.00**

Salt & pepper shakers, sm, watering can, white w/blue & gold trim, pr **$40.00**

Salt & pepper shakers, sm, wheelbarrow, white w/blue flower & trim, pr **$15.00**

Salt & pepper shakers, sm, wheelbarrow, white w/blue flower, blue & gold trim, pr **$35.00**

Salt & pepper shakers, sm, Winnie & Smiley, white w/blue & brown trim, pr **$38.00**

Salt box, Fernware, yellow, marked USA....................**$35.00**

Saucer, Corn, marked #91 ....**$12.00**

Snack jar, lg matt black ball jar, white lid w/red lobster handle, tab handles on side of jar, marked #925......**$180.00**

Sock darner, white w/blue or pink, marked USA........**$30.00**

Sugar bowl, bucket, white w/floral decals & gilt.........**$60.00**

Sugar bowl, Clover Bud, marked USA.........................**$40.00**

Sugar bowl, Corn, marked #78 ....**$30.00**

Sugar bowl, Cottage, marked USA...............................**$130.00**

Sugar bowl, Flower & Fern, yellow.............................**$20.00**

Sugar bowl, fruit, marked Shawnee #83......................**$35.00**

Sugar bowl, Snowflake, yellow, open, marked USA ...**$15.00**

Sugar bowl, Sunflower, marked USA............................**$30.00**

Sugar shaker, White Corn, w/gold trim.......................**$90.00**

Teapot, Clover Bud, marked USA.................................**$70.00**

Teapot, elephant, gold trim, marked USA.................**$135.00**

Teapot, elephant, green, yellow or blue, marked USA .**$85.00**

Teapot, embossed rose, gold trim **$55.00**

Teapot, Granny Ann, floral decals w/gold trim, marked USA...**$140.00**

Teapot, Granny Ann, green apron, marked Pat Ann...**$70.00**

Teapot, Sunflower, marked USA....................................**$40.00**

Teapot, Tom Tom, blue & rose airbrushing, marked Tom The Piper's Son Pat USA..**$70.00**

Teapot, Tom Tom, white w/blue patches & gold trim, marked Tom The Piper's Son Pat USA **$140.00**

Teapot, 10-oz, Pennsylvania Dutch motif, #10.............**$70.00**

Teapot, 30-oz, Corn Line, gold trim, marked #75......**$150.00**

Utility jar, floral decals on low white basket w/blue rope trim, gold accents, lg open handle on lid, USA **$95.00**

Utility jar, tall white basket w/green rope trim, open handle on lid, marked USA...**$60.00**

Vase, cornucopia style on square base, white w/floral decals & gold trim, marked Shawnee USA #466 ....**$10.00**

Vase, elegant hand holding up scalloped vessel w/flared rim, lime green, marked USA................................**$26.00**

Vase, green w/embossed flowers, bulbous lower body w/cylindrical upper body, flared rim, handled, marked USA #875..**$6.00**

Vase, horizontally ribbed w/imprinted philodendron design, handles shaped like question marks, marked Shawnee #805 ....**$18.00**

Vase, lg ball shape w/flared rim, allover embossed floral design, handled, marked #827 ....**$30.00**

Vase, lg embossed bow on bulbous lower body w/fan-shaped upper body, decorative closed handles, marked USA #819 ....**$18.00**

Vase, lg flared upper body on bulbous lower body, allover burlap texture in green or yellow, marked Shawnee #890 ....**$14.00**

Vase, pitcher w/pineapple design on bulbous lower body, handled, various colors, marked Shawnee #839 ....**$18.00**

Vase, swan wrapped around lower bulbous body, flared rim, various colors, marked USA #806...................**$18.00**

Vase, tall cylindrical shape w/flared rim & round base, embossed tulips on stems w/leaves, yellow, marked USA **$7.00**

Vase, vertically ribbed pitcher shape w/scalloped rim, round base, dolphin handle, green, marked Shawnee #828 ....**$22.00**

Vase, white scalloped fan shape w/iris, marked USA **$7.00**

Vase, yellow wheat w/green leaves on white, marked USA #1267...**$15.00**

Vase, 2 doves hugging sides of vertically ribbed vessel w/flared & scalloped rim, yellow w/gold trim, marked USA #829 ....**$30.00**

Vase, 2 lg leaves on round base, marked Shawnee #823 .**$30.00**

Sheet Music

Flea markets are a good source for buying old sheet music, and prices are usually very reasonable. Most examples can be bought for less than $5.00. More often than not, it is collected for reasons other than its contents. Some of the cover art was done by well-known illustrators like Rockwell, Christy, Barbelle, and Starmer, and some collectors like to zero in on their particular favorite, often framing some of the more attractive examples. Black Americana collectors can find many good examples with Black entertainers being featured on the covers or with the music revolving around an ethnic theme.

You may want to concentrate on music by a particularly renowned composer, for instance George M. Cohan or Irving Berlin. Or you may find you enjoy covers featuring famous entertainers and movie stars from the forties through the sixties. At any rate, be critical of condition when you buy or sell sheet music. As is true with any item of paper, tears, dog ears, or soil will greatly reduce its value.

If you'd like a more thorough listing of sheet music and prices, we recommend *The Sheet Music Reference and Price Guide* by Anna Marie Guiheen and Marie-Reine A. Pafik and *The Collector's Guide to Sheet Music* by Debbie Dillon.

Values are for mint condition examples.

Ace in the Hole, Cole Porter, from movie Let's Face It, 1943 ....**$5.00**

Across the Alley From the Alamo, Joe Green, Stan Kenton photo cover, 1947 ....**$4.00**

Alfie, Hal David & Burt Bacharach, from Alfie, 1966.....**$5.00**

All Dressed Up w/a Broken Heart, Fred Patrick, Claude Reese & Jack Val, Buddy Clark photo cover, 1946.**$3.00**

Always True to You in My Fashion, Cole Porter, from musical Kiss Me Kate, 1948 ....**$5.00**

An Old Sombrero, Lew Brown & Ray Henderson, Vic Damone photo cover, 1947.....................................**$3.00**

And Russia Is Her Name, Harburg & Kern, 1943.........**$10.00**

And Then I Remember, Janis Moss Rosenburg, 1956....**$5.00**

At Last, Mack Gordon & Harry Warren, from movie Orchestra Wives, Ray Anthony photo cover, 1942 ....**$5.00**

At the Flying W, Allie Wrubel, Elliot Lawrence photo cover, 1948...**$3.00**

Baby Talk to Me, Lee Adams & Charles Strause, from movie Bye Bye Birdie, 1960 ....**$5.00**

Beloved, Be Faithful, Ervin Drake & Jimmy Shirl, signed photo cover of Russ Morgan, 1950 ....**$5.00**

Best Man, Roy Alfred & Fred Wise, King Cole Trio photo cover, 1946 ....**$5.00**

Big Spender, Cy Coleman & Dorothy Fields, from Sweet Charity, Shirley MacLaine photo cover, 1969 ....**$3.00**

Blue Eyes Crying in the Rain, Fred Rose, 1948 ....**$5.00**

Broken Promise, James Goldsborough, from movie Jamboree, The Four Coins photo cover, 1957................**$5.00**

Buttons & Bows, Livingston & Evans, from Paleface, Bob Hope & Jane Russell photo cover, 1948 ....**$5.00**

Careless Hands, Bob Hilliard & Carl Sigman, John Laurenz photo cover, 1949 ....**$3.00**

Catch a Falling Star, Paul Vance & Le Pockriss, Perry Como photo cover, 1957 ....**$5.00**

Chattanoogie Shoe Shine Boy, Harry Stone & Jack Stapp, 1950...**$3.00**

Cling a Little Closer, Parish & Kent, 1947 ....**$5.00**

Cold Cold Heart, Hank Williams, Tony Bennett photo cover, 1951 ....**$3.00**

Consider Yourself, Lionel Bart, from Oliver, 1960 ....**$5.00**

Crazy Heart, Danny Davis & Fred Rose, Danny Davis photo cover, 1951 ....**$3.00**

Curly Top, Ted Koehler & Ray Henderson, from movie Curly Top, Shirley Temple, John Boles & Rochelle Hudson cover, 1935 ....**$10.00**

Daddy's Little Girl, Bobby Burke & Horace Gerlach, Dick Todd photo cover, 1949 ....**$10.00**

Dance to the Music of the Ocarina, Irving Berlin, from musical Call Me Madam, Ethel Merman caricature on cover, 1950 ....**$10.00**

Day Dreaming, Gus Kahn & Jerome Kern, Bing Crosby photo cover, 1941 ....**$5.00**

Dearie, Bob Hilliard & Dave Mann, 1950 ....**$3.00**

Do It the Hard Way, Lorenz Hart & Richard Rodgers, from musical Pal Joey, 1940 ....**$5.00**

Don't Cry Joe, Joe Marsala, 1940................................**$3.00**

Don't Let Me Down, John Lennon & Paul McCartney photo cover, 1969 ....**$30.00**

Dreamer's Holiday, Kim Gannon & Mabel Wayne, Perry Como photo cover, 1949 ....**$5.00**

Eleventh Hour Melody, King Palmer & Carl Sigman, Al Hibbler photo cover, 1956..**$3.00**

Evelyn, Paul Weston & Sid Robin, Kay Kyser photo cover, 1948..**$5.00**

Extra, Extra, Irving Berlin, from Miss Liberty, 1949........**$5.00**

Faith Can Move Mountains, Ben Raleigh & Guy Wood, Johnnie Ray photo cover, 1952 ....**$5.00**

Follow the Fold, Jo Swerling, Abe Burrows & Frank Loesser, from musical Guys & Dolls, 1950...........................**$5.00**

Galway Bay, Dr Arthur Calahan, signed photo cover of Bing Crosby, 1947 ....**$10.00**

Gentle on My Mind, John Hartford, Glen Campbell photo cover, 1967 ....**$5.00**

Give a Little Whistle, Carolyn Leigh & Cy Coleman, from movie Wildcat, 1960 ....**$5.00**

Goodbye Old Girl, Richard Adler & Jerry Ross, from musical Damn Yankees, 1955 ....**$5.00**

Goodnight Irene, Huddie Ledbetter & John Lomax, The Weavers & Gordon Jenkins photo cover, 1950.......**$3.00**

Guy Is a Guy, Oscar Brand, Doris Day photo, 1952 ....**$5.00**

Halls of Ivy, Henry Russell & Vick Knight, 1950............**$5.00**

Haven't Got Time for the Pain, Jacob Brackman, Carly Simon photo cover, 1974......................................**$5.00**

He's Got the Whole World in His Hands, Geoff Love, Laurie London photo cover, 1957 ....**$2.00**

Heaven Is a Raft on a River, Robert & Helen Thomas, Jane Pickens photo cover, 1954 ....**$5.00**

Here's a Hand, Lorenz Hart & Richard Rodgers, from movie All's Fair, 1942 ....**$5.00**

Hey There, Richard Adler & Jerry Ross, from musical Pajama Game, 1954...**$5.00**

How Sweet It Is, Jackie Gleason & Irving Caesar, Jackie Gleason & Frankie Fontaine photo cover, 1963 ...**$10.00**

I Believe, Ervin Drake, Irvin Graham & Al Stillman, Frankie Laine photo cover, 1952 ....**$2.00**

I Don't Want To Be Hurt Anymore, McCarthy, Nat King Cole photo cover, 1962 ....**$3.00**

I Enjoy Being a Girl, Richard Rodgers & Oscar Hammerstein II, from movie Flower Drum Song, 1961.................**$5.00**

I Just Love You, Joe Pasternak & Nicholas Brodsky, Tony Martin photo cover, 1953..............................**$3.00**

I Need You Now, Jimmy Crane & Al Jacobs, Eddie Fisher photo cover, 1953 ....**$3.00**

I'd Be Lost w/out You, Sunny Skylar, Jimmy Palmer photo cover, 1946 ....**$3.00**

I'll Close My Eyes, Buddy Kaye & Billy Reid, signed photo cover of Sammy Kaye, 1945 ....**$3.00**

I'll Never Fall in Love Again, Jimmie Currie, Tom Jones photo cover, 1962 ....**$5.00**

I'm Not Your Steppin' Stone, The Monkees, 1966.......**$10.00**

I've Got a Sixpence, Desmond Cox, 1943 ....**$3.00**

I've Gotta Be Me, Walter Marks, from Golden Rainbow, Steve Lawrence & Eydie Gorme cover, 1967 ....**$3.00**

If I Ever Love Again,Carlyle & Dick Reynolds, 1949......**$3.00**

It's a Lovely Day Today, Irving Berlin, from musical Call Me Madam, Ethel Merman caricature on cover, 1950...**$10.00**

Jealous Heart, Jenny Lou Carson, Al Morgan photo cover, 1944..**$3.00**

Johnny Is the Boy for Me, Les Paul, Marcel Stillman & Paddy Roberts, Les Paul & Mary Ford photo cover, 1953..**$5.00**

Just For Now, Dick Redmond, from movie Whiplash, Dane Clark & Alexis Smith photo cover, 1948.................**$5.00**

Just Walking in the Rain, Johnny Bragg & Robert S Riley, 1953...**$3.00**

King's New Clothes, Frank Loesser, from movie Hans Christian Andersen, Danny Kaye photo cover, 1951.......**$5.00**

Kiss Me Sweet, Milton Drake, 1959.................................**$3.00**

Let Your Love Walk In, Joe Greene, De Castro Sisters photo cover, 1955 ....**$5.00**

Lily Belle, Dave Franklin & Irving Taylor, Eddie Cantor photo cover, 1945 ....**$5.00**

Little Red Monkey, Stephen Gale & Jack Jordan, Rosemary Clooney photo cover, 1953 ....**$3.00**

Love Thy Neighbor, Mack Gordon & Harry Revel, from movie We're Not Dressing, Bing Crosby & Carole Lombard cover, 1934 ....**$15.00**

Lullaby in Doll Land, John W Schaum, 1956.................**$3.00**

Make It w/You, David Gates, 1970................................**$3.00**

May You Always, Larry Markes & Dick Charles, Maguire Sisters photo cover, 1958 ....**$5.00**

Melody Of Love, Tom Glazer & H Engelmann, Four Aces photo cover, 1954 ....**$5.00**

Mockin' Bird Hill, Vaughn Horton, Les Paul & Mary Ford photo cover, 1949 ....**$5.00**

Money Isn't Everything, Richard Rodgers & Oscar Hammerstein II, from musical Allegro, 1951 ....**$5.00**

My Kingdom for a Kiss, Warren & Dubin, from Hearts Divided, Marion Davies photo, 1936 ....**$10.00**

My Sugar Is So Refined, Dee & Lippman, 1946 ....**$3.00**

Naughty Angeline, Allan Roberts & Lester Lee, Lawrence Welk photo cover, 1947.................................**$3.00**

Never So Beautiful, Jay Livingston & Ray Evans, from movie Here Comes the Girls, 1953.............................**$5.00**

No Can Do, Charles Tobias & Nat Simon, from musical Copacabana, 1945 ....**$10.00**

Noon at Midnight, Lou Holzer & Harry Kogen, 1935 ....**$5.00**

Now & Then There's a Fool Such As I, Trader, Harry Snow photo cover, 1952 ....**$5.00**

Oh You Sweet One, Dick Hardt & Moe Jaffe, Andrew Sisters & Russ Morgan photo cover, 1949.....................**$3.00**

Okalehau, Leo Robin & Ralph Rainger, from Waikiki Wedding, Bing Crosby & Shirley Ross cover, 1937 ....**$5.00**

On Top of Old Smokey, Peter Seeger, 1951 ....**$3.00**

One Day We Dance, Carolyn Leigh & Cy Coleman, from movie Wildcat, 1960.....................................**$5.00**

Pair of Blue Eyes, William Kernell, from movie Song O' My Heart, John McCormack photo cover, 1940 ....**$5.00**

Penguin at the Waldorf, Jimmy Eaton, Larry Wagner & Frank Shuman, 1947...**$5.00**

Peppermint Twist, Joey Dee & Henry Glover, 1961......**$5.00**

Please Mr Sun, Sid Frank & Ray Geton, signed photo cover of Johnnie Ray, 1951..................................**$5.00**

Prove It by the Things You Do, Allan Roberts & Doris Fisher, 1945 ....**$3.00**

Quicksilver, Irving Taylor, George Wyle & Eddie Pola, Bing Crosby photo cover, 1949.............................**$3.00**

Quiet Cathedral, Iris Mason & Hal Saunders, 1945........**$3.00**

Rainbow, Russ Hamilton, 1957.................................**$5.00**

Ready, Willing & Able, Al Rinker, Floyd Huddleston & Dick Gleason, from movie Young At Heart, 1954 ....**$5.00**

Remember Me I'm the One Who Loves You, Stuart Hamblen, 1950 ....**$3.00**

Rosalie, Cole Porter, from movie Rosalie, Nelson Eddy & Eleanor Powell photo cover, 1937 ....**$10.00**

Roses, Tim Spencer & Glenn Spencer, 1950 ....**$3.00**

Ruby, Mitchell Parish & Heinz Roemheld, from movie Ruby Gentry, Jennifer Jones photo cover, 1953.................**$5.00**

Sam's Song, Jack Elliot & Lew Quadling, Bing Crosby photo cover, 1950 ....**$3.00**

Say You're Mine Again, Charles Nathan & Dave Heisler, 1953...**$3.00**

Shoo-Shoo Baby, Phil Moore, from movie Beautiful But Broke, Andrew Sisters photo cover, 1943 ....**$5.00**

Sing To Me Guitar, Cole Porter, from movie Mexican Hayride, 1943 ....**$3.00**

Slow Poke, Pee Wee King, Redd Stewart & Chilton Price, signed photo cover of Pee Wee King & Redd Stewart, 1951...**$5.00**

Snowbird, Gene MacLellan, Anne Murray cover, 1970..**$3.00**

Some of These Days, Shelton Brooks, Sophie Tucker photo cover, 1937 ....**$25.00**

Something for the Boys, Cole Porter, from movie Something for the Boys, 1942 ....**$5.00**

Son of Old Hawaii, Gordon Beecher & Johnny Noble, Tony Martin photo cover, 1938.................................**$5.00**

Star of God, Fred E Weatherly & Eric Coates, 1942.......**$5.00**
Streets of Laredo, M Alexander, 1966 ....**$2.00**
Summer Wind, Johnny Mercer & Henry Mayer, Roger Williams, Perry Como & Wayne Newton photo cover, 1965.................**$3.00**
Sweet & Low, Joseph Barnby & Alfred Tennyson, Doring Sisters photo cover, 1935....................**$5.00**
Syncopated Clock, Leroy Anderson, 1946 ....**$5.00**
Take It From There, Leo Robin & Ralph Rainger, from Coney Island, Betty Grable photo cover, 1943 ....**$5.00**
Tea for Two, Irving Caeser & Otto Harbach, from movie No No Nanette, Anna Neagle photo cover, 1940..........**$5.00**
That Old Dream Peddler, Stewart & Delgado, 1947 ......**$5.00**
There Once Was a Man, Richard Adler & Jerry Ross, from musical Pajama Game, 1954....................**$5.00**
There's No Tomorrow, Al Hoffman, Leo Corday & Leon Carr, 1949 ....**$5.00**
This Time, Irving Caesar & Sydney Green, 1953 ....**$3.00**
Till My Love Comes to Me, Paul Francis Webster & Ray Heindorf, from movie Young at Heart, 1954..........**$5.00**
Tom, Dick or Harry, Cole Porter, from musical Kiss Me Kate, 1948....................**$5.00**
Travelin' Man, Jerry Fuller, 1961 ....**$5.00**
Tulips & Heather, Milton Carson, Perry Como photo cover, 1950....................**$3.00**
Ugly Duckling, Frank Loesser, from movie Hans Christian Anderson, Danny Kaye photo cover, 1951..............**$5.00**
Until, Jack Fulton, Bob Crosby & Hunter Kahler, Tommy Dorsey photo cover, 1945 ....**$3.00**
Vagabond Shoes, Sammy Gallop & David Saxon, Vic Damone photo cover, 1949 ....**$3.00**
Wabash Cannon Ball, William Kindt, Rex Allen photo cover, 1939.....................**$5.00**
Wait for Me Mary, Charlie Tobias, Nat Simon & Harry Tobias, 1942 ....**$5.00**
Walk Hand in Hand, Johnny Cowell, 1956 ....**$3.00**
Wasted Years, Wally Fowler, 1959.......................**$2.00**
Wayward Wind, Herb Newman & Stan Lebowsky, signed cover photo of Gogi Grant, 1956...........................**$4.00**
We're All Together Now, Leo Robin & Ralph Rainger, from movie Gulliver's Travels, 1939 ....**$5.00**
What Takes My Fancy, Carolyn Leigh & Cy Coleman, from movie Wildcat, 1960....................**$5.00**
When I Write My Song, Mossman & Anson, 1947.........**$5.00**

When the Moon Comes Over the Mountain, by Kate Smith, Howard Johnson & Harry Woods, photo of Kate on cover, 1922....................$15.00

Where in the World, Buddy Kaye & Carl Lampl, Mindy Carson photo cover, 1950 ....**$5.00**
Who'll Be the Next One To Cry Over You, Johnny S Black, 1959......................**$3.00**
Why Don't You Love Me, Hank Williams, signed photo cover of Hank Williams, 1950 ....**$5.00**
Wilhelmina, Mack Gordon & Josef Myrow, from movie Wabash Avenue, Betty Grable photo cover, 1950 ..**$5.00**

Would You, Arthur Freed & Herb Brown, Clark Gable & Jeanette MacDonald photo cover $15.00
Yellow Rose of Texas, Don George, Johnny Desmond photo cover, 1955 ....**$3.00**
You Gorgeous Dancing Doll, Russ Morgan, Paul Cunningham & Ira Schuster, 1940.......................**$3.00**
Young at Heart, Carolyn Leigh & Johnny Richards, Frank Sinatra photo cover, 1954......................**$5.00**
Zigeuner, Noel Coward, 1941 ....**$5.00**

Shell Pink Glassware

Here's something new to look for this year – lovely soft pink opaque glassware made by the Jeannette Glass Company for only a short time during the late 1950s. Prices, says expert Gene Florence, have been increasing by leaps and bounds! You'll find a wide variance in style from piece to piece, since the company chose shapes from several of their most popular lines to press in the satiny shell pink. Refer to *Collectible Glassware from the 40s, 50s, and 50s*, by Mr. Florence for photos and more information.

Ashtray, butterfly shape.................................**$15.00**
Bowl, wedding; 8", w/lid **$25.00**
Bowl, 10½ ", Holiday, footed **$40.00**
Cake stand, 10", Harp.................................**$30.00**
Candy jar, 5½ ", grapes, 4-footed, w/lid **$18.00**
Creamer, Baltimore Pear.............................**$14.00**
Pitcher, 24-oz, Thumbprint, footed...................**$27.50**
Relish, 12", Vineyard, octagonal, 4-part.....................**$40.00**

Stem, 8-oz, water goblet, Thumbprint **$12.50**
Tray, 12½ x9¾ ", Harp, handles **$50.00**
Tumbler, 5-oz, Thumbprint, footed **$8.00**
Vase, 7" **$35.00**

Shirley Temple

Born April 23, 1928, Shirley Jane Temple danced and smiled her way into the hearts of America in the movie *Stand Up and Cheer*. Many, many successful roles followed and by the time Shirley was eight years old, she was #1 at the box offices around the country. Her picture appeared in publications almost daily, and any news about her was news indeed. Mothers dressed their little daughters in clothing copied after hers and coifed them with Shirley hairdos.

The extent of her success was mirrored in the unbelievable assortment of merchandise that saturated the retail market. Dolls, coloring books, children's clothing and jewelry, fountain pens, paper dolls, stationery, and playing cards are just a few examples of the hundreds of items that were available. Shirley's face was a common sight on the covers of magazines as well as in the advertisements they contained, and she was featured in hundreds of articles.

Though she had been retired from the movies for nearly a decade, she had two successful TV series in the late fifties, *The Shirley Temple Story-Book* and *The Shirley Temple Show*. Her reappearance caused new interest in some of the items that had been so popular during her childhood, and many were reissued.

If you're interested in learning more about her, we recommend *Shirley Temple Dolls and Collectibles* by Patricia R. Smith and *Toys, Antique and Collectible,* by David Longest.

Book, Shirley Temple's Book of Fairy Tales, Saalfield, 2nd printing, 1936 ....$25.00
Book, Shirley Temple's Favorite Poems, 1936, EX **$30.00**

Bookmark, photo & 20th Century Fox logo on heavy cardboard, from Spain, minimum value **$10.00**
Charm, 1¼ ", painted celluloid figural, unmarked, 1930s, minimum value **$45.00**
Christmas card, marked Hallmark, dated 1935, VG.....**$22.50**
Cigar bands, each w/different picture, set of 7, M **$15.00**
Cigarette card, w/Joel McCrea, from Our Little Girl.......**$8.00**
Coloring book, My Book To Color, #1768, covers loose, pictures colored **$10.00**
Coloring book, This Is My Crayon Book, Saalfield, 1935, EX **$30.00**
Creamer, portrait & facsimilie signature in white on cobalt, M **$35.00**
Cutout, 4½ x6", from Wheaties cereal box, EX **$15.00**
Doll, 12", vinyl, dressed as Heidi, Ideal, MIB **$200.00**
Doll, 12", vinyl, green & white dress, original slip, marked Ideal, complete, MIB **$200.00**
Doll, 15", vinyl, dressed as Cinderella, all original, 1961, M **$300.00**
Doll, 15", vinyl, dressed as Heidi, all original, 1960, M .**$265.00**
Doll, 16", vinyl, in Stand Up & Cheer dress, 1973, MIB .**$200.00**
Doll, 18", composition, Hawaiian, body marked Shirley Temple, head marked Ideal, all original **$850.00**
Doll, 19", vinyl, flirty eyes, all original, 1957 ....**$450.00**
Doll, 8", vinyl, dressed as Stowaway, Ideal, 1982.......**$45.00**
Jewelry set, locket, bracelet & ring, marked Made by Originals of New York on card, M, minimum value.....**$50.00**
Lobby card, Kiss for Corliss, EX.................................**$15.00**
Lobby card, Mr Belvedere **$15.00**
Lobby cards, The Blue Bird, set of 5 ....**$75.00**
Magazine, Celebrity Doll Journal, 1985, M **$8.00**
Magazine, Family Circle, photo cover, May 1942, EX....**$4.00**
Magazine, Life, color cover w/her daughter, February 3, 1958 ....**$7.50**
Magazine, Movie Mirror, Shirley w/a Difference article, March 1939 ....**$15.00**
Magazine, Roxy Review, Shirley as Stowaway on cover, dated 1936 ....**$25.00**
Magazine, Shirley Temple Black cover, Peninsula, February 1977...**$6.00**
Magazine ad, for Calox Dentifrice, from Life, ½-page w/2 photos **$5.00**
Magazine ad, for movie, Kiss for Corliss, 1949, full-page.**$3.00**
Magazine ad, for movie, Adventure in Baltimore, black & white, from Life, full-page **$4.00**
Magazine ad, Quaker, for Cosmopolitan, 1937, ½-page.**$3.00**
Magazine ad, Woodbury Face Powder, from Good Housekeeping, full-page **$2.50**
Movie ad, for movie, Since You Went Away, from Life, full-page **$4.50**
Movie insert, 14x36", A Kiss for Corliss, EX.................**$35.00**
Mug, portrait & faux signature in white on cobalt, M .**$35.00**
Newspaper ad, doll giveaway w/purchase of appliance, dated 1936, minimum value **$10.00**
Paper dolls, Saalfield, #440, uncut **$95.00**
Paper dolls, 1930s, EX **$50.00**
Paperweight, picture under plastic, 1930s....................**$10.00**
Photo, 11x14", sepia portrait, 1930s, minimum value..**$15.00**

Photo, 8x10", black & white portrait, signed, 1930s....**$60.00**
Photo, 8x10", color portrait as teenager **$12.00**
Postcard, Shirley's home w/picture, Western Publishing,
    #810...**$4.50**
Poster, 27x41", Miss Annie Rooney, G......................**$40.00**
Pressbook, Little Miss Broadway, minimum value.......**$95.00**
Program, 11x8½ ", Tournament of Roses, 1939, 38-pg.**$20.00**
Sewing pattern, Simplicity #2717, wardrobe for 12" doll,
    1958, minimum value **$15.00**
Sheet music, But Definitely, from movie Poor Little Rich
    Girl, EX...**$15.00**
Sheet music, Goodnight My Love, from movie Stowaway,
    EX..**$18.00**
Sheet music, Shirley Temple Song Album #2, EX........**$20.00**
Song album, 1930s, EX..**$25.00**
Song book, 8x12", Shirley Temple's Favorite Songs, Robbins
    Music Music Corp, 1937, 40-page, EX **$50.00**
Song sheet, Together, printed by Cambell, Connelly & Co of
    London, copyright 1944, minimum value...............**$8.00**
Stationery, 1930s, MIB **$65.00**
Tablet, 1930s, EX **$25.00**
Tablet cover, in pink dress w/short curls, 1935.............**$3.50**

Treasure board, Saalfield #8806, 1959....................**$20.00**
Video, Kiss & Tell, EX **$25.00**

Silhouette Pictures

These novelty pictures are familiar to everyone. Even today a good number of them are still around, and you'll often see them at flea markets and co-ops. They were very popular in their day and never expensive, and because they were made for so many years (the twenties through the fifties), many variations are available. Though the glasses in some are flat, others were made with curved glass. Backgrounds may be foil, a scenic print, hand tinted, or plain.

Sometimes dried flowers were added as accents. But the characteristic common to them all is the subject matter reverse painted on the glass. People (even complicated groups), scenes, ships, and animals were popular themes. Though quite often the silhouette was done in solid black to create a look similar to the 19th-century cut silhouettes, colors were sometimes used as well.

In the twenties, making tinsel art pictures became a popular pastime. Ladies would paint the outline of their subjects on the back of the glass and use crumpled tinfoil as a background. Sometimes they would tint certain areas of the glass, making the foil appear to be colored. This type is popular with with today's collectors.

If you'd like to learn more about this subject, we recommend _The Encyclopedia of Silhouette Collectibles on Glass_ by Shirley Mace.

Convex Glass

Colonial couple admiring swans, 5x4", full color, Benton
    Glass Co...**$12.00**

**Colonial couple in parlor setting, 5x4", vining plant on
    stand & lamp painted on glass, ca 1942..........$15.00**
Colonial couple seated at table having a glass of soda, 8x6",
    black on cream, Benton Glass Co.........................**$30.00**
Colonial lady lighting candles, 8x6", red on cream, Benton
    Glass Co...**$50.00**
Colonial lady playing piano, 5x4", black on cream, Benton
    Glass Co...**$15.00**
Colonial man pouring woman a glass of tea in a landscape,
    6x4", black figures on full-color ground, Benton Glass
    Co...**$18.00**
Couple building snowman, 5x4", black figures w/full-
    color sky & snow-capped mountains, Benton Glass
    Co **$20.00**
Courting couple on fence, 5x4", full-color landscape
    beyond, Benton Glass Co....................................**$18.00**

Horse & rider jumping fence, 8x6", full-color landscape beyond, Benton Glass Co......................................$35.00

Kittens watching ducks in a pond, 5x4", black on cream, Benton Glass Co $20.00

Little girl pushing stroller, 5x4", black on white background, Benton Glass Co $20.00

Mother & son in a garden landscape, 8x6", full-color background, Dearest Mother & poem upper left, Benton Glass Co......................................$20.00

Mountainous landscape w/house, 5x4", bridge in foreground, full color, Benton Glass Co $12.00

Oriental lady seated in a landscape, 4½ " dia, hand painted, full color, Edna Lewis Studio......................$12.00

Portrait of a woman surrounded by white lace, 8x6", Benton Glass Co, stamped 1941 Donald Art Co, NY.........$20.00

Scotty dog on hind legs swatting at a butterfly, 5x4", black on cream, Benton Glass Co..................................$20.00

Flat Glass

Autumn Bouquet, 11x7", earth tones, Reliance, signed Smith Frederick......................................$30.00

Baby in bonnet reaches for butterfly, 10x7", tinsel art .$15.00

Colonial couple playing in snow, 5x4", full-color cabin & mountain in background, Benton Glass Co .$20.00

Colonial couple admiring swans, 5x4", full color, Benton Glass Co......................................$12.00

Colonial couple seated at table having a glass of soda, 8x6", black on cream, Benton Glass Co........................$30.00

Colonial girl, 5" dia, black on gold foil background, Peter Watson's Studio......................................$15.00

Colonial man offering woman a rose, series of 4, titled Amourettes, 5x5", full color, copyright C&A Richards 1931 ....$25.00

Colonial man w/parasol, titled Lucky April Showers, 4x3", black on cream, Reliance $15.00

Couple carving hearts in a tree, titled Hearts, 10x8", silver foil background, Deltex Products Co..................$35.00

Couple embracing beside gate, Good Night, 6x4", Buckbee-Brehm Co, dated 1933......................................$20.00

Courting couple in a landscape, 9x7". black on cream West Coast Picture Co......................................$20.00

Courting couple on bridge, 10x4", black figures & full-color figures on gold foil background, Flowercraft........$20.00

Floral bouquet, 5x3½ ", hand painted to resemble butterfly wing colors, Reliance......................................$12.00

Gentleman holding bouquet for woman in swing, 10x8", black on silver foil, Deltex Products Co...............$35.00

Horse-drawn carriage w/figures, titled Tally Ho, 3x4", black on cream, Reliance......................................$10.00

Hunters in canoe, 12½ x9½ ", black image on full-color background, unmarked $35.00

Jack & The Beanstalk, 11x7", full color, Reliance........$35.00

John Alden & Priscilla, They Were Up To Date Too, 5x4", black figures on full-color interior scene, Newton Mfg Co......................................$12.00

Lady mailing letter, titled The Answer, 6x4", Buckbee-Brehm Co, 1930......................................$18.00

Lady w/parasol & 2 children in full-color circular inset, 5x8", white background, Art Publishing Co..................$12.00

Lady w/whippet, 7x10", full color, Art Publishing Co, stamped Stock No 290 on back $15.00

Little boy w/dog praying beside his bed, 3x4", West Coast Picture Co......................................$15.00

Little girl chasing dog, 4x4", dried wildflowers in the background, Fisher & Flowercraft $14.00

Little girl watering flowers, 5x6", black on cream, Reliance, marked T-1......................................$20.00

Red Riding Hood, 11x7", full color, Reliance..............$35.00

Windmill scene, 3½ x5", stream in foreground & house beyond, full color, Art Publishing Co, dated Feb 21, 1934......................................$8.00

Silver Flatware

You may have inherited a set of silver flatware with a few pieces missing, or you may become interested in collecting a pattern simply because you find yourself drawn to its elegance and the quality of its workmanship. Whatever the reason, if you decide to collect silver flatware, many matching services advertise in the trade papers listed in the back of this book.

Popular patterns are the most expensive, regardless of their age, due simply to collector demand. Monogrammed pieces are hard to sell and are worth only about half price.

Afterglow, cocktail fork, Oneida................................$17.00

Afterglow, cream soup, Oneida $20.00

Afterglow, gravy ladle, Oneida $42.00

American Classic, cream soup, Easterling $15.00

American Classic, luncheon fork, Easterling $15.00

American Classic, salad fork, Easterling $15.00
American Classic, seafood fork, Easterling..................$18.00
American Classic, tablespoon, Easterling $30.00
American Classic, teaspoon, Easterling........................$15.00
American Victorian, cocktail fork, Lunt $8.00
American Victorian, luncheon fork, Lunt $15.00
American Victorian, luncheon knife, Lunt..................$15.00
American Victorian, teaspoon, Lunt..........................$8.00
Amnerican Victorian, salad fork, Lunt $17.50
Angelique, gravy ladle, International..........................$30.00
Angelique, luncheon fork, International.....................$18.00
Angelique, luncheon knife, International...................$18.00
Angelique, salad fork, International...........................$22.00
Angelique, serrated cake knife, International $30.00
Angelique, tablespoon, International.........................$40.00
Angelique, teaspoon, International $15.00
Avalon, bouillon, International $25.00
Avalon, cold meat fork, International.........................$125.00
Baronial, sardine fork, Gorham.................................$95.00
Baronial, seafood fork, Gorham.................................$22.00
Baronial, soup ladle, Gorham....................................$300.00
Baronial, stuffing spoon, Gorham..............................$275.00
Botticelli, cocktail fork, Frank Whiting......................$22.00
Botticelli, cream soup, Frank Whiting $29.00
Botticelli, luncheon fork, Frank Whiting $29.00
Botticelli, luncheon knife, Frank Whiting...................$26.00
Bridal Rose, beef fork, Alvin....................................$95.00
Bridal Rose, berry spoon, Alvin, lg...........................$275.00
Bridal Rose, berry spoon, Alvin, sm $175.00
Bridal Rose, demitasse spoon, Alvin.........................$25.00
Bridal Rose, gravy ladle, Alvin..................................$175.00
Bridal Rose, individual butter spreader, Alvin $35.00
Bridal Rose, master butter spreader, Alvin................$110.00
Bridal Rose, meat fork, Alvin $195.00
Bridal Rose, pickle fork, long, Alvin..........................$125.00
Bridal Rose, sugar spoon, Alvin $95.00
Bridal Rose, 5 o'clock spoon, Alvin...........................$18.00
Buckingham, ice cream fork, Gorham........................$28.00
Buckingham, iced teaspoon, Gorham $25.00
Buttercup, butter spreader, Gorham..........................$75.00
Buttercup, cocktail fork, Gorham $20.00
Buttercup, gravy ladle, Gorham................................$95.00
Buttercup, jelly server, Gorham $75.00
Buttercup, luncheon fork, Gorham............................$30.00
Buttercup, macaroni server, Gorham $375.00
Buttercup, sardine fork, Gorham...............................$150.00
Buttercup, sauce ladle, Gorham................................$75.00
Buttercup, seafood fork, Gorham..............................$18.00
Buttercup, sugar spoon, Gorham..............................$35.00
Buttercup, sugar tongs, Gorham...............................$75.00
Buttercup, teaspoon, Gorham...................................$20.00
Buttercup, tomato server, Gorham $150.00
Buttercup, vegetable serving fork, Gorham $295.00
Cambridge, bouillon, Gorham $20.00
Cambridge, chocolate spoon, Gorham.......................$26.00
Cambridge, ice cream fork, Gorham $32.00
Cambridge, ice spoon, Gorham.................................$250.00
Cambridge, sardine fork, Gorham $75.00

Cambridge, strawberry fork, Gorham..........................$25.00
Campridge, cold meat fork, Gorham...........................$95.00
Canterbury, luncheon fork, Towle..............................$28.00
Canterbury, luncheon knife, Towle $28.00
Caramel, individual butter spreader, hollow handle,
    Wallace..$20.00
Caramel, luncheon fork, Wallace................................$25.00
Caramel, luncheon knife, Wallace $20.00
Caramel, salad fork, Wallace......................................$25.00
Caramel, teaspoon, Wallace $18.00
Carpenter Hall, dinner fork, Towle.............................$32.00
Carpenter Hall, luncheon knife, Towle $28.00
Carpenter Hall, place spoon, Towle............................$24.00
Chantilly, berry spoon, Gorham $195.00
Chantilly, cake knife, hollow handle, Gorham $65.00
Chantilly, cream soup, Gorham $32.00
Chantilly, demitasse spoon, Gorham..........................$13.00
Chantilly, dessert spoon, Gorham..............................$30.00
Chantilly, dinner fork, Chantilly.................................$43.00
Chantilly, dinner knife, Gorham.................................$32.00
Chantilly, gravy ladle, Gorham..................................$68.00
Chantilly, gumbo, Gorham..$35.00
Chantilly, iced teaspoon, Gorham $27.50
Chantilly, luncheon fork, Gorham..............................$23.00
Chantilly, luncheon knife, Gorham.............................$28.00
Chantilly, olive fork, Gorham....................................$45.00
Chantilly, round soup spoon, Gorham........................$30.00
Chantilly, serving fork, Gorham.................................$175.00
Chantilly, teaspoon, Gorham.....................................$20.00
Charles II, fish server, Dominick & Haff $250.00
Chateau Rose, cream soup, Alvin $18.00
Chrysanthemum, berry spoon, Durgin, lg..................$250.00
Chrysanthemum, cheese scoop, Dugrin......................$250.00
Chrysanthemum, gravy ladle, Durgin.........................$225.00
Chrysanthemum, ice cream server, Durgin...............$375.00
Chrysanthemum, sugar spoon, Durgin........................$75.00

**Continental, service for 6 w/4 serving pieces, Georg
    Jensen, 62 troy oz.....................................$2,750.00**
Damask Rose, cocktail fork, Oneida...........................$10.00
Damask Rose, luncheon fork, Oneida.........................$16.00
Damask Rose, teaspoon, Oneida $8.00
Dresden, master berry spoon, Whiting.......................$95.00

English King, dinner knife, Steiff $75.00
English King, gravy ladle, Steiff $35.00
English King, ice cream fork, Steiff................... $85.00
English King, iced teaspoon, Steiff $75.00
Florentine Lace, cream soup, Reed & Barton.............. $35.00
Florentine Lace, individual butter spreader, Reed & Barton.. $22.00
Florentine Lace, salad fork, Reed & Barton............... $40.00
Florentine Lace, tablespoon, Reed & Barton............... $58.00
Fountainbleau, dinner fork, Gorham.................... $55.00
Fountainbleau, dinner knife, Gorham $95.00
Fountainbleau, luncheon fork, Gorham $35.00
Fountainbleau, luncheon knife, Gorham................. $85.00
Fountainbleau, teaspoon, Gorham $25.00
Francis I, fish fork, Reed & Barton $55.00
Francis I, fruit spoon, Reed & Barton $45.00
Francis I, parfait spoon, Reed & Barton $55.00
Francis I, place spoon, Reed & Barton $35.00
French Renaissance, luncheon knife, Reed & Barton.. $25.00
French Renaissance, pickle fork, Reed & Barton........ $28.00
French Renaissance, pie server, Reed & Barton $38.00
French Renaissance, salad fork, Reed & Barton $25.00
French Renaissance, sugar shell, Reed & Barton $25.00
French Renaissance, tablespoon, Reed & Barton........ $48.00
French Renaissance, teaspoon, Reed & Barton........... $18.00
Frontenac, gravy ladle, International $80.00
Frontenac, iced teaspoon, International $26.00
Frontenac, pickle fork, International $45.00
Frontenac, sugar spoon, International.................. $55.00
Georgian Maid, citrus spoon, International............. $20.00
Georgian Maid, dinner fork, International.............. $22.00
Georgian Maid, dinner knife, International............. $20.00
Georgian Maid, gumbo, International................... $20.00
Georgian Rose, cream soup, Reed & Barton.............. $24.00
Georgian Rose, dinner fork, Reed & Barton $28.00
Georgian Rose, salad fork, Reed & Barton.............. $25.00
Georgian Rose, teaspoon, Reed & Barton................ $13.00
Grande Baroque, letter opener, Wallace................ $35.00
Grande Baroque, luncheon fork, Wallace................ $27.00
Grande Baroque, luncheon knife, Wallace $25.00
Grande Baroque, sauce ladle, Wallace.................. $65.00
Grande Baroque, teaspoon, Wallace.................... $18.00
Hamilton, olive spoon, Alvin $36.00
Hannah Hull, butter spreader, hollow handle, Tuttle.. $29.00
Hannah Hull, cream soup, Tuttle....................... $37.00
Hannah Hull, luncheon fork, Tuttle.................... $37.00
Hannah Hull, luncheon knife, Tuttle $32.00
Hannah Hull, salad fork, Tuttle....................... $37.00
Hepplewhite, dessert spoon, Reed & Barton $24.00
Hepplewhite, luncheon fork, Reed & Barton............. $24.00
Hepplewhite, luncheon knife, Reed & Barton............ $20.00
Hepplewhite, salad fork, Reed & Barton................ $22.00
Horizon, bake potato server, Easterling $30.00
Horizon, citrus spoon, Easterling $18.00
Horizon, cocktail fork, Easterling $14.00
Horizon, cream soup, Easterling....................... $18.00
Horizon, demitasse spoon, Easterling.................. $12.00
Horizon, dessert spoon, Easterling $18.00

Horizon, ice cream fork, Easterling $18.00
Horizon, luncheon fork, Eesterling.................... $48.00
Horizon, salad fork, Easterling....................... $14.00
Horizon, teaspoon, Easterling $12.00
Hunt Club, demitasse spoon, Gorham................... $9.00
Hunt Club, iced teaspoon, Gorham..................... $12.00
Hunt Club, master butter spreader, Hunt Club $15.00
Imperial Queen, cold meat fork, Whiting $100.00
Imperial Queen, lettuce fork, Whiting................. $95.00
Imperial Queen, luncheon fork, Whiting................ $25.00
Intermezzo, bread knife, National $22.00
Intermezzo, cream soup, National $12.00
Intermezzo, grill fork, National $14.00
Intermezzo, salad fork, National $15.00
Intermezzo, sugar shell, National..................... $10.00
Intermezzo, teaspoon, National $10.00
Kenmore, bouillon, Alvin $8.00
Kenmore, cocktail fork, Alvin $10.00
Kenmore, demitasse spoon, Alvin $8.00
Kenmore, dinner fork, Alvin $48.00
Kenmore, gravy ladle, Alvin $25.00
Kenmore, iced teaspoon, Alvin $14.00
Kenmore, master butter spreader, Alvin................ $16.00
King Albert, bake potato server, Whiting.............. $26.00
King Albert, citrus spoon, Whiting.................... $20.00
King Albert, dessert spoon, Whiting................... $16.00
King Albert, dinner fork, Whiting..................... $18.00
King Albert, gravy ladle, Whiting..................... $28.00
King Cedric, cold meat fork, Oneida................... $32.00
King Cedric, salad fork, Oneida....................... $14.00
King Cedric, teaspoon, Oneida $12.00
King Christian, bread knife, Wallace $22.00
King Christian, cream soup, Wallace $15.00
King Christian, dinner knife, Wallace $18.00
King Christian, luncheon fork, Wallace $18.00
King Christian, luncheon knife, Wallace $16.00
King Christian, salad fork, Wallace $16.00
King Christian, teaspoon, Wallace $8.00
King's Court, dessert spoon, Whiting $24.00
King's Court, luncheon fork, Whiting $15.00
King's Court, serving spoon, Whiting $32.00
La Comtesse, baked potato server, Reed & Barton...... $30.00
La Comtesse, dessert spoon, Reed & Barton............. $27.00
La Comtesse, serving spoon, Reed & Barton $27.00
Lancaster, asparagus server, Gorham $300.00
Lancaster, bonbon, Gorham............................ $45.00
Lancaster, bouillon, Gorham.......................... $20.00
Lancaster, cracker scoop, Gorham..................... $325.00
Lancaster, dessert spoon, Gorham..................... $25.00
Lancaster, jelly knife, Gorham....................... $150.00
Lancaster, sauce ladle, Gorham $55.00
Lancaster, seafood fork, Gorham...................... $20.00
Lily, berry spoon, Whiting........................... $155.00
Lily, butter fork, Whiting........................... $125.00
Lily, cocktail fork, Whiting......................... $45.00
Lily, dinner knife, Whiting.......................... $40.00
Lily, punch ladle, Gorham............................ $215.00
Lily, salad fork, Whiting............................ $60.00

Lily, tablespoon, Whiting.............................$75.00
Lily, 5 o'clock spoon, Whiting.....................$25.00
Lily of the Valley, cold meat fork, Whiting $85.00
Lily of the Valley, luncheon fork, Whiting $48.00
Lily of the Valley, 5 o'clock spoon, Whiting $22.00
Louis XV, cocktail fork, Whiting $18.00
Louis XV, master berry spoon, gold washed, Whiting .$85.00
Lucerne, luncheon knife, Wallace.................$25.00
Madame Jumel, salad fork, Whiting................$25.00
Madame Jumel, teaspoon, Whiting................$15.00
Mademoiselle, dessert spoon, International $20.00
Mademoiselle, luncheon fork, International...........$15.00
Mademoiselle, luncheon knife, International...........$15.00
Mademoiselle, salad fork, International...............$15.00
Majestic, bouillon, Alvin $30.00
Majestic, butter pick, Alvin $75.00
Majestic, cold meat fork, Alvin...................$100.00
Majestic, dinner knife, Alvin......................$28.00
Majestic, gravy ladle, Alvin........................$100.00
Majestic, lettuce fork, Alvin $95.00
Majestic, seafood fork, Alvin $20.00
Marie Antoinette, bouillon, Dominick & Haff $15.00
Marie Antoinette, cocktail fork, Dominick & Haff $15.00
Marie Antoinette, demitasse spoon, Dominick & Haff .$10.00
Marie Antoinette, luncheon fork, Dominick & Haff.....$25.00
Martha Washington, dinner fork, Watson.............$32.00
Martha Washington, salad fork, Watson.............$20.00
Melrose, tablespoon, Gorham $65.00
New Margaret, dinner fork, International..................$27.00
New Margaret, dinner knife, International $27.00
New Margaret, gumbo, International $22.00
New Margaret, salad fork, International $22.00
No 10, bouillon, Dominick & Haff.................$20.00
No 10, cold meat fork, Dominick & Haff..................$100.00
No 10, fish slice, Dominick & Haff $225.00
No 10, ice cream spoon, Dominick & Haff.................$35.00
No 10, master berry spoon, Dominick & Haff $100.00
No 10, tomato server, Dominick & Haff...................$125.00
Old Colonial, bouillon, Towle $25.00
Old Colonial, iced teaspoon, Towle $55.00
Old Colonial, lettuce fork, Towle $175.00
Old Orange Blossom, luncheon knife, Alvin $55.00
Old Orange Blossom, teaspoon, Alvin $18.00
Olympian, coffee spoon, Steiff....................$40.00
Olympian, olive fork, Steiff........................$125.00
Orange Blossom, bouillon, Alvin....................$35.00
Orange Blossom, ice cream spoon, Alvin $55.00
Orange Blossom, master berry spoon, Alvin $275.00
Orange Blossom, sugar shell, Alvin...............$95.00
Orange Blossom, tomato server, Alvin...............$275.00
Pansy, dinner fork, International $28.00
Patrician, dinner fork, Gorham $45.00
Poppy, dessert spoon, Gorham....................$30.00
Poppy, dinner fork, Gorham......................$40.00
Poppy, luncheon fork, Gorham $30.00
Poppy, master berry spoon, Gorham $80.00
Poppy, teaspoon, Gorham $23.00
Prelude, cocktail fork, International $16.00

Prelude, cream soup, International.............$20.00
Prelude, demitasse spoon, International $10.00
Prelude, dinner fork, International..................$30.00
Prelude, gravy ladle, International.................$50.00
Prelude, iced teaspoon, International..................$16.00
Prelude, luncheon fork, International................$22.00
Prelude, luncheon knife, International..............$17.00
Prelude, place spoon, International..................$27.00
Prelude, salad fork, International....................$22.00
Prelude, tablespoon, International..................$49.00
Princess Patricia, dessert spoon, Durgin...............$18.00
Princess Patricia, dinner fork, Durgin.................$20.00
Princess Patricia, dinner knife, Durgin................$18.00
Princess Patricia, teaspoon, Durgin..................$10.00
Renaissance, cold meat fork, Dominick & Haff........$150.00
Renaissance, luncheon fork, Dominick & Haff..........$40.00
Repousse, gravy ladle, Kirk......................$80.00
Repousse, lemon fork, Kirk.......................$35.00
Repousse, sugar shell, Kirk......................$40.00
Rococo, bouillon, Dominick & Haff $20.00
Rococo, chocolate spoon, Dominick & Haff............$20.00
Rococo, gravy ladle, Dominick & Haff.................$85.00
Rococo, ice cream spoon, Dominick & Haff.........$22.00
Rococo, parfait spoon, Dominick & Haff $25.00
Rococo, sugar sifter, Dominick & Haff $75.00
Romance of the Sea, cream soup, Wallace $35.00
Romance of the Sea, jelly spoon, Wallace.................$35.00
Romance of the Sea, lemon fork, Wallace.............$35.00
Romance of the Sea, salad fork, Wallace $40.00
Rose, cream soup, Kirk.............................$29.00
Rose, dinner fork, Wallace $25.00
Rose, luncheon fork, Kirk $29.00
Rose, luncheon knife, Kirk $27.00
Rose, teaspoon, Kirk................................$20.00
Royal Rose, luncheon fork, Wallace $29.00
Royal Rose, luncheon knife, Wallace $27.00
Royal Rose, salad fork, Wallace $29.00
Royal Rose, teaspoon, Wallace $22.00
Shell & Thread, teaspoon, Steiff..................$65.00
St Dunstan Chased, cocktail fork, Gorham $25.00
St Dunstan Chased, dinner knife, Gorham...............$40.00
St Dunstan Chased, fruit knife, Gorham..............$30.00
St Dunstan Chased, iced teaspoon, Gorham.............$30.00
St Dunstan Chased, luncheon knife, Gorham.............$35.00
Versailles, cheese scoop, Gorham $200.00
Versailles, demitasse spoon, Gorham $40.00
Versailles, dessert spoon, Gorham.................$55.00
Versailles, dinner fork, Gorham $80.00
Versailles, dinner knife, Gorham..................$80.00
Versailles, iced teaspoon, Gorham $75.00
Versailles, luncheon fork, Gorham $70.00
Versailles, salad fork, Gorham $55.00
Versailles, service for 12 w/11 serving pieces, Gorham, 146 troy oz $3,700.00
Versailles, sugar shell, Gorham...................$70.00
Versailles, tablespoon, Gorham $75.00
Versailles, teaspoon, Gorham......................$16.00
Vine, luncheon fork, Tiffany $135.00

Violet, bouillon spoon, Whiting......................$35.00
Violet, chipped beef fork, Whiting $65.00
Violet, luncheon fork, Whiting.....................$35.00
Violet, luncheon knife, Whiting $55.00
Violet, tablespoon, Whiting...........................$55.00
Violet, teaspoon, Whiting...............................$20.00
Virginia, fruit spoon, Dominick & Haff $18.00
Waltz of Spring, butter spreader, flat handle, Wallace .$20.00
Waltz of Spring, iced teaspoon, Wallace.....................$25.00
Waltz of Spring, luncheon fork, Wallace.....................$25.00
Waltz of Spring, luncheon knife, Wallace $22.00
Watteau, master salt spoon, Durgin...............$40.00
Watteau, sugar shell, Durgin..........................$40.00
Wedgwood, salad fork, International $35.00
Wellesley, bouillon, International $22.00
Wellesley, dessert spoon, International $27.00
Wellesley, luncheon fork, International...........$27.00
Wellesley, luncheon knife, International.........$25.00
Wellesley, salad fork, International..................$27.00
Winthrop, dinner fork, Tiffany.........................$65.00
Winthrop, dinner knife, Tiffany $70.00
Winthrop, gumbo, Tiffany................................$75.00
Winthrop, luncheon knife, Tiffany.................$55.00

Silverplated Flatware

When buying silverplated flatware, avoid pieces that are worn or have been monogrammed. Replating can be very expensive. Matching services often advertise in certain trade papers and can be very helpful in helping you locate the items you're looking for. One of the best sources we are aware of is *The Antique Trader*; they're listed with the trade papers in the back of this book.

If you'd like to learn more about the subject, we recommend *Silverplated Flatware, Revised Fourth Edition*, by Tere Hagan.

Adoration, dinner fork, International..........................$12.00
Adoration, salad fork, International $10.00
Adoration, teaspoon, International $7.00
Aldine, cold meat fork, Aurora $25.00
Aldine, dinner fork, Aurora $12.00
Aldine, pickle fork, Aurora $12.00
Aldine, tablespoon, Aurora $15.00
Aldine, teaspoon, Aurora..............................$8.00
American Beauty Rose, dinner knife, Rockford..........$25.00
American Beauty Rose, luncheon fork, Rockford........$12.00
American Beauty Rose, salad fork, Rockford $10.00
American Beauty Rose, teaspoon, Rockford $10.00
Arcadian, bouillon spoon, Rogers Smith & Co............$22.00
Arcadian, dinner knife, Rogers Smith & Co..................$25.00
Arcadian, master butter knife, Rogers Smith & Co $15.00
Arcadian, teaspoon, Rogers Smith & Co......................$15.00
Autumn, demitasse spoon, Rogers...............$8.00
Autumn, dinner knife, Rogers $12.00
Autumn, teaspoon, Rogers $8.00
Berkshire, cold meat fork.............................$30.00

Berkshire, dinner fork...................................$18.00
Berkshire, salad fork......................................$20.00
Berkshire, soup ladle....................................$80.00
Berkshire, teaspoon.......................................$12.00

Bradford, dinner fork...$8.00
Cardinal, ice cream spoon, Wallace.........................$12.50
Centennial, dinner fork, International $12.00
Centennial, dinner knife, International......................$12.00
Centennial, luncheon fork, International...................$10.00
Centennial, tablespoon, International.......................$10.00
Chateau, dinner knife, William Rogers $12.00
Chateau, ice cream spoon, William Rogers...............$12.00
Chateau, luncheon fork, William Rogers...................$12.00
Chateau, master butter knife, William Rogers...............$7.00
Columbia, cocktail fork, Rogers.................................$15.00
Columbia, dinner knife, Rogers.................................$30.00
Columbia, iced teaspoon, Rogers $18.00
Columbia, luncheon knife, Rogers............................$12.50
Columbia, teaspoon, Rogers......................................$15.00
Eternally Yours, gravy ladle, International $30.00
Eternally Yours, ice cream fork, International............$12.50
Eternally Yours, salad fork, International $10.00
Eternally Yours, teaspoon, International $7.00
Flair, cocktail fork, International..................................$10.00
Flair, iced teaspoon, International $10.00
Flair, luncheon fork, International $10.00
Flair, tablespoon, International....................................$12.00
Flair, youth spoon, International...................................$7.00
Forever, dinner knife, Oneida.....................................$12.00
Forever, iced teaspoon, Oneida..................................$10.00
Forever, luncheon knife, Oneida................................$12.00
Forever, soup spoon, Oneida..$8.00
Glenrose, dinner fork, William Rogers $18.00
Glenrose, dinner knife, William Rogers......................$25.00
Glenrose, teaspoon, William Rogers..........................$12.00
Grape, dinner fork, Williams $12.00
Grape, pickle fork, Williams $12.50
Grape, tablespoon, Williams $12.50
Grape, teaspoon, Williams $10.00

Greenwich, teaspoon..$5.00
Grosvenor, cocktail fork, Oneida..............................$12.00
Grosvenor, dinner knife, Oneida...............................$15.00
Grosvenor, luncheon fork, Oneida $15.00
Grosvenor, salad fork, Oneida...................................$12.00

Grosvenor, sugar tongs, Oneida $20.00
Isabella, gravy ladle, William Rogers & Son.................$32.00
Isabella, salad fork, William Rogers & Son..................$10.00
Isabella, teaspoon, William Rogers & Son....................$7.00
Lady Caroline, dinner fork, Gorham $12.00
Lady Caroline, dinner knife, Gorham $12.00
Lady Caroline, gravy ladle, Gorham $35.00
Lady Caroline, tablespoon, Gorham $12.50
Lady Caroline, teaspoon, Gorham $8.00
Laurel Mist, cold meat fork, International $25.00
Laurel Mist, dinner knife, International $12.00
Laurel Mist, salad fork, International $10.00
Laurel Mist, soup spoon, International $7.00
Laurel Mist, teaspoon, International.........................$7.00
Love, dinner knife, International............................$12.00
Love, salad fork, International..............................$10.00
Love, tablespoon, International..............................$10.00
Love, teaspoon, International................................$7.00

Moselle, dinner fork, International.......................$20.00
Moselle, dinner knife, International.........................$35.00
Moselle, ice cream spoon, International......................$20.00
Moselle, tablespoon, International...........................$18.00
Moselle, teaspoon, International.............................$15.00
Nenuphar, dinner fork, International.........................$15.00
Nenuphar, dinner knife, International........................$25.00
Nenuphar, fruit spoon, International.........................$10.00
Nenuphar, ice cream fork, International $15.00
Newport, cocktail fork, Rogers $12.00
Newport, dinner fork, Rogers $15.00
Newport, iced teaspoon, Rogers $12.00
Newport, tablespoon, Rogers $15.00
Oxford, gravy ladle, Rogers.................................$30.00
Oxford, individual butter spreader, Rogers $8.00
Oxford, tablespoon, Rogers $12.00
Oxford, teaspoon, Rogers....................................$10.00
Persian, salad fork, Meriden Britannia $10.00
Persian, tablespoon, Meriden Britannia $12.50
Persian, teaspoon, Meriden Britannia $7.00
Queen Bess, cocktail fork, Oneida $8.00
Queen Bess, demitasse spoon, Oneida $5.00
Queen Bess, dinner fork, Oneida $8.00
Queen Bess, salad fork, Oneida..............................$7.00
Queen Bess, teaspoon, Oneida................................$5.00
Queen's Grace, demitasse spoon, Gorham $8.00
Queen's Grace, dinner fork, Gorham..........................$12.00
Queen's Grace, salad fork, Gorham $10.00
Queen's Grace, soup spoon, Gorham $7.50
Queen's Grace, teaspoon, Gorham.............................$8.00
Rosemont, dinner fork, Gorham $12.00
Rosemont, individual butter spreader, Gorham $8.00
Rosemont, pickle fork, Gorham...............................$15.00

Rosemont, teaspoon, Gorham..................................$7.50
Royal Lace, dinner fork, Oneida $12.00
Royal Lace, salad fork, Oneida $10.00
Royal Lace, tablespoon, Oneida..............................$12.00
Royal Lace, teaspoon, Oneida................................$7.00
Sheraton, dinner knife, Oneida..............................$10.00
Sheraton, gravy ladle, Oneida...............................$25.00
Sheraton, luncheon fork, Oneida $8.00
Sheraton, soup spoon, Oneida................................$6.00
Signature, dinner fork, International.......................$10.00
Signature, salad fork, International........................$10.00
Signature, soup spoon, International........................$7.00
Spring Garden, demitasse spoon, International $8.00
Spring Garden, dinner fork, International...................$12.00
Spring Garden, luncheon fork, International $10.00
Spring Garden, salad fork, International $10.00
Wisteria, iced teaspoon, Reed & Barton......................$10.00
Wisteria, salad fork, Reed & Barton.........................$10.00
Wisteria, teaspoon, Reed & Barton...........................$7.00

Slot Machines

Coin-operated gambling machines have been around since before the turn of the century. There are many types. One-arm bandits, 3-reelers, uprights, trade stimulators, and bell machines are some of the descriptive terms used to describe them. Until the Johnson Act was signed by Harry Truman in 1951, the slot machine industry was thriving. This bill prohibited the shipment of slots into states where they were illegal and banned them from all military installations in the United States. One by one nearly every state in the union outlawed gambling devices, and soon the industry was practically non-existent.

Today, it is legal to own an 'antique' slot machine in all but eight states: Alabama, Connecticut, Hawaii, Indiana, South Carolina, Tennessee, and Nebraska and Rhode Island (who's views are uncertain.) Check your state's laws before you buy; the age of allowable machines varies from fifteen to thirty years.

Values of slots range from several hundred to thousands of dollars. If you decide to invest in this hobby, you'll need to study a good book on the subject. One we would recommend is *An American Premium Guide to Jukeboxes and Slot Machines* by Jerry Ayliffe.

Bally Spark Plug, counter-top model, 1934, EX original condition $2,750.00
Buckley Bones, counter-top model, ca 1936, EX original condition $5,000.00
Caille Dictator, ca 1934, EX original condition $2,750.00
Caille Dough Boy, ca 1935, EX original condition .$1,250.00
Field 5 Jacks, counter-top model, ca 1931, VG original condition $650.00
Groetchen Twin Falls, console model, ca 1938, EX original condition $650.00
Jennings Bank Chief, 1939, VG original condition .$1,250.00
Jennings Club Chief, 1945, EX original condition ..$1,250.00

Jennings Golf-a-Rola, console model, ca 1940, EX original condition **$1,450.00**

Jennings Prospector, console model, ca 1948, VG original condition **$850.00**

Mills Castle Front, 25½ ", restored **$1,750.00**

Mills Club, console model, ca 1937, EX original **$1,700.00**

Mills Club Royale, console model, ca 1945, NM original condition **$1,950.00**

Mills Melon, ca 1948, EX original condition **$1,750.00**

Mills Silent Golden, Roman head on front, ca 1932, VG original condition **$1,750.00**

Mills 5¢ Poinsettia, EX original condition **$1,000.00**

Pace Deluxe Cherry, 1945, EX original condition ..**$1,500.00**

Pace Rocket, ca 1940, EX original condition **$1,150.00**

Skelly Candy Boy, ca 1925, EX original condition .**$2,350.00**

Watling Baby Lincoln, 1928, EX original condition.**$2,000.00**

Watling Treasury, ca 1936, EX original condition ..**$4,000.00**

Snow Domes

Snow dome collectors buy them all, old and new. The older ones (from the thirties and forties) are made in two pieces, the round glass globe that sits on a separate base. They were made here as well as in Italy, and today this type is being imported from Austria and the Orient.

During the fifties, plastic snow domes made in West Germany were popular as souvenirs and Christmas toys. Some were half-domes with blue backs; others were made in bottle shapes or simple geometric forms.

There were two styles produced in the seventies. Both were made of plastic. The first were designed as large domes with a plastic figure of an animal, a mermaid, or some other character draped over the top. In the other style, the snow dome itself was made in an unusual shape.

Snow domes have become popular fun-type collectibles, and Nancy McMichael has written an illustrated book called *Snowdomes*, which we recommend if you'd like to read more about the subject. Also refer to *The Collector's Guide to Snow Domes* by Helene Guarnaccia.

Advertising, Newsweek on red bars & globe of world, lg, 1990 ....**$65.00**

Advertising, White Star Trucking, gold crown in glass globe on black base **$65.00**

Angel (head & shoulders) in plastic dome w/3 sm feet on white base **$10.00**

Capitol building in clear glass globe on black ceramic base, 1940s **$45.00**

Character, Felix the Cat, Determined Productions, Standing Ovations, 1987..**$15.00**

Character, Little Mermaid, clear plastic dome on blue base, Disney Collection, Bully, Germany..........................**$18.00**

Character, Marilyn Monroe, lg, clear glass dome on black base..**$35.00**

Figural, Santa w/deer over his shoulder, dome in tummy, plastic..**$18.00**

Figural, skull shape over much of dome containing bats, Bats in My Belfry on red plastic base **$18.00**

Figural, snowman w/dome in center section, ceramic, Applause, 1988..**$18.00**

Figural, tiger rests on top of plastic dome that contains tiger in jungle scene, plastic **$18.00**

George Washington Masonic National Memorial, emblem on oil-filled glass globe on white plastic base w/blue lettering..**$40.00**

Ghost on spring atop pumpkin in sm glass dome on black base..**$8.00**

Major League Baseball Team insignia in plastic dome on sm white base, any team **$8.00**

Rudolph the Red-Nosed Reindeer, glass globe on red base, Driss, Chicago, NM label **$45.00**

Saint (unidentified) w/children in plastic dome **$10.00**

Skull, lights up (battery operated) in glass globe on orange& black painted wooden base, Silvestri **$22.00**

Souvenir, Capital Building & Washington DC in plastic dome on white base, common **$10.00**

Souvenir, Kansas, pine trees & buffalo in plastic dome on white base **$10.00**

Souvenir, Mount Rushmore, Black Hills SD, sm plastic dome on white base..**$10.00**

Souvenir, Niagara Falls, black Bakelite base.........$35.00
Souvenir, Niagara Falls scene in plastic dome w/pencil
  sharpener in yellow base **$12.00**
Souvenir, pink flamingos in glass dome that rests on pink
  plastic ashtray base marked Florida......................**$40.00**

**Souvenir, Salt Lake City, skyline & mountains in rect-
  angular container...$10.00**
Souvenir, St Louis Arch & buildings in plastic dome on
  white base **$8.00**
WWII, soldier in glass globe on black base, 1940s **$45.00**

Soda Bottles

The earliest type of soda bottles were made by soda
producers and sold in the immediate vicinity of the bottling company. Many had pontil scars, left by a rod that
was used to manipulate the bottle as it was blown. They
had a flat bottom rather than a 'kick-up,' so for transport,
they were laid on their side and arranged in layers. This
served to keep the cork moist, which kept it expanded,
tight, and in place. Upright the cork would dry out,

shrink, and expel itself with a 'pop,' hence the name
'soda pop.'

Until the thirties, the name of the product or the bottler was
embossed in the glass or printed on a paper label (sometimes
pasted over reused returnable bottles). Though a few paper
labels were used as late as the sixties, nearly all bottles produced
from the mid-thirties on had painted-on (pyro-glazed) lettering,
and logos and pictures were often added. Imaginations ran ram-
pant. Bottlers waged a fierce competition to make their soda
logos eye catching and sales inspiring. Anything went! Girls, airplanes, patriotic designs, slogans proclaiming amazing health
benefits, even cowboys and Indians became popular advertising
ploys. This is the type you'll encounter most often today, and
collector interest is on the increase. Look for interesting, multicolored labels, rare examples from small-town bottlers, and
those made from glass other than clear or green. If you'd like to
learn more about them, we recommend *The Official Guide to
Collecting Applied Color Label Soda Bottles* by Thomas E. Marsh.

Paper labels were used to some extent from the thirties into
the sixties, sometimes pasted over reused returnable bottles.

Embossed Soda Bottles

Abilena Natural Cathartic Water, 10", shouldered cylinder
  w/blob top...**$6.00**
AM&B Co, 8½", AM&B Co, The Waco TX, Registered Mon-
  terrey... on aqua glass, applied lip.........................**$10.00**
B&C San Francisco, cylindrical, cobalt, applied top....**$35.00**
Billings EL Sacramento CA Geiser Soda, 7½", aqua.......**$7.50**
California Bottle Works, 7", T Blauth 407 K Street Sacra-
  mento, cylindrical, light green glass w/applied top.**$5.50**
Clarke & White New York, 7½", olive green glass w/applied
  top..**$32.00**
Consumers Bottling Co Key West FL, 7", cylindrical, clear
  glass w/blob top **$5.50**
Dr Pepper Good for Life, 6½-oz, 10-2-4 O'clock, clear glass
  w/crown top...**$4.00**
Eagle, 7", eagle on front, green w/applied top..............**$8.00**
Hawaiian Soda Works, 7½", name & place on light green
  glass w/applied top **$12.50**
Jackson Napa Soda, 7", cylindrical, light green glass
  w/applied lip...**$3.50**
Macomb Bottling Works, 6-oz, clear, Macomb IL..........**$8.00**

**Mendocin Bottling Works, AL Reynolds, 7", light
  green..$7.50**

Oakland Pioneer Soda Water Co, Oakland CA, 7½ ", clear glass **$4.00**

Priest Natural Soda, 7½ ", cylindrical, lg letters on light green glass **$12.00**

Sequoia Soda Works, Angels CA, 7½ ", aqua glass........**$5.00**

Still Shasta, 11½ ", cylindrical, embossed letters above a paper label on clear glass w/crown top.................**$3.50**

Yuba Bottling Works, 8", cylindrical, aqua....................**$5.00**

Painted-Label Soda Bottles

Alkalaris, 7-oz, Alkalaris Water, Natural Club Soda, clear.**$15.00**

Apollo, 12-oz, Apollo Made w/Sterilized water & human figure on clear glass...**$15.00**

Barney's Club, 7-oz, Beverages on green glass..............**$6.00**

Berkey's, 7-oz, Drink Berkey's Beverages on clear **$6.00**

Bob's Cola, 7-oz, Drink Bob's Cola Good for Thirst on clear glass **$6.00**

Chero, 6-oz, Chero Perfect Cola on clear glass, embossed swirls at shoulder...**$6.00**

Crush, 6½-oz, Orange Crush Company Bottle in diamond on amber glass w/embossed verticle ribs **$8.00**

Double Dry, 10-oz, Double Dry banner on shield logo on green glass...**$8.00**

Heads-Up, 7-oz, Heads-Up Lithiated...Mansfield OH on green glass...**$8.00**

Jack Frost Jr, 7-oz, Jack Frost Jr on clear glass..............**$6.00**

Jet, 8-oz, Jet Hits the Spot & plane on clear glass **$25.00**

Joe Louis Punch, 7-oz, Joe Louis Punch on clear **$10.00**

Manhattan, 7-oz, Manhattan Brewery & factory scene on clear glass **$10.00**

Mr Newport, 8-oz, Mr Newport Beverages & horse on clear glass **$20.00**

Penn State, 7-oz, Penn State Tonic Water on clear glass.**$6.00**

Pops, 12-oz, Pops Root Beer on amber glass **$20.00**

River Side, 10-oz, River Side Beverages & river landscape on clear glass **$10.00**

Sir Walter, 8-oz, Sir Walter & man's portrait in reserve on clear glass **$15.00**

Sparkle Springs, 7-oz, Sparkle Springs & swimmers on green glass **$20.00**

Sun Crest, King Size, 1964..**$5.00**

Taylor Maid, 7-oz, Taylor Maid & lady holding bottle on clear glass **$8.00**

Turner's, 7-oz, Turner's Club Soda on clear glass..........**$6.00**

Virginia Dare, 7-oz, Virginia Dare & girl's portrait on clear glass **$8.00**

Soda Fountain Collectibles

This is an area of collecting related to the advertising field, but of course zeroing in on items such as glassware once used to serve ice cream sundaes and malts, soda dispensers, ice cream dippers, straw holders, and signs that display products such as were sold at ice cream parlors and soda fountains.

While some items such as the dispensers, the straw holders, and some of the dippers have become very expensive, you'll be able to find other interesting items at low prices, so whether you're wanting to recreate a vintage soda fountain in your family room or simply buying to resell, you should be able to do very well.

If you want more pricing information, we recommend *Huxford's Collectible Advertising* by Sharon and Bob Huxford.

Bottle, seltzer; Dr pepper, Cheerio-Memphis, EX......**$150.00**

Bottle opener, Orange Crush **$25.00**

Canister, Horlick's Malted Milk, 10", aluminum, product name encircled w/scalloped border, slip lid, NM.**$70.00**

Clock, Canada Dry, 16" square, plastic face w/metal frame, logo in center, VG..**$37.50**

Clock, Dr Pepper, 15" square, logo under hands, EX.**$85.00**

Cone mold, Icy Pi **$130.00**

Cup, Armour's Vigoral **$25.00**

Dipper, Benedict Indestructo Disher #14, MIB.........**$225.00**

Dipper, Gilchrist #31...**$40.00**

Dipper, Indestructo #4, round....................................**$50.00**

Dish, banana split; Bowman etched on clear glass.$25.00

Dish, banana split; clear glass, footed **$17.50**

Dish, ice cream; Purity Ice Cream, Maddock's China..**$50.00**

Dispenser, Cherry Smash, 16x9", ceramic potbelly shape, Our Nation's Beverage, original pump, EX.........**$350.00**

Dispenser, Green River Syrup, 11x9x8", logo on river scene, painted metal base w/glass top, held 1-gal bottle, G.**$45.00**

Fan, Moxie, 10x8", cardboard, Frances Pritchard holding glass of Moxie, EX...**$55.00**

Flyer, Blue Ribbon Fountain Specialties, 12x9", 4 pages of soda fountain supplies, VG **$35.00**

Fountain glass, Cleo-Cola $30.00
Fountain glass, Dr Brown's Celery Tonic $37.50
Fountain glass, Lucky Mondae Siren $12.50
Fountain glass, Seven-Up, green................................$17.50
Hat, soda jerk's; Orange Crush, 14" long, paper, orange & blue print on white $8.00
Malted milk container, Borden's Malted Milk, clear glass jar w/enameled label, tin lid, EX..............................$120.00
Malted milk container, Borden's, painted tin, EX......$100.00
Malted milk container, National Dairy, aluminum, cylindrical, slight paint loss, denting on lid....................$160.00
Menu board, Crown Beverage, vertical cardboard rectangle w/logo at top & menu below, EX.........................$32.00
Menu board, Dr Pepper, tin, logo at top, EX..............$35.00
Menu board, Nu Grape, tin, product name & bottle above board, rounded corners, EX $42.00
Menu board, 7-Up, chalk type w/slanted bottle & 7-Up logo atop, rounded corners, NM $45.00
Mixer, Hamilton Beach #10.....................................$55.00
Mug, A&W Root Beer, 4", clear glass, EX....................$5.00
Mug, Hires Root Beer, ceramic, Hires boy lifting mug, Mettlach, EX $150.00
Mug, Richardson's Root Beer embossed on clear glass.$15.00
Plate, Hood's Sarsaparilla, 9", cardboard, 2 birds on front, testimonials on back, EX $25.00
Push bar, 7-Up, 3x30", porcelain, Fresh Up w/Seven-Up in red, EX $45.00
Stein, Murray's (Root Beer) $125.00
Straw dispenser, Hires Root Beer $750.00
Straw holder, green, w/lid $400.00
Straw holder, wide-ribbed glass, original top & insert .$100.00
Tray, Hershey's Ice Cream, 13" square, ice cream & peaches on red background, scratches, G............$125.00
Tumbler, Moxie, 4", Licensed Only for Serving, NM ...$40.00
Wafer holder, Reliance $110.00

Souvenir Spoons

Before the turn of the century, collecting silver spoons commemorating towns, states, fairs, holidays, and famous people became popular. Huge quantities were produced, and many are now found on the antiques and collectibles circuit, still interesting to collectors. There are many types of spoons; some are gold-washed, some enameled. Handles may be figural, representing something especially noteworthy about a particular area or state (for instance, a gold miner from Nevada or a salmon from Washington), or they may have a cut-out design. Indians and nudes are unusual, and along with the more interesting designs – past presidents, war memorials, or fraternal emblems, for instance – usually carry the higher price tags.

Bermuda, Bermuda lettered in bowl, enameled sea horse on handle..$8.00
Birmingham AL, Birmingham Alabama lettered in bowl, raised flowers & leaves on handle.................$16.00
Boise ID, plain bowl, state seal on handle...................$7.50

Buffalo NY, McKinley Monument embossed in bowl, embossed buffalo on handle................................$12.50
Chicago IL, plain bowl, Columbian Expo & bust of Columbus on handle $18.00

Christmas scene in bowl, saint & bell on handle.$25.00
Cincinnati OH, etched fountain in bowl, heavy floral design on front handle, simple design on reverse...........$14.00
Clearwater FL, plain bowl, alligator on handle...........$30.00
Concord MA, plain bowl, cutout of a minute man on handle $7.50
Crater Lake OR, plain bowl, cutout of Crater Lake on handle...$7.50
Denmark, girl on rock enameled on handle $9.50
Denver CO, Denver lettered in bowl, etched flowers on handle...$14.50
El Paso TX, plain bowl, cutout of San Jacinto Plaza on handle $12.50
Elm City, Elm City lettered in bowl, fancy scroll design on handle...$7.50
Fairbanks AK, Mt McKinley in bowl, various scenes on handle...$35.00
Hot Springs AR, Hot Springs Arkansas lettered in bowl, fancy scroll design on handle $14.00
Indianapolis, IN, Soldiers' & Sailors' Monument (illustrated)..$25.00
Indianapolis IN, Central Avenue Church etched in bowl, heavy scroll design on front handle, few scrolls on reverse $16.50
Iowa, Iowa lettered in bowl, fancy scrolls & monogramed M on front handle, few scrolls on reverse.................$12.50
Irish Fair, 4-leaf clover & Irish Fair in bowl, harp & scroll design on handle.......................................$6.00
Jackson MS, Jackson lettered in bowl, enameled flowers on twisted handle...$7.50
Jamestown ND, Jamestown lettered in bowl, state seal & eagle on front handle, 1906 on reverse.................$16.50
Kansas City MO, Convention Hall in bowl, various scenes on handle $30.00
Kansas City MO, post office embossed in bowl, state seal & mule on front handle, scroll design on reverse $12.50
Laguna Beach CA, plain bowl, Laguna Beach & painter's palette on front handle, brushed finish on reverse.$7.50
Lake Manitou, Lake Manitou lettered in bowl, 1901 & scroll design on handle $14.50

Las Vegas NV, donkey loaded w/wood in bowl, twisted design on handle **$18.50**

Los Angeles CA, cutout of City Hall on handle..............**$6.00**

Mayville WI, Mayville, lettered in bowl, embossed flowers on handle **$14.50**

Mexico, Mexico & eagle embossed on handle...............**$9.50**

Milwaukee WI, embossed library auditorium in bowl, simple line design on handle **$16.50**

Montana, plain bowl, flower cutouts & Montana lettered on handle **$7.50**

New Orleans LA, Jackson Monument embossed in bowl, bust of Old Hickory on front handle, wreath design on reverse **$12.50**

New York NY, plain bowl, cutout of Empire State Building on handle..**$9.50**

Niagara Canada, Niagara Falls lettered in bowl, enameled seal & maple leaf on handle **$14.50**

Omaha NE, Omaha lettered in bowl, grapes, leaves & vines on handle **$9.50**

Palm Beach FL, palm trees in bowl & on front handle, Poinciana Hotel on reverse...**$38.00**

Palm Springs CA, plain bowl, embossed mountains & palm trees on front handle, brushed finish on reverse....**$7.50**

Philadelphia PA, Liberty Bell & house on handle..........**$9.50**

Plymouth MA, plain bowl, 1620 Plymouth & cutout of ship on handle..**$9.50**

Portland OR, Mt Hood in relief in bowl, state seal & frog umbrella on handle, scroll on back.......................**$18.50**

Reno NV, dice, slot machine & Reno on handle **$7.50**

Salt Lake City UT, Mormon Tabernacle etched in bowl, plain handle **$14.00**

San Francisco CA, plain bowl, cutout of Chinatown on front handle, brushed finish on reverse..........................**$6.00**

Santa Cruz CA, Santa Cruz lettered in bowl, scroll design on handle..**$12.50**

Spokane WA, etching of Spokane Falls in bowl, embossed daisies on front handle, floral design on reverse..**$14.00**

St Augustine FL, plain bowl, cutout of Lightner Museum on handle..**$7.50**

St Paul MN, State Capitol etched in bowl, simple design on front & back handle **$11.50**

Statue of Liberty, NY (illustrated) **$25.00**

Syracuse NY, Syracuse lettered in bowl, raised floral design on handle..**$12.00**

Tacoma WA, etching of Mt Tacoma in bowl, Indian head & corn on handle...**$25.00**

Topeka KS, Capitol building embossed in bowl, grapes & leaves on front handle, few scrolls on reverse **$12.50**

Toronto Canada, enameled leaves on handle..............**$20.00**

Washington DC, Capitol building in bowl, George Washington & various scenes on handle............................**$28.00**

Space Collectibles

Even before the first man landed on the moon, the idea of space travel had always intrigued us. This is an area of collecting that is right now attracting lots of interest and includes not only serious documentary material, but games, toys, puzzles, and models as well.

Astronaut USA, jigsaw type, Jaymar, 1960s, MIB **$5.00**

Belt, Space Cadet, on original 7x13" card, M.............**$32.50**

Coloring book, Rockets, Jets, & Space in Action To Color, Merrill Publishers, 1953, M **$20.00**

Coloring book, Space Cadet, Saalfield, 1953, NM.......**$12.50**

Dart gun, 10", plastic, marked Buzz Corry.................**$60.00**

Figure, Johnny Apollo Astronaut, jointed, Marx, NM in good box **$38.00**

Figurine, 3", metallic light purple plastic spaceman, marked Premier Products Co, ca 1950s, VG **$30.00**

Film reel, The American in Orbit, John Glen & Friendship 7, black & white 8mm, Castle Films, #190, MIB........**$25.00**

Game, Space Race Cards, 1950s, MIB.........................**$10.00**

Goblet, Apollo Moon Landing, gas station premium..**$20.00**

Goggles, 8", Space Patrol, marked Hale Nass, 1953, M on card $30.00

Gumball machine, 16x9½ " dia, colorful rocket-formed plastic w/decals, 1950s, EX.......................................$120.00

Gun, Atomic Ray, full-color lithographed tin, marked Japan, NM $20.00

Gun, 7", Space Siren, red plastic w/silver trim, Ideal, 1950s, EX...$45.00

Kite, Little Boy, Hi-Flyer, 1950s, M $22.00

Model, Gemini Capsule, Revell, 1965, MIB..................$60.00

Pencil set, Apollo 11 Man on Moon graphics & date, set of 24, M in package..$20.00

Playset, Commander Comet Colorforms, EX................$50.00

Playset, Galaxy Laser Team, w/2" tall figures, marked Tim Mee Toys, ca 1970s, 25-piece, M in package........$12.50

Playset, navigator compass & badge, 1950s, M on card.$15.00

Playset, Star Battle, w/4" figures, marked Processed Plastic Co, ca 1970s, 5-piece, M in package $12.50

Playset, US Space Base, w/2 suited astronauts, marked Famus Corp, M on card $6.00

Puzzle, Rand McNally moon map, marked Selchow & Righter, 1970, MIB...$30.00

Puzzle, 19x19", Moon Mission, Fairchild Co, 750-piece, in original 12x12" box, NM....................................$30.00

Record, First Man on the Moon, commemorative of Apollo 11 flight, July 1969, MGM Merchandising Corporation, ca 1969, VG $7.50

Record, 78 rpm, Destination Moon, Capitol label, 1950, original sleeve, M $25.00

Rocket, 14", Apollo X, red & white plastic, battery-operated flashing nose cone, marked Hong Kong, MIB......$45.00

Rocket, 18", Apollo 12, battery operated, boxed, EX.$100.00

Satellite, 9" dia, lithographed metal, marked Cragstan, battery operated, EX $65.00

Space capsule, lithographed tin Friendship 7 figural, friction type, EX $45.00

Transfers, full-color designs, Japan, 1950s, set of 48 assorted, M in package...$6.00

Sports Collectibles

When the baseball card craze began sweeping the country a decade ago, memorabilia relating to many types of sports began to interest sports fans. Ticket stubs, uniforms, autographed baseballs, sports magazines, and game-used bats are prized by baseball fans, and some items, depending on their age or the notoriety of the player or team they represent, may be very valuable. Baseball and golfing seem to be the two sports most collectors are involved with, but basketball is gaining ground. There are several books on the market you'll want to read if you're personally interested in either: *Value Guide to Baseball Collectibles* by Don Raycraft and Craig Raycraft, *Collector's Guide to Baseball Memorabilia* by Don Raycraft and Stew Salowitz, and *The Encyclopedia of Golf Collectibles* by John M. Olman and Morton W. Olman.

See also Autographs; Baseball Cards; Hartland; Magazines; Pin-Back Buttons; Puzzles; View Master.

Bank, ceramic baseball cap form, LA Dodgers, EX.....$15.00

Bank, 3", Miami Dolphins decal on plastic cube w/figural dolphin holding coin, marked Super Bowl Champs, EX $15.00

Bank, 3" dia, plastic baseball on square black plastic base, Phillies team facsimile signatures, mid-1960s........$35.00

Baseball mitt, Reggie Jackson, Rawlings, XFG-12, EX.$20.00

Bat, aluminum, marked Ted Williams' Approved Little League Bat, ca 1960, NM....................................$20.00

Bat, regulation size, wood Louisville Slugger w/facsimile Johnny Bench signature, M $35.00

Book, Baseball Injuries & Training Tips, by Mickey Cobb, signed, 1974, NM $28.00

Book, Boys' Life Book of Baseball Stories, 1964, EX..$22.50

Book, Out of the Bunker & Into the Trees, 1st edition, 1960, 189 pages, hardcover, w/dust jacket, EX..............$15.00

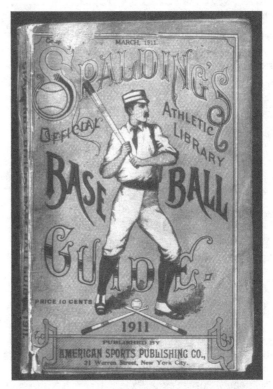

Book, Spalding's Official Athletic Library Baseball Guide, 1911, 400+ pages, color cover, EX.....$250.00

Book, Where Have You Gone Joe DiMaggio?, by Maury Allen, 1975, EX...$17.50

Booklet, Swimming & Diving, Kellogg Sports Library, 1930s, 46-page, EX $7.50

Booklet, Ted Williams' Baseball Basics, 1970s, 20-page, EX $12.00

Booklet, 1976 Famous Slugger Yearbook, promotional item from sporting goods stores, M...............................$7.00

Bottle caps, NFL teams, Gatorade, 1970s, set of 14, M.$10.00

Cards, NFL Official Football Quiz, Fleer, 1970s, set of 21, M.$5.00

Cup, 5½ ", Billy Williams & Chicago Cubs graphics on plastic, 7 Eleven promotion, dated 1972, M...................$1.50

Decal, 4½ ", St Louis Cardinals, 1950s....................$15.00
Doll, OJ Simpson, Shindana Toys, 1974, MIB............**$90.00**
Figurine, 4", Pete Rose, Starting Lineup Series, Kenner, 1988, 1 of set of 124, MIB **$35.00**
Figurine, 5½ ", Michael Jordan, marked Official NBA Product, on 8x9" card, M...**$12.50**
Film, 8mm, Sugar Ray Robinson versus Rocky Graziano, Castle, 1950s, NM..**$20.00**
Keychain, Robert Clemente 1960s Topps card, M **$8.00**
Match book, uniformed Joe DiMaggio at bat, DiMaggio's Grotto, San Francisco, 1939, M **$12.50**
Media guide, Braves, 1975, NM **$12.50**
Media guide, Dodgers, 1979, NM...................................**$6.00**
Media guide, St Louis Cardinals, 1978, M.......................**$8.00**
Nodder, Cleveland Indian, on green base, Japan, M..**$75.00**
Nodder, Cleveland Indian, reproduction made in Taiwan, 1970, M **$15.00**
Nodder, 4½" New York Yankees, Japan, 1960s, M......**$12.50**
Nodder, 6", Redskins, NFL & Japan stickers, reproduction mad in Taiwan, 1960s, EX.......................................**$55.00**
Pen, 8", wood Louisville bat figural w/Mickey Mantle signature, 1950s, NM...**$35.00**
Pennant, Baltimore Colts, blue, 1970, M **$20.00**
Photo, Chicago Cubs Team, 9x12", sepia, by Baseball Magazine Company, offer to subscribers, 1945, NM **$50.00**
Photo, Muhammad Ali in tux as Sportsman of the Year, December 23, 1974, M..**$45.00**
Photo, 6x8", Mickey Mantle, framed, 1950s, M............**$45.00**
Plate, Hall of Fame, 1978, Joss, Mathews, MacPhal; limited edition, 1 of 1000, pewter, M....................................**$60.00**
Poster, Reggie Jackson, candy bar premium, 1970s, M **$45.00**
Press pin, 1979, All-Star Game, Seattle **$45.00**
Press pin, 1981, All-Star Game, Cleveland....................**$30.00**
Program, Harlem Globetrotters, color photo w/faux signatures, 1975, M **$20.00**
Program, World Series 1966, Los Angeles Dodgers, unscored, EX...**$50.00**

Puzzle, 16x20", Joe Namath as quarterback of New York Jets, American Publishing, copyright 1971, 500-piece, MIB **$25.00**
Record, Instant Replay, Willie Mays, Mattel, 1971, w/illustration, M...**$35.00**
Sign, Hall of Fame Autograph Sessions, Cooperstown, New York, 1983, NM **$38.00**
Stamp album, 11x14", NFL picture sticker set, 1971, M...**$20.00**
Standee, 8½ x10½ ", Roger Staubach, Dallas Cowboys, cardboard, advertising Pizza Hut pro football calendar, 1977, NM..**$7.00**
Statue, 6", Mickey Mantle porcelain figurine on wood base, Sports Impressions, MIB.......................................**$38.00**
Statue, 6", Ty Cobb figural, bust portrait on 3x3" base, marked National Baseball Hall of Fame, 1963, 1 of set of 20, EX...**$50.00**
Ticket, Phantom World Series, 1982, Chicago White Sox, Game 4, M..**$17.50**
Ticket, World Series, 1973, Shea Stadium, EX.............**$35.00**
Ticket, 18th Indianapolis International 500 Mile Sweepstakes, May 30, 1930, M..**$20.00**
Tumbler, Ron Jaworski & Philadelphia Eagles, dated 1981, M **$5.00**
Wiffle ball set, Therman Munson on box, 1970s, M **$17.50**

Stanford Corn

Teapots, cookie jars, salt and pepper shakers, and other kitchen and dinnerware items modeled as ears of yellow corn with green shucks were made by the Stanford company, who marked most of their ware. The Shawnee company made two very similar corn lines; just check the marks to verify the manufacturer.

Butter dish **$45.00**
Cookie jar **$85.00**

Creamer & sugar bowl...**$45.00**
Pitcher, 7½ " **$55.00**
Relish tray...**$35.00**
Salt & pepper shakers, pr...**$25.00**
Spoon rest **$25.00**
Teapot...**$60.00**

Stangl Birds

The Stangl Pottery Company of Flemington and Trenton, New Jersey, made a line of ceramic birds which they introduced in 1940 to fullfill the needs of a market no longer able to access foreign imports, due to the onset of WWII. These bird figures immediately attracted a great deal of attention, and at the height of their production, sixty decorators were employed to hand paint the birds at the plant, and the overflow was contracted out and decorated in private homes. After WWII, inexpensive imported figurines once again saturated the market, and for the most part, Stangl curtailed their own production, though the birds were made on a very limited basis until as late as 1977.

For the most part, all the birds were marked. A four-digit number was used to identify the species, and some pieces were signed by the decorator. An 'F' indicates a the bird that was decorated at the Flemington plant.

Detailed information and a complete listing is available in *The Collectors Handbook of Stangl Pottery* by Norma Rehl.

Allen Hummingbird, #3634 ....$75.00
Bird of Paradise, #3408, sm......................................$120.00
Blue Jay, #3716, w/peanut $550.00
Blue-Headed Vireo, #3448.......................................$80.00
Bluebird, #3276.......................................$110.00
Bluebirds, #3276D.......................................$150.00
Broadbill Hummingbird, #3629.......................................$140.00
Cerulean Warbler, #3458 ....$100.00

Chestnut-Backed Chickadee, #3811.....................$100.00
Chickadees, #3581D $225.00
Cockatoo, #3405, sm.......................................$65.00
Cockatoo, #3580, med $150.00
Cockatoos, #3405D, old.......................................$175.00
Cockatoos, #3405D, revised $150.00
Flying Duck, #3443, blue-green.......................................$325.00
Gazing Duck, #3250, terra rose, green $75.00
Goldfinches, #3635 ....$235.00
Grey Cardinal, #3596 ....$85.00
Hen, #3446, yellow.......................................$175.00
Hummingbirds, #3599D.......................................$300.00
Kingfisher, #3406, light blue or blue-green.................$85.00

Lovebird, #3400, revised.......................................$70.00
Oriole, #3402, revised.......................................$75.00
Orioles, #3402D, revised $125.00
Painted Bunting, #3452.......................................$125.00
Parula Warbler, #3583.......................................$65.00
Prothonatary Warbler, #3447.......................................$85.00
Red Starts, #3490D.......................................$210.00
Red-Faced Warbler, #3594.......................................$80.00
Red-Headed Woodpeckers, #3752D, red matt..........$250.00
Reiffer's Hummingbird, #3628.......................................$150.00
Rivoli Hummingbird, #3627, w/red flower...............$150.00
Rooster, #3445, yellow $175.00
Rufous Hummingbird, #3585.......................................$70.00
Standing Duck, #3250, Granada Gold $65.00
Western Tanagers, #3750D.......................................$390.00
Wilson Warbler, #3597.......................................$55.00
Wren, #3401, revised $65.00
Wrens, #3401D.......................................$125.00
Yellow Warbler, #3850 ....$100.00

Stangl Dinnerware

The Stangl Company of Trenton, New Jersey, grew out of the Fulper company that had been established in Flemington early in the 1800s. Martin Stangl, president of the company, introduced a line of dinnerware in the 1920s. By 1954, 90% of their production centered around their dinnerware lines. Until 1942, the clay they used was white firing, and decoration was minimal, usually simple one-color glazes. In 1942, however, the first of the red-clay lines that have become synonomous with the Stangl name was created. Designs were hand carved into the greenware, then hand painted. More than one hundred different patterns have been cataloged. From 1974 until 1978, a few lines previously discontinued on the red clay were reintroduced with a white clay body. Soon after '78, the factory closed.

If you'd like more information on the subject, read *The Collector's Handbook of Stangl Pottery* by Norma Rehl and *The Collector's Encyclopedia of American Dinnerware* by Jo Cunningham.

Amberglo, cruet, w/stopper $25.00
Amberglo, gravy boat $10.00
Amberglo, gravy boat, w/underplate..........................$20.00
Americana, cream soup $4.00
Antique Gold, server, 10", center handle $15.00
Apple Delight, snack plate, 8¼ "...............................$3.50
Bella Rose, server, center handle..............................$10.00
Blueberry, bowl, 10".......................................$40.00
Blueberry, bowl, 12".......................................$50.00
Blueberry, cup & saucer.......................................$15.00
Blueberry, lug soup $15.00
Blueberry, plate, dinner size, 10".............................$16.50
Colonial, chop plate, 12½ " $12.00
Country Garden, bowl, divided vegetable $35.00
Country Garden, bowl, 8" $30.00
Country Garden, coaster, 5" $7.00

Country Garden, cup & saucer $12.00
Country Garden, plate, 10".......................................$15.00
Dahlia, cup & saucer $7.00
Dahlia, plate, 6"..$4.50
Fairlawn, server, center handle................................$10.00
Fruit & Flower, cup & saucer $14.00
Fruit & Flower, gravy boat $18.00
Fruits, bowl, salad; 10" $40.00
Fruits, pitcher, ½-pt...$15.00
Golden Blossom, plate, 10"......................................$4.50
Golden Harvest, coffee warmer...............................$12.00
Golden Harvest, cup $5.00
Golden Harvest, egg cup $8.00
Golden Harvest, plate, 10"..$7.50
Golden Harvest, plate, 8" $5.00
Magnolia, salt & pepper shakers, pr.........................$15.00
Orchard Song, coaster, 5"..$5.00

Orchard Song, gravy boat, 9" $16.00
Orchard Song, salt & pepper shakers, pr (illus-
trated) $15.00
Orchard Song, server, center handle $14.00
Orchard Song, snack plate, 8", w/off-center cup ring ...$5.00
Sgraffito, server, center handle $11.00
Sportsman's Ware, ashtray, 10⅝", mallard, oval..........$38.00
Star Flower, plate, 6"..$4.00
Thistle, bowl, vegetable; 7¼ x10½ ", divided..............$16.00
Thistle, bowl, 8" $25.00
Thistle, cup & saucer $6.50
Thistle, lug soup...$7.00
Wild Rose, celery $18.00
Wild Rose, creamer..$10.00

Star Trek Memorabilia

Trekkies, as fans are often referred to, number nearly 40,000 today, hold national conventions, and compete with each other for choice items of Star Trek memorabilia, some of which may go for hundreds of dollars.

The Star Trek concept was introduced to the public in the mid-1960s through a TV series which continued for many years in syndication. An animated cartoon series (1977), the release of six major motion pictures (1979 through 1989), and the success of 'Star Trek, The Next Generation,' television show (Fox network, 1987) all served as a bridge to join two generations of loyal fans.

Its success has resulted in the sale of vast amounts of merchandise, both licensed and unlicensed, such as clothing, promotional items of many sorts, books and comics, toys and games, records and tapes, school supplies, and party goods. Many of these are still available at flea markets around the country. An item that is 'mint in box' is worth at least twice as much as one in excellent condition but without its original packaging.

Book, Star Trek Color & Activity, Whitman, 1979, softcover, NM..$6.00
Book, Star Trek Punch-Out & Play Album, Saalfield, 1975, softcover, NM $20.00
Book, Starfleet Technical Manual, Ballantine, 1st printing, softcover, NM $40.00
Book, The Klingon Dictionary, expanded version, M ...$6.00
Book & record set, A Mirror..., Peter Pan, 1979, M $10.50

Book & record set, Passage to Moauv, 1979, NM ..$10.00
Calendar, The Next Generation, 1992, NM $10.00
Calendar, The Wrath of Khan, 1983, M $17.50
Colorforms, Star Trek Adventure Set, EX $25.00
Coloring book, Saalfield, Mr Spock cover, 1975, 40 pages, NM $18.00
Communicator, marked Official Starfleet, Playmates, light-up w/sounds, MIB...$18.00
Decanter, Spock figural, Grenadier, 1979, MIB...........$75.00

Figure, 12½ ", Ilia, Mego, M in VG box..................$45.00
Figure, 12½ ", Mr Spock, Mego, NMIB $75.00
Figure, 8", Captain Kirk, Mego, M in package $60.00

Greeting card, 10", Starfleet Achievement Award, dated 1976, M in original envelope....................................**$4.00**

Greeting card, 12", punch-out Vulcan ears, dated 1976, M in original envelope **$4.00**

Keychain, Starship Enterprise figural, Smithsonian Exclusive, NM **$11.00**

Kite, Enterprise & Klingon cruiser, Hi-Flier, 48", M in package **$15.00**

Magazine, Star Trek IV Official Movie, 1986, EX **$10.00**

Matchbook, Star Trek: The Motion Picture, M **$3.00**

Phaser, marked Official Starfleet Defensive Weapon, Playmates, 1992, MIB...**$24.00**

Poster, Star Trek: The Motion Picture, 1-sheet, M........**$35.00**

Program, Star Trek: The Motion Picture, M....................**$7.50**

Program, 20th-Anniversary, Spokane WA, 1986, EX....**$15.00**

Promotion, inflatable Enterprise, for movie, M............**$45.00**

Puzzle, Kirk outside Enterprise, Whitman, frame tray, 1979, M in package...**$6.00**

Sheet, twin size, characters, Enterprise & color graphics, 1976, M...**$25.00**

Sticker, Spock, The Motion Picture, Aviva, puffy type, M in package..**$8.00**

Tablet, Kirk w/phaser gun, Enterprise in background, 1967, NM **$24.00**

Tote bag, Star Trek: The Motion Picture, 1979, M **$22.50**

Vehicle, Klingon cruiser, Corgi, painted die-cast metal, M in package **$22.50**

View-Master set, Mr Spock's Time Trek, Sawyer, 1974, 3 reels w/16-page booklet, NM...............................**$12.00**

Star Wars Trilogy

In the late seventies, the movie 'Star Wars' became a box office hit, most notably for its fantastic special effects and its ever-popular theme of space adventure. Two more movies followed, 'The Empire Strikes Back' in 1980 and 'Return of the Jedi' in 1983. After the first movie, an enormous amount of related merchandise was released. A large percentage of these items was action figures, made by the Kenner company who included the logo of the 20th Century Fox studios (under whom they were licensed) on everything they made until 1980. Just before the second movie, Star Wars creator, George Lucas, regained control of the merchandise rights, and items inspired by the last two films can be identified by his own Lucasfilm logo. Since 1987, Lucasfilm, Ltd., has operated shops in conjunction with the Star Tours at Disneyland theme parks.

What to collect? First and foremost, buy what you yourself enjoy. But remember that condition is all important. Look for items still mint in the box. Using that as a basis for evaluation, if the box is missing, deduct at least half. If a major accessory or part is gone, the item is basically worthless. Learn to recognize the most desirable, most valuable items. There are lots of Star Wars bargains yet to be had!

Bank, R2-D2, Roman Ceramics, 1977, MIB **$45.00**

Book, Chewbacca Activity, Random House, 1979, M..**$10.00**

Catalog, Kenner Toy Company, Star Wars toys only, color, 1979, 17-page, M...**$40.00**

Collector case, 14½ ", Darth Vader bust figural, black plastic, w/room for 31 figures, Kenner, ca 1980, MIB.......**$22.00**

Cookie jar, R2-D2, ceramic, M **$125.00**

Doll, 12", Ben Obi-Wan Knobi, w/removable cape & light saber, Kenner, MIB...**$200.00**

Doll, 12", Stormtrooper, w/laser rifle, Kenner, MIB ..**$180.00**

Doll, 15", Darth Vader, cape & light saber, MIB........**$150.00**

Doll, 18", Chewbacca, stuffed, Kenner, MIB **$60.00**

Figure, 4", Rancor Keeper, olive pants w/no shirt, w/removable hood & stick, plastic, Kenner, 1984, MIB........**$5.00**

Figure, 2", Wickett, brown w/cream tummy, removable hood & spear, Kenner, 1984, M on card **$8.00**

Figure, 3", Chief Chirpa, removable brown hood & staff, Kenner, 1983, M on card **$6.00**

Figure, 3¼ ", Ben Obi-Wan Knobi, molded plastic, removable cape & retractable light saber, Kenner, 1977, M on card.......**$80.00**

Figure, 3¼ ", Luke Skywalker X-Wing Pilot, orange w/white helmet & laser pistol, Kenner, 1978, M on card....**$25.00**

Figure, 3¾ ", Greedo, green w/laser pistol, Kenner, 1978, M on card...**$40.00**

Figure, 3⅝", Princess Leia Organa, w/removable helmet, combat poncho, belt & laser pistol, Kenner, 1984, M on card.**$12.00**

Figure, 3⅞", Admiral Ackbar, tan vest on white, lobster head, black stick accessory, Kenner, 1983, M on card **$7.00**

Figure, 3⅞", Imperial Commander, w/black hat & laser pistol, Kenner, 1980, M on card................................**$12.00**

Figure, 3⅞", Teebo, light & dark gray striped plastic, removable hood, horn & axe, Kenner, 1984, MIB **$6.00**

Figure, 4", Biker Scout, black w/white armour & laser pistol, Kenner, 1983, M on card................................**$10.00**

Figure, 4", Bossk, yellow w/olive-green head & laser rifle, Kenner, 1980, M on card......................................**$15.00**

Figure, 4", C-3PO, metallic gold, removable limbs & papoose, Kenner, 1980, M on card......................**$12.00**

Figure, 4", Han Solo, in navy vest w/brown pants, laser pistol, Kenner, 1980, M on card.................................**$25.00**

Figure, 4", Lando Calrissian, light blue w/dark blue pants & cape, laser pistol, Kenner, 1980, M on card.........**$12.50**

Figure, 4¼ ", Chewbacca, brown w/silver bandolier & laser gun, marked SW-A3, Kenner, 1977, M on card.....**$60.00**

Figure paint kit, Empire Strikes Back, Leia, Craft Master, M on card...**$30.00**

Fun Poncho, Ben Cooper, 20th Century Fox, 1977, M in package...$35.00

Game, Escape From Death, VG **$7.00**
Model, Star Wars Landspeeder, wood, Japan, MIB......**$55.00**
Mug, Chewbacca figural head, marked Sigma, MIB **$25.00**

Playset, Creature Cantina, Kenner, 1979, NM in G box...$65.00

Playset, Dagobah, gray w/brown tree stump, 3 action levers, mud puddle, 2 containers, Kenner, 1981, MIB **$45.00**

Playset, Death Star Space Station, original box, EX.....**$75.00**

Playset, Imperial Attack Base, 17x10", revolving cannon & control room, 3 action levers, Kenner, 1978, MIB .**$65.00**

Playset, Jabba the Hutt, 11x5¼", grayish-brown platform w/2 doors, w/3 figures, Kenner, 1983, MIB.................**$32.00**

Playset, Jabba the Hutt Dungeon, 13x11", crane w/hood & branding iron, gray base, w/4 figures, Kenner, 1983, MIB **$30.00**

Playset, Land of the Ewoks, 22x16", tan platform supported by 3 trees, moving elevator, net & litter, Kenner, 1983, MIB **$40.00**

Playset, Patrol Dewback, 10½", green & white lizard, posable limbs & trap door back, brown saddle, Kenner, 1979, MIB **$20.00**

Playset, Taun-Taun, 9¾" long, gray & white w/brown horns, posable limbs, trap door in back, Kenner, 1980, MIB **$22.50**

Scissors, Return of the Jedi, marked Butterfly Originals, M on card...**$10.00**

Shampoo bottle, Yoda plastic figural, M **$10.00**

Sticker set, 20th-Century Fox, 1977, M **$5.00**

Vehicle, Darth Vader Tie-Fighter, 9¾ x11¾", removable wings, laser lights up, Kenner, 1978, MIB.............**$65.00**

Vehicle, Land Speeder, 9½ x6", brown w/chrome grills, 3 jets & windshield, Kenner, 1978, MIB **$50.00**

Vehicle, Millenium Falcon, 20½ x16½", off-white w/gray laser cannon, Kenner, 1979, MIB.........................**$80.00**

Vehicle, Speeder Bike, 8¾", light brown w/black engine, Kenner, 1983, MIB **$15.00**

Vehicle, Twin-Pod Cloud Car, die-cast metal, Kenner, M in package **$45.00**

Vehicle, X-Wing Fighter, die-cast metal, Kenner Series 1, M in package **$55.00**

Steiff Animals

These stuffed animals originated in Germany around the turn of the century. They were created by Margarete Steiff, whose company continues to operate to the present day. They are identified by the button inside the ear and the identification tag (which often carries the name of the animal) on their chest. Over the years, variations in the tags and buttons help collectors determine approximate dates of manufacture.

Teddy bear collectors regard Steiff bears as some of the most valuable on the market. When assessing the worth of a bear, they use some general guidelines as a starting basis, though other features can come into play as well. For instance, bears made prior to 1912 that have long gold mohair fur start at a minimum of $75.00 per inch. If the bear has dark brown or curly white mohair fur instead, the price may go as high as $135.00. From the 1920 to 1930 era, the price would be about $50.00 minimum per inch. A bear (or any other animal) on cast iron or wooden wheels starts at $75.00 per inch; but if the tires are hard rubber, the value is much lower, at $27.00 per inch.

It's a fascinating study which is well covered in *Teddy Bears and Steiff Animals, First and Second Series,* by Margaret Fox Mandel.

Alligator, 12", multicolor mohair, green plastic eyes, felt spines, toes & open mouth, no ID, EX.................**$90.00**

Bear, 10", Zotty, long frosted mohair, ball jointed, glass eyes, 1950s, EX **$235.00**

Bear, 15", tan mohair, glass eyes, fully jointed, growler, 1965, NM **$275.00**

Bear, 20", beige mohair, glass eyes, w/hump, growler, EX **$525.00**

Bear, 8½ ", tan mohair, hump, squeaker, w/button, 1950s, NM **$625.00**

Beaver, 3½ ", tan mohair, bristly back, felt paws, ears, feet & tail, plastic eyes, no ID, light wear, EX.................**$38.00**

Boar, 6x9", bristly mohair, sheared snout, plastic tusks, glass eyes, twine tail, all ID, M **$130.00**

Camel, 6", mohair w/velvet legs & face, bead eyes, twin tail, straw stuffing, chest tag, M.................................**$90.00**

Cat, 10" long, Fiffy, tabby-striped mohair w/plain center band on back, swivel head, glass eyes, 1950s, M..........**$250.00**

Cat, 11", Grisley, black mohair, swivel head, jointed limbs, glass eyes, red boots, w/button, NM...................**$120.00**

Cat, 5½ ", Tom Cat, black hair, green plastic eyes, stitched nose, w/button, 1960s, commonly found, M **$75.00**

Cat, 6½ ", gray & white mohair, green glassy eyes, not jointed, squeaker, no ID, VG **$15.00**

Cat, 9", Cattie, tabby striped draylon, green plastic eyes, floss nose & mouth, sitting, 1973, M.....................**$65.00**

Cow, 5", white & gold mohair, googly glass eyes, felt horns, red collar w/bell, no ID, EX.................................**$90.00**

Deer, 8", Bambi, velvet w/mohair insets on chest, ears & tail, glass eyes, not jointed, w/button, VG **$85.00**

Dog, 11", Revue Susi, long & short blond mohair airbrushed in gold, black & white eyes, original squeaker, NM **$125.00**

Dog, 5½ ", Scotty, thick black mohair, swivel head, glassine eyes, floss nose, leather collar w/bell, w/button, 1950s, NM **$200.00**

Dog, 5x7", Peky, pekingese, orange mohair, glass eyes, swivel head, not jointed, squeaker, chest tag, EX .**$55.00**

Dog, 6½ ", Laika, Husky, white mohair airbrushed in gold, glass eyes, floss nose & mouth, w/button...........**$300.00**

Dog, 7", Doxy, dachshund, brown & gold mohair, swivel head, glass eyes, not jointed, straw filled, no ID..**$50.00**

Dog, 8x10", Tessie, Schnauzer, gray mohair, glass eyes, swivel head, not jointed, red tongue & collar, squeaker, no ID **$110.00**

Dog, 9½ ", poodle, gray mohair, glass eyes, red collar w/bell, red tongue, swivel head, jointed, no ID...**$65.00**

Dog, 9x17", Waldi, orange & gold mohair, embroidered nose & claws, painted mouth, green collar, chest tag, M...............**$215.00**

Donkey, 10x19", Grissy, white w/black spots, black mane, glass eyes, chest tag, M...........**$70.00**

Dormouse, 3x8", Dormy, brown draylon, mohair tail, glass eyes, recumbent, w/button, NM **$90.00**

Duck, 4", yellow mohair, w/orange felt beak & feet, brown tail, plastic eyes, all ID, M **$55.00**

Duck, 4½ ", multicolor mohair, felt beak & feet, no identification, VG...............**$38.00**

Elephant, 6", gray mohair w/felt pads, pink felt nose, plastic tusks & googly eyes, not jointed, w/button, EX .**$110.00**

Elephant, 6x8", gray mohair & felt pads, plastic tusks, glass googly eyes, red blanket, w/button & tag, M **$130.00**

Fawn, 9x18", tan & white mohair, glass eyes, not jointed, reclining, w/button, NM **$195.00**

Fish, 11" long, multicolor mohair, felt peach mouth, lg plastic eyes, w/button, EX **$70.00**

Giraffe, 20", orange & white mohair, glass eyes, w/button, EX **$190.00**

Horse, 9½ ", Ferdy, brown & white mohair, plastic eyes, red harness, w/chest tag, M...............**$98.00**

Kangaroo, 5", Linda, brown mohair, plastic eyes, unjointed, plastic baby in pouch, w/tag, EX...............**$125.00**

Lamb, 11", white wooly mohair, glass eyes, squeaker, w/button, EX...............**$110.00**

Lamb, 4", Lamby, white wooly mohair, glass eyes, w/red ribbon & bell, EX...............**$60.00**

Lamb, 8", Cosy Lamby, white draylon w/pink velvet ears, glass eyes, w/button, EX **$75.00**

Lion, 6x10", tan & brown mohair, glass eyes, painted toes, reclining, no ID, some wear, VG...............**$140.00**

Lion, 8" long, yellow & brown mohair, plastic eyes, straw filled, reclining, no ID, VG...............**$95.00**

Llama, 11", multicolor mohair, plastic eyes, straw filled, w/button, EX...............**$230.00**

Lobster, 12" long, red, cream & orange mohair, black bead eyes, no ID, EX...............**$180.00**

Monkey, 10", Jocko, brown mohair, white beard, felt face, ears & paws, glass eyes, squeaker, EX...............**$110.00**

Monkey, 12", brown mohair w/felt face, glass eyes, jointed, w/button, EX...............**$95.00**

Parrot, 12", multicolor mohair, wire feet, green plastic eyes, straw filled, w/button, M...............**$145.00**

Pelican, 6", yellow mohair, felt beak, leathery inside mouth & teeth, glass googly eyes, no ID, NM...............**$180.00**

Pig, 12" long, pink draylon & cotton, felt nose & mouth, blue glass eyes, w/button, NM...............**$100.00**

Pony, 10", brown draylon, white hooves mane & tail, felt mouth, w/button, EX...............**$90.00**

Rabbit, 11", Sassy, pink & white mohair, swivel head, not jointed, squeaker, M...............**$88.00**

Rabbit, 18", Lulac, tan mohair, glass googly eyes, swivel head, jointed limbs, EX...............**$175.00**

Rabbit, 3", brown mohair, w/ribbon & bell, sitting, not jointed, M...............**$45.00**

Rabbit, 7", Manni, white & brown mohair, glass eyes, felt mouth, swivel head, no ID, NM...............**$95.00**

Raccoon, 20" long, mohair & synthetic, brown plastic eyes, imitation leather nose, w/button, EX...............**$95.00**

Rhino, 7½ ", Nosy, green mohair, felt ears, tail & pads, googly eyes, new-style chest tag, M...............**$55.00**

Rooster, 6", multicolor mohair, felt tail & feet, black bead eyes, EX...............**$60.00**

Seal, 8" long, white mohair w/blue spots, pink nose, brown mouth, plastic eyes, w/button, NM...............**$88.00**

Skunk, 4", black & white mohair, black velvet underside, unjointed, 1958-63, NM **$125.00**

Squirrel, 3½ ", white mohair, plastic eyes, VG.............**$48.00**

Tiger, 4½ " long, striped mohair, swivel head, glass eyes, jointed limbs, no ID, EX...............**$95.00**

Wolf, 9x10", brown mohair, plastic eyes, w/button, rare, NM...............**$585.00**

Zebra, 8x8", black & white striped mohair, plastic eyes, squeaker, no ID, EX...............**$80.00**

String Holders

Before Scotch tape made string obsolete, every household and business had a string holder of sorts. Some were made of cast iron, for heavy duty office work or for use in general stores and groceries. Others were frivolous and decorative, perhaps modeled as a human face or a big red apple, and made of various materials such as plaster or ceramic.

Ball-type, cast iron, hinged, ca 1910, EX....................$110.00
Beehive form, 5½ x6½ ", cast iron, dated 1861-66, EX.$60.00
Betty Boop, 10", chalkware w/hole in mouth for string, EX $135.00
Bird, ceramic, yellow on green string nest..................$30.00
Boy w/top hat & pipe, chalkware, EX paint...............$40.00
Chef's face, lg, ceramic, gold trim..............................$65.00
Compote shape w/embossed leaves, 10", cast iron, tall finial on lid $125.00

Girl w/hat, chalkware, EX paint...........................$45.00
Girl's head, ceramic..$50.00
Group of 3 girls, ceramic, Japan.................................$25.00
Lacy, cast iron, 2-part $45.00
Postem Beverages, 5x11½ " dia, tin, Pat 1915, EX.......$55.00
Sailor, chalkware, eyes looking sideways, w/pipe......$35.00
Spanish lady, lg, chalkware, EX...................................$85.00
Strawberry w/face, chalkware, EX................................$30.00

Wood sphere, 5½", varnished, 3 ivory inlays $95.00

Swanky Swigs

These glass tumblers ranging in size from 3¼ " to 4¾ " were originally distributed by the Kraft company who filled them with their cheese spread. They were primarily used from the 1930s until sometime during the war, but they were brought out soon after and used to some extent until the late 1970s. Many were decorated with fired-on designs of flowers, 'Bustling Betty' scenes (assorted chores being done by a Gibson-type Betty), 'Antique' patterns (clocks, coal scuttles, lamps, kettles, coffee grinders, spinning wheels, etc.), animals (in their 'Kiddie Cup' line), or solid colors of red, yellow, green, and blue (Fiesta ware look-alikes).

Even the lids are collectible and are valued at a minimum of $3.00, depending on condition and the advertising message they convey.

For more information, we recommend *Collectible Glassware of the 40s, 50s, and 60s* and *The Collector's Encyclopedia of Depression Glass, Revised Eleventh Edition*, both by Gene Florence.

Antique pattern, coffeepot & trivet, 3¼ ", black..........$10.00
Antique pattern, spinning wheel & bellows, 3¼ ", red.$10.00
Bear & pig, 3¾ ", blue..$4.00
Bicentennial, 3¾ ", yellow, red & green, 1975 ....$5.00

Bustling Betty, 3¾ ", all colors, each........................$4.00
Carnival, 3½ ", yellow, red, green or blue.....................$5.50
Cornflowers #1, 3½ ", light blue....................................$4.50
Cornflowers #1, 4½ ", light blue..................................$14.50
Cornflowers #2, 3½ ", dark blue....................................$3.50
Cornflowers #2, 3½ ", red or yellow $3.50
Cornflowers #2, 3¼ ", light blue....................................$8.50
Daisies, 3¾ ", red, white & green..................................$3.00
Daisies, 3¾ ", red & white $24.00
Dog & rooster, 3¾ ", orange..$4.00
Forget-Me-Nots, 3¼ ", yellow $10.00
Jonquils, 3½ ", yellow $4.50

Jonquils, 4½ ", yellow $14.50
Tulips #3, 3¾ ", dark blue.................................$3.50
Tulips #3, 3¾ ", red..$3.50
Tulips #3, 4½ ", dark blue...............................$14.50
Tulips in pots #1, 3½ ", green, w/label.............$10.00
Tulips in pots #1, 3½ ", red $4.00
Tulips in pots #1, 4½ ", green $14.00
Tulips in pots #2, 3½ ", black..........................$24.00
Violets, 3½ ", purple..$4.50

Syracuse Dinnerware

Until 1970 the Onondaga Pottery Company produced many lines of beautiful china dinnerware for home use. Located in Syracuse, New York, they are still in business, but the tablewares they make today are for commercial use only (hotels, restaurants, airlines, etc.). They marked their china with the trade name Syracuse, and in 1966 they adopted that name in order to more easily identify with the fine chinaware lines for which they had become famous.

Each piece is marked with a dating code that will help you determine just when your pattern was produced. In her book _Lehner's Encyclopedia of U.S. Marks on Pottery, Porcelain, & Clay_, Lois Lehner gives the details of this code. Nine columns of information and mark facsimiles are given as well, and if you're interested in learning more about Syracuse china, this is probably the best source available for study.

Apple Blosson, plate, 8" $20.00
Arcadia, creamer & sugar bowl.........................$65.00
Arcadia, demitasse cup & saucer $25.00
Arcadia, plate, 7"..$18.00
Arcadia, rimmed soup $25.00
Avalon, salad plate...$18.00
Baroque Gray, salad plate, 8"............................$18.00
Bombay, creamer & sugar bowl, ivory w/gold trim....$65.00
Bombay, vegetable bowl, ivory w/gold trim, w/lid.....$95.00
Briarcliff, cream soup.......................................$25.00
Briarcliff, cup & saucer $28.00
Briarcliff, fruit bowl, sm...................................$20.00
Carvel, platter, 14"..$65.00
Carvel, vegetable bowl $55.00
Celeste, cup & saucer $35.00
Celeste, salad plate $16.50
Clover, cereal bowl, 5½ "...................................$8.00
Clover, dinner plate, 10"...................................$10.00
Clover, gravy boat w/attached tray......................$20.00
Clover, platter, 14" $20.00
Coralbel, plate, 10¼ ".......................................$30.00
Countess, gravy boat $45.00
Coventry, luncheon plate..................................$15.00
Coventry, salad plate $10.00
Edmonton, bread & butter plate $8.00
Edmonton, dinner plate, 10".............................$10.00
Edmonton, sugar bowl, w/lid.............................$15.00

Gardinia, dinner plate.......................................$25.00
Indian Tree, cereal bowl $20.00
Jackstraws, cup & saucer...................................$16.00
Jackstraws, dinner plate....................................$10.00
Jackstraws, plate, 8"..$8.00
Jackstraws, soup or cereal bowl $8.00
Jefferson, gravy boat...$65.00
Jefferson, rimmed soup $25.00
Lyric, vegetable bowl, footed.............................$55.00
Madame Butterfly, bread & butter plate $14.50
Madame Butterfly, vegetable bowl, oval.............$27.50
Meadow Breeze, platter, 14"............................$125.00
Meadow Breeze, salad plate..............................$16.50
Oriental, luncheon plate, 9"...............................$8.00
Oriental, platter, 13½ "....................................$35.00
Riviera, dinner plate, 12".................................$25.00
Riviera, platter, 14"...$45.00
Romance Maroon, dinner plate, 9¾ "................$30.00
Rose Marie, vegetable bowl $45.00
Royal Court, plate, 10¼ "..................................$50.00
Serene, celery dish...$18.00
Serene, creamer & sugar bowl...........................$15.00
Serene, cup & saucer..$20.00
Serene, divided vegetable bowl..........................$20.00
Serene, pitcher..$20.00
Serene, platter, 11¼ ".......................................$20.00
Serene, salt & pepper shaker, pr $15.00
Sherwood, bread & butter plate..........................$7.00
Sherwood, cake plate, 10".................................$42.00
Sherwood, luncheon plate, 8".............................$10.00

Silhouette, cup & saucer, demitasse $17.50
Silhouette Flirtation, bread & butter plate $6.00
Silhouette Flirtation, dinner plate, 10½ " $15.00
Stansbury, dinner plate, 10" $10.00
Stansbury, platter, 12".......................................$25.00
Stansbury, soup plate $10.00
Suzanne, cup & saucer $35.00
Suzanne, gravy boat...$75.00
Victoria, dinner plate, 10"..................................$15.00
White w/Gold Band, celery dish, 9½ " $30.00
White w/Gold Band, dinner plate, 10"...................$15.00
White w/Gold Band, saucer..................................$5.00
Woodbine, dinner plate......................................$18.00

Telephones

Where better can the advancement of technology be portrayed than by comparing the large wood and metal wall phones of the late 1870s to the very small plastic portables of today. We've listed a few of the older styles, but remember the values we give you are retail. If you're buying to resell, you'll want to examine them and try to determine how much refurbishing you'll need to do. Many times dealers who specialize in old telephones will pay only 25% to 35% of retail.

Novelty phones have been popular for the past fifteen years or so, and many of them are now being seen on the secondary market. Especially good are character- and advertising-related models.

American Telecom, 1972, EX **$35.00**
Automatic Electric, metal w/cradle on top, nickel bands on
    hand set & dial, all original.................................**$165.00**
Automatic Electric, 3-slot coin-operated type, EX **$185.00**
Automatic Electric Model 34, desk type, Bakelite w/brass
    trim **$275.00**
Bell System, candlestick type, operator's issue............**$85.00**
Gray, pay phone, brass direction plate, early, M.......**$285.00**
Kellogg Master Phone, wall type, Deco style w/deep
    grooves, M...**$300.00**
Kellogg Red Bar, 1933 Streamline, chrome w/black trim, all
    original **$300.00**
National Cash Register, EX...**$125.00**
Northern Electric, wide desk type, chrome, 1930s **$260.00**
Sears & Roebuck, wall type, oak..................................**$200.00**
Stromberg-Carlson, non-dial desk type, EX original..**$115.00**
Western Electric, candlestick type, w/dial, all brass, all origi-
    nal...**$425.00**
Western Electric, oval base, non-dial cradle type........**$45.00**

**Western Electric Universal, wall type, Bakelite
handset, M..$275.00**

Novelty

Apple, 4" red plastic apple shape w/hinged top, push-button pad inside, Apple Phone, Touchtone **$35.00**

**Charlie the Tuna, 10", plastic, StarKist Foods, Inc,
1980s, M $50.00**
Crayon, 9", standing crayon form w/'Crayon Communicator'
    on label, marked Made by Tote, 1983...................**$40.00**
Garfield, reclining figural, EX.......................................**$59.00**
Kermit, 11½", frog reclining in chair, foot cradles receiver,
    1983 ....**$275.00**
Piano, 3x7¼", baby grand, push-button dial keyboard,
    marked Columbia Telecommunications **$59.00**
Pizza Baker, full-figured mustached man in white apron on
    round base w/'Pizza Inn,' in original box.............**$85.00**
Poppin' Fresh, 14", plastic advertising figure, 1980s, M.**$90.00**
Punchy, 11", comic figural for Hawaiian Punch, plastic,
    1980s, NM..**$150.00**
Raid Bug, 9", bug figural, push-button keys, NM **$95.00**
Ronald McDonald, 10", plastic figural, 1985, NM........**$90.00**
Snoopy & Woodstock, 14", figural, marked American
    Telecommunications...**$275.00**
TV Guide, 8½", numeral 1 w/TV Guide logo, NM.......**$60.00**

Televisions

If you're too young to remember what the very early TV sets looked like, screens were very small. Some measured only 7" – a few even less. In 1938 a miniature unit designed to be held in the hand was on display in London. It had an earphone to amplify the sound, and the screen was a tiny 2" square. By the late forties, luxurious home entertainment consoles were available, complete with glide-out turntables, hidden radios mounted on fold-out doors, and a big 10" 'direct view' screen, all for less than $500.00.

Today pre-WWII TVs sometimes sell for as much as $4,000.00. Unusual cabinet models from the forties may go as high as $300.00. Generally, any kind of vintage TV with a screen less than 14" is very collectible. Supply, demand, and of course, condition are the most important price-assessing factors. Our values are given for sets in fine condition and in working order.

If you'd like to see photos of these and many more fascinating early TVs (and learn what they're worth as well), we recommend *Classic TVs, Pre-War Through 1950s,* by Scott Wood.

Admiral, 10", Bakelite console, #20X122, 1950.........**$350.00**
Admiral, 7", Bakelite table-top model w/scarce Chinese grill #19A11, 1948.....................................**$200.00**
Admiral, 7", brown Bakelite, #17T1, 1948.................**$125.00**
Arvin, 8", metal w/limed oak front, #4080T, 1950.....**$150.00**

Automatic, 7" high, portable w/built in magnifier, #TV-P490, 1949 ....$225.00
Crosley, 7", portable, #9-425, 1949 ....**$175.00**
Delco, 7", wood, #71A, 1948.......................................**$175.00**
Fada, 10", w/magnifier, #799, 1947 ....**$150.00**
General Electric, 10", Bakelite portable, #800, 1948..**$200.00**
General Electric, 17", metal cabinet, #17T027, 1956....**$85.00**
Hallicrafters, 12", leatherette, #716, 1950....................**$150.00**
Hallicrafters, 7", blonde model, #T505, 1947 ....**$150.00**
Meck, 7", mahogany, #XA-701, 1941 ....**$200.00**
Motorola, 17", Bakelite, 1951 ....**$60.00**
Motorola, 19", 1st lg-screen color TV, #TS 905, 1954, minimum value **$1,000.00**
Motorola, 8", plastic grill cloth, 1949 ....**$100.00**
National, 7", mahogany, #7W, 1949..............................**$200.00**
Philco, 10", consolette, #49-1040, 1949........................**$75.00**
Philco, 7", black Bakelite, #50-702, 1950....................**$225.00**
Pilot, 3", w/magnifier attachment, #TV-37, 1949........**$250.00**
RCA, 12", metal cabinet, #2T51, 1950 ....**$100.00**
RCA, 7", blonde model, #621-TS, '46, mininum value.**$700.00**
Sentinel, 7", portable, leatherette, #400TV, 1948 ....**$200.00**
Silvertone, 8", upright portable, leatherette, #9115....**$150.00**
Sparton, mirror in lid, #4900, 1949 ....**$225.00**
Temple, 7", mahogany w/built-in magnifier, #1776 ..**$300.00**
Zenith, porthole console, 1949 ....**$150.00**

Thimbles

Collectors relate several reasons for their fascination with these small basic tools of needlework. First, many are very beautiful – tiny works of art in their own right. Enameling, engraving, and embossing are seen on thimbles made of metals such as gold, silver, brass, and pewter; and there are china thimbles that have been hand painted.

Many were made as souvenirs or as keepsake gifts to mark a special occasion. In the 19th century when social functions for ladies often revolved around their needlework projects, a fine, fancy thimble was a status symbol. Some collectors are intrigued by the inscriptions they find. Many suggest a glimpse into a thimble's history. For instance, 'Mother, 12-25-01' inside a lovely gold thimble conjures up a scene around a turn-of-the-century Christmas tree and a loving child presenting a special gift to a cherished parent.

Others simply like the older thimbles because to them they evoke a bit of nostalgia for a bygone era. But new thimbles are collectible as well. Bone china thimbles from England commemorating Charles' and Diana's marriage, Olympiad XXIII done in blue and white Jasperware by Wedgwood, hand-decorated examples with a 'Christmas 1982' message, and Norman Rockwell thimbles by Gorham are just a few examples of those that are 'new' yet very collectible.

If you'd like to read more about them and see hundreds shown in large, full-color photographs, we recommend *Antique and Collectible Thimbles and Accessories* by Averil Mathis.

Abalone & brass, Mexico..**$10.00**
Alabaster, floral decoration, unmarked **$12.00**
Brass, allover barbed-wire design, unmarked..............**$12.50**
Brass, allover pyramid design, unmarked.....................**$12.50**
Brass, decorative arches on band, unmarked **$10.00**
Brass, fluted band, unmarked **$6.50**
Brass, raised grape & leaf design, unmarked...............**$10.00**
Brass, solid band w/floral edge, unmarked **$10.00**
Brass, souvenir from 1982 World's Fair, unmarked.....**$10.00**
Brogan, sterling silver w/leaf design engraved in band, marked USA **$24.00**
Brogan, sterling silver w/scroll design engraved in band, marked USA **$42.00**
China, hand-painted flowers, marked USA **$6.00**

Cloisonne, unmarked $8.00
Glass, etched bells, marked USA **$10.00**
Glass, etched grapes, scalloped edge, marked USA....**$12.00**

Goldsmith-Stern, sterling silver, scroll design on gold band, marked USA **$55.00**

Goldsmith-Stern, sterling silver w/leaf & grape design on band, marked USA **$50.00**

Metal, mother & child in oval inset, marked USA.......... **$6.00**

Pewter, For a Good Girl, unmarked **$12.50**

Pewter, souvenir from Missouri Ozarks, unmarked **$6.00**

Pewter, souvenir from 1982 World's Fair, figural stein, unmarked **$6.00**

Pewter, 1980 Collector Circle Member, unmarked **$6.00**

Simons Brothers, sterling silver, Christmas 1982, marked USA **$50.00**

Simons Brothers, sterling silver, ornate floral decor on gold band, marked USA **$55.00**

Simons Brothers, sterling silver w/birds & flowers engraved on band, marked USA **$60.00**

Simons Brothers, sterling silver w/house engraved in band, marked USA **$42.00**

Simons Brothers, sterling silver w/sm panels on band, marked USA **$20.00**

Stern Brothers, sterling silver w/propeller design on band, marked USA **$24.00**

Waite-Thresher, sterling silver, scroll design on gold band, marked USA **$55.00**

Webster, sterling silver w/dogwood embossed on band, marked USA $55.00

Tiffin Glass

This company was originally founded in 1887 in Tiffin, Ohio, and later became one of several that was known as the U.S. Glass Company. U.S. Glass closed in the early sixties, and the plant reopened in 1963 under the title of the Tiffin Art Glass Company.

They have made many lovely lines of tableware and decorative items, but they are probably most famous for their black satin glass which was produced in the twenties.

Adam, champagne, pink **$30.00**
Bookmar, goblet **$20.00**
Bookmar, sherbet, tall **$16.00**

Byzantine, decanter, yellow, w/stopper.................... **$225.00**
Byzantine, plate, 10½" **$35.00**
Cadena, champagne, 6½", yellow **$32.00**
Cadena, goblet, water; 7½", yellow **$27.50**
Canterbury, claret, citron **$17.50**
Canterbury, goblet, iced tea; citron **$15.00**
Canterbury, sherbet, citron, tall **$12.50**
Cerice, bud base, 10½" **$45.00**
Cerice, champagne, 6" **$18.50**
Cerice, cocktail **$18.50**
Cerice, creamer & sugar bowl on tray **$95.00**
Cerice, goblet, iced tea; footed **$24.00**
Cerice, plate, 12" **$45.00**
Cerice, sundae **$18.00**
Cherokee Rose, bud vase, 10½" **$48.00**
Cherokee Rose, bud vase, 8" **$30.00**
Cherokee Rose, champagne, #17403 .... **$20.00**
Cherokee Rose, cocktail **$22.50**
Cherokee Rose, plate, 14" **$45.00**
Cherokee Rose, plate, 8" **$18.50**
Cherokee Rose, sugar bowl.................................... **$22.50**
Classic, champagne... **$25.00**
Classic, cocktail **$35.00**
Classic, plate, 7½" **$17.50**
Copen Blue, cigarette holder **$65.00**
Copen Blue, cornucopia vase, 8¼" **$75.00**
Empire, plate, 8", Twilight...................................... **$17.50**
Fairfax, goblet, iced tea; platinum trim..................... **$15.00**
Fairfax, plate, 8", platinum trim............................... **$10.00**
Fairfax, sherbet, tall, platinum trim **$12.00**
Flanders, cup & saucer.. **$35.00**
Flanders, goblet, iced tea; yellow **$25.00**
Flanders, plate, dinner; 10½", yellow **$35.00**
Flanders, plate, 6", smooth rim **$10.00**
Flanders, plate, 8", scalloped................................. **$12.00**
Flanders, wine, yellow... **$30.00**
Fontaine, champagne, green or pink......................... **$30.00**
Fontaine, cup & saucer, Twilight.............................. **$125.00**
Fontaine, goblet, water; pink **$40.00**
Fontaine, plate, 8", green or pink **$15.00**
Fontaine, saucer, green.. **$8.00**
Fontaine, sherbet, low, Twilight **$30.00**
Fontaine, tumbler, juice; green **$30.00**
Fuchsia, champagne, hollow stem............................ **$22.00**
Fuchsia, cocktail.. **$18.00**
Fuchsia, cordial.. **$40.00**
Fuchsia, goblet, iced tea; 12-oz, footed.................... **$28.00**
Fuchsia, goblet, water... **$25.00**
Fuchsia, sherbet, low.. **$14.00**
Fuchsia, wine **$35.00**
Julia, plate, 10¼", amber....................................... **$18.00**
June Beau, champagne.. **$12.00**
June Beau, goblet, 8".. **$17.00**
June Night, champagne goblet................................ **$24.00**
June Night, cocktail.. **$20.00**
June Night, goblet, iced tea; 6½" **$22.00**
June Night, goblet, water; #358.............................. **$25.00**
La Fleur, plate, 8½", topaz..................................... **$12.00**

Night lamp, 6", Twilight (rare in this color), #9441.$45.00

Palais Versailles, comport, gold trim $100.00
Persian Pheasant, champagne.....................................$24.00
Persian Pheasant, cordial..$40.00
Persian Pheasant, wine, 6" $35.00
Princeton, champagne..$12.00
Rambling Rose, goblet, iced tea...................................$23.00
Rambling Rose, goblet, water $23.00
Rambling Rose, relish, 3-compartment, round............$17.50
Rambling Rose, sherbet, low..$16.00
Rosalind, plate, 10½"..$35.00
Sylvan, cheese comport, green $15.00
Sylvan, cup & saucer, pink...$35.00
Tiffin Rose, champagne, 5⅞"...$22.00
Tiffin Rose, cordial, 5⅛" $35.00
Tiffin Rose, wine, 6⅜"...$25.00

Vase, 12", Kilarney Green & crystal Cellini stem,
1950 ....$175.00

Wall pocket, 15" overall, golden tan glass vase in
wrought iron vine-&-flower framework.........$75.00
Wistaria, cordial, #17477..$45.00
Wistaria, goblet, water..$25.00
Wistaria, plate, 8"...$15.00
Wistaria, tumbler, juice..$25.00

Tinware

Before Pyrex became the material of choice for pie plates, measuring cups, and other kitchenware items, many were made of tin. Of course, it was very durable, so many exampes, especially from the '20s through the '40s, are still around. Some collectors enjoy using their tinware in their vintage kitchens, while others display it on shelves with other old pieces, some vintage advertising, and perhaps an old cookbook.

Cake pan, raised Santa face in bottom, 9" dia $55.00
Candle holder, Christmas; flower shape, clips on tree, set of
    12 ....$30.00
Candle holder, dark gray, push up, ring-shaped handle on
    side, 3½x5½", EX...$75.00
Colander, pierced triangles, pedestal base, side handles, lg,
    EX...$22.00
Comb holder, embossed decoration, w/mirror & side pock-
    ets..$38.00
Cup, measuring; Rumford Baking powder...................$30.00
Ladle, pierced, 17" long..$20.00
Lamp, miner's spout type, Beall Bros, 3" w/4" spout..$48.00
Lamp, petticoat; double whale oil burners, filler spout w/old
    cork, strap handle, 4x2½"......................................$135.00
Lamp filler, dark gray w/2-section spout, 5x5½" $85.00
Mug, embossed designs, child's size $35.00
Pan, lady finger; 6 fluted long oval cups fastened to heavy
    tin straps $48.00
Pitcher, MK Fairbanks & Co, Pure Refined Lard, 2½"..$28.00

Spittoon, removable top, side handle, early, 6" base ..**$40.00**

Sugar shaker, 4", light rust.......................................**$35.00**
Syrup pitcher, hinged lid w/rolled tin lift, wide strap handle,
    4½x4½", EX **$60.00**
Teakettle, Kreamer, slant spout, flat bail, 4x4½".........**$60.00**
Wash boiler, w/lid, 12" long **$60.00**

Tire Ashtrays

Manufacturers of tires issued miniature versions that contained ashtray inserts that were usually embossed with an advertising message; some were used as souvenirs from World's Fairs as well. The inserts themselves were often made of clear glass, but other colors were also used, and once in awhile you'll find a tin one. The tires themselves were usually black, but you may find one in another color. For ladies or non-smokers, some miniature tires contained a pin tray.

Compass/key chain combination, 2⅛" dia, Japan..........**$2.50**
Dunlop Gold Seal 78, glass insert.................................**$15.00**
Firestone Champion Ground-Grip Gum-Dipped Tractor Tire,
    6¼" dia, glass insert, 1930s-40s **$25.00**
Firestone Giant Steel Radials, red & white logo on glass
    insert **$35.00**
Firestone Gum-Dipped 32x6, 6" dia, tan glass insert, ca late
    1920s...**$30.00**
Firestone Heavy-Duty 6.00x18, 4" dia, Century of Progress: Firestone Chicago 1934, glass insert, red or blue tire......**$50.00**

Firestone Heavy-Duty 6.00x18, 5¾" dia, Century of Progress: Firestone Chicago 1934, amber glass insert **$50.00**
Firestone Hi-Type Cushion, metal insert, 1920s..........**$50.00**

Goodyear Heavy-Duty Cushion Hard Rubber Tire (solid truck tire), 4½" dia, green glass insert, ca 1920.....**$50.00**
Miller Tires, 7" dia, glass insert, 8 cigarette rests, EX...**$40.00**
Seiberling Patrican Deluxe 4-Ply, 3½" dia, green glass insert,
    1930s **$20.00**

Toothbrush Holders

These figural novelties have been made in the likenesses of many storybook personalities, and today all are very collectible, especially those representing popular Disney characters. Most are made of bisque and are decorated over the glaze. Condition of the paint is an important consideration when trying to arrive at an evaluation.

Bugs Bunny, plastic, Warner Bros **$39.00**
Donald, Mickey & Minnie; 4½", Donald in middle hugging
    others, copyright Disney, Made in Japan, M.......**$275.00**
Donald Duck, 2 Donald figures stand side by side, facing
    opposite directions, WDE, ca 1930, M.................**$250.00**
Donald Duck, 5", Donald looking sideways w/mouth open,
    copyright Walt E Disney, M **$250.00**
Little Orphan Annie, 3½x3", Annie & Sandy sit on a couch,
    M..**$125.00**
Lone Ranger, composition, 1938, EX............................**$68.00**
Mickey & Minnie, 3½", seated on sofa w/sm Pluto at feet,
    Walt Disney Enterprises, ca 1930, M **$225.00**
Mickey & Pluto, Mickey holds handkerchief to Pluto's nose,
    Walt Disney, M..**$250.00**
Skippy, EX...**$85.00**
Snow White, 1938..**$150.00**
3 Little Pigs, 2 playing musical instruments, center pig sits
    facing backwards laying bricks, Walt Disney, M .**$170.00**

3 Little Pigs, 3½", Fifer Pig, Practical Pig & Fiddler Pig, Walt Disney Enterprises, ca 1930, G $125.00

Toothpick Holders

One reason these are so popular with collectors is their small size – and it's one of the reasons that so many have survived to the present day. Once a common accessory on any dining table, around the turn of the century, many were relegated to the back of the china cupboard and eventually became family heirlooms. Because they're so highly collected, many have been reproduced, so be sure of what you're buying. Knowing your dealer can be very helpful. Many that look 'old' have been made recently by several small glass studios such as Degenhart, Boyd, St. Clair, and Mosser.

Besides glass, toothpick holders have been made in china, some to match dinnerware patterns, some modeled as figures of animals or people, and some simply as novelties. Silverplated styles were made during Victorian times, and other materials have been used as well.

Acorn, peachblow, gold trim	$125.00
Apollo	$20.00
Arched Ovals, ruby stained	$32.50
Banded Portland, Maiden's Blush	$45.00
Beatty Honeycomb, blue	$45.00
Bird w/Basket, amber	$37.50
Britannic, ruby stained	$65.00
Bulging Loops, green	$35.00
Bull's Eye & Fan, green	$42.50
Cat on Pillow holds Daisy & Button bowl, amber	$65.00
Champion, green	$55.00
Coin Dot, ruffled top, amberina	$250.00
Colorado, 2¾", cobalt w/gold feet	$35.00
Cord & Pleat, cobalt	$88.00
Crysanthemum Leaf	$55.00
Diamond Peg, custard w/rose design	$75.00
Empress, green w/gold	$215.00
Fine Cut, hat shape, blue	$30.00
Fleur-de-Lis shape	$22.00
Frisco	$70.00
Galloway, rose stained	$60.00

Gatling gun, 3", amber	$40.00
Harvard, custard	$35.00
Idyll, apple green	$80.00
Illinois	$30.00
Kentucky, square, emerald green	$88.00
Lacy Medallion, green w/gold, has been reproduced	$32.00

Masonic	$75.00
Menagerie Fish, amber	$68.00
Nearcut	$25.00
Nestor, blue	$65.00
Paddle Wheel	$45.00
Paneled Grape	$45.00
Priscilla, Findlay	$30.00
Prize	$42.50
Quartered Block	$45.00
Queen's Necklace	$60.00
Ribbed Pillar, frosted cranberry spatter	$60.00
Scalloped Swirl, ruby stained	$55.00
Scrolled Shell, milk glass w/hand-painted design	$30.00
Sunflower Patch	$55.00
Tennessee	$55.00

Texas	$25.00
Trophy, emerald green	$20.00
Twist, blue opalescent	$45.00
Vermont, green w/gold	$65.00

Toys

Toy collecting has long been an area of very strong activity, but over the past decade it has really expanded. Many of the larger auction galleries have cataloged toy auctions, and it isn't uncommon for scarce 19th-century toys in good condition go for $5,000.00 to $10,000.00 and up. Toy shows are common, and there are clubs, newsletters, and magazines that cater only to the needs and wants of toy collectors. Though once buyers ignored toys less than thirty years old, in more recent years, even some toys from the eighties are sought after.

Condition has more bearing on the value of a toy than any other factor. A used toy in good condition with no major flaws will still be worth about half (in some cases much less) than one in mint (like new) condition. Those mint and in their original boxes will be worth much more than the same toy without its box.

There are many good toy guides on the market today including: *Teddy Bears and Steiff Animals* by Margaret Fox

Mandel; *Toys, Antique and Collectible,* and *Character Toys and Collectibles,* both by David Longest; *Modern Toys, American Toys 1930 to 1980,* by Linda Baker; *Collecting Toys, Collecting Toy Trains* and *Collecting Toy Soldiers,* all by Richard O'Brien; *Toys of the Sixties* by Bill Bruegman; and *Collector's Guide to Tootsietoys* by David E. Richter.

See also Barbie Collectibles; Breyer Horses; Bubble Bath Containers; Cracker Jack Collectibles; Disney Collectibles; Fast Food Toys and Figurines; Halloween Costumes; Hartland; Liddle Kiddles; Male Action Figures; Paper Dolls; Star Trek Memorabilia; and Star Wars Trilogy.

Airplanes

Auburn Rubber, A-11 Light Bomber, 4" wingspan, M.**$35.00**
Auburn Rubber, No 586 Army Pursuit Plane, marked US 1X2755 on wings, M............................**$25.00**
Barclay, BA7, 195 Aeroplane, 3¾", single engine transport, marked US Army, M............................**$35.00**
Chein, Mechanical Aquaplane, 8½", #39, no insignia, w/boat-like pontoons, M............................**$250.00**
Cruver Company, A-24, Dauntless, 1/72 scale WWII identification, 1942, EX............................**$22.00**

Girard, Whiz Sky Fighter, 9", stenciled tin, red, yellow, gold & blue, clockwork, EX $350.00
Hubley, H27, Crusader, 5⅛" wingspan, #427, twin engine, twin boom, marked TAT NC-31, M............................**$50.00**
Hubley, H33, Hellcat, 9¼" wingspan, plastic, M............**$20.00**
Hubley, H8, USN 3-B-4, 5⅛" wingspan, die-cast metal, retractable landing gear, M............................**$30.00**
Ideal, Yankee Scout, 17" long, gold paint, removable 19½" span wing, replaced stabilizer, G............................**$500.00**
J Toy Company, Flying Jet Plane Boeing 747P, 13", battery operated, 5 actions, 1960s, M............................**$180.00**
Kansas Toy & Novelty, KTA2 cabin plane, 3⅝"x3", high wing, Army Air Corps insignia, 8 oval windows, cast propeller, M............................**$28.00**
Kilgore, N4, 4", open cockpit monoplane, cast iron, M.**$225.00**

Leominster, C-47 Skytrain, 1/72 scale, WWII identification, 1943, EX............................**$50.00**
Lincoln White Metal, A2, 2½x2½", 3-motor, outboard engines mounted in wings, metal wheels, M........**$55.00**
M-T Company, Boeing 727 Jet Plane, 12½", battery operated, 3 actions, 1960s, M **$180.00**
Marx, Akron Zeppelin, 28", 1930s, EX........................**$140.00**
Marx, Army Dive Bomber, #482, tin, EX..................**$200.00**
Marx, Crop Duster, M............................**$60.00**
Marx, DC-6, transport plane, plastic, EX..................**$120.00**
Marx, Pioneer Air Express, 25½" wingspan, lithographed tin, high wing monoplane, EX **$100.00**
Metal Cast, Aeroplane, 4½" wingspan, #66, 2-engine lead, ca 1940s, M............................**$10.00**
Nomura, Zero, 14", friction, G **$150.00**
Ohio Art, Coast Guard Seaplane, 10" wings, 1950s, M.**$100.00**
Ralstoy, Cabin Plane, 3⅝"x3½", high wing, cowled radial engine, 2 doors, 6 windows, Made in USA, M......**$40.00**
Schuco US Zone Germany, Micro Jet, 5½", #1030, 1950s, M............................**$160.00**

Steelcraft, US Mail Plane, lg, pressed steel, restored to original color, replaced decals $325.00
T-N Company, F-14-A Navy Jet Fighter, 13", battery operated, 6 actions, 1960s, EX..................................**$300.00**
TN, Ford, 15", friction, EX **$90.00**

Tootsietoy, Corsair CV-240 twin engine, VG $30.00
TPS Company, Spad XIII S-7 Stunt Biplane, 9", battery operated, 3 actions, 1960s, EX..................................**$165.00**
TWA Multiaction DC-7C Airliner, 22½", Yonezawa, battery operated, 7 actions, 1960s, EX............................**$300.00**
West Germany, Cessna, 12", friction, EX....................**$80.00**
Wyandotte, Military Air Transport, 13" wingspan, M............................**$50.00**
Wyandotte, Stratocruiser, 13" wingspan, M.................**$75.00**

Battery Operated

It is estimated that approximately 95% of the battery-operated toys that were so popular from the forties through the sixties came from Japan. The remaining 5% were made in the United States by other companies. To market these toys in America, many distributorships were organized. Some of the largest were Cragstan, Linemar, and Rosko. But even American toy makers such as Marx, Ideal, Hubley, and Daisy sold them under their own names, so the trademarks you'll find on Japanese battery-operated toys are not necessarily that of the manufacturer, and it's sometimes just about impossible to determine the specific company that actually made them. After peaking in the sixties, the Japanese toy industry began a decline, bowing out to competition from the cheaper die-cast and plastic toy makers.

Remember that it is rare to find one of these complex toys that have survived in good, collectible condition. Batteries caused corrosion, lubricants dried out, cycles were interrupted and mechanisms ruined, rubber hoses and bellows aged and cracked, so the mortality rate was extremely high. A toy rated good, that is showing signs of wear but well taken care of, is generally worth about half as much as the same toy in mint (like new) condition. Besides condition, battery-operated toys are rated on scarcity, desirability, and the number of 'actions' they preform. A 'major' toy is one that has three or more actions, while one that does only one or two is considered 'minor.' These, of course, are worth much less.

Alps, Antique Gooney Car, 9", 4 actions, 1960s, M ...**$120.00**

Alps, Bunny the Magician, 14½", 5 actions, card-ribbon appratus for card trick, 1950s, EX **$285.00**

Alps, Busy Housekeeper, 8½", 4 actions, 1950s, EX..**$240.00**

Alps, Dandy the Happy Drumming Pup, 8½", 6 actions, w/detachable drum & cymbals, 1950s, EX..........**$150.00**

Alps, Drumming Polar Bear, 12", 3 actions, 1960, M.**$160.00**

Alps, Fred Flintstone Bedrock Band, 9½", 4 actions, 1962, EX **$375.00**

Alps, Happy Santa 1-Man Band, 9", 6 actions, w/cymbals & stand, 1950s, M **$240.00**

Alps, Hooty the Happy Owl, 9", 6 actions, 1960s, M .**$140.00**

Alps, Mexicali Pete Drum Player, 10½", 3 actions, 1960s, EX **$270.00**

Alps, Polar Bear, 8", 3 actions, 1970s, M **$80.00**

Alps, Shaggy the Friendly Pup, 8", 3 actions, 1960, M .**$60.00**

Alps, Teddy the Rhythmical Drummer, 11", 3 actions, 1960s, M...**$160.00**

Alps, Walking Itchy Dog, 9", 5 actions, 1950s, M **$100.00**

Alps, Yo-Yo Clown, 9", 3 actions, w/plastic yo-yo, 1960s, EX **$165.00**

Bandai, Air Control Tower, 11x37" span (extended), 4 actions, w/airplane & helicopter, 1960s, M.........**$440.00**

Bandai, Comic Road Roller, 9", 4 actions, 1960s, M ..**$120.00**

Bandai, Merry Ice Cream Truck, 10½", 5 actions, 1960s, EX **$120.00**

Bandai, Pete the Space Man, 5", Walking Mate Series, minor action, 1960s, M **$100.00**

Bandai, Thunder Jet Boat, 9¾", 3 actions, 1950s, EX .**$195.00**

Cragstan, Space Patrol Tank, 9", 5 actions, w/detachable jet plane, 1950s, EX..**$150.00**

Cragstan Crapshooter, 9½", 3 actions, 1950s, MIB.$180.00

Cragstan Western Locomotive, 12" long, 4 actions, 1950s, M..**$120.00**

Daisy, Tank-Daisymatic No 64 Rapid Fire Tank, 8", 4 actions, 1960s, M...**$200.00**

Daiya Company, Space Tank, 8", 4 actions, '50s, EX **$150.00**

GW Company, Suzy-Q Automatic Ironer, 7", 4 actions, 1950s, EX...**$135.00**

K Company, Anti-Aircraft Jeep, 9½", 5 actions, 1950s, M.**$180.00**

Kanto Toy, Pacific Piping Express Locomotive, 14", 4 actions, 1960s, EX **$120.00**

KKS Company, Fire Patrol Boat, 12", 3 actions, 1950s, EX **$135.00**

KO Company, Love-Beetle-Volks, 10" long, 3 actions, 1960s, M..**$120.00**

Lehmann, Rigi Ski Lift #900, Made in Western Germany, MIB..$45.00

Linemar, Ball Playing Dog, 9", 3 actions, 1950s, M ...**$240.00**

Linemar, Busy Secretary, 7½", 7 actions, 1950s, EX...**$225.00**

Linemar, Crawling Baby, 8½", 1940s, M **$100.00**

Linemar, Military Police Car, 8½", 6 actions, 1950s, EX.**$135.00**

Linemar, NBC Television Truck, 9" long, 5 actions, 1950s, EX **$360.00**

Linemar, Traveler Bear, 8", 3 actions, 1950s, EX........**$120.00**

Linemar, 14", Air Defense Pom-Pom Gun, battery operated, 5 actions, 1950s, M.....................................**$240.00**

lps, Hot Rod Limousine, 10½", 4 actions, 1960s, EX .**$270.00**

M Company, Electro Train Transcontinental, 20½" long, 3 actions, 3-piece, 1950s, M **$140.00**

M-T Company, Bixy Bizzy Friendly Bug, 6¼", 3 actions, 1950s, M **$120.00**

M-T Company, Circus Fire Engine, 11", 4 actions, 1960s, M..**$240.00**

M-T Company, Desert Patrol Jeep, 11" long, 4 actions, w/turret gunner, 1960s, M.................................**$180.00**

M-T Company, Good-Time Charlie, 12", 7 actions, 1960s, M **$180.00**

M-T Company, Mickey Mouse Trolley, 11", 3 actions, 1960s, EX **$210.00**

M-T Company, Musical Comic Jumping Jeep, 12" long, 6 actions, 1970s, M..**$120.00**

M-T Company, Papa Bear, Reading & Drinking in His Old Rocking Chair, 10", 4 actions, 1950s, EX............**$180.00**

M-T Company, River Queen Sidewheeler, 13½", 3 actions, 1950s, M **$200.00**

M-T Company, Santa Copter, 8½", 3 actions, '60s, EX .**$100.00**

M-T Company, Snoopy Sniffer, 8", 4 actions, '60s, M..**$80.00**

M-T Company, Spirit of 1776, 15¾", #4406, 5 actions, 1976, M...**$60.00**

M-T Company, Wagon Master, 18", 4 actions, 1960s, M.**$20.00**

M-T Company, Western Locomotive, 10½" long, 4 actions, 1950s, M **$80.00**

Marsusan, Tugboat, 13½" long, 3 actions, 1950s, M ..**$220.00**

Marx, Alley the Exciting New Roaring Stalking Alligator, 17½", 5 actions, 1960s, EX...................................**$225.00**

Marx, Brewster Rooster, 9½", 5 actions, 1950s, M **$240.00**

Marx, Nutty Mad Indian, 12", 4 actions, 1960s, EX....**$120.00**

Marx, Tugboat, 6½" long, 1950s, EX.........................**$75.00**

Mignon, Gama Mercedes Benx 220 SE Sedan, 9", 3 actions, 1960s, M **$280.00**

Nihonkogei, Golden Locomotive, 10½", 1950s, M.......**$60.00**

Poynter Products, Poverty Pup Bank, 4½", 3 actions, 1966, M...**$120.00**

S-H Company, Old-Fashioned Car, 10", 4 actions, 1950s, M **$80.00**

SAN Company, Shooting Bear, 10", 6 actions, 1950, EX .**$240.00**

T-N Company, Battery Locomotive, 10", #123, 3 actions, 1950s, M...**$60.00**

T-N Company, Bingo Clown, 13", 3 actions, 1950, EX.**$225.00**

T-N Company, Jolly Drumming Bear, 7", 4 actions, 1950s, EX...**$90.00**

T-N Company, Shaking Classic Car, 7", 4 actions, 1960s, EX **$75.00**

T-N Company, Shoe Maker Bear, 8½", 3 actions, 1960s, EX **$165.00**

T-N Company, Slurpy Pup, 6½", 4 actions, 1960s, EX.**$75.00**

T-N Company, Space Patrol Car, 9½", 4 actions, 1950s, EX **$450.00**

Tada Company, Space Ship X-8, 9" dia, 4 actions, 1960s, EX **$150.00**

TPS Company, Climbing Linesman, 24", 3 actions, 1950s, EX **$300.00**

Y Company, Bubble Blowing Bunny, 7", 4 actions, 1950s, M...**$180.00**

Y Company, Cragstan Mother Goose, 8¼", 6 actions, 1960s, M...**$160.00**

Y Company, Jumbo, Bubble Blowing Elephant, 7¼", 3 actions, plastic bowl for bubble solution, 1950s, EX...........**$90.00**

Y Company, Lighted Freight Train, 25½" long, 4 actions, 5 pieces w/8-section track, 1950s, M.....................**$120.00**

Y Company, Moon Oribiter, 4" long, w/6 sections of track & trestles, 1960s, EX **$135.00**

Y Company, Piggy Barbecue, 9½", 5 actions, w/chef's hat & lithographed tin fried egg, 1950s, M...................**$260.00**

Y Company, Tank M-107 US Army, 6", 4 actions, w/4 missiles, 1950s, EX...**$150.00**

Y Company, Tom-Tom Indian, 10", 4 actions, '61, M.**$160.00**

Y Company, Tubby the Turtle, 7", 3 actions, 1950, M .**$100.00**

Y-M Company, Astro Dog, 11", 3 actions, 1960s, EX.**$135.00**

Yada, Drum Monkey, 8", 3 actions, 1970s, M **$80.00**

Z Company, Old Ford Touring Car, 10", 4 actions, 1950s, M **$80.00**

Dakin

This is a California-based company that for many years has been producing plush animals. But in the late 1960s, they began to make a line of hollow plastic figures. They ranged in size from about 6" to 9," some had cloth costumes. Popular cartoon characters licensed by Disney, Hanna-Barbera, and Warner Brothers are among the most avidly searched for today, and when found in mint condition may reach $100.00 or more, though most are in the $20.00 to $50.00 range.

Ape Goofy Gram..**$45.00**

Banana Splits, Snorky the Elephant, 7", Hanna-Barbera, 1970, VG **$100.00**

Barney (Flintstones), EX..**$20.00**

Bugs Bunny, sm, marked Dakin, 1976, EX $25.00
Cool Cat, 9", w/fabric clothes, 1968, EX.....................$35.00
Daffy Duck, 7", 1975, EX.......................................$20.00
Donald Duck, 8", vinyl, removable jacket, marked Walt Disney Productions on head, 1973, M $30.00
Dream Doll Aloha Alice, 15", stuffed nylon net w/painted features, vinyl hair, grass skirt, original tag, 1956, M...$12.00
Dumbo, EX $22.00
Elephant, Dream Pet series, stuffed cloth, sitting & wearing beret, tag missing, NM......................................$10.00
Elmer Fudd, 6½", w/removable cloth & felt clothes, 1978, M in package $35.00

Elmer Fudd, 8", vinyl w/cloth suit, 1970, VG........$25.00
Fred Flintstone, M in package...................................$40.00
Fred Flintstone, 8", 1970, EX.................................$28.00
Goober Gorilla, Dream Pet Series, stuffed cloth, w/original paper tag, NM $15.00
Honolulu Harry Turtle, Dream Pet series, no tag, NM .$12.00
Merlin the Magic Mouse, 8", VG.............................$10.00

Merlin the Magic Mouse Goofy Gram, 1974, NM ..$25.00

Mickey Mouse, 8", cotton suit & vinyl shoes, 1975, common, EX..$20.00
Minnie Mouse, 6", plastic & vinyl, removable clothes, original tag, 1973, common, EX $20.00
Olive Oyl, sm, marked Dakin, 1976, NM $20.00
Pink Panther, NM...$32.00
Pinocchio, 8", jointed, molded-on gloves, slip-on shoes, cotton suit, original tag, 1975, M....................$45.00
Pluto, M $25.00
Red Bull Goofy Gram $55.00
Road Runner, sm, M $25.00
Road Runner, 9", 1968, EX.................................$17.50
Smokey Bear, bank, 8½", jointed, on tree stump, cloth clothing, w/accessories, 1970s, w/tag, M $75.00
Speedy Gonzales Goofy Gram................................$20.00
Sylvester the Cat, w/whiskers, 1969, EX.....................$20.00
Tweety Bird, bank, 1976, EX................................$40.00
Tweety Bird, 6", jointed, original cardboard tag, 1969, M in package $35.00
Whitecap Dolphin, Dream Pet series, stuffed cloth, w/sailor cap & original paper tag, NM........................$15.00
Wile E Coyote, 7", jointed, 1968, M $25.00
Yosemite Sam, 7", jointed, removable hat, 1960s, M...$30.00

Farm Toys

Since the decade of the twenties, farm machinery manufacturers have contracted with many of the leading toy companies to produce scale models of their machines. Most were made on a 1/16 scale, but other sizes have been made as well.

Cattle truck, Hubley, ca 1947, M.................................$90.00
Disc harrow, 4½", Auburn Rubber, M..........................$25.00
Harvester, 5½", Auburn Rubber, open top, M..............$25.00
Plow, bottom; International Harvester, Ertl, M............$25.00
Plow, David Bradley 2-Furrow, 4¾", Auburn Rubber, M.$20.00
Seeder, Reliable Front-Lift, 5", Auburn Rubber, M.......$20.00
Semi, 22¼", Grain Hauler, Tonka #550, 1952, G $120.00
Semi, 22¼", Livestock Hauler, Tonka #500, G $135.00
Spreader, Ertl, w/metal beater, M.............................$40.00
Spreader, manure; David Bradley, 4¾", Auburn Rubber, M...$20.00
Spreader, 10½", McCormick-Deering, steel w/black rubber tires, Made in USA, 1950s, EX $90.00
Tractor, Ertl #656, M $20.00
Tractor, John Deere Model A, 5", Auburn Rubber, M..$30.00
Tractor, Minneapolis-Moline Z, 4", Auburn Rubber, M $30.00
Tractor, Motor Express w/Trailer, 19", Hubley, 500 series, black rubber tires, M..............................$265.00
Tractor, 21½", Marx, Mechanical Tractor w/Earth Grader, ca 1950, M...$120.00
Tractor, 3", Case, Kansas Toy & Novelty #25, tow loop, lg front & sm rear open-spoke metal wheels, M.......$40.00
Tractor, 3½", Judy Co., solid rubber, late 1940s, M $25.00
Tractor, 4", Ideal, plastic, 1948, M............................$25.00
Tractor, 8", Kingsbury, mechanical, w/driver, G $250.00

Tractor, 8", Tru-Scale, red & white, NM..............$50.00

Trailer, Graham-Bradley, 4¾", Auburn Rubber, 4-wheel, M...**$25.00**

Trailer, 4⅝", Arcade #288, 1929, VG.......................**$52.50**

Trailer, 6⅜", Arcade #286, 1929, M.......................**$80.00**

Wagon, 10", Wolverine, plastic, 1950s, EX.................**$75.00**

Wagon, 10" long, SLIK, 1952, NM.....................$175.00

Fisher-Price

Since the thirties, Fisher-Price has been one of the best-known manufacturers of toys in this country. If your toy has any plastic parts at all, you can be certain that it was made after 1949. Toys made before 1962 carry the black and white rectangular logo.

Bossy Bell, #656, NM...**$45.00**

Bouncy Racer, #8, EX...**$60.00**

Buddy Bullfrog, #728, EX......................................**$85.00**

Bunny Basket Cart, #301, M..................................**$80.00**

Bunny Cart, #401, EX+..**$325.00**

Cement Mixer, #926, G.......................................**$225.00**

Chick & Cart, #407, EX...**$65.00**

Cookie Pig, #476, NM...**$50.00**

Crackling Hen, #120, white, M...............................**$80.00**

Donald Duck Doughboy, 13½", 1941, EX..............**$475.00**

Donald Duck Xylophone, #177, VG.......................**$150.00**

Fido Zilo, #707, EX..**$95.00**

Gabby Goofies, #775, M..**$50.00**

Happy Hippo, #151, NM......................................**$140.00**

Huffy Puffy Train, #999, w/4 cars, EX....................**$125.00**

Lady Bug, #658, EX...**$40.00**

Mother Goose, #164, NM.......................................**$50.00**

Musical Duck, #795, EX-......................................**$110.00**

Musical Sweeper, #230, EX...................................**$125.00**

Playful Puppy, #626, EX...**$48.00**

Playland Express, #192, M....................................**$170.00**

Pluto Pop-Up, #440, VG..**$75.00**

Pony Chime, #137, EX..**$60.00**

Poodle Zilo, #739, VG..**$90.00**

Pudgy Pig, #478, EX..**$50.00**

Quacky Family #799, EX+.......................................**$70.00**

Sleepy Sue, #495, NM..**$58.00**

Snorky Fire Engine, #168, w/all figures, M.............**$165.00**

Teddy Bear Zilo, #777, EX...............................$125.00

Timmy Turtle, #150, EX..**$125.00**

Tiny Teddy, #635, NM..**$55.00**

Wiggily Woofer, #640, M......................................**$100.00**

Guns

One of the best-selling kinds of toys ever made, toy guns were first patented in the late 1850s. Until WWII, most were made of cast iron, though other materials were used on a lesser scale. After the war, cast iron became cost prohibitive, and steel and die-cast zinc were used. By 1950 most were made either of die-cast material or plastic. Hundreds of names can be found embossed on these little guns, a custom which continues to the present time. Because of their tremendous popularity and durability, today's collectors can find a diversity of models and styles, and prices are still fairly affordable.

See also Western Heroes.

Actoy, Buckeroo, 8", single-shot western style, VG.....**$15.00**

BJ Crossman, Spud Gun No 504, die-cast metal, marked Hollywood California, M.....................................**$15.00**

Buckle Gun, Mattel, figural derringer, push latch to fire caps, 1958, boxed, NM...**$17.50**

Daisy, Buzz Barton Special No 195, BB gun, EX.......**$100.00**
Daisy, Cinematic Picture Pistol, ca mid-1940s, M **$85.00**
Daisy, Red Ryder BB Model #111, EX+ **$80.00**
Daisy, Red Ryder Cork Carbine, plastic stock, NM.....**$50.00**
Daisy, Targetter No 118, 10¼", automatic, EX............**$25.00**
Daisy, Zooka Pop Pistol, EX **$60.00**

G-Man Automatic, sparkles when wound, Marx, VG..$30.00

Hubley, Chief, 7", single-shot western style, VG **$10.00**
Hubley, Coyote, die-cast metal, NM **$38.00**
Hubley, Dick, 4⅛", cast iron cap automatic, marked Made in USA, 1940, M...**$30.00**
Hubley, Junior Police 32, 5¼", cast iron cap pistol, marked Pat'd 2088891, 1940, M **$45.00**
Hubley, Pioneer, die-cast metal, NM **$48.00**
Hubley, Remington .36, die-cast metal, M...................**$55.00**
Kenton, Jax, 4", cast iron cap pistol, marked Pat Sept 11-23, 1930, M...**$30.00**
Kenton, Persuader, 6⅜", cast iron cap pistol, marked Made in USA Pat Appld For, 1939, NM **$60.00**
Kenton, 6⅛", cast iron cap pistol, marked Pat Sept 11-23, 1935, M...**$35.00**
Kilgore, American, 9⅜", revolving cylinder, repeater type, VG..**$125.00**
Kilgore, Big Buck, 8¼", single shot, VG **$25.00**
Kilgore, Buck, 6¼", single-shot western style, VG.......**$20.00**
Kilgore, Cavalier, 4½", cast iron cap automatic, marked Pat Appld For Made in USA, 1935, NM.......................**$40.00**
Kilgore, H-Bar-O, 7½", cast iron cap pistol, marked Made in USA, NM **$60.00**
Kilgore, Police, 5¼", Bakelite-framed cap automatic, 1940, NM **$45.00**
Kilgore, Ranger, 8½", repeater style, VG **$60.00**
Leslie Henry, Derringer, cap gun, M...........................**$35.00**
Lone Star Company, James Bond 100-Shot Repeater Cap Pistol w/silencer, 9", 1961, EX **$255.00**
Marx, Automatic Repeater Paper Pop Pistol, aluminum, #74, NM **$25.00**
Marx, Click Pistol, #32, EX **$20.00**
Marx, Glaze Away Dart Pistol, #G23, EX....................**$18.00**
Marx, Sparkling Space Gun, M....................................**$75.00**

Mattel, Burp Gun, 13", aluminum, die-cast metal & plastic, 1956, EX...**$50.00**
Mattel, Fanner, 9", revolving changer, western, VG **$35.00**
National, Wild West, 6½", cast iron cap pistol, marked Made in USA, 1930, VG **$30.00**
Nichols, Cowman, 8½", western style, VG **$30.00**
Nichols, Rancho, 6", single-shot western style, VG+ ...**$40.00**

Pirate, 9½", zinc w/cast iron hammers & trigger, double barrel, Hubley, 1941, EX $85.00
Stevens, Buffalo Bill, 7¾", cast iron cap pistol, marked Made in USA, 1940, EX...**$50.00**
Stevens, Stevens 6-Shot Rapid Load, 6½", cast iron cap pistol, marked Made in USA, 1932, VG.....................**$40.00**
Stevens, Western Boy, 7¾", repeater style, VG...........**$80.00**

Super-Numatic, 7", paper buster, LMCO, EX $25.00
Woodhaven Metal Stamping Company, Tin Tin Gun, 3x5", turn crank to make noise, NM **$20.00**
Wyandotte, Police Chief, gun & leather shoulder holster set, ca late 1940s, EX..**$20.00**
Wyandotte, Sheriff, 7½", single shot, VG.....................**$20.00**
Wyandotte, W-Dot Ranch, 8", tin clicker type, VG......**$25.00**
Wyandotte, Water Pistol #41, M.................................**$20.00**

Model Kits

Though several companies were involved in manufacturing model kits, perhaps the largest of these was Aurora. The Aurora Plastics Corporation began on a very small scale in the early 1950s and immediately found a ready market for the model airplanes and ships which they sold through hobby stores and retail chains. But the company soon expanded and during the fifties and sixties went on to become the world's leading manufacturer of quality figure model kits, producing kits for assembling figures of TV heroes, presidents, sports legends, and movie monsters. If this is an area you find yourself interested in, you'll want a copy of the book *Aurora, History and Price Guide,* by Bill Bruegman. (Note: Models mint in box are worth approximately twice as much as one 'built up' or already assembled. If the original box is present, add about 50% to the value of the assembled model.)

Addar, General Aldo, Planet of Apes, kit #104, 1974 ..**$25.00**

AMT, Corvette Hardtop/Convertible, NM in box..$25.00

AMT, Fred Flintstone Family Sedan, kit #496, 1974.....**$45.00**
AMT, Spaceship Set, kit #6677, 1984 ....**$27.50**
AMT, USS Enterprise Without Lights, kit #951, 1976 ...**$50.00**
Aurora, Apache Warrior, kit #401, 1961 ....**$150.00**
Aurora, Blackbeard, kit #463, 1965...........................**$140.00**
Aurora, Cave Bear, kit #738, 1972 ....**$35.00**
Aurora, Dimetrodon, kit #745, 1974 ....**$30.00**
Aurora, Forgotten Prisoner, kit #422, 1966...............**$240.00**
Aurora, Frankenstein's Flivver, kit #465, 1964 ....**$240.00**
Aurora, Godzilla, kit #469, 1964 ....**$360.00**
Aurora, Hulk, kit #421, 1966.....................................**$135.00**

Aurora, Hunchback of Notre Dame, kit #481, made from 1969 to 1972................$50.00

Aurora, Jerry West, kit #865, 1965 ....**$90.00**
Aurora, Jungle Swamp, kit #740, 1972......................**$60.00**
Aurora, Land of Giants Spaceship, kit #830, 1969 ....**$265.00**
Aurora, Orion, kit #252, 1975.....................................**$40.00**
Aurora, Red Knight, various issues **$30.00**
Aurora, Spiderman, kit #477, 1966............................**$150.00**
Aurora, Spindrift, kit #255, 1975 ....**$55.00**
Aurora, Vampire, kit #452, 1966 ....**$150.00**
Hawk, Beach Bunny Catchin' Rays, kit #542, 1964 .....**$45.00**
Hawk, Woodie on a Surfari, kit #165, 1970 ....**$30.00**
Lindberg, Krimson Terror, kit #272, 1965...................**$60.00**
Monogram, Frankenstein, kit #6700, Aurora reissue....**$25.00**
Monogram, Super Fuzz, Fred Flypogger, kit #104, '65.**$150.00**
MPC, Batman, kit #1702, Aurora reissue, 1984 ....**$20.00**
MPC, Darth Vader, kit #1916, 1978-80.........................**$20.00**
MPC, Spiderman, kit #1931, 1978 ....**$20.00**
Multiple, Automatic Baby Feeder, kit #955, 1965 ....**$20.00**
Multiple, Saw the Lady in Half, kit #1258, 1966..........**$45.00**
Multiple, Torture Chair, kit #980, 1966......................**$120.00**
Pyro, Der Baron, kit #166, 1970 ....**$35.00**
Remco, Flintsones Sports Car, kit #450, 1961..............**$90.00**
Remco, Flintstones Paddy Wagon, kit #452, 1961 ....**$90.00**
Revell, Busby, Afghan Yak, kit #2006, 1959, Dr Seuss **$60.00**
Revell, Flash Gordon & Martian, kit #1450, 1965........**$90.00**
Revell, James Bond 007's Moonraker, MIB **$20.00**
Revell, Surfink, kit #1306, 1965.................................**$60.00**
Ryro, Surf's Up, kit #176, 1970...................................**$40.00**

Monsters

TV shows like Land of the Giants, Lost in Space, Munsters, Addams Family, Twilight Zone, and Outer Limits have spawned some great monster toys that collectors are zeroing in on today. Universal Studios are responsible for some as well, and it's not just the monster figures that are collectible but board games, puzzles, Halloween costumes, coloring books, and gum cards too.

Creature from the Black Lagoon, board game, Hasbro, 1963, EX in 10x9", box **$100.00**
Dracula, doll, 9", Remco, 1979, NM............................**$25.00**
Dracula Mystery Game, 4 playing pieces, spinner board, Hasbro, 1963, EX in 10x19" box **$65.00**
Frankenstein, jigsaw puzzle, depicts fight w/Wolfman, Jamar, 1963, EX in 7x10" box...............................**$35.00**
Frankenstein, patch, 12", iron-on cloth, 1960s, M........**$12.00**
Frankenstein Monster, 14", T-N Company, battery operated, 6 actions, 1960s, M..**$280.00**
Godzilla, coloring book, marked Toho, 1977, NM **$12.50**
Godzilla, coloring book, 8x11", black & white photo section, Toho Co Ltd & Resource Publisher, 1977, EX.......**$20.00**
Godzilla, 10½", Bullmark Company, battery operated, 5 actions, 1960s, EX **$450.00**
Godzilla Monster, 11½", Marusan Company, battery operated, 3 actions, 1970s, M **$140.00**
Gomora Monster, 8", Bullmark Company, battery operated, w/plastic missiles, 1960s, EX................................**$165.00**

Mighty Kong, 11", Marx, battery operated, 5 actions, 1950s, EX **$240.00**

Wolfman, notebook binder, 12x12", vinyl, 1963, EX...**$20.00**

Premiums

From the early thirties until the advent of TV, kids hurried home to tune in their favorite radio show. They were glued to the set for the thirty-minute program, and these bigger-and-better-than-life heroes were a very real part of their lives. They agonized over cliff-hanger episodes and were always vastly relieved when Tom Mix (or whoever) was rescued from the 'bad guys' the very next day. These radio superstars were made even more real to the children through the premiums they could obtain for nothing more than a box top or an inner label and a few pennies for postage. Secret manuals, signet rings, decoders, compasses, flashlights, pocketknives, and badges were just a few of the items available. Who could have known that by the nineties, some of these would be worth hundreds of dollars! Even premiums issued in recent years have value.

See also Character Collectibles.

Amos & Andy, puzzle, M...............................**$65.00**

Archie & Veronica, popping heads, 1½" head on 1½" spring-loaded base, M, each...............................**$10.00**

Babes in Toyland, table decoration set, Alco Wrap premium, 1961, M **$35.00**

Blondie & Dagwood, booklet, Go To Leisureland, Westinghouse, 1940, M...............................**$14.00**

Buck Jones, ring, Buck Jones Club, EX...............................**$48.00**

Buck Rogers, badge, Flight Commander Whistle, EX..**$75.00**

Buck Rogers, charm bracelet, EX...............................**$92.50**

Buck Rogers, instruction sheet, Ring of Saturn, EX.....**$45.00**

Buck Rogers, ring, birthstone & initial, EX...............................**$185.00**

Buffalo Bill Jr, ring, relief portrait on top, brass-colored metal, TV premium, M...............................**$30.00**

Cap'n Crunch, sea cycle, plastic kit snaps together, 6x5" assembled, w/Cap'n & Seadog figures, MIB **$29.00**

Captain Midnight, badge, American Flag Loyalty, 1940, EX...............................**$45.00**

Captain Midnight, Detect-O-Scope, 1941, M **$72.00**

Captain Midnight, magnifier, Code-O-Graph, 1945, EX .**$82.50**

Captain Midnight, Whirlwind Whistling ring, 1941, EX.**$92.50**

Casper, ring, Post Toasties Corn Flakes, 1949, M **$10.00**

Cheetos Cheese Mouse, figural eraser, 2", EX.............**$12.00**

Chicken Delight, musical menu record, cardboard 33⅓ rpm, Chicken Delight Twist, NM **$12.00**

Chitty Chitty Bang Bang, car, 2-tone plastic w/cardboard wings, 1968, NM...............................**$20.00**

Cisco Kid, badge, western hat w/chain, 1950s, M **$24.00**

Coca Puffs' Sonny the Cuckoo Bird, 3" figural eraser w/2½x3½" replica of box, on 4x5" card, M...........**$18.00**

Coco Wheats, badge, Radio Club on microphone form, M...............................**$30.00**

Dick Daring, puzzle, Quaker premium, in original mailing envelope, M...............................**$65.00**

Dick Tracy, badge, Republic Pictures, EX...............**$52.50**

Dick Tracy, ring, Post Toasties Corn Flakes, 1948, M..**$30.00**

Dr Seus, McElligot's Pool Book, Crest, 1975, NM........**$12.00**

Frito Bandito, eraser, 2", figural pink rubber, Frito Lay, 1960s, EX...............................**$7.50**

Frogman, 3" plastic baking soda-powered figure, issued in boxes of Raisin Bran, 1950s, 3 in the series, each, from $5 to...............................**$15.00**

Gene Autry, ring, plastic, Dell Comics, EX...............**$35.00**

Gnome Mobile, 2" green plastic figure attached to trapeze bar, potato chip premium, 1960s, M...............**$15.00**

Henry, ring, tin, Post Toasties, dated 1949, M **$15.00**

Honeybee, spoon hanger, 2" bee figure, Nabisco, 1950s-60s, M...............................**$10.00**

Hopalong Cassidy, ring, Bar 20 Compass, M...............**$30.00**

Howdy Doody, key chain, Howdy flashes to Poll Parrot, 1950s, M...............................**$18.00**

Howdy Doody, puppet, 15", cardboard, Mars Candy, 1950s, M...............................**$60.00**

Jack Armstrong, ring, Secret Egyptian Coder Siren, Wheaties, late 1930s, M...............................**$78.00**

Jungle Book, souvenir booklet, pop-up, 1967, M........**$28.00**

Kellogg's, model, balsa wood airplane, Pep War Plane series, ca 1945, M, each...............................**$25.00**

Little King, ring, tin, Post Grape Nuts, M...............**$8.00**

Little Orphan Annie, Pep pin, M...............................**$12.00**

Lone Ranger, badge, Bond Bread Safety Club, '38, M.**$30.00**

Lone Ranger, belt, glow-in-the-dark style, 1941, M **$96.00**

Lone Ranger, pedometer, 1943, Cheerios, M **$30.00**

Lum & Abner, booklet, Family Almanac & Helpful Hints, 1936, NM **$10.00**

Olive Oyl, Pep pin, M...............................**$7.00**

Orphan Annie, clicker, Secret Guard, 1942, M...........**$42.00**

Orphan Annie, comic book, Puffed Wheat, 1938, NM...............................**$15.00**

Orphan Annie, manual, Captain Sparks' Flight Manual, 1941, NM **$45.00**

Orphan Annie, ring, w/embossed portrait, 1934, M....**$60.00**

Pancho, mask, paper, Tip Top Bread, EX...............**$15.00**

Peabody & Sherman, flicker picture, Wheat Hearts, 1960, M in package **$10.00**

Popeye, ring, metal, Post Toasties, '49, M in package.**$48.00**

Quiz Kids, postcard, 3½x5½", black & white chromolithograph, Alka-Seltzer, ca 1950, VG.................$6.50

Rin Tin Tin, ring, plastic, TV premium, 1950s, M........$18.00

Rip Masters, ring, plastic, 1950s, M.....................$12.00

Roy Rogers, ring, microscope, Quaker Oats, 1947, M.$76.00

Sergeant Preston, knife, skinning; M...........................$54.00

Sky King, ring, Magni-Glo, EX.............................$75.00

Smoky Stover, ring, Post Toasties, 1948, EX.................$7.50

Straight Arrow, manual, Secrets of Indian Lore, EX.....$28.00

Straight Arrow, ring, Magic Cave, 1988 reissue, M.......$40.00

Sunbrite, badge, Junior Nurse Corps, brass, M...........$10.00

Superman, pin, Read Superman Action Comics Magazine, 1940s, M...$45.00

Tillie the Toiler, ring, Post Toasties, 1949, M.............$10.00

Tom Corbett, decoder, cardboard, 1950s, M.............$50.00

Tom Corbett, ring, Parallo-Ray Gun, Kellogg's, 1950, M.$20.00

Tom Corbett, ring, Rocket Scout, Kellogg's, 1950, M.....$20.00

Tom Mix, arm patch, Tom Mix Bar on checkerboard design, predominately red, 1947, M.................................$44.00

Tom Mix, badge, Straight Shooters, Ralston, EX.........$45.00

Tom Mix, bandanna, w/brand, EX.........................$68.00

Tom Mix, book, Life of Tom Mix, Ralston Straight Shooters, EX...$65.00

Tom Mix, bracelet, w/4 charms, EX.........................$70.00

Tom Mix, charm, contains genuine gold ore under plastic dome, 1940, M..$42.00

Tom Mix, ID bracelet, M.......................................$54.00

Tom Mix, medal, Straight Shooters, silver, M..............$65.00

Tom Mix, pocketknife, Straight Shooters, Ralston, EX.$65.00

Twinkles & His Pals, Little Golden Record, 7x8" Twinkles & his jungle friends on sleeve, scarce, EX.................$35.00

Ramp Walkers

Though ramp-walking figures were made as early as the 1870s, ours date from about 1935 on. They were made in Czechoslovakia from the twenties through the forties and in this country during the fifties and sixties by Marx, who made theirs of plastic. John Wilson of Watsontown, Pennsylvania, sold his worldwide. They were known as 'Wilson Walkies' and stood about 4½" high. But the majority has been imported from Hong Kong.

Astro & Rosie, Marx, M..$80.00

Black cat w/red ball, EX..$15.00

Brer Rabbit, Marx, M..$30.00

Donald Duck, w/wheelbarrow, Marx, 1960s, NM.......$40.00

Duck, yellow...$15.00

Duck w/3 babies walking behind, NM......................$28.00

Elephant, M...$20.00

Flintstones, Fred & Barney, Marx, EX......................$37.50

Flintstones, Pebbles & Dino, Marx, EX.....................$65.00

Hap & Hop (soldiers), 2¾", light wear.......................$25.00

Jungle animal w/rider, plastic, Marx, 1970s, M, any....$25.00

Kangaroo, M in package..$30.00

Little King & guard, ca 1956, EX.............................$60.00

Mickey Mouse, M...$40.00

Penguin, wood & composite, Wilson, EX..................$25.00

Popeye, pushing wheelbarrow spinach can, late '50s...$50.00

Rider on horse, Marx, MIB....................................$35.00

Santa & Mrs Claus, M...$40.00

Santa w/open bag, Marx, M....................................$40.00

Workman w/barrel, M..$22.50

Yogi Bear & Huckleberry Hound, 3¾", Made in Hong Kong $50.00

2 (of the 3) Pigs, Marx, M......................................$40.00

Robots

As early as 1948, Japanese toy manufacturers introduced their toy robots. Some of the best examples were made in the fifties, during the 'golden age' of battery-operated toys. They became more and more complex, and today some of these in excellent condition may bring well over $1,000.00. By the sixties, more and more plastic was used in their production, and the toys became inferior.

Acrobat Robot, 4½", S-H Company, battery operated, 3 actions, M..$80.00

Attacking Martian Robot, 11½", S-H Company, battery operated, 7 actions & 2 cycles, 1950s, M...................$240.00

Busy Robot, Japan, wheelbarrow missing, VG.........$150.00

Cragstan Astronaut, 13½", lithographed tin & plastic, NM in original box $1,200.00

Cragstan's Mr Robot, 10½", Y Company, battery operated, 4 actions, 1960s, G..................................$300.00

Electric Remote Control Robot, 7½", M-T Company, battery operated, 4 actions, 1950s, G..............................$400.00

Engine Robot, 9½", S-H Company, battery operated, 4 actions, 1960s, M..................................$120.00

Excavator Robot, 10", S-H Company, battery operated, 4 actions, 1960s, EX..................................$270.00

Fighting Robot, 11", lithographed tin, battery operated, yellow light on head, EX..................................$225.00

Golden Roto Robot, 8½", S-H Company, battery operated, 5 actions, 1960s, M..................................$180.00

I'm Robot, 4", push puppet, silver-colored plastic on round base, marked Kohner Brothers Inc, 1970s, EX......$35.00

Lost in Space, 16", marked Remco, original box, EX .$200.00

Mars Explorer, 9½", S-H Company, battery operated, 7 actions, 1950s, EX..................................$200.00

Mechanic Robot, 12", Y Company, battery operated, 5 actions, 1960s, EX..................................$180.00

Mr Atom the Electronic Walking Robot, 17", Advance Doll & Toy Co, battery operated, 6 actions, 1950s, EX..................................$750.00

Mr Machine, 20", plastic w/moving arms & legs, mouth opens & he makes noise, Ideal, 1977, EX............$25.00

Mr Sandman, 11", Wolverine, EX................................$325.00

Radar Robot, 12", S-H Company, battery operated, 5 actions, 1970s, M..................................$140.00

Radar Robot, 8", battery-operated eyes light up, marked Japan, EX..................................$400.00

Robert the Robot, 14", crank action w/voice, remote control, Ideal, 1950s, EX $165.00

Robot-7, 4", bullet-shaped tin wind-up, Japan, EX......$20.00

Robotron RT-2, 14½", w/smoking device..............$28.00

Smoking Robot, 10", M-T Company, plastic, battery operated, 4 actions, 1960s, M $120.00

Sparking Robot, 7", silver plastic w/square head & torso, SY, Japan, VG $110.00

Super Giant Robot, 15½", S-H Company, battery operated, 6 actions, 1960s, M..................................$240.00

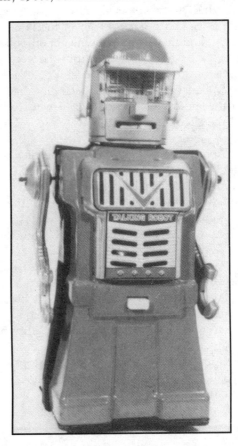

Talking Robot, 11¼", Yonezawa, painted & lithographed tin & plastic, speaks individual sentences, VG+..................................$550.00

Turn Signal Robot, 11", T-N Company, battery operated, 5 actions, 1960s, M..................................$320.00

Venus Robot, 5½", blue plastic w/red arms & tin litho face, remote control, KO Japan, 1960s, EX..................$400.00

Vision Robot, 11¾", S-H Company, battery operated, 5 actions, 1960s, M..................................$280.00

X-70 Robot, 12¼", T-N Company, battery operated, 5 actions, 1960s, EX..................................$750.00

Zem-21 Star Team Humanoid, 10", chrome w/green rubber head, Ideal, 1977, MIB..................................$20.00

Ships

Atwood Motors, California Amazon Side-Wheeler, plastic & metal, 1950s, EX..................................$300.00

Barclay, battleship, #373, M $55.00

Buddy L, 49 LST, 12", M..................................$65.00

Ideal, destroyer, 15", plastic, M..................................$250.00

Manoil, submarine, #79, lead alloy, M..................................$25.00

Marx, Mosquito Fleet Putt Putt Boat, EX..................$120.00

Remco, Mighty Matilda Aircraft Carrier, 35", M..........$150.00

Renwal, Viking Ship, 17", #245, ca 1955, EX $125.00

Thomas Toys, Battleship, 5½", plastic, EX.....................$4.50

Thomas Toys, Swamp Buggy, #487, plastic, w/motor, M .$20.00

Tootsietoy, battleship, Midget series, M..................$5.00

Slot Car Racers

Kids in the '70s were really into slot car racing. Any family with boys had a track set up in the family room or the basement, and that's where the neighborhood kids congregated. Slot cars ranged in size from the very small HO scale models up to some that were about 10" long. Transformers supplied the track with electricity that was conducted to the motors of the cars via a wire receptor that completed the circuit.

HO Scale, Aurora AFT, #1919, Magna-Traction Datsun Baja Pickup, NM...**$10.00**

HO Scale, Aurora AFT, Volkswagon Thing, NM.........**$10.00**

HO Scale, Aurora AFX, #1902, Porsche, white w/green stripes, yellow circles & #2, M **$12.00**

HO Scale, Aurora AFX, #1904, Dodge Charger Stock Car, yellow w/black hood & #11, M **$15.00**

HO Scale, Aurora AFX, #1904, Plymouth Road Runner, red & blue w/#43, EX..**$15.00**

HO Scale, Aurora AFX, #1905, Ferrari 512M, blue w/white trim & #2, M **$14.00**

HO Scale, Aurora AFX, #1927, Corvette, chrome w/red stripe, M...**$12.00**

HO Scale, Aurora AFX, #1975, Chevelle Stocker, orange w/#17, M..**$15.00**

HO Scale, Aurora AFX, Baja Bug Volkswagon, w/case, M...**$15.00**

HO Scale, Aurora AFX, blue, #3, M.........................$22.00

HO Scale, Aurora AFX, Plymouth Roadrunner, #43, NM...**$20.00**

HO Scale, Aurora AFX, Shadow, M **$10.00**

HO Scale, Aurora AFX, 1929 Model A Woodie, w/case, M...**$15.00**

HO Scale, Aurora Model Motoring, McLaren, Elva, 1960s, M...**$15.00**

HO Scale, Aurora T-Jet, #1374, Ford GT, MIB **$32.50**

1/32 Scale, Cox, Ford GT, w/instructions, MIB...........**$70.00**

1/32 Scale, Eldon, Ferrari P-3, red, EX **$20.00**

1/32 Scale, Eldon, 1968 Charger, VG.......................**$60.00**

1/32 Scale, Marx, 1957 Corvette, EX.........................**$35.00**

1/32 Scale, Revell, Hi-Bank Raceway Set, w/Cougar & Fire Bird, MIB **$120.00**

1/32 Scale, Revell, Mustang Fastback, EX **$40.00**

1/32 Scale, Strombecker, Chaparral, EX.....................**$40.00**

1/32 Scale, Strombecker, Lola, M.............................**$45.00**

1/32 Scale, Strombecker, Lotus, EX **$38.00**

1/64 Scale, Ertl, #1869, Cannonball Run Ferrari, die-cast metal, 1981, M on card.....................................**$20.00**

1/64 Scale, Ertl, #1942, Richard Petty #43 Stock Car, die-cast metal, 1980s, M on card....................................**$45.00**

Teddy Bears

Though the top-of-the-line collectible bears are those made by Steiff, there have been several other companies whose teddies are just about as high on many collectors' want lists. Hermann, Ideal, and Schuco are just a few, and even high-quality bears produced during the past ten years have collector potential; so with that in mind, hang on to the more modern bears as well.

American, 12", black & white mohair, straw stuffed, plastic eyes, floss nose, felt pads, squeaker, 1940s, EX .**$100.00**

American, 13", jointed, long rust mohair, straw & kapok stuffed, tin decal eyes, velveteen pads, growler, ca 1930, NM **$275.00**

American, 14", rust color cotton plush, open/close painted inset eyes, pompom nose, ca 1920-40.................**$150.00**

American, 16", jointed, burnished gold long-pile mohair, straw stuffed, sm eyes, worn felt pads, music box, ca 1930 ....**$325.00**

American, 23", jointed, thick gray mohair, oversize head, lg amber glass eyes, straw stuffed, ca 1930, EX.....**$375.00**

American, 24", gold cotton plush, straw & reprocessed cotton stuffed, glass eyes, white felt pads, squeaker, ca 1930, EX..**$285.00**

American, 25", gold & brown cotton plush, clothes sewn as body, inset painted vinyl snout, glass eyes, mid-1940s, EX...**$45.00**

American, 5", jointed, tan mohair, felt pads w/airbrushed claws, sewn nose & mouth, Character tag, '60s....**$40.00**

Animal Fair, 9", synthetic fleece w/foam-stuffed head, pellet-stuffed body, plastic eyes, felt nose, 1974, EX........**$6.00**

Animal Toys Plus, 16", brown plush, plastic eyes, felt nose, mouth & tongue, removable clothes, 1979, NM ...**$18.00**

Berg, 5¾", bright gold wool & cotton plush, plastic eyes, floss nose & mouth, marked Made in Austria on tag, 1946 on..**$50.00**

Character Novelty, 22", synthetic plush, styrofoam pellet stuffed, red felt mouth & black nose, glass eyes, ca 1970, EX..**$35.00**

Clemens, 9", unjointed, white mohair w/self-fabric vest, mohair pads, original blue rayon ribbon at neck, ca 1960 ....**$65.00**

Dakin, 12", Misha, 1980 Olympic mascot, stuffed plush made-to-body suit, Olympic belt printed on, M ...**$35.00**

Eden Toys, 14", thick gold plush, nylon fiber stuffed, floss nose & felt mouth, velveteen pads, ca 1975, missing eye, VG...**$18.00**

England, 12", golden yellow, jointed limbs, glass eyes, tags on feet read: Made...for Kaufmann's 5th Ave, 1940s, EX..**$80.00**

German, 15", jointed, excelsior stuffed, button eyes, w/hump, ca 1900s, EX...................................**$375.00**

German, 16", jointed, light gold mohair, straw stuffed, clear glass eyes, hump, 1920s, minimum value..........**$500.00**

Hermann, 5", long golden-tan mohair, on all fours, jointed neck, plastic eyes, floss nose & mouth, felt pads, ca 1970s..**$75.00**

Ideal, 12", light strawberry blonde mohair w/inset snout, straw & cotton stuffed, glass eyes, plastic snout, 1950, EX..**$75.00**

Ideal, 14", tan & cream plush, painted vinyl face, sleep eyes w/bristle eyelashes, ca 1955, VG **$25.00**

Japan, 11", wire jointed, sparse gold mohair, straw stuffed, tiny glass eyes, skinny limbs, squeaker, original bow, NM **$65.00**

Japan, 8", jointed, rayon velour, straw stuffed, glass eyes, thread nose & mouth, original collar w/rivet, ca 1930, M..**$65.00**

Knickerbocker, 15", tan wooly plush, hard stuffed head w/plastic eyes, felt nose on inset snout, original tag, 1960 ....**$25.00**

Knickerbocker, 15", unjointed, brown plush, painted vinyl face & ears w/closed eyes, ca 1955, VG **$25.00**

Merrythought, 15", jointed, gold mohair, straw & cotton stuffed, plastic eyes, embroidered claws, growler, 1984, NM **$85.00**

Schuco, 2½", caramel mohair, w/tag marked West Germany, M..**$250.00**

Sebastian, 24", finely carved wood face & paws, fully jointed, designed by Raikes for Applause, 1985, sold for $90, now...$250.00

Steiff, 10½", jointed, gold mohair, straw stuffed, glass eyes, 4 claws, vertical floss nose, long feet, 1950s, NM..**$325.00**

Steiff, 11½", replica of 1938 panda, jointed, mohair, felt pads, self-standing feet, squeeze voice box, 1984-85, NM **$175.00**

Steiff, 13", jointed, gold mohair, straw stuffed, glass eyes, slight hump, long arms, sloped snout, 1950s, EX.**$375.00**

Twyford, 12½", jointed, gold mohair, straw & cotton stuffed, red felt pads, plastic eyes, embroidered nose, ca 1960, EX..**$125.00**

Unknown manufacturer, 10", Hot-Cha, black long-pile mohair, kapok & straw stuffed, glass eyes, squeaker, ca 1929, EX **$200.00**

Unknown manufacturer, 11½", various patchwork gray wool fabrics, wire jointed, straw stuffed, glass eyes, 1920s, EX..**$185.00**

Unknown manufacturer, 13", extra-long gold mohair, straw stuffed, clear glass eyes, squeaker, ca 1930, EX .**$275.00**

Unknown manufacturer, 16½", long-pile white mohair, straw & cotton stuffed, amber glass eyes, clipped nose, 1940s, M..**$175.00**

Unknown manufacturer, 23", drum major, gold plush head on made-to-body outfit, straw stuffed, glass eyes, ca 1920, NM **$450.00**

Unknown manufacturer, 24", mohair, straw stuffed, shoe button eyes, swivel head, jointed limbs, hump on back, repaired $300.00

Unknown manufacturer, 4", jointed, champagne mohair, straw stuffed, glass eyes, inset snout, cotton pads, squeaker, 1930s..**$125.00**

Unknown manufacturer, 4½", wire jointed, bright gold mohair, straw stuffed, amber glass eyes, floss nose, ca 1950 ....**$75.00**

Unknown manufacturer, 9", jointed, sparce gold mohair on pink backing, straw stuffed, glass eyes, squeaker, ca 1920-30 ....**$125.00**

Toy Soldiers

For a thoroughly definitive book on this subject, you must get a copy of Richard O'Brien's book, *Collecting Toy Soldiers*. It covers them all, from plastic dimestore soldiers to those he calls 'connoisseur category.' In our listings, values are given for Britians in excellent condition; all others are for mint condition examples. A soldier in only 'very good' shape is one that has obviously seen use, has signs of wear and aging, but retains most of its paint and has a generally good appearance. In this condition, it would be worth only half of mint value. Grades in between would be evaluated accordingly.

Barclay, B002, cowboy on horse $24.00
Barclay, B005, flagbearer, tin helmet, short stride $22.00
Barclay, B013, sniper, kneeling, firing, long stride, tin helmet, M...$20.00
Barclay, B018, soldier, charging, short stride...............$15.00
Barclay, B038, West Point cadet, long stride...............$16.00
Barclay, B048, Indian chief $14.00
Barclay, B059, Marine, long stride $16.00
Barclay, B074, soldier bomb thrower $15.00
Barclay, B086, sharpshooter, standing, short stride $18.00
Barclay, B091, soldier, w/gas mask & rifle, charging ..$16.00
Barclay, B104, lying wounded, tin helmet $14.00
Barclay, B110, cook holding roast $26.00
Barclay, B147, soldier wireless operator $31.00
Barclay, B158, man passenger, overcoat over arm......$10.00
Barclay, B163, boy...$11.00
Barclay, B170, shoeshine boy......................................$12.00
Barclay, B176, boy skater...$11.00
Barclay, B186, policeman, arm raised $16.00
Barclay, B189, mailman..$14.00
Barclay, B195, Santa Claus on skis..............................$46.00
Barclay, B1954, pirate..$15.00
Barclay, B199, man pulling children on sled $50.00
Barclay, B202, kneeling, firing rifle..............................$35.00
Barclay, B206, prone machine gunner $18.00
Barclay, B211, marching, rifle slung $22.00
Barclay, B219, 2-soldier crew at radar equipment, pod foot series $23.00
Barclay, B223, 2-soldier crew, AA gun, pod foot series .$24.00
Barclay, B234, soldier charging, pod foot series..........$13.00
Barclay, B239, Marine, pod foot series........................$14.00
Barclay, B244, aviator, pod foot series........................$12.00
Barclay, B261, soldier w/bazooka, pod foot series $13.00
Barclay, B269, firing bazooka, pod foot series $60.00
Barclay, B287, mailman, pod foot series $9.00
Barclay, B294, groom, pod foot series $10.00
Barlcay, B275, policeman, pod foot series $9.00
Benton, BT24, masked bandit, left hand pointing rearward, plastic..$5.00
Benton, BT60, bugler, WWII helmet, plastic, October 1, 1949..$5.00
Britains, #121, Royal West Surry Infantrymen, standing, firing, third version..$16.00
Britains, #1258, Knights in Armour, herald, w/trumpet.$32.00
Britains, #1349, Royal Canadian Mounted Police, trooper, mounted, summer dress, ca 1934-66 ....$20.00
Britains, #137, Royal Army Medical Service, doctor.....$25.00
Britains, #141, French Infantry of the Line, trooper, slope arms, late version...$25.00

Britains, #1426, St John Ambulance, stretcher-bearer..$25.00
Britains, #162, Boy Scout Encampment, saluter...........$28.00
Britains, #196, Greek Evzones, black vest, slope arms, postwar, each $17.00
Britains, #2009, Belgian Grenadiers in Greatcoats, trooper, slope arms $16.00

Britains, #2011, Royal Air Force, 22 pieces, EX paint $300.00

Britains, #207, Officers & Petty Officers of the Royal Navy, Midshipman or Petty Officer, each $20.00
Britains, #2098, Venezuelan Military School Cadets, slope arms $30.00
Britains, #230, US Sailors, blue jackets, set of 8, each.$15.00
Britains, #429, Scots Guards & the Life Guards in Winter Dress, trooper, on foot $14.00
Britains, #69, Pipes of Scots Guards, piper, pre-1942..$22.00
Britains, #706a, British Infantry, service dress, ca 1935, set of 8, each..$9.00
Britains, #7250, Detail Contemporary British Troops, Scots Guards, plastic, ca 1971, set of 6 ....$25.00
Britains, #77, Gordon Highlanders, piper, round base, early prewar...$24.00
Britains, #88, Seaforth Highlanders, running, plug-in hand & rifle, first version $40.00
Britains, #94S, Fort Range British Foot Guards, marching, slope arms, 1950-59 ....$10.00
Britains, H301, Herald Khaki Infantry in Battledress, infantryman, at attention, plastic, marked Britain ...$6.00
Britains, H603, Herald Cowboys & Indians, cowboy, kneeling, firing gun, marked Hong Kong.......................$3.00
Britains, H605, Herald Cowboys & Indians, cowboy, standing, firing twin guns, marked Britain $4.00
Britians, #2082, Goldstream Guards, trooper at attention.$13.00
Grey Iron, F5, horse, American Family series $7.00
Grey Iron, G002, Colonial foot officer.......................$25.00
Grey Iron, G008, cadet officer $25.00
Grey Iron, G025, US Doughboy, port arms, early $17.00
Grey Iron, G038, US Calvary officer $35.00
Grey Iron, G047, Indian brave, shielding eyes $22.00
Grey Iron, G053, cowboy..$13.00
Grey Iron, G063, US Sailor, blue, early $17.00
Grey Iron, G093, knight in armor $16.00
Grey Iron, G108, Foreign Legion officer $28.00
Grey Iron, H11, milkman, American Family series $12.00
Grey Iron, R10, burro, American Family series...........$15.00
Grey Iron, T10, newsboy, American Family series $12.00

Johillco, J173, Infantryman, slope arms, WWI helmet ...**$8.00**
Johillco, J48, kneeling Indian, firing bow & arrow **$9.00**
Johillco, J79, Scots Guards, marching **$8.00**
Jones, J003, German, machine gunner, prone **$140.00**
Jones, J012, seated w/rifle **$76.00**
Jones, J022, seated w/phone **$90.00**
Jones, J029, standing, firing rifle **$90.00**
Jones, J037, farmer **$13.00**
Manoil, M005, parade, stocky version **$16.00**
Manoil, M015, drummer, vertical drum **$35.00**
Manoil, M023, sailor, hollow base **$44.00**
Manoil, M031, cowboy, second version **$18.00**
Manoil, M053, wounded soldier, lying **$16.00**
Manoil, M060, aviator **$20.00**
Manoil, M068, field doctor, crawling **$60.00**
Manoil, M079, bicycle dispatch rider **$26.00**
Manoil, M103, anti-tank gun, squared shield **$30.00**
Manoil, M111, soldier trench mortar **$25.00**
Manoil, M121, firefighter, white **$75.00**
Manoil, M130, girl, Happy Farm series **$9.00**
Manoil, M167, farmer, water pump, Happy Farm series **$22.00**
Manoil, M175, sniper, thin, ca late 1945 ....**$28.00**
Manoil, M189, soldier in poncho **$39.00**
Manoil, M207, cowboy rider, My Ranch Corral series .**$10.00**
Manoil, M215, cow feeding, My Ranch Corral series ...**$12.00**
Manoil, M220, sm horse, My Ranch Corral series **$25.00**
Manoil, M61, hostess, green **$60.00**
Marx, Daniel Boone, 54mm, soft plastic, 9-piece set,
each **$30.00**
Marx, Fort Apache Frontiersmen, 60mm, vinyl, each **$5.00**
Marx, Robin Hood, except Richard Greene, each **$14.00**
Marx, Spacemen, 70mm, soft plastic, without helmet, ca
1950s **$10.00**
Marx, Super Circus, 40mm, soft plastic, each **$12.00**
Marx, War of 1812 Sailors, 60mm, soft plastic, each ...**$20.00**
Marx, Wild Animals, 3", soft plastic, each **$3.00**
Marx, 21Ma, French Infantry **$8.00**
Marx, 25Ma, German Infantry **$8.00**
Marx, 35Ma, tank commander, standing........................**$8.00**
Timpo, WW2011, Cowboys & Indians, cowboy, mounted,
firing rifle at side...**$16.00**
Timpo, 9000, US Infantry, GI, at ease...........................**$16.00**

Trains

Lionel is a name that is almost synonymous with toy trains. The Lionel company was the one that introduced the O guage to the public in 1915, and it became the industry's standard for years to come. Some of their best toys came from the period of 1923 to 1940, when in addition to their trains they also brought out an extensive line of special sets. They bought out their competitors, the Ives corporation, in 1928, and except for the years from 1929 until 1934 when the nation was crippled by financial collapse and during WWII, they remained a giant industry. Sales began to decline in the fiftes, but even today, Lionel trains are being made in limited numbers.

Some of the other toy companies whose trains you may encounter are American Flyer, Marx, Buddy L, Tootsietoy, Unique, and Manoil. All these companies are included in *American Premium Guide to Electric Trains* by Richard O'Brien.

American Flyer C2009, S gauge gondola, Texas & Pacific on
light green, Pike Master, 1962-64, EX **$8.00**
American Flyer 1097, 0 gauge locomotive, lithographed tin,
orange, green & red w/nickel trim, EX **$145.00**
American Flyer 1114, 0 gauge caboose, American Flyer
lettered in white on red w/green stripes, brass trim,
EX **$60.00**
American Flyer 24422, S gauge reefer, Great Northern on
light green, Pike Master, 1965-66, EX **$80.00**
American Flyer 24631, S gauge caboose, AFL, yellow,
knuckle coupler, Pike Master, 1959-61, EX..........**$12.00**
American Flyer 26782, trestle set, EX...........................**$45.00**
American Flyer 293, S gauge steam locomotive, NYNH &
Hartford, Pacific, knuckle coupler, 1953-58, EX ...**$55.00**
American Flyer 3150, 0 gauge baggage car, 2-tone orange
w/nickel & brass trim, EX..**$72.00**
American Flyer 4042, standard gauge observation car,
maroon, EX **$120.00**
American Flyer 484, 0 gauge caboose, EX **$30.00**
American Flyer 632, S gauge hopper, Virginian, link coupler,
1946-49, EX..**$40.00**
American Flyer 719, S gauge coal dump car, CB&Q on
maroon, link coupler, 1950-54, EX **$65.00**
American Flyer 9100, S gauge tank car, Gulf, knuckle cou-
pler, 1979, M **$30.00**
Auburn Rubber, 1574, dump car, 5¼", pre-WWII, M .**$15.00**
Auburn Rubber 525, train set, locomotive-tender, coal car,
gondola, caboose & 3 trainsmen, ca 1958, M **$80.00**
Barclay 335, 3-Piece Train Set, New York Central Railroad,
locomotive, tender & observation car, ca post WWII,
M **$20.00**
Buddy L 54, 2" gauge rock car, red, 1929-31, VG **$150.00**
Dorfan, 0 gauge pullman, Seattle & Dorfan Lines on red
w/brass trim, 1924-33, EX..**$72.00**
Dorfan 494, 0 gauge observation car, green & maroon
w/brass trim, 1924-33, EX..**$90.00**
Dorfan 800, wide gauge gondola, 1924-33, EX **$110.00**
Ives 11, 0 gauge steam locomotive, black boiler & cab, 3
separate boiler bands, w/tender, 1914-16, EX **$145.00**
Ives 123, 0 gauge lumber car, 9" long, maroon, load held by
4 chains, 1925-28, EX..**$50.00**
Ives 131, 0 gauge baggage car, lithographed steel, Ives Rail-
way Baggage Express on orange, 1930, EX..........**$55.00**
Ives 1810, 0 gauge locomotive, green body w/red roof &
yellow trim, box cab, brass pantograph, electric, 1931-
32, EX **$95.00**
Ives 20-192, standard gauge box car, American Flyer body
on 2 4-wheel Ives trucks, brass plates, sliding doors,
1928-29 ....**$175.00**
Ives 203, transformer, EX **$10.00**
Ives 3245, standard gauge locomotive, stamped steel, center
cab, die-cast wheels, nickel tires, electric, '29, VG .**$500.00**

Ives 54, 0 gauge gravel car, hand-painted tin body, 4 cast iron wheels, 1903-04, EX..................................$100.00

Kansas Toy & Novelty 36, locomotive, 4½", lead alloy, 1923-1930s, M..................................**$20.00**

Lionel HO-301-16, HO gauge cargo bin, EX.................**$5.00**

Lionel HO-431, HO gauge landscape set, 1959, M......**$20.00**

Lionel HO-602, HO scale steam locomotive, 1960, M.**$50.00**

Lionel HO-713, HO gauge pullman car, Santa Fe, 1961, EX **$15.00**

Lionel HO-809, HO gauge helium car, 1961, M..........**$38.00**

Lionel HO-819-225, HO gauge work caboose, Santa Fe, 1960, M..................................**$26.00**

Lionel HO-865-300, HO gauge gondola w/crates, 1963, M..................................**$26.00**

Lionel 1029, transformer, 25 watt, 1936, M..................**$5.00**

Lionel 1043, transformer, 60 watt, 1953, M **$20.00**

Lionel 1120, 027 gauge steam locomotive, Scout, 1950, M..................................**$50.00**

Lionel 1122-100, 027 gauge switch control, 1957, M **$5.00**

Lionel 113, standard gauge station, 1931-34, VG.......**$275.00**

Lionel 125, whistle station, gray on green base, 1950-55, M..................................**$50.00**

Lionel 1615, 027 steam locomotive switcher, w/#1615 tender, EX..................................**$140.00**

Lionel 162, standard gauge dump truck, red, 1930, EX.**$60.00**

Lionel 1701, 027 gauge coach, streamliner, chrome, 1935, M..................................**$40.00**

Lionel 1877, 0 gauge horse car, 1959, M **$90.00**

Lionel 192, railroad control tower, 1959-60, EX.........**$125.00**

Lionel 202, 027 gauge diesel locomotive, Alco A, orange w/black letters, 1957, M **$100.00**

Lionel 2036, 027 gauge steam locomotive, w/#6466 tender, 1950, M..................................**$100.00**

Lionel 213, standard gauge cattle car, orange body w/green roof, 1926-40, EX **$175.00**

Lionel 218, 027 gauge diesel locomotive, Alco AB, ATSF, 1961, EX..................................**$80.00**

Lionel 221, 027 gauge steam locomotive, gray, EX ...**$120.00**

Lionel 2443, 0 gauge observation car, brown sheet metal, 1956, M..................................**$90.00**

Lionel 247, 027 gauge steam locomotive, B&O, '59, M.**$50.00**

Lionel 256, freight shed, 1950-53, M...........................**$50.00**

Lionel 263E, 0 gauge steam locomotive, gun metal gray, 1936, EX **$350.00**

Lionel 338, standard gauge observation car, Mojave, M..**$110.00**

Lionel 397, standard gauge diesel coal loader, blue motor cover, 1948-57, M..................................**$110.00**

Lionel 422, standard gauge observation car, Tempel, light blue body w/dark blue roof, 1930, EX................**$500.00**

Lionel 456, coal ramp & hopper car, 1950-55, EX.....**$100.00**

Lionel 5104, 0 gauge lane changeover, 1963, M...........**$1.00**

Lionel 514R, standard gauge refrigerator car, ivory body w/peacock roof, 1929, EX..................................**$125.00**

Lionel 529, 0 gauge pullman car, green, 1926, M........**$50.00**

Lionel 58, 027 gauge locomotive rotary snowplow, green shell w/white cab, 1959-61, EX..................................**$600.00**

Lionel 614, 027 gauge diesel locomotive, Alaska Railroad, blue w/yellow structure on roof, 1959-60, M......**$270.00**

Lionel 618, 0 gauge observation streamliner, black & chrome, 1935, M **$90.00**

Lionel 6445, 0 gauge Fort Knox Gold car, silver w/4 clear windows, shows gold bullion, 1961, M................**$80.00**

Lionel 646, 0 gauge steam locomotive, w/tender, 1954, EX **$125.00**

Lionel 700E, 0 gauge electric locomotive, New York Central, dark green, 1913-16, EX **$375.00**

Lionel 8, standard gauge locomotive, 1920s, red, VG .**$150.00**

Lionel 9210, 0 gauge automobile car, Baltimore & Ohio, 1970-72, M..................................**$26.00**

Lionel 962, turnpike set, plastic, 1958, 24 pieces, M ...**$20.00**

Marx, station, 5x10x13⅝", Glendale Freight Depot, lithographed tin, w/lamppost & mechanical gate, NM **$40.00**

Marx 10, HO gauge diesel locomotive switcher, blue w/yellow stripe, NM..................................**$20.00**

Marx 11874, HO gauge box car, plastic, Great Northern in white letters on green, NM..................................**$3.00**

Marx 1235, caboose, 7", tin, Southern Pacific in white letters on silver, 4 wheels, NM..................................**$6.00**

Marx 28233, HO gauge hopper, plastic, Virginian in white letters on brown, NM..................................**$5.00**

Marx 320, HO gauge work caboose, Monon in white letters on red, w/boom, NM..................................**$9.00**

Marx 3903, HO gauge caboose, Union Pacific in white letters on red, w/bay window, NM..................................**$3.00**

Marx 78450, HO gauge tank car, plastic, GATX & Hooker in black letters on gray, NM..................................**$3.00**

Marx 956, caboose, 7", tin, Nickel Plate Road in black & white letters on red & gray, 4 wheels, NM...........**$10.00**

Revell 4060, HO gauge caboose, Union Pacific, NM...**$15.00**

Tootsietoy, caboose, M..................................**$15.00**

Tootsietoy, gondola, DB&Co, black, M.......................**$15.00**

Tootsietoy, locomotive, Union Pacific, M...................**$30.00**

Tootsietoy, stock car, Pioneer Stock Shippers lettered on side, M..................................**$15.00**

Unique 1950, locomotive, 10", lithographed tin, Unique Lines lettered in white, electric, w/reverse & headlight, NM **$40.00**

Transformers

The first Transformers appeared on the toy shelves of America in 1984. Originally there were 28, 18 of which were Autobots, cars that became heroic warriors who desperately tried to terminate the evil Decepions (the other 10). These became so popular that the line was expanded to contain more than 200 different figures. Hasbro discontinued the Transformers late in 1990, but today their fans continue to clamor for more, and recently a new, limited edition series has been produced.

Autobot, Groundshaker, M...**$27.50**

Autobot, Hot House, M **$10.00**

Autobot, Inferno, MIB...**$25.00**

Autobot, Ironworks, M **$10.00**

Autobot, Tanker Truck, M..................................$22.50
Constructicon, Mixmaster, 1984, EX.....................$8.00
Constructicon, Scavenger, MOC...........................$10.00
Deception, Air Strike Control, set of 4, MIB.............$15.00
Deception, Airwave, M.....................................$10.00

Deception, Apeface, EX $14.00
Deception, Greaspit, M.....................................$10.00
Deception, Skywalker, M $32.00
Dino Bot, Slag, 1984, MOC $30.00
Insecticon, Bombshell, 1984, EX.........................$12.50
Insecticon, Kickback, 1984, M............................$15.00
Landmine, M...$18.00
Legends, Bumblebee, M $28.00
Legends, Grimlock, M......................................$35.00
Legends, Jazz, M $35.00
Legends, Starscream, M $38.00
Mini Car, Cosmos, 1985, MIB $10.00
Mini Car, Powerglide, 1985, EX...........................$8.00
Optimus Prime, M...$75.00
Quickmix, 1987, MIB..$10.00
Runamucker, 1986, MIB $25.00
Scattershot, M..$18.00

Vehicles

These are the types of toys that are intensely dear to the heart of many a collector. Having a beautiful car is part of the American dream, and over the past eighty years, just about as many models, makes, and variations have been made as toys for children, as the real vehicles for adults. Novices and advanced collectors alike are easily able to find something to suit their tastes as well as their budgets.

One area that is right now especially volatile covers those fifties and sixties tin scale-model autos imported by manufacturers from Japan, U.S. Zone Germany, and England. Since these are relatively modern, you'll still be able to find some at yard sales and flea markets at reasonable prices.

Auburn Rubber, open racer, 4¾", boat tail, no side pipes, M $40.00

Bandai, '50 BMW 600 Isetta, 9", friction, EX $200.00
Bandai, '58 Buick Century, 8", friction, NM $125.00
Bandai, '59 Austin Healey 100 Six Convertible, 8", friction, NM...$145.00
Bandai, Chevrolet Corvette, 8", friction, 1965, M.......$125.00
Bandai, Ford Thunderburd Sedan, 8", friction, '59, M.$80.00
Bandai, Lotus Elite, 8½", friction, 1950s, M $45.00
Bandai, Oldsmobile Toronado, 11", battery operated, 1966, M...$150.00
Bandai, Pontiac Firefird, 10", friction, 1967, M............$75.00
Bandai, Vespa, 9", friction, 1960s, M $125.00
Bandai, Volkswagen, 10½", battery operated, '60s, M.$75.00
Banner, LaFrance Fire Truck, 4", plastic, 1950, M........$10.00
Banner, Station Wagon, 4", Oldsmobile, 1948, M........$10.00
Barclay, '35 DeSoto Airflow, 5¼", M.........................$35.00
Barclay, Ambulance, 3½", w/sm cross, #194, M..........$40.00
Barclay, Armored Army Truck, 2⅞", #152, M.............$18.00
Barclay, Beer Truck, #377, w/barrels, M $35.00
Barclay, Cannon Truck, 4", w/movable cannon, M.....$40.00
Barclay, Hospital Truck, 2", ca 1968, M....................$12.00
Barclay, Milk Truck, 3⅝", #377, black rubber tires, M.$45.00
Barclay, Pepsi-Cola Truck, 2", 1960s, M $10.00
Barclay, Police Car, 3⅝", #317, die-cast metal, M $30.00
Barclay, Race Car, 2", no fenders, ca 1968, M.............$6.00
Barclay, Racer, 3½", w/tail fin, marked USA, M...........$35.00
Barclay, Racer, 5½", closed cockpit, M......................$35.00
Barclay, Sedan, 1⅝", 2-door style, 1960s, M..............$6.00
Barclay, Streamline Racer, 4⅜", #303, M.....................$3.00
Barclay, Volkswagen, 2", 1960s, M $6.00
Beaut Manufacturing, Police Car, 3¾", M $15.00
Best Toy & Novelty, Coupe, 3⅝", #93, streamlined style w/grid-pattern grille, open windows, rubber tires, M..........$32.00
Best Toy & Novelty, Racer, 4", #85, w/lg square fin, wood hubs w/rubber tires, 12 exhaust ports, M $20.00
Buddy L, Texaco Tanker, 25", gas station promo, M .$180.00
Buddy L, Trencher, #400, 1928-31, G $500.00
CAW Novelty, Sport Roadster, 3½", Packard, driver in open top, no windshield, horizontal grille, metal wheels, M..$40.00
CAW Novelty, Streamline Coupe, 3", #30, V-pattern grille, hood ornament, 4 open windows, sm rear fin, rubber wheels, M..$32.00
Champion, Convertible, futuristic-streamline style, black wood wheels, M...$150.00
Champion, Race Car, 5½", w/2 riders, M $250.00
Courtland, Dump Truck, 10½", friction type, w/dual rear wheels, M..$135.00
Courtland, Side-Dump Tractor-Trailer, 13", non-friction, EX $80.00
Daisy No 61 Cement Mixer, 11", plastic, battery operated, M in VG box..$95.00
Dinky, Bentley, M..$80.00
Dinky, Dodge Fire Rescue Truck, M $75.00
Dinky, Euclid Truck, M......................................$22.00
Dinky, Ford Escort, M..$15.00
Dinky, Ford Taurus, M $35.00
Dinky, Fordson Flatbed Truck, EX $30.00
Dinky, Taxi, M..$50.00

Dyna-Mo, Dump Truck, 2¾", open windows, hinged body w/realistic load of coal, dual rear wheels, M **$16.00**

Erie, Ford Pickup Truck, 5", high sides, sm rear window, M **$60.00**

Erie, Packard Roadster, 6", painted metal, M **$60.00**

Ertl, Fire Truck, 22", #9, M...**$30.00**

Ertl, Fire Truck, 7", cast iron, EX.................................**$100.00**

Ertl, Shell Tanker, 20", M...**$55.00**

Firestone, '35 Ford Sedan, 4⅞", 2-dr humpback style, M .**$60.00**

Girard, Fire Chief Car, 15", G......................................**$175.00**

Grey Iron, Airflow Sedan, 1½", M.................................**$40.00**

Grey Iron, Coupe, 1½", M **$40.00**

Hess, Tanker Truck, plastic, promotional, '68, MIB ..**$225.00**

Hess, Tanker Truck, plastic, 1985, MIB **$40.00**

Hess, Training Van, plastic, 1980, MIB.......................**$150.00**

Hot Wheels, Beach Patrol, #3922, 1983, M...................**$8.00**

Hot Wheels, Cat Dump Truck, #1171, 1980, NM **$5.00**

Hot Wheels, Custom Firebird, #6212, 1968, EX **$27.50**

Hot Wheels, Dune Daddy, #6967, 1973, EX.................**$40.00**

Hot Wheels, El Ray Special, #8273, 1974, EX..............**$25.00**

Hot Wheels, Funny Money, #6005, 1972, NM..............**$37.50**

Hot Wheels, Greased Gremlin, #2502, 1979, EX...........**$3.50**

Hot Wheels, Hoss Boss, #6407, 1971, NM....................**$38.00**

Hot Wheels, Indy Eagles, McLaren M6A, #6255, w/matching button, M on card.........................$40.00

Hot Wheels, Lotus Turbine, #6262, 1969, M **$28.00**

Hot Wheels, Mighty Maverick, #6414, 1970, EX **$28.00**

Hot Wheels, Mutt Mobile, #6185, 1971, NM................**$38.00**

Hot Wheels, Paramedic Van, #7661, 1975, EX............**$17.50**

Hot Wheels, Police Cruiser, #6963, 1974, NM.............**$32.50**

Hot Wheels, Real Riders Super Scraper, #4350, EX **$6.50**

Hot Wheels, Rescue Squad, #2204, 1981, M **$25.00**

Hot Wheels, Shell Shocker, #2518, 1986, EX.................**$2.50**

Hot Wheels, Spoiler Sport, #9641, 1977, NM.................**$7.50**

Hot Wheels, Tough Customer, #7655, 1975, NM.........**$24.00**

Hot Wheels, Tow Truck, #6450, 1970, NM...................**$35.00**

Hubley, Air Compress Truck, 7", ca 1950s, M.............**$75.00**

Hubley, Auto, die-cast metal w/black plastic wheels, ca 1950s, M...**$25.00**

Hubley, Bell Telephone Truck, 3¾", G **$90.00**

Hubley, Crash Car, 4¾", white rubber tires, M **$230.00**

Hubley, Jaguar Roadster, 9", 1950s, EX.....................**$80.00**

Hubley, Kiddietoy Motorcycle, 5", plastic, M.............**$30.00**

Hubley, Kiddietoy Racer, 6½", #457, die-cast metal w/rubber tires, M...**$55.00**

Hubley, Log Truck, #469, M..**$140.00**

Hubley, Pipe Truck, 9½", #803, ca 1950s, M..............**$70.00**

Hubley, Telephone Truck, plastic, M **$50.00**

Hubley, Wrecker, 4½", rubber wheels, 1930, EX......**$100.00**

Ideal, Cadillac Sedan, 4", plastic, 4-door, 1948, M......**$35.00**

Ideal, Ford Pickup Truck, 4", plastic, M **$35.00**

Jane Francis, Gulf Truck, 5", #447, die-cast metal w/tin cover, ca 1945, M...**$35.00**

Japan, Cadillac El Dorado, 28", friction, marked Ichiko, 1967, EX **$400.00**

Japan, Chevrolet Wagon, 12", friction, marked SY, 1959, EX **$90.00**

Japan, Chrysler, 8", friction, Yonezawa, 1955, EX **$200.00**

Japan, Dodge Yellow Cab, 12", friction, marked TN, 1968, EX **$125.00**

Japan, Ford Convertible, 11½", friction, marked Haji, 1956, G **$400.00**

Japan, Ford Fairlane Skyliner, 9", friction, marked Sankei Gangu, 1959, M...**$125.00**

Japan, Ford Mustang Convertible, 13½", battery operated, marked Yonezawa, 1965, EX **$125.00**

Japan, Lincoln Hardtop Convertible, 11", friction, marked Yonezawa, 1960, EX..**$150.00**

Japan, Lincoln Sedan, 12", friction, marked Yonezawa, 1955, EX **$325.00**

Japan, Mercedes Benz 250 SE, 14½", battery operated, marked Yanoman, 1960s, EX **$155.00**

Japan, Mercury Cougar Hardtop, 10", battery operated, marked Taiyo, 1967, M...**$65.00**

Japan, Plymouth Sedan, 12", friction, marked Ichiko, 1961, EX **$250.00**

Japan, Studebaker, 9", friction, Yoshiya, 1954, G **$150.00**

Keystone, Hydraulic Dump Truck, 26", #62, G.........**$300.00**

Kingsbury, Wrecker, 13", pressed steel, wind-up, G.**$250.00**

Lincoln Toys, Dump Truck, 7", Ontario, Canada, M....**$50.00**

Manoil, Gasoline Truck, #103, M **$20.00**

Manoil, Sport Car, #719, M **$20.00**

Manoil, Towing Truck, #714, M **$20.00**

Marx, Army Staff Car, 9", plastic, friction, M **$50.00**

Marx, Dump Truck, #1084, M.......................................**$60.00**

Marx, Fanny Farmer Candy Truck, plastic, M **$70.00**

Marx, Jeep, 11", NM...**$100.00**

Marx, Pet Shop Delivery Truck, 10", 1950s, EX **$75.00**

Marx, Side Dump Truck, #T-475, ca 1940, NM.........**$100.00**

Marx, Sparkling Hot Rod Racer, 8", plastic wind-up, 1950s, M **$75.00**

Matchbox, '11 Maxwell Roadster, #14, Models of Yesteryear, 1965, M...**$28.00**

Matchbox, '12 Packard Landaulet, #11, Models of Yesteryear, 1963, M...**$25.00**

Matchbox, '12 Simplex, #9, Models of Yesteryear, 1967, M **$40.00**

Matchbox, '26 Type 35 Bugatti, #6, Models of Yesteryear, 1961, M...**$28.00**

Matchbox, '36 Jaguar SS100, #1, Models of Yesteryear, 1977, M **$24.00**

Matchbox, '57 Chevy, #4, 1981, M $5.00
Matchbox, Atkinson Grit-Spreading Truck, #70, '65, M.$12.00
Matchbox, Beach Buggy, #30, 1971, M........................$5.00
Matchbox, BMW, #45, 1976, M.................................$9.00
Matchbox, Boss Mustang, #44, 1972, M........................$4.00
Matchbox, Cement Mixer, #3, 1953, M.......................$32.00
Matchbox, Citroen SM, #51, 1972, M $8.00
Matchbox, Container Truck, #42, 1977, M.....................$8.00
Matchbox, Daf Girder Truck, #58, 1968, M....................$8.00
Matchbox, Datsun 260Z, #67, 1978, M.........................$4.00
Matchbox, Dodge Charger MKIII, #52, 1970, M.............$7.00
Matchbox, Dodge Dumper Truck, #48, 1967, M...........$8.00
Matchbox, Excavator, #32, 1981, M $20.00
Matchbox, Ferrari, #70, 1981, M................................$4.00
Matchbox, Ford Capri, #54, 1971, M............................$8.00
Matchbox, Ford Escort RS2000, #9, 1978, M..................$5.00
Matchbox, Ford Refuse Truck, #7, 1967, M..................$10.00

Matchbox, Frehauf Grain Truck, M $65.00
Matchbox, Guildsman, #40, 1971, M............................$9.00
Matchbox, Hell Raiser, #55, 1975, M............................$5.00
Matchbox, Mercedes Tourer, #6, 1974, M $8.00
Matchbox, MGA Sports Car, #19, 1959, M...................$25.00
Matchbox, Mod Tractor, #25, 1972, M $6.00
Matchbox, Opel Diplomat, #36, 1966, M.......................$8.00

Matchbox, Pinocchio Truck, Lesney Corp, 1979, VG $23.50
Matchbox, Pontiac, #16, 1981, M $4.00
Matchbox, Prime Mover, #15, 1955, M $40.00
Matchbox, Road Dragster, #19, 1971, M.......................$7.00
Matchbox, Rolls-Royce Silver Shadow MKII, #39, M $7.00
Matchbox, Volkswagen 1200 Sedan, #25, 1958, M $50.00
Matchbox, Wildcat Dragster, #8, 1971, M....................$12.00

Matchbox, 1911 Model T Ford, #1, Models of Yesteryear, 1964, M $20.00

Nylint, Ford Tow Truck, 11", red & white, working wench, VG paint $70.00
Nylint, Hydraulic Dump Truck, 13½", #6100, NM $100.00
Nylint, Jalopy, 9⅝", #6800, M $65.00
Nylint, Lawn & Garden Service Truck, 20", #1200, w/12-piece tool set, G..$170.00
Nylint, Texaco Service Van, 12", #8300, EX $125.00
Rainbow, '35 Oldsmobile Sedan, 5", 4-door, M $55.00
Renwal, Gasoline Truck, #49, plastic, M $65.00
Slik-Toy, Sedan, 6", #9604, M....................................$25.00
Slik-Toy, Tank Truck, 6", #9607, M.............................$25.00
Smitty, Lumber Trailer, 17", #404T, NM.....................$300.00
Smitty, Stake Truck, 23½", #210, 14 wheels, EX $375.00
Steelcraft, Tank Truck, 25½", sheet metal, G $160.00

Structo, Emergency Truck, NM $85.00
Structo, Package Delivery Truck, #603, 1950s, M $120.00
Structo, Wrecker Truck, #822, wind-up, 1955, NM....$100.00
Sun Rubber, '40 Dodge, 4½", #12001, 4-door, M.........$25.00
Sun Rubber, Racer, 4⅜", #505, open, w/2 drivers, M ..$25.00
Sun Rubber, Scout Car, 6¾", #12014, w/4 gunners, 1946, M $35.00
Sun Rubber, Town Car, 5⅜", Brewster-type limo, #1015, w/driver, M...$30.00
Tonka, Cement Mixer Truck, 15½", #120, NM $100.00
Tonka, Dump Truck & Sand Loader, 23¼", #116, G ...$80.00
Tonka, Jeep Wrecker, 11", #375, 1964, M $75.00

Tonka, Military Jeep, 10½", #251, 1963, M **$60.00**
Tonka, Rescue Squad Van, 13¾", #105, EX...............**$150.00**
Tonka, Servi-Car, 9⅛", #201, 1962, M **$65.00**
Tonka, Tractor-Carry-All Trailor, 30½", 1949, EX.......**$120.00**
Tonka, Utility Hauler, 12", #175, M...............................**$150.00**
Tonka, Wrecker, 9½", #68, 1964, NM **$55.00**
Tootsietoy, Chevrolet El Camino Pickup Truck, 6", 1960,
    NM **$30.00**
Tootsietoy, Chrysler 300, 6", 2-door hardtop, 1955, M.**$25.00**
Tootsietoy, Corvette Roadster, 4", 1954-55, M.............**$25.00**
Tootsietoy, Ford Fairlane 500 Convertible, 3", '57, EX.**$18.00**
Tootsietoy, Ford Model A Sedan, #4665, EX...............**$45.00**
Tootsietoy, Ford Ranch Wagon, 3", 1954, M................**$32.00**
Tootsietoy, GMC Greyhound Scenicruiser Bus, 6", 1957,
    M **$40.00**
Tootsietoy, Lancia Racer, 6", 1956, M **$15.00**
Tootsietoy, Mack Long Distance Cargo Van, #0803, semi-
    trailer, tin top, ca 1933-36, EX................................**$90.00**
Tootsietoy, Nash Metropolitan Convertible, 3", '54, M.**$28.00**
Tootsietoy, Oil Tank Truck, #235, ca 1940-41, M........**$27.00**
Tootsietoy, Pontiac Chieftain Deluxe Coupe Sedan, 4", 1950,
    M **$30.00**
Tootsietoy, Rambler Super Cross-Country Station Wagon, 4",
    6-cylinder style, 1960, M...**$38.00**
Tootsietoy, Triumph TR3 Roadster, 3", 1956, M...........**$20.00**
Williams, Mack Truck, 3½", turned steel hub & starred axle
    peens, EX **$65.00**
Wyandotte, Army Truck, 22", EX...............................**$150.00**
Wyandotte, Coupe, 6", ca 1940, M................................**$50.00**
Wyandotte, Ice Truck, #348, marked ICE on sides, ca 1940,
    NM **$100.00**
Wyandotte, Sedan, 6", ca 1940, M **$60.00**

Wyandotte, Sportsman's Convertible, 12", VG in
    box **$185.00**
Wyandotte, Wrecker, 10", wood wheels, 1930s, NM...**$80.00**

Wind-Ups

Wind-up toys, especially comic character or personality-related, are greatly in demand by collectors today. Though most were made through the years of the thirties through the fifties, they carry their own weight against much earlier toys and are considered very worthwhile investment items. Mechanisms vary, some are key wound while others depended on lever action to tighten the main-spring and release the action of the toy. Tin and celluloid were used in their manufacture, and although it is sometimes possible to repair a tin wind-up, experts advise against putting your money into a celluloid toy whose mechanism is not working, since the material is too fragile to tolerate the repair.

Buffalo Toys, Aero Speeders, 10", carousel w/3 planes,
    screw-rod spring drive, 1920s, EX **$210.00**
Chein, Army Drummer, 7", plunger activated, '30s, EX.**$180.00**

Chein, bear w/hat, ca 1938, EX.............................**$50.00**
Chein, Cabin Cruiser, 9", 1940s, M................................**$40.00**
Chein, Marine, 6", hand on belt, 1950s, M **$200.00**
Chein, Pig, 4½", 1940s, M..**$75.00**
Courtland, City Meat Market Delivery Sedan, 2¾x7¼x3¼",
    #4000, M...**$100.00**
Courtland, ESSO Gasoline Tractor-Trailer, 3¼x13x3", #2000,
    EX **$100.00**
Courtland, Lawn Mower, 24", #15, 1950-51, M **$45.00**
Courtland, No 51 Steam Shovel, 10x16x4", #5200, M..**$90.00**

Gama, Sailor & Bum, 7", tin lithograph, German, VG,
    either one..**$120.00**
German, Bird in a Cage, 3½", M....................................**$120.00**
Girard, Goble the Gobbling Goose, M.......................**$240.00**
Irwin, Cinderella & Prince, 5", #7000, plastic, '50s,
    M..**$135.00**

Japan, cat & ball, 1950s, NM in very poor box $35.00
Japan, Clown in Hoop, 6½", EX $225.00
Kagran, Howdy Doody Air-O-Doodle Circus Train, 16" long, 1950s, M $180.00
Kellerman, Armored Vehicle, 4", 1930s, M................$110.00
Lakeside, Stan Laurel, 5", 1960s, M............................$40.00
Lehmann, Tom, 8", climbing monkey, G $140.00
Linemar, Babes in Toyland, 6½", lithographed tin Indian on roller skates, 1950s, M $320.00
Linemar, Dipsy Car, Donald Duck, 6" long, 1950s, EX .$525.00

Linemar, Donald Duck, 4x4", riding tricycle, NM.$1,000.00
Linemar, Donald Duck, Whirling Tail, 5", 1950, M....$400.00
Linemar, Mickey Mouse, 5½", tin, vibrates, '50s, EX .$510.00
Linemar, Minnie Mouse Knitter, 7", lithographed tin, 1950s, EX $500.00
Linemar, Pluto w/Whirling Tail, 4", 1950s, M $235.00
Linemar, Popeye Turnover Tank, 6", 1950s, EX $450.00
Marx, Daredevil Motor Drome, 5½x9" dia, w/2" wind-up car, 1930s, M $200.00
Marx, Donald Duck, 7", hard plastic, 1960s, M..........$100.00
Marx, Figaro, 4¾", tin, 1940, M $300.00
Marx, Goofy w/Whirling Tail, 8", plastic, 1950s, M...$200.00
Marx, Hopping Barney Rubble, 4", 1962, EX.............$300.00
Marx, Howdy Doody, 5", plays banjo & moves head, lithographed tin, ca 1950, EX..............................$300.00
Marx, Pluto, plastic w/spinning metal tail, 1950s, M..$220.00
Marx, Porky Pig, 8", holds umbrella, raises hat, lithographed tin, 1939, EX.......................................$335.00
Marx, Racing Car, 12", lithographed tin w/plastic driver, ca 1950, M...$225.00
Marx, Rooster w/Wagon, lithographed tin, 1930s, M...$120.00

Marx, Space Satellite w/Launching Station, 9x12" base, w/plastic accessories, 1950s, M..........................$100.00
Marx, Tom Tom Jungle Boy, lithographed tin, M......$150.00
Marx, Walt Disney's Friction Go-Mobile, 6", 1960s, M..$220.00
Mavco Company, Mickey Mouse Scooter Jockey, 6", all plastic, 1950s, EX......................................$240.00
Occupied Japan, Donald Race Car, celluloid, M........$450.00

Ohio Art, car, 3", #G-3 1960 marked on plate, G ..$35.00
Ohio Art, Traffic Control, 19x13" base, w/3½" long tin wind-up cars, 1950s, M $80.00
Schuco US Zone Germany, Mercer Auto, 7½", #1225, NM $175.00
Shuco, Donald Duck, 6", German, #984, EX.............$525.00

Toyodo, chicken & man, 7", G+ $500.00
TPS, Fishing Bear, 7½", 1950s, M..............................$200.00
TPS, Skating Chef, 6", 1950s, EX................................$225.00
Unique Art, Gertie, Galloping Goose, 9½", 1930s, EX .$225.00

Wyandotte, Acrobatic Monkeys, 10", VG- $50.00

Trading Cards

Modern collector cards are really just an extension of a hobby that began well before the turn of the century. Advertising cards put out by the food and tobacco companies of that era sometimes featured cute children, their pets, stage stars, battle scenes, presidential candidates, and so forth. Some cards were included with the products they advertised, and some were simply stacked on the grocer's counter for his customers to pick up when they visited his store. Collectors gathered them up and pasted them in scrapbooks. In the twentieth century, candy and bubble gum companies came to the forefront. Sports figures have become popular, so have fictional heroes, TV and movie stars, Disney characters, Barbie dolls, and country singers!

For more information, we recommend *Collector's Guide to Trading Cards* by Robert Reed.

Action/Panini, Barbie, 1922, series of 196, each ......$.25
Ad Trix, Tales of the Vikings, 1960, series of 66, each..**$1.50**
Bowman, Antique Autos, 1953, series of 48, each $5 to .**$12.00**
Bowman, Magic Pictures, 1955, series of 40, each **$1.00**
Bowman, Movie Stars, 1948, series of 36, each $10 to.**$20.00**
Bowman, Power for Peace, 1954, series of 96, each.....**$1.50**
Bowman, US Naval Victories, 1954, series of 48, each..**$6.00**
Comic Images, Capt'n America, 1990, series of 45, each.**$.35**
Comic Images, Frazetta, 1991, series of 90, each.............**$.25**
Comic Images, Heavy Metal, 1991, series of 90, each .....**$.15**
Comic Images, Punished, 1990, series of 50, each...........**$.35**
Comic Images, Wolverine, 1988, series of 50, each.........**$.50**
Crown, Desert Storm (II), 1991, series of 10, each ....**$.35**
Diamond, My Little Pony, 1986, series of 200, each ....**$.15**
Donruss, All Pro Skateboard, 1977, series of 44, each.....**$.25**
Donruss, CB Convoy, 1978, series of 44, each.................**$.35**
Donruss, Choppers /Hot Bikes, 1972, series of 66, each.**$.50**
Donruss, Dark Crystal, 1982, series of 78, each ....**$.25**
Donruss, Disneyland, 1965, series of 66, each...............**$2.50**
Donruss, Idiot Cards, 1961, series of 66, each **$1.00**

Donruss, Magnum PI, 1983, series of 66, each................**$.25**
Donruss, Marvel Super Heroes, 1966, series of 66, each.**$2.00**
Donruss, Saturday Night Fever, 1978, series of 66, each.**$.20**
Donruss, Space 1999, 1976, series of 66, each ....**$.30**
Donruss, Truckin', 1973, series of 44, each.....................**$.35**
Donruss, Voyage to the Bottom of the Sea, 1964, series of 66, each................**$2.50**
Dynamic, Believe It Or Not, 1962, series of 35, each....**$5.50**
Eclipse, Bush League, 1991, series of 100, each ....**$.35**
Eclipse, Early Jazz Greats, 1991, series of 36, each..........**$.35**
Eclipse, Rise & Fall of the Soviet Union, 1991, series of 36, each................**$.35**
Ed-U-Cards, Civil War Generals, 1982, series of 36, each.**$2.50**
Ed-U-Cards, Lone Ranger, 1950, series of 120, each......**$8.00**
Ed-U-Cards, New York World's Fair, 1964, series of 24, each................**$1.00**
Ed-U-Cards, US Presidents, 1976, series of 36, each......**$1.75**
Epic, Saturday Serials (II), 1991, series of 40, each..........**$.35**
Fleer, Beautiful People, 1978, series of 50 w/14 stickers, each................**$.50**
Fleer, Cops & Robbers, 1930, series of 35, each $6 to .**$25.00**
Fleer, Hollywood Slapstickers, 1975, series of 66, each ..**$.50**
Fleer, Kustom Cars II, 1975, series of 10 w/39 stickers, each **$1.00**
Fleer, Pac Man, 1980, series of 54, each ....**$.35**
Fleer, Pirates Bold, 1961, series of 66, each...................**$4.50**
Fleer, Race USA, 1972, series of 74, each.......................**$2.50**
Fleer, Weird-Ohs, 1965, series of 66, each.....................**$1.50**
Goudey, Boy Scouts, 1933, series of 48, each $15 to..**$20.00**
Goudey, Sea Raiders, 1933, series of 48, each.............**$14.00**
Goudey, Sky Birds, 1941, series of 24, each **$12.50**
Hassan, Artic Scenes, 1916, series of 25, each **$3.50**
Hassan, Indian Life in '60s, 1910, series of 50, each......**$4.50**
Helmar, Costumes & Jewelry, 1912, series of 50, each..**$6.00**
Impel, Terminator 2, 1991, series of 140, each ....**$.25**
Impel, Trading Card Treats, 1991, series of 36, each.......**$.25**
Leaf, Garrison's Gorillas, 1967, series of 72, each...........**$1.50**
Leaf, Good Guys & Bad Guys, 1966, series of 72, each.**$1.00**
Monty, Stars, 1988, series of 54, each ....**$.75**
Monty, Webster, 1985, series of 100, each ....**$.30**
Mutoscope, They'll Do It Every Time, 1942, series of 32, each................**$2.00**
Newport Products, Battleship Gum, 1938, series of 50, each $15 up to **$20.00**
Nu-Card, Rock & Roll Stars, 1959, series of 64, each.....**$4.50**
Nu-Cards, Horror Monsters, green, 1961, series of 66, each.**$3.50**
Pacific, Operation Desert Storm, 110 in series, each.......**$.20**
Philadelphia Gum, James Bond, Goldfinger, 1965, series of 66, each................**$4.00**
Philadelphia Gum, Super Heroes Stickers, 1967, series of 55, each................**$2.00**
Space Ventures, Moon-Mars, 1991, series of 36, each .....**$.75**
Star Pics, All My Children, 1991, series of 72, each ....**$.20**
Star Pics, Saturday Night Live Card Art, 1992, series of 150, each................**$.25**
Starline, Hollywood Walk of Fame, 1992, series of 250, each ....**$.25**
Top Pilot, Blue Angels, 1991, series of 14, each ....**$.75**

Top Pilot, Combat Helicopters, 1991, series of 14, each .**$.40**
Top Pilot, Thunderbirds, 1991, series of 14, each............**$.40**
Top Pilot, War Birds, 1990, series of 31, each **$1.00**
Topps, Animals of the World, 1954, series of 100, each $3
  up to **$6.00**

Topps, Batman, 1966, series of 38, each $4.00
Topps, Bring 'Em Back Alive, 1954, series of 100, each **$5.00**
Topps, Cats, 1983, series of 55, each................................**$.15**
Topps, Dallas Cowboy Cheerleaders, 1981, series of 30,
  each..**$.75**
Topps, Davy Crockett, 1956, green, series of 80, each..**$4.50**
Topps, Fabian, 1959, series of 55, each..........................**$1.75**
Topps, Fighting Marines, 1953, series of 96, each.........**$4.50**
Topps, Flipper, 1966, series of 30, each $60 up to......**$70.00**
Topps, Funny Foldees, 1955, series of 66, each **$5.00**
Topps, Green Hornet, 1966, series of 44, each..............**$4.50**
Topps, Hysterical History, 1979, series of 66, each ....**$.50**
Topps, King Kong, 1976, series of 55 w/11 stickers, each
  sticker 75¢, each card ....**$.50**
Topps, Look 'N See, 1952, series of 135, each..............**$4.25**
Topps, Lost in Space, 1966, series of 55, each..............**$6.00**
Topps, Monster Greetings, 1965, series of 60, each **$1.00**
Topps, Partridge Family III, 1971, series of 88, each.....**$2.00**
Topps, Planet of the Apes, 1969, series of 44, each......**$2.50**
Topps, Rambo, 1985, series of 66 w/22 stickers, each....**$.25**
Topps, Soupy Sales, 1965, series of 66, each.................**$4.00**
Topps, Sports Cars, 1961, series of 66 w/20 stickers, each
  sticker $4.50, each card **$3.00**
Topps, Stars Wars Mexicana, 1977, series of 66, each...**$1.00**
Topps, Tarzan's Savage Fury, 1955, series of 60,
  each...**$8.00**
Topps, Wacky Packages, 1967, series of 44, each.........**$5.50**
Wells Lamont, Red Ryder, 1952, series of 6, each **$10.00**
WS Co, Army, Navy & Aircorps, 1942, series of 48,
  each..**$8.50**
WS Co, Heroes of the Sea, 1939, series of 24, each **$4.00**
WS Co, Nightmare of Warfare, 1941, series of 48,
  each..**$9.50**

Trolls

The legend of the Troll originated in Scandinavia. Ancient folklore has it that they were giant, supernatural beings, but in more modern times, they're portrayed as dwarfs or imps who live in underground caverns. During the seventies there was a TV cartoon special called *The Hobbit* and a movie, *The Lord of the Rings*, that caused them to become popular; as a result, books, puzzles, posters, and dolls of all types were available on the retail market. In the early eighties, Broom Hilda and Irwin Troll were featured in a series of books as well as Saturday morning cartoons, and today trolls are enjoying a strong comeback.

The three main manufacturers of the 'vintage' trolls are Dam Things (Royalty Des. of Florida), Uneeda (Wishnicks), and A/S Nyform of Norway. Some were made in Hong Kong and Japan as well, but generally these were molded of inferior plastic.

The larger trolls (approximately 12") are rare and very desirable to collectors, and the troll animals, such as the giraffe, horse, cow, donkey, and lion made by Dam, are bringing premium prices.

Baseball player, 6", 1960s, NM......................................**$40.00**

Caveman, 3", marked Ughie, Ughie $15.00
Dam, bank, 7½", vinyl w/jointed neck, green mohair
  wig, marked USA Feeler, promotional item, 1967,
  M **$30.00**
Dam, Good Luck Graduate, 3", vinyl w/gray & black hair,
  original clothes, 1965, M..**$20.00**
Dam, Lover Boy-Nik, vinyl w/mohair, original clothes &
  cap, marked Dam on back, M..............................**$15.00**
Dam, Nite Out Troll, 3", vinyl w/glued-on mohair, brown
  eyes, sequin earrings & necklace, original clothes, 1964,
  M **$15.00**

**Dam, Santa, 12", vinyl w/jointed neck, white hair, inset
green eyes, marked on foot, EX $125.00**

Dam, Sappy Claws, M.................................$25.00

Dam, 5½", vinyl w/chartreuse hair & blue eyes, original felt
clothing & leather shield, 1965, M $20.00

Hong Kong, Vampire, 3", vinyl w/jointed neck & fangs,
marked Made in Hong Kong, 1966, M $15.00

Ideal, 14", cloth body w/vinyl head & hands, inset glassene
eyes, marked Scandinavian Enterprises, M............$90.00

Leprechaun Limited, Brother Bear, 7", vinyl w/jointed neck,
inset glassene eyes, comes w/passport, 1970, M ..**$80.00**

Roy Des of Florida, 2½", vinyl w/yellow hair, very pointed
ears, felt clothes w/silver collar, 1960s, M.............$20.00

Shekter, monkey, 8", vinyl w/jointed neck, lg inset eyes,
original clothes, marked on foot, 1966, M............$75.00

Uneeda, Batman, 3", vinyl w/inset blue eyes, stapled-on
clothes, w/mask, 1966, M......................$25.00

Uneeda, Wishnik, 3", Sock-It-to-Me, painted black eye, original clothes, EX $12.50

Uneeda, Wishnik, 6", vinyl w/jointed neck, lavender hair,
NM $25.00

Uneeda, 3", vinyl w/red mohair, lg yellow eyes, Gardentime
dress, 1966, NM..................................$15.00

Unmarked, cow, 3", unjointed vinyl w/lg inset glassene
eyes, EX $50.00

Unmarked, elephant, 3", vinyl w/long hair, inset glassene
eyes, M..$60.00

Unmarked, Hawaiian Troll, 3", vinyl, marked '64 on back,
M $15.00

Unmarked, monster, 3", all vinyl w/painted features & hair,
1-piece outfit missing, EX.....................$30.00

Unmarked, Santa, 4½", unjointed vinyl w/rooted beard &
hair, painted inset eyes, suit & cap w/bell, M.......$60.00

Unmarked, 3", vinyl w/jointed neck, protruding bump on
neck for hanging, M..........................$15.00

Vissin, Viking, 7", molded tooth & helmet, glued-on rabbit
fur beard, original clothes, marked Denmark, M..**$55.00**

TV Shows and Movies

Since the early days of TV and the movies right up to
the present time, hit shows have inspired numerous toys
and articles of memorabilia. If they were well established,
manufacturers often cashed in on their popularity through
the sale of more expensive items such as toys and dolls; but
more often than not, those less established were promoted
through paper goods such as books, games, and paper
dolls, just in case their fame turned out to be short lived.

Already in some of the tradepapers specializing in
toys, you see dealers speculatively offering Roger Rabbit
memorabilia for sale, and the same is true of Indiana
Jones, The Equalizer, and Ninja Turtles. So with an eye to
the future (possibly the *near* future), see if you can pick
the shows that will generate the collectibles you need to
be hanging on to.

See also Beatles Collectibles; Character and Promo-
tional Drinking Glasses; Character Collectibles; Dionne
Quintuplets; Elvis Presley Memorabilia; Games; Halloween
Costumes; Movie Stars; Paper Dolls; Puzzles; Shirley Tem-
ple; Star Trek Memorabilia; Star Wars Trilogy; Toys; and
Western Heroes.

Addams Family, magazine, Monster World #9, July .$10.00

Alf, air freshner, w/hanger, M.......................$5.00

Alf, key chain, M......................................$3.00

Alf, paint set, M......................................**$6.00**

All in the Family, cookbook, softcover paperback, Popular
library, 1972, 250-page, EX....................$17.50

Ben Casey, book, 7x10", Ben Casey Film Stories, marked KK
Publications & Bing Crosby Productions, issue #1, 1962,
EX..$20.00

Ben Casey, diary, cardboard w/metal clasp & key, 1962,
NM $35.00

Bionic Woman, trailer, 16mm, 30-second promotion....$5.00

Black Hole, Colorforms, M............................**$12.50**

Bonanza, mug, lithographed tin, 1960s, EX $10.00

Bonanza, tablet, 8x10", Lorne Greene cover, NM $10.00

Captain Kangaroo, badge, tin, 1960s, M $40.00

Captain Kangaroo, coloring book, 1957, NM $10.00

Captain Kangaroo, magic slate, NM $10.00

Captain Kangaroo, tablet, 1950s $7.50

Charlie's Angels, paint-by-number set, 15x11x1½", Sabrina, Kelly & Chris on lid, Hasbro & Spelling-Goldberg, 1977, M $20.00

Cheyenne, record, 45rpm, RCA Victor Bluebird label, Clint Walker full-color portrait on sleeve, 1950s, EX $20.00

CHIPS, figure, 5" long, motorcycle w/rider, marked Fleetwood Toys, ca 1978, M on card $6.50

Crazy Like a Fox, photo, 5x7", Jack Warden & John Rubinstein, black & white, EX $2.00

Creature From the Black Lagoon, key chain, 1", yellow plastic figural w/loop for brass chain, ca 1950s, EX $20.00

Daktari, tablet, ca 1960s, NM $15.00

Dr Kildare, notebook, dated 1962 ....$15.00

Dr Kildare, playset, Medical Kit, Hasbro, 1963, NM $50.00

Dragnet, whistle, plastic, NM $7.50

Emergency, hard hat, plastic, 1970s, M $40.00

Family Affair, tablet, 8x10", Anissa Jones (Buffy) w/Mrs Beasley full-color cover, late 1960s, M $20.00

Flintstones, coloring book, Flintstones Meet Gruesome, dated 1965, NM $30.00

Flintstones, mold, 2", embossed face, for ice cubes $5.00

Flintstones, plate, 7½", colorful graphics on plastic, marked Boonton Molding Co, NM $25.00

Flintstones, sleeping bag, dated 1974, EX $45.00

Flintstones, spoon, silver plated, 30th Birthday Anniversary, marked Perfection, MIB $17.50

Flipper, coloring book, 8x11", marked Whitman & Ivan Tors Films Inc, color covers, EX $20.00

Flying Nun, coloring book, Artcraft, 1968, NM $12.50

Full House, photo, 8x10", cast w/Xmas tree, 1988, NM .$3.00

Garrison's Gorillas, coloring book, Whitman, '68, EX .$15.00

Gemini Man, record, 33⅓ rpm, Gemini Man, Power Records label, marked Universal City Studios, original jacket, ca 1976 ....$20.00

Green Acres, tractor, die-cast metal replica w/Green Acres on sides, Ertl, 1960s, EX $37.50

Grizzly Adams, coloring book, marked Rand McNally, dated 1978, NM $15.00

Grizzly Adams, waste basket, lithographed tin, EX $15.00

Gunsmoke, badge, 2x1½", die-cut US Marshal on silver metal, M on card, James Arness' photo, 1959 ....$37.50

Hogan's Heroes, tablet, 8x10", color cover, M $18.00

I Dream of Jeannie, comic book, 7x10", Dell Publishing Vol 1 #1, April 1966, Sidney Productions Inc, EX $37.50

Incredible Hulk, Colorforms, 1978, NM $25.00

Incredible Hulk, mold, Play-Doh, M $5.00

Incredible Hulk, mug, plastic, Deka, 1977, NM $10.00

Incredible Hulk, playing cards, 1979, M on card $12.50

Incredible Hulk, switchplate, Monogram Products, M on card $5.00

Incredible Hulk, utility belt, Remco, 1978, MIB $10.00

Jetsons, book, Great Pizza Hunt, Wonder Books, 1976 .$6.00

Jetsons, coloring book, Whitman, 1963, EX $27.50

Journey to the Center of the Earth, coloring book, Whitman, 1968, EX $25.00

Knight Rider, photo, 7x9", David Hasselhoff, black & white, EX $6.00

Land of the Giants, coloring book, 8x10", marked Whitman & Kent Productions w/1969 copyright, VG $25.00

Laverne & Shirley, activity book, Playmore, 1983, NM $15.00

Leave It to Beaver, coloring book, Saalfield, 1958, EX.$150.00

Leave It to Beaver, tray, 10" dia, lithographed family photo on tin w/facsimile signature, 1983, M $15.00

Lethal Weapon 2, tie tac, M $7.50

M*A*S*H, dog tags, set of 2, M on card $22.50

M*A*S*H, key chain, marked Goodbye-Farewell-Amen 1972-1983 on plastic, M $10.00

Magnum PI, flashlight, 3½", black & white plastic w/sticker, Ja-Ru & Universal City Studios, M on card $20.00

Man From UNCLE, coloring book, 8x11", marked Watkins-Strathmore & Metro-Goldwyn-Mayer, 1965, EX $37.50

Mr Ed, hand puppet, Mattel, 1962, M $35.00

Mr Ed, photo, 8x10", glossy black & white of cast, inscribed, ca 1962, EX $50.00

My Favorite Martian, coloring book, Saalfield, #1148, 128 pages, EX $20.00

My Favorite Martian, magic set, Martian Magic Tricks, Gilbert, 1964, EX $75.00

Our Gang, coloring book, Saalfield, 1938, EX $38.00

Our Gang, photo, 5x7", cast members, marked Hal Roach Studios, late 1920s-early 1930s, EX $50.00

Partridge Family, coloring book, Artcraft, 1970, EX $15.00

Pee-Wee Herman, plastic figure w/scooter & helmet, Matchbox, M on card..$18.00

Peter Gun, record, 33⅓ rpm, Jazz From Peter Gun, Columbia label, photo cover, ca 1959, VG $20.00

Planet of the Apes, activity book, 1967, M $7.50

Planet of the Apes, dart set, 1968, MIB $28.00

Planet of the Apes, gum card box, 3½x8x2", graphics from movie, 1960s, empty, EX $35.00

Planet of the Apes, hobby kit, snap-together plastic, Addar Products, 1973, M in NM box $40.00

Raiders of the Lost Ark, playset, Streets of Cairo, for 3¾" figures, Kenner, MIB...$25.00

Raiders of the Lost Ark, playset, Wells of Souls, for 3¾" figures, Kenner, MIB...$35.00

Ramar of the Jungle, playsuit, jacket & skirt set, NM ..$55.00

Rin Tin Tin, activity book, 17x9½", Paint by Number, Transogram, 1956, VG...$32.50

Rin Tin Tin, book, 8½x7½", One of the Family, marked Whitman Cozy-Corner Book, 1953, 24-page, EX ..$20.00

Rin Tin Tin, canteen, G $15.00

Robin Hood, badge, embossed portrait & birthstone, ca 1956, M...$50.00

Robin Hood, hat, 12x5½", green & tan suede w/logo, Richard Greene portrait on brim, 1950s, missing feather, NM $45.00

Saturday Night Live, book, 8x11", softcover, 1977, M...$12.50

Sergeant Bilko, gun & holster set, w/arm patch & badge, marked Halco, 1956, MIB...$200.00

Sergeant Preston, book, 6½x8", Sergeant Preston of Royal Canadian Mounted Police, Rand McNally Elf Book, 1956, VG...$8.50

Sergeant Preston & Yukon King, coloring book, 1953, EX $35.00

Silver Spoons, photo, 7x9", cast shot, black & white, EX $3.00

Six Million Dollar Man, play set, Mission Control, for 12" figures, Kenner, MIB...$80.00

Space Angel, coloring book, Saalfield, 1963, EX $22.50

Sword in the Stone, coloring book, M.........................$10.00

Three's Company, sticker set, 1978, M $12.50

V, figurine, 11", enemy visitor, marked LJN #4500, 1984, M in package $25.00

Virginian, iron-on transfer, M...$7.50

Voyage to the Bottom of the Sea, coloring book, Whitman, 1965, 128-page, NM $48.00

Wacky Races, coloring book, Whitman, 1968, VG $18.00

Wagon Train, record, 78 rpm, Golden Records label, Ward Bond black & white photo on sleeve, EX.............$10.00

Wild Wild West, school tablet, 8x10", Ross Martin full-color photo cover, ca 1969, M...$37.50

Wild Wild West, tablet, Robert Conrad cover, M.........$25.00

Wizard of Oz, chalkboard, We're Off To See the Wizard, M $45.00

Wizard of Oz, coin, 1⅜", Cowardly Lion on dark blue plastic, 1967, MGM, marked Lion Trick on back, EX ..$20.00

Wizard of Oz, coloring book, The Story of the Wizard of Oz, Whitman, 1939, EX $35.00

Wizard of Oz, mask, paper, marked Einson-Freeman, dated 1939, EX...$30.00

Wizard of Oz, paint book, 10½x15", Whitman #663, HE Valely illustrations, 1939, 40-page, NM.................$87.50

Wizard of Oz, tin, Swifts Peanut Butter, color lithographed tin w/bail handle, EX...$85.00

TV Guides

TV Guides go back to the early 1950s, and granted, those early issues are very rare; but what an interesting, very visual way to chronicle the history of TV programing. For insight into *TV Guide* collecting, we recommend *The TV Guide Catalog* by Jeff Kadet, the *TV Guide* Specialist.

1953, December 18, Bob Hope cover, NM $20.00

1953, May 1, Eve Arden cover, NM $35.00

1953, October 2, Red Skelton cover, EX $25.00

1954, February 26, Liberace cover, EX $10.00

1954, June 11, Alan Young & Ben Blue cover, NM.....$25.00

1954, October 9, Lucille Ball cover, EX.......................$60.00

1955, January 1, Loretta Young cover, EX...................$12.50

1955, June 4, Eddie Fisher cover, EX...........................$7.00

1955, October 8, Burns & Allen cover, NM.................$22.50

1956, April 21, Nanette Fabray cover, EX....................$5.00

1956, December 8, Victor Borge cover, NM.................$7.50

Welcome Back Kotter, Sweat-Hog Calculator, #650, Remco, 1976, M on card....................................$15.00

1956, September 8, Elvis Presley cover, NM $175.00

1957, December 7, Dinah Shore cover, EX $7.00

1957, June 8, Lassie cover, NM $12.50

1958, December 27, David & Rick Nelson cover, NM. $50.00

1958, February 22, Rosemary Clooney cover, NM $8.00

1958, June 14, Robert Young & Jane Wyatt cover, NM. $10.00

1958, September 20, special fall preview issue, EX $35.00

1959, July 25, John Russell as The Lawman cover, NM... $17.50

1959, March 21, Ann Sothern cover, NM $12.50

1959, October 24, Jay North as Dennis the Menace cover, EX $35.00

1960, April 23, cast of Laramie cover, EX $27.50

1960, January 2, cast of Gunsmoke cover, EX $12.00

1960, September 10, Dick Clark cover, NM $12.50

1961, December 9, Dick Van Dyke & Mary Tyler Moore cover, NM $35.00

1961, January 21, Barbara Stanwick cover, NM $8.00

1961, May 20, Walter Brennan & Richard Crenna of Real McCoys cover, EX $5.00

1961, September 23, Mitch Miller cover, NM $10.00

1962, January 20, Chuck Conners, 'Rifleman' cover, NM $25.00

1962, March 24, Dick Powell cover, NM $8.00

1962, May 26, Fred MacMurray of My 3 Sons cover, EX. $5.00

1962, October 13, Jackie Gleason cover, EX $4.00

1963, January 26, Martin Milner & George Maharis of Route 66 cover, NM $35.00

1963, May 25, Lawrence Welk cover, EX $5.00

1963, November 9, Carol Burnette cover, EX $5.00

1963, September 7, Irene Ryan & Donna Douglas cover, EX $10.00

1964, April 11, cast of My Favorite Martian cover, EX... $5.00

1964, February 1, Danny Kaye cover, NM $7.00

1964, July 18, James Drury & Doug McClure of Virginian cover, NM $9.00

1964, November 21, Jim Nabors, Gomer Pyle cover, NM. $10.00

1965, April 24, Andy Griffith cover, EX $12.00

1965, October 23, Chuck Conners cover, NM $10.00

1966, April 23, Andy Williams cover, NM $5.00

1966, December 3, cast of Rat Patrol cover, NM $20.00

1966, January 15, Bill Cosby & Robert Culp of I Spy cover, NM $12.50

1967, February 25, Phyllis Diller cover, M $4.00

1967, June 10, Smothers Brothers cover, NM $15.00

1967, October 14, Johnny Carson cover, NM $10.00

1968, April 13, Carl Betz cover, EX $7.50

1968, January 27, Elizabeth Montgomery cover, NM... $10.00

1968, September 7, cast of Family Affair cover, EX $2.50

1969, August 30, Johnny Cash cover, M $4.00

1969, December 6, Doris Day cover, NM $15.00

1969, February 8, cast of Mission Impossible cover, EX. $6.00

1969, June 14, Glen Campbell cover, EX $4.00

1970, August 15, Johnny Carson by Rockwell, EX $9.00

1970, January 24, Tom Jones cover, NM $7.50

1970, May 9, David Frost cover, NM $5.00

1970, October 10, Hershal Bernardi of Arnie, NM $3.00

1971, April 17, Paul Newman cover, NM $5.00

1971, February 13, Goldie Hawn cover, M $4.00

1971, July 10, Cookie Monster cover, EX $3.00

1971, November 27, Joanne Woodward cover, EX $2.00

1972, June 17, Julie London cover, EX $3.00

1972, March 18, Sonny & Cher cover, EX $5.00

1972, November 4, John Wayne cover, NM $8.00

1973, June 16, cast of Maude cover, M $5.00

1973, March 3, William Conrad cover, NM $3.50

1973, November 17, Frank Sinatra cover, NM $5.00

1974, April 13, Waltons cover, NM $3.00

1974, August 24, Susan Blakely cover, EX $2.00

1974, November 10, A Very Special Week, 8 stars w/portraits of Bob Hope, Elvis, Sammy Davis Jr, Dean Martin & more, EX $4.00

1974, November 9, Sophia Loren cover, M $3.00

1975, August 2, Mike Douglas cover, NM $2.50

1975, February 22, Telly Savalas cover, EX $2.00

1975, November 15, David Soul & Michael Glazer of Starsky & Hutch cover, NM $8.00

1976, February 14, Red Foxx cover, NM $5.00

1976, May 22, cast of Laverne & Shirley cover, NM $6.00

1976, September 11, Bob Dylan cover, NM $15.00

1977, January 29, Wonder Woman cover, NM $10.00

1977, May 21, Farrah Fawcett of Charlie's Angels cover, NM $12.50

1977, October 8, Marie & Donnie Osmond cover, EX $3.00

1978, April 8, cast of Alice cover, NM $3.00

1978, June 17, Valerie Harper cover, NM $3.00

1978, November 25, Suzanne Somers cover, NM $7.50

1979, April 21, Walter Cronkite cover, NM $3.00

1979, July 28, Lou Ferrigno & Bill Bixby of Incredible Hulk cover, NM $6.00

1979, May 26, Ken Howard cover, NM $3.00

1980, August 2, Real People cover, M $4.00

1980, February 9, Olympics cover, M $3.00

1980, October 11, World Series cover, M $3.00

1981, January 17, Ronald Reagan cover, M $3.00

1981, May 9, Larry Hagman & Patrick Duffy of Dallas cover, M **$7.00**

1981, November 14, Loretta Lynn cover, M.................**$3.00**

1982, April 10, Tom Brokaw cover, M.........................**$3.00**

1982, September 18, Victoria Principal cover, M...........**$4.00**

1983, April 9, Elvis Presley cover, M.........................**$7.00**

1983, October 8, Willie Nelson & Anne Murray, NM.....**$7.00**

1984, December 15, Connie Sellecca, Priscilla Presley, & Jaclyn Smith cover, M **$4.00**

1984, January 14, Emmanuel Lewis cover, M.................**$3.00**

1984, March 31, Teri Copley cover, M.........................**$3.00**

1985, April 27, cast of Family Ties cover, M.................**$4.00**

1985, December 7, Cybill Shepherd cover, M.................**$5.00**

1985, September 14, special fall preview cover, M......**$11.00**

1986, December 27, Heather Locklear of Dynasty, M ...**$3.00**

1986, May 10, cast of Cheers cover, M **$4.00**

1986, October 25, Kim Novak cover, M **$3.00**

1987, February 7, Ann-Margaret cover, M **$4.00**

1987, July 4, Barbara Walters cover, M.........................**$3.00**

1987, June 20, Markie Post cover, M...........................**$4.00**

1988, April 9, Harry Hamlin cover, M.........................**$3.00**

1988, January 9, Emma Samms cover, M.......................**$4.00**

1988, September 17, Olympics cover, M **$4.00**

1989, January 14, cast of Moonlighting cover, M...........**$4.00**

1989, June 3, Oprah Winfrey cover, M.........................**$3.00**

1989, November 11, Richard Chamberlain cover, M......**$3.00**

1990, December 29, cast of Murphy Brown cover, M ...**$4.00**

1990, February 10, Hottest TV Couples cover, M...........**$4.00**

1990, June 23, Arsenio Hall cover, M **$3.00**

1991, April 20, Burt Reynolds & Marilu Henner, M **$3.00**

1991, July 13, Michael Landon cover, M.......................**$3.00**

1991, November 23, Madonna cover, M.......................**$3.00**

1992, May 23, Jerry Seinfeld cover, M **$3.00**

1992, September 5, Joan Lunden cover, M...................**$3.00**

1993, February 1, Jessica Lang cover, M.....................**$3.00**

Twin Winton

A California-based company founded by twins Ross and Don, the company called Twin Winton Ceramics had its beginnings in the mid-thirties. The men remained active in the ceramic industry until 1975, designing and producing animal figures, cookie jars and matching kitchenware items. One of their most successful lines was mugs, pitchers, bowls, lamps, ashtrays, and novelty items modeled after the mountain boys in Paul Webb's cartoon series.

If you'd like more information, read *The Collector's Encyclopedia of California Pottery* by Jack Chipman. See also Cookie Jars.

Bank, Friar, light brown w/Thou Shalt Not Steal lettered in white, 1960-70s, in-mold mark.............................**$25.00**

Decanter, Robin Hood, multicolored high-gloss glaze by Don Winton, manufactured by Winfield **$20.00**

Figurine, 2¾", sitting elf, underglazed **$15.00**

Figurine, 3¼", bashful boy elf **$15.00**

Figurine, 4", lg-eyed girl w/freckles & pigtails, painted underglaze Burke Winton mark.........................**$15.00**

Figurine, 4", sitting elf, lg feet, Burke Winton mark....**$15.00**

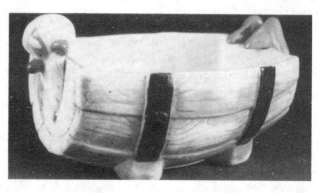

Ice bucket, Hillbilly, in-mold mark, horizontal banded half barrel w/bearded man's head & feet protruding from ends **$35.00**

Mug, figural handle of boy in yellow & light blue underglaze...**$25.00**

Napkin holder, Ranger Bear, woodtone finish w/lightly painted detailing, unmarked **$25.00**

Pitcher, Hillbilly, banded barrel shape w/spout & hillbilly figural handle **$35.00**

Pitcher, Open Range, cowboy figural handle, embossed horse on side, brown tones.............................**$45.00**

Salt & pepper shakers, Hillbilly, head emerging from keg form, pr...**$12.00**

Table lamp, Hillbilly, sleeping figure on moonshine keg, figural, ca 1949 ....**$65.00**

Tankard, Hillbilly, tall, hillbilly figural handle.............**$25.00**

Universal Dinnerware

This pottery incorporated in Cambridge, Ohio, in 1934, the outgrowth of several smaller companies in the area. They produced many lines of dinnerware and kitchenware items, most of which were marked. They're best known for their Ballerina dinnerware (simple modern shapes in a variety of solid colors) and Cat-tail (See Cat-tail Dinnerware). The company closed in 1960.

Ballerina, creamer...**$10.00**

Ballerina, plate, dinner **$8.00**

Ballerina, plate, 6"...**$2.50**

Ballerina, salt & pepper shakers, pr **$10.00**

Ballerina, tidbit, 2-tier...**$12.00**

Ballerina, 3-piece mixing bowl set **$55.00**

Ballerina Mist, bowl, 9", decal of white flowers w/black stems...**$10.00**

Calico Fruit, bowl, mixing; 6"...................................**$13.50**

Calico Fruit, bowl, mixing; 7½".................................**$15.00**

Calico Fruit, bowl, mixing; 9".....................................**$17.50**

Calico Fruit, custard cup, 5-oz...................................**$4.00**

Calico Fruit, pitcher, utility **$22.00**

Calico Fruit, pitcher, w/lid...**$32.50**

Cattail, custard cup, 5-oz **$5.50**

Fruits & Flowers, plate, serving $15.00
Hollyhocks, bowl, salad $18.00
Iris, pie baker...$15.00

Iris, plate, dinner $5.00
Iris, refrigerator jug (illustrated) $20.00
Largo, plate, dessert; 6"...$3.00
Largo, salt & pepper shakers, pr....................................$6.00
Rambler Rose, shaker, utility...$6.00
Red Poppy, plate, utility; 11½".....................................$10.00
Rose, plate, dinner; on Laurella shape $6.00
Rose, plate, sm, on Old Holland shape.........................$4.00
Windmill, bowl, utility; w/lid $6.00
Woodvine, bowl, flat soup $4.00
Woodvine, bowl, vegetable; oval $8.00
Woodvine, gravy boat $10.00

Valentines

Valentines that convey sentimental messages are just the type of thing that girls in love tuck away and keep. So it's not too hard to find examples of these that date back to the early part of the century. But there are other kinds of valentines that collectors search for too – those with Black themes and Disney characters, advertising and modes of transportation, 3-dimensionals, and mechanicals. Look for artist signed cards; these are especially prized.

Angel in garden w/fountain, 8", 3 levels, Victorian, marked
    Germany...$20.00
Boy & dog fold-out, 5", multicolor, Victorian, marked Ger-
    many...$18.00

**Children & hearts, 7x5", embossed paper w/applied
paper lace**...$8.50
George Washington fold-out, 5" $12.50

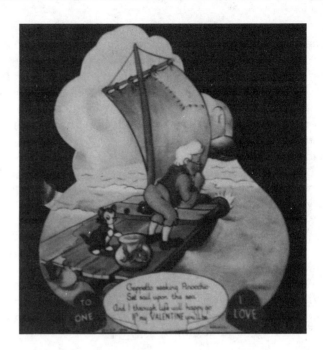

**Geppetto on raft, 7½x6", mechanical, Walt Disney Pro-
ductions, 1939, VG**..$15.00
Golfer w/Zeppelin $16.00
Heart in center w/honeycomb, 8"...............................$22.50
Heart w/honeycomb, 5" $18.00
Horse & wagon, children writing, 10", 2 honeycombs.$35.00
Wax figure of lady in fabric flower arch, 6½x4x2⅝" ...$50.00
2 angels w/honeycomb, 10½".......................................$22.50
2 girls w/honeycomb, 8" $20.00

Van Briggle

This pottery was founded in Colorado Springs around the turn of the century by Artus Van Briggle who had previously worked at Rookwood. After his death in 1904, his wife, Anne, took over the business which she controlled until it sold in 1913. The company has continued to operate up to the present time.

Because many of the original designs were repeated down through the years, it is often very difficult to determine when some pieces were produced. There are several factors to consider. Until late 1907, pieces were marked with the 'double A' logo, 'Van Briggle,' and the date. The 'double A' logo was in constant use until the mid-fifties, and a few marks still indicated the date; others contained a design number. Many times 'Colorado Springs' was included as well. Earlier pieces had glazed bottoms, but from 1921 until 1930, the bottoms were left unglazed. From 1922 until 1929, 'U.S.A.' was added to the Colorado Springs designation. Pieces made from 1955 to 1968 were usually marked 'Anna Van Briggle' with no 'double A' logo, but it does appear again on those made after '68.

Colors are another good indicator of age. Until 1930, colors were limited to turquoise, blue, maroon, brown, green, and yellow (in blended effects or in combination).

In 1946, the mulberry was lightened, and the shade was named 'Persian Rose.' It was a popular until 1968. 'Mountain Craig Brown,' used from about 1915 until the mid-thirties, was one of their most famous glazes. It was a warm brown color with a green overspray. (This effect has been reproduced in recent years.) 'Moonglow' (white matt) has been in constant production since 1950, and their turquoise matt was made from the very early years on. High-gloss colors of brown, blue, black, and green were introduced in the mid-fifties, though matt colors were still favored. Other colors have been made in addition to those we've mentioned.

Still another factor that can be helpful is the type of clay that was used. Dark clays (including terra cotta) indicate a pre-1930 origin. After that time, the body of the ware was white.

If you'd like more information, we recommend *The Collector's Encyclopedia of Van Briggle Art Pottery* by Richard Sasicki & Josie Fania. *Lehner's Encyclopedia of U.S. Marks on Pottery, Porcelain, and Clay* by Lois Lehner is another good source.

Bookends, owl figural, dark blue, marked, pr...........**$250.00**
Bookends, polar bears, Persian Rose w/blue **$275.00**
Bowl, Ming Turquoise, oak leaf & acorn, 1920s..........**$75.00**
Candlestick, Goldenrod (dark yellow), 1915 ....**$300.00**
Creamer, 2½", Persian Rose, paper label.....................**$35.00**
Figurine, donkey, 4x3", dark dray **$60.00**
Figurine, horse, recumbent, white, Colorado Springs, late 1980s...**$45.00**
Figurine, 3x4", elephant, raised trunk, sienna brown..**$70.00**
Figurine, 7½", seated lady holding shell, turquoise...**$150.00**
Flower frog, duck form, dark green, unmarked **$40.00**
Lamp, leopard, Persian Rose, original shade, artist signed, NM **$225.00**
Lamp, 11", Ming Blue, 2 racing deer **$185.00**
Lamp, 6", ginger jar shape, original butterfly shade ..**$225.00**
Mug, dark green w/no decoration, Colorado Springs, #753, ca 1909-12 ....**$300.00**
Plaque, 7", peacock, turquoise w/some red on tail, 1908-11, #807 ....**$260.00**

Vase, bud; 7½", Mountain Craig Brown...............$175.00

Vase, sm, med green w/blue overspray, sm ear handles, bowl form, Colorado Springs mark, 1935-45.........**$50.00**
Vase, turquoise w/embossed long-stem flowers on slim form, Colorado Springs, #786, 1920s...................**$175.00**
Vase, 2¾", butterflies on Persian Rose, dated 1915 ...**$200.00**
Vase, 3", butterflies on turquoise, ca 1950 ....**$65.00**
Vase, 3¼", Persian Rose, ca 1920, #310 ....**$65.00**
Vase, 4", blue & green, 1908-11, #654 ....**$195.00**
Vase, 6½", dragonflies on turquoise, 1920s...............**$325.00**

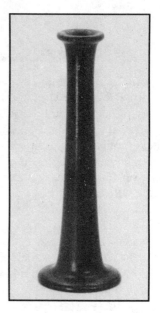

Vase, 9½", leaves & buds on maroon, 1917........$245.00

Vending Machines

Coin-operated machines that were used to sell peanuts, gumballs, stamps, even sandwiches were already popular by the turn of the century. But they saw their heaviest use from the first decade of the 20th century until about 1940. Some of the better-known vending machine manufacturers were Ad-Lee, Columbus, Exhibit, Northwestern, and Victor.

Values are determined in part by condition. Original paint and decals are certainly desirable, but because these machines were often repainted by operators while they were still in use, collectors often allow a well-done restoration. There are variations that bear on value as well, such as color, special features and design.

Advance E-Z, 16", gum vending, cast iron & glass w/original decals, VG **$500.00**
Caille Teddy Bear, gum vendor, ca 1910, EX.........**$2,500.00**
Columbus Model 21, ca 1920, EX orig **$235.00**
Hance Electric Vendor, ca 1920, EX original **$650.00**
Mills, match vending, ca 1910, EX orig **$995.00**
Premier, card vending, 1950, EX original **$85.00**
Regal, candy vending, ca 1935, EX original **$85.00**
Simmons Model A, ca 1930, EX original **$175.00**
Tomb Thumb, ca 1920, EX original...........................**$115.00**

Zeno, porcelain case, gum vending, lettered front, ca 1910, EX original..**$400.00**
Zeno, wood cabinet, gum vending, EX original........**$650.00**

Vernon Kilns

Founded in Vernon, California, in 1930, this company produced many lines of dinnerware, souvenir plates, decorative pottery, and figurines. They employed several well-known artists whose designs no doubt contributed substantially to their success. Among them were Rockwell Kent, Royal Hickman, and Don Blanding, all of whom were responsible for creating several of the lines most popular with collectors today.

In 1940, they signed a contract with Walt Disney to produce a line of figurines and several dinnerware patterns that were inspired by Disney's film *Fantasia*. The figurines were made for a short time only and are now expensive.

The company closed in 1958, but Metlox purchased the molds and continued to produce some of their best-selling dinnerware lines through a specially established 'Vernon Kiln' division.

Most of the ware is marked in some form or another with the company name and, in some cases, the name of the dinnerware pattern.

If you'd like to learn more, we recommend *The Collector's Encyclopedia of California Pottery* by Jack Chipman.

Bel-Air, ashtray..**$3.00**
Brown Eyed Susan, platter, 12" dia..............................**$12.00**
Brown-Eyed Susan, pitcher, 11½"..............................**$45.00**
California Ivy, casserole, 9", w/lid..............................**$25.00**
California Ivy, relish, 7", divided..............................**$12.00**
California Ivy, sugar bowl, w/lid..............................**$12.00**
California Ivy, tumbler, 6"..............................**$15.00**
Casual California, mug, green..............................**$15.00**
Early California, lug soup, 5"..............................**$12.00**
Gingham, bowl, divided vegetable..............................**$20.00**
Gingham, bowl, mixing; 8"..............................**$25.00**
Gingham, bowl, mixing; 9"..............................**$30.00**
Gingham, bowl, nested set of 5..............................**$75.00**
Gingham, casserole, w/lid..............................**$25.00**
Gingham, coffee carafe..............................**$28.00**
Gingham, cup & saucer..............................**$9.00**
Gingham, plate, 6¼"..............................**$30.00**
Gingham, plate, 9½"..............................**$9.00**
Gingham, sugar bowl, w/lid..............................**$12.00**
Hawaiian Flowers, tumbler, iced tea..............................**$20.00**
Heavenly Days, platter, 13½"..............................**$15.00**
Homespun, bowl, vegetable; 9"..............................**$14.00**
Homespun, bowl, 9"..............................**$19.00**
Homespun, chop plate, 13"..............................**$22.00**
Homespun, coaster, 3¾"..............................**$8.00**
Homespun, creamer & sugar bowl, open..............................**$8.00**
Homespun, egg cup..............................**$20.00**
Homespun, pitcher, 24-oz..............................**$15.00**
Homespun, plate, 6"..............................**$4.00**

Homespun, plate, 7"..............................**$5.00**
Homespun, platter, 10¼", oval..............................**$17.50**

Homespun, salt & pepper shakers, pr..............................**$9.00**
Homespun, sugar bowl, round, w/lid..............................**$10.00**
Homespun, tumbler, 14-oz..............................**$17.50**
Lei Lani, chop plate, 14", marked Blanding..............................**$45.00**
Monterey, salt & pepper shakers, pr..............................**$15.00**
Organdie, bowl, 5½"..............................**$7.00**
Organdie, creamer..............................**$8.00**
Organdie, cup & saucer..............................**$12.00**
Organdie, gravy boat..............................**$18.00**
Organdie, pitcher, 24-oz..............................**$20.00**
Organdie, plate, 10"..............................**$10.00**
Organdie, plate, 7"..............................**$3.50**
Organdie, salt & pepper shakers, pr..............................**$12.00**
Organdie, soup, flat..............................**$12.00**
Organdie, sugar bowl..............................**$9.00**
Plate, souvenir, North Carolina, multicolor..............................**$15.00**
Plate, souvenir; Carlsbad Cavern, brown..............................**$10.00**
Plate, souvenir; MacArthur, maroon..............................**$18.00**

Plate, souvenir; St Augustine, red..............................**$15.00**
Santa Fe, ashtray, red..............................**$16.00**

Sherwood, bowl, divided vegetable; oval $6.00
Tam O'Shanter, bowl, divided vegetable; oval $25.00
Tam O'Shanter, butter dish, ¼-lb..............................$35.00
Tam O'Shanter, carafe, w/stopper $45.00
Tam O'Shanter, creamer & sugar bowl $10.00
Tam O'Shanter, pitcher, 8¼" $25.00
Tam O'Shanter, plate, 10¼x6½"...............................$15.00
Tam O'Shanter, plate, 14"..$15.00
Tam O'Shanter, salt & pepper shakers, pr $20.00

View-Master Reels and Packets

William Gruber was the inventor who introduced the View-Master to the public at the New York World's Fair and the Golden Gate Exposition held in California in 1939. Thousands of reels and packets have been made since that time on every aspect of animal life, places of interest, and entertainment.

Over the years the company has changed ownership five times. It was originally Sawyer's View-Master, G.A.F. (in the mid-sixties), View-Master International (1981), Ideal Toy, and most recently Tyco Toy Company. The latter three companies produced it strictly as a toy and issued only cartoons, making the earlier non-cartoon reels and the 3-reel packets very collectible.

Sawyer made two cameras so that the public could take their own photo reels in 3-D. They made a projector as well, so that the homemade reels could be viewed on a large screen. 'Personal' or 'Mark II' cameras with their cases usually range in value from $100.00 to $200.00; rare viewers such as the blue 'Model B' start at about $100.00, and the 'Stereo-Matic 500' projector is worth $175.00 to $200.00. Most single reels range from $1.00 to $5.00, but some early Sawyer's & G.A.F.'s may bring as much as $25.00 each, and character-related reels sometimes even more.

Airplanes of the World $40.00
Alf, M $5.00
Annapolis US Navel Academy....................................$12.50
Apollo Moon Landing..$12.50
Bad News Bears, 1977..$10.00
Beautiful Washington, DC $10.00
Bedknobs & Broomsticks, 1971, M............................$17.50
Black Hole, 1979 ....$8.00
Blondie & Dagwood, 1966..$25.00
Brothers Grimm Fairy Tales $10.00
Buffalo Bill Jr, 1950s, VG..$15.00
Captain America, 1977, M...$10.00
Captain Kangaroo, M...$17.50
Charlie Brown's Summer Fun, 1978, M $8.00
CHIPS, 1981...$18.00
Close Encounters of the Third Kind, M......................$10.00
Conquest of Space 1968 ....$20.00
Coronation of Queen Elizabeth, 1950s, M..................$25.00
Cypress Gardens, 1950s, M $10.00
Daktari, 1968, M..$40.00
Denmark, 1950s, M..$10.00

Dr Shrinker & Wonderbug, 1977, VG.........................$12.50
Dr Strange, 1968, M...$10.00
Dr Strange, 1979, M...$15.00
Eight Is Enough, 1980..$15.00
Famous Stamps, 1972, M..$18.00

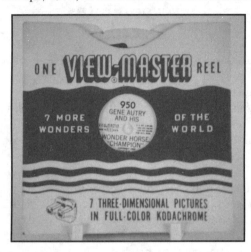

Gene Autry & His Wonder Horse Champion, #950,
  M $15.00
Godzilla, 1978, M...$18.00
Green Hornet $75.00
Happy Days, 1974, M..$15.00
Huckleberry Hound & Yogi Bear, 1960, M $25.00
Indiana Jones, 1980s, M...$8.00
Japan, 1960s, M..$8.00
Jetsons, 1981...$17.50
King Kong, 1976...$20.00
Kiss, M $30.00
Laugh In, 1968, M $30.00
Lost in Space $50.00
Love of Benji, 1977, M...$7.50
M*A*S*H, 1978...$22.00
Man From UNCLE $36.00
Mannix $14.00
Mickey Mouse in Clock Cleaners, 1971, M.................$20.00
Mork & Mindy, M..$12.00
Pee-Wee's Playhouse, 1988, M $7.00
Roadrunner, 1967, M $14.00
Rookies $10.00
Run Joe Run, 1978 ....$15.00
Scenic USA, 1960s, M...$7.50
Six Million Dollar Man, 1974, M................................$15.00
Star Trek Next Generation, M......................................$7.00
Top Cat, 1962...$27.50
US Space Port, 1968...$26.00
Voltron, M $10.00
Welcome Back Kotter, 1977, M..................................$10.00
Wrestling Superstars, 1985, M $7.00

Vistosa Dinnerware

This was a solid color line of dinnerware made from 1938 until sometime in the middle forties in an effort to compete with the very successful Fiesta line by Homer Laughlin. Vistosa was produced by Taylor, Smith, and Taylor, who like HLC were also located in the famous East Liverpool/Newell, Ohio, pottery district. Though T.S. & T. duplicated several of Fiesta's popular early glazes (mango red, cobalt blue, light green, and deep yellow), they completely lost out on the design. Instead of the wonderful Art Deco shapes the public evidently favored in combination with the primary colors, Vistosa's evoked more country charm than sophistication because of the dainty 5-petal flower molded into the handles and lid finials.

Vistosa is relatively scarce, but collectors find the same features that spelled doom for the line in the early forties more appealing today, and its scarcity only adds fun to the hunt. Red is the most desirable color, and you may have to pay a little more to get it.

Bowl, flat soup..$25.00
Bowl, fruit; 5¾"...$10.00
Bowl, salad; footed..$95.00
Bowl, vegetable; 8½".......................................$30.00
Chop plate, 11"..$20.00
Chop plate, 13"..$30.00
Creamer...$12.00
Cup & saucer...$15.00
Egg cup..$22.50
Pitcher, water; cobalt & red $75.00
Pitcher, water; other colors $60.00
Plate, 6"...$4.00
Plate, 9"..$10.00
Salt & pepper shakers, pr................................$20.00
Sugar bowl..$15.00

Teapot $95.00

W. S. George Dinnerware

From the turn of the century until the late 1950s, this East Palestine, Ohio, company produced many lines of dinnerware. Some were in solid colors, but the vast majority were decaled. Most of the lines were marked. If you'd like

more information, we recommend *The Collector's Encyclopedia of American Dinnerware* by Jo Cunningham.

Blossoms, cup & saucer, on Lido shape.......................$10.00
Blossoms, sugar bowl w/lid, on Lido shape $14.00
Bluebird, plate, 6", on Derwood shape.......................$12.00
Blushing Rose, salt & pepper shakers, Lido shape, pr.$15.00

Bouquet, plate, dinner; 10".......................................$6.00
Breakfast Nook, plate, 9", on Rainbow shape...............$8.00
Flower Rim, plate, dinner (illustrated) $6.00
Iroquois Red, creamer, on Ranchero shape $10.00
Iroquois Red, sugar bowl, on Ranchero shape...........$16.00
Mexi-Lido, bowl, vegetable $20.00
Peach Blossom, plate, 8", on Lido shape.....................$6.00
Petalware, plate, 9", dark green $3.00
Petalware, platter, 11", light green $8.00
Petit Point Rose, plate, dinner; 10", Fleurette shape......$8.00
Poppy, platter, 11½", on Rainbow shape $12.00
Rainbow, cup, on Rainbow shape..................................$8.00
Rainbow, plate, 8", on Rainbow shape..........................$4.00
Rainbow, saucer, yellow, on Rainbow shape $3.00
Ranchero, gravy boat, 2-spout, gray w/gold specks....$10.00
Roses, bowl, soup; 8", on Bolero shape.........................$6.00
Rosita, creamer, on Ranchero shape.............................$8.00
Shortcake, coffee server $45.00
Shortcake, salt & pepper shakers, on Lido shape, pr.$16.00
Tiny Flowers, egg cup, on Lido shape $12.00
Wheat, coffee server..$38.00

Wade Porcelain

If you've attended many flea markets, you're already very familiar with the tiny Wade animals, most of which are 2" and under. Wade made several lines of animal figures, but the most common were made as premiums for the Red Rose Tea company; and though most sell for $3.50 to $7.00 or so, some (Colt and the Gingerbread Man for instance) may bring $20.00 or so. A few larger animals were made as well, and these often sell for more than $100.00.

The Wade company dates to 1810. The original kiln was located near Chesterton in England. The tiny pottery merged with a second about 1900 and became known as the George Wade Pottery. They continued to grow and to absorb smaller nearby companies and eventually manufactured a wide range of products from industrial ceramics to

Irish porcelain giftware. In 1990 Wade changed its name to Seagoe Ceramics Limited.

If you'd like to learn more, we recommend *The World of Wade* by Ian Warner and Mike Posgay.

Addis shaving mug, various colored designs **$22.50**
Blow-up Disney, Bambi **$120.00**
Blow-up Disney, Lady, 1961-65 ....**$180.00**
British Character set, Pearly King, 1962..............**$160.00**
Disney hat box, Dumbo **$85.00**
Flower jug, 9", Gothic design................................**$80.00**
Guinness promotional figurine, Tony Weller, 1968...**$160.00**
Happy Families, adults, all sets, 1978-86, each..........**$12.00**
Janny Walker water jug, ca 1960 ....**$35.00**
Man in the Boat, 1978-84 ....**$60.00**
Nat West Panda money box, 1989...........................**$30.00**
Nod, figurine, 2½", 1951.....................................**$140.00**
Noddy series, Big Ears, 1958-60..........................**$150.00**
Piggy Bank Family, Lady Hillary, 7" **$35.00**
Piggy Bank Family, Maxwell, 6¾"..........................**$28.00**
Piggy Bank Family, Woody, 5" **$25.00**

Pitcher, 6", Harvestware, hand-painted flowers & vines, copper lustre band & handle................$30.00
Plaque, 12½" dia, peony design...............................**$75.00**
Red Rose Tea figurine, Three Bears, 1971-79 ....**$22.00**
Sea Gull Boat, 1961 ....**$70.00**
Shamrock Pottery, cottage, ca 1959............................**$40.00**
Spirit container, Chick, 3⅜", 1961 ....**$35.00**

Tankard, souvenir; Nelson's Column, Trafalgar Square, ca 1950s **$12.00**

Thomas the Tank, Engine miniature, 1985-87.............**$45.00**
Winkyn, figurine, 2¾", 1951.......................................**$140.00**
Yachts, wall plaque, 1955, set of 3.............................**$300.00**

Wallace China

Although they made decaled lines and airbrush-stencil patterns as well, this California pottery (1931-1964) is most famous for their 'Westward Ho' package of housewares. There were three designs, 'Rodeo,' 'Boots and Saddle,' and 'Pioneer Trails,' all created by western artist Till Goodan.

Today anything related to the West is highly collectible, and as a result, values have drastically accelerated on many items that only a few months ago tended to be sometimes overlooked on the secondary market. Any dinnerware line with a Western or Southwestern motif has become extremely popular.

Jack Chipman's book, *The Collector's Encyclopedia of California Pottery*, has a chapter on Wallace China.

Ashtray, Boots & Saddle.......................................**$50.00**
Ashtray, Christmas Greetings from Wallace China Co, round, ca 1950, stamped mark............................**$45.00**
Ashtray, commemorative of Los Angeles' Biltmore Hotel, dated 1949, stamped mark **$40.00**
Ashtray, Rodeo..**$75.00**
Bowl, cereal; 5¾", Rodeo **$25.00**
Bowl, sm, restaurant china, stamped mark, Desert Ware.**$15.00**
Bowl, 6¾", restaurant china, 1955, Chuck Wagon.......**$15.00**
Creamer, Boots & Saddle..**$35.00**

Cup & saucer, Rodeo...**$60.00**
Pitcher, Rodeo...**$125.00**
Plate, bread & butter; 7¼", Rodeo (illustrated) $30.00
Plate, dinner; Hibiscus..**$10.00**
Plate, dinner; 10¾", Rodeo (illustrated) $45.00
Platter, 11½", Mission Palm Tree................................**$45.00**
Salt & pepper shakers, range size, Rodeo, pr............**$200.00**
Salt & pepper shakers, Rodeo, pr **$60.00**
Saucer, Rodeo **$15.00**
Sugar bowl & creamer, Rodeo.................................**$150.00**

Wall Pockets

A few years ago there were only a handful of really avid wall pocket collectors, but today many are finding them intriguing. They were popular well before the turn of the century. Roseville and Weller included at least one and sometimes several in many of their successful lines of art pottery, and other American potteries made them as well. But many were imported from Germany, Czechoslovakia, China, and Japan. By the 1950s, they were passe.

Some of the most popular today are the figurals. Look for the more imaginative and buy the ones you like—these are light-hearted collectibles. If you're buying to resell, look for those designed around animals, large exotic birds, children, luscious fruits, or those that are especially eyecatching. Appeal is everything.

Baby's face, 5", little girl w/blond bangs wearing pink ruffled bonnet, rosy cheeks, #S688B **$25.00**
Basket of flowers, 9", multicolored **$15.00**
Bird, sm, white, green & yellow **$10.00**
Bird w/nest, beige, brown, yellow, blue & orange, Czechoslovakia **$20.00**
Birdhouse, blue w/pink roof **$10.00**

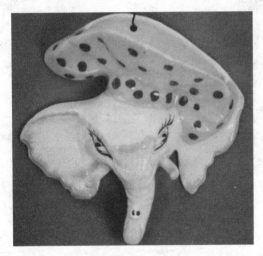

Elephant head in polka-dot hat **$50.00**
Flowers, 6x4¼", rose, blue, green & yellow **$12.00**
Indian's face, 8", in profile wearing headdress **$30.00**
Leaf, 9x7", beige & pink w/gold highlights, marked #721 USA California Originals **$25.00**
Little girl's face, 5¼", light brown curly hair & big brown eyes looking left, blue hat w/white feather **$25.00**
Oriental girl w/pigtail, 5", pink, rust & black **$12.00**
Oriental lady's face, 6½", red flower in curly blue hair, red cheeks & lips, Japan **$30.00**
Parrot, 9x4", multicolored, made in Japan **$36.00**
Potbelly stove, 7", white, green, pink & yellow, USA . **$15.00**
Windmill & trees, glossy white, orange, yellow & green, hand painted, Japan **$30.00**
Wishing well, pink **$12.50**

Watch Fobs

Strap-type watch fobs have been issued by the thousands by companies advertising farm machines, traps, guns, ammunition, heavy equipment, and products of many types.

Some are relatively common and are worth only about $3.00 to $10.00, but others may go for $100.00 or more. To learn more about their values, we recommend _Collecting Watch Fobs_ by John M. Kaduck.

Allis-Chalmers, 19 Diesel, bronze, bulldozer shape, 1950s **$20.00**
American Gopher Shovels, silver, embossed steam shovel, 1960s **$50.00**
Atlas Life Insurance, Atlas holding world, brass **$16.00**
Bastian Bros, bronze w/red enamel center, 1912 .... **$60.00**
Bridge & Iron Workers, silver w/blue rim, 1950s **$15.00**

Bryan, brass, bust portraits of he & Kern **$25.00**
Buick, colorful enamel, 1920s **$45.00**
Case, 7th National Watch Fob Show, multicolored metal, 1971 .... **$20.00**
Caterpillar, bronze, lettering above embossed bulldozer, 1930s **$20.00**
Caterpillar, silver, CAT logo above bulldozer w/raised shovel **$10.00**
Damrow Brothers Cheese, brass w/blue border **$22.50**
Denver Rock Drill Mfg, brass, rock drill shape **$57.50**
Diamond T Trucks, silver, lettering arched above frontal view of embossed truck on round disk, 1960s **$15.00**
Euclid Earth Moving Equipment, silver, lettering over tractor above wagon pulling dirt, 1950s **$15.00**
Fairchild's Flour, boy selling newspapers, celluloid, EX colors **$27.50**
Ford, celluloid center, 1960-70 .... **$12.00**
Franklin D Roosevelt, silver w/celluloid picture, 1940 .... **$25.00**
Galion Motor Graders, bronze 1950s **$12.00**
Gillette Heavy Duty Tires & Tubes, silver, bear walking through upright tire, 1950s **$30.00**
GM Diesel Power, bronze, GM logo over embossed figural motor, 1950s **$15.00**
Heinz 57, silver, This Charm Entitles Wearer to 57 Varieties of Good Luck & Happiness **$30.00**
Herman's US Army Shoes, round, celluloid center w/shield logo **$25.00**
Huber, brass, roller embossed on front **$22.50**
Ingersoll Rand, bronze, man w/jackhammer **$15.00**
International Harvester, bronze, embossed bulldozer moving dirt, 1960s **$10.00**
John Deere, bronze figural deer, 1920s **$60.00**
Joy Silver Streak Dual-Valve Rock Drills, silver **$15.00**

K of C state convention, bronze w/colorful enameled symbol, Hannibal Missouri, 1914.................................**$15.00**

Keen Kutter, red paint on silver................................**$50.00**

Loom Lodge, enameled **$20.00**

Lorain Shovels, bronze, embossed steam shovel.........**$30.00**

Mack (Trucks), bronze, embossed bulldog on round disk, 1960s..**$15.00**

Macobar Heavy Mud Weight for Oil Well Drilling, silver-colored metal **$15.00**

Malleable Range, silver, 1910.....................................**$35.00**

Michigan Tractor Shovels, bronze, 1950s **$10.00**

Miller Tire, brass, embossed tire around man's arm....**$48.00**

National Sportsman, brass, deer & gun **$25.00**

Oliver Corp, brass, tractor shape **$35.00**

Piper Heidsieck Chewing Tobacco, silver, seal of US, piper w/bagpipe on back...**$35.00**

Poggemeyer Clothes, silver w/celluloid flag insert......**$32.00**

Polarine, silver, 1920s..**$35.00**

Studebaker, silver, 1930s...**$50.00**

Tractor, Allis-Chalmers, 19 Diesel, bronze, bulldozer shape, 1950s **$20.00**

Witherspoon-McMullen Livestock Commission, porcelain, multicolor paint...**$27.50**

Wizard Shoes, round, celluloid center w/mirror on reverse, 1908 ....**$35.00**

Yoeman, porcelain, bow & arrow in red & green.......**$18.00**

1933 Century of Progress, aerial view **$42.50**

Watch Pottery

The Watt Pottery operated in Crooksville, Ohio, from 1922 until sometime in 1935. The ware they produced is easily recognized and widely available today. It appeals to collectors of country antiques, since the body is yellowware and its decoration simple. Several pieces of Watt pottery were featured in *Country Living* magazine a few years ago, and it was this exposure that seemed to catapult it onto the collectibles market.

Several patterns were made: Apple, Autumn Foliage, Cherry, Dutch Tulip, Morning-Glory, Pansy, Rooster, Tear Drop, Starflower, and Tulip among them. All were executed in bold brush strokes of primary colors. Some items you'll find will also carry a stenciled advertising message, made for retail companies as premiums for their customers.

For further study, we recommend *Watt Pottery, An Identification and Price Guide,* by Sue and Dave Morris.

Apple, baker, 5¾x8½", #96, w/lid **$125.00**

Apple, bean pot, 6½x7½", #76, w/lid, 2-handled **$135.00**

Apple, bowl, cereal or salad; 2¼x6½", #52 ....**$35.00**

Apple, bowl, mixing; 4½x8", #8, ribbed.....................**$45.00**

Apple, bowl, mixing; 5x9", #9....................................**$55.00**

Apple, bowl, 6½x8¾", #601, w/lid, ribbed................**$125.00**

Apple, casserole on stand, 5¼x8½", #3/19................**$265.00**

Apple, chip & dip set, sm 2x5" bowl & lg 3¾x8" bowl, #120/#110 ....**$250.00**

Apple, cookie jar, 8x8½", #503.............................**$300.00**

Apple, ice bucket, 7¼x7½"..**$225.00**

Apple, pitcher, 5½x5¾", #15 ....**$55.00**

Apple, salt & pepper shakers, 4½x2½", hourglass shape, holes depict S&P, pr **$200.00**

Apple (Double), baker on stand, 5½x8½", #96, w/lid.**$225.00**

Apple (Double), bowl, 4x9", #73................................**$85.00**

Apple (Double), creamer, 4¼x4½", #62 ....**$125.00**

Apple (Open), bowl, mixing; 4½x8", #8 ....**$125.00**

Apple (Reduced Decoration), bowl, mixing; 6½", #63.**$65.00**

Autumn Foliage, baker, 5¾x8½", #96, w/lid...............**$90.00**

Autumn Foliage, bowl, cereal; 1¾x6", #94 ....**$25.00**

Autumn Foliage, bowl, 3x7¾", #600, ribbed..............**$30.00**

Autumn Foliage, bowl, 6", ribbed..............................**$35.00**

Autumn Foliage, creamer, 4¼x4½", #62 ....**$55.00**

Autumn Foliage, mug, 3¾x3", #501 ....**$125.00**

Autumn Foliage, pie plate, 1½x9", #33......................**$80.00**

Autumn Foliage, pitcher, 5½x5¾", #15 ....**$35.00**

Autumn Foliage, refrigerator dish, 3x7½", #02, rare ..**$165.00**

Autumn Foliage, salt & pepper shakers, 4½x2½", hourglass shape, holes depict S&P, pr **$145.00**

Banded (Blue & White), bowl, mixing; 2¾x5"............**$25.00**

Banded (Blue & White), casserole, 4½x8¾", w/lid......**$55.00**

Banded (Brown), creamer, 4¼x4½", #62....................**$55.00**

Banded (Brown), plate, salad; 7½", #102 .... $25.00
Banded (Light Blue & White), bowl, mixing; 7x7¾" ... $35.00
Banded (White), bowl, 2½x5" $25.00
Banded (White), pitcher, 7x7¾" $45.00
Brown Basketweave, bean pot, 6½x7½", w/lid $50.00
Brown Basketweave, mug, 3¾x3¼", #801/#806 .... $10.00
Butterfly, bowl, 4x7", very rare $85.00
Cherry, bowl, berry; #4 .... $25.00
Cherry, bowl, cereal; #52 .... $25.00
Cherry, cookie jar, 7½x7", #21 .... $160.00
Cherry, pitcher, 8x8½", #17 .... $125.00
Dogwood, plate, bread; 6½" dia $55.00
Dogwood, platter, 15", #31 .... $110.00
Dutch Tulip, bean pot, 6½x7½", #76, w/lid $225.00
Dutch Tulip, bowl, 6½x8½", #67, w/lid $175.00
Dutch Tulip, pitcher, 5½x5¾", #15 .... $85.00
Eagle, canister, 7¼x7", #72, no lid $150.00
Eagle, pitcher, 8x8½", w/ice lip $185.00
Kitch-N-Queen, bowl, mixing; 5x9", #9, ribbed $35.00
Kitch-N-Queen, cookie jar, #503 .... $125.00
Kla-Ham'rd, pie plate, 1½x9", #43-13 .... $35.00
Kla-Ham'rd, pitcher, 7x8", #43-14 .... $55.00
Morning Glory, bowl, 4½x8", #8 .... $60.00
Morning Glory, cookie jar, 10¾x7½", #95 .... $275.00
Morning Glory, creamer, 4¼x4½", #97 .... $100.00
Morning Glory, sugar bowl, 4¼x5x3", #98 .... $175.00
Pansy (Cut-Leaf), bowl, individual serving; 2x5½", bull's eye
   w/red swirls $25.00
Pansy (Cut-Leaf), pitcher, 6½x6¾" $75.00
Pansy (Cut-Leaf), plate, individual spaghetti; 1½x8" $40.00
Pansy (Cut-Leaf), saucer, 6½", bull's eye w/red swirls . $20.00
Pansy (Old), cookie jar, 7½x7", w/crosshatching $140.00
Pansy (Old), pitcher, 8x8½", #17 .... $125.00
Pansy (Old), platter, 15", w/crosshatching $125.00
Pansy (Raised), casserole, individual; 3¾x7½" long, w/lid,
   stick handle $175.00
Pansy (Raised), creamer, 3x5½" $85.00
Rooster, bowl, 4x5", #05, raised bands, w/lid $135.00
Rooster, bowl, 4x9½" $75.00
Rooster, creamer, 4¼x4½", #62 .... $85.00
Rooster, ice bucket, 7¼x7½", w/lid $185.00
Rooster, nesting bowl set, #66/#67/#68 .... $180.00
Rooster, pitcher, 5½x5¾", #15 .... $75.00

Rooster, pitcher, 6½", #16 .... $125.00
Starflower, bowl, berry; 1½x5¾" $35.00

Starflower, bowl, 4x9½", #73 .... $55.00
Starflower, grease jar, 5x4½", #47 .... $175.00
Starflower, mug, 4½x2¾", #501, barrel shape $85.00
Starflower, pie plate, 1½x9", #33 .... $125.00
Starflower, salt & pepper shakers, 4x2½", barrel shape,
   green bands, pr $150.00
Starflower, tumbler, 4½x4", #56, tapered sides $225.00
Starflower (Green-on-Brown), bowl, spaghetti; #39 .... $90.00
Starflower (Green-on-Brown), pitcher, 5½x5¾", #15 ... $75.00
Starflower (Green-on-Brown), platter, 15", #31 .... $110.00
Starflower (Pink-on-Green), bowl, berry; 1¾x5" $35.00
Starflower (Pink-on-Green), casserole, 8¾", w/lid $125.00
Starflower (White-on-Blue), bowl, spaghetti; 13", #39 . $175.00
Tear Drop, bowl, 3x7", #66 .... $45.00
Tear Drop, cheese crock, 8x8¼", #80 .... $275.00
Tear Drop, individual bean server, 2¼x3½", #75 .... $25.00
Tear Drop, pitcher, 5½x5¾", #15 .... $45.00
Tulip, bowl, mixing; 2x5¾", #603, ribbed $65.00
Tulip, bowl, mixing; 5¾x8½", #65 .... $80.00
Tulip, bowl, 5½x7¾", #600, ribbed, w/lid $200.00
Tulip, creamer, 4¼x4½", #62 .... $95.00
Tulip, pitcher, 6½x6¾", #16 .... $125.00
White Daisy, casserole, 5x8¾" $55.00
White Daisy, cup & saucer $75.00
White Daisy, plate, salad; 8½" $65.00
Woodgrain, bowl, chip & dip; 2¾x11¼", #611W $75.00
Woodgrain, pitcher, 7½x6", #614W $75.00
Yellow Morning Glory, casserole, 4x8½", #94, w/lid ... $95.00

Weil Ware

Though the Weil company made dinnerware and some kitchenware, their figural pieces are attracting the most collector interest. They were in business from the 1940s until the mid-fifties, another of the small but very successful California companies whose work has become so popular today. They dressed their 'girls' in beautiful gowns of vivid rose, light dusty pink, turquoise blue and other lovely colors enhanced with enameled 'lacework' and flowers, sgraffito, sometimes even with tiny applied blossoms. Both paper labels and ink stamps were used to mark them, but as you study their features, you'll soon learn to recognize even those that have lost their labels over the years. Four-number codes and decorators' initials are also common.

If you want to learn more, we recommend *The Collector's Encyclopedia of California Pottery* by Jack Chipman.

Bowl, cream soup; Rose $6.00
Bowl, divided vegetable; Rose $12.00
Bowl, salad; sm, Rose $4.00
Coffee server, Bamboo $20.00
Comport, sweets; Rose $12.50
Cup & saucer, Rose $6.00
Dish, 10½" square, divided, Dogwood $7.50
Figurine, boy w/wheelbarrow, #4005 .... $28.00
Figurine, lg, girl w/chin lifted, sgraffito on skirt $45.00
Figurine, 11", girl w/sm bowl, simple $25.00

Gravy boat, Rose...**$17.50**
Planter, 11", girl figural, #1899, artist signed, simple...**$30.00**
Planter, 8", lady's head w/fan, hand-painted...............**$45.00**

Planter/vase, lady's head w/fan, hand-painted roses...$45.00

Plate, 10", Rose...**$6.00**
Vase, 8½", Ming Tree, w/coralene.................................**$35.00**

Wall pocket/vase, 9¾", little girl w/elbow on vase.$28.00

Weller

Though the Weller Pottery has been closed since 1948, they were so prolific that you'll be sure to see several pieces anytime you're 'antiquing.' They were one of the largest of the art pottery giants that located in the Zanesville, Ohio, area, using locally dug clays to produce their wares. In the early years, they made hand-decorated vases, jardinieres, lamps, and other decorative items for the home, many of which were signed by notable artists such as Fredrick Rhead, John Lessell, Virginia Adams, Anthony Dunlavy, Dorothy England, Albert Haubrich, Hester Pillsbury, E.L. Pickens, and Jacques Sicard, to name only a few. Some of their early lines were First and Second Dickens, Eocean, Sicardo, Etna, Louwelsa, Turada, and Aurelian. Portraits of Indians, animals of all types, lady golfers, nudes, and scenes of Dickens stories were popular themes, and some items were overlaid with silver filigree. These lines are rather hard to find at this point in time, and prices are generally high; but there's plenty of their later production still around; and most pieces are relatively inexpensive.

If you'd like to learn more, we recommend *The Collector's Encyclopedia of Weller Pottery* by Sharon and Bob Huxford.

Ardsley, bud vase, 7½", cattails & water lily decoration on green...**$45.00**
Art Nouveau, bank, 8", corn figural, unmarked........**$275.00**
Art Nouveau, ewer, 14½", floral decoration on pastel, slim form, ornate handle, marked **$350.00**
Art Nouveau, vase, 4½", ear of corn form...................**$95.00**
Atlas, bowl, 4", tan w/cream interior, 5-pointed star-shaped rim...**$45.00**
Atlas, star dish, 2", ivory 5-pointed, script mark.........**$25.00**
Atlas, vase, 10½", blue w/ivory interior, 5-pointed star shape, marked...**$65.00**
Baldin, vase, 9½", apple decoration on bulbous form, twig handles **$225.00**
Blo' Red, vase, 3½", golden tan mottle on dark red, sm handles, marked...**$50.00**
Blo' Red, vase, 7", golden tan mottling on dark red, ink stamp **$70.00**
Blossom, wall vase, 7½", floral decoration on brown .**$60.00**
Bonito, bowl, 3" high, floral decoration on cream, blue band at base, signed CF, marked **$85.00**
Bonito, bowl, 3½" high, floral on cream, signed CF....**$75.00**
Bonito, vase, 11", floral decoration on ivory, handles, artist signed, marked...**$250.00**
Bonito, vase, 7", floral decoration on ivory, blue trim at rim & foot, upturned handles, artist signed...............**$150.00**
Bouquet, pitcher, 9½", yellow floral decoration on blue, marked...**$60.00**
Bouquet, vase, 9", pink floral decoration on blue, cylindrical w/sm foot, in-mold mark **$35.00**
Brighton, figurine, 5", bluebird on stump, tail up **$275.00**
Brighton, figurine, 6", flamingo, unmarked...............**$225.00**
Brighton, figurine, 7x11½", pheasant.........................**$450.00**
Cactus, figurine, 4", camel, brown, recumbent **$75.00**
Cactus, figurine, 4", elephant, brown, marked..........**$110.00**
Cactus, figurine, 4½", duck, green, marked **$85.00**
Cactus, figurine, 5", Pan w/lily, brown, marked **$75.00**
Cameo, basket, 7½", embossed white floral decoration on green, script mark...**$30.00**
Cameo, vase, 7", embossed white floral decoration on green, script mark...**$25.00**

Clarmont, candle holders, 8", stylized floral decoration on dark brown, marked, pr **$175.00**

Classic, bowl, 8", white, reticulated design at flared rim, script mark................................**$40.00**

Classic, wall pocket, 6", green, reticulated design at top, script mark................................**$80.00**

Classic, window box, 4", green, reticulated design at rim, script mark................................**$70.00**

Claywood, mug, 5", floral decoration on brown & ivory w/brown band at rim & base, unmarked...........**$100.00**

Claywood, vase, 5½", brown spider web pattern on ivory, cylindrical, unmarked **$75.00**

Coppertone, fan vase, 8", brown & green 'copper-like' appearance, flower form w/frog each side.........**$450.00**

Coppertone, vase, 6½", brown & green 'copper-like' appearance, flared cylinder w/sm foot, unmarked........**$150.00**

Cornish, candle holders, 3½", berry & leaf decoration on brown, in-mold script mark, pr............**$40.00**

Cornish, vase, 6", berry & leaf decoration on blue, sm handles, unmarked................................**$30.00**

Darsie, candle holders, 3½", berry & leaf decoration on brown, in-mold script mark...............**$65.00**

Darsie, vase, 5½", blue w/embossed swags & tassels, scalloped rim, in-mold script mark **$35.00**

Darsie, vase, 9½", green w/embossed swags & tassels, in-mold script mark.........................**$65.00**

Decorated Creamware, mug, 5", decalcomania **$75.00**

Decorated Creamware, mug, 5", hand-painted floral decoration, unmarked.....................................**$125.00**

Decorated Creamware, pitcher, 5", decalcomania **$100.00**

Delsa, vase, 5", pink floral decoration on white, sm handles, footed, marked....................................**$30.00**

Elberta, bowl, 3½" high, peachy-tan shaded to green, 3-part, marked................................**$50.00**

Elberta, vase, 4", peachy-tan shaded to green, classic form, marked................................**$30.00**

Elberta, vase, 8", peachy-tan shaded to green, slightly waisted, marked................................**$45.00**

Eocean, vase, 6", floral decoration on gray shaded to cream, artist signed, tub handles...................**$210.00**

Eocean, vase, 8", berries & leaves, artist signed, NM .**$375.00**

Eocean, vase, 8", lg stork, sgn F (Ferrell), flattened, footed, handled **$1,000.00**

Etna, vase, 11", floral decoration on shaded gray, handles, marked................................**$300.00**

Etna, vase, 4½", lizard applied to side of gourd form, impressed mark....................................**$450.00**

Etna, vase, 6½", floral decoration on pastel shaded gourd form, marked................................**$125.00**

Etna, vase, 7", floral decoration on pastel shaded background **$15.00**

Etna, vase, 7", floral decoration on pastel shaded classic form, marked................................**$150.00**

Flask, 4", All's Well, ivory w/brown details **$135.00**

Flask, 6", Never Dry, ivory w/brown details............**$135.00**

Flemish, towel bar, 11½", bluebirds over, 3 roses..**$1,100.00**

Fleron, bowl, 3" high, green w/lavender highlights & interior, vertical ribs, folded rim, marked Hand Made **$45.00**

Florenzo, basket, 5½", floral decoration on ivory w/green & brown trim, ink mark................................**$55.00**

Florenzo, planter, 3½", floral decoration on ivory w/green & brown trim, square shape, marked.......................**$35.00**

Floretta, ewer, 10½", vintage decoration on brown, straight sides, double-circle mark **$135.00**

Floretta, vase, 7½", floral decoration on brown, angle handles, footed, double-circle mark.........................**$125.00**

Geode, vase, 5", blue stars & streaks on ivory, bulbous form, sm neck, marked **$200.00**

Gloria, vase, 12½", iris decoration on green, marked..**$85.00**

Goldenglow, bowl, 3½x16", dark golden tan w/embossed floral decoration, sm handles, unmarked.............**$60.00**

Goldenglow, bud vase, 8½", dark golden tan w/embossed floral decoration, 3-legged, in-mold script mark...**$35.00**

Goldenglow, candle holder, 3½", dark golden tan, triple, in-mold script mark................................**$40.00**

Greenbriar, pitcher, 10", marble-like mottling **$160.00**

Greenbriar, vase, 6", marble-like mottling, classic form, unmarked **$55.00**

Hobart, figure of a lady, 11½", shaded pink, standing in fluted bowl $300.00

Hudson, vase, 9½", flowers on blue to green background, signed S Timberlake......................$395.00

Lavonia, vase, 10", embossed floral decoration on pink to green, slim cylindrical form, paper label............$150.00

Lido, cornucopia, 5", cream to peach, script mark......$20.00

Lido, vase, 7", blue shaded to green flower form, marked..$30.00

Lonhuda, vase, 4½", floral decoration on brown, integral handles, artist signed, shield mark.......................$200.00

Lorbeek, wall pocket, 8½", glossy lavender-pink, 'folded' triangular shape, marked..$100.00

Louwelsa, candle holder, 4½", floral on brown, artist signed MH, marked..$145.00

Louwelsa, candle holder, 9", floral decoration on brown, slim form, artist signed, half-circle mark............$115.00

Louwelsa, ewer, 12", floral decoration on brown, artist signed, marked...$350.00

Louwelsa, vase, 11", floral decoration on brown, slim form, angle handles, signed V Adams, marked............$260.00

Louwelsa, vase, 2", floral decoration on brown, squat shape w/integral handles, half-circle mark......................$85.00

Louwelsa, vase, 3", floral decoration on blue, sm neck bulbous w/integral handle, half-circle mark............$400.00

Louwelsa, vase, 5", floral decoration on brown, shouldered form, half-circle mark....................................$115.00

Malvern, vase, 5½", floral decoration on green to brown, gourd form, script mark......................................$25.00

Malvern, wall pocket, 11", floral decoration on green to brown, unmarked...$65.00

Manhattan, pitcher, 10", dark green floral decoration on green, marked...$100.00

Manhattan, vase, 9", dark green leaves decoration on med green, marked...$85.00

Novelty, bluebird, 2½", unmarked.................................$175.00

Novelty, butterfly, 3", unmarked.................................$175.00

Novelty, dragonfly, 3¼", unmarked............................$175.00

Novelty, kangaroo & pouch, 5½", brown, pouch forms ash receiver, unmarked..$85.00

Novelty, Three Pigs ashtray, 4", pigs beside tray, brown, unmarked...$70.00

Oak Leaf, basket, 7½", oak leaf on brown, twig handle, marked...$60.00

Oak Leaf, vase, 6", oak leaf on blue, script mark........$20.00

Patra, basket, 5½", floral-decorated band, brown textured bowl w/green trim at rim & foot, marked............$90.00

Patra, nut dish, 3", floral decoration on brown textured ground, green handle & trim, marked...................$35.00

Patra, vase, 4½", floral decoration on brown textured ground, green handles, marked............................$40.00

Patrician, vase, 5", tan w/green runs, 2 goose-head handles, unmarked...$30.00

Patrician, vase, 6", green mottle w/goose-head handles, marked...$60.00

Raydance, vase, 7½", white w/embossed leaf-spray decoration, upturned handles, marked..........................$35.00

Raydance, vase, 9", blue w/embossed floral decoration at base, sm upturned handles, marked.....................$60.00

Sicardo, bowl vase, 8½", Art Nouveau lilies..........$1,100.00

Softone, bud vase, double; 9", pink, 2 tubes in 'V' form, script mark...$28.00

Softone, ewer, 5", pink w/embossed linear 'swag-like' decoration..$35.00

Souvenir, pin tray, 2½", applied rose at side of ruffled tray, marked...$100.00

Souvenir, vase, 3", St Louis 1904, unmarked............$200.00

Stellar, vase, 5", white stars on black bulbous shape, script mark..$150.00

Stellar, vase, 6", white stars on blue, marked...........$150.00

Sydonia, fan vase, 5½", blue mottle to green, marked.$60.00

Sydonia, planter, 4", blue mottle shaded to green.......$35.00

Teapot, 5", Gold-Green, ink mark.............................$75.00

Teapot, 6", pink w/gold diamond band & trim, gold stamped mark...$75.00

Turkis, vase, 5", drip glaze on maroon, bulbous........$30.00

Turkis, vase, 5", drip glaze on maroon, upturned handles, marked...$45.00

Turkis, vase, 5½", drip glaze on maroon, angle handles, marked...$90.00

Utility ware, pitcher, 5½", brown, cylindrical, angle handles, marked...$45.00

Utility ware, teapot, 4", brown, simple shape.............$35.00

Utility ware, teapot, 6½", pineapple form, marked....$170.00

Utility ware, tumbler, 4", brown, marked...................$12.00

Wild Rose, vase, 6½", open white floral decoration on green, marked...$25.00

Wild Rose, vase, 9½", open white floral decoration on pink, handles, marked...$35.00

Woodcraft, vase, 9", w/rare applied blackbird ...$350.00

Woodrose, bowl, 2½x8½", pink flower decoration on brown 'wooden' tub form, handles, unmarked................$60.00

Woodrose, wall vase, 5½", pink flower decoration on brown 'wooden' tub form, marked.................................$90.00

Zona, pitcher, 8½", kingfisher panels, natural colors.$200.00

Western Heroes

No friend was ever more true, no brother more faithful, no acquaintance more real to us than our favorite cowboys of radio, TV, and the silver screen. They were upright, strictly moral, extremely polite, and tireless in their pursuit of law and order in the American West. How unfortunate that such role models are practically extinct nowadays.

This is an area of strong collector interest right now, and prices are escalating. Some collectors prefer one cowboy hero over the others and concentrate their collections on that particular star. Some unlikely items are included in this specialized area – hair tonic bottles, cookie jars, wallets, and drinking mugs, for instance.

For more infomation and some wonderful pictures, we recommend *Toys, Antique and Collectible,* and *Character Toys and Collectibles, First and Second Series,* all by David Longest.

See also Big Little Books; Character Watches; Games; Puzzles; Paper Dolls; Pin-back Buttons; and Toys (Premiums and Guns).

Annie Oakley, rifle, 32", marked Daisy Lever Pop Rifle, gold, VG **$75.00**

Bat Masterson, cane, black wood w/silver handle, w/instructions, NM **$35.00**

Bill Elliot, tablet, EX **$20.00**

Billy the Kid, gun, 6¾", marked Stevens, repeater, VG **$85.00**

Billy the Kid, gun, 8", marked Service Manufacturing Company, repeater, VG..**$30.00**

Buffalo Bill, gun, 8", marked Stevens, VG....................**$30.00**

Buffalo Bill & Calamity Jane, coloring book, Whitman, 1957, EX...**$25.00**

Buffalo Bill Cody, figure, 3¾", Gabriel, #31634, jointed plastic, w/carbine, ca early 1980s, M........................**$15.00**

Butch Cavendish, figure, 3¾", Gabriel, #31632, jointed plastic, w/pistol, ca 1981, M **$15.00**

Cisco Kid, coloring book, 13¾x10½", full-color cover photo, Saalfield, 1953, EX...**$40.00**

Cisco Kid, hobby horse, marked Ride 'Em Cisco Kid, 1950s, M..**$70.00**

Cisco Kid, neckerchief, w/nickeled metal sombrero stamped slide, M..**$20.00**

Cisco Kid, tee shirt, 1950s, NM **$38.00**

Daniel Boone, magic slate, Fess Parker & graphics on cardboard, NM..**$15.00**

Davy Crockett, coonskin hat, M...................................**$32.00**

Davy Crockett, gun, Buffalo Rifle, Hubley, cap shooter, M...**$100.00**

Davy Crockett, gun, 8", tin clicker-type pistol, VG......**$20.00**

Davy Crockett, knife, marked Frontier & Imperial Knife Company, 1950s, EX..**$35.00**

Davy Crockett, pillow case, M **$10.00**

Davy Crockett, plate, 9½", brown graphics on ivory ground, marked Royal China, dated 1955, M.....................**$40.00**

Davy Crockett, powder horn, marked Daisy, M..........**$40.00**

Davy Crockett, record, 33⅓ rpm, marked Walt Disney Productions, 1971, w/24-page booklet, EX.................**$8.00**

Davy Crockett, record, 45 rpm, Ballad of Davy Crockett, Columbia, Fess Parker on sleeve, ca 1955, EX......**$20.00**

Davy Crockett, rifle, 35", Daisy Pop-Lever Rifle, VG ...**$75.00**

Davy Crockett, tie clip & cuff links, copper-colored metal, M **$35.00**

Davy Crockett, toy watch, M on card **$35.00**

Davy Crockett, wall plaque, 7½" oval, embossed bust, marked Miller Studio Inc, ca 1955, EX..................**$45.00**

Davy Crockett, wallet, 4x5", brown vinyl, marked Walt Disney, ca 1955, EX...**$20.00**

Gene Autry, bicycle horn, ca 1950, M **$50.00**

Gene Autry, boots, red & white western style w/2x3" full-color portrait on sides, late 1940s-50s, EX............**$75.00**

Gene Autry, cap pistol, pearl handles, Kenton, NM **$70.00**

Gene Autry, cap pistol, 8½", silver cast iron w/orange plastic grips, marked Kenton Toys, late 1940s, VG.........**$75.00**

Gene Autry, coloring book, Whitman, 1975, NM **$25.00**

Gene Autry, coloring book, 8x11", ca 1950s, VG **$15.00**

Gene Autry, guitar, marked Emenee, ca 1950s, EX **$65.00**

Gene Autry, gun, 7½", Buss Henry, full grip, gold & nickel, western style, VG **$45.00**

Gene Autry, hankerchief, 15½x16", outline portrait on white cloth w/facsimile signature, 1940s-50s, EX...........**$37.50**

Gene Autry, marionette, 18", 1940s, EX **$210.00**

Gene Autry, paint book, Merrill Publishing, 1940, EX.**$45.00**

Gene Autry, program, 1st Annual Fort Madison Rodeo, 1948, M...**$30.00**

Gene Autry, record, 45 rpm, Frosty the Snow Man, Columbia label, ca 1940s, VG **$5.00**

Gene Autry, records, 45rpm, Merry Christmas, Columbia Records, 1950, set of 4 in original sleeves, original box, EX..**$35.00**

Gene Autry, ring, bent horseshoe nail w/Flying A logo, 1950s, EX...**$75.00**

Gene Autry, song book, Song Hits, 1941, NM **$17.50**

Gene Autry, tablet, 9x5½", color cover w/facsimile signature, 1950s, M..**$30.00**

Gene Autry, wallet, 3½x4½", graphics on vinyl w/facsimile name, early 1950s, EX....................................**$30.00**

Hoot Gibson, lariat, M **$80.00**

Hopalong Cassidy, alarm clock, metal, ca 1950s, EX.**$100.00**

Hopalong Cassidy, autograph album, embossed portrait on leatherette, EX..**$75.00**

Hopalong Cassidy, binoculars, plastic, ca 1950, EX **$45.00**

Hopalong Cassidy, birthday card, 6¼x4¼", mechanical w/revolving scenic wheel on front, marked Buzza, early '50s **$37.50**

Hopalong Cassidy, book, Two Young Cowboys, Whitman Cozy-Corner Book, 1951, EX................................**$25.00**

Hopalong Cassidy, bottle, 9½", Hair Trainer, 1950, w/original contents, NM **$50.00**

Hopalong Cassidy, Butternut Bread wrapper, EX........**$20.00**

Hopalong Cassidy, coloring book, William Bond cover, Samuel Lowe, EX **$50.00**

Hopalong Cassidy, cowgirl suit, EX **$120.00**

Hopalong Cassidy, figure, 3", painted cast iron **$20.00**

Hopalong Cassidy, flashlight, portrait w/Morse code on sides, no siren, screw-off top, Topper Toys, EX **$150.00**

Hopalong Cassidy, greeting card, w/Santa Claus, marked Buzza, M **$40.00**

Hopalong Cassidy, gun, Repeating Cap Pistol, portrait & fac-simile signature, All Metal Products Co, MIB **$75.00**

Hopalong Cassidy, gun, 9", marked Wyandotte, repeater in nickel & gold, VG **$85.00**

Hopalong Cassidy, lobby card, Heart of the West, portrait w/Gabby Hayes, 1936, EX **$25.00**

Hopalong Cassidy, magazine ad, Alden's Hoppy wear, 2 color, 1-page, 1950, EX **$10.00**

Hopalong Cassidy, magazine ad, Rollfast Bicycles, 1-page, ca 1950s, unframed, EX **$25.00**

Hopalong Cassidy, milk bottle, 1-qt, Morland Dairy, graphics on clear glass, NM **$40.00**

Hopalong Cassidy, milk bottle stopper, portrait & My Favorite on paper circle, EX **$15.00**

Hopalong Cassidy, mug, marked WS George, EX **$20.00**

Hopalong Cassidy, napkins, set of 25, M in package .. **$35.00**

Hopalong Cassidy, party invitation, marked Buzza, 1950s, EX **$12.00**

Hopalong Cassidy, pencil case, cardboard w/3-section sliding tray, EX **$80.00**

Hopalong Cassidy, pencil case, 8", hard plastic gun shape, black & white portrait on hinged lid, unmarked, empty, EX **$62.50**

Hopalong Cassidy, photo, black & white glossy, scene from Bar 20 Rides Again, 1935, M **$10.00**

Hopalong Cassidy, plate, 9½", Hoppy on Topper on white china, marked WS George, 1950s, NM **$32.50**

Hopalong Cassidy, postcard, Happy Birthday, Savings Rodeo Club, EX **$14.00**

Hopalong Cassidy, radio, Arvin Table-N, red $500.00
Hopalong Cassidy, record, 45 rpm, Billy & the Bandit, in original sleeve, EX **$35.00**

Hopalong Cassidy, record, 78 rpm, Hopalong Cassidy & the 2-Legged Wolf, marked Bozo Approved, sleeve missing, EX **$45.00**

Hopalong Cassidy, tumbler, 5", milk glass w/ fired-on black design $28.00
Hopalong Cassidy, tumbler, 6", Hoppy twirling rope, Breakfast Milk & verse on back, milk glass, flared top, ring base **$40.00**

Hopalong Cassidy, wallet, embossed name on leather w/metal steer's head on exterior panels, EX **$140.00**

Hopalong Cassidy, 2-ring school binder, w/portrait on Topper & name on front, EX **$60.00**

Kit Carson, cap gun, 8¼", marked Kilgore, repeater, nickel & gold metal, VG **$25.00**

Kit Carson, cap pistol, marked Kilgore, EX **$38.00**

Lone Ranger, badge, Jr Deputy on 6-point star, NM ... **$25.00**

Lone Ranger, coloring book, Whitman, 1959, EX **$30.00**

Lone Ranger, figure, 3¾", Gabriel, #31630, jointed plastic, 1981, M **$15.00**

Lone Ranger, figure, 9½", Gabriel, #23620, fully-jointed plastic, cloth clothes, M **$35.00**

Lone Ranger, game, Hi-Yo-o-o-o Silver, Parker Brothers, 1938, VG $35.00
Lone Ranger, gun, 10", marked Actoy, repeater type in nickel & brass, VG **$70.00**

Lone Ranger, gun, 8", tin clicker pistol, w/celluloid insert grips, VG **$50.00**

Lone Ranger, gun, 8¼", marked Kilgore, repeater, VG .**$65.00**

Lone Ranger, hat, Lone Ranger Hi! Yo! Silver! inscribed on white felt w/red trim, 1940s, M............**$45.00**

Lone Ranger, neckerchief, 17x17x26" triangle, printed image on blue cloth, 1930s, EX............**$62.50**

Lone Ranger, premium coupon, for comic book, 1939, NM............**$10.00**

Lone Ranger, rifle, 32", Marx-Winchester Lever, VG....**$50.00**

Lone Ranger, scrapbook, Whitman, 1950s, EX............**$35.00**

Lone Ranger, stamp set, marked Stamp Kraft, dated 1939, boxed, EX............**$40.00**

Lone Ranger, toothbrush holder, horse & rider figural, painted composition, VG............**$38.00**

Lone Ranger, toy pedometer, metal, VG............**$38.00**

Lone Ranger & Lassie, banner, 1940s, EX............$25.00

Lone Ranger & Tonto, puzzle, 200 pieces, American Publishing Corp............$15.00

Matt Dillon, badge, US Marshall, M............**$30.00**

Matt Dillon, gun, 11½", marked Halco #45, break-top repeater, VG............**$150.00**

Matt Dillon, gun, 9", marked Leslie Henry, portrait on grip, VG............**$65.00**

Maverick, gun & holster set, wrist type w/single-shot cap gun, dated 1959, M on card............**$160.00**

Red Ryder, frame-tray puzzle, 11x14", Fred Harman art, marked Jaymar & Slesinger, 1951............**$37.50**

Red Ryder, holster, leather, no gun, VG............**$20.00**

Red Ryder & Little Beaver, wall plaque, 4¼x5½x1", relief images in plaster, marked Slesinger, 1940s............**$37.50**

Rifleman, patch, 2x4", Chuck Conners black & white photo on red & yellow ground, marked Arlington Hat, 1958, VG............**$37.50**

Rifleman, rifle, marked Hubley, 1959, NM in box.....**$400.00**

Rifleman, tablet, Chuck Conners cover, EX............**$10.00**

Roy Rogers, bandana, lg, M............**$40.00**

Roy Rogers, coloring book, 11x8", Roy Rogers Rodeo Days, Whitman #1220, 1962, NM............**$35.00**

Roy Rogers, gun, marked Lone Star, steer's head on grips, VG............**$85.00**

Roy Rogers, gun, 2½", marked Tuck-A-Way Derringer, nickel & gold metal, VG............**$35.00**

Roy Rogers, harmonica, M in package............**$75.00**

Roy Rogers, key chain, silver bullet, M in package.....**$15.00**

Roy Rogers, mug, hard plastic bust figural, marked F&F Mold & Die Company, ca 1950s, M............**$30.00**

Roy Rogers, mug, 3", glazed china, 1950s, EX............**$60.00**

Roy Rogers, playset, Roy Rogers Chuck Wagon, 13" long, Ideal, 1950s, EX............**$135.00**

Roy Rogers, playset, Roy Rogers Stage Coach Wagon Train, 14" long, plastic, wind-up, 1950s, MIB............**$250.00**

Roy Rogers, rifle, 26", marked Marx, ca 1950s, EX......**$65.00**

Roy Rogers, song book, Roy Rogers Guitar Folio, ca 1954, 20-page, NM............**$12.50**

Roy Rogers, spurs, sold by Sears, 1954, boxed, NM..**$150.00**

Roy Rogers, tablet, 8x10", picture cover, G............**$20.00**

Roy Rogers, yo-yo, M in package............**$20.00**

Roy Rogers & Trigger, bandana, red cloth, EX............**$35.00**

Straight Arrow, bandana, Nabisco radio premium, 1949, EX............**$35.00**

Tin Mix, poster, Safety Patrol, 1947, NM............**$32.50**

Tom Mix, cigar box label, 6x10", colorful, 1920s, EX..**$50.00**

Tom Mix, manual, Ralston Purina, 1944, EX............**$48.00**

Tom Mix, spurs, glow-in-the-dark, EX............**$45.00**

Tonto, figure, 9½", Gabriel, #23621, fully-jointed plastic, cloth clothes, M............**$45.00**

Tonto, puppet, vinyl, 1966, NM............**$25.00**

Wild Bill Hickok, gun, 9", repeater, marked Leslie Henry, VG............**$45.00**

Wild Bill Hickok, postcard, 3½x5¼", glossy black & white photo w/facsimile signature, 1950............**$30.00**

Wyatt Earp, badge, marked Marshall on tin, NM.........**$20.00**

Wyatt Earp, badge, US Marshall, w/Hugh O'Brian photo, 1950s, M............**$35.00**

Wyatt Earp, color & stencil set, Transogram, '59, NM.**$38.00**

Wyatt Earp, crayon & stencil set, 10x11½x1¼", Life & Legend of Wyatt Earp, Transogram, 1958, EX............**$62.50**

Wyatt Earp, gun, 9", repeater, marked Actoy, VG.......**$40.00**

Wyatt Earp, outfit, US Marshall, marked Pla-Master, M.**$75.00**

Wyatt Earp, puzzle, 14½x11½", Hugh O'Brian full-color portrait, Whitman, 1958, frame tray, EX............**$37.50**

Wyatt Earp, record, 45 rpm, The Legend of Wyatt Earp, RCA Victor, original picture sleeve, VG............**$3.50**

Zorro, belt buckle, 1¾x2¾", metal die-cut Zorro on horse on pearlized ground, marked WDP, ca 1960, EX......**$58.00**

Zorro, playset, mask & whip, marked M Shimmel Sons, 1950s, M on card..**$70.00**

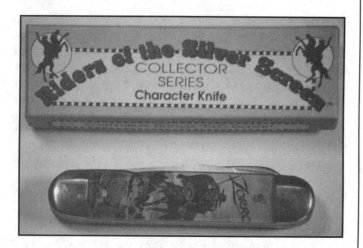

Zorro, pocketknife, Riders of the Silver Screen Collector Series, Camillus, MIB..................**$45.00**
Zorro, puppet, cloth & vinyl, ca 1960s, EX................**$15.00**

Westmoreland Glass

Before the turn of the century, this company was known as the Specialty Glass Works and was located in East Liverpool, Ohio, where they produced tableware as well as utilitarian items. They moved to Grapeville, Pennsylvania, in 1890 and added many more decorative glassware items to their inventory. Carnival glass was their mainstay before the years of the twenties, but they're most famous today for their milk glass, black glass, and colored glass tableware patterns.

Early pieces carried paper labels, but by the 1960s, the mark was embossed in the glass itself. The superimposed 'WG' mark was the first of the embossed marks; the last was a circle containing 'Westmoreland' around the outside with a large 'W' in the center.

For more information, we recommend *Westmoreland Glass* by Philip J. Rosso, Jr., and Phil Rosso.

See also Animal Dishes; Carnival Glass.

Beaded Edge, plate, 7", milk glass, hand-painted fruit.**$18.00**
Beaded Edge, tumbler, milk glass w/hand-painted fruit, footed...**$15.00**
Beaded Grape, ashtray, 5", milk glass **$12.00**
Beaded Grape, candy dish, milk glass, footed, w/lid..**$22.00**
Beaded Grape, honey dish, 5", milk glass, w/lid.........**$28.00**
Beaded Grape, puff box, hand-painted roses & bows on milk glass...**$32.00**
Black Glass, plate, 8½", Mary Gregroy-style children hand-painted in white, each.......................................**$45.00**
Della Robbia, bowl, 12", colored fruit, footed **$85.00**
Della Robbia, bowl, 13½", gold fruit, rolled edge **$65.00**
Della Robbia, candy dish, milk glass, footed..............**$32.50**
Della Robbia, creamer & sugar bowl, colored fruit.....**$35.00**
Della Robbia, creamer & sugar bowl, milk glass.........**$20.00**

Della Robbia, goblet, 6", milk glass, plain..................**$18.00**
Dolphin, compote, 6x8", pink, #1049.........................**$48.00**
English Hobnail, candy dish, milk glass, 3-footed.......**$30.00**
English Hobnail, cup & saucer, milk glass...................**$15.00**
English Hobnail, goblet, 8-oz, milk glass....................**$14.00**
English Hobnail, ivy ball, milk glass...........................**$20.00**
Lotus, salt & pepper shakers, pr.................................**$35.00**
Old Quilt, butter dish, ¼-lb, milk glass **$32.00**
Old Quilt, candlesticks, 4", milk glass, pr...................**$22.00**
Old Quilt, celery vase, 6½", milk glass.......................**$22.00**
Old Quilt, cruet, milk glass, w/stopper.......................**$20.00**
Old Quilt, fan vase, milk glass....................................**$22.00**
Old Quilt, jardiniere, 6½", milk glass, cupped............**$42.50**
Old Quilt, pickle dish, 10", milk glass........................**$30.00**
Old Quilt, salt & pepper shakers, milk glass, pr..........**$22.00**
Old Quilt, sherbet, milk glass, low foot **$22.50**
Old Quilt, sugar bowl, milk glass................................**$22.00**
Old Quilt, sweetmeat, milk glass, w/lid, footed **$25.00**
Old Quilt, vase, 9", milk glass, straight sides, footed ..**$48.00**
Panelled Grape, basket, oval, milk glass, split handle .**$30.00**
Panelled Grape, butter dish, 1-lb, milk glass, round ...**$60.00**
Panelled Grape, butter dish, ¼-lb, milk glass **$32.00**
Panelled Grape, canape set, milk glass, 3 pieces **$68.00**
Panelled Grape, candelabra, milk glass, 3-light........**$200.00**

Panelled Grape, candlestick, 4", octagonal, milk glass, pr **$22.50**
Panelled Grape, candy dish, milk glass, 3-toed, pansy decoration on lid..**$50.00**
Panelled Grape, compote, milk glass, 9" (illustrated) **$60.00**
Panelled Grape, creamer, individual size, milk glass ..**$10.00**
Panelled Grape, cup & saucer, milk glass...................**$18.00**
Panelled Grape, epergne, 11", milk glass, 2-piece **$160.00**
Panelled Grape, mayonnaise, milk glass, footed.........**$22.00**
Panelled Grape, pitcher, 1-qt, milk glass....................**$25.00**
Panelled Grape, planter, 3x8½", milk glass.................**$35.00**
Panelled Grape, planter, 5x9", milk glass...................**$38.00**
Panelled Grape, plate, 8½", milk glass **$24.00**
Panelled Grape, salt & pepper shakers, milk glass, footed, pr...**$18.00**
Panelled Grape, sauce boat, milk glass, w/undertray .**$65.00**
Panelled Grape, spooner, 6", milk glass......................**$30.00**
Panelled Grape, tumbler, 12-oz, milk glass.................**$20.00**

Panelled Grape, vase, 9", milk glass............................$25.00
Panelled Grape, wine, 2-oz, milk glass $16.00
Rose & Bows, wedding bowl, milk glass $75.00
Thousand Eye, bowl, 11¼", ruby & marigold flash $18.00
Thousand Eye, sherbet, 4¼", crystal $12.00
Thousand Eye, sherbet, 4¼", purple & marigold flash .$15.00
Wildflower & Lace, bowl, fruit; 10" $22.50

Wheaton Bottles

Of interest to bottle collectors and political buffs as well, Wheaton bottles were first produced in the late 1960s. The first canteen-shaped presidential bottle commemorated J.F.K., and it was followed by a complete series, one for each of our country's former leaders. They were designed with a well-detailed relief portrait on one side and a famous quote or slogan on the back. Colors varied; some were iridescent. Production was turned over to the Wheaton Historical Association in 1974, who limited their bottles to about 5,000 each. Then in 1976, the molds went to the Millville Art Glass Company.

Other series were made as well and include: Great Americans, Astronauts, Christmas, Political Campaigns, American Patriots, and American Military Leaders. Most of these are worth well under $15.00. In 1984, miniature bottles (3") called Mini-Presidentials were made, one for each president. Some Wheaton bottles have been reproduced by Viking and are so marked. The originals are marked 'Wheaton, NJ, First Edition,' or 'Wheaton Hand-Made, First Edition, Millville, NJ.'

Abraham Lincoln, from $20 up to................................$25.00
Andrew Jackson, from $30 up to................................$35.00
Andrew Johnson, from $10 up to...............................$15.00
Calvin Coolidge, from $20 up to................................$25.00
Chester A Arthur, from $30 up to $35.00
Eisenhower, from $15 up to.......................................$20.00
FDR (Franklin Delano Roosevelt), from $20 up to $25.00
Franklin Pierce, from $30 up to $35.00
Franklin Pierce, second version, from $30 up to.........$35.00
George Bush, from $10 up to $15.00
George Washington, from $12 up to............................$15.00
Gerald R Ford, from $10 up to....................................$15.00
Grover Cleveland, from $20 up to...............................$25.00
Harry S Truman, ruby red, from $30 up to $35.00
Herbert Hoover, from $10 up to.................................$15.00

Ike (General), from $15 up to $20.00

James Buchanan, from $10 up to................................$15.00
James Garfield, from $30 up to...................................$35.00
James K Polk, from $30 up to.....................................$35.00
James Madison, from $30 up to..................................$35.00
James Monroe, from $50 up to....................................$60.00
Jimmy Carter, from $10 up to $12.00
John Adams, from $20 up to.......................................$25.00
John F Kennedy, light blue, from $75 up to.............$100.00
John Quincy Adams, from $35 up to..........................$40.00
John Tyler, from $15 up to..$25.00
John Tyler, second version, from $20 up to.................$25.00
Lyndon B Johnson, from $15 up to $20.00
Martin Van Buren, from $30 up to..............................$35.00
Millard Fillmore, from $30 up to.................................$35.00
Richard Nixon, from $15 up to $20.00
Ronald Reagan, from $10 up to $15.00
Rutherford B Hayes, from $35 up to $40.00
Rutherford B Hayes, second or corrected version, from $30 up to..$35.00
Teddy Roosevelt, royal blue, from $15 up to...............$20.00
Thomas Jefferson, from $20 up to $25.00
Ulysses S Grant, from $15 up to $20.00
Warren G Harding, from $20 up to $25.00
William H Harrison, from $10 up to............................$15.00
William Howard Taft, from $20 up to $25.00
William McKinley, from $30 up to..............................$35.00
Woodrow Wilson, from $10 up to...............................$15.00
Zachary Taylor, from $30 up to $35.00
Zachary Taylor, second version, from $30 up to.........$35.00

World's Fair Collectibles

Souvenir items have been issued since the mid-1800s for every world's fair and exposition. Few fairgoers have left the grounds without purchasing at least one. Some of the older items were often manufactured right on the fairgrounds by glass or pottery companies who erected working kilns and furnaces just for the duration of the fair. Of course, the older items are usually more valuable, but even souvenirs from the past fifty years are worth hanging onto.

Philadelphia, 1926

Badge, 2", red, white & blue ribbon holds sm Liberty Bell, Gimbel Brothers..$15.00
Box, jewelry; 3x8x5", wooden w/signing of Declaration of Independence scene on glass lid, exposition marks & dates, NM..$37.50
Bust of George Washington, 3¾", base metal, Sesquicentennial medallion on front...$16.50
Pin-back button,¾x1", Sesquicentennial 1776-1926 on Liberty Bell shape, silvery metal w/enameling, EX....$17.50

Chicago, 1933

Ashtray, 3¼", copper on metal, in original box, VG........$15.00

Ashtray, 5x4" oval, silverplated w/Hall of Science Building embossed in center.................**$10.00**

Cigarette case, marbleized celluloid on steel, Travel & Transportation Building on lid.........................**$37.50**

Fountain pen, 5", marbled celluloid w/1933 Century of Progress sticker, silver metal clip, Japan, NM.................................**$25.00**

Pin-back button, I'm From Ohio, red, white & blue enameling, EX...............................**$10.00**

Puzzle, Expo scene, in original box, NM.................**$28.00**

Stamps, 3¼x4¾" overall, blue & white w/1933 Century of Progress, comet logo, block of 10, unused..........**$20.00**

Tea ball, 1", chrome w/2¼" saucer, Expo medallion at end of 3" chain...**$10.00**

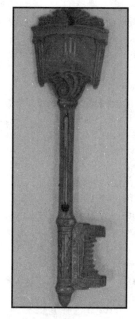

Thermometer, 7¾", figural key, silver metal.......$20.00

New York, 1939

Pin, Westinghouse Pavillion Robot, 3-dimensional, gilt tin w/red & black enameling, NM..............**$22.50**

Pin-back button, ⅝", I Was There, Trylon & Perisphere in center, blue, white & orange enameling, EX........**$17.50**

Tie clasp, Trylon & Perisphere in open ring, gilt w/black enameling, NM...**$8.50**

San Francisco, 1939

Compact, 2¾" square, Exposition Tower & Gateway night scene in blue enamel border, MIB.........................**$75.00**

Pin-back button, Golden Gate International Exposition, 5 fair buildings, gilt & blue enamel, NM...................**$15.00**

Poster stamp, 2", Pagent of the Pacific w/map motif, Let's Get Associated series, M...**$2.50**

Seattle, 1962

Pin-back button, 1¾", I Was There, Space Needle, Seattle 1962, red, white & blue enameling, EX...............**$15.00**

Slides, 2x2", Official Souvenir, sealed set of 4 in original printed package, M.................................**$4.00**

Tumbler, 6¾", fired-on fair scenes, set of 6 ....$60.00

New York, 1964

Ashtray, 6¾x4¾", smoky glass, Bell System Pavillion in multicolor enamel...**$9.00**

Booklet, Progressland, presented by General Electric & Walt Disney, EX...**$25.00**

Charm, sterling Unisphere form w/blue & orange enameling, NM...**$15.00**

Game, New York World's Fair Inventions, 1963, EX...**$15.00**

Mug, coffee; I Was a Coffee Hound at the New York World's Fair, comic dog's head, multicolor enameling, M...**$15.00**

Plate, 7", black glass, Unisphere in center, 6 fair views along border, multicolor enameling.............................**$15.00**

Puzzle, Milton Bradley, 1964, in original box, EX.......**$17.50**

Salt & pepper shakers, 2¾x2" dia, Unisphere form, blue & white ceramic w/plastic stoppers, EX...................**$30.00**

Tray, 6¾x5", black glass, Bell System display in multicolor enamel **$8.00**

Tray, 6x4½", copper plated w/9 embossed fair buildings & attractions, EX...**$8.50**

Auction Houses

Many of the auction galleries we've listed here have appraisal services. Some, though not all, are free of charge. We suggest you contact them first by phone to discuss fees and requirements.

A-1 Auction Service
P.O. Box 540672
Orlando, FL 32854
407-841-6681
Specializing in American antique sales

Alderfer Auction Company
501 Fairground Rd.
Hatfield, PA 19440
215-368-5477 or FAX 215-368-9055

America West Archives
Anderson, Warren
P.O. Box 100
Cedar City, UT 84721
801-586-9497
Quarterly 26-page illustrated catalog includes auction section of scarce and historical early western documents, letters, autographs, stock certificates, and other important ephemera. Subscription: $10 per year

Andre Ammelounx
The Stein Company
P.O. Box 136
Palatine, IL 60078
708-991-5927 or FAX 708-991-5947
Specializing in steins, catalogs available

Anthony J. Nard & Co
US Rt. 220
Milan, PA 18831
717-888-9404 or FAX 717-888-7723

Arman Absentee Auctions
P.O. Box 174
Woodstock, CT 06281
203-928-5838
Specializing in American glass, Historical Staffordshire, English soft paste, paperweights

Autographs of America
Anderson, Tim
P.O. Box 461
Provo, UT 84603
Free sample catalog of hundreds of autographs for sale

Barrett Bertoia Auctions & Appraisals
2413 Madison Avenue
Vineland, NJ 08360
609-692-4092
Specializing in antique toys and collectibles

Berman's Auction Gallery
33 West Blackwell St.
Dover, NJ 07081
201-361-3110

Bider's
241 S Union St.
Lawrence, MA 01843
508-688-4347 or 508-683-3944
Antiques appraised, purchased, and sold on consignment

Bob Koty Professional Auctioneers
Koty, Bob & Clara
P.O. Box 625
Freehold, NJ 07728
908-780-1265

Brian Riba Auctions, Inc.
P.O. Box 53, Main St.
S Glastonbury, CT 06073
203-633-3076

Butterfield & Butterfield
7601 Sunset Blvd.
Los Angeles, CA 90046
213-850-7500

Butterfield & Butterfield
220 San Bruno Ave.
San Francisco, CA 94103
415-861-7500

C.E. Guarino
Box 49
Denmark, ME 04022

Castner Auction & Appraisal Service
Leon Castner, President
6 Wantage Ave.
Branchville, NJ 07826
201-948-3868

Charles E. Kirtley
P.O. Box 2273
Elizabeth City, NC 27096
919-335-1262
Specializing in World's Fair, Civil War, political, advertising, and other American collectibles

Chase Gilmore Art Galleries
724 W Washington
Chicago, IL 60606
312-648-1690

Christie's
502 Park Ave.
New York, NY 10022
212-546-1000

Cincinnati Art Gallery
635 Main St.
Cincinnati, OH 45202
513-381-2128
Specializing in American art pottery, American and
European fine paintings, watercolors

Col. Doug Allard
P.O. Box 460
St. Ignatius, MT 59865

Collectors Auction Services
326 Seneca St.
Oil City, PA 16301
814-677-6070
Specializing in advertising, oil and gas, toys, rare
museum and investment-quality antiques

David Rago
P.O. Box 3592, Station E
Trenton, NJ 08629
609-397-9374
Gallery: 17 S Main St.
Lambertville, NJ 08530
Specializing in American art pottery and Arts & Crafts

Don Treadway Gallery
2128 Madison Rd.
Cincinnati, OH 45208
513-321-6742 or FAX 513-871-7722
Member: National Antique Dealers Association, American
Art Pottery Association, International Society of Appraisers,
and American Ceramic Arts Society

Douglas Auctioneers
Douglas B. Bilodeau
R.R. 5
S Deerfield, MA 01373
413-665-3530 or FAX 413-665-2877
Year-round sales, specializing in antiques, estates, fine art,
appraising

Doyle, Auctioneers & Appraisers
R.D. 3, Box 137
Osborne Hill Road
Fishkill, NY 12524
914-896-9492
Thousands of collectibles offered: call for free calendar of events

Duane Merrill
32 Beacon St.
S Burlington, VT 05403
802-878-2625

Du Mouchelles
409 E Jefferson Ave.
Detroit, MI 48226
313-963-6255 or FAX 313-963-8199

Dunning's Auction Service, Inc.
755 Church Rd.
Elgin, IL 60123
312-741-3483 or FAX 708-741-3589

Dynamite Auctions
Franklin Antique Mall & Auction Gallery
1280 Franklin Ave.
Franklin, PA 16323
814-432-8577 or 814-786-9211

Early Auction Co.
123 Main St.
Milford, OH 45150

F.B. Hubley & Co., Inc.
364 Broadway
Cambridge, MA 02139
617-876-2030

Fredericktowne Auction Gallery
Thom Pattie
5305 Jefferson Pike
Frederick, MD 21701
301-473-5566 or 800-962-1305

Freeman/Fine Arts of Philadelphia
Leslie Lynch, ASA
1808-10 Chestnut St.
Philadelphia, PA 19103
215-563-9275 or FAX 215-563-8236

Garth's Auctions, Inc.
2690 Stratford Rd.
Box 369, Delaware, OH 43015
614-362-4771

Glass-Works Auctions
James Hagenbuch
102 Jefferson
East Greenville, PA 18041
215-679-5849
America's leading auction company in
early American bottles and glass

Greenberg Auctions
7566 Main St.
Sykesville, MD 21784
Specializing in trains: Lionel, American
Flyer, Ives, Marx, HO

Guernsey's
136 E 73rd St.
New York, NY 10021
212-794-2280
Specializing in carousel figures

Gunther's International Auction Gallery
P.O. Box 235
24 S Virginia Ave.
Brunswick, MD 21716
301-834-7101 or 800-274-8779
Specializing in political, Oriental rugs, art,
bronzes, antiques, the unusual

Gustave White Auctioneers
P.O. Box 59
Newport, RI 02840
401-847-4250

Hake's Americana & Collectibles
Specializing in character and personality collectibles along
with all artifacts of popular culture for over 20 years. To
receive a catalog for their next 3,000-item mail/phone bid
auction, send $5 to Hake's Americana
P.O. Box 1444M
York, PA 17405

Hanzel Galleries, Inc.
1120 S Michigan Ave.
Chicago, IL 60605
312-922-6234

Harmer Rooke Galleries
3 E 57th St.
New York, NY 10022
212-751-1900 or FAX 212-758-1713

Harris Auction Galleries
8783-875 N Howard St.
Baltimore, MD 21201
301-728-7040

Iroquois Auction Gallery
Box 66
Port Henry, NY 12974
518-546-7003

Jack Sellner
Sellner Marketing of California
P.O. Box 308
Fremont, CA 94536
415-745-9463

James D. Julia
P.O. Box 210, Showhegan Rd.
Fairfield, ME 04937

James R. Bakker Antiques, Inc.
James R. Bakker
370 Broadway
Cambridge, MA 02139
617-864-7067
Specializing in American paintings,
prints, and decorative arts

Jim Depew Galleries
1860 Piedmont Rd.
NE Atlanta, GA 30324
404-874-2286

L.R. 'Les' Docks
Box 691035
San Antonio, TX 78269-1035
Providing occasional mail-order record auctions, rarely
consigned; the only consignments considered are
exceptionally scarce and unusual records

Leslie Hindman Auctions
215 W Ohio St.
Chicago, IL 60610
312-670-0010 or FAX 312-670-4248

Litchfield Auction Gallery
Clarence W. Pico
425 Bantam Rd., P.O. Box 1337
Litchfield, CT 06759
203-567-3126 or FAX 203-567-3266

Lloyd Ralston Toys
447 Stratford Rd.
Fairfield, CT 06432

Lubin Galleries, Inc.
Irwin Lubin
30 W 26th St.
New York, NY 10010
212-924-3777 or FAX 212-366-9190

Manion's International Auction House, Inc.
P.O. Box 12214
Kansas City, KS 66112

Mapes Auctioneers & Appraisers
David W. Mapes
1600 Vestal Parkway West
Vestal, NY 13850
607-754-9193 or FAX 607-786-3549

Maritime Auctions
R.R. 2, Box 45A
York, ME 03909
207-363-4247

Marvin Cohen Auctions
Box 425, Routes 20 & 22
New Lebanon, NY 12125
518-794-7477

Mid-Hudson Auction Galleries
One Idlewild Ave.
Cornwall-on-Hudson, NY 12520
914-534-7828 or FAX 914-534-4802

Milwaukee Auction Galleries, Ltd.
4747 W Bradley Rd.
Milwaukee, WI 53223
414-355-5054

Morton M. Goldberg Auction Galleries, Inc.
547 Baronne St.
New Orleans, LA 70113
504-592-2300 or FAX 504-592-2311

Noel Barrett Antiques & Auctions
P.O. Box 1001
Carversville, PA 18913
215-297-5109

Northeast Auctions
Ronald Bourgeault
694 Lafayette Rd.
Hampton, NH 03842
603-926-9800 or FAX 603-926-3545

Nostalgia Co.
21 S Lake Dr.
Hackensack, NJ 07601
201-488-4536

Nostalgia Galleries
657 Meacham Ave.
Elmont, NY 11003
516-326-9595
Auctioning items from almost every area of
the collectibles field, catalogs available

Parker's Knife Collector Service
P.O. Box 23522
5950 'C' Shallowford Rd.
Chattanooga, TN 37422
615-892-0448 or 800-247-0599
FAX 615-892-4165

Paul McInnis
356 Exeter Rd.
Hampton Falls, NH 03844
603-778-8989

Pennypacker Auction Center
1540 New Holland Rd.
Reading, PA 19807

Phillips Fine Art & Auctioneers
406 E 79th St.
New York, NY 10021

Rex Stark Auctions
49 Wethersfield Rd.
Bellingham, MA 02019

Richard A. Bourne Co., Inc.
Estate Auctioneers & Appraisers
Box 141
Hyannis Port, MA 02647
617-775-0797

Richard W. Oliver, Inc.
Plaza One, Rt. 1
Kennebunk, ME 04043
207-985-3600 or FAX 207-985-7734
Outside Maine: 800-992-0047

Richard Opfer Auctioneering, Inc.
1919 Greenspring Dr.
Timonium, MD 21093
301-252-5035

Richard W. Withington, Inc.
R.D. 2, Box 440
Hillsboro, NH 03244
603-464-3232

Roan, Inc.
Box 118, R.D. 3
Cogan Station, PA 17728

Robert W. Skinner, Inc.
Auctioneers & Appraisers
Rt. 117
Bolton, MA 01740
617-779-5528

Sanders & Mock Associates, Inc.
Mark Hanson
P.O. Box 37
Tamworth, NH 03886
603-323-8749 or 603-323-8784

Sloan's
Ben Hastings
4920 Wyaconda Rd.
Rockville, MD 20852
301-468-4911

Smith House
P.O. Box 336
Eliot, ME, 03903
207-439-4614 or FAX 207-439-8554
Specializing in toys

South Bay Auctions, Inc.
485 Montauk Highway
E Moriches, NY 11940
516-878-2909 or FAX 516-878-1863

Sotheby Parke Bernet, Inc.
980 Madison Ave.
New York, NY 10021

Sotheby's Arcade Auction
1334 York Ave. at 72nd St.
New York, NY 10021
212-606-7409

TSACO (The Stein Auction Company) East
Ron Fox
416 Throop St.
N Babylon, NY 11704
Telephone and FAX 516-669-7232

Weschler's
Adam A. Weschler & Son
905 E St. NW
Washington, DC 20004

Willis Henry Auctions
22 Main St.
Marshfield, MA 02050

Winter Associates, Inc.
Regina Madigan
P.O. Box 823
Plainville, CT 06062
207-793-0288 or 800-962-2530

Wolf's Auctioneers
1239 W 6th St.
Cleveland, OH 44113
216-575-9653 or 800-526-199
FAX 216-621-8011

Woody Auction Company
P.O. Box 618
Douglass, KS 67039
316-746-2694

Clubs, Newsletters and Other Publications

There are hundreds of clubs and newsletters available to collectors today, some are generalized and cover the entire realm of antiques and collectibles, while others are devoted to a specific interest such as toys, coin-operated machines, character collectibles, or railroadiana. You can obtain a copy of most newsletters simply by requesting one. If you'd like to try placing a 'for-sale' ad or a mail bid in one of them, see the introduction for suggestions on how your ad should be composed.

AB Bookman's Weekly
P.O. Box AB
Clifton, NJ 07015
201-772-0020 or FAX 201-772-9281
$80 per year bulk mail USA ($75 per year Canada or Foreign). $125 per year 1st class mail (USA, Canada, and Mexico). Foreign Air Mail: Inquire. Sample copies: $10. AB Bookman's Yearbook: $20. All advertising and subscriptions subject to acceptance

Abingdon Pottery Collectors Newsletter
Abingdon Pottery Club
Penny Vaughan, President
212 S. Fourth
Monmouth, IL 61462
309-734-2337

Action Toys Newsletter
P.O. Box 31551
Billings, MT 59107
406-248-4121

The Akro Agate Gem
Akro Agate Art Association
Joseph Bourque
P.O. Box 758
Salem, NH 03079

The Aluminist
Aluminum Collectors
Dannie Woodard
P.O. Box 1347
Weatherford, TX 76086
817-594-4680

America West Archives
Warren Anderson
P.O. Box 100
Cedar City, UT 84721
26-page illustrated catalogs issued quarterly. Has both fixed-price and auction sections offering early western documents, letters, stock certificates, autograph, and other important ephemera. Subscription: $10 per year

American Barb Wire Collectors Society
John Mantz
1023 Baldwin Rd.
Bakersfield, CA 93304
805-397-9572

American Carnival Glass News
Dennis Runk, Secretary
P.O. Box 235
Littlestown, PA 17340
717-359-7205

American Ceramic Circle Journal and Newsletter
American Ceramic Circle
Grand Central Station
P.O. Box 1495
New York, NY 10163

American Game Collectors Association
49 Brooks Ave.
Lewiston, ME 04240

American Lock Collectors Association Newsletter
Charles Chandler
36076 Grennada
Livonia, MI 48154
313-522-0920
Issued bimonthly. Subscription: $16 per year.

American Militaria Sourcebook and Directory
Terry Hannon
P.O. Box 245
Lyon Station, PA 19536-9986
800-446-0909 or FAX 215-682-1066

American Political Items Collectors
Tony Lee
P.O. Box 134
Monmouth Junction, NJ 08852

American Pottery Journal
P.O. Box 14255
Parkville, MO 64152
816-587-9179 or FAX 816-746-6924

American Quilter magazine
American Quilter's Society
P.O. Box 3290
Paducah, KY 42002-3290
$15 annual membership includes 4 issues.

The American STAR
American Scouting Traders Assn., Inc.
Dave Minnihan, President
P.O. Box 92
Kentfield, CA 94914-0092
415-665-2871

American Willow Report
Lisa Kay Henze, Editor
P.O. Box 900
Oakridge, OR 97463
Bimonthly newsletter, subscription: $15 per year, out of
country add $5 per year
Antique Advertising Association
P.O. Box 1121
Morton Grove, IL 60053
708-446-0904

Antique and Collectible News
P.O. Box 529
Anna, IL 62906
Monthly newspaper for auctions, antique shows,
collectibles and flea markets for the Midwest.
USA Subscription: $12 per year

Antique and Collectors Reproduction News
Mark Cherenka
Circulation Department
P.O. Box 71174
Des Moines, IA 50325
800-227-5531
Monthly newsletter showing differences between old origi-
nals and new reproductions; subscription: $32 per year

Antique Bottle Club of Northern Illinois
P.O. Box 571
Lake Geneva, WI, 53417

Antique Gazette
6949 Charlotte Pk., #106
Nashville, TN 37209
Monthly publication covering the antique and
collectibles market. Subscription: $16.95 per year

Antique Monthly magazine
Stephen C. Croft, Publisher
2100 Powers Ferry Rd.
Atlanta, GA 30339
404-955-5656 or FAX 404-952-0669
Subscription: $19.95 per year (11 issues)

Antique Press of Florida
12403 N Florida Ave.
Tampa, FL 33612
Subscription: $12 (6 issues) per year

Antique Souvenir Collectors' News
Gary Leveille, Editor
P.O. Box 562
Great Barrington, MA 01230

The Antique Trader Weekly
P.O. Box 1050 CB
Dubuque, IA 52004
Subscription: $28 (52 issues) per year; sample: 50¢

Antique Week
P.O. Box 90
Knightstown, IN 46148
Weekly newspaper for auctions, antique shows,
antiques, collectibles and flea markets. Write
for subscription information.

Antiques Americana
K.C. Owings, Jr.
P.O. Box 19
N Abington, MA 02351
617-857-1655
Specializing in paper collectibles

Antiques and Collecting
1006 S Michigan Ave.
Chicago, IL 60605
Monthly magazine with a wide variety of information and an extensive classified section. Subscription: $24 per year; sample: $2.95 (refundable with subscription order)

Appraisers Information Exchange
International Society of Appraisers
P.O. Box 726
Hoffman Estates, IL 60195
708-882-0706

Art Deco Reflections
Chase Collectors Society
Barry L. Van Hook, Director
2149 W. Jibsail Loop
Mesa, AZ 85202; 5524
602-838-6971

Arts and Crafts Quarterly
P.O. Box 3592, Station E
Trenton, NJ 08629
1-800-541-5787

Auction Block newspaper
P.O. Box 337
Iola, WI 54945
715-445-5000
Subscription: $8 per year

Auction Opportunities, Inc.
Doyle Auctioneers and Appraisers
109 Osborne Hill Rd.
Fishkill, NY 12524
800-551-5161
Subscription: $25 per year

The Autograph Review, bimonthly newsletter
Jeffrey Morey
305 Carlton Rd.
Syracuse, NY 13207
315-474-3516

Autographs and Memorabilia
P.O. Box 224
Coffeyville, KS 67337
316-251-5308
Six issues per year on movie and sports memorabilia

Automobile License Plate Collectors Newsletter
Gary Brent Kincade
P.O. Box 712
Weston, WV 26452
304-842-3773

Avon Times newsletter
c/o Dwight or Vera Young
P.O. Box 9868, Dept. P.
Kansas City, MO 64134
Inquires should be accompanied by LSASE

Barber Shop Collectibles Newsletter
Penny Nader
320 S Glenwood St.
Allentown, PA 18104
215-437-2534

Barbie Bazaar magazine
5617 Sixth Ave., Dept NY593
Kenosha, WI 53140
414-658-1004 or FAX: 414-658-0433
6 bimonthly issues for $25.95

Barbie Talks Some More!
Jacqueline Horning
7501 School Rd.
Cincinnati, OH 45249

The Baum Bugle
The International Wizard of Oz Club
Fred M. Meyer
220 N 11th St.
Escanaba, MI 49829

Beam Around the World
International Association of Jim Beam Bottle and Specialties Club
Shirley Sumbles, Secretary
5013 Chase Ave.
Downers Grove, IL 60515
708-963-8980

Beer Can Collectors News
Beer Can Collectors of America
Don Hicks, President
747 Merus Court
Fenton, MO 63026
314-343-6486 or FAX 314-343-6486

The Bell Tower
American Bell Association
Charles Blake
P.O. Box 172
Shoreham, VT 05770

Berry-Bits
Strawberry Shortcake Collectors' Club
Peggy Jimenez
1409 72nd St.
N Bergen, NJ 07047

Beyond the Rainbow Collector's Exchange
P.O. Box 31672
St. Louis, MO 63131

Big Little Times
Big Little Book Collectors Club of America
Larry Lowery
P.O. Box 1242
Danville, CA 94526
415-837-2086

Blue and White Pottery Club Newsletter
224 12th St. NW
Cedar Rapids, IA 52405
319-362-8116

Bojo
P.O. Box 1203
Cranberry Township, PA 16033-2203
412-776-0621 (9 AM to 9 PM E.T.)
Issues fixed-price catalog of Beatles and Rock 'n Roll memorabilia.

Bookmark Collector
Joan L. Huegel
1002 W. 25th St.
Erie, PA 16502
Quarterly newsletter: $5.50 per year ($6.50 in Canada);
sample copy: $1 plus stamp or LSASE

Books Are Everything
302 Martin Dr.
Richmond, KY 40475
Subscription: $25 (4 issues) per year in USA; $7.50 for sample

Bossons Briefs
International Bossons Collectors
Dr. Robert E. Davis, Executive Director
21 John Maddox Dr.
Rome, GA 30161
404-232-1266

Bridal Collector's Roster
Ann C. Bergin
P.O. Box 105
Amherst, NH 03031
603-673-1885

Buckeye Marble Collectors Club
Betty Barnard
472 Meadowbrook Dr.
Newark, OH 43055
614-366-7002

Bulletin
Doll Collectors of America
14 Chestnut Rd.
Westford, MA 01886
617-692-8392

Bulletin of the NAWCC
National Assn. of Watch and Clock Collectors, Inc.
Thomas J. Bartels, Executive Director
514 Poplar St., Columbia, PA 17512-2130
717-684-8621 or FAX 717-684-0878

California Pottery Newsletter
c/o Verlangieri Gallery
816 Main St., West
Cambria, CA 93428
800-292-2153

The Cambridge Crystal Ball
National Cambridge Collectors, Inc.
P.O. Box 416
Cambridge, OH 43725-0416
Dues: $15 for individual member and $3
for associate member of same household

The Candlewick Collector Newsletter
Virginia R. Scott
275 Milledge Terrace
Athens, GA 30306
404-548-5966

The Candy Gram
Candy Container Collectors of America
Douglas Dezso
864 Paterson, Ave.
Maywood, NJ 07607
201-845-7707

The Cane Collector's Chronicle
Linda Beeman
15 2nd St. NE
Washington, D.C. 20002
$30 (4 issues) per year

Captain's Log magazine
World Airline Historical Society
Paul F. Collins, President
3381 Apple Tree Lane
Erlanger, KY 41018
606-342-9039

Cast Iron Seat Collectors Association Newsletter
RFD #2, Box 40
Le Center, MN 56057
612-357-6142

Cat Collectors Club
33161 Wendy Dr.
Sterling Heights, MI 48310
Subscription: $18 per year (includes bimonthly
newsletter and catalogs); sample package: $4

Cat Talk
Marilyn Dipboye
31311 Blair Dr.
Warren, MI 48092
313-264-0285

Century Limited
Toy Train Collectors Society
160 Dexter Terrace
Tonawanda, NY 14150
716-694-3771

Chain Gang Key Chain Collector
P.O. Box 9397
Phoenix, AZ 85068
602-942-0043

Chicagoland Antique Advertizing
Slot Machine and Jukebox Gazette
Ken Durham, Editor
P.O. Box 2426
Rockville, MD 20852
20-page newsletter published twice a year.
Subscription: 4 issues for $10; sample: $5

Classic Amusements
Wordmarque Design Associates
12644 Chapel Rd.
Suite 204, Box 315
Clifton, VA 22024
Subscription: $36 (6 issues) per year in USA;
$42 in Canada

Clear the Decks
52 Plus Joker
Bill Coomer, Secretary
1024 S. Benton
Cape Girardeau, MO 63701
For collectors of playing cards, unusual and antique decks

Coca-Cola Collectors Club International
P.O. Box 49166
Atlanta, GA 30359
Annual dues: $25

Coin Machine Trader
Ted and Betty Salveson
569 Kansas SE, P.O. Box 602
Huron, SD 57350
605-352-3870

Coin-Op Newsletter
Ken Durham, Publisher
909 26th St., NW
Washington, DC 20037
Subscription (10 issues): $24; sample: $5

Collecting Tips Newsletter
c/o Meredith Williams
P.O. Box 633
Joplin, MO 64802
417-781-3855 or 417-624-2518
12 issues per year focusing on Fast Food collectibles

The Collector
Box 158
Heyworth, IL 61745
309-473-2466
Newspaper published monthly

Collector Glass News
P.O. Box 308
Slippery Rock, PA 16057
412-946-8126 or 412-794-6420
For collectors of promotional and fast food glassware

Collectors' Classified
William Margolin
P.O. Box 347
Hollbrook, MA 02343-0347
617-961-1463
Covers collectibles in general; 4 issues: $1

Collector's Digest
P.O. Box 23
Banning, CA 92220
714-849-1064
Subscription: $11 (6 issues) per year

Collector's Mart magazine
P.O. Box 12830
Wichita, KS 67277
Subscription: $23.95 per year; Add $15 in Canada

Collectors of Findlay Glass
P.O. Box 256
Findlay, OH 45839

Cookbook Gossip
Cookbook Collectors Club of America, Inc.
Bob and Jo Ellen Allen
231 E James Blvd., P.O. Box 85
St. James, MO 65559
314-265-8296

Cookie Crumbs
Cookie Cutter Collectors Club
Ruth Capper
1167 Teal Rd. SW
Dellroy, OH 44620
216-735-2839 or 202-966-0869

Cookie Jarrin' With Joyce: The Cookie Jar Newsletter
R.R. 2, Box 504
Walterboro, SC 29488

The Cookie Jar Collector's Club News
Louise Messina Daking
595 Cross River Rd.
Katonah, NY 10536
914-232-0383 or FAX 914-232-0384

The Co-Op Connections
Sagebrush Treasures
963 Williams
Fallon, NV 89406
Subscription $15 per year for 12 issues

Coors Pottery Newsletter
Robert Schneider
3808 Carr Pl. N
Seattle, WA 98103-8126

Costume Society of America Newsletter
55 Edgewater Dr., P.O. Box 73
Earleville, MD 21919
301-275-2329 or FAX 301-275-8936

Crown Jewels of the Wire Insulator Collector
John McDougald
P.O. Box 1003
St. Charles, IL 60174-1003
708-513-1544

The Courier
2503 Delaware Ave.
Buffalo, NY 14216
716-873-2594
A Civil War collector newsletter published bimonthly

The Cutting Edge
Glass Knife Collectors' Club
Adrienne S. Escoe, Editor
P.O. Box 342
Los Alamitos, CA 90720
Subscription: $3 (4 issues) per year; sample: 50¢

Daguerreian Society, Inc.
John F. Graff, President
P.O. Box 2129
Green Bay, WI 53406-2129

Dark Shadows Collectibles Classified
Sue Ellen Wilson
6173 Iroquois Trail
Mentor, OH 44060
216-946-6348
For collectors of both old and new series

Decoy Hunter Magazine
901 North 9th St.
Clinton, IN 47842
Subscription: $12 per year for 6 issues

Decoy Magazine
Joe Engers
P.O. Box 277
Burtonsville, MD 20866
301-890-0262

Depression Glass Daze
Teri Steel, Editor/Publisher
Box 57
Otisville, MI 48463
313-631-4593
The nation's marketplace for glass, china, and pottery

Dept. 56 Collectors: *The Village Press*
Roger and Khristine Bain, Publishers
1625 Myott Ave.
Rockford, IL 61103
Subscription: $20 (8 issues) per year; free sample copy

DISCoveries Magazine
Mark Phillips, Associate Editor
P.O. Box 255
Port Townsend, WA 98368-0255
Specializing in collectible records, international distribution

Doll Investment Newsletter
P.O. Box 1982
Centerville, MA 02632

Doll News
United Federation of Doll Clubs
P.O. Box 14146
Parkville, MO 64152

Doorstop Collectors of America
Doorstopper newsletter
Jeanie Bertoia
2413 Madison Ave.
Vineland, NJ 08630
609-692-4092
Membership $20.00 per year, includes 2 newsletters and convention. Send 2-stamp SASE for sample

Dunbar's Gallery
76 Haven St.
Milford, MA 01757
508-634-8697 or FAX 508-634-8698
Specializing in quality advertising, Halloween,
toys, coin-operated machines; holding cataloged
auctions occasionally, lists available.

Early American Industries Association
J. Watson
P.O. Box 2128, Dept. PR
Empire State Plaza Station
Albany, NY 12220
Providing information on early tools and trades

Eggcup Collectors' Corner
Joan George
67 Stevens Ave.
Old Bridge, NJ 08857
Subscription: $18 per year for 4 issues
Sample copies or back issues available at $5 each

Ephemera News
The Ephemera Society of America, Inc.
P.O. Box 37
Schoharie, NY 12157
518-295-7978

The Ertl Replica
Ertl Collectors Club
Mike Meyer, Editor
Highways 136 and 20
Dyersville, IA 52040
319-875-2000

Facets of Fostoria
Fostoria Glass Society of America
P.O. Box 826
Moundsville, WV 26041
Membership: $12.50 per year

Fair News
World's Fair Collectors' Society, Inc.
Michael R. Pender, Editor
P.O. Box 20806
Sarasota, FL 34238
Dues: $12 (12 issues) per year in USA
$13 in Canada; $20 for overseas members

Farm Antique News
Gary Van Hoozer
812 N Third St.
Tarkio, MO 64491
816-736-4528
Annual subscription: $14

Favorite Westerns and Serial World magazine
Westerns and Serials Fan Club
c/o Norman Kietzer
R.R. 1, Box 103
Vernon Center, MN 56090

The Federation Glass Works
Federation of Historical Bottle Clubs
Barbara A. Harms
14521 Atlantic
Riverdale, IL 60627
312-841-4068

The Fenton Flyer
National Fenton Glass Society
P.O. Box 4008
Marietta, OH 45750

Fiesta Collector's Quarterly
China Specialties, Inc.
19238 Dorchester Circle
Strongville, OH 44136
$12 (4 issues) per year

Figural Bottle Openers
Contact: Donna Kitzmiller
117 Basin Hill Road
Duncannon, PA 17020

Fire Collectors Club Newsletter
David Cerull
P.O. Box 992
Milwaukee, WI 53201

Flag Bulletin
Flag Research Center
P.O. Box 580
Winchester, MA 01890
617-729-9410

FLAKE, The Breakfast Nostalgia Magazine
P.O. Box 481
Cambridge, MA 02140
617-492-5004
Bimonthly illustrated issue devoted to one hot
collecting area such as Disney, etc., withletters,
discoveries, new releases, and ads.
Single issue: $4 ($6 foreign)
Annual: $20 ($28 foreign)
Free 25-word ad with new subscription

Flashlight Collectors of America Newsletter
Bill Utley
P.O. Box 3572
Downey, CA 90242
$12 (4 issues) per year

Flea Marketeer
P.O. Box 686
Southfield, MI 48037
313-351-9910 or FAX 313-351-9037

Folk Art Messenger
P.O. Box 17041
Richmond, VA 23226

Fox Hunt Newsletter
R. Atkinson Fox Society
Hugh Hetzer
209 Homevale Rd.
Reisterstown, MD 21136

Friends of Hoppy Club
Laura Bates
6310 Friendship Dr.
New Concord, OH 43762-9708
614-826-4850
Publishes newsletter

The Front Striker Bulletin
Bill Retskin
P.O. Box 18481
Asheville, NC 28814
704-254-4487 or FAX 704-254-1066
Quarterly newsletter for matchcover collectors,
$17.50 per year for 1st class mailing
+ $2 for new member registration

Game Times
American Game Collectors Association
Joe Angiolillo, President
4628 Barlow Dr.
Bartlesville, OK 74006

Garfield Collectors Society Newsletter
% David L. Abrams, Editor
744 Foster Ridge Rd.
Germantown, TN 38138-7036
901-753-1026

Gaudy Collector's Society
Suzanne Troll
P.O. Box 274
Gates Mills, OH 44040
For enthusiasts of Gaudy Welsh,
Gaudy Ironstone and Gaudy Dutch china

Gene Autry Star Telegram
Gene Autry Development Association
Chamber of Commerce
P.O. Box 158
Gene Autry, OK 73436

George Kamm Paperweights
24 Townsend Court
Lancaster, PA 17603
Specializing in paperweights; color brochure
published 4 to 5 times a year. $5 (1-time charge)

Ginny Doll Club News
Jeanne Niswonger
305 W Beacon Rd.
Lakeland, FL 33803
813-687-8015

Glass Chatter
Midwest Antique Fruit Jar and Bottle Club
P.O. Box 38
Flat Rock, IN 47234

Glass Collector's Digest
P.O. Box 553
Marietta, OH 45750-9979
800-533-3433
Subscription: $19 (6 issues) per year
Add $5 for Canada and foreign

Glass Shards
The National Early American Glass Club
P.O. Box 8489
Silver Spring, MD 20907

Golf Club Collectors Association Newsletter
c/o Dick Moore
640 E Liberty St.
Girard, OH 44420-2308

Gonder Pottery Collectors' Newsletter
c/o John and Marilyn McCormick
P.O. Box 3174
Shawnee KS 66203

Gone With the Wind Collectors Club Newsletter
8105 Woodview Rd.
Ellicott City, MD 21043
301-465-4632

Grandma's Trunk
P.O. Box 404
Northport, MI 49670
Subscription: $8 per year for 1st class or
$5 per year for bulk rate

Hall China Collector Club Newsletter
P.O Box 360488
Cleveland, OH 44136

Haviland Collectors International Foundation
Jean Kendall
Iowa Memorial Union, University of Iowa
Iowa City, IA 52242
319-335-3513

Headhunters Newsletter for head vase collectors
Maddy Gordon
P.O. Box 83H
Scarsdale, NY 10583
914-472-0200
Subscription: $16 (4 issues) per year

The Heisey News
Heisey Collectors of America
169 W Church St.
Newark, OH 43055
612-345-2932

Hello Again Old-Time Radio Show Collector
Jay A. Hickerson
P.O. Box 4321
Hamden, CT 06514
203-248-2887 or FAX 203-281-1322
Sample copy upon request with SASE

Hobby News bimonthly newsletter
J.L.C. Publications
Box 258
Ozone Park, NY 11416

Holly Hobbie Newsletter
Helen McCale
Route 3, Box 35
Butler, MO 64730

Hopalong Cassidy Newsletter
Hopalong Cassidy Fan Club
P.O. Box 1361
Boyes Hot Springs, CA 95416

Ice Screamer
c/o Ed Marks, Publisher
P.O. Box 5387
Lancaster, PA 17601
Published bimonthly, dues: $15 per year

The Illustrator Collector's News
Denis Jackson, Editor
P.O. Box 1958
Sequim, WA 98382
206-683-2559
Subscription: $17 per year

The Indian Trader
Martin Link
P.O. Box 1421
Scottsdale, AZ 85251

Inside Antiques monthly newsletter
Antique and Collectible News Service
Robert Reed, Editor
P.O. Box 204
Knightstown, IN 46148
317-345-7479

International Association of Dinnerware Matchers
P.O. Box 50125
Austin, TX 78763-0125
512-264-1054

International Brick Collectors Association Journal
International Brick Collectors Association
8357 Somerset Dr.
Prairie Village, KS 66207
913-341-8842

The International Carnival Glass Association
Lee Markley, Secretary
R.R. 1, Box 14
Mentone, IN 46539
219-353-7678
Publishes quarterly bulletin. $10 per family

International Club for Collectors of Hatpins
and Hatpin Holders
Lillian Baker
15237 Chanera Ave.
Gardena, CA 90249
Enclose SASE for information

International Perfume
and Scent Bottle Collectors Association
c/o Phyllis Dohanian
53 Marlborough St.
Boston, MA 02116-2099
617-266-4351

International Pin Collectors Club Newsletter
P.O. Box 430
Marcy, NY 13403
315-736-5651 or 315-736-4019

International Society of Antique Scale Collectors
Bob Stein, President
176 W. Adams St., Suite 1706
Chicago, IL 60603
312-263-7500
Publishes quarterly magazine

Just for Openers Newsletter
John Stanley
605 Windsong Lane
Durham, NC 27713
Quarterly newsletter covers all types of
bottle openers and corkscrews

Kit Builders and Glue Sniffers
Gordy's
2103 Sharon Copley Rd.
Medina, OH 44256
216-239-1657

Kitchen Antiques and Collectibles News Newsletter
KOOKS (Kollectors of Old Kitchen Stuff)
4645 Laurel Ridge Dr.
Harrisburg, PA 17110
Membership: $24 per year

The Lace Collector newsletter
Elizabeth M. Kurella
P.O. Box 222
Plainwell, MI 49080
616-685-9792
A quarterly publication for the study of old lace

The Laughlin Eagle
c/o Richard G. Racheter
1270 63rd Terrace South
St. Petersburg, FL 33705

Light Revival Restoration Newsletter
Tom Barnard
35 W Elm Ave.
Quincy, MA 02170
617-773-3255

The Link
National Cuff Link Society
Eugene R. Klompus
P.O. Box 346
Prospect Heights, IL 60070
708-632-0561
For collectors of cuff links and related accessories

Madame Alexander Fan Club Newsletter
Earl Meisinger
11 S 767 Book Rd.
Naperville, IL 60564

Maine Antique Digest monthly newspaper
Sam and Sally Pennington
P.O. Box 645
Waldoboro, ME 04572
207-832-7534

Majolica International Society Newsletter
Michael G. Strawser, President
Suite 103, 1275 First Ave.
New York, NY 10021

Marble Mania
Marble Collectors Society of America
Stanley Block
P.O. Box 222
Trumbull, CT 06611
203-261-3223

Martha's Kidlit Newsletter
Box 1488A
Ames, IA 50010
A bimonthly publication for children's books collectors.
Subscription: $25 per year

Matchbox USA
Charles Mack
62 Saw Mill Rd.
Durham, CT 06422
203-349-1655

McDonald's Collecting Tips
Meredith Williams
Box 633
Joplin, MO 64802.
Send SASE for information

McDonald's Collector Club Newsletter
c/o Tenna Greenberg
5400 Waterbury Rd.
Des Moines, IA 50312
515-279-0741

Medical Collectors Association Newsletter
Dr. M. Donald Blaufox, MD
1300 Morris Park Ave.
Bronx, NY 10461

The Milk Route
National Association of Milk Bottle Collectors, Inc.
Thomas Gallagher
4 Ox Bow Rd.
Westport CT 06880-2602
203-277-5244

Mini Thistle
Pairpoint Cup Plate Collectors of America
Box 52
E Weymouth, MA 02189

The Miniature Bottle Collector
Briscoe Publications
P.O. Box 2161
Palos Verdes Peninsula, CA 90274

Miniature Piano Enthusiast Club
Janice E. Kelsh
5815 N. Sheridan Rd., Suite 202
Chicago, IL 60660
312-271-2970

Model and Toy Collector Magazine
137 Casterton Ave.
Akron, OH 44303
216-836-0668 or FAX 216-869-8668

Modern Doll Club Journal
Jeanne Niswonger
305 W Beacon Rd.
Lakeland, FL 33803

Morgantown Newscaster
Morgantown Collectors of America
Jerry Gallagher and Randy Supplee
420 1st Ave. NW
Plainview, MN 55964
Subscription: $15 per year.
SASE required for answers to queries

The Mouse Club East (Disney collectors)
P.O. Box 3195
Wakefield, MA 01880
Family membership: $25 (includes newsletters
and 2 shows per year)

Movie Advertising Collector magazine
George Reed
P.O. Box 28587
Philadelphia, PA 19149

Mystic Knights of the Aladdin Lights
J.W. Courter
R.R. 1, Box 256
Simpson, IL 62985
Subscription: $20 (6 issues, postpaid 1st class)
per year with current buy-sell-trade information

NAOLH Newsletter
National Assn. for Outlaw and Lawman History
Hank Clark
P.O. Box 812
Waterford, CA 95386
209-874-2640

NAPAC Newsletter
National Association of Paper and Advertising Collectors
P.O. Box 500
Mount Joy, PA 17552
717-653-4300

National Association of Breweriana Advertising
c/o John Murray
475 Old Surrey Rd.
Hinsdale, IL 60521

National Blue Ridge Newsletter
Norma Lilly
144 Highland Dr.
Blountsville, TN 37617
Subscription: $12 (6 issues) per year

National Book Collector
National Book Collectors Society
65 High Ridge Rd., Suite 349
Stamford, CT 06095
Annual dues: $20 (includes 6 issues) per year in USA
$25 in Canada and foreign countries
Sample copy: $2

National Button Bulletin
National Button Society
Lois Pool, Secretary
2733 Juno Place
Akron, OH 44333-4137
216-864-3296

National Early American Glass Club
P.O. Box 8489
Silver Spring, MD 20907

National Ezra Brooks Bottle and Specialty Club Newsletter
420 W 1st St.
Kewanee, IL 61443

National Fantasy Fan Club (for Disney collectors)
Dept. AC, Box 19212
Irvine, CA 92713
Membership: $20 per year, includes newsletters,
free ads, chapters, conventions, etc.

National Graniteware News
National Graniteware Society
P.O. Box 10013
Cedar Rapids, IA 52410-0013

National Greentown Glass Association Newsletter
c/o Annette W. LaRowe, Secretary/Treasurer
P.O. Box 107
Greentown, IN 46936

National Imperial Glass Collectors' Society
P.O. Box 534, Bellaire, OH 43906. Dues: $12 per year (plus
$1 for each additional member in the same household),
quarterly newsletter, convention every June

*National Milk Glass Collectors' Society and Quarterly
Newsletter*
c/o Arlene Johnson, Treasurer
1113 Birchwood Dr.
Garland, TX 75043.
Please include SASE

National Reamer Collectors Association Quarterly Review
R.R. 3, Box 67
Frederic, WI 54837
715-327-4365

National Valentine Collectors Bulletin
Evalene Pulati
P.O. Box 1404
Santa Ana, CA 92702
714-547-1355

News and Views
The National Depression Glass Association
Anita Wood
P.O. Box 69843
Odessa, TX 79769
915-337-1297

Night Light (miniature lamp collectors)
c/o Bob Culver
38619 Wakefield Court
Northville, MI 48167
313-473-8575

Noritake News
David H. Spain
1237 Federal Ave. E
Seattle, WA 98102
206-323-8102

North America Torquay Society
Jerry and Gerry Kline, members
604 Orchard View Dr.
Maumee, OH 43537
Quarterly newsletter sent to members; information
and membership form requires LSASE

Novelty Salt and Pepper Club
c/o Irene Thornburg, Membership Coordinator
581 Joy Rd.
Battle Creek, MI 49017
Publishes quarterly newsletter and annual roster.
Annual dues: $20 in USA, Canada, and Mexico;
$25 for all other countries

Old Ivory Newsletter
Pat Fitzwater
P.O. Box 1004
Wilsonville, OR 97070
SASE for sample copy

Old Morgantown Topics
Old Morgantown Glass Collectors' Guild
Jerry Gallagher, President
420 1st Ave. NW
Plainview, MN 55964
507-534-3511

The Olympic Collectors Newsletter
Bill Nelson
P.O. Box 41630
Tucson, AZ 85717-1630

On the Lighter Side
Judith Sanders
Route 3, 136 Circle Dr.
Quitman, TX 75783
903-763-2795
Send SASE for information regarding vintage lighters

McCoy Publications
Kathy Lynch, Editor
P.O. Box 14255
Parkville, MO 64152
816-587-9179 or FAX 816-746-6924

Paper Collectors' Marketplace
470 Main St., P.O. Box 128
Scandinavia, WI 54977
715-467-2379
Subscription: $17.95 (12 issues) per year in USA
Canada and Mexico add $15 per year

Paper Doll News
Ema Terry
P.O. Box 807
Vivian, LA 71082

Paper Pile Quarterly
P.O. Box 337
San Anselmo, CA 94979-0337
415-454-5552
Subscription: $12.50 per year in USA and Canada

Paperback Parade
c/o Gryphon Publications
P.O. Box 209
Brooklyn, NY 11228-0209
Magazine for paperback readers and collectors.
Subscription: $30 (6 issues) per year, third class; sample: $6

Paperweight Collector's Bulletin
Paperweight Collector's Association, Inc.
150 Fulton Ave.
Garden City Park, NY 11040
516-741-3090 or FAX 506-741-3985

Peanuts Collector Club Newsletter
Peanuts Collector Club
Andrea C. Podley
P.O. Box 94
N Hollywood, CA 91603

Peanut Papers
Planter's Peanuts Collectors Club
804 Hickory Grade Rd.
Bridgeville, PA 15017
412-221-7599

The Pen and Quill
Universal Autograph Collectors Club
P.O. Box 6181
Washington, DC 20044-6181

Pen Fancier's Club
1169 Overcash Dr.
Dunedin, FL 34698
Publishes monthly magazine of pens and mechanical
pencils; Subscription: $45 per year; sample: $4

The Pencil Collector
American Pencil Collectors Society
Robert J. Romey, President
2222 S Millwood
Wichita, KS 67213
316-263-8419

Pepsi-Cola Collectors Club Newsletter
Pepsi-Cola Collectors Club
Bob Stoddard
P.O. Box 1275
Covina, CA 91722
714-593-8750
Membership: $15

Perfume and Scent Bottle Collectors
Jeane Parris
2022 E Charleston Blvd.
Las Vegas, NV 89104
Membership: $15 USA or $30 foreign (includes quarterly
newsletter). Information requires SASE

Phoenix Bird Discoveries
Joan Oates
685 S Washington
Constantine, MI 49042
Membership: $10 per year
Includes newsletter published 3 times a year

Pickard Collectors Club
Alicia Miller
300 E. Grove St.
Bloomington, IL 61701
309-828-5533

Pie Birds Unlimited
Lillian M. Cole
14 Harmony School Rd.
Flemington, NJ 08822

Plantation Galleries International Newsletter
6400 Davison Rd.
Burton, MI 48509
313-743-5258 or FAX 313-743-5791
Subscription: $24.95 per year

The Plastic Candy Dispenser Newsletter
Sue Sternfeld
90-60 Union Turnpike
Glendale, NY 11385
Information on Pez containers

Plate-O-Holic
Plate Collector's Stock Exchange
478 Ward St. Extension
Wallingford, CT 06492
203-265-1711

Playing Card Collectors Association (PCCA) Bulletin
P.O. Box 783
Bristol, WI, 53014
414-857-9334

The Pokey Gazette
Steve Santi
19626 Ricardo Ave.
Hayward, CA 94541
510-481-2586

Police Collector News
Mike Bondarenko, Publisher
R.R. 1, Box 14
Baldwin, WI 54002

Political Bandwagon
Larry L. Krug
18222 Flower Hill Way, #299
Gaithersburg, MD 20879
Published monthly. Free with $24 annual membership in
American Political Items Collectors (you also receive *The
Keynoter* magazine 3 times a year).

Positively PEZ
Crystal and Larry LaFoe
3851 Gable Lane Dr., Apt. 513
Indianapolis, IN 46208

Postcard History Society Bulletin
John H. McClintock, Director
P.O. Box 1765
Manassas, VA 22110
703-368-2757

Pottery Lovers Newsletter
Pottery Lovers Reunion
Pat Sallaz
4969 Hudson Dr.
Stow, OH 44224

Powder Puff
P.O. Box Letter S
Lynbrook, NY 11563
Subscription: $25 (4 issues, USA or Canada) per year

Precious Collectibles magazine for Precious Moments
figurine collectors, *The Ornament Collector* magazine for Hallmark and other ornaments, and the *Collectors' Bulletin* magazine
for all Limited Edition collectibles.
Rosie Wells Enterprises, Inc.
R.R. 1, Canton, IL 61520

Quint News
Dionne Quint Collectors
P.O. Box 2527
Woburn, MA 01888
617-933-2219

Red Wing Collectors Newsletter
Red Wing Collectors Society, Inc.
David Newkirk
R.R. 3, Box 146
Monticello, MN 55362

Roseville's of the Past
Jack Bomm, Editor
P.O. Box 1018
Apopka, FL 32704-1018
Subscription: $19.95 per year for 6 to 12 newsletters

Roy Rogers-Dale Evans Collectors Association
Nancy Horsley
P.O. Box 1166
Portsmouth, OH 45662

Royal Bayreuth International Collectors' Society
Howard and Sara Wade
P.O. Box 325
Orrville, OH 44667

Royal Doulton International Collectors Club Newsletter
c/o Royal Doulton, Inc.
P.O. Box 1815
Somerset, NJ 08873
908-356-7929 or 800-582-2102

Schoenhut Newsletter
Schoenhut Collectors Club
Robert Zimmerman
45 Louis Ave.
W Seneca, NY 14224

Scoop News
Margaret Alves
84 Oak Ave.
Shelton, CT 06484.
Issued bi-monthly;
send $1 for sample copy

Scottie Sampler and fellowship group Wee Scotts
P.O. Box 1512
Columbus, IN 47202

Scout Memorabilia
R.J. Sayers
P.O. Box 629
Brevard, NC 28712

Scouting Collectors Quarterly
National Scouting Collectors Society
806 E Scott St.
Tuscola, IL 61953

Sebastian Miniatures Collectors Society News
Cyndi Gavin McNally
c/o Lance Corp.
321 Central St.
Hudson, MA 01749
508-568-1401 or FAX 508-568-8741

SFPCS Newsletter
Southern Folk Pottery Collectors Society
Roy Thompson
1224 Main St.
Glastonbury, CT 06033
203-633-3121 or 203-659-3695

Shawnee Pottery Collectors' Club
P.O. Box 713
New Smyrna Beach, FL 32170-0713
Monthly nationwide newsletter. SASE (c/o Pamela Curran) required
when requesting info. Optional: $3 for sample of current newsletter

The Shirley Temple Collectors News
8811 Colonial Rd.
Brooklyn, NY 11209
Dues: $20 per year; checks paybable to Rita Dubas

The Shot Glass Club of America
Mark Pickvet, Editor
P.O. Box 90404
Flint, MI 48509
Non-profit organization publishes 12 newsletters per year.
Subscription: $6; sample: $1

The Silent Film Newsletter
Gene Vazzana
140 7th Ave.
New York, NY 10011
Subscription $18, send $2.50 for sample copy

The Silver Bullet newsletter
Terry and Kay Klepey
P.O. Box 553
Forks, WA 98331
206-327-3726
Subscription: $12 per year; sample copy available for $4;
also licensed mail order seller of memorabilia and appraiser

Singing Wires
Telephone Collectors International, Inc.
George W Howard
19 N Cherry Dr.
Oswego, IL 60543
708-554-8154

The Ski Country Collector Bottle Club
1224 Washington Ave.
Golden, CO 80401
Informational newsletter on decanters

Sleepy Eye Newsletter
Jim Martin
P.O. Box 12
Monmouth, IL 61462
309-734-4933 or 309-734-2703

Smurf Collectors Club
24ACH, Cabot Rd. W
Massapequa, NY 11758
Membership includes newsletters. LSASE for information

Snow Biz
c/o Nancy McMichael
P.O. Box 53262
Washington, D.C. 20009
Quarterly newsletter with information on snow domes
(subscription: $10 per year); also collector's club

Society for the Advancement of Space Activities
SASA
Michael S. Mitchell
P.O. Box 192
Kents Hill, ME 04349-0192

Spoutings
Watt Pottery Collectors
Box 26067
Fairview Park, OH 44126
Supscription (4 issues): $10 per year

The Spur
National Bit, Spur and Saddle Collectors Association
P.O. Box 3098
Colorado Springs, CO 80934

The Stained Finger
The Society of Inkwell Collectors
Vince McGraw
5136 Thomas Ave. S
Minneapolis, MN 55410
612-922-2792

Statue of Liberty Collectors' Club
Iris November
P.O. Box 535
Chautauqua, NY 14722
216-831-2646

Steiff Life
Steiff Collectors Club
Beth Savino
c/o The Toy Store
7856 Hill Ave.
Holland, OH 43528
419-865-3899 or 800-862-8697

Stein Line
Thomas A. Heiza, Publisher
P.O. Box 48716
Chicago, IL 60648-0716 or FAX 708-673-2634
Bimonthly newsletter concerning stein
sales, auctions, values, etc.

Stretch Glass Society
P.O. Box 770643
Lakewood, OH 44107
Membership: $8; quarterly newsletter, annual convention

Swatch Collectors
9595 Mt. Nebo Rd.
North Bend, OH 45052
513-941-5565

Table Topics
Table Toppers Club
1340 W Irving Park Rd.
P.O. Box 161, Chicago 60613
312-769-3184
Membership: $18 (6 issues) per year.
For those interested in table-top collectibles

Tea Leaf Reading
Tea Leaf Club International
P.O. Box 904
Mt. Prospect, IL 60056
Membership: $20 (single) or $25 (couple) per year

Tea Talk
Diana Rosen
419 N Larchmont Blvd. #225
Los Angeles, CA 90004
213-871-6901 or FAX 213-828-2444

Thimble Guild
Wynneth Mullins
P.O. Box 381807
Duncansville, TX 75138-1807

Tin Type
Tin Container Collectors Association
c/o Clark and Mary Beth Secrest
P.O. Box 4555
Denver, CO 80204

'TIQUES
Maxine/Stuart Evans
7 Rittner Lane
Old Bridge, NJ 08857
908-679-8212
FAX 908-679-1090

Tobacco Jar Newsletter
Society of Tobacco Jar Collectors
Charlotte Tarses, Treasurer
3011 Fallstaff Road #307
Baltimore, MD 21209
Dues: $30 per year ($35 outside of U.S.)

Toothpick Bulletin
National Toothpick Holder Collectors' Society
Judy Knauer, Founder
1224 Spring Valley Lane
W Chester, PA 19380

Torquay Pottery Collectors Society Newsletter
Torquay Pottery Collectors Society
Beth Pulsipher
Box 373
Schoolcraft, MI 49087
616-679-4195

Toy Gun Collectors of America Newsletter
Jim Buskirk, Editor and Publisher
312 Starling Way
Anaheim, CA 92807
Published quarterly, covers both toy and BB guns.
Dues: $15 per year

Toys and Prices magazine
700 E State St.
Iola, WI 54990-0001
715-445-2214 or FAX 715-445-4087
Subscription: $14.95 per year

The Trade Card Journal
Kit Barry
86 High St.
Brattleboro, VT 05301
802-254-2195
A quarterly publication on the social and
historical use of trade cards

Trainmaster newsletter
P.O. Box 1499
Gainesville, FL 32602
904-377-7439 or 904-373-4908
FAX 904-374-6616

UHL Collectors' Society
Steve Brundage, President
80 Tidewater Rd.
Hagerstown, IN 47346
Dale Blann, Vice President
R.R. 1, Box 136
Wheatland, IN 47597
For membership and newsletter information
contact either of the above

The Upside Down World of an O.J. Collector
The Occupied Japan Club
c/o Florence Archambault
29 Freeborn St.
Newport, RI 02840
Published bimonthly. Information requires SASE

Vernon Views
P.O. Box 945
Scottsdale, AZ 85252
Published quarterly beginning with the spring issue,
$6 per year

Vintage Clothing Newsletter
Terry McCormick
P.O. Box 1422
Corvallis, OR 97339
503-752-7456

Vintage Fashion and Costume Jewelry Newsletter/Club
P.O. Box 265
Glen Oaks, NY 11004
or call Davida Baron: 718-969-2320

Vintage Fashion Sourcebook
Kristina Harris
904 N 65th St.
Springfield, OR 97478-7021

Vintage Paperback Collecting Guide
Black Ace Books
1658 Griffith Park Blvd.
Los Angeles, CA 90026
213-661-5052 Information about terms, book fairs, auctions,
and references; available for $2 postpaid

Walking Stick Notes
Cecil Curtis, Editor
4051 E Olive Rd.
Pensacola, FL 32514
Quarterly publication with limited distribution

Watt's News
c/o Susan Morris and Jan Seeck
P.O. Box 708
Mason City, IA 50401
Subscription: $10 per year

Wedgwood Collectors Society Newsletter
P.O. Box 14013
Newark, NJ 07198

Westmoreland Glass Society
Jim Fisher, President
513 5th Ave.
Coralville, IA 52241
319-354-5011

The Working Class Hero Beatles Newsletter
3311 Niagra St.
Pittsburgh, PA 15213-4223
Published 3 times per year; send SASE for information

The Wrapper
Bubble Gum and Candy Wrapper Collectors
P.O. Box 573, St. Charles, IL 60174
708-377-7921

Zane Grey's West Society
Carolyn Timmerman
708 Warwick Ave.
Fort Wayne, IN 46825
219-484-2904

Zeppelin Collector
Zeppelin Collectors Club
c/o Aerophilatelic Federation
P.O. Box 1239
Elgin, IL 60121-1239
708-888-1907

Interested Buyers of Miscellaneous Items

In this section of the book we have listed hundreds of buyers who are actively looking to buy items from specific areas of interest. Don't expect a response from them unless you include an SASE (stamped self-addressed envelope) with your letter. If you'd rather they contact you by phone, give them your number and make sure you tell them to call collect. Describe your merchandise throughly and mention any marks; you can sometimes do a pencil rubbing to duplicate the mark exactly. Photographs are still worth a 'thousand words,' and photocopies are especially good if you're selling paper goods, patterned dinnerware, or even smaller 3-dimensional items. Be sure to read the Introduction for more suggestions about how to carry on a successful transaction by mail.

Buyers are listed alphabetically under bold topics. A line in italics indicates only the specialized interests of the particular buyer whose name directly follows it. Recommended reference guides not available from the Nostalgia Publishing Company may be purchased directly from the authors whose addresses are given in this section.

Abingdon
Vintage Charm
P.O. Box 26241
Austin, TX 78755

Advertising
Tin lithographed pot scrapers
Keith and Kevin Boline
BCC Enterprises
7811- 35th Ave. NE
Salem, OR 97303
503-393-0321

Also Coca-Cola
Jeff Bradfield
90 Main St.
Dayton, VA 22821

Porcelain signs and light-up clocks
Mike Bruner
6980 Walnut Lake Rd.
W Bloomfield, MI 48323
313-661-8241

Gas station items
Peter Capell
1838 W Grace St.
Chicago, IL 60613-2724

Upright tobacco tins; no Prince Albert, Half and Half Bond Street, Velvet or Edgeworth
Dennis and George Collectibles
304 Lake Montebello Dr.
Baltimore, MD 31318
410-889-3964

Vinyl figurals
Suzan Hufferd
6625 Sunbury Dr.
Indianapolis, IN 46241
317-630-7180 or 317-487-6352

Signs, trays, calendars, etc.
Steve Ketcham
P.O. Box 24114
Minneapolis, MN 55424
612-920-4205

Signs and tins
Doug Moore
57 Hickory Ridge Cir.
Cicero, IN 46034
317-877-1741

Soda Pop, especially Coca-Cola and Pepsi
Craig and Donna Stifter
511 Aurora Ave., #117
Naperville, IL 60540

Porcelain door push plates
Edward Foley
P.O. Box 572
Adamstown, PA 19501
717-484-4779

Henry F. Hain III Antiques and Collectibles
2623 N 2nd St.
Harrisburg, PA 17110

Terri Mardis-Ivers
1104 Shirlee
Ponca City, OK 74601

African Art and Oceanic Art
Scott Nelson
Box 6081
Santa Fe, NM 87502
505-986-1176

Airline Memorabilia
Richard R. Wallin
Box 1784
Springfield, IL 62705

Aluminum
Author of book
Dannie Woodard
P.O. Box 1346
Weatherford, TX 76086
817-594-4680

American Dinnerware
Russel Wright, Eva Zeisel, Homer Laughlin
Charles Alexander
221 E 34th St.
Indianapolis, IN 46205
317-924-9665

American Flags
Early, vintage
Robert Banks
18901 Gold Mine Ct.
Brookerville, MD 20833
301-774-7850

American Indian
Especially prehistoric artifacts
Author of book
Lar Hothem
P.O. Box 458
Lancaster, OH 43130

Animal Dishes
Author of book
Everett Grist
6503 Slater Rd., Suite H
Chattanooga, TN 37412-3955
615-855-4032

Robert and Sharon Thoerner
15549 Ryon Ave.
Bellflower, CA 90706

Architectural Items
John and Barbara Michel
Americana Blue
200 E 78th St., 18E
New York City, NY 10021
212-861-6094

Art Deco
Mark Bassett
P.O. Box 771233
Lakewood, OH 44107

DLK Nostalgia and Collectibles
P.O. Box 5112
Johnstown, PA 15904

Art Glass, Contemporary
Especially Boyd, Summit, and Moser
Chip and Dale Collectibles
3500 S Cooper
Arlington, TX 76015

Art Glass
Mark Bassett
P.O. Box 771233
Lakewood, OH 44107

American and European
Mirko Melis
4589 Longmoor Rd.
Mississauga, Ontario
Canada L5M 4H4
905-820-8066

Durand
Ed Meschi
R.R. 3, Box 550
Monroeville, NJ 08343
609-358-7293

Art Nouveau
Antique and Art Galleries, Ltd.
109 N Main St.
Bentonville, AR 72712
501-273-7770

Autographs
American West Archives
P.O. Box 100
Cedar City, UT 84720

Antiques Americana
K.C. Owings, Jr.
P.O. Box 19
N Abington, MA 02351
617-857-1655

Autumn Leaf
Edits newsletter
Gwynneth Harrison
P.O. Box 1
Mira Loma, CA 91752-0001
909-685-5434
Buys and appraises

Avon Collectibles
Author of book
Bud Hastin
P.O. Box 43690
Las Vegas, NV 89116

Tammy Rodrick
Stacey's Treasures
R.R. #2, Box 163
Sumner, IL 62466

Badges
Police and fireman
Gene Matzke
2345 S 28th St.
Milwaukee, WI 53215-2925
414-383-8995

Banks
Phil Helley
Old Kilbourn Antiques
629 Indiana Ave.
Wisconsin Dells, WI 53965

Marked Ertl
Homestead Collectibles
P.O. Box 173
Mill Hall, PA 17751

Barb Wire
John Mantz
American Barb Wire Collectors Society
1023 Baldwin Rd.
Bakersfield, CA 93304

Barber Shop Collectibles
Burton Handelsman
18 Hotel Dr.
White Plains, NY 10605
914-428-4480

Barware
Specializing in vintage cocktail shakers
Stephen Visakay
P.O. Box 1517
W Caldwell, NJ 07707-1517

Specializing in gambling-related items
Robert Eisenstadt
P.O. Box 020767
Brooklyn, NY 11202-0017

Battersea Boxes
John Harrigan
1900 Hennepin
Minneapolis, MN 55403
612-872-0226
Buy and sell

Batman
Colleen Garmon Barnes
114 E Locust
Chatham, IL 62629

Beer Cans
Steve Gordon
G & G Pawnbrokers
1325 University Blvd. E
Langley Park, MD 30783

Beer Steins
Tammy Rodrick
Rt. 2, Box 163
Sumner, IL 62466

Bells
Unusual; no cow or school
Author of book
Dorothy Malone Anthony
802 S Eddy
Ft. Scott, KS 66701

Billikens
Judy Knauer
1224 Spring Valley Lane
W Chester, PA 19380
601-431-3477

Black Americana
Judy Posner
R.D. 1, Box 273
Effort, PA 18330
Pre-1950s items

Jan Thalberg
23 Mountain View Dr.
Weston, CT 06883

Black Cats
Shafford only
Doug Dezso
864 Paterson Ave.
Maywood, NJ 07607

Black Glass
Author of book
Marlena Toohey
703 S Pratt Pkwy.
Longmont, CO 80501
303-678-9726

Blue and White Stoneware
Also Flemish
G & T Antiques
50 Broadmoor Dr.
Wabash, IN 46992
219-563-5682

Blue Willow
Tammy Rodrick
Rt. 2, Box 163
Sumner, IL 62466

Bobbin' Heads by Hartland
Patrick Flynn
Minne Memories
122 Shadywood Ave.
Mankato, MN 56001

Boats and Motors, Miniature
Dave Hoover
1023 Skyview Dr.
New Albany, IN 47150

Bohemian Glass
Tom Bradshaw
325 Carol Dr.
Ventura, CA 93303
805-653-2723 or 310-450-6486

Bookmarks
Joan L. Huegel
1002 W 25th St.
Erie, PA 16502

Books
Children's illustrated
Noreen Abbott Books
2666 44th Ave.
San Francisco, CA 94116

Hippie, beat and counterculture paperbacks
Black Ace Books
1658 Griffith Park Blvd.
Los Angeles, CA 90026

Vintage paperbacks
Buck Creek Books
838 Main St.
Lafayette, IN 47901

Paperback originals
For Collectors Only
2028B Ford Pkwy #136
St. Paul, MN 55116

American Indian archaeology
Lar Hothem
P.O. Box 458
Lancaster, OH 43130

Children's
Nerman's Books
410-63 Albert St.
Winnipeg, Manitoba
Canada R3B 1G4

Children's
My Bookhouse
27 S Sandusky St.
Tiffin, OH 44883
419-447-9842

Little Golden Books
Steve Santi
19626 Ricardo Ave.
Hayward, CA 94541

Little Blue Books
Judy Wilson
10125 River Acres Rd.
Scott, AR 72142

Bottles
Commercial perfumes and samples
Luc A. De Broqueville
8650 S Western 2623
Dallas, TX 75206

Bitters, figurals, inks, barber, etc.
Steve Ketcham
P.O. Box 24114
Minneapolis, MN 55424
612-920-4205

Dairy and milk
O.B. Lund
13009 S 42nd St.
Phoenix, AZ 85044

Painted-label soda
Author of book
Thomas Marsh
914 Franklin Ave.
Youngstown, OH 44502

Dairy and milk
Author of book
John Tutton
R.R. 4, Box 929
Front Royal, VA 22630
703-635-7058

Breweriana
DLK Nostalgia and Collectibles
P.O. Box 5112
Johnstown, PA 15904

Steve Gordon
G & G Pawnbrokers
1325 University Blvd. E
Langley Park, MD 20783

Breyer Figures
Terri Mardis-Ivers
1104 Shirlee
Ponca City, OK 74601

British Pottery
Susie Cooper, Mabel Lucie Atwell, Jazz Age
David J. Ehrhard
Psycho-Ceramic Restorations
10642½ Hillhaven Ave.
Tujunga, CA 91042

British Royal Commemoratives
Audrey Zeder
6755 Coralite St. S
Long Beach, CA 90808

Brush McCoy Pottery
Authors of book
Steve and Martha Sanford
230 Harrison Ave.
Campbell, CA 95008
408-978-8408

Buggy Steps
John W. Waddell
P.O. Box 664
Mineral Wells, TX 76067

Button Hooks
All types
Richard Mathes
P.O. Box 1408
Springfield, OH 45501-1408
Has duplicates to sell or trade; single
items or entire collections

Buttons
Also buckles
Tender Buttons
143 E 6nd St.
New York, NY 10021

Calendar Plates
Dated before 1950
Elizabeth M. Stout
152 Hwy. F
Defiance, MO 63341

California Perfume Company
Not common; especially marked Goetting Co.
Dick Pardini
3107 N El Dorado St., Dept. G
Stockton, CA 95204-3412

California Raisins
Larry De Angelo
516 King Arthur Dr.
Virginia Beach, VA 23464

Cambridge Glassware
John and Peggy Scott
4640 S Leroy
Springfield, MO 65810

Cameras
Wooden, detective and stereo; also old brass lenses
John A. Hess
P.O. Box 3062
Andover, MA 01810

Also accessories and 3-D projectors
Harry Poster
P.O. Box 1883
S Hackensack, NJ 07606
201-410-7525

Candy Containers
Glass
Jeff Bradfield
90 Main St.
Dayton, VA 22821

Glass
Doug Dezso
864 Paterson Ave.
Maywood, NJ 07607

Pre-WWII, holidays, papier-mache
Marjorie Geddes
P.O. Box 5875
Aloha, OR 97007

Linda Vines
P.O. Box 721
Upper Montclair, NJ 07043
201-746-5206

Carnival Chalkware
Author of book
Thomas G. Morris
503-779-3164

Carnival Glass
Helen Greguire
716-392-2704

Cast Iron
Door knockers, sprinklers and figural paperweights
Craig Dinner
P.O. Box 4399
Sunnyside, NY 11104

Especially marked cookware
David G. Smith
11918 2nd St.
Perrysburg, NY 14129

Cat Figurines
Also china and glassware with cats
Marjorie Geddes
P.O. Box 5875
Aloha, OH 97007

Ceramic Arts Studio
Author of book
BA Wellman
#106 Cordaville Rd.
Ashland, MA 01721-1002

Cereal Boxes and Premiums
Scott Bruce, Mr. Cereal Box
P.O. Box 481
Cambridge, MA 02140

Tammy Rodrick
Rt. 2, Box 163
Sumner, IL 62466

Character Collectibles
Gumby
Colleen Garmon Barnes
114 E Locust
Chatham, IL 62629

Author of book
Bill Bruegman
Toy Scouts, Inc.
137 Casterton Ave.
Akron, OH 44303

Premiums, early Disney, Western heroes
Ron Donnelly
P.O. Box 7047
Panama City Beach, FL 32413

Dick Tracy
Larry Doucet
2351 Sultana Dr.
Yorktown Heights, NY 10598

The Garfield Collectors Society
David L. Abrams
7744 Foster Ridge Rd.
Germantown, TN 38138-7036

Reddy Kilowatt
Lee Garmon
1529 Whittier St.
Springfield, IL 62704

Dark Shadows memorabilia
Steve Hall
P.O. Box 960398
Riverside, GA 30296-0398

The Lone Ranger
Terry and Kay Klepey
c/o The Silver Bullet Newsletter
P.O. Box 553
Forks, WA 98331

Peanuts and Schultz Collectibles
Author of book
Freddi Margolin
P.O. Box 512P
Bay Shore, NY 11706

Tom Mix
Author of book
Merle 'Bud' Norris
1324 N Hague Ave.
Columbus, OH 43204-2108

Lil' Abner
Kenn Norris
P.O. Box 4830
Sanderson, TX 79848-4830
Roy Rogers and Dale Evans

Author of book
Robert W. Phillips
1703 N Aster Pl.
Broken Arrow, OK 74012-1308

Betty Boop
Leo A. Mallette
2309 Santa Anita Ave.
Arcadia, CA 91006-5154

Terri Mardis-Ivers
1104 Shirlee
Ponca City, OK 74601

Michael Paquin
That Toy Guy
57 N Sycamore St.
Clifton Heights, PA 19018

Especially Disney
Judy Posner
R.D. 1, Box 273
Effort, PA 18330

Dionne Quintuplets
Jimmy Rodolfos
P.O. Box 2527
Woburn, MA 01888

Tammy Rodrick
Rt. 2, Box 163
Sumner, IL 62466

Especially premiums
Bruce Thalberg
23 Mountain View Dr.
Weston, CT 06883

Betsy McCall and friends
Marci Van Ausdall
666-840 Spring Creek Dr.
Westwood, CA 96137

Norm Vigue
62 Barley St.
Stoughton, MA 02072
617-344-5441

Chase
Barry Van Hook
2149 W Jibsail Loop
Mesa, AZ 85202
602-838-6971

Children's Dishes
German, English and French
Majorie Geddes
P.O. Box 5875
Aloha, OR 97007
Also English Carlton Ware and Shelly in
all-over floral patterns

China
From Depression era
Jay Adams
245 Lakeview Ave., Ste. 208
Clifton, NJ 07011
201-365-5907

Discontinued patterns
Classic Tableware
P.O. Box 4265
Stockton, CA 95204
209-956-4645
Specializing in Castleton, Lenox,
Spode, Syracuse, Fostoria

Matching service
Old China Patterns Ltd.
P.O. Box 290
Fineview, NY 13640
315-482-3829
Specializing in English and American companies;
Shelley, Haviland, Mikasa

Especially Shelly
Shrader's Antiques
Fred and Lila Shrader
2025 Hyw. 199
Crescent City, CA 95531
707-458-3525

Christmas
Jackie Chamberlain Antiques
P.O. Box 20842
Wickenburg, AZ 85358
602-684-2296

*Aluminum trees (all colors), unusual color
wheels and motorized stands*
Ted Haun
2426 N 700 East
Kokomo, IN 46901-9343

Especially German-marked items and other holiday items
Linda Vines
P.O. Box 721
Upper Montclair, NJ 07043
201-746-5206

Clarice Cliff Pottery
Louis and Susan Meisel
141 Prince St.
New York, NY 10012

Cleminson
Marilyn Whittingham
7290 Thunderbird Lane
Stanton, CA 90680

Clocks
All types
Bruce A. Austin
40 Selborne Chase
Fairport, NY 14450
716-223-0711

The Clock Doctor
Steve Gabany, Ph.D.
585 Woodbine
Terre Haute, IN 47803-1759

Comic character
Author of book
Howard S. Brenner
106 Woodgate Terrace
Rochester, NY 14625

Novelty animated and non-animated
Carole S. Kaifer
P.O. Box 232
Bethania, NC 27010

Tammy Rodrick
Rt. 2, Box 163
Sumner, IL 62466

Clothing
Vintage; also accessories
Leah and Walt Bird
P.O. Box 4502
Medford, OR 97501

Cocktail Shakers
Arlene Lederman Antiques
150 Main St.
Nyack, NY 10960

Steven Visakay
P.O. Box 1517
W Caldwell, NJ 07007-1517

Comic Strip Art
David H. Begin
138 Lansberry Ct.
Los Gatos, CA 95032

Cookie Jars
Joe Devine
1411 3rd St.
Council Bluffs, IA 51503
712-232-5233 or 712-328-7305

Judy Posner
R.D. 1, Box 273
Effort, PA 18330

Corkscrews
Antique and unusual
Paul P. Luchsinger
104 Deer Run
Williamsville, NY 14221

Cowan
Mark Bassett
P.O. Box 771233
Lakewood, OH 44107

Cracker Jack Items
Phil Helley
Old Kilbourn Antiques
629 Indiana Ave.
Wisconsin Dells, WI 53965

Wes Johnson, Sr.
106 Bauer Ave.
Louisville, KY 40207

Credit Cards and Related Items
Walt Thompson
Box 2541
Yakima, WA 98907-2541

Crystal
Discontinued patterns
Classic Tableware
P.O. Box 4265
Stockton, CA 95204
209-956-4645

Matching service
Old China Patterns Ltd.
P.O. Box 290
Fineview, NY 13640
315-482-3829

Cuff Links
Also related items
National Cuff Link Society
Eugene R. Klompus
P.O. Box 346
Prospect Heights, IL 60070
708-632-0561

Also buckles
Tender Buttons
143 E 6nd St.
New York, NY 10021

Currier and Ives Prints
Original only
Rudisill's Alt Print Haus
Barbara and John Rudisill
24305 Waterview Dr.
Worton, MD 21678
410-778-9290

Cut Glass
Ron Damaska
738 9th Ave.
New Brighton, PA 15066
412-843-1393

Dakins
Suzan Hufferd
6625 Sunbury Dr.
Indianapolis, IN 46241
317-630-7180 or 317-487-6352

Decanters
Homestead Collectibles
P.O. Box 173
Mill Hall, PA 17751

Decorative Arts
Turn of the century
Carl Heck
Box 8416
Aspen, CO 81612
303-925-8011

Depression Glass
Jay Adams
245 Lakeview Ave., Ste. 208
Clifton, NJ 07011
201-365-5907

Dale Armstrong
7307 N State Rd. 39
Lizton, IN 46149
317-994-5125

Mail order only
Glass Connection
312 Babcock Dr.
Palantine, IL 60067
708-359-3839

H.E. Gschwend
1421 Camden St.
Pekin, IL 61554
309-347-1679

John and Peggy Scott
4640 S Leroy
Springfield, MO 65810

Dan Tucker
Toledo, OH; 419-478-3815 or
Tavares, FL (winter)
904-742-2638

Also Elegant glassware
Bobby's Past Time
301 N Main
Mt. Vernon, MO 65712
417-466-7645

Documents
David M. Beach
Paper Americana
P.O. Box 2026
Goldenrod, FL 32733

Especially Civil War items
K.C. Owings, Jr.
P.O. Box 19
N Abington, MA 02351

Gordon Totty
Scarce Paper Americana
347 Shady Lake Pkwy.
Baton Rouge, LA 70810
504-766-8625

Dolls
Joan Faulkner
1149 Buchanan
Plainfield, IN 46168
317-839-6092

Cabbage Patch
Mari Forquer
P.O. Box 714
Cleveland, GA 30528

Skookum
Barry Friedman
22725 Garzota Dr.
Valencia, CA 91355

Pre-World War II
Marjorie Geddes
P.O. Box 5875
Aloha, OR 97007
Also German snow babies and Kewpies

Captain Action
Michael Paquin
That Toy Guy
57 N Sycamore St.
Clifton Heights, PA 19018

Dollhouse Furniture and Accessories
Marian Schmuhl
7 Revolutionary Ridge Rd.
Bedford, MA 10730

Door Knockers
Craig Dinner
P.O. Box 4399
Sunnyside, NY 11104

Dr. Seuss
Michael Gessel
P.O. Box 748
Arlington, VA 22216

Dragonware
Susie Hibbard
2570 Walnut Blvd. #20
Walnut Creek, CA 94596

Egg Cups
Majorie Geddes
P.O. Box 5875
Aloha, OR 97007

Egg Timers
Jeannie Greenfield
310 Parker Rd.
Stoneboro, PA 16153

Elegant Glassware
John and Shirley Baker
673 W Township Rd. #118
Tiffin, OH 44883

Elvis Presley
Author of book
Rosalind Cranor
P.O. Box 859
Blacksburg, VA 24063

Enamelware
Linda Hicks
3055 E Lake
Gladwater, TX 75647

Ephemera
Author of book
Warren R. Anderson
American West Archives
P.O. Box 100
Cedar City, UT 84721
801-586-9497

Holiday theme
Chris Russell and The Halloween Queen
4 Lawrance St., Rt. 10
Winchester, NH 54559

Exit Globes
Mike Bruner
6980 Walnut Lake Rd.
W Bloomfield, MI 48323
313-661-8241

Expositions
D.D. Woollard, Jr.
11614 Old St. Charles Rd.
Bridgeton, MO 63044
314-739-4662

Fans
Early electric, prior to 1960
Rick Hackman
P.O. Box 212
Delaware, NJ 07833; 908-475-5456
Also sells

Farm Collectibles
Farm Antique News
Gary Van Hoozer
812 N Third St.
Tarkio, MO 64491-0812

Fast Food Collectibles
Authors of book
Joyce and Terry Losonsky
7506 Summer Leave Lane
Columbia, MD 21046-2455

Bill and Pat Poe
Poe-Pourri
220 Dominica Cir. E
Niceville, FL 32578-4068

Suzan Hufferd
6625 Sunbury Dr.
Indianapolis, IN 46241
317-630-7180 or 317-487-6352

Fast Food Glasses
Tammy Rodrick
Rt. 2, Box 163
Sumner, IL 62466

Fiesta
Fiesta Plus
Mick and Lorna Chase
380 Hawkins Crawford Rd.
Cookeville, TN 38501
615-372-8333
Also Harlequin, Riviera and other Homer Laughlin patterns;
Franciscan, Lu Ray, Russel Wright, and Metlox

Dan Tucker
Toledo, OH; 419-478-3815 or
Tavares, FL (winter)
904-742-2638

Figural Ceramics
Teapots, shakers, kitchen items, etc.
Richard and Carol Silagyi
CS Antiques and Jewelry
P.O. Box 151
Wyckoff, NJ 07430

Figurines
Designed by Erich Stauffer (child-like)
Joan Oates
685 S Washington
Constantine, MI 49042
Buy and sell

Fire-King
Author of book
April M. Tvorak
HCR #34, Box 25B
Warren, PA 18851

Fireworks and 4th of July
Dennis C. Manochio
4th of July Americana and Fireworks Museum
P.O. Box 2010
Saratoga, CA 95070

Fishing Collectibles
Dave Hoover
1023 Skyview Dr.
New Albany, IN 47150
Publishes fixed price catalog

T.C. Wills
103 Virginia St.
Dyess AFB, TX 79607

Flashlights
Bill Utley
P.O. Box 3572
Downey, CA 90242

Florence Ceramics
John and Peggy Scott
4640 S Leroy
Springfield, MO 65810

Fountain Pens
Pen Fancier's Club
1169 Overcash Dr.
Dunedin, FL 34698

Franciscan Dinnerware
Franciscan Dinnerware Matching Service
323 E Matilija, Ste. 112
Ojai, CA 93023
Mail order only; buy and sell

Frank Lloyd Wright and Prairie School
Richard A. Haussmann
25 Hampton Rd.
Montgomery, IL 60538-2321
708-896-8287

Frankart
Barry Van Hook
2149 W Jibsail Loop
Mesa, AZ 85202
602-838-6971

Frankoma
Phyllis and Tom Bess
14535 E 13th St.
Tulsa, OK 74108

Fraternal Organizations
Masonic ironstone
Susan and Larry Hirshman
540 Siskiyou Blvd.
Ashland, OR 97520

Masonic and Shriner
David Smies
Box 522
Manhattan, KS 66502
913-776-1433

Odd Fellows
Greg Speiss
230 E Washington
Joliet, IL 60433
815-722-5639

Fruit Jars
Especially old, odd or colored jars
John Hathaway
Rte. 2, Box 220
Bryant Pond, ME 04219
Also old jar lids and closures

Fry Glass
Ron Damaska
738 9th Ave.
New Brighton, PA 15066
412-843-1393

Furniture
Dale Armstrong
7307 N State Rd. 39
Lizton, IN 46149
317-994-5125

Mission, Stickley and Roycroft
Bruce A. Austin
40 Selborne Chase
Fairport, NY 14450
716-223-0711

Joan Faulkner
1149 Buchanan
Plainfield, IN 46168
317-839-6092

18th and 19th-century American
Oveda Mauer Antiques
34 Greenfield Ave.
San Anselmo, CA 94960

Mission
Douglass White
P.O. Box 540672
Orlando, FL 32854
407-841-6681

Gambling and Gambling-Related Items
Robert Eisenstadt
P.O. Box 020767
Brooklyn, NY 11202-0017

Games
Phil McEntee
Where the Toys Are
45 W Pike St.
Canonsburg, PA 15317

TV and other characters
Norm Vigue
62 Barley St.
Stoughton, MA 02072
617-344-5441

Gasoline Globes, Pumps and Signs
Author of book
Scott Benjamin
P.O. Box 611
Elyria, OH 44036
216-365-9534
Also service station promotionals

Peter Capell
1838 W Grace St.
Chicago, IL 60613-2724

Geisha Girl Porcelain
Elyce Litts
P.O. Box 394
Morris Plains, NJ 07950

Glass Animals
Author of book
Lee Garmon
1529 Whittier St.
Springfield, IL 62704

Glass Knives
Editor of newsletter
Adrienne Esco
P.O. Box 342
Los Alamitos, CA 90720
310-430-6479

Glass Shoes
Author of book
The Shoe Lady
Libby Yalom
P.O. Box 852
Adelphi, MD 20783

Glassware
Antique
Dale Armstrong
7307 N State Rd. 39
Lizton, IN 46149
317-994-5125

Kitchen, Pyrex, Corningware, etc.
Author of book
April M. Tvorak
HCR #34, Box 25B
Warren, PA 18851

Glidden Pottery
David Pierce
27544 Black Rd.
P.O. Box 248
Danville, OH 43014
614-599-6394

Goebel
Friar Tuck and Cardinals
Carol and Jim Carlton
8115 S Syracuse St.
Englewood, CO 80112
303-773-8616

Goofus Glass
Rare or unusual
Dan Gandolfo
3 S 577 Elizabeth Ave.
Warrenville, IL 60555
708-393-9115

Gone with the Wind Collectibles
Author of book
Patrick McCarver
5453 N Rolling Oaks Dr.
Memphis, TN 38119

Ron Donnelly
P.O. Box 7047
Panama City Beach, FL 32413

Graniteware
Helen Greguire
716-392-2704

American gray
Keith and Kevin Boline
BCC Enterprises
7811- 35th Ave. NE
Salem, OR 97303
503-393-0321

Griswold
Author of book
Denise Harned
P.O. Box 330373
Elmwood, CT 06133-0373

Hall
H.E. Gschwend
1421 Camden St.
Pekin, IL 61554
309-347-1679

Dan Tucker
Toledo, OH; 419-478-3815 or
Tavares, FL (winter)
904-742-2638

Hallmark Ornaments
Susan K. Holland
6151 Main St.
Springfield, OR 97478

Author of book
Rosie Wells Enterprises, Inc.
R.R. #1
Canton, IL 61520

Halloween
Jackie Chamberlain Antiques
P.O. Box 20842
Wickenburg, AZ 85358
602-684-2296

Specializing in costumes
Craig Reid
P.O. Box 881
Post Falls, ID 838-54-0881

Chris Russell and The Halloween Queen
4 Lawrance St., Rt. 10
Winchester, NH 54559
Also other holidays

Linda Vines
P.O. Box 721
Upper Montclair, NJ 07043
201-746-5206

Handcuffs and Leg Irons
David Pierce
27544 Black Rd.
P.O. Box 248
Danville, OH 43104
614-599-6394

Joseph M. Tanner
3024 E 35th St.
Spokane, WA 99223
509-448-8457
Buy, sell, and trade

Hatpins and Hatpin Holders
Author of book
Lillian Baker
15237 Chanera Ave.
Gardena, CA 90249

Head Vases
Tammy Rodrick
Rt. 2, Box 163
Sumner, IL 62466

Historical Staffordshire China
Also Liverpool, Gaudy Dutch and Spatterware
Richard G. Marden
Box 524
Wolfeboro, NY 03894
603-569-3209

Holly Hobbie and Friends
Holly Hobbie Club of America
Helen McCale
R.R. 3, Box 35
Butler, MO 64730

Homer Laughlin China
Author of book
Darlene Nossaman
5419 Lake Charles
Waco, TX 76710

Dreamland and Holland
Aletha Barlow
Rte. 1, Box 8
Clearmont, MO 64431
816-729-4688

Hull
Mirror Brown
Bill and Connie Sloan
Rte. 32, Box 629
Pt. Pleasant, PA 18950

Hummels
Fred and Lila Shrader
Shrader Antiques
2025 Hwy. 199
Crescent City, CA 95531
707-458-3525

Look-alikes marked Stauffer, Japan
Joan Oates
685 S Washington
Constantine, MI 49042
616-435-8353

Ice Cream Molds
Jackie Chamberlain Antiques
P.O. Box 20842
Wickenburg, AZ 85358
602-684-2296

Ice Cream Scoops
Lillian M. Cole
14 Harmony School Rd.
Flemington, NJ 08822
908-782-3198

Illustrator Art
Louis Wain cats
Jackie Durham
909 26th St. NW
Washington, D.C. 20037

Icart etchings and Maxfield Parrish prints
Ed Meschi
R.R. 3, Box 550
Monroeville, NJ 08343
609-358-7293
Also American oil paintings

Maxfield Parrish Prints & Items
L.C. Stroup
P.O. Box 3009
Paducah, KY 42002-3009

Imperial Porcelain
Geneva D. Addy
P.O. Box 124
Winterset, IA 50273

Paul Webb series
Carol and Jim Carlton
8115 S Syracust St.
Englewood, CO 80112
303-773-8616

Insulators
Len Linscott
3557 Nicklaus Dr.
Tutusville, FL 32780

Mike Bruner
6980 Walnut Lake Rd.
W Bloomfield, MI 48323
313-661-8241

Irish Belleek
Richard K. Degenhardt
Sugar Hollow Farm
124 Cypress Point
Henderson, NC 28739
704-696-9750

Irons and Pressing Devices
D&R Farm Antiques
4545 Hwy. H
St. Charles, MO 63301
314-258-3790

Jewell Tea
Bobby's Past Time
301 N Main
Mt. Vernon, MO 65712
417-466-7645

Jewelry
Joan Faulkner
1149 Buchanan
Plainfield, IN 46168
317-839-6092

Mexican silver
Richard Haigh
P.O. Box 29888
Richmond, VA 23242

Antique and estate
Mirko Melis
4589 Longmoor Rd.
Mississauga, Ontario
Canada L5M 4H4
905-820-8066

Kay Finch
Doris Frizzell
5687 Oakdale Dr.
Springfield, IL 62707

Kentucky Derby and Horse Racing
B.L. Hornback
707 Sunrise Lane
Elizabethtown, KY 42701

Knives
Author of book
Jim Sargent
Books Americana, Inc.
Florence, AL 35630

Dennis Stapp
7037 Haynes Rd.
Georgetown, IN 47122

Lace
The Lace Merchant Newsletter
Elizabeth M. Kurella
P.O. Box 222
Plainwell, MI 49080

Labels
Cerebro
P.O. Box 1221
Lancaster, PA 17603
1-800-695-2235

Cigar Labels and Boxes
David M. Beach
Paper Americana
P.O. Box 2026
Goldenrod, FL 32733

Also can, crate, firecracker, and all pre-1920s
D. Freiberg
P.O. Box 327
E Prospect, PA 17317-0327

Ladies' Compacts
Author of book
Roselyn Gerson
P.O. Box Letter S
Lynbrook, NY 11563

Lori Landgrebe
2331 E Main St.
Decatur, IL 62521

Elyce Litts
P.O. Box 394
Morris Plains, NJ 07950

Lalique
John R. Danis
11028 Raleigh Ct.
Rockford, IL 61111
815-963-0757 or FAX 815-877-6042

Lamps
Specializing in Aladdin
Author of book
J.W. Courter
R.R. 1, Box 256
Simpson, IL 62985

William Durham and William Galaway
615 S State St.
Belvidere, IL 61008
815-544-0577
Specializing in parts and restoration

Oveda Mauer Antiques
34 Greenfield Ave.
San Anselmo, CA 94960

Law Enforcement, Crime-Related Memorabilia
Antiques of Law and Order
Tony Perrin
H.C. 7, Box 53A
Mena, AR 71953

Especially restraints, badges and photos
Gene Matzke
2345 S 28th St.
Milwaukee, WI 53215-2925
414-383-8995

Lefton
Loretta De Lozier
1101 Polk St.
Bedford, IA 50833

License Plate Attachments
Edward Foley
P.O. Box 572
Adamstown, PA 19501
717-484-4779

License Plates
Richard Diehl
5965 W Colgate Pl.
Denver, CO 80227

Liddle Kiddles
Cindy Sabulis
3 Stowe Dr., #1S
Shelton, CT 06484

Lighters
Bill Majors
P.O. Box 9351
Boise, ID 83707

Jack Seiderman
1631 NW 114 Ave.
Bembroke Pines, FL 33026-2539
Issues catalogs

Lightning Rod Balls
Mike Bruner
6980 Walnut Lake Rd.
W Bloomfield, MI 48323
313-661-8241

Magic and Escape Art
Especially Houdini-related items
Joseph M. Tanner
3024 E 35th St.
Spokane, WA 99223
509-448-8457
Buy, sell and trade

Magazines
Mad and related collectibles
Jim McClane
232 Butternut Dr.
Wayne, NJ 07470

Monster from 1950s-'70s, from movies (not comics)
Steve Dolnick
P.O. Box 69
E Meadow, NY 11554
516-486-5085

National Geographic
Author of book
Don Smith's National Geographic Magazines
3930 Rankin St.
Louisville, KY 40214
502-366-7504

Marbles
Author of book
Everett Grist
6503 Slater Rd., Suite H
Chattanooga, TN 37412-3955
615-855-4032

Marilyn Monroe
Colleen Garmon Barnes
114 E Locust
Chatham, IL 62629

Matchcovers
Bill Retskin
P.O. Box 18481
Asheville, NC 22814

Match Holders
Ron Damaska
738 9th Ave.
New Brighton, PA 15066
412-843-1393

Match Safes
George Sparacio
R.D. #2, Box 139C
Newfield, NJ 08344

Militaria
Especially US Navy
Ron M. Willis
Heartland of Kentucky Decanters and Steins
P.O. Box 428
Lebanon Jct., KY 40150
502-833-2827

Moorcroft
John Harrigan
1900 Hennepin
Minneapolis, MN 55403
612-872-0226
Buy and sell

Morgantown
Literature, catalogs and glass
Editor of newsletter
Jerry Gallagher
420 1st Ave. NW
Plainview, MN 55964
507-534-3511

Mourning Collectibles
Postmortem, memorial, photography and ephemera
Steve DeGenaro
P.O. Box 5662
Youngstown, OH 44504
216-759-7737

Mouse Traps
Boyd Nedry
728 Buth Dr.
Comstock Park, MI 49321

Music Boxes
Anything related to antique mechanical music
Mechantiques
26 Barton Hill
E Hampton, CT 06424
203-267-8682
Also monkey organs, musical clocks and watches, band organs, coin pianos, orchestrions, player organs, mechanical birds, automata, and phonographs with horns

Niloak
Fred and Lila Shrader
Shrader Antiques
2025 Hwy. 199
Crescent City CA 95531
707-458-3525
Also Shelley Dinnerware

Nodders
Doug Dezso
864 Paterson Ave.
Maywood, NJ 07607

Occupied Japan
The Occupied Japan Club and Newsletter
% Florence Archambault
29 Freeborn St.
Newport, RI 02840
401-846-9024

Oil Company Collectibles
Author of book
Scott Benjamin
P.O. Box 611
Elyria, OH 44036
216-365-9534

Orientalia
Susie Hibbard
2570 Walnut Blvd. #20
Walnut Creek, CA 94596

Padlocks
Charles Chandler
36076 Grennada
Livonia, MI 48154

Joseph M. Tanner
3024 E 35th St.
Spokane, WA 99223
509-448-8457

Paperweights

19th-century glass
Tom Bradshaw
325 Carol Dr.
Ventura, CA 93303
805-653-2723 or 310-450-6486

Antique and modern; leading artist and Baccarat
George Kamm
24 Townsend Ct.
Lancaster, PA 17603
717-872-7858

Specifically Blue Bell
Author of book
Jackie Linscott
3557 Nicklaus Dr.
Tutusville, FL 32780

Contemporary and antique
The Paperweight Shop
Betty Schwab
2507 Newport Dr.
Bloomington, IL 61704
309 662-1956

Pen Delfin Rabbit Figurines

George Sparacio
R.D. #2, Box 139C
Newfield, NJ 08344

Pencil Sharpeners

Martha Hughes
4128 Ingalls St.
San Diego, CA 92103

Pennsbury Pottery

B A Wellman
#106 Cordaville Rd.
Ashland, MA 01721-1002

Perfume Bottles

Especially commercial, Czechoslovakian, Lalique, Baccarat,
Victorian, crown top, facties, miniatures
Monsen and Baer
310 Maple Ave. West, Ste. 115
Vienna, VA 22180
703-938-2129
Buy, sell and accept consignments for auctions

Pewter

Oveda Mauer Antiques
34 Greenfield Ave.
San Anselmo, CA 94960
415-454-6439
Also hearthware

Pez

Sue Sternfeld
90-60 Union Turnpike
Glendale, NY 11385

Pfaltzgraff

Gourmet, Gourmet Royal
Bill and Connie Sloan
Rte. 32, Box 629
Pt. Pleasant, PA 18950

Phoenix and Consolidated

Author of book
Jack D. Wilson
P.O. Box 81974
Chicago, IL 60681-0974

Phoenix Bird Chinaware

Joan Oates
685 S Washington
Constantine, MI 49042
616 435-8353
P.O. Box 81974
Chicago, IL 60681-0974
Buy and Sell; 1994 newsletters (2) $8

Ron Damaska
738 9th Ave.
New Brighton, PA 15066
412-843-1393

Photographica

Any pre-1900
John A. Hess
P.O. Box 3062
Andover, MA 01810

Pie Birds

Also funnels
Lillian M. Cole
14 Harmony School Rd.
Flemington, NJ 08822
908-782-3198

Joe Devine
1411 3rd St.
Council Bluffs, IA 51503
712-232-5322 or 712-328-7305

Pink Pigs

Also Pink-Paw Bears
Geneva Addy
P.O. Box 124
Winterset, IA 50273

Pin-Up Art
Original art only
Louis and Susan Meisel
141 Prince St.
New York, NY 10012

Playing Cards
Ray Hartz
P.O. Box 1002
Westerville, OH 43081
614-891-6296

Political
Before 1960
Michael Engel
29 Groveland St.
Easthampton, MA 01027

Pins, banners, ribbons, etc.
Paul Longo Americana
Box 490
Chatham Rd., South Orleans
Cape Cod, MA 02662
508-255-5482

The Political Bandwagon Newspaper
P.O. Box 348
Leola, PA 17540

Pond Sailboats
English and American; 1890-1950s
Louis and Susan Meisel
141 Prince St.
New York, NY 10012

Postcards
Jeff Bradfield
90 Main St.
Dayton, VA 22821

Author of book
Margaret Kaduck
P.O. Box 26076
Cleveland, OH 44126

Holiday theme
Chris Russell and The Halloween Queen
4 Lawrance St., Rt. 10
Winchester, NH 54559

Pottery
Niloak, Camark, Ouachita, Ozark,
Hy-Long, Marie, Mussel Shoals
Arkansas Pottery Co.
P.O. Box 7617
Little Rock, AR 72217
Buying and selling; also Arkansas memorabilia in celluloid

American Art Pottery
Mark Bassett
P.O. Box 771233
Lakewood, OH 44107

Especially Hull and Roseville
Bobby's Past Time
301 N Main
Mt. Vernon, MO 65712
417-466-7645

Colorado (Broadmoor), Coors, Lonhuda, and Denver White
Carol and Jim Carlton
8115 S Syracuse St.
Englewood, CO 80112
303-773-8616

Joe Devine
1411 3rd St.
Council Bluffs, IA 51503
712-232-5322 or 712-328-7305

John Harrigan
1900 Hennepin
Minneapolis, MN 55403

Author of book on Van Briggle
Scott H. Nelson
Box 6081
Santa Fe, NM 87502
505-986-1176

American companies
Betty Thomas
2600 Sherman Dr.
Kokomo, IN 46902
317-453-1178
Also Fiesta, Hall and Jewell T

Especially Fulper, Newcomb, Teco, Grueby, Marblehead
Douglass White
P.O. Box 540672
Orlando, FL 32854
407-841-6681

Powder Jars
John and Peggy Scott
4640 S Leroy
Springfield, MO 65810

Precious Moments®
Author of book
Rosie Wells Enterprises, Inc.
R.R. #1
Canton, IL 61520

Primitives and Country Collectibles
Lana Henry
1147 Terrace Ave.
Jasper, IN 47546
812-634-9819

Purinton Pottery
P.O. Box 708
Mason City, IA 50401

Purses
Veronica Trainer
P.O. Box 40443
Cleveland, OH 44140

Puzzles
Mechanical, dexterity types
Thomas M. Rogers Jr.
1466 W Wesley Rd.
Atlanta, GA 30327

Quilts
Artisons
Rte. 1, Box 20-C
Mentone, AL 35984
205-634-4037

Radio Premiums
Phil Helley
Old Kilbourn Antiques
629 Indiana Ave.
Wisconsin Dells, WI 53965

Doug Moore
57 Hickory Ridge Cir.
Cicero, IN 46034
317-877-1741

Radios
Antique Radio Labs
James Fred
Rte. 1, Box 41
Cutler, IN 46920
Buy, sell and trade; repairs radio equipment
using vaccuum tubes

Author of book
Harry Poster
P.O. Box 1883
S Hackensack, NJ 07606
201-410-7525
Also televisions, related advertising items, old tubes, cameras, 3-D viewers and projectors, View-Master and Tru-View reels and accessories

Railroadiana
Any item; especially china and silver
Grandpa
1701 Wynkoop St.
Denver, CO 80202
303-892-1177

Also steamship and other transportation memorabilia
Fred and Lila Shrader
Shrader Antiques
2025 Hwy. 199
Crescent City, CA 95531
707-458-3525

Records
Especially 78s
L.R. 'Les' Docks
Box 691035
San Antonio, TX 78269-1035
Write for want list

Reddy Kilowatt
Lee Garmon
1529 Whittier St.
Springfield, IL 62704

Red Wing Stoneware
Keith and Kevin Boline
BCC Enterprises
7811- 35th Ave. NE
Salem, OR 97303
503-393-0321

Road Maps
Oil company or states
Noel Levy
P.O. Box 595699
Dallas, TX 75359-5699

Robinson Ransbottom
Tammy Rodrick
Rt. 2, Box 163
Sumner, IL 62466

Rowland and Marsellus
David Ringering
Salem, OR 97301
503-585-8253
Also other souvenir and historical china with scenes of tourist attractions from 1890 through the 1930s

Roselane Sparklers
Lee Garmon
1529 Whittier St.
Springfield, IL 62704

Rosemeade
NDSU research specialist
Bryce Farnsworth
1334 14½ St. S
Fargo, ND 58103
701-237-3597

Royal Copley
Author of book
Joe Devine
1411 3rd St.
Council Bluffs, IA 51503
712-323-5233 or 712-328-7305
Buy, sell or trade

Royal Doulton Tobies
John Harrigan
1900 Hennepin
Minneapolis, MN 55403
612-872-0226
Buy and sell

Royal Haeger and Royal Hickman
Lee Garmon
1529 Whittier St.
Springfield, IL 62704

Ruby Glass
Author of book
Naomi L. Over
8909 Sharon Lane
Arvada, CO 80002
303-424-5922

Russel Wright
Author of book
Ann Kerr
P.O. Box 437
Sidney, OH 45365

Salesman Samples
Cast iron stoves
D & R Farm Antiques
4545 Hwy. H
St. Charles, MO 63301
314-258-3790

Saloon Memorabilia
Author of book
Richard M. Bueschel
414 N Prospect Manor Ave.
Mt. Prospect, IL 60056
phone or FAX 708-253-0791

Backbars
Greg Speiss
230 E Washington
Joliet, IL 60433
815-722-5639
Also fireplace mantels

Salt and Pepper Shakers
Joe Devine
1411 3rd St.
Council Bluffs, IA 51503
712-232-5233 or 712-328-7305

Pattern glass
Authors of book
Mildred and Ralph Lechner
P.O. Box 554
Mechanicsville, VA 23111

Figural or novelty
Judy Posner
R.D. 1, Box 273
Effort, PA 18330

Salts, Open
M.A. Geddes
P.O. Box 5875
Aloha, OR 97007

Schoolhouse Collectibles
Kenn Norris
P.O. Box 4830
Sanderson, TX 79848-4830

Scottie Dog Collectibles
Wee Scots, Inc.
Donna Newton
P.O. Box 1512
Columbus, IN 47202

Scouting Collectibles
Author of book
R.J. Sayers
P.O. Box 629
Brevard, NC 28712

Sebastians
Blossom Shop Collectibles
112 N Main St.
Farmer City, IL 61842
800-842-2593

Sewing Collectibles
Leah and Walt Bird
P.O. Box 4502
Medford, OR 97501

Pre-1930s
Marjorie Geddes
P.O. Box 5875
Aloha, OR 97007

Sewing Machines
Toy only
Authors of book
Darryl and Roxana Matter
P.O. Box 65
Portis, KS 67474-0065

Shaving Mugs
David Giese
1410 Aquia Dr.
Stafford, VA 22554

Occupational
Ed Meschi
R.R. 3, Box 550
Monroeville, NJ 08343
609-358-7293

Occupational
Burton Handelsman
18 Hotel Dr.
White Plains, NY 10605
914-428-4480

Shawnee Pottery
John Hathaway
Rt. 2, Box 220
Bryant Pond, ME 04219

Sheet Music
Mt. Washington Antiques
3742 Kellogg Ave.
Cincinnati, OH 45226
513-231-6584 or 513-321-0919
Buy and sell

Shirley Temple
Gen Jones
294 Park St.
Medford, MA 02155

Shooting Gallery Targets
John and Barbara Michel
Americana Blue
200 E 78th St., 18E
New York City, NY 10021
212-861-6094

Shot Glasses
Author of book
Mark Pickvet
P.O. Box 90404
Flint, MI 48509

Silhouette Pictures (20th Century)
Author of book
Shirley Mace
Shadow Enterprises
P.O. Box 61
Cedar, MN 55011-066

Snow Babies
Linda Vines
P.O. Box 721
Upper Montclair, NJ 07043
201-746-5206

Snow Domes
Author of book
Nancy McMichael, Editor
P.O. Box 53262
Washington, DC 20009

Soakies
Sue Sternfeld
90-60 Union Turnpike
Glendale, NY 11385

Soda Fountain Collectibles
Harold and Joyce Screen
2804 Munster Rd.
Baltimore, MD 21234
410-661-6765

Space-Related Memorabilia
Michael Mitchell
P.O. Box 192
Kents Hill, ME 04349-0192
207-897-6855

Sports Collectibles
Paul Longo Americana
Box 490
Chatham Rd., South Orleans
Cape Cod, MA 02662
508-255-5482

Robert Edward Auctions
P.O. Box 1923
Hoboken, NJ 07030
201-792-9324 or FAX 201-792-2469
Catalogs available

Sports Cards
Sally S. Carver
179 South St.
Chestnut Hill, MA 02167

Sports Pins
Tony George
22431 - B160 Antonio Pky, #252
Rancho Santa Margarita, CA 92688
714-589-6075

Sprinkler Bottles
Richard and Carol Silagyi
CS Antiques and Jewelry
P.O. Box 151
Wyckoff, NJ 07430

Carol and Jimmy Walker
501 N 5th St.
Waelder, TX 78959
512-665-7166

St. Louis, MO
Tower Grove Antiques
3308 Meramec
St. Louis, MO 63118

Stangl
Birds, dinnerware, artware
Popkorn Antiques
Bob Perzel
P.O. Box 1057
4 Mine St.
Flemington, NJ 08822
908-782-9631

Statue of Liberty
Mike Brooks
7335 Skyline
Oakland, CA 94611

Star Trek and Star Wars
Craig Reid
P.O. Box 881
Post Falls, ID 83854-0881

Sterling Silver
Also silverplate and souvenir spoons
Margaret Alves
84 Oak Ave.
Shelton, CT 06484

Also baby and souvenir spoons
Marjorie Geddes
P.O. Box 5875
Aloha, OR 97007
Also tea-related items

Stocks and Bonds
Author of book
Warren R. Anderson
American West Archives
P.O. Box 100
Cedar City, UT 84721
801-586-9497

Paul Longo Americana
Box 490
Chatham Rd., South Orleans
Cape Cod, MA 02662
508-255-5482

Strawberry Shortcake
Geneva D. Addy
P.O. Box 124
Winterset, IA 50273

Stringholders
Al Little
P.O. Box 288
Antioch, IL 60002

Swanky Swigs
M. Fountain
201 Alvena
Wichita, KS 67203
316-943-1925

Target Balls
Mike Bruner
6980 Walnut Lake Rd.
W Bloomfield, MI 48323
313-661-8241

Tea Leaf Ironstone
William Durham and William Galaway
615 S State St.
Belvidere, IL 61008
815-544-0577

Teapots and Tea-Related Items
Tina Carter
882 S Mollison
El Cajon, CA 92020

Telephones
Antique to modern; also parts
Phoneco
207 E Mill Rd.
P.O. Box 70
Galesville, WI 54630

The Three Stooges
Soitenly Stooges Inc.
Harry S. Ross
P.O. Box 72
Skokie, IL 60076

Tiffin Glassware
John and Shirley Baker
673 W Township Rd. #118
Tiffin, OH 44883

Tiffany
Lamps, windows, paintings, etc.
Carl Heck
Box 8416
Aspen, CO 81612
303-925-8011

Tire Ashtrays
Jeff McVey
1810 W State St., #427
Boise, ID 83702

Tobacco Collectibles
Any related items
Chuck Thompson
P.O. Box 11652
Houston, TX 77293

Toothpick Holders
Antique, souvenir
Judy Knauer
1224 Spring Valley Lane
W Chester, PA 19380
601-431-3477

Torquay Pottery
Jerry and Gerry Kline
604 Orchard View Dr.
Maumee, OH 43539
419-893-1226

Toasters
Helen Greguire
716-392-2704

Toys
Aurora model kits, and especially toys from 1948-1972
Author of book
Bill Bruegman
137 Casterton Dr.
Akron, OH 44303

Especially tin or cast iron
Jeff Bradfield
90 Main St.
Dayton, VA 22821

Tonka Toys
Doug Dezso
864 Paterson Ave.
Maywood, NJ 07607

DLK Nostalgia and Collectibles
P.O. Box 5112
Johnstown, PA 15904
Also football cards and miscellaneous

Cast iron cookware
D & R Farm Antiques
4545 Hwy. H
St. Charles, MO 63301
314-258-3790

Model kits other than Aurora
Gordy Dutt
Box 201
Sharon Center, OH 42274-0201

Especially die-cast vehicles
Mark Giles
P.O. Box 821
Ogallala, NE 69153-0821

Lionel, American Flyer, Marx and other makes of trains
Author of book
Bruce Greenberg
Greenberg Publishing Company, Inc.
Sykesville, MD 21784
410-795-4749

Phil Helley
Old Kilbourn Antiques
629 Indiana Ave.
Wisconsin Dells, WI 53965

Tin litho, paper on wood, comic character, penny and
Schoenhut
Wes Johnson, Sr.
106 Bauer Ave.
Louisville, KY 40207

Terri Mardis-Ivers
1104 Shirlee
Ponca City, OK 74601

Disney, Buddy-L, cast iron and wind-ups
Doug Moore
57 Hickory Ridge Cir.
Cicero, IN 46034
317-877-1741

Especially transformers and robots
David Kolodny-Nagy
3701 Connecticut Ave. NW #500
Washington, DC 20008
202-364-8753

Phil McEntee
Where the Toys Are
45 W Pike St.
Canonsburg, PA 15317

Slot race cars from 1960s-70s
Gary T. Pollastro
4156 Beach Dr. SW
Seattle, WA 98116

Charlie Reynolds
Reynolds Toys
2836 Monroe St.
Falls Church, VA 22042
703-533-1322

Tammy Rodrick
Rt. 2, Box 163
Sumner, IL 62466

Especially from 1950s-60s
Rick Rowe, Jr.
Childhood, The Sequel
HC 1, Box 788
Saxon, WI 54559

Especially character and space
Norm Vigue
62 Barley St.
Stoughton, MA 02072
617-344-5441

Steiff
Linda Vines
P.O. Box 721
Upper Montclair, NJ 07043; 201-746-5206

Walkers, ramp-walkers, and wind-ups
Randy Welch
1100 Hambrooks Blvd.
Cambridge, MD 21613

Trade Cards
Rudisill's Alt Print Haus
Barbara and John Rudisill
24305 Waterview Dr.
Worton, MD 21678
410-778-9290

Trade Catalogs
Richard M. Bueschel
414 N Prospect Manor Ave.
Mt. Prospect, IL 60065
708-253-0791

Architectural related
Greg Speiss
230 E Washington
Joliet, IL 60433
815-722-5639

Tramp Art
Also folk carvings and primitive arts
Artisons
Rte. 1, Box 20-C
Mentone, AL 35984
205-634-4037

Trolls
Roger Inouye
2622 Valewood Ave.
Carlsbad, CA 92008-7925

Tammy Rodrick
Rt. 2, Box 163
Sumner, IL 62466

TV Guides
TV Guide Specialists
Jeff Kadet
P.O. Box 20
Macomb, IL 61455

Twin Winton
Joe Devine
1411 3rd St.
Council Bluffs, IA 51503
712-232-5233 or 712-328-7305

Typewriter Ribbon Tins
Hobart D. Van Deusen
28 the Green
Watertown, CT 06795
203-945-3456

Typewriters
Jerry Propst
P.O. Box 45
Janesville, WI 53547-0045

Valentines
Katherine Kreider
Kingsbury Productions
4555 N Pershing Ave., Ste. 33-138
Stockton, CA 95207
209-467-8438

Van Briggle
Dated examples
Author of book
Scott H. Nelson
Box 6081
Santa Fe, NM 87502
505-986-1176
Also UND (University of North Dakota)

Vaseline Glass
Terry Fedosky
Rte. 1, Box 118
Symsonia, KY 42082

Vernon Kilns
Maxine Nelson
873 Marigold Ct.
Carlsbad, CA 92009

View-Master and Tru-View
Also Tru-View
Harry Poster
P.O. Box 1883
S Hackensack, NJ 07606
201-410-7525

Roger Nazeley
4921 Castor Ave.
Philadelphia, PA 19124

Walter Sigg
3-D Entertainment
P.O Box 208
Smartswood, NJ 07877

Wade
Author of book
Ian Warner
P.O. Box 93022
Brampton, Ontario
Canada L6Y 4V8

Warwick
Authors of book
Pat and Don Hoffman Sr.
1291 N Elmwood Dr.
Aurora, IL 60506

Walking Sticks and Canes
Bruce Thalberg
23 Mountain View Dr.
Weston, CT 06883

Watch Fobs
Author of book
Margaret Kaduck
P.O. Box 260764
Cleveland, OH 44126

Watches
Character and personality
Author of book
Howard S. Brenner
106 Woodgate Terrace
Rochester, NY 14625

Character, 1930s to mid-1950s
Ron Donnelly
P.O. Box 7047
Panama City Beach, FL 32413

All brands and character
James Lindon
5267 W Cholla St.
Glendale, AZ 85304
602-878-2409

Antique pocket and vintage wristwatches
Maundy International
P.O. Box 13028-SF
Shawnee Mission, KS 66282
800-235-2866

Swatch
Timesavers
Box 400
Algonquin, IL 60102

Swatch
W.B.S. Marketing
P.O. Box 3280
Visalia, CA 93278

Watt Pottery
Susan Morris
P.O. Box 708
Mason City, IA 50401

Western Americana
Author of book
Warren R. Anderson
American West Archives
P.O. Box 100
Cedar City, UT 84720
801-586-9497

Barry Friedman
22725 Garzota Dr.
Valencia, CA 91355

Especially Civil War items
K.C. Owings, Jr.
P.O. Box 19
N Abington, MA 02351

Gordon Totty
Scarce Paper Americana
347 Shady Lake Pkwy.
Baton Rouge, LA 70810
504-766-8625

Westmoreland
Betty Thomas
2600 Sherman Dr.
Kokomo, IN 46902
317-453-1178
Westmoreland Glass Society Inc.

Jim Fisher
513 5th Ave.
Coralville, IA 52241

Windmill Weights
Artisons
Rte. 1, Box 20-C
Mentone, AL 35984
205-634-4037

Wizard of Oz
Lori Landgrebe
2331 E Main St.
Decatur, IL 62521

World's Fairs
D.D. Woollard, Jr.
11614 Old St. Charles Rd.
Bridgeton, MO 63044
314-739-4662

Yard Long Prints
Also Long Ladies
Author of book
William Keagy
P.O. Box 106
Bloomfield, IN 47424
812-384-3471

Authors of Book
Charles and Joan Rhoden
605 N Main
Georgetown, IL 61846
217-662-8046

Yellow Ware
Also Spongeware
John and Barbara Michel
Americana Blue
200 E 78th St., 18E
New York City, NY 10021
212-861-6094

Index

This catalog contains over 200 titles that we recommend on antiques & collectibles. These titles were chosen from several leading publishers in this field. These are the titles that we are currently stocking, and would be happy to fill your order within 24 hours of receipt. So please look over the next few pages and if there are titles that are of interest to you, simply fill out the order form on the back page and send it to:

Nostalgia Publishing • P.O. Box 277 • La Center, KY 42056

General Antiques

Garage Sale & Flea Market Annual
2nd Edition

This deluxe, hardbound book gives descriptions and values of nearly 25,000 collectibles most likely to be discovered on your garage sale and flea market outings. In addition to hundreds of sharp photos, this resourceful guide offers suggestions on how to conduct your own sales, establish yourself as a flea market dealer, and how to buy and sell by mail.

#3818, 8½ x 11, 512 Pgs., HB..............$24.95

Flea Market Trader • 9th Edition
Edited by Bob & Sharon Huxford

This is the only guide on the market which introduces you to collectibles that are just becoming popular, while keeping you attuned to those already well-established collectible fields. It features many categories you can't find in any other price guide. Nearly 10,000 listings are divided into both general and specific categories, alphabetically arranged.

#3817, 5½ x 8½, 432 Pgs., PB..............$ 12.95

Schroeder's Antiques Price Guide
Twelfth Edition

More than 45,000 items in almost 500 categories are listed along with hundreds of sharp original photos that illustrate not only the rare and unusual, but the common collectibles as well – not postage stamp photos, but large close-up shots that show important details clearly. Each subject is represented with histories and background information.

#3737, 8½ x 11, 608 Pgs., PB..............$12.95

Kovel's Antiques & Collectibles Price List
26th Edition • by Ralph & Terry Kovel

Included in this 26th Anniversary edition are up-to-date prices for virtually every category of antiques and collectibles. More than 50,000 current values, hundreds of factory marks and identifying logos, and more than 500 photos are included.

#2361, 5½ x 8½, 864 Pgs., PB..............$13.00

Glassware & Bottles

Avon Bottle Collectibles Encyclopedia
13th Edition • by Bud Hastin

This is THE guide to collectible Avon bottles and products. This 13th edition features the most popular items for Avon bottle collectors. It contains over 600 pages with thousands of photographs and items with information, circa date and current values.

#3744, 6 x 6, 620 Pgs., PB..............$19.95

Bottle Pricing Guide
3rd Edition • by Hugh Cleveland

This revised 3rd edition of Hugh Cleveland's popular bottle guide features over 4,000 bottles listed alphabetically. It contains hundreds of photos including Avons, medicine bottles, Jim Beam bottles, bitters, and a revised value guide.

#1128, 5½ x 8½, 251 Pgs., PB..............$7.95

Cambridge Glass, 1930-1934

We were excited when The Cambridge Collectors of America Inc. brought us four old Cambridge catalogs to be reprinted. These catalogs have over 3,400 etchings of Cambridge Glass and are combined and cased. Updated current values are included.

#1006, 11 x 8½, 254 Pgs., PB..............$14.95

Children's Glass Dishes, China & Furniture
by Doris Lechler

This large hardbound book has over 2,500 children's accessories illustrated. Includes Depression glass, pattern glass, Heisey & Imperial glass, miniature furniture and much more.

#2310, 8½ x 11, 240 Pgs., HB..............$19.95

Cambridge Glass 1949-1953

The Cambridge Collectors of America Inc. have once again compiled an edition of catalog reprints. This edition is a companion volume to the previous Cambridge guide. Thousands of pieces of the popular Cambridge Glass are illustrated and current values are included.

#1007, 8½ x 11, 304 Pgs., PB..............$14.95

Children's Glass Dishes, China & Furniture
2nd Series • by Doris Lechler

This 2nd series has no repeats of items in the first series and includes approximately 2,000 children's items and current values.

#1627, 8½ x 11, 208 Pgs., HB..............$19.95

Collector's Encyclopedia of Akro Agate Glassware
by Gene Florence

This marbleized glass that was produced from 1911 to 1951 has now won the hearts of collectors. The many that have been searching for this book will be glad to know it's back in print and all values have been updated.

#2352, 8½ x 11, 80 Pgs., PB..............$14.95

The Collector's Encyclopedia of American Art Glass
By John Shuman

This book combines beautiful full color photos with an extensive text. Complete descriptions, original catalog and advertising material make this book the most informative available.

#1810, 8½ x 11, 336 Pgs., HB..............$29.95

Collector's Encyclopedia of Children's Dishes
by Margaret & Kenn Whitmyer

Featuring over 500 color photos, this hardbound edition includes recent repros & reissues, catalog reprints and current values for each piece.

#3312, 8½ x 11, 278 Pgs., HB..............$19.95

Collector's Encyclopedia of Fry Glass
by Fry Glass Society

Collectors of Depression-era glassware look for the opalescent reamers and opaque green kitchenware made during the early 30's. This encyclopedia has some of the most complete history and background information ever published on any glass subject. This book is produced with 80% of its photography in full color. Includes current prices.

#1961, 8½ x 11, 224 Pgs., HB..............$24.95

Collector's Encyclopedia of Heisey Glass 1925-1938
by Neila Bredehoft

This encyclopedia has 32 pages of full color. Original sales catalogs #14B, 212, and 109 are reprinted featuring 1000's of pieces of glass plus current values.
#1664, 8½ x 11, 464 Pgs., HB..............$24.95

Covered Animal Dishes
by Everett Grist

Included are over 200 beautiful, full color photos that include nearly 600 different dishes. Some very interesting text is provided and of course current values. Mr. Grist has spent a lifetime dealing in antiques and collectibles including covered animal dishes. Collectors and dealers alike will welcome this book.
#1843, 8½ x 11, 120 Pgs., PB $14.95

Electric Lighting of the 20's & 30's
Edited by James Edward Black

Lamps of Jeanette, Handel, Moe Bridges, Art Deco, wicker, floor, & table. Fine catalog reprints and photos with hundreds of lamps priced. Features black and white photographs with some color.
#1979, 8½ x 11, 124 Pgs., PB $12.95

The Collector's Encyclopedia of Pattern Glass
by Mollie Helen McCain

This author is one of the country's most recognized authorities on pattern glass. This comprehensive volume contains hundreds of illustrations of patterns and a complete pricing system for the glass.
#1380, 5½ x 8½, 541 Pgs., PB..................$12.95

400 Trademarks on Glass
by Arthur G. Peterson

This definitive text will be of lasting interest and value to collectors of glassware for years to come. This scholarly study of trademarks on glass has been summarized in concise and convenient form for excellent identification of glass.
#3471, 5½ x 8½, 54 Pgs., PB..................$9.95

1000 Fruit Jars Priced and Illustrated
by Bill Schroeder

This is the fifth edition of what is probably the best selling jar and bottle book ever published. This little book shows an illustration of each embossing on the front of the jar. Each jar has such information as size, color, closure and value.
#1782, 5½ x 8½, 76 Pgs., PB..................$5.95

Quality Electric Lamps, A Pictorial Price Guide
by Arthur G. Peterson

Hundreds of full color examples of quality electric lamps are featured in full color. This book will help you identify and price the lamps in your collection, or it might help you identify that lamp you have been looking for. Collectors will enjoy this release.
#3423, 8½ x 11, 188 Pgs., HB..................$39.95

Standard Carnival Glass Price Guide
9th Edition • by Bill Edwards

Hundreds of patterns and pieces of carnival glass are listed and priced in this value guide by popular glass author Bill Edwards. Many illustrations are provided for identification. This easy to use price guide to carnival glass is ideal for the advanced collector as well as the novice.
#3740, 8½ x 11, 64 Pgs., PB $9.95

Colors in Cambridge
by National Cambridge Society

The National Cambridge Society has banded together to produce this beautiful book. They photographed more Cambridge Glass than has ever been put into one book. This full color book has many pieces illustrated with complete history of the company. Also included are current values.
#1523, 8½ x 11, 128 Pgs., HB..............$19.95

Czechoslovakian Glass & Collectibles
by Dale & Diane Barta & Helen M. Rose

This title not only includes the most beautiful glass but also includes purses, jewelry, pottery, porcelain, china, lamps and other collectibles made in Czechoslovakia. Full color photos, histories, descriptions, dates, and current values are also included. The authors have traveled and researched this collectible for several years.
#2275, 8½ x 11, 152 Pgs., PB..................$16.95

Electric Lighting of the 20's & 30's, Vol. 2
by James Edward Black

Volume 2 contains no repeats of the first volume and is produced to be a companion to Volume I. Lamps included are Handel, Jeanette, boudoir, floor, hanging, wall, and many more. This book also contains current values. Lamp collectors will want both editions of this popular series.
#2115, 8½ x 11, 110 Pgs., PB..................$12.95

Fostoria
by Ann Kerr

Until now never has there been a more complete manuscript to the popular hand pressed, molded, and blown shapes of Fostoria. This all new book includes color photographs plus line drawings and a host of catalog reprints to aid in identifying facts, histories, dates colors, sizes, and details are included. The current values are listed for each piece and all colors.
#3725, 8½ x 11, 232 Pgs., PB..................$24.95

Imperial Glass Identification & Value Guide

The popular glassware of the Imperial Glass Company has become a very collectible item in recent years. This guide combines several of the company's early catalogs and gives the glassware current market values. Glass dealers and collectors will love this large edition.
#1008, 8½ x 11, 212 Pgs., PB..................$14.95

The Opalescent Glass Price Guide
by Bill Edwards

This handy guide contains scores of color photos and is the 1st book on the subject to list prices for virtually every pattern, color and shape made from 1890-1940.
#2347, 8½ x 11, 64 Pgs., PB..................$9.95

The Standard Old Bottle Price Guide
by Carlo & Dorothy Sellari

The authors, well-known authorites on collectible bottles, produced this listing of thousands of old bottles with current values. They have included hundreds of excellent photographs for ease of identification.
#1922, 8½ x 11, 176 Pgs., PB $14.95

The Standard Encyclopedia of Carnival Glass
4th Edition • by Bill Edwards

This is the most comprehensive carnival glass book available today. This large format, deluxe hardbound edition features hundreds of full color photographs and lots of information on patterns, available colors, manufacturers, and much more. The value guide is now bound within this edition at no additional charge.
#3739, 8½ x 11, 288 Pgs., HB..................$24.95

Bedroom & Bathroom Glassware of the Depression Years

by Kenn & Margaret Whitmyer

Collectors have now begun buying this glassware made during the mid 20's to mid 30's. Over 300 beautiful, full-color photographs containing 1,000's of items are included. Current values are given for each piece.
#2016, 8½ x 11, 256 Pgs., HB $19.95

Collector's Encyclopedia of Depression Glass

11th Edition • by Gene Florence

Depression glass collectors have recently reported that glass collecting has never been better, and prices are still rising. This 11th Edition has been completely revised and many new finds have been added. A special section is included to expose re-issues and fakes.
#3724, 8½ x 11, 224 Pgs., HB $19.95

Kitchen Glassware of the Depression Years

4th Edition • by Gene Florence

A revised 4th edition features all the new finds that have turned up since the 3rd edition. Gene Florence also added many new group shots as well as updated the values on all the popular pieces in each color. It features over 3,000 pieces of glass listing size, color, pattern description & current values.
#2024, 8½ x 11, 224 Pgs., HB $19.95

Pocket Guide To Depression Glass

8th Edition • by Gene Florence

This popular guide has been completely revised with all values being updated. Full color presentation and the same easy-to-use format with bold photographs make pattern identification simple. Also includes a section on re-issues and fakes.
#3322, 5½ x 8½, 160 Pgs., PB $9.95

Collectible Glassware of the 40's, 50's, 60's...

2nd Edition • by Gene Florence

Produced in the same easy-to-use format as Florence's *Collector's Encyclopedia of Depression Glass*, with large full-color photos of 1000's of pieces with current values, descriptions and company histories.
#3719, 8½ x 11, 192 Pgs., HB $19.95

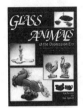

Glass Animals of the Depression Era

by Lee Garmon & Dick Spencer

Probably the most popular items collected out of the Depression glass family are the many different glass animals. This book represents an in-depth look at the animal and figurine production during the Depression Era, and also features a section on reissues that have been produced.
#3318, 8½ x 11, 240 Pgs., HB $19.95

Very Rare Glassware of the Depression Years

by Gene Florence

Are you still wondering if that piece of Depression glass that you found is rare and possibly valuable? This set of 3 *Very Rare Glassware of the Depression Years* may be just what you need to identify and evaluate that glassware. These editions are just jam-packed with new finds presented in full color. Each is a companion volume to the other with all new photos and prices presented in each series.

1st Series, **#1848, 8½ x 11, 128 Pgs., HB** **$24.95**

2nd Series, **#2140, 8½ x 11, 144 Pgs., HB** **$24.95**

3rd Series, **#3326, 8½ x 11, 144 Pgs., HB** **$24.95**

Pottery, Porcelain & China

Blue & White Stoneware

by Kathryn McNerney

Blue & white pitchers, crocks and bowls have increased in popularity and price making this guide a must for collectors. This full-color guide has 100's of photos, descriptions and values.
#1312, 5½ x 8½, 160 Pgs., PB $9.95

Blue Willow Revised 2nd edition

by Mary Frank Gaston

Completely rephotographed in full color, this revised edition has been expanded to include over 400 photos, complete descriptions, updated values and a special marks section.
#1959, 8½ x 11, 192 Pgs., PB $14.95

Collecting Yellowware

by Lisa McAllister & John Michel

Filled with over 300 color photos, the comprehensive chapters include molds, pitchers, miniatures, figural and more. Current values and a special marks section make this a great reference guide.
#3311, 8½ x 11, 128 Pgs., PB $16.95

Collector's Encyclopedia to Blue Ridge Dinnerware

by Betty and Bill Newbound

This fact-filled resource combines interesting historical information with over 200 beautiful color photos and many in black and white. In addition to the 690 patterns and shapes and over 70 marks featured, there are special sections on animals and figures, ashtrays and commemorative items, and even glassware to match the pottery.
#3815, 8½ x 11, 176 Pgs., HB $19.95

Blue Ridge Dinnerware, Revised 3rd Edition

by Betty & Bill Newbound

Expanded to a larger format, this 3rd editon has 100's of color photos of new finds and known pieces. Includes updated values, a complete marks section and many old company catalogs.
#1958, 8½ x 11, 160 Pgs., PB $14.95

Collectible Vernon Kilns

by Maxine Feek Nelson

A new generation of collectors has emerged eagerly seeking the colorful wares of this California pottery. A thorough history, a marks section, and hundreds of color photographs make this identification and value guide indispensable to collectors and dealers alike.
#3816, 8½ x 11, 256 Pgs., PB $24.95

Collector's Encyclopedia of American Dinnerware

by Jo Cunningham

This comprehensive dinnerware book featuring 100's of pieces in color and black & white. Includes backstamps, advertising, loads of company info and current values.
#1373, 8½ x 11, 336 Pgs., HB $24.95

Collector's Encyclopedia of California Pottery

by Jack Chipman

California Pottery has far too long been a missing chapter in the annals of collectible American ceramics. In fact, it has been one of the least documented of all collectibles. But not anymore. Over 26 different companies are represented, each containing company histories, background information and a marks section.
#2272, 8½ x 11, 168 Pgs., HB $24.95

Collector's Encyclopedia of Cookie Jars
by Fred & Joyce Roerig
The authors have brought to you what very well could be the last word on this subject. 1,000's of full-color examples are beautifully photographed in this 312 page encyclopedia. Each photograph includes complete descriptions, manufacturers, sizes, histories and, of course, current values.
#2133, 8½ x 11, 312 Pgs., HB..................$24.95

Collector's Encyclopedia of Cookie Jars
Book II • by Fred & Joyce Roerig
Beautiful, color photographs of over 1,000 collectible cookie jars with current values. The jars range from the novelty to the exquisite artist made limited editions. Informative text, current values, beautiful photos, plu the fact that there are no repeats of *Book I*, will make this new edition a great buy for pottery and cookie jar collectors.
#3723, 8½ x 11, 400 Pgs., HB..................$24.95

Collector's Encyclopedia of Figural & Novelty Salt & Pepper Shakers
by Melva Davern

Thousands of figural and novelty shakers are photographed in color – animals, clowns, birds, children, and more. Each encyclopedia features large photos and an easy-to-use format to help aid in identification. Huggers, nesters, longfellows, turn-abouts, go-withs and one piece shakers are explored as well as the traditional two piece set. These two volumes will give you an extensive amount of reference material on ceramic, plastic, metal, chalkware, china, and glass salt & pepper shakers, both foreign and domestic. All with a current value guide.

Volume I, #1634, 8½ x 11, 160 Pgs., PB.................$19.95
Volume II, #2020, 8½ x 11, 216 Pgs., PB...............$19.95

Collector's Encyclopedia of Limoges Porcelain
2nd Edition • by Mary Frank Gaston
This revised edition features 100's of beautiful pieces in full color. All are described and valued in this beautiful hardbound volume.
#2210, 8½ x 11, 224 Pgs., HB..................$24.95

Collector's Encyclopedia of Majolica
by Mariann Katz-Marks
Over the past 10 years Mariann Katz-Marks has authored two books on Majolica Pottery. Now in this third book we have included over 500 beautiful, full color photos & of course, all the values have been updated to reflect the latest trends of this collectible.
#2334, 8½ x 11, 192 Pgs., HB..................$19.95

Collector's Encyclopedia of McCoy Pottery
by Sharon & Bob Huxford
The most popular pottery authors have written this informative resource. This guide has 121 color photos featuring 100's of pieces of McCoy pottery with current values.
#1358, 8½ x 11, 248 Pgs., HB..................$19.95

Collector's Encyclopedia of Noritake
by Joan Van Patten
This Japanese china is becoming more and more popular with collectors. Prefaced by a short history of the company, this full color guide has over 450 photos and a large marks section. A current value guide is bound within the book.
#1447, 8½ x 11, 200 Pgs., HB $19.95

Collector's Encyclopedia of Fiesta
7th Edition • by Sharon & Bob Huxford
Revised and updated with several new finds being added, this expanded edition is in full color with over 1,000 pieces of Fiesta illustrated.
#2209, 8½ x 11, 190 Pgs., HB..................$19.95

Collector's Encyclopedia of Flow Blue China
by Mary Frank Gaston
This hardbound edition features 436 illustrations in full color and 168 different marks. An excellent background section is also included with this current value and identification guide.
#1439, 8½ x 11, 160 Pgs., HB $19.95

Collector's Encyclopedia of Homer Laughlin China
by Joanne Jasper
Over 175 full color photos of this beautiful china from 1900-1950 with histories, sizes, dates, and values. This is the first book devoted to the dinnerware of Homer Laughlin.
#3431, 8½ x 11, 208 Pgs., HB $24.95

Collector's Encyclopedia of Hull Pottery
by Brenda Roberts
Over 2,500 items are illustrated and described in this hardbound volume. Descriptions of 116 Hull lines with an in-depth history of the pottery as well as a current value guide make this an excellent resource.
#1276, 8½ x 11, 208 Pgs., HB................$19.95

Collector's Encyclopedia of Nippon I, II, III
by Joan Van Patten

Joan Van Patten has compiled the most complete series ever published on Nippon porcelain. This porcelain is becoming more valuable each day and collectors will want to keep up with this ever changing market. With this series they will be able to do just that, because each volume contains useful information, photographs and current values. Each volume features over 700 illustrations that are not included in the other volumes. The complete set contains over 2,000 items illustrated in full color. The set has over 3,000 listings, most of them pictured, and all with current values.

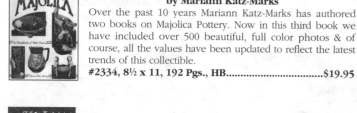

Volume I, #3837, 8½ x 11, 238 Pgs., HB...............$24.95
Volume II, #2089, 8½ x 11, 256 Pgs., PB..............$24.95
Volume III, #1665, 8½ x 11, 336 Pgs., PB.............$24.95

Collector's Encyclopedia of Noritake
2nd Series • by Joan Van Patten
A companion volume to the first, this beautiful book includes current values, tips on photographing your collection, buying and selling through the mail, over 1,000 full color photos and complete histories & descriptions. 1993 values.
#3432, 8½ x 11, 264 Pgs., HB $24.95

Collector's Encyclopedia of Occupied Japan
by Gene Florence

Gene Florence has been collecting & researching Occupied Japan collectibles about 20 years and is regarded as the foremost authority in this field. Each volume has 1000's of items with descriptions and current values. Complete this five volume set and have all the updated information available on this subject.

Volume I, #1037, 8½ x 11, 107 Pgs., PB.............$14.95
Volume II, #1038, 8½ x 11, 112 Pgs., PB.............$14.95
Volume III, #2088, 8½ x 11, 144 Pgs., PB.............$14.95
Volume IV, #2019, 8½ x 11, 128 Pgs., PB.............$14.95
Volume V, #2335, 8½ x 11, 128 Pgs., PB $14.95

Collector's Encyclopedia of Roseville Pottery I & II
by Sharon & Bob Huxford

This complete set has over 4,000 items illustrated in beautiful full color and a completely illustrated marks section. With this set, one will be able to learn about the history of Roseville as well as having a beautiful full-color identification and value guide.

Volume I, #1034, 8½ x 11, 192 Pgs., HB...$19.95
Volume II, #1035, 8½ x 11, 208 Pgs., HB .$19.95
Price Guide, #3357, 8½ x 11, 32 Pgs., PB ...$9.95

Collector's Encyclopedia of Van Briggle Art Pottery
by Richard Sasicki & Josie Fania

A comprehensive guide with over 400 color photos of more than 800 pieces, it includes info on the company history, production, identification and dating, and catalogs, all with current values.
#3314, 8½ x 11, 144 Pgs., HB.....................$24.95

Collector's Guide to Country Stoneware & Pottery
by Don & Carol Raycraft

Featuring 182 beautiful, full-color photos. All types of jugs and crocks are identified, described and evaluated.
#3452, 5½ x 8½, 160 Pgs., PB.....................$11.95

Collector's Guide to Shawnee Pottery
by Duane & Janice Vanderbilt

A refreshing book for the Shawnee collector. There are over 400 full color photos including 120 cookie jars. Many items in this book have never been pictured or listed in any other guides. Also includes catalog pages and current values. The cookie jar section alone will make this a highly sought after edition.
#2339, 8½ x 11, 160 Pgs., HB.....................$19.95

Collector's Encyclopedia of Niloak Pottery
by David Edwin Gifford

This work corrects much misinformation about Niloak pottery and features over 750 pieces, many in full color. Also includes a complete marks section with dates. This is far more than just a value guide.
#3313, 8½ x 11, 255 Pgs., HB $19.95

Collector's Encyclopedia of RS Prussia
by Mary Frank Gaston

This volume contains 575 full-color photos of this porcelain. Complete descriptions and a large marks section are also included to help the collector in identification.
#1311, 8½ x 11, 216 Pgs., HB $24.95

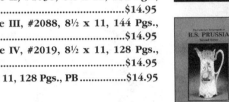

Collector's Encyclopedia of RS Prussia
2nd Series • by Mary Frank Gaston

This 2nd series contains no repeats of the 1st book. Beautiful porcelain is once again featured in full color with well over 700 pictures.
#1715, 8½ x 11, 230 Pgs., HB $24.95

Collector's Encyclopedia of RS Prussia
3rd Series • by Mary Frank Gaston

This long-awaited 3rd Series is complete and features over 600 beautiful color photos. A complete marks section is included in chronological order for ease in identification. The special features such as the mold identification chart, artists signatures section, and indexes will help collectors quickly identify, date, and evaluate their pieces. There are no repeats in any of the three volumes.
#3726, 8½ x 11, 224 Pgs., HB $24.95

Collector's Encyclopedia of Russel Wright Designs
by Ann Kerr

Russel Wright designs, including dinnerware, furniture, housewares and accessories, are extremely collectible. This book includes 100's of photos in full color and black and white with a complete marks section and current value guide.
#2083, 8½ x 11, 192 Pgs., HB $19.95

Collector's Guide to Weller Pottery
by Sharon & Bob Huxford

This reference work features 175 full-color photos, loads of information and current values. It's the most informative identification guide available on the subject.
#2111, 8½ x 11, 392 Pgs., HB $29.95

Collector's Guide to Country Stoneware & Pottery
2nd Series • by Don & Carol Raycraft

This makes a great companion to the first series. 100's of pieces in full color with current values, descriptions, dates, and sizes.
#2077, 8½ x 11, 120 Pgs., PB $14.95

Collector's Guide to Harker Pottery
by Neva W. Colbert

Complete histories, tips about collecting, displaying and caring for your collection are all included. With over 100 full color photographs and a current value for each piece, this is the most complete guide available on this popular pottery.
#3433, 8½ x 11, 128 Pgs., PB $17.95

Collector's Guide to Hull Pottery
by Barbara Burke
Covers the 13 dinnerware lines produced by Hull from the early 1960's to 1985. More than 650 listings with color photos, actual catalog reprints and a current value guide make this an invaluable reference.
#3434, 8½ x 11, 168 Pgs., PB $16.95

An Illustrated Guide to Cookie Jars
by Ermagene Westfall
Cookie jars were made by many companies in many shapes, styles, and sizes. This full-color identification guide has 100's of jars with important info such as maker, marks, and current values.
#1425, 5½ x 8½, 160 Pgs., PB $9.95

Head Vases, Identification & Value Guide
by Kathleen Cole
This book has over 200 photographs in full-color. Each vase is identified by company, number, date and size. Also included is the current value for all vases listed. Collectors of pottery and porcelain will welcome this release.
#1917, 8½ x 11, 144 Pgs., PB $14.95

Red Wing Collectibles
by Dan & Gail DePasquale & Larry Peterson
This companion volume features 100's of items not featured in *Red Wing Stoneware*. Beautiful, full color examples fill this identification and value guide.
#1670, 5½ x 8½, 160 Pgs., PB $9.95

Red Wing Stoneware
by Dan & Gail DePasquale & Larry Peterson
Kitchen stoneware, crocks, jugs, churns and other items are presented in full-color. Includes special section on marks and 100's of photos help to identify pieces.
#1440, 5½ x 8½, 168 Pgs., PB $9.95

Watt Pottery – An Identification & Value Guide
by Sue & Dave Morris
This popular book contains a history of the pottery and includes over 350 full color photos with dimensions, marks, and current values. Also features unusual and one-of-a-kind pieces.
#3327, 8½ x 11, 160 Pgs., HB $19.95

Shawnee Pottery – An Identification & Value Guide
by Jim & Bev Mangus
Jim & Bev Mangus have been long time collectors and authorities on this subject. They have included over 1,200 of the most beautiful full color photographs that have ever been published. The manuscript is arranged in a simple and easy-to-use format, and collectors will absolutely love it. Included in these photographs are lamps, miniatures, bathroom accessories, planters, vases, wall pockets, and much more. Many have never been shown elsewhere in print.
#3738, 8½ x 11, 272 Pgs., HB $24.95

DeBolt's Dictionary of American Pottery Marks
by Gerald DeBolt
Over 2,000 marks from whiteware, porcelain, and ironstone from the 1860's to the 1960's. An excellent reference to identify one piece or an entire collection. No values.
#3435, 8½ x 11, 288 Pgs., PB $17.95

An Illustrated Value Guide to Cookie Jars
Book II • by Ermagene Westfall
With the ever increasing popularity of cookie jars, Mrs. Westfall has authored an all-new book as a companion volume to her first. Book II contains so many photos and listings it was enlarged to a 8½ x 11 format. It contains over 650 full color photos of 1,000's of jars, each with complete descriptions and current values.
#3440, 8½ x 11, 240 Pgs., PB $19.95

Luckey's Hummel Figurines & Plates
10th Edition • by Carl Luckey
This is the only guide which reflects the drastic price changes that occur annually. Many more rare pieces are included as well as illustrations and information on soon-to-be released pieces. Foremost authority Carl Luckey has made this guide the standard for the collector.
#3854, 8½ x 11, 443 Pgs., PB $22.95

Lehner's Encyclopedia of U.S. Marks on Pottery, Porcelain & Clay
by Lois Lehner
This book represents about 15 years of intensive work on the part of the author. It contains over 1,900 companies with over 8,000 marks, logos, symbols, etc. divided about equally among the old folk potters, studio potters, dinnerware manufacturers, distributors and decoration companies.
#2379, 8½ x 11, 636 Pgs., HB $24.95

Salt & Pepper Shakers
Volumes I, II, III, & IV
by Helene Guarnaccia
Salt & Pepper shakers were made in every size and shape imaginable. These identification guides contain full color photos, complete descriptions, interesting facts, dates, plus current values. Virtually every type of shaker is included.

Volume I, #1632, 5½ x 8½, 160 Pgs., PB $9.95
Volume II, #1888, 8½ x 11, 192 Pgs., PB $14.95
Volume III, #2220, 8½ x 11, 152 Pgs., PB $14.95
Volume IV, #3443, 8½ x 11, 240 Pgs., PB $18.95

Dolls & Toys

Advertising Dolls
by Joleen Robison & Kay F. Sellers
Advertising dolls have gained popularity with doll lovers everywhere. This guide illustrates and gives current values for 100's of advertising dolls including Aunt Jemima, Campbell Kids, the Uneeda Biscuit Boy, Kellogg's dolls, plus much more! Over 300 pages packed with interesting information and values.
#2382, 5½ x 8½, 328 Pgs., PB $9.95

Antique & Collectible Marbles
by Everett Grist
This 3rd revised edition has been totally updated. There are 100's of full color examples with interesting comments and current values to virtually every type of marble ever produced. A listing of collectors, clubs, dealers, glass-grinders and marble restorers, plus a section on valuing marbles make this a must for the marble collecting enthusiasts!
#2333, 5½ x 8½, 96 Pgs., PB $9.95

Barbie Fashion, Volume I, 1959-1967
by Sara Sink Eames
This style book shows the clothes and accessories of these popular dolls. Included are complete histories of the wardrobes of Barbie doll, her friends and her family from 1959 to 1967. This deluxe, large format book features hundreds of full color illustrations, complete descriptions and current values.
#2079, 8½ x 11, 256 Pgs., PB $24.95

Chatty Cathy Dolls
by Kathy & Don Lewis
This informative guide will delight doll collectors everywhere. It gives the collector/dealer as mush detailed information on these wonderful dolls as possible. Presented in full color are hundreds of dolls, clothing outfits, furniture, patterns and accessories that are still in existence. Interesting, well written history as well as essential details about the entire Chatty Cathy family combined with current values for every doll make this book a great collector's reference.
#3810, 5½ x 8½, 128 Pgs., PB $15.95

Collectible Male Action Figures
by Paris & Susan Manos
Male action figures and dolls have become more collectible and the need for a good book on the subject increased until two of our popular doll authors filled that need with this informative book. Nearly 250 full color photographs of 100's of dolls with complete listings and values are included.
#2021, 8½ x 11, 112 Pgs., PB..................................$14.95

Collector's Encyclopedia of Barbie Dolls and Collectibles
by Sibyl DeWein & Joan Ashabraner
Because of popular demand, we have reprinted this detailed and informative publication. With 100's of photos of Barbie doll and her family and friends, this comprehensive book contains information gained from years of intensive research.
#1529, 8½ x 11, 312 Pgs., HB $19.95

Encyclopedia of Toys & Banks
Edited by L-W Publishing
A very nice book on old toys and banks. Everything from Cast Iron to Tin to Wind Ups to Autos and more. Very large selection of cast iron and still banks.
#2046, 8 x 11, 208 Pgs., PB....................................$14.95

Collecting Toy Trains #3
Identification and Value Guide
by Richard O' Brien
This new 3rd edition has added hundreds of new photos and listings. Lionel, Marx, American Flyer, Ives, Buddy L, plus others. This guide includes engines, cars and accessories with descriptions, prices and photos.
#2293, 8½ x 11, 224 Pgs., HB $22.95

The Collector's Guide to Miniature Teddy Bears
by Cynthia Powell
This fun and fascinating volume is THE comprehensive reference on tiny Teds. Informative and well-researched, the text uncovers the most complete information on small Schucos, as well as Steiff miniatures, top artist Teds, and other rare little bears. Nearly 400 colorful, quality photos with current values and patent drawings make this the ultimate Teddy treasure-hunter's picture book.
#3728, 8½ x 11, 160 Pgs., PB $17.95

Collector's Guide to Tootsietoys
by David Richter
These toys have become hot items at the shows across the country. This book has over 300 pictures that are full size to the toy, wheel identification and separate chapters on each subject such as airplanes, trains, ships, cars, etc.
#2151, 8½ x 11, 152 Pgs., PB $16.95

Black Dolls 1820-1991
An Identification & Value Guide
by Myla Perkins
Myla Perkins' book contains over 1,400 dolls photographed, identified, documented and described. This book includes papier-maché dolls from the 1800's, china dolls from 1" to 20", bisque dolls, including Jumeaus, composition dolls, topsy-turvy dolls, cloth dolls, plastic and vinyl dolls.
#3310, 8½ x 11, 344 Pgs., PB $17.95

Character Toys & Collectibles
by David Longest
This guide has over 400 full-color photos of toys and collectibles. Included in this deluxe edition are: Disney characters, radio characters, space and super heroes, western heroes, Popeye, Orphan Annie and other comic characters, puppets, windups, tin, plastic and rubber toys.
#1514, 8½ x 11, 184 Pgs., HB $19.95

Character Toys & Collectibles
2nd Series • by David Longest
This series has over 600 full-color photos with no repeats of the first edition. It features a character toy hall of fame with such notables as: Felix, Barney Google, Mutt and Jeff, Uncle Wiggley, Betty Boop, Li'l Abner, and more. This series employs the same easy-to-use format as the first book and has current values plus updates of all the values in the first book.
#1750, 8½ x 11, 256 Pgs., HB $19.95

Collector's Encyclopedia of Madame Alexander Dolls 1965-1990
by Patricia Smith
Mrs. Smith has been an avid doll collector for many years and has authored over 30 different doll reference value guides. This particular encyclopedia has been in the works for a number of years. Loaded with a wealth of information, it could be the last word on the subject.
#2211, 8½ x 11, 264 Pgs., HB $24.95

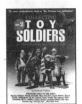

Collecting Toy Soldiers #2
An Identification & Value Guide
by Richard O' Brien
Many newly-discovered early American makers have been added, with their soldiers shown in depth. In the American dimestore area, many new finds are shown, as well as such "new" companies as Wilton, H.B. Toys and Paul Paragine.
#3386, 8½ x 11, 627 Pgs., PB..................................$29.95

Collecting Toys #6
A Collector's Identification & Value Guide
by Richard O' Brien
This is the most comprehensive book on toys ever published. A complete revision and update of the fantastic 5th edition. Thousands of new listings and photos have been added to the existing information. 520 pages loaded with illustrations, many in full color.
#3446, 8½ x 11, 586 Pgs., PB..................................$22.95

The Collector's Encyclopedia of Disneyana
by David Longest & Michael Stern
This is the definitive guide to collecting the golden age of Disneyana, containing more than 860 full color photos of common, rare unusual and highly collectible items. Toys included represent items from the 1930's through the early 1960's with a heavy concentration on Micky Mouse items.
#2338, 8½ x 11, 224 Pgs., HB $24.95

A Historical, Rarity, Value Guide
Fisher-Price® 1931-1963
by John Murray & Bruce Fox
Two of the country's foremost collectors of antique Fisher-Price toys trace the history of Fisher-Price and its evolving toy lines from 1931 to date, concentrating on the 30's, 40's 50's and early 60's. Their book contains nearly 75 black and white and 150 color photographs.
#2358, 8½ x 11, 224 Pgs., PB...............................$24.95

Grist's Machine Made & Contemporary Marbles
by Everett Grist

Machine made and contemporary marbles have really become a hot item at flea markets and antique shows in recent months. This book has over 100 full color photographs containing hundreds of marbles. Also included is a very interesting text with complete descriptions and values.
#2278, 5½ x 8½, 96 Pgs., PB $9.95

Madame Alexander Collector Dolls
by Patricia Smith

Madame Alexander Dolls are the most popular limited edition dolls manufactured today. A complete reference and value guide, this large, 8½ x 11 hardbound title now includes current values bound in the book. Included are over 600 photos and a wealth of information. After 16 years, it is still one of our bestselling doll books.
#1067, 8½ x 11, 328 Pgs., HB $19.95

Matchbox Toys 1948 to 1993
by Dana Johnson

This book provides current values and information on the popular series of diecast vehicles produced by Lesney Products and Matchbox® International Limited, and its beautiful full color photographs make it a picture book as well. Over 400 detailed photos are included with complete descriptions and current values. Virtually every Matchbox® toy made from 1948 to present is included.
#3732, 8½ x 11, 160 Pgs., PB $18.95

Modern Collector's Dolls
I, II, III, IV, V & VI
by Patricia Smith

This series is considered to be the finest and most complete set of identification and value guides ever produced for modern dolls. Each book features 1,200 different photographs and up to 2,000 current values, making the five book series a must for the advanced doll collector and dealer. Dolls from 1935 through 1983 are included in this series with a total of 5,700+ photographs and 8,000+ values. There are no duplicates in any of the five volumes. This deluxe 8½ x 11, hardbound set has over 1,600 pages of modern dolls. Virtually every doll company is represented with photos and current values. Foreign dolls are covered extensively in addition to sections on trolls and puppets.

Volume I, #2185, 8½ x 11, PB $17.95
Volume II, #2186, 8½ x 11, PB $17.95
Volume III, #2187, 8½ x 11, PB $17.95
Volume IV, #2188, 8½ x 11, PB.................$17.95
Volume V, #2189, 8½ x 11, PB $17.95
Volume VI, #3733, 8½ x 11, HB $24.95

Stern's Guide to Disney Collectibles
by Michael Stern

Mickey Mouse and his friends are the most sought after Disney collectibles because everyone of every age identifies with them. Their popularity continues to grow among collectors. Our 8½ x 11, full-color edition is packed full of Disney memorabilia. This book will assist you in dating & pricing your various pieces.
#1886, 8½ x 11, 128 Pgs., PB $14.95

Stern's Guide to Disney Collectibles
2nd Series • by Michael Stern

This second series contains no repeats of the first, hundreds of examples of Disney collectibles in full color and current values. Over 240 beautiful color photographs including virtually every type of Disney collectible from the Golden Age to modern merchandise.
#2139, 8½ x 11, 152 Pgs., PB..................................$14.95

The Collector's Guide to Ideal Dolls
by Judith Izen

Readers will recognize dolls they played with or wished for in their youth as they view the over 500 full color photos of the most enduring and beloved dolls of this century. Included are names, dates, descriptions, marks, photos, catalog numbers, original retail prices, and the current market prices. Virtually everything a collector could ask for is included in this guide.
#3727, 8½ x 11, 256 Pgs., PB...............................$18.95

Madame Alexander Collector's Dolls
Price Guide #19
by Patricia Smith

This full color guide is anxiously awaited each year by collectors of America's most popular dolls. The values are revised annually to reflect today's market and can be used alone or as a companion volume to Smith's other Madame Alexander books.
#3822, 8½ x 11, 88 Pgs., PB.....................................$9.95

Modern Collector's Dolls Update
1993 Edition • by Patricia Smith

Patricia Smith's Modern Collector's Dolls Series I-IV contains over 8,000 values & this book completely revises each of those values. This update can be used with any of the Modern Collector's Dolls books or it can be used independently, either way it's a bargain at $9.95. Each doll listing contains name, size, date and current values so one can quickly evaluate their dolls.
#3472, 8½ x 11, 96 Pgs., PB.....................................$9.95

Modern Toys 1930-1980
by Linda Baker

This full color guide has thousands of toys with full descriptions and wonderful photographs. Crammed full of toys made from 1930 to 1980 with current values. This deluxe edition contains all American toy manufacturers and their products from the Depression thru Star Wars era.
#1540, 8½ x 11, 267 Pgs., HB $19.95

Patricia Smith's Album of All Bisque Dolls
by Patricia Smith

This all new guide is produced in full color including over 200 dolls. Each color photograph includes size, description, histories, any important information and current values. Most doll collectors will enjoy finding the little dolls in this album. Hopefully going through this book will help each collector better appreciate their collection.
#2344, 8½ x 11, 104 Pgs., PB $14.95

Patricia Smith's Doll Values
10th Series • by Patricia Smith

This new edition includes over 450 full color photos. Practically every doll manufacturer is represented. Over 6,000 dolls are featured and described with current values, histories, tips and a wealth of facts to help in identification.
#3824, 5½ x 8½, 320 Pgs., PB $12.95

Riding Toys

Many color photos of wagons, tricycles, scooters, sleds, irish mails, ride-ons, mobos, and rocking horses. Covering pre 1900's and later. Also included in this book are many catalog pages for reference and pricing. The price guide has current values.
#3448, 8½ x 11, 194 Pgs., PB..................................$29.95

Story of Barbie
by Kitturah B. Westenhouser

The Story of Barbie is the most comprehensive history ever written of the world's most famous doll. This interesting text covers the insights and innovations that have made Barbie what she is today. Over 300 color photos, many never before published, illustrate this entertaining book which reveals the labor and genius required to make Barbie a continued success.
#3826, 8½ x 11, 184 Pgs., HB $19.95

Teddy Bears and Steiff Animals
by Margaret Fox Mandel
With teddy bears becoming more collectible each day, Mrs. Mandel filled the need for a good book on the entire field of Teddy Bears and Steiff Animals. Over 500 full color photographs of bears and animals from 1903-1980 are included in this complete identification and value guide.
#1513, 5½ x 8½, 288 Pgs., PB $9.95

Teddy Bears and Steiff Animals
2nd Series • by Margaret Fox Mandel
Hundreds of bears and animals are featured in full color in this 8½ x 11, hardbound book. Lots of information and a current value guide are included. There is no repeat material from the first book.
#1817, 8½ x 11, 200 Pgs., PB $19.95

Teddy Bears and Steiff Animals
3rd Series • by Margaret Fox Mandel
Each book in this series contains over 300 photos not repeated in any of the other books. This third series includes 100's of examples of teddy bears, Steiff animals & Annalee figures all photographed in color. Includes complete histories, interesting facts, dates, sizes & current values.
#2084, 8½ x 11, 224 Pgs., PB $19.95

Antique & Collectible Thimbles
by Averil Mathis
Now with this complete book one will be able to identify and evaluate their collectible thimbles. Over 700 items are featured in full color in this beautiful value guide.
#1712, 8½ x 11, 184 Pgs., HB $19.95

Art Nouveau & Art Deco Jewelry
by Lillian Baker
This guide to Art Nouveau & Art Deco jewelry is by America's best known jewelry author. Hundreds of pieces are described and illustrated in color with values for each item. It is full of information about the Art Nouveau and Art Deco movement.
#1278, 5½ x 8½, 176 Pgs., PB $9.95

Identification & Value Guide
Collecting Comic Character Clocks & Watches
by Howard Brenner
This is the first and only price guide to deal with those timepieces that we all treasured as youngsters. They are all illustrated with full descriptions, makers, dates and values. Many are in full color. Not only is it a great reference tool for the collector but it's also a trip down memory lane.
#1797, 8½ x 11, 136 Pgs., PB $14.95

Collector's Encyclopedia of Compacts
by Laura M. Mueller
Over 700 items are featured in the most beautiful color photos ever published. Original advertisements add a special touch to this historical overview. Every item is described in detail including size, date of manufacture, marks, and a current collector value. The enjoyable text written by a longtime collector and dealer provides a glossary of terms, a bibliography, and a comprehensive index.
#3722, 8½ x 11, 320 Pgs., HB $24.95

Hatpins & Hatpin Holders
by Lillian Baker
This full color identification and value guide is filled with useful information. The beautiful photographs are accompanied by descriptions, sizes and circa dates. An easy-to-use value guide is included. This book is an excellent addition to any jewelry or antique collectors library.
#1424, 5½ x 8½, 160 Pgs, PB $9.95

Toys, Antique & Collectible
by David Longest
With over 10,000 listings and values this book is a must for both the new as well as the advanced collector. From the old cast iron toys of yesteryear to the newer modern toys of the 50's & 60's, this book has it all.
#2028, 8½ x 11, 240 Pgs., PB $14.95

The Wonder of Barbie
by Paris and Susan Manos
This book, by the authors of World of Barbie, studies this collecting phenomenon and provides information, values, and photographs of dolls and accessories from 1976 to 1986.
#1808, 5½ x 8½, 134 Pgs., PB $9.95

The World of Barbie Dolls
by Paris and Susan Manos
This edition has 100's of dolls illustrated in full color. Containing Barbie, Ken, Skipper and other friends and family as well as cases, houses, furniture and accessories. This pocket size guide is perfect for the collector on the go! Over 140 pages of Barbies, related items and current values fill this book.
#1430, 5½ x 8½, 144 Pgs., PB $9.95

Antique Purses
Revised 2nd Edition • by Richard Holiner
Richard Holiner has included all the color photos that were in the first edition & added at least that many more to complete this revised second edition. This value guide features hundreds of purses in full color.
#1748, 8½ x 11, 208 Pgs, PB $19.95

Collecting Rhinestone & Colored Jewelry
An Identification and Value Guide
3rd Edition • by Maryanne Dolan
Rhinestones are becoming more and more valuable! Several hundred pieces have been added to the existing photos with all new prices. This also includes colored stones. The "Designers' Marks" section has now been greatly expanded.
#3806, 8½ x 11, 330 Pgs, PB...................................$22.95

Complete Price Guide To Watches
14th Edition • by Shugart & Gilbert
This 14th edition has over 1,000 packed pages with over 7,400 illustrations, 35,000+ current values and 8 pages of full color. The wristwatch section alone has 6,320 illustrations with prices for each. It's professional standard for watch collectors and dealers.
#3831, 5½ x 8½, 1,064 Pgs, PB $19.95

Fifty Years of Fashion Jewelry
by Lillian Baker
More than 75 individual designer-name examples with many full color photos are included in this exciting value guide. Over 400 individual pieces of jewelry are represented from over 25 different collections.
#1716, 8½ x 11, 192 Pgs., HB $19.95

Answers To Questions About Old Jewelry
3rd Edition • by Jeanenne Bell
This popular book by Jeanenne Bell has been expanded in this new edition with approximately 1,500 photos, many in full color. Each photo is fully described and valued. It also includes information on how to determine whether it's authentic or synthetic. Each period includes information on what influenced the jewelry of that time.
#2390, 5½ x 8½, 445 Pgs., PB $14.95

100 Years of Collectible Jewelry
by Lillian Baker

In this comprehensive guide to collectible and antique jewelry, 100's of pieces of jewelry are photographed in beautiful full color and are presented with authoritative descriptions and current market values.
#1181, 5½ x 8½, 170 Pgs, PB $9.95

Twentieth Century Fashionable Plastic Jewelry
by Lillian Baker

This complete encyclopedia includes great photos, a glossary of terms and types of plastic jewelry, new conceptions and historical footnotes. Virtually every aspect of this prized plastic jewelry is covered in detail, including full descriptions with dates, nomenclature and current values.
#2348, 8½ x 11, 240 Pgs, HB $19.95

Identification & Value Guide To Cameos
by Ed Aswad & Michael Weinstein

For hundreds of years, cameos have been treated as decorations for clothing, fingers and necks with little thought as to the care that went into their making. This is the first reference guide to bring these beautifully handcarved pieces of art to the forefront with full descriptions and detailed photography of over 100 cameos.
#2195, 5½ x 8½, 184 Pgs., PB. $12.95

Vintage Vanity Bags & Purses
by Roselyn Gerson

A complete pictorial reference guide, it is the definitive source for history, values, patents, origins, composition, and manufacturers of these many whimsical yet functional accessories. Over 300 gorgeous color photos in additon to hundreds of vintage ads feature all types of bags – from the traditional box-shape bags.
#3830, 8½ x 11, 272 Pgs., HB. $24.95

American Premium Guide To Pocket Knives & Razors
3rd Edition • by Jim Sargent

Jim Sargent has added hundreds of photos of rare knives. The collector will also find additional sections on Pal and Browning knives with photos & full descriptions. All existing values have been updated. Other manufacturers include: Winchester, Queen, Western States and Keen Kutter.
#2368, 8½ x 11, 474 Pgs., PB. $22.95

Early Archaic Indian Points & Knives
by Robert Edler

Each of the over 40 types of archaic points are beautifully illustrated and include detailed histories. Also included is a complete section on how Indian points and tools were originally made.
#2015, 8½ x 11, 120 Pgs., PB, No Values $14.95

Flint Blades & Projectile Points of the North American Indian
by Lawrence Tully

Lawrence Tully has been studying Indian artifacts for over 40 years and he included all his knowledge into this book. Each artifact pictured is photographed to actual size and there are 100's of good sharp photos. This is without a doubt the last word to the many artifacts of the North American Indian.
#1668, 8½ x 11, 240 Pgs., HB, ...$24.95

Indian Axes & Related Stone Artifacts
by Lar Hothem

This value guide to these primitive axes and stone artifacts is filled with photos and explains the basics, the how-to's and the identification of axe collecting. Both history of Indian axes and the future of axe collecting are included.
#1964, 8½ x 11, 224 Pgs., HB $14.95

Modern Guns Identification & Values
by Russell & Steve Quertermous

This huge collection features 480 pages crammed full of valuable information and photographs that are indispensable to gun lovers. Over 2,250 models of rifles, handguns and shotguns from 1900 to the present are described and priced in excellent and very good condition with suggested retail prices for those models still in production.
#3320, 8½ x 11, 480 Pgs., PB..............................$12.95

North American Indian Ornamental & Ceremonial Artifacts
by Lar Hothem

144 pages with over 400 photos, descriptions and values. Featured are: Effigy stones, Birdstones, Bannerstones, Gorgets, Pendants, Celts, Beadwork, Quiltwork, Trade Ornaments, Pipes plus much more.
#2192, 8½ x 11, 133 Pgs., PB..............................$19.95

Antique Tools: Our American Heritage
by Kathryn McNerney

A much needed reference, this guide to old tools is filled with information on both the common and unusual tools of the past. Fully illustrated, this quality paperback includes current values and descriptions.
#1868, 5½ x 8½, 156 Pgs...$9.95

Arrowheads & Projectile Points
by Lar Hothem

Projectile points of American Indians have long been objects of interest to students and historians. Recently they have come to be valuable to collectors as well. This book has 100's of photos of points, information about origin, methods of production, sizes, values and a section on detecting fakes.
#1426, 5½ x 8½, 224 Pgs., PB. $7.95

Indian Artifacts of The Midwest
by Lar Hothem

This publication is loaded with all types of artifacts coming from the midwest. It includes a comprehensive text and is much more than just a value guide. Hundreds of photos are included to help in identification.
#2279, 8½ x 11, 208 Pgs., PB..............................$14.95

Keen Kutter Collectibles
by Jerry & Elaine Heuring

Probably the most respected trade name from yesterday's hardware companies was Keen Kutter. Any item marked with this famous logo is sought by today's collector. From hammers & axes through razors, scissors & knives this book covers almost every item that was marked Keen Kutter. This book is well illustrated & contains current values.
#2023, 8½ x 11, 128 Pgs., PB..............................$14.95

North American Indian Artifacts
5th Edition • by Lar Hothem

All values based on the 1991 Allard Auction. This is the guide for collectors and historians on all aspects of North American Indian artifacts. Over 2,300 items listed, described and valued, fully illustrated with many in color.
#3805, 8½ x 11, 512 Pgs., PB..............................$22.95

The Standard Knife Collector's Guide
2nd Edition • by Roy Ritchie & Ron Stewart

This complete revised 2nd edition includes virtually all knife manufacturers both old and new plus commemoratives, and serves as a general price guide to 1,000's of knives. Many photographs and line drawings are also included to aid the collector. The authors are the publishers of the monthly newsletter *The Whittler*.
#3325, 5½ x 8½, 608 Pgs., PB $12.95

Pocket Guide to Handguns
Pocket Guide to Rifles
Pocket Guide to Shotguns
by Steve & Russell Quertermous

Each one of these three volumes contains hundreds of illustrations, dates, histories, facts, and current values for guns currently still in production. The handy 5½ x 8½ size makes these guides perfect to carry along to shows, auctions, and other gun selling events. So if you are interested in rifles, handguns, or shotguns, now you can choose the book that most interests you.

Handguns, #3734, 5½ x 8½, 192 Pgs., PB $9.95
Rifles, #3735, 5½ x 8½, 192 Pgs., PB.....................$9.95
Shotguns, #3736, 5½ x 8½, 192 Pgs., PB.................$9.95

Primitives Our American Heritage
1st & 2nd Series • by Kathryn McNerney

Primitives are becoming more and more popular and demanding premium prices. These two books are a wonderful look at life in days gone by featuring identification and value guides on such primitive items as tools, furniture and household goods. Each guide includes hundreds of black & white photographs with no repeats, plus current values. Loaded with information, this set is a must for primitive collectors and dealers.

1st Series, #2164, 5½ x 8½, 190 Pgs., PB...$9.95
2nd Series, #1759, 8½ x 11, 160 Pgs., PB .$14.95

Furniture

American Oak Furniture
by Kathryn McNerney

This book has over 440 photos with current values for each piece. Benches, stools, bookcases, desks, chairs, beds, dressers, store accessories and much more are featured in this informative and beautiful volume on American oak furniture.
#1457, 5½ x 8½, 176 Pgs., PB $9.95

American Oak Furniture
Book II • by Kathryn McNerney

American Oak Furniture, Book II is produced to be a companion volume to the first book and not intended to replace it nor have any repeats of that title. This book includes detailed photographs, descriptions, dates, sizes, important facts, and current values, all written in Kathryn's colorful, personal style.
#3716, 5½ x 8½, 224 Pgs., PB $12.95

The Book of Country
Volume I & II • by Don & Carol Raycraft

The Raycrafts have loaded these books with wonderful country collectibles. Over 200 color photos are in each volume. Furniture, baskets, tins, toys and stoneware are just a few of the categories.

Volume I, #1666, 8½ x 11, 160 Pgs., PB...$19.95
Volume II, #1960, 8½ x 11, 160 Pgs., PB..$19.95

Furniture of the Depression Era
by Robert & Harriett Swedberg

This is the first and only book to date that deals exclusively with furniture made during the 1920's, 30's & 40's. When one reads this book he will learn what type of furniture was made, why it was made, how it was made, the year it was made, the value today and much more.
#1755, 8½ x 11, 144 Pgs., HB $19.95

Pine Furniture, Our American Heritage
by Kathryn McNerney

Since colonial times, pine furniture has held its own distinctively respected place in our heritage. Kathryn McNerney presents excellent references to pine furniture. This value guide features beautiful black and white photographs with detailed descriptions of the pieces featured. A short history of the furniture is also included.
#1965, 8½ x 11, 152 Pgs., PB $14.95

Antique Oak Furniture
by Conover Hill

Probably the most collectible furniture available today is oak. Quarter sawn golden oak was the furniture of the era from 1900 to 1930. *Antique Oak Furniture* is the first and foremost value guide on the market today. It contains over 900 pictures and current values.
#1118, 8½ x 11, 124 Pgs., PB $7.95

Collector's Encyclopedia of American Furniture
Volume I • by Robert & Harriett Swedberg

First in a series of furniture books, Volume I contains the dark woods of the nineteenth century including mahogany, cherry, rosewood, and walnut. This beautiful furniture has been photographed in full color with complete descriptions and current values.
#2132, 8½ x 11, 128 Pgs., HB $24.95

Collector's Encyclopedia of American Furniture
Volume II • by Robert & Harriett Swedberg

This volume contains oak, ash, and elm furniture of the Depression era, none of which is included in the first volume. Over 450 full color photos make this a very informative edition and companion to Volume I.
#2271, 8½ x 11, 144 Pgs., HB $24.95

Collector's Encyclopedia of American Furniture
Volume III • by Robert & Harriett Swedberg

This is the first book of its kind featuring country furniture of the 18th & 19th centuries. Over 350 full color photos are included containing virtually every country furniture category. Each beautifully illustrated piece contains important facts, histories, dates, and current values. This edition is the final book in the series.
#3720, 8½ x 11, 128 Pgs., HB $24.95

Collector's Guide To Country Furniture
by Don & Carol Raycraft

This price guide features over 100 full-color illustrations with lots of information and values. This first volume contains furniture, baskets, folk art, small decorative items, furniture trends, and a special section on detecting authentic country furniture.
#1437, 5½ x 8½, 112 Pgs., PB $9.95

Collector's Guide To Country Furniture
Book II • by Don & Carol Raycraft

It has been four years since Don & Carol Raycraft wrote their first book on country furniture. After many hours of research they released Book II which has hundreds of full color photos. This companion volume includes the everyday fun-type of collectible, not museum-type funiture.
#1842, 8½ x 11, 112 Pgs., PB $14.95

Victorian Furniture
by Kathryn McNerney
With the same pleasant style and format of her other books, Kathryn McNerney presents a detailed informative look at this beautiful style of furniture. Useful information and an abundance of photographs are included in this fully illustrated, handy value guide.
#1885, 5½ x 8½, 256 Pgs., PB $9.95

Victorian Furninture
Book II • by Kathryn McNerney
This new companion volume to the first book, which was published in 1981, features hundreds of exceptional pieces, each described in detail and priced. This handy, informative guide provides useful information and current values for antique dealers and collectors as well as over 500 great photos to showcase the romantic world of Victorian furniture.
#3829, 5½ x 8½, 272 Pgs., PB $9.95

Paper Collectibles & Records

American Premium Record Guide 1900-1965
by Les Docks
The #1 reference for collectors of old records. Thousands upon thousands of listings from over 7,500 artists. 1,500 photos of labels. Jazz, Big Bands, Blues, Rhythm & Blues, Country & Western, Hillbilly, Rock & Roll, Rock-a-Billy, etc. 78's & 45's, LPs and EPs.
#2386, 8½ x 11, 400 Pgs., PB $22.95

Collector's Guide To Post Cards
by Jane Wood
Over 2,000 post cards are included in this illustrated value guide. It contains 16 pages of full color and features post cards on the subjects of Christmas, Easter, railroad, children, military, and many more. An interesting and informative look at this collectible field.
#1441, 8½ x 11, 176 Pgs., PB $9.95

Comic Book Price Guide
22nd Edition • by Robert Overstreet
Since 1970 the Overstreet Price Guide has been known and accepted as the most comprehensive & reliable source of information in the comic book market. Every known American comic book from 1901 to present is listed and all major artists are pointed out. The information in this guide is as complete as 20 years of research can allow.
#2249, 5½ x 8½, 520 Pgs., PB $15.00

Florence's Standard Baseball Card Price Guide
6th Edition • by Gene Florence
This guide is so easy to use, the advanced collector, beginner or even a child can find a card in seconds. With over 60,000 listings in alphabetical order, it has become a best seller in its field. A color section showing the front and back of the card identifies cards throughout the years.
#3731, 5½ x 8½, 592 Pgs., PB $9.95

Price Guide To Cookbooks
by Colonel Bob Allen
Allen has formed an extensive collection and has been studying and researching cookbooks for many years. This comprehensive study, loaded with histories, dates and current values, features a wealth of information about cookbooks and booklets over the years.
#2081, 8½ x 11, 216 Pgs., PB $14.95

Huxford's Old Book Value Guide
6th Edition
This informative annual guide lists 25,000 titles with current values. More than just a price guide – you'll find actual buyers listed by the subject matter they are looking for, so it's a selling guide as well.
#3820, 8½ x 11, 392 Pgs., HB $19.95

Maxfield Parrish
A Price Guide
This book has 120 pages with 40 pages of full color photos. There are over 932 items plus book plates listed & priced. This book will help anyone who is just starting to collect Maxfield Parrish and it will also help price and identify items that you already have.
#3473, 5½ x 8½, 112 Pgs., PB $12.95

Price Guide To Cookbooks & Recipe Leaflets
by Linda Dickinson
This author has been collecting and studying the history of cookbooks for years and now has completed a very needed price guide to thousands of cookbooks. Included are many large photos to aid the collector in identification. The cookbooks are arranged in alphabetical order to make locating simple.
#2080, 5½ x 8½, 190 Pgs., PB $9.95

Collector's Guide to Trading Cards
by Robert Reed
This book contains current values for over 90,000 cards from the 1880's to present, plus over 925 different sets of American cards. Also included are over 400 full color photographs to aid in identification. The easy-to-use format is arranged alphabetically from A-Team to Zorro. The author has written articles on this subject for a wide range of publications and is considered an authority.
#3438, 8½ x 11, 224 Pgs., PB $17.95

Sheet Music Reference & Price Guide
by Marie-Reine A. Pafik & Anna Marie Guiheen
This full color price guide lists the song titles alphabetically with as much information as is available to make identifying quick and simple. You don't have to be able to read music to be an enthusiast of this beautiful and fanciful art form. From Dixie to Jazz, Blues to Ragtime, this is a most enjoyable book.
#2346, 8½ x 11, 296 Pgs., PB $18.95

Miscellaneous

Advertising Playing Cards
by Everett Grist
This colorful book includes nothing but advertising playing cards. The author has been collecting cards for several years and has bought and sold over 10,000 decks. Included are hundreds of photos with the bulk of the cards from 1940-1970.
#2280, 8½ x 11, 232 Pgs., PB $16.95

American Sterling Silver Flatware
1830's-1990's
Featuring patterns and values of thousands of pieces from the early silversmiths to current manufacturers. Also includes historical information on all companies.
#3418, 8½ x 11, 230 Pgs., PB $22.95

Antique Advertising Encyclopedia
Volume I • by Ray Klug
This book has long been considered the authority on advertising collectibles. Includes tins, trays, signs and much more. If you are an antique advertising enthusiast, you must have this book for reference and pricing.
#1520, 8 x 10, 327 Pgs., PB $17.95

Antique Advertising Encyclopedia
Volume II • by Ray Klug
A very lovely book on advertising with 117 pages in full color. This book is good for the hard-to-find items and very expensive items. If you can't find it in volume one, chances are that you will find it here.
#1687, 8 x 10, 240 Pgs., HB $39.95

Antique Brass & Copper
by Mary Frank Gaston

Brass and copper collectibles are sought after in today's market and this book will help both the buyer and seller make accurate evaluations. Over 500 full color examples are included, each containing complete descriptions and current values.
#2269, 8½ x 11, 208 Pgs., PB...................................$16.95

Black Collectibles
by P. J. Gibbs

Over 500 color photos including advertising items, containers, dolls, entertainment, figural images, folk art, literary collectibles, novelties and souvenirs, pictorial images, toys and more are included in this volume with current values.
#1714, 8½ x 11, 296 Pgs., PB...................................$19.95

Collectible Aluminum
by Everett Grist

Everett Grist has compiled an informative guide including over 430 photographs featuring hand wrought, forged, cast, and hammered aluminum. Everything from ashtrays to smoking stands, jewelry to tables and hundreds of seving pieces. All sizes & shapes are featured.
#3718, 8½ x 11, 160 Pgs., PB...................................$16.95

Collectible Cats: An Identification & Value Guide
by Marbena "Jean" Fyke

This is a comprehensive value guide to cats made of wood, bronze, glass and china; cat jewelry; black cats of the 1940's; Garfield; prints & paintings; salt & pepper shakers; kitchen items; and a large miscellaneous section. This fun, colorful guide features over 500 photos with complete descriptions & current values.
#3445, 8½ x 11, 160 Pgs., PB...................................$18.95

Collector's Encyclopedia of Granite Ware
by Helen Greguire

This comprehensive work includes pattern and color descriptions, shades of color, enameling types, names and makers, age, construction, popularity, care and preserving instructions and more. Over 180 color photographs make this a truly necessary guide to investing in this collectible.
#2018, 8½ x 11, 416 Pgs., HB $24.95

Collector's Guide to Antique Radios
2nd Edition • by Marty & Sue Bunis

This all-new revised 2nd edition includes over 5,000 model numbers & over 600 full color photos not found in the 1st edition. This new edition covers literally 1,000's of sets made between the years of 1920-1960. Collectors will enjoy the easy-to-use format with the radios listed alphabetically by company. All manufacturers are included with complete descriptions.
#2336, 8½ x 11, 216 Pgs., PB...................................$17.95

Collector's Guide to Coca-Cola Items
Volume I • by Al Wilson

A very nice book by one of the foremost authorities on Coca-Cola collectibles. From signs to trays to calendars to toys to thermometers, it is all in this book. Fine quality all color pictures. Also includes 1992 current values.
#1677, 5 x 8, 96 Pgs., PB...$10.95

Collector's Guide to Country Baskets
by Don & Carol Raycraft

This book has interesting information and hundreds of photos on this popular collectible, with current values.
#1537, 5½ x 8½, 128 Pgs., PB $9.95

Antique Iron
by Kathryn McNerney

Included in this identification and value guide are farm tools, furniture, kitchen items, toys, banks and many more cast iron collectibles. Over 400 different photos fill this informative value guide.
#1880, 5½ x 8½, 232 Pgs., PB $9.95

Christmas Collectibles
2nd Edition • by Margaret & Kenn Whitmyer

The authors have added several hundred photographs to the first book, updated all the values, and added new information. Features an interesting history of Kris Kringle and Santa Claus and an overview of Christmas items are now demanding huge prices at antique shows across the country.
#3717, 8½ x 11, 304 Pgs., HB $24.95

Christmas Ornaments, Lights & Decorations
by George W. Johnson

This book lists information on identifying, storage, repairing, histories, types and much more. Over 750 full color photographs with the name of the item, interesting facts and current values are all listed.
#1752, 8½ x 11, 320 Pgs., HB $19.95

Collecting Antique Bird Decoys and Duck Calls
2nd Edition • by Carl F. Luckey

The author has traveled throughout the country researching this reference guide and has photographed over 230 decoys and approximately 100 calls. Along with the photos are full descriptions and values. Each is identified as to its maker, school of carving, etc.
#3361, 8½ x 11, 240 Pgs., PB...................................$22.95

Collector's Encyclopedia of Granite Ware
Book 2 • by Helen Greguire

Helen Greguire has collected granite ware for many years and is considered an expert in her field. This second book, which has no repeats of her first book and makes the perfect companion volume, features many more unusual colors and shapes as well as rarities never before photographed. With over 1,000 pieces featured in full color.
#3430, 8½ x 11, 384 Pgs., HB $24.95

Collector's Guide to Art Deco
by Mary Frank Gaston

The distinctive lines of Art Deco come alive in this full color value guide. The 318 color photos are divided into categories including Clocks, Dress Accessories, Lamps, Smoking Accessories, Statues, Tablewares, and Vases.
#1916, 8½ x 11, 136 Pgs., PB...................................$14.95

Collector's Guide to Coca-Cola Items
Volume II • by Al Wilson

Coca-Cola collectibles are one of the more popular collectibles on the market today. Al Wilson is one of the foremost authorities of this popular collectible. Included in this new Volume II is virtually every Coca-Cola category. This book is produced in full color and contains current values.
#1824, 5½ x 8½, 96 Pgs., PB $10.95

Collector's Guide to Hopalong Cassidy Memorabilia
by Joseph J. Caro

There are several hundred items in this book ranging from Advertising to Toys to Playsuits with many items in between. The author is a very respected Hoppy collector and has been collecting since 1977. Mr. Caro has collected over 600 items of "Hoppy" memorabilia. Rare and common items are pictured in this book.
#3458, 8½ x 11, 190 Pgs., PB...................................$17.95

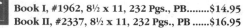

Collector's Guide to Decoys
Books I & II • by Bob & Sharon Huxford

These books cover miniature, decorative, factory and artists' decoys. Actual prices, characteristics and conditions are listed with hundreds of color and black and white photographs. These two volumes will be a valuable addition to any sports enthusiast's library and will help in dating and pricing a collection. Both advanced and beginning collectors will enjoy these books.

Book I, #1962, 8½ x 11, 232 Pgs., PB........$14.95
Book II, #2337, 8½ x 11, 232 Pgs., PB $16.95

Collector's Guide to Keywind Coffee Tins
by James H. Stahl
Over 1,200 one pound coffee tins are pictured and priced. This is the only book you will ever need if you are a collector of coffee tins. It shows over 150 coffee tins in full color; the rest in fine quality black and white, and includes a history of the coffee tin.
#2250, 8 x 11, 172 Pgs., PB.....................$19.95

The Encyclopedia of Golf Collectibles
by Mort & John Olman
This book is a comprehensive guide dealing with the identification, dating and valuation of all sorts of golf memorabilia from clubs and balls to books, paintings, prints and more. Among its features are over 2,000 items fully illustrated, names of craftsmen, manufacturers, artists and authors.
#1559, 8½ x 11, 328 Pgs., PB.................$14.95

Goldstein's Coca-Cola Collectibles
by Shelly Goldstein
If you have any interest in Coca-Cola memorabilia, you will want and need this full color price guide. Previously offered as a four volume set, we have taken these four volumes and combined them into one book. This edition is a must for both the serious collector and the novice.
#2215, 8½ x 11, 128 Pgs., PB.................$16.95

A Guide To Easter Collectibles
by Juanita Burnett
This pictorial guide is designed for the beginning or advanced collector, with many categories covering a time span from the 1800's to the present. History, care instructions and tips on dating your collection, color photos and current values are included.
#2340, 8½ x 11, 128 Pgs., PB.................$16.95

Kitchen Antiques 1790-1940
by Kathryn McNerney
This outstanding reference includes over 650 photographs containing virtually every kitchen item since the 1790's. Every kitchen item picture or listing in this book contains complete descriptions, sizes, dates, histories and of course a current value guide.
#2216, 8½ x 11, 224 Pgs., PB $14.95

Pictorial Price Guide to Metal Lunch Boxes
by Larry Aikins
This is the book everyone has been waiting for. Almost every metal lunch box that was ever made is included in this full color publication. Over 800 boxes pictured. Every box has a front and back view plus a photo of the thermos. You must have this book!
#3334, 5 x 8, 218 Pgs., PB.....................$19.95

Old Lace & Linens Including Crochet
Identification & Value Guide • by Maryanne Dolan
This reference guide features the intricate artwork found in handstitched items over the past century. Featuring tablecloths, centerpieces, doilies, collars, bedspreads, napkins, pillowcases, hand & tea towels plus more. Fully illustrated.
#2041, 5½ x 8½, 200 Pgs., PB $10.95

Collector's Guide to Transistor Radios
by Marty & Sue Bunis
This book includes information on over 2,000 different transistor radios representing over 248 companies. Over 200 full color photographs are included with complete descriptions and current values. The authors have put a special emphasis on radios from 1954 – 1965.
#3730, 5½ x 8½, 144 Pgs., PB $15.95

Decoys
by Gene & Linda Kangas
The scope of this manuscript is very complex and includes every aspect of decoy collecting. This is much more than just an identification and value guide. This full color hardbound book includes 600+ photographs with chapters on North American Indian decoys, non-native decoys, transportation, influences and decoy painting, care & maintenance, decoratives, miniatures, fish decoys and much much more!
#2276, 11 x 8½, 336 Pgs., HB $24.95

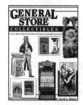

Doorstops
Identifications & Values • by Jeanne Bertoia
Collectors will learn detection of reproductions and care and preservation as well as history, manufacturers, designers, and pointers in valuing doorstops. Figural examples include Uncle Sam, black mammies, art deco ladies and more. Over 300 color photographs are included.
#1629, 5½ x 8½, 176 Pgs., PB $9.95

General Store Collectibles
by David L. Wilson
This identification and value guide features an interesting text with more than 500 knock-out color photos of store fixtures, showcases, advertising items, patent medicines, dye cabinets, coffee mills, and much more from the shelves, counters, and walls of the old general store.
#3819, 8½ x 11, 192 Pgs., HB $24.95

Huxford's Collectible Advertising
by Bob & Sharon Huxford
Thousands of listings and hundreds of photos are included with the bulk of them produced in full color. The format is amazingly simple and the book very easy to use. Each item is described in full so that even subtle variations are easy to spot; condition, an all-important factor to consider as you evaluate your collectibles, is well defined.
#3319, 8½ x 11, 144 Pgs., PB.................$17.95

Jukeboxes & Slot Machines
Plus Gum Balls, Arcade, Trade Stimulators
3rd Edition • by Jerry Ayliffe
Includes Wurlitzer, Seeburg, Rockola, AMI, Mills, Fey, Caille, Jennings, Pace, Watling, Northwestern, Columbus, Advance, Leebold, Master plus many more.
#2332, 5½ x 8½, 400 Pgs., PB $14.95

Jukeboxes: A Blast From the Past
Edited by Scott Wood
You will never find another book on jukeboxes with this many photos and prices. Over 100 jukeboxes in beautiful color. Wurlitzer and AMI to Seeburg, Rockola and more. Also includes some wall boxes and speakers.
#3388, 5 x 8, PB $14.95

Old Fishing Lures & Tackle
3rd Edition • by Carl Luckey
This very popular book has now added over 400 lures to the existing photos and illustrations in the 2nd edition. Many more manufacturers have been added and all prices have been updated. Tremendous job...very well written and illustrated.
#2194, 8½ x 11, 472 Pgs., PB.................$22.95

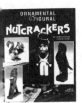

Ornamental & Figural Nutcrackers
by Judith Rittenhouse

At long last, a book about decorative nutcrackers covering their history from the very earliest use to the production of colorful and elaborate figurals of today. Over 100 color photos of over 150 nutcrackers, along with a variety of illustrations. Basic types of nutcrackers, their composition, dating and pricing are discussed.

#3321, 8½ x 11, 144 Pgs., PB....................$16.95

Evolution of the Pedal Car
Volume I • Edited by Neil S. Wood

Includes Pedal Cars and other riding toys from 1884 to 1970's. Contains old catalog pages and color photos of private collections. This is possibly the hottest new collectible in the antique market today. With the aid of this book you will keep in touch with realistic prices for any pedal car you will find.

#2060, 8 x 11, 218 Pgs., PB....................$29.95

Evolution of the Pedal Car
Volume II • Edited by Neil S. Wood

Same format as volume one with completely different information and photos. Includes pedal cars, sleds, scooters, tricycles and more from pre 1900's to 1980's. A must book for your pedal car library.

#2197, 8 x 11, 185 Pgs., PB....................$29.95

Evolution of the Pedal Car
Volume III • Edited by Neil S. Wood

The best one yet! Another completely different book on pedal cars. This book is on pedal cars from pre 1900 to 1990's. Add this one to your other two books on pedal cars and you shouldn't have to look any further.

#2388, 8 x 11, 250 Pgs., PB....................$29.95

Silverplated Flatware
Revised Fourth Edition • by Tere Hagan

This 4th edition has been expanded to 372 pages with updated values. As in the previous edition, each pattern has current values for the fork, knife and spoon with each illustration. A price code remains in the front of the book for the other pieces in each pattern. Over 1,500 patterns are included in this fully illustrated guide.

#2096, 8½ x 11, 372 Pgs., PB....................$14.95

The Book of Moxie
by Frank N. Potter

This huge book by America's Moxie expert is full of information about the company, its products, advertising and collectibles. Hundreds of vintage photographs plus hundreds of color photos of collectible items are included. Moxie, a bitterish concoction of gentian root extract and about 20 other flavorings was once the nation's No. 1 soft drink.

#1811, 8½ x 11, 304 Pgs., HB $29.95

300 Years of Housekeeping Collectibles
by Linda Campbell Franklin

You already know her *300 Years of Kitchen Collectibles*; this new collector's guide is just as comprehensive and exciting with well illustrated sections on Laundering, House Cleaning, Closeting, Bathrooms. You'll know what all those "Whatzzit" gadgets were used for. 216 pages loaded with illustrations and full descriptions.

#3359, 8½ x 11, 216 Pgs., PB....................$22.95

Value Guide To Baseball Collectibles
by Don & Craig Raycraft

Until the publication of this *Value Guide To Baseball Collectibles* there have been few sources for collectors seeking detailed & current information about baseball related memorabilia. Now you can even locate a value for a copy of *Newsweek* magazine from the 1930's with Carl Hubbell on the cover. The authors have been serious collectors of baseball memorabilia for 15 years.

#2349, 8½ x 11, 216 Pgs., PB....................$16.95

Pepsi-Cola Collectibles
Volume I • by Bill Vehling & Michael Hunt

Pepsi-Cola collectibles are now as popular as Coca-Cola items. You need this book to find the price of the items you have just purchased or are looking for. Very accurate pricing on trays to openers to jewelry to signs to coolers. Includes current values.

#1800, 8 x 11, 150 Pgs., PB....................$14.95

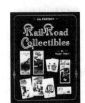

Pepsi-Cola Collectibles
Volume II • by Bill Vehling & Michael Hunt

Another fine book by the experts in the Pepsi-Cola field. Completely different items found in this book than are pictured in volume one. Aprons to carriers to fans to magazine ads, this book will price them for you.

#2142, 8 x 11, 192 Pgs., PB....................$17.95

Railroad Collectibles
Revised 4th Edition • by Stanley Baker

Stanley Baker, the well-known & popular collector of America's railroad memorabilia has completely revised his popular value guide. This edition has new illustrations and is completely updated. From dining car china to switch keys this book is invaluable to thousands of railroad buffs. It is not only a must but is considered *the* book on the subject.

#2026, 8½ x 11, 200 Pgs., PB....................$14.95

R. Atkinson Fox, His Life & Works
by Rita C. Mortenson

A very nice book on the history of R. Atkinson Fox with pictures and prices. Eight pages of full color with the rest of the book in fine black and white. One of the fastest growing collectibles in the art field today.

#2247, 8 x 11, 150 Pgs., PB....................$17.95

R. Atkinson Fox
Volume II • by Rita C. Mortenson

The second volume that everyone has been waiting for. Completely different from volume one. Anyone interested in the works of R. Atkinson Fox will want this book.

#3350, 8 x 11, 308 Pgs., PB....................$24.95

Sterling Silver, Silverplate & Souvenir Spoons
Edited by Neil S. Wood

A very nice book to identify and price your silver, silverplate and souvenir spoons. Includes everything from flatware to thimbles to napkin rings to match boxes.

#1875, 8 x 11, 188 Pgs., PB....................$12.95

300 Years of Kitchen Collectibles
3rd Edition • by Linda C. Franklin

Four years ago, Linda Franklin decided to take the extra time to move this reference work to a much higher plane. The number of illustrations, listings and the size of the book has doubled. (Patent date charts and a recipe index are also included.) Now in a large format.

#2299, 8½ x 11, 640 Pgs., PB....................$22.95

Wanted To Buy
4th Edition

The perfect reference book for both selling your collectibles and determining the actual current market value, because it lists actual buyers along with the price they're willing to pay. This book creates a marketplace for both the collectors and dealers.

#3444, 5½ x 8½, 416 Pgs., PB $9.95

NOSTALGIA PUBLISHING ORDER FORM

Name _____
(please print)

Address _____

City _____ State ____ Zip _____

Method of Payment

☐ Check   ☐ VISA   ☐ MasterCard

Cardholder's Name _____

Card # _____ Expiration Date _____

POLICY

- **Send check or charge card information with order.**
- **NO OPEN ACCOUNTS**
- **Postage & Handling: Add $2.00 for 1st book & .30¢ for each additional book.**
- **We will ship your order the day we receive it.**
- **Mail order only – no showroom.**
- **Due to high postage rates we only accept orders from U.S. customers.**

ITEM #	QTY	TITLE	PRICE	TOTAL

Send Order To:

Nostalgia Publishing Co., Inc.
P.O. Box 277
La Center, KY 42056

SUBTOTAL	
Postage & Handling: Add $2.00 for 1st book & .30¢ for each additional book	
TOTAL ENCLOSED	

This form may be photocopied